TEACHER'S EDITION

Houghton Mifflin Harcourt

collections

GRADE 7

Program Consultants:

Kylene Beers

Martha Hougen

Carol Jago

William L. McBride

Erik Palmer

Lydia Stack

bio.

Printed in the U.S.A.

ISBN 978-0-544-08705-7

2 3 4 5 6 7 8 9 10 0914 22 21 20 19 18 17 16 15 14 13

4500431989   A B C D E F G

collections

Teacher's Edition Table of Contents

Kylene Beers Nationally known lecturer and author on Reading and Literacy; 2011 recipient of the Conference on English Leadership Exemplary Leader Award; coauthor of *Notice and Note: Strategies for Close Reading*; former President of the National Council of Teachers of English. Dr. Beers is the nationally known author of *When Kids Can't Read: What Teachers Can Do* and coeditor of *Adolescent Literacy: Turning Promise into Practice*, as well as articles in the *Journal of Adolescent and Adult Literacy*. Former editor of *Voices from the Middle*, she is the 2001 recipient of NCTE's Richard W. Halley Award, given for outstanding contributions to middle-school literacy. She recently served as Senior Reading Researcher at the Comer School Development Program at Yale University as well as Senior Reading Advisor to Secondary Schools for the Reading and Writing Project at Teachers College.

Martha Hougen National consultant, presenter, researcher, and author. Areas of expertise include differentiating instruction for students with learning difficulties, including those with learning disabilities and dyslexia; and teacher and leader preparation improvement. Dr. Hougen has taught at the middle school through graduate levels. Recently her focus has been on working with teacher educators to enhance teacher and leader preparation to better meet the needs of all students. Currently she is working with the University of Florida at the Collaboration for Effective Educator Development, Accountability, and Reform Center (CEEDAR Center) to improve the achievement of students with disabilities by reforming teacher and leader licensure, evaluation, and preparation. She has led similar efforts in Texas with the Higher Education Collaborative and the College & Career Readiness Initiative Faculty Collaboratives. In addition to peer-reviewed articles, curricular documents, and presentations, Dr. Hougen has published two college textbooks: *The Fundamentals of Literacy Assessment and Instruction Pre-K–6* (2012) and *The Fundamentals of Literacy Assessment and Instruction 6–12* (2014).

Carol Jago Teacher of English with 32 years of experience at Santa Monica High School in California; author and nationally known lecturer; and past President of the National Council of Teachers of English. Currently serves as Associate Director of the California Reading and Literature Project at UCLA. With expertise in standards assessment and secondary education, Ms. Jago is the author of numerous books on education, including *With Rigor for All* and *Papers, Papers, Papers*, and is active with the California Association of Teachers of English, editing its scholarly journal *California English* since 1996. Ms. Jago also served on the planning committee for the 2009 NAEP Framework and the 2011 NAEP Writing Framework.

William L. McBride Curriculum Specialist. Dr. McBride is a nationally known speaker, educator, and author who now trains teachers in instructional methodologies. He is coauthor of *What's Happening*, an innovative, high-interest text for middle-grade readers, and author of *If They Can Argue Well, They Can Write Well*. A former reading specialist, English teacher, and social studies teacher, he holds a masters in reading and a doctorate in curriculum and instruction from the University of North Carolina at Chapel Hill. Dr. McBride has contributed to the development of textbook series in language arts, social studies, science, and vocabulary. He is also known for his novel *Entertaining an Elephant*, which tells the story of a veteran teacher who becomes reinspired with both his profession and his life.

Erik Palmer Veteran teacher and education consultant based in Denver, Colorado. Author of *Well Spoken: Teaching Speaking to All Students* and *Digitally Speaking: How to Improve Student Presentations*. His areas of focus include improving oral communication, promoting technology in classroom presentations, and updating instruction through the use of digital tools. He holds a bachelor's degree from Oberlin College and a master's degree in curriculum and instruction from the University of Colorado.

Lydia Stack International ESL consultant. Director of the Screening and Assessment Center in the San Francisco Unified School District. Her areas of expertise are English language teaching strategies, ESL standards for students and teachers, and curriculum writing. Her teaching experience includes 25 years as an elementary and high school ESL teacher. She is past president of TESOL. Her awards include the James E. Alatis Award for Service to TESOL and the San Francisco STAR Teacher Award. Her publications include *On Our Way to English*; *Wordways*; *Games for Language Learning*; and *Visions: Language, Literature, Content*.

Additional thanks to the following Program Reviewers

Rosemary Asquino	Carol M. Gibby	Linda Beck Pieplow
Sylvia B. Bennett	Angie Gill	Molly Pieplow
Yvonne Bradley	Mary K. Goff	Mary-Sarah Proctor
Leslie Brown	Saira Haas	Jessica A. Stith
Haley Carroll	Lisa M. Janeway	Peter Swartley
Caitlin Chalmers	Robert V. Kidd Jr.	Pamela Thomas
Emily Colley-King	Kim Lilley	Linda A. Tobias
Stacy Collins	John C. Lowe	Rachel Ukleja
Denise DeBonis	Taryn Curtis MacGee	Lauren Vint
Courtney Dickerson	Meredith S. Maddox	Heather Lynn York
Sarah Easley	Cynthia Martin	Leigh Ann Zerr
Phyllis J. Everette	Kelli M. McDonough	
Peter J. Foy Sr.	Megan Pankiewicz	

FLEXIBILITY

Blended classroom?   Flipped?   Traditional approach?

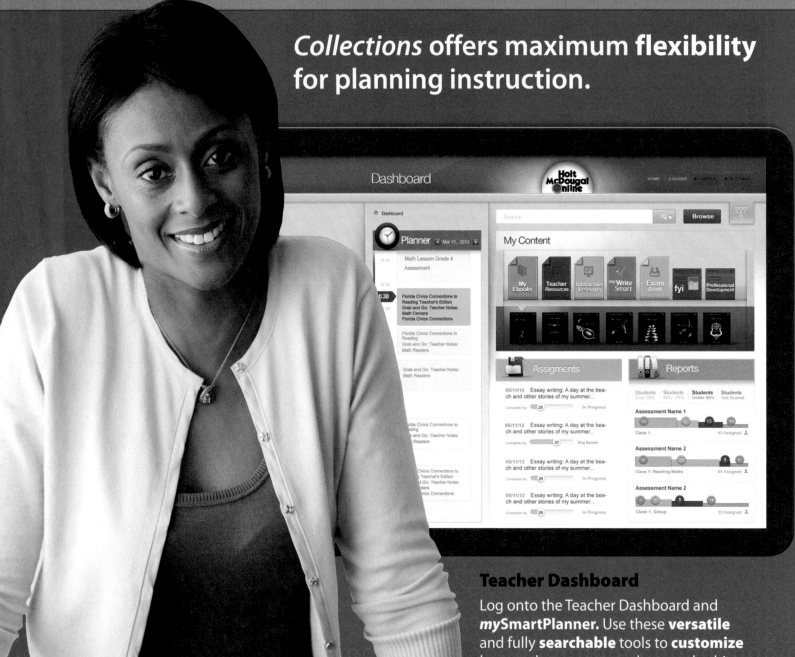

Collections offers maximum **flexibility** for planning instruction.

Teacher Dashboard

Log onto the Teacher Dashboard and *my*SmartPlanner. Use these **versatile** and fully **searchable** tools to **customize** lessons that engage students and achieve your instructional goals.

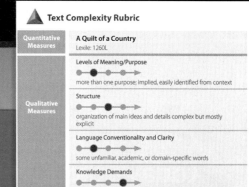

Text Complexity Rubric

Quantitative Measures	A Quilt of a Country
	Lexile: 1260L

Qualitative Measures

Levels of Meaning/Purpose

more than one purpose; implied, easily identified from context

Structure

organization of main ideas and details complex but mostly explicit

Language Conventionality and Clarity

some unfamiliar, academic, or domain-specific words

Knowledge Demands

extensive knowledge of history required

Text Complexity Rubrics

help you identify dimensions of complex text.

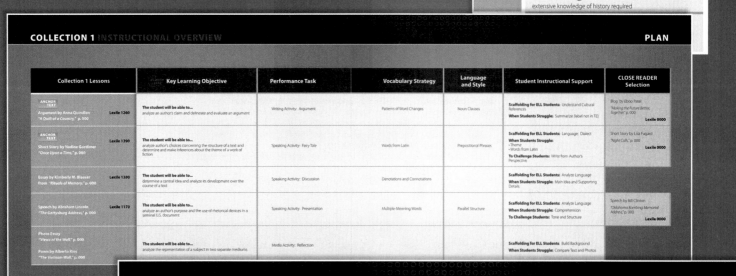

COLLECTION 1 INSTRUCTIONAL OVERVIEW

PLAN

Collection 1 Lessons	Key Learning Objective	Performance Task	Vocabulary Strategy	Language and Style	Student Instructional Support	CLOSE READER Selection
ANCHOR TEXT Argument by Anna Quindlen "A Quilt of a Country," p. 000 — Lexile 1260	The student will be able to... analyze an author's claim and delineate and evaluate an argument	Writing Activity: Argument	Patterns of Word Changes	Noun Clauses	Scaffolding for ELL Students: Understand Cultural References When Students Struggle: Summarize (label not in TE)	Blog by Eboo Patel "Making the Future Better, Together," p. 000 Lexile 0000
ANCHOR TEXT Short Story by Nadine Gordimer "Once Upon a Time," p. 000 — Lexile 1390	The student will be able to... analyze author's choices concerning the structure of a text and determine and make inferences about the theme of a work of fiction	Speaking Activity: Fairy Tale	Words from Latin	Prepositional Phrases	Scaffolding for ELL Students: Language; Dialect When Students Struggle: • Theme • Words from Latin To Challenge Students: Write from Author's Perspective	Short Story by Lisa Fugard "Night Calls," p. 000 Lexile 0000
Essay by Kimberly M. Blaeser from "Rituals of Memory," p. 000 — Lexile 1380	The student will be able to... determine a central idea and analyze its development over the course of a text	Speaking Activity: Discussion	Denotations and Connotations		Scaffolding for ELL Students: Analyze Language When Students Struggle: Main Idea and Supporting Details	
Speech by Abraham Lincoln "The Gettysburg Address," p. 000 — Lexile 1170	The student will be able to... analyze an author's purpose and the use of rhetorical devices in a seminal U.S. document	Speaking Activity: Presentation	Multiple-Meaning Words	Parallel Structure	Scaffolding for ELL Students: Analyze Language When Students Struggle: Comprehension To Challenge Students: Tone and Structure	Speech by Bill Clinton "Oklahoma Bombing Memorial Address," p. 000 Lexile 0000
Photo Essay "Views of the Wall," p. 000 Poem by Alberto Rios "The Vietnam Wall," p. 000	The student will be able to... analyze the representation of a subject in two separate mediums	Media Activity: Reflection			Scaffolding for ELL Students: Build Background When Students Struggle: Compare Text and Photos	

Print planning

pages show the integrated Table of Contents and all assets in the **Student Edition** and the **Close Reader.**

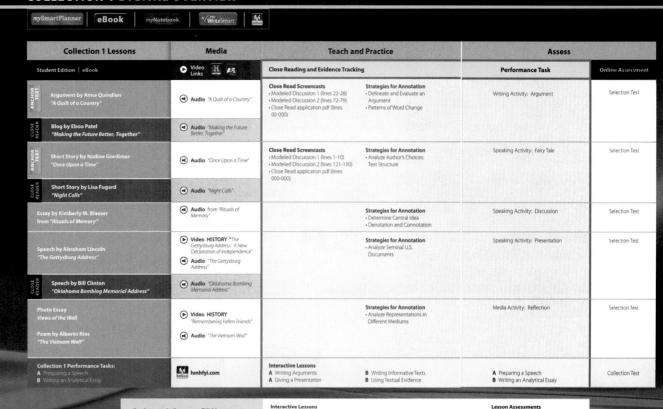

COLLECTION 1 DIGITAL OVERVIEW

mySmartPlanner | eBook | myNotebook | myWriteSmart | fyi

Collection 1 Lessons	Media	Teach and Practice		Assess	
Student Edition | eBook	Video Links	Close Reading and Evidence Tracking		Performance Task	Online Assessment
ANCHOR TEXT Argument by Anna Quindlen "A Quilt of a Country"	Audio "A Quilt of a Country"	Close Read Screencasts • Modeled Discussion 1 (lines 22-28) • Modeled Discussion 2 (lines 72-79) • Close Read application pdf (lines 00-000)	Strategies for Annotation • Delineate and Evaluate an Argument • Patterns of Word Change	Writing Activity: Argument	Selection Test
CLOSE READER Blog by Eboo Patel "Making the Future Better, Together"	Audio "Making the Future Better, Together"				
ANCHOR TEXT Short Story by Nadine Gordimer "Once Upon a Time"	Audio "Once Upon a Time"	Close Read Screencasts • Modeled Discussion 1 (lines 1-10) • Modeled Discussion 2 (lines 121-130) • Close Read application pdf (lines 000-000)	Strategies for Annotation • Analyze Author's Choices; Text Structure	Speaking Activity: Fairy Tale	Selection Test
CLOSE READER Short Story by Lisa Fugard "Night Calls"	Audio "Night Calls"				
Essay by Kimberly M. Blaeser from "Rituals of Memory"	Audio from "Rituals of Memory"		Strategies for Annotation • Determine Central Idea • Denotation and Connotation	Speaking Activity: Discussion	Selection Test
Speech by Abraham Lincoln "The Gettysburg Address"	Video HISTORY "The Gettysburg Address: A New Declaration of Independence" Audio "The Gettysburg Address"		Strategies for Annotation • Analyze Seminal U.S. Documents	Speaking Activity: Presentation	Selection Test
CLOSE READER Speech by Bill Clinton "Oklahoma Bombing Memorial Address"	Audio "Oklahoma Bombing Memorial Address"				
Photo Essay Views of the Wall Poem by Alberto Rios "The Vietnam Wall"	Video HISTORY "Remembering Fallen Friends" Audio "The Vietnam Wall"		Strategies for Annotation • Analyze Representations in Different Mediums	Media Activity: Reflection	Selection Test
Collection 1 Performance Tasks: A Preparing a Speech B Writing an Analytical Essay	hmhfyi.com	Interactive Lessons A Writing Arguments A Giving a Presentation	B Writing Informative Texts B Using Textual Evidence	A Preparing a Speech B Writing an Analytical Essay	Collection Test

For Systematic Coverage of Writing and Speaking & Listening Standards	Interactive Lessons Writing as a Process Participating in Collaborative Discussions	Lesson Assessments Writing as a Process Participating in Collaborative Discussions

ENGAGEMENT

Digital natives?   Media enthusiasts?   Writers?

Collections engages learners with today's digital tools.

Voices and images

from **A&E®, bio.®,** and **HISTORY®** transport students to different times and places.

***my*Notebook**

stores students' annotations and notes for use in **Performance Tasks.**

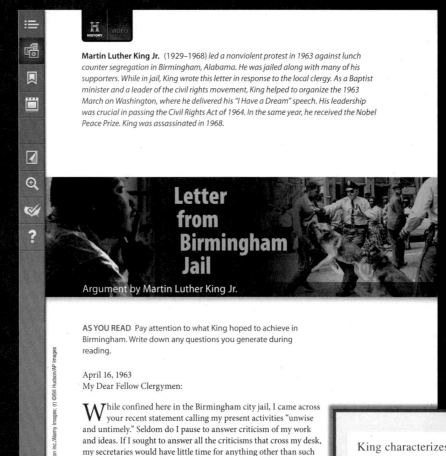

Online Tools

allow students to annotate critical passages for discussion and writing, by using **highlighting, underlining,** and **notes.**

Martin Luther King Jr. (1929–1968) *led a nonviolent protest in 1963 against lunch counter segregation in Birmingham, Alabama. He was jailed along with many of his supporters. While in jail, King wrote this letter in response to the local clergy. As a Baptist minister and a leader of the civil rights movement, King helped to organize the 1963 March on Washington, where he delivered his "I Have a Dream" speech. His leadership was crucial in passing the Civil Rights Act of 1964. In the same year, he received the Nobel Peace Prize. King was assassinated in 1968.*

Letter from Birmingham Jail

Argument by Martin Luther King Jr.

AS YOU READ Pay attention to what King hoped to achieve in Birmingham. Write down any questions you generate during reading.

April 16, 1963
My Dear Fellow Clergymen:

While confined here in the Birmingham city jail, I came across your recent statement calling my present activities "unwise and untimely." Seldom do I pause to answer criticism of my work and ideas. If I sought to answer all the criticisms that cross my desk, my secretaries would have little time for anything other than such correspondence in the course of the day, and I would have no time for constructive work. But since I feel that you are men of genuine
10   good will and that your criticisms are sincerely set forth, I want to try to answer your statement in what I hope will be patient and reasonable terms.

I think I should indicate why I am here in Birmingham, since you have been influenced by the view which argues against "outsiders coming in." I have the honor of serving as president of the Southern Christian Leadership Conference, an organization

Student Note

King characterizes his critics as "men of goodwill" to suggest that an understanding can be reached with them.

✓ Save to Notebook   Delete   Save

*my*Notebook

King characterizes his critics as "men of goodwill" to suggest that an understanding can be reached with them.

Letter from Birmingham Jail   **319**

Credits: (l) ©CSU Archives/Everett Collection Inc./Alamy Images; (r) ©Bill Hudson/AP Images

Informational text

on **fyi** is linked to each collection topic and is **curated** and **updated** monthly.

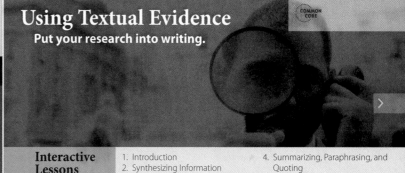

Available in Your eBook

Digital Collections

for **writing, speaking,** and **listening** provide opportunities for in-depth instruction and practice in key 21st-century skills.

Available in Your eBook

Media Lessons

prompt students to read **news reports, literary adaptations, ads,** and **websites** as complex texts.

PREPARATION

Close reading strategies?   Conversations about text?

Collections prepares students for rigorous expectations.

Background *The Hmong (hmông) are an ethnic group from southern China, Laos, Vietnam, and Thailand. In the 1970s, war and conflict caused many of the Hmong people in Laos to flee to refugee camps in Thailand. Author* **Kao Kalia Yang** *(b. 1980) was born in one of these camps. She moved with her family, including her older sister Dawb, to Minnesota in 1987. Four other siblings were born in the United States, where all the Yang children received their educations.*

from

The Latehomecomer

Memoir by Kao Kalia Yang

SETTING A PURPOSE As you read, notice the challenges and the opportunities that life in a new country presents Kao Kalia Yang and her family. How does Yang react to her situation?

We had been in America for almost ten years. I was nearly fifteen, and Dawb had just gotten her driver's license. The children were growing up. We needed a new home—the apartment was too small. There was hardly room to breathe when the scent of jasmine rice and fish steamed with ginger mingled heavily with the scent of freshly baked pepperoni pizza—Dawb's favorite food. We had been looking for a new house for nearly six months.

It was in a poor neighborhood with houses that were
10 ready to collapse—wooden planks fallin[g]
away, sloping porches—and huge, old tr[ees]
realty sign in the front yard, a small pat[ch]
of the white house. It was one story, wit[h]
and a single wide window framed by bla[ck]
black door. There was a short driveway

(c) ©Houghton Mifflin Harcourt; (b) ©Der Yang

Anchor Texts

drive each collection and have related selections in the **Close Reader.**

Close Reading Screencasts

provide **modeled conversations** about text at point of use in your **eBook.**

I was feeling a strong push to reinvent myself. Without my realizing, by the time high school began, I had a feeling in the pit of my stomach that I had been on simmer for too long. I wanted to bubble over the top and douse the confusing fire that burned in my belly. Or else I wanted to turn the stove off. I wanted to sit cool on the burners of life, lid on, and steady. I was ready for change, but there was so little in my life that I could adjust. So life took a blurry seat.

These images give the impression the narrator is uncomfortable.

Background *A member of the Standing Rock Sioux,* **Susan Power** *was born in 1961 and grew up in Chicago. She spent her childhood listening to her mother tell stories about their American Indian heritage. These stories later served as inspiration for Power's writing. As a young girl, Power made frequent visits with her mother to local museums—trips that inspired her memoir "Museum Indians."*

Museum Indians

Memoir by Susan Power

CLOSE READ
Notes

Close Reader

allows students to apply standards and practice close reading strategies in a consumable **print** or **digital** format.

1. **READ ▶** As you read lines 1–16, begin to cite text evidence.

- Underline a metaphor in the first paragraph that describes the mother's braid.
- Underline a metaphor in the second paragraph that describes the mother's braid differently.
- In the margin, note the adjectives the narrator uses to describe the braid.

A snake coils in my mother's dresser drawer; it is thick and black, glossy as sequins. My mother cut her hair several years ago, before I was born, but she kept one heavy braid. It is the three-foot snake I lift from its nest and handle as if it were alive.

"Mom, why did you cut your hair?" I ask. I am a little girl lifting a sleek black river into the light that streams through the kitchen window. Mom turns to me.

"It gave me headaches. Now put that away and wash your hands for lunch."

10 "You won't cut *my* hair, will you?" I'm sure this is a whine.

"No, just a little trim now and then to even the e

I return the dark snake to its nest amon

arranging it so that its thin tail hides

thick
black
glossy

SUCCESS

Collections scaffolds assessment demands in the classroom.

Performance Tasks
create opportunities for students to respond **analytically** and **creatively** to complex texts.

myWriteSmart
provides a **collaborative** tool to revise and edit **Performance Tasks** with peers and teachers.

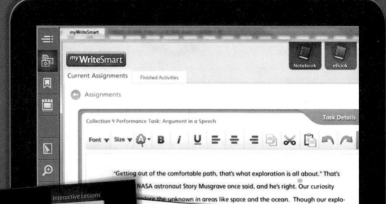

myWriteSmart

Current Assignments | Finished Activities

Assignments

Collection 4 Performance Task: Argument in a Speech | Task Details

Font ▼ Size ▼ A ▼ B *i* U ≡ ≡ ≡ ≡ ✂ ▢ ↶ ↷

"Getting out of the comfortable path, that's what exploration is all about." That's
NASA astronaut Story Musgrave once said, and he's right. Our curiosity
...lore the unknown in areas like space and the ocean. Though our explo-
...advances in medicine

Interactive Lessons
If you need help...
• Writing Arguments
• Using Textual Evidence

COLLECTION 1
PERFORMANCE TASK

Write an Argument

This collection focuses on how and why Europeans came to the Americas and what happened as they settled in unfamiliar environments. In turn, Relocating to the Americas dramatically changed settlers' lives. In turn, the settlers changed the Americas through their interaction with its land and its native populations. Look back at the anchor text, "Of Plymouth Plantation," and at other texts you have read in this collection. Synthesize your ideas about them by writing an argument. Your argument should persuade readers to agree with your claim about how immigration changed America, and how America changes those who come here.

COMMON CORE

W 1a–e Write arguments to support claims in an analysis of substantive topics or texts, using valid reasoning and relevant and sufficient evidence.

W 9 Draw evidence form literary or informational texts to support analysis, reflection, and research.

An effective argument
- identifies a central issue or question
- states a precise claim in response to the question
- develops the claim with valid reasons and relevant evidence, such as examples and quotations from the texts
- anticipates opposing claims and counters them with well-supported counterclaims
- establishes clear, logical connections among claims, counterclaims, reasons, and evidence
- includes an introduction, a logically structured body including transitions, and a conclusion
- maintains an appropriate tone based on its audience and context
- follows the conventions of written English

myNotebook

PLAN

Analyze the Text Think about the following questions as they relate to the anchor text, "Of Plymouth Plantation":
- Why did European settlers come to the New World?
- When settlers came to explore and settle the Americas, how did it change their lives?
- What changes did these settlers bring to the Americas?

Choose one question to address in your argument. Then, select three texts from this collection—including "Of Plymouth Plantation"—that provide evidence for your position. These texts might present similar or different views from each other.

ACADEMIC VOCABULARY
As you share your ideas about the role of immigration in American society, be sure to use these words.

adapt
coherent
device
displace
dynamic

Collection Performance Task   **103**

COLLECTION 6 TASK A
ARGUMENT

	Ideas and Evidence	Organization	Language
ADVANCED	• The introduction is memorable and persuasive; the claim clearly states a position on a substantive topic. • Valid reasons and relevant evidence from the texts convincingly support the writer's claim. • Counterclaims are anticipated and effectively addressed with counterarguments. • The concluding section effectively summarizes the claim.	• The reasons and textual evidence are organized consistently and logically throughout the argument. • Varied transitions logically connect reasons and textual evidence to the writer's claim.	• The writing reflects a formal style and an objective, or controlled, tone. • Sentence beginnings, lengths, and structures vary and have a rhythmic flow. • Spelling, capitalization, and punctuation are correct. • Grammar and usage are correct.
COMPETENT	• The introduction could do more to capture the reader's attention; the claim states a position on an issue. • Most reasons and evidence from the texts support the writer's claim, but they could be more convincing. • Counterclaims are anticipated, but the counterarguments need to be developed more. • The concluding section restates the claim.	• The organization of reasons and textual evidence is confusing in a few places. • A few more transitions are needed to connect reasons and textual evidence to the writer's claim.	• The style is informal in a few places, and the tone is defensive at times. • Sentence beginnings, lengths, and structures vary somewhat. • Several spelling and capitalization mistakes occur, and punctuation is inconsistent. • Some grammatical and usage errors are repeated in the argument.
	• The introduction is ordinary; the claim identifies an issue, but the writer's position is not clearly stated. • The reasons and evidence from the texts are not always logical or relevant. • Counterclaims are anticipated but not addressed logically. • The concluding section includes an incomplete summary of the claim.	• The organization of reasons and textual evidence is logical in some places, but it often doesn't follow a pattern. • Many more transitions are needed to connect reasons and textual evidence to the writer's position.	• The style becomes informal in many places, and the tone is often dismissive of other viewpoints. • Sentence structures barely vary, and some fragments or run-on sentences are present. • Spelling, capitalization, and punctuation are often incorrect but do not make reading the argument difficult. • Grammar and usage are incorrect in many places, but the writer's ideas are still clear.
	The introduction is missing. ...ignificant supporting reasons and ...vidence from the texts are missing. ...ounterclaims are neither ...ticipated nor addressed. ...e concluding section is missing.	• An organizational strategy is not used; reasons and textual evidence are presented randomly. • Transitions are not used, making the argument difficult to understand.	• The style is inappropriate, and the tone is disrespectful. • Repetitive sentence structure, fragments, and run-on sentences make the writing monotonous and hard to follow. • Spelling and capitalization are often incorrect, and punctuation is missing. • Many grammatical and usage errors change the meaning of the writer's ideas.

604   Collection 6

Common Core Assessment

print and **online** resources provide instruction in three steps: **Analyze the Model, Practice the Task,** and **Perform the Task.**

STEP 2 — PRACTICE THE TASK

Should a business have the right to ban teenagers?

You will read:

▶ A NEWSPAPER AD
Munchy's Promise

▶ A BUSINESS ANALYSIS
Munchy's Patrons in July–October

▶ A STUDENT BLOG
Munchy's Bans Students!

▶ A NEWSPAPER EDITORIAL
A Smart Idea Can Save a Business

You will write:

▶ AN ARGUMENTATIVE ESSAY
Should a business have the right to ban teenagers?

Unit 1: Argumentative Essay **9**

Mr. Jones,
Here is the analysis of
July vs. October data.
Your Accountant,
Hector Ramirez, CPA

...sis

Munchy's Patrons in October

- minors
- adults

73%

Monthly Sales

- minors
- adults

September   October

...hart.
...wn in the graph?
...wo forms of data.

Unit 1: Argumentative Essay **11**

...y studies on sleep deprivation have ...only thing that might improve. An ...ositively affect a student's mood ...says that when he was in school, ...nd were better rested. With ...hers and students would get along

...agers should take affirmative ...otherwise adjust to the reality of ...m to research done in the 1990s, ...nd wake patterns in adolescents ...Experts talked, and California ...stened. She introduced House ..., the "ZZZ's to A's Act," to ...earlier than 8:30 A.M.

...ng again. It's 7:00 A.M. You say to ...nd I've got plenty of time to get ...e a huge difference in your mood

You use an effective transition to create cohesion and signal the introduction of another reason. Your language is formal and non-combative. You remain focused on your purpose.

You anticipated and addressed an opposing claim that is likely to occur to your audience. Your answer to the opposing claim is well-supported with valid evidence.

Smooth flow from beginning to end. Clear conclusion restates your claim. Your evidence is convincing. Excellent use of conventions of English. Good job!

...ool should start later? If so, which data was the most

Unit 1: Argumentative Essay **7**

Graphics

enhance instruction, making **Common Core Assessment** unique and effective.

Common Core Enrichment App

provides instant feedback for **close reading practice** with appeal for today's students.

COLLECTION 1
Bold Actions

Collection Overviews

Each collection suggests different starting points, as well as overviews of digital resources and instructional topics for selections.

COLLECTION PERFORMANCE TASKS

Annotated Student Edition Table of Contents

Topical Organization

Each collection reflects an engaging topic that connects selections for discussion and analysis, so students can explore several dimensions of the topic.

COMMON CORE

COLLECTION 1

Bold Actions

Close Reader

Image credits: ©Kevin C. Downs/Photolibrary/Getty Images

KEY LEARNING OBJECTIVES
- Make inferences.
- Determine theme.
- Analyze plot, conflict, and setting.
- Analyze myths.
- Analyze alliteration.
- Analyze poetic form.
- Cite evidence.
- Determine central idea and details.
- Analyze and compare news stories.
- Determine author's purpose.

eBook *Explore It!*

▶ **Video Links**

HISTORY **A&E**

eBook *Read On!*
Novel list and additional selections

 Visit hmhfyi.com for current articles and informational texts.

Common Core State Standards

Each collection addresses a range of **Common Core State Standards,** ensuring coverage of the Reading Literature and Reading Informational Texts standards.

Close Reader

The **Close Reader** provides selections related to the collection topic for additional practice and application of close reading skills and annotation strategies.

COLLECTION 2
Perception and Reality

COLLECTION PERFORMANCE TASKS

Student Edition + Close Reader

In each collection, the collection topic is explored in both the **Student Edition** and **Close Reader** selections. This page shows how the two components are integrated.

Annotated Student Edition Table of Contents

Anchor Texts

Complex and challenging, the anchor texts provide a cornerstone for exploring the collection topic, while also being integral to the Collection Performance Task. Close Reader selections relate to the Student Edition anchor texts.

Variety of Genres

Both the Student Edition and the Close Reader include a variety of genres of literary texts, informational texts, and media. The genre of each selection is clearly labeled.

COMMON CORE

COLLECTION **2**

Perception and Reality

Close Reader

KEY LEARNING OBJECTIVES
Summarize a story.
Identify elements of a folk tale.
Analyze influence of setting on characters.
Analyze use of figurative language.
Analyze use of sound devices.
Analyze poetic form.

Identify and analyze drama elements.
Compare script and performance.
Summarize informational text.
Analyze text features.
Analyze visual media.

Image credits: ©Todd Davidson/Images.com/Corbis

eBook *Explore It!*

 Video Links  HISTORY A+E

eBook *Read On!*
Novel list and additional selections

 fyi hmhfyi.com Visit hmhfyi.com for current articles and informational texts.

Collection Performance Tasks

One or two Collection Performance Tasks present a cumulative task in which students draw on their reading and analysis of the collection's selections as well as additional research.

COLLECTION 3
Nature at Work

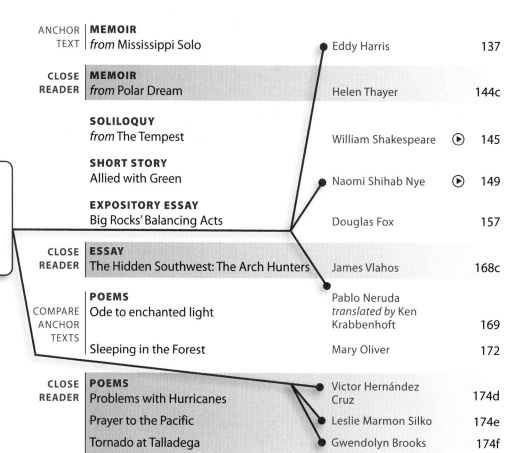

Cultural Diversity

To enrich students' perspectives, both the Student Edition and the Close Reader include selections by writers from diverse cultures.

COLLECTION PERFORMANCE TASKS

Image Credit: ©Franz Pritz/Picture Press/Getty Images

Annotated Student Edition Table of Contents

Classic and Contemporary Texts

Students read the works of world-renowned masters and current popular authors.

Text-Dependent Questions

Both the Student Edition and the Close Reader include text-dependent questions that require students to re-enter the text and cite text evidence to support their claims.

COMMON CORE

COLLECTION 3

Nature at Work

Close Reader

Image credits: ©Franz Pritz/Picture Press/Getty Images

eBook *Explore It!*

 Video Links  eBook *Read On!* Novel list and additional selections **Visit hmhfyi.com** for current articles and informational texts. hmhfyi.com

KEY LEARNING OBJECTIVES
Identify elements of Shakespearean language.
Analyze a soliloquy.
Determine theme.
Analyze figurative language.

Compare and contrast poetic forms.
Identify features of a memoir.
Analyze author's style.
Analyze structure in an expository essay.

eBook

The eBook, both Student Edition and Teacher's Edition, is your entryway to a full complement of digital resources.

COLLECTION 4
Risk and Exploration

Focus on Argument

Through a range of informational texts—including speeches, commentaries, and essays—students analyze claims and supporting evidence.

Annotated Student Edition Table of Contents

Complex Texts

With rich themes, distinctive language, stylistic elements, and high knowledge demands, complex texts from all genres challenge students to grow as readers and thinkers.

COMMON CORE

COLLECTION **4**

Risk and Exploration

Close Reader

Image credits: ©PhotoSpin, Inc/Alamy; (bg) ©Corbis

eBook *Explore It!*

▶ Video Links **HISTORY** **A+E** | eBook *Read On!* Novel list and additional selections | **fyi** hmhfyi.com Visit **hmhfyi.com** for current articles and informational texts.

KEY LEARNING OBJECTIVES	
Analyze extended metaphor.	Analyze tone.
Analyze imagery.	Analyze cause-and-effect relationships.
Determine central ideas and details.	Trace and evaluate an argument.
Analyze sound reasoning.	

Digital Resources

From video links to additional selections and informational texts, a range of digital resources in the eBook complements and enriches students' reading.

The Stuff of Consumer Culture

Annotated Student Edition Table of Contents

Compare Texts

To enrich the analysis and discussion of each text, students compare and contrast selections, exploring elements such as authors' choices, themes, and the structure of arguments.

COMMON CORE

COLLECTION 5

The Stuff of Consumer Culture

Close Reader

KEY LEARNING OBJECTIVES
Determine theme.
Analyze elements of science fiction.
Compare and contrast poetic forms.
Make inferences.
Draw conclusions about graphic aids.
Analyze author style.
Analyze cause-and-effect organization.

eBook *Explore It!*

▶ Video Links

eBook *Read On!*
Novel list and additional selections

 Visit hmhfyi.com
for current articles and informational texts.

Image credits: ©Michael Blann/Getty Images and Guy Jarvis/Houghton Mifflin Harcourt

 HISTORY® and A&E®

Adding the images and voices that make selections and historical periods come alive, these video assets are available at point of use in the eBook.

Contemporary Selections

21st-century selections offer current perspectives on how to improve society.

Grade 7

Annotated Student Edition Table of Contents

Media Analysis
Lessons based on media provide opportunities for students to apply analysis and techniques of close reading to other kinds of texts.

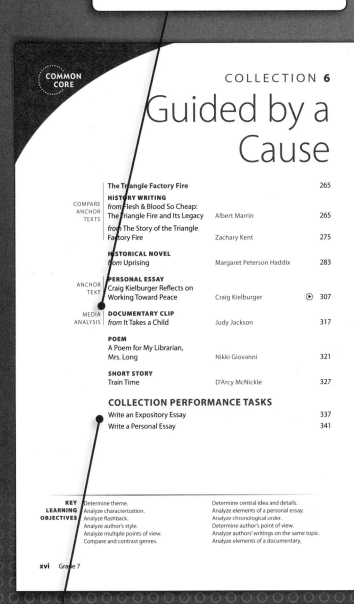

COMMON CORE

COLLECTION 6

Guided by a Cause

KEY LEARNING OBJECTIVES
Determine theme.
Analyze characterization.
Analyze flashback.
Analyze author's style.
Analyze multiple points of view.
Compare and contrast genres.

Determine central idea and details.
Analyze elements of a personal essay.
Analyze chronological order.
Determine author's point of view.
Analyze authors' writings on the same topic.
Analyze elements of a documentary.

Close Reader

Image credits: ©Mohd Shahrizan Hussin/Shutterstock

eBook *Explore It!*

⏵ Video Links | **eBook** *Read On!* Novel list and additional selections | **fyi** Visit hmhfyi.com for current articles and informational texts.

Collection Performance Tasks
Collection Performance Tasks require students to develop a variety of writing and speaking products, working through the process of planning, producing, revising, and presenting for each task.

fyi
The fyi website at hmhfyi.com provides additional contemporary informational texts to enhance each collection. Updated regularly, this site expands background knowledge, discussion, and research.

Student Resources

COMMON CORE

Information, Please

When students have questions, they can turn to Student Resources for answers. This section includes information about Performance Tasks, the nature of argument, vocabulary and spelling, and grammar, usage, and mechanics.

Word Knowledge

The Glossaries provide definitions for selection, academic, and domain-specific vocabulary, conveniently compiled in a single location.

DIGITAL OVERVIEW

Connecting to Your World

Every time you read something, view something, write to someone, or react to what you've read or seen, you're participating in a world of ideas. You do this every day, inside the classroom and out. These skills will serve you not only at home and at school, but eventually (if you can think that far ahead!), in your career.

The digital tools in this program will tap into the skills you already use and help you sharpen those skills for the future.

Start your exploration at my.hrw.com

Start with the Dashboard

Get one-stop access to the complete digital program for *Collections* as well as management and assessment tools.

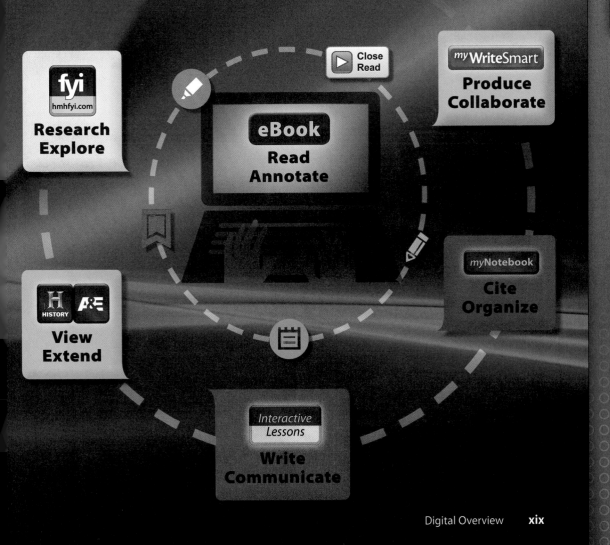

fyi hmhfyi.com
Research Explore

HISTORY | **A&E**
View Extend

Close Read

eBook Read Annotate

Interactive Lessons
Write Communicate

my **WriteSmart**
Produce Collaborate

*my*Notebook
Cite Organize

COMMON CORE

Writing and Speaking & Listening

Communication in today's world requires quite a variety of skills. To express yourself and win people over, you have to be able to write for print, for online media, and for spoken presentations. To collaborate, you have to work with people who might be sitting right next to you or at the other end of an Internet connection.

Comprehensive Standards Coverage

Twelve digital collections provide thorough coverage of all Writing and Speaking and Listening Common Core State Standards.

Available Only in Your eBook

Interactive Lessons

The interactive lessons in these collections will help you master the skills needed to become an expert communicator.

Choosing Relevant Evidence

Choose the pieces of evidence that support the reason shown and drag them into the box.

Tip ⌄

Reality stars are often placed in situations that cause them to grow or change in a positive way.

One contestant who participated in a fashion reality show remarked, "The show made me a better designer." ✓

The winner of one cooking show won a million dollars.

According to Nielsen ratings for this season, 17 of the top 50 most popular TV shows for viewers between the ages of 18-49 were reality shows.

68% of former contestants on a popular weight-loss show have maintained their goal weight for five years post-show.

You've got it! This quotation shows how one contestant experienced personal growth.

Writing Arguments

**Learn how to build
a strong argument.**

COMMON CORE **W 1, W 10**

**Interactive
Lessons**

1. Introduction
2. What Is a Claim?
3. Support: Reasons and Evidence
4. Building Effective Support
5. Creating a Coherent Argument
6. Persuasive Techniques
7. Formal Style
8. Concluding Your Argument

Student-Directed Lessons

Though primarily intended for individual student use, these interactive lessons also offer opportunities for whole-class and small-group instruction and practice.

Writing Informative Texts

**Shed light on complex ideas
and topics.**

COMMON CORE **W 2, W 10**

**Interactive
Lessons**

1. Introduction
2. Developing a Topic
3. Organizing Ideas
4. Introductions and Conclusions
5. Elaboration
6. Using Graphics and Multimedia
7. Precise Language and Vocabulary
8. Formal Style

Writing Narratives

**A good storyteller can
always capture an audience.**

COMMON CORE **W 3, W 10**

**Interactive
Lessons**

1. Introduction
2. Narrative Context
3. Point of View and Characters
4. Narrative Structure
5. Narrative Techniques
6. The Language of Narrative

DIGITAL COLLECTIONS

Writing as a Process

Get from the first twinkle of an idea to a sparkling final draft.

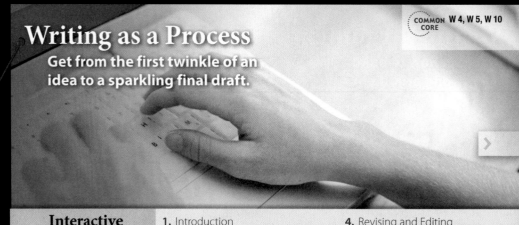

COMMON CORE W 4, W 5, W 10

Interactive Lessons

1. Introduction
2. Task, Purpose, and Audience
3. Planning and Drafting
4. Revising and Editing
5. Trying a New Approach

Teacher Support

Each collection in your teacher eBook includes

- support for English language learners and less-proficient writers
- instructional and management tips for every screen
- a rubric
- additional writing applications

Producing and Publishing with Technology

Learn how to write for an online audience.

COMMON CORE W 6

Interactive Lessons

1. Introduction
2. Writing for the Internet
3. Interacting with Your Online Audience
4. Using Technology to Collaborate

Conducting Research

There's a world of information out there. How do you find it?

COMMON CORE W 6, W 7, W 8

Interactive Lessons

1. Introduction
2. Starting Your Research
3. Types of Sources
4. Using the Library for Research
5. Conducting Field Research
6. Using the Internet for Research
7. Taking Notes
8. Refocusing Your Inquiry

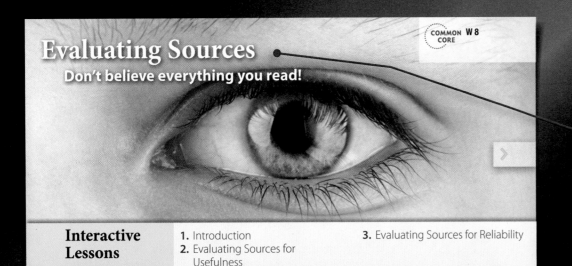

Evaluating Sources
Don't believe everything you read!

COMMON CORE **W 8**

Interactive Lessons	1. Introduction	3. Evaluating Sources for Reliability
	2. Evaluating Sources for Usefulness	

Authentic Practice of 21st-Century Skills

Students have ample opportunities to evaluate real websites, engage in digital collaboration, conduct Web research, and critique student discussions.

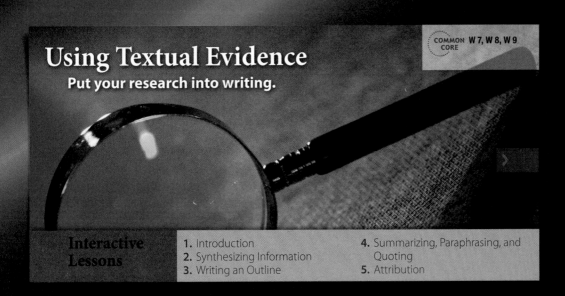

Using Textual Evidence
Put your research into writing.

COMMON CORE **W 7, W 8, W 9**

Interactive Lessons	1. Introduction	4. Summarizing, Paraphrasing, and Quoting
	2. Synthesizing Information	5. Attribution
	3. Writing an Outline	

Participating in Collaborative Discussions
There's power in putting your heads together.

COMMON CORE **SL 1**

Interactive Lessons	1. Introduction	4. Speaking Constructively
	2. Preparing for Discussion	5. Listening and Responding
	3. Establishing and Following Procedure	6. Wrapping Up Your Discussion

Analyzing and Evaluating Presentations

COMMON CORE SL 2, SL 3, SL 6

Media-makers all want your attention. What are they trying to tell you?

Interactive Lessons		
	1. Introduction	4. Tracing a Speaker's Argument
	2. Analyzing a Presentation	5. Rhetoric and Delivery
	3. Evaluating a Speaker's Reliability	6. Synthesizing Media Sources

Giving a Presentation

COMMON CORE SL 4, SL 6

Learn how to talk to a roomful of people.

Interactive Lessons		
	1. Introduction	3. The Content of Your Presentation
	2. Knowing Your Audience	4. Style in Presentation
		5. Delivering Your Presentation

Using Media in a Presentation

COMMON CORE SL 5

If a picture is worth a thousand words, just think what you can do with a video.

Interactive Lessons		
	1. Introduction	3. Using Presentation Software
	2. Types of Media: Audio, Video, and Images	4. Practicing Your Presentation

DIGITAL SPOTLIGHT

eBook | myNotebook | fyi hmhfyi.com | my WriteSmart

Supporting Close Reading, Research, and Writing

Understanding complex texts is hard work, even for experienced readers. It often takes multiple close readings to understand and write about an author's choices and meanings. The dynamic digital tools in this program will give you opportunities to learn and practice this critical skill of close reading—and help you integrate the text evidence you find into your writing.

Integrated Digital Suite

The digital resources and tools in *Collections* are designed to support students in grappling with complex text and formulating interpretations from text evidence.

Learn How to Do a Close Read

An effective close read is all about the details; you have to examine the language and ideas a writer includes. See how it's done by accessing the **Close Read Screencasts** in your eBook. Hear modeled conversations about anchor texts.

Close Read Screencasts

For each anchor text, students can access modeled conversations in which readers analyze and annotate key passages.

of the birds, how they soared and glided overhead. He pointed out the slow, graceful sweep of their wings as they beat the air steadily, without fluttering. Soon Icarus was sure that he, too, could fly and, raising his arms up and down, skirted over the white sand and even out over the waves, letting his feet touch the snowy foam as the water thundered and broke over the sharp rocks. Daedalus watched him proudly but

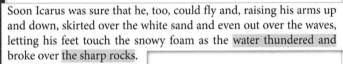

Soon Icarus was sure that he, too, could fly and, raising his arms up and down, skirted over the white sand and even out over the waves, letting his feet touch the snowy foam as the water thundered and broke over the sharp rocks.

There might be a sense of danger here.

Daedalus watched him proudly but with misgivings. He called Icarus to his side and, putting his arm round the boy's shoulders, said, 'Icarus, my son, we are about to make our flight. No human being has ever traveled through the air before, and I want you to listen carefully to my instructions.

DIGITAL
SPOTLIGHT

Annotate the Texts

Practice close reading by utilizing the powerful annotation tools in your eBook. Mark up key ideas and observations using highlighters and sticky notes.

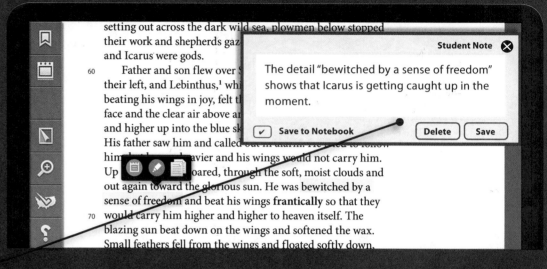

Digital Tools for Close Reading

Annotation tools allow students to note central ideas and details about an author's craft. Students can save their annotations to *my*Notebook, tagging them to particular performance tasks.

Collect Text Evidence

Save your annotations to your notebook. Gathering and organizing this text evidence will help you complete performance tasks and other writing assignments.

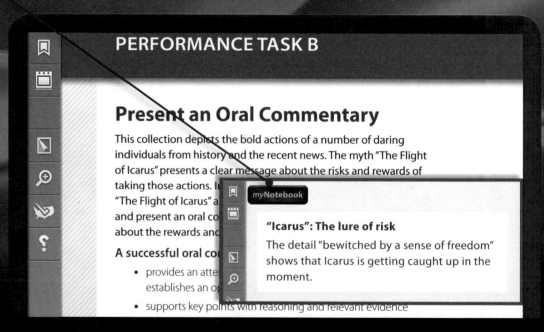

hmhfyi.com

Find More Text Evidence on the Web

Tap into the *FYI* website for links to high-interest informational texts about collection topics. Capture text evidence from any Web source by including it in your notebook.

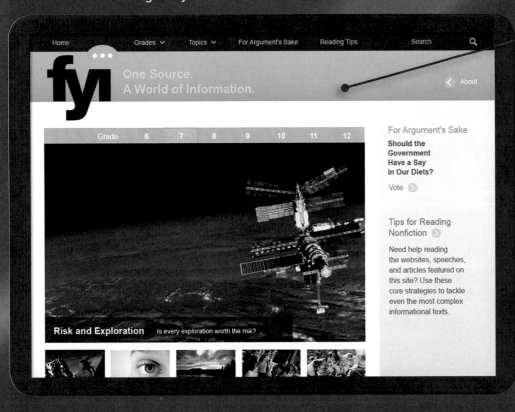

High-Interest Informational Text

Updated monthly, *FYI* features links to reputable sources of informational text.

Integrate Text Evidence into Your Writing

Use the evidence you've gathered to formulate interpretations, draw conclusions, and offer insights. Integrate the best of your text evidence into your writing.

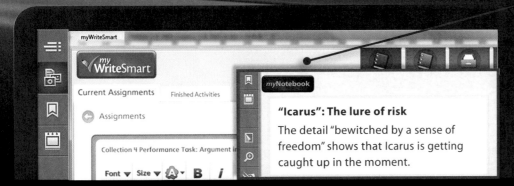

Tools for Writing

Assign and manage performance tasks in *my*WriteSmart. Students can use the annotations they've gathered and tools for writing and collaboration to complete each task.

COMMON CORE

Correlation of *Collections*, Grade 7, to the English Language Arts Common Core State Standards

The grade 7 standards on the following pages define what students should understand and be able to do by the end of the grade. They correspond to the College and Career Readiness (CCR) anchor standards below by number. The CCR and grade-specific standards are necessary complements—the former providing broad standards, the latter providing additional specificity—that together define the skills and understandings that all students must demonstrate.

College and Career Readiness Anchor Standards for Reading

Common Core State Standards

KEY IDEAS AND DETAILS

1. Read closely to determine what the text says explicitly and to make logical inferences from it; cite specific textual evidence when writing or speaking to support conclusions drawn from the text.

2. Determine central ideas or themes of a text and analyze their development; summarize the key supporting details and ideas.

3. Analyze how and why individuals, events, and ideas develop and interact over the course of a text.

CRAFT AND STRUCTURE

4. Interpret words and phrases as they are used in a text, including determining technical, connotative, and figurative meanings, and analyze how specific word choices shape meaning or tone.

5. Analyze the structure of texts, including how specific sentences, paragraphs, and larger portions of the text (e.g., a section, chapter, scene, or stanza) relate to each other and the whole.

6. Assess how point of view or purpose shapes the content and style of a text.

INTEGRATION OF KNOWLEDGE AND IDEAS

7. Integrate and evaluate content presented in diverse formats and media, including visually and quantitatively, as well as in words.

8. Delineate and evaluate the argument and specific claims in a text, including the validity of the reasoning as well as the relevance and sufficiency of the evidence.

9. Analyze how two or more texts address similar themes or topics in order to build knowledge or to compare the approaches the authors take.

RANGE OF READING AND LEVEL OF COMPLEXITY

10. Read and comprehend complex literary and informational texts independently and proficiently.

Reading Standards for Literature

Common Core State Standard	Student Edition /Teacher's Edition

KEY IDEAS AND DETAILS

1. Cite several pieces of textual evidence to support analysis of what the text says explicitly as well as inferences drawn from the text.

   Student Edition
   15, 16, 36, 73, 108, 126, 127–130, 131–134, 154, 171, 173, 174, 179–182, 214, 244, 246, 248, 256, 325, 334

   Teacher's Edition
   3, 4, 5, 6, 7, 8, 9, 10, 11, 12, 13, 14, 15, 16, 18a, 31, 32, 34, 36, 40, 42, 63, 65, 67, 69, 72, 73, 74, 95, 96, 97, 98, 99, 100, 103, 108, 112, 113, 114, 115, 116, 118, 119, 121, 124, 126, 149, 150, 151, 153, 154, 170, 172, 173, 174, 174a, 192, 213, 214, 214b, 242, 243, 244, 245, 246, 248, 249, 250, 253, 254, 256, 284, 285, 287, 288, 289, 291, 294, 296, 297, 299, 300, 302, 321, 322, 323, 325, 327, 328, 330, 331, 332, 334

2. Determine a theme or central idea of a text and analyze its development over the course of the text; provide an objective summary of the text.

   Student Edition
   35, 36, 42, 68, 69, 75, 76, 108, 126, 148, 153, 154, 214, 247, 248, 255, 256, 304, 324, 325, 333, 334

   Teacher's Edition
   31, 32, 33, 34, 35, 36, 38a, 42, 63, 64, 66, 67, 68, 69, 75, 108, 126, 149, 151, 152, 153, 154, 156a, 172, 174b, 214, 247, 248, 248a, 250, 251, 253, 254, 255, 256, 304, 321, 322, 323, 324, 325, 331, 332, 333, 334

3. Analyze how particular elements of a story or drama interact (e.g., how setting shapes the characters or plot).

   Student Edition
   15, 16, 35, 36, 68, 69, 107, 108, 125, 126, 154, 255, 256, 303, 304, 333, 334

   Teacher's Edition
   3, 4, 6, 7, 9,10, 12, 13, 14, 15, 16, 18a, 31, 33, 35, 36, 38a, 63, 64, 66, 67, 68, 69, 70a, 93, 94, 96, 97, 99, 100, 101, 103, 106, 107, 108, 110a, 113, 114, 115, 116, 117, 118, 119, 120, 121, 122, 123, 124, 125, 126, 154, 156a, 249, 250, 253, 254, 255, 256, 258a, 284, 286, 292, 296, 297, 298, 300, 302, 303, 304, 328, 329, 330, 331, 332, 333, 334, 336a, 336b

CRAFT AND STRUCTURE

4. Determine the meaning of words and phrases as they are used in a text, including figurative and connotative meanings; analyze the impact of rhymes and other repetitions of sounds (e.g., alliteration) on a specific verse or stanza of a poem or section of a story or drama.

   Student Edition
   36, 41, 42, 69, 73, 75, 76, 107, 108, 147, 148, 153, 154, 171, 173, 174, 179–182, 214, 244, 246, 247, 248, 256, 324, 325

   Teacher's Edition
   6, 36, 40, 41, 42, 42a, 45, 65, 69, 72, 73, 74, 75, 76, 76a, 95, 97, 98, 103, 105, 107, 108, 148a, 150, 151, 152, 153, 154, 170, 173, 174, 174a, 174b, 195, 197, 213, 214, 214a, 242, 243, 244, 246, 247, 248, 249, 256, 289, 299, 321, 322, 323, 324, 325, 326a, 327, 332

Common Core State Standard	Student Edition /Teacher's Edition
5. Analyze how a drama's or poem's form or structure (e.g., soliloquy, sonnet) contributes to its meaning.	**Student Edition** 41, 42, 73, 75, 76, 108, 125, 126, 147, 148, 171, 173, 174, 179–182, 244, 246, 247, 248, 324, 325 **Teacher's Edition** 40, 41, 42, 42a, 72, 73, 74, 75, 76, 76a, 108, 111, 112, 113, 114, 115, 116, 117, 118, 119, 121, 122, 124, 125, 126, 126b, 148a, 170, 171, 172, 173, 175, 214b, 242, 243, 244, 245, 246, 247, 248, 321, 323, 324, 325, 326a
6. Analyze how an author develops and contrasts the points of view of different characters or narrators in a text.	**Student Edition** 154, 303, 304, 334 **Teacher's Edition** 154, 156a, 172, 174, 174a, 283, 287, 290, 291, 292, 295, 298, 303, 304, 306a, 334

INTEGRATION OF KNOWLEDGE AND IDEAS

Common Core State Standard	Student Edition /Teacher's Edition
7. Compare and contrast a written story, drama, or poem to its audio, filmed, staged, or multimedia version, analyzing the effects of techniques unique to each medium (e.g., lighting, sound, color, or camera focus and angles in a film).	**Student Edition** 126 **Teacher's Edition** 126, 126a
8. (Not applicable to literature)	
9. Compare and contrast a fictional portrayal of a time, place, or character and a historical account of the same period as a means of understanding how authors of fiction use or alter history.	**Student Edition** 303, 304 **Teacher's Edition** 284, 285, 288, 289, 290, 294, 296, 297, 300, 301, 303, 304, 306a

RANGE OF READING AND LEVEL OF TEXT COMPLEXITY

Common Core State Standard	Student Edition /Teacher's Edition
10. By the end of the year, read and comprehend literature, including stories, dramas, and poems, in the grades 6–8 text complexity band proficiently, with scaffolding as needed at the high end of the range.	**Student Edition** 3–16, 93–108, 111–126, 169–174, 241–248, 249–256 **Teacher's Edition** 3A, 3–16, 63A, 69, 93A, 93–108, 111A, 111–126, 169A, 169–174, 241A, 241–248, 249A, 249–256

Reading Standards for Informational Text

Common Core State Standard	Student Edition /Teacher's Edition

KEY IDEAS AND DETAILS

1. Cite several pieces of textual evidence to support analysis of what the text says explicitly as well as inferences drawn from the text.

Student Edition
49, 50, 142, 166, 190, 198, 210, 229, 230, 237, 238, 274, 278, 280, 314

Teacher's Edition
20, 21, 22, 24, 26, 27, 43, 44, 45, 46, 47, 48, 49, 50, 77, 78, 81, 137, 138, 139, 142, 148, 157, 159, 161, 162, 163, 166, 185, 186, 187, 188, 190, 194, 195, 196, 198, 203, 204, 207, 208, 210, 221, 222, 223, 224, 225, 226, 227, 228, 229, 230, 231a, 233, 234, 236, 237, 238, 240a, 266, 267, 272, 273, 274, 275, 276, 278, 280, 307, 308, 309, 312, 314, R16, R23

2. Determine two or more central ideas in a text and analyze their development over the course of the text; provide an objective summary of the text.

Student Edition
23, 27, 29, 30, 85, 86, 142, 165, 166, 198, 209, 210, 229, 230, 238, 274, 278, 280, 314, R16–R22, R23–R29

Teacher's Edition
20, 21, 22, 23, 24, 25, 26, 27,29, 30, 52a, 79, 80, 82, 83, 84, 85, 86, 142, 146, 148, 163, 165, 166, 192, 198, 202, 205, 206, 209, 210, 222, 223, 226, 227, 229, 230, 231a, 235, 238, 240a, 266, 267, 268, 269, 270, 271, 272, 274, 278,280, 310, 314, 316a, R16, R18, R19, R21, R22, R23

3. Analyze the interactions between individuals, events, and ideas in a text (e.g., how ideas influence individuals or events, or how individuals influence ideas or events).

Student Edition
30, 50, 141, 142, 165, 166, 209, 210, 279, 280, 313, 314, R16–R22

Teacher's Edition
30, 50, 137, 138, 140, 141, 142, 144a, 157, 159, 160, 161, 162, 163, 164, 165, 166, 168a, 202, 203, 204, 205, 206, 208, 209, 210, 212a, 223, 224, 225, 226, 227, 228, 229, 230, 231a, 238, 278, 279, 280, 308, 311, 313, 314, 316a, R16, R18, R19, R21, R22, R23

CRAFT AND STRUCTURE

4. Determine the meaning of words and phrases as they are used in a text, including figurative, connotative, and technical meanings; analyze the impact of a specific word choice on meaning and tone.

Student Edition
85, 86, 141, 142, 166, 190, 197, 198, 237, 238, R23–R29

Teacher's Edition
45, 77, 78, 81, 83, 85, 86, 137, 139, 141, 142, 144a, 146, 147, 148, 157, 162, 166, 190, 196, 197, 198, 200a, 206, 225, 231, 233, 235, 236, 237, 238, 240a, 242, 312, R16, R23

CORRELATION

Common Core State Standard	Student Edition /Teacher's Edition
5. Analyze the structure an author uses to organize a text, including how the major sections contribute to the whole and to the development of the ideas.	**Student Edition** 23, 27, 29, 30, 85, 86, 165, 166, 189, 190, 197, 198, 209, 210, 229, 230, 238, 278, 313, 314, R16–R22, R23–R29 **Teacher's Edition** 20, 21, 22, 23, 24, 25, 26, 27, 29, 30, 77, 78, 81, 83, 85, 86, 88a, 145, 147, 148, 157, 158, 159, 160, 161, 162, 163, 164, 165, 166, 168a, 186, 187, 188, 189, 190, 192a, 193, 197, 198, 201, 203, 204, 207, 208, 209, 210, 212a, 221, 223, 224, 225, 226, 229, 230, 238, 240a, 271, 275, 276, 277, 278, 282a, 307, 308, 310, 311, 313, 315, 315a, R16–R22, R23, R26
6. Determine an author's point of view or purpose in a text and analyze how the author distinguishes his or her position from that of others.	**Student Edition** 30, 49, 50, 166, 210, 274, 279, 280, 313, 314, 320, R23–R29 **Teacher's Edition** 30, 30a, 43, 44, 47, 48, 49, 50, 52a, 166, 185, 198, 210, 266, 267, 268, 269, 272, 274, 275, 276, 279, 280, 282a, 308, 309, 312, 313, 314, 320, R23

INTEGRATION OF KNOWLEDGE AND IDEAS

7. Compare and contrast a text to an audio, video, or multimedia version of the text, analyzing each medium's portrayal of the subject (e.g., how the delivery of a speech affects the impact of the words).	**Student Edition** 190, 320 **Teacher's Edition** 190, 192a, 320
8. Trace and evaluate the argument and specific claims in a text, assessing whether the reasoning is sound and the evidence is relevant and sufficient to support the claims.	**Student Edition** 27, 30, 189, 190, 197, 198, 238, 314, R23–R29 **Teacher's Edition** 24, 25, 26, 27, 30, 186, 187, 188, 189, 190, 192a, 193, 194, 195, 196, 197, 198, 238, 316a, R23, R24, R26, R28, R29
9. Analyze how two or more authors writing about the same topic shape their presentations of key information by emphasizing different evidence or advancing different interpretations of facts.	**Student Edition** 30, 279, 280 **Teacher's Edition** 30, 30a, 279, 280, 282a

RANGE OF READING AND LEVEL OF TEXT COMPLEXITY

10. By the end of the year, read and comprehend literary nonfiction in the grades 6–8 text complexity band proficiently, with scaffolding as needed at the high end of the range.	**Student Edition** 43–50, 157–166, 275–280, 307–314 **Teacher's Edition** 43A, 43–50, 157A, 157–166, 265A, 275–280, 307A, 307–314, R16, R23

College and Career Readiness Anchor Standards for Writing

Common Core State Standards

TEXT TYPES AND PURPOSES

1. Write arguments to support claims in an analysis of substantive topics or texts, using valid reasoning and relevant and sufficient evidence.

2. Write informative/explanatory texts to examine and convey complex ideas and information clearly and accurately through the effective selection, organization, and analysis of content.

3. Write narratives to develop real or imagined experiences or events using effective technique, well-chosen details, and well-structured event sequences.

PRODUCTION AND DISTRIBUTION OF WRITING

4. Produce clear and coherent writing in which the development, organization, and style are appropriate to task, purpose, and audience.

5. Develop and strengthen writing as needed by planning, revising, editing, rewriting, or trying a new approach.

6. Use technology, including the Internet, to produce and publish writing and to interact and collaborate with others.

RESEARCH TO BUILD AND PRESENT KNOWLEDGE

7. Conduct short as well as more sustained research projects based on focused questions, demonstrating understanding of the subject under investigation.

8. Gather relevant information from multiple print and digital sources, assess the credibility and accuracy of each source, and integrate the information while avoiding plagiarism.

9. Draw evidence from literary or informational texts to support analysis, reflection, and research.

RANGE OF WRITING

10. Write routinely over extended time frames (time for research, reflection, and revision) and shorter time frames (a single sitting or a day or two) for a range of tasks, purposes, and audiences.

Writing Standards

Common Core State Standard	Student Edition /Teacher's Edition	Digital Collection/Lesson
TEXT TYPES AND PURPOSES		
1. Write arguments to support claims with clear reasons and relevant evidence.	**Student Edition** 57–60, 127–130, 154, 210, 215–218, 314, 334, R2–R3 **Teacher's Edition** 30, 57–60, 127–130, 210, 215–218, 280, 334, R2	**Writing Arguments** • Introduction • What Is a Claim? • Support: Reasons and Evidence • Building Effective Support • Creating a Coherent Argument • Persuasive Techniques • Formal Style • Concluding Your Argument

Common Core State Standard	Student Edition /Teacher's Edition	Digital Collection/Lesson
a. Introduce claim(s), acknowledge alternate or opposing claims, and organize the reasons and evidence logically.	**Student Edition** 57–60, 127–130, 215–218, R2–R3 **Teacher's Edition** 57–60, 127–130, 215–218, R2	**Writing Arguments** • What Is a Claim? • Creating a Coherent Argument
b. Support claim(s) with logical reasoning and relevant evidence, using accurate, credible sources and demonstrating an understanding of the topic or text.	**Student Edition** 57–60, 127–130, 215–218, R2–R3 **Teacher's Edition** 57–60, 127–130, 215–218, R2	**Writing Arguments** • Support: Reasons and Evidence • Building Effective Support
c. Use words, phrases, and clauses to create cohesion and clarify the relationships among claim(s), reasons, and evidence.	**Student Edition** 57–60, 127–130, 215–218, R2–R3 **Teacher's Edition** 57–60, 127–130, 215–218, R2	**Writing Arguments** • Creating a Coherent Argument
d. Establish and maintain a formal style.	**Student Edition** 57–60, 127–130, 215–218, R2–R3 **Teacher's Edition** 57–60, 127–130, 215–218, R2	**Writing Arguments** • Formal Style
e. Provide a concluding statement or section that follows from and supports the argument presented.	**Student Edition** 57–60, 127–130, 215–218, R2–R3 **Teacher's Edition** 57–60, 127–130, 215–218, R2	**Writing Arguments** • Concluding Your Argument
2. Write informative/explanatory texts to examine a topic and convey ideas, concepts, and information through the selection, organization, and analysis of relevant content.	**Student Edition** 42, 50, 126, 131–134, 179–182, 190, 214, 230, 248, 259–262, 280, 337–340, 341–344, R4–R5 **Teacher's Edition** 50, 131–134, 179–182, 190, 214, 230, 248, 259–262, 337–340, 341–344, R4	**Writing Informative Texts** • Introduction • Developing a Topic • Organizing Ideas • Introductions and Conclusions • Elaboration • Using Graphics and Multimedia • Precise Language and Vocabulary • Formal Style **Using Textual Evidence** • Writing an Outline

Common Core State Standard	Student Edition /Teacher's Edition	Digital Collection/Lesson
a. Introduce a topic clearly, previewing what is to follow; organize ideas, concepts, and information, using strategies such as definition, classification, comparison/contrast, and cause/effect; include formatting (e.g., headings), graphics (e.g., charts, tables), and multimedia when useful to aiding comprehension.	**Student Edition** 131–134, 179–182, 259–262, 337–340, 341–344, R4–R5 **Teacher's Edition** 131–134, 179–182, 259–262, 337–340, 341–344, R4	**Writing Informative Texts** • Developing a Topic • Organizing Ideas • Introductions and Conclusions • Using Graphics and Multimedia
b. Develop the topic with relevant facts, definitions, concrete details, quotations, or other information and examples.	**Student Edition** 131–134, 179–182, 259–262, 337–340, 341–344, R4–R5 **Teacher's Edition** 131–134, 179–182, 259–262, 337–340, 341–344, R4	**Writing Informative Texts** • Elaboration
c. Use appropriate transitions to create cohesion and clarify the relationships among ideas and concepts.	**Student Edition** 131–134, 179–182, 259–262, 337–340, 341–344, R4–R5 **Teacher's Edition** 131–134, 179–182, 259–262, 337–340, 341–344, R4	**Writing Informative Texts** • Organizing Ideas
d. Use precise language and domain-specific vocabulary to inform about or explain the topic.	**Student Edition** 131–134, 179–182, 259–262, 337–340, 341–344, R4–R5 **Teacher's Edition** 131–134, 179–182, 259–262, 337–340, 341–344, R4	**Writing Informative Texts** • Precise Language and Vocabulary
e. Establish and maintain a formal style.	**Student Edition** 131–134, 179–182, 259–262, 337–340, 341–344, R4–R5 **Teacher's Edition** 131–134, 179–182, 259–262, 337–340, 341–344, R4	**Writing Informative Texts** • Formal Style
f. Provide a concluding statement or section that follows from and supports the information or explanation presented.	**Student Edition** 131–134, 179–182, 259–262, 337–340, 341–344, R4–R5 **Teacher's Edition** 131–134, 179–182, 259–262, 337–340, 341–344, R4	**Writing Informative Texts** • Introductions and Conclusions

Common Core State Standard	Student Edition /Teacher's Edition	Digital Collection/Lesson
3. Write narratives to develop real or imagined experiences or events using effective technique, relevant descriptive details, and well-structured event sequences.	**Student Edition** 16, 36, 53–56, 174, 175–178, 256, 304, 325, R6–R7 **Teacher's Edition** 16, 36, 53–56, 175–178, 256, 304, 325, R6	**Writing Narratives** • Introductions • Narrative Context • Point of View and Characters • Narrative Structure • Narrative Techniques • The Language of Narrative
a. Engage and orient the reader by establishing a context and point of view and introducing a narrator and/or characters; organize an event sequence that unfolds naturally and logically.	**Student Edition** 53–56, 175–178, R6–R7 **Teacher's Edition** 53–56, 175–178, R6	**Writing Narratives** • Narrative Context • Point of View and Characters • Narrative Structure
b. Use narrative techniques, such as dialogue, pacing, and description, to develop experiences, events, and/or characters.	**Student Edition** 53–56, 175–178, R6–R7 **Teacher's Edition** 53–56, 175–178, R6	**Writing Narratives** • Narrative Techniques • The Language of Narrative
c. Use a variety of transition words, phrases, and clauses to convey sequence and signal shifts from one time frame or setting to another.	**Student Edition** 53–56, 175–178, R6–R7 **Teacher's Edition** 53–56, 175–178, R6	**Writing Narratives** • Narrative Structure
d. Use precise words and phrases, relevant descriptive details, and sensory language to capture the action and convey experiences and events.	**Student Edition** 53–56, 175–178, R6–R7 **Teacher's Edition** 53–56, 175–178, R6	**Writing Narratives** • The Language of Narrative
e. Provide a conclusion that follows from and reflects on the narrated experiences or events.	**Student Edition** 53–56, 175–178, R6–R7 **Teacher's Edition** 53–56, 175–178, R6	**Writing Narratives** • Narrative Structure

Common Core State Standard	Student Edition /Teacher's Edition	Digital Collection/Lesson

PRODUCTION AND DISTRIBUTION OF WRITING

4. Produce clear and coherent writing in which the development, organization, and style are appropriate to task, purpose, and audience. (Grade-specific expectations for writing types are defined in standards 1–3 above.)

Student Edition
53–56, 57–60, 126, 127–130, 131–134, 154, 175–178, 179–182, 210, 215–218, 248, 256, 259–262, 304, 314, 325, 334, 337–340, 341–344, R2–R3, R4–R5, R6–R7

Teacher's Edition
30, 30a, 53–56, 57–60, 126, 127–130, 131–134, 154, 175–178, 179–182, 210, 248, 256, 259–262, 304, 320, 325, 334, 337–340, 341–344, R2, R4, R6

Writing as a Process
• Task, Purpose, and Audience

5. With some guidance and support from peers and adults, develop and strengthen writing as needed by planning, revising, editing, rewriting, or trying a new approach, focusing on how well purpose and audience have been addressed. (Editing for conventions should demonstrate command of Language standards 1–3 up to and including grade 7.)

Student Edition
53–56, 57–60, 127–130, 131–134, 175–178, 179–182, 215–218, 259–262, 304, 337–340, 341–344

Teacher's Edition
53–56, 57–60, 127–130, 131–134, 175–178, 179–182, 215–218, 259–262, 304, 337–340, 341–344

Writing as a Process
• Introduction
• Task, Purpose, and Audience
• Planning and Drafting
• Revising and Editing
• Trying a New Approach

6. Use technology, including the Internet, to produce and publish writing and link to and cite sources as well as to interact and collaborate with others, including linking to and citing sources.

Student Edition
30, 50, 92, 259–262, 337–340, 341–344

Teacher's Edition
30, 30a, 92, 259–262, 337–340, 341–344

Producing and Publishing with Technology
• Introduction
• Writing for the Internet
• Interacting with Your Online Audience
• Using Technology to Collaborate

RESEARCH TO BUILD AND PRESENT KNOWLEDGE

7. Conduct short research projects to answer a question, drawing on several sources and generating additional related, focused questions for further research and investigation.

Student Edition
36, 69, 86, 166, 190, 198, 215–218, 259–262, 337–340, R8–R9

Teacher's Edition
36, 42, 86, 88a, 166, 190, 198, 215–218, 230, 259–262, 337–340, R8

Conducting Research
• Introduction
• Starting Your Research
• Types of Sources
• Using the Library for Research
• Conducting Field Research
• Using the Internet for Research
• Refocusing Your Inquiry
Using Textual Evidence
• Synthesizing Information

Common Core State Standard	Student Edition /Teacher's Edition	Digital Collection/Lesson
8. Gather relevant information from multiple print and digital sources, using search terms effectively; assess the credibility and accuracy of each source; and quote or paraphrase the data and conclusions of others while avoiding plagiarism and following a standard format for citation.	**Student Edition** 57–60, 131–134, 190, 198, 210, 215–218, 259–262, 337–340, R8–R11 **Teacher's Edition** 42, 52a, 57–60, 88a, 131–134, 190, 198, 210, 215–218, 230, 259–262, 280, 337–340, R8	**Conducting Research** • Types of Sources • Using the Library for Research • Using the Internet for Research **Evaluating Sources** • Introduction • Evaluating Sources for Usefulness • Evaluating Sources for Reliability **Using Textual Evidence** • Summarizing, Paraphrasing, and Quoting • Attribution
9. Draw evidence from literary or informational texts to support analysis, reflection, and research.	**Student Edition** 57–60, 69, 108, 126, 127–130, 142, 179–182, 214, 304, 314, 334 **Teacher's Edition** 57–60, 108, 126, 127–130, 179–182, 214, 305, 334	**Writing Informative Texts** • Elaboration **Conducting Research** • Taking Notes **Using Textual Evidence** • Introduction • Synthesizing Information • Summarizing, Paraphrasing, and Quoting
a. Apply *grade 7 Reading standards* to literature (e.g., "Compare and contrast a fictional portrayal of a time, place, or character and a historical account of the same period as a means of understanding how authors of fiction use or alter history").	**Student Edition** 108, 126, 214, 334 **Teacher's Edition** 108, 126, 214, 334	
b. Apply *grade 7 Reading standards* to literary nonfiction (e.g., "Trace and evaluate the argument and specific claims in a text, assessing whether the reasoning is sound and the evidence is relevant and sufficient to support the claims").	**Student Edition** 142, 154, 210, 314 **Teacher's Edition** 142, 154, 210, 314	

RANGE OF WRITING

Common Core State Standard	Student Edition /Teacher's Edition	Digital Collection/Lesson
10. Write routinely over extended time frames (time for research, reflection, and revision) and shorter time frames (a single sitting or a day or two) for a range of discipline-specific tasks, purposes, and audiences.	**Student Edition** 50, 53–56, 57–60, 126, 127–130, 131–134, 154, 174, 175–178, 179–182, 210, 215, 248, 256, 259–262, 304, 314, 325, 334, 337–340, 341–344 **Teacher's Edition** 50, 53–56, 57–60, 126, 127–130, 131–134, 154, 174, 175–178, 179–182, 210, 215, 248, 249A, 256, 259–262, 304, 305, 314, 325, 334, 337–340, 341–344	**Writing as a Process** • Task, Purpose, and Audience **Writing Arguments** **Writing Informative Texts** **Writing Narratives** **Using Textual Evidence**

College and Career Readiness Anchor Standards for Speaking and Listening

Common Core State Standards

COMPREHENSION AND COLLABORATION

1. Prepare for and participate effectively in a range of conversations and collaborations with diverse partners, building on others' ideas and expressing their own clearly and persuasively.

2. Integrate and evaluate information presented in diverse media and formats, including visually, quantitatively, and orally.

3. Evaluate a speaker's point of view, reasoning, and use of evidence and rhetoric.

PRESENTATION OF KNOWLEDGE AND IDEAS

4. Present information, findings, and supporting evidence such that listeners can follow the line of reasoning and that the organization, development, and style are appropriate to task, purpose, and audience.

5. Make strategic use of digital media and visual displays of data to express information and enhance understanding of presentations.

6. Adapt speech to a variety of contexts and communicative tasks, demonstrating command of formal English when indicated or appropriate.

Speaking and Listening Standards

Common Core State Standard	Student Edition/Teacher's Edition	Digital Collection/Lesson
COMPREHENSION AND COLLABORATION		
1. Engage effectively in a range of collaborative discussions (one on one, in groups, and teacher led) with diverse partners on *grade 7 topics, texts, and issues*, building on others' ideas and expressing their own clearly.	**Student Edition** 76, 148, 198, 238, R12–R13 **Teacher's Edition** 42a, 76, 148, 174b, 192a, 198, 200a, 238, R12	**Participating in Collaborative Discussions** • Introduction • Preparing for Discussion • Establishing and Following Procedure • Speaking Constructively • Listening and Responding • Wrapping Up Your Discussion
a. Come to discussions prepared, having read or researched material under study; explicitly draw on that preparation by referring to evidence on the topic, text, or issue to probe and reflect on ideas under discussion.	**Student Edition** 198, 238, R12–R13 **Teacher's Edition** 76, 198, 200a, R12	**Participating in Collaborative Discussions** • Preparing for Discussion
b. Follow rules for collegial discussions, track progress toward specific goals and deadlines, and define individual roles as needed.	**Student Edition** 198, 238, R12–R13 **Teacher's Edition** 76, 198, 200a, R12	**Participating in Collaborative Discussions** • Establishing and Following Procedure
c. Pose questions that elicit elaboration and respond to others' questions and comments with relevant observations and ideas that bring the discussion back on topic as needed.	**Student Edition** 198, 238, R12–R13 **Teacher's Edition** 76, 198, 200a, R12	**Participating in Collaborative Discussions** • Speaking Constructively • Listening and Responding

Common Core State Standard	Student Edition/Teacher's Edition	Digital Collection/Lesson
d. Acknowledge new information expressed by others and, when warranted, modify their own views.	**Student Edition** 198, 238, R12–R13 **Teacher's Edition** 76, 198, 200a, R12	**Participating in Collaborative Discussions** • Wrapping Up Your Discussion
2. Analyze the main ideas and supporting details presented in diverse media and formats (e.g., visually, quantitatively, orally) and explain how the ideas clarify a topic, text, or issue under study.	**Student Edition** 23, 29, 30, 92,126, 319, 320 **Teacher's Edition** 20, 21, 22, 25, 29, 30, 90, 91, 92, 92a, 126, 319, 320, 320a	**Analyzing and Evaluating Presentations** • Introduction • Analyzing a Presentation
3. Delineate a speaker's argument and specific claims, evaluating the soundness of the reasoning and the relevance and sufficiency of the evidence.	**Student Edition** 190, 320, R14–R15 **Teacher's Edition** 190, 192a, 200, 320, R14	**Analyzing and Evaluating Presentations** • Identifying a Speaker's Claim • Tracing a Speaker's Argument

PRESENTATION OF KNOWLEDGE AND IDEAS

Common Core State Standard	Student Edition/Teacher's Edition	Digital Collection/Lesson
4. Present claims and findings, emphasizing salient points in a focused, coherent manner with pertinent descriptions, facts, details, and examples; use appropriate eye contact, adequate volume, and clear pronunciation.	**Student Edition** 16, 42, 57–60, 86, 166, 198, 215–218, 259–262, 280, 320, R14–R15 **Teacher's Edition** 16,42, 57–60, 76, 86, 154, 166, 198, 200a, 215–218, 259–262, 280, R14	**Giving a Presentation** • Introduction • The Content of Your Presentation • Style in Presentation • Delivering Your Presentation
5. Include multimedia components and visual displays in presentations to clarify claims and findings and emphasize salient points.	**Student Edition** 57–60, 92, 215–218, 259–262, 320 **Teacher's Edition** 57–60, 92, 215–218, 259–262	**Using Media in a Presentation** • Introduction • Types of Media: Audio, Video, and Images • Using Presentation Software • Building and Practicing Your Presentation
6. Adapt speech to a variety of contexts and tasks, demonstrating command of formal English when indicated or appropriate. (See grade 7 Language standards 1 and 3 for specific expectations.)	**Student Edition** 57–60, 148, 215–218, 259–262, 280 **Teacher's Edition** 57–60, 69, 70a, 76, 148, 215–218, 259–262, 280	**Participating in Collaborative Discussions** • Speaking Constructively **Giving a Presentation** • Style in Presentation

College and Career Readiness Anchor Standards for Language

Common Core State Standards

CONVENTIONS OF STANDARD ENGLISH

1. Demonstrate command of the conventions of standard English grammar and usage when writing or speaking.

2. Demonstrate command of the conventions of standard English capitalization, punctuation, and spelling when writing.

KNOWLEDGE OF LANGUAGE

3. Apply knowledge of language to understand how language functions in different contexts, to make effective choices for meaning or style, and to comprehend more fully when reading or listening.

VOCABULARY ACQUISITION AND USE

4. Determine or clarify the meaning of unknown and multiple-meaning words and phrases by using context clues, analyzing meaningful word parts, and consulting general and specialized reference materials, as appropriate.

5. Demonstrate understanding of word relationships and nuances in word meanings.

6. Acquire and use accurately a range of general academic and domain-specific words and phrases sufficient for reading, writing, speaking, and listening at the college and career readiness level; demonstrate independence in gathering vocabulary knowledge when considering a word or phrase important to comprehension or expression.

Language Standards

Common Core State Standard	Student Edition/Teacher's Edition
CONVENTIONS OF STANDARD ENGLISH	
1. Demonstrate command of the conventions of standard English grammar and usage when writing or speaking.	**Student Edition** 18, 38, 52, 88, 156, 168, 200, 212, 240, 306, 316, 326, 336, R30–R54 **Teacher's Edition** 52, 88, 156, 168, 200, 212, 240, 306, 316, 326, 336, R30, R38, R40
a. Explain the function of phrases and clauses in general and their function in specific sentences.	**Student Edition** 18, 52, 88, 168, 200, 212, 240, 306, 326, R30, R47–R50 **Teacher's Edition** 52, 88, 168, 200, 212, 240, 306, 326, R38, R40, R50
b. Choose among simple, compound, complex, and compound-complex sentences to signal differing relationships among ideas.	**Student Edition** 18, 156, R30, R32, R44–R45, R46, R50–R51 **Teacher's Edition** 156, R30
c. Place phrases and clauses within a sentence, recognizing and correcting misplaced and dangling modifiers.*	**Student Edition** 316, 326, 336, R30, R44–R45, R47–R50 **Teacher's Edition** 316, 326, 336, R30, R46

Common Core State Standard	Student Edition/Teacher's Edition
2. Demonstrate command of the conventions of standard English capitalization, punctuation, and spelling when writing.	**Student Edition** 38, 110, 192, 258, 282, R30, R33–R36, R60–R63 **Teacher's Edition** 38, 110, 258, 282, R30
a. Use a comma to separate coordinate adjectives (e.g., *It was a fascinating, enjoyable movie* but not *He wore an old[,] green shirt*).	**Student Edition** 38, R30 **Teacher's Edition** 38, R30
b. Spell correctly.	**Student Edition** 110, 258, R30, R55, R60–R63 **Teacher's Edition** 110, 258, R30, R55

KNOWLEDGE OF LANGUAGE

Common Core State Standard	Student Edition/Teacher's Edition
3. Use knowledge of language and its conventions when writing, speaking, reading, or listening.	**Student Edition** 57–60, 144, 192, 232, R30 **Teacher's Edition** 57–60, 144, 232, R30
a. Choose language that expresses ideas precisely and concisely, recognizing and eliminating wordiness and redundancy.*	**Student Edition** 144, 232 **Teacher's Edition** 144, 232

VOCABULARY ACQUISITION AND USE

Common Core State Standard	Student Edition/Teacher's Edition
4. Determine or clarify the meaning of unknown and multiple-meaning words and phrases based on *grade 7 reading and content,* choosing flexibly from a range of strategies.	**Student Edition** 17, 37, 51, 70, 87, 109, 155, 167, 191, 199, 211, 239, 257, 281, 315, 335, R55, R57, R59 **Teacher's Edition** 17, 37, 51, 70, 78, 81, 87, 109, 117,155, 167, 191, 199, 206, 211, 212a, 231, 239, 257, 281, 315, 335, R55
a. Use context (e.g., the overall meaning of a sentence or paragraph; a word's position or function in a sentence) as a clue to the meaning of a word or phrase.	**Student Edition** 17, 51, 87, 191, R55–R56 **Teacher's Edition** 17, 51, 78, 81, 87, 109, 117, 191, 206, 212a, 231, 315, R55
b. Use common, grade-appropriate Greek or Latin affixes and roots as clues to the meaning of a word (e.g., *belligerent, bellicose, rebel*).	**Student Edition** 17, 37, 70, 87, 167, 199, 211, 281, R55, R56–R57 **Teacher's Edition** 17, 37, 70, 87, 109, 167, 199, 211, 281, R55

Common Core State Standard	Student Edition/Teacher's Edition
c. Consult general and specialized reference materials (e.g., dictionaries, glossaries, thesauruses), both print and digital, to find the pronunciation of a word or determine or clarify its precise meaning or its part of speech.	**Student Edition** 17, 87, 109, 155, 191, 211, 315, 335, R55, R59–R60 **Teacher's Edition** 87, 109, 117, 155, 191, 211, 212a, 315, 335, R55
d. Verify the preliminary determination of the meaning of a word or phrase (e.g., by checking the inferred meaning in context or in a dictionary).	**Student Edition** 70, 191, 239, 257, R55, R59–R60 **Teacher's Edition** 70, 191, 212a, 239, 257, 281, 315, R55
5. Demonstrate understanding of figurative language, word relationships, and nuances in word meanings.	**Student Edition** 51, 143, 239, 305, R55–R59 **Teacher's Edition** 51, 109, 143, 239, 289, 299, 305, R55
a. Interpret figures of speech (e.g., literary, biblical, and mythological allusions) in context.	**Student Edition** 143, R55 **Teacher's Edition** 143, R55
b. Use the relationship between particular words (e.g., synonym/antonym, analogy) to better understand each of the words.	**Student Edition** 239, 305, R55, R58–R59 **Teacher's Edition** 109, 203, 239, R55
c. Distinguish among the connotations (associations) of words with similar denotations (definitions) (e.g., *refined, respectful, polite, diplomatic, condescending*).	**Student Edition** 51, R55, R58 **Teacher's Edition** 51, R55
6. Acquire and use accurately grade-appropriate general academic and domain-specific words and phrases; gather vocabulary knowledge when considering a word or phrase important to comprehension or expression.	**Student Edition** 2, 53, 57, 62, 109, 127, 136, 167, 175, 179, 184, 199, 211, 215, 220, 231, 239, 257, 259, 264, 315, 335, 337, 341, R55, R55–R63 **Teacher's Edition** 2, 53, 57, 62, 109, 127, 136, 167, 175, 179, 184, 199, 211, 215, 220, 231, 239, 257, 259, 264, 315, 335, 337, 341, R55–R63

Complex Text:
What It Is and What It Isn't . . . or Don't Let a Good Poem Get You Down

By Carol Jago

Do you sometimes think that what your teacher asks you to read is too hard? Let me tell you a secret. Those poems and passages can be tough for your teacher as well. Just because a text isn't easy doesn't mean there is something wrong with it or something wrong with the reader. It means you need to do more than skim across the words on the page. Reading complex text takes effort and focused attention. Do you sometimes wish writers would just say what they have to say simply? I assure you that writers don't use long sentences and unfamiliar words to annoy their readers or make readers feel dumb. They employ complex syntax and rich language in order to express complex ideas.

Excellent literature and nonfiction—the kind you will be reading over the course of the year—challenges readers in various ways. Sometimes the background of a story or the content of an essay is so unfamiliar that it is difficult to understand why characters are behaving as they do or to follow the argument a writer is making. By persevering, reading like a detective, and following clues in the text, you will find that your store of background knowledge grows. As a result, the next time you read about this subject, the text won't seem nearly as hard. The more you read, the better a reader you will become.

Good readers aren't put off by challenging text. When the going gets rough, they know what to do. Let's take vocabulary, a common measure of text complexity, as an example. Learning new words is the business of a lifetime. Rather than shutting down when you meet a word you don't know, take a moment to think about the word. Is any part of the word familiar to you? Is there something in the context of the sentence or paragraph that can help you figure out its meaning? Is there someone or something that can provide you with a definition? When reading literature or nonfiction from a time period other than our own, the text is often full of words we don't know. Each time you meet those words in succeeding readings you will be adding to your understanding of the word and its use. Your brain is a natural word-learning machine. The more you feed it complex text, the larger a vocabulary you'll have.

Have you ever been reading a long, complicated sentence and discovered that by the time you reached the end you had forgotten the beginning? Unlike the sentences we speak or dash off in a note to a friend, complex text is often full of sentences that are not only lengthy but also constructed in intricate ways. Such sentences require readers to slow down and figure out how phrases relate to one another as well as who is doing what to whom. Remember, rereading isn't cheating. It is exactly what experienced readers know to do when they meet dense text on the page. On the pages that follow you will find stories and articles that challenge you at the sentence level. Don't be intimidated. With careful attention to how those sentences are constructed, their meaning will unfold right before your eyes.

> "Your brain is a natural word-learning machine. The more you feed it complex text, the larger a vocabulary you'll have."

Another way text can be complex involves the density of the ideas in a passage. Sometimes a writer piles on so much information that you think your head might explode if you read one more detail or one more qualification. At times like this talking with a friend can really help. Sharing questions and ideas, exploring a difficult passage together, can help you tease out the meaning of even the most difficult text. Poetry is often particularly dense and for that reason it poses particular challenges. A seemingly simple poem in terms of vocabulary and length may express extremely complex feelings and insights. Poets also love to use mythological and Biblical allusions which contemporary readers are not always familiar with. The only way to read text this complex is to read it again and again.

You are going to notice a range of complexity within each collection of readings. This spectrum reflects the range of texts that surround us: some easy, some hard, some seemingly easy but in fact hard, some seemingly hard but actually easy. Whatever their complexity, I think you will enjoy these readings tremendously. Remember, read for your life!

Understanding the Common Core State Standards

What are the English Language Arts Common Core State Standards?

The Common Core State Standards for English Language Arts indicate what you should know and be able to do by the end of your grade level. These understandings and skills will help you be better prepared for future classes, college courses, and a career. For this reason, the standards for each strand in English Language Arts (such as Reading Informational Text or Writing) directly relate to the College and Career Readiness Anchor Standards for each strand. The Anchor Standards broadly outline the understandings and skills you should master by the end of high school so that you are well-prepared for college or for a career.

How do I learn the English Language Arts Common Core State Standards?

Your textbook is closely aligned to the English Language Arts Common Core State Standards. Every time you learn a concept or practice a skill, you are working on mastering one of the standards. Each collection, each selection, and each performance task in your textbook connects to one or more of the standards for English Language Arts listed on the following pages.

The English Language Arts Common Core State Standards are divided into five strands: Reading Literature, Reading Informational Text, Writing, Speaking and Listening, and Language.

©Blend/Getty Images

Strand	What It Means to You
Reading Literature (RL)	This strand concerns the literary texts you will read at this grade level: stories, drama, and poetry. The Common Core State Standards stress that you should read a range of texts of increasing complexity as you progress through high school.
Reading Informational Text (RI)	Informational text encompasses a broad range of literary nonfiction, including exposition, argument, and functional text, in such genres as personal essays, speeches, opinion pieces, memoirs, and historical and technical accounts. The Common Core State Standards stress that you will read a range of informational texts of increasing complexity as you progress from grade to grade.
Writing (W)	For the Writing strand you will focus on generating three types of texts—arguments, informative or explanatory texts, and narratives—while using the writing process and technology to develop and share your writing. The Common Core State Standards also emphasize research and specify that you should write routinely for both short and extended time frames.
Speaking and Listening (SL)	The Common Core State Standards focus on comprehending information presented in a variety of media and formats, on participating in collaborative discussions, and on presenting knowledge and ideas clearly.
Language (L)	The standards in the Language strand address the conventions of standard English grammar, usage, and mechanics; knowledge of language; and vocabulary acquisition and use.

Common Core Code Decoder

The codes you find on the pages of your textbook identify the specific knowledge or skill for the standard addressed in the text.

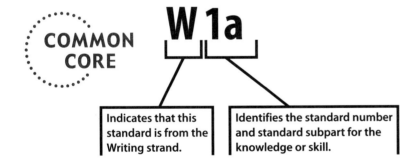

COMMON CORE

W 1a

Indicates that this standard is from the Writing strand.

Identifies the standard number and standard subpart for the knowledge or skill.

English Language Arts
Common Core State Standards

Listed below are the English Language Arts Common Core State Standards that you are required to master by the end of grade 7. We have provided a summary of the concepts you will learn on your way to mastering each standard. The CCR anchor standards and grade-specific standards for each strand work together to define college and career readiness expectations—the former providing broad standards, the latter providing additional specificity.

College and Career Readiness Anchor Standards for Reading

Common Core State Standards

KEY IDEAS AND DETAILS

1. Read closely to determine what the text says explicitly and to make logical inferences from it; cite specific textual evidence when writing or speaking to support conclusions drawn from the text.

2. Determine central ideas or themes of a text and analyze their development; summarize the key supporting details and ideas.

3. Analyze how and why individuals, events, and ideas develop and interact over the course of a text.

CRAFT AND STRUCTURE

4. Interpret words and phrases as they are used in a text, including determining technical, connotative, and figurative meanings, and analyze how specific word choices shape meaning or tone.

5. Analyze the structure of texts, including how specific sentences, paragraphs, and larger portions of the text (e.g., a section, chapter, scene, or stanza) relate to each other and the whole.

6. Assess how point of view or purpose shapes the content and style of a text.

INTEGRATION OF KNOWLEDGE AND IDEAS

7. Integrate and evaluate content presented in diverse formats and media, including visually and quantitatively, as well as in words.

8. Delineate and evaluate the argument and specific claims in a text, including the validity of the reasoning as well as the relevance and sufficiency of the evidence.

9. Analyze how two or more texts address similar themes or topics in order to build knowledge or to compare the approaches the authors take.

RANGE OF READING AND LEVEL OF TEXT COMPLEXITY

10. Read and comprehend complex literary and informational texts independently and proficiently.

Reading Standards for Literature, Grade 7 Students

The College and Career Readiness Anchor Standards for Reading apply to both literature and informational text.

Common Core State Standards	What It Means to You
KEY IDEAS AND DETAILS	
1. Cite several pieces of textual evidence to support analysis of what the text says explicitly as well as inferences drawn from the text.	You will use information from the text to support its main ideas—both those that are stated directly and those that are suggested.
2. Determine a theme or central idea of a text and analyze its development over the course of the text; provide an objective summary of the text.	You will analyze a text's main ideas and themes by showing how they unfold throughout the text. You will also summarize the main idea of the text as a whole without adding your own ideas or opinions.
3. Analyze how particular elements of a story or drama interact (e.g., how setting shapes the characters or plot).	You will analyze how different parts of a story or drama affect each other.
CRAFT AND STRUCTURE	
4. Determine the meaning of words and phrases as they are used in a text, including figurative and connotative meanings; analyze the impact of rhymes and other repetitions of sounds (e.g., alliteration) on a specific verse or stanza of a poem or section of a story or drama.	You will analyze specific words, phrases, and patterns of sound in the text to determine what they mean and how they contribute to the text's larger meaning.
5. Analyze how a drama's or poem's form or structure (e.g., soliloquy, sonnet) contributes to its meaning.	You will analyze how the form of a drama or poem affects its meaning.
6. Analyze how an author develops and contrasts the points of view of different characters or narrators in a text.	You will analyze how an author contrasts the perspectives of different characters or the points of view of narrators in a text.
INTEGRATION OF KNOWLEDGE AND IDEAS	
7. Compare and contrast a written story, drama, or poem to its audio, filmed, staged, or multimedia version, analyzing the effects of techniques unique to each medium (e.g., lighting, sound, color, or camera focus and angles in a film).	You will compare and contrast how events and information are presented in visual and non-visual texts.

Common Core State Standards	What It Means to You
8. (Not applicable to literature)	
9. Compare and contrast a fictional portrayal of a time, place, or character and a historical account of the same period as a means of understanding how authors of fiction use or alter history.	You will recognize and analyze how an author draws from and uses historical source material.
RANGE OF READING AND LEVEL OF TEXT COMPLEXITY	
10. By the end of the year, read and comprehend literature, including stories, dramas, and poems, in the grades 6–8 text complexity band proficiently, with scaffolding as needed at the high end of the range.	You will read and understand grade-level appropriate literary texts by the end of grade 7.

Reading Standards for Informational Text, Grade 7 Students

Common Core State Standards	What It Means to You
KEY IDEAS AND DETAILS	
1. Cite several pieces of textual evidence to support analysis of what the text says explicitly as well as inferences drawn from the text.	You will cite information from the text to support its main ideas—both those that are stated directly and those that are suggested.
2. Determine two or more central ideas in a text and analyze their development over the course of the text; provide an objective summary of the text.	You will analyze the development of at least two of a text's main ideas by showing how they progress throughout the text. You will also summarize the text as a whole without adding your own ideas or opinions.
3. Analyze the interactions between individuals, events, and ideas in a text (e.g., how ideas influence individuals or events, or how individuals influence ideas or events).	You will analyze the ways in which individuals, events, and ideas in the text interact with one another.

Common Core State Standards	What It Means to You

CRAFT AND STRUCTURE

4. Determine the meaning of words and phrases as they are used in a text, including figurative, connotative, and technical meanings; analyze the impact of a specific word choice on meaning and tone.

You will analyze specific words and phrases in the text to determine both what they mean and how they affect the text's tone and meaning as a whole.

5. Analyze the structure an author uses to organize a text, including how the major sections contribute to the whole and to the development of the ideas.

You will examine the major sections of a text and analyze how each one contributes to the whole.

6. Determine an author's point of view or purpose in a text and analyze how the author distinguishes his or her position from that of others.

You will understand the author's point of view and analyze how the author sets his or her position apart from others.

INTEGRATION OF KNOWLEDGE AND IDEAS

7. Compare and contrast a text to an audio, video, or multimedia version of the text, analyzing each medium's portrayal of the subject (e.g., how the delivery of a speech affects the impact of the words).

You will compare and contrast text to an audio, video, or multimedia version of the text.

8. Trace and evaluate the argument and specific claims in a text, assessing whether the reasoning is sound and the evidence is relevant and sufficient to support the claims.

You will evaluate the strength of the author's claims and reasoning and identify any faults or weaknesses in them.

9. Analyze how two or more authors writing about the same topic shape their presentations of key information by emphasizing different evidence or advancing different interpretations of facts.

You will compare and contrast at least two different authors' treatments of the same subject.

Reading Standards for Informational Text, Grade 7, continued

Common Core State Standards	What It Means to You

RANGE OF READING AND LEVEL OF TEXT COMPLEXITY

10. By the end of the year, read and comprehend literary nonfiction in the grades 6–8 text complexity band proficiently, with scaffolding as needed at the high end of the range.	You will demonstrate the ability to read and understand grade-level appropriate literary nonfiction texts by the end of grade 7.

College and Career Readiness Anchor Standards for Writing

Common Core State Standards

TEXT TYPES AND PURPOSES

1. Write arguments to support claims in an analysis of substantive topics or texts, using valid reasoning and relevant and sufficient evidence.

2. Write informative/explanatory texts to examine and convey complex ideas and information clearly and accurately through the effective selection, organization, and analysis of content.

3. Write narratives to develop real or imagined experiences or events using effective technique, well-chosen details, and well-structured event sequences.

PRODUCTION AND DISTRIBUTION OF WRITING

4. Produce clear and coherent writing in which the development, organization, and style are appropriate to task, purpose, and audience.

5. Develop and strengthen writing as needed by planning, revising, editing, rewriting, or trying a new approach.

6. Use technology, including the Internet, to produce and publish writing and to interact and collaborate with others.

RESEARCH TO BUILD AND PRESENT KNOWLEDGE

7. Conduct short as well as more sustained research projects based on focused questions, demonstrating understanding of the subject under investigation.

8. Gather relevant information from multiple print and digital sources, assess the credibility and accuracy of each source, and integrate the information while avoiding plagiarism.

9. Draw evidence from literary or informational texts to support analysis, reflection, and research.

RANGE OF WRITING

10. Write routinely over extended time frames (time for research, reflection, and revision) and shorter time frames (a single sitting or a day or two) for a range of tasks, purposes, and audiences.

Writing Standards, Grade 7 Students

Common Core State Standards	What It Means to You
TEXT TYPES AND PURPOSES	
1. Write arguments to support claims with clear reasons and relevant evidence.	You will write and develop arguments with clear reasons and strong evidence that include
a. Introduce claim(s), acknowledge alternate or opposing claims, and organize the reasons and evidence logically.	a clear organization of claims and counterclaims
b. Support claim(s) with logical reasoning and relevant evidence, using accurate, credible sources and demonstrating an understanding of the topic or text.	strong, accurate support for claims
c. Use words, phrases, and clauses to create cohesion and clarify the relationships among claim(s), reasons, and evidence.	use of cohesive words, phrases, and clauses to link information
d. Establish and maintain a formal style.	a formal style
e. Provide a concluding statement or section that follows from and supports the argument presented.	a strong concluding statement that summarizes the argument
2. Write informative/explanatory texts to examine a topic and convey ideas, concepts, and information through the selection, organization, and analysis of relevant content.	You will write clear, well-organized, and thoughtful informative and explanatory texts with
a. Introduce a topic clearly, previewing what is to follow; organize ideas, concepts, and information, using strategies such as definition, classification, comparison/contrast, and cause/effect; include formatting (e.g., headings), graphics (e.g., charts, tables), and multimedia when useful to aiding comprehension.	a clear introduction and organization, including headings and graphic organizers (when appropriate)
b. Develop the topic with relevant facts, definitions, concrete details, quotations, or other information and examples.	sufficient supporting details and background information

Common Core State Standards	What It Means to You
c. Use appropriate transitions to create cohesion and clarify the relationships among ideas and concepts.	cohesive transitions to link ideas
d. Use precise language and domain-specific vocabulary to inform about or explain the topic.	precise language and relevant vocabulary
e. Establish and maintain a formal style.	a formal style
f. Provide a concluding statement or section that follows from and supports the information or explanation presented.	a strong conclusion that restates the importance or relevance of the topic
3. Write narratives to develop real or imagined experiences or events using effective technique, relevant descriptive details, and well-structured event sequences.	You will write clear, well-structured, detailed narrative texts that
a. Engage and orient the reader by establishing a context and point of view and introducing a narrator and/or characters; organize an event sequence that unfolds naturally and logically.	draw your readers in with a clear topic that unfolds logically
b. Use narrative techniques, such as dialogue, pacing, and description, to develop experiences, events, and/or characters.	use narrative techniques to develop and expand on events and/or characters
c. Use a variety of transition words, phrases, and clauses to convey sequence and signal shifts from one time frame or setting to another.	use a variety of transition words to clearly signal shifts between time frames or settings
d. Use precise words and phrases, relevant descriptive details, and sensory language to capture the action and convey experiences and events.	use precise words and sensory details that keep readers interested
e. Provide a conclusion that follows from and reflects on the narrated experiences or events.	have a strong conclusion that reflects on the topic

PRODUCTION AND DISTRIBUTION OF WRITING

4. Produce clear and coherent writing in which the development, organization, and style are appropriate to task, purpose, and audience. (Grade-specific expectations for writing types are defined in standards 1–3 above.)	You will produce writing that is appropriate to the task, purpose, and audience for whom you are writing.

Common Core State Standards	What It Means to You
5. With some guidance and support from peers and adults, develop and strengthen writing as needed by planning, revising, editing, rewriting, or trying a new approach, focusing on how well purpose and audience have been addressed.	With help from peers and adults, you will revise and refine your writing to address what is most important for your purpose and audience.
6. Use technology, including the Internet, to produce and publish writing and link to and cite sources as well as to interact and collaborate with others, including linking to and citing sources.	You will use technology to share your writing and to provide links to other relevant information.

RESEARCH TO BUILD AND PRESENT KNOWLEDGE

7. Conduct short research projects to answer a question, drawing on several sources and generating additional related, focused questions for further research and investigation.	You will conduct short research projects to answer a question using multiple sources and generating topics for further research.
8. Gather relevant information from multiple print and digital sources, using search terms effectively; assess the credibility and accuracy of each source; and quote or paraphrase the data and conclusions of others while avoiding plagiarism and following a standard format for citation.	You will effectively conduct searches to gather information from different sources and assess the strength of each source, following a standard format for citation.
9. Draw evidence from literary or informational texts to support analysis, reflection, and research. a. Apply *grade 7 Reading standards* to literature (e.g., "Compare and contrast a fictional portrayal of a time, place, or character and a historical account of the same period as a means of understanding how authors of fiction use or alter history"). b. Apply *grade 7 Reading standards* to literary nonfiction (e.g. "Trace and evaluate the argument and specific claims in a text, assessing whether the reasoning is sound and the evidence is relevant and sufficient to support the claims").	You will paraphrase, summarize, quote, and cite primary and secondary sources to support your analysis, reflection, and research.

RANGE OF WRITING

10. Write routinely over extended time frames (time for research, reflection, and revision) and shorter time frames (a single sitting or a day or two) for a range of discipline-specific tasks, purposes, and audiences.	You will write for many different purposes and audiences both over short and extended periods of time.

College and Career Readiness Anchor Standards for Speaking and Listening

Common Core State Standards
COMPREHENSION AND COLLABORATION
1. Prepare for and participate effectively in a range of conversations and collaborations with diverse partners, building on others' ideas and expressing their own clearly and persuasively.
2. Integrate and evaluate information presented in diverse media and formats, including visually, quantitatively, and orally.
3. Evaluate a speaker's point of view, reasoning, and use of evidence and rhetoric.
PRESENTATION OF KNOWLEDGE AND IDEAS
4. Present information, fi ndings, and supporting evidence such that listeners can follow the line of reasoning and the organization, development, and style are appropriate to task, purpose, and audience.
5. Make strategic use of digital media and visual displays of data to express information and enhance understanding of presentations.
6. Adapt speech to a variety of contexts and communicative tasks, demonstrating command of formal English when indicated or appropriate.

Speaking and Listening Standards, Grade 7 Students

Common Core State Standards	What It Means to You
COMPREHENSION AND COLLABORATION	
1. Engage effectively in a range of collaborative discussions (one-on-one, in groups, and teacher-led) with diverse partners on grade 7 topics, texts, and issues, building on others' ideas and expressing their own clearly.	You will actively participate in a variety of discussions in which you
a. Come to discussions prepared, having read or researched material under study; explicitly draw on that preparation by referring to evidence on the topic, text, or issue to probe and refl ect on ideas under discussion.	have read any relevant material beforehand and have come to the discussion prepared
b. Follow rules for collegial discussions, track progress toward specific goals and deadlines, and defi ne individual roles as needed.	work with others to establish goals and processes within the group

Common Core State Standards	What It Means to You
c. Pose questions that elicit elaboration and respond to others' questions and comments with relevant observations and ideas that bring the discussion back on topic as needed.	ask and respond to questions and make observations that bring the discussion back to topic as needed
d. Acknowledge new information expressed by others and, when warranted, modify their own views.	respond to different perspectives and adjust your own views if necessary
2. Analyze the main ideas and supporting details presented in diverse media and formats (e.g., visually, quantitatively, orally) and explain how the ideas clarify a topic, text, or issue under study.	You will analyze main ideas and details of various media and relate them to a topic under study.
3. Delineate a speaker's argument and specific claims, evaluating the soundness of the reasoning and the relevance and suffi ciency of the evidence.	You will evaluate a speaker's argument and identify any false reasoning or evidence.

PRESENTATION OF KNOWLEDGE AND IDEAS

4. Present claims and findings, emphasizing salient points in a focused, coherent manner with pertinent descriptions, facts, details, and examples; use appropriate eye contact, adequate volume, and clear pronunciation.	You will organize and present information to your listeners in a logical sequence and engaging style that is appropriate to your task and audience.
5. Include multimedia components and visual displays in presentations to clarify claims and findings and emphasize salient points.	You will use digital media to enhance and add interest to presentations.
6. Adapt speech to a variety of contexts and tasks, demonstrating command of formal English when indicated or appropriate.	You will adapt the formality of your speech appropriately.

College and Career Readiness Anchor Standards for Language

Common Core State Standards

CONVENTIONS OF STANDARD ENGLISH

1. Demonstrate command of the conventions of standard English grammar and usage when writing or speaking.

2. Demonstrate command of the conventions of standard English capitalization, punctuation, and spelling when writing.

KNOWLEDGE OF LANGUAGE

3. Apply knowledge of language to understand how language functions in different contexts, to make effective choices for meaning or style, and to comprehend more fully when reading or listening.

VOCABULARY ACQUISITION AND USE

4. Determine or clarify the meaning of unknown and multiple-meaning words and phrases by using context clues, analyzing meaningful word parts, and consulting general and specialized reference materials, as appropriate.

5. Demonstrate understanding of word relationships and nuances in word meanings.

6. Acquire and use accurately a range of general academic and domain-specific words and phrases sufficient for reading, writing, speaking, and listening at the college and career readiness level; demonstrate independence in gathering vocabulary knowledge when considering a word or phrase important to comprehension or expression.

Language Standards, Grade 7 Students

Common Core State Standards	What It Means to You
CONVENTIONS OF STANDARD ENGLISH	
1. Demonstrate command of the conventions of standard English grammar and usage when writing or speaking.	You will correctly understand and use the conventions of English grammar and usage, including
a. Explain the function of phrases and clauses in general and their function in specific sentences.	explaining the function of phrases and clauses
b. Choose among simple, compound, complex, and compound-complex sentences to signal differing relationships among ideas.	using a variety of sentence structures
c. Place phrases and clauses within a sentence, recognizing and correcting misplaced and dangling modifiers.	correctly placing phrases and clauses in sentences

Common Core State Standards	What It Means to You
2. Demonstrate command of the conventions of standard English capitalization, punctuation, and spelling when writing.	You will correctly use the conventions of English capitalization, punctuation, and spelling, including
a. Use a comma to separate coordinate adjectives (e.g., *It was a fascinating, enjoyable movie* but not *He wore an old[,] green shirt*).	commas
b. Spell correctly.	spelling

KNOWLEDGE OF LANGUAGE

3. Use knowledge of language and its conventions when writing, speaking, reading, or listening.	You will apply your knowledge of language in different contexts by
a. Choose language that expresses ideas precisely and concisely, recognizing and eliminating wordiness and redundancy.	choosing precise and concise language to avoid wordiness or stating the same thing more than once

VOCABULARY ACQUISITION AND USE

4. Determine or clarify the meaning of unknown and multiple-meaning words and phrases based on *grade 7 reading and content,* choosing flexibly from a range of strategies.	You will understand the meaning of grade-level appropriate words and phrases by
a. Use context (e.g., the overall meaning of a sentence or paragraph; a word's position or function in a sentence) as a clue to the meaning of a word or phrase.	using context clues
b. Use common, grade-appropriate Greek or Latin affixes and roots as clues to the meaning of a word (e.g., *belligerent, bellicose, rebel*).	using Greek or Latin roots
c. Consult general and specialized reference materials (e.g., dictionaries, glossaries, thesauruses), both print and digital, to find the pronunciation of a word or determine or clarify its precise meaning or its part of speech.	using reference materials
d. Verify the preliminary determination of the meaning of a word or phrase (e.g., by checking the inferred meaning in context or in a dictionary).	inferring and verifying the meanings of words in context

Common Core State Standards	What It Means to You
5. Demonstrate understanding of figurative language, word relationships, and nuances in word meanings.	You will understand figurative language, word relationships, and slight differences in word meanings by
a. Interpret figures of speech (e.g., literary, biblical, and mythological allusions) in context.	interpreting figures of speech in context
b. Use the relationship between particular words (e.g., synonym/antonym, analogy) to better understand each of the words.	analyzing relationships between words
c. Distinguish among the connotations (associations) of words with similar denotations (definitions) (e.g., *refined, respectful, polite, diplomatic, condescending*).	distinguishing among words with similar definitions
6. Acquire and use accurately grade-appropriate general academic and domain-specific words and phrases; gather vocabulary knowledge when considering a word or phrase important to comprehension or expression.	You will learn and use grade-appropriate vocabulary.

©Kevin C. Downs/Photolibrary/Getty Images

Bold Actions

"Be bold, take courage . . . and be strong of soul."

—Ovid

PLAN

CONNECTING WORD AND IMAGE

ASK STUDENTS to discuss how the collection opener image and the collection quotation work together to create a connection.

PERFORMANCE TASK PREVIEW

Point out to students that they will complete two performance tasks at the end of the collection. The performance tasks will require them to further analyze the selections in the collections and to synthesize ideas about these analyses. Students will present their findings in a variety of products.

ACADEMIC VOCABULARY

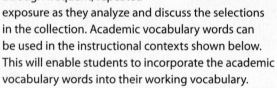
View It!
Professional Development Podcast:
Academic Vocabulary

Students can acquire facility with the academic vocabulary words through frequent, repeated exposure as they analyze and discuss the selections in the collection. Academic vocabulary words can be used in the instructional contexts shown below. This will enable students to incorporate the academic vocabulary words into their working vocabulary.

- Collaborative Discussion sections at the end of each selection
- Analyzing the Text questions for each selection
- Selection-level Performance Tasks
- Vocabulary instruction exercises (for Critical Vocabulary and/or for Vocabulary Strategy)
- Language Conventions
- End-of-collection Performance Task for all selections in the collection

ASK STUDENTS to review the Academic Vocabulary word list for this collection. You may wish to pronounce each word aloud so students hear the correct pronunciation. Then, discuss the definitions and the related forms for each word. Remind students that they will encounter these five academic vocabulary words throughout the collection.

Bold Actions

In this collection, you will explore what it means to face challenges fearlessly, even if it means failing in the attempt.

hmhfyi.com

COLLECTION
PERFORMANCE TASK Preview
After reading the selections in this collection, you will have the opportunity to complete two performance tasks:

• In one, you will write a short story with a main character who boldly attempts to overcome a tremendous challenge.

• In the second, you will write and present an oral commentary about the rewards and risks of undertaking bold actions.

ACADEMIC VOCABULARY
Study the words and their definitions in the chart below. You will use these words as you discuss and write about the texts in this collection.

Word	Definition	Related Forms
aspect (ăs´pəkt) *n.*	a characteristic or feature of something	aspectual
cultural (kul´chər-əl) *adj.*	of or relating to culture or cultivation	agriculture, culture, cultured, multicultural
evaluate (ĭ-văl´yōō-āt´) *v.*	to examine something carefully to judge its value or worth	evaluation, evaluator, evaluative
resource (rē´sôrs´) *n.*	something that can be used for support or help	resources, resourceful, natural resources
text (tĕkst) *n.*	a literary work that is regarded as an object of critical analysis	textbook, textual, texture, textile

2

USING COLLECTIONS YOUR WAY

Use the following information, along with the charts on the following pages, to help you decide how you want to introduce the collection. Based on your teaching style, your students' interests, or your instructional goals, you may want to structure this collection in various ways. You may choose different entry points each time you teach the collection.

"I love teaching traditional literature."

This retelling of the classic Greek myth about Icarus contains many of the elements common to traditional literature.

Background Today we think of myths as stories that have been passed down through countless generations. In the ancient civilization of Greece, myths were the basis of an elaborate system of beliefs. Myths explained their mystifying world and offered wisdom on how to live in it. The myth of Daedalus and his son Icarus is one example.

The Flight of Icarus

Greek Myth retold by Sally Benson

SETTING A PURPOSE As you read, pay close attention to the choices Icarus and his father make. What do these choices reveal? Write down any questions you may have while reading.

When Theseus escaped from the labyrinth, King Minos flew into a rage with its builder, Daedalus, and ordered him shut up in a high tower that faced the lonely sea. In time, with the help of his young son, Icarus, Daedalus managed to escape from the tower, only to find himself a prisoner on the island. Several times he tried by bribery to stow away on one of the vessels sailing from Crete, but King Minos kept strict watch over them, and no ships were allowed to sail without being carefully searched.

Daedalus was an ingenious artist and was not discouraged by his failures. "Minos may control the land and sea," he said, "but he does not control the air. I will try that way."

He called his son, Icarus, to him and told the boy to gather up all the feathers he could find on the rocky shore.

The Flight of Icarus   31

Background This adventure story features a cutter-rigged sailboat. Cutter-rigged boats are small sailing yachts, each with a single mast for the main sail and smaller sails up front. Cutters are equipped with a cabin that usually includes a small kitchen, called a galley. Author **Theodore Taylor** (1921–2006) wrote many stories about self-reliant characters who face great challenges. His best-known book, The Cay, depicts the struggles of a young shipwrecked sailor.

Rogue Wave

Short Story by Theodore Taylor

SETTING A PURPOSE Pay attention to the details and events that make this story an adventure. As you read, think about how the author builds a sense of excitement and anticipation throughout the short story.

A killer wave, known to mariners as a "rogue wave," was approaching a desolate area of Baja California below Ensenada. It had been born off the east coast of Australia during a violent storm; it had traveled almost 7,000 miles at a speed of 20.83 miles an hour. Driven by an unusual pattern of easterly winds, it was a little over 800 feet in length and measured about 48 feet from the bottom of its trough to its crest. On its passage across the Pacific, it had already killed thirteen people, mostly fishermen in small boats, but also an entire French family of five aboard a 48-foot schooner . . .

Melissa "Scoot" Atkins went below into the *Old Sea Dog's* tiny galley, moving down the three steps of the companionway, closing the two solid entry doors behind her, always a good

Rogue Wave   3

"I love to concentrate on contemporary literature."

This adventure story about two siblings battling to survive a marine disaster is a classic example of the contemporary short story genre.

"I like to teach by comparing texts."

This Compare Media feature presents three different perspectives on a real-life news story: an online news article, an online opinion piece, and a television news film clip.

COMPARE MEDIA

Background A compelling event in the news can trigger controversy. Through television, the Internet, and print articles, journalists and the general public voice their opinions and ask heated questions that may not have easy answers.

SETTING A PURPOSE In this lesson, you'll analyze media about a 16-year-old's attempt to become the youngest person to sail solo around the world, an event that sparked worldwide controversy.

MEDIA ANALYSIS

Covering Issues in the News

Parents of Rescued Teenage Sailor Abby Sunderland Accused of Risking Her Life
Online News Article by Paul Harris

Ship of Fools
Editorial by Joanna Weiss

Was Abby Too Young to Sail?
TV News Interview by CBS News

Compare Media   19

COLLECTION 1 DIGITAL OVERVIEW

mySmartPlanner | **eBook** | **my**Notebook | **my** WriteSmart | **fyi** hmhfyi.com

Collection 1 Lessons	Media	Teach and Practice
**Student Edition	eBook**	▶ **Video Links** HISTORY A&E	**Close Reading and Evidence Tracking**
ANCHOR TEXT Short Story by Theodore Taylor "Rogue Wave"	🔊 **Audio** "Rogue Wave"	**Close Read Screencasts** • Modeled Discussion 1 (lines 75–82) • Modeled Discussion 2 (lines 154–161) • Close Read application PDF (lines 351–362) **Strategies for Annotation** • Make Inferences • Analyze Story Elements: Plot and Setting • Latin Roots
CLOSE READER Short Story by Eleanora Tate "Big Things Come in Small Packages"	🔊 **Audio** "Big Things Come in Small Packages"	
Online News Article by Paul Harris "Parents of Rescued Teenage Sailor Abby Sunderland Accused of Risking Her Life"	🔊 **Audio** "Parents of Rescued Teenage Sailor Abby Sunderland Accused of Risking her Life"	**Strategies for Annotation** • Analyze Structure • Trace and Evaluate an Argument
Editorial by Joanna Weiss "Ship of Fools"	🔊 **Audio** "Ship of Fools"	
TV News Interview by CBS News "Was Abby Too Young to Sail?"		
CLOSE READER Essay by Robert Medina "Finding Your Everest"	🔊 **Audio** "Finding Your Everest"	
ANCHOR TEXT Greek Myth retold by Sally Benson "The Flight of Icarus"	▶ **Video HISTORY** *The Seven Deadly Sins: Pride* 🔊 **Audio** "The Flight of Icarus"	**Close Read Screencasts** • Modeled Discussion (lines 35–47) • Close Read application PDF (lines 63–75) **Strategies for Annotation** • Determine Theme • Analyze Story Elements: Myth • Noun Suffixes -*ty* and -*ity*
CLOSE READER Greek Myth retold by Olivia Coolidge "Arachne"	🔊 **Audio** "Arachne"	
Poem by Stephen Dobyns "Icarus's Flight"	🔊 **Audio** "Icarus's Flight"	**Strategies for Annotation** • Analyze Form: Poetry
Informational Text by Patricia and Fredrick McKissack "Women in Aviation"	🔊 **Audio** "Women in Aviation"	**Strategies for Annotation** • Draw Conclusions • Determine Author's Purpose • Connotations and Denotations
Collection 1 Performance Tasks: **A** Write a Short Story **B** Present an Oral Commentary	**fyi** hmhfyi.com	**Interactive Lessons** **A** Writing Narratives **B** Writing Arguments **B** Giving a Presentation

For Systematic Coverage of Writing and Speaking & Listening Standards	**Interactive Lessons** Writing as a Process Participating in Collaborative Discussions

Assess		Extend	Reteach
Performance Task	**Online Assessment**	**Teacher eBook**	**Teacher eBook**
Writing Activity: Movie Outline	Selection Test	**Analyze Story Elements: Plot and Conflict > Interactive Whiteboard Lesson** > Plot and Conflict	**Analyze Story Elements: Plot and Setting > Level Up Tutorial >** Setting: Effect on Plot
Media Activity: Blogs	Selection Test	**How to Create a Blog > Interactive Lessons** > Producing and Publishing with Technology	**Analyze Presentations of Information**
Writing Activity: Graphic Comic	Selection Test	**Analyze Story Elements: Characterization >Interactive Whiteboard Lesson >** Character Development **Interactive Graphic Organizer** > Freeform Web	**Determine Theme >Level Up Tutorial >** Theme
Speaking Activity: Oral Response	Selection Test	**Analyze Form: Scansion >Level Up Tutorial** > Rhythm	**Analyze Form: Poetry >Interactive Whiteboard Lessons >** Form in Poetry **Interactive Graphic Organizer >** Comparison-Contrast Chart
Writing Activity: Report	Selection Test	**Determine Facts and Opinions Determine Central Idea and Details Evaluate Online Sources > Interactive Whiteboard Lessons >** Doing Research on the Web	**Determine Author's Purpose > Level Up Tutorials >** Author's Purpose
A Write a Short Story **B** Present an Oral Commentary	Collection Test		

Lesson Assessments
Writing as a Process
Participating in Collaborative Discussions

Collection 1 Lessons	Key Learning Objective	Performance Task
ANCHOR TEXT **Short Story by Theodore Taylor** **"Rogue Wave," p. 3A**　　**Lexile 980L**	**The student will be able to . . .** identify, analyze, and make inferences about the elements of plot in a short story.	Writing Activity: Movie Outline
Online News Article by Paul Harris　**Lexile 1110L** **"Parents of Rescued Teenage Sailor Abby Sunderland Accused of Risking Her Life," p. 19A**	**The student will be able to . . .** analyze and compare news stories about the same event from various sources.	Media Activity: Blogs
Editorial by Joanna Weiss　　**Lexile 1120L** **"Ship of Fools," p. 19A**		
TV News Interview by CBS News **"Was Abby Too Young to Sail?" p. 19A**		
ANCHOR TEXT **Greek Myth retold by Sally Benson**　**Lexile 1110L** **"The Flight of Icarus," p. 31A**	**The student will be able to . . .** analyze the elements of a myth and to determine two or more themes.	Writing Activity: Graphic Comic
Poem by Stephen Dobyns **"Icarus's Flight," p. 39A**	**The student will be able to . . .** understand how the elements of form and the use of alliteration emphasize ideas and meaning in a poem.	Speaking Activity: Oral Response
Informational Text by Patricia and Fredrick McKissack　**Lexile 1150L** **"Women in Aviation," p. 43A**	**The student will be able to . . .** identify, analyze, and draw conclusions about an author's purpose for writing informational texts.	Writing Activity: Report

Collection 1 Performance Tasks:
A Write a Short Story
B Present an Oral Commentary

Vocabulary Strategy	Language and Style	Student Instructional Support	CLOSE READER Selection
Latin Roots	Sentence Structure	**Scaffolding for ELL Students:** Language Awareness **When Students Struggle:** Plot and Suspense **To Challenge Students:** Discuss Themes	Short Story by Eleanora Tate "Big Things Come in Small Packages," p. 18b **Lexile 900L**
		Scaffolding for ELL Students: Analyze Language: Words Related to *danger* **When Students Struggle:** • Reasons For/Against • Claims and Reasons	Essay by Robert Medina "Finding Your Everest," p. 30b **Lexile 1160L**
Noun Suffixes -ty and -ity	Commas and Coordinate Adjectives	**Scaffolding for ELL Students**: Analyze Language: Description	Greek Myth retold by Olivia Coolidge "Arachne," p. 38b **Lexile 1250L**
		Scaffolding for ELL Students: Determine Meaning of Words and Phrases: Alliteration **When Students Struggle:** Rhythm in Poetry	
Connotations and Denotations	Subordinate Clauses	**Scaffolding for ELL Students**: Expand Vocabulary **When Students Struggle:** Author's Purpose	

ANCHOR TEXT

Rogue Wave

Short Story by Theodore Taylor

Why This Text?

Understanding the elements of plot and learning to make inferences to "read between the lines" helps students experience fiction more fully and deepens their experience with all great works of literature. This lesson explores the interaction of plot elements in an adventure story.

▶ **View It!**

Professional Development Podcast:
Text-Dependant Analysis

Key Learning Objective: The student will be able to identify, analyze, and make inferences about the elements of plot in a short story.

For practice and application:

Big Things Come in Small Packages
Short Story by Eleanora E. Tate

Close Reader selection:
"Big Things Come in Small Packages"
Short Story by Eleanora E. Tate

Common Core Standards

RL 1 Cite textual evidence.
RL 3 Analyze how elements of a story interact.
SL 4 Present claims and findings.
W 3 Write narratives.
L 1b Choose among simple, compound, complex, and compound-complex sentences.
L 4a Use context as a clue to the meaning of a word or phrase.
L 4b Use Greek or Latin affixes and roots as clues to word meanings.
L 4c Consult general reference manuals.

Text Complexity Rubric

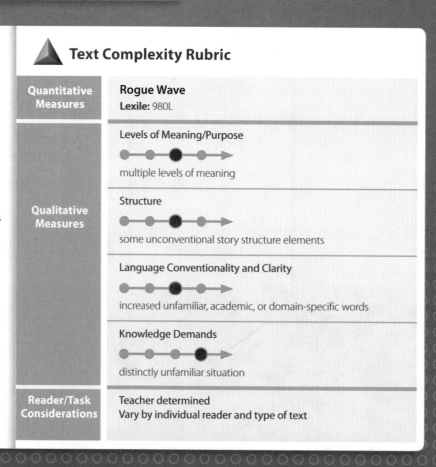

Quantitative Measures

Rogue Wave
Lexile: 980L

Qualitative Measures

Levels of Meaning/Purpose
multiple levels of meaning

Structure
some unconventional story structure elements

Language Conventionality and Clarity
increased unfamiliar, academic, or domain-specific words

Knowledge Demands
distinctly unfamiliar situation

Reader/Task Considerations
Teacher determined
Vary by individual reader and type of text

Background Have students read the background and author information. Explain that this short story contains many nautical terms specific to sailing in a recreational sailboat. Point out that while knowing all the terms is not necessary for appreciating the story, it may be helpful for students to consult a dictionary or manual of nautical terms as they read. Finally, explain that the custom among sailors is to refer to boats using the female pronouns *she* and *her*, which Theodore Taylor follows in the story.

SETTING A PURPOSE Direct students to use the Setting a Purpose prompt to focus their reading. Remind them to write any questions they have as they read.

Analyze Story Elements: Plot and Setting (LINES 1–10, 11–16)

COMMON CORE RL 1, RL 3

Explain to students that most stories follow a series of events, called the **plot.** The first part of a plot is called the **exposition,** where the author introduces the **setting,** or time and place of the action, and the characters. Point out that in this story, the author has chosen to provide background information before introducing the first character.

A **ASK STUDENTS** to reread lines 1–10. Why might the author include this information? *(The author is showing that there is a possible threat to people who might be sailing in the area of Baja California. This hints at possible impending danger to sailors in the area.)*

Point out that the author introduces one of the characters at the beginning of the second paragraph and adds details that hint at the setting.

B **CITE TEXT EVIDENCE** Have students reread lines 11–16 to cite text evidence that identifies the setting. *(The author uses nautical terms, such as galley and companionway, and the phrase "always a good idea in offshore sailing." These suggest that the setting is the ocean on the* Old Sea Dog, *a "thirty-foot Baba type" sailboat.)*

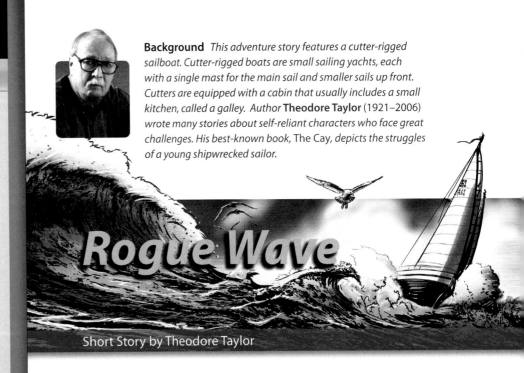

Background *This adventure story features a cutter-rigged sailboat. Cutter-rigged boats are small sailing yachts, each with a single mast for the main sail and smaller sails up front. Cutters are equipped with a cabin that usually includes a small kitchen, called a galley. Author* **Theodore Taylor** *(1921–2006) wrote many stories about self-reliant characters who face great challenges. His best-known book,* The Cay, *depicts the struggles of a young shipwrecked sailor.*

Rogue Wave

Short Story by Theodore Taylor

SETTING A PURPOSE Pay attention to the details and events that make this story an adventure. As you read, think about how the author builds a sense of excitement and anticipation throughout the short story.

> *A killer wave, known to mariners as a "rogue wave," was approaching a desolate area of Baja California below Ensenada. It had been born off the east coast of Australia during a violent storm; it had traveled almost 7,000 miles at a speed of 20.83 miles an hour. Driven by an unusual pattern of easterly winds, it was a little over 800 feet in length and measured about 48 feet from the bottom of its trough to its crest. On its passage across the Pacific, it had already killed thirteen people, mostly fishermen in small boats, but also an*
> 10 *entire French family of five aboard a 48-foot schooner . . .*

Melissa "Scoot" Atkins went below into the *Old Sea Dog's* tiny galley, moving down the three steps of the companionway, closing the two solid entry doors behind her, always a good

(t) ©Don Romero/Romero Fine Portraiture

Rogue Wave **3**

Modeled Discussions

Have students click the *Close Read* icons in their eBooks to access two screencasts in which readers discuss and annotate the following key passages:

- It was already too late . . . (lines 75–82)
- He fought back tears of frustration . . . (lines 154–161)

As a class, view and discuss at least one of these videos. Then have students pair up to do an independent close read of an additional passage—"A big sailboat, beating south . . ." (lines 351–362).

Analyze Story Elements: Plot and Setting (LINES 17–36)

COMMON CORE · RL 1, RL 3

Explain to students that authors include details in the text that help the reader picture the setting. These details can also influence the events and characters.

 CITE TEXT EVIDENCE Have students reread lines 17–36 and use details in the story to describe the setting. What makes the setting a potentially dangerous place? *(Sample answer: The boat is surrounded by seawater. Sunlight glitters off the waves, as the boat glides over the swells. But the beautiful setting is also dangerous—the characters are all alone on the ocean, which can be a deadly force of nature.)*

CRITICAL VOCABULARY

swell: The author uses *swells* to describe the motion of the ocean's surface. *Swells* is a more specific word than *waves,* because swells are longer, rolling waves that cover a vast area.

ASK STUDENTS how the swells might affect the *Old Sea Dog* as she sails over them. *(The boat is probably gently rising and falling on the swells as it moves through the water.)*

deck: Scoot is in the galley, which is part of the boat's interior cabin below deck.

ASK STUDENTS to explain what Scoot would have seen if she were standing on the boat's deck. *(Scoot would be standing on the top surface of the boat, where sailors stand to sail the boat. She would see the boat's sails, the sun, and the ocean swells.)*

---

idea in offshore sailing. The three horizontal hatch boards that were on top of the doors were also firmly in place, securing the thirty-foot Baba type against sudden invasion of seawater.

C *Rogues and sneakers have been around since the beginning of the oceans, and the earliest sea literature makes note of "giant" waves. The U.S. Navy manual* Practical Methods for
20 Observing and Forecasting Ocean Waves *says, "In any wave system, after a long enough time, an exceptional high one will occur. These monstrous out-sized waves are improbable but still possible and the exact time of occurrence can never be predicted." Naval hydrography[1] studies indicate that waves 15 to 25 feet high qualify for "sneaker" or "sleeper" status; the freak rogue is up to 100 feet or over. As waters slowly warm they seem to be occurring more frequently. In 1995 the* Queen Elizabeth 2 *(the QE2), the great British passenger liner, encountered a 95-foot rogue south of Newfoundland. More than 900 feet long, the*
30 *QE2 rode over it, but her captain said it looked like they were sailing into the White Cliffs of Dover.*

Sullivan Atkins, Scoot's oldest brother, was steering the cutter-rigged boat on a northerly course about fifteen miles off desolate Cabo Colnett, south of Ensenada. Under a brilliant sun, the glittering blue Pacific rose and fell in long, slick **swells,** a cold light breeze holding steady.

Below **deck** Scoot was listening to Big Sandy & His Fly-Rite Boys doing "Swingin' West," and singing along with them while slicing leftover steak from last night's meal. They'd
40 grilled it on a small charcoal ring that was mounted outboard on the starboard side[2] at the stern, trailing sparks into the water. The *Sea Dog* had every blessed thing, including a barbecue pit, she marveled.

Scoot was learning how to be a deep-water sailor. She was fourteen years old and pretty, with dark hair. Though small in size, not even five feet, she was strong. She'd started off with eight-foot Sabots. On this trip, her first aboard the *Sea Dog,* she'd manned the wheel for most of the three days they'd been under way. She'd stood four-hour watches at night. Sully was a
50 good teacher.

swell
(swĕl) *n.*
A *swell* is a long, unbroken wave.

deck
(dĕk) *n.* The *deck* is the platform on a ship or boat where people stand.

---

[1] **hydrography:** the scientific description and analysis of the earth's surface waters.

[2] **outboard on the starboard side:** positioned outside and on the right side of the boat.

4 Collection 1

SCAFFOLDING FOR ELL STUDENTS

Language Awareness Using a whiteboard, project lines 1–10.

- Highlight in yellow: killer wave, mariners, "rogue wave," 800 feet in length, 48 feet from bottom of its trough to its crest.
- Underline the words as shown above and discuss how they relate to a story about sailing.
- Highlight the last sentence of the passage in green and discuss.

ASK STUDENTS what could happen if a rogue wave suddenly hit a small boat.

It was one of those perfect days to be out, Sully thought: the three Dacron sails belayed and whispering, white bow waves singing pleasant songs as the fiberglass hull, tilting to starboard, sliced through the ocean. It was a day filled with goodness, peace, and beauty. They'd come south as far as Cabo Colnett, turning back north only an hour ago. They'd sailed from Catalina Island's Avalon Harbor, the *Sea Dog's* home port, out in the channel off Los Angeles. Sully had borrowed the boat from a family friend, Beau Tucker,
60 a stockbroker with enough money to outfit it and maintain it properly. Built by Ta-Shing, of Taiwan, she was heavy and sturdy, with a teakwood deck and handsome teakwood interior, and the latest in **navigation** equipment. Sully had sailed her at least a dozen times. He'd been around boats, motor and sail, for many of his nineteen years. He thought the *Old Sea Dog* was the best, in her category, that he'd ever piloted.

As he was about to complete a northeast tack, Sully's attention was drawn to a squadron of seagulls diving on
70 small fish about a hundred yards off the port bow, and he did not see the giant wave that had crept up silently behind the *Sea Dog*. But a split second before it lifted the boat like a carpenter's chip, he sensed something behind him and glanced backward, toward the towering wall of shining water.

It was already too late to shout a warning to Scoot so she could escape from the cabin; too late to do anything except hang on to the wheel with both hands; too late even to pray. He did manage a yell as the *Sea Dog* became vertical. She rose up the surface of the wall stern first and then pitch-poled
80 violently, end over end, the bow **submerging** and the boat going upside down, taking Sully and Scoot with it, the forty-foot mast, sails intact, now pointing toward the bottom.

Scoot was hurled upward, legs and arms flying, her head striking the after galley bulkhead and then the companionway steps and the interior deck, which was now the ceiling. She instantly blacked out.

Everything loose in the cabin was scattered around what had been the overhead. Water was pouring in and was soon lapping at Scoot's chin. It was coming from a four-inch
90 **porthole** that had not been dogged securely and a few other smaller points of entry.

D **navigation**
(năv´ĭ-gā´shən) *n.*
The *navigation* of a ship or boat is the act of guiding it along a planned course.

submerge
(səb-mûrg´) *v.*
When something *submerges*, it becomes covered by water.

porthole
(pôrt´hōl) *n.* A *porthole* is a circular window on a boat or ship.

Rogue Wave 5

A killer wave, known to mariners as a "rogue wave," was approaching . . . it was a little over 800 feet in length and measured about 48 feet from the bottom of its trough to its crest. On its passage across the Pacific, it had already killed thirteen people, mostly fishermen in small boats, but also an entire French family of five aboard a 48-foot schooner . . .

CLOSE READ

Make Inferences (LINES 63–67)   RI 1

Explain to students that as they read they can make **inferences,** or logical guesses based on details in the text and their own knowledge. Making inferences helps them to understand aspects of a story that are not directly described by the author. To support their inferences, they should **cite textual evidence,** or provide specific information from the text.

D **CITE TEXT EVIDENCE** Have students reread lines 63–67 and use the textual evidence to support an inference about Sully's abilities as a sailor. (*Sully had sailed the* Old Sea Dog *many times already and been around boats most of his life. People with a lot of experience at something are usually experts. So, Sully seems to be an expert sailor. He'd be very capable to handle trouble at sea.*)

CRITICAL VOCABULARY

navigation: The *Old Sea Dog* is an impressive sailing vessel with the "latest in navigation equipment."

ASK STUDENTS why this feature would make Sully feel confident and safe in the middle of the ocean. (*If the boat has the best navigation equipment, it is easy to navigate, or reliably steer and direct its coarse.*)

submerge: Suddenly, the front end, or bow, of the *Old Sea Dog* is submerged when the rogue wave hits.

porthole: Water is pouring into the galley from a porthole that has not been locked, or "dogged."

ASK STUDENTS to explain why an open porthole would be a problem for a boat that is submerged. (*Portholes are windows in a boat's cabin. If the boat is submerged, and a porthole is open, then water will come into the boat's cabin.*)

Analyze Story Elements: Plot and Conflict (LINES 94–107)

COMMON CORE RL 1, RL 3

Explain to students that in most stories, characters must solve or deal with a problem. This problem is called the **conflict,** a struggle between opposing forces. The sudden appearance of the rogue wave has created an **external conflict**—a struggle with an outside force.

E **CITE TEXT EVIDENCE** Have students reread lines 94–107 and use text evidence to identify the external conflict. *(The rogue wave has tipped over the* Sea Dog. *Judging by the locked cabin doors that Sully can't open, Scoot is trapped inside the cabin. He concludes that the cabin is probably filling with water. So, the external conflict is Sully's struggle to get inside the cabin to free his sister. For Scoot, the conflict is the same—she must find a way out.)*

Determine Meanings

COMMON CORE RL 1, RL 4

(LINES 94–101)

Explain to students that a **simile** is a figure of speech that makes a comparison between two unlike things using the word *like* or *as.* Point out that the author uses a number of similes in this story to help create vivid images for the reader.

F **CITE TEXT EVIDENCE** Have students reread lines 94–101 and identify the simile. Then ask them to explain the effect this choice of words creates in describing the setting. *(The simile "like a cork" suggests that the* Sea Dog *is a now a small object floating helplessly in the water. It has the effect of underscoring how alone and helpless Sully and Scoot are now.)*

Sully's feet were caught under forestay sailcloth, plastered around his face, but then he managed to shove clear and swim upward, breaking water. He looked at the mound of upside-down hull, bottom to the sky, unable to believe that the fine, sturdy *Sea Dog* had been flipped like a cork, perhaps trapping Scoot inside. Treading water, trying to collect his thoughts, he yelled, "Scoot," but there was no answer. Heart pounding, unable to see over the mound of the hull, he circled
100 it, thinking she might have been thrown clear. But there was no sign of her.

> **Maneuvering his body, he pulled on the handles. The doors were jammed.**

He swam back to the point of cabin entry, took several deep breaths, and dove. He felt along the hatch boards and then opened his eyes briefly to see that the doors were still closed. She *was* still inside. Maneuvering his body, he pulled on the handles. The doors were jammed, and he returned to the surface for air.

He knew by the way the boat had already settled that there was water inside her. Under usual circumstances, the hull
110 being upright, there would be four feet, nine inches of hull below the waterline. There would be about the same to the cabin overhead, enabling a six-foot-person to walk about down there.

Panting, blowing, Sully figured there was at least a three-foot air pocket holding the *Sea Dog* on the surface, and if Scoot hadn't been knocked unconscious and drowned, she could live for quite a while in the dark chamber. How long, he didn't know.

G 120 In the blackness, water continued to lap at Scoot's chin. She had settled against what had been the deck of the galley alcove, her body in an upright position on debris. Everything

6 Collection 1

not tied down or in a locker was now between the overhead ribs. Wooden hatch covers[3] from the bilges were floating in the water and the naked bilges were exposed. Just aft of her body, and now above it, was the small diesel engine as well as the batteries. Under the water were cans of oil, one of them leaking. Battery acid might leak, too. Few sailors could imagine the nightmare that existed inside the *Sea Dog.* Scoot's pretty face was splashed with engine oil.

130 Over the next five or six minutes, Sully dove repeatedly, using his feet as a fulcrum, and using all the strength that he had in his arms, legs, and back, in an effort to open the doors. The pressure of the water defeated him. Then he thought about trying to pry the doors open with the wooden handle of the scrub brush. Too late for that, he immediately discovered. It had drifted away, along with Scoot's nylon jacket, her canvas boat shoes—anything that could float.

Finally he climbed on top of the keel, catching his breath, resting a moment, trying desperately to think of a way to enter 140 the hull. Boats of the Baba class, built for deep-water sailing, quite capable of reaching Honolulu and beyond, were almost sea-tight unless the sailors made a mistake or unless the sea became angry. The side ports were supposed to be dogged securely in open ocean. Aside from the cabin doors, there was no entry into that cabin without tools. He couldn't very well claw a hole through the inch of tough fiberglass.

He thought about the hatch on the foredeck, but it could only be opened from inside the cabin. Then there was the skylight on the top of the seventeen-foot cabin, used for 150 ventilation as well as a sun source; that butterfly window, hinged in the middle, could be opened only from the inside. Even with scuba gear, he couldn't open that skylight unless he had tools.

He fought back tears of frustration. There was no way to reach Scoot. And he knew what would happen down there. The water would slowly and inevitably rise until the air pocket was only six inches; her head would be trapped between the surface of the water and the dirty bilge. The water would torture her, then it would drown her. Seawater has no heart,

---

[3] **Wooden hatch covers:** door-like coverings made of wood that fit over openings on the deck or hull of a boat.

CLOSE READ

Analyze Story Elements: Plot and Setting (LINES 119–137)
COMMON CORE RL 1, RL 3

Point out now that while the overall setting is still the middle of the ocean, Scoot and Sully are each in their own settings.

G CITE TEXT EVIDENCE Ask students to reread lines 119–137, which begins on the previous page, and identify the two settings. Have them explain how these two settings now impact the plot. *(Sully is outside the capsized boat, where there is plenty of light and air. But he wants to get into the boat to free his sister. Scoot is below in the darkness with limited air. She wants to get out to the surface. So, the settings separate the two characters, underscoring the external conflict.)*

Make Inferences (LINES 124–129)
COMMON CORE RL 1, RL 3

The author directly describes the scene inside the cabin, where an unconscious Scoot rests, as a "nightmare." He includes details that suggest that Scoot has more to worry about than just the flooding water and dwindling oxygen.

H CITE TEXT EVIDENCE Have students reread lines 124–129 and identify evidence in the text that suggests the added danger. *(The water is becoming toxic. Oil is dripping into it, and the battery could leak acid. These liquids are poisonous, so Scoot is threatened by these additional, unseen dangers.)*

Strategies for Annotation ✎ 🖫 *Annotate it!*

Make Inferences
COMMON CORE RL 1

Have students locate the five sentences in lines 124–129. Encourage them to use their eBook annotation tools to do the following:

- Highlight in yellow the text that directly describes Scoot's situation.
- Underline clues that help you make inferences about additional dangers.
- Review your annotations and use them to make inferences about these details. *(Scoot is trapped with oil and possibly battery acid leaking into the water. These are harmful chemicals, so they add to the danger.)*

her body, and now above it, was the small diesel engine as well as the batteries. Under the water were 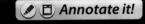cans of oil, one of them leaking. Battery acid might leak, too. Few sailors could imagine the nightmare that existed inside the *Sea Dog.* Scoot's pretty face was splashed with engine oil.

Make Inferences

COMMON CORE **RL 1**

(LINES 175–185)

Explain that the author provides details that hint at Scoot's ability to take care of herself in tough situations.

🅘 **CITE TEXT EVIDENCE** Ask students to reread lines 175–185 and identify details that support an inference about how Scoot might deal with the situation she is in. *(The author tells us Scoot was always "spunky." Her reaction to Sully's teasing and her determination to go offshore sailing show she is persistent, fearless, and unflinching. Although she is small, she is energetic and strong. People like this often persevere and overcome challenges, so Scoot will use her strength and spunk to get out and won't stop trying until she does.)*

160 no brain. The *Sea Dog* would then drop to the ocean floor, thousands of feet down, entombing her forever.

Maybe the best hope for poor Scoot was that she was already dead, but he had to determine whether she was still alive. He began pounding on the hull with the bottom of his fist, waiting for a return knock. At the same time, he shouted her name over and over. Nothing but silence from inside there. He wished he'd hung on to the silly scrub brush. The wooden handle would make more noise than the flesh of his fist.

Almost half an hour passed, and he finally broke down
170 and sobbed. His right fist was bloody from the constant pounding. Why hadn't *he* gone below to make the stupid sandwiches? Scoot would have been at the wheel when the wave grasped the *Sea Dog*. His young sister, with all her life to live, would be alive now.

They'd had a good brother-sister relationship. He'd teased her a lot about being pint-sized and she'd teased back, holding her nose when he brought one girl or another home for display. She'd always been spunky. He'd taken her sailing locally, in the channel, but she'd wanted an offshore cruise for
180 her fourteenth birthday. Now she'd had one, unfortunately.

Their father had nicknamed her Scoot because, as a baby, she'd crawled so fast. It was still a fitting name for her as a teenager. With a wiry body, she was fast in tennis and swimming and already the school's champion in the hundred-yard dash.

Eyes closed, teeth clenched, he kept pounding away with the bloody fist. Finally he went back into the ocean to try once more to open the doors. He sucked air, taking a half-dozen deep breaths, and then dove again. Bracing his feet against the
190 companionway frames, he felt every muscle straining, but the doors remained jammed. He was also now aware that if they did open, more water would rush in and he might not have time to find Scoot in the blackness and pull her out. But he was willing to take the gamble.

Scoot awakened as water seeped into her mouth and nose. For a moment she could not understand where she was, how she got there, what had happened …Vaguely, she remembered the boat slanting steeply downward, as if it were suddenly diving, and she remembered feeling her body going up.

APPLYING ACADEMIC VOCABULARY

evaluate	resource	text

As you discuss the plot of the story, incorporate the following Collection 1 academic vocabulary words: *evaluate, resource,* and *text.* Ask students what **resource** they might use to better understand nautical terms in the **text.** As students read about how Scoot and Sully try to solve their problems, have the students **evaluate** the effectiveness of each solution the characters try.

200 That's all she remembered, and all she knew at the moment was that she had a fierce headache and was in chill water in total darkness. It took a little longer to realize she was trapped in the *Sea Dog's* cabin, by the galley alcove. She began to feel around herself and to touch floating things. The air was thick with an oil smell. Then she ran her hand over the nearest solid thing—a bulkhead. *That's strange,* she thought—her feet were touching a pot. She lifted her right arm and felt above her—the galley range. The galley range above her? *The boat was upside down.* She felt for the companionway steps and found the
210 entry doors and pushed on them; that was the way she'd come in. The doors didn't move.

Sully crawled up on the wide hull again, clinging to a faint hope that a boat or ship would soon come by; but the sun was already in descent, and with night coming on, chances of rescue lessened with each long minute. It was maddening to have her a few feet away and be helpless to do anything. Meanwhile the hull swayed gently, in eerie silence.

Scoot said tentatively, "Sully?" Maybe he'd been drowned. Maybe she was alone and would die here in the foul water.
220 She repeated his name, but much more loudly. No answer. She was coming out of shock now and fear icier than the water was replacing her confusion. To die completely alone? It went that way for a few desperate moments, and then she said to herself, *Scoot, you've got to get out of here! There has to be some way to get out . . .*

9

Analyze Story Elements: Plot and Conflict

COMMON CORE RL 1, RL 3

(LINES 239–258, 245–249)

Explain to students that the introduction of obstacles in the rising action helps build **suspense,** or the growing feeling of tension and excitement that readers feel as they follow a character's struggle with the conflict. Explain further that there are two kinds of conflicts: **external conflicts,** which are struggles with outside forces, such as another character or a force of nature, and **internal conflicts,** which are struggles characters have with their own thoughts.

K **CITE TEXT EVIDENCE** Have students reread 239–258 and identify how Sully and Scoot have overcome the first big obstacle in their way. (*Neither Scoot nor Sully was sure that the other person was still alive. Now that they know this, they've overcome one hurdle in their way.*)

L **ASK STUDENTS** to reread lines 245–249 and explain how this quick exchange between the characters helps build suspense. (*The urgent back and forth between Scoot and Sully, who are suddenly energized and hopeful, creates a feeling of excitement. The reader is suddenly excited for the characters.*)

WHEN STUDENTS STRUGGLE . . .

To guide students' comprehension of plot elements that create tension, have students work in pairs to fill out a chart like the one shown. Explain that the chart will help them to link feelings of tension or excitement to story events.

Have pairs fill in the chart as they reread lines 245–249, and discuss their reactions to the story event. Explain that as they read they can ask questions, such as *What parts of the story are most exciting? Why do they make me feel that way?*

Sully clung to the keel with one hand, his body flat against the smooth surface of the hull. There was ample room on either side of the keel before the dead-rise, the upward slope of the hull. The *Sea Dog* had a beam of ten feet. Unless a wind and
230 waves came up, he was safe enough in his wet perch.

Scoot again wondered if her brother had survived and if he was still around the boat or on it. With her right foot she began to probe around the space beneath her. The pot had drifted away, but her toes felt what seemed to be flatware. That made sense. The drawer with the knives and forks and spoons had popped out, spilling its contents. She took a deep breath and ducked under to pick out a knife. Coming up, she held the knife blade, reaching skyward with the handle . . .

Eyes closed, brain mushy, exhausted, Sully heard a faint
240 tapping and raised up on his elbows to make sure he wasn't
K dreaming. No, there was a tapping from below. He crawled back toward what he thought was the source area, the galley area, and put an ear to the hull. *She was tapping!* He pounded the fiberglass, yelling, "Scoot, Scooot, Scooot . . ."

Scoot heard the pounding and called out, "Sully, I'm here, I'm here!" Her voice seemed to thunder in the air pocket.

Sully yelled, "Can you hear me?"

Scoot could only hear the pounding.
"Help me out of here . . ."

250 Ear still to the hull, Sully shouted again, "Scoot, can you hear me?" No answer. He pounded again and repeated, "Scoot, can you hear me?" No answer. The hull was too thick and the slop of the sea, the moan of the afternoon breeze, didn't help.

Though she couldn't hear his voice, the mere fact that he was up there told her she'd escape. Sully had gotten her out of jams before. There was no one on earth that she'd rather have as a rescue man than her oldest brother. She absolutely knew she'd survive.

Though it might be fruitless, Sully yelled down to the galley
260 alcove, "Listen to me, Scoot. You'll have to get out by yourself. I can't help you. I can't break in. Listen to me, I know you're in water, and the best way out is through the skylight. You've got

WHEN I READ . . .	I FELT . . .
Sully hears Scoot tapping and starts trying to yell to her. She yells back, but they can't hear each other's voices.	*excited, frustrated*

to dive down and open it. You're small enough to go through it . . ." She could go through either section of the butterfly window. "Tap twice if you heard me!"

She did not respond, and he repeated what he'd just said, word for word.

No response. No taps from below.

270 Scoot couldn't understand why he didn't just swim down and open the doors to the cabin, release her. That's all he needed to do, and she'd be free.

> **No response.**
> **No taps from below.**

Sully looked up at the sky. "Please, God, help me, help us." Ⓜ It was almost unbearable to know she was alive and he was unable to do anything for her. Then he made the decision to keep repeating: "Listen to me, Scoot. You'll have to get out by yourself. I can't break in. Listen to me, the best way out is through the skylight. You've got to dive down and open it. You're small enough to go through it . . ."

He decided to keep saying it the rest of the day and into 280 the night or for as long as it took to penetrate the hull with words. *Skylight! Skylight!* Over and over.

He'd heard of mental telepathy but had not thought much about it before. Now it was the only way to reach her.

Scoot finally thought that maybe Sully was hurt, maybe helpless up on that bottom, so that was why he couldn't open the doors and let her out. That had to be the reason—Sully up there with broken legs. *So I'll have to get out on my own,* she thought.

Over the last two days, when she wasn't on the wheel she 290 had been exploring the *Sea Dog,* and she thought she knew all the exits. Besides the companionway doors, which she knew she couldn't open, there was the hatch on the foredeck for access to the sails; then there was the skylight, almost

CLOSE READ

Make Inferences

COMMON CORE **RL 1**

(LINES 272–281)

Explain to students that Sully is making a decision to do something by repeating the same words over and over.

Ⓜ **ASK STUDENTS** to reread lines 272–281 and make an inference about how Sully's actions might help both Scoot and Sully himself. *(Sully thinks that his repeating the words to Scoot might reach her through mental telepathy. But, the repetition of words is also likely helping Sully, because it makes him feel less powerless. Earlier in the paragraph, Sully actually prays. This repetition of words may comfort him like a prayer.)*

Make Inferences

COMMON CORE **RL 1**

(LINES 303–312)

Explain to students that the author is providing many details about Scoot's thought process and abilities in an emergency.

 CITE TEXT EVIDENCE Have students reread lines 303–312 and cite evidence that supports an inference about Scoot's abilities. *(Scoot is levelheaded, calm, and resourceful, even in an emergency situation. She clearly thinks through a number of solutions to her problem. She remembers the emergency flashlight and reasons that it's waterproof. She calculates how much time she will have to unscrew the dogs. She even has the presence of mind to let Sully know she is still alive.)*

Analyze Story Elements:
Plot and Setting (LINES 314–319)

COMMON CORE **RL 3**

Explain to students that the author is using an aspect of the outdoor, ocean setting to reinforce a continually worsening obstacle.

O **ASK STUDENTS** to reread lines 314–319 and identify the obstacle and how it is related to the setting. *(Sully is noting that there are three hours until sundown. The approaching nighttime is like a deadline for him and Scoot. If she doesn't get out by then, they could be in much worse trouble.)*

---

in the middle of the long cabin. Sully had opened it, she remembered, to air out the boat before they sailed. As she clung to a light fixture by the alcove, in water up to her shoulders, something kept telling her she should first try the butterfly windows of the skylight. The unheard message was compelling—*Try the skylight.*

300   Sully's voice was almost like a recording, a mantra, saying the same thing again and again, directed down to the position of the galley.

Scoot remembered that an emergency flashlight was bracketed on the bulkhead above the starboard settee, and she assumed it was waterproof. From what Sully had said, Beau Tucker took great care in selecting emergency equipment. It might help to actually see the dogs on the metal skylight frame. She knew she wouldn't have much time to spin them loose. Maybe thirty or forty seconds before she'd have to surface for breath. Trying
310   to think of the exact position of the upside-down flashlight, she again tapped on the hull to let her brother know she was very much alive.

He pounded back.

Sully looked at his watch. Almost four-thirty. About three hours to sundown. Of course, it didn't make much difference to Scoot. She was already in dank night. But it might make a difference if she got out after nightfall. He didn't know what kind of shape she was in. Injured, she might surface and drift away.
320   The mantra kept on.

Scoot dove twice for the boxy flashlight, found it, and turned it on, suddenly splitting the darkness and immediately feeling hopeful. But it was odd to see the *Sea Dog's* unusual overhead, the open hatchways into the bilge and the debris floating on the shining water, all streaked with lubricants; odd to see the toilet upside down. She held the light underwater and it continued to operate.

Every so often, Sully lifted his face to survey the horizon, looking for traffic. He knew they were still within sixteen or
330   seventeen miles of the coast, though the drift was west. There was usually small-boat activity within twenty miles of the shore—fishermen or pleasure boats.

Strategies for Annotation   ✎ 🗐 *Annotate it!*

Analyze Story Elements:
Plot and Setting

COMMON CORE **RL 1, RL 3**

Have students locate lines 314–319. Encourage them to use their eBook annotation tools to do the following:

- Highlight in yellow the text that describes the obstacle.
- Underline the text that explains why these details are a threat to Sully and Scoot.
- Review your annotations and explain how this text evidence helps build suspense. *(Time is running out for Scoot and Sully. If it gets dark, Scoot may never get rescued.)*

Sully looked at his watch. Almost four-thirty. About three hours to sundown. Of course, it didn't make much difference to Scoot. She was already in dank night. But it might make a difference if she got out after nightfall. He didn't know what kind of shape she was in. Injured, she might surface and drift away.

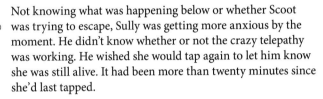

Scoot worked herself forward a few feet, guessing where the skylight might be, and then went down to find the butterfly windows, the flashlight beam cutting through the murk. It took a few seconds to locate them and put a hand on one brass dog. She tried to turn it, but it was to tight for her muscles and she rose up to breathe again.

340 Not knowing what was happening below or whether Scoot was trying to escape, Sully was getting more anxious by the moment. He didn't know whether or not the crazy telepathy was working. He wished she would tap again to let him know she was still alive. It had been more than twenty minutes since she'd last tapped.

Scoot had seen a toolbox under the companionway steps and went back to try to find it. She guessed there'd be wrenches inside it, unless they'd spilled out. Using the flashlight again, she found the metal box and opened it. Back to the surface to breathe again, and then back to the toolbox to extract a wrench. 350 With each move she was becoming more and more confident.

A big sailboat, beating south, came into Sully's view; but it was more than two miles away and the occupants—unless he was very lucky—would not be able to spot the *Sea Dog's* mound and the man standing on it, waving frantically.

Four times Scoot needed to dive, once for each dog; and working underwater was at least five times as difficult as trying to turn them in usual circumstances. She'd aim the light and rest it to illuminate the windows. Finally, all the dogs

Rogue Wave **13**

TEACH

CLOSE READ

Analyze Story Elements: Plot and Setting (LINES 339–354)

COMMON CORE RL 1, RL 3

Explain to students that now the rising action is moving at a faster pace, as time is running out for Scoot and Sully. The author jumps back and forth between the two settings, showing what each character is experiencing.

Ⓟ ASK STUDENTS to reread lines 339–354 to identify details that are increasing the suspense, and have the students explain how these details create tension and excitement for the reader. *(Sully is getting very anxious. Meanwhile, Scoot is working away, growing more confident. The situation is getting very bad, although there is some hope. But the hope caused by the sighting of the other boat fades, adding to Sully's frustration. These details seem to make the plot move more quickly because we want to find out what will happen.)*

Rogue Wave **13**

Analyze Story Elements: Plot and Setting (LINES 363–372)

COMMON CORE RL 1, RL 3

Explain to students that the suspense in a story often builds to a breaking point. This point in the plot is called the **climax**—the story's most interesting moment when the conflict is finally resolved.

 CITE TEXT EVIDENCE Have students reread lines 363–372 and cite evidence that indicates this is the **climax** of the story. *(Sully is finally giving up hope. Scoot is on her sixth dive. She gives one final push "with all her strength" and the skylight finally opens. Scoot is almost out of breath—about to lose consciousness— but she has resolved her conflict.)*

Make Inferences

COMMON CORE RL 1, RL 3

(LINES 383–387)

Explain that in the moments of the story right after the climax, called the **resolution,** Sully has one last exchange with the captain of the *Red Rooster.*

R **ASK STUDENTS** to reread the exchange and explain why Stevens responds in the way he does. *(Sully answers Stevens's question with just two words: "rogue wave." Stevens winces and nods because that is all he needs to hear—a rogue wave is so sudden and destructive, it goes without saying that it causes massive problems.)*

COLLABORATIVE DISCUSSION Have students pair up and discuss the specific details and events in the plot that made this story so exciting. Encourage students to jot down notes as they talk. Then have them share their ideas with the class and discuss others' reactions to the story.

ASK STUDENTS to share any questions they generated in the course of reading and discussing the selection.

---

were loose and she rose once again. This time, after filling her
360 lungs to bursting, she went down and pushed on the starboard window. It cracked a little, but the outside sea pressure resisted and she had to surface again.

Q Sully sat down, almost giving up hope. How long the air pocket would hold up was anybody's guess. The boat had settled at least six inches in the last two hours. It might not last into the night.

On her sixth dive Scoot found a way to brace her feet against the ceiling ribs. She pushed with all her strength, and this time the window opened. Almost out of breath, she quickly
370 pushed her body through and the *Old Sea Dog* released her. Treading water beside the hull, she sucked in fresh air and finally called out, "Sully …"

He looked her way, saw the grin of triumph on the oil-stained imp face, and dived in to help her aboard the derelict.

Shivering, holding each other for warmth all night, they rode and rocked, knowing that the boat was sinking lower each hour.

Just after dawn, the *Red Rooster,* a long-range sports fishing boat out of San Diego bound south to fish for wahoo
380 and tuna off the Revilla Gigedo Islands, came within a hundred yards of the upside-down sailboat and stopped to pick up its two chattering survivors.

R The *Red Rooster's* captain, Mark Stevens, asked, "What happened?"

"Rogue wave," said Sully. That's what he planned to say to Beau Tucker as well.

Stevens winced and nodded that he understood.

The *Old Sea Dog* stayed on the surface for a little while longer, having delivered her survivors to safety; then her air
390 pocket breathed its last and she slipped beneath the water, headed for the bottom.

COLLABORATIVE DISCUSSION How and when did this adventure tale "hook" you? As it unfolded, what events helped to keep you anxious about what would happen? With a partner, review "Rogue Wave" to point out and discuss the parts that helped to create excitement and anticipation.

TO CHALLENGE STUDENTS . . .

Theme Explain to students that a story's theme is a message or lesson about life that a writer shares with the reader. Have students work in small groups and use examples from the text to discuss the unpredictability of and devastation caused by the rogue wave.

Analyze Story Elements: Plot and Setting RL 3

The power of a story, such as "Rogue Wave," comes from its action and events. Most stories follow a series of events, also known as the **plot.** A story centers around the **conflict,** the struggle between opposing forces. As the characters struggle to resolve a conflict, the plot builds **suspense,** the growing tension and excitement felt by the reader. Most plots have five stages:

- The **exposition** introduces the characters and presents the setting and conflict.
- The **rising action** presents complications that intensify.
- The **climax** is the story's moment of greatest interest—the point where the conflict is resolved.
- In the **falling action,** the story begins to draw to a close.
- The **resolution** reveals the final outcome of the conflict.

Often the plot is influenced by the **setting,** or the time and place of the action. For example, the setting can cause plot complications. In "Rogue Wave," Sully notes that as evening comes, the fading light could hamper his rescue efforts. To understand the influence of setting on the plot in "Rogue Wave," find details that tell where and when the events are happening. Use those details to visualize the setting and follow the action.

Make Inferences RL 1

Authors do not always fully describe every aspect of a story, setting, or character. They do, however, provide clues that help you to make **inferences,** logical guesses based on facts and one's own knowledge and experience. You make an inference by text combining evidence with what you know.

To support your inferences, you may need to **cite textual evidence,** or provide specific information from the text. For example, you can identify story details that indicate a character's feelings, as shown in the chart. Using a chart like this one can help you make inferences throughout a text.

Detail from the Text
In lines 37–39, Scoot is listening to music and singing along.

My Own Experience
When I sing along to a song, I usually feel happy.

My Inference
Scoot feels happy to be sailing with her brother.

TEACH

CLOSE READ

Analyze Story Elements: Plot and Setting RL 3

Discuss the terms and the five stages of a plot. Have volunteers name at least one example of each stage from the story. Then discuss the information about how setting can influence plot.

Work with students to analyze the plot and identify how suspense is created. Explain that

- with each additional obstacle, the suspense is usually heightened.
- details of setting such as, the oncoming sundown and the flooding cabin, build suspense.
- as students read a story, they should notice each time they wonder "What happens next?"

Make Inferences RL 1

Help students understand that making inferences is a way to figure out things that are not directly described in a text. To demonstrate making an inference, point out that when you see someone crying, you can infer that the person is sad. You don't need to be told. Discuss the chart and how to use details from the text and your own experiences to make an inference about Scoot. Then work with students to use a chart, like the one shown, to make additional inferences about other plot elements.

Strategies for Annotation   **Annotate it!**

Analyze Story Elements: Plot and Setting

COMMON CORE RL 1, RL 3

Share these strategies for guided or independent analysis:

- Highlight in yellow details about the setting that prove to be an obstacle.
- Underline details that show how the character deals with the obstacle.

Over the next five or six minutes, Sully dove repeatedly, <u>using his feet as a fulcrum</u>, and <u>using all the strength that he had in his arms, legs, and back</u>, in an effort to open the doors. The pressure of the water defeated him. Then <u>he thought about trying to pry the doors open with the wooden handle of the</u>

Analyzing the Text COMMON CORE RL 1, RL 3

Possible answers:

1. *Scoot has scary thoughts about whether Sully is okay. Fear takes over her, but only for a few moments. Then she turns her attention to getting out. People who act like this in the face of disaster are brave and resilient.*

2. *By providing details of the dangers of rogue waves, it underscores the threat to Scoot and Sully and suggests the conflict that they will soon have to resolve—surviving the sudden strike of a rogue wave.*

3. *Sully has just been thinking about his sister and their loving relationship. He has pounded his fists bloody, trying to contact her. He jumps in the water for one final time. He is scared and desperate.*

4. *Sully knows roughly their location in the ocean. He also knows that small boats might be in the area. This shows that he is knowledgeable and that rescue might be close. There is still hope for Sully and Scoot.*

5. ***Scoot's complications:*** *1. the flooding, upturned, dark cabin; 2. a headache; 3. concern about Sully and inability to hear him; 4. dwindling air; 5. the locked skylight.*
   Sully's complications: *1. his inability to see or hear Scoot; 2. his inability to get inside the capsized cabin; 3. fears of what could happen to Scoot; 4. guilt about putting Scoot in danger; 5. the sinking hull and the oncoming sunset.*

6. *The two settings are outside on the Sea Dog's upturned hull, and below in the upturned cabin. Shifting between these settings builds suspense by alternating between the obstacles each character encounters.*

7. *The climax is the moment when Scoot finally unfastens the dogs of the skylight and pushes through to the ocean. It's suspenseful because we know she is exhausted and running out of air. Meanwhile, up above, Sully has almost given up hope. The situation seems desperate.*

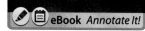

eBook *Annotate It!*

Analyzing the Text COMMON CORE RL 1, RL 3, W 3, SL 4

Cite Text Evidence Support your responses with evidence from the text.

1. **Infer** Reread lines 218–225. What inference can you make about Scoot's personality, based on these lines?

2. **Connect** How does the information in lines 17–31 help establish the conflict?

3. **Infer** Reread lines 186–194. Describe Sully's emotions at this point.

4. **Infer** Reread lines 328–332. What inference does the author want you to make at this point?

5. **Compare** Fill out a chart like this one to trace the conflicts or complications Scoot and Sully encounter in the story. Review the story events in the text, expanding the chart as necessary to cover the key happenings.

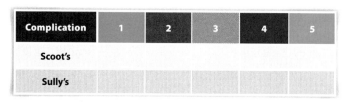

Complication	1	2	3	4	5
Scoot's					
Sully's					

6. **Analyze** Identify the two settings in this story. How does the author's shifting between these settings help build suspense?

7. **Evaluate** Describe the climax of the story. What makes this moment so suspenseful? Explain.

PERFORMANCE TASK

Writing Activity: Movie Outline
Think about how "Rogue Wave" could be adapted as an action movie. Write a four-paragraph movie outline showing how it could be done. Use your completed outline to "pitch"—or present persuasively—your movie idea to a partner or group. In your outline, be sure to include:

- a description of the opening scene that establishes the characters, setting, and conflict.
- a description of each important scene in the plot.
- suggestions for how to shoot each scene to convey the suspense.

Assign this performance task.

PERFORMANCE TASK COMMON CORE W 3, SL 4

Writing Activity: Movie Outline Have students work independently. Direct them to review "Rogue Wave" and use the main plot elements to organize their outlines. Suggest that they search online for sample movie outlines, or treatments, to use as examples of how to describe movie scenes. When finished, encourage students to use their completed outlines to pitch their idea to a partner or small group, explaining why the movie should be made.

Critical Vocabulary

COMMON CORE L 4a, L 4b, L 4c

swell   deck   navigation   submerge   porthole

Practice and Apply Complete each sentence to show that you understand the meaning of the boldfaced vocabulary word.

1. I can see the water's motion by watching how a **swell** . . .

2. One reason to be on the **deck** of a boat is . . .

3. Sailors need tools for **navigation,** such as . . .

4. When the tide comes in on the beach, it could **submerge** . . .

5. There was a **porthole** in our room on the boat, so we . . .

Vocabulary Strategy: Latin Roots

A **root** is a word part that came into English from an older language. Roots from ancient language of Latin appear in many English words. Often, by identifying Latin roots, you can figure out the meanings of words that seem unfamiliar. For example, the chart shows two words from "Rogue Wave." Each contains a Latin root having to do with the sea.

Word	Latin Root	Root's Meaning
mariners	mar	sea
navigation	nav	ship

Mariners are sea sailors, which comes from the Latin root *mar.* The Latin root *nav,* from which *navigation* comes, appears in words having to do with ships and sailing, such as *navy* (a fleet of ships) and *naval* (having to do with navies). By identifying the roots *mar* and *nav,* you can make a good guess about the meanings of longer words that include them. Relying on a resource such as a print or online dictionary also can help you confirm your ideas.

Practice and Apply Read each sentence. Identify the words with the Latin roots *mar* and *nav.* Tell what each word means. Use a print or online dictionary to check your ideas.

1. Sailors in the navy may spend time in submarines.

2. Mariners long ago navigated using the stars.

3. Using navigation equipment, fishermen found a region of rich marine life.

4. Boats set out from the marina to sail up the river, which is navigable to the waterfalls.

Critical Vocabulary

COMMON CORE L 4a, L 4b, L 4c

Possible answers:

1. *rises and falls on the ocean.*

2. *to move the boat's wheel or rudder to steer it.*

3. *a map and a compass.*

4. *any sand castles that have been built near the water.*

5. *could see the other boats in the harbor.*

Vocabulary Strategy: Latin Roots

Answers:

1. *navy:* fleet of ships; *submarines:* sea vessels that travel underwater

2. *mariners:* sea sailors; *navigated:* directed a ship's course

3. *navigation:* the act of directing a ship's course; *marine:* having to do with the sea

4. *marina:* docks by the sea for boats and supplies; *navigable:* able to be sailed through

---

Strategies for Annotation   ✏ 🗐 *Annotate it!*

Latin Roots

COMMON CORE L 4b

Have students locate the sentences containing *navy* and *naval* in lines 19–26. Encourage them to use their eBook annotation tools to do the following:

- Highlight each word.
- Underline the Latin root in each word.
- Use the Latin root in each word to make a good guess about its meaning and write an annotation.

"giant" waves. *The U.S. <u>Nav</u>y manual* Practical Methods for Observing and Forecasting Ocean Waves says, *"In any wave system, after a long enough time, an exceptional high one will . . . still possible and the exact time of occurrence can never be predicted." <u>Nav</u>al* hydrography studies indicate that wave

navy: a fleet of military ships

Language Conventions: Sentence Structure

COMMON CORE L 1b

Tell students that the examples in the chart show the building blocks of a simple sentence—the basic type of sentence. Invite volunteers to come up with examples of other simple sentences and identify the complete subject and complete predicate in each. *(Sample answers: Rogue waves are very destructive. Complete subject: Rogue waves; Complete predicate: are very destructive. Sully and Scoot almost died in a serious maritime accident. Complete subject: Sully and Scoot; Complete predicate: almost died in a serious maritime accident.)* Then have volunteers use these simple sentences to form compound sentences, using either conjunctions or a semicolon. *(Rogue waves are very destructive, so Sully and Scoot almost died in a serious maritime accident.)*

Sample answers:

1. *Rogue waves are frightening, and they are unpredictable giants.*

2. *A rogue wave can be very tall, and it can travel thousands of miles.*

3. *Sailors know about the sea's dangers, so they follow safety rules.*

4. *Life at sea has its risks, but it also has beauty.*

5. *Sailors prepare for dangerous weather, or they risk dying at sea.*

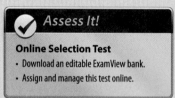

Assess It!

Online Selection Test
- Download an editable ExamView bank.
- Assign and manage this test online.

Language Conventions: Sentence Structure

COMMON CORE L 1b

A **clause** is a group of words that has the two main parts of a sentence—a complete subject and a complete predicate. A **complete subject** includes all the words that identify the person, place, thing, or idea that the sentence is about. The **complete predicate** includes all the words that tell or ask something about the subject.

Complete Subject	Complete Predicate
The *Sea Dog*	had every blessed thing.
Sully	was a good teacher.

A **simple sentence** contains just one main clause.

Sully looked at his watch.

In this sentence, the complete subject is *Sully* and the complete predicate is *looked at his watch*.

A **compound sentence** contains two or more main clauses that are joined either by a comma and coordinating conjunction, such as *and, but, or, for, so, yet,* and *nor,* or are joined by a semicolon.

She pushed with all her strength, and this time the window opened.

In this compound sentence, the simple sentence *She pushed with all her strength* is combined with the sentence *this time the window opened,* using a comma and the coordinating conjunction *and.*

She found the entry doors; they were closed.

In this compound sentence, a semicolon is used to connect two simple sentences.

Practice and Apply Create a compound sentence by joining the two simple sentences with either a comma and a coordinating conjunction or a semicolon.

1. Rogue waves are frightening. They are unpredictable giants.

2. A rogue wave can be very tall. It can travel thousands of miles.

3. Sailors know about the sea's dangers. They follow safety rules.

4. Life at sea has its risks. It also has beauty.

5. Sailors prepare for dangerous weather. They risk dying at sea.

INTERACTIVE WHITEBOARD LESSON

Analyze Story Elements: Plot and Conflict

COMMON CORE
RL 1,
RL 3

Learn the Skill ▶ What Is Conflict?

What Is Conflict?
Click to explore different types of conflicts.

Conflict in Literature

A **conflict** is a struggle between two opposing forces in the plot of a story. A conflict can be external (against an outside force) or internal (within the character).

Conflict in Literature · External: Against Character(s) · External: Against Nature

TEACH

Before having students complete their outlines as part of the Performance Task, review these points about conflict:

- Every story centers around a **conflict,** a struggle between opposing forces.
- An **external conflict** is a struggle against an outside force, such as nature, a physical obstacle, or another character.
- Ask volunteers to name examples of a few external conflicts, such as a knight fighting against an evil king or characters trying to survive a tornado.
- An **internal conflict** is one that occurs within a character. An internal conflict is a struggle inside a character's mind.
- Ask volunteers to name examples of a few internal conflicts, such as deciding to keep a found wallet or deciding to turn it in to the police, or a character struggling with a choice between a friend and doing the right thing.

COLLABORATIVE DISCUSSION

Have students work in pairs to review the story "Rogue Wave" and identify examples of both kinds of conflict. Ask students to cite evidence from the text to discuss how the author establishes each conflict and how these conflicts help build suspense in the story.

Analyze Story Elements: Plot and Setting

COMMON CORE
RL 3

RETEACH

Use a story map to review the five stages of a plot (Exposition, Rising Action, Climax, Falling Action, and Resolution), filling in the map with events from "Rogue Wave."

- Then give an example of another story in which the setting has an effect on the plot, such as "A lava flow from an erupting volcano threatens the lives of the people in the village below."
- Ask students to name other ways in which the sample setting could affect the plot. *(Sample answer: Ash falling from the erupting volcano covers the roads, making escape more difficult.)*
- Discuss how obstacles like this create suspense, making the reader want to find out what happens next.

LEVEL UP TUTORIALS Assign the following *Level Up* tutorial: **Setting: Effect on Plot**

? EXIT X

Setting: Effect on Plot TUTORIAL PRACTICE

Setting: Effect on Plot

Say you're writing a story about someone throwing the game-winning touchdown pass. Would it be important to discuss the time and place of a story? How about the events that led up to the winning pass?

The **setting**, or the time and place in which the story occurs, helps shape stories. Often, the setting can also affect the **plot**, or the series of events that make up a story.

The setting of a story is important.

The setting sometimes affects the plot.

1 2 3 4 5 6 7 8 9 ..9

CLOSE READING APPLICATION

Students can apply the skill to another short story of their own choosing. Have them work independently to identify the main plot elements. Then have them list ways in which the setting has an effect on the plot. Ask: *How does the writer use aspects of the setting to introduce obstacles? How do these obstacles help create suspense?*

Big Things Come in Small Packages

Short Story by Eleanora E. Tate

Why This Text

Students often read a short story without understanding that the elements of a story interact. The setting of a story, for example, may shape the characters or plot—or both. Stories such as this one by Eleanora E. Tate may explicitly describe the setting, characters, and plot, or they may provide clues to help the reader make inferences, supported by textual evidence. With the help of the close-reading questions, students will recognize how the setting influences the characters and plot. This close reading will lead students to develop their understanding of how particular elements of a short story interact.

Background Have students read the background and the information about the author. Introduce the selection by telling students that Eleanora E. Tate is a powerful storyteller who writes books and short stories "so that everyone of every ethnic group can read about the proud history and culture of African Americans." As a folklorist, Tate imbues her writing with African American lore and sayings, as seen in her popular book *Don't Split the Pole: Tales of Down-Home Folk Wisdom.*

SETTING A PURPOSE Ask students to pay close attention to how the elements of the story interact. When did they first understand the conflict that needs to be resolved in the story?

Common Core Support

- cite several pieces of textual evidence
- make inferences drawn from the text
- analyze how particular elements of a story interact
- analyze how setting shapes the characters or plot

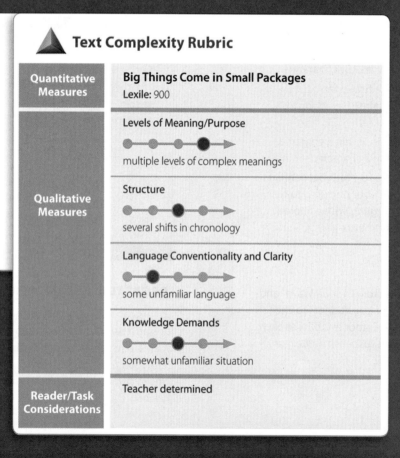

Text Complexity Rubric

Quantitative Measures

Big Things Come in Small Packages
Lexile: 900

Qualitative Measures

Levels of Meaning/Purpose

multiple levels of complex meanings

Structure

several shifts in chronology

Language Conventionality and Clarity

some unfamiliar language

Knowledge Demands

somewhat unfamiliar situation

Reader/Task Considerations

Teacher determined

Strategies for CLOSE READING

Analyze Story Elements: Plot and Setting

Students should read this short story carefully all the way through. Close-reading questions at the bottom of the page will help them focus on a thorough analysis of how particular story elements interact, specifically on how the setting influences the characters and plot. As they read, students should record comments about the text in the side margins.

WHEN STUDENTS STRUGGLE . . .

To help students understand the major structural elements in a fictional narrative, have them work in a small group to fill out a story map, such as the one shown below, as they analyze the story.

CITE TEXT EVIDENCE For practice in tracking how the particular story elements interact, have students cite text evidence to complete the story map.

> *Setting:*
>
> *Where: Morehead City, North Carolina*
>
> *When: 1970s and present*

> *Major Characters: Tucker Willis ("Tugboat"), narrator (LaShana Mae), and Richard Etheridge*
>
> *Minor Characters: Mr. Nibbles, narrator's mother, Tucker's parents*

> *Plot/Problem: Tucker is called names by the other kids because of his small size.*

> *Event 1:*
> *Tucker meets Richard, who nicknames him "Tugboat."*

> *Event 2:*
> *Tucker tries to save Mr. Nibbles from drowning, but thinks he is going to die.*

> *Event 3:*
> *Richard helps in the rescue, and he and Tucker save Mr. Nibbles.*

> *Outcome: Tucker becomes a hero for having saved Mr. Nibbles, and the name-calling stops. Tucker discovers that Richard had really died in 1900 and had been the Keeper of the Pea Island Lifesaving Service.*

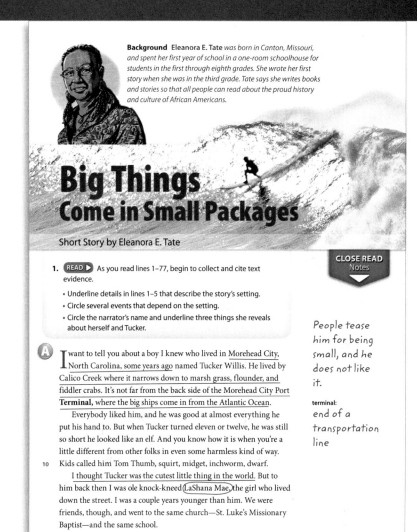

Background Eleanora E. Tate *was born in Canton, Missouri, and spent her first year of school in a one-room schoolhouse for students in the first through eighth grades. She wrote her first story when she was in the third grade. Tate says she writes books and stories so that all people can read about the proud history and culture of African Americans.*

Big Things Come in Small Packages

Short Story by Eleanora E. Tate

1. **READ ▷** As you read lines 1–77, begin to collect and cite text evidence.

   • Underline details in lines 1–5 that describe the story's setting.
   • Circle several events that depend on the setting.
   • Circle the narrator's name and underline three things she reveals about herself and Tucker.

CLOSE READ
Notes

I want to tell you about a boy I knew who lived in Morehead City, North Carolina, some years ago named Tucker Willis. He lived by Calico Creek where it narrows down to marsh grass, flounder, and fiddler crabs. It's not far from the back side of the Morehead City Port Terminal, where the big ships come in from the Atlantic Ocean.

Everybody liked him, and he was good at almost everything he put his hand to. But when Tucker turned eleven or twelve, he was still so short he looked like an elf. And you know how it is when you're a little different from other folks in even some harmless kind of way.

10   Kids called him Tom Thumb, squirt, midget, inchworm, dwarf.

I thought Tucker was the cutest little thing in the world. But to him back then I was ole knock-kneed LaShana Mae, the girl who lived down the street. I was a couple years younger than him. We were friends, though, and went to the same church—St. Luke's Missionary Baptist—and the same school.

People tease him for being small, and he does not like it.

terminal:
end of a transportation line

3

---

1. **READ AND CITE TEXT EVIDENCE** Explain to students that Tate explicitly identifies the setting at the beginning of the story, establishing how the time and place will shape the characters and plot.

   A ASK STUDENTS to determine how Tate establishes the setting to shape the characters and plot by citing specific textual evidence in lines 1–77. *Responses may include references to evidence in lines 1–5, 12, 19–21, 27–30, 34–36, 39–40, and 53.*

   Critical Vocabulary: terminal (line 5) Have students explain the meaning of "terminal" as it is used here. Ask students what means of transportation have terminals at the end of their lines. *Students should be able to cite these modes of transportation: bus, train, and subway lines.*

Back in those days, in the 1970s, young boys and girls didn't hang out as boyfriend and girlfriend like kids do now. Plus, I was just a skinny girl with braids and braces. Kids called me Wires because of those braces, and boy, did it ever make me mad! So Tucker and I had a
20　lot in common, and lots of times we talked about the things kids called us, especially when we went fishing.

B　Even though being called those names hurt, Tucker gave up fighting the kids who said them. Fighting didn't help. The name-callers were all too big for him to beat up. So after a while, he learned to ignore the teasing. Most times he laughed it off. He was a tough little dude. But oh mercy, how he hated those names!

One day Tucker did something that made everybody stop calling him names he didn't like. I think it helped him grow a few inches, too.

You need to know a few things about this boy before I tell you
30　what changed things around. Tucker could do almost anything that any other kid his age could do. He was a hotshot shortstop on the Little League baseball team. He could jump like a flea on the basketball court. He was smart in school. He was in the Boy Scouts. He could swim like a fish—and I even surf!

He looked like a Tootsie Roll to me in that big ocean. Yeah, I had a name for him, too. I called him Tootsie Roll, but never to his face. I just kept it to myself. And when I called him that in my head, I didn't mean it in a bad way.

Tucker could do some fishing. He especially liked to fish his folks'
40　little **pier** alongside their house. In the summertime he'd lie on his stomach on the pier and catch some of the biggest flounder to come out of Calico Creek. Instead of a rod and reel, he used a handful of fishing line, a hook baited with shrimp, and a sinker to keep the bait from floating on the surface.

He'd dangle that shrimp an inch or two off the bottom, right in front of a flounder's nose. Sometimes we'd fish together on his pier, and I wouldn't catch diddlysquat, not even a pinfish, not even a lizard fish, nothing. But ole Tootsie Roll could catch 'em.

I tried fishing the way he did, but most of the time I used a rod
50　and reel cause I thought the way Tucker did it was country. I still couldn't catch anything, not in Calico Creek. I did all right when I fished at the pier in Atlantic Beach.

pier:
a platform
over the water

That's how I'd see Tucker surfing. He even got teased about surfing, because not many black kids we knew surfed. Shoot, as much as we all loved the water, not a whole lot of us even knew how to swim. I didn't. Not until Tucker taught me later on.

He and his dad or mom would fish out on their own little pier all night sometimes with a Coleman lantern[1] for light. His folks used regular rods and reels. I never fished out there at night with them
60　because the mosquitoes and the gnats would about eat me up.

Plus, my momma liked to tell me that they used to do baptizing in that creek, which was okay. But then Momma'd say, "LaShana Mae, you watch out about being around that creek by yourself at night. The people who got baptized there and who've passed on come back to that creek as spirits in the middle of the night when the moon's full. They'll be singing and celebrating and shouting and praising, and they don't want to be **disturbed.** Unless you wanna join in with 'em."

Me being a scared little kid, you can believe that Momma didn't have to worry about me going out to *nobody's* Calico Creek by myself
70　at night. But sometimes I'd go to my window at night and look out to see if anybody was celebrating the way she said. All I ever saw were grown folks fishing. Sometimes somebody would holler when they caught a big one. After I got grown I understood that Momma told me that story to try to help me stay out of trouble. She was worried I'd drown or get into some kind of foolishness. Well, it worked. I knew that it was easy to get into trouble when you're out someplace where you're not supposed to be.

disturbed:
bothered

---

[1] **Coleman lantern:** a lamp that burns pressurized kerosene to give light.

---

2. **◀ REREAD** Reread lines 6–26. In the margin, describe the conflict Tucker faces. Circle the text that foreshadows a future event.

3. **READ ▶** As you read lines 78–116, continue to cite textual evidence.
- Circle text that creates suspense about a major event in the plot that will take place.
- Underline text that suggests that his meeting with Richard was important to Tucker.
- In the margin, make an inference about Tucker's attitude toward Richard.

4

5

Critical Vocabulary: pier (line 40) Have students share their definitions of "pier." Ask them to provide a homophone (a word that sounds the same but has a different meaning and spelling) for the word. *Students should be able to cite the word "peer," but not "pear," which has a slightly different pronunciation.*

FOR ELL STUDENTS It will be difficult for ELL students to understand the central idea of this section if they do not know the meaning of a few key words and phrases. Make sure that they understand that "calling someone names" actually means "to call them bad names." Describe what "braids," "braces," and "wires" are.

ASK STUDENTS to make the connection between the narrator's braces and her nickname, *Wires*.

2. **REREAD AND CITE TEXT EVIDENCE** Remind students that writers include textual details that foreshadow, or hint at, future events.

B **ASK STUDENTS** to point out the text that foreshadows an event that will resolve the conflict.

3. **READ AND CITE TEXT EVIDENCE**

C **ASK STUDENTS** to make inferences drawn from the text and from their margin notes that suggest why the meeting with Richard is important to Tucker and what Tucker's attitude is toward Richard. *Students should cite examples in lines 97–98, 103–104, and 115–116.*

Critical Vocabulary: disturbed (line 67) Have students share their definitions of *disturbed* as Tate uses it here. What does the narrator's mother mean when she says that the spirits "don't want to be disturbed"? *She means that they don't want to be bothered, or annoyed, by her daughter.*

CLOSE READ
Notes

Anyway, what happened to change all the name-calling started when Tucker was on his pier trying to catch a flounder. He noticed a
80 man standing on the Moten Motel dock just a few yards from him. The man had a thick white mustache and Vandyke beard and wore a blue-and-gold military-style jacket and cap. I wasn't there, so I didn't see him, but that's what Tucker told me.

When the man waved, Tucker, being a friendly kind of kid, waved back. They struck up a conversation. The man said his name was Richard and that he was staying at the motel for a few days. His home was in Manteo, on Roanoke Island, not far from the Outer Banks, where he worked with the U.S. Lifesaving Service.

Tucker figured what he meant was that he was with the U.S. Coast
90 Guard. Tucker was pretty knowledgeable about the coast guard, but he had never heard of this lifesaving service. Tucker asked the man if he liked to fish. Richard said yes. He'd been a commercial fisherman before he became a captain in the lifesaving service. As a lifesaver, he said, he and his men went into the ocean in the middle of hurricanes and nor'easters[2] to save passengers and crew members whose ships were sinking.

C Of course, anything about water fascinated Tucker, so he must have asked this Richard a million questions. Richard didn't seem to mind, though. He said he didn't get to talk to kids much anymore.

D 100 Richard said a good crewman had to be strong, an excellent swimmer, a quick thinker, and in good physical health, have good eyesight, and understand how dangerous the sea can be. He told so many stories about lifesaving that Tucker wished he could enlist right away, and said so. He had the right **qualifications**—other than being too young, of course. And too short.

Richard told him it wasn't the size of a person that got the job done. It was how bad the person wanted to do it. How were those huge ships two and more stories high able to move into the Morehead City port and back out to sea? Most couldn't do it without little
110 tugboats pushing and pulling them in, Richard said. A tugboat could bring in a ship many times its size.

Richard said that Tucker would make a good tugboat and one day might even grow to be a big ship. He thanked Tucker for the conversation, said maybe they'd meet again, and then the man

qualifications:
abilities and accomplishments

Tucker is fascinated by Richard's knowledge and reassured by his kindness.

[2] **nor'easters:** storms with winds blowing from the northeast.

6

wandered off back toward the motel. Tucker said for the rest of the afternoon, he thought over what Richard had said.

A few days later, Tucker decided to go with his dad to the Atlantic Beach pier to fish. His daddy worked there as a cook. For some reason I couldn't go that day. I've always wished I had. Tucker said he took
120 his surfboard too, in case fishing got slow. It was early morning, but a hot July wind blew in from the southwest, making the waves choppy and sandy. The tide was going out. Hardly anybody was on the pier, which was another hint that the fish might not be biting. Tucker said only one guy was in the water, floating on a red raft like a huge jellyfish.

After a good hour had passed and he hadn't got a bite, Tucker left his rod and reel with his father in the pier restaurant's kitchen and went surfing. After he swam out far enough, he climbed onto his surfboard and rode a wave in. When he glanced back at the pier,
130 guess who he saw? His new friend, Richard, on the pier, clapping for him. At least this time he had on shorts and a regular shirt. Tucker said he bet Richard had about burnt up in that heavy uniform the other day.

Richard hollered, "Do it, Tugboat! Pull that ole wave in!"

Tugboat? Tucker said he frowned until he remembered Richard's story about tugboats. So he waved back and swam out to pull in another one, passing the man on the raft. The man said, "You're

4. **◄ REREAD** Reread lines 100–116. Explain the significance of Richard's statement that "Tucker would make a good tugboat and one day might even grow to be a big ship." Cite specific text evidence to support your explanation.

Richard is reassuring Tucker that his size would not interfere with his ability to save someone's life at sea. He explained that Tucker has the main requirement for the job, strong desire. He is also giving Tucker hope that he may grow taller someday.

5. **READ ►** As you read lines 117–183, continue to cite textual evidence.
   • In the margin, take notes about how suspense is built in this section.
   • Circle the paragraph that is most likely the story's climax.

7

Critical Vocabulary: qualifications (line 104) Have students give examples of *qualifications* that team members need to have to be on a basketball or soccer team. *Students should be able to draw on their own knowledge and experience to brainstorm a list of qualifications, such as strength and coordination, that members of these teams need to have.*

4. **REREAD AND CITE TEXT EVIDENCE**

D **ASK STUDENTS** to explain how Richard's statement that "Tucker would make a good tugboat and one day might even grow to be a big ship" reveals Richard's attitude about Tucker. *Students should cite specific textual evidence as they point out that Richard believes Tucker has great potential. He is trying to reassure Tucker that he is qualified for the job and that his ability to rescue someone at sea would not be impaired by his size.*

5. **READ AND CITE TEXT EVIDENCE**

E **ASK STUDENTS** to read their margin notes to a partner and then work together to find and cite specific text examples of how suspense is built into this section, leading to the climax of the story. *Students should cite that the possibility of the drowning and the storm builds suspense, leading to the climax, the moment before the rescue when Tucker thinks he is going to die.*

> # " He thrashed around in the water screaming that he couldn't swim. "

kinda little to be way out here, ain't ya, squirt?" Tucker just shook his head and kept going.

(F) 140   Tucker pulled in four more waves until he noticed a tall purple thunderhead rising up on the southwest horizon. That cloud meant a storm was probably on its way, but Tucker figured he had at least half an hour before the wind kicked up the waves and blew the cloud in and the rain began. Tucker wasn't afraid of a thing, but his common sense and his folks had told him to always leave away from water when storms and lightning came along. It's hard to get grown without having common sense, because being stupid can get you killed sometimes.

The possibility of drowning builds suspense.

(E)   Keeping an eye on the horizon, Tucker went on pulling in those
150   waves until a huge one arched up behind his back and crashed down on him. Tucker disappeared.

Wipeout. No big deal for Tucker, though. He popped right up in the water and grabbed his board, which was tied to his ankle. He was all right. But the man on the raft wasn't. He thrashed around in the water screaming that he couldn't swim.

Now someone's life is in real danger.

As that big black cloud spread across the sky toward them, the wind and waves grew rougher. Wanting to help the man, but concerned about his own safety, Tucker hesitated, then straddled his surfboard and, using his hands for oars, paddled toward the raft.

Now Tucker is in danger.

160   He'd have time to get the guy's raft back to him and then head in. But as Tucker passed, the man lunged at the surfboard, knocking Tucker off.

And then this guy grabbed hold of Tucker! Wrapped up in that big bear's arms and legs, with the sea getting choppier, Tucker said he knew he was about to die. He began to pray.

But something lifted Tucker up through the water and onto his surfboard, where he was able to catch his breath. That's when he saw his friend Richard in the water, too! Have mercy! Richard was hauling that raft toward the man. With two big heaves, Richard snatched that
170   guy straight up out of the water and onto the raft.

Richard yelled, "Let's push and pull it, Tugboat! Push and pull it in!"

Somehow Tucker and Richard pushed and pulled that raft—with the guy glued to it—close enough to shore that the man was able to wade in the rest of the way. Four or five people splashed into the water and helped them onto the beach and into the pier house. One of the helpers was a reporter on vacation.

As soon as everybody was inside the pier house, the rain poured down. An arrow of lightning whizzed across the pier into the water
180   and lit up the whole ocean. That's when Tucker said he got scared, seeing that lightning. He'd have been fried alive, you know. The guy Tucker rescued was named Nibbles. Mr. Nibbles was so grateful that he gave Tucker a hundred dollars right on the spot.

The reporter interviewed everybody and took pictures of Tucker, Nibbles, and Tucker's dad, who almost had a heart attack when he heard what happened. When the reporter asked how such a small boy was able to rescue a big, grown man, Tucker said, "'Cause I'm a tugboat, like Richard said. We pull the big ones in."

But when Tucker turned around to point out Richard, he couldn't
190   find him.

Getting help releases some of the suspense.

We know the man is okay.

6. **◄ REREAD AND DISCUSS** Reread lines 140–148. With a partner, discuss the details that build suspense. What do you think these details foreshadow? Support your answer with explicit textual evidence.

7. **READ ►** As you read lines 184–237, continue to cite textual evidence.
   • In the margin, explain how Tucker's conflict is resolved.
   • Then, summarize what Tucker learns about Richard in lines 216–237.

8

9

FOR ELL STUDENTS Direct students to lines 140–148. Ask them to reread this passage and to point out the storm-related vocabulary: *thunderhead, cloud* (line 141) *storm* (line 142), *wind, blew* (line 143), *rain* (line 144), and *lightning* (line 146). Ask students to define these weather words by using the context of the story. If students have difficulty explaining the meaning of the words, invite them to draw pictures or to use gestures to define them.

6. **REREAD AND DISCUSS USING TEXT EVIDENCE**

(F) ASK STUDENTS to work with a partner to cite specific text evidence that builds suspense and might foreshadow the climax. *Students should cite textual evidence from lines 140–148 to show that the approaching storm builds tension, creating suspense, and foreshadows the "stormy weather ahead," in the form of near-drowning, for Tucker and Mr. Nibbles.*

7. **READ AND CITE TEXT EVIDENCE**

(G) ASK STUDENTS to read their margin notes to a partner, and then create one summary that briefly states what Tucker learns about Richard. *Students should cite textual evidence from lines 206–207 and 216–237.*

CLOSE READ
Notes

Tucker is a local hero when he rescues a grown man from the sea.

The reporter's story about Tucker's rescue was in the local paper, then got picked up by the Associated Press and went all over the world. CBS TV even flew him and his folks to New York to be on its morning show. Afterwards, back home in Morehead City, strangers stopped Tucker on the street, in stores, even came to his home. They wanted to see the little "tugboat" that hauled in that big man, and get his autograph.

200   Businesses up and down Arendell Street put up WELCOME HOME, TUGBOAT! posters in their windows. And there was a parade. Tucker was a hero! He and the mayor rode on the back of a big ole white Cadillac convertible and waved at everybody. I was so proud that I almost forgot and hollered out, "Way to go, Tootsie Roll!" but I caught myself in time.

  Everybody—even local folks—called Tucker Tugboat after that, including us kids. We'd never seen a real live hero close up before, especially one our age. It wasn't cool anymore to tease him with those other names. Funny how things can turn right around, isn't it?

No one makes fun of Tucker anymore.

  And you know what? Tucker grew to be six feet five. He played on the North Carolina Central University Eagles basketball team, joined
210   the U.S. Coast Guard, and lives in Kill Devil Hills, North Carolina, on the Outer Banks.

Plus, he grew tall after all.

  But there's something Tucker never figured out. When he first told people that Richard was the real hero, nobody believed him. Apparently nobody but Tucker had seen Richard—not even Mr. Nibbles.

  There's more. When Tucker went into the pier gift shop to spend some of his rescue money, he picked up a book about the coast guard. He was thumbing through it when he stopped at an old-timey picture of some black men wearing jackets like Richard's. They were standing
220   in front of a building on the Outer Banks. Below it was a picture of—yes, Richard! Mustache, beard, jacket, everything!

  Tucker read, "History of the Pea Island Lifesaving Service. Captain Richard Etheridge was Keeper of the Pea Island Lifesaving Service, a forerunner of part of what is now the U.S. Coast Guard. This unique, all African American, courageous lifesaving crew, and those who followed, saved hundreds of shipwrecked passengers' lives by plunging into the stormy seas and bringing their charges back to safety."

Richard was the head of a lifesaving service and died in 1900.

10

CLOSE READ
Notes

  Tucker said he shot out of that gift shop toward the restaurant to
230   show his dad the book to prove his case, but what he read next made him stop: "Captain Etheridge, born in 1844 on Roanoke Island in North Carolina, died in 1900."

  Tucker said he read that date fifteen or twenty times before it started to sink in. Nineteen Hundred? Richard Etheridge had been dead for almost one hundred years. How was it possible a dead man helped him save that guy? Unless Richard was a ghost. He'd been talking to, and swimming with—a ghost?

  You can believe Tucker hit up the library that very next day and searched for as much information as he could find on Richard
240   Etheridge. There wasn't much, but what he read was that Richard Etheridge was all those great things he had read about and that he still died in 1900.

H   A few years later, when Tucker's folks visited the North Carolina Aquarium on Roanoke Island, <u>Tucker found Richard Etheridge's grave and monument. Etheridge's headstone was marked 1844–1900.</u> That's when Tucker stopped talking about Richard being involved in the rescue. Unless somebody asked.

  So now, if you run into Tucker "Tugboat" Willis, ask him about the rescue, and he'll tell you. Then, real carefully, ask if he ever met
250   Richard Etheridge. He'll tell you yes, he did, and what he learned. What he learned was that it pays to be polite to everybody you meet, like Tucker was to a man named Richard. You never know when that person might help you.

  And every time Tucker tells me the story, he tells it to me the same way I told it to you. Seeing how Tucker turned out proves that some mighty things that help folks out in some mighty big ways can come in some mighty small packages.

  It also proves that good things come to those who wait, like I did. (I know, because I'm Mrs. LaShana Mae Willis, Tugboat's wife.)

8. **READ ▶** As you read lines 238–275, continue to cite textual evidence.

- Underline the reason Tucker stops talking about Richard's involvement in the rescue (lines 243–247).
- Circle what you learn about the narrator.

11

WHEN STUDENTS STRUGGLE . . .

To help students understand how the setting shapes the events and the role Richard plays in the story, ask them to reread lines 212–237. Invite them to work with a small group to discuss how this passage gives insight into the setting, characters, and plot of the story.

FOR ELL STUDENTS A phrasal verb (a verb that is followed by a preposition, which gives the verb another meaning) may be difficult for ELL students to comprehend. Make sure that students understand the actual meaning of "shot out" (left very quickly), "hit up" (went to) and "run into" (meet by coincidence).

ASK STUDENTS to use each of these phrasal verbs in a sentence.

8. **READ AND CITE TEXT EVIDENCE** Although Tucker most likely believes that Richard Etheridge participated in the rescue, he stops including Richard's involvement in the rescue until somebody asks about him.

H **ASK STUDENTS** to cite textual evidence that suggests why Tucker stops talking about Richard's involvement in the rescue of Mr. Nibbles. *Students should cite that when Tucker sees Richard Etheridge's grave and monument, confirming that Richard had died in 1900, he stops talking about Richard's participation in the rescue because people might doubt Tucker's sanity if he says he was helped by someone who has been dead for a century.*

CLOSE READ Notes

I 260   There really was a man named Richard Etheridge, a professional fisherman who was born in 1844 on Roanoke Island off North Carolina. A member of the Thirty-sixth U.S. Colored Troops of the Union Army, he fought at the Battle of New Market Heights in Virginia during the Civil War. And in 1880, Etheridge was hired as the Keeper of the Pea Island Lifesaving Station on the Barrier Islands (the Outer Banks) of North Carolina. The station continued to set a high standard of performance with its all-black personnel until 1947, when the Coast Guard closed down the facilities.

        No one made any formal recognition of the Pea Island surfmen's daring sea rescues until 1996. In March of that year, Etheridge and his men were finally acknowledged **posthumously** in formal ceremonies in Washington, D.C., with a Gold Lifesaving Medal from the United States Coast Guard. Etheridge and his wife and daughter are buried on the grounds of the North Carolina Aquarium in Manteo, which maintains an exhibit on these brave men.

posthumously:
after death

270

9. ◀ **REREAD AND DISCUSS** Reread lines 260–275. With a partner, discuss the inclusion of the historical facts at the end of a fictional story. Does it add anything to the story or is it unnecessary?

SHORT RESPONSE

Cite Text Evidence Was Tucker the hero that everyone thought him to be, or was Richard mostly responsible for the rescue? **Cite text evidence** to support your opinion.

Tucker was a hero. He decided to save Mr. Nibbles, despite knowing he was in danger himself. Even if Richard was really there, Tucker "wasn't afraid of a thing." He still had to fight the storm and struggle hard to help rescue Mr. Nibbles. If Richard was only in Tucker's imagination, he certainly was a hero and accomplished an amazing feat.

12

---

9. ⬛ **REREAD AND DISCUSS USING TEXT EVIDENCE**

I ASK STUDENTS to cite specific text evidence and line numbers to support what interest historical facts add to the story. *Students should cite text evidence from lines 260–275.*

Critical Vocabulary: posthumously (line 271) Discuss why the author uses the word "posthumously" when discussing the awards given to the Pea Island surfmen. *The surfmen were only recognized for their service many years after their death.*

SHORT RESPONSE

Cite Text Evidence Student responses will vary, but students should cite evidence from the text to support their positions. Students should:

- explain whether Tucker or Richard was truly the hero.
- give reasons for their point of view.
- cite specific evidence from the text to support their reasons.

TO CHALLENGE STUDENTS . . .

For more context about Richard Etheridge and the Pea Island Lifesaving Service, students can conduct print, online, or multimedia research to write a report about Etheridge and his all–African American Pea Island lifesavers and their daring rescues on North Carolina's Outer Banks.

ASK STUDENTS to do some preliminary research to find an aspect of the topic that interests them. Possible topics for their research might include:

- Etheridge's role as the keeper of the Pea Island station,
- the rescue of the *E.S. Newman* by the Pea Island lifesavers in 1896,
- the Roanoke Island Freedmen and the Pea Island Life-Saving Station.

With the class, discuss the following elements of a research report after students have chosen a topic.

Plan Your Research

- Write questions about your topic.
- Research your topic and take notes.
- Organize your notes.
- Write an outline based on your notes.

Write Your Report

- Keep your purpose and audience in mind.
- Write a first draft, revise your report, and proofread it.
- Reread your report and check that your bibliography is accurate.

Publish and Share

- Make a final copy of your report.
- Publish and share it.

ASK STUDENTS what they hope to discover as they research their report. How is the information they find similar to, yet different from, the story and facts shared by Tate?

DIG DEEPER

1. With the class, return to Question 6, Reread and Discuss. Have students share the results of their discussion.

ASK STUDENTS whether they were pleased with the outcome of their partner discussions. Have each pair share the details they chose that created suspense in the plot. How did these details create tension and excitement for the reader? Then ask each pair to share their discussion about a future event these details foreshadowed. What textual evidence did pairs cite to support their opinion about this future plot development?

- Guide each pair to tell whether his or her partner cited any textual details (or evidence) with which he or she did not agree. If so, what was it? How did the partners resolve their differences of opinion?

- Encourage partners to explain how they decided on the event (or plot development) in the story that was foreshadowed by the details of the growing storm. What compelling evidence did they find to support their choice?

- After partners have shared the results of their discussion, ask whether another pair shared any ideas they wish they had thought of.

2. With the class, return to Question 9, Reread and Discuss. Have students share the results of their discussion.

ASK STUDENTS whether they were satisfied with the outcome of their partner discussions. Have each pair share their agreed-upon opinion about the inclusion of the historical facts at the end of the fictional story. What convincing evidence did pairs cite from the story to support their opinion?

- Encourage pairs to tell whether their partner cited any compelling textual evidence to support the opposite position. If so, why wasn't the evidence strong enough to become the agreed-upon opinion? How did the pairs resolve any conflicts or disagreements?

- After partners have shared the results of their discussion, ask whether another pair's findings convinced them that the opposite opinion had merit. Did it change their opinion?

ASK STUDENTS to return to their Short Response answer and to revise it based on the class discussion about citing convincing textual evidence to support an opinion.

CLOSE READING NOTES

mySmartPlanner — Create lesson plans and access resources online.

COMPARE MEDIA

MEDIA Covering Issues in the News

Online News Article, Editorial, and TV News Interview

Why These Texts?

Students regularly encounter news stories in their daily lives. This lesson explores the same news story as covered in three different forms of media, offering a variety of perspectives and opinions. By learning to analyze news stories in different media, students will become more savvy consumers of news.

Key Learning Objective: The student will be able to analyze and compare news stories about the same event from various sources.

For practice and application:

Background At approximately 29,000 feet above sea level, Mount Everest is the highest mountain in the world. More than five thousand people have reached the summit of Mount Everest since the first successful climb in 1953 by Edmund Hillary and Tenzing Norgay. However, the climb is extremely dangerous; more than 200 people have died attempting to reach the top.

Finding Your Everest

Essay by Robert Medina

Close Reader selection:
"Finding Your Everest"
Essay by Robert Medina

COMMON CORE Common Core Standards

RI 1 Cite textual evidence.
RI 2 Determine central ideas and details.
RI 3 Analyze interactions between individuals, events, and ideas.
RI 5 Analyze the structure an author uses to organize a text.
RI 6 Determine an author's point of view or purpose.
RI 8 Trace and evaluate an argument.
RI 9 Analyze how two or more authors write about the same topic.
SL 2 Analyze main ideas and details presented in diverse media.
W 1 Write arguments.
W 4 Produce clear and coherent writing.
W 6 Use technology to produce and publish writing.

▲ Text Complexity Rubric

	Parents of Rescued Teenage Sailor ... **Lexile:** 1110L	Ship of Fools **Lexile:** 1120L	Was Abby Too Young to Sail? **Lexile:** N/A
Quantitative Measures			
Qualitative Measures	Levels of Meaning/Purpose single level of simple meaning	Levels of Meaning/Purpose single level of simple meaning	Levels of Meaning/Purpose more than one purpose; implied, easily identified from context
	Structure organization of main ideas and details complex, but clearly stated and generally sequential	Structure implicit problem-solution text structure	Structure largely simple graphics, supplementary to understanding of the media
	Language Conventionality and Clarity some unfamiliar language	Language Conventionality and Clarity more complex sentence structure	Language Conventionality and Clarity mainly conversational language
	Knowledge Demands some specialized knowledge required	Knowledge Demands some specialized knowledge required	Knowledge Demands some specialized knowledge required
Reader/Task Considerations	Teacher determined Vary by individual reader and type of text		

CLOSE READ

Background Have students read the background information about news pieces. Explain that students are going to read and watch news pieces about Abby Sunderland, a 16-year-old American girl who in 2010 attempted to sail around the world by herself. Abby's trip was cut short when her sailboat was hit by a storm in the Indian Ocean. Abby's story raised a range of emotions around the world, from admiration to fear to anger.

SETTING A PURPOSE Direct students to use the Setting a Purpose text to focus their reading and viewing. Remind them to generate questions as they read and view.

Background *A compelling event in the news can trigger controversy. Through television, the Internet, and print articles, journalists and the general public voice their opinions and ask heated questions that may not have easy answers.*

SETTING A PURPOSE In this lesson, you'll analyze media about a 16-year-old's attempt to become the youngest person to sail solo around the world, an event that sparked worldwide controversy.

MEDIA ANALYSIS

Covering Issues
in the News

Parents of Rescued Teenage Sailor Abby Sunderland Accused of Risking Her Life
Online News Article by Paul Harris

Ship of Fools
Editorial by Joanna Weiss

Was Abby Too Young to Sail?
TV News Interview by CBS News

(t) ©Richard Hartog/AP Images; (tc) ©Eric Hoarau/TAAF/AFP/Getty Images; (bc) ©Charles Krupa/AP Images; (b) ©BBC Motion Gallery

SCAFFOLDING FOR ELL STUDENTS

Analyze Language In a word web, display words and phrases from the two news articles that are all related to the *danger* Abby Sunderland faced, such as *risking her life, save her life, sink, emergency beacon, search and rescue, difficult conditions,* etc. Discuss the meaning of each word and phrase. Then explain how these words are related.

ASK STUDENTS what kinds of dangers a teenager might meet on a solo sailboat trip around the world.

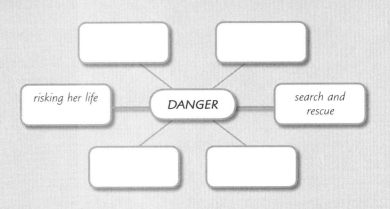

risking her life — DANGER — search and rescue

Analyze Structure

(LINES 1–4)

COMMON CORE RI 1, RI 2, RI 5, SL 2

Explain to students that journalists use the **5 Ws and H** questions as an outline for writing a news story. The questions are *who, what, when, where, why,* and *how.* Journalists then use this information to organize their writing. Answering each question contributes to the development of the article.

(A) CITE TEXT EVIDENCE Have students reread lines 1–4 and tell who and what the online news article is about. *(It is about a teenage girl who was rescued after she attempted to sail around the world by herself.)*

MEDIA

Parents of Rescued Teenage Sailor Abby Sunderland Accused of Risking Her Life

Sailing experts condemn family for allowing 16-year-old American girl to attempt a solo round-the-world voyage

Paul Harris, New York
The Observer, June 12, 2010

A teenage girl attempting to sail solo around the world was rescued yesterday in a remote spot of the Indian Ocean, bringing to a successful conclusion the dramatic bid to save her life.

Sixteen-year-old American Abby Sunderland was picked up from her stricken vessel by a dinghy[1] launched from the French fishing boat *Ile de la Reunion.*[2]

Her father, Laurence Sunderland, speaking to reporters outside their California home, said his daughter was safe and
10 well: "She got out of her vessel with the clothes on her back, and we are just really excited and ecstatic that Abigail is in safe hands. She was in good spirits . . . she talked to her mother."

However, the same cannot be said of Sunderland's yacht, *Wild Eyes.* The vessel was apparently pounded by gigantic waves that had destroyed its mast,[3] which in turn knocked out her satellite communications equipment. The yacht was then effectively left floundering midway between Africa and Australia. It is likely to be allowed to sink.

Sunderland had activated an emergency beacon[4] which
20 started a huge search and rescue operation involving Australia, America, and France. Numerous ships became involved in the hunt, as well as a chartered jet which spotted the teenager late on Thursday. Sunderland was able to radio the plane and report that she was fit and had food and water supplies.

---

[1] **dinghy:** a small open boat carried as a lifeboat on a larger boat.
[2] *Ile de la Reunion:* the French fishing boat carrying the dinghy that picked up Abby is a large ocean-going ship, 180 feet long, 23 feet wide, and weighing 1295 tons.
[3] **mast:** the tall, vertical pole that supports the sail and rigging of a ship.
[4] **beacon:** a radio or transmitter that emits a guidance signal.

APPLYING ACADEMIC VOCABULARY

aspect	resource

As you discuss the news piece, incorporate the following Collection 1 academic vocabulary words: *aspect* and *resource*. Ask students to tell what **aspect** of Abby's trip was most concerning to them. Have them name some of the **resources** Abby had on her sailboat to help keep her safe.

The rescue itself was not without incident as rough seas saw the captain of the French boat fall into the water. "He was fished out in difficult conditions," said a statement from the French territory of Reunion Island.

30 B Though the search for Sunderland ended happily, it has caused a debate on the wisdom of such young sailors making dramatic and dangerous journeys. Sunderland was following the achievement of her brother, Zac, who had made the solo journey around the world at the age of 17, becoming the youngest person in the world to do so.

Abby Sunderland on her sailboat *Wild Eyes* in Ensenada, Mexico, during her attempt at a solo round-the-world voyage

©Richard Hartog/AP Images

Many critics of Sunderland—and her parents—have criticized the decision to let her go on such a journey. "It's not something that a 16-year-old should be able to decide—whether they're capable of doing it. It's potentially 40 irresponsible for the parents," Michael Kalin, junior director of San Francisco's St Francis Yacht Club, told the Associated Press.

Other top figures from the world of sailing joined in the criticism. "In Abby's case she was lucky. It's only a matter of time until we end up with a tragedy on our hands," said Derrick Fries, a world sailing champion and author of *Learn to Sail.*

CLOSE READ

Analyze Structure

 COMMON CORE RI 1, RI 2, RI 5, SL 2

(LINES 30–35, 36–47)

At this point in the news article, the focus shifts from the recounting of Abby Sunderland's rescue to the debate in the media her voyage created. Here the **central idea,** or the most important idea about a topic, shifts from focusing on Abby's voyage, to reactions to Abby's voyage.

B ASK STUDENTS to reread lines 30–35 and identify the central idea introduced in this section of the article. *(This section introduces the debate sparked by Abby's voyage over the wisdom of young sailors making "dramatic and dangerous journeys.")*

Explain to students that **supporting details** can be facts, statistics, and anecdotes that tell more about, or support, a central idea.

C CITE TEXT EVIDENCE Have students reread lines 36–47 and identify supporting details that provide more information about the central idea. *(Many critics, including experts, criticized the decision to let Abby go on the voyage. The director of a yacht club suggested it wasn't Abby's decision to make, and a world sailing champion thought Abby was lucky to survive.)*

Strategies for Annotation   🖊 📋 **Annotate it!**

Analyze Structure

COMMON CORE RI 2, RI 5, SL 2

Have students locate lines 43–47. Encourage them to use their eBook annotation tools to do the following:

- Highlight in yellow *What* this paragraph is about—the central idea.
- Highlight in green a *Who* detail that supports this idea.
- On a note, write the central idea in your own words.

Other top figures from the world of sailing joined in the criticism. "In Abby's case she was lucky. It's only a matter of time until we end up with a tragedy on our hands," said Derrick Fries, a world sailing champion and author of *Learn to Sail.*

Analyze Structure

COMMON CORE · RI 1, RI 5, SL 2

(LINES 57–62)

Point out that news stories often tell about why something happened.

 CITE TEXT EVIDENCE Ask students to reread lines 57–62 and tell why Abby's family believed that she should have been allowed to go on the sailing trip. *(Abby's family believed that Abby was highly experienced and skilled; they believe challenge is healthy for an adventurous child; they believe many parents are overprotective.)*

Such opinions by professionals have been echoed on blogs and comments on news articles as members of the public
50 have called the Sunderlands irresponsible and careless. One commentator on the *Los Angeles Times* website summed up the view of many: "Abby Sunderland was on the wrong type of boat (a racing yacht) in the wrong location (the southern Indian Ocean) at the wrong time of year (winter in the southern hemisphere). Other than those minor details, it was a well-planned voyage."

But the family have robustly defended themselves. They have pointed out that Abby is a highly experienced and highly skilled sailor. They have even used the debate to criticize the
60 too-careful tendency of much modern parenting advice and said that a certain amount of risky challenge was healthy for an adventurous child.

"I never questioned my decision in letting her go. In this day and age we get overprotective with our children," Laurence Sunderland said. "Look at how many teenagers die in cars every year. Should we let teenagers drive cars? I think it'd be silly if we didn't."

WHEN STUDENTS STRUGGLE...

To guide students' understanding of the information presented in the news piece, have pairs of students work together to make a two-column chart to list reasons given in the text that explain why Abby should and should not have been allowed to make the solo sailboat trip. Students can then look at their chart and discuss their own opinions.

Reasons For	Reasons Against
She had a radio.	It's not something a child should be able to decide.
She had food and water supplies.	

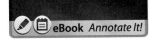

Analyze Structure

COMMON CORE RI 2, RI 5, SL 2

In a **news report,** whether it's online, in print, or broadcast on television, journalists commonly use the **5 Ws and H questions**—*who, what, when, where, why,* and *how*—as an outline for writing the news story. Following this structure helps to ensure that writers have covered the necessary details. In turn, readers can use the 5 *Ws* and *H* questions to determine the main idea and supporting details of a news story. The **central idea** is the most important idea about a topic that a writer conveys, and the **supporting details** are the examples, facts, statistics, and anecdotes that provide a basis for the central idea.

Analyzing the Media

COMMON CORE RI 2, RI 5, SL 2

Cite Text Evidence Support your responses with evidence from the text.

1. **Summarize** Review the news story and fill out a chart like this one to record the story's 5 *Ws* and *H*.

5 W's and H Questions	
Who is the story about?	
What happened to this person?	
When did it happen?	
Where did it happen?	
Why did it happen?	
How did it happen?	

2. **Infer** What is the central idea of this article? Cite details from the article to support your answer.

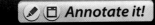

PRACTICE & APPLY

Analyze Structure

COMMON CORE RI 2, RI 5, SL 2

Help students understand the terms. Discuss whether the news report they just read answers all of the 5 *Ws* and *H* questions. Then have them explain how answering these questions helped the journalist to write the story. *(Answering all of these questions makes sure that the reader understands everything about the news event and what people thought of it.)*

Analyzing the Media

COMMON CORE RI 2, RI 5, SL 2

Possible answers:

1. ***Who:*** *A 16-year-old girl and her family;* ***What:*** *She gets rescued while attempting to sail around the world by herself;* ***When:*** *In 2010;* ***Where:*** *In the Indian Ocean;* ***Why:*** *Her sailboat was disabled by a big storm;* ***How:*** *A fishing boat picked her up.*

2. *The central idea of this article is that many people do not think that Abby should have been able to go on this trip by herself, but her parents disagree. Details that support this idea include the following: experts and other members of the public said that the girl should not have been able to go by herself; her parents said that she was skilled enough to sail alone and that risky challenges are good for adventurous children.*

Strategies for Annotation   Annotate it!

Analyze Structure

COMMON CORE RI 2, RI 5, SL 2

Have students locate lines 8–12. Encourage them to use their eBook annotation tools to do the following:

*   Highlight in yellow *Who* this paragraph is about.
*   Highlight in green *Where* this person is.
*   Review annotations and, in a note, tell how this paragraph supports the article's central idea.

Her father, Laurence Sunderland, speaking to reporters outside their Californian home, said his daughter was safe and well: "She got out of her vessel with the c... and we are just really excited and ecstatic... hands. She was in good spirits . . . she tal...

> That her parents were happy Abby made the trip even though others may disagree with their choice is supported here by showing that they were relieved she was safe.

TEACH

CLOSE READ

COMMON CORE RI 1, RI 2, RI 5, RI 8

Trace and Evaluate an Argument (LINES 7–9, 19–23)

Explain to students that an **editorial** is an opinion piece that appears in the part of a newspaper that has other opinions. An **opinion** is a statement of belief or feeling. It is not a fact. A **fact** is a statement that can be proved. Facts can be used to support a person's opinions.

 ASK STUDENTS to reread the sentence on lines 7–9 and identify if the statement is a fact or an opinion. *(It is an opinion because it cannot be proved. It is a statement of the writer's beliefs.)*

Explain that an editorial can include a claim. A **claim** is the writer's position or opinion. To prove a claim, a writer must provide reasons and evidence. **Reasons** are statements that explain a person's beliefs or actions. **Evidence** includes the facts, statistics, quotations, or anecdotes that support each reason.

CITE TEXT EVIDENCE Have students reread lines 19–23, state the writer's claim, and identify reasons that support that claim. *(The writer's claim is that letting Abby go on her solo voyage was a foolish and dangerous decision by Abby's parents. The writer gives reasons, such as the danger the rescue workers were exposed to and talks about the "uninspiring" image of Abby alone surrounded by threatening waves.)*

MEDIA

Ship of Fools

Protecting a 16-year-old sailor, not enabling dangerous dreams, is a parent's responsibility

Joanna Weiss, Globe Columnist
The Boston Globe, June 15, 2010

'I THINK it's a parent's job to realize their kids' dreams," Abby Sunderland's father told the *Los Angeles Times* last winter. This was just before he waved his 16-year-old daughter off on what was to be a six-month voyage alone on a small boat, her effort to become the youngest person to sail around the world nonstop and unassisted.

Here's a proposed rule of thumb: any record that requires more than 10 syllables to explain does not need to be broken. At any rate, Abby did not succeed. A massive storm
10 in the Indian Ocean knocked out her mast, launching a massive international rescue effort. She has since abandoned her 40-foot boat and boarded a French fishing vessel, from where she has resumed her blog.

Actually, she has a panoply of interlinked blogs,[1] set up to track and promote her journey, including one that sold T-shirts and shoes with an "Abby 16" logo. They're flooded now with comments offering gratitude and praise, calling her a role model and an inspiration.

So this is the definition of bravery now? Embarking[2] on
20 unnecessary risk that jeopardizes the lives of rescue workers? When I thought of a 16-year-old bobbing alone in the Indian Ocean, surrounded by 25-foot waves, I didn't feel inspired. I felt sad. And when I thought about her parents, I felt furious.

Abby's fans would call me a naysayer,[3] I gather from their posts, and tell me I lack a spirit of adventure. And I'll admit that parenthood requires one to overcome a certain intolerance[4] for risk. I can't watch my 5-year-old daughter climb the monkey bars without feeling like I'm going to have a coronary. God knows what I'll do when she starts driving.

---

[1] **panoply (păn´ə plē) of interlinked blogs:** an array of blogs that are linked together.
[2] **Embarking:** setting out.
[3] **naysayer:** one who opposes or takes a negative view.
[4] **intolerance:** condition or quality of not accepting.

APPLYING ACADEMIC VOCABULARY

cultural	evaluate	text

As you discuss the editorial, incorporate the following Collection 1 academic vocabulary words: *cultural, evaluate,* and *text.* Ask students to discuss the **cultural** influences on decisions like the one Abby Sunderland's parents made. Ask them to point to examples of these influences cited in the **text.** Then ask them to **evaluate** the writer's overall claim.

30   But parenthood also requires you to invoke[5] maturity where your child lacks it, whether it's telling her that she's too small to slide down the fireman's pole or that her sailing journey will have to wait until she's old enough to come to her senses. It involves helping her figure out the difference between a dream and a fantasy.

    Perhaps someone should have stepped in to impose some parenting standards on the Sunderlands; last summer, a court in the Netherlands stopped a 13-year-old girl from making her own unadvised solo sail. Better yet, we could give up a

40 culture that treats accomplishment as a race and turns risk into its own reward. Abby Sunderland couldn't drive without a learner's permit, but her journey on the high seas got her fawning press[6] and endorsement deals. Now, some fans on her site have offered their own money to recover her lost boat. One pledged to play an extra $5 a day in the lottery, just in case.

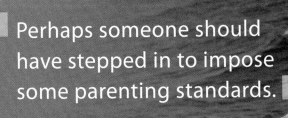

> Perhaps someone should have stepped in to impose some parenting standards.

    When will he realize he's simply a pawn in the Sunderlands' audience-building scheme? From onboard the French fishing vessel, Abby has declared, *quelle surprise*,[7] that she's writing a book. Her father also disclosed that he's been

50 shopping a reality show with the working title "Adventures in Sunderland." (What good fortune this family has, to have a name that lends itself to puns.)

---

[5] **invoke:** to call (a higher power) for assistance or support.

[6] **fawning press:** favor-seeking press.

[7] *quelle surprise*: What a surprise!

Ship of Fools   **25**

©Comstock/Getty Images

TEACH

CLOSE READ

Trace and Evaluate an Argument (LINES 36–45)

COMMON CORE   RI 2, RI 5, RI 8

The writer is suggesting that society has a certain responsibility to intercede in situations like Abby's.

H   CITE TEXT EVIDENCE Have students reread lines 36–45 and name a reason that the writer presents to support her claim that someone should have stepped in to impose some parenting standards on Abby Sunderland's parents. *(A court in the Netherlands stopped another teenage girl from making her own unadvised solo sail; Abby couldn't drive without a learner's permit, but she could sail without conforming to any rules.)*

WHEN STUDENTS STRUGGLE . . .

To guide students' understanding of claims and reasons, have pairs of students reread lines 30–35. Have them work together to make a two-column chart to list the claim and reasons the author makes about parenthood. Have students continue to use the chart as they read and view.

Claim	Reasons
Parents need to be invoking maturity where children lack it.	*It helps children figure out the difference between a dream and a fantasy.*

Trace and Evaluate an Argument (LINES 63–69)

COMMON CORE RI 1, RI 2, RI 5, RI 8

Tell students that a writer may also make counterarguments. A **counterargument** is a response to a differing opinion. By addressing the counterargument, the writer more fully develops his or her opinion and ideas.

CITE TEXT EVIDENCE Have students reread lines 63–69 and cite a counterargument to some people's opinion that Abby was a hero. *(The writer argues that being the youngest person to do something shouldn't be confused with being the first to do something; she feels that Abby was very lucky to have survived.)*

Childhood fame is always some mix of the child's dream and the parents'; so it was with Jessica Dubroff, the 7-year-old who died in 1996, trying to pilot a plane across the country.

With the growing temptations of book deals and TV series, the balance may be shifting even more. We'll surely hear more from Jordan Romero, the 13-year-old who just became the youngest person to climb Mount Everest. We

60 probably haven't heard the last of the Heenes of Colorado,[8] who at least had the sense not to actually put their child inside the Mylar balloon.

But while there's clearly a market for immature stars, we shouldn't confuse "youngest" with significant "first," and we shouldn't call these publicity stunts anything but what they are. Abby Sunderland may find a way to convert her misadventures into lingering fame. But while she seems to be a skilled junior sailor, calm in the face of danger, that doesn't make her a hero. It just makes her very, very lucky.

[8] **Heenes of Colorado:** a reference to a widely reported incident in 2009 in which a six-year-old boy was said to have floated away in a helium balloon. The report turned out to be false.

Strategies for Annotation   ✎ 🖉 *Annotate it!*

Analyze Structure

COMMON CORE RI 2, RI 5

Have students locate lines 63–69. Encourage them to use their eBook annotation tools to do the following:

- Highlight in yellow a counterargument that the writer makes.
- Highlight in green the writer's claim.
- Underline reasons the writer includes to show the counterargument is wrong.

But while there's clearly a market for immature stars, 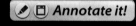 we shouldn't confuse "youngest" with significant "first," and we shouldn't call these publicity stunts anything but what they are. Abby Sunderland may find a way to convert her misadventures into lingering fame. But while she seems to be a skilled junior sailor, calm in the face of danger, that doesn't make her a hero. It just makes her very, very lucky.

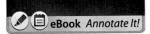 **eBook** *Annotate It!*

Trace and Evaluate an Argument

COMMON CORE RI 2, RI 5, RI 8

An **editorial** is an opinion piece that usually appears in the opinion and commentary section of a newspaper. An editorial is a type of argument in which the writer expresses one or more opinions about an issue and uses facts to support those opinions. A **fact** is a statement that can be proved. An **opinion** is a statement of belief or feeling. Like an argument, an editorial can include a **claim,** which is the writer's position or opinion; **reasons and evidence** that support the claim; and **counterarguments,** or responses to differing opinions.

Analyzing the Media

Cite Text Evidence Support your responses with evidence from the text.

1. **Cite Evidence** Reread the editorial and fill in a chart like this one to cite the facts and opinions you find.

Type of Evidence	Examples
Facts	
Opinions	

2. **Identify** Which sentence in the editorial represents the writer's claim?

3. **Analyze** In the first quote, Abby's father says, "I think it's a parent's job to realize their kids' dreams." What is the editorial writer's counterargument to this statement?

4. **Summarize** What point does the editorial writer make in lines 41–62?

5. **Evaluate** How effectively does the editorial writer convey her opinion? Evaluate how clearly and convincingly the writer presents her evidence and ideas and concludes the editorial.

Ship of Fools **27**

PRACTICE & APPLY

Trace and Evaluate an Argument

COMMON CORE RI 2, RI 5, RI 8

Help students with the terms. Discuss whether the editorial made a convincing counterargument to Abby's father's statement that it is a parent's job to realize their kids' dreams. Have students cite three reasons the author of "Ship of Fools" gives to support her claim that letting Abby take a solo voyage was foolish and dangerous. *(Parenting requires invoking maturity where a child lacks it. The Sunderlands used Abby's voyage to create an audience for media projects. Being the youngest to do something does not have the same significance as being the first.)*

Analyzing the Media

COMMON CORE RI 1, RI 2, RI 5, RI 8

Possible answers:

1. *Facts: Abby tried a solo voyage; A storm knocked out her mast; She abandoned her boat; A court in the Netherlands stopped a teen from taking a solo sailing trip. Opinions: It's a parent's job to realize their kids' dreams; Parents must invoke maturity where their child lacks it; Someone should have imposed parenting standards on the Sunderlands.*

2. *Protecting a 16-year-old sailor, not enabling dangerous dreams, is a parent's responsibility.*

3. *The writer's counterargument is that parenthood requires you to invoke maturity where your child lacks it.*

4. *The writer points out that Abby and her family were trying to get endorsement, book, and TV deals.*

5. *The writer conveys her opinion well. Her arguments are supported with facts. She concludes with the strong point that despite her skills, Abby was not a hero.*

Strategies for Annotation  *Annotate it!*

Trace and Evaluate an Argument

COMMON CORE RI 5, RI 8

Have students locate lines 46–52. Encourage them to use their eBook annotation tools to do the following:

- Highlight opinions in yellow.
- Highlight facts in green.
- Review the annotations and explain how this text evidence helps readers understand the editorial.

The examples support the opinion that the Sunderlands were trying to get publicity.

...ize he's simply a pawn in the Sunderlands' audience-building scheme? From onboard the French fishing vessel, Abby has declared, *quelle surprise,* that she's writing a book. Her father has also declared that he's been shopping a reality show with the working title "Adventures in Sunderland." (What good fortune this family has , to have a

Ship of Fools **27**

AS YOU VIEW Direct students to use the information in this section to help them understand the TV interview they are about to watch. Remind them to generate questions as they view.

COLLABORATIVE DISCUSSION Have students work in small groups to view and discuss the director's use of the different onscreen techniques and how they affect the viewer. Then have them compare the information to the other news pieces and discuss what is accomplished in the news report that cannot be done in the two print texts. Students may want to make a three-column chart to help them compare the information and insights they gathered from each news piece.

ASK STUDENTS to share any questions they generated in the course of viewing and discussing the TV interview.

MEDIA

Was Abby Too Young to Sail?

TV News Interview by Harry Smith, CBS News

Running Time: 3:40 minutes

AS YOU VIEW The news interview you are about to view was first broadcast June 11, 2010, on the CBS Morning News as news broke that Abby Sunderland had been found in the Indian Ocean and was being rescued. In the segment you are about to view, journalist Harry Smith interviews the Sunderland family. Video clips of Abby and her sailboat before the trip are included.

► NEW YORK   ► THOUSAND OAKS, CA

EARLY SHOW   BREAKING NEWS

FOUND ALIVE!
BOATS HEADING TO RESCUE TEEN SAILOR

COLLABORATIVE DISCUSSION Consider the choices the director makes about arranging the split-screen and including media features such as video clips. What is the effectiveness and impact of using video segments while the interviewees are speaking? What new information or insights do you learn from the interview about Abby's voyage and her preparedness? Discuss these choices and questions with your group and cite segments from the newscast to support your ideas.

©BBC Motion Gallery

Analyze Structure

In a **TV news interview,** a journalist asks questions of and discusses issues with one or more people who may be experts, eyewitnesses, informed persons, or others close to the subject of the news interview. An interview includes video of the discussion between the interviewer and interviewee and may also include video or visuals of related information that tell the viewer more about the subject. The visual elements usually illustrate or emphasize important information by showing rather than telling what happened. These images can create positive or negative views of the topic or individuals.

When gathering information from a television interview, note the questions and listen carefully to the information provided in each interviewee's response.

Analyzing the Media

 COMMON CORE   RI 2, RI 5, SL 2

| Cite Text Evidence | Support your responses with evidence from the media. |

1. **Identify** As you view the interview, use a chart like the one shown below to record information provided by each interviewee.

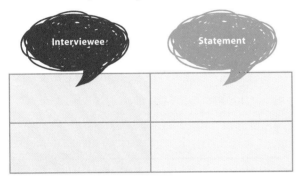

2. **Interpret** What overall impression of the Sunderland family does the interview create? Cite specific examples from the interview to support your response.

3. **Analyze** The video segments of Abby that appear at certain points during the interview were recorded before her trip. How do these video segments and the video overall characterize Abby?

Analyze Structure

 COMMON CORE   RI 2, RI 5, SL 2

Discuss the elements and structure of TV news interviews with students. Have them point out who is being interviewed in "Was Abby Too Young to Sail?" Then have them tell why the interviewees were good choices for the TV interview. *(They are members of Abby's family. They know her very well and know about the trip she was making.)*

Analyzing the Media

COMMON CORE   RI 2, RI 5, SL 2

Possible answers:

1. *Interviewee: Abby's father; Statement: He believed Abby is relieved that the rescue mission had found her; He believed that Abby had proven to him that she was qualified to do what she set out to do; Interviewee: Abby's mother; Statement: Abby is very resilient; The storm was just another challenge for her to meet; Interviewee: Abby's brother; Statement: Abby had the correct safety gear for this trip.*

2. *The interview makes them seem very confident about Abby's abilities and supportive of her trip. They told about how she had proven that she was qualified, how she was ready and equipped for challenges, and that she had the right safety gear to protect her in case of emergency.*

3. *The video segments of Abby show her sailing. They give the viewer the feeling that she is a very competent sailor.*

Analyze Ideas in Diverse Media

 COMMON CORE RI 2, RI 3,
RI 5, RI 6,
RI 8, RI 9,
SL 2

Remind students that news can be reported in a variety of different media. Each type has special characteristics that make it different and able to achieve its purpose.

Have students explain what advantage the TV interview had over the news article and editorial. *(The TV interview included footage that showed what Abby's family is like in person, including their reactions to the questions, so that viewers could see it for themselves and form their own opinions. It also included footage of Abby sailing that gave the viewer a good idea about her abilities.)*

Analyzing the Media

 COMMON CORE RI 2, RI 3,
RI 5, RI 6,
RI 8, RI 9,
SL 2, W 6

Possible answers:

1. **News Article:** *Purpose: to inform; Central Idea: There is a debate about whether Abby should have been allowed to go on her trip; Support: The article provides quotes from experts and Abby's parents;* **Editorial:** *Purpose: to persuade and to express thoughts or feelings; Claim: It is a parent's responsibility to protect his or her child; Evidence: The editorial provides counterarguments to Abby's parents' claim that she was capable of making the trip;* **TV News Interview:** *Purpose: to inform and to entertain; Central Idea: Abby's family thinks that she was capable of making the trip; Support: The answers include reasons such as that she was a capable and proven sailor and that she had the proper safety equipment.*

2. *The editorial emphasized the idea that it is a parent's responsibility to protect a child from dangerous dreams. It attempted to change a reader's view from thinking that Abby was a hero to thinking she was reckless.*

3. *The TV interview let us know what Abby's family looked like and gave some more information on the reasons they let her go. The footage also showed what Abby's boat looked like and her ability as a sailor.*

Analyze Ideas in Diverse Media

 COMMON CORE RI 2, RI 3, RI 5,
RI 6, RI 8, RI 9,
SL 2

You've just read coverage of a single topic in three different formats—a news article, an editorial, and a television interview—by different writers who provide their own unique evidence and interpretations of Abby Sunderland's rescue.

To analyze the information from these varied sources, examine the purpose and the ideas presented in each. The writer's purpose is his or her reason for writing the report or story: to inform, to persuade, to entertain, or to express thoughts or feelings. Often there is more than one purpose.

Analyzing the Media

 COMMON CORE RI 2, RI 3, RI 5,
RI 6, RI 8, RI 9,
SL 2, W6

Cite Text Evidence   Support your responses with evidence from the media.

1. **Analyze** Use a chart like this one to analyze the purpose and key information presented in each of the selections.

Type	News Article	Editorial	TV News Interview
Purpose			
Central Idea(s) or Claim(s)			
Support or Evidence			

2. **Synthesize** What idea about Abby's trip is emphasized in the editorial but not in the other two reports? How does this emphasis change your view of Abby's story?

3. **Analyze** What did you learn from the news interview that you did not learn from the articles? Cite specific evidence from each media piece to support your answer.

PERFORMANCE TASK

 my WriteSmart

Media Activity: Blog With your classmates, create a class blog to discuss what you think would be an appropriate age to pursue such an undertaking. To build the blog, map out your home page and plan one or more discussion threads.

Begin the blog by writing your own opinion of Abby's solo adventure. Was it foolish or wise for someone her age to attempt such a trip alone? Refer to any of the three news pieces for evidence. Encourage classmates to post to the blog.

Assign this performance task.  my WriteSmart

PERFORMANCE TASK

 COMMON CORE W1, W4,
W6

Media Activity: Blogs Have students work in teams.

- Remind them that good blogs are visually appealing and have structures that are easily navigated.
- Encourage them to make several different drafts of their home page before deciding on the one that works best.

Analyze Presentations of Information

COMMON CORE
RI 6,
RI 9

RETEACH

Explain to students that different authors can write about the same topic, but often these authors have different reasons for writing, or **author's purposes.** Depending on the author's purpose, a writer will choose different types of texts, each with its own goals and structure. Review the following to illustrate the differences between two types of texts.

- **Informative/Explanatory** The goal of informative or explanatory text is to present facts about a topic. The facts are used as evidence to support a central idea. Authors of this kind of text want to inform, for example, by presenting facts about Abby Sunderland's voyage, or to explain, by reporting why Abby's voyage stirred up a lot of debate.

- **Argument** The goal of texts that present an argument is to provide reasons and evidence to support a claim. An opinion essay is an example of this type of writing. In "Ship of Fools," the author argued that Abby Sunderland's parents used poor judgment.

- To compare two different texts about the same topic, look at the structure of each text, as well as the author's purpose for writing it. Is one author presenting an opinion while the other author is reporting facts? What does each author want the reader to take away from the text?

COLLABORATIVE DISCUSSION

Work with students to develop a chart that tells about the similarities and differences between a news article and an editorial on the same subject. Have them discuss the different purposes for each type of text, as well as the different kinds of information provided in each one.

How to Create a Blog

COMMON CORE
W 4,
W 6

TEACH

Explain to students that a **blog** enables writers to share their ideas about a topic over the Internet with a broad audience. It can also enable blog writers to benefit from readers' comments on their writing.

Before students begin working on their blog in the Performance Task, discuss the following:

- **Determine discussion threads.** Include a separate **discussion thread**—a chain of related posts—for each different idea discussed. Take notes on all the team's ideas before voting to select the best ones.

- **Map out a home page.** Sketch the home page, visually representing how users will link to the different threads. Discuss and vote on what other information to include.

- **Assign roles.** Make a plan to complete all the team's goals by specific deadlines. Divide the work equally. One person might research websites that can host the blog. Another might make a logo for the home page. Make sure any images used are not copyrighted. In addition, one person should be responsible for writing the first post within each thread.

- **Build the blog.** With the assistance of a school technology coordinator, assemble and launch the blog on a school or blogging website.

PRACTICE AND APPLY

Students can work with a team to plan and produce their blog. Once they have launched their blog, have students take turns posting messages several times a week. After a few weeks, have students evaluate what they might add or change to make their blog more user-friendly and current.

 INTERACTIVE LESSON Have students complete the tutorials in this lesson: **Producing and Publishing with Technology.**

Finding Your Everest

Essay by Robert Medina

Why This Text

Students often read the text of an argumentative essay without a complete grasp of the author's ideas and evidence. Arguments such as this one by Robert Medina may have several central ideas and reasoning that become clear only with careful study. With the help of the close-reading questions, students will trace and evaluate the argument about the risks and rewards of mountain climbing for a 13-year-old boy. This close reading will lead students to develop a coherent understanding of the argument as well as the counterargument that Medina presents.

Background Have students read the background information about Mount Everest, the highest peak on Earth. Introduce the selection by sharing this anecdote: When asked why he kept trying to climb Mount Everest, the English mountaineer George Mallory is said to have replied, "Because it was there." Whether or not this is the main reason for the more than five thousand climbs to the summit of Mount Everest since the first successful ascent in 1953 by Edmund Hillary and Tenzing Norgay, one thing is clear. Mount Everest is there to challenge its climbers.

SETTING A PURPOSE Ask students to pay close attention to the structure of this essay. How soon into the essay does Medina present the argument "for" Jordan's climb and the counterargument "against" it?

Common Core Support

- cite several pieces of textual evidence
- determine two or more central (or main) ideas in a text
- trace and evaluate an argument
- assess claims, reasoning, and evidence in a text

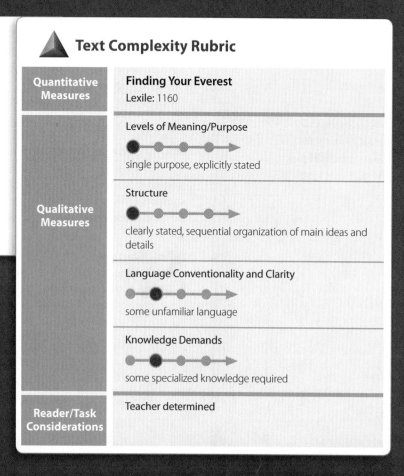

Text Complexity Rubric

	Finding Your Everest
Quantitative Measures	Lexile: 1160

Levels of Meaning/Purpose

single purpose, explicitly stated

Structure

clearly stated, sequential organization of main ideas and details

Language Conventionality and Clarity

some unfamiliar language

Knowledge Demands

some specialized knowledge required

Reader/Task Considerations — Teacher determined

Strategies for CLOSE READING

Trace and Evaluate an Argument

Students should read this essay carefully all the way through. Close-reading questions at the bottom of the page will help them focus on a thorough analysis of the argument as well as the counterargument. As they read, students should record comments or questions about the text in the side margins.

WHEN STUDENTS STRUGGLE . . .

To help students follow the reasons Medina cites to support a claim made by Paul Romero and a counterclaim made by several mountaineers and medical experts, have students work in a small group to fill out charts, such as the ones shown below, as they analyze the essay.

CITE TEXT EVIDENCE For practice in tracing an argument and counterargument, ask students to cite evidence that Medina gives to support each reason.

CLAIM: *The risks of climbing Everest are not too great for 13-year-old Jordan.*

SUPPORT:

Reason 1: *He is up to the challenge physically and mentally.*

Reason 2: *He is well prepared for the climb.*

Reason 3: *His parents will be climbing with him.*

Reason 4: *His young brain is more resilient, according to some medical experts.*

COUNTERCLAIM: *The risks are too great for 13-year-old Jordan.*

SUPPORT:

Reason 1: *He does not have the cognitive ability to make life-and-death decisions or to truly understand what he is signing on for.*

Reason 2: *Such a high climb will harm his body.*

Reason 3: *He has his whole life to climb Everest.*

Reason 4: *It is just a publicity stunt and not worth the risk.*

Background *At approximately 29,000 feet above sea level, Mount Everest is the highest mountain in the world. More than five thousand people have reached the summit of Mount Everest since the first successful climb in 1953 by Edmund Hillary and Tenzing Norgay. However, the climb is extremely dangerous; more than 200 people have died attempting to reach the top.*

Finding Your Everest

Essay by Robert Medina

CLOSE READ
Notes

1. **READ ▶** As you read lines 1–33, begin to collect and cite text evidence.
   - Circle the most important information you learn about Jordan Romero in lines 1–13.
   - Explain in the margin what is meant by "the seven summits."
   - Underline details in lines 22–33 that explain what Jordan achieved.

(A) Can parents go too far in supporting their children's dreams? This is a question people sometimes ask when they hear the story of the teenage mountain climber, Jordan Romero. Between the ages of 10 and 15, Jordan climbed the highest mountain on every continent—and his father and stepmother climbed them with him. They call themselves Team Jordan.

Paul Romero, Jordan's father, was taken by surprise when his 9-year-old son firmly announced his intention to climb "the seven summits." Jordan had seen a mural at school, showing the seven

10 peaks that make up this **pantheon** of mountains. When he told his father what he wanted to do, Paul Romero's jaw dropped. Paul Romero is an experienced mountaineer, so he knew what was involved. He also knew his son.

"The seven summits" refers to the tallest mountain on each continent.

pantheon:
a very famous group

13

1. **READ AND CITE TEXT EVIDENCE** Explain that Medina poses a question ("Can parents go too far in supporting their children's dreams?") to open his essay. Such a provocative question "grabs" the reader's attention, and in this case, states the topic the essay will argue.

(A) ASK STUDENTS to determine how Medina begins to answer his question by citing specific textual evidence in lines 1–33. *Responses may include references to evidence in lines 1–6, 14–21, 22–33.*

Critical Vocabulary: pantheon (line 10) Have students share their definitions of *pantheon*. Ask how *pantheon* fits into Jordan's "dream." *His "dream" is to climb "the seven summits," the highest and most famous mountain on each continent.*

CLOSE READ
Notes

Climbing mountains is not just fun. It's hard work.

persevered:
continued in spite of difficulties

controversy:
a dispute between opposing sides

(B) "We've always taught him to just think big and we'll try to make it happen," Paul Romero said. But, as Romero later noted, there was a fine line between encouraging his son and pushing him too far. The father began by training his son so that he could "begin to even understand what mountaineering was—that there's this long, hard, dirty, un-fun hours and days and weeks of carrying packs and long,
20 extensive, brutal travel, and all this type of stuff just before you can even think of climbing a mountain."

Jordan **persevered**, though, and in July 2006, when he was 10 years old, Jordan and his family climbed 19,300-foot-high Mount Kilimanjaro, the highest peak on the African continent. This was the first rung in the amazing ladder that Jordan Romero had set out to climb. Over the next five and a half years, Team Jordan climbed Mount Elbrus in Russia (2007), Mount Aconcagua in South America (2007), Mount McKinley in North America (2008), Mount Carstensz Pyramid in Indonesia (2009), Mount Everest in Asia (2010), and
30 Vinson Massif in Antarctica (2011). In many of these climbs, Jordan set a world record as the youngest ever to climb the peak. When he completed the seven summits at 15, he was the youngest person ever to accomplish that feat.

(C) It was the Mount Everest ascent—when Jordan was only 13 years old—that has created the greatest **controversy.** Jordan's feat, as the youngest person to reach "the top of the world" was publicized

around the world. "How Young Is Too Young?" asked one newspaper headline. Many mountain climbers and medical experts questioned whether a 13-year-old boy could climb so high (Mount Everest is
40 almost 30,000 feet high) without physically harming his body. Dr. Michael Bradley of the National Institute of Health noted, "Most 13-year-olds don't have the wiring to make **cognitive** life-and-death decisions and are not truly able to understand what they're signing on for." Another physician, Dr. Peter Hackett, reported that there are conflicting opinions about the effects on a young brain. Some theories say that a young brain is more resilient; others say that it may be more vulnerable.

(D) Many climbers take exception to the publicity surrounding Team Jordan. Everest climber Todd Burleson summed it up by saying, "He's
50 got his whole life to climb Everest. Being the youngest boy to climb is a fashionable, celebrity-oriented sort of thing. But it's not about the mountains. It's like trying to get your PhD at ten."

(E) Paul Romero claims that he is fully aware of the risks. There is a fine line between encouraging Jordan and pushing him too far, he says. He talked about the point where Jordan might have "reached his maximum mentally, physically, and where the risk has become too high." He said, "Jordan has just not even come close to that point yet."

And what about Jordan, now that he has accomplished his goal of climbing the seven summits before his 16th birthday? Unsurprisingly,

CLOSE READ
Notes

cognitive:
using reason to understand and make judgments

Paul Romero claims that Jordan is up to the challenge and not at risk.

---

2. **◀ REREAD** Reread lines 14–21. In the margin, restate in your own words what Paul Romero says about mountaineering.

3. **READ ▶** As you read lines 34–52, continue to cite textual evidence.
- Underline the medical claim (a position or opinion) about the dangers of mountain climbing to a 13-year-old.
- Circle the medical claim that offers a counterargument, or response, to the dangers of mountain climbing to a 13-year-old.
- Underline the opinion given by another mountain climber.

4. **◀ REREAD AND DISCUSS** Reread lines 49–52. With a small group, discuss whether the evidence Todd Burleson cites is sufficient to support his opinion that Jordan and his family are just publicity seekers.

5. **READ ▶** As you read lines 53–68, continue to cite textual evidence.
- In the margin, restate the claim that Paul Romero makes in lines 53–57.
- Circle the main idea in lines 58–65.
- Underline the details that support the main idea.

14

15

---

2. **REREAD AND CITE TEXT EVIDENCE**

(B) ASK STUDENTS to explain the reason for Romero's statement about the difficulties of mountaineering. *He is trying to inject some reality into his son's dream.*

3. **READ AND CITE TEXT EVIDENCE**

(C) ASK STUDENTS to find and cite specific examples of the risks involved for a 13-year-old boy. *Students should cite examples in lines 34–52.*

Critical Vocabulary: persevered (line 22) Have students share examples of times when they have persevered in a situation. *Students should cite examples of learning a difficult subject, sport, or musical instrument.*

Critical Vocabulary: controversy (line 35) Why does Medina use the word *controversy* to introduce the counterargument? *It is the perfect word to use to present the opposing claim.*

4. **REREAD AND DISCUSS USING TEXT EVIDENCE**

(D) ASK STUDENTS to appoint a reporter for each group to cite specific text evidence and line numbers to support their position about the sufficiency of Todd Burleson's evidence. *Students should cite evidence from lines 49–52.*

5. **READ AND CITE TEXT EVIDENCE**

(E) ASK STUDENTS to read their margin notes to a partner and then write one response that summarizes Paul Romero's viewpoint in lines 53–57, incorporating his central idea. *Students should see that he says that he realizes the risks but is encouraging Jordan, not pushing him beyond his mental and physical limits.*

Critical Vocabulary: cognitive (line 42) Have students explain *cognitive* as it is used here. Ask how it fits in with the counterargument given by a medical expert. *The doctor says, "'Most 13-year-olds don't have the wiring'" to make judgments about "'life-and-death decisions.'"*

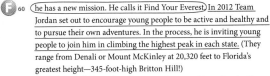

CLOSE READ Notes

Some may say that Jordan and his family are only trying to attract attention.

F 60 he has a new mission. He calls it Find Your Everest In 2012 Team Jordan set out to encourage young people to be active and healthy and to pursue their own adventures. In the process, he is inviting young people to join him in climbing the highest peak in each state. (They range from Denali or Mount McKinley at 20,320 feet to Florida's greatest height—345-foot-high Britton Hill!)

"I feel good about what my parents have taught me about setting goals," Jordan says. And now he wants to spread that message to others.

6. ◀ **REREAD** Reread lines 58–68. Make a note in the margin about how people might react to Jordan's new mission, considering the response to his earlier climbs.

SHORT RESPONSE

Cite Text Evidence The article opens with the question, "Can parents go too far in supporting their children's dreams?" Review your reading notes, and answer the question as it relates to the Romeros, evaluating the strength of the claims offered. Be sure to **cite text evidence** in your response.

Answers will vary. Some students may believe that Jordan Romero's parents have gone too far in allowing him to realize his dream of climbing the seven highest mountains on Earth. The claims made by many medical experts suggest that most 13-year-olds do not have the ability to make "cognitive life-and-death decisions." While some doctors claim that a young brain is more resilient, many doctors think that climbing the highest summits will damage a young body. Furthermore, some climbers suggest that Jordan and his parents are just publicity seekers hoping to gain celebrity status.

16

---

6. REREAD AND CITE TEXT EVIDENCE

F **ASK STUDENTS** to write a response that states why people might be in favor of Jordan's new mission and why others might not. *Students should cite textual evidence from lines 58–68 to offer a "for" and "against" position.*

FOR ELL STUDENTS (line 60) Explain that *mission* is a multiple-meaning word. Ask students if they know at least two meanings of the word. *One meaning is that of a goal or special task; another is that of a church.* Have students tell which meaning is used here. *Here, it means "a goal or special task."*

SHORT RESPONSE

Cite Text Evidence Students should:

- explain whether or not they believe that the Romeros have gone too far in supporting Jordan's dream.
- give reasons for their point of view.
- cite specific evidence from the text to support their reasons.

TO CHALLENGE STUDENTS . . .

For more context about Mount Everest, including how it was formed and what makes it such a difficult and dangerous mountain to climb, students can view the brief video "Mountain Building," a part of the *How the Earth Was Made* series, in their eBooks.

ASK STUDENTS what they have learned about the formation of mountains and why the Himalayas, the highest mountain system on Earth, which includes Mount Everest, is such a forbidding mountain range. *Students should recognize that Mount Everest, the world's tallest peak, rising 29,000 feet above sea level, might be a risky mountain to climb for a 13-year-old boy.*

DIG DEEPER

With the class, return to Question 4, Reread and Discuss. Have students share the results of their discussion.

ASK STUDENTS whether they were satisfied with the outcome of their small-group discussions. Have each group share whether or not they agreed with the claim made by Todd Burleson, an Everest climber, that Jordan and his family are just publicity seekers looking to achieve celebrity status. Invite each group to share the majority opinion of the group. What compelling evidence from the essay did each group cite to support its opinion?

- Encourage students to tell whether there was any compelling textual evidence cited by Burleson to support his position and how that evidence (or lack of it) may have prompted them to agree (or disagree) with his point of view.

- Have groups disclose how they decided whether or not the evidence was sufficient. Did everyone in the group agree as to what made the evidence sufficient? How did the group resolve any conflicts or differing opinions?

- Invite groups to reveal whether there was any convincing evidence cited by group members holding the minority opinion. If so, why didn't it sway the group's opinion?

- After students have shared the results of their group's discussion, ask whether another group shared any findings they wished they had brought to the table.

ASK STUDENTS to return to their Short Response answer and to revise it based on the class discussion.

*my***SmartPlanner** Create lesson plans and access resources online.

ANCHOR TEXT # The Flight of Icarus

Greek Myth retold by Sally Benson

Why This Text?

Students often encounter universal themes that have their roots in mythology—lessons about human nature that were important not only to the ancient peoples but also to people of today. After reading the myth of Icarus, students will better understand references to someone who "flies too close to the sun."

Key Learning Objective: The student will be able to analyze the elements of a myth and to determine two or more themes.

For practice and application:

Background *Many Greek myths are about characters who stray beyond the limits set by Greek gods and goddesses or who ignore their warnings. In this myth, Arachne (ərăk'nē), a weaver, pits herself against Athena (ə-thē'nə), the goddess of wisdom and of crafts, particularly weaving.*

Arachne

Greek Myth retold by Olivia E. Coolidge

Close Reader selection
"Arachne"
a Greek myth retold by Olivia Coolidge

COMMON CORE Common Core Standards

RL 1 Cite textual evidence.
RL 2 Determine a theme and analyze its development.
RL 3 Analyze how elements of a story interact.
RL 4 Determine the meaning of words and phrases.
W 3 Write narratives.
W 7 Conduct short research projects.
L 2a Use a comma to separate coordinate adjectives.
L 4b Use Greek or Latin affixes and roots as clues to word meanings.

▲ Text Complexity Rubric

Quantitative Measures	**The Flight of Icarus** Lexile: 1110L
Qualitative Measures	**Levels of Meaning/Purpose** ●─●─**●**─●─➤ multiple levels of meaning (multiple themes)
	Structure ●─●─**●**─●─➤ somewhat complex story concepts
	Language Conventionality and Clarity ●─**●**─●─●─➤ some figurative language
	Knowledge Demands ●─●─**●**─●─➤ increased amount of cultural and literary knowledge useful
Reader/Task Considerations	Teacher determined Vary by individual reader and type of text

TEACH

CLOSE READ

Background Have students read the background information about myths and their role in ancient Greek civilization. Tell students that Greek myths have also become an important part of our culture. In their reading or in viewing other media, students are likely to come across references to mythological characters like Icarus. Also point out that the first lines of this myth refer to another mythological character called Theseus. Theseus escaped from a fierce monster in King Minos's labyrinth, setting the stage for the myth students are about to read.

SETTING A PURPOSE Direct students to use the Setting a Purpose question to focus their reading. Remind them to also write any questions they have as they read.

Analyze Story Elements: Myth (LINES 10–12)

COMMON CORE RL 1, RL 3

Tell students that a **myth** is a traditional story that attempts to answer basic questions about human nature or the natural world. In a myth, events occur that cannot happen in real life, and characters also have unusual or even supernatural powers.

(A) CITE TEXT EVIDENCE Ask students what we have learned so far about Daedalus. What evidence in the text hints that he may have unusual or supernatural powers? (*We have learned that Daedalus is resourceful and ingenious. The lines "but he does not control the air. I will try that way," hint at unusual powers, since there was no air travel in the time of the ancient Greeks.*)

Determine Theme

COMMON CORE RL 1, RL 2

(LINES 4–12)

Explain that the **theme** of a literary text is a message about life or human nature. In a myth, the theme often reveals what is important to a culture. The first step in determining the theme of a myth is to determine what the characters want.

(B) ASK STUDENTS to reread lines 4–12 and to identify what Daedalus and Icarus want? (*They want to escape from the island of Crete.*)

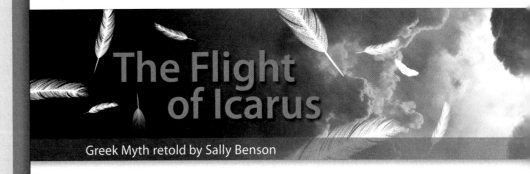

The Flight of Icarus

Greek Myth retold by Sally Benson

(l) ©xzoex/Shutterstock; (bg) ©Alegria/Shutterstock; (r) ©Igor Zh/Shutterstock

Background *Today we think of myths as stories that have been passed down through countless generations. In the ancient civilization of Greece, myths were the basis of an elaborate system of beliefs. Myths explained their mystifying world and offered wisdom on how to live in it. The myth of Daedalus and his son Icarus is one example.*

SETTING A PURPOSE As you read, pay close attention to the choices Icarus and his father make. What do these choices reveal? Write down any questions you may have while reading.

When Theseus escaped from the labyrinth, King Minos flew into a rage with its builder, Daedalus, and ordered him shut up in a high tower that faced the lonely sea. In time, with the help of his young son, Icarus, Daedalus managed to escape from the tower, only to find himself a prisoner on the island. Several times he tried by bribery to stow away on one of the vessels sailing from Crete, but King Minos kept strict watch over them, and no ships were allowed to sail without being carefully searched.

10 Daedalus was an ingenious artist and was not discouraged by his failures. "Minos may control the land and sea," he said, "but he does not control the air. I will try that way."

He called his son, Icarus, to him and told the boy to gather up all the feathers he could find on the rocky shore.

Close Read Screencasts   ▶ View It!

Modeled Discussions

Have students click the *Close Read* icons in their eBooks to access a screencast in which readers discuss and annotate the passage about Icarus's first flight and Daedalus's warning to him (lines 35–47).

As a class, view and discuss this video. Then have students pair up to do an independent close read of an additional passage—Icarus flies too high and begins to lose his feathers (lines 63–75).

TEACH

Determine Theme

COMMON CORE   RL 1, RL 2

(LINES 15–29, 39–47)

Tell students that, once they have discovered what the characters want, the next step in determining the theme of a myth is to learn what they do to reach that goal.

C ASK STUDENTS to reread lines 15–29 and summarize what Daedalus does to help himself and his son escape from the island. *(He makes two sets of wings from melted wax and feathers. He intends that he and his son will fly away from the island.)*

The final step in determining the theme is to analyze how well the characters succeed at reaching their goal, and why.

D CITE TEXT EVIDENCE Have students reread lines 39–47 and cite the specific evidence that suggests Daedalus's plan will not go well. *("Daedalus watched him proudly but with misgivings"; "No human being has ever traveled through the air before"; "if you fly too low, the fog and spray will clog your wings, and if you fly too high, the heat will melt the wax that holds them together.")*

CRITICAL VOCABULARY

moderate: Daedalus warned his son to keep at a moderate height, neither too high nor too low.

ASK STUDENTS why Daedalus gave his son this warning to be moderate. What does this suggest about one theme of the myth? *(If Icarus flew too low, his wings would clog; if he flew too high, the wax would melt. The warning suggests that one theme of the myth is the value of moderation.)*

prowess: Point out that Icarus and Daedalus wanted to test their prowess before setting out across the sea.

ASK STUDENTS to describe the prowess that this flight required. *(It required the ability to control height and direction and the strength to keep flying for as long as it took to cross the sea.)*

C As thousands of gulls soared over the island, Icarus soon collected a huge pile of feathers. Daedalus then melted some wax and made a skeleton in the shape of a bird's wing. The smallest feathers he pressed into the soft wax and the large ones he tied on with thread. Icarus played about on the beach
20 happily while his father worked, chasing the feathers that blew away in the strong wind that swept the island and sometimes taking bits of the wax and working it into strange shapes with his fingers.

It was fun making the wings. The sun shone on the bright feathers; the breezes ruffled them. When they were finished, Daedalus fastened them to his shoulders and found himself lifted upwards, where he hung poised in the air. Filled with excitement, he made another pair for his son. They were smaller than his own, but strong and beautiful.

30 Finally, one clear, wind-swept morning, the wings were finished, and Daedalus fastened them to Icarus's shoulders and taught him how to fly. He bade him watch the movements of the birds, how they soared and glided overhead. He pointed out the slow, graceful sweep of their wings as they beat the air steadily, without fluttering. Soon Icarus was sure that he, too, could fly and, raising his arms up and down, skirted over the white sand and even out over the waves, letting his feet touch the snowy foam as the water thundered and broke over the sharp rocks. Daedalus watched him proudly but
D 40 with misgivings. He called Icarus to his side and, putting his arm round the boy's shoulders, said, "Icarus, my son, we are about to make our flight. No human being has ever traveled through the air before, and I want you to listen carefully to my instructions. Keep at a **moderate** height, for if you fly too low, the fog and spray will clog your wings, and if you fly too high, the heat will melt the wax that holds them together. Keep near me and you will be safe."

He kissed Icarus and fastened the wings more securely to his son's shoulders. Icarus, standing in the bright sun, the
50 shining wings dropping gracefully from his shoulders, his golden hair wet with spray, and his eyes bright and dark with excitement, looked like a lovely bird. Daedalus's eyes filled with tears, and turning away, he soared into the sky, calling to Icarus to follow. From time to time, he looked back to see that the boy was safe and to note how he managed his wings in his flight. As they flew across the land to test their **prowess** before

moderate
(mŏd´ər-ĭt) *adj.* When something is kept moderate, it is kept within a certain limit.

prowess
(prou´ĭs) *n.* Prowess is the strength and courage someone has.

SCAFFOLDING FOR ELL STUDENTS

Analyze Language: Description Paying attention to the author's vivid descriptive language will help English learners visualize the events in the myth. Project lines 15–19 on a whiteboard. Invite volunteers to highlight the details that help them picture how Daedalus made the wings.

ASK STUDENTS to describe in their own words how the wings were made.

setting out across the dark wild sea, plowmen below stopped
their work and shepherds gazed in wonder, thinking Daedalus
and Icarus were gods.

60   Father and son flew over Samos and Delos, which lay on
their left, and Lebinthus,[1] which lay on their right. Icarus,
beating his wings in joy, felt the thrill of the cool wind on his
face and the clear air above and below him. He flew higher
and higher up into the blue sky until he reached the clouds.
His father saw him and called out in alarm. He tried to follow
him, but he was heavier and his wings would not carry him.
Up and up Icarus soared, through the soft, moist clouds and
out again toward the glorious sun. He was bewitched by a
sense of freedom and beat his wings **frantically** so that they
70   would carry him higher and higher to heaven itself. The
blazing sun beat down on the wings and softened the wax.
Small feathers fell from the wings and floated softly down,
warning Icarus to stay his flight and glide to earth. But the
enchanted boy did not notice them until the sun became so
hot that the largest feathers dropped off and he began to sink.
Frantically he fluttered his arms, but no feathers remained
to hold the air. He cried out to his father, but his voice was
submerged in the blue waters of the sea, which has forever
after been called by his name.

80   Daedalus, crazed by **anxiety**, called back to him, "Icarus!
Icarus, my son, where are you?" At last he saw the feathers

frantic
(frăn´tĭk) *adj.* If you
do something in
a frantic way, you
do it quickly and
nervously.

anxiety
(ăng-zī´ĭ-tē) *n.*
Anxiety is an uneasy,
worried feeling.

---

[1] **Samos . . . Delos . . . Lebinthus:** (sā´mŏs´ . . . dē´lŏs´ . . . lŭbĭn´thŭs´): small Greek
islands in the eastern Aegean Sea.

©Houghton Mifflin Harcourt

APPLYING ACADEMIC VOCABULARY

aspect	cultural

As you discuss the elements and theme of the myth, incorporate the
following Collection 1 academic vocabulary words: *aspect* and *cultural*.
Ask students what **aspects** of the characters and plot are typical of myths.
Discuss what we can learn from this myth about the **cultural** values of the
ancient Greeks and about our own culture.

Analyze Story Elements: Myth

COMMON CORE   RL 1, RL 2, RL 3

(LINES 57–63, 60–79)

Remind students that myths typically include events
that cannot happen in real life and characters with
unusual abilities.

E CITE TEXT EVIDENCE Ask students to cite
specific evidence in the text that illustrates these two
aspects of a myth. *(Daedalus and Icarus are able to fly.
The people watching from below think they are gods.)*

Recall also that myths often show the values of the
culture in which the myth was first told.

F ASK STUDENTS to reread lines 60–79 and ask
them to identify the cause of Icarus's fall and what his
failure reveals about the cultural values of the ancient
Greeks. *(He falls because he flies higher and higher,
"bewitched by a sense of freedom." Finally, the sun melts
the wax on his wings, just as his father had warned. This
tells us that the Greeks valued moderation and knowing
your place—not trying to be like the gods.)*

CRITICAL VOCABULARY

frantic: The author tells us that Icarus beat his
wings frantically in order to fly higher and higher.

ASK STUDENTS how the author's use of the word
frantically helps us to picture the scene. *(It helps us
to visualize Icarus in a very excited state, beating his
wings faster and faster.)*

anxiety: Earlier in the text (line 65) Daedalus "called
out in alarm." Now, after seeing his son fly too high,
he is "crazed by anxiety."

ASK STUDENTS to describe the change in
Daedalus's feelings. How does *alarm* differ from
anxiety? *(Alarm is a sudden feeling that something
may be wrong or a warning; anxiety is a nervous
state—an intense worry or fear that something will
go wrong.)*

Determine Theme COMMON CORE RL 1, RL 2

(LINES 88–95)

Remind students that, to determine the theme of a myth, they should consider whether the characters succeeded or failed at achieving their goal—and why.

C **CITE TEXT EVIDENCE** Have students reread lines 88–95, keeping Daedalus's original goal in mind. Ask them whether he succeeded or failed and what this might reveal about a life lesson or theme. *(His original goal was to escape from Crete. He succeeded at that goal but "his victory over the air was bitter to him" because he had lost his son. This suggests the theme "know your place"—don't soar too high or try to be like the gods.)*

COLLABORATIVE DISCUSSION Have students work in small groups to discuss the "bold and risky moves" made by both Daedalus and Icarus. Suggest that they consider whether each character's actions were worth the risk he took. Encourage students to jot down notes as they talk. Then have each group share their ideas with the class.

ASK STUDENTS to share any questions they generated in the course of reading and discussing the selection.

---

floating from the sky, and soon his son plunged through the clouds into the sea. Daedalus hurried to save him, but it was too late. He gathered the boy in his arms and flew to land, the tips of his wings dragging in the water from the double burden they bore. Weeping bitterly, he buried his small son and called the land Icaria in his memory.

G Then, with a flutter of wings, he once more took to the
90 air, but the joy of his flight was gone and his victory over the air was bitter to him. He arrived safely in Sicily, where he built a temple to Apollo and hung up his wings as an offering to the god, and in the wings he pressed a few bright feathers he had found floating on the water where Icarus fell. And he mourned for the birdlike son who had thrown caution to the winds in the exaltation of his freedom from the earth.

COLLABORATIVE DISCUSSION In the last sentence, the author says that Icarus "had thrown caution to the winds"—he had made a bold and risky move. How had both Icarus and Daedalus made bold and risky moves? Share your ideas with your group.

Strategies for Annotation 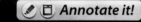 Annotate it!

Determine Theme COMMON CORE RL 2

Share these strategies for guided or independent analysis:
- Highlight in yellow evidence that Daedalus reached his goal.
- Highlight in blue the evidence that reveals how well he succeeded.
- On a note, record the life lesson or big idea that this evidence leads you to.

Then, with a flutter of wings, he once more took to the air, but the joy of his flight was gone and his victory over the air was bitter to him. He arrived safely in Sicily . . . And he mourned for the birdlike son who had thrown caution to the winds in the exaltation of his freedom from the earth.

Big idea: don't soar too high or try to be like the gods

Analyze Story Elements: Myth

 COMMON CORE RL 3

"The Flight of Icarus" is a **myth,** a traditional story that attempts to answer basic questions about human nature, origins of the world, mysteries of nature, and social customs. A myth is also a form of entertainment that people have enjoyed since ancient times. Most myths share these elements:

- gods and other supernatural beings with special powers
- supernatural events and settings
- a lesson about life or human nature

Myths may also explain the origins of natural phenomena, such as volcanoes or constellations, or warn against the consequences of human error. Often, myths reveal the values that are of greatest cultural importance to a society, such as honesty, cleverness, and moderation, which means acting within reasonable limits. Myths were used to guide ancient people's behavior in a way that reflected these values and beliefs.

Explain how each of these statements is true for "The Flight of Icarus":
- In a myth, events occur that cannot happen in real life.
- A mythical character has unusual abilities.
- A myth shows the values of a culture.

Determine Theme

 COMMON CORE RL 2

A **theme** is a message about life or human nature that a writer shares with the reader. An example of a theme might be "beauty fades" or "greed can lead to ruined lives." Authors might state a theme directly. More often, however, a reader must analyze the story events and characters' actions to infer, or make logical guesses about, the theme.

A myth often contains more than one theme, and often the theme reflects the cultural values of the society in which the myth was first told. By analyzing the behavior of mythic characters in unusual situations, we can learn lessons about the traits that mattered to a culture. This chart provides helpful questions for determining a myth's likely themes.

Your answers to the third question can lead you to ideas about life lessons or other big ideas—the themes—in a myth.

Finding the Theme of a Myth	1. What do the characters want?	2. What do the characters do to reach that goal?	3. How well do they succeed, and why?

CLOSE READ

Analyze Story Elements: Myth

 COMMON CORE RL 3

Help students understand the definition and characteristics of a myth. Then discuss their responses to the activity at the end of the lesson.

- In a myth, events occur that cannot happen in real life. *(Possible answer: In this myth, a man and his son are able to fly, using wings that the man made of wax and feathers.)*
- A mythical character has unusual abilities. *(Possible answer: Both Icarus and Daedalus are able to fly.)*
- A myth shows the values of a culture. *(Possible answer: The lesson seems to be to stay in the middle and not fly too high or too low. Flying high would make Icarus too much like a god, which was probably seen as being against the laws of nature to the Greeks. It also seems to be saying "don't get ahead of yourself," suggesting the Greeks prized humility and good sense.)*

Determine Theme

 COMMON CORE RL 2

Review the definition of a theme, emphasizing that in a myth the theme often reflects the cultural values of the society in which it was told.

Review the three steps for finding the theme shown in the chart. Have students review the myth to answer the questions, and share their responses.

Strategies for Annotation  *Annotate it!*

Analyze Story Elements: Myth

 COMMON CORE RL 3

Have students use their eBook annotation tools to analyze the text. Ask them to do the following:

- Reread lines 56–59 and highlight in yellow the evidence that shows supernatural abilities.
- Highlight in blue the evidence that suggests the values of the ancient Greek culture.

As they flew across the land to test their prowess before setting out across the dark wild sea, plowmen below stopped their work and shepherds gazed in wonder, thinking Daedalus and Icarus were gods.

PRACTICE & APPLY

Analyzing the Text

COMMON CORE RL 1, RL 2, RL 3, RL 4

Possible answers:

1. *Daedalus is reacting with frustration, because he has tried every way possible, including bribery, to escape from the island with no success.*

2. *The advice suggests that the ancient Greeks valued moderation.*

3. *The sentence suggests that the people watching from below thought that Daedalus and Icarus were gods. It suggests that one theme of the myth is, "Don't get above yourself and try to be like the gods."*

4. *When Icarus first tries the wings, he riskily "lets his feet touch the snowy foam," and his father watches "with misgivings." Daedalus offers specific instructions about not flying too high or too low, which are hints that his son, whose eyes show excitement, may be too thrilled to obey.*

5. *The words and phrases* up and up, soared, glorious, sense of freedom, higher and higher, *and* heaven *suggest the thrill that Icarus experiences. The words* bewitched *and* frantically *suggest that he cannot control his urge to fly higher.*

6. *Someone who flies too close to the sun reaches for thrills, power, or a goal in a self-destructive way. Like Icarus, the person reached for greatness and was punished for his misguided ways.*

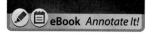

Analyzing the Text

COMMON CORE RL 1, RL 2, RL 3, RL 4, W 3, W 7

Cite Text Evidence   Support your responses with evidence from the text.

1. **Infer** Reread lines 1–9. How do you think Daedalus is reacting to his situation at this point?

2. **Interpret** Think about Daedalus's advice to Icarus in lines 41–47. What do these lines suggest about the kind of behavior that ancient Greeks valued?

3. **Interpret** Reread lines 56–59. What does the sentence suggest about one of the themes of this myth?

4. **Cite Evidence** What text clues does the author provide to hint at the outcome of Icarus's flight?

5. **Analyze** Reread lines 67–71, and identify descriptive words and phrases. What do these descriptions suggest about Icarus's experience?

6. **Connect** People today may refer to someone "who flew too close to the sun" as a cautionary tale. What does this expression mean and what does it have to do with the myth of Icarus? Explain.

PERFORMANCE TASK

Writing Activity: Graphic Comic
"The Flight of Icarus" begins with references to Theseus and his escape from the labyrinth built by Daedalus. Retell your own version of the myth in the form of a graphic comic. In this kind of text, both verbal and visual elements work together.

- Research retellings of the myth of Theseus and the Minotaur.

- Redo the text of the myth in your own words. Try to keep any character speeches or descriptions as brief as possible.
- Make sure that the words don't crowd the art space.
- Plan how your characters will look. Use any descriptions you find in the text version of the myth to help you.
- Do a rough sketch of your ideas before creating finished pages.

Assign this performance task.

PERFORMANCE TASK

COMMON CORE W 3, W 5, W 7

Writing Activity: Graphic Comic Have students work independently to research retellings and sketch their ideas.

- Suggest that they look at a variety of graphic novels as examples of the format.
- Have pairs of students review and comment on each other's sketches before they create final pages.

Critical Vocabulary

COMMON CORE L 4b

moderate   prowess   frantic   anxiety

Practice and Apply Answer each question with *yes* or *no*. With your group, use examples and reasons to explain your answers.

1. Are most professional basketball players of **moderate** height?

2. Is **prowess** related to pride?

3. Is it possible to speak in a **frantic** way?

4. Would you look forward to having **anxiety**?

Vocabulary Strategy: Noun Suffixes *-ty* and *-ity*

A **suffix** is a word part that appears at to the end of a word or root. Readers can use their knowledge of suffixes to figure out word meanings. Some suffixes signal that a word is a naming word, or **noun.** Notice the word with a noun suffix in this sentence from "The Flight of Icarus."

> Daedalus, crazed by anxiety, called back to him, "Icarus! Icarus, my son, where are you?"

The word *anxiety* ends with the suffix *-ty*, which signals that *anxiety* is a noun. Another form of the suffix is *-ity*. These suffixes add the meaning "state or condition of" to a word.

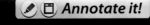

Anxiety means "the state of feeling anxious."

The suffix *-ty* changes the adjective into a noun.

> The word *anxious* is an **adjective,** a word that modifies a noun or a pronoun.

Practice and Apply The bold words in these items are adjectives. Change each adjective into its noun form by using the suffix *-ty* or *-ity*. Consult a resource, such as a print or online dictionary, for words that are unfamiliar.

1. Things that are **similar** are alike. A likeness is a _____.

2. Something that is **frail** may break. It has _____.

3. A **loyal** friend can be trusted. Friends share _____.

4. **Cruel** words hurt. Their speaker shows _____.

5. To be free from danger is to feel **secure.** This freedom is called _____.

The Flight of Icarus   **37**

PRACTICE & APPLY

Critical Vocabulary

COMMON CORE L 4b

Possible answers:

1. *No. Most professional basketball players are extremely tall.*

2. *Yes, because if you have prowess, you have great skill and the ability to accomplish things, which would make most people proud.*

3. *Yes. If you're upset, you might speak very quickly and erratically.*

4. *No. I don't like the feeling of being worried or scared, which is how anxiety makes me feel.*

Vocabulary Strategy: Noun Suffixes *-ty* and *-ity*

Answers:

1. *similarity*

2. *frailty*

3. *loyalty*

4. *cruelty*

5. *security*

Strategies for Annotation ✎ 📖 Annotate it!

Vocabulary Strategy: Noun Suffixes *-ty* and *-ity*

COMMON CORE L 4b

Have students locate the sentence on lines 80–81. Encourage them to use their eBook annotation tools to do the following:

- Highlight the word that contains the ending *-ty* or *-ity*.
- Underline the ending.
- In a note, write the meaning of the word.
- Consult a resource, such as a print or online dictionary, to confirm the answer.

> Daedalus, crazed by anxiety, called back to him, "Icarus! Icarus, my son, where are you?"

> anxiety: state of feeling anxious or nervous

The Flight of Icarus   **37**

Language Conventions: Commas and Coordinate Adjectives

COMMON CORE L 2a

Tell students that the left side of the chart in the lesson shows examples of phrases with coordinate adjectives, or adjectives of equal effect, which are set apart by a comma. The examples in the right side are phrases containing adjectives that do not have an equal effect and therefore do not require a comma. Ask volunteers to come up with additional examples, such as the ones shown here, for each side of the chart. Use the tests suggested in the lesson to confirm each example.

Comma Needed	No Comma Needed
tall, dark stranger; *slow, easy* pace; *shallow, murky* water	*great big* smile; *angry old* man; *silly little* girl

Possible Answers:

1. *bright, sparkling sun*

2. *shining, feathery wings*

3. *golden, flowing hair*

4. *bright, intelligent eyes*

5. *lovely, soaring bird*

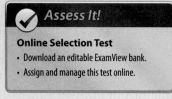

Assess It!

Online Selection Test
- Download an editable ExamView bank.
- Assign and manage this test online.

Language Conventions: Commas and Coordinate Adjectives

COMMON CORE L 2a

Writers use **adjectives** to modify, or describe, nouns. Often, a writer will use more than one adjective to modify the same noun, such as in this phrase from "The Flight of Icarus": *one clear, wind-swept morning.*

Notice that the adjectives *clear* and *wind-swept* are separated by a comma. These are called **coordinate adjectives,** adjectives of equal effect that modify the same noun. Here is another example from the story: *the slow, graceful sweep of their wings.*

The comma acts like the word *and* between the coordinate adjectives. When you write, you can use a comma to replace *and*. Sometimes, however, two or more adjectives that modify the same noun do not have equal effect. Then no comma is needed.

Comma Needed	No Comma Needed
dark, stormy night	**little red** schoolhouse
fierce, angry cries	**usual afternoon** nap
crowded, noisy city	**tired old** dog

You can determine whether adjectives modify equally with these tests:
- Swap the position of the adjectives. If the sentence makes sense, the adjectives modify equally: *the stormy, dark night*
- Insert the word *and* between the adjectives. If the sentence still reads well, the adjectives modify equally: *the dark **and** stormy night*

Practice and Apply Find the nouns *sun, wings, hair, eyes,* and *bird* in this sentence from "The Flight of Icarus." Write two coordinate adjectives to describe each noun, using commas where needed. Consult resources such as a print or online dictionary for words that are unfamiliar to you.

> Icarus, standing in the bright sun, the shining wings dropping gracefully from his shoulders, his golden hair wet with spray, and his eyes bright and dark with excitement, looked like a lovely bird.

INTERACTIVE WHITEBOARD LESSON
Analyze Story Elements: Characterization

COMMON CORE
RL 3

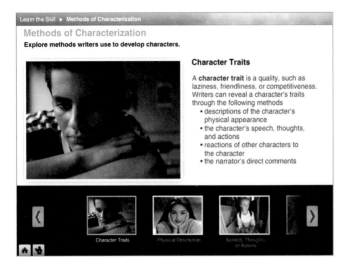

TEACH

Use the whiteboard lesson to review the methods that writers use to develop characters. Discuss how the author of "The Flight of Icarus" used these methods to develop the character of Icarus.

- **Description of physical appearance** *(his golden hair wet with spray, and his eyes bright and dark with excitement; looked like a lovely bird)*
- **Character's speech, thoughts, and actions** *(beating his wings in joy, felt the thrill of the cool wind on his face)*
- **Reactions of other characters** *(Daedalus watched him proudly but with misgivings.)*
- **Narrator's direct comments** *(…the birdlike son who had thrown caution to the wind in the exaltation of his freedom from the earth.)*

PRACTICE AND APPLY

As students apply what they have learned about character development in their graphic comics for the Performance Task, suggest that they use an Interactive Graphic Organizer, such as a Freeform Web, to list the traits of Theseus they want to show. Have them work with partners to plan the best ways to show these traits.

INTERACTIVE GRAPHIC ORGANIZER Have students use this interactive graphic organizer: **Freeform Web**

Determine Theme

COMMON CORE
RL 2

RETEACH

Review the definition of **theme**: a message about life or human nature that a writer shares with the reader. Explain that the theme of a story is not just what the story is about. Use this example:

- **What "The Flight of Icarus" is about:** A man and his son attempt to escape from an island by flying.
- **Theme of "The Flight of Icarus:"** Practice moderation; do not aspire to be like the gods.

Review the chart on Student Book page 35. Discuss how the answer to the third question, "How well do they succeed, and why?" leads to the theme of the myth. *(Icarus does not succeed because he ignores his father's warning to be moderate and flies toward heaven, like a god. Daedalus succeeds in escaping the island, but his success is bitter because he has lost his son.)*

LEVEL UP TUTORIALS To give students additional practice in determining theme, assign the following *Level Up* tutorial: **Theme**

CLOSE READING APPLICATION

Students can apply the skill to another myth of their choice. Have them work independently to use the three questions for finding the theme of a myth to guide them.

Arachne

Greek Myth retold by Olivia E. Coolidge

Why This Text

Students may read the text of a myth without a thorough grasp of the theme or of the way in which the elements of the myth interact. For example, a myth such as this one will share a message about life or human behavior, but students may not understand that this is the theme. With the help of the close-reading questions, students will see how the theme reflects the cultural values of the ancient Greeks, who first told the myth. This close reading will help students develop an awareness of the elements of a myth and of how these elements interact.

Background Have students read the background of this Greek myth and explain that Greek mythology is filled with stories about mortals who pit themselves against the gods and about the consequences of their behavior or defiance. Introduce the selection by telling students that Elizabeth E. Coolidge (1908-2006) is a famous mythographer. An expert on Greek mythology, some of her most popular books—*Greek Myths* and *The Trojan War*—retell many of the famous Greek stories.

SETTING A PURPOSE Ask students to pay attention to the theme and to how the elements of the myth interact. When did they first understand that the theme grew out of the conflict in the myth?

Common Core Support

- cite several pieces of textual evidence

- determine a theme and analyze its development over the course of a text

- analyze how particular elements of a story interact

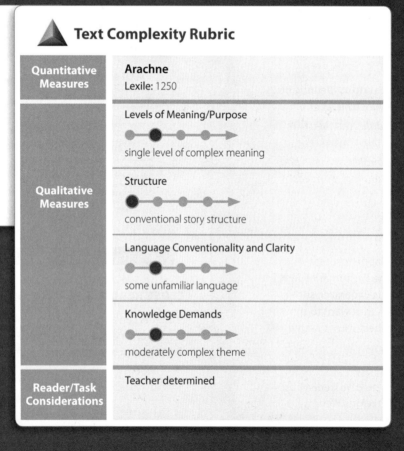

Text Complexity Rubric

Quantitative Measures	**Arachne** Lexile: 1250
Qualitative Measures	Levels of Meaning/Purpose — single level of complex meaning
	Structure — conventional story structure
	Language Conventionality and Clarity — some unfamiliar language
	Knowledge Demands — moderately complex theme
Reader/Task Considerations	Teacher determined

Strategies for CLOSE READING

Determine Theme

Students should read this myth carefully all the way through. Close-reading questions at the bottom of the page will help them determine the theme (the message about life or human nature) and analyze the way elements of a myth interact, including how characters influence plot events. As they read, students should record comments or questions about the text in the side margins.

WHEN STUDENTS STRUGGLE . . .

To help students determine the theme of the myth, have them work in a small group to fill out a chart such as the one shown below as they analyze the myth.

CITE TEXT EVIDENCE The theme of a Greek myth, such as this one about Arachne, is the central idea that expresses an important message about life or human nature. In a myth or story, the theme is an idea, such as "pride goes before a fall," that is revealed through the writer's presentation of characters or plot events. For practice in determining the theme of this myth, track the goal of the characters, what they do to reach that goal, and how well they succeed, and why.

Finding the Theme of a Myth

What do the characters want?	What do the characters do to reach that goal?	How well do they succeed, and why?
Arachne wants to be viewed as great a weaver as Athene, a god. Athene does not want Arachne to put herself on a pedestal with the gods.	They engage in a contest to see who is the better weaver—a mortal or a god.	They prove to be nearly equal in skill, but Arachne remains proud and arrogant, insulting Athene. Athene transforms Arachne into a spider because her pride and disdain have caused her to overstep her bounds.

Background *Many Greek myths are about characters who stray beyond the limits set by Greek gods and goddesses or who ignore their warnings. In this myth, Arachne (ərăk'nē), a weaver, pits herself against Athene (ə-thē'nē), the goddess of wisdom and all crafts, particularly weaving.*

Arachne

Greek Myth retold by Olivia E. Coolidge

CLOSE READ
Notes

1. **READ ▶** As you read lines 1–37, begin to collect and cite text evidence.

   • Underline details that describe Arachne's skill.
   • Circle details that reveal Arachne's personality.

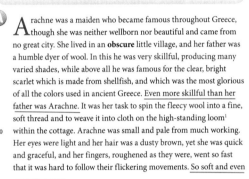

Ⓐ   Arachne was a maiden who became famous throughout Greece, though she was neither wellborn nor beautiful and came from no great city. She lived in an **obscure** little village, and her father was a humble dyer of wool. In this he was very skillful, producing many varied shades, while above all he was famous for the clear, bright scarlet which is made from shellfish, and which was the most glorious of all the colors used in ancient Greece. Even more skillful than her father was Arachne. It was her task to spin the fleecy wool into a fine, soft thread and to weave it into cloth on the high-standing loom[1]

10 within the cottage. Arachne was small and pale from much working. Her eyes were light and her hair was a dusty brown, yet she was quick and graceful, and her fingers, roughened as they were, went so fast that it was hard to follow their flickering movements. So soft and even

obscure:
not well-
known

[1] **high-standing loom:** a tall frame used to hold threads in a vertical position as other threads are woven through horizontally.

17

1. **READ AND CITE TEXT EVIDENCE** Explain to students that Coolidge opens her retelling of the myth with details that describe Arachne's skill at weaving and also reveal her personality, or character traits, which will shape events in the myth.

   Ⓐ **ASK STUDENTS** to determine how Coolidge describes Arachne's skill and character traits, both positive and negative, by citing specific textual evidence in lines 1–37. *Responses may include references to evidence in lines 1–4, 7–16, and 17–37.*

   Critical Vocabulary: obscure (line 3) Have students explain the meaning of *obscure* as it is used here. Ask how *obscure* plays a role in the setting and how it contrasts with Arachne's character traits. *Although Arachne comes from a little-known village, she becomes known all over Greece because of her skill. Her fame becomes so great that it shapes her disdainful attitude and leads to the conflict and contest between Arachne and Athene.*

was her thread, so fine her cloth, so gorgeous her embroidery, that soon her products were known all over Greece. No one had ever seen the like of them before.

At last Arachne's fame became so great that people used to come from far and wide to watch her working. Even the graceful nymphs would steal in from stream or forest and peep shyly through the dark
20 doorway, watching in wonder the white arms of Arachne as she stood at the loom and threw the shuttle² from hand to hand between the hanging threads, or drew out the long wool, fine as a hair, from the distaff³ as she sat spinning. "Surely Athene herself must have taught her," people would murmur to one another. "Who else could know the secret of such marvelous skill?"

B Arachne was used to being wondered at, and she was immensely proud of the skill that had brought so many to look on her. Praise was all she lived for, and it displeased her greatly that people should think anyone, even a goddess, could teach her anything. Therefore when she
30 heard them murmur, she would stop her work and turn round indignantly to say, "With my own ten fingers I gained this skill, and by hard practice from early morning till night. I never had time to stand looking as you people do while another maiden worked. Nor if I had, would I give Athene credit because the girl was more skillful than I. As for Athene's weaving, how could there be finer cloth or

indignantly:
in a manner that expresses anger over an injustice

---
² **shuttle:** a piece of wood holding the thread that is to be woven horizontally through the vertical threads on a loom.
³ **distaff:** a short rod for holding wool that is to be spun into a thread.

---

2. **REREAD** Reread lines 26–37. Explain why Arachne is so indignant. What character traits does Arachne reveal with this behavior? Support your answer with explicit textual evidence.

Arachne is angered when people say Athene taught her to weave.
Arachne's behavior indicates that she is proud and ungrateful.

3. **READ** As you read lines 38–67, continue to cite textual evidence.
- Underline the advice the old woman gives Arachne.
- In the margin, restate Arachne's response to the woman's advice.
- In the margin, describe Arachne's reaction when she finds out she's speaking to Athene.

18

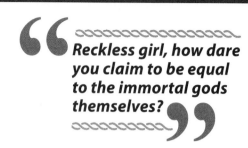

> **Reckless girl, how dare you claim to be equal to the immortal gods themselves?**

more beautiful embroidery than mine? If Athene herself were to come down and compete with me, she could do no better than I."

One day when Arachne turned round with such words, an old woman answered her, a grey old woman, bent and very poor, who
40 stood leaning on a staff and peering at Arachne amid the crowd of
D onlookers. "Reckless girl," she said, "how dare you claim to be equal to the immortal gods themselves? I am an old woman and have seen much. Take my advice and ask pardon of Athene for your words. Rest content with your fame of being the best spinner and weaver that mortal eyes have ever beheld."

"Stupid old woman," said Arachne indignantly, "who gave you a right to speak in this way to me? It is easy to see that you were never good for anything in your day, or you would not come here in poverty and rags to gaze at my skill. If Athene resents my words, let her
50 answer them herself. I have challenged her to a contest, but she, of course, will not come. It is easy for the gods to avoid matching their skill with that of men."

At these words the old woman threw down her staff and stood erect. The wondering onlookers saw her grow tall and fair and stand
C clad in long robes of dazzling white. They were terribly afraid as they realized that they stood in the presence of Athene. Arachne herself flushed red for a moment, for she had never really believed that the goddess would hear her. Before the group that was gathered there she would not give in; so pressing her pale lips together in **obstinacy** and
60 pride, she led the goddess to one of the great looms and set herself before the other. Without a word both began to thread the long

Arachne rejects the woman's advice and insults her.

obstinacy:
unwillingness to change one's behavior or attitude

19

---

2. **REREAD AND CITE TEXT EVIDENCE**

B **ASK STUDENTS** to "unpack" Arachne's prideful behavior and indignation. How does it reveal her disdainful attitude? *Instead of being humbled by all the praise she receives, she has become indignant toward those who say that Athene has taught her to spin.*

3. **READ AND CITE TEXT EVIDENCE**

C **ASK STUDENTS** to read their margin notes to a partner and then create one response that describes Arachne's reaction when she discovers that she is speaking to Athene in lines 53–67, citing textual evidence.

Critical Vocabulary: indignantly (line 31) Have students share their definitions of *indignantly*. Ask how *indignantly* reveals Arachne's character traits. *It shows her haughty attitude toward her skill and her anger toward those who would say that Athene had taught her.*

Critical Vocabulary: obstinancy (line 59) Encourage students to cite textual examples of Arachne's obstinacy and to describe what this behavior says about her. *Students should be able to point to her refusal to take the old woman's advice about begging Athene's forgiveness for her prideful speech and behavior.*

FOR ELL STUDENTS Explain to students that *poor* (line 39), *right* (line 47), *threw* (line 53), *red* (line 57), *hear, there* (line 58), and *would, pale* (line 59) are examples of homophones, words that sound alike but have different meanings and spellings. Ask students if they know what each of these words means. Then have them make a list of the words, writing the homophone beside each word. *Students should be able to list these homophones:* pour, write, through, read, here, their, wood, *and* pail.

Arachne challenges Athene to a competition to see who is a more talented weaver.

woolen strands that hang from the rollers, and between which the shuttle moves back and forth. Many skeins lay heaped beside them to use, bleached white, and gold, and scarlet, and other shades, varied as the rainbow. Arachne had never thought of giving credit for her success to her father's skill in dyeing, though in actual truth the colors were as remarkable as the cloth itself.

70   Soon there was no sound in the room but the breathing of the onlookers, the whirring of the shuttles, and the creaking of the wooden frames as each pressed the thread up into place or tightened the pegs by which the whole was held straight. The excited crowd in the doorway began to see that the skill of both in truth was very nearly equal, but that, however the cloth might turn out, the goddess was the quicker of the two. A pattern of many pictures was growing on her loom. There was a border of twined branches of the olive, Athene's favorite tree, while in the middle, figures began to appear. As they looked at the glowing colors, the spectators realized that Athene was weaving into her pattern a last warning to Arachne. The central figure was the goddess herself

80 competing with Poseidon for possession of the city of Athens; but in the four corners were mortals who had tried to **strive** with gods and pictures of the awful fate that had overtaken them. The goddess ended a little before Arachne and stood back from her marvelous work to see what the maiden was doing.

strive:
compete

---

4. **◀ REREAD** Reread lines 38–45. What does the old woman's advice suggest about the theme, or central idea, of the myth?

The old woman's advice suggests that human beings should not overstep their bounds.

---

5. **READ ▶** As you read lines 68–112, continue to cite textual evidence.

• Underline the warning that Athene weaves into her cloth for Arachne.
• Circle the insult Arachne weaves into her cloth for Athene.
• In the margin, explain what happens to Arachne at the end of the myth.

20

An ancient Greek statue of Athene

    Never before had Arachne been matched against anyone whose skill was equal, or even nearly equal to her own. As she stole glances from time to time at Athene and saw the goddess working swiftly, calmly, and always a little faster than herself, she became angry instead of frightened, and an evil thought came into her

90 head. Thus as Athene stepped back a pace to watch Arachne finishing her work, she saw that the maiden had taken for her design a pattern of scenes which showed evil or unworthy actions of the gods, how they had deceived fair maidens, resorted to trickery, and appeared on earth from time to time in the form of poor and humble people. When the goddess saw this insult glowing in bright colors on Arachne's loom, she did not wait while the cloth was judged, but stepped forward, her grey eyes blazing with anger, and tore Arachne's work across. Then she struck Arachne across the face. Arachne stood there a moment, struggling with anger,

100 fear, and pride. "I will not live under this insult," she cried, and seizing a rope from the wall, she made a noose and would have hanged herself.

21

---

4. **REREAD AND CITE TEXT EVIDENCE**

D **ASK STUDENTS** to explain how the old woman's advice to Arachne may express the theme of the myth. How does it signify a message about human behavior? *Students should cite textual evidence from lines 38–45 as they point out that the advice suggests that human beings should not be proud, nor overstep their bounds.*

5. **READ AND CITE TEXT EVIDENCE**

E **ASK STUDENTS** to read their margin notes to a partner and then collaborate to find and cite text examples from lines 68–112 to explain what happens to Arachne at the end of the myth. *Students should recognize that Arachne's disdainful, insulting behavior causes Athene to transform her into a spider.*

Critical Vocabulary: strive (line 81) Encourage students to explain *strive* as it is used here. Why does Coolidge use this word? *She may wish to emphasize the theme of not overstepping one's bounds.*

FOR ELL STUDENTS Explain that *from time to time* (line 87) is an idiomatic phrase (or expression), in which the words together have a meaning that differs from the dictionary definition of the individual words. Ask students if they know what this idiomatic expression means. *Students should be able to point out that it means "at intervals," "occasionally," or "once in a while."* Ask students to look for other idiomatic phrases (or expressions) and cite them in the margin. *Possible answers include* **from far and wide** *(line 18) and* **steal in** *(line 19).*

CLOSE READ
Notes

descendants:

people who come after

Arachne is turned into a spider.

The goddess touched the rope and touched the maiden. "Live on, wicked girl," she said. "Live on and spin, both you and your **descendants.** When men look at you they may remember that it is not wise to strive with Athene." At that the body of Arachne shriveled up, and her legs grew tiny, spindly, and distorted. There before the eyes of the spectators hung a little dusty brown spider on a slender thread.

110 All spiders descend from Arachne, and as the Greeks watched them spinning their thread wonderfully fine, they remembered the contest with Athene and thought that it was not right for even the best of men to claim equality with the gods.

(E)

6. ◀ **REREAD AND DISCUSS** With a small group, discuss what Arachne does to so enrage Athene and whether or not her punishment is justified. Cite text evidence in your discussion.

SHORT RESPONSE

Cite Text Evidence   What lessons about human behavior does this myth teach? Review your reading notes, and be sure to **cite text evidence** from the myth in your response.

The myth teaches that humans should not be prideful and arrogant. Arachne does not listen to the advice to "Rest content with your fame of being the best spinner and weaver that mortal eyes have ever beheld." Arachne's boasting and rude treatment of Athene lead Athene to accept Arachne's challenge. Arachne's pride causes her to insult Athene and causes Athene to turn her into a spider.

22

---

6. **REREAD AND DISCUSS USING TEXT EVIDENCE**

(F) **ASK STUDENTS** to appoint a reporter for each group to cite specific textual evidence and line numbers to support their position about whether or not Arachne's punishment is justified. *Students should cite specific textual evidence from lines 68–112.*

Critical Vocabulary: descendants (line 105) Have students share their definitions of *descendants*. Then ask them to compare the meanings of the words *descendants* and *ancestors*.

SHORT RESPONSE

Cite Text Evidence   Students should:

- explain the larger lesson about human behavior this myth teaches.
- give reasons for their point of view.
- cite specific evidence from the text to support their reasons.

TO CHALLENGE STUDENTS . . .

For more context about the Greek myth of Arachne, and for additional information about Greek mythology, history, or culture, students can do print, online, or multimedia research to write a chapter for a book about the context in which the ancient Greek myths were created and told.

ASK STUDENTS to work with a small group to do some preliminary research to find an interesting topic for their chapter, explaining that the completed chapters will be combined into a class book. Possible topics might include:

- special heroes of Greek mythology and their attributes, including the goddess Athene.
- how Greek myths expressed the values and beliefs of ancient Greek culture and society.
- heroes, gods, and monsters of Greek myths.
- brief history of ancient Greece, perhaps focusing on conflicts or culture.

With the class, discuss the elements of writing a chapter after students have chosen a topic, eliciting these points:

Plan your group research

- choose a group recorder
- make a list of questions about your topic
- research your topic and take notes
- organize your notes
- write an outline based on your notes

Write your group chapter

- keep your purpose and audience in mind
- write a first draft and title your chapter
- illustrate your chapter
- revise your writing and proofread the revision
- make a final copy and combine it with the other groups' chapters to publish and share a class book.

Students might also wish to view the following videos: "Greek Gods," "Spartans Deconstructed," or "The Peloponnesian War," which are part of the program *Ancient Greece*, in their eBooks.

DIG DEEPER

With the class, return to Question 6, Reread and Discuss. Have students share the results of their discussion.

ASK STUDENTS whether they were satisfied with the outcome of their group discussions. Have each group share what the majority opinion was of the group. What convincing evidence did the group cite from the myth to support its opinion?

- Encourage students to tell whether there was any convincing evidence cited by group members holding the minority opinion. If so, why didn't it sway the group's position on the judgment meted out by Athene?

- Have groups explain how they decided that the punishment was (or was not) justified. Did everyone in the group agree? How did the group use the skills of conflict resolution to clear up any disagreements or disputes?

- After students have shared the results of their individual group's discussion, ask whether another group shared any findings that would have swayed their opinion.

ASK STUDENTS to return to their Short Response answer and to revise it based on the class discussion, revising their specific textual evidence if needed.

CLOSE READING NOTES

Icarus's Flight

Poem by Stephen Dobyns

Why This Text?

Students will often encounter poetry in their studies and, from time to time, in their own reading. Understanding poetic form and elements will deepen their appreciation of the poet's art. This lesson focuses on poetic form and on how alliteration contributes to a poem's meaning.

Key Learning Objectives: The student will understand how the elements of form and the use of alliteration emphasize ideas and meaning in a poem.

COMMON CORE Common Core Standards

RL 1 Cite textual evidence.

RL 2 Determine a theme or central idea.

RL 4 Analyze the impact of repetitions of sounds of a poem.

RL 5 Analyze how a poem's form contributes to its meaning.

W 2 Write informative/explanatory texts.

SL 1 Engage in collaborative discussions.

SL 4 Present claims and findings; use appropriate eye contact, adequate volume, and clear pronunciation.

▲ Text Complexity Rubric

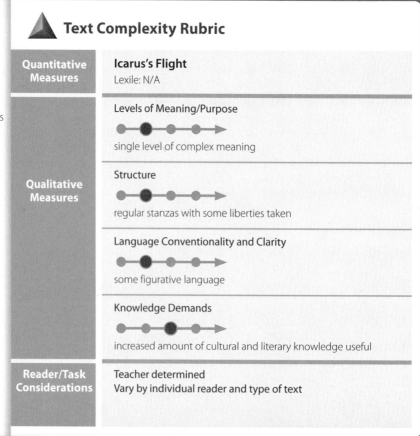

Quantitative Measures	**Icarus's Flight** Lexile: N/A
Qualitative Measures	**Levels of Meaning/Purpose** single level of complex meaning
	Structure regular stanzas with some liberties taken
	Language Conventionality and Clarity some figurative language
	Knowledge Demands increased amount of cultural and literary knowledge useful
Reader/Task Considerations	Teacher determined Vary by individual reader and type of text

CLOSE READ

Background Have students read the background and poet information. Explain that the story of Icarus has been the subject of many other poems, stories, songs, and paintings. Icarus is usually depicted as a young teen, who, like most young people, possesses a naïve and bold confidence about his own mortality. In this poem, Stephen Dobyns depicts Icarus as having a great deal more insight into his actions during his fatal flight than is commonly found in traditional retellings of the myth. To share more about the poet, Stephen Dobyns, point out that not only does Dobyns feel he must work at the craft of poetry every day, but that being a poet also requires a love of reading of all kinds of books, but especially "good books." As for his own writing, he says that poems can begin for him at any time or place during a day. An idea might wake him in the middle of the night, or it might come to him while swimming laps in a pool.

SETTING A PURPOSE Direct students to use the Setting a Purpose prompt to focus their reading. Tell students to write any questions they generate during reading.

SCAFFOLDING FOR ELL STUDENTS

Determine Meaning of Words and Phrases: Alliteration Point out how the use of alliteration, the repetition of consonant sounds at the beginning of words, helps give the poem rhythm. Display and read aloud lines 9–10, emphasizing the rhythm. Highlight in yellow the words that stand out because of their alliterative sounds.

ASK STUDENTS to replace one instance of *flew* with *soared*, and one instance of *far* with *high*. Then reread the poem aloud. Discuss how the rhythm and pace of the poem changes.

Background *From ancient times to present, writers have been fascinated by the characters of myths. They have featured famous mythic characters in such forms as dramas, stories, and poetry. Whether powerful or weak, noble or flawed, these characters have a hold on writers' imaginations. "Icarus's Flight" is a poem that reflects a poet's fascination with the myth of Icarus, the son of Daedalus who flew too close to the sun.*

Icarus's Flight

Poem by Stephen Dobyns

Stephen Dobyns (b. 1941) *has written numerous, critically acclaimed poetry collections. While he is also the author of other popular works of fiction, including novels and mysteries, he considers himself first and foremost a poet. In fact, he has claimed that he thinks of poetry twenty-four hours a day and that being a successful poet requires constant focus on the craft. Dobyns has also taught writing at a number of colleges throughout the United States.*

A

SETTING A PURPOSE As you read this poem, think about the way the poet portrays Icarus and his true intention.

(t) ©eAlisa/Shutterstock; (b) ©Isabel Bize

his liberty. You say he flew too far?

He flew just far enough. He flew precisely

Analyze Form: Poetry (LINES 1–8)

 COMMON CORE RL 1, RL 5

Explain to students that a poem's **form** is the way in which the words and lines are arranged on the page. Form also includes the way in which related ideas are grouped together into **stanzas,** the groups of two or more lines that form a unit in a poem.

Ⓐ CITE TEXT EVIDENCE Have students reread lines 1–8, and identify the number of lines in each stanza, whether the lines rhyme, and how end punctuation is used in each line. What is the effect of these elements of form on the meaning? *(This part is divided into two stanzas of four lines in each. The lines do not rhyme. The sentences extending across lines and stanzas pull the reader along, from one line to the next.)*

Determine Meaning of Words and Phrases: Alliteration (LINES 10–16)

 COMMON CORE RL 1, RL 4

Inform students that **alliteration** is the repetition of consonant sounds at the beginning of words. Poets use alliteration to give the poem **rhythm,** which is the pattern of sounds similar to beats in music. Alliteration also helps direct attention to certain words.

Ⓚ CITE TEXT EVIDENCE Have students reread line 10 to "around him" in line 16. Ask them to identify the alliterative words *(flew, flutter, flight, far, forever)* and explain how these words affect the poem. *(The repeating consonant sounds emphasize these words, helping to create the image of flight and distance.)*

COLLABORATIVE DISCUSSION Have partners discuss their ideas about what Icarus really wanted and whether he achieved it. Remind them to cite evidence from the text to support their ideas.

ASK STUDENTS to share any questions they generated in the course of reading and discussing this selection.

Icarus's Flight

Ⓐ   What else could the boy have done? Wasn't
flight both an escape and a great uplifting?
And so he flew. But how could he appreciate
his freedom without knowing the exact point

5   where freedom stopped? So he flew upward
and the sun dissolved the wax and he fell.
But at last in his anticipated plummeting
he grasped the confines of what had been

      his liberty. You say he flew too far?
Ⓑ 10 He flew just far enough. He flew precisely
to the point of wisdom. Would it
have been better to flutter ignorantly

      from petal to petal within some garden
forever? As a result, flight for him was not
15 upward escape, but descent, with his wings
disintegrating around him. Should it matter

      that neither shepherd nor farmer with his plow
watched him fall? He now had his answer,
laws to uphold him in his downward plunge.
20 Cushion enough for what he wanted.

COLLABORATIVE DISCUSSION According to the poet, what did Icarus really want? Do you think Icarus achieved it? Discuss your ideas with a partner.

WHEN STUDENTS STRUGGLE . . .

Explain to students that reading a poem aloud often helps reveal the rhythm. Have students work in small groups to take turns reading the poem aloud to each other. Point out that it helps to read to the end of each thought, pausing at the end of sentences and questions rather than at the end of each line.

Analyze Form: Poetry

COMMON CORE RL 5

Poetry is a type of literature in which words are carefully chosen and arranged to create certain effects. **Form** in poetry is the way the words are arranged on the page. Here are two basic elements of form in poetry:

- The **line** is the main unit of all poems. Poets play with line length to emphasize meaning and to create rhythm. **Rhythm** is a pattern of stressed and unstressed syllables in a line of poetry, similar to the rhythmic beats in music.
- Lines are arranged in a group called a **stanza.** A single stanza may express a separate idea or emotion, but each stanza contributes to the overall meaning of a poem.

Crafting a poem's form involves careful choices of words, rhythms, and sounds. To understand how form can help create an effect such as rhythm in a poem, ask yourself these questions.

 How long are the lines?

 Do the lines rhyme?

 Do the sentences always end at the end of a line?

How many lines are in each stanza?

Determine Meaning of Words and Phrases: Alliteration

COMMON CORE RL 4

Poetry is often created to be spoken and heard. Reading a poem aloud can give readers a better sense of the feeling and sounds that the poet intended.

Poets often choose different words for their sounds. **Alliteration** is the repetition of consonant sounds at the beginning of words. It can establish rhythms in a poem that create feelings or emphasize ideas and images.

Read aloud these lines from "Icarus's Flight." Listen for the alliterative sounds. What do the repeated sounds suggest to you? How do they create rhythm and add emphasis to ideas or images in text?

> **As a result, flight for him was not**
> **upward escape, but descent, with his wings**
> **disintegrating around him. Should it matter**

Notice how the alliterative words of *descent* and *disintegrating* not only emphasize similar sounds, but they create a sense of falling *downward*—another word that begins with the same sound.

TEACH

CLOSE READ

Analyze Form: Poetry

COMMON CORE RL 5

Have students work with a partner to examine the poem's form and answer the questions. Have them describe how the form affects the poem. *(Possible answer: There are four lines in each stanza. Each line is about the same length. There is a pattern of asking questions that introduces ideas, helps organize the speaker's thoughts, and gives the poem rhythm.)*

Determine Meaning of Words and Phrases: Alliteration

COMMON CORE RL 4

Have partners take turns reading the poem aloud. As one partner reads, have the other jot down repeated consonant sounds at the beginning of words. Ask how this use of language contributes to the meaning and feeling of the poem. *(Possible answer: Repeated words and sounds provide rhythm and emphasize the actions described in the poem. They help the reader understand the poet's view of Icarus's flight.)*

Strategies for Annotation *Annotate it!*

Determine Meaning of Words and Phrases: Alliteration

COMMON CORE RL 4

Have students use their eBook annotation tools to analyze the text. Ask them to do the following:

- Highlight in yellow the questions.
- Underline alliterative words.
- On a note, record difficult or confusing words or phrases.
- Review their annotations and explain how alliteration contributes to the meaning of the poem.

What else could the boy have done? Wasn't <u>flight</u> both an escape and a great uplifting? And so he <u>flew</u>. But how could he appreciate his <u>freedom</u> without knowing the exact point

 confusing words and phrases: great uplifting

PRACTICE & APPLY

Analyzing the Text

COMMON CORE RL 1, RL 2, RL 4, RL 5

Possible answers:

1. *It pulls the reader along, connecting the stanzas and giving the poem an almost vertical motion downward. This seems to suggest the downward descent of Icarus's flight.*

2. *The exact point where freedom stopped is the moment in which Icarus's wings failed, and he was about to begin his descent.*

3. *flew and flutter are alliterative; the poet chose those words to emphasize the contrast between strong and weak flight.*

4. *The poet means that Icarus succeeded because by flying to that point, he learned what freedom was. He achieved "precisely" the "wisdom" of understanding both freedom and mortality at the same time.*

5. *Alliterative words:* him, he, had, his. *The poet uses these words to emphasize the idea that Icarus has finally attained what he wanted.*

6. *This poem changed my perception of Icarus from thinking of him as a young boy who forgot to heed his father's warning and loses his life, to someone who becomes fully aware of his actions and in failure actually gains wisdom and freedom.*

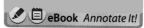 eBook *Annotate It!*

Analyzing the Text

COMMON CORE RL 2, RL 4, RL 5, W 2, SL 4

Cite Text Evidence   Support your responses with evidence from the text.

1. **Identify**   Look closely at how certain sentences of the poem extend from one stanza into the next one. What effect is created by extending a sentence into the next line or into the next stanza?

2. **Analyze**   Examine the question in lines 3–5. Based on what you know about the Icarus myth, where is the "exact point where freedom stopped"? How would you answer this question?

3. **Analyze**   Look at the third stanza and identify the alliterative words. What idea does this alliteration emphasize or draw attention to?

4. **Interpret**   What does the poet mean by the two sentences in lines 10 and 11?

5. **Analyze**   Find the sentence that begins within line 18 and read it aloud. What examples of alliteration do you see? Why do you think the poet uses alliteration here?

6. **Compare**   Consider what you already knew about the mythological character, Icarus, before reading this poem. How does this poem cause your perception of Icarus to change? Explain.

PERFORMANCE TASK

Speaking Activity: Oral Response
The poet asks a number of questions throughout the poem, as if speaking directly to readers. What is the purpose of these questions? Do they cause you to consider Icarus's actions in a new light? Share your views in an oral response.

- Think about the questions and views the poet presents.
- Identify evidence from the poem to support your views.
- Make sure your points are clear and convincing. Use verbal and nonverbal techniques to enhance your points.

Assign this performance task.

PERFORMANCE TASK

COMMON CORE W 2, SL 4

Oral Response   Have students review the poem.

- Ask them to list the questions the poet includes in the poem. Then, have them try to answer each question, citing examples from the poem.
- Have them organize their ideas, using a hierarchy chart, to support their views on the effectiveness of these questions.
- Remind them to use appropriate eye contact, volume, and clear pronunciation when speaking.

Analyze Form: Scansion

COMMON CORE
RL 4,
RL 5

TEACH

Explain to students that **rhythm** in a poem is like the beat in music. It is a regular pattern of sound that is created by stressing some words or syllables and not others. Poets intentionally arrange words into rhythms that convey feelings and meaning.

- Explain that **scansion** is the process of marking the stressed and unstressed words or syllables in a poem to find its rhythm. Display and read aloud the following sentence, pointing out that the boldfaced words are stressed:

    The **time** to **act** is **now**!

- Explain that a repeated pattern of rhythm is called **meter.** Point out that in the meter in the example sentence, every other word is stressed.

- Explain that another way to mark up the rhythm of a line of poetry is by placing an acute accent (´) over the stressed words and a breve (˘) over the unstressed syllables.

- Display the sentence again, marking it as shown.

    The time to act is now!

 LEVEL UP TUTORIALS Assign the following *Level Up* tutorial: **Rhythm**

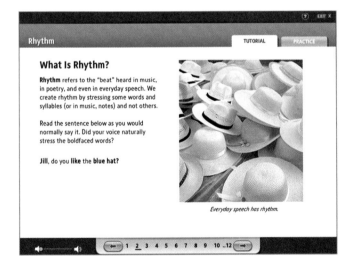

PRACTICE AND APPLY

Have partners work together to mark the stressed and unstressed syllables in the first stanza of "Icarus's Flight." Have them identify its rhythm and meter, and discuss how they affect the poem's meaning.

 INTERACTIVE WHITEBOARD LESSON
Analyze Form: Poetry

COMMON CORE
RL 5,
SL 1

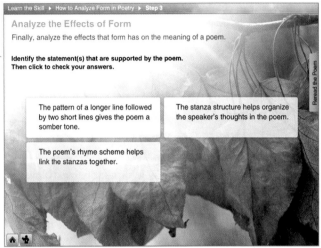

RETEACH

Review with students that the **form,** or structure, of a poem is the way in which the words and **lines,** the main units of a poem, are arranged on the page. Form also includes the way in which related ideas are grouped together into **stanzas.**

- Poets use different forms to suite the types of thoughts and feelings they wish to convey.

- For example, a poet might use many short lines with no stanzas to create a feeling of energy and movement. They might alternate between long and short lines to play with rhythm and to emphasize some ideas over others.

- By analyzing the lengths of lines and the organization of the poem into stanzas, readers can understand and better appreciate a poet's ideas.

COLLABORATIVE DISCUSSION

Have pairs of students pick three poems by the same poet, either in a book or in an online collection. Have partners use an Interactive Graphic Organizer, such as a Comparison-Contrast Chart, to list how the poet uses lines and stanzas in each poem. Then have students discuss the effects that the different forms have on rhythm and meaning in each poem.

 INTERACTIVE GRAPHIC ORGANIZER Have students use this interactive graphic organizer: **Comparison-Contrast Chart**

mySmartPlanner Create lesson plans and access resources online.

Women in Aviation

Informational Text by Patricia and Fredrick McKissack

Why This Text?

Students encounter informational text almost daily. Understanding why an author writes a particular piece and how the author's choices reveal that purpose helps students be more analytical readers. This lesson explores an author's purpose for writing and has students support the conclusions they draw as they read.

► View It!

Professional Development Podcast:

Informational Text

Key Learning Objective: Students will be able to identify, analyze, and draw conclusions about an author's purpose for writing informational texts.

COMMON CORE Common Core Standards

RI 1 Cite textual evidence.
RI 2 Determine two or more central ideas.
RI 3 Analyze interactions between individuals, events, and ideas.
RI 4 Determine the meaning of words and phrases.
RI 6 Determine an author's purpose.
W 2 Write informative/explanatory texts.
W 6 Use technology to produce/publish writing.
W 8 Gather information from print and digital sources.
W 10 Write routinely.
L 1a Explain the function of phrases and clauses.
L 4a Use context as a clue to the meaning of a word or phrase.
L 5c Distinguish among connotations of words with similar denotations.

▲ Text Complexity Rubric

Quantitative Measures	**Women in Aviation** Lexile: 1150L
	Levels of Meaning/Purpose ●—●—●—●—→ single purpose, explicitly stated
Qualitative Measures	**Structure** ●—●—●—●—→ organization of main ideas and details complex, but clearly stated and generally sequential
	Language Conventionality and Clarity ●—●—●—●—→ less straightforward sentence structure
	Knowledge Demands ●—●—●—●—→ somewhat complex social studies concepts
Reader/Task Considerations	Teacher determined Vary by individual reader and type of text

CLOSE READ

Background Have students read the background and author information. Explain that aviation—the operation of aircraft—dates back to the first balloon flights in the late 1700s. In the 1890s, the first gliders, airplane-like aircraft without engines, were flown. But it was not until 1903 that the Wright brothers made the first successful flight in an engine-powered aircraft, the airplane. Airplane flight really "took off" during and after World War I (1914–1918), which saw a more widespread use of airplanes for military purposes.

SETTING A PURPOSE Direct students to use the Setting a Purpose question to focus their reading. Remind them to generate questions as they read.

Determine Author's Purpose (LINES 1–8)

 COMMON CORE RI 1, RI 6

Explain to students that authors write for a reason—the **author's purpose.** Authors of informational texts often write to inform or explain, presenting facts and other information about a topic.

A **CITE TEXT EVIDENCE** Ask students to reread lines 1–8 and cite evidence that helps them identify the authors' purpose. *(The purpose is to inform, because the authors include information about women aviators in the early days of aviation in America. The authors also explain that despite prejudice, some women and African Americans still dreamt of becoming aviators.)*

Cite Evidence and Draw Conclusions (LINES 9–15)

 COMMON CORE RI 1

Explain that as they read, students can **draw conclusions,** or make judgments about or take positions on, a topic. They should base these conclusions on evidence, experience, and reasoning. To support their conclusions, readers should cite **textual evidence** in the form of facts and details.

B **CITE TEXT EVIDENCE** Ask students to reread lines 9–15 and identify evidence that supports a conclusion that the earliest women aviators were brave and accomplished. *(The detail "a number of women…gained fame for their skill and daring" supports this, as do the facts about Sophie Blanchard and other European women aviators.)*

Background *In the early 1900s, flying in "aeroplanes"—fixed-winged, self-propelled flying machines—was a bold undertaking. Male pilots were dashing heroes. However, female aviators—especially African American women—had to struggle for acceptance.* **Patricia and Fredrick McKissack** (b. 1944; b. 1939) *have written over 100 biographies and nonfiction books, most focusing on the achievements of African Americans.*

Women in Aviation

Informational Text by Patricia and Fredrick McKissack

(t) Houghton, Mifflin, Harcourt; (l) ©Tobias Helbig/Getty Images; (bg) ©Digital Vision/Getty Images; (cl) ©Apic/Hulton Archive/Getty Images; (cr) ©Fotosearch/Archive Photos/Getty Images; (r) ©Bettmann/Corbis

SETTING A PURPOSE As you read, pay attention to the details that describe what it was like for a woman to become a pilot during this period. What obstacles did each pilot face? Write down any questions you may have while reading.

Americal aviation was from its very beginnings marred with sexist and racist assumptions. It was taken for granted that women were generally inferior to men and that white men were superior to all others. Flying, it was said, required a level of skill and courage that women and blacks lacked. Yet despite these prevailing prejudices, the dream and the desire to fly stayed alive among women and African-Americans.

10 The story of women in aviation actually goes back to the time of the hot-air balloons. A number of women in Europe and America gained fame for their skill and daring. Sophie Blanchard made her first solo balloon flight in 1805. She grew in fame and was eventually named official aeronaut of the empire by Napoleon. By 1834, at least twenty women in Europe were piloting their own balloons.

SCAFFOLDING FOR ELL STUDENTS

Expand Vocabulary Using a whiteboard, project the second paragraph of the text. Highlight in yellow: *aviation, flight, aeronaut,* and *piloting.* Discuss how all these words are similar, as they are all words related to flying aircraft, and how they are all related to the topic of this selection. As needed, review the meaning of each word.

ASK STUDENTS if an aeronaut might pilot an airplane. Have them explain why or why not.

For more context and historical background, students can view the video "Bessie Coleman" in their eBooks.

Determine Author's Purpose (LINES 25–33)

COMMON CORE RI 1, RI 6

Explain to students that authors can have more than one purpose for writing. For example, in an informational text, a writer might include fun details or interesting facts in order to entertain the reader as well as to inform.

C **ASK STUDENTS** to reread lines 25–33 and identify details that both entertain and inform. *(Sample answer: The quotation from Harriet Quimby "Flying is easier than voting." was said with "a smile and a wink." This detail adds some humor to the piece, making it both informative and fun to read.)*

CRITICAL VOCABULARY

inundate: The author is describing how Harriet Quimby was often surrounded by male reporters who found her both attractive and entertaining.

ASK STUDENTS how a woman aviator might feel to be inundated with questions by a large group of reporters. *(She might feel crowded or overwhelmed, and several people might be asking her questions at the same time.)*

Though she did not fly, Katherine Wright was a major supporter of her brothers' efforts. Orville so appreciated his sister's help that he said, "When the world speaks of the Wrights, it must include my sister. . . . She inspired much of 20 our effort."

Although Raymonde de la Roche of France was the first woman in the world to earn her pilot's license, Harriet Quimby held the distinction of being the first American woman to become a licensed pilot.

On August 1, 1911, Quimby, who was described as a "real beauty" with "haunting blue-green eyes," strolled off the field after passing her pilot's test easily. To the male reporters who **inundated** her with questions, Quimby fired back answers with self-confidence. Walking past a group of women who had 30 come to witness the historic event, Quimby was overheard to quip with a smile and a wink: "Flying is easier than voting." (The Woman's Suffrage Amendment wasn't passed until 1920.)

As difficult as it was for women to become pilots in significant numbers, it was doubly hard for African-Americans, especially black women. That's why Bessie Coleman, the first African-American to earn her pilot's license, is such an exciting and important figure in aviation.

Bessie Coleman was born in 1893 in Atlanta, Texas, 40 the twelfth of thirteen children. Her mother, who had been a slave, valued education and encouraged all of her children to attend school in order to better themselves. The encouragement paid off, because Coleman graduated from high school, a feat not too many black women were able to accomplish in the early 1900s.

Bessie Coleman refused to accept the limitations others tried to place on her. She attended an Oklahoma college for one semester but ran out of money. Accepting the offer of one of her brothers to come live with him and his family 50 in Chicago, Coleman found a job as a manicurist. She fully intended to return to school after saving enough money. But she never did. While in Chicago she learned about flying and made a new set of goals for herself. She wanted to be a pilot.

Coleman learned about flying from reading newspaper accounts of air battles during World War I. She tried to find a school that would accept her as a trainee. But no American instructor or flying school was willing to teach her.

inundate
(ĭn´ŭn-dāt´) *v.* To *inundate* is to give a huge amount of something.

WHEN STUDENTS STRUGGLE . . .

While it may be clear to students that the authors' main purpose in this informational text is to inform, they may struggle determining other purposes.

As students read, have pairs fill in a chart to track choices that the authors make that are evidence of other purposes. Explain that as they read they can ask questions, such as: *What effect does this information have on me? Does it make the text fun to read? Does it help explain something?*

When the war ended, a friend, Robert S. Abbott, the founder of the *Chicago Defender*, one of the most popular
60 black-owned and -operated newspapers in the country, suggested that Coleman go to France, where racial prejudice was not as **restrictive** as it was in America. Even though the United States was the birthplace of flight, it was slower than other countries to develop an organized aviation program. European leaders immediately saw the commercial and military advantages of a strong national aviation program. Bessie knew from her reading that both French and German aircraft were among the best in the world.

restrictive
(rĭ-strĭk´tĭv) *adj.*
When something is *restrictive*, it is limiting in some way.

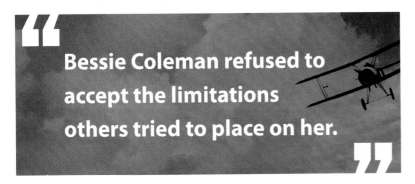

Bessie Coleman refused to accept the limitations others tried to place on her.

Coleman had also read about Eugene Jacques Bullard, the
70 well-decorated[1] and highly honored native of Georgia who had become the first African-American to fly an airplane in combat as a member of the French Lafayette Flying Corps during World War I. Other blacks had gone to Europe to get their training, too. Coleman realized that if she were ever going to get a chance to fly, she, too, would have to go to France. But she didn't have any money to get there, and besides, she couldn't speak a word of French.

For almost two years, Coleman worked part-time as a manicurist and as a server in a Chicago chili parlor and saved
80 every penny to finance her trip to France. Meanwhile she learned to speak French, so when the time came, she'd be able to understand her instructors.

---

[1] **well-decorated:** term used to describe a person in the military who has received many awards.

CLOSE READ

Analyze the Meanings of Words and Phrases

COMMON CORE RI 1, RI 4

(LINES 74–77)

Tell students that an author's choice of words can affect the meaning and tone of a passage. Explain that **tone** is the author's attitude toward a topic, or the way the author sounds, such as angry, outraged, or amused.

D **CITE TEXT EVIDENCE** Have students reread lines 74–77 and identify words that suggest a more conversational, informal tone. Ask what this might reveal about the authors' attitude toward Bessie Coleman. *(The words "and besides, she couldn't speak a word of French" have a more conversational tone. This suggests a familiarity and understanding of Coleman by the authors, almost as if they were talking about someone they actually know and admire.)*

CRITICAL VOCABULARY

restrictive: The authors are explaining how prejudices that held back African Americans in the United States were not as common in France.

ASK STUDENTS to describe how a restrictive policy in the United States affected Bessie Coleman. *(The unwillingness of American instructors and flying schools to teach African American women was restrictive to Coleman because it prevented her from pursuing her dream of becoming a pilot.)*

The Authors' Choices	What These Details Reveal About Their Purpose
Male reporters crowd around Harriet Quimby, and she jokes with them.	*The authors want to entertain with an interesting detail.*
	They also want to explain how Quimby dealt with sexist attitudes towards women.

(r) ©Tobias Helbig/Getty Images; (bg) ©Digital Vision/Getty Images

Cite Evidence and Draw Conclusions

 COMMON CORE RI 1

(LINES 86–88)

Point out to students that while the overall topic of this informational text is women in aviation, the authors chose to focus on just two women aviators—Harriet Quimby and Bessie Coleman.

E ASK STUDENTS to reread lines 86–88 and to think about the information they had read earlier about Harriet Quimby. Ask them what conclusion they can draw about the significance of these two aviators. *(Both aviators were "firsts" to become aviators: Quimby was the first woman, and Coleman was the first African American woman. The conclusion can be made that the experiences of people who are "first" at something reveal the struggle and determination that it takes to succeed.)*

Aviator Bessie Coleman posed for this photograph in 1920.

In 1921, Coleman made it to France, where she found an instructor who was one of Tony Fokker's chief pilots. Fokker, the famous aircraft manufacturer, said Coleman was a "natural talent." On June 15, 1921, Coleman made history by becoming the first black woman to earn her wings, thus joining the ranks of the handful of American women fliers.

90   Returning to the United States determined to start a flying school where other African-American pilots could be trained, Coleman looked for ways to finance her dream. There were very few jobs in the aviation industry for women or blacks. She soon learned that there was little or no support for a black woman who wanted to start a flying school. To call attention to aviation and to encourage other women and African-Americans to take part in the new and growing field,

©Michael Ochs Archives/Getty Images

46   Collection 1

Cite Text Evidence and Draw Conclusions

 COMMON CORE RI 1

Have students locate the first paragraph. Encourage them to use their eBook annotation tools to do the following:

- Highlight in yellow the text that describes Coleman's achievements.
- Underline text that indicates why the achievements were important.
- Review your annotations and explain how this text helps you draw a conclusion. *(A person who is a first in a field is important because that person overcame obstacles that no one else had.)*

an instructor who was one of Tony Fokker's chief pilots. Fokker, the famous aircraft manufacturer, said Coleman was a "natural talent." On June 15, 1921, Coleman made history by becoming the <u>first black woman</u> to earn her wings, thus joining the ranks of the handful of American women fliers.

F Coleman gave flying **exhibitions** and lectured on aviation. She thrilled audiences with daredevil maneuvers, just as Quimby had done before her.

Along with racism, Coleman encountered the burden of sexism, but she made believers out of those who doubted her skill. "The color of my skin," she said, "[was] a drawback at first. . . . I was a curiosity, but soon the public discovered I could really fly. Then they came to see *Brave Bessie*, as they called me."

The strict rules and regulations that govern aviation today didn't exist during the first three decades of flying. For example, it wasn't uncommon for aviators to ignore safety belts and fly without parachutes. One of these simple
110 safety **precautions** might have saved the lives of both Harriet Quimby and Bessie Coleman.

On a July morning in 1912, Quimby, and a passenger named William P. Willard, set out to break an over-water speed record. When Quimby climbed to five thousand feet, the French-made Blériot monoplane[2] suddenly nosed down. Both Quimby and Willard were thrown from the plane and plunged to their deaths in the Boston Harbor.

The *New York Sun* used the opportunity to speak out against women fliers:

120 Miss Quimby is the fifth woman in the world killed while operating an aeroplane (three were students) and their number thus far is five too many. The sport is not one for which women are physically qualified. As a rule they lack strength and presence of mind and the courage to excel as aviators. It is essentially a man's sport and pastime.

Fourteen years later, Bessie Coleman died in a similar accident. With almost enough savings to start her school, Coleman agreed to do an air show in Florida on May Day
130 for the Negro Welfare League of Jacksonville. At 7:30 P.M. the night before, Coleman, accompanied by her publicity agent, William Wills, took her plane up for a test flight. When she reached an altitude of about five thousand feet, her plane flipped over. Coleman was thrown from the plane and

---

[2] **monoplane:** an airplane with only one pair of wings.

exhibition
(ĕk´sə-bĭsh´ən) *n.*
An *exhibition* is an organized presentation or show.

precaution
(prĭ-kô´shən) *n.*
A *precaution* is an action taken to avoid possible danger.

TEACH

CLOSE READ

Determine Author's Purpose (LINES 97–99)

COMMON CORE · RI 1, RI 6

Point out that an author's choice of words often helps reveal a purpose for writing a certain section of text.

F **CITE TEXT EVIDENCE** Have students reread lines 97–99 and ask them to identify words that reveal the authors' purpose in this section. What do these word choices reveal about the authors' purpose? (*The words "thrilled audiences" and "daredevil maneuvers" suggest excitement and courageousness. The authors want to show how fearless and entertaining Coleman and Quimby were as aviators. These choices by the authors are both informative and entertaining. They also help create a more vivid description for the reader.*)

CRITICAL VOCABULARY

exhibition: The authors are explaining how Bessie Coleman became well known by performing as an aviator and public speaker.

ASK STUDENTS to describe what they might have seen at one of Bessie Coleman's exhibitions. (*Sample answer: I might see Coleman flying upside down in her airplane above a large crowd on the ground.*)

precaution: Early aviation was a particularly dangerous endeavor as pilots flew in relatively unstable aircraft, sitting in open-air cockpits.

ASK STUDENTS to describe why a safety belt would be a good precaution for an aviator in an open-air cockpit. (*Sample answer: It would hold them securely to their seats so that they couldn't fall out of the aircraft.*)

APPLYING ACADEMIC VOCABULARY

aspect	cultural	evaluate

As you discuss the text, incorporate the following Collection 1 academic vocabulary words: *cultural, aspect,* and *evaluate*. Ask students what **aspects** of life in America created **cultural** obstacles for women who wanted to become pilots. As students read, have them **evaluate** how effectively the authors present the achievements of the first women aviators.

Determine Author's Purpose (LINES 137–145)

COMMON CORE RI 1, RI 6

Explain that Amelia Earhart was famous for being the first woman, and second person, to make a solo airplane flight across the Atlantic Ocean. This 1932 flight from Canada to France made Earhart one of the most famous people in the world. Earhart's interest in flying was sparked when she was just ten years old and saw an aviation exhibition, much like the ones in which Bessie Coleman and Harriet Quimby performed.

H **ASK STUDENTS** to reread lines 137–145 and explain why the authors chose to include a quote from Amelia Earhart at the end of the selection. *(The authors included a quote from Amelia Earhart because she was one of the most famous women aviators from the early 1900s and was a pioneer of aviation; Earhart's quote underscores the authors' point that all women aviators had to overcome cultural obstacles to pursue their dreams.)*

COLLABORATIVE DISCUSSION Have groups of students discuss the obstacles that early female pilots overcame, using examples from the text. Encourage them to jot down notes as they talk. Then have them share their ideas with the class and evaluate how effectively the women featured in the text achieved their goals.

ASK STUDENTS to share any questions they generated in the course of reading and discussing the selection.

plunged to her death April 30, 1926. Wills died seconds later when the plane crashed.

Once again critics used the tragedy to assert that neither women nor blacks were mentally or physically able to be good pilots. "Women are often penalized by publicity for their every

140 mishap," said Amelia Earhart, the most famous female pilot in aviation history. "The result is that such emphasis sometimes directly affects [a woman's] chances for a flying job," Earhart continued. "I had one manufacturer tell me that he couldn't risk hiring women pilots because of the way accidents, even minor ones, became headlines in the newspapers."

Although Bessie Coleman died tragically, her plans to open a flight training school for blacks were continued by those she had inspired.

COLLABORATIVE DISCUSSION What obstacles did Quimby, Coleman, and other early female pilots face that their male counterparts did not face? In a group, share ideas about what motivated these women to achieve in spite of difficulties.

Determine Author's Purpose

 COMMON CORE RI 6

An **author's purpose** is the reason the author wrote a particular work. Usually an author writes for one or more purposes, as shown in this chart:

Author's Purpose	Examples of Written Works
To inform or explain	encyclopedia entries, informational articles, how-to articles, biographies, and other factual, real-world examples
To persuade	editorials, opinion essays and blogs, advertisements, and other works in which the author shares an opinion and tries to persuade readers to agree
To entertain	stories, novels, plays, essays, and literary works that engage the reader with qualities such as humor, suspense, and intriguing details
To express thoughts or feelings	poems, personal essays, journals and other texts in which the author shares insights, emotions, and descriptions

To determine an author's purpose in informational texts, examine the the facts and quotations. An author may have a main purpose for writing, as well as other purposes. For example, "Women in Aviation" provides facts, so it is written mainly to inform. But the authors have other purposes, too, revealed by their word choices and their examples.

Cite Evidence and Draw Conclusions

 COMMON CORE RI 1

When you **draw conclusions,** you make judgments or take a position on a topic. To support conclusions, readers cite **textual evidence**—information from the text in the form of facts and details. To draw conclusions in an informational text, follow these steps:

- Look for statements in the text that support your conclusion.
- Consider your own experience and knowledge about the topic.
- Make a judgment based on evidence and your own knowledge.

Informational texts contain details readers can use as textual evidence. For example, here's a quote from "Women in Aviation" that describes Katherine Wright, the sister of famous aviators Orville and Wilbur Wright:

> "When the world speaks of the Wrights, it must include my sister. . . . She inspired much of our effort."

Katherine Wright wasn't a pilot. However, based on this text, what conclusion can you draw about her contribution to the Wright brothers' achievements?

Women in Aviation **49**

CLOSE READ

Determine Author's Purpose

 COMMON CORE RI 6

Discuss the definition of author's purpose with students, asking volunteers for reasons that writers might have for writing different types of text. Review the different author's purposes listed in the chart, and ask volunteers to name titles of the various genres listed for each author's purpose.

Help students determine an author's purpose in an informational text. Explain that

- an author usually has one main purpose for the piece as a whole, and other secondary purposes
- details, such as facts, quotations, opinions, word choices, can reveal an author's purpose
- as students read, they should track these details to figure out an author's purpose

Cite Evidence and Draw Conclusions

 COMMON CORE RI 1

Explain that drawing conclusions is a way to add up information to make judgments or to decide how one feels about a text. To do this, readers should cite textual evidence to support their conclusions. Have students draw a conclusion about Katherine Wright's contributions to her brothers' achievements. (*Sample answer: She inspired her brothers' accomplishments.*)

Strategies for Annotation 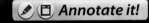 ✎ 🖸 *Annotate it!*

Determine Author's Purpose

 COMMON CORE RI 1, RI 6

Share these strategies for guided or independent analysis (lines 34–48):

- Highlight in yellow details that suggest that the authors' purpose is to inform.
- Underline details that suggest the authors' purpose is to persuade.
- Draw a conclusion about the text supported by the evidence. (*Sample answer: Because she was the first African American woman aviator, Bessie Coleman is a good example of a pioneering female aviator.*)

As difficult as it was for women to become pilots in significant numbers, it was doubly hard for African-Americans, especially black women. That's why Bessie Coleman, the first African American to earn her pilot's license, is such an exciting and important figure in aviation.

PRACTICE & APPLY

Analyzing the Text
COMMON CORE RI 1, RI 3, RI 6

Possible answers:

1. *Their purpose is to inform readers that American aviation had a history of unfairness to women and minorities. The phrase "marred with sexist and racist assumptions" supports this.*

2. *Harriet Quimby was an attractive, self-confident woman with a sense of humor. Evidence of this is the description of her appearance, her interaction with the reporters, and her comment to the other women.*

3. ***Textual Evidence:** Coleman worked for two years to finance her trip and also learned French. **Experience:** Reaching a goal requires making a plan and sticking to it. **Conclusion:** Coleman showed patience and determination in overcoming obstacles to reach her goal.*

4. *Both were pioneers in aviation. Both had the self-confidence to overcome male prejudice. Both were probably courageous risk takers who enjoyed the thrill of flight.*

5. *By including facts and details about prejudice and sexist attitudes of the time, the authors were expressing their thoughts and feelings about the size of the challenges faced by early women and African American aviators.*

6. *The authors want readers to see early female pilots, especially African American female pilots, as heroic. The authors provide convincing support, such as quotations from the women and from news reports. The authors also select interesting details, such as Quimby's self-confident manner and Coleman's learning French.*

Analyzing the Text
COMMON CORE RI 1, RI 3, RI 6, W 2, W 6, W 10

Cite Text Evidence   Support your responses with evidence from the text.

1. **Cite Evidence** Based on the first sentence in "Women in Aviation," what do you think the author's purpose might be? Which words or phrases indicate this purpose?

2. **Interpret** Reread lines 26–33. What impression do the authors create of Harriet Quimby by using facts and quotations?

3. **Draw Conclusions** Reread lines 69–82. What conclusion can you draw about Bessie Coleman's personality, based on the information in these paragraphs? Fill out a chart to show how you came to your conclusion. Use chart headings like these:

Textual Evidence	My Experience	Conclusion

4. **Compare** In what ways were Harriet Quimby and Bessie Coleman probably most alike? Explain.

5. **Analyze** You've learned that authors may have more than one purpose in mind for a text. For "Woman in Aviation," it's clear that the authors' main purpose is to inform. What secondary purpose do you think is evident in the text?

6. **Evaluate** What do you think is the most important idea the authors want to convey about the efforts of women aviators in the early 20th century? Support your view with evidence from "Women in Aviation."

PERFORMANCE TASK

Writing Activity: Report Do further research on one of the figures from "Women in Aviation." Then present your research in the form of a report.

- Use text, online, and digital resources such as encyclopedias, web searches, and other texts to find facts and details.

- Include details about the pilot's achievements and their importance.

- Be sure to include additional quotes either directly from or about the aviator you chose.

Assign this performance task.

PERFORMANCE TASK
COMMON CORE W 2, W 6, W 10

Writing Activity: Report Have students work in small groups to choose and research a woman aviator from the early 20th century.

- Direct them to reread the selection to generate questions they would want to answer.

- See page 64 for further instruction on evaluating credible online sources.

Critical Vocabulary

COMMON CORE L 4a, L 5c

inundate   restrictive   exhibition   precaution

Practice and Apply Which of the two situations best matches the meaning of the vocabulary word? Explain your choice.

1. inundate
  a. More than 400 customers call the hot line one morning.
  b. One two visitors come to a museum.

2. restrictive
  a. The gate to the park is locked at six o'clock.
  b. The gate to the park has a rusty lock.

3. exhibition
  a. A crowd gathered at a store advertising a one-day sale.
  b. The crowd watched a holiday cooking demonstration.

4. precaution
  a. The state lets voters send in their ballots before Election Day.
  b. The state requires motorcyclists to wear safety helmets.

Vocabulary Strategy:
Connotations and Denotations

A word's **denotation** is its literal, dictionary meaning. A word's **connotation** comes from the ideas and feelings associated with the word. The authors of "Women in Aviation" chose words based on connotation and denotation.

> On August 1, 1911, Quimby, who was described as a "real beauty" with "haunting blue-green eyes," strolled off the field after passing her pilot's test easily.

Notice how the specific word choice of *strolled* suggests an easy, confident way of walking. This paints a picture of an accomplished young pilot. Words can have a positive or a negative connotation. The context of a phrase, sentence, or paragraph can help you determine the connotation of a word.

Practice and Apply For each item that follows, choose the word you think better expresses the meaning of the sentence. Use a print or online dictionary to help you with unfamiliar words. Then write the reason for your choice.

1. Bessie Coleman refused to give up. She was (**stubborn, determined**).

2. Early pilots performed stunts. The pilots were (**daring, reckless**).

3. Women had barriers. Yet female pilots (**followed, pursued**) their dreams.

4. Coleman died as a pioneer. Her efforts (**inspired, helped**) future generations.

Critical Vocabulary

COMMON CORE L 4a, L 5c

Answers: **1.** *a,* **2.** *a,* **3.** *b,* **4.** *b*

Vocabulary Strategy:
Connotations and Denotations

Sample answers: 1. determined; Determined *has a positive connotation of working toward a goal, while* stubborn *has a slightly more negative connotation.* **2.** daring; Daring *connotes courage and bravery, while* reckless *suggests the person is foolhardy and lives carelessly.* **3.** pursued; Pursued *has a slightly stronger connotation of striving for a goal than* followed. **4.** inspired; Inspired *connotes that Coleman did more than just helped. She actually motivated others.*

Strategies for Annotation   ✏️ 📖 *Annotate it!*

Connotations and Denotations

COMMON CORE L 4a, L 5c

Have students locate the sentence that contains *thrilled, daredevil,* and *maneuvers* in lines 97–99 of the selection. Encourage them to use their eBook annotation tools to do the following:

- Highlight each word.
- Use the context or a print or digital dictionary to determine each word's meaning.
- Make an annotation explaining why each word choice is better than other synonyms such as *entertained, exciting,* and *stunts.*

Coleman gave flying exhibitions and lectured on aviation. She thrilled audiences with daredevil maneuvers, just as Quimby had done before her.

> *Maneuvers* is a better word choice than *stunts* because it suggests that Bessie was very skillful and talented.

PRACTICE & APPLY

Language Conventions: Subordinate Clauses

Tell students that the examples show two types of clauses: independent clauses and subordinate clauses. Point out that the word *independent* means that something can be on its own and does not need anything to help make it complete. *Subordinate* means that something is subject to the control of something else. Tell students they can think of a subordinate clause as needing the help of another clause to make it a complete thought. Point to the list of subordinate clauses and ask volunteers to use each one in a sentence with an independent clause. Discuss why the first half of the sample sentence is a subordinate clause and the second half, after the comma, is an independent clause.

Sample answers:

1. *Because flying was a new and exciting sport, crowds gathered to watch air shows.*

2. *Accidents were common until aviation was regulated.*

3. *Military pilots returned to jobs flying planes when World War I ended.*

4. *Although Bessie Coleman died tragically, her life inspired other African Americans to become pilots.*

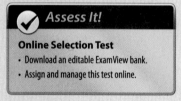

✓ Assess It!

Online Selection Test
- Download an editable ExamView bank.
- Assign and manage this test online.

Language Conventions: Subordinate Clauses

Think of clauses as building blocks for sentences. A sentence is an **independent clause** because it can stand alone and express a complete thought. A **subordinate clause** cannot stand alone in a sentence because it is subordinate to, or dependent on, a main clause. Subordinate clauses are also called **dependent clauses.**

Subordinate Clause	Independent Clause
Because it's stormy,	the flight is delayed.
We'll take off,	when the skies are clear.

You can recognize a subordinate clause because it begins with a **subordinating conjunction.** Common subordinating conjunctions are *after, although, as, because, before, even though, if, since, so that, though, unless, until, when, where,* and *while.*

The subordinating conjunction *even though* introduces the subordinating clause in this sentence from "Women in Aviation":

> **Even though the United States was the birthplace of flight, it was slower than other countries to develop an organized aviation program.**

When you write, be careful not to confuse a subordinate clause with a complete sentence; a subordinate clause cannot stand alone. A subordinate clause can appear anywhere in a sentence. If you position it before the independent clause, set it off with a comma.

Practice and Apply Write a complete sentence, using each of these subordinate clauses. You can review the text of "Women in Aviation" for details to include.

1. because flying was a new and exciting sport

2. until aviation was regulated

3. when World War I ended

4. although Bessie Coleman died tragically

Determine Facts and Opinions

COMMON CORE

RI 2

TEACH

Most informational writing contains both facts and opinions. Explain to students that a **fact** is a statement that can be proved, or verified, while an **opinion** is a statement that expresses a writer's belief, feelings, or thoughts, and cannot be proved.

- Use the following example from the text (lines 108–111) to review how to distinguish fact from opinion: *For example, it wasn't uncommon for aviators to ignore safety belts and fly without parachutes. One of these simple safety precautions might have saved the lives of both Harriet Quimby and Bessie Coleman.*

- Explain that the first sentence is a fact, which can be proved by consulting sources about the use of safety equipment in the early days of airplane aviation.

- The second sentence is more of an opinion, because it expresses the authors' belief that this equipment "might" have saved the two pilots' lives.

- Point out, however, that it is likely that the authors could have **substantiated** this opinion, or established it by evidence, by providing verifiable facts about the effectiveness of safety belts and parachutes.

PRACTICE AND APPLY

Display lines 34–38 of the selection. Have volunteers identify examples of facts and opinions in the passage. *(Facts: It was difficult for women to become pilots and especially difficult for African Americans to do so. Bessie Coleman was the first African American woman to earn her pilot's license. Opinion: Bessie Coleman is an exciting and important figure in aviation.)* Have students explain why these details are either facts or opinions. You might point out that the opinion in the passage is eventually substantiated by additional evidence in the rest of the selection.

Determine Central Idea and Details

COMMON CORE

RI 2

TEACH

Explain that in "Women in Aviation," the McKissacks include **supporting details** to support, or tell more about, **central ideas**—the most important ideas about a topic. Supporting details can be used to support the central idea of an entire text or the central idea of a single paragraph. Explain that one type of supporting detail is the use of **quotations,** words taken verbatim from a source or from a person who lived through an event.

- In historical writing, quotations can be taken from a variety of sources, including interviews, first-hand accounts, news articles, and personal writings.

- Have students reread lines 25–33 of the selection. Help them identify the quotations—both the shorter phrases from newspaper reporters and the sentence spoken by Harriet Quimby herself. Point out that quotations are always set off by **quotation marks.**

- Discuss how Quimby's own words and the phrases used by reporters help support the central idea that Quimby was self-confident, even when confronted by male reporters who may have been more interested in writing about her appearance.

- Then work with students to identify another central idea, such as that early women aviators struggled to overcome great obstacles, and discuss how it is developed throughout the story. Have students identify details that support this claim. *(Sexist attitudes, such as the opinion that women didn't posses enough physical strength to fly, made it hard for women to get flying instruction. As an example of a woman overcoming this obstacle, Bessie Coleman had to save money to move to other countries to learn to fly.)*

PRACTICE AND APPLY

Display lines 137–145. Ask volunteers to identify the central idea of the paragraph and to explain how the quotation from Amelia Earhart is a particularly effective supporting detail. *(Central Idea: Critics of the time maintained that women and African Americans were not suitable for aviation. Support: The authors support this with a quote from Amelia Earhart. This is particularly effective as it gives the exact words of a notable figure in aviation who experienced similar bias.)*

INTERACTIVE WHITEBOARD LESSON
Evaluate Online Sources

COMMON CORE
W 8

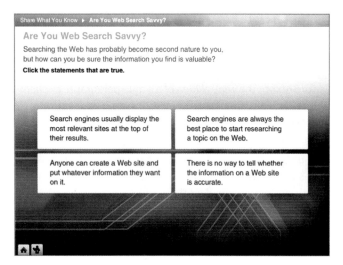

Share What You Know ▶ Are You Web Search Savvy?

Are You Web Search Savvy?

Searching the Web has probably become second nature to you, but how can you be sure the information you find is valuable?

Click the statements that are true.

Search engines usually display the most relevant sites at the top of their results.

Search engines are always the best place to start researching a topic on the Web.

Anyone can create a Web site and put whatever information they want on it.

There is no way to tell whether the information on a Web site is accurate.

TEACH

Before having students complete their research as part of the Performance Task, review how to evaluate online sources:

- Point out that when doing online research, it is important to evaluate the credibility and accuracy of any online source to ensure the information is authoritative and reliable.

- **Step 1: Analyze Sources** Ask questions: *Who is the author of the website content and what makes the author a legitimate authority? Why was the site created? When was the site last updated? Are statements of fact supported by examples and evidence? Is the site produced by a government office, a respected periodical, or an expert on the subject?*

- **Step 2: Check for Bias** Ask yourself if the creator of the site is trying to present a specific point of view or sell a product or service.

- **Step 3: Verify Facts** Use other reliable sources to confirm the information you find on a site. The more credible sources that show the same facts, the more likely the facts are accurate.

COLLABORATIVE DISCUSSION

Have students work in small groups to conduct online research on an early woman aviator. Have groups compare their results and discuss the credibility of their online sources, using the above steps as a guide.

DETERMINE AUTHOR'S PURPOSE

COMMON CORE
RI 6

Review that writers always have a reason for writing a piece—the author's purpose.

- Review the four main reasons for writing: to inform or to explain; to persuade; to entertain; to express thoughts or feelings.

- Explain that clues in the text help reveal the author's purpose. For example, a text with many facts and statistics is evidence that the author's purpose is to inform. A text with jokes is likely intended to entertain.

- Select a variety of texts, such as a humorous personal narrative, how-to books or websites, news stories, textbook chapters, and editorial opinion pieces.

- Read sample passages from each text with students and ask volunteers to identify the author's purpose and cite evidence from the text that reveals this purpose.

LEVEL UP TUTORIALS Assign the following *Level Up* tutorial: **Author's Purpose**

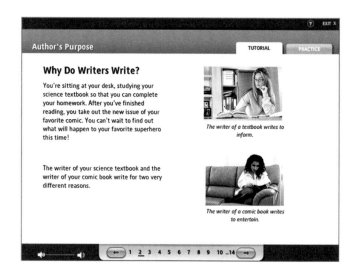

Author's Purpose

TUTORIAL   PRACTICE

Why Do Writers Write?

You're sitting at your desk, studying your science textbook so that you can complete your homework. After you've finished reading, you take out the new issue of your favorite comic. You can't wait to find out what will happen to your favorite superhero this time!

The writer of a textbook writes to inform.

The writer of your science textbook and the writer of your comic book write for two very different reasons.

The writer of a comic book writes to entertain.

1 **2** 3 4 5 6 7 8 9 10 ..14

CLOSE READING APPLICATION

Students can apply the skill to another piece of writing of their own choosing. Have them work independently to determine the author's purpose, citing evidence from the text.

PERFORMANCE TASK A

Write a Short Story

Short stories such as "Rogue Wave" often present characters that take bold actions in order to overcome great challenges. In the following activity, you can use "Rogue Wave" and other texts in the collection as models for writing your own short story in which a main character or characters take bold actions in the face of a seemingly overwhelming challenge.

COMMON CORE

W 3a–e Write narratives.
W 4 Produce clear and coherent writing.
W 5 Develop and strengthen writing.
W 10 Write routinely.

A successful short story narrative

- introduces and develops characters and a setting
- establishes, develops, and resolves a conflict
- contains a plot with a well-structured and logical sequence
- uses dialogue, pacing, and relevant descriptive details
- utilizes transitions to convey sequence
- provides a conclusion that flows from the story events and reflects a theme, or message, about life

PLAN

Establish Story Elements A short story is a narrative that describes experiences and events that you imagine. Plan the characters and events of your story by following these steps.

- Brainstorm ideas for your characters. What does your main character look like? How does the character act, speak, and relate to other characters? Who are the other characters in the story?
- Determine the setting—the time and place where the story occurs. Brainstorm ideas for events that will cause your character to confront his or her fear.
- Establish the conflict—the struggle between opposing forces that the main character must overcome. How does this challenge give your main character the opportunity to take bold actions? What seems overwhelming about the challenge? Write your ideas in short sentences, such as, "A girl finds out she is braver than she thought."

***my*Notebook**

Use the annotation tools in your eBook to mark up key details that you might want to include. Save each detail to your notebook.

ACADEMIC VOCABULARY

As you plan, write, and review your draft, try to use the academic vocabulary words.

aspect
cultural
evaluate
resource
text

PERFORMANCE TASK A

WRITE A SHORT STORY

COMMON CORE W 3a-e, W 4, W 5, W 10

Introduce students to the Performance Task by reading the introductory paragraph with them and reviewing the criteria for what makes a good short story. Remind students that a story becomes more interesting when the characters seem real and when their problems are ones with which readers can identify.

PLAN

ESTABLISH STORY ELEMENTS

View It!

Professional Development Podcast:

Performance Tasks

Share with students that good stories focus on characters who face a conflict. When choosing the plot for their stories, students can think about external and internal challenges. Point out that challenges can range from physical ones, such as struggling to survive in a disaster, to more thoughtful ones, such as overcoming a fear about speaking in front of an audience.

List Plot Events Fill out a plot diagram to plan your story.

- Use the exposition to introduce the characters, setting, and conflict.
- Introduce obstacles that the characters have to overcome in the rising action. Think about how these obstacles build suspense and draw out bold actions in the main character.
- At the climax, tell the most important or exciting event. This is where the suspense comes to a peak—your character is about to overcome the challenge.
- Finally, end with the falling action and resolution to show how the conflict is resolved. Consider what you might be saying about bravery or resourcefulness in extreme situations.
- As you plan, keep pacing in mind. In a well-paced story, the action transitions smoothly from one event to the next.

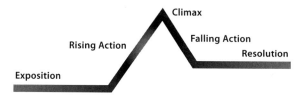

Decide on a Point of View Think about the point of view you want to use in your narrative. Consider how you want the story narrated.

- When a story is told from the first-person point of view, the narrator is a character in the story and uses first-person pronouns such as *I*, *me*, and *we*.
- In a story told from the third-person point of view, such as "Rogue Wave," the narrator is not a character. The narration is told using pronouns such as *he*, *she*, *it*, and *they*.

Consider Your Purpose and Audience Who will read or listen to your short story? What effect do you want the story to have on readers? Do you want simply to entertain them? To inspire them? To make them think? Keep the audience and purpose in mind as you prepare to write.

Write Your Short Story Review your plot diagram as you begin your draft.

- Introduce the main character and setting, engaging your audience with action and dialogue that set up the conflict.
- Establish your point of view by introducing a narrator.
- Create the sequence of events, building suspense with transition words and phrases that clearly show the order of events and signal any shifts in setting.
- Use precise words and phrases and sensory language to create a vivid picture.
- Tell how the conflict is resolved. Clearly show how bold actions fuel the struggle and how the character or characters finally overcome the challenge.
- Leave the audience with a message to reflect on—a life lesson or theme that may be implied.

*my*WriteSmart

Write your rough draft in *my*WriteSmart. Focus on getting your ideas down, rather than perfecting your choice of language.

Review Your Draft Work with a partner to determine if you have achieved your purpose and effectively told your story to your audience. Consider the following during your review:

- Make sure the exposition grabs the audience's attention.
- If necessary, rewrite dialogue to sound like everyday speech.
- Examine the development of your characters. Are their personalities and actions believable?
- Add sensory details to more fully describe the setting.
- Delete any details and events that do not help the plot build to a climax.

*my*WriteSmart

Have your partner or a group of peers review your draft in *my*WriteSmart. Ask your reviewers to note any scenes that do not help build suspense.

Create a Finished Copy Finalize your short story and choose a way to share it with your audience:

- Present your short story in an author's reading to the class.
- Submit your story to the school literary magazine or other online or print literary magazines.

Collection Performance Task A **55**

PERFORMANCE TASK A

WRITE YOUR SHORT STORY

View It!

Professional Development Podcast:
Writing Narratives at the Secondary Level

Remind students that before writing they should decide upon the kind of narrator they want to use in their stories. Students can ask themselves questions such as the following:

- Should the story be told by one of the characters? First-person narrators give a very personal feel to a story but tell it from only one person's point of view.
- Or should the story be told by someone who is not a character? Third-person narrators have the advantage of being able to tell about all of the characters' thoughts and feelings.

REVIEW YOUR DRAFT

Remind students that when they revise their stories, they should think about these goals: 1) Find places to add details about the characters, including dialogue and description, and 2) make the plot more entertaining by adding sensory details and making sure that the action builds to create suspense.

CREATE A FINISHED COPY

Students can present their stories to the class. Remind them that when reading a story aloud, it is important to deliver it in a way that helps to bring the story to life.

PERFORMANCE TASK A

LANGUAGE

Have students look at the chart and identify how they did on the Performance Task in each of the three main categories. Prompt students to check the impact of their word choices and vivid details. Ask students to think about one way they could improve their writing in each of the categories and discuss how they would improve upon their writing the next time they write a story.

	Ideas and Evidence	Organization	Language
ADVANCED	• An engaging conflict is clearly established, developed, and resolved. • The setting is skillfully established and developed and helps shape the conflict. • Characters are compelling and believable. • Dialogue and description are used effectively.	• Event sequence is smooth, is well structured, and creates suspense. • The plot builds to a strong, satisfying conclusion. • Pacing is clear and effective. • Transition words and phrases effectively convey sequence and indicate shifts in setting. • The conclusion clearly reflects a theme, or message, about life.	• The story has a consistent and effective point of view. • Words and phrases are precise and vivid. • Sensory language reveals the setting and characters. • Spelling, capitalization, and punctuation are correct. • Grammar and usage are correct.
COMPETENT	• A conflict is introduced, developed, and resolved, but it could better engage the readers. • The setting is established but could be more developed to shape the characters and conflict. • Characters have some believable traits but may need development. • Dialogue and description could be more interesting.	• Event sequence is generally well structured but includes some extraneous events. • The plot builds to a conclusion. • Pacing is somewhat uneven and confusing. • Transition words and phrases convey sequence but don't indicate shifts in setting. • The conclusion could more clearly reflect a theme, or message, about life.	• The story has a consistent point of view. • Descriptive words and phrases and sensory language are used but could be more vivid and revealing of characters. • Few spelling, capitalization, and punctuation errors occur. • Some grammatical and usage errors are repeated in the story.
LIMITED	• A conflict is introduced but not developed or resolved; it does not engage the reader. • The setting is unclear and does not affect the characters or conflict. • Characters are somewhat clear but undeveloped. • Dialogue and description are insufficient or uninteresting.	• Events are not well structured, are too numerous, or distract from the plot. • The conclusion is unsatisfying, with little suspense, and does not follow from the events. • Pacing is distracting or choppy. • Few transition words and phrases are used. • The conclusion does not reflect a theme, or message, about life.	• The story's point of view is inconsistent. • Precise words and sensory language are mostly lacking. • Spelling, capitalization, and punctuation are often incorrect but do not make reading the story difficult. • Grammar and usage are incorrect in many places, but the writer's ideas are still clear.
EMERGING	• A conflict is not identifiable. • The setting is not described. • Characters are unclear and underdeveloped. • Dialogue and descriptions are not included.	• Event sequence is not evident. • There is no clear conclusion. • There is no evidence of pacing. • No transition words and phrases are used.	• The story's point of view is never clearly established. • Precise words and phrases and sensory language are lacking. • Spelling, capitalization, and punctuation are incorrect throughout, making reading difficult. • Many grammatical and usage errors change the meaning of the writer's ideas.

COLLECTION 1
PERFORMANCE TASK B

Interactive Lessons
If you need help . . .
• Writing Arguments
• Giving a Presentation

Present an Oral Commentary

COMMON
CORE

W 1a–e Write arguments.
W 8 Gather relevant information.
W 9 Draw evidence from literary or informational texts.
W 10 Write routinely.
SL 4 Present claims and findings.
SL 5 Include multimedia components and visual displays.
SL 6 Adapt speech to a variety of contexts and tasks.
L 3 Use knowledge of language and its conventions.

This collection depicts the bold actions of a number of daring individuals from history and the recent news. The myth "The Flight of Icarus" presents a clear message about the risks and rewards of taking those actions. In the following activity, you will draw from "The Flight of Icarus" and other texts in the collection to prepare and present an oral commentary, or an expression of your opinion, about the rewards and risks associated with bold actions.

A successful oral commentary

- provides an attention-grabbing introduction that clearly establishes an opinion
- supports key points with reasoning and relevant evidence pulled from a variety of solid, credible sources
- uses appropriate eye contact, adequate volume, and clear pronunciation
- includes visuals to emphasize salient points
- concludes by leaving the audience with a lasting impression

PLAN

Clarify Understanding Review the selections in this collection about people and characters that took bold actions.

- Determine the various opinions or messages expressed about the rewards and risks associated with bold actions.
- Identify the reasons and evidence given to support these opinions and messages. In some of the selections, the reasons and evidence may not be directly stated.

Form an Opinion Decide whether you think the rewards of bold actions are worth the risks. Make a list of the reasons for your opinion.

Do Research Gain a better understanding of the topic.

- Search for solid, credible evidence for both sides of the argument.
- Find facts, details, and examples that support your opinion.

myNotebook

Use the annotation tools in your eBook to find evidence to support your ideas. Save each piece of evidence to your notebook.

ACADEMIC VOCABULARY

As you plan and present your commentary, be sure to use the academic vocabulary words.

aspect
cultural
evaluate
resource
text

PERFORMANCE TASK B

PRESENT AN ORAL COMMENTARY

COMMON CORE

W 1a-e, W 8, W 9, W 10, SL 4, SL 5, SL 6, L 3

Introduce students to the Performance Task by reading the introductory paragraph with them and reviewing the criteria for what makes a good oral commentary. Remind students that it is important for an oral commentary to be written well, but that it is equally important for it to be delivered well.

PLAN

CLARIFY UNDERSTANDING

Remind students that opinions need to be supported by reasons and evidence. Before students begin writing, they should check the information in their graphic organizers.

- Does the listed evidence support the reasons for the opinion?
- Is the evidence credible?

- Understand the counterclaim that might keep your audience from agreeing with you.
- Identify any visuals, such as pictures or graphs, that illustrate your ideas.

Organize Your Ideas Think about how you will organize the text of your commentary. A graphic organizer, such as a hierarchy chart, can help you to present your ideas logically.

Consider Your Purpose and Audience Who will listen to your report? What do you want your audience to think? Think about that audience as you prepare your commentary. Your tone and word choices may be different for a group of classmates or friends than it would be for a group of adults.

PRODUCE

my **WriteSmart**

Write your rough draft in *my*WriteSmart. Focus on getting your ideas down, rather than perfecting your choice of language.

Draft Your Commentary Although you will be presenting your opinion in a spoken commentary, you will need to write a full draft of your commentary before presenting it to your audience.

- Begin by introducing the topic and stating your opinion. Include an attention-grabbing lead, such as a question, story, startling fact, or quote.
- Express your reasons and support them with credible sources. Use the information in your graphic organizer to help you organize your reasons and evidence logically.
- Recognize opposing opinions and explain why you disagree.
- Use words and phrases such as *because*, *therefore*, and *for that reason* that will make your opinion clearer and more coherent.
- Bring your commentary to a conclusion. Summarize your opinion, repeating the most important reasons and evidence, to leave your audience with a lasting impression.

PRODUCE

DRAFT YOUR COMMENTARY

▶ *View It!*

Professional Development Podcast:

Teaching Argument

Remind students that the goal of their oral commentaries will be to present a clear, well-supported opinion to an audience of listeners. As they write, tell students to "hear" the argument in their heads as if they were the people listening in the audience. Have students consider the following:

- Is the argument well laid out?
- Is it convincing?
- Are the reasons presented in a logical manner?

Prepare Visuals Consider using multimedia and visual displays to emphasize your key points.

- Be sure you have a clear purpose for each visual. Think about how the audience might react.
- Choose images that are inspiring or thought-provoking.
- Check that all visuals are large and clear enough that everyone in the audience can read them.

REVISE

Practice Your Commentary Once you have a draft you like, use it to present your commentary aloud. Try speaking in front of a mirror, or make a recording of your commentary and listen to it. Then practice with a partner.

- Use your voice effectively. Speak loudly, varying your pitch and tone.
- Maintain eye contact. Look directly at individuals in your audience.
- Use gestures and facial expressions to emphasize ideas and express emotion.

Evaluate Your Commentary Work with your partner to determine whether your commentary is effective. Make adjustments to the draft based on your evaluation.

- Check that your opinion is clear and logically supported with relevant and accurate reasons and evidence.
- Check that your commentary keeps your audience's attention and concludes with a statement that sums up your opinion.

my WriteSmart

Have your partner or a group of peers review your draft in *my*WriteSmart. Ask your reviewers to note any reasons that do not support your opinion or lack sufficient evidence.

PRESENT

Deliver Your Commentary Finalize your oral commentary and present it to the class. You might also want to use these additional formats to present it:

- Use a computer presentation program to create an interactive version of your commentary.
- Make a video recording of yourself presenting your commentary, and share it on your class or school website.

REVISE

PRACTICE YOUR COMMENTARY

Have students work with a partner to help them revise their commentaries. Students can take turns listening to each other's commentaries and offering suggestions to make them more effective. Remind students that when evaluating their partner's commentary, they should think about: 1) how clearly their opinions are stated; 2) how well their opinions are supported; and 3) how well the commentary is delivered.

PRESENT

DELIVER YOUR COMMENTARY

Students may want to create multimedia presentations using computer software. They can create slides to accompany and support the points they make in their presentations.

PERFORMANCE TASK B

ORGANIZATION

Have students look at the chart and identify how they did on the Performance Task in each of the three main categories. In particular, have students look at how well they organized the reasons and evidence in their commentaries. If students videotaped their presentations, they can use the recordings to critique themselves.

ORAL COMMENTARY

	Ideas and Evidence	Organization	Language
ADVANCED	• The introduction immediately grabs the audience's attention; the speaker clearly states his or her opinion. • Logical reasons and relevant evidence from the texts and multiple, credible sources convincingly support the speaker's opinion. • The opposing opinion is anticipated and effectively addressed. • The conclusion effectively summarizes the opinion and leaves a lasting impression.	• The reasons and evidence are organized consistently and logically throughout. • Varied transitions logically connect reasons and evidence to the speaker's opinion. • Visuals and graphic aids are visible, well organized, and support key points. • Visuals and graphic aids are drawn from multiple, credible print and digital sources.	• The commentary reflects a formal speaking style. • The speaker uses precise and concise language. • Sentence beginnings, lengths, and structures vary and have a rhythmic flow. • Grammar, usage, and mechanics are correct.
COMPETENT	• The introduction could do more to grab the reader's attention; the speaker states an opinion. • Most reasons support the speaker's opinion but could be more convincing; most reasons are supported with evidence from the texts and research sources. • The opposing opinion is anticipated but could be more effectively refuted. • The conclusion restates the opinion.	• The organization of reasons and evidence is confusing in some places. • A few more transitions are needed to clarify the relationships between ideas. • Visuals and graphic aids could be clearer and more complete; they don't always support important points. • Visuals and graphic aids are drawn from just a few sources.	• The style becomes informal in a few places. • The speaker's use of language could be more precise and concise. • Sentence beginnings, lengths, and structures vary somewhat. • Some grammatical usage errors are repeated in the report.
LIMITED	• The introduction is ordinary; the speaker's opinion is unclearly stated. • The reasons are not always logical or relevant. • The speaker uses poor, unclear evidence from just a few sources. • The opposing opinion is anticipated but not logically addressed. • The conclusion provides an incomplete or unclear summary of the opinion.	• The organization of reasons and evidence is logical in some places, but it often doesn't follow a pattern. • Many more transitions are needed to connect reasons and evidence to the speaker's opinion. • Few visuals or graphic aids are used; those used are unclear, poorly organized, and don't support important points.	• The style frequently becomes informal. • Language used is vague, unnecessarily wordy, and unclear in many places. • Sentence structures barely vary, and some fragments or run-on sentences are present. • Grammar and usage are incorrect in many places, but the ideas are clear.
EMERGING	• The introduction is confusing and contains no opinion. • Supporting reasons are missing. • The speech contains no evidence from the texts or research sources. • The opposing opinion is neither anticipated nor addressed. • The concluding section is missing.	• There is no logical organization; reasons and evidence are presented randomly. • No transitions are used, making the commentary difficult to understand. • No visuals or graphic aids are used.	• The style is inappropriate. • Language used makes the commentary confusing. • Repetitive sentence structure, fragments, and run-on sentences make the commentary hard to follow. • Many grammatical and usage errors change the meaning of ideas.

©Todd Davidson/Images.com/Corbis

Perception and Reality

❝ *Now* I do not know whether it was then
I dreamt I was a butterfly, or whether I am now a butterfly,
dreaming I am a man. ❞

—Chuang Tzu

61

CONNECTING WORD AND IMAGE

ASK STUDENTS to discuss how the collection opener image and the collection quotation work together to create a connection.

PERFORMANCE TASK PREVIEW

Point out to students that they will complete two performance tasks at the end of the collection. The performance tasks will require them to further analyze the selections in the collections and to synthesize ideas about these analyses. Students will present their findings in a variety of products.

ACADEMIC VOCABULARY

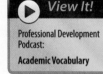

View It!

Professional Development Podcast:

Academic Vocabulary

Students can acquire facility with the academic vocabulary words through frequent, repeated exposure as they analyze and discuss the selections in the collection. Academic vocabulary can be used in the instructional contexts shown below. This will enable students to incorporate the academic vocabulary words into their working vocabulary.

- Collaborative Discussion at the end of each selection
- Analyzing the Text questions for each selection
- Selection-level Performance Task
- Vocabulary instruction (for Critical Vocabulary and/or for Vocabulary Strategy)
- Language Conventions
- End-of-collection Performance Task for all selections in the collection

ASK STUDENTS to review the Academic Vocabulary word list for this collection. You may wish to pronounce each word aloud so students hear the correct pronunciation. Then, discuss the definitions and the related forms for each word. Remind students that they will encounter these five academic vocabulary words throughout the collection.

Perception and Reality

hmhfyi.com

In this collection, you will explore how things in life are not always how we perceive them to be.

COLLECTION

PERFORMANCE TASK Preview

After reading the selections in this collection, you will have the opportunity to complete two performance tasks:

- In one, you will write an essay expressing your opinion of the saying, "Seeing is believing," using evidence from the literature to support your opinion.

- In the second, you will write an expository essay explaining how a single action can dramatically change a person's perception.

ACADEMIC VOCABULARY

Study the words and their definitions in the chart below. You will use these words as you discuss and write about the texts in this collection.

Word	Definition	Related Forms
abnormal (ăb-nôr´məl) *adj.*	not typical, usual, or regular; not normal	normal, normalcy, normality, normalize, paranormal, subnormal
feature (fē´-chər) *n.*	a prominent or distinctive part, quality, or characteristic	feature article, featured, featureless, featuring, text feature
focus (fō´kəs) *v.*	to direct toward a specific point or purpose	autofocus, focused, refocus, unfocused
perceive (pər-sēv´) *v.*	to become aware of something directly through any of the senses	misperceive, misperception, perception, unperceived
task (tăsk) *n.*	an assignment or work done as part of one's duties	multitask, taskmaster

62

USING COLLECTIONS YOUR WAY

Use the following information, along with the charts on the following pages, to help you decide how you want to introduce the collection. Based on your teaching style, your students' interests, or your instructional goals, you may want to structure this collection in various ways. You may choose different entry points each time you teach the collection.

"I like to use digital products as a starting point."

Julian Beever is an English, Belgium-based chalk artist who creates trompe-l'oeil chalk drawings on pavement surfaces, making images look three-dimensional and playing with his viewers' sense of reality.

Julian Beever (b. 1959) *creates unusual chalk drawings on public sidewalks. Beever started drawing pavement art as a way to make money while traveling. Since then, he has gained international recognition. Beever chooses to draw on sidewalks so that everyone can have access to his art. He says, "My work appeals literally to the man (and woman) in the street and is not confined in galleries or limited by the gallery system."*

MEDIA ANALYSIS

Pavement Chalk Art

Public Art by Julian Beever

SETTING A PURPOSE Beever has developed a special technique of using distortion to unequally magnify images in his work. When seen from one special angle, these images come together to create the illusion that his "anamorphic" drawings are truly three dimensional. Viewed this way, his drawings seem to come to life.

Beever's pavement art gives viewers the impression that they are entering a very real, physical place that exists in the drawings. As you view the two drawings, think about what it would be like to be a passerby who suddenly walks across—or into—one of Beever's works. Write down any questions you have as you view.

Pavement Chalk Art **89**

Background *When* **Cory Doctorow** (b. 1971) *first saw the movie Star Wars at the age of six, he was inspired to rewrite the entire story as a self-made book. The movie sparked his desire to be a science fiction writer. Publishing his first story at 17, Doctorow has since produced many science fiction novels, short stories, and magazine articles. The author has an online presence as a blogger and makes most of his books available online for free.*

Another Place, Another Time

Short Story by Cory Doctorow

SETTING A PURPOSE Science-based ideas are important in this story. As you read, think of the significance of these ideas to the characters—especially to Gilbert.

Gilbert hated time. What a tyrant it was! The hours that crawled by when his father was at sea, the seconds that whipped past when he was playing a brilliant game in the garden with the Limburgher children. The eternity it took for summer to arrive at the beach at the bottom of the cliffs, the flashing instant before the winter stole over them again and Father took to the sea once more.

"You can't hate *time*," Emmy said. The oldest of the three Limburghers and the only girl, she was used to talking younger boys out of their foolishness. "It's just *time*."

Gilbert stopped pacing the tree house floor and pointed a finger at her. "That's where you're wrong!" He thumped the book he'd taken out of his father's bookcase, a book fetched

Another Place, Another Time **93**

"I love to concentrate on contemporary literature."

This short story, taken from *The Chronicles of Harris Burdick*, is a contemporary fantasy that deals with fictional children and how they navigate time.

Background *Brain scientists* **Susana Martinez-Conde** *and* **Stephen L. Macknik** *study how the human visual system responds to and perceives the world around us. They see science at work behind magicians' techniques. A good magician relies on the inner workings of the brain to create all kinds of sensory illusions. By studying how these tricks work, scientists are learning more about the brain. Their work has led them to start a new area of science that they call neuromagic.*

Magic and the Brain

Magazine Article by Susana Martinez-Conde and Stephen L. Macknik

SETTING A PURPOSE As you read, think about the term *neuromagic* and its usefulness as a new field of scientific study. Write down any questions you may have during reading.

The spotlight shines on the magician's assistant. The woman in the tiny white dress is a luminous beacon of beauty radiating from the stage to the audience. The Great Tomsoni announces he will change her dress from white to red. On the edge of their seats, the spectators strain to focus on the woman, burning her image deep into their retinas. Tomsoni claps his hands, and the spotlight dims ever so briefly before reflaring in a blaze of red. The woman is awash in a flood of redness.

Whoa, just a moment there! Switching color with the spotlight is not exactly what the audience had in mind. The magician stands at the side of the stage, looking pleased at his little joke. Yes, he admits, it was a cheap trick; his favorite kind, he explains devilishly. But you have to agree, he did turn her dress red—along with the rest of her. Please, indulge him

Magic and the Brain **77**

"I want to challenge my students to the utmost."

This article from *Scientific American* challenges readers with technical language and fascinating scientific explanations for how our brain processes magic.

mySmartPlanner | **eBook** | **myNotebook** | **myWriteSmart** | **fyi** hmhfyi.com

Collection 2 Lessons	Media	Teach and Practice	
**Student Edition	eBook**	▶ Video Links HISTORY A&E	**Close Reading and Evidence Tracking**	
Folk Tale retold by **Virginia Hamilton** **"The People Could Fly"**	🔊 **Audio** "The People Could Fly"	**Close Read Screencasts** · Modeled Discussion (lines 23–30) · Close Read application PDF (lines 71–81)	**Strategies for Annotation** · Analyze Story Elements: Folk Tale · Summarize Text · Latin Suffixes
CLOSE READER — Short Story by **David Yoo** **"Heartbeat"**	🔊 **Audio** "Heartbeat"		
EXEMPLAR — Poem by **W. B. Yeats** **"The Song of Wandering Aengus"**	🔊 **Audio** "The Song of Wandering Aengus"		**Strategies for Annotation** · Determine the Impact of Rhyme · Analyze Form: Sonnet
Poem by **William Shakespeare** **"Sonnet 43"**	▶ **Video** HISTORY *Biography: William Shakespeare* 🔊 **Audio** "Sonnet 43"		
Magazine Article by **Susana Martinez-Conde and Stephen L. Macknik** **"Magic and the Brain"**	▶ **Video** HISTORY *Steve Cohen's Lost Magic* 🔊 **Audio** "Magic and the Brain"		**Strategies for Annotation** · Analyze Structure: Text Features · Summarize Text · The Greek Prefix *neuro-*
CLOSE READER — Science Writing by **Reynaldo Vasquez** **"Saving the Lost"**	🔊 **Audio** "Saving the Lost"		
Public Art by **Julian Beever** *Pavement Chalk Art*			
Short Story by **Cory Doctorow** **"Another Place, Another Time"**	🔊 **Audio** "Another Place, Another Time"		**Strategies for Annotation** · Determine Meaning of Words and Phrases · Analyze Story Elements: Character · Reference Aids
ANCHOR TEXT — Drama by **Lucille Fletcher** *Sorry, Wrong Number*	🔊 **Audio** *Sorry, Wrong Number*	**Close Read Screencasts** · Modeled Discussion (lines 53–75) · Close Read application PDF (lines 872–898)	**Strategies for Annotation** · Analyze Form: Drama
CLOSE READER — Novel Excerpt by **Charles Dickens** from *A Christmas Carol* Drama Excerpt by **Israel Horovitz** Graphic Story by **Marvel Comics**	🔊 **Audio** from *A Christmas Carol*		
Collection 2 Performance Tasks: **A** Write an Opinion Essay **B** Write an Expository Essay	**fyi** hmhfyi **hmhfyi.com**	**Interactive Lessons** **A** Writing Arguments **A** Using Textual Evidence	**B** Writing Informative Texts **B** Writing as a Process

For Systematic Coverage of Writing and Speaking & Listening Standards	**Interactive Lessons** Writing an Argument Analyzing and Evaluating Presentations

Assess		Extend	Reteach
Performance Task	**Online Assessment**	**Teacher eBook**	**Teacher eBook**
Speaking Activity: Dramatic Reading	Selection Test	**Prepare for a Dramatic Reading > Interactive Lessons >** Giving a Presentation	**Analyze Story Elements: Folk Tale >Interactive Graphic Organizers >** Comparison-Contrast Chart
Speaking Activity: Discussion	Selection Test	**Analyze Form >Interactive Whiteboard Lesson >** Form in Poetry	**Determine Meanings >Level Up Tutorial >** Figurative Language
Speaking Activity: Demonstration	Selection Test	**Conduct Online Research > Interactive Lessons >** Conducting Research **> Interactive Lessons >** Evaluating Sources	**Analyze Structure: Text Features >Level Up Tutorial >** Informational Text
Media Activity: Poster	Selection Test	**Analyze Media: Perspective and Illusion > Interactive Graphic Organizer >** Comparison-Contrast Chart	**Analyze Diverse Media**
Writing Activity: Character Profile	Selection Test	**Analyze Story Elements: Character and Setting >Interactive Graphic Organizer >** Comparison-Contrast Chart	**Analyze Story Elements: Character >Level Up Tutorial >** Methods of Characterization
Writing Activity: Character Analysis	Selection Test	**Compare and Contrast: Text and Media > Interactive Graphic Organizer >** Venn Diagram	**Analyze Form: Drama >Level Up Tutorial >** Elements of Drama
A Write an Opinion Essay **B** Write an Expository Essay	Collection Test		

Lesson Assessments
Writing an Argument
Analyzing and Evaluating Presentations

Collection 2 Lessons	Key Learning Objective	Performance Task
ANCHOR TEXT **Folk Tale retold by Virginia Hamilton** **"The People Could Fly," p. 63A** **Lexile 430L**	**The student will be able to . . .** identify elements of a folk tale and summarize the story.	Speaking Activity: Dramatic Reading
EXEMPLAR **Poem by W. B. Yeats** **"The Song of Wandering Aengus," p. 71A** **Poem by William Shakespeare** **"Sonnet 43," p. 71A**	**The student will be able to . . .** learn how to analyze a poem's form as well as the use of figurative language and sound devices to understand their effects on meaning.	Speaking Activity: Discussion
Magazine Article by Susana Martinez-Conde and Stephen L. Macknik **"Magic and the Brain," p. 77A** **Lexile 1340L**	**The student will be able to . . .** analyze how text features contribute to a text and to summarize text objectively.	Speaking Activity: Demonstration
Public Art by Julian Beever *Pavement Chalk Art,* **p. 89A**	**The student will be able to . . .** analyze the purposes of public art and the techniques Beever uses to create the illusion of 3-dimensionality.	Media Activity: Poster
Short Story by Cory Doctorow **"Another Place, Another Time," p. 93A** **Lexile 1060L**	**The student will be able to . . .** identify and analyze how setting affects characters' traits, motivations, and actions.	Writing Activity: Character Profile
ANCHOR TEXT **Drama by Lucille Fletcher** *Sorry, Wrong Number,* **p. 111A**	**The student will be able to . . .** analyze the elements of a drama and make comparisons between a script and a performance.	Writing Activity: Character Analysis

Collection 2 Performance Tasks:
A Write an Opinion Essay
B Write an Expository Essay

Vocabulary Strategy	Language and Style	Student Instructional Support	CLOSE READER Selection
Latin Suffixes		**Scaffolding for ELL Students:** Analyze Story Elements: Folk Tales **When Students Struggle:** Analyze Characters	Short Story by David Yoo "Heartbeat," p. 70b **Lexile 840L**
		Scaffolding for ELL Students: Analyze Language: Idioms **When Students Struggle:** Paraphrase Poetry	
The Greek Prefix *neuro-*	Adverb Clauses	**Scaffolding for ELL Students**: Vocabulary Strategy **When Students Struggle:** Summarize Central Ideas **To Challenge Students:** Evaluate Ideas	Science Writing by Reynaldo Vasquez "Saving the Lost," p. 88b **Lexile 920L**
		Scaffolding for ELL Students: Vocabulary Support **When Students Struggle:** Concept Support	
Reference Aids	Spell Correctly	**Scaffolding for ELL Students**: Analyze Language **When Students Struggle:** • Symbols • Determine Meanings of Words and Phrases **To Challenge Students:** Analyze Theme	
		Scaffolding for ELL Students: Analyze Form: Drama **When Students Struggle:** Visualize Onstage Action **To Challenge Students:** Analyze Story Elements	from *A Christmas Carol*, p. 126b Novel Excerpt by Charles Dickens **Lexile 730L** Drama Excerpt by Israel Horovitz, Graphic Story by Marvel Comics

my SmartPlanner Create lesson plans and access resources online.

ANCHOR TEXT EXEMPLAR

The People Could Fly

Folk Tale retold by Virginia Hamilton

Why This Text?

Folk tales and other folklore show students connections among history, culture, and literature. By reading folk tales, students broaden their understanding and appreciation of literature from the oral tradition. This lesson leads students to analyze and summarize the elements of a folk tale.

Key Learning Objective: The student will be able to identify elements of a folk tale and summarize the story.

For practice and application:

Close Reader selection:
"Heartbeat"
Short Story by David Yoo

COMMON CORE Common Core Standards

RL 1 Cite textual evidence.

RL 2 Determine a theme and provide a summary.

RL 3 Analyze story elements.

RL 4 Determine the meaning of words and phrases.

RL 10 Read grade 6–8 literature proficiently.

W 7 Conduct short research projects to answer a question.

W 9 Draw evidence from texts to support analysis, reflection, and research.

SL 6 Adapt speech to a variety of contexts and tasks.

L 4b Use Greek or Latin affixes and roots as clues to word meanings.

L 4d Verify the meaning of a word or phrase by checking context.

▲ Text Complexity Rubric

Quantitative Measures	**The People Could Fly** **Lexile:** 430L
Qualitative Measures	**Levels of Meaning/Purpose** single level of complex meaning
	Structure conventional story structure
	Language Conventionality and Clarity figurative, less accessible language
	Knowledge Demands some cultural and literary knowledge useful
Reader/Task Considerations	Teacher determined Vary by individual reader and type of text

TEACH

CLOSE READ

Background Have students read the background and information about the author. Tell them that Virginia Hamilton created a narrator, the person who tells a story, who sounds like an African American storyteller from the days of slavery. Point out that folk tales come from an oral tradition—they were told aloud long before they were written down. Explain that the narrator uses speech rhythms and language like that of a storyteller speaking to an audience. Students can imagine themselves as listeners as they read the story.

SETTING A PURPOSE Direct students to use the Setting a Purpose prompt to focus their reading. Remind them to generate questions as they read.

Analyze Story Elements: Folk Tales (LINES 1–9)

COMMON CORE RL 1, RL 3

Tell students that **folk tales** are stories passed down by word of mouth from generation to generation. Explain that folk tales often feature supernatural events and characters with supernatural abilities.

 CITE TEXT EVIDENCE Ask students to reread lines 1–9 to identify supernatural abilities that seem likely to be important in the story. (*Some of the African people had the magical power to fly, though they shed their wings after being captured.*)

Summarize Text

COMMON CORE RL 2

(LINES 10–18)

Tell students that a **summary** of a folk tale is a brief retelling that includes the most important details about the setting, characters, and events.

 ASK STUDENTS to reread lines 10–18 and tell what seems most important to remember about the characters who "could no longer breathe the sweet scent of Africa." (*Once the people were in the land of slavery, some still had the secret power of flying, though they looked like everyone else.*)

Background *Between the 1600s and 1800s, millions of Africans were taken forcibly to the Americas as enslaved people. Their labor spurred the growth of large-scale farming in the colonies. Despite the hardships of oppression, these people nurtured a strong sense of tradition, passing stories from generation to generation.* **Virginia Hamilton** (1934–2002) *grew up listening to such stories. As an adult, she put many of them into writing and wrote a number of her own books about African American history and culture.*

The People Could Fly

Folk Tale by Virginia Hamilton

SETTING A PURPOSE As you read, think about what this folk tale says about the importance of hope in the lives of oppressed people.

They say the people could fly. Say that long ago in Africa, some of the people knew magic. And they would walk up on the air like climbin' up on a gate. And they flew like blackbirds over the fields. Black, shiny wings flappin' against the blue up there.

Then, many of the people were captured for Slavery. The ones that could fly shed their wings. They couldn't take their wings across the water on the slave ships. Too crowded, don't you know.

10   The folks were full of misery, then. Got sick with the up and down of the sea. So they forgot about flyin' when they could no longer breathe the sweet scent of Africa.

  Say the people who could fly kept their power, although they shed their wings. They kept their secret magic in the land

---

Close Read Screencasts   ▶ View It!

Modeled Discussions

Have students click the *Close Read* icons in their eBooks to access a screencast in which readers discuss and annotate the following key passage:

• The slaves labored in the fields . . . did move faster. Had to. (lines 23–30)

As a class, view and discuss the video. Then have students pair up to do an independent close read of an additional passage—"Say the next day . . . And they too rose on the air" (lines 71–81).

Summarize Text
COMMON CORE RL 2

(LINES 33–40)

Tell students that a **conflict** in a story is a struggle between opposing forces. Explain that the conflict sets up the story action and is important to include in a summary.

C ASK STUDENTS to reread the two paragraphs beginning on line 33 and sum up the conflict shown. *(The conflict is between the cruel Overseer and the young mother named Sarah. When she doesn't quiet her baby, the Overseer whips it.)*

CRITICAL VOCABULARY

croon: The young mother, Sarah, does not even try to croon to her baby to soothe it.

ASK STUDENTS how Sarah's crooning to the child might have soothed it. *(Soft singing to a young child usually calms the child, especially when the crooning is done by the child's mother.)*

SCAFFOLDING FOR ELL STUDENTS

Analyze Story Elements: Folk Tales Using a whiteboard, project the four sentences that begin on line 24. Invite volunteers to mark up the lines:

- Underline the words that tell who is described.
- Highlight in yellow the words that describe that person.

ASK STUDENTS What is the owner of the slaves compared to? What do those comparisons help you understand?

---

of slavery. They looked the same as the other people from Africa who had been coming over, who had dark skin. Say you couldn't tell anymore one who could fly from one who couldn't.

20 One such who could was an old man, call him Toby. And standin' tall, yet afraid, was a young woman who once had wings. Call her Sarah. Now Sarah carried a babe tied to her back. She trembled to be so hard worked and scorned.

The slaves labored in the fields from sunup to sundown. The owner of the slaves callin' himself their Master. Say he was a hard lump of clay. A hard, glinty coal. A hard rock pile, wouldn't be moved. His Overseer[1] on horseback pointed out the slaves who were slowin' down. So the one called Driver cracked his whip over the slow ones to make them move faster. That whip was a slice-open cut of pain. So they did

30 move faster. Had to.

Sarah hoed and chopped the row as the babe on her back slept.

Say the child grew hungry. That babe started up bawling too loud. Sarah couldn't stop to feed it. Couldn't stop to soothe and quiet it down. She let it cry. She didn't want to. She had no heart to **croon** to it.

"Keep that thing quiet," called the Overseer. He pointed his finger at the babe. The woman scrunched low. The Driver cracked his whip across the babe anyhow. The babe hollered

40 like any hurt child, and the woman fell to the earth.

The old man that was there, Toby, came and helped her to her feet.

"I must go soon," she told him.

"Soon," he said.

Sarah couldn't stand up straight any longer. She was too weak. The sun burned her face. The babe cried and cried, "Pity me, oh, pity me," say it sounded like. Sarah was so sad and starvin', she sat down in the row.

"Get up, you black cow," called the Overseer. He pointed

50 his hand, and the Driver's whip snarled around Sarah's legs. Her sack dress tore into rags. Her legs bled onto the earth. She couldn't get up.

Toby was there where there was no one to help her and the babe.

croon
(krōon) *v.* When someone *croons*, that person hums or sings softly.

---

[1] **Overseer** (ō′vər-sē′ər): a person who directs the work of others; a supervisor. During the time of slavery, the overseer was usually a white man.

The owner of the slaves callin' himself their Master. Say he was a hard lump of clay. A hard, glinty coal. A hard rock pile, wouldn't be moved. His Overseer on horseback pointed out

"Now, before it's too late," panted Sarah. "Now, Father!"

"Yes, Daughter, the time is come," Toby answered. "Go, as you know how to go!"

He raised his arms, holding them out to her. *"Kum . . . yali, kum buba tambe,"* and more magic words, said so quickly,
60 they sounded like whispers and sighs.

The young woman lifted one foot on the air. Then the other. She flew clumsily at first, with the child now held tightly in her arms. Then she felt the magic, the African mystery. Say she rose just as free as a bird. As light as a feather.

The Overseer rode after her, hollerin'. Sarah flew over the fences. She flew over the woods. Tall trees could not **snag** her. Nor could the Overseer. She flew like an eagle now, until she was gone from sight. No one dared speak about it. Couldn't believe it. But it was, because they that was there
70 saw that it was.

snag
(snăg) *v.* If you *snag* something, you catch it quickly and unexpectedly.

Say the next day was dead hot in the fields. A young man slave fell from the heat. The Driver come and whipped him. Toby come over and spoke words to the fallen one. The words of ancient Africa once heard are never remembered completely. The young man forgot them as soon as he heard them. They went way inside him. He got up and rolled over on the air. He rode it awhile. And he flew away.

The People Could Fly **65**

Analyze Story Elements: Folk Tales (LINES 64–70)

 COMMON CORE RL 1, RL 3, RL 4

Tell students that a folk tale may be told in **dialect,** which is the form of language spoken in a particular place or by a particular culture. Explain that the use of dialect can put readers in the scene and help them hear how the narrator and characters sound.

D **CITE TEXT EVIDENCE** Direct students to find examples of dialect in lines 64–70 and tell how it affects readers. (*The narrator says* Say *instead of* They say; *drops the final* g *in* hollering; *and says* they that was there *instead of* those who were there. *The reader imagines a folksy speaker talking naturally and sincerely.*)

CRITICAL VOCABULARY

snag: Even tall trees could not snag the flying woman named Sarah.

ASK STUDENTS how the word *snag* as used here contrasts with the description in lines 49–52. Have them tell how Sarah is snagged in the earlier description. (*Sarah is now free and soaring, instead of sitting heavily on the ground because her legs and dress were snagged by a whip.*)

APPLYING ACADEMIC VOCABULARY

feature	focus

As you discuss the author's use of language, incorporate the following Collection 2 academic vocabulary words: *feature* and *focus*. Tell students to **focus** on word choice, figurative comparisons, and dialect. Talk about how these **features** create a clear, sharp storytelling voice.

Summarize Text

COMMON CORE RL 2

(LINES 98–109)

Tell students that when they summarize a story, they should include information about the most important characters and events.

(E) ASK STUDENTS to reread lines 98–109. Have them summarize what is most important to recall about old Toby and the people who could fly. *(The slave old Toby is a seer. He still remembers the ancient magical words that cause all the people who could fly to rise into the air to freedom. Old Toby flies, too, taking care of them.)*

CRITICAL VOCABULARY

shuffle: The slaves join hands as if in a ring-sing, but they don't shuffle in a circle. Instead, they rise into the air.

ASK STUDENTS to describe people shuffling in a ring-sing and give ideas why the author might have included this detail. *(In a ring-sing, people join hands to form a circle. They take little sliding steps while singing. The author includes this detail to show a feature of culture among slaves and to contrast it with the change that happens as the people rise to freedom.)*

plantation: The people fly above the plantation, "way over the slavery land."

ASK STUDENTS what the plantation probably represents to the African Americans who told this folk tale. *(The plantation is a place of bondage, sorrow, and pain that the people remember as part of their history.)*

WHEN STUDENTS STRUGGLE . . .

Help students focus on old Toby's significance in this folk tale. Direct partners to find each of the following descriptions in the text and decide together what the details show about old Toby:

- (lines 41–42, lines 53–54)
- (lines 55–60, lines 72–73)
- (lines 78–80, lines 91–97, lines 106–109)

Partners may list their ideas in a chart.

She flew clumsily at first, with the child now held tightly in her arms. 🙶

Another and another fell from the heat. Toby was there. He cried out to the fallen and reached his arms out to them. *"Kum*
80 *kunka yali, kum . . . tambe!"* Whispers and sighs. And they too rose on the air. They rode the hot breezes. The ones flyin' were black and shinin' sticks, wheelin' above the head of the Overseer. They crossed the rows, the fields, the fences, the streams, and were away.

"Seize the old man!" cried the Overseer.

"I heard him say the magic *words*. Seize him!"

The one callin' himself Master come runnin'. The Driver got his whip ready to curl around old Toby and tie him up. The slave owner took his hip gun from its place. He meant to
90 kill old black Toby.

But Toby just laughed. Say he threw back his head and said, "Hee, hee! Don't you know who I am? Don't you know some of us in this field?" He said it to their faces. "We are ones who fly!"

And he sighed the ancient words that were a dark promise. He said them all around to the others in the field under the whip, *". . . buba yali . . . buba tambe . . ."*

(E) There was a great outcryin'. The bent backs straightened up. Old and young who were called slaves and could fly joined
100 hands. Say like they would ring-sing. But they didn't **shuffle** in a circle. They didn't sing. They rose on the air. They flew in a flock that was black against the heavenly blue. Black crows or black shadows. It didn't matter, they went so high. Way above the **plantation**, way over the slavery land. Say they flew away to *Free-dom.*

And the old man, old Toby, flew behind them, takin' care of them. He wasn't cryin'. He wasn't laughin'. He was the seer. His gaze fell on the plantation where the slaves who could not fly waited.

shuffle
(shŭf´əl) *v.* When you *shuffle*, you move with short sliding steps.

plantation
(plăn-tā´shən) *n.* A *plantation* is a large farm or estate on which crops are raised.

Character: Old Toby	
What He Is Like	**What He Does**
kind helpful fatherly brave remembers the ancient ways has magical powers	recites magic words to rescue Sarah and others who can fly laughs at slave owner flies to freedom takes care of the flying group

110   *"Take us with you!"* Their looks spoke it, but they were afraid to shout it. Toby couldn't take them with him. Hadn't the time to teach them to fly. They must wait for a chance to run.

    "Goodie-bye!" the old man called Toby spoke to them, poor souls! And he was flyin' gone.

    So they say. The Overseer told it. The one called Master said it was a lie, a trick of the light. The Driver kept his mouth shut.

    The slaves who could not fly told about the people who could fly to their children. When they were free. When they

120 sat close before the fire in the free land, they told it. They did so love firelight and *Free-dom*, and tellin'.

    They say that the children of the ones who could not fly told their children. And now, me, I have told it to you.

COLLABORATIVE DISCUSSION Sarah, Toby, and the others hold onto hope in the most difficult of circumstances. With a partner, discuss what this folk tale says about the nature of hope.

The People Could Fly   **67**

TEACH

CLOSE READ

Summarize Text   COMMON CORE RL 2

(LINES 110–115)

Tell students that a story's conflict is usually resolved by its end. Explain that this part of the plot, called the **resolution,** is the final part of a story summary.

F **ASK STUDENTS** to reread lines 110–115 and suggest a final sentence of this story summary. *(The people who could fly escape to freedom, but those who couldn't remain enslaved, with only the hope of escape.)*

Analyze Story Elements: COMMON CORE RL 1, RL 2, RL 3
Folk Tale (LINES 118–123)

Tell students that a folk tale reveals what is important to the cultural group that first told it. Values such as cleverness and courage are often features of folk tales.

G **CITE TEXT EVIDENCE** Ask students to reread lines 118–123 and identify and discuss details that reveal values that are important to those who told this story. *(The sentence "They did so love firelight and Free-dom, and tellin'" shows that people used stories to pass down values such as hope, love of freedom, connections to one's past and future, and triumph over oppression.)*

COLLABORATIVE DISCUSSION Have student pairs discuss the message of hope in this folk tale. Then have them share their ideas with the class as a whole.

ASK STUDENTS to share any questions they generated in the course of reading and discussing the selection.

Strategies for Annotation   🖊 📘 *Annotate it!*

Analyze Story Elements: COMMON CORE RL 2, RL 3
Folk Tale

Have students locate the last two paragraphs of the story. Encourage them to use the eBook annotation tools to do the following:

- Highlight in yellow the sentences that reveal the cultural values of the people who tell this story.
- Underline specific details that support this.
- Add a note that summarizes these lines to show the most important information.

    The slaves who could not fly told about the people who could fly to their children. When they were free. When they sat close before the fire in the free land, they told it. They did <u>so love firelight</u> and <u>Free-dom</u>, and <u>tellin'</u>.

    They say that the children of the ones who could not fly told their children. And now, me, I have told it to you.

The People Could Fly   **67**

TEACH

CLOSE READ

Analyze Story Elements: Folk Tale **RL 3**

Talk with students about the term *oral tradition,* sharing ideas about how a story that is passed down by word of mouth differs from one that is written. Discuss the term *dialect,* and have students give ideas about why dialect is common in stories in the oral tradition.

Have students work in small groups of three. Each group member will choose one feature of folk tales and locate examples of the feature in the story. Then have the groups discuss their findings.

- supernatural events set in the past: *(The setting is a plantation during the days of slavery. Characters fly.)*
- characters with supernatural abilities: *(Old Toby can make people fly.)*
- life lesson: *(People can draw on hope and their inner strength to escape evil.)*

Summarize Text **RL 2**

Help students recognize that the sample first sentence of the summary corresponds to the "Title and Genre" entry in the story map. Have them suggest a next sentence that gives information about the setting. *(It takes place on a plantation during slavery times.)*

Use the graphic organizer to point out that this folk tale, like many others, has a straightforward plot that includes these parts: conflict, events, climax, and resolution. Students should jot down the most important information that belongs in each frame.

Analyze Story Elements: Folk Tales **RL 3**

Folk tales are stories passed down by word of mouth from generation to generation. "The People Could Fly" is a folk tale that would have been around a long time as an oral tradition before it was finally recorded.

Folk tales can vary from culture to culture, but often have these elements:

- supernatural events set in the distant past
- talking animals or other characters with supernatural abilities
- lessons about what is important to the culture of origin

Folk tales are often told using **dialect**—a form of language that is spoken in a particular place or by a particular group of people—to suggest real people talking. In "The People Could Fly," Virginia Hamilton uses dialect to suggest the folksy speech of the African American storyteller. The use of dialect helps to draw the reader or listener more fully into the setting.

Choose one of the listed features of folk tales. Tell how the feature is shown in "The People Could Fly."

Summarize Text **RL 2**

A **summary** of a story is a brief retelling that gives only the most important details. When you summarize a story, you use your own words to answer the basic questions *who? when and where?* and *what happens?* A story map like the one shown can help you organize your answers.

Title and Genre (kind of story):	Setting:

Conflict:

Main Events (several events in order):

Outcome/Resolution:

Here is a possible first sentence of a summary of the story you have read:

> **"The People Could Fly" is a folk tale that originated among people held captive as slaves.**

What would you write as the next sentence of the summary?

Strategies for Annotation 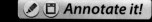 Annotate it!

Summarize Text **RL 2**

Share these strategies for guided or independent analysis:

- Identify a segment of the story in which an important event occurs (e.g. lines 55–64).
- Highlight in yellow the names of the characters.
- Underline details about them and their actions.
- Add a note that summarizes the information in as few words as possible.

> "Now, before it's too late," panted Sarah. "Now, Father!"
>
> "Yes, Daughter, the time is come," Toby answered. "Go, as you know how to go!"
>
> He raised his arms, holding them out to her. "*kum buba tambe,*" and more magic words, said so...

When Sarah asked Toby for help, he held out his arms to her and said the magic words that sent her into the air holding her baby.

 **eBook** *Annotate It!*

Analyzing the Text

COMMON CORE RL 2, RL 3, RL 4, W 7, W 9

Cite Text Evidence Support your responses with evidence from the text.

1. **Interpret** Folk tales often feature lessons that are important to a culture or group of people. What is the lesson of this folk tale? How would enslaved Africans have perceived the lesson as being important?

2. **Summarize** Early in the folk tale, the narrator says, "The folks were full of misery, then." Review the first half of the tale to find details about the conditions under which the slaves lived. Then in your own words, describe these conditions.

3. **Summarize** Fill out a story map for "The People Could Fly." Use your completed map to summarize the plot of the folk tale. Compare your summary with that of a classmate.

4. **Analyze** Reread lines 1–10 to identify examples of dialect. What effect does the use of dialect achieve at the beginning of the story?

5. **Analyze** Reread lines 23–30. What is the Master compared to? What is the whip compared to? Why might the author have included these figurative comparisons?

6. **Analyze Theme** Reread lines 98–105. What theme is expressed in this paragraph?

PERFORMANCE TASK

Speaking Activity: Dramatic Reading With a small group, do a dramatic reading of "The People Could Fly," using the text of the folk tale as a script. Follow these tips for preparing and performing:

- Rehearse the reading several times.
- Make sure your voices fit the personalities of the characters you portray.
- Deliver lines with the appropriate emotion.
- Keep in mind how the tale begins somberly but builds in intensity.

 Assign this performance task.

PERFORMANCE TASK

COMMON CORE RL 10, SL 6

Speaking Activity: Dramatic Reading Here are three ideas for assigning parts:

- Students may divide the text into parts, one student reading each part.
- Several students may divide the narration, and one student may read the dialogue spoken by the different characters.
- Partners may share a segment, devising a method for giving a lively reading.

PRACTICE & APPLY

Analyzing the Text

COMMON CORE RL 1, RL 2, RL 3, RL 4

Possible answers:

1. *The lesson is that even in the worst of circumstances, people have the power within themselves to hold onto hope and the promise of freedom. This lesson would have been critical for enslaved people as they dreamed about rising above their hardships.*

2. *Slaves suffered with sickness on the ships to America. At the plantations, they did back-breaking work all day. Cruel men watched them, and the Driver whipped them when they slowed down, even while some carried hungry infants.*

3. *Story Map:* **Title and Genre:** *"The People Could Fly," African American folk tale.* **Setting:** *plantation during slavery era.* **Characters:** *Toby; Sarah; the Overseer; Driver.* **Conflict:** *Overseer and Driver treat slaves with brutality.* **Main Events:** *(1) Africans slaves lose their memory of flying. (2) Sarah hoes with the crying baby on her back. (3) The Driver whips the baby and Sarah. (4) Toby enables Sarah and the baby to fly away. (5) Toby helps more slaves to find their power of flight.* **Outcome/Resolution:** *Toby and the people who can fly escape to freedom. The slaves who remain tell the story of what they saw.* **Sample Plot Summary:** *Some of the slaves have a secret power inherited from their African ancestors, the ability to fly. After the slave driver whips a young mother, named Sarah, and her baby, she reaches her breaking point. An old man named Toby recites magic words that enable Sarah to fly away with her baby. Toby helps other slaves fly away, telling those who remain they must find their own way to freedom.*

4. *Examples of dialect: Say that; climbin', flappin'; Too crowded, don't you know. Use of dialect establishes the narrator's voice as a storyteller from the times of slavery.*

5. *The Master was a "hard lump of clay. A hard glinty coal. A hard rock pile." The whip was "a slice-open cut of pain." These comparisons are vivid, helping the reader experience the unfeeling, immovable Master and the hurtful whip.*

6. *The theme is soaring hope leading to freedom.*

PRACTICE & APPLY

Critical Vocabulary

COMMON CORE L 4d

Answers:

1. *The word* croon *goes with* song, *because when you croon a song, you sing it softly.*

2. *The word* plantation *goes with* farm, *because a plantation is a big farm, particularly one in the South of the United States.*

3. *The word* snag *goes with* thorn, *because a thorn is sharp and could snag—catch or tear—something, like skin or clothing.*

4. *The word* shuffle *goes with* feet, *because shuffling is taking little steps without lifting your feet.*

Vocabulary Strategy: Latin Suffixes

COMMON CORE L 4b

1. *misery*
2. *transportation*
3. *posture*
4. *defiance*
5. *creative*

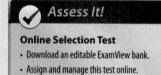

✓ Assess It!

Online Selection Test
• Download an editable ExamView bank.
• Assign and manage this test online.

Critical Vocabulary

COMMON CORE L 4b, L 4d

croon   snag   shuffle   plantation

Practice and Apply Identify the Vocabulary word that is tied in meaning to the italicized word in each question. Provide reasons for your choices.

1. Which word goes with *song*? Why?
2. Which word goes with *farm*? Why?
3. Which word goes with *thorn*? Why?
4. Which word goes with *feet*? Why?

Vocabulary Strategy: Latin Suffixes

A **suffix** is a word part added to the end of a root or base word to form a new word. Readers can use their knowledge of suffixes to analyze words and find familiar parts to determine the meaning of a word. Many suffixes in English words come from Latin. Look at the meanings of the suffixes in the chart.

Suffix	Example Words
-ure	exposure, lecture
-ery/-ary	nursery, military
-ence/-ance	violence, reliance
-ive/-ative	selective, talkative
-ion/-ation	tension, imagination

For example, notice the word with a Latin suffix in this sentence from "The People Could Fly."

> His gaze fell on the plantation where the slaves who could not fly waited.

You can see that *plantation* is made of the base word *plant* and the suffix *-ation*. The meaning of *plantation* is "a farm where crops are planted."

Practice and Apply Choose a suffix from the chart to complete each word. Use a print or online dictionary to find the meanings of unfamiliar words and to confirm your answers.

1. To be enslaved is to live in **mis**_____.
2. Human flight is an unusual form of **transport**_____.
3. The people stood up and straightened their **post**_____.
4. When confronting evil, story characters show **defi**_____.
5. The solutions in folk tales may be magical and **creat**_____.

Strategies for Annotation ✏ 🖸 *Annotate it!*

Latin Suffixes

COMMON CORE L 4b

Give students practice identifying words with the Latin suffixes in a passage from the story, such as lines 6–12. Encourage them to use their eBook annotation tools to:

• Highlight the suffix in yellow.
• Underline the part of the word before the suffix.
• Note whether the suffix is attached to a base word or a word root.
• Give a meaning for the word, using the suffix as a clue.

> The folks were full of <u>misery</u>, then. Got sick with the up and down of the sea. So they forgot about flyin' when they could no longer breathe the sweet scent of Africa.

Prepare for a Dramatic Reading

COMMON CORE
SL 6

TEACH

Use these ideas to help students prepare for the Performance Task.

Give an expressive reading of the last two paragraphs of the folk tale. Then point out that the narrator is also the storyteller, reminding listeners that this folk tale comes from the oral tradition. Help students to prepare their dramatic reading by imagining themselves as a storyteller addressing listeners sitting "close before the fire in the free land."

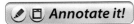 **Annotate it!**

Together, choose one segment to analyze for an oral reading using the eBook Annotation tools.

- Have students read the segment softly to themselves while listening for the storyteller's voice.
- Together, decide on the words to emphasize, and underline them.
- Decide on the places to pause. Highlight with yellow for a short pause. Highlight with green for a longer pause.
- Add notes about the emotion to express with one's voice and face, along with any gestures to make.

For example

> or black shadows. It didn't matter, they went so high. Way
> above the plantation, way over the slavery land. Say they flew
> away to Free-dom.

PRACTICE AND APPLY

Choose another segment for students to review and annotate independently. Then invite volunteers to read aloud. Emphasize the need for multiple rehearsals for an oral performance. Repeated practice enables readers to focus on expression and also gives them confidence.

 INTERACTIVE WHITEBOARD LESSON Have students complete the tutorials in this lesson: **Giving a Presentation**.

Analyze Story Elements: Folk Tale

COMMON CORE
RL 3

RETEACH

Review common features of a **folk tale** by listing each of these terms and discussing how it is connected to "The People Could Fly."

- *oral tradition* (stories passed down by speaking, not writing)
- *supernatural abilities* (abilities that no real person could have)
- *supernatural events* (things that can't happen in real life)
- *life lesson* (what is important and valuable)
- *culture of origin* (the group that first told the tale)

Offer each of the following folk tale descriptions, and have students identify the common features of folk tales in each one:

- In Native American tales, Coyote is a trickster character who tries to trick people but is often tricked himself.
- Two hundred years ago, children in Italy listened to stories about a girl whose father was a wolf.
- In a folk tale from Japan, the gentleness of a poor servant girl so impresses a rich farmer's son that she becomes his bride.

CLOSE READING APPLICATION

Guide students to another folk tale, and have them read it independently. Ask: *How can you tell this is a folk tale? What features does it share with the folk tale "The People Could Fly"?* Have pairs of students work together to compare and contrast the features in each tale using a Comparison-Contrast Chart. Then have students use their completed charts to discuss the two folk tales and what each one reveals about its culture of origin.

 INTERACTIVE GRAPHIC ORGANIZER Have students use this Interactive Graphic Organizer: **Comparison-Contrast Chart.**

Heartbeat

Short Story by David Yoo

Why This Text

Students may read a short story without a complete understanding of the story's theme or central idea, or of how particular elements of a story interact. The setting of a story, for example, may influence the characters or plot—or both—and may contribute to the shaping of the theme. Stories such as this one by David Yoo may explicitly state the theme or imply it. With the help of the close-reading questions, students will determine the theme or central idea and use it to provide an objective summary of the text.

Background Have students read the background and the biographical information about the author. Introduce the selection by telling students that David Yoo is a Korean American writer known for his true-to-life stories and his young-adult novels that mix humor with brutal honesty about being different. In his memoir, *The Choke Artist*, Yoo demonstrates his endearing ability to laugh at himself, revealing the insecurities we all feel, but hate to admit.

SETTING A PURPOSE Ask students to pay attention to the development of the theme or central idea and to the way that story elements interact. At what point do students begin to identify the theme or central idea—that of trying to pretend to be more than what you are?

Common Core Support

- cite several pieces of textual evidence
- determine the theme or central idea in a text
- provide an objective summary of a text
- analyze how particular elements of a story interact

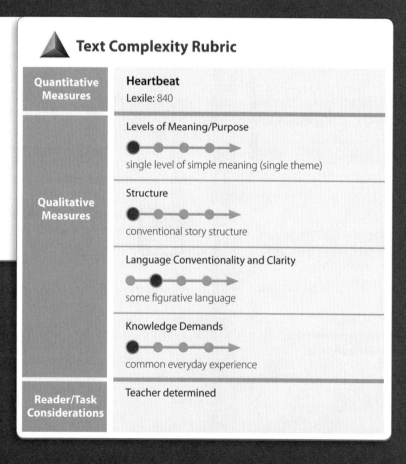

Text Complexity Rubric

Quantitative Measures	**Heartbeat** Lexile: 840
Qualitative Measures	**Levels of Meaning/Purpose** single level of simple meaning (single theme)
	Structure conventional story structure
	Language Conventionality and Clarity some figurative language
	Knowledge Demands common everyday experience
Reader/Task Considerations	Teacher determined

Strategies for CLOSE READING

Summarize Text

Students should read this short story carefully all the way through. Close-reading questions at the bottom of the page will help them focus on the theme and on how particular elements of the story interact and will help them write an objective summary of the text after they have read it. As they read, students should record comments or questions about the text in the side margins.

WHEN STUDENTS STRUGGLE ...

To help students write an objective summary of the story, have them work in a small group to fill out a story map such as the one shown below.

CITE TEXT EVIDENCE For practice in writing an objective summary, free of their opinions, ask students to trace the development of the theme over the course of the text and to analyze how the story elements interact.

> **Setting:** A cold region of the United States in winter

> **Major Characters:** Heartbeat (Dave)
> **Minor Characters:** Sarah, Heartbeat's parents

> **Plot/Problem:** A skinny 16-year-old boy nicknamed "Heartbeat" decides to wear several layers of clothing to appear bigger and stronger in order to impress a girl.

> **Event 1:** Heartbeat tries everything to look bigger and stronger, but nothing works.

> **Event 2:** He begins to wear extra layers of clothing to look bigger. The kids stop calling him Heartbeat.

> **Event 3:** At a party he is so hot that he sheds his extra layers of clothing, but he leaves them behind by mistake.

> **Outcome:** After he sheds his clothes at the party, Heartbeat realizes that in the spring, he will have to stop wearing so many layers, so he might as well just be himself now.

Background Born in 1974, **David Yoo** has often felt like an outsider. While attending an international school in Korea, he was the only Korean American student among German and Saudi Arabian classmates. When his family moved to Connecticut, he again encountered few Asian peers. He published his first book, Girls for Breakfast, when he was twenty-nine. The book is a humorous account of a Korean-American teenage hero's efforts to fit in at a suburban American high school.

Heartbeat

Short Story by David Yoo

CLOSE READ Notes

1. **READ ▶** As you read lines 1–36, begin to collect and cite text evidence.
   - Underline adjectives that describe Heartbeat.
   - In the margin, summarize how Heartbeat tries to gain weight.
   - Circle text that reveals how Heartbeat feels when he tries to gain weight.

My nickname's "Heartbeat," because my friends swear that you can actually see the pulse on my bare chest. I've always been skinny. Everyone assumes I'm a weakling because I'm so thin (I prefer "lean and mean" or "wiry"), despite being a three-sport athlete. I decided to do something about it this fall when Sarah, the girl I have a crush on, said, "Oh my gosh . . . you are so skinny." She was visibly repulsed by my sunken chest as I stepped off the soccer bus after practice. I silently vowed to do everything within my power to become the "after" picture. I was sixteen years old, but looked like I was eleven.

 For the rest of fall, I did countless push-ups and curled free weights until I couldn't bend my arms. I got ridiculously strong and defined, but I wasn't gaining weight. I wanted to be thicker. I didn't care about getting stronger if nobody could tell. I did research, and started lifting heavier weights at lower reps and supplemented my meals with weight-gainer shakes, egg whites, boiled yams, and tubs of

Heartbeat works out, eats a huge amount, and moves less.

25

---

1. **READ AND CITE TEXT EVIDENCE** Explain that as they read, students may want to note the most important idea on the page to include in a summary of Heartbeat's efforts to gain weight. Remind students that a brief objective summary answers the questions: *Who? When and Where?* and *What happens?*

A **ASK STUDENTS** to read their margin notes to a partner and then write one response that objectively summarizes what Heartbeat does to try to gain weight, citing specific textual evidence from lines 11–22.

FOR ELL STUDENTS Clarify for your ELL students that *skinny* (lines 3 and 6) and *lean* (line 4) are adjectives that describe someone who is thin. Explain that these words have a similar meaning and are called synonyms.

ASK STUDENTS to look for other synonyms of *skinny* in the text and cite them in the margin.

CLOSE READ
Notes

cottage cheese. I forced myself to swallow the daily caloric intake equivalent of three overweight men and still wasn't able to increase my mass. (I have a ridiculously fast metabolism.) Over Christmas
20 break I cut out all useless movement, like Ping-Pong and staircases, because I'm like a sieve—the 83 calories in a mini-Snickers bar is **moot** because I waste 90 chewing it.

moot:
of little or no value

B I returned to school in January (depressed), because I was still Heartbeat in everyone's eyes. I constantly weighed myself. At least once an hour, no matter where I was, I'd find a bathroom so I could take off my shirt and flex in the mirror for a couple of minutes. I was so (frustrated) that nothing was working—but the frustration didn't last. I was sitting in study hall two weeks ago when Sarah said the magic words: "Have you been working out, (Dave?) You look bigger." I
30 couldn't tell if she was being **sarcastic**. I went home and inspected myself in the mirror. I did look bigger!

sarcastic:
bitter and mocking
futile:
serving no useful purpose

But then I realized the reason: I'd accidentally worn *two* T-shirts under my rugby shirt that day. It was just an illusion. I was **futilely** stuffing my face and religiously pumping iron and failing to alter my appearance, and now I'd stumbled on the simplest solution to looking bigger. I felt like I was reborn.

I went to school the next day wearing <u>two T-shirts</u> under my turtleneck. I felt solid. By the end of last week, I was wearing <u>three</u>

---

2. ◀ **REREAD** Reread lines 23–31. Circle the narrator's real name. How does he think his classmates perceive him? Support your answer with explicit textual evidence.

Heartbeat says that everyone thinks he's a weakling. He says Sarah is
"visibly repulsed" by his body. He can't tell if Sarah is being sarcastic
when she says he looks bigger.

3. **READ** ▶ As you read lines 37–75, continue to cite textual evidence.
   • Underline the number of T-shirts Heartbeat wears.
   • Circle Heartbeat's interpretation of the way his classmates feel when they see him wearing extra layers.

26

CLOSE READ
Notes

<u>T-shirts</u> under my rugby shirt. This Monday I tucked <u>four T-shirts</u>
40 under my plaid button-down. It gave me traps that didn't exist. My
C Q-tip-sized shoulders transformed into NBA-grapefruit deltoids.[1] (I could tell my classmates subtly regarded me differently. It was respect.)
D Sarah gave me a look I'd never seen before, as if she felt . . . *safer around me.* I was walking down the hallway at the end of the day and must have twisted awkwardly because suddenly my zipper literally exploded, and all my T-shirts spilled out of my pants. Luckily, the hallway was empty and I was wearing a belt.

I realized I had artificially outgrown my clothes. My button-downs were so tight that a few seconds after jamming the extra layers
50 into my pants, the pressure would suddenly bunch the cloth up in random places so it looked like I had a goiter[2] on my shoulder or something. I complained to my parents over dinner last night. "I don't fit into anything anymore," I said. "It reflects poorly on you guys. You could get arrested."

"What are you talking about? You look the same as always. You're still my little boy," my dad replied, putting me in a headlock and giving me a noogie. I glared at him.

"I need a new ski jacket," I said. It was true. I could barely clap my hands with all the layers I was wearing. I was getting out of control at
60 this point. The <u>four T-shirts</u> under my wool sweater were smushing my lungs together like a male girdle. It was a small price to pay; nobody called me Heartbeat anymore, I reminded myself.

After dinner I went to a party. Even though it was winter, I opted to hang out on the back porch as much as possible because it was so

---

[1] **traps…deltoids:** traps (short for trapezius) are large, flat upper-back muscles; deltoids are triangular muscles that connect the top of the shoulder to the arm.
[2] **goiter:** swollen thyroid gland often visible at the bottom of the neck.

27

---

2. ⬤ REREAD AND CITE TEXT EVIDENCE

B ASK STUDENTS to infer what Heartbeat means when he thinks: "I was still Heartbeat in everyone's eyes." What does it suggest about how he thinks his classmates view him? *He thinks they still perceive him as being a scrawny weakling. Even Sarah may be using sarcasm when she says he looks bigger. Students should support their answer with evidence from lines 23–31.*

3. ⬤ READ AND CITE TEXT EVIDENCE

C ASK STUDENTS to evaluate whether Heartbeat's interpretation of his classmates' new perception of him is accurate. *Students should recognize that he thinks that his classmates are viewing him with a newfound respect, citing evidence from lines 41–44.*

Critical Vocabulary: moot (line 22), **sarcastic** (line 30), and **futile** (line 33) Ask students to share their definitions of these words and use them in a summary of lines 19–36.

WHEN STUDENTS STRUGGLE . . .

To help students understand how particular elements of a story interact, guide them to reread lines 37–75 to recognize how the specific setting (the party) influences the main character (Heartbeat) and the events of the plot (what happens as a result of his wearing extra layers to the party). Have students work with a small group to discuss how this section highlights the interaction of story elements.

FOR ELL STUDENTS Direct ELL students to reread lines 37–75. Ask them to point out the clothing vocabulary: *T-shirts* (line 37), *turtleneck* (line 38), *rugby shirt* (line 39), *button-down* (line 40), *zipper* (line 45), *pants* (line 46), *belt* (line 47), *layers* (line 49), *ski jacket* (line 58), *girdle* (61), *long-sleeves* (line 70), *wool sweater, sweatpants* (line 71), and *tube socks* (lines 71–72).

ASK STUDENTS to define these words related to clothing. If students have difficulty, ask them to point to the articles of clothing on students who are wearing them or to draw pictures of the items.

hot inside. Being indoors was like a sauna, but Sarah was in the basement so I headed that way. We were talking and she noticed that I was dripping with perspiration. "You're trembling," she said, touching my shoulder. She thought I was nervous talking to her and probably thought it was cute, but in reality I was on the verge of passing out

70 because I was wearing four tight T-shirts and two long-sleeves under my wool sweater, not to mention the sweatpants tucked into my tube socks to add heft to my (formerly chicken-legs) quads. She squeezed my biceps.[3]

"Jeez, Dave, how many layers are you wearing?"

I couldn't even feel her squeezing them.

"I have to go," I said, excusing myself to another corner of the basement. Everyone was smushed together. It was so hot everyone except me was hanging out in T-shirts and tank tops. I was sopping

claustrophobic:
uncomfortable in closed spaces

and delirious and felt **claustrophobic**. My chest was cold because I
80 had four drenched T-shirts underneath my sweater. It looked like I was breaking out with Ebola[4] or something. When I coughed people turned away from me in fear. *Abandon ship, abandon ship!* I had no choice but to take some layers off. I lurched to the bathroom. My arms were ponderously heavy as I pulled off the sweater. Just lifting my arms exhausted me, and I had to stop midway and take a rest by sitting on the edge of the tub, gasping. I slowly peeled off the layers, one at a time. I took off my pants and peeled off my sweatpants, too, down to my undies. I dried myself off with a wash cloth. My red T-shirt had bled onto the three white Ts because of the sweat, so they
90 now were faded pink tie-dyes. I hoisted the bundle of clothes and was

[3] **quads...biceps:** quads (short for quadriceps) are long muscles in the front of the thigh; biceps are the large muscles in the front of the upper arm.
[4] **Ebola:** deadly virus that causes high fever and bleeding.

4. ◄ **REREAD AND DISCUSS** Reread lines 37–44. Dave says, "…my classmates subtly regarded me differently. It was with respect." With a small group, discuss whether Dave's assessment of his classmates' response is reality-based or a product of his imagination.

5. **READ** ► As you read lines 76–113, continue to cite textual evidence.
   • Underline adjectives Heartbeat uses to describe himself.
   • In the margin, summarize how Heartbeat feels when he sheds his layers at the party.

28

"I was sopping and delirious and felt claustrophobic."

Heartbeat feels happy and free when he takes off his layers.

He wants Sarah to like him as he is. He could not wear all the layers in the spring.

shocked at the weight. I jammed them into the closet. I'd retrieve them later, before I left. I put my sweater back on without anything underneath. After two weeks of constricting my air supply and range of motion by wearing upwards of six layers, I was amazed at how much freedom I had with my arms. I felt like dancing for the first time in my life. I suddenly realized what I really looked like at this party: a padded, miserable, and frustrated puffball, burning up in all my layers. All this because I hated my nickname?

I got home and realized I'd left my bundle of wet clothes back at
100 the party. I took this as a sign. My days of wearing extra layers was officially over. Had Sarah fallen for the padded me, she'd be falling for someone else. Besides, winter wasn't going to last forever, and I couldn't just revert back to wearing just one set of clothes like a normal human being come spring. The change in my outward appearance would be the equivalent of a sheared sheep. From now on, I was going to just be me.

That was last night. *I'm not disgustingly thin*, I constantly remind myself. I am wiry. I'm lean and mean.

29

---

4. **REREAD AND DISCUSS USING TEXT EVIDENCE**

D **ASK STUDENTS** to appoint a reporter for each group to cite specific textual evidence and line numbers to support their position about Dave's (Heartbeat's) interpretation of his classmates' "subtle" change in attitude toward him. *Students should cite evidence from lines 37–44 to support their opinion.*

5. **READ AND CITE TEXT EVIDENCE**

E **ASK STUDENTS** to read their margin notes to a partner and write one response that best summarizes the causes for Dave's shedding of his layers at the party and the effects, or results, of his actions. *Students should cite evidence from lines 77–83, 93–98, and 99–106.*

Critical Vocabulary: claustrophobic (line 79) Have students define *claustrophobic* in context. Why does the author use the word to describe why Dave sheds his layers? *Yoo may be creating an image to suggest that Dave is shedding his skin.*

FOR ELL STUDENTS Explain that *winter* (line 102) and *spring* (line 104) signify two of the four seasons of the year and that *night* (line 107) represents a time of day. Ask students to define these words, either through words or pictures. Then review the days of the week and the months of the year using a print or an online calendar as a prop. Write each day and month on the board, saying each one and having students repeat.

ASK STUDENTS to look through the text for other words that name the seasons, the times of the day, the months of the year, and holidays, citing each word in the margin.

CLOSE READ
Notes

Outside it's snowing again. There's a party tonight, and my friends
110   are on their way to pick me up. I don't know what to wear, so I lay out
four different outfits on the floor as if they're chalk outlines of people.
A car horn honks ten minutes later and I still haven't decided on an
outfit. Maybe I'll just wear all of them.

6. ◀ REREAD As you reread lines 76–113, make notes in the margin
about why Heartbeat decides he is done wearing extra layers. Then
reread the story's final line. Do you think Heartbeat's essential
personality has changed? Support your answer with explicit textual
evidence.

*He uses the same kind of humor and is making fun of himself, as he
has throughout the story.*

SHORT RESPONSE

Cite Text Evidence   Write a brief summary of the plot of "Heartbeat." Review
your reading notes, and use your own words to answer *who? when and where?*
and *what happens?* **Cite text evidence** to support your response.

*Heartbeat is a sixteen-year-old boy who hates his nickname. He says
his classmates assume he's a weakling, and Sarah is repulsed by how
skinny he is. After he tries to put on weight by eating a lot and lifting
weights, he wears more layers of clothing—gradually realizing that it
is a ridiculous solution. He thinks his body looks strange, and he is
uncomfortable all of the time. When he sheds his extra layers, he is
relieved. He understands he was silly to try to change because of a
nickname, and he wants people to like him the way he is.*

30

---

6. **REREAD AND CITE TEXT EVIDENCE**

F **ASK STUDENTS** to read their margin notes to a partner or a
small group and then create one response that best states why
Dave (Heartbeat) decides to stop wearing layers. *Students should
cite specific textual evidence from lines 93–106.* Have students
evaluate the meaning and effectiveness of the last line of the
story, citing evidence and line numbers to support their position
about whether or not Dave has really changed.

SHORT RESPONSE

Cite Text Evidence   Student responses will vary, but students
should cite evidence from the text in order to write an objective
summary of the story. Students should:

• explain the theme or central idea of the story.

• cite evidence to show the interaction of story elements.

• answer these questions in their summary: *Who? When and where?*
and *What happens?*

70f   Collection 2

TO CHALLENGE STUDENTS . . .

For more context about health and fitness, encourage students to
conduct print, online, or multimedia research to write a "how-to"
guide to fitness, including information and graphics about diet
and exercise.

ASK STUDENTS to work with a small group to do some
preliminary research to find an aspect of the topic that interests
them. Possible topics for their "how-to" fitness guide might
include:

• How to build total fitness

• How to use strength training to build lean muscle tissue

• How to use exercise and nutrition to burn calories

• How to build power, strength, and stamina

• How to use health-and-fitness equipment, step by step

After students have chosen a topic, discuss these guidelines for
writing a "how-to" guide, reminding students that the purpose of
such a guide is to tell the audience how to do something.

GUIDELINES FOR "HOW-TO" WRITING

• Explain your information clearly.

• Present step-by-step instructions in a logical way.

• Give directions that are easy to follow.

• Use time-order or spatial words to help your reader complete
the steps of the process.

• Include graphics to help you explain.

Students might also wish to view one of the hundreds of videos
about fitness, strength training, and nutrition.

ASK STUDENTS what they hope to discover as they research
their "how-to" fitness guide. How is the information they find
similar to, yet different from, the facts and information about
nutrition and fitness shared by Yoo in his story?

DIG DEEPER

With the class, return to Question 4, Reread and Discuss. Have students share the results of their discussion.

ASK STUDENTS whether they were pleased with the outcome of their small-group discussions. Have each group share what the majority opinion was of the group. How did most of the group members react to Dave's (Heartbeat's) interpretation of his classmates' newfound respect for him? Is this newfound respect Dave perceives based on reality, or is it a figment of Dave's imagination? What compelling evidence did the groups cite from the text to support their opinion, or point of view?

- Encourage groups to tell whether there was any convincing evidence cited by group members who held a different opinion from most of the group. If so, why didn't this opinion sway the group?

- Have groups explain how they decided whether or not they had found sufficient textual evidence to support their opinion. Did everyone in the group agree as to what made the evidence sufficient? How did the group resolve any conflicts or disagreements? What conflict-resolution techniques did the group use to resolve any differences?

- After students have shared the results of their group discussion, ask whether another group shared any ideas or findings they wish they had brought to the table. Did the group's findings convince them that the opposite view was reasonable and had merit? Did it change their opinion? Why or why not?

ASK STUDENTS to return to their Short Response answer and to revise it based on the class discussion. What important details or evidence can they add to their summary? What unnecessary details can they delete?

CLOSE READING NOTES

PLAN

The Song of Wandering Aengus

Sonnet 43

Poem by William Butler Yeats

Poem by William Shakespeare

Why These Texts?

The form of a poem is integral to its meaning. Understanding a poem's form deepens a reader's experience of a poem. This lesson focuses on figurative language and sound devices in poems and how they affect meaning in a poem.

View It!

Professional Development Podcast:

Text-Dependent Analysis

Key Learning Objective: The student will learn how to analyze a poem's form, as well as the use of figurative language and sound devices, to understand their effects on meaning.

 ## Common Core Standards

RL 1 Cite evidence to support analysis.
RL 2 Determine theme.
RL 4 Analyze the impact of rhymes and other repetitions of sounds on a specific verse or stanza of a poem.
RL 5 Analyze how a poem's form contributes to its meaning.
SL 1 Engage in a collaborative discussion.
SL 4 Present claims and findings; use appropriate eye contact, adequate volume, and clear pronunciation.
SL 6 Adapt speech.

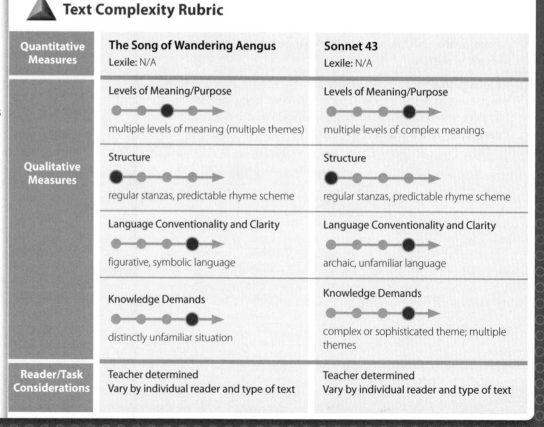

Text Complexity Rubric

	The Song of Wandering Aengus	Sonnet 43
Quantitative Measures	Lexile: N/A	Lexile: N/A
Qualitative Measures	Levels of Meaning/Purpose — multiple levels of meaning (multiple themes)	Levels of Meaning/Purpose — multiple levels of complex meanings
	Structure — regular stanzas, predictable rhyme scheme	Structure — regular stanzas, predictable rhyme scheme
	Language Conventionality and Clarity — figurative, symbolic language	Language Conventionality and Clarity — archaic, unfamiliar language
	Knowledge Demands — distinctly unfamiliar situation	Knowledge Demands — complex or sophisticated theme; multiple themes
Reader/Task Considerations	Teacher determined. Vary by individual reader and type of text	Teacher determined. Vary by individual reader and type of text

mySmartPlanner Create lesson plans and access resources online.

TEACH

CLOSE READ

Background Have students read the background and information about the poets. Explain that many poems are inspired by the experience of love and loss. Like the myth of Aengus, Yeats's poem "The Song of Wandering Aengus" tells of a man in search of a loved one in hopes of spending the rest of his life in happiness with her. Shakespeare's "Sonnet 43" also highlights these themes, describing the speaker's own emotional state as he longs for an absent loved one. It is a part of a series of sonnets by Shakespeare that are all connected by these same themes.

SETTING A PURPOSE Direct students to use the Setting a Purpose question to focus their reading. Remind them to write down questions as they read.

SCAFFOLDING FOR ELL STUDENTS

Analyze Language: Idioms Explain to students that poets sometimes use idioms to expand meaning or express an idea in a more thoughtful way. Point out that an **idiom** is a phrase that has a meaning different from the meaning of its individual words. Display lines 1–4 on the board or on a device. Read the lines aloud. Highlight in yellow the phrase "a fire was in my head." Discuss how the literal meaning, that the speaker's head is on fire, does not make sense.

ASK STUDENTS What might it feel like if a person in a poem about love had a fire in his head? *(The person would have a feeling of passion.)*

COMPARE TEXTS

Background *"The Song of Wandering Aengus" was inspired by Aengus, the Irish god of love and inspiration. In the original myth, Aengus falls in love with a girl he has dreamed about, but when he is unable to find her, he becomes ill. His parents go searching for her, and after three years the couple is finally united.*

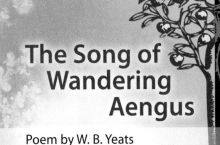

The Song of Wandering Aengus
Poem by W. B. Yeats

Sonnet 43
Poem by William Shakespeare

William Butler Yeats (1865–1934) *was an Irish poet and playwright, and one of the most notable literary figures of the 20th century. As a boy, Yeats made frequent trips to a rural region in Ireland called Sligo. There he enjoyed local stories about Irish heroes, heroines, and magical creatures. In Yeats's later life as a poet and playwright, the region and its folklore inspired his poetry and drama. "The Song of Wandering Aengus" is an example of this inspiration.*

William Shakespeare (1564–1616) *was an English playwright, poet, and actor. While Shakespeare is widely regarded as the greatest playwright in the English language, he was just as influential as a poet. He began writing poetry when theaters shut down during an outbreak of the plague in London. Adapting and refining the sonnet form, he produced 154 of his own sonnets. Now the Shakespearean sonnet is itself a unique poetic form.*

SETTING A PURPOSE As you read, think about what each poem has to say about the absence of a loved one. How does each poem convey a sense of loss and longing?

I went out to the hazel wood,

Because a fire was in my head,

And cut and peeled a hazel wand,

And hooked a berry to a thread;

CLOSE READ

Determine the Impact of Rhyme (LINES 1–16)

COMMON CORE RL 1, RL 4, RL 5

Explain to students that poets constantly play with **diction,** or word choice, as they write. They choose words not only for their meaning, but also for their sound. Explain that one example of this is a poet's use of **rhyme,** the repetition of sounds at the end of words. Rhyme can help emphasize ideas and create a musical quality. The most common type of rhyme in a poem is **end rhyme,** in which rhyming words come at the end of lines.

A **CITE TEXT EVIDENCE** Have students reread lines 1–16 aloud. Ask students to identify examples of rhyme and explain its effect on the poem. *(Possible answers: head/ thread, out/ trout, aflame/ name, hair/ air are end rhymes. The rhyming words create rhythm and help give the poem a rhythm of a folk song, which adds a mystical feel.)*

Determine Meanings

COMMON CORE RL 4, RL 5

(LINES 17–24)

Explain to students that poets often use figurative language to compare things, emphasize ideas, or give an emotional effect. **Figurative language** is a way of using words to express ideas that are not literally true. Yeats uses the following types of figurative language in this poem.

- A **simile** is a comparison between two unlike things using the words *like* or *as.*
- A **metaphor** is a comparison of two unlike things without the words *like* or *as.*
- **Personification** is giving human qualities to an animal, object, or idea.

K **ASK STUDENTS** to reread lines 17–24. Have them tell what the poet means by the metaphors "silver apples of the moon" and "golden apples of the sun." *(night and day)* Then have them explain the meaning of lines 17–24. *(When Aengus finds his love, they will be together until the end of time.)*

The Song of Wandering Aengus
by W. B. Yeats

A

I went out to the hazel wood,
Because a fire was in my head,
And cut and peeled a hazel wand,
And hooked a berry to a thread;
5   And when white moths were on the wing,
And moth-like stars were flickering out,
I dropped the berry in a stream
And caught a little silver trout.

When I had laid it on the floor
10 I went to blow the fire aflame,
But something rustled on the floor,
And someone called me by my name:
It had become a glimmering girl
With apple blossom in her hair
15 Who called me by my name and ran
And faded through the brightening air.

B

Though I am old with wandering
Through hollow lands and hilly lands,
I will find out where she has gone,
20 And kiss her lips and take her hands;
And walk among long dappled[1] grass,
And pluck till time and times are done,
The silver apples of the moon,
The golden apples of the sun.

---

[1] **dappled:** marked with many spotted colors or light.

APPLYING ACADEMIC VOCABULARY

focus	perceive

As you discuss the poem, incorporate the following Collection 2 academic vocabulary words: *focus* and *perceive*. Have students explain how the **focus** of the poem shifts at different points, and how the speaker, or person who "talks" to the reader, **perceives** life with or without love.

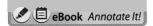 **eBook** *Annotate It!*

Determine the Impact of Rhyme

COMMON CORE RL 4, RL 5

A poem is a combination of sound and meaning. Poets choose their words carefully, since word choice, or **diction,** affects a poem's meaning and the way it sounds. **Rhyme** is the repetition of sounds at the end of words, as in *more* and *roar*. Words rhyme when their accented vowels and the letters that follow have identical or similar sounds.

Poets use rhyme for a number of purposes:

to make a poem songlike or playful

to emphasize sounds that suggest feelings

to create rhythms that help convey sensory feelings, such as a sense of motion

End rhyme refers to words that rhyme at the ends of lines of poetry. For example, the second and fourth lines from "The Song of Wandering Aengus" contain end rhymes:

> I went out to the hazel wood,
> Because a fire was in my head,
> And cut and peeled a hazel wand,
> And hooked a berry to a thread;

The end rhymes are *head/thread*. Reread the first stanza of the poem to listen for and identify a second pair of end rhymes.

Analyzing the Text

COMMON CORE RL 1, RL 4, RL 5

Cite Text Evidence   Support your responses with evidence from the text.

1. **Summarize** What are the primary actions that take place in each of the three stanzas of the poem?

2. **Identify Patterns** Find end rhymes and other examples of repetition in the second stanza. What effects do those forms of repetition have? Do they emphasize a particular meaning?

3. **Interpret** What is the quest of Aengus in this poem?

4. **Analyze** What words suggest that Aengus is chanting a song?

The Song of Wandering Aengus   **73**

PRACTICE & APPLY

Determine the Impact of Rhyme

COMMON CORE RL 4, RL 5

Review the information about the use of rhyme in a poem and its effect on meaning and **rhythm,** or the pattern of stressed and unstressed syllables in a line of poetry. Guide students to find another example of rhyme in the first stanza of "The Song of Wandering Aengus." *(out/trout)* Then have partners reread the poem and discuss the impact of the rhyme.

Analyzing the Text

COMMON CORE RL 1, RL 4, RL 5

Possible answers:

1. *In the first stanza, Aengus makes a fishing rod and catches a silver trout. In the second stanza, the trout turns into a girl who calls his name and runs away. In the third stanza, he is old and dreams of finding the girl.*

2. *The end rhymes in the second stanza are* aflame/name *and* hair/air. *The poet repeats the word* floor, *the /f/ in* floor, fire, aflame, faded; *and the /g/ in* glimmering girl. *The sounds create a musical rhythm. They also create images of a glowing fire, suggesting a feeling of burning love and the sudden disappearance of this love, almost into thin air* (hair/air).

3. *The line "Because a fire was in my head" suggests a burning desire for something. That something turns out to be his quest for love, embodied by the trout-girl.*

4. *The lines have a repeating pattern of rhythm and rhyme, like in a chant. Every other syllable is stressed to create a steady rhythm, and end rhymes, such as* head/thread *and* out/trout *give it the feeling of a song or chant.*

Strategies for Annotation   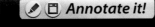 *Annotate it!*

Determine the Impact of Rhyme

COMMON CORE RL 4, RL 5

Have students use their eBook annotation tools to identify rhyme in "The Song of Wandering Aengus." Ask them to do the following:

- Highlight in yellow the rhyming words in the first stanza.
- Highlight in blue the rhyming words in the second stanza.
- Highlight in green the rhyming words in the third stanza.
- Identify any patterns in rhyme.

Discuss how these rhyming patterns give the poem a chanting, folk song quality.

> Though I am old with wandering
>
> Through hollow lands and hilly lands,
>
> I will find out where she has gone,
>
> And kiss her lips and take her hands;

The Song of Wandering Aengus   **73**

TEACH

CLOSE READ

 For more context and historical background, students can view the video "Biography: William Shakespeare" in their eBooks.

Analyze Form: Sonnet
COMMON CORE RL 1, RL 4, RL 5

(LINES 1–4)

Explain that a poem's **form** is the arrangement of words and lines. Explain that traditional forms of poetry have fixed rules for the number of lines, how the lines are grouped, and the pattern of end rhymes, called the **rhyme scheme**. A **sonnet** is a traditional form that has 14 lines, a specific rhyme scheme, and a set rhythmic pattern, or meter. **Meter** is the regular pattern of stressed and unstressed syllables.

C CITE TEXT EVIDENCE Reread lines 1–4 aloud. Have students count the number of syllables in each line, and the meter, or the stressed and unstressed syllables. *(There are 10 syllables in lines 1 and 3, and 11 syllables in lines 2 and 4. Each line follows a pattern of one stressed syllable and one unstressed syllable.)*

Determine Meanings
COMMON CORE RL 1, RL 4, RL 5

(LINES 13–14)

Tell students that "Sonnet 43" makes use of conflicting ideas, or paradox. **Paradox** is a statement that has seemingly contradictory ideas. Point out line 1 when the speaker says he sees best when asleep, a time when our eyes are closed, and we don't "see" at all.

D CITE TEXT EVIDENCE Have students identify examples of paradox in lines 13–14 and explain how they deepen the poem's meaning. *("days are as dark as night and nights bright days"; The speaker's days are dark because he is sad when he cannot dream of his beloved. Nights are light because he sees his love in his dreams.)*

COLLABORATIVE DISCUSSION Have partners discuss how effectively the poets express their feelings. Then have them share their ideas with the larger group.

ASK STUDENTS to share any questions they generated in the course of reading and discussing this selection.

Sonnet 43
by William Shakespeare

When most I wink, then do mine eyes best see,
For all the day they view things unrespected;[1]
But when I sleep, in dreams they look on thee,
And, darkly bright, are bright in dark directed.
5 Then thou, whose shadow shadows doth make bright,
How would thy shadow's form form happy show
To the clear day with thy much clearer light,
When to unseeing eyes thy shade shines so!
How would, I say, mine eyes be blessèd made
10 By looking on thee in the living day,
When in dead night thy fair imperfect shade
Through heavy sleep on sightless eyes doth stay!
   All days are nights to see till I see thee,
    And nights bright days when dreams do show thee me.

COLLABORATIVE DISCUSSION Each of these two poems is, in a sense, a love poem. With a partner, discuss how effectively each poet expresses his feelings about love and loss.

---

[1] **they view things unrespected:** during the day the poet's eyes are looking at things that are insignificant or unimportant.

WHEN STUDENTS STRUGGLE...

To guide students' comprehension of the poem, help them understand the language. Display the poem. Work with students to paraphrase the poem line by line. Have them fill in a chart like the one shown and use it to explain the meaning of the poem.

When I most wink, then mine eyes best see,	I see best when I am asleep.
For all the day they view things unrespected;	All day, I look at things that are unimportant.

©Nicemonkey/Shutterstock

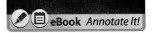 **eBook** Annotate It!

Analyze Form: Sonnet
COMMON CORE RL 4, RL 5

The deliberate arrangement of words is the mark of a well-crafted poem. The **form** of a poem is the arrangement of its words and lines on a page. One established form is a 14-line poem called a **sonnet.** The sonnet is a form that originated in Italy but was altered by English poets, especially William Shakespeare. The Shakespearean sonnet is named for the best-known user of the form.

A Shakespearean sonnet has these features:

- The whole poem develops a single idea.
- The idea is developed in three parts, each made of four lines.
- The **rhyme scheme** is the pattern of end rhymes: a-b-a-b, c-d-c-d, e-f-e-f, g-g. The matching letters refer to the pairs of end rhymes.
- The final pair of lines, called a **couplet,** completes the poet's message with a strong impact and helps focus the reader's attention on the theme.

A sonnet may also have a specified **meter,** which is a regular pattern of stressed and unstressed syllables. Notice where the stress falls in this line of the poem.

> When most I wink, then do mine eyes best see,

Look again at the sonnet you have just read. How does the punctuation at the end of the lines show how the ideas are organized?

Analyzing the Text
COMMON CORE RL 2, RL 4, RL 5

Cite Text Evidence Support your responses with evidence from the text.

1. **Identify Patterns** Explain what you notice about the rhyme scheme of this poem.

2. **Summarize** A **paradox** is a statement that seems to contradict itself. What paradox presented in the first line is developed throughout the sonnet? (Note that the word *wink* means "to close one's eyes to sleep.")

3. **Interpret** Reread the final couplet. Restate its message in your own words.

4. **Analyze** Reread line 5. How should it be read aloud to express its meaning?

PRACTICE & APPLY

Analyze Form: Sonnet
COMMON CORE RL 4, RL 5

Review the features of a Shakespearean sonnet. Discuss how the punctuation at the end of the lines helps the reader identify the sonnet's three parts.

Then have students reread each part of "Sonnet 43" and explain the ideas developed in each. *(In the first part, the speaker declares that he is happy at night because he can see his love in his dreams. In the second part, the speaker wonders how his love would appear in the daylight, after appearing so brightly at night. In the third part, the speaker imagines how happy he would be to see his love by day.)*

Analyzing the Text
COMMON CORE RL 2, RL 4, RL 5

Possible answers:

1. *This sonnet has the rhyme scheme a-b-a-b, c-d-c-d, e-f-e-f, g-g: see/unrespected/thee/directed; bright/show/light/so; made/day/shade/stay; thee/me.*

2. *The line "When most I wink, then do mine eyes best see" means that the speaker sees best when he is asleep. This is the paradox developed throughout the poem—that seeing is sharpest when there's darkness, which usually prevents sight. This image emphasizes the poet's longing for an absent loved one.*

3. *"All days are nights" because the speaker will be in darkness without seeing his beloved. "And nights bright days" because the speaker will see his beloved in his dreams.*

4. *When read aloud, a pause between* shadow *and* shadows *suggests the meaning that even darkness will shed bright light on the beloved.*

Strategies for Annotation
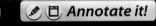 Annotate it!

Analyze Form: Sonnet
COMMON CORE RL 4, RL 5

Have students use their eBook annotation tools to identify the rhyme scheme of "Sonnet 43." Ask them to do the following:

- Highlight each set of rhyming words. Use different colors for each set.
- Review your highlights. On a note, assign the lines that are highlighted in yellow the letter *a.* Assign the lines highlighted in green the letter *b.*
- Continue in the same way for the remaining verses.
- Identify the pattern in the rhyme scheme.

When most I wink, then do mine eyes best see,

For all the day they view things unrespected;

But when I sleep, in dreams they look on thee,

And, darkly bright, are bright in dark directed.

rhyme scheme: abab

Determine Meanings

 COMMON CORE RL 4, RL 5

Review the examples of figurative language. Discuss how they contribute to the meaning and feeling of the poem. Ask students to provide additional examples of each type of figurative language in the poems. Then discuss the question, having students support their answers with evidence from the text. *("All days are nights to see till I see thee"; the speaker compares day to night because he feels lonely during the day when he cannot dream of his beloved.)*

Analyzing the Text

 COMMON CORE RL 4, RL 5

Possible answers:

1. *In the Yeats poem, not every line has an end rhyme. In each stanza, the 2nd and 4th lines and the 6th and 8th lines share end rhymes. In the sonnet, every line has an end rhyme, using the standard rhyme scheme for sonnets: a-b-a-b, c-d-c-d, e-f-e-f, g-g.*

2. *In the Yeats poem, the metaphor for love is a fish "that got away." The girl first appears as a trout. The fishing metaphor is introduced in the first stanza, with the images of fishing such as "a hazel wand" and "I dropped the berry in the stream/And caught a little silver trout." The rest of the poem extends the metaphor as the fish becomes a girl, who then disappears, or "gets away." In "Sonnet 43," the extended metaphor of shades and shadows creates a paradox. The shadow of the loved one can "make shadows bright." The loved one's "shade shines so!"*

3. *It is easy to speak the words, as the consistent pattern of rhythm feels like regular speech. The Yeats poem almost sounds like a chant or a song. And the sonnet's meter creates a similar rhythmic pattern.*

Determine Meanings

 COMMON CORE RL 4, RL 5

Figurative language is the use of words in imaginative ways to express ideas that are not literally true. Poets use figurative language to convey meaning and achieve certain effects. This chart shows three common types of figurative language with examples from "The Song of Wandering Aengus."

Types of Figurative Language	Examples	Effect
Simile is a comparison between two unlike things using the words *like* or *as*.	*moth-like stars,* line 6	The twinkling stars look like moths fluttering.
Metaphor is a comparison of two unlike things without the words *like* or *as*.	*a fire was in my head,* line 2	A feverish, uneasy feeling is likened to a fire in the head.
Personification gives human qualities to an animal, object, or idea.	*And someone called me by my name,* line 12	The trout is given the human quality of speech.

The figurative language in "Sonnet 43" seems subtler than that in the Yeats poem. In Shakespeare's sonnet, which words help create a metaphor for the absence of the poet's loved one?

Analyzing the Text

 COMMON CORE RL 2

Cite Text Evidence Support your responses with evidence from the texts.

1. **Identify Patterns** What is the rhyme scheme of the Yeats poem and how does it differ from the rhyme scheme of "Sonnet 43"?

2. **Compare** An **extended metaphor** compares two unlike things at length and in a number of ways, sometimes throughout an entire work. In each poem, the poet uses an extended metaphor. What is the metaphor in each poem and what words does the poet use to extend it?

3. **Analyze** Read each poem aloud to hear and feel the unstressed and stressed syllables in each line. What qualities does the meter contribute to each poem? Explain.

PERFORMANCE TASK

Speaking Activity: Discussion With a small group, discuss which speaker of these two poems seems more affected by what he perceives. To prepare for your discussion:

- Consider what each speaker is longing for.
- Think about the words used to express the speaker's longing in each poem.

PERFORMANCE TASK

 COMMON CORE SL 1a–d, SL 4, SL 6

Assign this performance task.

Speaking Activity: Discussion As students compare and contrast how the speakers express feelings, have them record ideas in a Venn diagram.

- They can use the completed diagram as a guide for their discussion.
- Remind them to use appropriate eye contact, adequate volume, and clear pronunciation when speaking.
- Point out to students that because this is a discussion with classmates, they can use more informal language.

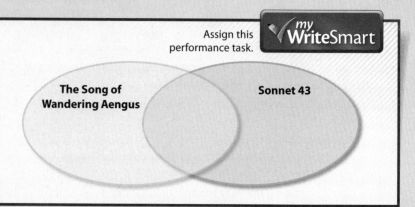

The Song of Wandering Aengus   Sonnet 43

INTERACTIVE WHITEBOARD LESSON
Analyze Form

COMMON CORE
RL 5

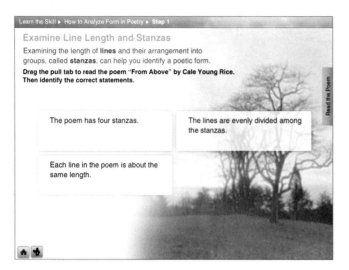

Learn the Skill ▶ How to Analyze Form in Poetry ▶ Step 1

Examine Line Length and Stanzas

Examining the length of **lines** and their arrangement into groups, called **stanzas**, can help you identify a poetic form.

Drag the pull tab to read the poem "From Above" by Cale Young Rice. Then identify the correct statements.

The poem has four stanzas.

The lines are evenly divided among the stanzas.

Each line in the poem is about the same length.

TEACH

Review with students that the form of a poem is the arrangement of its words and lines. Form may also involve patterns of rhythm and rhyme.

Explain that students can focus on these steps when analyzing form to compare and contrast two poems:

1. Examine line length and stanzas. A **line** is the core unit of a poem. A **stanza** is a group of two or more lines.
2. Look for a **rhyme scheme,** or pattern of end rhymes, in a poem.
3. Identify whether each poem is traditional or conventional. A **traditional** poem follows fixed rules for the number of lines and stanzas and for the pattern of rhyme. A **conventional** poem does not follow fixed rules. Its words and lines may be arranged in different ways.
4. Analyze the effects the form has on meaning in each poem. Think about how ideas are linked together, the feeling you get when reading the poem, and how the speaker's thoughts are organized into stanzas.

PRACTICE AND APPLY

Have students work in groups to apply the steps to another pair of poems: a poem with alternating end rhymes, such as the Yeats poem, and another sonnet. Have groups compare their results.

Determine Meanings

COMMON CORE
RL 4

RETEACH

Review that **figurative language** is a way of using words in imaginative ways to express ideas that are not literally true.

- A **simile** is a comparison between two unlike things using the words *like* or *as*.
- A **metaphor** is a comparison of two unlike things without the words *like* or *as*.
- **Personification** is giving human qualities to an animal, object, or idea.

Give simple examples of each, prompting students with relevant questions. For example:

- *My brother was as cold as ice.* What two things are being compared? Does the example include the words *like* or *as*? What type of figurative language is this?

 LEVEL UP TUTORIALS Assign the following *Level Up* tutorial: **Figurative Language**

Figurative Language   TUTORIAL   PRACTICE

Figurative Language

When a writer uses words according to their dictionary definition, he or she is using **literal language**. Click the top image to see literal language used to describe the sky.

Click this image

When a writer uses words in an imaginative way to express meanings beyond the literal meanings, he or she is using **figurative language**. Figurative language is sometimes referred to as *figures of speech*. Click the bottom image for an example of figurative language.

Click this image

1 2 3 4 5 6 7 8 9 10 ..11

CLOSE READING APPLICATION

Student partners can work together to apply the skill to another poem or poems they have read. Have them work together to find at least two examples of each type of figurative language. They can list their examples in a three-column chart. Then have pairs explain the examples and their meanings in a group discussion.

Magic and the Brain

*my*SmartPlanner Create lesson plans and access resources online.

Magazine Article by Susana Martinez-Conde and Stephen L. Macknik

Why This Text?

While this text is complex and technical, it also involves a high-interest topic. It is an example of how complex, scientific information can connect to students' lives and interests. The lesson will guide students to use organizational text features to better understand such complex texts.

View It!

Professional Development Podcast:

Text Complexity

For practice and application:

Saving the Lost

Close Reader selection
"Saving the Lost"
Science Writing by Reynaldo Vasquez

Key Learning Objective: The student will be able to analyze how text features contribute to a text and to summarize text objectively.

COMMON CORE Common Core Standards

RI 1 Cite textual evidence.
RI 2 Provide an objective summary of the text.
RI 4 Determine the meaning of technical words and phrases; analyze the impact of word choice.
RI 5 Analyze the structure used to organize a text, including text features.
W 7 Conduct short research projects.
W 8 Gather relevant information from print and digital sources.
SL 4 Present claims and findings.
L 1a Explain the function of adverb clauses.
L 4a Use context as a clue to the meaning of a word or phrase.
L 4b Use common Greek affixes as clues to the meaning of a word.
L 4c Consult print and digital reference materials to determine/clarify meaning.
L 6 Acquire and use accurately domain-specific words and phrases.

▲ Text Complexity Rubric

	Magic and the Brain
Quantitative Measures	**Lexile:** 1340L
	Levels of Meaning/Purpose two topics
Qualitative Measures	**Structure** genre traits specific to science text
	Language Conventionality and Clarity many unfamiliar, high academic, and complex domain-specific words
	Knowledge Demands complex science concepts
Reader/Task Considerations	Teacher determined Vary by individual reader and type of text

TEACH

CLOSE READ

Background Have students read the background and information about the authors. Tell students that the two scientists study the nervous system, which has to do with the nerves in the human body. Explain that nerves transmit signals to and from the brain and all of the body's muscles and organs.

SETTING A PURPOSE Direct students to use the Setting a Purpose prompt to focus their reading. Remind students to write down questions that arise as they read.

Analyze Structure: Text Features (TITLE)

COMMON CORE **RI 4, RI 5**

Point out to students that the **title** is the name that is attached to a piece of writing. The title is sometimes called a **heading.** Explain that the title is just one type of **text feature,** or an element that helps organize or call attention to important information. Note that this title is accompanied by a photograph, a visual element that both clarifies the title's meaning and draws readers into the text.

 ASK STUDENTS to explain how the title and the visual elements that accompany it introduce the text. *(The title states the topic so readers know what the article is about. The photograph emphasizes the magic aspect of the article; the lines of electricity create a little excitement and raise curiosity.)*

Analyze the Meanings of Words and Phrases (LINES 1–9)

COMMON CORE **RI 1, RI 4**

Explain that the authors begin the article with an **anecdote,** or a brief account of an event. Tell students that authors use anecdotes to make a point or to provide information in an entertaining and/or memorable way.

 CITE TEXT EVIDENCE Ask students to identify words and phrases that make the anecdote especially vivid. Have them tell what effect the word choices have on this opening paragraph. *(Vivid words and phrases include: "tiny white dress," "luminous beacon of beauty radiating," "burning her image," and "a blaze of red." The vivid details help make readers feel as if they are witnessing the event.)*

Background *Brain scientists* **Susana Martinez-Conde** *and* **Stephen L. Macknik** *study how the human visual system responds to and perceives the world around us. They see science at work behind magicians' techniques. A good magician relies on the inner workings of the brain to create all kinds of sensory illusions. By studying how these tricks work, scientists are learning more about the brain. Their work has led them to start a new area of science that they call* neuromagic.

Magic and the Brain

Magazine Article by Susana Martinez-Conde and Stephen L. Macknik

SETTING A PURPOSE As you read, think about the term *neuromagic* and its usefulness as a new field of scientific study. Write down any questions you may have during reading.

The spotlight shines on the magician's assistant. The woman in the tiny white dress is a luminous beacon of beauty radiating from the stage to the audience. The Great Tomsoni announces he will change her dress from white to red. On the edge of their seats, the spectators strain to focus on the woman, burning her image deep into their retinas. Tomsoni claps his hands, and the spotlight dims ever so briefly before reflaring in a blaze of red. The woman is awash in a flood of redness.

10   Whoa, just a moment there! Switching color with the spotlight is not exactly what the audience had in mind. The magician stands at the side of the stage, looking pleased at his little joke. Yes, he admits, it was a cheap trick; his favorite kind, he explains devilishly. But you have to agree, he did turn her dress red—along with the rest of her. Please, indulge him

©Comstock/Getty Images

SCAFFOLDING FOR ELL STUDENTS

Vocabulary Strategy Using a whiteboard, project lines 36–40. Highlight the words *responsiveness* and *stimulus.* Help students use the following strategy to figure out unfamiliar words:

- Look for familiar word parts, such as *respons*, which indicates that *responsiveness* is related to *respond*, or "answer."
- Try to get meaning from the context: a *stimulus* is something that the neural system responds to.
- Use a dictionary to confirm or clarify meaning.

ASK STUDENTS to identify another unfamiliar word in the passage and use the same strategy.

CLOSE READ

Analyze Structure: Text Features (LINES 21–25, FOOTNOTES)

COMMON CORE · RI 1, RI 4, RI 5, L 4a

Explain that words in **boldface type**—dark, heavy print—are also text features. Boldface words call attention to important words or ideas.

 CITE TEXT EVIDENCE Ask students to identify the words in boldface type as well as the associated definitions in the margins, and identify how they impact the reading of the text. *(The boldface words* neural *and* neuroscientists *are Critical Vocabulary words. Their definitions make the text easier to understand, as they are placed where the words first occur.)*

Tell students that **footnotes,** or notes at the bottom of a page, provide definitions or additional information.

 CITE TEXT EVIDENCE Have students locate the word *intuitive* on line 22. Ask them to use the context, or the words and phrases surrounding it that provide hints about its meaning, to try to determine the word's meaning. Then have them use the footnote to confirm the meaning and restate the ideas in their own words. *(Thompson has a natural ability to understand how to use science to make his trick work.)*

CRITICAL VOCABULARY

neural: The authors refer to neural processes that take place in people's brains as they watch a trick.

neuroscientist: The authors note that neuroscientists can learn from magicians.

ASK STUDENTS what kinds of neural processes engaged during a magic show might be of interest to a neuroscientist. *(The brains of spectators at a magic show would be using neural processes that send and receive signals from the eyes. Learning how this works might be of interest to a neuroscientist.)*

neuron: Neurons have a "firing rate" that scientists can measure.

ASK STUDENTS to explain what is meant by the "firing rate" of a neuron. *(Neurons send messages, so "firing rate" has to do with how many messages or how quickly neurons are sending messages back and forth to the brain.)*

---

and direct your attention once more to his beautiful assistant as he switches the lights back on for the next trick. He claps his hands, and the lights dim again; then the stage explodes in a supernova of whiteness. But wait! Her dress really has turned 20 red. The Great Tomsoni has done it again!

The trick and its explanation by John Thompson (aka the Great Tomsoni) reveal a deep intuitive[1] understanding of the **neural** processes taking place in the spectators' brains—the kind of understanding that we **neuroscientists** can appropriate for our own scientific benefit. Here's how the trick works. As Thompson introduces his assistant, her skintight white dress wordlessly lures the spectators[2] into assuming that nothing— certainly not another dress—could possibly be hiding under the white one. That reasonable assumption, of course, is 30 wrong. The attractive woman in her tight dress also helps to focus people's attention right where Thompson wants it—on the woman's body. The more they stare at her, the less they notice the hidden devices in the floor, and the better adapted their retinal neurons[3] become to the brightness of the light and the color they perceive.

All during Thompson's patter after his little "joke," each spectator's visual system is undergoing a brain process called neural adaptation. The responsiveness of a neural system to a constant stimulus (as measured by the firing rate of the 40 relevant neurons) decreases with time. It is as if neurons actively ignore a constant stimulus to save their strength for signaling that a stimulus is changing. When the constant stimulus is turned off, the adapted neurons fire a "rebound" response known as an after discharge.

In this case, the adapting stimulus is the redlit dress, and Thompson knows that the spectators' retinal neurons will rebound for a fraction of a second after the lights are dimmed. The audience will continue to see a red afterimage in the shape of the woman. During that split second, a trap door in 50 the stage opens briefly, and the white dress, held only lightly in place with fastening tape and attached to invisible cables leading under the stage, is ripped from her body. Then the lights come back up.

neural
(nŏŏr´əl) *adj.* Anything that is *neural* is related to the nervous system.

neuroscientist
(nŏŏr´ō-sī´ən-tĭst) *n.* A *neuroscientist* is a person who studies the brain and the nervous system.

[1] **intuitive** (ĭn-tōō´ĭ-tĭv): having the ability to know or understand something without evidence.
[2] **spectators:** the people who are watching the event.
[3] **retinal neurons** (rĕt´n-əl nŏŏr´ŏnz´): the cells in the retina of the eye that convert light into images.

78 Collection 2

APPLYING ACADEMIC VOCABULARY

focus	perceive	task

As you discuss the selection, incorporate the following Collection 2 academic vocabulary words: *focus, perceive,* and *task.* Help students understand the magic tricks described by clarifying what spectators **focus** on and what they perceive, and how what they **perceive** differs from reality. Discuss how giving a **task** to magic show viewers or test subjects affects what they see or don't see.

VISUAL ILLUSIONS
FOOLING MIND OR EYE?

An illusion created by an image like this one often induces a false sense of flowing movement in the concentric rings (start at the center dot in the pictures). But does the illusion originate in the mind or in the eye? The evidence was conflicting until the authors and their colleagues showed in October that the illusory motion is driven by microsaccades—small, involuntary eye movements that occur during visual fixation. Knowing the roles of eye and mind in magic can be used as experimental tools **neuroscience**.

neuroscience
(no͞or´ō-sī´əns) *n.*
Neuroscience is any of the sciences that study the nervous system.

60 Two other factors help to make the trick work. First, the lighting is so bright just before the dress comes off that when it dims, the spectators cannot see the rapid motions of the cables and the white dress as they disappear underneath the stage. The same temporary blindness can overtake you when you walk from a sunny street into a dimly lit shop. Second, Thompson performs the real trick only after the audience thinks it is already over. That gains him an important cognitive advantage—the spectators are not looking for a trick at the critical moment, and so they slightly relax their scrutiny.

The New Science of Neuromagic

Thompson's trick nicely illustrates the essence of stage magic. Magicians are, first and foremost, artists of attention and awareness. They manipulate the focus and intensity of human attention, controlling, at any given instant, what

Magic and the Brain   **79**

CLOSE READ

Analyze Structure: Text Features (SIDEBAR)

COMMON CORE **RI 5**

Tell students that **sidebars** are boxes that appear alongside or within an article to provide additional information related to the text. Sidebars often contain additional **graphic aids,** such as charts, graphs, or photographs.

E **ASK STUDENTS** to reread the sidebar and explain how the text and graphic aid enhance the information of the main text. *(The sidebar explains how neuroscientists investigated and determined whether a visual illusion originates in the eye or in the brain. The photograph shows the painting that creates the illusion.)*

CRITICAL VOCABULARY

neuroscience: The authors, who are neuroscientists, are actually studying magic to learn about how people's brains work.

ASK STUDENTS to tell what magic and neuroscience have in common. *(Both are concerned with how the brain works. In magic, people try to "fool" the brain; in neuroscience, people try to understand the brain.)*

Strategies for Annotation   ✐ 🖺 *Annotate it!*

Analyze Structure: Text Features

COMMON CORE **RI 2, RI 5**

Have students use their eBook annotation tools to analyze the text. Ask students to:

- Highlight in green the central idea of the sidebar.
- Write a note that briefly states the central idea.
- Write another note that explains how this information fits in with the rest of the text.

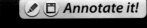

their colleagues showed in October that the illusory motion is driven by microsaccades—small, involuntary eye movements that occur during visual fixation. Knowing the roles of

Neuroscientists were able to determine that the origin of the visual illusion originated in the eye. Studying magic in the same way can be a tool for neuroscientists

Magic and the Brain   **79**

(Spiral) ©Atypeek Design/Shutterstock; (human eye) © Corbis RF

Summarize Text (LINES 85–94) COMMON CORE **RI 2**

Explain that to **summarize** is to retell a text's central, or main, ideas in your own words. When readers summarize, they should be **objective,** or not include their own opinions or judgments about the text. Tell students that stopping to summarize a paragraph or a section as they read can help them remember information.

F **ASK STUDENTS** to reread lines 85-94 and identify the central idea. Then have them summarize the paragraph. *(Central idea: Scientists and magicians have different aims, yet they can learn from each other. Sample summary: Neuroscientists try to understand the brain's cognitive functions. Magicians try to find cognitive weaknesses. Neuroscientists could use magicians' techniques to explore brain functions further.)*

CRITICAL VOCABULARY

cynic: The authors say that a cynic would not approve of their research.

ASK STUDENTS why a cynic would not approve of the authors' research. *(Because a cynic is skeptical or critical of others, it would be likely that a cynic would point out that such research is unnecessary.)*

---

we are aware of and what we are not. They do so in part by
70 employing bewildering combinations of visual illusions (such as afterimages), optical illusions (smoke and mirrors), special effects (explosions, fake gunshots, precisely timed lighting controls), sleight of hand, secret devices and mechanical artifacts ("gimmicks").

 Neuroscience is becoming familiar with the methods of magic.

But the most versatile instrument in their bag of tricks may be the ability to create cognitive illusions. Like visual illusions, cognitive illusions mask the perception of physical reality. Yet unlike visual illusions, cognitive illusions are not sensory in nature. Rather they involve high-level functions
80 such as attention, memory and causal inference. With all those tools at their disposal, well-practiced magicians make it virtually impossible to follow the physics of what is actually happening—leaving the impression that the only explanation for the events in magic.

 Neuroscientists are just beginning to catch up with the magician's facility in manipulating attention and cognition. Of course the aims of neuroscience are different from those of magic, the neuroscientist seeks to understand the brain and neuron underpinnings of cognitive functions, whereas the
90 magician wants mainly to exploit cognitive weaknesses. Yet the techniques developed by magicians over centuries of stage magic could also be subtle and powerful probes in the hands of neuroscientists, supplementing and perhaps expanding the instruments already in experimental use.

Neuroscience is becoming familiar with the methods of magic by subjecting magic itself to scientific study—in some cases showing for the first time how some of its methods work in the brain. Many studies of magic conducted so far confirm what is known about cognition and attention from earlier
100 work in experimental psychology. A **cynic** might dismiss such efforts: Why do yet another study that simply confirms what is

cynic
(sĭn′ĭk) *n.* A *cynic* is a person who has negative opinions about other people and what they do.

WHEN STUDENTS STRUGGLE...

Remind students that summarizing is a strategy that can help them understand and remember complex text. Explain that using a graphic organizer to record central ideas and supporting details will help them summarize. Model rereading the paragraph in lines 95–109 and identifying its central idea. *(Neuroscientists are studying magic to learn how its methods work in the brain.)* Have students record the central idea in a graphic organizer like the one shown. Next have them reread the paragraph, identify details that support the central idea, and add them to the chart.

already well known? But such criticism misses the importance and purpose of the studies. By investigating the techniques of magic, neuroscientists can familiarize themselves with methods that they can adapt to their own purposes. Indeed, we believe that cognitive neuroscience could have advanced faster had investigators probed magicians' intuitions earlier. Even today magicians may have a few tricks up their sleeves that neuroscientists have not yet adopted.

110 By applying the tools of magic, neuroscientists can hope to learn how to design more robust experiments and to create more effective cognitive and visual illusions for exploring the neural bases of attention and awareness. Such techniques could not only make experimental studies of cognition possible with clever and highly attentive subjects; they could also lead to diagnostic and treatment methods for patients suffering from specific cognitive deficits—such as attention deficits resulting from brain trauma, ADHD (attention-deficit hyperactivity disorder), Alzheimer's disease, and the like. The

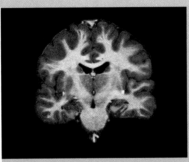

Diagnosing a Brain Disorder Physicians and scientists use Magnetic Resonance Imaging (MRI) as shown above on the left to make detailed scans of the body's internal structures. The MRI scan on the right highlights regions of the brain most affected by Alzheimer's disease.

Brain Regions and Alzheimer's Disease

- The hippocampus is the region where the disease may start.
- In the temporal lobe, the advancing disease affects memory, hearing and language.
- The cerebral cortex thins as the disease progresses, judgement worsens and language is impaired.

Central Idea 1

Supporting Detail 1

Supporting Detail 2

Supporting Detail 3

CLOSE READ

Analyze Meanings of Words and Phrases

 COMMON CORE **RI 1, RI 4, L 4a**

(LINES 110–116)

Tell students that authors choose words carefully to convey certain meanings. Ask students to reread lines 110–116 and to consider the use of the word *robust*.

G CITE TEXT EVIDENCE Have students reread the first six lines of the paragraph and identify context clues that might help them determine the meaning of *robust*. As needed, have students confirm the meaning with a print or digital dictionary. Have them discuss the effect of the use of the word *robust*. *(The phrase "more effective" suggests that* robust *describes something better or stronger.* Robust *has a sense of being both strong and healthy, in the sense of an experiment being well thought out or very thorough.)*

Analyze Structure: Text Features (SIDEBAR)

 COMMON CORE **RI 5**

Direct students' attention to the sidebar.

H ASK STUDENTS to reread the sidebar and explain how it adds or contributes to the topic. *(The main text above the graphic aid mentions using new experimental techniques that could lead to diagnosing or treating certain disorders. The graphic aid gives an example of how brain research is used to explore Alzheimer's disease.)*

Summarize Text

COMMON CORE **RI 2**

(LINES 124–134)

Explain that stopping to summarize a paragraph as students read can help them clarify meaning and better comprehend the central idea.

 ASK STUDENTS to summarize the paragraph. If students need support, have them first identify the central idea and then the supporting details. *(Sample summary: Misdirection is the act of turning spectators' attention away from a secret action. Overt misdirection is a direct request to spectators to focus on something.)*

120 methods of magic might also be put to work in "tricking" patients to focus on the most important parts of their therapy, while suppressing distractions that cause confusion and disorientation.

Magicians use the general term "misdirection" to refer to the practice of diverting the spectator's attention away from a secret action. In the lingo of magic, misdirection draws the audience's attention toward the "effect" and away from the "method," the secret behind the effect. Borrowing some terms from cognitive psychology, we have classified misdirection as 130 "overt" and "covert." The misdirection is overt if the magician redirects the spectator's gaze away from the method—perhaps simply by asking the audience to look at a particular object. When the Great Tomsoni introduces his lovely assistant, for instance, he ensures that all eyes are on her.

> ## Magicians use the general term 'misdirection' to refer to the practice of diverting the spectator's attention.

"Covert" misdirection, in contrast, is a subtler technique; there, too, the magician draws the spectator's attentional spotlight—or focus of suspicion—away from the method, but without necessarily redirecting the spectator's gaze. Under the influence of covert misdirection, spectators may be looking 140 directly at the method behind the trick yet be entirely unaware of it.

Cognitive neuroscience already recognizes at least two kinds of covert misdirection. In what is called change blindness, people fail to notice that something about a scene is different from the way it was before. The change may be expected or unexpected, but the key feature is that observers

---

Strategies for Annotation

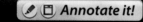 ✎ 🖹 *Annotate it!*

Summarize Text

COMMON CORE **RI 2**

Have students use their eBook annotation tools to analyze the text in lines 124–134. Ask students to do the following:

- Highlight in green the central idea.
- Underline one or two important details that support the central idea.
- In a note, write an objective summary of the paragraph.

Magicians use the general term "misdirection" to refer to the practice of diverting the spectator's attention away from a secret action. In the lingo of magic, misdirection draws the audience's attention toward the "effect" and away from the "method," the secret behind the effect.

> Misdirection is the act of turning spectators' attention away from a secret action. Magicians call this drawing attention to the "effect" and away from the "method."

do not notice it by looking at the scene at any one instant in time. Instead the observer must compare the postchange state with the prechange state.

150   Inattentional blindness differs from change blindness in that there is no need to compare the current scene with a scene from memory. Instead people fail to notice an unexpected object that is fully visible directly in front of them. Psychologist Daniel J. Simons invented a classic example of the genre. Simons and psychologist Christopher F. Chabris, both then at Harvard University, asked observers to count how many times a "team" of three basketball players pass a ball to each other, while ignoring the passes made by three other players. While they concentrated on counting, half of the
160 observers failed to notice that a person in a gorilla suit walks across the scene (the gorilla even stops briefly at the center of the scene and beats its chest!). No abrupt interruption or distraction was necessary to create this effect; the counting task was so absorbing that many observers who were looking directly at the gorilla nonetheless missed it.

Controlling Awareness in the Wired Brain

The possibilities of using magic as a source of cognitive illusion to help isolate the neural circuits responsible for specific cognitive functions seem endless. Neuroscientists recently borrowed a technique from magic that made
170 volunteer subjects incorrectly link two events as cause and effect while images of the subjects' brains were recorded. When event A precedes event B, we often conclude, rightly or wrongly, that A causes B. The skilled magician takes advantage of that predisposition by making sure that event A (say, pouring water on a ball) always precedes event B (the ball disappearing). In fact, A does not cause B, but its prior appearance helps the magician make it seem so. Cognitive psychologists call this kind of effect illusory correlation.

       In an unpublished study in 2006 Kuhn and cognitive
180 neuroscientists Ben A. Parris and Tim L. Hodgson, both then at the University of Exeter in England, showed videos of magic tricks that involved apparent violations of cause and effect to subjects undergoing functional magnetic resonance imaging. The subjects' brain images were compared with those of a control group: people who watched videos showing no

CLOSE READ

Analyze Structure: Text Features (HEADING)

COMMON CORE RI 2 RI 4, RI 5

Point out that this is the second heading in this article. A **heading,** like a title, is another text feature that organizes information for readers. Headings tell what a section of text is about.

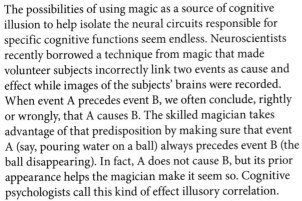 **ASK STUDENTS** to reread the heading and use it to tell what the section is about and explain how it represents a new kind of information. *(The previous section was about neuromagic and how neuroscientists are using magicians' techniques to understand the brain. This heading reveals that the next section of text will deal with controlling the brain rather than just understanding it.)*

CLOSE READ

Summarize Text

COMMON CORE RI 2

(LINES 166–199)

Tell students that, in a longer article, it is sometimes useful to summarize a section instead of each paragraph. Guide students to turn the heading above line 166 into a question *("How can we control awareness in the wired brain?").*

(K) ASK STUDENTS to reread and summarize the last section of the article, using the heading-turned-question as a guide. *(Sample summary: Scientists are using the illusion techniques of magic to learn more about cognitive functions. In one study, illusory correlation causes subjects to misidentify causes and effects. In another study, scientists were able to see the particular part of the brain that was active while subjects watched magic tricks. Using the techniques of magicians may allow scientists to understand and possibly even control the brain's specific areas of function.)*

COLLABORATIVE DISCUSSION Have individuals review the text on the page where the term *neuromagic* is introduced (heading above line 65). Encourage students to jot notes about what the term means and whether it is useful or not. Then, when students discuss the term with small group members, tell them to cite text evidence to support their opinions or conclusions.

ASK STUDENTS to share any questions they generated in the course of reading and discussing the selection.

---

apparent causal violations. The investigators found greater activation in the anterior cingulate cortex among the subjects who were watching magic tricks than among the controls. The finding suggests that this brain area may be important for
190 interpreting causal relationships.

The work of Kuhn and his colleagues only begins to suggest the power of the techniques of magic for manipulating attention and awareness while studying the physiology of the brain. If neuroscientists learn to use the methods of magic with the same skill as professional magicians, they, too, should be able to control awareness precisely and in real time. If they correlate the content of that awareness with the functioning of neurons, they will have the means to explore some of the mysteries of consciousness itself.

COLLABORATIVE DISCUSSION The authors have invented the term *neuromagic.* Why do they think it is a useful term? Talk about your ideas with other group members.

TO CHALLENGE STUDENTS . . .

Evaluate Ideas In the last section of the article, the authors state that the possibilities of using the techniques of magic in neuroscience "seem endless." They go on to suggest, "If neuroscientists learn to use the methods of magic with the same skill as professional magicians, they, too, should be able to control awareness precisely and in real time."

ASK STUDENTS to closely reread this section of the article. Challenge them to brainstorm some of the "endless" possibilities—for good or for ill—that might result from scientists being able to control human awareness. Have them sort their ideas into two categories—those that would benefit society and those that might be harmful—and share them with the class.

Analyze Structure: Text Features COMMON CORE RI 4, RI 5

Text features are elements of a text that help organize and call attention to important information. Informational texts such as "Magic and the Brain" often contain one or more text features, such as those shown in the chart.

Text Features in Informational Texts	
titles, headings, subheadings	The **title** of a piece of writing is the name that is attached to it. It often identifies the topic of the whole text and is sometimes referred to as a **heading. Subheadings** appear at the beginning of sections within the text and indicate the focus of that section.
sidebar	A **sidebar** is a box alongside or within an article that provides additional information that is related to the article's main text.
boldface type	**Boldface type** is dark, heavy print that is used to draw attention to unfamiliar vocabulary.
footnotes	**Footnotes,** which appear at the bottom of the page, provide definitions or additional information about terms in the text.

Graphic aids, such as maps, charts, diagrams, graphs, and pictures are visual text features that can help you understand ideas or processes.

Text features may be used to highlight **technical language**—terms used in a specialized field such as science or technology. If there is no definition for a technical term, use context to determine its meaning. You can confirm the meaning in such resources as print or online dictionaries and encyclopedias.

Look at the top of page 79 of "Magic and the Brain." Identify the text feature that appears there.

Summarize Text COMMON CORE RI 2

When you **summarize** a text, you briefly retell the central ideas in your own words. An **objective summary** reports what the original writer intended, without opinions or unnecessary details. Do not include opinions or commentary. Use headings and subheadings to help you organize ideas.

To summarize a paragraph, find and restate the main idea. To summarize a section, turn the heading into a question. Answer the question using the main idea and important details in the paragraph. To summarize an article, combine your section summaries. Add a sentence to sum up the central idea of the whole article.

Reread lines 1–20 of "Magic and the Brain." How would you complete a summary of that section?

TEACH

CLOSE READ

Analyze Structure: Text Features COMMON CORE RI 4, RI 5

Review the role and examples of text features. Have students point out examples of text features in the article and tell how or what each text feature adds to the text. Pose these questions to guide discussion:

- Does this text feature organize information, call attention to it, or both? How?
- Does this text feature emphasize information in the text or *add to* information in the text?
- Does this text feature use technical language—terms used in a special field, such as science?

Answer to final question: *sidebar*

Summarize Text COMMON CORE RI 2

Explain that students summarize when they relate the events of a movie, telling only main events, or "big ideas." Point out that a text summary is similar because they tell central ideas in their own words.

Sample summary of lines 1–20: *The Great Tomsoni says he will change his assistant's dress from white to red. He dims the lights, the stage is flooded in red light, and everything, including the dress, is red. He claims it was just a joke and directs the audience's attention back to the dress. Again he dims the lights. This time the stage is flooded in white light, but the dress is still red.*

Strategies for Annotation  *Annotate it!*

Analyze Structure: Text Features COMMON CORE RI 4, RI 5

Share these strategies for guided or independent analysis:

- Highlight headings in yellow.
- Underline boldface words, including those in footnotes.
- For each highlighted or underlined feature, write a note that restates the feature's important idea or tells briefly what the feature adds to the text. *(This section explores a new type of science called neuromagic.)*

The New Science of Neuromagic

Thompson's trick nicely illustrates the essence of stage magic. Magicians are, first and foremost, artists of attention

PRACTICE & APPLY

Analyzing the Text

COMMON CORE RI 2, RI 4, RI 5

Possible answers:

1. *Stage magicians use two types of misdirection: "overt" and "covert." With overt misdirection, the magician tells the audience to look at a particular object. "Covert" misdirection is subtler because spectators may be looking unknowingly at the method behind the trick yet be totally unaware of it. One kind of covert misdirection is change blindness, in which the viewer can't compare two scenes and therefore doesn't see the change. Another kind is inattentional blindness, in which people simply don't see something because they're focusing on something else.*

2. *The authors found that the illusion of motion doesn't originate in the brain, but in tiny movements of the eye. They solved an ongoing scientific puzzle about the roles of eye and brain.*

3. *"The wired brain" refers to neural circuits in the brain, the nerve connections responsible for cognitive functions.*

4. *The aim of a magician is to use the functions of the brain and the eyes to fool and entertain people. The aim of neuroscientists is to study and understand the functions of these organs as they process illusions in order to explore the mysteries of consciousness itself.*

5. *The most surprising aspect is that the subjects did not notice the person in the gorilla suit as they counted.*

6. *A visual illusion causes people to misperceive reality by changing what they sense with their eyes. A cognitive illusion causes people to misperceive reality because of how the brain works as it attends, remembers, and thinks.*

7. *The authors believe that experiments on attention and awareness should incorporate magicians' techniques because they could help scientists understand how the brain works in both highly attentive people and in people with attention deficits. More understanding might lead to being better able to diagnose or treat people with attention deficits.*

 eBook *Annotate It!*

Analyzing the Text

COMMON CORE RI 2, RI 4, RI 5, W 7, SL 4

Cite Text Evidence Support your responses with evidence from the text.

1. **Summarize** Reread lines 124–141. Write a summary of these paragraphs to explain how magic tricks work through the techniques of "misdirection."

2. **Draw Conclusions** Reread the sidebar on page 79. What discovery did the authors make about the origin of illusion? Why is it important?

3. **Interpret** Reread the heading on page 83. Use the information in that section to explain what is meant by "the wired brain."

4. **Summarize** Reread lines 85–94. In your own words, describe how the aims of a magician might differ from those of a neuroscientist.

5. **Infer** Reread lines 154–165. What is the most surprising detail about the counting task that is performed by the test subjects?

6. **Compare** Reread lines 65–80. What is the difference between a cognitive illusion and a visual illusion?

7. **Synthesize** Reread lines 110–123. Why do the authors want neuroscientists to use "tools of magic"?

PERFORMANCE TASK

Speaking Activity: Demonstration
Do research to find an easily performed "magic trick" that is based on a science principle. Follow the step-by-step directions for the trick and practice performing it. Determine the principle that makes the trick work. Then demonstrate the trick in a performance for your classmates. Follow these suggestions during the demonstration:

- If necessary, perform the trick a second time, but more slowly, indicating whatever you're doing to distract their attention.
- At the end of the performance, explain the principle at work in the trick and how it relates to the article "Magic and the Brain."
- Invite feedback. Discuss with your classmates whether the demonstration increases their understanding of neuromagic.

Assign this performance task.

PERFORMANCE TASK

COMMON CORE W 7, SL 4, L 6

Speaking Activity: Demonstration Suggest that students work with partners to take the roles of magician and assistant. Provide this additional guidance:

- Encourage students to search for videos as they conduct research. Videos will help them understand the visual showmanship involved in the trick.
- When students explain their tricks, encourage them to use technical terms from the article such as "visual illusion" and "cognitive illusion."

Critical Vocabulary

neural	neuroscientist	neuron	neuroscience	cynic

Practice and Apply Answer each question.

1. How is a **neural** network like and different from a computer network?

2. How is a **neuroscientist** like and different from a brain surgeon?

3. How is a **neuron** like and different from a blood cell?

4. How is **neuroscience** like and different from medical science?

5. How is a **cynic** like and different from a critic?

Vocabulary Strategy: The Greek Prefix *neuro-*

A **root** is a word part that came into English from an older language, such as ancient Latin or Greek. The Greek word for "cord" or "nerve" was *neuron*. The Greek root *neuro* appears as a prefix at the start of many English words about nerves and the nervous system.

This sentence comes from "Magic and the Brain"; notice the two words with the prefix *neuro-*:

> The responsiveness of a neural system to a constant stimulus (as measured by the firing rate of the relevant neurons) decreases with time.

Restate the sentence replacing each word with *neuro* with another term that includes *nerve* or *nervous*.

Practice and Apply Use the context and your knowledge of the root *neuro* to write a likely meaning for each bold word. Use a print or online dictionary to look up unfamiliar words or word parts and to confirm word meanings.

1. A patient with an abnormal tingling in one arm may consult a **neurologist.**

2. Some snakes paralyze their prey by injecting a **neurotoxin.**

3. People with a **neuromuscular** disorder may have difficulty with tasks such as unscrewing a jar lid.

4. The **neurosurgeon** removed a tumor from the patient's brain.

PRACTICE & APPLY

Critical Vocabulary

Possible answers:

1. *A neural network is a system of nerves. A computer network is a system of electronic devices. Both handle high-speed signals to transmit messages or move data.*

2. *Both a neuroscientist and a brain surgeon work with the nervous system. A neuroscientist studies how the brain works; a brain surgeon performs surgery on the brain.*

3. *Neurons and blood cells are both cells. A neuron is a cell in the nervous system that transmits signals to and from the brain. A blood cell is a cell in the circulatory system that carries oxygen to and from the heart.*

4. *Neuroscience and medical science are both concerned with the body. Neuroscience focuses on how the brain and nervous system work; medical science focuses on the treatment of illness affecting organs and bodily functions.*

5. *A cynic and a critic both make judgments, but a cynic is less trusting and more negative than a critic.*

Vocabulary Strategy: The Greek Prefix *neuro-*

Possible answers:

The responsiveness of a nervous system to a constant stimulus (as measured by the firing rate of the relevant nerve cells) decreases with time.

1. *neurologist: a medical doctor who treats nerve disorders*

2. *neurotoxin: a substance that damages nerves*

3. *neuromuscular: having to do with the nerves that control muscle movement*

4. *neurosurgeon: a medical doctor who operates on parts of the nervous system such as the brain*

Strategies for Annotation ✎ 🗐 *Annotate it!*

Vocabulary Strategy: The Greek Prefix *neuro-*

Have students locate the various words in the selection that contain the Greek prefix *neuro-*. Encourage them to use their eBook tools to do the following:

- Highlight in yellow each word with the prefix *neuro-* or *neur-*.
- Underline the prefix in each.
- Write notes for each explaining how you used the root to infer the word's meaning.

The trick and its explanation by John Thompson (aka the Great Tomsoni) reveal a deep intuitive understanding of the **neural** processes taking place in the spectators' brains—the kind of understanding that we **neuroscientists** can

> A scientist is someone who studies, so a neuroscientist must study nerves.

Language Conventions: Adverb Clauses

 COMMON CORE L 1a

Review that an adverb answers the questions *When? Where? How?* or *To what extent?* about a verb, an adjective, or another adverb. Provide these examples as review:

- *When?* She went to school <u>yesterday</u>.
- *Where?* She went to school <u>somewhere</u>.
- *How?* She went to school <u>slowly</u>.
- *To what extent?* She went to school <u>rather</u> slowly. (*slowly* is also an adverb; *rather* tells to what extent she went slowly)

Emphasize that an adverb clause functions in the same way as a one-word adverb does. Point out that the subordinating conjunctions are signal words. Help students see that these are all familiar words.

Answers:

1. *adverb clause: After the magician's "little joke,"; modifies the verb* took place; *tells when*

2. *adverb clause: as any the magician had ever performed; modifies the adjective* complicated; *tells how or to what extent*

3. *adverb clause: where they usually performed their act; modifies the adverb* here; *tells where (i.e., tells where "here" is)*

4. *adverb clause: Before the assistant left the stage; modifies the verb* handed; *tells when*

Assess It!

Online Selection Test
- Download an editable ExamView bank.
- Assign and manage this test online.

Language Conventions: Adverb Clauses

 COMMON CORE L 1a

An **adverb** is a part of speech that modifies a verb, an adjective, or another adverb. It answers the question *When? Where? How?* or *To what extent?* A **clause** is a group of words that contains a subject and a predicate—the two main parts of a complete sentence. An **adverb clause** is a subordinate clause that completes the same task as an adverb: it modifies a verb, an adjective, or another adverb.

Adverb clauses start with a connecting word called a **subordinating conjunction,** such as *after, although, as, because, before, even though, if, since, so that, though, unless, until, when, where, while.* Notice the subordinating conjunction and adverb clause in this sentence from "Magic and the Brain."

> **When the constant stimulus is turned off, the adapted neurons fire a "rebound" response known as an afterdischarge.**

The phrase *When the constant stimulus is turned off* modifies the verb *fire* in the rest of the sentence. The clause tells when the "neurons fire." It begins with the subordinating conjunction *when.*

When you write, be careful not to confuse an adverb clause with a complete sentence; an adverb clause cannot stand alone. If you position an adverb clause before the main clause, set it off with a comma.

Sentence Fragment	Complete Sentence
Because not enough research had been done	The science of magic could not be used in medicine because not enough research had been done.
After the lights on stage flashed	After the lights on stage flashed, a set of cables switched the dresses worn by the assistant.

Practice and Apply Identify the adverb clause in each of these sentences and tell whether it modifies a verb, an adjective, or an adverb. Tell which question the adverb clause answers: *When? Where? How?* or *To what extent?*

1. After the magician's "little joke," the real illusion took place.

2. The trick was as complicated as any the magician had ever performed.

3. The magician and his assistant stood here, where they usually performed their act.

4. Before the assistant left the stage, the magician handed her his hat.

Conduct Online Research

COMMON CORE
W 7,
W 8

TEACH

Explain to students that finding information on the Internet is easy. The hard part is weeding out the unreliable, useless, or just plain bad information from the reliable, useful, and good information. Provide these tips for conducting keyword searches for the Performance Task:

- Avoid very broad topics or keywords. For this Performance Task, the search string "magic trick" would bring an overwhelming list of results. Narrow the search string to a specific type of magic trick; perhaps "sleight of hand."

- Be specific, but not *too* specific. The search string "how-to video on sleight of hand trick with coins" would yield some good results, but you might also miss out on some good sites that don't include videos or that are about sleight of hand tricks with other materials.

As students conduct searches, provide these tips for evaluating the validity or assessing the relevance of websites:

- If the website is primarily a site that sells things, it is unlikely to be a good source of information.

- If the website is maintained by an organization or professional association, what is the group and what is its mission?

- If the website or blog is maintained by a person, check the person's credentials. For this Performance Task, if he or she is a professional magician, the information is *likely* to be valid, but readers should still use their good judgment.

PRACTICE AND APPLY

Have students apply these tips as they conduct their magic trick research. Or, you may wish to have them complete the Interactive Lessons "Conducting Research" and/or "Evaluating Sources." Monitor students' research, and ask probing questions to help shape their search strings or evaluate websites.

 INTERACTIVE LESSON Have students complete the tutorials in these lessons: **Conducting Research, Evaluating Sources**

Analyze Structure: Text Features

COMMON CORE
RI 5

RETEACH

Review the following list of text features with students and talk about what each one is. As needed, point to examples of each type of text feature in "Magic and the Brain" or another magazine article or informational text.

- **titles, headings, subheadings** (organizational items that label sections of text and tell what a section is about)

- **sidebars** (a box beside or within text that provides additional information)

- **boldface type** (a text treatment that calls attention to important words or ideas)

- **footnotes** (definitions or additional information at the bottom of a page)

- **graphic aids** (visual elements such as maps, charts, diagrams, graphs, and photographs)

 LEVEL UP TUTORIALS Assign the following *Level Up* tutorial: **Informational Text**

CLOSE READING APPLICATION

Students can apply their knowledge of text features and how to use them to other pieces of informational text. Have them work independently to fill in a chart with examples of each kind of text feature that appears in the text and how it helps them to locate and understand the information.

Text Feature	Example	What it does
sidebar		
heading		

As students read, suggest that they ask themselves questions such as these:

- Does this feature emphasize something in the text or add information to the text?

- What important idea or information does this feature provide?

- How does this feature add or contribute to my understanding of this topic?

Saving the Lost

Science Article by Reynaldo Vasquez

Why This Text

Students may find it difficult to identify and follow the central ideas of science articles. This difficulty may be compounded if students are not familiar with scientific terms and technical concepts that are common in such articles. With the help of the close-reading questions, students will identify and then summarize some of the central ideas in this science article. This close reading will lead students to understand how the central ideas are developed, forming a coherent argument.

Background Have students read the background information about the scientist in the article. Point out that medicine has provided incredible benefits to modern society, improving the health and extending the lives of most people. However, modern medicine also presents doctors and scientists with difficult medical challenges and ethical dilemmas. People with serious brain injuries, for example, may prove to be conscious in unexpected ways.

SETTING A PURPOSE Ask students to pay attention to the major steps in Owen's research. How does the author use these as central ideas for his article?

 COMMON CORE Common Core Support

- cite multiple pieces of text evidence
- determine central ideas in a text
- provide an objective summary of the text
- determine the meaning of words as they are used in the text
- analyze the structure of a text

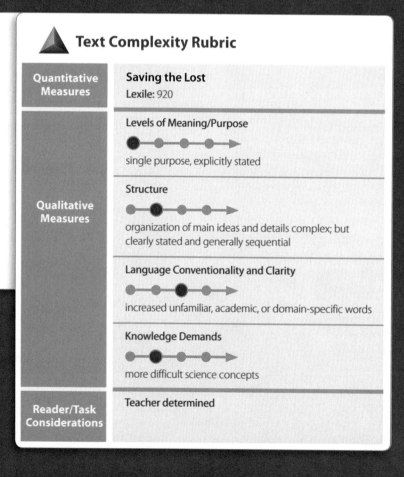

Text Complexity Rubric

Quantitative Measures	Saving the Lost
	Lexile: 920

Qualitative Measures

Levels of Meaning/Purpose

single purpose, explicitly stated

Structure

organization of main ideas and details complex; but clearly stated and generally sequential

Language Conventionality and Clarity

increased unfamiliar, academic, or domain-specific words

Knowledge Demands

more difficult science concepts

Reader/Task Considerations	Teacher determined

Strategies for CLOSE READING

Summarize Text

Students should read this science article carefully all the way through. Close-reading questions at the bottom of the page will help them focus on a thorough analysis of central ideas. As they read, students should jot down comments or questions about the text in the margins.

WHEN STUDENTS STRUGGLE . . .

To help students summarize "Saving the Lost," have them work in small groups to fill out a chart like the one shown below.

CITE TEXT EVIDENCE For practice in summarizing text, ask students to write a central idea of the article, cite text evidence in support of the idea, and then summarize the idea.

Central Idea	Textual Evidence
Many patients in a vegetative state may in fact be conscious.	A brain scan of one patient "lit up like a Christmas tree."
	When asked to think about playing tennis, another patient's brain showed the same response as that of a healthy person.
	Five out of another 54 patients also showed a normal brain response when asked to imagine playing tennis.
	A patient was able to alter his brain activity to give yes/no answers to questions.

Summary: A scientist named Adrian Owen has used neuroimaging technology to study the brains of patients in a vegetative state. He found that some patients' brains respond to questions and directions the same way that healthy people's brains do. This proved to Owen that some of these patients are in fact conscious and capable of communication.

Background *Adrian Owen is a groundbreaking British scientist whose research has been reported in documentaries, on radio and television shows, and in newspapers and magazines. This article presents the remarkable discoveries Owen brought to light as he studied the brain activity of a special group of people.*

Saving the Lost

Science Article by Reynaldo Vasquez

CLOSE READ
Notes

1. **READ ▶** As you read lines 1–14, begin to collect and cite text evidence.
   - Circle the question at the beginning of the article.
   - Underline the central idea in the first paragraph, and paraphrase the idea in the margin.
   - Underline the central idea in the second paragraph, and restate it in the margin.

How can we understand what a person who cannot respond is thinking or feeling? People in a *vegetative state* are those who have come out of a coma and appear to be awake with open eyes and sleep patterns. However, they do not show any awareness of who they are or where they are. They cannot speak and do not respond to sounds, hunger, or pain. The actual condition of patients in a vegetative state mostly remained a secret until Adrian Owen made some startling discoveries.

In the late 1990s, British scientist Owen realized that the technology of *neuroimaging*—producing images of brain activity without surgery—supported what scientists already knew. Different parts of the brain process different kinds of thoughts. Owen's concern was that neuroimaging was breaking no new ground. He wanted to find a real use for it.

Adrian Owen discovered new facts about people who are in a vegetative state.

Owen wanted to find a way to make neuroimaging more useful.

31

---

1. **READ AND CITE TEXT EVIDENCE** Point out that the author begins the article with a simple but puzzling question that catches the reader's attention. Also, he phrases the question in "friendly," nonscientific language, thus inviting a wide audience to continue reading.

Ⓐ **ASK STUDENTS** to explain how they identified the central idea of the first paragraph. What clues in the underlined sentence suggest that this sentence expresses the central idea? *The word* actual *makes it clear that the condition of patients wasn't what people expected. Also, Owen made some "startling" discoveries about the patients' condition.*

CLOSE READ
Notes

> STRANGE AS IT SOUNDS, SCIENTISTS KNOW THE PART OF THE BRAIN THAT SHOWS ACTIVITY IN HEALTHY PEOPLE WHEN THEY IMAGINE PLAYING TENNIS. IT IS ALWAYS THE SAME.

rehabilitation:
therapy to restore good health

Time-order words or phrases let the reader follow the events in order.

In 1997, Owen and his team began testing a patient who was in a vegetative state. They scanned her brain as they showed her familiar faces, and "it lit up like a Christmas tree." Based on these results, the patient was given intense **rehabilitation**—whereas in many cases, people in a vegetative state are simply kept alive. She has since sent a letter to thank Owen, realizing that without the brain scan, she too would have been written off.

Owen continued his research, and in 2006 he made another breakthrough. He took brain scans of a woman patient as he asked her to imagine playing tennis. Strange as it sounds, scientists know the part of the brain that shows activity in healthy people when they imagine playing tennis. It is always the same. It was the same in his patient, too. He asked his patient to imagine walking through her home. Her brain showed activity in the exact same spot as healthy

2. ◀ REREAD Reread lines 9–14. Summarize Adrian Owen's challenge and the medical mystery he hoped to solve. Support your answer with explicit textual evidence.

Adrian Owen, a British scientist, looked for a real use for neuroimaging, and he wanted to find out about the actual condition of people who are in a vegetative state.

3. READ ▶ As you read lines 15–33, continue to cite textual evidence.
- Circle the time-order words or phrases that signal the sequence of events.
- In the margin, explain the advantage of using chronological order to organize the text.

32

people would if they thought of walking through the rooms of their homes. Owen believed that this showed that the patient was conscious. Some researchers agreed with Owen, while others disagreed. They believed that the response was an involuntary reaction to the final words that Owen said to the patient.

Owen did not give up. With a team from Belgium, he tested 54 other patients. Of these, five responded in the same way as his previous patient. Then they reached a huge breakthrough studying "patient 23." He had been in a vegetative state for five years following a car accident. The scientists discovered that patient 23 was able to give "yes" and "no" answers by changing his brain activity. They asked him questions with answers that the **technicians** couldn't know, and that weren't given away by any clues.

"Is your father's name Thomas?"
"No."
"Is your father's name Alexander?"
"Yes."
"Do you have any brothers?"
"Yes."
"Do you have any sisters?"
"No."

When Owen published his discovery in 2010, there was an immediate response from the media and the scientific community. A Canadian university offered a huge amount of funding for Owen to continue his research there.

The questions Owen asked did not include clues, and the technicians could not have know the answers.

technician:
a person with training in a technical process

Owen's discovery prompted an offer from a university to fund his research.

4. ◀ REREAD Reread lines 22–33. Summarize the events that took place in 2006. Support your answer with explicit textual evidence.

Owen found that a patient reacted to a prompt the same way as a healthy person would. He believed that it proved that the patient was conscious, though some other researchers did not agree.

5. READ ▶ Read lines 34–60. Underline each central idea, and in the margin, write at least one supporting detail.

33

2. REREAD AND CITE TEXT EVIDENCE

Ⓑ **ASK STUDENTS** to discuss Owen's implied criticism of neuroimaging in the 1990s. What was neuroimaging being used for then? *Scientists were using the technology to confirm what they already knew.* What was Owen's new idea? *He wanted to use neuroimaging to study the brains of patients in a vegetative state.*

3. READ AND CITE TEXT EVIDENCE

Ⓒ **ASK STUDENTS** how the phrase *based on these results* establishes a sequence of events. *The phrase* based on these results *implies that the results lead to some sort of action.*

FOR ELL STUDENTS Some students will know that a *state* is a part of a country. It can also mean the condition of something.

Critical Vocabulary: rehabilitation (line 18) Have students share their definitions of *rehabilitation*, and ask volunteers to use the noun in a sentence.

4. REREAD AND DISCUSS USING TEXT EVIDENCE

Ⓓ **ASK STUDENTS** to state the two central ideas of the paragraph. *One central idea is that the patient's brain responded to directions the same way as a healthy person's brain. Another central idea is that not everyone believed this was a sign of consciousness.*

5. READ AND CITE TEXT EVIDENCE

Ⓔ **ASK STUDENTS** to debate whether the sentence beginning "Then they reached . . ." or the sentence beginning "The scientists discovered . . ." better states that paragraph's central idea. *Students should point out that the second sentence explains the breakthrough mentioned in the first sentence. Also, the following series of questions and answers supports the idea in the second sentence.*

Critical Vocabulary: technician (line 40) Have students name different fields in which a technician might work. Then have volunteers use the word in sentences for two or three different kinds of technicians.

CLOSE READ
Notes

Owen believes that his work could help thousands of patients in the United States.

There are neuroscientists who do not agree with Owen's conclusions and who argue about the point at which consciousness can be said to exist. Owen is not interested in such details. In the United States, there are tens of thousands of people in vegetative states. Owen thinks that perhaps one-fifth of these people could be able to communicate. He would like to see that possibility become
60   a reality.

6. ◀ REREAD AND DISCUSS Reread lines 34–49. With a small group, discuss the reasons the author includes dialogue in this passage.

SHORT RESPONSE

Cite Text Evidence Using specific details from the text, write a short summary of Owen's work and its possible consequences. **Cite text evidence** to support your response.

Owen worked with patients in a vegetative state. He discovered that neuroimaging could be used to monitor changes in brain activity— one patient was able to give answers to yes/no questions, leading Owen to believe that some patients in a vegetative state are conscious. Although some neuroscientists do not agree with his conclusions, Owen believes that his discovery could help thousands of patients in a vegetative state to communicate.

34

---

6. REREAD AND DISCUSS USING TEXT EVIDENCE

(F) ASK STUDENTS from each group to reach a consensus on reasons why the author might have included the dialogue. How does the author use the dialogue to structure the final section of the article? *Students should recognize that the dialogue provides an immediate, dramatic conclusion to the story of Owen's research—technicians are actually having a conversation with a person in a vegetative state.*

SHORT RESPONSE

Cite Text Evidence Students' responses should include text evidence in their summaries. They should:

- explain that Owen used neuroimaging to study the brains of patients in a vegetative state.
- explain that some patients' brains responded to directions and questions in the same way that healthy people's brains respond.
- describe how Owen's research has been received by others.

TO CHALLENGE STUDENTS . . .

To better understand the context of Owen's work, students can research the history of how patients in a vegetative state have been viewed and treated over the last century.

ASK STUDENTS to discuss why it took so long for medical researchers to apply neuroimaging technology to patients in a vegetative state. In what ways can widely accepted "truths" block the way of medical innovations and other breakthroughs? *As Owen's case shows, when the experts in a field of medicine think they know something, they may not bother to investigate whether it is in fact true. Since everyone believed that patients in a vegetative state were unconscious, nobody thought to use neuroimaging to test the hypothesis.*

DIG DEEPER

With the class, return to Question 2, Reread. Have groups share their responses to the question.

ASK STUDENTS about the challenges Owen faced.

- Ask students to describe some of the challenges presented by the patients themselves. *People in a vegetative state cannot speak or move. Nor do they respond to noises, pain, or hunger. So it seemed impossible to communicate with them.*
- Have students discuss some of the challenges that came from other scientists in Owen's field. *At the time, researchers were using neuroimaging to study the brains of healthy people, so it took a leap even to think of applying the technology to patients in a vegetative state. Later, when Owen published his results, other researchers were skeptical. Some thought that the patients' brains were showing involuntary responses to Owen's directions. Others thought Owen's results did not prove the patients were actually conscious.*

ASK STUDENTS to return to their Short Response answer and revise it based on the class discussion.

COMPARE MEDIA

MEDIA **Pavement Chalk Art**

Art by Julian Beever

Why This Media?

Students usually encounter art in museums. This lesson will explore the public pavement art created by Julian Beever. By learning about public art and the techniques Beever uses to produce it, students will be better able to appreciate an artist's purpose and messages when they see a work of art.

Key Learning Objective: The student will be able to analyze the purposes of public art and the techniques Beever uses to create the illusion of three-dimensionality.

COMMON CORE **Common Core Standards**

SL 2 Analyze the main ideas and supporting details presented in diverse media.

SL 5 Integrate multimedia and visual displays into presentations.

W 6 Use technology to publish writing.

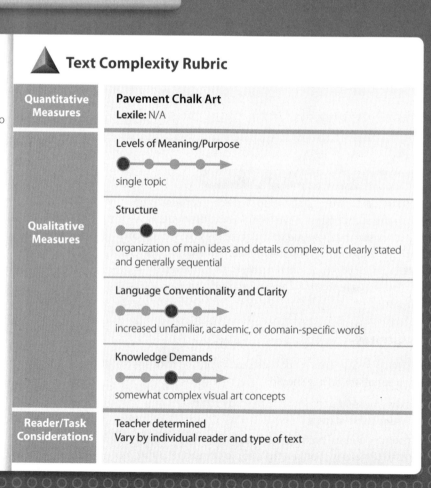

▲ Text Complexity Rubric

Quantitative Measures	**Pavement Chalk Art** **Lexile:** N/A
Qualitative Measures	**Levels of Meaning/Purpose** single topic
	Structure organization of main ideas and details complex; but clearly stated and generally sequential
	Language Conventionality and Clarity increased unfamiliar, academic, or domain-specific words
	Knowledge Demands somewhat complex visual art concepts
Reader/Task Considerations	Teacher determined Vary by individual reader and type of text

Julian Beever Have students read the background about the artist Julian Beever. Point out that Beever uses a technique called "anamorphosis" to create his drawings. This technique involves doing a drawing in a distorted, stretched form so that from one particular viewpoint, the distortion is resolved into the correct shape and form. It allows Beever to create the illusion of solid or hollow forms going in to, coming out of, or standing on the ground.

SETTING A PURPOSE Direct students to use the Setting a Purpose prompt to focus their viewing. Remind them to write down any questions they have as they read and view.

Julian Beever (b. 1959) *creates unusual chalk drawings on public sidewalks. Beever started drawing pavement art as a way to make money while traveling. Since then, he has gained international recognition. Beever chooses to draw on sidewalks so that everyone can have access to his art. He says, "My work appeals literally to the man (and woman) in the street and is not confined in galleries or limited by the gallery system."*

MEDIA ANALYSIS

Pavement Chalk Art

Public Art by Julian Beever

SETTING A PURPOSE Beever has developed a special technique of using distortion to unequally magnify images in his work. When seen from one special angle, these images come together to create the illusion that his "anamorphic" drawings are truly three dimensional. Viewed this way, his drawings seem to come to life.

Beever's pavement art gives viewers the impression that they are entering a very real, physical place that exists in the drawings. As you view the two drawings, think about what it would be like to be a passerby who suddenly walks across—or into—one of Beever's works. Write down any questions you have as you view.

(bg) ©olivier/Shutterstock; (r) ©Rex Features/AP Images

Pavement Chalk Art **89**

SCAFFOLDING FOR ELL STUDENTS

Vocabulary Support The selection contains many words that may not be familiar to ELL students, for example *distortion*, *images*, and *three-dimensional*. Have students use the context of the As You View sections and the drawings to determine the meanings on their own or with guiding questions from the teacher.

AS YOU VIEW Tell students that they will be looking at one of Beever's drawings. Explain that artists use different techniques to make their images come to life. Have students read the As You View section to help them focus their viewing on how Beever uses lines to help create his illusion. Discuss how Beever uses the technique called **perspective** to create the sense of three-dimensionality.

Analyze Diverse Media SL 2

Explain to students that artists like Beever have an audience in mind when they create their art. The **audience** is the group of people who will view an artist's work.

ASK STUDENTS how Beever's audience differs from the audience of most artists. Then ask why he may have chosen this audience. *(Beever's audience is normal people who just happen to be walking along the street. Beever chose this audience because he wanted his audience to be surprised. If his art were in a museum, the audience would be expecting to see it.)*

A Slight Accident in a Railway Station

AS YOU VIEW Artists make choices about the works they produce and the techniques they use to create those works. **Perspective** is the technique that artists use to give the illusion of three-dimensional space on a two-dimensional surface, which in Beever's case is the sidewalk. One way that Beever creates this illusion is through his use of lines. Beever uses thick and thin as well as long and short lines to frame the stairway in the drawing. Notice how the lines make the stairs look thinner the farther away they seem to get from the viewer.

©Julian Beever

WHEN STUDENTS STRUGGLE . . .

After students read the As You View section, discuss the meaning of *perspective* with them. You may want to show students some of M. C. Escher's artwork as an example of how other artists play with perspective to create illusions.

Meeting Mr. Frog

AS YOU VIEW In addition to lines, Beever uses colors and shadows to create the illusion that we are seeing something real. Artists can use color to create mood and to create images that imitate life. Notice how the colors Beever uses at the top of the frog seem brighter or lighter. He uses shadows, or shading, at the bottom of the drawing where the frog sits on the lily pad. Color and shadow work together to give the whole image a sense of shape and depth.

COLLABORATIVE DISCUSSION Beever's drawings focus on the sudden collision of perception and reality. With a partner, discuss your reactions to one of Beever's drawings.

CLOSE READ

AS YOU VIEW Tell students that they will be looking at another one of Beever's drawings. Explain that artists also use color and shading to make their images come to life. Have students read the As You View section to help them focus their viewing on the ways Beever uses these elements.

Analyze Diverse Media   COMMON CORE SL 2

Explain to students that artists like Beever also have a message in mind when they create art. The **message** is the idea or point that an artist wants to convey to the audience.

ASK STUDENTS how Beever's use of color and shadows helps him to convey the message that everything you see is not what you think it is. *(By using color and shading, Beever creates forms that seem so realistic that viewers mistake them for the real thing.)*

COLLABORATIVE DISCUSSION Have pairs work together to discuss how they reacted to Beever's drawings and why each of Beever's drawings would be confusing to a passerby. What is real about them? What is unreal? Accept all reasonable responses.

ASK STUDENTS to share any questions they generated in the course of viewing and discussing the artwork.

APPLYING ACADEMIC VOCABULARY

abnormal	focus	perceive

As you discuss Beever's drawings, incorporate the following Collection 2 academic vocabulary words: *abnormal, focus,* and *perceive.* Ask students to tell what part of the drawing they **focus** on. What do they **perceive** there? What might seem **abnormal** about Beever's art and where he creates it?

Analyze Diverse Media SL 2

Explain to students that artists, like writers, create their works with an audience in mind. Have students compare how visual artists, such as Beever, and writers might convey a message. *(Visual artists use visual elements such as line, color, and shape to craft their messages. Writers use words to convey their messages.)* Then discuss how Beever's audience differs from the kinds of audiences most artists create their works for. *(Beever's art reaches people who are not expecting to view art. They are not necessarily people who usually go to museums—their viewing of Beever's work is usually accidental and, therefore, a surprising experience.)*

Analyzing the Media SL 2

Possible answers:

1. *The colors are dark, forming shadows that help create a sense of depth. The shadow below the man suggests he is airborne. The vertical lines that narrow toward the train platform also create depth, giving the sense that the man, who is drawn mainly with curving and non-linear lines, is falling.*

2. *"A Slight Accident in a Railway Station" uses perspective to give the stairs the illusion that they are receding into the sidewalk; lines help to create a sense of space by making the stairs seem like they extend into a space in the sidewalk; color and shadow give the drawing a sense of realism and form; distorted forms create the illusion of three-dimensionality.*

3. *The drawings are different in several ways. "A Slight Accident in a Railway Station" recedes into the ground. It also creates a sense of motion and energy. "Meeting Mr. Frog" projects out of the ground. It is very still and whimsical.*

4. *Because he places his work in public spaces, all of Beever's work conveys the message that art should be experienced everywhere by everyone, not just by those who enter an art museum. Another message is that what we see is not always what is true reality. The drawings playfully trick the viewer.*

Analyze Diverse Media SL 2

Art is created with an audience in mind. The **audience** is the group of people who view an exhibit or performance. Because Beever produces art that is viewed in public outdoor spaces, his audience is everyday passersby.

Artists also have a **message,** an idea or point, that they want to convey through their art. Beever uses various artistic elements and techniques, such as lines, perspective, and distortion, to convey his message and to make his illusions come to life.

Analyzing the Media SL 2, SL 5, W 6

 Support your responses with evidence from the media.

1. **Analyze** How do the colors and lines in "A Slight Accident in a Railway Station" create a feeling of movement and make the image seem real?

2. **Analyze** Choose one of Beever's drawings. Tell how Beever uses the elements of line, color, perspective, shadow, and distortion to create effects, As shown in the graphic below, explain what effect each element creates.

Element Effect

3. **Compare** Both drawings create the illusion of depth. What are some ways the two drawings are different?

4. **Synthesize** Why do you think Beever chooses to create this style of art to put in public spaces? What message or messages does Beever convey through his art?

PERFORMANCE TASK

Media Activity: Poster Working in small groups, create a poster or a flyer that announces an exhibit of Beever's art in a city. Use your favorite design software program to lay out your work, including images and text.

- Highlight the effectiveness of Beever's drawings as public art.

- Promote the advantages of having sidewalk art in a city.
- Present your completed flyer or poster to the other groups, explaining what you intend to communicate with it and how you accomplished that goal.

Assign this performance task.

PERFORMANCE TASK SL 5, W 6

Media Activity: Poster Have students work in small groups. Posters should promote the art and highlight its advantages as public art. Have students:

- include images that engage their audience and convey their message.
- use different forms of media and visual aids to help with their posters, such as photo editing, design/layout, and/or illustration software.

Analyze Media: Perspective and Illusion

SL 2

TEACH

Explain to students that artists use different design elements instead of words to help them convey their messages. The following basic elements are used to help give meaning to visuals:

- **Lines** are strokes or marks. They can be thick or thin, long or short, smooth or jagged. They can focus attention and create a feeling of depth. They can frame an object, direct a viewer's eye, or create a sense of motion.
- **Shape** is the external outline of an object. Shape can emphasize visual elements and add interest.
- **Color** can be used to create a mood and to make things look real. By using color and shadow together, artists can give an image a sense of shape and depth.
- **Texture** is the surface quality or appearance of an object. For example, an object's texture can be rough, wet, or shiny. Texture can also be used to make an object seem real. For example, wallpaper patterns can create a sense of depth, smoothness, or roughness, even though the texture is only visual and cannot be felt.

PRACTICE AND APPLY

Have students search online for other images created by Julian Beever. Have them tell how the artist uses the design elements you discussed to help create the illusion of reality. Students can compare and contrast two of Beever's other drawings using an interactive Comparison-Contrast Chart to list the ways the visual techniques are used in each drawing.

INTERACTIVE GRAPHIC ORGANIZER Have students use this Interactive Graphic Organizer: **Comparison-Contrast Chart**

Analyze Diverse Media

SL 2

RETEACH

Remind students that artists create art with an audience in mind. Point out that the **audience** is the person or group of people who will view an artist's work. Perhaps most often, the audience comes to a museum to see the art. But in some cases, like with Julian Beever's art, artists seek out a different audience.

Point out that artists, like writers, have **messages** they want to convey. Writers use words to convey their messages, but artists use design elements to convey their messages.

Discuss the following descriptions of pieces of art. Have students identify the likely audience and message:

- an outdoor sculpture of a baseball player in front of a ballpark
- a painting of a beautiful mountain in a museum
- a mural of a community working together on the wall of a city building

CLOSE VIEWING APPLICATION

Students can apply the skill to other works of art. Have them work independently to find other examples of different forms of visual art online, including paintings, computer-rendered artwork, sculpture, and mixed media installations. Ask: *Who is the artist's audience? What message does the artist want to convey to viewers?*

*my*SmartPlanner   Create lesson plans and access resources online.

Another Place, Another Time

Short Story by Cory Doctorow

Why This Text?

When students understand the elements of fiction, they can analyze and discuss literature—a skill that will serve them in school, when they read for enjoyment, and when they view and discuss movies and television shows. This lesson explores the elements of character, setting, and symbolism in a science fiction story.

Key Learning Objective: The student will be able to identify and analyze how setting affects characters' traits, motivations, and actions.

 COMMON CORE

Common Core Standards

RL 1 Cite text evidence.
RL 2 Determine a theme and provide a summary.
RL 3 Analyze interactions among story elements.
RL 4 Determine word meaning; analyze impact of repeated sounds.
RL 5 Analyze how structure contributes to meaning.
W 9a Apply grade 7 reading standards to literature.
L 2b Use correct spelling.
L 4a Use context as a clue to the meaning of a word or phrase.
L 4c Consult general and specialized reference materials.
L 5b Use the relationship between particular words to understand each of the words.
L 6 Gather vocabulary knowledge.

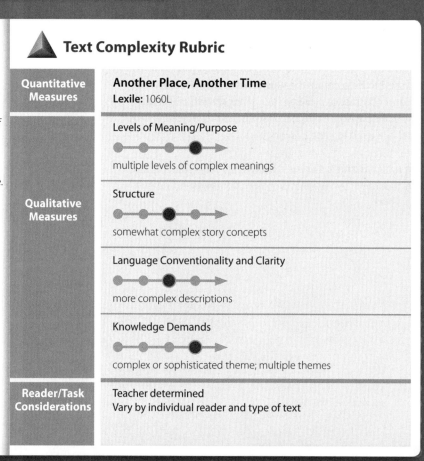

Text Complexity Rubric

Quantitative Measures	**Another Place, Another Time** **Lexile:** 1060L
Qualitative Measures	**Levels of Meaning/Purpose** multiple levels of complex meanings
	Structure somewhat complex story concepts
	Language Conventionality and Clarity more complex descriptions
	Knowledge Demands complex or sophisticated theme; multiple themes
Reader/Task Considerations	Teacher determined Vary by individual reader and type of text

Background Have students read the background and information about the author. Explain that this short story is featured in a collection of stories titled *The Chronicles of Harris Burdick*. The collection is based on a series of text-free illustrations by Chris Van Allsburg, titled *The Mysteries of Harris Burdick*. The illustration that served as the basis of "Another Place, Another Time" is featured on page 102 in the student edition. If students enjoy this selection, suggest that they explore *The Chronicles of Harris Burdick* for further reading or *The Mysteries of Harris Burdick* to inspire their own imaginations and their own writing projects.

SETTING A PURPOSE Direct students to use the Setting a Purpose prompt to focus their reading. In addition, remind students to generate questions as they read.

Analyze Story Elements: Character (LINES 1–7)

 COMMON CORE RL 3

Explain to students that one story element can often reveal information about another story element. For instance, **setting,** the time and place of the action, can influence the **characters,** the people, animals, or other creatures who take part in the story. In this section, the character Gilbert's interpretation of each setting reveals much about him.

Ⓐ ASK STUDENTS to reread the first paragraph, identify the different settings that Gilbert is thinking of, and discuss what these settings reveal about Gilbert. *(Time flies by for Gilbert when he is in the summer garden setting, playing with his friends. This shows he is fun-loving and playful. Time crawls slowly by when he is waiting for his father's return in the winter setting of the beach at the bottom of the cliffs. This shows Gilbert loves his father, but he is lonely without his father.)*

Background *When* **Cory Doctorow** *(b. 1971) first saw the movie Star Wars at the age of six, he was inspired to rewrite the entire story as a self-made book. The movie sparked his desire to be a science fiction writer. Publishing his first story at 17, Doctorow has since produced many science fiction novels, short stories, and magazine articles. The author has an online presence as a blogger and makes most of his books available online for free.*

Another Place, Another Time

Short Story by Cory Doctorow

SETTING A PURPOSE Science-based ideas are important in this story. As you read, think of the significance of these ideas to the characters—especially to Gilbert.

Gilbert hated time. What a tyrant it was! The hours that crawled by when his father was at sea, the seconds that whipped past when he was playing a brilliant game in the garden with the Limburgher children. The eternity it took for summer to arrive at the beach at the bottom of the cliffs, the flashing instant before the winter stole over them again and Father took to the sea once more.

"You can't hate *time*," Emmy said. The oldest of the three Limburghers and the only girl, she was used to talking
10 younger boys out of their foolishness. "It's just *time*."

Gilbert stopped pacing the tree house floor and pointed a finger at her. "That's where you're wrong!" He thumped the book he'd taken out of his father's bookcase, a book fetched

 Ⓐ

Another Place, Another Time **93**

SCAFFOLDING FOR ELL STUDENTS

Analyze Language Have students reread the first two sentences of the story. Explain that time is an important idea in the story, but it is presented in ways that students might not be familiar with. Discuss what students know and think of time. Then discuss how in different situations time seems to move slowly or quickly.

ASK STUDENTS When you are playing an exciting game, does time go quickly or slowly? Why? *(It goes quickly because I'm having fun.)* When you are very hungry and waiting for dinner, does time go quickly or slowly? Why? *(It goes slowly because I'm hungry and want to eat right away.)*

Analyze Story Elements: RL 3
Character (LINES 31–44)

Explain to students that all stories have a **main character,** the character whose problem or goal drives the plot. Point out that authors often reveal information about characters by showing how they interact with each other.

Ⓑ **CITE TEXT EVIDENCE** Ask students to reread lines 31–44 and identify the main character and the problem that is being explained. Ask them to cite evidence from the text that reveals his state of mind here and what the other characters may think about him. *(The main character is Gilbert. As he struggles to explain his ideas to Emmy and the twins, their reactions show that they are at first frustrated with him. Emmy and Gilbert are both smart, but Gilbert can frustrate his friends with his ideas.)*

CRITICAL VOCABULARY

eloquence: The author uses the word *eloquence* to describe Emmy as she rolls her eyes.

ASK STUDENTS if Emmy's earlier reply to Gilbert, "That's stupid," would be an example of eloquence. Why? *(No. Eloquence suggests a way of speaking or acting that is effective and persuasive, but Emmy's words seem harsh and confrontational.)*

---

home from London, heavy and well made and swollen with the damp air of the sea-crossing home to America. He hadn't read the book, but his tutor, sour Señor Uriarte, had explained it to him the day before while he was penned up inside, watching summer whiz past the study's windows. "Time isn't just time! Time is also space! It's also a dimension." Gilbert
20 thumped the book again for emphasis, then opened it to the page he'd marked with a wide blade of sawgrass.

"See this? This is a point. That's one dimension. It doesn't have length or depth. It's just a dot. When you add another dimension, you get *lines.*" He pointed at the next diagram with a chewed and dirty fingernail. "You can go back and you can go forward, you can move around on the surface, as though the world were a page. But you can't go up and down, not until you add another dimension." He pointed to the diagram of the cube, stabbing at it so hard, his finger dented the page. "That's
30 three dimensions, up and down, side to side, and in and out."

Emmy rolled her eyes with the **eloquence** of a thirteen-year-old girl whose tutor had already explained all this to her. Gilbert smiled. Em would always be a year older than he was, but that didn't mean he would always be dumber than she was.

"And Mr. Einstein, who is the smartest man in the whole history of the world, he has proved—absolutely *proved*—that time is just *another dimension*, just like space. Time is what happens when you can go up and down, side to side, in and
40 out, and *before and after.*"

Em opened her mouth and closed it. Her twin brothers, Erwin and Neils, snickered at the sight of their sister struck dumb. She glared at them, then at Gilbert. "That's stupid," she said.

"You're calling *Einstein* stupid?"

"Of course not. But you must not understand him properly. Space is space. Time is time. Everyone knows that."

Gilbert pretended he hadn't heard her. "But here's the part no one knows: why can we move through space in any
50 direction—"

"You can't go up!" Em said, quickly.

"You got up into my tree house," he said, putting a small emphasis on *my.* "And you could go back *down,* too."

eloquence
(ĕl′ə-kwəns) *n.* If someone behaves or speaks with *eloquence*, he or she uses persuasive, powerful expression.

APPLYING ACADEMIC VOCABULARY

abnormal	feature	focus

As you discuss the characters and settings in "Another Place, Another Time," incorporate the following Collection 2 academic vocabulary words: *feature, focus,* and *abnormal.* Ask students how characters change when **features** of the setting change. Ask students how the author keeps the reader's **focus** on the element of time. Finally, ask students how the **abnormal** events toward the end of the story allow new insight into the characters.

Emmy, who was a better fighter than any of them, put her fists on her hips and mimed *Make me*. He pretended he didn't see it.

"Why can we move through space in *almost* any direction, but time only goes in one direction, at one speed? Why can't we go faster? Slower? Backwards?"

60 "Sideways?" Neils said. He didn't speak often, but when he did, what he said was usually surprising.

"What's sideways in time?" his twin asked.

Neils shrugged. "Sideways is sideways."

"This is dumb," Emmy declared, but Gilbert could see that she was getting into the spirit of the thing—starting to understand how it had made him all so angry.

Outside Gilbert's house the summer roared past like a three-masted schooner before a gale,[1] with all sails bellied out. Inside the study, the hours crawled by. And then, in between, there
70 were the breakfasts and dinners with Gilbert's father, who was home for the summer, whose kind eyes were set into an ever-growing net of wrinkles and bags, who returned from his winter voyages each year a little thinner, a little more frail.

"And what did you learn today, my boy?" he said, as he tucked in to the mountain of lentils and beans made by the housekeeper, Mrs. Curie (who was so old that she had actually once served as Father's nanny and changed his diapers, which always made Gilbert giggle when he thought of it). Father was a strict vegetarian and swore by his diet's life-enhancing
80 properties, though that didn't seem to stop him from growing older and older and older.

Gilbert stopped fussing with his lentils, which he didn't like very much. "Geography," he said, looking at his plate. "We're doing the lowlands." He looked out at the sunset, the sun racing for the other side of the planet, dragging them all back toward the winter. "Belgium. Belgium, Belgium, Belgium."

His father laughed and smacked his hands on his thighs. "Belgium! Poor lad. I've been **marooned** there once or twice.
90 Land of bankers and cheese-makers. Like hitting your head, Belgium, because it feels so good when you stop. What else?"

maroon
(mə-roōn´) *v.* To *maroon* is to abandon or leave someone in a place that is hard to get away from.

[1] **three-masted schooner before a gale:** a vessel with three sails, moving fast because of a forceful wind.

CLOSE READ

Determine Meaning of Words and Phrases

COMMON CORE RL 1, RL 4

(LINES 82–87)

Explain to students that a **symbol** is a person, a place, an object, or an activity that stands for something beyond itself. Point out that throughout the story, the author uses different symbols to emphasize time's significance to Gilbert. Also point out that, often, symbols are open to interpretation. Two different readers might determine that the same symbol represents two different things, but as long as an interpretation is supported in the text and makes sense within the story, the interpretation can be valid.

C CITE TEXT EVIDENCE Have students reread lines 82–87 and identify a symbol that suggests the passing of time. Ask them to use text evidence to explain what it reveals about Gilbert. *(The sunset is a symbol that suggests time passing. Gilbert seems to be struggling with the idea of time—and his inability to control it. The idea that the sun is "dragging them all back toward winter" shows that he is concerned with the passing of time, as winter means his father will leave.)*

CRITICAL VOCABULARY

maroon: Gilbert's father was marooned in Belgium.

ASK STUDENTS to describe what it might feel like to be marooned somewhere. When might Gilbert feel marooned? *(Being marooned is probably lonely and frightening. Gilbert might feel marooned when he has to study on beautiful days.)*

Strategies for Annotation 🖊 📋 *Annotate it!*

Determine Meaning of Words and Phrases

COMMON CORE RL 4

Have students reread lines 82–87. Encourage them to use their eBook annotation tools to do the following:

- Highlight in yellow the details that suggest a symbol of time.
- Underline details that reveal Gilbert's feelings.
- Write a note to describe what the symbol reveals about Gilbert.

"We're doing the lowlands." He looked out at the sunset, the

sun racing for the other side of the planet, 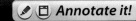 dragging them

all back toward the winter. "Belgium. Belgium, Belgium

Belgium."

> Gilbert feels dread about the coming winter, so he is unhappy about time moving too quickly.

Analyze Story Elements: Character (LINES 94–122)

COMMON CORE RL 1, RL 3

Explain to students that authors use many techniques to give readers an understanding of each character's **character traits**—the qualities shown by a character. Point out that a character trait might be physical, such as eye color, or a trait could be an expression of personality, such as shyness. Point out that one way to show a character's traits is through **dialogue,** or the words that the character and other characters speak.

 CITE TEXT EVIDENCE Have students reread lines 94–122 and cite evidence in the text that reveals some of Gilbert's and his father's character traits. *(Gilbert's words show him to be inquisitive and focused on his struggle with time. His father seems patient and loving, as he listens, asks questions, and even adds more information for Gilbert to think about. This reveals a loving relationship. The author also describes a physical character trait of Gilbert's father—"furry eyebrows.")*

CRITICAL VOCABULARY

judicious: Gilbert's father is listening to Gilbert go on and on about time—a topic that Gilbert is clearly obsessed with.

ASK STUDENTS why Gilbert's father nods judiciously when Gilbert talks about his tutor. *(Gilbert is trying to get his father to take his side. His father responds to him in a fair, even way, showing he understands Gilbert's concern while respecting the tutor's authority.)*

"I *want* to do more physics, but Señor says I don't have the math for it."

His father nodded **judiciously**. "He would know. Why physics?"

"Time," he said, simply. They'd talked of time all summer, in those few hours when Gilbert wasn't with his tutor and when Father wasn't sitting at his desk working at his accounts, or riding into town to huddle over the telephone, casting his
100 will over place and time, trying to keep his ships and their cargos in proper and correct motion.

"Why time, Gil? You're eleven, son! You've got lots of time! You can worry about time when you're an old man."

Gilbert pretended he hadn't heard. "I was thinking of more ways that time is like space. If I was at sea, standing on the deck of a ship, I could see a certain ways before me, and if I turned around, I could see a small ways behind me. But the horizon cuts off the view in both directions. Time is like that. I can think back a certain ways, and the further back I
110 try to remember, the fuzzier it gets, until I can't see at all. And I can see forward—we'll have cobbler soon, go to bed, wake tomorrow. But no further."

His father raised his furry eyebrows and smiled a genuine and delighted smile. "Ah, but things separated by time affect each other the way that events separated by space can't. A star dying on the other side of the universe, so far away that its light hasn't yet had time enough to crawl all the way to us, can't have any effect on us. But things that happened hundreds of years ago, like the planting of the seed that grew the oak
120 that made this table . . ." He rattled his saucer on it, making his coffee sway like a rough chop. He waggled his eyebrows again.

"Yikes," Gilbert said. That hadn't occurred to him. "What if time moved in every direction and at every speed—could you have a space where events at the far end of the galaxy affected us?" He answered his own question. "Of course. Because the events could travel backwards in time—or, uh . . ." He fumbled, remembered Neils. "Sideways." He swallowed.

"What's sideways in time?"
130 He shrugged. "Sideways is sideways," he said.

judicious
(jōō-dĭsh´əs) *adv.* If you are *judicious*, you have good judgment.

> ## WHAT IF TIME MOVED IN EVERY DIRECTION AND AT EVERY SPEED?

His father laughed until tears rolled down his cheeks, and Gilbert didn't have the heart to tell him that the phrase had been Neils's, because making his father laugh like that was like Christmas and his birthday and a day at the beach all rolled into one.

And then his father took him down to the ocean, down the rough goat trail cut into the cliff, as surefooted as a goat himself. They watched the sun disappear behind the waves, and then they moved among the tidepools, swirling their

140 hands in the warm, salty water to make the bioluminescent[2] speck-size organisms light up like fireworks. They sat out and watched the moon and the stars, lying on their backs in the sand, Gilbert's head in the crook of his father's arm, and he closed his eyes and let his father tell him stories about the sea and the places he went in the long, lonely winters, while the waves went *shhh, shhh,* like the whisper of the mother who'd died giving birth to him.

Then they picked their way back up the cliff by moonlight that was so bright, it might have been day, a blue-white noon

150 in shades of gray, and his father tucked him up into bed as if he were three years old, smoothing the covers and kissing him on the forehead with a whiskery kiss.

As he lay along a moment that stretched sleepily out like warm taffy, suspended on the edge of sleep, the thought occurred to him: *What if space moved in only one direction, in two dimensions, like time?*

---

[2] **bioluminescent** (bī´ō-lōō´mə-nĕs´ənt): visible light, caused by chemical reactions, that emits from a living organism.

CLOSE READ

Analyze Story Elements: Character (LINES 131–135)

 COMMON CORE RL 1, RL 3

Explain that a **character's motivation** is the reason for a character's behavior.

E **CITE TEXT EVIDENCE** Have students reread lines 131–135 and cite details that reveal one of Gilbert's motivations. *(Gilbert loves to make his father laugh. It shows how deeply he loves his father. He feels safe and cared for with his father.)*

Determine Meaning of Words and Phrases

 COMMON CORE RL 4

(LINES 136-147)

Explain to students that an author sometimes uses a **simile**—a figure of speech that makes a comparison between two unlike things using the word *like* or *as*—to make explicit comparisons.

F **ASK STUDENTS** how the author used a simile to reveal the sea as a symbol. *(Gilbert is sad at this moment, thinking about his father's imminent departure. But the author is using the sea as a symbol for Gilbert's lost mother, calming him.)*

Strategies for Annotation   🖊 🗐 *Annotate it!*

Analyze Story Elements: Character

COMMON CORE RL 3

Have students reread lines 131–135. Encourage them to use their eBook annotation tools to do the following:

- Underline clues that reveal his father's character traits.
- Highlight the details that reveal Gilbert's motivations.
- Describe Gilbert's character traits when he is in his father's presence. *(Gilbert feels happy and secure.)*

His father laughed until tears rolled down his cheeks, and

Gilbert didn't have the heart to tell him that the phrase had

been Neils's, because making his father laugh like that was like

Christmas and his birthday and a day at the beach all rolled

into one.

CLOSE READ

Determine Meaning of Words and Phrases

COMMON CORE RL 1, RL 4

(LINES 157–171)

Emphasize for students that the author repeatedly describes the weather in this passage and that weather is often used in fiction to create different kinds of **moods**, or the feelings or atmosphere that a writer creates for the reader.

Ⓖ CITE TEXT EVIDENCE Have students reread lines 157–171 and identify references to weather. Ask them to describe the effect the weather has on the setting and on Gilbert. *(References to weather: "while the wind and rain howled outside the window" and "adding logs against the unseasonal winds outside." The author uses the unseasonably cold, turbulent weather to symbolize that something is not quite right. This aspect of the setting creates a mood of dread—that perhaps something bad is about to happen.)*

WHEN STUDENTS STRUGGLE...

To guide students' understanding of the author's use of weather as a symbol, have students work in pairs to fill out a chart like the one shown. Explain that the chart will help them identify ways that the author uses symbols to reveal information about the plot. Have pairs fill in the chart as they read and discuss how the details help identify symbols.

The year passed. For so long as Gilbert could remember, summer's first messenger had been the postmaster, Mr. Ossinger, who rode his bicycle along the sea road to the house
160 to deliver his father's telegram advising of his expected arrival in port and the preparations to be made for him. Mrs. Curie usually signed for the letter, then knocked on the study door to deliver it into Gilbert's eager hands.

But this year, while the wind and rain howled outside the window, and Señor Uriarte plodded through the formation of igneous rock,[3] Mrs. Curie did not come and deliver the letter, rescuing him from geography. She didn't come to the door, though Señor had finished rocks and moved on to algebra and then to Shakespeare. Finally, the school day ended. Gilbert left
170 Señor stirring through the coals of the study fire, adding logs against the unseasonal winds outside.

Gilbert floated downstairs to the kitchen as though trapped in a dream that compelled him to seek out the housekeeper, even though some premonition told him to hide away in his room for as long as possible.

From behind, she seemed normal, her thin shoulders working as she beat at the batter for the night's cake, cranking the mixer's handle with slow, practiced turns. But when the door clicked shut behind him, she stopped working the
180 beater, though her shoulders kept working, shuddering, rising, falling. She turned her face to him and he let out a cry and took a step back toward the door. It was as though she had been caught by an onrush of time, one that had aged her, turning her from an old woman to an animated corpse. Every wrinkle seemed to have sunk deeper, her fine floss hair hung limp across her forehead, her eyes were red and leaked steady rills of tears.

She took a step toward him, and he wanted to turn and run, but now he was frozen. So he stood, rooted to the
190 spot, while she came and took him up in her frail arms and clutched at him, sobbing dry, raspy sobs. "He's not coming home," she whispered into his ear, the whiskers on her chin tickling at him. "He's not coming home, Gilbert. Oh, oh, oh." He held her and patted her and the time around him seemed to crawl by, slow enough that he could visualize every sweet moment he'd had with his father, time enough to visualize

---

[3] **igneous rock** (ĭg´nē-əs rŏk): rock formed when melted rock, called magma, cools and solidifies above or below the earth.

Detail	What it reveals
But this year, the wind and rain howled outside.	*Unlike past happier summers, the weather suggests something bad. It seems to represent darkness and death.*

every storm his father had ever narrated to him. Had all that time and more before Señor Uriarte came downstairs for his tea and found them in the kitchen. He gathered up frozen
200 Gilbert and carried him to his bedroom, removed his shoes, and sat with him for hours until he finally slept.

When morning dawned, the storm had lifted. Gilbert went to his window to see the stupid blue sky with its awful yellow sun and realized that his father was now gone forever and ever, to the end of time.

Emmy and her brothers were queasy of him for the first week of summer, playing with him as though he were made of china or tainted with plague. But by the second week, they were back to something like normal, scampering up the trees and down
210 the cliffs, ranging farther and farther afield on their bicycles.

Most of all, they were playing down at the switchyards, the old rail line that ran out from the disused freight docks a few miles down the beach from their houses. Señor and Mrs. Curie didn't know what to do with him that summer, lacking any direction from Father, and so Gilbert made the most of it, taking the Limburghers out on longer and longer trips, their packs bursting with food and water and useful tools: screwdrivers, crowbars, cans of oil.

Someone probably owned the switchyard, but whoever
220 that was, he was far away and had shown no interest in it in Gilbert's lifetime. It had been decades since the freighters came into this harbor and freight trains had taken their cargos off into the land on the rusted rails. The rusted padlocks on the utility sheds crumbled and fell to bits at the lightest touch from the crowbars; the doors squealed open on their ancient hinges.

Inside, the cobwebby, musty gloom yielded a million treasures: old time-tables, a telegraph rig, stiff denim coveralls with material as thick as the hall carpet at home, ancient
230 whiskey bottles, a leather-bound journal that went to powder when they touched it, and . . .

A handcar.[4]

"It'll never work," said Emmy. "That thing's older than the dinosaurs. It's practically rusted through!"

---

[4] **handcar:** a small, open railroad car that is propelled by a hand pump.

CLOSE READ

Analyze Story Elements: Character (LINES 211–231)

COMMON CORE **RL 3**

Reiterate for students that characters often behave differently in different settings. In addition, children behave differently when adults are not present, compared with when they are.

H **ASK STUDENTS** how the characters' freedom from adult supervision affects their behavior? How does Gilbert "make the most of" this time in his life? *(The children are very brave, and they take actions, such as breaking into the utility sheds, that they would probably not take if adults were present. Gilbert takes advantage of this time by adventuring away from home farther and for longer periods of time.)*

Make Inferences (LINES 230–232)

COMMON CORE **RL 1**

Explain to students that authors use many techniques to emphasize important ideas, such as setting ideas apart from the rest of the text. Students can use this textual evidence to support inferences, or good guesses, about information that is not directly stated in the text.

I **CITE TEXT EVIDENCE** Ask students to identify how the author sets apart text in this section. What inference about the handcar does this text evidence support? *(By placing the first mention of the handcar on another line preceded by an unfinished line, the author shows it will be important. It's likely that the handcar will be a significant story element.)*

Analyze Story Elements: Character (LINES 235–249)

COMMON CORE RL 1, RL 3

Explain to students that sometimes authors explicitly describe a character's traits. More often, however, they provide evidence of character traits and expect readers to **infer,** or make good guesses about, them.

J CITE TEXT EVIDENCE Have students reread the section and identify ways in which the author shows that the children are determined. *(Gilbert keeps trying to move the handcar, while the other children watch. He moves it a little at a time. Each time gives him more hope. He applies oil. Emmy "leans in" and "doesn't mind" that the car almost crushes her foot. They are all staring at the car "as if to say, 'Where have you been all my life?'" This shows they are drawn to it and determined to get it going.)*

Gilbert pretended he hadn't heard her. He wished he could move the car a little closer to the grimy windows. It was almost impossible to make sense of in the deep shadows of the shed. He pushed hard on the handle, putting his weight into it. It gave a groan, a squeal, and another groan. Then it moved
240 an inch. That was a magic inch! He got his oilcan and lavishly applied the forty-weight oil to every bearing he could find. Neils and Erwin held the lamp. Emmy leaned in closer. He pushed the handle again. Another groan, and a much higher squeal, and the handle sank under his weight. The handcar rumbled forward, almost crushing Emmy's foot—if she hadn't been so quick to leap back, she'd have been crippled. She didn't seem to mind. She, her brothers, and Gilbert were all staring at the handcar as if to say, "Where have you been all my life?"

> **"THE HANDCAR RUMBLED FORWARD, ALMOST CRUSHING EMMY'S FOOT."**

250 They christened it *Kalamazoo* and they worked with oil and muscle until they had moved it right up to the doorway. It cut their fingers to ribbons and turned their shins into fields of bruises, but it was all worth it because of what it promised: motion without end.

The track in the switchyard went in two directions. Inland, toward the nation and its hurrying progress and its infinite hunger for materials and blood and work. And out to sea, stretching out on a rockbed across the harbor, to the breakers where the great boats that were too large for
260 the shallow harbor used to tie up to offload. Once they had bullied *Kalamazoo* onto the tracks—using blocks, winches, levers, and a total disregard for their own safety—they stood to either side of its bogey handle and stared from side to side. Each knew what the others were thinking: Do we pump for the land, or pump for the sea?

"Tomorrow," Gilbert said. It was the end of August now, and lessons would soon begin again, and each day felt like something was drawing to a close. "Tomorrow," Gilbert said. "We'll decide tomorrow. Bring supplies."

That night, by unspoken agreement, they all packed their treasures. Gilbert laid out his sailor suit—his father bought him a new one every year—and his book about time and space and stuffed a picnic blanket with Mrs. Curie's preserves, hardtack bread, jars of lemonade, and apples from the cellar. Mrs. Curie—three quarters deaf—slept through his raid. Gilbert then went to his father's study and took the **spyglass** that had belonged to his grandfather, who had also been lost at sea. He opened the small oak box holding Grandad's **sextant**, but as he'd never mastered it, he set it down. He took his father's enormous silver-chased[5] turnip watch, and tried on his rain boots and discovered that they fit. The last time he'd tried them on, he could have gotten both feet into one of them. Time had passed without his noticing, but his feet had noticed.

He hauled the bundles out to the hedgerow at the bottom of the driveway, and then he put himself to bed and in an instant he was asleep. An instant later, the sun was shining on his face. He woke, put on his sailor suit, went downstairs, and shouted hello to Mrs. Curie, who smiled a misty smile to see him in his sailor suit. She gave him hotcakes with butter and cherries from the tree behind Señor's shed, a glass of milk and a mountain of fried potatoes. He ate until his stomach wouldn't hold any more, said goodbye to her, and walked to the bottom of the hedgerow to retrieve his secret bundle. He wrestled it into his bike's basket and wobbled down to the Limburghers' gate to meet his friends, each with a bundle and a bike.

The half-hour ride to the switchyard took so little time that it was over even before Gilbert had a chance to think about what he was doing. Time was going by too fast for thoughts now, like a train that had hit its speed and could now only be perceived as a blur of passing cars and a racket of wheels and steam.

spyglass
(spī´glăs´) n. A spyglass is a small telescope.

sextant
(sĕk´stənt) n. A sextant is an instrument used to determine location by measuring the position of the stars and sun.

---

[5] **silver-chased:** Silver-chasing is a technique used in engraving silver. The silver is moved, rather than removed, with a small pointed tool and mallet to create a design or texture.

TEACH

CLOSE READ

Analyze Story Elements: Character (LINES 270–284)
COMMON CORE RL 3

Remind students that things rarely "just happen" in literature. Authors show things happening and characters doing things either to advance the plot or to give us insight regarding character traits and character motivations.

K **ASK STUDENTS** to reread lines 270–284 and determine Gilbert's motivation for bringing each item. Were his motivations purely practical, or did he bring any of the items for sentimental reasons? *(The practical items that Gilbert takes include the picnic blanket full of food, the spyglass, and the turnip watch. The food will nourish him on his journey. The watch will help him keep track of time. The spyglass will help him see where he is going. However, the watch, spyglass, and sailor suit also have sentimental value. They are symbols of his lost father (sailor suit and watch) and grandfather (spyglass). So, his motivations are not purely practical. He wants to bring his father's memory with him.)*

CRITICAL VOCABULARY

spyglass: Gilbert brings "the spyglass that had belonged to his grandfather, who had also been lost at sea."

ASK STUDENTS to explain why the author might have chosen to use the term *spyglass* instead of the term *telescope*. *(Spyglass is more old-fashioned, underscoring the object's connection to the past, and making it another symbol of time.)*

sextant: Gilbert chose not to bring his grandfather's sextant because he had never learned to use it.

ASK STUDENTS why a sextant might have been helpful had Gilbert taken it. *(He would have been able to figure out his location during the journey.)*

TEACH

CLOSE READ

102 Collection 2

WHEN STUDENTS STRUGGLE . . .

Students may be unfamiliar with what a *handcar* is. Explain that in this particular story, there are two significant clues that can help them clarify the meaning. Have students reread the footnote for the word *handcar*, on page 99 of the Student Edition. Then, have them use the illustration to further clarify the meaning.

Kalamazoo was still beaded with dew as they began to unload their bundles onto its platform. Gilbert set his down at the end farthest from the sea, and Emmy set hers down at the end farthest from the land, and when they stood to either side of the pump handle, it was clear that Emmy wanted to push for the land while Gilbert wanted to push them out to sea.
310 Naturally.

Emmy looked at Gilbert and Gilbert looked at Emmy. Gilbert took out his grandfather's spyglass, lifted off the leather cap from the business end, extended it, and pointed it out to sea, sweeping from side to side, looking farther than he'd ever seen. Wordlessly, he held it out to Emmy, who turned around to face the bay and swept it with the telescope. Then she handed it off to Neils and Erwin, who took their turns.

Nothing more had to be said. They leaned together into the stiff lever that controlled *Kalamazoo's* direction of travel,
320 threw it into position, and set to pumping out to sea.

What the spyglass showed: waves and waves, and waves and waves, and, farther along, the curvature of the planet itself as it warped toward Europe and Africa and the rest of the world. It showed a spit of land, graced with an ancient and crumbling sea fort, shrouded in mist and overgrown with the weeds and trees of long disuse. And beyond it, waves and more waves.

The gentle sea breeze turned into a stiff wind once they'd pumped for an hour, the handcart at first rolling slowly on the complaining wheels. Then, as the rust flaked off the axles
330 and the bearings found their old accommodations, they spun against one another easily. The pumping was still hard work, and even though they traded off, the children soon grew tired and sore and Emmy called for a rest stop and a snack.

As they munched their sandwiches, Gilbert had a flash. "We could use this for a sail," he said, nudging his picnic blanket with one toe. Neils and Erwin—whose shorter arms suffered more from the pumping labor—loved the idea, and set to rigging a mast from their fishing poles and the long crowbar they'd lashed to *Kalamazoo's* side. Emmy and Gilbert
340 let them do the work, watching with the wisdom of age, eating sandwiches and enjoying the breeze that dried their sweat.

CLOSE READ

Determine Meaning of Words and Phrases

 COMMON CORE RL 1, RL 4

(LINES 304–310)

Explain to students that here the author is using the land and sea both as symbols and as literal destinations to establish what Gilbert wants.

L CITE TEXT EVIDENCE Have students reread lines 304–310. Ask them to identify what Emmy and Gilbert each want at this moment, while keeping in mind that Emmy is the older of the two. Then ask students to explain what this may reveal about the significance of the symbols of the land and the sea in this story. *(Emmy is older and perhaps more responsible. She chooses land, as it seems to represent the safety of the adult world—a place of "hurrying progress and infinite hunger" and a place of "work," as indicated earlier in the story. Gilbert wants to go to the sea, a symbol of the lost love of his parents, of the adventures and imagination of childhood.)*

Analyze Story Elements: Character (LINES 321–333)

 COMMON CORE RL 3

Explain to students that both the spyglass and the handcar are tools that help the children see and set their course very clearly. They use each to change their setting.

M ASK STUDENTS to reread this passage and tell how the settings of the handcar and the sea ahead of them help focus the children's motivation. *(They all want to head for the infinite possibilities of the sea on the handcar that moves more and more easily, even though it is tiring work. Through the spyglass they see the infinite waves and the last signs of the finite world— an ancient, decaying fort.)*

As they started up again, *Kalamazoo* seemed as refreshed from the rest as they were, and it rolled more easily than ever, the sail bellied out before the mast. When Gilbert and Emmy stopped to trade pumping duties back to the twins, *Kalamazoo* continued to roll, propelled by the stiff wind alone. All four children made themselves comfortable at the back of the pump car and allowed the time and the space to whip past them as they would.

350 "We're moving through space like time," Gilbert said.

Emmy quirked her mouth at him, a familiar no-nonsense look that he ignored.

"We are," he said. "We are moving in a straight line, from behind to in front, at a rate we can't control. Off to the sides are spaces we could move through, but we're not. We're on these rails, and we can't go sideways, can't go back, can't go up or down. We can't control our speed. We are space's slaves. This is just how we move through time."

Emmy shook her head. Neils seemed excited by the idea, 360 though, and he nudged his twin and they muttered in their curious twinnish dialect to one another.

The sea fort was visible with the naked eye now, and with the spyglass, Gilbert could make out its brickwork and the streaks of guano that ran down its cracked walls. The rails ran right up to the fort—last used as a customs inspection point— and past it to the hidden docks on the other side of the spit.

"Better hope that the wind shifts," Emmy said, holding a wetted finger up to check the breeze.

"Otherwise we're going to have a devil of a time pumping 370 ourselves home in time for supper."

Gilbert drew out the turnip watch, which he'd set this morning by the big grandfather clock in the front hall, carefully winding its spring. He opened its face and checked the second hand. It seemed to be spinning a little more slowly, but that could have been his imagination. According to the watch, it was nearly eleven, and they'd been on the rails for three hours.

"I think we'll make the fort in time for lunch," he said.

At the mention of food, Neils and Erwin clamored for 380 snacks, and Emmy found them cookies she'd snitched from the big jar in the Limburgher kitchen.

TO CHALLENGE STUDENTS ...

Analyzing Theme What is Gilbert's take on time? Corey Doctorow has Gilbert explain how time is a fourth dimension, as laid out in the theories of scientist Albert Einstein. Doctorow himself has said that he had difficulty grasping all the science in this story, so he consulted real scientists while he wrote it. Suggest that students briefly research student-friendly online sources on Einstein's theories of relativity and what they say about time. Then have students work in small groups to discuss Gilbert's grasp of the theory and how his explanation early in the story plays out in the events at the end.

Gilbert looked at the watch for a moment. The second hand had stopped moving. He held it up to his ear, and it wasn't precisely ticking any longer, but rather making a sound like a truck-wheel spinning in spring mud. He closed the lid again, and held it so tight that the intricate scrolling on the case dug into his palm.

Time passed.

And then it didn't.

390 And then it did again.

"Oh!" said Neils and Erwin together.

> " GILBERT LOOKED AT THE WATCH FOR A MOMENT. THE SECOND HAND HAD STOPPED MOVING. "

To either side of the car, stretching into infinity, were more tracks, running across the endless harbor, each with its own car, its own sail, its own children. Some were edging ahead of them. Some were going backwards. A racket overhead had them all look up at once, at the tracks there, too, the rails and the cars and the Limburghers and the Gilberts in them. Some children were older. Some were younger. One Gilbert was weeping. One was a girl.

400 Gilbert waved his hand, and a hundred Gilberts waved back. One made a rude gesture.

"Oh!" said Emmy. To her right, another Emmy was offering her a sandwich. She took it and handed over the last of her cookies and Emmy smiled at herself and said thank you as politely as you could wonder.

"Sideways is sideways," Neils and Erwin said together. Emmy and Gilbert nodded.

CLOSE READ

Analyze Story Elements: Character (LINES 392–407)

COMMON CORE RL 3

Suddenly, the setting changes significantly—to a different reality. The children are still safely on the handcar, but around them, everything extends to infinity.

N **CITE TEXT EVIDENCE** Have students reread lines 392–407 and discuss the effect that the change in setting has on the children. Ask how each child reacts and what that reveals about him or her. *(The children seem unfazed but happy to see the strange sights around them. Gilbert waves to the other children, including duplicates of his grieving self and his feminine self. Emmy also seems happy as she accepts the cookie and smiles to herself. The twins stay constant, repeating the same line that they had earlier in the story.)*

Strategies for Annotation 🖊 📖 Annotate it!

Analyze Story Elements: Character

COMMON CORE RL 3

Have students reread lines 400–405. Encourage them to use their eBook annotation tools to do the following:

- Underline any clues that show how the setting has changed.
- Highlight in yellow details that reveal how Gilbert and Emmy react.
- Write a note to describe Emmy and Gilbert's character traits.

Gilbert waved his hand, and a hundred Gilberts waved back. One made a rude gesture.

"Oh!" said Emmy. To her right, another Emmy was offering her a sandwich. She took it and handed over the last of her cookies and Emmy smiled at herself and said thank you as politely as you could wonder.

Gilbert is intrigued and happy.
Emmy is still polite but also happy.

Analyze Story Elements: **COMMON CORE** RL 3
Character (LINES 414–421)

In the end, Gilbert makes a bold move to leave the other children behind and set out on his own.

 CITE TEXT EVIDENCE Ask students to reread the last three paragraphs and identify what Gilbert does and explain what this action reveals about him. *(Gilbert has been on a mission to fulfill a dream—to break free of the tyranny of time. That has been his motivation. He now sees his chance to step into the timeless realm of infinite possibility. Emmy responds with a playful gesture, which shows she's like a supportive big sister. Gilbert leaps onto the other handcar. It is an easy leap. He remains a dreamer and a searcher—but this time, all on his own.)*

COLLABORATIVE DISCUSSION Have groups of students discuss Gilbert's interest in the dimension of time. Point out that Gilbert's interest in time is connected to Einstein's idea that the experience of time can be relative. For Gilbert, time is relative to events, actions, and settings—his experience of it varies as these elements change. Then have them share their ideas with the class as a whole. Accept all reasonable responses.

ASK STUDENTS to share any questions they generated in the course of reading and discussing the selection.

Gilbert pulled out his spyglass and looked ahead at the fort. All the rails converged on it, but without ever meeting. 410 And some stretched beyond. And out there, somewhere, there was time like space and space like time. And somewhere there was a father on a ship that weathered a storm rather than succumbed to it.

Gilbert turned to his friends and shook each of their hands in turn. Neils was crying a little. Emmy gave Gilbert a friendly punch in the shoulder and then a hug.

There was another *Kalamazoo* to the right, and Gilbert was pretty sure he could easily make the leap from his car to it. And then to the next car, and the next. And beyond, into 420 the infinite sideways.

If there was an answer, he'd find it there.

COLLABORATIVE DISCUSSION Why is Gilbert so interested in the dimension of time? Talk about your ideas with other group members. Discuss how time interacts with and changes Gilbert.

Analyze Story Elements: Character

COMMON CORE RL 3

The characters of "Another Place, Another Time" bring amazingly complex happenings down to a human level. **Characters** are the people, animals, or other creatures who take part in a story. A short story often has a **main character,** whose problem or goal drives the plot. The behavior and action of all the characters affects what happens. In addition, the **setting** of the story, or the time and place of the action, can affect the characters' traits, motivations, and actions.

When you analyze how characters act and change throughout a story, consider the chart below.

Character traits are the qualities shown by a character. Traits may be physical (blond hair) or expressions of personality (fearlessness).	The writer may directly state the character's traits, or you may have to infer traits based on the character's words, thoughts, actions, appearance, or relationships.
Character motivations are the reasons for a character's behavior.	To understand a character's obvious or hidden desires and goals, notice what makes the character take or avoid action.

Think about the main character, Gilbert, in "Another Place, Another Time." Use one or two words to describe his traits. How do the setting and events change him as the story unfolds?

Determine Meaning of Words and Phrases

COMMON CORE RL 4

A **symbol** is a person, a place, an object, or an activity that stands for something beyond itself. Often, a symbol represents an important idea or concept, such as freedom, love, or loneliness. For example, a dove is often a symbol of peace. Characters, objects, conflicts, and settings can serve as symbols for important ideas in a story.

You can identify symbols and determine their meanings by analyzing details in the text.

- Look for people, places, things, or actions that the writer emphasizes or mentions frequently.
- Think about the importance of these details to the characters.

The sea setting is a major feature in "Another Place, Another Time." The sea stands for at least one idea or feeling that is important to Gilbert. Reread lines 138–147 of the story. What might the sea represent for Gilbert here?

CLOSE READ

Analyze Story Elements: Character

COMMON CORE RL 3

Discuss the literary terms and what to consider when analyzing characters. Have volunteers identify the main character and other characters in the story. Then, discuss examples of the characters' traits, especially in different settings. Finally, discuss the main character's motivation and how Gilbert's pursuit of his goal changes him in the story.

Determine Meaning of Words and Phrases

COMMON CORE RL 4

Discuss the definition of the term *symbol*. Using familiar symbols in school, such as the flag, discuss what each represents. Then ask volunteers to identify symbols they encountered in the story, such as the symbol of the sea. Discuss what these symbols represent and how they make the story more compelling and satisfying to read.

Strategies for Annotation 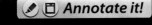 *Annotate it!*

Analyze Story Elements: Character

COMMON CORE RL 3

Share these strategies for guided or independent analysis:

- Highlight in yellow details about the setting that affect a character's motivations.
- Underline details that show characters taking action.
- On a note, jot down your insights regarding the character's motivations for taking the action.

"You got up into my tree house," he said, putting a small emphasis on *my*. "And you could go back *down*, too."

Emmy, who was a better fighter than any of them, put her fists on her hips and mimed *Make me*. He pretended he didn't see it.

PRACTICE & APPLY

Analyzing the Text

COMMON CORE RL 1, RL 2, RL 3, RL 4, RL 5

Possible answers:

1. *The title directly reveals the character's interest in time and its interplay with place. These ideas are further developed in the first paragraph of the story, when we see that Gilbert is keenly aware that time seems to move more quickly in some places than others. Gilbert's interest in the interplay between space and time is one of his primary motivations.*

2. *Words used to describe time include:* tyrant, crawled, whipped, eternity, flashing instant. *These descriptions suggest that time—or at least our perception of it—is imposed upon us and entirely outside our control. It is part of the nature of humanity to be caught in time.*

3. *Einstein claimed that time was similar to space, implying that one might travel back in time. At the beginning of the story this is an interesting idea to Gilbert, but his father's death further increases its appeal. If Gilbert could travel backward in time, he might be with his father—and his mother—once more.*

4. *Gilbert feels trapped in and by time. His observation that the rails limit the children's movements through space helps reiterate his understanding of time. It also sets up a clear point of reference for the following section in which the bounds of both space and time fall away.*

5. *Gilbert is still struggling to come to terms with his father's death. He wants to see his father again, and in these lines we see his belief that this may be possible.*

6. *Symbol: handcar; What it represents (in outer ovals of web): freedom, power, self-directed movement, hope, determination. The handcar symbolizes the children's newfound ability first to determine their own direction in space from just two choices and later to determine their own direction through both time and space from an unlimited list of possibilities. The handcar symbolizes freedom from the bounds of both space and time.*

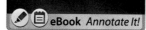 **eBook** *Annotate It!*

Analyzing the Text

COMMON CORE RL 1, RL 2, RL 3, RL 4, RL 5, W 9a

Cite Text Evidence Support your responses with evidence from the text.

1. **Infer** What does the story title have to do with the setting and the main character's motivations?

2. **Interpret** Reread lines 1–7. What words or phrases describe time? What do these descriptions suggest about the story's **theme,** the message about life or human nature?

3. **Cite evidence** How might Albert Einstein be a motivating factor in Gilbert's quest?

4. **Infer** Reread lines 353–358. What does this speech reveal about Gilbert and how he perceives reality?

5. **Interpret** Examine lines 408–413.. What do these lines suggest about Gilbert's emotional state at this point of the story?

6. **Synthesize** Use a web like the one shown to explore symbolism in the story. In the central circle, write *handcar, father's watch,* or the name of something else from the story that works as a symbol. Fill out the web by recording your ideas about what the symbol represents.

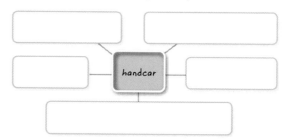

PERFORMANCE TASK

Writing Activity: Character Profile
With a partner, find and record references to the passage of time that connect to key experiences for Gilbert. For each important reference, also note what is happening to Gilbert. Together, write a one-page character profile of Gilbert, including details that answer these questions:

- What are Gilbert's personal traits?
- What motivates Gilbert's actions?
- What life-changing events occur in his life?
- When and where is he at the start of the story? At the end?
- How has he changed by the end of the story?

Assign this performance task.

PERFORMANCE TASK

COMMON CORE RL 1, RL 2, W 9a

Writing Activity: Character Profile Have students work with a partner to complete their character profiles of Gilbert. For this work, they should review the story and:

- use each new setting as a clue that new character traits might come to the surface.

- use each new event in the story as a clue to character motivations.

Critical Vocabulary

COMMON CORE L 4c, L 6

eloquence   maroon   judicious   spyglass   sextant

Practice and Apply Complete each sentence to show that you understand the meaning of the vocabulary word.

1. Everyone was impressed by the **eloquence** of . . .

2. The sailors were **marooned** on . . .

3. Before the travelers set out, they were **judicious** about . . .

4. The way to use a **spyglass** is to . . .

5. Sailors long ago needed a **sextant** to . . .

Vocabulary Strategy: Reference Aids

A **dictionary** is a valuable resource for anyone who is checking and expanding their vocabulary. The searching and browsing methods differ for print and digital dictionaries, but users can find the same basic information about each entry word.

- pronunciation
- part of speech label
- one or more definitions
- related forms

> **in·tri·cate** (ĭn´trĭ-kĭt) *adj.* **1.** Having many complexly arranged elements; elaborate. **2.** Difficult to understand, analyze, or solve for having many interconnected elements. —**in´tri·cate·ly** *adv.* —**in´tri·cate·ness** *n.*

Synonyms are words with similar meanings. The dictionary entry shown for *intricate* includes a synonym within the definition: *elaborate*. Some dictionaries provide a list of synonyms after an entry. A **thesaurus** is a reference aid that lists synonyms. Writers can use a print or digital thesaurus to help find the exact word they need.

> **intricate** *adj.* complicated, complex, elaborate, involved, convoluted

Practice and Apply Find the sentence with *judiciously* in line 94 of "Another Place, Another Time." Look up the word *judicious* and find the related form in an available dictionary and thesaurus. Use your own words to tell what the sentence means. Then rewrite the sentence using an appropriate synonym.

Another Place, Another Time **109**

PRACTICE & APPLY

Critical Vocabulary

COMMON CORE L 4a, L 4b, L 4c

Sample answers:

1. *Everyone was impressed by the eloquence of the speaker, whose words moved some listeners to tears.*

2. *The sailors were marooned an island with no fresh water, and no rescue ship was in sight.*

3. *Before the travelers set out, they were judicious about packing only the clothes they could carry in backpacks.*

4. *The way to use a spyglass is to hold it up to one eye and look through it so that distant objects appear close.*

5. *Sailors long ago needed a sextant to determine their location in the open sea.*

Vocabulary Strategy: Reference Aids

Sample answer:

The sentence His father nodded judiciously *means that his father nodded with an expression on his face that showed he was thinking wisely and agreeing with the judgment of the tutor. Sample restatement with a synonym:* His father nodded thoughtfully.

Strategies for Annotation   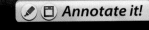 *Annotate it!*

Critical Vocabulary

COMMON CORE L 4a, L 4c, L 5b

Have students locate the first two lines of the story. Encourage them to use their eBook annotation tools to do the following:

- Highlight the word *tyrant* in yellow.
- Use the context of the sentence to make a guess at the word's meaning.
- Confirm the meaning in a dictionary.
- Use a thesaurus to find a synonym and add it to a note.

Gilbert hated time. What a tyrant it was! The hours tha
crawled by when his father was at sea, the seconds that

> Synonym
> oppressor
> dictator

Another Place, Another Time **109**

Language Conventions: Spell Correctly

 COMMON CORE L 2b

Tell students that the examples in the chart show just a few examples for each category. Invite volunteers to come up with familiar examples for each category. *(Possible answers: geographical names: your town's name, your school's name, your state's name; personal titles and names: your name, students' names, Principal Smith, President Obama; proper adjectives: Italian, French, American, Canadian; abbreviations: St., Rd., Mrs., Ms.)*

Answers:

1. *Doctorow, Kalamazoo*

2. *Limburgher, Erwin*

3. *Uriarte, Mrs., Atlantic Ocean*

4. *Professor, Newtonian*

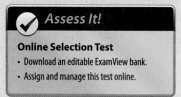

✓ *Assess It!*

Online Selection Test
- Download an editable ExamView bank.
- Assign and manage this test online.

Language Conventions: Spell Correctly

 COMMON CORE L 2b

When you proofread your writing for accuracy, you should check the spelling of every word. If you are using computer software to write, you will find that the spellchecker catches most misspellings—but not all. So, you still need to check the spelling in your work. In particular, be attentive to the spelling of proper nouns, proper adjectives, personal titles, and abbreviations, which are less likely to be corrected by a spellchecker.

Read these sentences from "Another Place, Another Time."

> He thumped the book he'd taken out of his father's bookcase, a book fetched home from London, heavy and well made and swollen with the damp air of the sea-crossing home to America. He hadn't read the book, but his tutor, sour Señor Uriarte, had explained it to him the day before . . .

Note the capitalization and spelling of the geographical names *London* and *America*; a personal title, *Señor*; and a proper name, *Uriarte*.

The chart shows categories of words to check for correct spelling and capitalization.

Category	Examples
geographical names	Madagascar, Kaskaskia River, Cincinnati, Sagamore Boulevard
personal titles and names	Madame Thibeau, Professor Moriarty, Señorita Madariaga
proper adjectives	Parisian, Colombian, Shakespearean, Einsteinian
abbreviations	Mme., Mr., Dr., Ave., Sq., Blvd.

Practice and Apply These sentences include errors in spelling and capitalization. In each sentence, identify the misspellings and write the words correctly. Refer to "Another Place, Another Time" and to other reference resources to check spellings.

1. Cory Docorow, the author of "Another Place, Another Time," tells how the children named the handcar *Kamalazoo*.

2. In this story, Gilbert is friends with Emmy Limberger and her twin brothers, Neils and Irwin.

3. Gilbert's tutor, Señor Uriate, and his housekeeper, Mme. Curie, care for him when his father is crossing the Altantic ocean.

4. Profesor Einstein's book leaves a deep impression on Gilbert, who wants to understand how the newtonion view of the universe has changed.

Analyze Story Elements: Character and Setting

RL 3

TEACH

Remind students that the **settings** in a story—or the times and places of the action—can affect the characters.

- Ask students how their own behavior and feelings can change from one place to another. For example, they'd likely feel one way on a beach on a hot summer afternoon than they would at a bus stop on a cold, rainy evening in winter. Their reasons, or **motivations,** for their behavior would be different in each setting.
- Point out that these feelings and actions are similar to the **traits** and motivations of story characters.
- As story characters encounter different settings, their traits and motivations can change. The settings affect the characters, and their reactions reveal information about them.
- In works of fiction, the evidence of these changes is revealed by the dialogue, descriptions, and details in the text.
- Discuss how in "Another Place, Another Time," Gilbert behaved differently when he was by the ocean with his father than when he was in the tree house with his friends.

CLOSE READING APPLICATION

Have pairs of students work together to identify different settings in "Another Place, Another Time." Have them use a graphic organizer such as a Comparison-Contrast Chart to track how Gilbert changes in each setting. Have them list details about each setting that seem to affect Gilbert and list how each setting reveals different traits and motivations for Gilbert. Have students share their completed charts with another pair of students and discuss what the changes in setting reveal about Gilbert.

 INTERACTIVE GRAPHIC ORGANIZERS Have students find graphic organizers for comparing and contrasting, such as the **Comparison-Contrast Chart.**

Analyzing Story Elements: Character

RL 3

RETEACH

Review the terms *character, main character, character traits,* and *character motivations*. Point out that all main characters and most secondary characters have traits and motivations that can be identified in a number of ways.

- **Direct Characterization** An author might directly describe a character's traits and motivations.
- **Indirect Characterization** Often, authors reveal character traits and motivations indirectly. They include information that helps the reader **infer,** or guess, what a character is like. These indirect hints include details, such as the character's physical appearance, speech, thoughts, and actions as well as other characters' reactions to a character.

 LEVEL UP TUTORIALS Assign the following *Level Up* tutorial: **Methods of Characterization**

COLLABORATIVE DISCUSSION

Have small groups of students work together to find examples of both direct and indirect characterization of three or four characters from the story. Have each group member pick a character to analyze by rereading the text and writing down examples of characterization. Then have students come together to discuss the different ways that Corey Doctorow created interesting, believable characters.

ANCHOR TEXT EXEMPLAR

Sorry, Wrong Number

*my*SmartPlanner — Create lesson plans and access resources online.

Drama by Lucille Fletcher

Why This Text?

As regular viewers of dramas, students can also develop as readers of drama and enhance their understanding of how works of fiction are structured for audiences. This lesson leads students to analyze a written script for dramatic elements and explore the ways in which a play and a film are similar and different.

Key Learning Objective: Students will be able to analyze the elements of a drama and make comparisons between a script and a performance.

For practice and application:

A Christmas Carol

Close Reader selection
A Christmas Carol
Novel Excerpt by Charles Dickens; Drama Excerpt by Israel Horovitz; Graphic Story from Marvel Comic

 COMMON CORE

Common Core Standards

RL 1 Make inferences.
RL 2 Provide a summary.
RL 3 Analyze story elements.
RL 4 Determine meanings of words and phrases.
RL 5 Analyze how a drama's structure contributes to its meaning.
RL 7 Compare and contrast a drama to its filmed version.
RL 10 Read and comprehend dramas.
W 2 Write explanatory texts.
W 4 Produce clear and coherent writing.
W 9a Apply grade 7 Reading standards to literature.
W 10 Write routinely.
L 4a Use context as a clue to meaning.
L 4c Consult reference materials to clarify meaning.
SL 2 Analyze the main ideas and supporting details in diverse media and formats.

Text Complexity Rubric

Quantitative Measures	**Sorry, Wrong Number** **Lexile:** N/A
Qualitative Measures	**Levels of Meaning/Purpose** single level of simple meaning (single theme)
	Structure simple, linear chronology
	Language Conventionality and Clarity increased, clearly assigned dialogue
	Knowledge Demands some cultural and literary knowledge useful
Reader/Task Considerations	Teacher determined Vary by individual reader and type of text

Background Have students read the background and information about the author. Provide further explanation of mid-twentieth century communication:

- Telephone numbers were literally dialed, as in the rotary phone shown.
- There was no voice messaging. If a phone was in use, a caller heard a short series of beeps, called a busy signal.
- Each phone number began with a two-letter abbreviation; for example, the phone exchange "Murray Hill" in this play was MU.
- Callers dialed the number for Information to talk to a live operator who looked up phone numbers.

SETTING A PURPOSE Direct students to use the Setting a Purpose prompt to focus their reading. Remind them to write down any questions they have as they read.

Analyze Form: Drama   COMMON CORE RL 5

(CAST OF CHARACTERS)

Tell students that a play, or **drama,** is a form of literature meant to be performed by actors in front of an audience. The script for a play begins with a list of all the characters in the play, called the **cast of characters.** Explain that in this play, the main character is Mrs. Stevenson, and the other characters have supporting roles.

Ⓐ ASK STUDENTS what they can predict about the action of the play from the Operator and Information listings. *(Mrs. Stevenson will talk to seven different telephone operators over the course of the action.)*

Background *Long before cell phones, telephone service went over wires. People called the operator, who connected them to a number. Occasionally, malfunctions resulted in "crossed" wires, allowing a caller to hear other people's phone conversations.* **Lucille Fletcher** (1912–2000) *wrote novels, radio plays, stage plays, and screenplays. She is best remembered for her radio play* Sorry, Wrong Number, *which was first broadcast in 1943. The play became a sensation, capturing the imaginations of mystery fans around the world.*

Sorry, Wrong Number

Drama by Lucille Fletcher

SETTING A PURPOSE A drama is mainly intended to be performed for an audience. As you read, pay attention to the stage directions to help you imagine the plot events as if they were being performed by live actors. Write down any questions you have while reading.

Cast of Characters

Mrs. Stevenson	4th Operator
1st Operator	5th Operator
1st Man	Information
2nd Man	Hospital Receptionist
Chief Operator	Western Union
2nd Operator	Sergeant Duffy
3rd Operator	A Lunchroom-Counter Attendant

Ⓐ

(br) ©Mihai Simonia/Shutterstock; (bg) ©PhotoHouse/Shutterstock

Close Read Screencasts   ▶ *View It!*

Modeled Discussion

Have students click the *Close Read* icons in their eBooks to access a screencast in which readers discuss and annotate the following key passage:

> **Operator.** Ringing Murray Hill 4–0098. ... **George.** Yes, sir. (lines 53–75)

As a class, view and discuss the video. Then have students pair up to do an independent close read of an additional passage: **Operator.** Ringing the Police Department. ... *(the curtain falls.)* (lines 872–898)

Analyze Form: Drama

COMMON CORE **RL 1, RL 5**

(LINES 1–15, 28–29)

Point out the typography conventions used in the script:

- Italic type, often in parentheses, denotes **stage directions**—unspoken instructions about how the drama is to be performed. The letters *L* and *R* denote "stage left" and "stage right," when facing the audience.
- Roman type labels the characters' names within stage directions.
- Roman type is used for **dialogue,** the words spoken by the characters. The character's name in boldface type precedes his or her lines of dialogue.

B **CITE TEXT EVIDENCE** Have students find the descriptive details in the stage directions that tell what is lit and what is in darkness onstage. *(Mrs. Stevenson in her bed is in the center of the stage, lit by a table lamp. The left and right sections of the stage are dark.)*

Tell students that readers of a play can use the stage directions to visualize the characters and imagine how they sound.

C **ASK STUDENTS** to give ideas about Mrs. Stevenson's character based on the description in lines 28–29. *(She is a "querulous, self-centered neurotic." That means she is nervous, demanding, and possibly not likable.)*

B **Scene:** *As the curtain rises, we see a divided stage, only the center part of which is lighted and furnished as* Mrs. Stevenson's *bedroom. Expensive, rather fussy furnishings. A large bed, on which* Mrs. Stevenson, *clad in a bedjacket, is lying. A nighttable close by, with phone, lighted lamp, and pill bottles.*
10 *A mantel, with clock, R. A closed door, R. A window, with curtains closed, rear. The set is lit by one lamp on nighttable. Beyond this central set, the stage on either side is in darkness.*

Mrs. Stevenson *is dialing a number on the phone as the curtain rises. She listens to the phone, slams down the receiver in irritation. As*
20 *she does so, we hear the sound of a train roaring by in the distance. She reaches for her pill bottle, pours herself a glass of water, shakes out a pill, swallows it, then reaches for the phone again, dials the number nervously.* Sound: *Number being dialed on the phone. Busy signal.*

C **Mrs. Stevenson** (*a querulous, self-centered neurotic*). Oh, *dear!*
30 (*Slams down receiver. Dials* Operator. *A spotlight, L. of side flat, picks up out of peripheral darkness the figure of* 1st Operator *sitting with headphones at small table.*)

Operator. Your call, please?

Mrs. Stevenson. Operator? I've been dialing Murray Hill 4-0098 for the last three quarters of an hour and the line is always busy.
40 But I don't see how it *could* be busy

that long. Will you try it for me, please?

Operator. Murray Hill 4-0098? One moment, please. (*She makes gesture of plugging in call through a switchboard.*)

Mrs. Stevenson. I don't see how it could be busy all this time. It's my husband's office. He's working late
50 tonight and I'm all alone here in the house. My health is very poor and I've been feeling so nervous all day.

Operator. Ringing Murray Hill 4-0098. (Sound: *Phone buzz. It rings three times. Receiver is picked up at the other end. Spotlight picks up a figure of a heavy-set man seated at a desk with a phone on R. side of dark periphery of stage. He is*
60 *wearing a hat. Picks up phone.*)

Man. Hello.

Mrs. Stevenson. Hello? (*a little puzzled*) Hello. Is Mr. Stevenson there?

Man (*into phone, as though he has not heard*). Hello. (*louder*) Hello. (*Spotlight on L. now moves from* Operator *to another man,* George—*a killer type, also wearing*
70 *a hat, but standing as in a phone booth.*)

2nd Man (*slow heavy quality, faintly foreign accent*). Hello.

1st Man. Hello? George?

George. Yes, sir.

Mrs. Stevenson (*louder and more imperious, to phone*). Hello. Who's this? What number am I calling, please?

SCAFFOLDING FOR ELL STUDENTS

Analyze Form: Drama Using a whiteboard, project lines 1–15 of the play, which gives stage directions. Invite volunteers to mark up the lines:

- Highlight in yellow the names of the props on the set. Discuss what each one looks like and where it is located onstage.
- Underline the words that describe Mrs. Stevenson. Clarify any unfamiliar words.

ASK STUDENTS What do you see when the curtain rises?

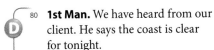

1st Man. We have heard from our client. He says the coast is clear for tonight.

George. Yes, sir.

1st Man. Where are you now?

George. In a phone booth.

1st Man. Okay. You know the address. At eleven o'clock, the private patrolman goes around to the bar on Second Avenue for a beer. Be sure that all the lights downstairs are out. There should be only one light visible from the street. At eleven-fifteen, a subway train crosses the bridge. It made a noise in case her window is open and she should scream.

Mrs. Stevenson (*shocked*). Oh— *hello!* What number is this, please?

George. Okay. I understand.

1st Man. Make it quick. As little blood as possible. Our client does not wish to make her suffer long.

George. A knife okay?

1st Man. Yes. A knife will be okay. And remember—remove the rings and bracelets, and the jewelry in the bureau drawer. Our client wishes it to look like simple robbery.

George. Okay—I get—(*Spotlight suddenly goes out on George. Sound: A bland buzzing signal. Spotlight goes off on 1st Man.*)

Mrs. Stevenson (*clicking phone*). Oh! (*Bland buzzing signal continues. She hangs up.*) How awful! How unspeakably—(*She lies back on her pillows, overcome for a few seconds, then suddenly pulls herself together, reaches for phone. Sound: Dialing. Phone buzz. Spotlight goes on at 1st Operator's switchboard. 1st and 2nd Man exit as unobtrusively as possible, in darkness.*)

Operator. Your call, please?

Mrs. Stevenson (*unnerved and breathless, into phone*). Operator, I—I've just been cut off.

Operator. I'm sorry, madam. What number were you calling?

Mrs. Stevenson. It was supposed to be Murray Hill 4-0098, but it wasn't. Some wires must have crossed—I was cut into a wrong number. And I've just heard the most dreadful thing—a—a murder—and (*imperiously*) you'll simply have to retrace that call at once, Operator.

Operator. I beg your pardon, madam, I don't quite—

Mrs. Stevenson. Oh, I know it was a wrong number and I had no business listening, but these two men—they were cold-blooded fiends and they were going to murder somebody—some poor innocent woman who was all alone—in a house near a bridge. And we've got to stop them—

Operator (*patiently*). What number were you calling, madam?

Mrs. Stevenson. That doesn't matter. This was a *wrong* number.

CLOSE READ

Analyze Form: Drama

COMMON CORE RL 1, RL 3, RL 5

(LINES 80–96, 110–125)

Tell students that, like other forms of literature, this play has a series of events called a **plot**. The first part of the plot, called the **exposition**, gives audiences the basic information about the **conflict**—the struggle between opposing forces—that will drive the rest of the plot.

D **ASK STUDENTS** to reread lines 80–96 to tell what the audience and Mrs. Stevenson learn at the same time. (*A murder of a woman is being planned by two men, one working for a client and the other named George, the hired killer.*)

Tell students that the lighting and dialogue help audiences understand that different characters onstage are each in a different **setting**—the time and place of the events.

E **CITE TEXT EVIDENCE** Have students find the details in lines 110–125 that describe what the audience sees onstage. (*Spotlights go off the two men. Then one spotlight lights the 1st Operator's switchboard. Mrs. Stevenson, still in bed, is no longer overhearing the men's phone conversation but is speaking to the Operator.*)

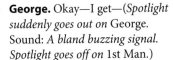

Scene: *As the curtain rises, we see a divided stage, only the center part of which is lighted and furnished as Mrs. Stevenson's bedroom. Expensive, rather fussy furnishings. A large bed, on which* Mrs. Stevenson, *clad in a bedjacket, is lying. A nighttable close by, with phone, lighted lamp, and pill bottles. A mantel, with clock, R. A closed door, R. A window, with curtains closed, rear. The set is lit by one lamp on nighttable. Beyond this central set, the stage on either side is in darkness.*

Analyze Form: Drama

COMMON CORE RL 1, RL 3, RL 5

(LINES 176–182, 194–200)

Explain that stage directions help actors know what emotions to convey and help readers visualize those emotions.

F **CITE TEXT EVIDENCE** Have students reread lines 176–182 and note the stage directions that reveal how Mrs. Stevenson feels. Ask them why she might feel that way. *(As she wipes her forehead with a handkerchief, she is "glancing uneasily for a moment toward the window." That uneasy glance reveals that she is worried about what might be happening outside.)*

Point out that the **conflict** in a drama or other fictional work is the problem that the characters try to resolve. Efforts to resolve the conflict create the action of the plot and build **suspense,** the feeling of growing tension and excitement felt by readers and viewers of a play.

G **ASK STUDENTS** to reread lines 194–200 to tell about Mrs. Stevenson's conflict and her attempts to resolve it. *(The conflict is set up when Mrs. Stevenson overhears plans for a murder. She is desperate for the operator to trace the call to find the men and apprehend them.)*

And *you* dialed it. And we've got to find out what it was—immediately!

Operator. But, madam—

Mrs. Stevenson. Oh, why are you
160 so stupid? Look—it was obviously a case of some little slip of the finger. I told you to try Murray Hill 4-0098 for me—you dialed it but your finger must have slipped and I was connected with some other number. I could hear them, but they couldn't hear me. I simply fail to see why you couldn't make that same mistake again—on purpose.
170 Why you couldn't *try* to dial Murray Hill 4-0098 in the same careless sort of way—

Operator (*quickly*). Murray Hill 4-0098? I will try to get it for you, madam.

F **Mrs. Stevenson** (*sarcastically*). *Thank you.* (*She bridles, adjusts herself on her pillows, reaches for a handkerchief and wipes her*
180 *forehead, glancing uneasily for a moment toward the window. Sound of ringing and busy signal.*)

Operator. I'm sorry. Murray Hill 4-0098 is busy.

Mrs. Stevenson (*frantically clicking receiver*). Operator—Operator!

Operator. Yes, madam?

Mrs. Stevenson (*angrily*). You *didn't* try to get that wrong number
190 at all. I asked explicitly and all you did was dial correctly.

Operator. I'm sorry. What number were you calling?

Mrs. Stevenson. Can't you forget **G** what number I was calling and do something specific? I want to trace that call. It's my civic duty—it's *your* civic duty—to trace that call and to apprehend those dangerous
200 killers. And if *you* won't—

Operator (*glancing around wearily*). I will connect you with the Chief Operator.

Mrs. Stevenson. *Please!* (*Sound of ringing.* Operator *puts hand over mouthpiece of phone, gestures into darkness.*)

Operator (*a half whisper*). Miss Curtis, will you pick up on
210 seventeen, please? (Miss Curtis, *Chief Operator, enters. Middle-aged, efficient, pleasant. Wearing headphone.*)

Miss Curtis. Yes, dear. What's the trouble?

Operator. Somebody wanting a call traced. I can't make head nor tail of it.

Miss Curtis (*sitting down at desk*
220 *as* Operator *gets up*). Sure, dear. (*She makes gesture of plugging in her headphone, coolly and professionally.*) This is the Chief Operator.

Mrs. Stevenson. Chief Operator? I want you to trace a call. Immediately. I don't know where it came from, or who was making it, but it's absolutely necessary
230 that it be tracked down. It was about a murder, a terrible, cold-

blooded murder of a poor innocent woman—tonight, at eleven-fifteen.

Chief Operator. I see.

Mrs. Stevenson (*high-strung, demanding*). Can you trace it for me? Can you track down those men?

240 **Chief Operator.** It depends, madam.

Mrs. Stevenson. Depends on what?

Chief Operator. It depends on whether the call is still going on. If it's a live call, we can trace it on the equipment. If it's been disconnected, we can't.

Mrs. Stevenson. Disconnected?

Chief Operator. If the parties have 250 stopped talking to each other.

Mrs. Stevenson. Oh, but of course they must have stopped talking to each other by *now*. That was at least five minutes ago.

Chief Operator. Well, I can try tracing it. (*She takes a pencil out of her hair.*) What is your name, madam?

Mrs. Stevenson. Mrs. Elbert 260 Stevenson. But listen—

Chief Operator (*writing*). And your telephone number?

Mrs. Stevenson (*more irritated*). Plaza 4-2295. But if you go on wasting all this time—(*She glances at clock on the mantel.*)

Chief Operator. And what is your reason for wanting this call traced?

Mrs. Stevenson. My reason? Well, 270 for heaven's sake, isn't it obvious? I overhear two men planning to murder this woman—it's a matter for the police!

Chief Operator. Have you told the police?

Mrs. Stevenson. No. How could I?

Chief Operator. You're making this check into a private call purely as a private individual?

280 **Mrs. Stevenson.** Yes. But meanwhile—

Chief Operator. Well, Mrs. Stevenson, I seriously doubt whether we could make this check for you at this time just on your say-so as a private individual. We'd have to have something more official.

Mrs. Stevenson. Oh, for heaven's 290 sake! You mean to tell me I can't report a murder without getting tied up in all this red tape? It's perfectly idiotic. All right, then I *will* call the police. (*She slams down the receiver. Spotlight goes off two* Operators.) Ridiculous! (*Sound of dialing as* Mrs. Stevenson *dials phone and two* Operators *exit unobtrusively in darkness. On* R. 300 *of stage, spotlight picks up a* 2nd Operator, *seated like first, with headphone at table—same one vacated by* 1st Man.)

2nd Operator. Your call, please?

Mrs. Stevenson (*very annoyed*). The Police Department—please.

CLOSE READ

Analyze Form: Drama

 COMMON CORE · RL 1, RL 3, RL 5

(LINES 235–266, 289–304)

Tell students that once the conflict sets the plot in motion, the events that occur are called the **rising action.**

(H) ASK STUDENTS to reread lines 235–266 and give ideas about why rising action is a fitting term to describe what is happening. (*As Mrs. Stevenson tries to explain what she wants to the Chief Operator, her panic starts to rise. The suspense builds for the audience, too, because it's clear that the call can't be traced, and precious time is passing.*)

Point out that stage directions help readers visualize how characters are entering and exiting the scene.

(I) CITE TEXT EVIDENCE Have students reread lines 289–304 and tell what the audience sees as Mrs. Stevenson dials the phone. (*The table to the right that was hidden in darkness is now lit with a spotlight, and a new character, 2nd Operator, is seated at it.*)

APPLYING ACADEMIC VOCABULARY

perceive	task

As you discuss the dramatist's techniques, incorporate the following Collection 2 academic vocabulary words: *perceive* and *task.* Talk about the dramatist's **tasks:** to build suspense using dialogue and to lead audiences to **perceive** events onstage as if they are happening in a real-life setting.

Analyze Form: Drama

COMMON CORE   RL 1, RL 3, RL 5

(LINES 337–349)

Explain that suspense is building as Mrs. Stevenson keeps trying to persuade others that a murder is going to occur.

J **CITE TEXT EVIDENCE** Ask students to reread lines 337–349 to identify words that show Duffy's reaction to Mrs. Stevenson's call. Ask them what effect the dramatist wants to create. *(Duffy "relaxes, sighs, starts taking lunch from bag." He says "Yes, ma'am," in a voice that shows he's not impressed. The effect is to build tension, because the audience knows that Mrs. Stevenson is right, but she can't seem to explain the situation convincingly.)*

2nd Operator. Ringing the Police Department. (*Ring twice. At table L. spotlight now picks up* Sergeant
310   Duffy, *seated in a relaxed position. Just entering beside him is a young man in a cap and apron, carrying a large brown-paper parcel, delivery boy for a local lunch counter. Phone is ringing.*)

Lunchroom Attendant. Here's your lunch, Sarge. They didn't have no jelly doughnuts, so I got French crullers, okay?

320   **Duffy.** French crullers. I got ulcers. Whyn't you make it apple pie? (*picks up phone*) Police Department, Precinct 43, Duffy speaking.

Lunchroom Attendant (*anxiously*). We don't have no apple pie, either, Sarge.

Mrs. Stevenson. Police Department? Oh. This is Mrs.
330   Stevenson—Mrs. Elbert Smythe Stevenson of 53 North Sutton Place. I'm calling to report a murder. (Duffy *has been examining lunch, but double-takes suddenly on above.*)

Duffy. Eh?

Mrs. Stevenson. I mean, the murder hasn't been committed yet, I just overheard plans for it
340   over the telephone—over a wrong number the operator gave me. (Duffy *relaxes, sighs, starts taking lunch from bag.*) I've been trying to trace the call myself, but everybody is so stupid—and I guess in the end

you're the only people who could *do* anything.

Duffy (*not too impressed*). Yes, ma'am. (Attendant *exits.*)

350   **Mrs. Stevenson** (*trying to impress him*). It was perfectly *definite* murder. I heard their plans distinctly. (Duffy *begins to eat sandwich, phone at his ear.*) Two men were talking, and they were going to murder some woman at eleven-fifteen tonight—she lived in a house near a bridge.

Duffy. Yes, ma'am.

360   **Mrs. Stevenson.** There was a private patrolman on the street who was going to go around for a beer on Second Avenue. And there was some third man, a client, who was paying to have this poor woman murdered. They were going to take her rings and bracelets— and use a knife. Well, it's unnerved me dreadfully—and I'm not well.

370   **Duffy.** I see. (*He wipes his mouth with a paper napkin.*) When was all this, ma'am?

Mrs. Stevenson. About eight minutes ago. Oh—(*relieved*)—then you *can* do something? You *do* understand.

Duffy. And what is your name, ma'am? (*He reaches for a pad of paper.*)

380   **Mrs. Stevenson** (*impatiently*). Mrs. Stevenson. Mrs. Elbert Stevenson.

Duffy. And your address?

Mrs. Stevenson. 53 North Sutton Place. *That's* near a bridge. The Queensboro Bridge, you know— and *we* have a private patrol-man on *our* street. And Second Avenue—

Duffy. And what was that number you were calling?

Mrs. Stevenson. Murray Hill 4-0098. (Duffy *writes it down.*) But that wasn't the number I overheard. I mean Murray Hill 4-0098 is my husband's office. (Duffy, *in exasperation, holds his pencil poised.*) He's working late tonight and I was trying to reach him to ask him to come home. I'm an invalid, and it's the maid's night off, and I *hate* to be alone even though he says I'm perfectly safe as long as I have the telephone right beside my bed.

Analyze Form: Drama

COMMON CORE RL 3, RL 5

(LINES 384–405)

Tell students that a dramatist uses dialogue to move the action along and to provide information to the audience.

K ASK STUDENTS to reread lines 384–405 and tell what Mrs. Stevenson is revealing to the audience as she speaks to Duffy. *(She herself lives in a place like the one described by the murder planners. She is all alone because her husband is not home and it's the maid's night off. The woman who is to be murdered is also alone in her house.)*

Determine Meaning of Words and Phrases

COMMON CORE RL 4, L 4a, L 4c

(LINE 401)

Point out line 401, where Mrs. Stevenson says she is an invalid.

L ASK STUDENTS to use the context of surrounding words to determine the meaning of *invalid*. As needed, have students confirm the meaning in a digital or print dictionary. Then ask students what the word *invalid* suggests about how Mrs. Stevenson perceives herself. *(She sees herself as ill, helpless, and always requiring care from others.)* Point out that this usage of the word *invalid* was more common at the time that this play was first performed. Discuss how it would no longer be an appropriate way to categorize someone in a similar situation today.

Strategies for Annotation

✏️ 🗐 *Annotate it!*

Analyze Form: Drama

COMMON CORE RL 3, RL 5

Have students use their eBook annotation tools to annotate the text, focusing on what the audience hears and sees as Mrs. Stevenson and Duffy interact.

- Highlight in yellow the stage directions that tell what Duffy is doing.
- Add a note to describe Duffy's expression as he does each thing.
- Add a note to describe how Mrs. Stevenson sounds as she speaks the dialogue.

Mrs. Stevenson. Murray Hill 4-0098. *(Duffy writes it down.)* But that wasn't the number I overheard. I mean Murray Hill 4-0098 is my husband's office.

(Duffy, in exasperation, holds his pencil poised.) He's working late tonight and I was trying to reach him to ask him an invalid and

Duffy: bored or resigned
Mrs. Stevenson: rushing, with anxiety

Analyze Form: Drama

COMMON CORE · RL 1, RL 3, RL 5

(LINES 415–439)

Point out that the characters' gestures and postures onstage reveal what they are thinking and feeling.

M CITE TEXT EVIDENCE Direct students to scan lines 415–439 to identify words that show what Duffy is doing. Ask what his actions reveal about him. *(Duffy "yawns slightly"; "reaches for a paper cup of coffee"; "He begins to remove the top of the coffee container"; "puts down the phone to work on the cup." His actions show that he is unconcerned about Mrs. Stevenson's report and has no intention of getting involved.)*

Duffy (*stolidly*). Well, we'll look into it, Mrs. Stevenson, and see if we can check it with the telephone company.

410 **Mrs. Stevenson** (*getting impatient*). But the telephone company said they couldn't check the call if the parties had stopped talking. I've already taken care of that.

Duffy. Oh—yes? (*He yawns slightly.*)

M

Mrs. Stevenson. Personally, I feel you ought to do something far more immediate and drastic than 420 just check the call. What good does checking the call do if they've stopped talking? By the time you track it down, they'll already have committed the murder.

Duffy (*he reaches for a paper cup of coffee*). Well, we'll take care of it, lady. Don't worry. (*He begins to remove the top of the coffee container.*)

430 **Mrs. Stevenson.** I'd say the whole thing calls for a complete and thorough search of the whole city. (Duffy *puts down the phone to work on the cup as her voice continues.*) I'm very near a bridge, and I'm not far from Second Avenue. And I know I'd feel a whole lot better if you sent around a radio car to *this* neighborhood at once.

440 **Duffy** (*picks up phone again, drinks coffee*). And what makes you think the murder's going to be committed in your neighborhood, ma'am?

Mrs. Stevenson. Oh, I don't know—the coincidence is so

horrible. Second Avenue—the bridge—

Duffy. Second Avenue is a very long street, ma'am. And do you 450 happen to know how many bridges there are in the city of New York? How do you know there isn't some little house out on Staten Island— on some little Second Avenue you never heard about? (*He takes a long gulp of coffee.*) How do you know they were even talking about New York at all?

Mrs. Stevenson. But I heard 460 the call on the New York dialing system.

Duffy. How do you know it wasn't a long-distance call you overheard? Telephones are funny things. (*He sets down coffee.*) Look, lady, why don't you look at it this way? Supposing you hadn't broken in on that telephone call? Supposing you'd got your husband the way 470 you always do? Would this murder have made any difference to you then?

Mrs. Stevenson. I suppose not. But it's so inhuman—so cold-blooded—

Duffy. A lot of murders are committed in this city every day, ma'am. If we could do something to stop 'em, we would. But a clue of 480 this kind that's so vague isn't much more use to us than no clue at all.

Mrs. Stevenson. But surely—

Duffy. Unless, of course, you have some reason for thinking this call

---

Strategies for Annotation ✎ 🗏 Annotate it!

Analyze Form: Drama

COMMON CORE · RL 3, RL 5

Have students use their eBook annotation tools to annotate Duffy's actions in lines 415–429.

- Highlight in yellow the words that indicate what Duffy is doing.
- Add notes to describe how his actions contradict the words he speaks.

Duffy. Oh—yes? (*He yawns slightly.*)

Mrs. Stevenson. Personally, I feel you ought to do something far more immediate and drastic…

Duffy (*he reaches for a paper cup of coffee*). Well, we'll take care of it, lady. Don't worry. (*He begins to remove the top of the coffee container.*)

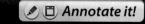

Duffy isn't listening closely and has no intention to help Mrs. Stevenson.

is phony, and that someone may be planning to murder *you*?

Mrs. Stevenson. *Me?* Oh, no—I hardly think so. I mean—why should anybody? I'm alone all day and night. I see nobody except my maid Eloise—she's a big two-hundred-pound woman too lazy to bring up my breakfast tray—and the only other person is my husband Elbert. He's crazy about me—adores me—waits on me hand and foot. He's scarcely left my side since I took sick twelve years ago—

Duffy. Well, then, there's nothing for you to worry about, is there? (*The* Lunchroom-Counter Attendant *has entered. He is carrying a piece of apple pie on a plate and points it out to* Duffy *triumphantly.*) And now, if you'll just leave the rest of this to us—

Mrs. Stevenson. But what will you *do?* It's so late—it's nearly eleven o'clock.

Duffy (*firmly*). We'll take care of it, lady.

Mrs. Stevenson. Will you broadcast it all over the city? And send out squads? And warn your radio cars to watch out—especially in suspicious neighborhoods like mine. (*The* Attendant, *in triumph, has put the pie down in front of* Duffy.)

Duffy (*more firmly*). Lady, I *said* we'd take care of it. Just now I've got a couple of other matters here on my desk that require my immediate—

Mrs. Stevenson. Oh! (*She slams down the receiver hard.*) Idiot! (*Duffy listening at the phone, hangs up and shrugs, then attacks his pie as spotlight fades out. Mrs. Stevenson, in bed, looks at the phone nervously.*) Why did I do that? Now he'll think I *am* a fool. (*She sits tensely, then throws herself back against the pillows, lying there a moment, whimpering with self-pity.*) Oh, why doesn't Elbert come home? *Why* doesn't he? (*We hear sound of train roaring by in the distance. She sits up, reaching for phone. Sound of dialing operator. Spotlight picks up* 2nd Operator, *seated* R.)

Operator. Your call, please?

Mrs. Stevenson. Operator—for heaven's sake—will you ring that Murray Hill 4-0098 number again? I can't think what's keeping him so long.

Operator. Ringing Murray Hill 4-0098. (*rings—busy signal*) The line is busy. Shall I—

Mrs. Stevenson (*nastily*). I can hear it, you don't have to tell me it's busy! (*Slams down receiver. Spotlight fades off on* 2nd Operator. Mrs. Stevenson *sinks back against the pillows again, whimpering to herself fretfully. She glances at the clock, then, turning, punches her pillows up, trying to make herself comfortable. But she isn't and she whimpers to herself as she squirms restlessly in bed.*) If I could get out of this bed for a little while. If I could get a breath of fresh air—or

Sorry, Wrong Number **119**

CLOSE READ

Analyze Drama: Form
COMMON CORE RL 1, RL 3, RL 5

(LINES 487–498, 537–539)

Review that a dramatist, the person who writes a drama, uses dialogue to reveal character. The audience uses what the character says to **make inferences,** or good guesses, about what the character doesn't say.

N **ASK STUDENTS** to reread lines 487–498 and tell what they can infer about Mrs. Stevenson that she herself doesn't seem to realize. *(Mrs. Stevenson says that she can't imagine anyone wanting to kill her. Yet she goes on to name two people who might have reason to: her maid and her husband.)*

Tell students that in a staged drama, sound effects may be used to show elements of the time and place of the action—the setting.

O **CITE TEXT EVIDENCE** Direct students to identify the sound effect in lines 537–539 and tell about its significance. *(The "train roaring by in the distance" is a reminder that the murderers are planning to use the sound of a train to muffle the victim's screams.)*

Determine Meaning of Words and Phrases
COMMON CORE RL 4

(Lines 535, 557, 562)

Draw students' attention to forms of the word *whimper* in the stage directions. Have them demonstrate whimpering.

P **ASK STUDENTS** what the word *whimper* suggests about Mrs. Stevenson. *(She feels frustrated and can't cope with setbacks. She's like a helpless child.)*

TEACH

CLOSE READ

Analyze Form: Drama

(LINES 567–581, 630–643)

Tell students that as the rising action of the plot continues, the main character tries to deal with obstacles that prevent her from resolving the conflict.

Q ASK STUDENTS to describe the new obstacle Mrs. Stevenson encounters in lines 567–581 and how she handles it. *(Now the phone rings, but nobody is on the other end. She handles this problem poorly, just shouting "Hello" repeatedly and slamming down the receiver.)*

Explain that the telephone is the most important prop in the play. In some ways it is like a character interacting with Mrs. Stevenson.

R ASK STUDENTS to reread lines 630–643 to visualize how Mrs. Stevenson is interacting with the phone. Volunteers may say Mrs. Stevenson's lines as they pantomime using a telephone like hers.

---

just lean out the window—and see the street. (*She sighs, reaches for pill bottle, and shakes out a pill. As she does, the phone rings and she darts for it instantly.*) Hello, Elbert? Hello. Hello. Hello. Oh—what's the *matter* with this phone? *Hello? Hello?* (*Slams down the receiver and stares at it tensely. The phone rings again. Once. She picks it up.*) Hello? Hello! Oh, for heaven's sake, who *is* this? Hello. Hello. *Hello.* (*Slamming down the receiver, she dials the operator. Spotlight comes on L. showing* 3rd Operator, *at spot vacated by* Duffy.)

3rd Operator. Your call, please?

Mrs. Stevenson (*very annoyed and imperious*). Hello, Operator, I don't know what's the matter with this telephone tonight, but it's positively driving me crazy. I've never seen such inefficient, miserable service. Now, look. I'm an invalid, and I'm very nervous, and I'm *not* supposed to be annoyed. But if this keeps on much longer—

3rd Operator (*a young, sweet type*). What seems to be the trouble, madam?

Mrs. Stevenson. *Everything's* wrong. The whole world could be murdered for all you people care! And now my phone keeps ringing!

Operator. Yes, madam?

Mrs. Stevenson. Ringing and ringing and ringing every five seconds or so, and when I pick it up there's no one there!

Operator. I'm sorry, madam. If you'll hang up, I'll test it for you.

Mrs. Stevenson. I don't want you to test it for me, I want you to put through that call—whatever it is— at once.

Operator (*gently*). I'm afraid that's not possible, madam.

Mrs. Stevenson (*storming*). Not possible? And why, may I ask?

Operator. The system is automatic, madam. If someone is trying to dial your number, there's no way to check whether the call is coming through the system or not—unless the person who is trying to reach you complains to his particular operator.

Mrs. Stevenson. Well, of all the stupid, complicated—And meanwhile *I've* got to sit here in my bed, *suffering* every time that phone rings, imagining everything!

Operator. I'll try to check it for you, madam.

Mrs. Stevenson. Check it! Check it! That's all anybody can do. Of all the stupid, idiotic—(*She hangs up.*) Oh, what's the use! (3rd Operator *fades out of spotlight as* Mrs. Stevenson's *phone rings again. She picks up the receiver.*) Hello! *Hello!* Stop ringing, do you hear me? Answer me? What do you want? Do you realize you're driving me crazy? (*Spotlight goes on* R. *We see a* Man *in eyeshade and shirtsleeves at a desk with a phone and telegrams.*) Stark, staring—

WHEN STUDENTS STRUGGLE . . .

To help students visualize the onstage action, guide partners to create a diagram of the stage, showing the bed in the center, a desk to the right (Stage Right), and a desk to the left (Stage Left). Suggest that they read aloud Mrs. Stevenson's spoken parts in lines 570–581 and 630–643 and label the desks to understand who is entering and exiting the stage at the same time.

Western Union (*dull, flat voice*). Hello. Is this Plaza 4-2295?

Mrs. Stevenson (*catching her breath*). Yes. Yes. This is Plaza 4-2295.

650 **Western Union.** This is Western Union. I have a telegram here for Mrs. Elbert Stevenson. Is there anyone there to receive the message?

Mrs. Stevenson (*trying to calm herself*). I am Mrs. Stevenson.

Western Union (*reading flatly*). The telegram is as follows: "Mrs. Elbert Stevenson, 53 North Sutton Place, New York, New York.
660 Darling. Terribly sorry. Tried to get you for last hour, but line busy. Leaving for Boston eleven P.M. tonight on urgent business. Back tomorrow afternoon. Keep happy. Love. Signed, Elbert."

Mrs. Stevenson (*breathlessly, aghast, to herself.*) Oh, no—

Western Union. That's all, madam. Do you wish us to deliver a copy of
670 the message?

Mrs. Stevenson. No—no, thank you.

Western Union. Thank you, madam. Goodnight. (*He hangs up the phone. Spotlight on* Western Union *immediately out.*)

Mrs. Stevenson (*mechanically, to phone*). Goodnight. (*She hangs up slowly, suddenly bursting into*)
680 No—no—it isn't true! He couldn't do it! Not when he knows I'll be all alone! It's some trick—some

fiendish—(*We hear the sound of a train roaring by outside. She half rises in bed, in panic, glaring toward the curtains. Her movements are frenzied. She beats with her knuckles on the bed, then suddenly stops and reaches for the phone.*
690 *Spotlight picks up* 4th Operator, *seated L.*)

Operator (*coolly*). Your call, please?

Mrs. Stevenson. Operator—try that Murray Hill 4-0098 number for me just once more, please.

Operator. Ringing Murray Hill 4-0098. (*Call goes through. We hear ringing at the other end, ring
700 after ring.*)

Mrs. Stevenson. He's gone. Oh, Elbert, how could you? How could you? (*She hangs up, sobbing pityingly to herself, turning restlessly. Spotlight goes out on* 4th Operator.) But I can't be alone tonight, I can't! If I'm alone one more second— (*She runs her hands wildly through her hair.*) I don't care what he
710 says, or what the expense is, I'm a sick woman—I'm entitled! (*With trembling fingers she picks up the receiver again and dials* Information. *The spotlight picks up* Information Operator, *seated R.*)

Information. This is Information.

Mrs. Stevenson. I want the telephone number of Henchley Hospital.

720 **Information.** Henchley Hospital? Do you have the address, madam?

CLOSE READ

Analyze Drama: Form

COMMON CORE · RL 1, RL 3, RL 5

(LINES 656–665, 683–689)

Remind students that a dramatist uses dialogue to move the action along.

S ASK STUDENTS to reread what the man from Western Union says beginning in line 656 and tell what new obstacle is being presented. (*Mrs. Stevenson's husband is not coming home tonight, and she now must deal with being alone.*)

Point out that stage directions help readers visualize the action and imagine the emotions that audiences experience.

T CITE TEXT EVIDENCE Direct students to reread the stage directions in lines 683–689. Have them identify the words that convey emotion. (*"Panic," "frenzied," and "beats with her knuckles on the bed" show that Mrs. Stevenson is out of control with frustration and terror. The "sound of a train roaring by outside" is like a scream that adds to the feeling of terror.*)

TEACH

CLOSE READ

Analyze Form: Drama

 COMMON CORE RL 3, RL 5

(LINES 759–795)

Tell students that Mrs. Stevenson is now attempting to handle the obstacle of facing the night alone.

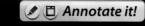 **ASK STUDENTS** to reread the conversation between Mrs. Stevenson and the Woman at Henchley Hospital and to tell how the dialogue builds suspense. *(The dialogue creates tension because Mrs. Stevenson's growing panic is contrasted with the businesslike manner of the Woman. Time is passing, the murder is about to be committed, and Mrs. Stevenson still can't get anyone to help her.)*

Invite volunteers to read the dialogue aloud to convey the contrast in emotions between the characters.

Mrs. Stevenson. No. It's somewhere in the Seventies. It's a small, private, and exclusive hospital where I had my appendix out two years ago. Henchley. H-E-N-C—

Information. One moment, please.

Mrs. Stevenson. Please—hurry.
730 And please—what's the time?

Information. I don't know, madam. You may find out the time by dialing Meridan 7-1212.

Mrs. Stevenson (*irritated*). Oh, for heaven's sake, couldn't you—?

Information. The number of Henchley Hospital is Butterfield 7-0105, madam.

Mrs. Stevenson. Butterfield
740 7-0105. (*She hangs up before she finishes speaking and immediately dials the number as she repeats it. Spotlight goes out on* Information. *Phone rings. Spotlight picks up* Woman *in nurse's uniform, seated at desk L.*)

Woman (*middle-aged, solid, firm, practical*). Henchley Hospital, good evening.

750 **Mrs. Stevenson.** Nurses' Registry.

Woman. Who was it you wished to speak to, please?

Mrs. Stevenson (*high-handed*). I want the Nurses' Registry at once. I want a trained nurse. I want to hire her immediately. For the night.

Woman. I see. And what is the nature of the case, madam?

Mrs. Stevenson. Nerves. I'm very
760 nervous. I need soothing—and companionship. My husband is away and I'm—

Woman. Have you been recommended to us by any doctor in particular, madam?

Mrs. Stevenson. No. But I really don't see why all this catechizing is necessary. I want a trained nurse. I was a patient in your hospital
770 two years ago. And, after all, I *do* expect to pay this person—

Woman. We quite understand that, madam. But registered nurses are very scarce just now and our superintendent has asked us to send people out only on cases where the physician in charge feels it is absolutely necessary.

Mrs. Stevenson (*growing
780 hysterical*). Well, it is absolutely necessary! I'm a sick woman. I'm very upset! Very! I'm alone in this house—and I'm an invalid—and tonight I overheard a telephone conversation that upset me dreadfully. About a murder—a poor woman who was going to be murdered at eleven-fifteen tonight. In fact, if someone doesn't come
790 at once, I'm afraid I'll go out of my mind!

Woman (*calmly*). I see. Well, I'll speak to Miss Phillips as soon as she comes in. And what is your name, madam?

Mrs. Stevenson. When do you expect Miss Phillips in?

Strategies for Annotation ✏️ 🗒️ *Annotate it!*

Analyze Form: Drama

COMMON CORE RL 3, RL 5

Have students use their eBook annotation tools to annotate Mrs. Stevenson's dialogue in lines 759–791 as if preparing to play the role.

- Highlight in yellow words to emphasize.
- Add notes to describe how she speaks and what gestures she makes.

Have students compare their annotations and take turns reading segments aloud expressively.

Mrs. Stevenson. Nerves. I'm very nervous. I need soothing—and companionship. My husband is away and I'm—. . .

almost breathless, gripping phone tightly with both hands

Mrs. Stevenson. No. But I really don't see why all this catechizing is necessary. I want a trained nurse. I was a patient in your hospital two years ago. And, after all, I do expect to pay this person—

Woman. I really don't know, madam. She went out to supper at 800 eleven o'clock.

Mrs. Stevenson. Eleven o'clock. But it's not eleven yet. (*She cries out.*) Oh, my clock *has* stopped. I *thought* it was running down. What time is it? (Woman *glances at wristwatch.*)

Woman. Just fourteen minutes past eleven. (*Sound of phone receiver being lifted on same line as* 810 Mrs. Stevenson's. *A click.*)

Mrs. Stevenson (*crying out*). What's *that?*

Woman. What was what, madam?

Mrs. Stevenson. That—that click just now—in my own telephone? As though someone had lifted the receiver off the hook of the extension phone downstairs.

Woman. I didn't hear it, madam. 820 Now, about this—

Mrs. Stevenson (*scared*). But I *did.* There's someone in this house! Someone downstairs in the kitchen! And they're listening to me now—they're (*She puts hand over her mouth, hangs up the phone, and sits in terror, frozen, listening.*) I won't pick it up, I won't let them hear me. I'll be quiet—and they'll 830 think—(*with growing terror*) But if I don't call someone now while they're still down there, there'll be no time! (*She picks up the receiver. There is a bland, buzzing signal. She dials the operator. On the second ring, spotlight goes on* R. *We see* 5th Operator.)

Operator (*fat and lethargic*). Your call, please?

Sorry, Wrong Number **123**

CLOSE READ

Analyze Drama: Form

COMMON CORE **RL 3**

(LINES 821–837)

Tell students that the rising action of the plot is almost at the point of greatest tension, called the **climax.**

V **ASK STUDENTS** to reread Mrs. Stevenson's dialogue beginning on line 821 and tell how audiences are probably reacting at this point in the play. *(People at a live performance of this drama are probably biting their knuckles or shading their eyes because the tension is almost unbearable. They've strongly suspected that Mrs. Stevenson is the intended murder victim, and now that someone is downstairs, they know for sure.)*

TO CHALLENGE STUDENTS . . .

Analyzing Story Elements Have students work in small groups to discuss how this drama might be different if it were written today, with modern characters, a modern setting, and current technology. How could a dramatist use modern technology to create a similarly suspenseful conflict? How might changes in language and cultural sensibilities since the original version was written be reflected in the modern version? Have students refer to examples from the original version to compare and contrast a possible modern version.

Analyze Form: Drama

COMMON CORE RL 1, RL 3, RL 5

(LINES 850–871, 895–898)

Explain that the play is approaching the climax. At the climax, audiences know how the main conflict will be resolved.

W **ASK STUDENTS** to reread lines 850–871 and tell why this is the climax of the play. *(Mrs. Stevenson is desperately trying to overcome the final obstacle— the murderer in her house—by calling the police. Her screams and the shadow rushing in the darkness create an emotional peak. Her silence tells the audience that the conflict has been resolved with her murder.)*

Tell students that the tension eases during the **falling action,** the events following the climax and leading to the last event of the plot, called the **resolution.** Explain further that the term **irony** can name a situation in which the audience knows something that a character doesn't know.

X **CITE TEXT EVIDENCE** Have students tell what George says and does at the resolution of the plot. Ask what is ironic about that remark and action. *(George says, "Sorry, wrong number," and hangs up. The audience knows that his victim had been trying to use the phone as a lifeline, doing nothing but calling "wrong numbers"—never finding the connection that would prevent her death.)*

COLLABORATIVE DISCUSSION Have students pair up and discuss how they would present this drama if it were to be viewed, or if it were only to be heard. Suggest that they also tell what they as directors would look for when casting the part of Mrs. Stevenson, and what would make a strong performance.

ASK STUDENTS to share any questions they generated in the course of reading and discussing the selection.

840 **Mrs. Stevenson** (*a desperate whisper*). Operator—I—I'm in desperate trouble—

Woman. I cannot hear you, madam. Please speak louder.

Mrs. Stevenson (*still whispering*). I don't dare. I—there's someone listening. Can you hear me now?

Operator. Your call, please? What number are you calling, madam?

850 **Mrs. Stevenson** (*desperately*). You've got to hear me! Oh, please! You've got to help me! There's someone in this house—someone who's going to murder me! And you've got to get in touch with the—(*Click of receiver being put down on* Mrs. Stevenson's *line. She bursts out wildly.*) Oh—there it is—he's put it down! He's coming!
860 (*She screams.*) He's coming up the stairs! (*She thrashes in the bed. The phone cord catching in the lamp wire, the lamp topples, goes out. Darkness. Hoarsely.*) Give me the Police Department (*We see on the dark C. stage the shadow of the door opening.* Mrs. Stevenson *screams.*) The police! (*On stage, there is the swift rush of a shadow advancing to*
870 *the bed—the sound of her voice is choked out as*)

Operator. Ringing the Police Department. (*Phone is rung. We hear the sound of a train beginning to fade in. On the second ring,* Mrs. Stevenson *screams again, but the roaring of the train drowns out her voice. For a few seconds we hear nothing but the roaring of the*
880 *train, then, dying away, the phone at Police Headquarters ringing. Spotlight goes on* Duffy, L. *stage.*)

Duffy. Police Department. Precinct 43. Duffy speaking. (*Pause. Nothing visible but darkness on C. stage*) Police Department. Duffy speaking. (*Now a flashlight goes on, illuminating the open phone to one side of* Mrs. Stevenson's
890 *bed. Nearby hanging down, is her lifeless hand. We see the second man,* George *in black gloves, reach down and pick up the phone. He is breathing hard.*)

George. Sorry, wrong number. (*He replaces the receiver on the hook quietly and exits as* Duffy *hangs up with a shrug and the curtain falls.*)

X

COLLABORATIVE DISCUSSION *Sorry, Wrong Number* was originally performed as a radio play. With a partner, discuss how you would translate this drama into a radio or stage production. How would you direct the actors to bring the mystery story to life in performance?

Analyze Form: Drama

 COMMON CORE RL 3, RL 5

The play you have just read is a **drama,** a form of literature meant to be performed by actors in front of an audience. Like other forms of literature, a drama presents a series of events, called the **plot,** and establishes the time and place of those events, called the **setting.** The plot centers on a **conflict,** a struggle between opposing forces, and unfolds through the characters' words and actions.

Unlike other forms of literature, a drama usually includes the following elements:

- **cast of characters**—a list of all the characters in the drama; the cast appears at the beginning of the drama.
- **dialogue**—the words that the characters say; the character's name precedes his or her lines of dialogue.
- **stage directions**—instructions for how the drama is to be performed in front of an audience; the instructions are often set in parentheses.

Because dramas are primarily meant to be performed, reading the script requires you to focus on the dialogue and stage directions to picture the action and understand the drama's meaning. Use a graphic organizer to keep track of the plot as you read and to help you analyze how the elements of the drama interact.

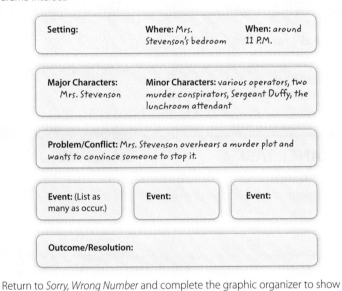

| Setting: | Where: *Mrs. Stevenson's bedroom* | When: *around 11 P.M.* |

| Major Characters: *Mrs. Stevenson* | Minor Characters: *various operators, two murder conspirators, Sergeant Duffy, the lunchroom attendant* |

Problem/Conflict: *Mrs. Stevenson overhears a murder plot and wants to convince someone to stop it.*

| Event: (List as many as occur.) | Event: | Event: |

Outcome/Resolution:

Return to *Sorry, Wrong Number* and complete the graphic organizer to show the Plot Events and Outcome/Resolution.

CLOSE READ

Analyze Form: Drama

 COMMON CORE RL 3, RL 5

Review the boldfaced terms by having students use each in a sentence that tells about the play *Sorry, Wrong Number.*

After students read the items in the graphic organizer, help them to review the play to summarize the main events of the plot. Suggest that they begin with Mrs. Stevenson's attempt to have operators trace the call she has overheard. For example:

Plot Events (in order)

(1) Mrs. S. learns that she can't order a trace. (2) Mrs. S. tells Police Sergeant Duffy about the call, but he doesn't take her seriously. (3) Growing ever more anxious, Mrs. S. keeps trying to call her husband, but the line is always busy. (4) Western Union tells Mrs. S. that her husband won't be home. (5) With rising panic, Mrs. S. calls a hospital to try to get a nurse. (6) Mrs. S. overhears someone in the house. In terror, she tries to call the police. (7) George murders Mrs. S.

Outcome/Resolution:

George hangs up the dead woman's phone after saying, "Sorry, wrong number."

Strategies for Annotation   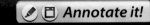 *Annotate it!*

Analyze Form: Drama

 COMMON CORE RL 3, RL 5

Share these strategies for guided or independent analysis:

- To summarize the main events, divide the play into segments based on transitions in the action.
- Highlight in yellow the start and end of each segment.
- For each segment, jot notes to sum up the action and conversation.
- Write a summarizing note to answer, "What happens?"

Department. *(Ring twice. At table L. spotlight now picks up* Sergeant Duffy, *seated in a relaxed position. Just entering beside him . . .*

. . . his pie as spotlight fades out. Mrs. Stevenson, *in bed, looks at the phone nervously.)* Why did I do that? Now he'll think I *am* a fool.

Analyzing the Text

COMMON CORE RL 1, RL 2, RL 3, RL 5, RL 7, RL 10

Possible answers:

1. She is lying in bed with pill bottles within reach. After slamming down the phone, she takes a pill. These actions reveal a character who is bedridden, possibly for a medical reason, and seems very nervous.

2. Sergeant Duffy initially reacts with interest, but he quickly loses interest. He is "not too impressed" and seems preoccupied with his food. When Mrs. Stevenson realizes that he is not going to take her fears seriously, she slams down the phone and says, "Idiot!"

3. **Exposition:** Mrs. Stevenson is bedridden and trying to call someone when she accidentally overhears a murder plot.
Rising Action: She makes call after call trying but failing to enlist the help of operators, the police, and a hospital.
Climax: Mrs. Stevenson hears an intruder and knows that she is the intended murder victim. The murderer kills her.
Falling Action: Sergeant Duffy answers Mrs. Stevenson's final call.
Resolution: The murderer delivers the title line of the play and hangs up.

4. The sound of the train in the opening scene foreshadows the plotters' mention of a train that will muffle screams. During Mrs. Stevenson's talk with Sergeant Duffy, she gives details about her own location, which match those of the murder victim.

5. Mrs. Stevenson knows that the murder will be committed in a location very similar to her own, but she doesn't perceive herself as the victim until it's too late. She also can't imagine anyone having a reason to want her dead. No one she calls takes her fears seriously—everyone perceives her as a worrier.

Speaking and Listening

COMMON CORE RL 7, SL 2

Have students watch the film clip, which can be found in their eBook. Then have them locate the corresponding section of the script for the stage play. See Extend & Reteach at the end of this selection for further instruction on comparing and contrasting a stage drama to its film version.

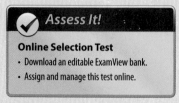

eBook *Annotate It!*

Analyzing the Text

COMMON CORE RL 1, RL 2, RL 3, RL 5, RL 7, RL 10, W 2, W 4, W 9a, W 10, SL 2

Cite Text Evidence Support your responses with evidence from the text.

1. **Infer** Reread the stage directions in lines 16–27. What do Mrs. Stevenson's actions reveal about her physical condition?

2. **Cause/Effect** Reread lines 328–531. How does Sergeant Duffy react to Mrs. Stevenson's call and how does his reaction affect Mrs. Stevenson?

3. **Summarize** Create a plot diagram like the one shown. Then place the events of *Sorry, Wrong Number* in their correct position on the diagram.

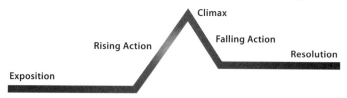

4. **Analyze** When a writer provides hints that suggest future events in a story, it's called **foreshadowing.** Go back through the drama and find examples of foreshadowing. For each example, provide a description of what eventually happens.

5. **Analyze and Evaluate** How do the setting and other details from the drama show that perception and reality do not always match up?

Speaking and Listening

Watch the clip from the film version of *Sorry, Wrong Number.* How is seeing the drama as a film different from reading it? With a partner, discuss the differences between the use of stage directions in the drama and the filmmakers' use of film techniques to create suspense and a feeling of terror.

PERFORMANCE TASK

Writing Activity: Character Analysis Write a three-paragraph character analysis of Mrs. Stevenson. Support your analysis with examples of her actions, as expressed in the dialogue and stage directions. Try to answer these questions.

- How does she perceive herself?

- How does she perceive other people such as the operators, police sergeant, and hospital workers?
- What parts of her personality might have been misunderstood or allow her to be misunderstood by others?
- How do her actions affect the drama's plot?

Assign this performance task.

PERFORMANCE TASK

COMMON CORE RL 3, W 2, W 4, W 9a, W 10

Writing Activity: Character Analysis Provide guidance for planning the writing:

- In the center of a web graphic organizer, write the name of the main character and her role in the drama.

- In the surrounding circles, write details about her traits and qualities, how others perceive her, and how she interacts with others.

Compare and Contrast: Text and Media

COMMON CORE

RL 7

TEACH

Explain to students that a play and a film share certain elements, including *settings, characters, a plot,* and *dialogue.* Review the terms, and then ask why the dramatic element of *suspense* belongs in any discussion of *Sorry, Wrong Number. (The suspense builds throughout the play. Suspense is the tense feeling that grows stronger as we wait for the outcome.)*

Emphasize that dramatists and filmmakers combine visual and sound techniques in different ways.

- **In a play,** the action is driven by dialogue, with help from the stage directions. The settings are usually limited to sets that would be built for a stage.
- **On film,** the action is recorded and often seems real. Audiences usually aren't aware of the sources of lighting, sound, and special effects, as they would be with a play. Settings are often in actual real-world locations, such as a city street, although often films are shot on sets, too.
- A movie version of a play is usually more detailed and realistic in presentation—it is one person's vision of the play's plot transferred to screen.

PRACTICE AND APPLY

Film Clip: 90 minutes

Encourage multiple viewings of the film clip and rereadings of the similar scene in the script. Provide these questions to prompt discussion of similarities and differences. Suggest that students jot down notes in a Venn Diagram.

- How do the settings differ?
- How is the main character in the film like and different from the character you pictured while reading?
- How is suspense created in the script? In the film?
- What do you notice about the dialogue in each form?
- What is alike and different about the visual and sound techniques used onstage and onscreen?
- What seems most different about reading a script and viewing a film?

 INTERACTIVE GRAPHIC ORGANIZER Have students use this Interactive Graphic Organizer: **Venn Diagram.**

Analyze Form: Drama

COMMON CORE

RL 5

RETEACH

Help students understand the ways in which drama and other forms of fiction are alike:

- Review the names of story elements in both drama and fiction by displaying these terms and questions and having students match the term with the question it answers:
  o *characters, setting, plot*
  o *When and where? What happens? Who?*
- Define *conflict* as the struggle or problem that sets the plot in motion. Have students give examples of conflicts in stories they have recently viewed or read.
- Then use a plot diagram, such as the one in Analyzing the Text, and details from *Sorry, Wrong Number* to review the five main parts of a plot.

Ask questions that will prompt discussion of the unique features of drama; for example: *Why are stage directions needed? How does an actor know what words to say? Why is dialogue so important in a play?*

 LEVEL UP TUTORIALS Assign the following *Level Up* tutorial: **Elements of Drama**

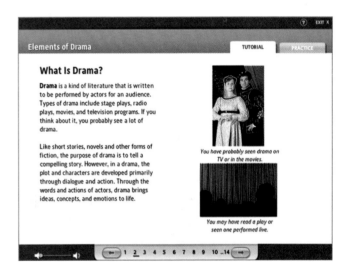

CLOSE READING APPLICATION

Guide students to locate a script for a short drama and to read it with a partner. Possible search term: "One-act plays." Have partners identify the elements of the drama that are shared with other works of fiction and the features that are shared only with other works of drama.

Comparing Versions of A Christmas Carol

A Christmas Carol

A Christmas Carol: Scrooge and Marley

A Christmas Carol

Novel by Charles Dickens

Drama by Israel Horovitz

Graphic Story by Marvel Comics

Why This Text

Students will read the same scene from *A Christmas Carol* presented in three genres: as an excerpt from the novel, as a scene from a play, and as part of a graphic story. With the help of close-reading questions, students will analyze the characters and the benefits of each genre. This will lead students to an understanding of how different genres can present a story.

Background Have students read the background about the novel *A Christmas Carol*. Tell students that Charles Dickens was the most popular novelist of his time, and wrote 15 novels and hundreds of short stories and articles. Dickens was a social reformer. He campaigned for children's rights and for the poor. When he toured America he was a vocal opponent of slavery.

SETTING A PURPOSE Ask students to compare and contrast each genre. What advantages does each genre have?

COMMON CORE

Common Core Support

- cite several pieces of textual evidence
- analyze how particular elements of a drama interact
- compare and contrast genres

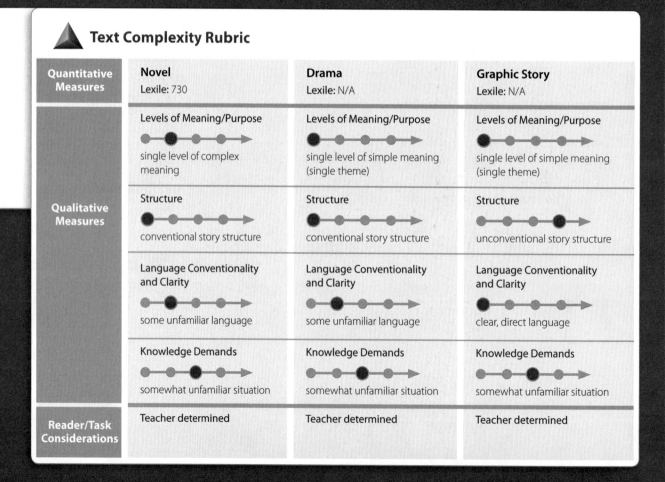

▲ Text Complexity Rubric

	Novel	Drama	Graphic Story
Quantitative Measures	Lexile: 730	Lexile: N/A	Lexile: N/A
Qualitative Measures	Levels of Meaning/Purpose — single level of complex meaning	Levels of Meaning/Purpose — single level of simple meaning (single theme)	Levels of Meaning/Purpose — single level of simple meaning (single theme)
	Structure — conventional story structure	Structure — conventional story structure	Structure — unconventional story structure
	Language Conventionality and Clarity — some unfamiliar language	Language Conventionality and Clarity — some unfamiliar language	Language Conventionality and Clarity — clear, direct language
	Knowledge Demands — somewhat unfamiliar situation	Knowledge Demands — somewhat unfamiliar situation	Knowledge Demands — somewhat unfamiliar situation
Reader/Task Considerations	Teacher determined	Teacher determined	Teacher determined

Strategies for CLOSE READING

Compare and Contrast Genres

Students should read each version of the scene carefully all the way through. Close-reading questions at the bottom of the page will help them understand how the elements of the story interact in each genre. As they read, students should jot down comments or questions about the text in the margins.

WHEN STUDENTS STRUGGLE . . .

To help students compare and contrast how each genre presents a specific scene from *A Christmas Carol*, have them work in small groups to fill out a chart like the one shown below.

CITE TEXT EVIDENCE For practice in comparing how each genre presents the same scene, ask students to give text examples and identify the advantages of each.

Text Example	Advantage
Novel:	
"The spirit was as immovable as ever." (line 14)	The reader learns a lot about the character and his previous actions.
"It shrunk, collapsed, and dwindled down into a bedpost." (lines 29–30)	This "impossible" action can be described with well-chosen words.
Drama:	
Stage directions describe the setting.	The directions are sufficient for readers to visualize the setting.
The story is told through dialogue.	Dialogue brings the story alive.
Graphic Story:	
The story is illustrated.	Each frame advances the story; the illustrations show the setting, action, and characters' expressions.
Dialogue shown with lettering and speech balloons.	The combination of kinds of lettering and speech balloons can imply emotions and volume.

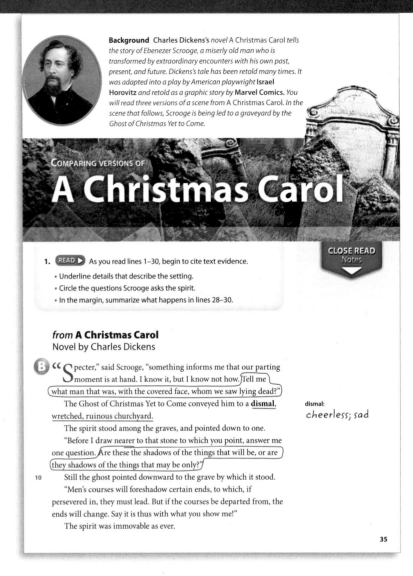

Background Charles Dickens's *novel* A Christmas Carol *tells the story of Ebenezer Scrooge, a miserly old man who is transformed by extraordinary encounters with his own past, present, and future. Dickens's tale has been retold many times. It was adapted into a play by American playwright* **Israel Horovitz** *and retold as a graphic story by* **Marvel Comics.** *You will read three versions of a scene from* A Christmas Carol. *In the scene that follows, Scrooge is being led to a graveyard by the Ghost of Christmas Yet to Come.*

COMPARING VERSIONS OF
A Christmas Carol

CLOSE READ Notes

1. **READ ▶** As you read lines 1–30, begin to cite text evidence.
   • Underline details that describe the setting.
   • Circle the questions Scrooge asks the spirit.
   • In the margin, summarize what happens in lines 28–30.

from **A Christmas Carol**
Novel by Charles Dickens

B "Specter," said Scrooge, "something informs me that our parting moment is at hand. I know it, but I know not how. Tell me what man that was, with the covered face, whom we saw lying dead?"

The Ghost of Christmas Yet to Come conveyed him to a **dismal**, wretched, ruinous churchyard.

The spirit stood among the graves, and pointed down to one.

"Before I draw nearer to that stone to which you point, answer me one question. Are these the shadows of the things that will be, or are they shadows of the things that may be only?"

10   Still the ghost pointed downward to the grave by which it stood.

"Men's courses will foreshadow certain ends, to which, if persevered in, they must lead. But if the courses be departed from, the ends will change. Say it is thus with what you show me!"

The spirit was immovable as ever.

dismal: cheerless; sad

35

1. **READ AND CITE TEXT EVIDENCE** Scrooge has seen his own grave in the future—and it is neglected. He begs the spirit to let him change his ways, and by doing so, change the way he will be remembered.

A ASK STUDENTS what happens in lines 28–30. *The spirit collapsed and turned into a bedpost.* What might this tell the reader about the spirit? *Students may suggest that the spirit is no longer interacting with Scrooge, which might imply that Scrooge's words have been heeded. They may also suggest that the spirit is simply in Scrooge's imagination and disappears after Scrooge has experienced all he needed to.*

Critical Vocabulary: dismal (line 4) Ask students to share their definitions of *dismal*. Ask them how the word choice contributes to the mood in the first paragraph.

CLOSE READ
Notes

Scrooge crept toward it, trembling as he went; and following the finger, read upon the stone of the neglected grave his own name—EBENEZER SCROOGE.

"Am I that man who lay upon the bed? No, Spirit! Oh no, no! Spirit! hear me! I am not the man I was. I will not be the man I must
20 have been but for this intercourse. Why show me this, if I am past all hope? Assure me that I yet may change these shadows you have shown
me, by an **altered** life."

For the first time the kind hand faltered.

"I will honor Christmas in my heart, and try to keep it all the year. I will live in the Past, the Present, and the Future. The spirits of all three shall strive within me. I will not shut out the lessons that they teach. Oh, tell me I may sponge away the writing on this stone!"

Ⓐ Holding up his hands in one last prayer to have his fate reversed, he saw an alteration in the phantom's hood and dress. It shrunk,
30 collapsed, and dwindled down into a bedpost.

altered:
changed

The spirit turned into a bedpost.

---

2. **◄ REREAD** Reread lines 1–30. What effect do Scrooge's repeated questions achieve?

The questions show his desperation. He is scared of the future and wants to know how he can stop it from happening. Repeating the questions shows he wants to change.

SHORT RESPONSE

Cite Text Evidence Scrooge is the only character who speaks in the scene. Which details show that the spirit is affected by what Scrooge says? **Cite text evidence** in your response.

The descriptions of the spirit's physical reactions convey that the spirit is affected by Scrooge. First, the spirit is unmoved by Scrooge, perhaps because Scrooge is too demanding. Then, the spirit's hand falters when Scrooge announces his sincere intention to change.

CLOSE READ
Notes

3. **READ ▶** As you read lines 1–28, continue to cite textual evidence.
- Underline every sentence that mentions Future's hand.
- Circle the special effects in the stage directions.
- In the margin, note an element in this drama that is not in the original story.

from **A Christmas Carol: Scrooge and Marley**
Drama by Israel Horovitz

Scrooge. Specter, something informs me that our parting moment is at hand. I know it, but I know not how I know it.
Ⓓ [FUTURE *points to the other side of the stage. Lights out on* CRATCHITS.[1] FUTURE *moves slowing, gliding.* SCROOGE *follows.* FUTURE *points opposite.* FUTURE *leads* SCROOGE *to a wall and a tombstone. He points to the stone.*]
Am *I* that man those ghoulish parasites[2] so gloated over? (*Pauses*) Before I draw nearer to that stone to which you point, answer me one question. Are these the shadows of things that will be, or the shadows
10 of things that MAY be, only?
Ⓒ [FUTURE *points to the gravestone.* MARLEY[3] *appears in light well* UPSTAGE. *He points to grave as well. Gravestone turns front and grows to ten feet high. Words upon it:* EBENEZER SCROOGE. *Much smoke billows now from the grave. Choral music here.* SCROOGE *stands looking up at gravestone.* FUTURE *does not at all reply in mortals' words, but points once more to the gravestone. The stone undulates and glows. Music plays, beckoning* SCROOGE. SCROOGE, *reeling in terror*]

The ghost of Scrooge's former partner Marley appears in this drama.

---

[1] **Crachits:** The family of Bob Crachit, Scrooge's clerk. He is mistreated and underpaid by Scrooge.
[2] **ghoulish parasites:** people who stole Scrooge's possessions and divided them up after he died.
[3] **Marley:** Scrooge's business partner, deceased at the time of the events in the drama. He appears to Scrooge as a ghost.

---

2. **REREAD AND CITE TEXT EVIDENCE**

Ⓑ ASK STUDENTS to refer to the questions they circled. What might Scrooge want to accomplish with these questions? *Students may say that he is hoping that the spirit will give him answers. They may also point out that Scrooge wants reassurance that he can change the future, and he tells the spirit of his intentions.*

Critical Vocabulary: altered (line 22) Have students compare the words *altered* and *changed*. Ask them if there is a slight difference of meaning. *Students may suggest that the word* altered *sometimes has a connotation of intentional change.*

SHORT RESPONSE

Cite Text Evidence Students should:
- cite details that explain the spirit's actions.
- explain what the spirit's actions imply.
- compare the spirit's gestures to infer a change in its attitude.

3. **READ AND CITE TEXT EVIDENCE**

Ⓒ ASK STUDENTS to consider which stage directions require special effects. What do the special effects add to the drama? *The gravestone turning and growing huge while smoke billows from the grave creates a terrifying setting, and as the gravestone undulates and glows it is clear why Scrooge is terrified.*

FOR ELL STUDENTS Encourage a volunteer student to guess the meaning of the expression *at hand*. Act out having something at hand to demonstrate why it means "near."

Sorry, Wrong Number

(14)

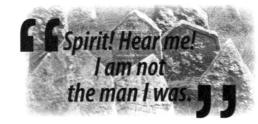

"Spirit! Hear me! I am not the man I was."

Oh, no, Spirit! Oh, no, no!

20 [FUTURE's *finger still pointing*]
Spirit! Hear me! I am not the man I was. I will not be the man I would have been but for this intercourse. Why show me this, if I am past all hope?
[FUTURE *considers* SCROOGE'S *logic. His hand wavers.*]
Oh, Good Spirit, I see by your wavering hand that your good nature intercedes for me and pities me. Assure me that I yet may change these shadows that you have shown me by an altered life!
[FUTURE's *hand trembles; pointing has stopped.*]
I will honor Christmas in my heart and try to keep it all the year.

30 I will live in the Past, the Present, and the Future. The Spirits of all Three shall strive within me. I will not shut out the lessons that they teach. Oh, tell me that I may sponge away the writing that is upon this stone!

Scrooge wants a sign that he can change his future.

F [SCROOGE *makes a desperate stab at grabbing* FUTURE's *hand. He holds it firm for a moment, but* FUTURE, *stronger than* SCROOGE, *pulls away.* SCROOGE *is on his knees, praying.*]

E Spirit, dear Spirit, I am praying before you. Give me a sign that all is possible. Give me a sign that all hope for me is not lost. Oh, Spirit, kind Spirit, I beseech thee: give me a sign . . .

4. **◄ REREAD AND DISCUSS** Reread lines 1–28. In a small group, discuss why Future stops pointing.

5. **READ ►** As you read lines 29–44, continue to cite textual evidence.
   • Underline the promise that Scrooge makes.
   • Circle the stage directions.
   • Note in the margin what Scrooge wants in lines 37–39.

38

40 [FUTURE *deliquesces,*[4] *slowly, g...*
robe drop gracefully to the groun...
nothing in them. They are morte...
SCROOGE *has his sign.* SCRO...
to black.]

[4] **deliquesces:** melts away; dissolves.

6. **◄ REREAD** Reread lines 34–36. What do the stage directions reveal about Scrooge's emotions? Cite textual evidence in your answer.

Scrooge "makes a desperate stab at" Future's hand because he wants a sign from him that things can change. Scrooge also kneels and prays, which indicates that he is humble and sincere.

SHORT RESPONSE

Cite Text Evidence How is this experience of reading a dramatization of *A Christmas Carol* different from reading the original story? Analyze elements such as stage directions and dialogue. Use your reading notes and be sure to **cite text evidence** in your response.

The additional details in the drama's stage directions make it easier to visualize the setting. For example, the smoke surrounding Scrooge's grave emphasizes how somber and spooky the scene is. The description of Scrooge's and Future's physical actions help me picture certain aspects of the scene. Also, the dialogue helps me understand that Scrooge is sorry for his behavior.

39

---

4. **REREAD AND DISCUSS USING TEXT EVIDENCE** Point out to students that Future has said nothing, but only gestured using his hand.

D ASK STUDENTS to explain Future's gestures. *First, Future points to the other side of the stage and then at a tombstone. When Scrooge asks if he is seeing a possible future, the spirit simply points again at the gravestone, and keeps pointing there until Scrooge promises to change. He then asks why he is shown the future if there is no way to alter it. The spirit's hand wavers, showing that Future hears Scrooge, and then it trembles again, revealing that Future is considering Scrooge's pleas.*

5. **READ AND CITE TEXT EVIDENCE**

E ASK STUDENTS what Scrooge is feeling in the graveyard. *He desperately wants to change so that the future he sees will not happen.* Ask what Scrooge means when he says, "Give me a sign that all is possible." *Knowing that the spirit will not talk, Scrooge wants the spirit to show him a sign that he can change the future.*

6. **REREAD AND CITE TEXT EVIDENCE**

F ASK STUDENTS what Scrooge does in lines 34–36. *He makes a desperate grab at Future's hand, holds it for a moment, then kneels and prays.* What does the word *desperate* tell you? *Scrooge is frantic for some response from the spirit.* Why is Scrooge kneeling and praying? *He is showing that he is humble and that he has no pride in begging for the spirit's help.*

SHORT RESPONSE

Cite Text Evidence Students' responses should include text evidence that supports their positions. They should:

• contrast the drama with the original story.
• analyze the stage directions and explain their effects.
• analyze the dialogue and what it reveals about Scrooge.

7. READ AND CITE TEXT EVIDENCE

G **ASK STUDENTS** what they can infer from the frames on this page. *Scrooge has seen a dead man, and the ghost takes Scrooge to a graveyard where it is probable that the dead man is buried.* Why does Scrooge suggest that the future can be changed? *He is concerned that he himself may be the dead man.*

8. REREAD AND CITE TEXT EVIDENCE

H **ASK STUDENTS** to describe the expressions on Scrooge's face. *Scrooge looks terrified. In the final frame on the page, he is shocked and distressed.* What do Scrooge's expressions reveal about his feelings? *He is scared of the ghost and of what he may learn. His expression of shock reveals that he has learned something that torments him.*

FOR ELL STUDENTS Point out that the word *indeed* is used to emphasize the truth of a statement. It can be replaced with *certainly* or *without question.*

9. READ AND CITE TEXT EVIDENCE Scrooge has been asking the ghost to assure him that he can change his ways and therefore his future, but has had no definite response.

I **ASK STUDENTS** why Scrooge grabs the ghost's hand. *He is trying to get a response from the ghost.* What happens when Scrooge grabs the ghost's hand? *The ghost shrinks and turns into a bedpost—he is no longer present. Scrooge is holding his own bedpost, as if he has awoken from a nightmare.*

CLOSE READ Notes

10. ◀ **REREAD AND DISCUSS** In a small group, discuss which was most effective in conveying the change in Scrooge: the text or the illustrations. Cite text evidence in your discussion.

SHORT RESPONSE

Cite Text Evidence Is the change in Scrooge's character most believable in the novel, the drama, or the graphic story? **Cite text evidence** in your response.

Answers may vary. Some students may say they think the change in Scrooge's character is most believable in the drama. Scrooge's dialogue, especially when he is pleading for a sign from the spirit, conveys how remorseful he feels. Likewise, the playwright reveals Scrooge's desperation for a chance to change in the stage directions.

42

10. REREAD AND DISCUSS USING TEXT EVIDENCE

🅙 **ASK STUDENTS** to assign a reporter for each group to present its response. *Some groups may suggest that the text is more effective as it tells the story, and devices such as the size and weight of the lettering show variations in emphasis; others may think that the illustrations tell the story adequately on their own. It's likely that some groups will point out that the text and illustrations work together to tell the story most effectively.*

SHORT RESPONSE

Cite Text Evidence Students' responses should include text evidence that supports their positions. They should:

- analyze the change in Scrooge's character.
- explain how the dialogue reveals Scrooge's motivations.
- determine which presentation they think most effectively portrayed Scrooge's change of character.

TO CHALLENGE STUDENTS . . .

It took Dickens only six weeks to write *A Christmas Carol*. When it was first published, it had a huge impact on the public. An American entrepreneur gave his employees an extra day's holiday after reading the story; within two months there were eight different theatrical productions playing in London; and two months after publication a publisher pirated the book.

ASK STUDENTS to research some of the effects Dickens's novel had. (These include the popularization of the phrase *Merry Christmas* and the use of the name *Scrooge* and the expression *Bah! Humbug!* A more meaningful effect was the change in the way Christmas was celebrated after Dickens's novel became such a hit—the importance of the holiday increased, and it was spent with family in merry moods.) Have students write a paragraph from their research, and compare what they find out.

DIG DEEPER

With the class, return to the Short Response on page 42. Have students share their responses.

ASK STUDENTS to cite the text evidence that led to their decision about the most effective presentation of the scene from *A Christmas Carol*.

- Have students explain how each genre presents the setting of the scene. *The novel describes the setting; the drama explains the setting in stage directions; the graphic story shows the setting in the illustrations.*
- Ask students how the story of Scrooge's character change is told in each genre. *The novel uses dialogue and descriptions to tell the story; the drama uses dialogue; the graphic story uses dialogue, description, and illustrations.*
- Have students describe the part of the story that had the greatest impact on them, and which of the versions was most effective.

ASK STUDENTS to return to their Short Response answer and revise it based on the class discussion.

COLLECTION **2**
PERFORMANCE TASK A

Interactive Lessons

If you need help . . .
• Writing Arguments
• Using Textual Evidence

Write an Opinion Essay

Folktales like "The People Could Fly" often make readers reflect on the ways we perceive our world. Consider the common saying "seeing is believing" and its meaning. After reading the texts in this collection, do you believe this saying is true? In this activity, you will draw from "The People Could Fly" and other texts in the collection to write an essay that states and supports your opinion.

A successful opinion essay

- contains an engaging introduction that clearly states the opinion, or claim
- supports the opinion with logical reasoning and relevant evidence
- presents and refutes opposing viewpoints
- uses language that effectively conveys ideas and adds interest
- concludes by leaving the audience with a lasting impression

COMMON CORE

RL 1 Cite textual evidence.
W 1a–f Write arguments.
W 4 Produce clear and coherent writing.
W 5 Develop and strengthen writing.
W 9 Draw evidence from literary or informational texts.
W 10 Write routinely.

PLAN

Form an Opinion Revisit the texts in the collection. Consider your answers to the following questions as you form your opinion:

- How do the characters or people perceive the things that happen?
- Why do the characters or people perceive things the way they do?
- How does this information relate to the meaning of the saying "seeing is believing"?

Gather Information Focus on the selection(s) that have information you can cite to support your opinion.

- Consider the points of view or opinions that are expressed in the selections.
- Make a list of the reasons you have the opinion, or claim, that you do.
- Identify evidence in the texts that supports your reasons.

***my*Notebook**

Use the annotation tools in your eBook to find evidence to support your opinion. Save each piece of evidence to your notebook.

ACADEMIC VOCABULARY

As you plan, write, and review your draft, be sure to use the academic vocabulary words.

abnormal
feature
focus
perceive
task

WRITE AN OPINION ESSAY

COMMON CORE
RL 1, W 1a–e, W 4, W 5, W 9, W 10

Introduce students to the Performance Task by reading the introductory paragraph with them and reviewing the criteria for what makes a good opinion essay. Remind students that an opinion essay needs to provide evidence to support the reasons for the writer's opinions.

PLAN

GATHER INFORMATION

Explain to students that as they plan their writing they should anticipate readers' opposing viewpoints. Students should write down opposing viewpoints and questions and prepare counterarguments to include in their essays. Point out that including counterarguments will make it harder for readers to disagree with students' opinions.

Organize Your Ideas Think about how you will organize your essay. A graphic organizer, such as a hierarchy chart, can help you to present your ideas logically.

Place your opinion in the top box, your reasons in the next row of boxes, and the evidence in the last row.

Consider Your Purpose and Audience Think about who will read or listen to your essay. What do you want them to understand? What ideas, reasons, or evidence will be most convincing to them? Keep these questions and your answers in mind as you prepare to write.

PRODUCE

WRITE YOUR ESSAY

View It!

Professional Development Podcast:

Teaching Argument

Explain to students that before they begin writing they should think about what kind of tone would be most convincing to a reader. Discuss the following questions with students:

- Would a light, humorous tone be convincing? Why or why not?
- Would a serious, formal tone be convincing? Why or why not?

PRODUCE

Write Your Essay Review the information in your graphic organizer as you begin your draft.

- Begin by introducing the topic and stating your opinion. Include an attention-grabbing lead, such as a quote, a story, or an interesting example from the texts.
- Write your reasons and support them with evidence, such as facts and examples. Use the information in your graphic organizer to help you organize your essay logically.
- Recognize opposing opinions and explain further why you disagree.
- Include words and phrases such as *because, therefore,* and *for that reason* that will link your opinion, reasons, and evidence and make your opinion clearer and more coherent.
- Establish and maintain a formal style and tone.
- Bring your essay to a conclusion. Summarize your opinion, repeating the most important reasons and evidence, and leave your audience with a lasting impression.

my **WriteSmart**

Write your rough draft in *my*WriteSmart. Focus on getting your ideas down, rather than perfecting your choice of language.

REVISE

Evaluate Your Draft Work with your partner to determine whether your essay is effective. Use the chart on the following page to help evaluate the substance and style of your essay.

- Check that your opinion is clear and logically supported with a number of reasons and evidence.
- Examine your evidence to make sure it is relevant. Look back at the selections to make sure you've accurately used text evidence to support your reasons.
- Check that your essay keeps your audience's attention and concludes with a statement that sums up your opinion.

my WriteSmart

Have your partner or a group of peers review your draft in *my*WriteSmart. Ask your reviewers to note any reasons or evidence that does not support your opinion.

PRESENT

Create a Finished Copy Finalize your essay and choose a way to share it with your audience. Consider these options:

- Present your essay as an oral report.
- Post your essay as a blog on a personal or school website.
- Present your ideas in a debate with someone who has an opposing opinion.

REVISE

EVALUATE YOUR DRAFT

Explain to students that they should reread their draft as if they were reading it for the first time. Tell students to ask themselves questions such as:

- Does the introduction clearly state my opinion?
- Are my reasons supported by good evidence?
- Have I left out anything that a reader would want to know?

PRESENT

CREATE A FINISHED COPY

Students with differing opinions can present their essays in a debate. After listening to each other's essays, allow time for students to question each other's reasoning. Remind students to take turns asking and answering questions, and to listen to each other's responses.

IDEAS AND EVIDENCE

Have students look at the chart and identify how they did on the performance task in each of the three main categories. In particular, discuss with students how convincingly they supported their opinions with logical reasons and relevant evidence from the texts. Ask students to name one way in which they might improve their writing the next time they are asked to write an opinion essay.

COLLECTION 2 TASK A
OPINION ESSAY

	Ideas and Evidence	Organization	Language
ADVANCED	• The introduction is engaging; it clearly states the writer's opinion about the statement. • Logical reasons and relevant evidence from the texts convincingly support the writer's opinion. • Opposing opinions are anticipated and effectively refuted. • The concluding section effectively summarizes the opinion and leaves a lasting impression.	• The reasons and evidence are organized logically and consistently throughout the essay. • Transitions logically connect reasons and evidence to the writer's opinion.	• The writing reflects a formal style and tone. • The use of clear, succinct language effectively conveys the writer's ideas. • Sentence beginnings, lengths, and structures vary and have a rhythmic flow. • Spelling, capitalization, and punctuation are correct. • Grammar and usage are correct.
COMPETENT	• The introduction could do more to grab the reader's attention; the introduction states the writer's opinion. • Most reasons and relevant evidence from the texts support the writer's opinion, but they could be more convincing. • Opposing opinions are anticipated, but they could be more effectively refuted. • The concluding section restates the opinion, but it is not very memorable.	• The organization of reasons and evidence is confusing in a few places. • A few more transitions are needed to connect reasons and evidence to the writer's opinion.	• The style and tone become informal in a few places. • Sentence beginnings, lengths, and structures vary somewhat. • Few spelling, capitalization, and punctuation mistakes occur. • Some grammatical and usage errors are repeated in the argument.
LIMITED	• The introduction is ordinary; the writer's opinion is not clearly stated. • The reasons and evidence are not always relevant or logical. • Opposing opinions are anticipated but not addressed logically. • The concluding section includes an incomplete summary of the opinion.	• The organization of reasons and evidence is generally logical, but it frequently doesn't follow a pattern. • Many more transitions are needed to connect reasons and evidence to the writer's opinion.	• The style and tone become informal in many places. • Sentence structures barely vary, and some fragments or run-on sentences are present. • Several spelling and capitalization mistakes occur, and punctuation is inconsistent. • Grammar and usage are incorrect in many places.
EMERGING	• The introduction is missing. • Supporting reasons and evidence are missing. • Opposing opinions are neither anticipated nor addressed. • The concluding section is missing.	• A logical organization is not used; reasons and evidence are presented randomly. • Transitions are not used.	• The style and tone are inappropriate for an opinion essay. • Repetitive sentence structure, fragments, and run-on sentences make the writing hard to follow. • Spelling and capitalization are often incorrect, and punctuation is missing. • Many grammatical and usage errors occur.

COLLECTION **2**
PERFORMANCE TASK B

Interactive Lessons

If you need help . . .
- **Writing Informative Texts**
- **Writing as a Process**

Write an Expository Essay

In *Sorry, Wrong Number* and other texts in this collection, you learned that a single action or event can dramatically change a person's perception. In the following activity, you will draw from *Sorry, Wrong Number* and "Another Place, Another Time" to write an expository essay that explains how this dramatic change occurs.

A successful expository essay

- provides an introduction that clearly states the topic and engages readers

- organizes central ideas and concepts logically to make important connections and distinctions

- includes facts, concrete details, definitions, quotations, and examples that support central ideas

- uses appropriate transitions to link ideas and precise language and techniques such as metaphor, simile, and analogy to clearly explain the topic

- provides a conclusion that follows from and supports the explanation presented

COMMON CORE

RL 1 Cite textual evidence.
W 2a–f Write informative/explanatory texts.
W 4 Produce clear and coherent writing.
W 5 Develop and strengthen writing.
W 8 Gather information.
W 10 Write routinely.

PLAN

Gather Information Review *Sorry, Wrong Number* and "Another Place, Another Time." Consider the following questions as you take notes, including examples, concrete details, and quotations, about the major events and actions that happen in each story:

- How do the main characters perceive the people and world around them?

- Which events cause the characters to change their perceptions?

- How does their change in perception affect their actions?

***my*Notebook**

Use the annotation tools in your eBook to mark up key details that you might want to include. Save each detail to your notebook.

ACADEMIC VOCABULARY

As you plan and write your essay, try to use the academic vocabulary words.

abnormal

feature

focus

perceive

task

PERFORMANCE TASK B

WRITE AN EXPOSITORY ESSAY

COMMON CORE
RI 1, W 2a–f, W 4, W 5, W 8, W 10

Introduce students to the Performance Task by reading the introductory paragraph with them and reviewing the criteria for what makes a good expository essay. Remind students that the purpose for an expository essay is to explain or inform.

PLAN

GATHER INFORMATION

Remind students that their essay needs to explain why something happens. As students look for evidence in the stories, have them look for cause-effect relationships. Point out that a cause-effect relationship doesn't always exist just because one event follows another. Students should look for evidence that the effect could not have happened if the first event had not caused it.

Organize Your Ideas Think about how you will organize and discuss your ideas. A graphic organizer, such as a three-column chart, can help you show the relationship between perceptions and events.

Characters' Perceptions	Event	How Perceptions Changed

Consider Your Purpose and Audience Think about who will read or listen to your essay and what you want them to understand. Keep this in mind as you prepare to write.

PRODUCE

WRITE YOUR ESSAY

Remind students to use their graphic organizers as a guide for their essays. Point out that relationships that cause the characters' perceptions to change should be clearly stated. Remind students that words like *because, as a result of,* and *therefore* can be used to express cause-effect relationships.

PRODUCE

Write Your Essay Review your notes and the information in your graphic organizer as you begin your draft.

- Introduce the topic clearly, previewing what is to follow in an interesting way. Include an unusual comment, fact, quote, or personal anecdote to grab the reader's attention.

- Develop your central idea and key points. Focus on the relationship between events and perceptions. Address what happens and why, using concrete details and relevant examples from the texts.

- Include transition words and phrases, such as *in addition* and *therefore* to clarify the relationship among ideas.

- Use a formal tone and precise language to explain your topic.

- Write a conclusion that follows from and supports your explanation.

my **WriteSmart**

Write your rough draft in *my*WriteSmart. Focus on getting your ideas down, rather than perfecting your choice of language.

REVISE

Review Your Draft Work with a partner to determine if you have explained your topic and ideas clearly. Use the chart on the following page to help evaluate the substance and style of your expository essay. Consider the following:

- Does the introduction grab the reader's attention? Are your topic and central idea clearly defined?
- Does each paragraph have one distinct key point? Is each point supported with concrete details, examples, or quotations from the texts?
- Are your ideas organized in a logical sequence? Do transition words help the reader follow along and reinforce logic?
- Do you use precise language that helps explain the topic?
- Does your conclusion support the information presented?

my WriteSmart

Have your partner or a group of peers review your draft in *my*WriteSmart. Ask your reviewers to note any ideas that are off topic.

PRESENT

Create a Finished Copy Finalize your essay and choose a way to share it with your audience. Consider these options:

- Present your essay as a speech to the class about people's changing perceptions as depicted in literature.
- Record yourself reading your essay as a video or audio recording, and post the recording on an approved video- or audio-sharing website.
- Post your essay as a blog on a personal or school website.
- Present your ideas about perception from the perspective of the main character in one of the stories.

REVISE

REVIEW YOUR DRAFT

Have students work with a partner to help them revise their essays. Students can take turns listening to each other's essays and offering suggestions to make them more effective. After students revise their essays, partners can reread them and discuss whether they need further revising.

PRESENT

CREATE A FINISHED COPY

Students may want to present their essays as a speech to the class. Have students practice their speech before presenting it to a class. Remind students to pause slightly after making important points, speak clearly, maintain good posture, and use expressive body language while speaking.

PERFORMANCE TASK B

ORGANIZATION

Have students look at the chart and identify how they did on the performance task in each of the three main categories. In particular, have students examine how clearly and logically they organized their essays and how effectively they used transitions. Partners can exchange essays and critique them for each other. Then, students can discuss ways to improve them.

EXPOSITORY ESSAY

	Ideas and Evidence	Organization	Language
ADVANCED	• The introduction is appealing and informative; a central idea clearly identifies the topic being explained in an engaging way. • The topic is well developed with relevant examples, concrete details, and interesting quotations drawn from the two selections. • The concluding section capably summarizes the information presented.	• The organization is effective and logical throughout the essay. • Transitions successfully connect related ideas.	• The writing reflects a formal style, with strong, precise language. • Sentence beginnings, lengths, and structures vary and have a rhythmic flow. • Spelling, capitalization, and punctuation are correct. • Grammar and usage are correct.
COMPETENT	• The introduction could do more to grab the reader's attention; the central idea identifies the topic being explained. • One or two key points could be better supported with more relevant examples, concrete details, and quotations from the two selections. • The concluding section summarizes the information presented.	• The organization is confusing in a few places. • A few more transitions are needed to connect related ideas.	• The style is inconsistent in a few places. • Language is too general in some places. • Sentence beginnings, lengths, and structures vary somewhat. • Few spelling, capitalization, and punctuation mistakes occur. • Some grammatical and usage errors are repeated in the essay.
LIMITED	• The introduction is only partly informative; the central idea only hints at a topic. • Most key points need more support in the form of relevant examples, concrete details, and quotations from the selections. • The concluding section partially summarizes the information presented.	• The organization is logical in some places but often doesn't follow a pattern. • More transitions are needed throughout to connect related ideas.	• The style becomes informal in many places. • Overly general language is used in many places. • Sentence structures barely vary, with some fragments or run-on sentences present. • Spelling, capitalization, and punctuation are often incorrect. • Grammar and usage are incorrect in many places.
EMERGING	• The introduction is missing. • Examples, details, and quotations from the selections are missing. • The essay lacks a concluding section.	• A logical organization is not used; information is presented randomly. • Transitions are not used, making the essay difficult to understand.	• The style is inappropriate for the essay. • Language is too general to convey the information. • Repetitive sentence structure, fragments, and run-on sentences make the writing monotonous and difficult to follow. • Spelling, capitalization, and punctuation are incorrect throughout. • Many grammatical and usage errors change the meaning of the writer's ideas.

© Franz Pritz/Picture Press/Getty Images

Nature at Work

❝Those who dwell . . . among the beauties and mysteries of the earth are never alone or weary of life.❞

—Rachel Carson

CONNECTING WORD AND IMAGE

ASK STUDENTS to discuss how the collection opener image and the collection quotation work together to create a connection.

PERFORMANCE TASK PREVIEW

Point out to students that they will complete two performance tasks at the end of the collection. The performance tasks will require them to further analyze the selections in the collection and to synthesize ideas about these analyses. Students will present their findings in a variety of products.

ACADEMIC VOCABULARY

View It!

Professional Development Podcast:
Academic Vocabulary

Students can acquire facility with the academic vocabulary words through frequent, repeated exposure as they analyze and discuss the selections in the collection. Academic vocabulary can be used in the instructional contexts shown below. This will enable students to incorporate the academic vocabulary words into their working vocabulary.

- Collaborative Discussion at the end of each selection
- Analyzing the Text questions for each selection
- Selection-level Performance Task
- Vocabulary instruction (for Critical Vocabulary and/or for Vocabulary Strategy)
- Language Conventions
- End-of-collection Performance Task for all selections in the collection

ASK STUDENTS to review the Academic Vocabulary word list for this collection. You may wish to pronounce each word aloud so students hear the correct pronunciation. Then, discuss the definitions and the related forms for each word. Remind students that they will encounter these five academic vocabulary words throughout the collection.

COLLECTION 3
Nature at Work

In this collection, you will explore the beauty, power, and mystery of nature.

hmhfyi.com

COLLECTION
PERFORMANCE TASK Preview

After reading the selections in this collection, you will have the opportunity to complete two performance tasks:

- In one, you will write a memoir about a natural setting that is meaningful to you.
- In the second, you will write a poetry analysis of poems about nature.

ACADEMIC VOCABULARY

Study the words and their definitions in the chart below. You will use these words as you discuss and write about the texts in this collection.

Word	Definition	Related Forms
affect (ə-fĕkt´) v.	to have an influence on or effect a change in something	affectation, affection, affective, affects, disaffected, unaffected
element (ĕl´ə-mənt) n.	a part or aspect of something	elemental, elementally, elementary, elements
ensure (ĕn-shŏŏr´) v.	to make sure or certain	ensured, ensuring
participate (pär-tĭs´ə-pāt´) v.	to be active and involved in something or to share in something	participant, participation, participator
specify (spĕs´ə-fī´) v.	to state exactly or in detail what you want or need	nonspecific, specific, specific gravity, specific heat

USING COLLECTIONS YOUR WAY

Use the following information, along with the charts on the following pages, to help you decide how you want to introduce the collection. Based on your teaching style, your students' interests, or your instructional goals, you may want to structure this collection in various ways. You may choose different entry points each time you teach the collection.

"I emphasize informational texts."

This online science article examines how scientists are learning more about earthquakes by examining giant balancing boulders that resist toppling over.

Douglas Fox *is a science, environmental, and technology writer who lives in northern California. His pursuit of science stories has led him to many exotic places, including Australia, Mauritius, Papua New Guinea, and Antarctica. In addition to writing, Fox sometimes takes photos for his stories, which have appeared in many scientific journals, magazines, and books.*

Big Rocks' Balancing Acts

Expository Essay by Douglas Fox

SETTING A PURPOSE In this article, you'll get familiar with a curiosity in nature. As you read, think about what makes these rock formations so unique and what people can learn from them. Write down any questions you have while reading.

Richard Brune was pretty dizzy the first time he shot photos while leaning out of a flying airplane.

The plane's door had been removed so Brune could ride with one leg outside. As the tiny propeller plane zigzagged over the desert, Brune leaned out over empty air. The 80 mile-per-hour headwind pummeled his face. He looked through his camera and snapped pictures of the rocky desert hundreds of feet below.

He got woozy after a few seconds, unsure which way was up. He learned to avoid that feeling by keeping his eyes on the shifting, slanting horizon whenever he could. And just in case he tumbled out of the plane, he wore a parachute. "It's not that bad," says Brune, who has done plenty of skydiving. "From 1,000 feet you've probably got at least nine or 10 seconds [of falling] before you really have to pull the rip cord."

Big Rocks' Balancing Acts **157**

"I stress the importance of language and style."

In this excerpt from his memoir, Eddy Harris lyrically recounts a revelatory experience during his solo canoe trip down the length of the Mississippi River.

Eddy Harris (b. 1956) *is a writer, adventurer, and seeker who spent his early years in New York City before moving to St. Louis. His first book, Mississippi Solo, chronicles the canoe trip he took down the entire length of the Mississippi River in the 1980s—a risky trip that this city dweller was unprepared for. He has also written about adventurous journeys in other southern regions and in Africa.*

from Mississippi Solo

Memoir by Eddy Harris

SETTING A PURPOSE Pay attention as you read to how the author recounts a special moment from his life while he canoed by himself down the Mississippi River. What makes his experience so meaningful for him?

Too many marvelous days in a row and you begin to get used to it, to think that's the way it's supposed to be. Too many good days, too many bad days—you need some break in the monotony of one to appreciate the other. If you only get sunshine, someone said, you end up in a desert.

I guess I'd had enough hard days to last me for a while, enough scary times to be able to appreciate the peaceful, easy, glorious days. On the way to Natchez,[1] I had another one, and I took full advantage of it to do absolutely nothing. No singing, no thinking, no talking to myself. Just feeling. Watching the river, noticing the changes in color, seeing the way it rises and falls depending on the wind and on what lies

[1] Natchez (năch′ĭz): a city in southwest Mississippi on the Mississippi River.

from Mississippi Solo **137**

"I want to challenge my students to the utmost."

This classic Shakespearean soliloquy, from what many believe to be Shakespeare's last great dramatic work, allows students to explore the language and poetry of the great English playwright.

Background The Tempest, *from which this excerpt is taken, is believed to be the last play Shakespeare wrote alone. In The Tempest, Prospero, the duke of Milan and a powerful magician, was exiled from Italy and left to die at sea by his brother, Antonio, and Alonso, the king of Naples. After twelve years, Fortune finally sends Antonio and Alonso within Prospero's reach. He conjures a powerful storm, the tempest, causing his enemies to shipwreck on his island. Prospero then seeks to use his magic to make these lords restore him to his rightful position.*

from The Tempest

Soliloquy by William Shakespeare

William Shakespeare (1564–1616) *is generally considered the greatest playwright in the English language. From about 1592 on, he performed in and wrote plays in London. The location most closely associated with him is the Globe Theatre, shown here. Most of Shakespeare's early plays are about historical figures, although he also wrote more light-hearted comedies. Later, Shakespeare penned his famous tragedies, including Hamlet and Macbeth.*

SETTING A PURPOSE In The Tempest, Prospero, who has learned to cast spells from a book of magic, rules over a mystical island. As you read, think about what Prospero plans to do with his power and what that means for his character.

from The Tempest **145**

mySmartPlanner | **eBook** | **myNotebook** | **myWriteSmart** | **fyi** hmhfyi.com

Collection 3 Lessons	Media	Teach and Practice
Student Edition | eBook	▶ Video Links HISTORY A&E	**Close Reading and Evidence Tracking**
ANCHOR TEXT **Memoir by Eddy Harris** from *Mississippi Solo*	🔊 **Audio** from *Mississippi Solo*	**Close Read Screencasts** • Modeled Discussion (lines 19–27) • Close Read application PDF (lines 93–100)	**Strategies for Annotation** • Analyze Meanings of Words and Phrases • Precise Language
CLOSE READER **Memoir by Helen Thayer** from *Polar Dream*	🔊 **Audio** from *Polar Dream*		
Soliloquy by William Shakespeare from *The Tempest*	▶ **Video HISTORY** *Biography: William Shakespeare* 🔊 **Audio** from *The Tempest*		**Strategies for Annotation** • Determine Meanings
Short Story by Naomi Shihab Nye "Allied with Green"	▶ **Video HISTORY** *Greening Lower Manhattan* 🔊 **Audio** "Allied with Green"		**Strategies for Annotation** • Determine Meanings of Words and Phrases • Determine Theme • Using a Glossary
Expository Essay by Douglas Fox "Big Rocks' Balancing Act"	🔊 **Audio** "Big Rocks' Balancing Act"		**Strategies for Annotation** • Analyze Structure: Essay • Prepositional Phrases
CLOSE READER **Informational Text by James Vlahos** "The Hidden Southwest: The Arch Hunters"	🔊 **Audio** "The Hidden Southwest: The Arch Hunters"		
Poem by Pablo Neruda "Ode to enchanted light" **Poem by Mary Oliver** "Sleeping in the Forest"	🔊 **Audio** "Ode to enchanted light" 🔊 **Audio** "Sleeping in the Forest"	**Close Read Screencasts** • Modeled Discussion1 "Ode to enchanted light" (lines 10–12) • Modeled Discussion2 "Sleeping in the Forest" (lines 1–5) • Close Read application PDF "Ode to enchanted light" (lines 13–15) "Sleeping in the Forest, (lines 12–18)	**Strategies for Annotation** • Analyze Form: Ode • Analyze Form: Lyric Poem
CLOSE READER **Poems by Leslie Marmon Silko, Victor Hernandez Cruz, and Gwendolyn Brooks** from *Poems About Nature*	🔊 **Audio** from *Poems About Nature*		
Collection 3 Performance Tasks: **A** Write a Memoir **B** Write a Poetry Analysis	**fyi** hmhfyi.com	**Interactive Lessons** **A** Writing Narratives	**B** Writing Informative Texts **B** Using Textual Evidence
	For Systematic Coverage of Writing and Speaking & Listening Standards	**Interactive Lessons** Conducting Research Evaluating Sources

Assess		Extend	Reteach
Performance Task	**Online Assessment**	**Teacher eBook**	**Teacher eBook**
Writing Activity: Analysis	Selection Test	**Determine the Meanings of Words and Phrases**	**Analyze Text: Memoir > Interactive Graphic Organizer >** Spider Map
Speaking Activity: Dramatic Reading	Selection Test	**Analyze Form**	**Determine Meanings of Words and Phrases**
Writing Activity: Essay	Selection Test	**Analyze Point of View > Interactive Whiteboard Lesson >** Analyze Point of View	**Determine Theme > Level Up Tutorial >** Theme
Speaking Activity: Oral Report	Selection Test	**Analyze Texts: Fact and Opinion**	**Analyze Structure: Essay > Level Up Tutorial >** Chronological Order; Cause-and-Effect Organization; Comparison-Contrast Organization
Writing Activity: Poem	Selection Test	**Determine Theme > Interactive Whiteboard Lesson >** Theme/Central Idea	**Determine Meanings of Words and Phrases > Level Up Tutorial >** Figurative Language
A Write a Memoir **B** Write a Poetry Analysis	Collection Test		

Lesson Assessments
Conducting Research
Evaluating Sources

Collection 3 Lessons	Key Learning Objective	Performance Task
ANCHOR TEXT **Memoir by Eddy Harris** from *Mississippi Solo,* p. 137A Lexile 830L	**The student will be able to . . .** identify features of a memoir and to analyze the author's style.	Writing Activity: Analysis
Soliloquy by William Shakespeare from *The Tempest,* p. 145A	**The student will be able to . . .** identify elements of Shakespearean language, interpret meaning, and analyze a soliloquy.	Speaking Activity: Dramatic Reading
Short Story by Naomi Shihab Nye "Allied with Green," p. 149A Lexile 900L	**The student will be able to . . .** determine the theme of a short story and to analyze word choice and style.	Writing Activity: Essay
Expository Essay by Douglas Fox "Big Rocks' Balancing Act," p. 157A Lexile 1060L	**The student will be able to . . .** analyze elements of an expository essay and its structure.	Speaking Activity: Oral Report
ANCHOR TEXT **Poem by Pablo Neruda** "Ode to enchanted light," p. 169A **Poem by Mary Oliver** "Sleeping in the Forest," p. 169A	**The student will be able to . . .** analyze poetic form and learn how poets use figurative language to express feelings and ideas.	Writing Activity: Poem

Collection 3 Performance Tasks:
A Write a Memoir
B Write a Poetry Analysis

Vocabulary Strategy	Language and Style	Student Instructional Support	CLOSE READER Selection
Figures of Speech	Precise Language	**Scaffolding for ELL Students:** Analyze Meanings of Words and Phrases **When Students Struggle:** Characterization	Memoir by Helen Thayer from *Polar Dream*, p. 144b **Lexile 1070L**
		Scaffolding for ELL Students: Determine Meanings	
Using a Glossary	Sentence Structure	**Scaffolding for ELL Students:** Imagery **When Students Struggle:** Figurative Language	
Latin Roots	Prepositional Phrases	**Scaffolding for ELL Students:** Analyze Language **When Students Struggle:** Summarize **To Challenge Students:** Analyze Media	Informational Text by James Vlahos "The Hidden Southwest: The Arch Hunters," p. 168b **Lexile 1060L**
		Scaffolding for ELL Students: Analyze Language **When Students Struggle:** Analyze Form	Poems by Leslie Marmon Silko, Victor Hernandez Cruz, and Gwendolyn Brooks from *Poems About Nature*, p. 174b

ANCHOR TEXT *from* **Mississippi Solo**

Memoir by Eddy Harris

*my*SmartPlanner   Create lesson plans and access resources online.

Why This Text?

Memoirs and other forms of autobiographical writing show how writers reflect on personal experiences. By analyzing a memoir, students tap into the writer's mind and build an understanding of the writer's craft. This lesson introduces students to the memoir genre and to how various choices create a writer's style.

Key Learning Objective: The student will be able to identify features of a memoir and analyze the author's style.

For practice and application:

Close Reader selection
from *Polar Dream*
Memoir by Helen Thayer

COMMON CORE Common Core Standards

RI 1 Cite textual evidence; make inferences.
RI 2 Determine central idea.
RI 3 Analyze the interaction between individuals, events, and ideas.
RI 4 Determine the meaning of words and phrases.
W 9 Draw evidence from informational texts to support analysis.
L 3a Choose language that expresses ideas precisely and concisely.
L 5a Interpret figures of speech in context.

▲ Text Complexity Rubric

	from Mississippi Solo
Quantitative Measures	**Lexile:** 830L
	Levels of Meaning/Purpose
	single topic
Qualitative Measures	Structure
	less conventional
	Language Conventionality and Clarity
	some figurative language
	Knowledge Demands
	everyday knowledge required
Reader/Task Considerations	Teacher determined
	Vary by individual reader and type of text

Eddy Harris Have students read the information about the author. Explain that the author had grown up along the Mississippi River in St. Louis and had long held a dream of canoeing its length—to experience the adventure, challenge himself, and make self-discoveries. The voyage from Lake Itasca in Minnesota to the Gulf of Mexico covers more than 2,300 miles.

SETTING A PURPOSE Direct students to use the Setting a Purpose question to focus their reading. Remind them to generate questions as they read.

Analyze Text: Memoir
COMMON CORE RI 1, RI 3
(LINES 6–8)

Tell students that a **memoir** is a form of autobiographical writing in which the author tells about personal experiences.

 CITE TEXT EVIDENCE Have students reread the full sentence in lines 6–8 and cite evidence that reveals this text to be a memoir. How have events already shaped the author's ideas about this day? *(The author uses the pronoun I and gives personal information about "hard days" and "scary times" in his past. This indicates he is writing about a personal experience. Previous events that created "hard days" make the author appreciate peaceful days.)*

Analyze the Meanings of Words and Phrases (LINE 10)
COMMON CORE RI 1, RI 4

Tell students that **style** is *how* an author writes, rather than *what* an author writes. Explain that an author's style includes ways of shaping sentences. Point out that this author's style includes **sentence fragments,** groups of words that are only parts of sentences.

B **CITE TEXT EVIDENCE** Direct students to locate sentence fragments in line 10 and to give ideas about why the author chose to write in this style. *("No singing, no thinking, no talking to myself. Just feeling." These fragments make a good connection to meaning—as if he's not even thinking connected thoughts.)*

Eddy Harris *(b. 1956) is a writer, adventurer, and seeker who spent his early years in New York City before moving to St. Louis. His first book, Mississippi Solo, chronicles the canoe trip he took down the entire length of the Mississippi River in the 1980s—a risky trip that this city dweller was unprepared for. He has also written about adventurous journeys in other southern regions and in Africa.*

from Mississippi Solo

Memoir by Eddy Harris

SETTING A PURPOSE Pay attention as you read to how the author recounts a special moment from his life while he canoed by himself down the Mississippi River. What makes his experience so meaningful for him?

Too many marvelous days in a row and you begin to get used to it, to think that's the way it's supposed to be. Too many good days, too many bad days—you need some break in the monotony of one to appreciate the other. If you only get sunshine, someone said, you end up in a desert.

I guess I'd had enough hard days to last me for a while, enough scary times to be able to appreciate the peaceful, easy, glorious days. On the way to Natchez,[1] I had another one, and I took full advantage of it to do absolutely nothing.
10 No singing, no thinking, no talking to myself. Just feeling. Watching the river, noticing the changes in color, seeing the way it rises and falls depending on the wind and on what lies

A

B

---
[1] **Natchez** (năch´ĭz): a city in southwest Mississippi on the Mississippi River.

from Mississippi Solo **137**

Close Read Screencasts   ▶ View It!

Modeled Discussions

Have students click the *Close Read* icon in their eBooks to access the screencast in which readers discuss and annotate the following key passage:

- "The river was like that to me. . . . like batter in a bowl." (lines 19–27)

As a class, view and discuss this video. Then have students work in pairs to do an independent close read of an additional passage—"I was more amazed than anything . . . nothing could happen to me." (lines 93–100)

CLOSE READ

Analyze the Meanings of Words and Phrases

COMMON CORE RI 1, RI 4

(LINES 13–25)

Tell students that the way an author describes things is another aspect of style. Point out that this author uses **personification,** a figurative comparison in which human qualities are given to something that is not human. Explain that personification is a form of **figurative language**—the imaginative use of words to express ideas that are not literally true, but are meaningful and can have an emotional impact.

ⓒ CITE TEXT EVIDENCE Tell students to reread lines 13–25, cite evidence of how the author personifies the river, and discuss the effect this comparison has on the text. *(The author says, "The river was talking to me"; "A comfortable buddy sharing a lazy day." "The river kept me company and kept me satisfied." "Then the river whispered, 'Get ready. Get ready.'" This language suggests a connection between the author and the river, as if the river is a human friend.)*

CRITICAL VOCABULARY

avalanche: The author compares a distant rainstorm to an avalanche.

ASK STUDENTS what feelings are suggested by the word *avalanche* and how a rainstorm might be like an avalanche. *(power and danger; A storm could be like an avalanche of rainwater falling from the sky.)*

insulate: The author describes passing through insulated air.

ASK STUDENTS to describe what insulated air feels like. *(It's warm because it's holding onto heat.)*

SCAFFOLDING FOR ELL STUDENTS

Analyze Meanings of Words and Phrases Using a whiteboard, project lines 13–25. Help students understand the figurative comparisons by guiding them to do the following:

- Underline the words that tell what is described.
- Highlight in yellow the words that tell what it is like.

ASK STUDENTS what this comparison helps them picture. *(The river is compared to a person, because it can talk and keep the writer company. It makes the river sound like a friend.)*

Have students use the eBook annotation tools while reading the text.

ⓒ on the river bed. Each change had something to say, and I listened to the river. The river was talking to me, changing colors from puce[2] to brown to thick, murky green. Saying nothing. The idle chatter you get when you walk with your favorite niece or nephew going no place in particular with nothing special on your minds and the little kid just jabbers away because it's comfortable and he feels like it. The river was
20 like that to me. A comfortable buddy sharing a lazy day.

Nothing else mattered then. Going someplace or not. Arriving in New Orleans or shooting past and landing in Brazil. I didn't care about anything. The river kept me company and kept me satisfied. Nothing else mattered.

Then the river whispered, "Get ready. Get ready."

The day turned gray and strange. Clouds rolled overhead in wild swirls like batter in a bowl. I could see the rainstorm forming off in the distance but swirling rapidly toward me like a dark gray **avalanche**. I felt the river dip down and up—a
30 shallow dale[3] in the water. I passed from the cool moisture surrounding me and into a pocket of thin air hot and dry. It was as though a gap had opened in the clouds and the sun streamed through to boil the water and heat up this isolated patch of river a scant[4] thirty yards long. My first thought was to shed a shirt and stay cool, but when I passed through the far curtain of the **insulated** air, I knew I had better do just the opposite. I drifted and donned my yellow rain suit and hood. The sky above grew serious and advanced in my direction with the speed of a hurricane. Looking for a place to land, I
40 scanned the shore. There was no shore. Only trees. Because of the heavy rains and high water, the shore had disappeared, and the new shoreline of solid earth had been pushed back through the trees and beyond the woods. How far beyond, I couldn't tell. I looked across to the other side of the river half a mile away. No way could I have made it over there. Halfway across and the wind would have kicked up and trapped me in the middle.

The leading edge of the storm came, and the first sprinkles passed over like army scouts. The wooded area lasted only
50 another hundred yards or so, and I thought I could easily get there before the rains arrived. I could then turn left and find

avalanche
(ăv´ə-lănch´) *n.* An *avalanche* is a large mass of snow, ice, dirt, or rocks falling quickly down the side of a mountain.

insulate
(ĭn´sə-lāt´) *v.* When you *insulate* something, you prevent the passage of heat through it.

---

[2] **puce** (py<u>oo</u>s): purplish brown.
[3] **dale:** valley.
[4] **scant:** just short of.

---

listened to the river. <u>The river</u> was talking to me, changing colors from puce to brown to thick, murky green. Saying nothing. The idle chatter you get when you walk with your favorite niece or nephew going no place in particular with nothing special on your minds and the little kid just jabbers away because it's comfortable and he feels like it. <u>The river was</u> like that to me. A comfortable buddy sharing a lazy day.

ground to pull out and wait out the storm. But the voice of the river came out and spoke to me teasingly but with a chill of seriousness down my spine. I could have ignored it, but as if reading my thoughts and not wanting me to fight it, the river grabbed the end of the canoe and turned me toward the trees. I thought I was looking for land. I wasn't. I was looking for shelter.

" The day turned gray and strange. "

The urge to get into the trees came on me quite suddenly
60 and really without thought or effort on my part. Almost an instinct.

No sooner had I ducked into the trees than the sky split open with a loud crash and a **splintery** crackle of lightning. I was not going to make it through the trees. The wind came in at hurricane strength. The tips of the trees bent way over and aimed toward the ground, like fishing rods hooked on a big one. Water flooded like the tide rushing upstream. The trees swooshed loudly as the leaves and branches brushed hard together. Branches fell. Rains came and poured down
70 bucketfuls.

The trees were tall and no more than three feet around. I maneuvered the canoe as best I could in the wind and rushing water, turned it to face upstream, and kept my back to the rain, which slanted in at a sharp angle. I reached out for the sturdiest tree I could get my arms around and I held on.

Water everywhere.[5] The river sloshed over the side and into the canoe. I tried to keep the stern pointed right into the flow so the canoe could ride the waves, but it didn't work. The canoe was twisted about, and water poured over the side. The

splinter
(splĭn´tər) v. To *splinter* means to break up into sharp, thin pieces.

D

---

[5] **Water everywhere:** The author is referring to the line "water, water, everywhere" from *The Rime of the Ancient Mariner*, a widely known poem about a sailor recounting supernatural events at sea.

from Mississippi Solo   **139**

CLOSE READ

Analyze the Meanings of Words and Phrases

 COMMON CORE RI 1, RI 4

(LINES 65–67)

Point out that the author uses descriptive language to help the reader share the experience of the storm. Tell students that a **simile** is a kind of figurative comparison in which unlike things are shown to be alike in some way. A simile includes the word *like* or *as*.

D **CITE TEXT EVIDENCE** Direct students to reread lines 65–67. Ask them to cite evidence of what the tips of the trees are compared to and to describe the impact this simile has on the text. *("The tips of trees bent way over" are "like fishing rods hooked on a big one." The simile deepens the description of the bending trees, creating an image of arched branches straining against a force, like a fishing rod strains when a big fish is hooked.)*

> **CRITICAL VOCABULARY**

splinter: The author describes the crash of thunder and the "splintery crackle" of lightning.

ASK STUDENTS what lightning made of splintery crackles might look like. *(The lines of lightning go off in different directions, like a network of cracks in crackled pottery or tree branches.)*

APPLYING ACADEMIC VOCABULARY

affect	element	participate

As you discuss the memoir, incorporate the following Collection 3 academic vocabulary words: *affect, element,* and *participate*. Ask students to discuss how Eddy Harris was **affected** by his experiences on the river. Ask what techniques he used to describe the river as a living being, able to **participate** with him in these events. Discuss the **elements** of a memoir that appear in this selection.

Analyze Text: Memoir

COMMON CORE **RI 3**

(LINES 85–100)

Tell students that the author of a memoir recalls particular events that have left a strong impression on him or her. A memoir describes how events have shaped the author's ideas about the experience being recounted.

E **ASK STUDENTS** to reread lines 85–100 and share ideas about why this particular episode is so memorable for the author and how events shaped his ideas about the episode. *(His reaction to the danger is surprising, even to him. He doesn't feel worried or fearful, but safe and protected, as if he's in a "cocoon." The storm has sparked a reaction in him—a feeling of calm—leading him to conclude that he is "one with the river.")*

CRITICAL VOCABULARY

ethereal: The author points out that something "so very definite" yet "so ethereal" urged him to seek safety in the trees.

ASK STUDENTS why the author contrasts the words *definite* and *ethereal*. *(He's trying to show that he doesn't know what the voice or intuition was. It was something he definitely heard or felt, but it was also something vague that he couldn't put his finger on.)*

COLLABORATIVE DISCUSSION Have student pairs reread segments of the memoir in order to talk with group members about the author's experience on the river. Suggest that students think about what new understanding Harris reached as a result of this experience.

ASK STUDENTS to share any questions they generated in the course of reading and discussing the selection.

---

80 rain was heavier than any I had ever been in or seen before. It really was more like a tropical storm. The heavy winds, the amount of water, the warmth of the air, and the cold rain. Only my neck was exposed to the rain. When the rain hit my neck, it ran under the rain suit and very cold down my back.

E The wind shifted as the storm came directly overhead. Water streamed straight down. I was drenched, and the canoe was filling up quickly. Anything in the canoe that could float was floating. If the rain continued for long or if the wind kept up strong and the rain kept spilling into the canoe, I would

90 sink. But I was not worried, hardly more than concerned. In fact I enjoyed the feeling of the water all around me and on me, enveloping me like a cocoon, and despite the drama I felt no real threat. I was more amazed than anything, trying to analyze the voice I had heard or whatever instinct or intuition it was that urged me to park in these trees. It had been something so very definite that I could feel it and yet so **ethereal** that I could not put my finger on it. So I stopped trying and just sat there patiently waiting and hugging my tree. I was one with this river, and nothing could happen to

100 me.

The storm slid forward, and the rain slanted in on my face. Then it moved on farther up the river to drench someone else. It was gone as suddenly as it had arisen. Only the trailing edge was left, a light rain that lasted almost until I reached Natchez.

ethereal
(ĭ-thîr´ē-əl) *adj.* If something is *ethereal*, it is light and airy.

COLLABORATIVE DISCUSSION What do you think made this experience on the river affect the author so strongly? Talk about your ideas with other group members.

TO CHALLENGE STUDENTS . . .

Characterization Point out that readers can learn a lot about Eddy Harris as a person from what he reveals in his memoir.

ASK STUDENTS to discuss in small groups what inferences they can make about Harris's character. Have students create a brief character sketch, including supporting evidence from the memoir.

Analyze Text: Memoir

COMMON CORE RI 3

A **memoir** is a form of autobiographical writing in which a writer shares his or her personal experiences and observations of significant events or people. Memoirs are often written in the first person. Authors of memoirs often

- "talk" to readers, using informal language and sharing personal feelings
- recall actual events and emphasize their reactions to them
- show how their experiences changed their attitudes and lives

What feature of a memoir appears in the first sentence of the excerpt from *Mississippi Solo*?

Analyze the Meanings of Words and Phrases

COMMON CORE RI 4

The author's **style** is the manner of writing—*how* something is said rather than what is said. Readers can analyze an author's style by making observations about these elements:

- word choice
- sentence types
- sentence length
- sentence fragments
- repetition of one or more words
- descriptive details

An author's style can be **formal,** using complex language and sentence structures, or **informal,** using simpler language, sentences, and fragments.

Figurative language is an imaginative use of words to express ideas that are not literally true but that are meaningful and can have an emotional impact. This chart shows three common kinds of figurative comparisons.

Comparison	Example	Effect
simile: a comparison of two unlike things using the word *like* or *as*	Clouds rolled overhead in wild swirls like batter in a bowl. (lines 26–27)	vivid image of changing sky
metaphor: a comparison of two unlike things that have qualities in common, without using *like* or *as*	. . . the far curtain of the insulated air . . . (lines 35–36)	warmth that is trapped inside a barrier
personification: the giving of human qualities to an animal, object, or idea	The river was talking to me . . . (line 14)	a feeling of connectedness

Find another example of a simile in this memoir. What does it help you understand?

TEACH

CLOSE READ

Analyze Text: Memoir

COMMON CORE RI 3

Explain that memoirs emphasize remembering particular personal experiences.

- Have students read the features of memoirs.
- Have students reread the lines 1–2 of the memoir and imagine that they are listening to the author speaking.
- Have students name features of a memoir in the sentence. *(The author talks in a familiar way. He uses an informal sentence structure and the pronoun* you *to mean "everyone." He reveals a personal view that life isn't supposed to be just "marvelous days.")*

Analyze the Meanings of Words and Phrases

COMMON CORE RI 4

Discuss Harris's use of language. Guide students to cite examples of sentence fragments, descriptive details, and word choice. Have students list words that describe his style. *(descriptive, informal, conversational, natural)*

To review figurative language, have students find the listed examples. Discuss how the examples impact the meaning and feeling, or **tone,** of the narrative.

Share ideas about additional similes students locate. *("sprinkles passed over like army scouts;" The comparison connects sparse drops that hint at the full "army" of rain to come.)*

Strategies for Annotation

 Annotate it!

Analyze the Meanings of Words and Phrases

COMMON CORE RI 4

Share these strategies for guided or independent analysis:

- Highlight in green figurative and descriptive language.
- Underline sentence fragments.
- Highlight any other technique you may notice in yellow.
- In a note, describe the effect of the language.

Nothing else mattered then. Going someplace or not. Arriving in New Orleans or shooting past and landing in Brazil. I didn't care about anything. The river kept me company and kept me satisfied. Nothing else mattered.

Then the river whispered, "Get ready. Get ready."

> Repetition reinforces his presence in the moment. It hints at something to come.

Analyzing the Text

COMMON CORE RI 1, RI 2, RI 3, RI 4

Possible answers:

1. *It's surprising that the author is "not worried," even though drowning or other harm seems possible. He is "more amazed than anything" at feeling protected by the river. His feeling of being "one with this river" is unexpected, because experiencing a severe storm while being vulnerable in a canoe usually creates the feeling of fear.*

2. *The author compares his figurative conversation with the river to a pleasant experience with a young niece or nephew jabbering away on a walk to "no place in particular." The comparison suggests a familiar, easy, friendly experience.*

3. *The author is in a relaxed, philosophical frame of mind, thinking about what is important in life. He reflects on "hard days" and "scary times" in the past, and he is appreciating the "peaceful, easy, glorious days" of the present.*

4. *The author is using personification to develop his idea that the river has human qualities. The river is talking to him and is warning him to prepare for danger.*

5. *In lines 81–82, the author strings together these fragments: "The heavy winds, the amount of water, the warmth of the air, and the cold rain." The author uses fragments here and elsewhere to reflect his thinking at the moment that he is experiencing events. Thoughts and images come to mind in incomplete sentences, as they often do in life. The author also uses fragments, which are more conversational, to create a more informal style.*

6. *Examples of figurative and descriptive language: "the sky split open with a loud crash"; "a splintery crackle of lightning"; the bent treetops were "like fishing rods hooked on a big one"; the rising water was "like the tide rushing upstream"; "trees swooshed loudly"; rain "poured down in bucketfuls." All of this imagery comes in a rush, suggesting a flood and conveying the sounds, sights, and feelings of the storm.*

 eBook *Annotate It!*

Analyzing the Text

COMMON CORE RI 1, RI 2, RI 3, RI 4, W 9

Cite Text Evidence Support your responses with evidence from the text.

1. **Interpret** Reread lines 85–100. What seems unexpected about the author's reactions during this experience?

2. **Compare** Reread lines 13–20 to find what the author compares to walking with a favorite niece or nephew. What does that comparison suggest?

3. **Cite Evidence** Reread lines 1–10. What does the author reveal about himself?

4. **Analyze** Reread line 25. What kind of figurative language is the author using, and what does it suggest about his connection to his environment?

5. **Analyze** Find an example of one or more sentence fragments. Why might the author have chosen to use fragments instead of complete sentences, and what does it suggest about the style of his writing?

6. **Analyze** Reread lines 62–70. What word choices and figurative language help you picture the scene?

PERFORMANCE TASK

Writing Activity: Analysis Look back through the memoir to list examples of how the author uses similes and personifies the river. Focusing on examples from your list, write a two- to four-paragraph literary analysis that explains how the author uses figurative language in this memoir.

- Support your main points by using quotes from the text as examples.
- Explain the meanings of the examples and how they contribute to important ideas of the memoir.
- Discuss what impressions you have about the author's writing style, based on his use of figurative language.

Assign this performance task.

PERFORMANCE TASK

COMMON CORE RI 4, W 9

Writing Activity: Analysis Help students develop a plan for their analyses by

- starting with a sentence that gives a central idea about the author's relationship with the river
- listing text examples of similes and personification to support that idea
- jotting down notes about the meanings of the figurative language and the effects they have on the reader

Critical Vocabulary

avalanche   insulate   splinter   ethereal

Practice and Apply Choose the situation that is the better match with the meaning of the vocabulary word. Give your reasons.

1. **avalanche**
   a. Snow fell for two days, covering the rooftops and streets.
   b. Snow on a mountainside suddenly loosened and slid.

2. **insulate**
   a. On a hot day, a car with closed windows heats up quickly.
   b. An old, drafty house is expensive to heat in winter.

3. **splinter**
   a. People stroll on the boardwalk that crosses the wetland.
   b. River water breaks up into many streams and smaller creeks.

4. **ethereal**
   a. The desert travelers came to an area with palm trees and shade.
   b. The desert travelers mistakenly thought they saw a lake ahead.

Vocabulary Strategy: Figures of Speech

An author may make an **allusion,** a reference to a famous person, place, event, or work of literature. Although an allusion is not explained, the reader may recognize its source and meaning, or may do research to learn about it. Look for the allusions in these examples:

> Poppa's shoe store closed after only a year, and he lost money. Poppa worked hard, but he just didn't have the Midas touch.

> All of my cousins were strong and good-looking; I was unhappily aware of my ugly duckling status from an early age.

In the first example, the phrase *the Midas touch* is an allusion to the Greek myth about King Midas, who was briefly able to turn everything he touched into gold. The second example includes an allusion to the fairy tale "The Ugly Duckling," by Hans Christian Andersen. In that tale, an odd-looking duckling endures abuse until it grows up to find its true family of beautiful swans.

Practice and Apply Reread the paragraph that begins on line 76 of the memoir. The first sentence of that paragraph is an allusion to a well-known quotation from the long poem *The Rime of the Ancient Mariner*, by Samuel Taylor Coleridge. Find the poem and identify the famous lines in Part II. What meaning from the poem might Harris have tried to connect to his own experience?

Critical Vocabulary

COMMON CORE L 5a

Answers:

1. *b*

2. *a*

3. *b*

4. *b*

Vocabulary Strategy: Figures of Speech

The line "Water everywhere" in this memoir may be an allusion to the lines in stanza nine of Part II of Coleridge's poem: "Water, water everywhere, / Nor any drop to drink." In the poem, these lines come at a part where the Mariner and his crew are stuck at sea with no wind, becoming more and more desperate for drinking water in the harsh sun. The line expresses the frustration that the sailors are surrounded by ocean water, but can drink none of it. In his memoir, Harris uses the allusion to underscore his situation—being surrounded by water both below (the river) and above (the rain). He is alone in a possibly desperate situation.

Language Conventions: Precise Language

Tell students that strong writing is concise—it has no unnecessary words. It is also precise, or sharply written—with concrete nouns and vivid verbs.

Possible answers:

1. *Cottony clouds sailed slowly overhead like ships.*

2. *A streak of lightning suddenly zigzagged from a gigantic cloud to the ground.*

3. *Thunder boomed, and the ground shook.*

4. *I scanned the area for shelter and dashed into a nearby building.*

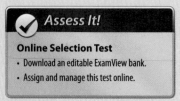

Assess It!

Online Selection Test
- Download an editable ExamView bank.
- Assign and manage this test online.

Language Conventions: Precise Language

When you write, choose words carefully to ensure that readers picture what you see and understand what you mean. Use precise words to express exact meanings and to be concise, using only necessary words. Compare these two sentences:

> I moved the canoe in the water, which was rushing very fast.

> I maneuvered the canoe in the rushing water.

You can tell that the second sentence is the stronger one. The word *maneuvered* is more precise than *moved*. In the clause *which was rushing very fast*, the words *very fast* are unnecessary because they repeat the meaning of *rushing*. The single word *rushing* conveys the same meaning.

This sentence appears in the excerpt from *Mississippi Solo*. Note how the author has used vivid language and precise words—*gap, streamed, boil, isolated patch, a scant thirty yards long*—to help the reader participate in the scene.

> It was as though a gap had opened in the clouds and the sun streamed through to boil the water and heat up this isolated patch of river a scant thirty yards long.

Practice and Apply Each of these sentences is not as strong as it could be. Rewrite the sentence to make it more precise and concise.

1. The clouds in the sky overhead moved very slowly and looked interesting.

2. All at once, a streak of lightning suddenly traveled down from a big cloud.

3. I heard the thunder, which was loud and shook the ground under my feet a lot.

4. I looked around for a place that would be safe and went into a building that was nearby.

Strategies for Annotation  Annotate it!

Language Conventions: Precise Language

COMMON CORE L 3a

Have students use their eBook annotation tools to analyze the Practice and Apply sentences. Ask them to do the following:

- Underline words that repeat meaning.
- Highlight in green other unnecessary words.
- Highlight in yellow words that could be made more precise.

> The clouds <u>in the sky overhead</u> moved very slowly and looked interesting.

Determine the Meaning of Words and Phrases

COMMON CORE

RI 4

TEACH

Explain that examining authors' sentences gives student writers ideas for shaping their own sentences. Display the term **syntax,** defining it as "the ways in which words, phrases, and clauses are put together to form grammatical sentences." Point out that word order is a main feature of syntax.

Tell students that there are many correct ways to order words within sentences, and the author's syntax choices reflect his or her style.

Display these sentences:

- You begin to get used to marvelous days if there are too many of them, and you begin to think they're supposed to happen.
- If you have too many marvelous days, you begin to get used to them, to think that all days are supposed to be like that.

Prompt students to identify the sentence structure of each example, identifying the differences in word order, meaning, emphasis, and effect between the sentences.

Direct students to compare the two displayed sentences to the first sentence in the memoir they have just read:

- Too many marvelous days in a row and you begin to get used to it, to think that's the way it's supposed to be.

Ask why the author might have chosen that syntax. *(It sounds informal, puts the emphasis on "marvelous days," and has an intriguing word order.)*

PRACTICE AND APPLY

As students draft their analyses for the Performance Task, tell them to use what they have learned about syntax when they discuss the author's style.

Analyze Text: Memoir

COMMON CORE

RI 3

RETEACH

Tell students that a **memoir** is a kind of nonfiction writing in which the writer recalls actual events he or she experienced. Review and discuss these features of a memoir:

- **First-person point of view:** The writer uses first-person pronouns, such as *I, me,* and *mine,* so readers can see events through his or her eyes.
- **Informal language:** The sentences sound like someone having a conversation.
- **Personal feelings and reactions:** The words describe how the person feels about the experience.
- **A changed attitude or new understanding:** The writer tells about the importance of an experience—how the experience leads to new ideas or insights that are significant to the writer.

Have students identify one or more of the listed features in each of these sentences:

- The first time I saw the little yellow house, I said to myself, "Someday I'm going to live there."
- Above all else, I felt at peace and grateful just to be alive.
- When that roller coaster began to plummet, I thought for sure I'd black out.

CLOSE READING APPLICATION

Students can apply the skill to another memoir from the school or classroom library. You might suggest the following: *An American Childhood* by Annie Dillard or *Red Scarf Girl* by Ji-li Jiang.

Tell students to read the memoir, or a portion of it, and to identify examples of the features discussed in the lesson. Ask students to record each example in a graphic organizer, such as a Spider Map. Then, ask them to include descriptions of the effectiveness of each feature and an explanation of how it shapes, or is shaped by, the events of the narrative.

INTERACTIVE GRAPHIC ORGANIZER
Spider Map

from Polar Dream

Memoir by Helen Thayer

Why This Text

Students may read a memoir without a complete understanding of the way elements of the text interact. Memoirs such as this one by the renowned explorer Helen Thayer may use figurative language or an introspective writing style that becomes clear only after the reader's examination of explicit textual evidence. With the help of the close-reading questions, students will develop an understanding of how the particular elements of a memoir are woven together to reveal the thoughts and emotions of the writer.

Background Have students read the background and the information about the author. Introduce the selection by telling students that Thayer has had a lifetime of adventures, including walking 4,000 miles across the Sahara Desert, kayaking 2,200 miles in the Amazon, and studying wild wolves for six months in the Canadian Yukon, actually living alongside a wolf den to study the pack's daily live. Tell them she has been honored by the White House and the National Geographic Society and was named "One of the Great Explorers of the 20th Century."

SETTING A PURPOSE Ask students to pay close attention to how this true story is told. How soon into the memoir did students begin to recognize that the writer was giving her own observations about an event that really happened to her?

Common Core Support

- cite multiple pieces of textual evidence

- analyze interactions between elements of an informational text

- determine the meaning of words and phrases, including figurative language, and analyze the impact of specific word choice on meaning and tone

- determine an author's point of view or purpose in a text

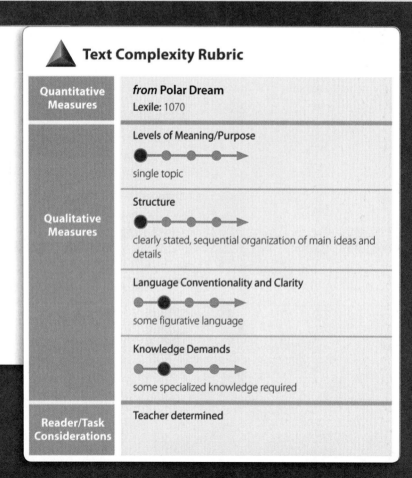

Text Complexity Rubric

Quantitative Measures

from Polar Dream
Lexile: 1070

Qualitative Measures

Levels of Meaning/Purpose

single topic

Structure

clearly stated, sequential organization of main ideas and details

Language Conventionality and Clarity

some figurative language

Knowledge Demands

some specialized knowledge required

Reader/Task Considerations

Teacher determined

Strategies for CLOSE READING

Analyze the Meanings of Words and Phrases

Students should read this memoir carefully all the way through. Close-reading questions at the bottom of the page will help them focus on a thorough analysis of the meanings of words and phrases, including figurative language and word choice, and of the author's style. As they read, students should record comments or questions about the text in the side margins.

WHEN STUDENTS STRUGGLE . . .

To help students analyze the meanings of words and phrases, especially of figurative language, have them work in small groups to fill out a chart such as the one shown below as they analyze the memoir.

CITE TEXT EVIDENCE For practice in "unpacking" the meaning of figurative language in a text and the comparison created by each figure of speech, have students cite specific textual evidence to complete the chart.

Comparison	Example	Effect
Simile:	"... my nerves were as tight as violin strings ..." (line 87)	creates a vivid image of her taut nerves about to snap
Metaphor:	"My hands were blistered clubs ..." (lines 1–2)	creates a vivid image of cold, swollen hands
Personification:	"... she was a tender, attentive mother caring for her cubs." (lines 128–129)	likens the polar bear to a human mother

Background Helen Thayer *is a decorated explorer and adventurer. Her achievements include being the first woman to walk across the Sahara Desert, kayaking 1,200 miles across two rivers in the Amazon, and walking 1,600 miles across the Gobi Desert in Asia. In 1988, at the age of 50, she became the first woman to walk and ski to the North Pole without a snowmobile or dogsled. She wrote about her adventure in* Polar Dream.

from
Polar Dream

Memoir by Helen Thayer

CLOSE READ
Notes

1. **READ ▶** As you read lines 1–64, begin to collect and cite evidence.
   - Circle the metaphor in the second sentence, and explain the meaning of it in the margin.
   - Underline items Thayer wears to stay warm.
   - Write in the margin why it's important for Thayer to stay hydrated.

A I woke at 5:30 A.M. after a restless night's sleep. My hands were blistered clubs and hurt every time I touched something. Overnight enormous blood blisters had formed to reach all the way down to the second joint of each finger except my left little finger, which had somehow escaped freezing. I knew I had to keep the blisters intact so that my hands wouldn't become raw and bleeding. It would be better to use my heavy mitts as much as possible even though they were clumsy. I thought back to the previous morning, remembering the crazy repacking of my sled with gear ending up in all the wrong
10 places as I just stood there not wanting to offend anyone. I decided what is done is done. One learns one's lessons the hard way sometimes and, besides, if that was to be the only problem of the whole expedition, then I would consider myself lucky.

Reaching over I painfully and slowly unzipped the tent door to inspect the new day. Just like yesterday. The wind had dropped. I looked out at cold, clear skies and a light northerly wind. Another

Her hands are unresponsive and feel wooden because of painful blisters.

45

1. READ AND CITE TEXT EVIDENCE

A ASK STUDENTS to read their margin notes to a partner and then write one response that explains the meaning of the metaphor in lines 1–2, citing specific textual evidence. *Students should explain that Thayer's hands are so cold, swollen, and unresponsive that she compares them to "blistered clubs," using a metaphor to create a striking image that appeals to the reader's sense of sight and touch.*

FOR ELL STUDENTS Have students reread lines 14–23. Point out the weather vocabulary: *wind* (line 15), *cold, clear* (line 16), *another beautiful ... day* (lines 16–17), *snowstorm* (line 18), and *frost* (line 21). Have students define these words by using context clues, or by drawing them or using gestures.

beautiful Arctic day. Charlie was up and looking at his empty bowl. I crawled out of my sleeping bag, creating a minor snowstorm as I brushed against the frost-covered tent roof while I pulled on my

20 jacket. I'm normally a morning person but there was something about the intense cold, the tent frost down my neck, and my sore hands that made that morning most unappealing. But it was time to greet Charlie and start the day.

Stepping out of the tent, still in my insulated blue camp booties, I checked the thermometer, minus 41 degrees. I looked around for bears or tracks and saw none, but I was surprised to notice that the shore ice with its jagged blocks and pinnacles ended only one hundred feet from my tent. In the settling light of last evening it had looked as if I was at least four hundred yards from the closest rough shore ice. It

30 was my first lesson in the **sly** nature of the changing Arctic light and the way it affected depth perception.

sly: clever; tricky

Charlie was bouncing up and down at the end of his chain looking well rested. I hugged him good morning as his soft tongue wiped across my face. I poured what looked like a pound of dog food into his bowl, which he attacked with gusto.

Now for my stove. I simply had to light it that morning. I needed water for the next leg of my journey and a hot breakfast would get my day started off right. I carefully put a pair of woollen gloves over my liners and with clenched teeth I forced my cruelly protesting fingers

40 to push the stove tube into the gasket at the top of the fuel bottle. Success. I lit it, put snow and ice into my two-quart pan, and soon had warm water. To conserve fuel, I heated water only to a temperature at which I could still put my finger into it.

It was only six o'clock, so I decided to have a leisurely breakfast of a bowl of granola, milk powder, coconut flakes, raisins, and butter mixed with warm water. I sat on my sled to enjoy the full effect of my first breakfast of the expedition only to find that after the third spoonful it was frozen. So much for leisurely breakfasts! I added more warm water and ate the rest as fast as possible. Then I melted enough

50 ice to fill two vacuum bottles with water and a carbohydrate powder.

Thayer wants to stay hydrated so she can be warm and energized.

The dry Arctic air holds little moisture, causing quick dehydration of the body, which, in turn, causes early fatigue and reduces the body's ability to keep warm, so fluid would be just as important as

food to keep my energy reserves up. I put my day's supply of crackers, cashews, walnuts, and peanut butter cups in my day food bag along with the two vacuum bottles and slipped everything down into the front of the sled bag. Then, remembering Charlie's appetite for crackers, I added a few more.

B Last to be packed was the tent. I was completely **engrossed** in
60 finding a way to twist the tent ice screws out of the ice so that my hands wouldn't scream in protest when suddenly I heard a deep, long growl coming from the depths of Charlie's throat. In a flash I looked at him and then in the direction in which he was staring. I knew what I would see even before I looked. A polar bear!

engrossed: absorbed; focused

It was a female followed by two cubs coming from Bathurst Island,[1] slowly, purposefully, plodding through the rough shore ice toward me. They were two hundred yards away. With a pounding heart I grabbed my loaded rifle and flare gun and carefully walked sideways a few steps to Charlie, who was snarling with a savagery that
70 caught my breath. Without taking my eyes off the bear, I unclipped Charlie from his ice anchor and, again walking sideways, I led him to the sled where I clipped his chain to a tie-down rope. The bear, now only 150 yards away, wasn't stopping. Her cubs had dropped back but she came on with a steady measured stride while I frantically tried to **D** remember all the Inuit[2] had told me. Keep eye contact, move sideways

---
[1] **Bathurst Island:** an uninhabited island that is part of the Canadian Arctic Archipelago.
[2] **Inuit:** a group of people belonging to the Eskimo family who live throughout the Canadian Artic.

2. **◄ REREAD AND DISCUSS** Reread lines 59–64. In a small group, discuss whether Thayer seems prepared for the situation that occurs.

3. **READ ►** As you read lines 65–103, continue to cite textual evidence.
   • Underline what Thayer was told to do if a polar bear approached her.
   • Circle figurative language that describes how Thayer feels during the encounter with the polar bear.
   • In the margin, explain what this figurative language conveys about Thayer.

46

47

Critical Vocabulary: sly (line 30) Have students share their definitions of *sly*. Ask them to provide two or more synonyms of the word *sly*, leading them to recognize that a synonym is a word that has the same (or nearly the same) meaning as that of another word. *Students should be able to cite the words* clever, tricky, *and* crafty, *among others.*

FOR ELL STUDENTS Point out the words *perception* (line 31), *conserve, temperature* (line 42), *fluid* (line 53), and *energy* (line 54). Explain, or ask a volunteer to explain, the meaning of each of the words. Point out that many Spanish-speaking students might recognize that these words are cognates for the Spanish words *percepción, conservar, temperatura, fluido,* and *energía.* Lead students to recognize that many scientific or technical terms have cognates in many languages.

2. **REREAD AND DISCUSS USING TEXT EVIDENCE**

B **ASK STUDENTS** to appoint a reporter for each group to cite textual evidence and line numbers about the level of Thayer's preparedness for the situation with the polar bear. *Students should cite evidence from lines 59–64 to support their position.*

3. **READ AND CITE TEXT EVIDENCE**

C **ASK STUDENTS** to read their margin notes to a partner and then produce one response that best describes how Thayer feels during her encounter with the polar bear. *Students should cite the simile that Thayer uses in lines 87–88 to convey the tension and anxiety she feels during her confrontation with the bear.*

Critical Vocabulary: engrossed (line 59) Have students share their definitions of *engrossed.* Why does she use the word to provide the backdrop for the imminent encounter with the bear? *She may want to show that she is surprised by the situation that is about to occur.*

CLOSE READ Notes

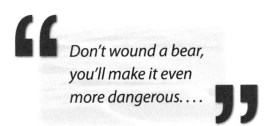

Don't wound a bear, you'll make it even more dangerous. . . .

or slightly forward, never backward, stay calm, don't show fear, stand beside a tent, sled, or other large object to make my five feet three inches appear as large as possible. Don't shoot unless forced to. Don't wound a bear, you'll make it even more dangerous, and never run.

80 Repeating to myself, "Stay calm, stay calm," I fired a warning shot to the bear's left. The loud explosion of the .338 had no effect. On she came. I fired a flare, landing it a little to her right. Her head moved slightly in its direction but she didn't stop. I fired another flare, this time dropping it right in front of her. She stopped, looked at the flare burning a bright red on the white ice, then looked at me. She was only one hundred feet away now.

Thayer is tense and nervous.

C By this time my nerves were as tight as violin strings and my heart could have been heard at base camp. The bear began to step around the flare, and I dropped another flare two feet in front of her. Again
90 she stopped, looked at the flare and at me. Then she fixed her tiny black eyes on Charlie, who was straining at the end of his chain, snapping and snarling trying to reach her. She looked back at her

rabid: *raging; uncontrollable*

cubs. I could sense her concern about Charlie's snarling, **rabid** act and her cubs. She waited for her cubs to catch up, then moved to my left in a half circle. In spite of my sore fingers I fired two more flares in quick succession, trying to draw a line between her and me. She stopped, then moved back toward my right. I fired two more flares and again she stopped. She seemed to want to cross the line of flares but was unsure of the result and of Charlie, so she elected to stay back.

48

100 She kept moving right in a half circle, still one hundred feet away. Finally, with a last long look she plodded north with her two new cubs trotting behind her, their snow-white coats contrasting with their mother's creamy, pale yellow color.

F The whole episode lasted fifteen minutes but seemed years long. I was a nervous wreck. My hands were shaking as I stood still holding my rifle and flare gun, watching the trio slowly move north. But in spite of the mind-numbing fear that still gripped me, I could feel deep down inside a real satisfaction. I now knew that I could stand up to a bear in the wild, stay calm enough to function and still remember the
110 words of wisdom from the Inuit. With Charlie's help I had passed my first test. The bear had been completely silent as it had approached and moved around me on paws thickly padded with fur on the undersides. I was thankful for Charlie's warning. Now he had stopped growling and snarling but still stood rigid, watching the bears as they zigzagged in and out of the rough ice hunting for the seals that lived in the cold waters beneath the ice. He seemed to hardly notice the giant hug I gave him. He was still on guard.

The bears were only about four hundred yards away but I decided to continue packing my tent and move around to stay warm, still
120 keeping a wary eye on the bears. I was getting cold. My fear and flowing adrenaline had kept me warm but I was beginning to shiver

Charlie made noise when the polar bear approached; Thayer had not heard her. Charlie keeps watch even after the immediate threat of the bear has passed.

CLOSE READ Notes

4. **◀ REREAD** Reread lines 65–86. The writer could have used many short sentences to retell the advice she received. What is the effect of retelling all the advice she received in three sentences?

Retelling the advice in this way creates the effect that she is thinking quickly and trying to retrieve any bit of advice that will help her.

5. **READ ▶** As you read lines 104–129, continue to cite textual evidence.

- Underline the emotions Thayer feels after the polar bear leaves.
- Make notes in the margin about why Thayer is grateful to Charlie.
- Circle words that describe the polar bear.

49

WHEN STUDENTS STRUGGLE . . .

To help students understand the interactions between particular elements in a text, such as how ideas influence individuals or events, or how individuals influence ideas or events, ask them to reread lines 65–103. Invite students to work in small groups to discuss how the advice given to Thayer by the Inuit about how to react, especially to remain calm, probably saved her life.

Critical Vocabulary: rabid (line 93) Have students explain *rabid* as Thayer uses it here. Why does she use the word to describe Charlie's actions toward the polar bear and her cubs? *Thayer probably wants to emphasize how savage polar dogs can be if provoked.*

4. **REREAD AND CITE TEXT EVIDENCE**

D ASK STUDENTS to reread the three sentences in lines 75–79, observing their sentence type and length to analyze the author's style. *Students should point out that all three sentences are imperative, showing her quick recall of the Inuit advice about what not to do if confronted by a polar bear, and that sentences 1 and 3 seem to have combined short, choppy sentences combined into a single sentence, evidencing Thayer's quick thinking and retrieval of the advice that could now save her life.*

5. **READ AND CITE TEXT EVIDENCE** Remind students that in a memoir, the author expresses his or her point of view, as well as personal thoughts and emotions.

E ASK STUDENTS to read their margin notes to a partner and then create a response about Thayer's feelings toward Charlie, showing why she is grateful to him. *Students should cite explicit textual evidence from lines 110–111 and 113–117.*

CLOSE READ
Notes

now. I finished packing and stood around until ten o'clock, keeping warm, until I was sure the bears had disappeared and weren't circling back to me. If I stayed out from the coast, keeping away from the rough ice, I hoped to make up the time I had lost. But as I started out I still thought about the bears. Even as frightened as I had been, it was a thrill to see a bear and her cubs in their natural environment. She was unafraid of me, powerful and dangerous, yet graceful. And she was a tender, attentive mother caring for her cubs.

6. **◀ REREAD** Reread lines 104–129. How does the author's specific word choice convey the importance of this experience to her? Support your answer with explicit textual evidence.

"Shaking" and "mind-numbing fear" are vivid words that emphasize the danger she faces. Thayer's use of words like "satisfaction" and "thrill" convey the pride she feels in how she handled the situation.

SHORT RESPONSE

Cite Text Evidence Analyze the way Thayer uses a particular style to convey the meaning of events in the text. Include examples of words and phrases as they are used in the text, such as figurative language and specific word choice. Be sure to review your reading notes and **cite text evidence** in your response.

At the beginning of the essay, Thayer uses a metaphor and specific descriptive details to convey the harsh conditions she faces. When the polar bear arrives, she groups a series of sentences together in a way that reveals the speed of her thinking. However, once the polar bear moves on, she describes the "thrill" she felt and "satisfaction" she experiences.

50

6. **REREAD AND CITE TEXT EVIDENCE**

F **ASK STUDENTS** to identify the author's specific word choice in describing how she felt after the experience with the polar bear. How does her word choice convey her ideas and emotions through specific language? *Students should cite textual evidence from lines 104–129 to support the idea that Thayer adapts her word choice and writing style to express her thoughts about (and pride in) her response to this episode.*

SHORT RESPONSE

Cite Text Evidence Students should cite specific textual evidence to support their analysis of Thayer's writing style to convey the meaning of events. Students should:

- analyze words, phrases, figurative language, and word choice.
- assess whether her style supports her meaning and tone.
- cite specific evidence from the text to support their reasons.

TO CHALLENGE STUDENTS . . .

For more context about the Arctic, the polar region at the northernmost part of the Earth, students can conduct print, online, or multimedia research to write a report about this frigid place and the skills needed to survive there.

ASK STUDENTS to do some preliminary research to find an aspect of the topic that interests them. Possible topics for their research might include:

- The Dangers Faced by Polar Explorers
- How Our Changing Climate Is Affecting the Arctic
- The Daily Life of the Inuit
- How Polar Bears Survive in the Arctic

With the class, discuss the following elements of a research report after students have chosen a topic:

- Plan Your Research
    Write questions about your topic.
    Research your topic and take notes.
    Organize your notes.
    Write an outline based on your notes.
- Write your Report
    Keep your purpose and audience in mind.
    Write a first draft, revise your report, and proofread it.
- Publish and Share
    Make a final copy of your report.
    Publish and share it.

ASK STUDENTS what they hope to discover as they research their report. How is the information they find similar to, yet different from, the autobiographical account of the Arctic shared by Thayer?

DIG DEEPER

With the class, return to Question 2, Reread and Discuss. Have students share the results of their discussion.

ASK STUDENTS whether they were pleased with the outcome of their group discussions. Have each group share its feelings about Thayer's preparedness for the situation with the polar bear. Encourage groups to tell whether they thought that Thayer had portrayed the event accurately. How did her style of writing, including her specific word choice, use of figurative language, and of varying sentence types and lengths, convey the telling of the event?

- Encourage each group to explain what the majority opinion of the group was concerning Thayer's level of preparedness. What compelling evidence did the group cite from the memoir to support this opinion?
- Guide students to tell whether there was any convincing evidence cited by group members holding a different opinion. If so, why didn't it sway the group's position?
- Have groups explain whether or not they had found sufficient evidence to support their opinion that she was prepared (or ill-prepared) for the encounter with the bear. Did everyone in the group agree as to what made the evidence sufficient? What conflict-resolution techniques did the group use to resolve any differences of opinion?
- After students have shared the results of their group's discussion, ask whether any other group had expressed an opinion that had differed from their own. Ask if the other group's opinion had merit. If so, why didn't it persuade the group to change its position?

ASK STUDENTS to return to their Short Response answer and revise it based on the class discussion.

CLOSE READING NOTES

*my*SmartPlanner Create lesson plans and access resources online.

from The Tempest

Soliloquy by William Shakespeare

Why This Text?

Reading this soliloquy by one of the most famous characters in Shakespearean drama exposes students to the language and dramatic techniques of a literary giant. This lesson helps students meet the challenge of interpreting Shakespearean vocabulary, grammar, sentence structure, and allusions.

> ▶ **View It!**
> Professional Development Podcast:
> **Text Complexity**

Key Learning Objective: The student will be able to identify elements of Shakespearean language, interpret meaning, and analyze a soliloquy.

COMMON CORE Common Core Standards

RL 1 Cite textual evidence.
RL 2 Determine a central idea.
RL 4 Determine meanings of words and phrases.
RL 5 Analyze how a soliloquy's form or structure contributes to its meaning.
SL 1 Engage in collaborative discussions.
SL 6 Adapt speech to a variety of contexts and tasks.

▲ Text Complexity Rubric

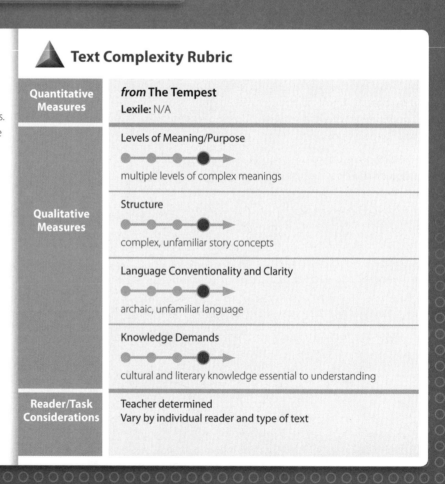

	from The Tempest
Quantitative Measures	**Lexile:** N/A
Qualitative Measures	Levels of Meaning/Purpose — multiple levels of complex meanings
	Structure — complex, unfamiliar story concepts
	Language Conventionality and Clarity — archaic, unfamiliar language
	Knowledge Demands — cultural and literary knowledge essential to understanding
Reader/Task Considerations	Teacher determined Vary by individual reader and type of text

TEACH

CLOSE READ

Background Have students read the background to this excerpt and the information about the playwright. Share this additional information about this soliloquy:

- Shakespeare makes allusions to Roman mythology. He often borrowed from earlier sources, and some of the lines in this soliloquy are nearly identical to lines in the Roman poet Ovid's famous work *Metamorphoses*. Educated members of Shakespeare's audiences may well have recognized the literary allusions.

- When Prospero begins this soliloquy, the play is nearing its end. Prospero has just sent away his servant, an airy spirit named Ariel, to bring back the characters who are under Prospero's spell. Prospero has just said, "Go release them, Ariel. / My charms I'll break, their senses I'll restore, / And they shall be themselves."

SETTING A PURPOSE Direct students to use the Setting a Purpose prompt to focus their reading. Remind them to generate questions as they read.

Analyze Form

◌ COMMON CORE RL 5

Tell students that Prospero is the main character in *The Tempest*. Point out the word *soliloquy* below the title, explaining that a **soliloquy** is a speech given by a character alone on the stage. In a soliloquy, the character reveals thoughts and plans.

A **ASK STUDENTS** to reread the Background section and suggest what goal Prospero has had throughout most of the play. Why might Shakespeare have chosen to have Prospero give a soliloquy toward the end of the play? *(By the end of the play, Prospero has used his magic to right the wrong that was done to him by Antonio and Alonso. Now, Shakespeare uses the soliloquy to reveal Prospero's thoughts about his actions and reveal how events have changed him.)*

Background *The Tempest, from which this excerpt is taken, is believed to be the last play Shakespeare wrote alone. In The Tempest, Prospero, the duke of Milan and a powerful magician, was exiled from Italy and left to die at sea by his brother, Antonio, and Alonso, the king of Naples. After twelve years, Fortune finally sends Antonio and Alonso within Prospero's reach. He conjures a powerful storm, the tempest, causing his enemies to shipwreck on his island. Prospero then seeks to use his magic to make these lords restore him to his rightful position.*

from
The Tempest

Soliloquy by William Shakespeare

William Shakespeare (1564–1616) *is generally considered the greatest playwright in the English language. From about 1592 on, he performed in and wrote plays in London. The location most closely associated with him is the Globe Theatre, shown here. Most of Shakespeare's early plays are about historical figures, although he also wrote more light-hearted comedies. Later, Shakespeare penned his famous tragedies, including* Hamlet *and* Macbeth.

SETTING A PURPOSE In *The Tempest*, Prospero, who has learned to cast spells from a book of magic, rules over a mystical island. As you read, think about what Prospero plans to do with his power and what that means for his character.

(t) ©Pixtal /Age Fotostock; (c) ©Petar Paunchev/Shutterstock; (b) ©Bettmann/CORBIS

from The Tempest **145**

SCAFFOLDING FOR ELL STUDENTS

Determine Meanings One way to make Shakespearean English accessible is to show how it is spoken. Video performances of Prospero's soliloquy in Act V Scene 1 are available online and through video sources. Search for the soliloquy by identifying the play, act, scene, and names of leading actors who have been filmed in the role, among them: Heathcote Williams, Michael Hordern, and Helen Mirren (as Prospera).

Have students read the text while watching the performance. Discuss the connection between words, meaning, and emotion.

For more context and historical background, students can view the video "Biography: William Shakespeare" in their eBooks.

Determine Meanings

COMMON CORE — RL 1, RL 4

(LINES 1–8)

Tell students that language is always changing and is not the same today as it was when Shakespeare wrote. Point out that in lines 1–8, Prospero is speaking to elves and other invisible spirits. His grammar, vocabulary, and word order are "Shakespearean."

 CITE TEXT EVIDENCE Tell students to reread lines 1–8 and cite the lines that might be stated this way in modern English: "You airy spirits leave no footprints on the sand as you chase the waves that come ashore." (*And ye that on the sands with printless foot / Do chase the ebbing Neptune, and do fly him / When he comes back*) Reread the lines aloud to help students appreciate the connection between rhythm and image.

Analyze Form (LINES 22–25)

COMMON CORE — RL 1, RL 3, RL 5

Tell students that after recalling the magical power he has used, Prospero, says "I'll break my staff." Explain that a staff is a stick, like a magic wand.

C CITE TEXT EVIDENCE Have students reread lines 22–25 and cite the words that show Prospero has undergone an important change. (*He says about his staff that he'll "Bury it certain fathoms in the earth" and also says, "I'll drown my book." He's giving up his powers by destroying his staff and his book of spells.*)

COLLABORATIVE DISCUSSION Have students take turns rereading segments of the soliloquy that show Prospero's special powers. Have them share ideas about what his final words reveal about him and his plans.

ASK STUDENTS to share any questions they generated in the course of reading and discussing the selection.

---

from **The Tempest**
ACT 5, Scene 1

Prospero. Ye elves of hills, brooks, standing lakes and groves,
And ye that on the sands with printless foot
Do chase the ebbing Neptune,[1] and do fly him
When he comes back; you demi-puppets that
5   By moonshine do the green sour ringlets make
Whereof the ewe not bites; and you whose pastime
Is to make midnight mushrooms, that rejoice
To hear the solemn curfew; by whose aid,
Weak masters[2] though ye be, I have bedimmed
10   The noontide sun, called forth the mutinous winds,
And 'twixt the green sea and the azured vault
Set roaring war—to the dread rattling thunder
Have I given fire, and rifted Jove's stout oak[3]
With his own bolt; the strong-based promontory
15   Have I made shake, and by the spurs plucked up
The pine and cedar; graves at my command
Have waked their sleepers, oped, and let 'em forth
By my so potent art. But this rough magic
I here abjure. And when I have required
20   Some heavenly music—which even now I do—
To work mine end upon their senses that
This airy charm[4] is for, I'll break my staff,
Bury it certain fathoms in the earth,
And deeper than did ever plummet sound
25   I'll drown my book.

COLLABORATIVE DISCUSSION What does Prospero plan to do with his source of power? What does that tell you about Prospero's character? Share your ideas with other group members.

[1] **ebbing Neptune:** Neptune was the mythical Roman god of water and the sea; "ebbing Neptune" suggests waves flowing away from shore. Like tiny seabirds on a beach, the elves chase the ocean waves as they flow away from the shore, and "fly" or run from them as they flow back to shore.

[2] **Weak masters:** supernatural spirits that do not work powerful evil.

[3] **rifted Jove's stout oak:** Jove was the mythical Roman king of the gods for whom the oak tree was sacred. Jove was identified with thunderbolts, too. Here the image is of lightning splitting the oak.

[4] **airy charm:** magical music.

Determine Meanings

COMMON CORE RL 4

The English language we use today is different from the language used by writers in the 1600s. To understand a Shakespearean play, you need to analyze how Shakespeare uses the language of his time to create rhythm and meaning. These elements all appear in the excerpt from *The Tempest*.

Grammar

Shakespeare used familiar pronouns such as *you, yourself, your,* and *yours,* but he also used other forms of *you: thou, thee, thy, thine,* and *ye.* Shakespeare used *my* or *mine* before a noun, but we no longer say phrases such as *mine eyes.*

Word Order

The positions of words and phrases in Shakespearean language can sound strange to modern ears. Prospero says:

> the strong-based promontory
> Have I made shake, and by the spurs plucked up
> The pine and cedar;

A modern English speaker might use this sentence structure: "I have made the strong-based promontory shake, and plucked up the pine and cedar by the spurs."

Vocabulary

Shakespeare's vocabulary included words that modern English speakers either no longer use or use differently. What is a "strong-based promontory"? It's the strong rocky base that holds the "spurs," or roots, of pine and cedar trees.

Blank Verse

Shakespeare wrote many of his plays, including *The Tempest*, in **blank verse,** or unrhymed iambic pentameter. In blank verse, the final words of the lines do not rhyme, and each line consists of ten syllables alternating unstressed and stressed.

Analyze Form

COMMON CORE RL 5

In a drama, a **soliloquy** is a speech given by a character alone on a stage. It is different from a **monologue,** which is a speech that is often directed to another character.

In soliloquys, characters seem to be thinking aloud, revealing thoughts, feelings, and plans. It is almost as if the characters are talking to themselves. In lines 18–19 of his soliloquy, Prospero announces his plan with the words, "But this rough magic / I here abjure." He is saying that he will no longer work his magic.

TEACH

CLOSE READ

Determine Meanings

COMMON CORE RL 4

Have students find an example of each element of Shakespearean language in the soliloquy.

Make these points about blank verse:

- The term *blank verse* describes any unrhymed poetry that has lines with a regular rhythm.
- Shakespearean blank verse has lines with five stressed syllables, often in this pattern: duh-DAH, duh-DAH, duh-DAH, duh-DAH, duh-DAH. This pattern is called iambic pentameter.
- Iambic pentameter is said to be most like natural English speech. Poets who use it usually introduce variations, so that the lines don't all sound alike.

Have students read aloud a ten-syllable line to listen for a pattern of stresses. Direct them to the soliloquy's last line and ask why it varies from iambic pentameter. (*"I'll drown my book" has only four single-syllable words. It stands out as a forceful final statement.*)

Analyze Form

COMMON CORE RL 5

Point out lines 18–19: "But this rough magic I here abjure." Help students recognize its significance:

- It is the only short sentence in the soliloquy, signaling an abrupt change.
- It follows descriptions of Prospero's powers.
- It leads to the close of the soliloquy and a major change for Prospero.

Strategies for Annotation ✏️ 🖥️ *Annotate it!*

Determine Meanings

COMMON CORE RL 4

Share these strategies for guided or independent analysis of the soliloquy:

- Highlight in yellow words that are no longer used in modern spoken English.
- Underline groups of words that would be positioned differently in modern English sentences.
- Add a note to restate the meaning in modern English.

The pine and cedar; graves at my command

Have waked their sleepers, oped, and let 'em forth

By my so potent art. But this rough magic

> With my powerful magic, I've commanded graves to open and the dead to come out.

PRACTICE & APPLY

Analyzing the Text

Possible answers:

1. *You fairies that by moonlight make the sour-tasting grassy rings that grazing sheep avoid.*

2. *solemn curfew; A curfew is a set time at night when something ends and others begin. Here, the "solemn curfew" is midnight.*

3. *He has dimmed the sun at noon, made stormy winds blow, and caused a terrible, destructive storm at sea. He has added lightning to thunder, and cut apart a stout oak tree with a lightning bolt. His spells have literally shaken the earth and caused the dead to rise from their graves.*

4. *"By my so potent art" means "using my powerful magic."*

5. *Blank verse gives the soliloquy its rhythm and makes it less like conversational dialogue and more like a poem. Prospero speaks like a poet reciting his lines with strong emotion.*

6. *In lines 1–8, Prospero might make fanciful gestures with his hands as he playfully describes the elves and fairies. In lines 9–18, he might take a bold posture and gesture more wildly as he forcefully describes the violent and powerful things he has done by magic. In lines 19–25, his voice may grow softer and he may take on a gentler, thoughtful appearance as he says that he is giving up magic forever—a significant admission for such a powerful man.*

7. *Words about sight, sound, and touch that describe characters and events, such as fairies playing with waves, lightning and thunder, shaking earth, and heavenly music help readers imagine the scene that Prospero is describing.*

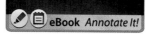 eBook *Annotate It!*

Analyzing the Text

Cite Text Evidence   Support your responses with evidence from the text.

1. **Interpret** In lines 4–6, Prospero refers to "green sour ringlets." These rings were said to be a poisonous trail made by fairies dancing in the night. (Today, a circle of mushrooms that sprouts overnight is still called a fairy ring.) How would you restate Prospero's words in modern English?

2. **Interpret** What words in lines 5–8 help you understand when fairies and other magical creatures were free to come out?

3. **Cause/Effect** In lines 9–18, Prospero vividly describes the powerful things he has accomplished with magic. What are some of the effects of his spells?

4. **Interpret** What does Prospero mean in line 18, when he says, "By my so potent art"?

5. **Analyze** Shakespeare wrote Prospero's soliloquy in blank verse. How does this form contribute to the meaning of the text?

6. **Draw Conclusions** How might an actor playing Prospero use his voice and gestures to convey the meanings of the text in these three main sections: lines 1–8, lines 9–18, lines 19–25?

7. **Evaluate** This excerpt from *The Tempest* includes many examples of imagery—the words and phrases that appeal to the five senses. Evaluate the impact the imagery has on your understanding of the text.

PERFORMANCE TASK

Speaking Activity: Dramatic Reading
Divide the lines of this soliloquy among the members of a small group so that each participant has several lines that express one idea or related ideas.

- Together, discuss and analyze the Shakespearean vocabulary and sentence structure.
- Use your analysis to rewrite Prospero's soliloquy in your own words.
- Then, as a group, deliver your version of the soliloquy to the class.

Assign this performance task.

PERFORMANCE TASK

Speaking Activity: Dramatic Reading Have students work in small groups. Suggest they use footnotes with the soliloquy, published versions of *The Tempest*, or glossaries of words commonly used by Shakespeare to help them. Have them practice their readings with a partner. As they perform, remind them to adapt their speech to changing meanings and words in the passage.

Analyze Form

COMMON CORE

RL 5

TEACH

Tell students that Prospero's soliloquy sounds like a poem because of its rhythmical pattern. Display these terms and definitions:

meter: the pattern of stressed and unstressed syllables in a line of poetry

foot: a unit of meter with one stressed syllable

iamb: a two-syllable foot with the second syllable stressed

tetrameter: a line with four feet

pentameter: a line with five feet

iambic tetrameter: four iambs in a line

iambic pentameter: five iambs in a line

Help students contrast the two iambic meters by showing foot divisions and stressed syllables in lines of poetry. Prompt students to use the listed terms to tell about the rhythms they hear:

As NIGHT | drew ON | and, FROM | the CREST

Of WOOD | ed KNOLLS | that RIDGED | the WEST

When I | have SEEN | the HUN | gry O | cean GAIN

Ad VAN | tage ON | the KING | dom OF | the SHORE

Emphasize that although a poem may have an identifiable meter, poets introduce variations in rhythms to connect sound to meaning and to avoid singsong sameness.

PRACTICE AND APPLY

Show students the symbols ´ and ˘. Explain that these symbols can be used above syllables to mark the pattern of stresses they hear.

Tell students to identify the feet and stresses in the following lines from Prospero's soliloquy: line 2, line 5, line 15, line 24.

And ye | that on | the sands | with print | less foot

By moon | shine do | the green | sour ring | lets make

Have I | made shake, | and by | the spurs | plucked up

And deep | er than | did ev | er plum | met sound

Determine Meanings

COMMON CORE

RL 4

RETEACH

Tell students that William Shakespeare is often called the greatest playwright who ever wrote in English, and his plays are still being performed. Point out that because Shakespeare wrote in an older form of English, readers may need footnotes and other help to clarify meaning. As readers become more accustomed to Shakespeare's language, they can also figure out likely meanings.

Display well-known quotations from Shakespeare's plays in order to help students make modern paraphrases of Shakespearean English. For example:

- "What's in a name? that which we call a rose by any other name would smell as sweet." *(Who cares what something is called? A rose would still smell sweet if it had a different name.)*

- "Lord, what fools these mortals be." *(Wow! These human beings sure are foolish.)*

- "Neither a borrower, nor a lender be; For loan oft loses both itself and friend." *(Don't borrow or lend money. A loan that's not paid back can end a friendship.)*

PRACTICE AND APPLY

Have students find this famous quotation in the soliloquy they have just read:

I'll break my staff,
Bury it certain fathoms in the earth,
And deeper than did ever plummet sound
I'll drown my book.

Guide students to make a line-by-line paraphrase. *(I'll destroy my magic wand. I'll bury it deep underground. And I'll throw my book of magic spells into the deep sea.)*

mySmartPlanner Create lesson plans and access resources online.

Allied with Green

Why This Text?

"Allied with Green" is an example of the type of complex text that students are increasingly expected to read and analyze. It is driven mainly by language and imagery rather than plot. Students determine the meaning of the story's figurative language and analyze the author's style and the effects it creates.

View It!

Professional Development Podcast:

Text Complexity

Key Learning Objective: The student will be able to determine the theme of a short story and to analyze word choice and style.

COMMON CORE

Common Core Standards

RL 1 Cite textual evidence.
RL 2 Determine and analyze theme.
RL 3 Analyze how elements of a story interact.
RL 4 Determine the meanings of words and phrases.
RL 6 Analyze points of view.
W 1 Write arguments.
W 4 Produce clear and coherent writing.
W 10 Write routinely.
SL 1 Engage in collaborative discussions.
L 1b Choose among compound, complex, and compound-complex sentences to signal differing relationships among ideas.
L 4c Consult reference materials to determine pronunciation or clarify meaning.

Text Complexity Rubric

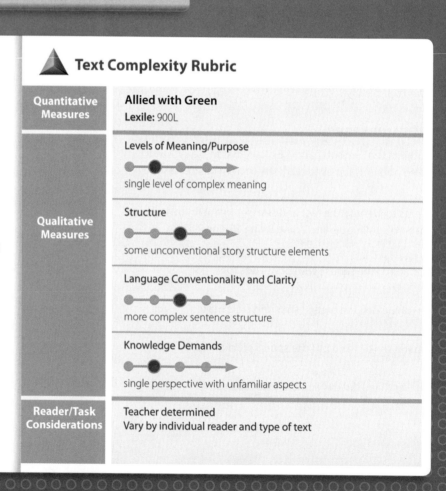

Quantitative Measures	Allied with Green
	Lexile: 900L

Levels of Meaning/Purpose

single level of complex meaning

Structure

some unconventional story structure elements

| Qualitative Measures | |

Language Conventionality and Clarity

more complex sentence structure

Knowledge Demands

single perspective with unfamiliar aspects

Reader/Task Considerations	Teacher determined
	Vary by individual reader and type of text

TEACH

Naomi Shihab Nye Have students read the information about the author. Point out that Naomi Shihab Nye is an accomplished poet as well as a writer of fiction, and her background as a poet is evidenced in the story. Encourage students to pay attention to the author's use of language and the images she creates with it.

SETTING A PURPOSE Direct students to use the Setting a Purpose question to focus their reading. Remind them to also generate their own questions as they read.

Determine Theme

COMMON CORE RL 1, RL 2

(TITLE; LINES 1–2)

Tell students that the **theme** of a story is a message about life or human nature that the author wants to convey. Often, readers must **infer,** or make a good guess about, the theme from evidence in the text. Explain that authors sometimes reveal the theme in the story's title, as well as in the words and actions of characters.

A **CITE TEXT EVIDENCE** Have students read the title and lines 1–2. Ask what it means to be "allied" and what "allied with green" might suggest about the story's theme. *(To be allied means to be mutually supportive or working together. The title suggests that the character is an ally or supporter of green.)* Ask students to cite evidence in lines 1–2 that supports this inference. *(When asked what she believes in, the first thing Lucy writes is "the color green.")*

SCAFFOLDING FOR ELL STUDENTS

Imagery Tell students that this author's style involves a great deal of **imagery,** or words that appeal to the senses. Using this imagery to form pictures in their minds will help students to better understand the story. Display lines 5–11 on a whiteboard. Invite students to highlight in yellow the words that help them picture what the author describes.

ASK STUDENTS to describe how they visualize the scene. Ask what the author means by "green" *(grasses and plants)* and why she says that green "seems to keep everything else going." *(People depend on the presence of plants.)* Encourage students to use this strategy as they read the rest of the story.

Naomi Shihab Nye (b. 1952) *was born to a Palestinian father and an American mother. During her adolescence, she lived in St. Louis, Missouri; Jerusalem; and San Antonio, Texas; and she has traveled extensively as an adult. Influenced by her heritage and the cultural diversity of the places she has known, Nye has written books of poetry as well as fiction for younger audiences.*

Allied with Green

Short Story by Naomi Shihab Nye

SETTING A PURPOSE As you read, consider the author's use of the word *green*. How is she using the term to describe something that Lucy, the story's main character, feels very strongly about?

For her paper on "What I Believe In," Lucy writes first "the color green."

That's how everything starts. A tiny shoot of phrase prickling the mind . . .

Then she runs around for a few days doing other things but noticing the green poking up between buildings, on sides of roads, in front of even the poorest homes, how pots of green lined on rickety front porches, hanging baskets of green on light posts downtown, the new meticulous xeriscape[1] beds of
10 puffy green grasses and plants alongside the river, are what seem to keep everything else going. If people could not see

---

[1] **xeriscape** (zĭr´ ĭ-skāp´): landscaping that saves water and protects the environment.

(t) ©Pixtal /Age Fotostock; (c) ©Petar Paunchev/Shutterstock; (b) ©Bettmann/CORBIS

Allied with Green **149**

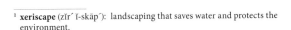

Then she runs around for a few days doing other things

but noticing the green poking up between buildings, on sides

of roads, in front of even the poorest homes, how pots of green

lined on rickety front porches, hanging baskets of green on

Allied with Green **149**

Determine the Meanings of Words and Phrases

COMMON CORE RL 1, RL 4

(LINES 15–17)

Explain that an author's **style** is his or her manner of writing—*how* something is said rather than *what* is said. Point out that this author's style includes frequent use of **figurative language,** comparisons or expressions that are not literally true. One example of figurative language is **personification,** or the assigning of human traits to animals, objects, or ideas.

 CITE TEXT EVIDENCE Ask students to reread lines 15–17 and cite the author's use of personification. *(The author assigns feelings to the color green, for example, "Green has had a terrible summer" and "green has had many second thoughts.")*

Ask how this use of personification reveals the narrator's feelings about plants. *(It shows that the narrator feels close to, or allied with, green (plants), as if she understands their feelings, as someone might understand the feelings of a friend.)*

CRITICAL VOCABULARY

addiction: Lucy was supposed to write a paper about addiction and she wrote about trimming plants.

ASK STUDENTS why Lucy considers trimming plants to be an addiction. *(Lucy feels that she is addicted to plants, or "green," because she loves plants and feels we are all dependent on them, the way an addict is dependent on a substance.)*

median: The author says that Lucy's father plants trees on medians as an apology.

ASK STUDENTS to explain what he is apologizing for and why he chooses medians for his planting. *(He is apologizing for driving on the highway every day. Since the median runs down the middle of the highway, he is trying to at least make the space a bit more beautiful.)*

green from the windows of the hospital, the hospital might fall down. She believes this.

Once she starts making a list, it will not stop.

Green has had a terrible summer. Threatened by the longest drought and highest heat in recorded history, green has had many second thoughts.

Lucy's family could only water with a sprinkler on Wednesday evenings between eight and ten. When she and
20 her mom wash lettuce, blueberries, peaches, they carry the plastic tubs of fruit water outside to pour onto a plant. It's ritual now. It's holy water. The city had a water waster hotline. It made the national news. You could turn people in for excessive watering.

Last semester, when asked to write a paper on **addictions,** Lucy wrote about trimming and got a C. Her teacher scrawled across the top of the paper, "What is this?" But Lucy often feels happiest with pruning shears in her hand, heading toward an overgrown jasmine vine.
30 It's a clear task, trimming. The longer you've done it, the more you know how it encourages green, in the long run. Also, you can have fine ideas while trimming. Queen's crown, germander, plumbago. *Snip, snip, snip.*

She knew it had been mentioned before, but thought she ought to include how cities assault their green for two reasons: money and greed. Later, feeling remorseful, or sickened by the new view, they name everything for green—Oak Meadows, Lone Pine. You could find it almost anywhere now.

Lucy's father demonstrated against developments when he
40 was in college. She had a faded black and white picture of him holding a NO! sign, his hair bushy and wild. Highways slashing through green space—he now drives one of those highways almost every day, feeling guilty. He plants free trees in scrappy **medians,** as an apology. Sometimes people steal them. When he planted four little palms in pots as a gift to Freddy's Mexican Restaurant, they got plucked from the soil overnight. Obviously some people were desperate for green. And surely, with all the population issues now, some developments were necessary, but look at what happened
50 before you knew it—hills sheared, meadows plucked, fields erased, the world turns into an endless series of strip centers— yo, Joni Mitchell! Joni sang about parking lots when the world

addiction
(ə-dĭk´shən) *n.* An *addiction* is a habit one is dependent on.

median
(mē´dē-ən) *n.* A *median* is a dividing area between opposing lanes of traffic on a highway or road.

WHEN STUDENTS STRUGGLE...

Tell students that the author's use of figurative language is very important in this story. Have students use a chart like the one below to track the use of figurative language and analyze its meaning in lines 11–13. Suggest that students continue filling in the chart for the rest of the story.

Expression	Meaning	Purpose
"the hospital might fall down"	The view of green plants from the windows keeps the patients' spirits up.	to show the importance of green plants in people's lives

had probably half the number it has now. Her dad told her that. She likes Joni Mitchell.

The boulevard wakes up when a strip of green is planted down its center.

The sad room smiles again when a pot of green is placed on a white tablecloth.

No one goes to Seattle to see the concrete.

60 An exhausted kid says, I'm going outside—sick of her mother's voice, she knows she will feel better with bamboo.

In Dallas people run around the lake or refresh themselves at the **arboretum**.

San Antonians send their kids to summer digging classes at the botanical gardens. The kids come home with broccoli. After a while.

Patience is deeply involved with green.

It's required.

So, why don't people respect green as much as they should?

70 This was the serious question growing small fronds and tendrils at the heart of Lucy's paper. She knew her teacher might turn a snide nose up at it. Oh, blah blah, isn't this rather a repeat of what you wrote last semester?

People took green for granted. They assumed it would always be skirting their ugly office buildings and residences

arboretum
(är´bə-rē´təm) *n.*
An *arboretum* is a
place where many
trees are grown
for educational or
viewing purposes.

Allied with Green **151**

CLOSE READ

Determine Theme

COMMON CORE **RL 1, RL 2**

(LINES 59–66)

Tell students they can infer a story's theme by analyzing statements made by a narrator or character.

C CITE TEXT EVIDENCE Have students reread lines 59–66, cite examples that reveal theme, and ask how they reveal theme. *("No one goes to Seattle to see concrete." "An exhausted kid . . . will feel better with bamboo." People "refresh themselves at the arboretum." They show people need green, so it must be protected.)*

Determine the Meanings of Words and Phrases

COMMON CORE **RL 2, RL 4**

(LINES 69–71)

Remind students that the author includes figurative language, which she uses to develop the theme.

D ASK STUDENTS to reread lines 69–71 and identify the figurative expression. Ask what comparison it makes and how this supports the theme. *(The phrase "the serious question growing small fronds and tendrils" compares Lucy's question to a plant. It supports the theme by reinforcing her belief in the value of plants.)*

CRITICAL VOCABULARY

arboretum: The author says that in Dallas people refresh themselves in the arboretum.

ASK STUDENTS why an arboretum is refreshing. *(An arboretum provides a sanctuary from city life.)*

Strategies for Annotation ✎ 🖥 *Annotate it!*

Determine the Meanings of Words and Phrases

COMMON CORE **RL 4**

Have students reread lines 69–71 and use their eBook annotation tools to do the following:

- Underline the example of figurative language.
- Use two different colors (yellow and green) to highlight the two things being compared.
- In a note, explain the meaning of the comparison.

So, why don't people respect green as much as they should?

This was the serious question growing small fronds and

tendrils at the heart of Lucy's paper.

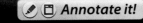

The question is compared to a plant—"growing small fronds and tendrils."

For more context and historical background, students can view the video "Greening Lower Manhattan" in their eBooks.

Determine the Meanings of Words and Phrases

  COMMON CORE **RL 2, RL 4**

(LINES 98–105)

Point out that the author concludes the story with a final figurative expression that also sums up the story's theme.

E **ASK STUDENTS** to reread lines 98–105. Have them analyze line 105 and explain what the author means by "carry a bucket." *(to tend and care for green plants)* Ask how this supports the story's theme. *(It suggests that we all must do our part to protect this valuable resource.)*

> **CRITICAL VOCABULARY**
>
> **obituary:** The author tells us that Lucy clipped Robert Isabell's obituary, or death notice, from the newspaper and kept it on her desk.
>
> **ASK STUDENTS** what Lucy might have learned from Isabell's obituary and why she kept it on her desk. *(She might have learned important facts about his life and accomplishments. She kept it because she admired him and felt inspired by him.)*

COLLABORATIVE DISCUSSION Have small groups of students discuss the author's use of the word *green*. Encourage them to write notes as they talk. Then have each group share their ideas with the class and discuss others' reactions to the author's word choice.

ASK STUDENTS to share any questions they generated in the course of reading and discussing the selection.

---

and so they didn't give it the attention it deserved. Somewhat like air. Air and green, close cousins.

Lucy truly loved the words *pocket park*.[2]

She loved community gardeners with purple bandannas
80 tied around their heads. She loved their wild projects—rosemary grown so big you could hide in it.

She loved roofs paved with grass.

She loved the man in New York City—Robert Isabell—who planted pink impatiens on the metal overhang of his building. He had started out as a florist, at seventeen, in Minnesota—green state in the summer, not so green in December. Then he moved to New York City and became a major party planner, incorporating flowers, lighting, tents, fabrics, to create magical worlds of festivity. He didn't attend
90 his own parties. He disappeared once he got everything set up. Sometimes he hid behind a giant potted plant to see what people liked. Lucy found his **obituary** in the newspaper, clipped it out, and placed it on her desk. She wished she could have worked for him just to learn how he put flowers together on tables, how he clipped giant green stalks and placed them effectively around a tent to make Morocco, Italy, the French Riviera. Transporting. Green could take you away.

E Save you. But you had to care for it, stroke it, devote yourself to it, pray to it, organize crews for it, bow down to it.
100 You had to say the simple holy prayer, rearranging the words any way you liked best—"Dig, Grow, Deep, Roots, Light, Air, Water, Tend."

Tend was a more important verb than most people realized.

You had to carry a bucket.

obituary
(ō-bĭch´ oo-ĕr´ē) *n.* An *obituary* is a public notice of a death.

COLLABORATIVE DISCUSSION What is unusual about the author's use of the word *green*, and why does she use it that way? Talk about your ideas with other group members.

---

[2] **pocket park:** a small park accessible to the general public.

APPLYING ACADEMIC VOCABULARY

affect	ensure

As you discuss the story, incorporate the following Collection 3 academic vocabulary words: *affect,* and *ensure*. Ask students how the author's use of imagery and figurative language **affects** their understanding of the story and its theme. Discuss why it is so important to the main character to **ensure** that green plants are valued and protected.

Determine Theme

In short stories like "Allied with Green," authors often use the characters to share a theme with the reader. A **theme** is a message about life or human nature. In works of fiction, themes are the "big ideas" that readers infer based on evidence from the text. The following statements are examples of themes that might be found in short stories:

- A person can gain more by giving than by taking.
- We may not appreciate what we have until it is gone.

Often the theme of a story is not stated directly. It's usually implied. You have to analyze the text to see what it reveals about the theme. To determine the theme, it is helpful to

- look at the title to see if it contains a significant idea
- analyze the characters' words and actions, especially how characters change
- evaluate whether the setting has special meaning to a character
- look for important statements by the narrator or a character

Determine the Meanings of Words and Phrases

An author's **style** is his or her manner of writing—*how* something is said rather than *what* is said—and it often corresponds to the genre of the writing. Style can be described with words such as *formal, journalistic, literary, flowery,* and *plain.*

Readers can analyze an author's style by making observations about the author's word choice and descriptive details, among other elements. An author may use **imagery**—words and phrases that appeal to the senses—to help readers imagine how things look, feel, smell, sound, and taste.

An author's style may also include **figurative language,** comparisons and expressions that are not literally true but give meaning in imaginative ways. One form of figurative language is **personification,** the giving of human qualities to animals, objects, or ideas. The author of "Allied with Green" uses personification to give human qualities to the color green and other objects.

Review "Allied with Green." How would you describe the style in which it's written?

Allied with Green **153**

TEACH

CLOSE READ

Determine Theme

Review that theme is a message about human nature or life. Discuss the list of tips and then have students review the story and cite examples for each tip.

- **Title:** *The title suggests that a character in the story is an ally, or supporter, of green.*
- **Character's words and actions:** *"For her paper on 'What I Believe In,' Lucy writes first 'the color green.'"* (lines 1–2)
- **Setting:** *The importance of the setting is shown in the way Lucy notices green wherever she goes (lines 5–11) and in how much pleasure she gets from tending her plants. (lines 30–33)*
- **Important statements by narrator:** *"You had to carry a bucket." (line 105)*

Discuss what the examples suggest about the theme. *(The theme has to do with Lucy's belief in the value of green, growing plants and her love of tending them.)*

Determine the Meanings of Words and Phrases

Review that style is an author's manner of writing and that an author's word choice can help readers analyze the style of a work. Review the definitions of imagery, figurative language, and personification. Discuss what Naomi Shihab Nye's frequent use of these elements reveals about her style. *(Her style can be described as literary or poetic.)*

Strategies for Annotation 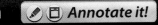 *Annotate it!*

Determine Theme

Have students review the story and use their eBook annotation tools to do the following:

- Highlight in yellow a character's words and actions that support the theme.
- Highlight in green important statements by the narrator.
- In a note, draw conclusions about the theme based on this evidence.

> For her paper on "What I Believe In," Lucy writes first "the color green."
>
> That's how everything starts. A tiny shoot of phrase prickling the mind . . .
>
> Then she runs around for a few days doing other things

Lucy sees, thinks about, and interacts with plants. It is central to her life, to all life.

Analyzing the Text

COMMON CORE RL 1, RL 2, RL 3, RL 4, RL 6

Possible answers:

1. The phrase means "a few words that are the start of an idea for a school paper." The author combines the image of a tiny shoot that prickles, which is the beginning of a green plant, with the beginning of an idea. The phrase "the color green" is what prickles her mind.

2. It shows that Lucy is a sensitive, perceptive person who cares very much about the importance of green plants.

3. The author compares the water used to wash fruit, and reused to water plants, to the holy water poured in a religious service. The water is precious and used in a kind of ritual to keep plants alive.

4. Her teacher, who didn't appreciate Lucy's previous paper on an addiction to trimming plants, is likely to "turn a snide nose up at" this one and say that Lucy hasn't come up with new ideas.

5. The narrator is making the point that development is a destructive force ("cities assault their green"; "Highways slashing through green space"; "hills sheared, meadows plucked, fields erased"). She is also making the point that people are often ambiguous about preserving green spaces—cities develop for greed and money, then people feel remorseful. Even Lucy's father feels a bit guilty about his lack of 100% commitment.

6. Plants give life even to inanimate things, like a boulevard and a room.

7. **Imagery:** "a faded black and white picture … his hair bushy and wild"; **Figurative Language:** "It's holy water"; "You had to carry a bucket." **Personification:** "Green has had a terrible summer"; "green has had many second thoughts"; "The sad room smiles."

8. People must respect and care for green plants of all kinds because "green" refreshes and sustains human life.

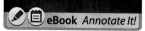 eBook *Annotate It!*

Analyzing the Text

COMMON CORE RL 1, RL 2, RL 3, RL 4, RL 6, W 1, W 4, W 10

Cite Text Evidence   Support your responses with evidence from the text.

1. **Interpret** In lines 3–4, the author uses the phrase "a tiny shoot of phrase prickling the mind" to describe how everything starts. What does the phrase mean?

2. **Infer** Once Lucy decides on the topic for her school assignment, she can't help but notice the green around her. What does this tell you about her character and how she feels about her topic?

3. **Interpret** Reread lines 18–22 to find what the narrator compares to holy water. What does that comparison suggest?

4. **Predict** Lucy chooses to write about the color green for her school assignment. Based on her teacher's reaction to her paper from last semester, what will her teacher's reaction to this topic probably be?

5. **Draw Conclusions** Reread lines 34–51. What point is the narrator making about developments?

6. **Analyze** What does the personification in lines 55–58 help the reader understand?

7. **Analyze** Use a chart like this one to list examples of imagery, figurative language, and personification that contribute to Naomi Shihab Nye's style.

Elements	Examples
Imagery	
Figurative Language	
Personification	

8. **Draw Conclusions** What is the theme of this story?

PERFORMANCE TASK

 my WriteSmart

Writing Activity: Essay Look back through "Allied with Green" to take notes on the points Lucy makes in favor of green. Adapt those ideas to develop a three- to four-paragraph persuasive essay in support of or against her position.

- Introduce your opinion.
- Specify support for your opinion with reasons and examples.
- Acknowledge a possible argument from an opponent and refute it.
- Conclude with a statement that summarizes your opinion and ties your ideas together.

Assign this performance task. my WriteSmart

PERFORMANCE TASK

COMMON CORE W 1, W 4, W 10, SL 1

Writing Activity: Essay Have individual students take notes and decide their position. Review the steps for writing a persuasive essay, emphasizing the need to support claims with clear reasons and evidence. Have pairs review each other's drafts and offer suggestions for revision, paying attention to the organization of the draft. Then, have pairs with opposing views take turns reading aloud their essays, followed by a group discussion about the issues.

Critical Vocabulary

COMMON CORE L 4c

addiction   median   arboretum   obituary

Practice and Apply Answer each question with *yes* or *no*. With your group, use examples and reasons to explain your answer.

1. Could someone have an **addiction** to chocolate? Why or why not?
2. Could a single-lane road have a **median?** Why or why not?
3. Is an **arboretum** like a garden? Why or why not?
4. Is an **obituary** like a biography? Why or why not?

Vocabulary Strategy: Using a Glossary

A **glossary** is a list of specialized terms and their definitions. A glossary can exist on its own, or it can be part of a larger text. A text may have more than one glossary if it refers to multiple types of specialized terms that a reader is not assumed to know. Here are more useful details about glossaries.

-   When a printed book contains a glossary, words are listed in the back of the book in alphabetical order.
-   A digital, or electronic, glossary allows readers to click on a word in the text to see its definition and hear its pronunciation.
-   A glossary may contain information about a word's pronunciation and part of speech.

Notice the parts of this glossary entry for the word *median*.

Practice and Apply This literature program contains multiple glossaries. Use the table of contents and the glossaries to answer the following questions.

1. In which glossary would you expect to find a listing for the Critical Vocabulary words that are highlighted in each selection?
2. Which glossary would you use to learn definitions for the literary terms that are used in the instruction?
3. According to the glossary, what is the part of speech for the word *obituary*?

Allied with Green **155**

PRACTICE & APPLY

Critical Vocabulary

COMMON CORE L 4c

Possible answers:

1. *Yes, because the word* addiction *can be used generally, as well as to name a medical condition.*
2. *No, a median runs through the center of a road; it can't run through a single lane.*
3. *Yes, an arboretum is like a garden because plants are on display in both; in an arboretum, the plants are trees.*
4. *Yes, an obituary tells about the life of a person, giving biographical information about someone who has just died.*

Vocabulary Strategy: Using a Glossary

Answers:

1. *Glossary of Critical Vocabulary*
2. *Glossary of Literary and Informational Terms*
3. *noun*

Strategies for Annotation 🖉 📄 *Annotate it!*

Using a Glossary

COMMON CORE L 4c

Have students locate the entry for *median* in the Glossary of Critical Vocabulary. Encourage them to use their eBook annotation tools to do the following:

-   Highlight the entry word in yellow.
-   Highlight the pronunciation in blue.
-   Highlight the part of speech in green.
-   Underline the definition.
-   In a note, use the word in a sentence that illustrates its meaning.

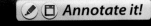

median (mē′dē-ən) *n.* A **median** is a dividing area between opposing lanes of traffic on a highway or road.

After the accident, one car had stopped on the median.

Allied with Green **155**

PRACTICE & APPLY

Language Conventions: Sentence Structure

  COMMON CORE L 1b

- Review the definitions of **compound sentence** and **coordinating conjunction,** and use the first chart to discuss the two ways to join independent clauses to form a compound sentence.
- Review the definitions of **complex sentence** and **subordinating conjunction.** Use the second chart to discuss how to join an independent clause and a subordinate clause to form a complex sentence.
- Then review the definition of a **compound-complex sentence** and the two examples.

Possible answers:

1. *Compound sentence: He planted four little palms in pots, but they were stolen. Compound-complex sentence: He planted four little palms in pots, but they were stolen because people were desperate for green.*

2. *Compound sentence: A pot of green is placed on a white tablecloth, and a sad room seems to smile. Compound-complex sentence: When a pot of green is placed on a white tablecloth, a sad room seems to smile, and everyone feels welcome.*

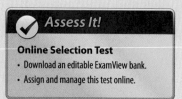

✓ Assess It!

Online Selection Test
- Download an editable ExamView bank.
- Assign and manage this test online.

Language Conventions: Sentence Structure

  COMMON CORE L 1b

When you combine two independent clauses, you make a **compound sentence.** There are two basic ways to combine clauses to make a compound sentence: (1) with a **coordinating conjunction,** such as *and, but,* and *or;* (2) with a semicolon.

Independent Clauses	Urban parks are calm places. City dwellers need them.
Compound Sentence	Urban parks are restful places, and city dwellers need them.
Independent Clauses	The color green suggests life. People are drawn to green.
Compound Sentence	The color green suggests life; people are drawn to green.

When you combine a subordinate clause with an independent clause, you make a **complex sentence.** A subordinate clause begins with a **subordinating conjunction,** such as *after, although, as, because, before, even though, if, since, so that, though, unless, until, when, where,* and *while.*

Independent Clause	Gardens give many rewards.
Subordinate Clause	although gardening requires patience
Complex Sentence	Although gardening requires patience, gardens give many rewards.

A **compound-complex sentence** combines two or more independent clauses and one or more subordinate clauses. Note the three clauses in each example:

> **When trees grow on city sidewalks, people must take care of them, or the trees will fail to thrive.**

> **People love the pocket park because it was green and quiet; they found peace there.**

Practice and Apply The following independent clauses are taken from "Allied with Green." For each independent clause, add more clauses to make a compound sentence and a compound-complex sentence. Then explain how each sentence type signals a different relationship between ideas.

1. He planted four little palms in pots.

2. A pot of green is placed on a white tablecloth.

INTERACTIVE WHITEBOARD LESSON

Analyze Point of View

COMMON CORE

RL 3,
RL 6

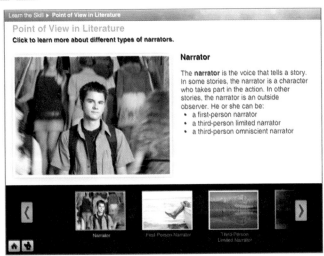

TEACH

Tell students that **point of view** is the vantage point from which a story is told. The writer's choice of a **narrator,** or the voice that tells the story, determines the point of view. When a story is told from the **first-person point of view,** the narrator is a character in the story and uses first-person pronouns. In a story told from the **third-person point of view,** the narrator is not a character and uses third-person pronouns.

Share and discuss these steps for analyzing point of view:

Step 1: Look at the Pronouns Does the narrator use first-person or third-person pronouns?

Step 2: Identify the Narrator Is the narrator an outside observer, or a character in the story?

Step 3: Analyze the Effects What do I learn about the narrator? What do I learn from the narrator about events and other characters? What is this narrator unable to tell me?

COLLABORATIVE DISCUSSION

Have students work in pairs to use the three steps above to analyze the point of view of "Allied with Green." Suggest that students pay particular attention to what we learn about Lucy from the narrator. Ask: What does the narrator want us to think about Lucy? Suggest that students take notes during the discussion, and have each pair share their analysis with the class. *(The narrator uses third-person pronouns, so the point of view is third person. The narrator uses beautiful imagery, descriptions of "green," and Lucy's feelings about "green," suggesting that the narrator shares Lucy's point of view.)*

Determine Theme

COMMON CORE

RL 2

RETEACH

Review with students that a **theme** is a big idea about life that the author of a story wants to convey. Emphasize that the theme is not the same as what the story is about. For example:

- "Allied with Green" is about a girl who is writing a paper on the importance of green.
- The theme of "Allied with Green" can be stated as *People must respect and care for green plants because "green" refreshes and sustains human life.*

Tell students that the theme of a story is often not stated and must be figured out from evidence in the story, such as the characters' words and actions and what the narrator tells us.

Read aloud each of the following lines from "Allied with Green." Discuss with students what each line reveals about the theme.

- "No one goes to Seattle for the concrete." (Line 59)
- "So, why don't people respect green as much as they should?" (Line 69)
- ". . . Green could take you away. Save you. But you had to care for it, stroke it, devote yourself to it . . ." (Lines 97–99)

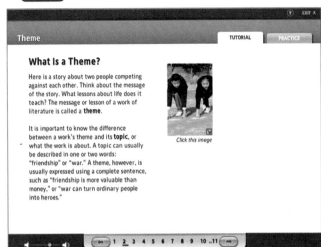

LEVEL UP TUTORIALS Assign the following *Level Up* tutorial: **Theme**

CLOSE READING APPLICATION

Students can apply the skill to another short story of their own choosing. Have students work independently to identify ways in which the author reveals the theme. Suggest that students take notes to record evidence that helps them infer the theme.

Big Rocks' Balancing Acts

*my*SmartPlanner — Create lesson plans and access resources online.

Expository Essay by Douglas Fox

Why This Text?

This essay takes an interesting approach to presenting complex technical concepts through the words and experiences of real scientists who are studying them. As they analyze the text, students will learn to understand how it is organized and to use organizational patterns to support comprehension.

Key Learning Objective: The student will be able to analyze elements of an expository essay and its structure.

For practice and application:

Close Reader selection
"The Hidden Southwest: The Arch Hunters"
Informational Text by James Vlahos

 ## Common Core Standards

RI 1 Cite textual evidence.
RI 2 Determine central ideas; provide an objective summary.
RI 3 Analyze the interactions in a text.
RI 4 Determine meanings of words and phrases.
RI 5 Analyze the structure an author uses to organize a text.
RI 6 Determine an author's purpose.
W 7 Conduct short research projects.
SL 4 Present claims and findings in a focused, coherent manner.
L 1a Explain the function of phrases.
L 4b Use Latin affixes and roots.
L 6 Acquire and use general academic and domain-specific words.

▲ Text Complexity Rubric

Quantitative Measures	**Big Rocks' Balancing Acts** **Lexile:** 1060L

Levels of Meaning/Purpose

single purpose and topic

Structure

more than one text structure; organization is complex but mostly explicit

Qualitative Measures

Language Conventionality and Clarity

some unfamiliar academic and domain-specific words

Knowledge Demands

somewhat complex science concepts

Reader/Task Considerations	Teacher determined Vary by individual reader and type of text

Douglas Fox Have students read the information about the author. Tell students that James Brune, the geologist mentioned in the essay, published an article in the journal *American Scientist* in 2007 titled "Gauging Earthquake Hazards with Precariously Balanced Rocks."

SETTING A PURPOSE Direct students to use the Setting a Purpose prompt to focus their reading. Remind them to write questions they have while reading.

Analyze Structure: Essay

COMMON CORE **RI 3, RI 5**

(LINES 1–2)

Explain that this selection is an **expository essay,** a short work of nonfiction that presents or explains information and ideas. Point out that all writers, whether they are writing fiction or nonfiction, want to grab readers' interest at the beginning. Direct students to lines 1–2.

 ASK STUDENTS what image the first sentence creates in their minds. Talk about why the author chose to begin the article in this way. *(The sentence describes a person leaning out of a flying airplane taking photos. The image is both a little startling and intriguing. It makes readers wonder what taking pictures from airplanes has to do with rocks.)*

Analyze Language

COMMON CORE **RI 1, RI 4**

(LINES 12–15)

Call attention to the words in quotation marks. Explain that these words are not dialogue, as in a story. In expository text, a **quotation** relates a real person's exact words. Note that the bracketed words were added by the author for clarity.

B **CITE TEXT EVIDENCE** Have students cite Richard Brune's exact words and tell what effect the quotation has on the text. *(The speaker's exact words are, "It's not that bad. From 1,000 feet you've probably got at least nine or 10 seconds before you really have to pull the rip cord." The quotation gives the text a personal "eyewitness" feel. It also gives the reader an idea of what Brune is like.)*

Douglas Fox *is a science, environmental, and technology writer who lives in northern California. His pursuit of science stories has led him to many exotic places, including Australia, Mauritius, Papua New Guinea, and Antarctica. In addition to writing, Fox sometimes takes photos for his stories, which have appeared in many scientific journals, magazines, and books.*

Big Rocks' Balancing Acts

Expository Essay by Douglas Fox

SETTING A PURPOSE In this article, you'll get familiar with a curiosity in nature. As you read, think about what makes these rock formations so unique and what people can learn from them. Write down any questions you have while reading.

A Richard Brune was pretty dizzy the first time he shot photos while leaning out of a flying airplane.

The plane's door had been removed so Brune could ride with one leg outside. As the tiny propeller plane zigzagged over the desert, Brune leaned out over empty air. The 80 mile-per-hour headwind pummeled his face. He looked through his camera and snapped pictures of the rocky desert hundreds of feet below.

He got woozy after a few seconds, unsure which way was
10 up. He learned to avoid that feeling by keeping his eyes on the shifting, slanting horizon whenever he could. And just in case he tumbled out of the plane, he wore a parachute. "It's not that bad," says Brune, who has done plenty of skydiving. "From 1,000 feet you've probably got at least nine or 10 seconds [of falling] before you really have to pull the rip cord."

©John Hoffman/Shutterstock

SCAFFOLDING FOR ELL STUDENTS

Analyze Language Using a whiteboard, project the first two paragraphs of the text (lines 1–8). Highlight the word *desert* and explain that it is the first of several words related to geology, or the study of the earth's physical structure. Use the photo and context to help students understand the meaning of *desert*. Provide these additional tips:

- Look at the words around an unfamiliar word to see if they help you understand the meaning.
- Look at any photographs or other graphics for clues to meaning.
- Look up the word in a print or online dictionary.

ASK STUDENTS to use this strategy as they read to determine the meanings of *geologist, earthquake, tremor, boulder, granite, gravel, quartz,* and *erode.*

Analyze Structure: Text Features

COMMON CORE RI 5

(PHOTO AND CAPTION; HEADING)

Tell students that photographs and captions are **text features,** elements that help organize or call attention to important information. Photographs and captions can clarify or add to the information in the text.

C **ASK STUDENTS** how the photograph and caption contribute to the text. *(The photograph gives a good visual example of a balanced rock and what little support it has. The caption tells how long the rock has been in that spot.)*

Point out the **heading** and tell students that this is another text feature that authors use to help organize information. A heading helps readers understand what the section is about.

D **ASK STUDENTS** what they expect to read about in this section, based on the heading. *(The section will probably explain something about Richard Brune's "odd hobby" of photographing balanced rocks.)*

It is estimated this balanced rock has occupied this spot in the Mojave Desert for 15,000 to 20,000 years.

Brune wasn't flying over the desert in southern California to be a daredevil. He was taking pictures of balanced rocks. Big, balanced rocks. Really awkward ones. The kind of rock that looks like it would tip over, roll down a hill and flatten a
20 car if someone were silly enough to lean against it.

ODD HOBBY

Richard and his dad, James Brune, have a passion for balanced rocks. James is a geologist, someone who studies the history and movement of the Earth as recorded in rocks, at the University of Nevada in Reno. He has spent 20 years looking for balanced rocks across the deserts of Nevada and California.

Richard, his son, isn't officially a scientist, but he is good with airplanes, parachutes, cameras, computers—all kinds of gadgets. When he was younger, he would camp in the
30 desert while his dad did scientific work there. Richard, now 46, has helped his dad study balanced rocks for 15 years, photographing them from the air and then hiking into the desert with his dad to find them.

"We've found literally thousands of these rocks," says James. Some of them stand up to 5 meters tall and weigh 15,000 kilograms—real car crushers!

©Douglas Fox

158 Collection 3

WHEN STUDENTS STRUGGLE . . .

To guide students' comprehension, have them work in pairs to fill out a chart, like the one to the right, for each section of the text. Tell students to pause after they read each section and ask themselves, "What is this section mostly about?" Have students reread the text if they need to, and restate the important ideas in their own words.

It sounds like an odd hobby, but James, the geologist, is serious about these rocks. He has also studied earthquakes for many years, and he believes that balanced rocks can tell
40 us something important about earthquakes.

STANDING STRONG

An earthquake's tremors can topple balanced rocks. So if you look at these rocks across California, you should find clues about where sizable earthquakes have happened.

In places that haven't experienced large earthquakes, you should find really delicate rocks—ones you could tip over with a finger. But in places that have seen more serious quakes, the only rocks left standing in the balance should be those that are far harder to tip over.

Geologists find these rocks so interesting because they
50 could give clues about the severity of earthquakes over thousands of years. In parts of California, records collected by scientists go back only about 150 years. Historical data on tremor intensities are important when determining how strong a bridge or dam needs to be to survive earthquakes.

HOW OLD IS OLD?

All of this depends, of course, on finding out how long the balanced rocks have been standing.

It's a basic question, really: How quickly does the land change? Maybe you've wondered it yourself. Have you ever walked down a path, kicked a rock and wondered how long
60 that rock had stood there before you knocked it down the hill? Maybe it was there for one year. Maybe 100 years. Perhaps even 10,000 years.

Or maybe you sat on a boulder and wondered who else had sat there. Was the boulder there when the first pioneers rolled their wagons by 200 years ago? Or maybe even when the very first humans arrived in North America 15,000 years ago?

Believe it or not, scientists have clever ways to figure this stuff out.

Earlier this year, Richard Brune went to the Mojave Desert
70 in southern California to find out how long some balanced rocks have been standing.

The desert slopes gently away from a mountain of globby shaped granite rocks. Gravel and lots of prickly plants cover

Section Heading	Important Ideas
Odd Hobby	James Brune is a geologist, a scientist who studies rocks. Richard, his son, works with him taking photographs. They've been studying balanced rocks for 15 years. James believes that we can learn about earthquakes from these rocks.

CLOSE READ

Analyze Structure: Essay (LINES 44–54)

COMMON CORE RI 1, RI 3, RI 5

Explain that authors use different **patterns of organization,** or ways of structuring the ideas and information in expository writing. An author might use one pattern throughout an essay, or different sections might follow different patterns. One pattern of organization is **cause and effect,** in which text is organized to show the relationship between causes and effects.

E **ASK STUDENTS** to reread lines 44–48 and identify the two causes and their effects in the paragraph. *(cause: no large earthquakes have occurred; effect: delicate, easy-to-tip balanced rocks can be found; cause: strong earthquakes have occurred; effect: only more solidly grounded rocks are found)*

Explain that sometimes an author uses a signal word or phrase, such as *because, so,* or *as a result,* to indicate a cause-and-effect relationship.

F **CITE TEXT EVIDENCE** Ask students to reread lines 49–54. Have students cite the signal word or phrase and the cause-and-effect relationship it indicates. *(signal word: "because"; cause: balanced rocks can give clues about the history of earthquakes; effect: geologists are interested in studying balanced rocks)*

Analyze Structure: Essay (LINES 92–95)

COMMON CORE RI 3, RI 5

The author presents another cause-and-effect relationship in lines 92–95. In this case, there is no signal word, and the relationship is implied.

 ASK STUDENTS to closely reread lines 92–95 and to explain the cause-and-effect relationship. *(cause: river water "chews away the weaker types of rock"; effect: the stronger types of rock are left behind, sometimes balancing on thin foundations)*

CRITICAL VOCABULARY

gully: Brune walks along the bottom of a gully, looking for balanced rocks.

ASK STUDENTS why balanced rocks would occur on the edge of a gully. *(A gully is formed by running water. The water forms a ditch by washing away sand or lightweight soil. That leaves the rocks behind.)*

bedrock: The author explains how the balanced rocks were probably formed from the bedrock beneath the desert floor.

ASK STUDENTS to relate the process in their own words. *(River water flows over the solid bedrock and cuts paths by wearing away the softer rock, leaving only the harder, stronger rock behind.)*

gradual: The process of water wearing away rock is a gradual one.

ASK STUDENTS to explain why the author uses *gradually* instead of *slowly*. *(Slowly means simply "not quick or fast." Gradually suggests something happening in steps, or little by little.)*

---

the ground. Richard has parked his Jeep at the end of a bumpy dirt road. He now walks on the sandy bottom of a winding **gully** with Dylan Rood, a geologist from Lawrence Livermore National Laboratory in California.

80   Speckled granite rocks stacked like giant brown marshmallows tower above the gully on both sides. Now and then, Richard and Rood spot a rock balanced on top of the stack, like a milk jug standing upside down.

> ## " Speckled granite rocks stacked like giant brown marshmallows tower above the gully. "

"Be careful," says Richard, as Rood approaches one rock. "That one could go off easily. It wouldn't take much."

Several minutes later, Rood climbs to another rock, this one the size of a TV, sitting on top of the marshmallows. "Woohoo!" he hollers to Richard. "Just with a thumb I can move it."

CARVED BY WATER

People often assume that rocks become balanced after falling on top of each other. But that wasn't the case for these

90   marshmallow stacks—there's nowhere the balanced rocks could have rolled from above.

Ⓖ   Instead, scientists think these balanced rocks were probably carved by water. As rivers cut gullies into the granite **bedrock** beneath the desert floor, water chews away the weaker types of rock, leaving only the stronger behind.

Imagine a house built of strong bricks and held together by weak cement—bedrock often has these strong and weak parts, although they aren't always visible. If the house is continuously exposed to running water, the cement will

100   **gradually** wear away. But the bricks will remain. And some of the bricks will be left stacked or balanced on top of each other—like the granite marshmallows in the gully.

gully
(gŭl´ē) *n.* A *gully* is a deep ditch cut in the earth by running water.

bedrock
(bĕd´rŏk´) *n.* Bedrock is the solid rock that lies under sand, soil, clay, and gravel.

gradual
(grăj´ōō-əl) *adj.* If something is *gradual*, it advances little by little.

Rood thinks that most of these rocks were carved out during the last Ice Age.[1] "There was a lot more water," he says. "There were big lakes all over the Mojave Desert." If that's true, it would mean these rocks have been standing like bowling pins in the desert for 15,000 to 20,000 years—four or five times longer than the pyramids of Egypt!

SUNBURNED ROCK

110 Rood and Richard plan to test this age estimate. Late one afternoon, a couple of days after their walk through the marshmallow gully, they find a refrigerator-sized boulder that looks ready to roll downhill.

Unlike a lot of the other balanced rocks they've seen, this one is on the side of a small mountain, in a place where it *could* have landed after rolling from somewhere higher up. But Richard and Rood have a way of knowing that it didn't. They can tell, in fact, that it's sitting within a few centimeters of where it was eroded out of the surrounding bedrock.

120 Rood points out a vein of brownish quartz crystals, several fingers thick, that runs through the bedrock a few meters behind the rock. That layer runs for 30 meters before disappearing. It is tilted, like the hour hand of a wall clock at 8 o'clock—but otherwise straight as an arrow. That same layer of quartz runs through the boulder. It is perfectly lined up with the layer in the bedrock. It would be a pretty unlikely **coincidence** if the boulder just rolled down the mountain and landed that way. This rock has to be sitting in its original birthplace.

Rood hangs a tape measure down the boulder, which is 130 6 feet tall.

He hammers a small piece off of the boulder every few inches from top to bottom. Back at the lab, he'll test these bits of rock to see how long each part of the boulder has been exposed to sunlight.

Rood measures this by using an accelerator-mass spectrometer, a monster machine the size of an 18-wheeler. He'll use this machine to measure tiny amounts—a few quadrillionths of a gram—of a rare radioactive form of the element beryllium.

coincidence
(kō-ĭnˊsĭ-dəns) *n.*
A *coincidence* is a sequence of events that although accidental seems to have been planned.

---

[1] **Ice Age:** a time in history when thick sheets of ice covered large areas of land.

CLOSE READ

Analyze Structure: Essay (LINES 109–112)

COMMON CORE · RI 1, RI 3, RI 5

Explain that even though an article or essay might have one overall pattern of organization, individual paragraphs or sections might use a different pattern. Information in this paragraph (lines 109–112) is organized in **chronological,** or time, order.

H **CITE TEXT EVIDENCE** Ask students to reread lines 109–112. Have students cite the words and phrases that indicate the passage of time or the order of events. *(The phrases "Late one afternoon" and "a couple of days after their walk" indicate when the event is occurring and that it happens after the walk in the gully that was described previously.)*

CRITICAL VOCABULARY

coincidence: The author describes how Rood and Richard know that the boulder did not roll or fall from somewhere else.

ASK STUDENTS to describe the coincidence that would have to have occurred for the boulder to simply roll or fall into position. *(The boulder, with its brownish "stripe" of quartz crystals, would have had to roll to a stop in just a certain way to line up exactly with the quartz crystals in the bedrock.)*

APPLYING ACADEMIC VOCABULARY

affect	ensure

As you discuss the selection, incorporate the following Collection 3 academic vocabulary words: *affect* and *ensure*. Talk about the erosion process and how flowing water **affects** bedrock, softer rock materials, and harder rock materials. Have students explain how the gradual process of erosion **ensures** that balanced rocks are left behind in the Mojave Desert.

Analyze Structure: Essay (LINES 140–148)

COMMON CORE RI 3, RI 5

Tell students that some causes have multiple effects. Here, Fox describes a cause-and-effect relationship related to how long a rock is exposed to sunlight. The second effect is not stated directly, but is implied.

ASK STUDENTS to closely reread lines 140–148 and to explain the cause and the two effects. *(cause: the sun's rays hit the rock; effect 1: beryllium-10 develops in its outer layer; effect 2: the presence or absence of beryllium-10 allows scientists to determine how long the rock has been exposed to sunlight)*

Analyze Language

COMMON CORE RI 1, RI 4

(LINES 140–148)

Tell students that authors of expository text may use **figurative language,** or words used in a way that is different from the literal meaning. They do this to help make complex technical concepts clear to readers.

CITE TEXT EVIDENCE Have students reread lines 140–148 and cite two examples of figurative language. Ask them to tell what each means and identify the author's purpose in using it. *("the rock is getting sunburned": The author compares the process of beryllium-10 forming in a rock to a person getting sunburned to help readers relate a complex process to something familiar. The expression "before running water chews it out of the desert floor" helps readers visualize how running water eats away at the rock.)*

This is one section of an accelerator-mass spectrometer, an enormous instrument scientists can use to analyze and collect data about rock samples.

140 This rare form, called beryllium-10, is created when cosmic rays from space hit the rock and split apart larger atoms of oxygen and nitrogen. You might say that when this happens, the rock is getting sunburned. As long as the rock is sitting out in the open, the cosmic rays are hitting it and beryllium-10 is forming in the outer 2 or so centimeters of the rock. But while the rock is buried underground—before running water chews it out of the desert floor—it's shaded from cosmic rays, so no beryllium-10 develops.

OLDEST PLACES

By measuring the sunburn—that is, the amount of
150 beryllium-10 in the rock fragments—scientists can tell how long ago the rock emerged from the surrounding bedrock.

James King-Holmes/Science Source/Photoresearchers

Strategies for Annotation  Annotate it!

Analyze Structure: Essay

COMMON CORE RI 3, RI 5

Have students use their eBook annotation tools to analyze the text. Ask students to do the following:

- In lines 140–148, highlight in yellow each cause.
- Highlight in green each effect.
- In notes, write down any implied effects.
- Reread the text to make sure you fully understand the cause-and-effect relationship.

happens, the rock is getting sunburned. As long as the rock is sitting out in the open, the cosmic rays are hitting it and beryllium-10 is forming in the outer 2 or so centimeters of the rock. But while the rock is buried underground—before running water chews it out of the desert floor—it's shaded from cosmic rays, so no beryllium-10 develops.

Rood has already used this method, called exposure dating, on one balanced rock in the Mojave Desert. He found that it had been freestanding for 18,000 years—about what he expected if the rock was carved out during the last Ice Age.

Scientists have used exposure dating all over the world. Deserts, usually the oldest places, change the slowest because there is little water to alter the landscape. Once a rock is standing, it can stay still for a long time because there is
160 hardly any water to erode it or wash it away. And during the winter, ice doesn't form inside cracks in the rock and slowly pry it apart.

In places with lots of water, things change quickly. Over the past 150 years, the Missouri River has shifted its winding path by three kilometers in some places, leaving its mark in the landscape.

Antarctica probably has the oldest, most unchanging landscapes on Earth. Ice covers most of the continent, but a few small areas remain ice-free. In one such place, called the
170 Olympus Range, you can sit on boulders that haven't moved in five or six million years! The rocks survived because Antarctica is a desert: It is so cold that it receives hardly any rain or snow. The continent was once warmer and wetter, but when it became cold and dry, it stayed that way.

ROCK TIPPING

Here in California, Rood and Richard need to know not only how long their **precariously** balanced rocks have been standing but also how hard they are to knock over.

These are tough questions. The best way to find out how firmly in place a rock is—simply push it over. But toppling
180 a rock that's been balanced for 18,000 years is sort of like chopping down one of the oldest redwood trees. No one wants to do it.

Once, though, Richard and James Brune had a chance to topple some rocks. They heard about a businessman who was building some houses in the desert and planned to knock over some balanced rocks that were in the way.

The Brunes convinced the developer to let them do it for him. They fastened a steel cable to each rock and used a gadget to measure exactly how much pulling was needed to bring
190 down the boulder. "It was kind of fun," admits James. "They

precarious
(prĭ-kâr´ē-əs) *adj.*
If something is *precarious*, it is dangerous and unstable.

Analyze Structure:
Essay (LINES 156–162; 167–174)

COMMON CORE RI 1, RI 2, RI 3, RI 5

Tell students that lines 156–162 describe a cause and three effects. Note that sometimes an effect is named first, and then the cause is identified.

K **CITE TEXT EVIDENCE** Have students identify the cause and its effects in this paragraph by citing the text. *(cause: in a desert, "there is little water to alter the landscape"; effect 1: change occurs very slowly; effect 2: a rock "can stay still for a long time"; effect 3: "ice doesn't form inside cracks in the rock and slowly pry it apart")*

Explain that identifying the cause-and-effect organization of a paragraph can help students determine the **central idea**—the most important idea in the paragraph or section of text.

L **CITE TEXT EVIDENCE** Ask students to reread lines 167–174 and cite an example of a word that reveals the cause-and-effect structure. *(The word* because *in the sentence "The rocks survived because Antarctica is a desert" reveals a cause-and-effect structure.)* What is the central idea of this paragraph, and how does the above sentence support it? *(The central idea is that Antarctica has the oldest, most unchanging landscapes on Earth. The sentence about Antarctica being a desert reinforces this idea, showing why the landscape is unchanging.)*

CRITICAL VOCABULARY

precarious: Some of the rocks are precariously balanced.

ASK STUDENTS to describe a rock that is *not* precariously balanced. *(A rock that is not precariously balanced would have a good, solid foundation under it. It would not be easily tipped over or rolled.)*

Analyze Structure: Essay (LINES 193–204)

COMMON CORE RI 3, RI 5

Once again, in lines 193–204, Fox uses an example to support the statement he makes in the first sentence in lines 193–194.

 ASK STUDENTS to explain what "less destructive" method Richard has found. Ask what pattern of organization the author uses to describe this method. *(Richard first takes photographs, then loads the photos into a computer and makes a virtual model. He can then run a computer program to learn how much force it takes to tip the rock, without actually moving it. The author uses chronological order in this description.)*

COLLABORATIVE DISCUSSION Have small groups of students review the aspects of geological research described in the essay and discuss what surprised them. Have each group summarize the main points of their discussion and share their conclusions with the class.

ASK STUDENTS to share any questions they generated in the course of reading and discussing the selection.

were 7 or 8 feet high and weighed many tons." And each landed with a satisfying thud.

Richard has also found less destructive ways to pull on rocks. Out in the Mojave Desert with Rood, he takes out a camera and begins photographing from all sides the refrigerator-sized boulder they're studying.

Back at home, he'll load the photos into a computer that will stitch the pictures into a three-dimensional model of the rock—a virtual rock.

200 Richard can then run that virtual rock through a computer program that shakes and knocks the rock down many times. By tipping that virtual rock they can ensure that the other one—the real rock—has a fighting chance to stay standing for another 18,000 years.

COLLABORATIVE DISCUSSION What surprising details does the author reveal about how geologists conduct their research? Discuss your ideas with a small group of classmates.

TO CHALLENGE STUDENTS . . .

Analyzing Media The opening scene and the author's frequent use of quotations from scientists, suggest that this essay could make a compelling documentary film.

ASK STUDENTS to work in small groups to discuss how they would create a documentary based on this essay. Tell students to consider the following:

- Camera angles: Which scenes would they shoot close-up? Which would be long shots, or "big picture" shots?
- Sound elements: What music would be effective? Where would they include interviews? Voice-overs?
- What special effects might enhance the film?

Analyze Structure: Essay

COMMON CORE RI 2, RI 3, RI 5

"Big Rocks' Balancing Acts" is an **expository essay,** which presents or explains information or ideas. To ensure that informational texts are clear to readers, writers choose a **pattern of organization,** a particular arrangement of ideas and information. Facts and details can be organized in a variety of ways. This chart shows a few common patterns of organization:

Pattern	What It Shows or Highlights	Signal Words or Phrases
chronological order	the order in which actions or events occur	*first, second, then, at the same time*
cause-and-effect order	the relationship between events and their causes	*because, and so, as a result, therefore*
compare-and-contrast order	the similarities and differences of two or more subjects	*like, by contrast, similarly, as opposed to, however*
spatial order	the arrangement of details according to their physical position or relationship	*top, bottom, above, in front of*

A pattern of organization may be used to organize an entire piece of writing or single paragraphs within a longer work. Reread lines 113–118. Identify the pattern of organization within that paragraph and the words or phrases that signal the organization.

Being able to identify patterns of organization can help readers find a writer's main, or central, idea, which is the most important idea in an essay. Often, the **central idea** is not directly stated but is implied by supporting details. As you read, use these strategies to identify and understand central ideas in an expository essay:

- Identify the specific topic of each paragraph or section.
- Examine the details the author includes in that section.
- Look for words that signal an organization.
- Ask what idea or message the details convey about the topic.

Where in "Big Rocks' Balancing Acts" does the author introduce the topic and central idea of the essay?

CLOSE READ

Analyze Structure: Essay

COMMON CORE RI 2, RI 3, RI 5

Guide students to understand and distinguish among the four organizational patterns shown in the chart. Provide this additional information:

- Chronological order means time order. An essay that relates events usually uses this pattern.
- Causes and effects help us understand how and why things happen. Essays that explain concepts or processes may use this pattern.
- To compare and contrast, the author needs at least two events or objects that have something in common.
- Authors use spatial order when they describe a place.

Emphasize that an author might organize a single paragraph in an essay using one of these patterns, even though the rest of the essay follows a different pattern. Have students reread the paragraph in lines 113–118 and identify the pattern and the words that signal it. *(compare-and-contrast; signal words: "Unlike," "But")*

Help students understand that the author introduces the topic, balancing rocks, at the end of the introduction, after describing Richard Brune's daring picture-taking. He introduces the central idea at the end of the next section, "Odd Hobby," when he explains that studying balanced rocks "can tell us something important about earthquakes." *(lines 39–40)*

Strategies for Annotation   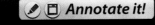 Annotate it!

Analyze Structure: Essay

COMMON CORE RI 3, RI 5

Share these strategies for guided or independent analysis:

- In paragraphs that describe cause-and-effect relationships, highlight in yellow the cause.
- Highlight in green the effect or effects.
- Reread the text to make sure you have found all of the cause-and-effect relationships and that you understand them fully.
- In a note, explain the ideas in your own words.

Imagine a house built of strong bricks and held together by weak cement—bedrock often has these strong and weak parts, although they aren't always visible. If the house is continuously exposed to running water, the cement will gradually wear away. But the bricks will remain. And some

PRACTICE & APPLY

Analyzing the Text

COMMON CORE RI 1, RI 2, RI 3, RI 4, RI 5, RI 6

Possible answers:

1. *The author uses spatial order in these lines as he describes the appearance of a particular rock and its surroundings. The measurements and the position words, such as "tilted," "straight," and "perfectly lined up" help reveal the pattern.*

2. *Geologist James Brune and his son Richard have been studying balanced rocks to learn about earthquakes.*

3. *Balanced rocks give clues about the severity of earthquakes in a region over thousands of years because delicate rocks remain only where no earthquakes have occurred. These clues are helpful in the construction of bridges or dams because builders know more about the likelihood and severity of tremors in the area.*

4. *The author compares bedrock to bricks held together with weak cement to help readers visualize how the action of water on rock wears away the weak parts and leaves bricks, or a stack of rocks, behind. The stacked rocks are compared to marshmallows to help readers visualize their shapes.*

5. *The author uses informal language and addresses readers directly, helping them to connect to their own experiences and curiosity.*

6. *These rocks have been balancing for a long time and should be left alone for the sake of natural beauty and for further study.*

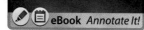 eBook *Annotate It!*

Analyzing the Text

 COMMON CORE RI 1, RI 2, RI 3, RI 4, RI 5, RI 6, W 7, SL 4

Cite Text Evidence   Support your responses with evidence from the text.

1. **Recognize and Analyze**   Under the heading "Sunburned Rock," examine lines 119–130. What pattern of organization is evident in these paragraphs? What details help you to recognize it?

2. **Summarize**   Reread from the beginning of the essay to the end of the section "Odd Hobby." In your own words, describe the most important idea the author of this expository essay wants readers to understand.

3. **Cite Evidence**   Reread the section "Standing Strong." Why is it worthwhile to study balanced rocks?

4. **Analyze**   Reread lines 96–102. What comparisons does the author make, and how are they helpful for readers?

5. **Draw Conclusions**   Reread lines 57–68. What might be the author's reason in using the pronoun *you* and presenting information in this way?

6. **Analyze**   What important idea from the essay is in the concluding sentence?

PERFORMANCE TASK

Speaking Activity: Oral Report   Choose a concept or term about geology from "Big Rocks' Balancing Acts" (for example: *earthquake tremors, granite, bedrock, accelerator-mass spectrometer, erosion, Ice Age,* or *geology* itself). Think of a question related to that term to explore, such as *"How many ice ages have taken place on Earth?"* Research your topic and present the findings to your class in a brief oral report.

- Find at least two informational print or online articles on the topic. Make sure these sources are credible and believable.
- List the most important ideas you want to present in your report.
- Begin your report with an introduction that specifies your topic clearly, establishes your central idea, and hooks listeners into listening further.
- Support your central idea or ideas with evidence from your research.

Assign this performance task.

PERFORMANCE TASK

COMMON CORE W 7, SL 4

Speaking Activity: Oral Report   Have students work individually or in pairs. Encourage students to spend time shaping their initial question so their research can be focused and efficient. Provide these tips for students' oral delivery: familiarize yourself with the material—do not simply read the report aloud; practice delivering your report in a room by yourself; if making eye contact makes you uncomfortable, look just over the heads of your audience.

Critical Vocabulary

gully	bedrock	gradual	coincidence	precarious

Practice and Apply Identify the vocabulary word that is tied in meaning to the italicized word in each question. Give your reasons.

1. Which word goes with *patience*? Why?

2. Which word goes with *drill*? Why?

3. Which word goes with *cliff*? Why?

4. Which word goes with *rainstorm*? Why?

5. Which word goes with *chance*? Why?

Vocabulary Strategy: Latin Roots

A **root** is a word part that came into English from an older language. You can check a print or digital dictionary to learn about roots; the entry for a word often gives details about the word's origin. Roots from Latin appear in many English words. This sentence comes from "Big Rocks' Balancing Acts":

> If the house is continuously exposed to running water, the cement will gradually wear away.

The word *gradually* contains a root, *grad*, from the Latin word *gradus*, which means "step" or "stage." You can see the root meaning in the different meanings of the word *grade*, which have to do with steps, stages, or levels. The root meaning also appears in the word *gradually*, which describes actions taken step by step. In the example sentence, the cement doesn't disappear all at once, but wears away in stages. By recognizing the root *grad*, you can make a good guess about the meanings of longer words that include it.

Practice and Apply Read each sentence. Identify the word with the Latin root *grad*. Tell what each word means. Use a print or digital dictionary to check your ideas.

1. After learning camera settings, we graduated to taking nature photos.

2. The hill has a gradient that is perfect for sledding.

3. Until astronomers understood that planets orbit the Sun, they had trouble explaining the retrograde motion of planets during part of the year.

4. The art appears to be red, but a closer look shows gradations of color.

5. Weathering and erosion slowly cause the degradation of mountains.

6. Some products last forever in landfills, while others are biodegradable.

PRACTICE & APPLY

Critical Vocabulary

Possible answers:

1. *gradual; Waiting for something to occur in stages requires patience.*

2. *bedrock; You need a drill to cut through bedrock.*

3. *precarious; Something that might fall from the edge of a cliff is balanced in a precarious way.*

4. *gully; Rain and flowing water can carve a gully in the earth.*

5. *coincidence; A coincidence happens by chance.*

Vocabulary Strategy: Latin Roots

Possible answers:

1. *graduated: moved on to the next step*

2. *gradient: amount of slope*

3. *retrograde: moving backward or in a direction opposite to what is expected*

4. *gradations: series of stages*

5. *degradation: the opposite of building up; breaking down*

6. *biodegradable: able to be broken down by bacteria or other life forms*

PRACTICE & APPLY

Language Conventions: Prepositional Phrases

Point out to students that prepositions, such as the examples shown, are common words that they use every day.

With the class, examine each of the following sentences. Guide students to identify the prepositional phrase, what the phrase modifies, and what it tells.

- One of the windows is open. *(modifies "One" and tells* which*)*
- The hinge on the door squeaks like a rusty gate. *(modifies "hinge" and tells* which; *modifies "squeaks" and tells* how*)*
- She stuffed her cold hands into her pockets and squeezed her fists into tight balls. *(modifies "stuffed" and tells* where; *modifies "squeezed" and tells* how *or to what extent)*

Possible answers:

- *Balanced boulders stand like bowling pins in the desert.*
- *The rocks were carved by water and have remained standing for a long time.*
- *In lands with little water, people can sit on ancient boulders.*

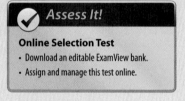

Assess It!

Online Selection Test
- Download an editable ExamView bank.
- Assign and manage this test online.

Language Conventions: Prepositional Phrases

A **preposition** is a part of speech that relates one word to another. These are just a few common prepositions: *about, across, against, at, before, beside, between, by, for, from, in, like, next to, of, on, on top of, over, through, to,* and *with.*

A **phrase** is a group of related words that acts like a single word in a sentence. A **prepositional phrase** acts like a **modifier,** a word that changes the sense of another word in a sentence. A prepositional phrase includes a preposition, its object (the noun or pronoun that follows the preposition), and any modifiers. These examples show how the prepositional phrase always modifies or relates to another word in a sentence, telling where, when, how, why, or to what extent.

modifies

The scientists fly over the southern California desert.

(The prepositional phrase *over the southern California desert* modifies *fly* and tells *where.*)

modifies

The scientists have a passion for balanced rocks.

(The prepositional phrase *for balanced rocks* modifies *passion* and tells *what kind.*)

modifies   *modifies*

One of them shoots photos from the plane.

(The prepositional phrase *of them* modifies *One* and tells *which.* The prepositional phrase *from the plane* modifies *shoots* and tells *where.*)

Writers use prepositional phrases to add information to their sentences. This sentence from "Big Rocks' Balancing Acts" has five prepositional phrases:

> **And some of the bricks will be left stacked or balanced on top of each other—like the granite marshmallows in the gully.**

Practice and Apply Use these prepositional phrases to build sentences that tell about information in "Big Rocks' Balancing Acts." Try to use more than one phrase in a sentence.

- in the desert
- with little water
- on ancient boulders
- by water
- like bowling pins
- for a long time

Strategies for Annotation   ✎ 🗐 *Annotate it!*

Language Conventions: Prepositional Phrases

Have students locate lines 3–8 of the essay and use their eBook annotation tools to do the following:

- Underline each prepositional phrase.
- Highlight the preposition in yellow.
- Highlight in green the word the phrase modifies.
- In a note, write what the phrase tells about the modified word.

The plane's door had been removed so Brune could ride with one leg outside. As the tiny propeller plane zigzagged over the desert, Brune leaned out over empty air. The 80 mile-per-hour headwind pummeled his face. He looked through his camera and snapped pictures of the rocky desert hundreds of feet below.

Analyze Texts: Fact and Opinion

COMMON
CORE

RI 3

TEACH

Tell students that most informational writing contains both facts and opinions. Explain that a **fact** is a statement that can be proved, or verified. An **opinion** is a statement that expresses a writer's belief, feelings, or thoughts; it cannot be proved. In general, facts are more reliable than opinions. However, some informational writing includes the opinions of experts, which are based on their experience and knowledge of the subject matter.

- Display the following text (lines 103–105):
  Rood thinks that most of these rocks were carved out during the last Ice Age. "There was a lot more water," he says. "There were big lakes all over the Mojave Desert."
- Explain that the first sentence is an opinion because it expresses the scientist's belief about when the balanced rocks were established. The word *thinks* is a clue. However, the opinion is based on his expert knowledge of the subject.
- The second and third sentences are facts that can be proved by consulting scientific sources.
- Point out that the opinions expressed by the geologist Rood are not necessarily those of the author Douglas Fox.

PRACTICE AND APPLY

Display lines 37–40 of the essay. Have students identify a fact, an author's opinion, and an expert opinion, and give reasons for their answers.

Fact: *He has also studied earthquakes for many years.*

Author's Opinion: *"It sounds like an odd hobby."*

Expert Opinion: *"He believes that balanced rocks can tell us something about earthquakes."*

Reasons: *The fact can be verified by checking the scientist's research and publications. The author's opinion is what Douglas Fox expresses about studying rocks as a hobby. The expert opinion is based on his many years of studying earthquakes.*

Tell students to be careful to distinguish between facts and opinions when they do research for their oral reports in the Performance Task.

Analyze Structure: Essay

COMMON
CORE

RI 3,
RI 5

RETEACH

Remind students that an expository essay presents or explains information or ideas. Explain that an author chooses one or more patterns of organization as a way to structure the information. Review the patterns in the chart shown in the skill lesson "Analyze Structure: Essay." Provide the following examples of topics that might use each type of organization. Talk about why each pattern of organization "fits" the topic.

- An expository essay tells about events before, during, and after a natural disaster in **chronological,** or time, order.
- An expository essay explores the **causes and effects** related to using more and less fertilizer on vegetable plants.
- An expository essay **compares and contrasts** life in New York City and in Los Angeles.
- An expository essay describes an award-winning school building using **spatial** order.

 LEVEL UP TUTORIALS Assign one or more of the following *Level Up* tutorials: **Chronological Order; Cause-and-Effect Organization; Comparison-Contrast Organization**

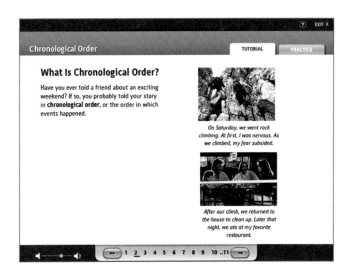

CLOSE READING APPLICATION

Students can apply their knowledge of patterns of organization to help them understand other pieces of expository text. For example, stop and ask students to identify the patterns in paragraphs or sections of a textbook they are using in class. Remind students to look for signal words as clues.

The Hidden Southwest: The Arch Hunters

Essay by James Vlahos

Why This Text

Students may read an essay without a complete understanding of the author's central idea and details that support it. Essays such as this one by James Vlahos may have more than one complex central idea, and a pattern of organization that is clarified only with careful study. With the help of the close-reading questions, students will determine the central ideas by examining the evidence, enabling them to develop a cohesive understanding of an informational text.

Background Have students read the background information that describes the rock formations in Canyonlands National Park in Utah. The landscape has been carved by erosion and weathering into an intricate maze of deep narrow canyons and other odd landforms such as mesas, buttes, and rock arches. Introduce the selection by sharing a description from Edward Abbey's book *Desert Solitaire*, in which he depicts the rocks in Canyonlands as "monolithic formations of sandstone."

SETTING A PURPOSE Ask students to pay close attention to the central ideas in this essay and to the interactions among individuals, ideas, and events in the text. How soon into the essay does Vlahos present the essay's central idea?

Common Core Support

- cite several pieces of textual evidence

- determine two or more central ideas in a text

- analyze the interactions among individuals, events, or ideas in a text

- analyze the structure an author uses to organize a text

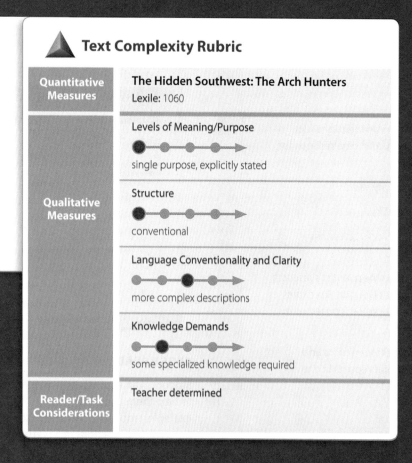

Text Complexity Rubric

Quantitative Measures

The Hidden Southwest: The Arch Hunters
Lexile: 1060

Qualitative Measures

Levels of Meaning/Purpose
single purpose, explicitly stated

Structure
conventional

Language Conventionality and Clarity
more complex descriptions

Knowledge Demands
some specialized knowledge required

Reader/Task Considerations
Teacher determined

Strategies for CLOSE READING

Determine the Central Idea

Students should read this essay carefully all the way through. Close-reading questions at the bottom of the page will help them focus on a thorough analysis of the central idea of the essay and on the details that support it. As they read, students should record comments or questions about the text in the side margins.

WHEN STUDENTS STRUGGLE . . .

To help students follow the central idea of the essay, they should work in a small group to fill out a chart such as the one shown below as they analyze the essay.

CITE TEXT EVIDENCE For practice in finding the central idea the writer develops over the course of the text, ask students to examine the details and evidence that support the central idea.

Central Idea: Rock arches are natural wonders that attract curious explorers.

Detail 1: Generations of explorers have been astounded by rock arches.

Detail 2: Rock arches are almost as iconic as Old Faithful and Half Dome.

Detail 3: People notice rock when it takes "flight in the sky," flouting physical laws.

Detail 4: The author and two other explorers search for the rock arch and are ecstatic when they find it.

Background *Canyonlands National Park in southeast Utah contains countless canyons, mesas, buttes, and other odd rock formations created by the Colorado and Green rivers. The environmental essayist Edward Abbey has described the park as "the most weird, wonderful, magical place on earth— there is nothing else like it anywhere." In this essay, you will discover the reason why some elite adventurers come to explore the park.*

The Hidden Southwest:
The Arch Hunters

Essay by James Vlahos

CLOSE READ
Notes

1. **READ** ▶ As you read lines 1–22, begin to collect and cite text evidence.

- Circle the repeated statement in lines 1–10.
- In the margin, state in your own words the central (or main) idea the repeated statement expresses.
- Underline the supporting details in lines 1–22 that develop the central idea.

A **B** The rock arch is lost. It's around here somewhere but could be anywhere; we've searched all morning and gotten nowhere. Picking my way through boulders and gnarled junipers, I reach the scalloped rim of a high mesa and peer over the edge. My stomach drops.

This part of Canyonlands National Park is known as the Needles District, a name too tidy to describe the slickrock chaos erupting from the valley below. There are knobs, blobs, towers, and fins, an array containing every shape of sculpted rock save the one we're

10 seeking. The arch is lost.

Two men join me on the overlook. The first wears a plaid Western shirt neatly tucked into blue Levi's. Leathery, all limbs and no body fat, he steps **nimbly** to the precipice. "Did you talk to Alex Ranney?" he is saying.

The writer cannot find the rock arch he is searching for.

nimbly: *gracefully*

51

---

1. **READ AND CITE TEXT EVIDENCE** Explain that the central idea is usually stated at the beginning or end of an essay, a paragraph, or a section of text; however, in this essay, the central idea of the first section (lines 1–10) is restated at the end, also.

A **ASK STUDENTS** to evaluate the effectiveness of the repetition of the sentence "The rock arch is lost" in lines 1–10. *Students should note that the repetition stresses the importance of the goal of the arch hunters to find the rock arch.*

Critical Vocabulary: nimbly (line 13) Have students explain "nimbly," as Vlahos uses it here. Why might the arch hunter need to step nimbly? *to keep from falling off the overlook*

FOR ELL STUDENTS Explain that a compound word usually consists of two words that are joined together to make one word. Point out that "Canyonlands" (line 6) and "slickrock" (line 7) are compound words.

ASK STUDENTS to look for other compound words in the text and cite them in the margin.

"I did," replies the second man. Wearing a khaki shirt, shorts, and mirrored sunglasses, he looks like a refugee from a Kalahari game drive.

"Did you get any more clues?" asks Western Shirt.

"Nope, Ranney was elusive," replies Sunglasses.

20 "Tight-lipped."

"Totally. He said, 'I want you to be able to find it yourself and get the thrill of discovery.'"

The rock formation we seek is a quadruple arch known as Klingon Battle Cruiser. The first recorded sighting wasn't until 1994 by Ranney, a canyoneer from Tucson, Arizona. Not on any map or trail, it has probably been glimpsed by fewer than a dozen people in the history of the park. Tom Budlong (Western Shirt) and Tom Van Bebber (Sunglasses) desperately want to add their names to the list. These guys are no casual tourists. Rather, they are arch hunters.

30 Few sights are as celebrated in—or as iconic of—the American West as the natural rock arch. Arches have astounded generations of desert wanderers, from Teddy Roosevelt, who camped below Rainbow Bridge in 1913, to Edward Abbey, who memorably **venerated** them in *Desert Solitaire*. America's spans are internationally recognizable wonders on par with Old Faithful and Half Dome, their shapes burned into the collective consciousness by countless photographs and films.

Rock shouldn't take flight in the sky; when it does, in scorn of known physical laws, people take notice. Arches National Park,

40 America's best known repository of spans, draws more than 800,000 visitors each year from around the world. Yet despite such obvious attraction, few consider searching outside park boundaries—even

venerate:
celebrate

---

though the Colorado Plateau has the highest density of rock arches worldwide. There are at least 2,000 stone spans scattered throughout the Four Corners states.

Budlong and Van Bebber belong to the world's **preeminent**, and perhaps only, arch-hunting club—NABS, the Natural Arch and Bridge Society. Its 110 members scour the globe by plane, boat, 4x4, and foot.

50 They prowl Antarctic islands, Algerian sands, and the canyons of the American Southwest. True explorers, they live for the moment of discovery: rounding a canyon bend to spot a miracle of natural engineering that perhaps nobody else in the world has ever seen.

In the case of Klingon Battle Cruiser, that moment of revelation is proving hard to come by. Van Bebber had invited me along on a week's worth of arch hunting, hoping I might catch the fever. This is not an encouraging start. He examines a map, scratches his chin, and sighs, "It's probably just right below us."

I leave the pair to study their charts and hike several hundred

60 yards along the rim. Looking down at an expanse of tawny rock, I realize I am gazing *through* it—through a yawning window at the tiny green dots of trees in the valley below. Nearby, I see three additional **portals**. "Over here!" I shout.

I step carefully from the canyon rim onto the top of the arch and feel a swirl of vertigo. After it subsides I take a second step, then a third, following a rock catwalk into blue sky. Reaching the apex I rotate slowly around, a full 360 degrees, the canyon bottom hundreds of feet straight below.

Worldwide, arches number in the tens of thousands, and probably no place is better suited to their formation than the Colorado Plateau.

70 The sandstone is porous and erosive. The geological strata are such that harder layers lie atop weaker ones; the softer rock erodes from

preeminent:
superior to
all others

Budlong and
Van Bebber
strive to
discover what
no one else
has seen.

portals:
entrances

---

2. ◀ REREAD Reread lines 1–22. Use the central idea and the supporting details to write a summary of the first two paragraphs.

The writer and two other men cannot find the rock arch they are looking for in Canyonlands National Park.

3. READ ▶ As you read lines 23–45, continue to cite textual evidence.

• Circle the specific reason the arch hunters are in the park.
• Underline the details that suggest that a rock arch is an extraordinary sight.

---

4. ◀ REREAD AND DISCUSS Reread lines 23–45. With a small group discuss the reasons why adventurers seek out rock arches.

5. READ ▶ As you read lines 46–88, continue to cite textual evidence.

• In the margin, paraphrase the reason why the writer says Budlong and Van Bebber are true explorers.
• Circle the sentences that show that the narrator has found the arch.
• Underline the sentences in lines 77–88 that reveal an unexpected discovery.

---

2. **REREAD AND CITE TEXT EVIDENCE**

B ASK STUDENTS to cite textual evidence that shows the central idea of the first two paragraphs and the details that support it. How might the repetition of the first sentence suggest that this is the central idea? *By repeating the statement that "The rock arch is lost," Vlahos is suggesting the importance of this idea. Students should cite evidence from lines 1–2 and 8–10.*

3. **READ AND CITE TEXT EVIDENCE** Vlahos states that when rock takes "flight in the sky . . . people take notice."

C ASK STUDENTS to cite details that suggest that a rock arch, which stands high in the sky, is an awesome sight. *Students should cite details from lines 23–24 and 30–45.*

Critical Vocabulary: venerate (line 33) Have students share their definitions of *venerate*. Ask how *venerate* fits into Vlahos's discussion of rock arches, which extend for miles. *The spans of rock arches are so huge that people have honored them.*

4. **REREAD AND DISCUSS USING TEXT EVIDENCE**

D ASK STUDENTS to appoint a reporter for each group to explain the arch hunters' motivations. *Students should cite evidence from lines 23–28, 30–35, and 38–45.*

5. **READ AND CITE TEXT EVIDENCE**

E ASK STUDENTS to read their margin notes to a partner and then write one response that best paraphrases Vlahos's assessment of Budlong and Van Bebber as being "true explorers." *Students should cite evidence from lines 46–52, and 54–59.*

Critical Vocabulary: preeminent (line 46) Ask students why Vlahos uses this word to support his claim that Budlong and Van Bebber are "true explorers". *He wants to show that they belong to the foremost arch-hunting club—perhaps the only one.*

Critical Vocabulary: portals (line 62) Have students explain the meaning and importance of *portals*.

CLOSE READ
Notes

below to leave an arch standing above. And finally, the plateau is in the midst of a rapid geological uplift. Cliff walls push higher while at the same time rivers and meltwater carve deeper and faster. The twin forces produce the critical fins and cracks.

A day after finding Klingon Battle Cruiser, I stand at the base of an **undulating** mass of slickrock, a natural staircase of narrow benches and tilted slopes. With Van Bebber's outstretched palms providing a necessary toehold on blank rock, I scramble up to the first
80   shelf. After walking along it until I find a low-angle passage, I clamber to the next level of the staircase, and the next. A few hundred yards upslope is my goal: the massive triangular portal of Cleft Arch. The only visible route up to the fourth and final bench, however, is too steep. Frustrated, I follow the shelf south and round a corner to make a startling discovery. Tucked under an overhang, invisible until I'm right upon it, is an Anasazi ruin with three well-preserved walls of neatly stacked stone. Arch hunting, I'm learning, often yields much more than the arches themselves.

undulating:
moving up and down like a wave

The sandstone, geological strata, and geological uplift cause rock arches to form in the Colorado Plateau.

6. ◀ **REREAD**   Reread lines 70–75. Write an explanation in the margin of the cause-and-effect connection between events in these lines.

SHORT RESPONSE

Cite Text Evidence   What is the central idea of the essay? Consider the important details the writer conveys about rock arches in the text. Review your reading notes, and **cite text evidence** in your response.

The central idea of the essay is that rock arches are natural wonders that attract curious explorers. Rock arches "take flight in the sky... in scorn of physical laws" so it is no wonder that they have "astounded generations of desert wanderers." The author, along with Budlong and Van Bebber, expend great effort to find a rock arch and express excitement when they do.

54

---

6. **REREAD AND CITE TEXT EVIDENCE**   Vlahos explains the process of rock-arch formation at the end of his essay, relating cause-and-effect events.

(F) ASK STUDENTS to read their margin notes to a partner and then explain the cause-and-effect relationship between the Colorado Plateau and the formation of rock arches. *Students should cite textual evidence from lines 70–75. The Colorado Plateau is probably the place best suited to the formation of rock arches.*

Critical Vocabulary: undulating   (line 77) Ask students for examples associating the word with natural disasters.

SHORT RESPONSE

Cite Text Evidence   Students should:

- explain what the central idea is of the essay.
- give reasons for their point of view.
- cite details and evidence from the text to support their viewpoint.

TO CHALLENGE STUDENTS . . .

For more context about rock arches, Canyonlands, and other national parks, students can research rock arches in national parks online.

ASK STUDENTS what they have learned about unusual rock formations and about the natural beauty of our national parks. *Students should report on the facts they have learned and the impression they were left with.*

DIG DEEPER

With the class, return to Question 4, Reread and Discuss. Have students share the results of their discussion.

ASK STUDENTS whether they were satisfied with the outcome of their small-group discussions. Have each group share the reasons they cited to explain the motivations of adventurers who seek out these unusual rock formations. What compelling evidence did the group cite to support their opinion?

- Guide students to tell whether there was any convincing evidence cited by group members who did not agree with the reasons given by the majority of the group. How did the group handle this difference of opinion?

- Have groups explain how they decided whether or not they had found enough textual evidence to support their ideas or opinion. Did everyone in the group agree as to what made the evidence sufficient? How did the group use conflict-resolution techniques to resolve disagreements?

- After students have shared the results of their group's discussion, ask whether they think another group shared any reasons they wished they had brought to the table.

ASK STUDENTS to return to their Short Response answer and to revise it based on the class discussion.

ANCHOR TEXT

Ode to enchanted light

Sleeping in the Forest

Poem by Pablo Neruda

Poem by Mary Oliver

Why These Texts?

Poetry can capture the beauty and awe of nature in a unique way, allowing the reader to see aspects of the world in a new way. This lesson focuses on different forms of poetry and the different ways in which poets express personal thoughts and feelings.

Key Learning Objective: The student will learn how to analyze poetic form and how poets use figurative language to express feelings and ideas.

For practice and application:

Poems About Nature

Close Reader selection
Poems About Nature
Poetry by Leslie Marmon Silko,
Victor Hernandez Cruz, and Gwendolyn Brooks

 COMMON CORE

Common Core Standards

RL 1 Cite textual evidence.
RL2 Determine a theme or central idea.
RL 4 Determine the meaning of words and phrases.
RL 5 Analyze how a poem's form contributes to its meaning.
RL 6 Analyze points of view of narrators in a text.
W 2 Write explanatory texts.
W 10 Write routinely.
SL 1 Engage in collaborative discussions.

Text Complexity Rubric

	Ode to enchanted light **Lexile:** N/A	Sleeping in the Forest **Lexile:** N/A
Quantitative Measures		
Qualitative Measures	Levels of Meaning/Purpose — multiple levels of meaning	Levels of Meaning/Purpose — multiple levels of meaning
	Structure — Complex structures, such as sonnets, villanelles, etc.	Structure — free verse, no particular patterns
	Language Conventionality and Clarity — figurative, less accessible language	Language Conventionality and Clarity — figurative, less accessible language
	Knowledge Demands — moderately complex theme	Knowledge Demands — experience includes unfamiliar aspects
Reader/Task Considerations	Teacher determined Vary by individual reader and type of text	Teacher determined Vary by individual reader and type of text

TEACH

CLOSE READ

Background Have students read the background and information about the poets. Tell students that, although these poets use different poetic forms and styles to write about nature, both express an appreciation for nature that causes us to consider our own feelings about nature and our relationship with it.

SETTING A PURPOSE Direct students to use the Setting a Purpose prompt to focus their reading. Remind them to write down questions as they read.

Background *The topic of nature is popular with poets around the world and throughout history. Two of the most important poets of the 20th century, Pablo Neruda and Mary Oliver, continue this tradition with their poems in this lesson. Neruda's poem "Ode to enchanted light" was written originally in Spanish. Its Spanish title is "Oda a la luz enchantada."*

Ode to enchanted light

Sleeping in the Forest

Poem by Pablo Neruda

Poem by Mary Oliver

Pablo Neruda (1904–1973) *was the pen name of Ricardo Eliecer Neftalí Reyes Basoalto. Born in a small town in Chile, Neruda began writing poetry as a child. While a student, he met Gabriela Mistral, a famous poet. She encouraged Neruda to continue writing. Neruda went on to write hundreds of poems and gain a worldwide reputation. He was awarded the Nobel Prize for Literature in 1971 for his lifetime of work.*

Mary Oliver (b. 1935) *was born in Maple Heights, Ohio. She spent a great deal of time in her younger years writing, reading, and walking through the woods where she grew up. Today, Oliver always walks with a notepad so she can write down her thoughts immediately. Oliver's first book of poems was published in 1962. Since then she has written many books and won many awards for her poetry.*

SETTING A PURPOSE As you read, think about how each poet portrays a meaningful experience in nature. Beyond the subject matter, how are the poems similar? How are they different? Write down any questions you have while reading.

Compare Texts **169**

Close Read Screencasts ▶ View It!

Modeled Discussions

Have students click the *Close Read* icons in their eBooks to access two screencasts in which readers discuss and annotate the following key lines from each poem:

- "A cicada sends . . ." ("Ode to enchanted light" lines 10–12)
- "I thought the earth . . ." ("Sleeping in the Forest" lines 1–5)

As a class, view and discuss at least one of these videos. Then have students work in pairs to do an independent close read of an additional passage—the last stanza from "Ode to enchanted light" (lines 13–15) or the last seven lines in "Sleeping in the Forest" (lines 12–18).

Analyze Form: Ode

COMMON CORE **RL 1, RL 5**

(LINES 1–15)

Explain to students that an **ode** is a type of traditional poem that expresses an appreciation for someone or something. It usually deals with serious themes, such as justice, truth, or beauty. There are many different types of odes, each following a different set of rules for lines, stanzas, and patterns of rhyme and rhythm.

(A) CITE TEXT EVIDENCE Have students reread the poem and cite text evidence that reveals this poem to be an ode. *(The poet is expressing appreciation for natural light shining through a tree. In the first stanza, phrases, such as "dropped from the top of the sky" and "like a green / latticework of branches," create a sense of the light moving in an enchanting, magical way. In the second stanza, the image of a cicada singing creates an image of celebratory song. Finally, the "glass overflowing" completes the celebration with an image of the abundance of natural beauty.)*

Determine Meaning

COMMON CORE **RL 1, RL 4**

(LINES 13–15)

Explain to students that poets often use figurative language to compare things, emphasize ideas, or give an emotional effect. **Figurative language** is a way of using words to express ideas that are not literally true. Discuss three common types of figurative language: A **simile** is a comparison of two unlike things using *like* or *as*. A **metaphor** is a comparison of two unlike things without the words *like* or *as*. **Personification** is giving human qualities to an animal, object, or idea.

(B) CITE TEXT EVIDENCE Ask students to reread the first stanza and to cite an example of figurative language in lines 3–5. *(simile: "light / like a green / latticework of branches")* Ask students to cite the text clue that helps them identify this example, explain what is being compared, and tell how this choice of words affects the meaning of the poem. *(The word* like *reveals this to be a simile. The light is being compared to a green latticework, or crisscross pattern. The simile creates the image of light broken up by the green leaves and branches of the tree, as seen from below. Depicting the light as broken up in this way creates an "enchanted" image of light dancing through the tree branches.)*

Ode to enchanted light

by Pablo Neruda
translated by Ken Krabbenhoft

Under the trees light
has dropped from the top of the sky,
light
like a green
5   latticework of branches,   **(B)**
shining
on every leaf,
drifting down like clean
white sand.

10   A cicada sends
its sawing song
high into the empty air.

The world is
a glass overflowing
15   with water.

©vovan/Shutterstock

SCAFFOLDING FOR ELL STUDENTS

Analyze Language Display the poem for students. Highlight the phrase, "light like a green latticework of branches." Explain to students that this is an example of figurative language, in which one thing is compared to another thing. Point out that the pattern of light through the trees is compared to latticework. Tell students that latticework is a pattern of crossing lines, similar to what is found in a screen or a spider's web. Encourage volunteers to draw images of patterns that are similar to latticework. Discuss how the branches of a tree might form a latticework pattern.

ASK STUDENTS to describe what sunlight shining through branches of a tree looks like. Use a prompt, such as "The light came through the branches. It looked like _____."

Analyze Form: Ode
COMMON CORE **RL 5**

Pablo Neruda's poem is an **ode,** a poem that deals with serious themes, such as justice, truth, or beauty. An ode praises or celebrates its subject, which is usually a person, event, thing, or element in nature.

The word *ode* comes from the Greek word *aeidein*, which means to sing or chant. Originally, the ode was written to be accompanied by music and dance. A traditional ode is a long poem with a formal structure, and due to its dignified nature, its language is often formal as well. Many modern poets experiment with the form to make it fresh and interesting for modern readers. What do you notice about the length and arrangement of lines in Neruda's poem?

Analyzing the Text
COMMON CORE **RL 1, RL 4, RL 5**

Cite Text Evidence   Support your responses with evidence from the text.

1. **Infer** What feelings are suggested in lines 1–9 of this poem? How does the poet suggest those feelings?

2. **Analyze** A cicada is an insect that makes a high-pitched, continual sound, usually in summer. Reread lines 10–12. What repeated first sounds, or **alliteration,** do you hear, and how are the sounds connected to the poem's meaning?

3. **Analyze and Evaluate** Does this poem meet the requirements of an ode? Why or why not?

Ode to enchanted light   **171**

PRACTICE & APPLY

Analyze Form: Ode
COMMON CORE **RL 5**

Review the definition of an ode. Have students tell what subject the poet is praising in "Ode to enchanted light." Next, review that, when analyzing the form of a poem, students should pay attention to how the poem is laid out on the page—line lengths, line breaks, how the lines are grouped, and any patterns of rhythm and rhyme. Using the question as a prompt, discuss how the form of this poem impacts its meaning. *(The poem is a mix of long and short lines—some just one word long—and one long stanza followed by two shorter stanzas of equal length. The first stanza creates a cascading, tumbling feeling—as if the words are falling down the page in the same way that light is tumbling through the trees. The second stanza has a regular pattern of rhythm—almost like the sound of a cicada. Finally, in the last stanza, the longer middle line emphasizes the image of the "glass overflowing.")*

Analyzing the Text
COMMON CORE **RL 1, RL 4, RL 5**

Possible answers:

1. *The lines suggest a feeling of calm, of being transfixed by the light dropping through the tree branches. The poet creates this feeling first with the setting, "Under the trees." Then, the phrase "a green/latticework of branches" compares the broken pattern of light to the crossed patterns of tree branches. This suggests a peaceful setting. He finishes the stanza with the image of the light as "drifting down like clean / white sand."*

2. *The /s/ sounds in "cicada sends / its sawing song" suggest the repetitious, raspy noise of a cicada itself.*

3. *Yes. The poem expresses an appreciation for how light enhances the beauty of sights and sounds in nature.*

Strategies for Annotation   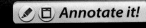 Annotate it!

Analyze Form: Ode
COMMON CORE **RL 5**

Have students use their eBook annotation tools to do the following:

- Count the number of lines in each stanza.
- Underline the repeating words.
- Highlight all repeating initial consonant sounds in yellow.
- Highlight repeating sounds within words in green.
- On a note, jot down any patterns in lines, stanzas, or rhythm. *(.)*

Under the trees <u>light</u>

has dropped from the top of the sky,

<u>light</u>

like a green

latticework of branches,

no set rhythmic pattern; suggests enchanting dance of light through branches of trees

TEACH

Analyze Form: Lyric Poem (LINES 1–14)

COMMON CORE RL 1, RL 2, RL 5, RL 6

Explain to students that a **lyric poem** is a poem that expresses the personal thoughts and feelings of a speaker. The **speaker,** or the person who is telling the poem, can be the poet or an invented character who has an experience that he or she is responding to.

Ⓐ CITE TEXT EVIDENCE Ask students to reread lines 1–8, identify the speaker, and explain what he or she is communicating to the reader. Which words reveal the speaker's message? *(The poem begins with the word I. This suggests that the poet could be the speaker, recounting a very personal experience in the forest. The phrase "thought the earth remembered me," suggests that the poet is talking about an intimate companion—someone who is holding her like a mother might hold a baby in the "dark skirts" of her lap.)*

Ⓑ CITE TEXT EVIDENCE Have students reread lines 9–14. Is the speaker comfortable in the natural world? What text evidence supports your answer? *(The speaker conveys the idea that, in the forest, the separation between her and the natural world dissolves. The speaker's thoughts are "light" and are in tune with the "small kingdoms" of animals.)*

Determine Meaning

COMMON CORE RL 1, RL 4

(LINES 9–11)

Remind students that poets often use figurative language to compare things, give emphasis to meaning, and create emotion.

Ⓒ ASK STUDENTS to identify the figurative language used in lines 9–11 *(simile)* and explain its effect on the meaning of the poem. *(The poet compares two unlike things: her thoughts to flying moths. The simile describes how close to nature she feels, and how her thoughts come and go like moths flying.)*

COLLABORATIVE DISCUSSION Have partners reread the first two lines of each poem to one another and discuss their ideas about each speaker's relationship to nature. Remind students to cite evidence from the poems to support their ideas.

Sleeping in the Forest
by Mary Oliver

Ⓐ

I thought the earth
remembered me, she
took me back so tenderly, arranging
her dark skirts, her pockets
5   full of lichens[1] and seeds. I slept
as never before, a stone
on the riverbed, nothing
between me and the white fire of the stars
but my thoughts, and they floated   Ⓒ
Ⓑ 10   light as moths among the branches
of the perfect trees. All night
I heard the small kingdoms breathing
around me, the insects, and the birds
who do their work in the darkness. All night
15   I rose and fell, as if in water, grappling[2]
with a luminous doom. By morning
I had vanished at least a dozen times
into something better.

COLLABORATIVE DISCUSSION Read the first two lines of each poem and compare the images they present. What do these lines say about the speaker's relationship to nature? Share your ideas with the students in your class.

---

[1] **lichens** (lī´kənz): fungi that grow together with algae and form a crust-like growth on rocks or tree trunks.
[2] **grappling:** struggling.

WHEN STUDENTS STRUGGLE...

Guide students in understanding the rhythm of the poem. Discuss how the line lengths vary and how the punctuation occurs within the lines. Reread lines 14–18 aloud. Point out how the different line breaks and punctuation affect the rhythm. Then rewrite the poem, changing the line breaks. Reread the lines again.

ASK STUDENTS to tell how reading the poem in this way changes the rhythm.

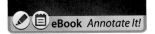

Analyze Form: Lyric Poem

"Sleeping in the Forest" is a **lyric poem,** a short poem in which a single speaker expresses personal thoughts and feelings. Lyric poetry is a broad category that includes traditional forms such as odes and sonnets, as well as **free verse,** a form that does not use formal structure or rhyme schemes. In fact, in ancient times, lyric poems were created to be sung. Although they aren't sung today, lyric poems do have some elements in common with songs, including

- a sense of rhythm and melody
- imaginative word choice, or **diction**
- the creation of a single, unified impression

What is the single, unified impression conveyed in this poem?

Analyzing the Text

 COMMON CORE RL 1, RL 4, RL 5

Cite Text Evidence   Support your responses with evidence from the text.

1. **Interpret** Reread the last sentence in the poem. What might the speaker mean by "something better"?

2. **Analyze** Reread lines 5–7. What is compared to "a stone / on the riverbed"? Where else does that image appear in the poem?

3. **Analyze and Evaluate** Identify examples of each of the elements of a lyric poem that appear in "Sleeping in the Forest." Do you think Oliver's poem is a good example of a lyric poem? Why or why not?

PRACTICE & APPLY

Analyze Form: Lyric Poem

 COMMON CORE RL 4, RL 5

Review the elements of lyric poetry with students and discuss the question. *(The single impression is of someone blissfully lying on the forest floor at night, listening to the sounds, sights, and feelings of the forest. It's an image of a child sleeping in his or her mother's arms.)* Then ask students to tell whether the poem is traditional or free verse. Have students provide an explanation for their answer. *(The poem is free verse. The arrangement of words and lines does not follow any fixed rules for number of lines, line length, or pattern of rhythm and rhyme.)*

Analyzing the Text

 COMMON CORE RL 1, RL 4, RL 5

Possible answers:

1. *Perhaps sleeping in the forest enriches the speaker so that she is a better person, at one with nature. Perhaps spending a night in the forest has sent the speaker into another realm, better than the world of daylight.*

2. *The sleeping speaker is compared to a stone on the riverbed; both lie still. The image of being in water is reinforced by these words elsewhere in the poem: "floated"; "rose and fell, as if in water."*

3. *The poem is intimate, expressing the speaker's thoughts and feelings about nature and life, as inspired by a blissful experience sleeping in a forest one night. While the poem is free verse and has no end rhymes, it does have a steady rhythm, suggestive of the breathing of an infant. Word choices such as "the white fires of the stars" and "small kingdoms breathing" are imaginative. It gives an impression of a child sleeping in its mother's arms.*

Strategies for Annotation   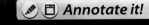 *Annotate it!*

Analyze Form: Lyric Poem

 COMMON CORE RL 4, RL 5

Share these strategies for guided or independent analysis:

- Highlight in blue imaginative word choices.
- On a note, jot down how the arrangement of lines creates rhythm and how the rhythm changes throughout the poem. *(The changing rhythm is almost like the in-and-out/rising-and-falling of gentle breathing while sleeping.*

I heard the small kingdoms breathing

around me, the insects, and the birds

who do their work in the darkness. All night

I rose and fell, as if in water, grappling

with a luminous doom. By morning

> The changing rhythm is like the in-and-out/ rising-and-falling of gentle breathing while sleeping.

Determine Meaning

COMMON CORE RL 1, RL 4

Discuss the examples of simile, metaphor, and personification. Then, ask students to reread "Ode to enchanted light" before answering the question. *(This is a simile. It uses the word* like *to compare the light to "clean white sand.")* Ask students to find additional examples of figurative language in each poem. Discuss the impact each one has on meaning and emotion.

Analyzing the Text

COMMON CORE RL 1, RL 4, RL 5, RL 6

Possible answers:

1. *"The world is a glass overflowing with water" is a metaphor comparing the world to an overflowing glass of water. The image suggests that the world, like overflowing water is clear, sparkling, fresh, life-giving, and abundant.*

2. *The earth is personified as a woman wearing dark skirts with pockets. Perhaps the poet is making a connection to the familiar concept of Mother Nature or an earth goddess from mythology, who lovingly cradles and nurtures the speaker during sleep.*

3. *In Neruda's poem, "drifting down like clean / white sand" is part of a simile comparing the light dropping through the trees to drifting sand. In Oliver's poem, "but my thoughts, and they floated / light as moths among the branches / of the perfect trees," is a simile comparing the speaker's thoughts to floating moths. One image conveys downward motion; the other conveys a feeling of floating upward.*

4. *In "Ode to enchanted light," the speaker's vision of light is the subject of the poem. Light is enchanting, or magical. In "Sleeping in the Forest," the speaker is in darkness, seeing only "the white fire of the stars." The phrase "luminous doom" suggests a negative or worrisome connection to something light or glowing.*

 **eBook** *Annotate It!*

Determine Meaning

COMMON CORE RL 1, RL 4

Through **figurative language,** words are used in an imaginative way to express ideas that are not literally true. The most common types are

 simile   a comparison between two unlike things using the word *like* or *as* (*friendship as sturdy as a tree*)

 metaphor   a comparison of two things that are basically unlike but have some qualities in common; a metaphor does not contain the word *like* or *as* (*a forest of confused thoughts*)

 personification   the giving of human qualities to an animal, object, or idea (*the trees stood guard*)

In the poem "Ode to enchanted light," the poet Pablo Neruda states that light is "drifting down like clean / white sand." What type of figurative language does this phrase represent?

Analyzing the Text

COMMON CORE RL 1, RL 4, RL 5, W2, W 10

Cite Text Evidence   Support your responses with evidence from the texts.

1. **Interpret** Reread lines 13–15 of "Ode to enchanted light." What type of figurative language is represented here, and what is the comparison being made? What feelings does this evoke in the reader?

2. **Analyze** What is personified in lines 1–5 of "Sleeping in the Forest"? Why might the poet have chosen to use this personification?

3. **Compare** Reread lines 8–9 of "Ode" and lines 9–11 of "Sleeping in the Forest." What similarities do you observe in the poets' use of language?

4. **Analyze** How do the images of light differ in these two poems?

PERFORMANCE TASK

 **WriteSmart**

Writing Activity: Poem Write a four-stanza poem to describe an experience with nature.

- Base the poem on your own experiences or on an imagined one.
- Experiment with figurative language.

- Consider expressing a theme or message about nature.
- As you create your poem, try reading it aloud to help you refine your choices of words or effects.

Assign this performance task. **WriteSmart**

PERFORMANCE TASK

COMMON CORE W 3, W 10

Writing Activity: Poem Have students work independently. Tell students to do the following: decide on the main message they want to convey; read and listen to other types of poems to help them choose a form that suits their message; decide who the speaker will be; choose words carefully, using imaginative words and figurative language; and use imagery.

INTERACTIVE WHITEBOARD LESSON
Determine Theme

COMMON CORE

RL 2, SL 1

TEACH

Explain that the **theme** of a poem is the main message about life or human nature that a poet communicates to the reader. The theme is often implied, rather than directly stated. Readers can identify the theme by paying attention to the words and details in a poem and by asking themselves, "What big message about life is the poet trying to tell me?"

Use the Interactive Whiteboard Lesson "Theme/Central Idea" to help students identify and explore theme in poetry.

Review the steps for identifying theme:

1. Examine clues in the text. What does the title tell you? How does the poet use figurative language to convey a message?
2. Use the clues to determine the theme.

COLLABORATIVE DISCUSSION

Have students work in groups to apply the steps to the example texts in the Interactive Whiteboard Lesson. Have students compare their results in a group discussion.

Analyze Narrator

COMMON CORE

RL 6

TEACH

Tell students that to understand a poem, the reader must understand the speaker. Explain that the **speaker** of a poem is the voice that "talks" to the reader. Tell students that, in a lyric poem, the speaker can be the poet, but doesn't have to be. They can identify the speaker by paying attention to the words and details in the poem.

Reread lines 1–5 of "Sleeping in the Forest." Tell students that the phrase "I thought the earth remembered me, she took me back so tenderly" suggests that the speaker is an adult who is doing something he or she has done before, and that he or she has feelings of intimacy, familiarity, and safety with the earth.

Point out that because the poem is told in the first-person singular—using pronouns such as *I, me,* and *my*—it is possible that the speaker is the poet, recounting an actual experience in the forest. Explain further, however, that as with many poems, it is almost impossible to tell who the speaker is for certain.

PRACTICE AND APPLY

Have students identify other details in the poem that help them understand who the speaker is and what the poem reveals about the speaker.

Have students discuss the following questions with a partner:

- Is there just one speaker? How do you know?
- What words and details suggest who the speaker is?
- What are the thoughts and feelings of the speaker? Do they change throughout the poem?
- Have you had similar experiences or felt the same way? How did they make you feel? How might you describe the experience in a poem?

Poems About Nature

Problems with Hurricanes

Victor Hernández Cruz

Prayer to the Pacific

Leslie Marmon Silko

Tornado at Talladega

Gwendolyn Brooks

Why These Texts

Because poetry, both in its form (lines and stanzas rather than sentences and paragraphs) and in its use of language (sound devices, imagery, and figurative language), is so different from prose, some students may have difficulty understanding it. With the help of the close-reading questions, students will analyze three poems, using the questions to enhance their comprehension. This close reading will lead students to develop a deeper understanding of not only the specific poems but also poetry in general.

Background Have students read the background information about nature being an inspiration for poets. Tell them that these three poems are all lyric poems—short poems in which a single speaker expresses his or her personal thoughts and feelings. In these poems, nature has been an inspiration to each of the poets. Their varied heritages have colored their styles and their individual responses to nature, but each adds insights into the world we live in.

SETTING A PURPOSE Ask students to read each poem carefully and slowly, noting how the poem sounds as well as what it says. Remind them to pay close attention to the author's tone and use of figurative language.

Common Core Support

- cite evidence from the text
- determine the meaning of words and phrases, including figurative language
- analyze how a poem's form contributes to its meaning

▲ Text Complexity Rubric

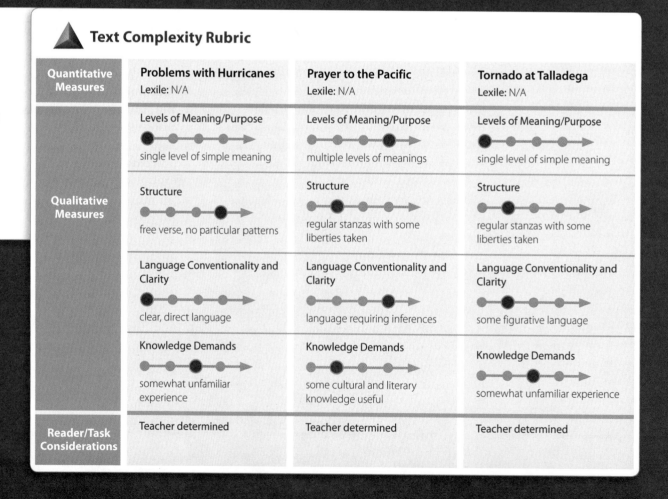

	Problems with Hurricanes	Prayer to the Pacific	Tornado at Talladega
Quantitative Measures	Lexile: N/A	Lexile: N/A	Lexile: N/A
Qualitative Measures	Levels of Meaning/Purpose — single level of simple meaning	Levels of Meaning/Purpose — multiple levels of meanings	Levels of Meaning/Purpose — single level of simple meaning
	Structure — free verse, no particular patterns	Structure — regular stanzas with some liberties taken	Structure — regular stanzas with some liberties taken
	Language Conventionality and Clarity — clear, direct language	Language Conventionality and Clarity — language requiring inferences	Language Conventionality and Clarity — some figurative language
	Knowledge Demands — somewhat unfamiliar experience	Knowledge Demands — some cultural and literary knowledge useful	Knowledge Demands — somewhat unfamiliar experience
Reader/Task Considerations	Teacher determined	Teacher determined	Teacher determined

Strategies for CLOSE READING

Determine Meaning

Students should read each poem carefully and slowly. Close-reading questions at the bottom of the page will help them determine the meaning of figurative language to better understand the poems. As they read, students should jot down comments or questions about the text in the margins.

WHEN STUDENTS STRUGGLE . . .

To help students cite text evidence in the poems, have them work in small groups to fill out a chart like the one shown below.

CITE TEXT EVIDENCE For practice in determining meaning, ask students to explain the meaning of the figurative language in the chart below.

Figurative Language	Meaning
If you are going out beware of mangoes And all such beautiful sweet things. ("Problems with Hurricanes," lines 32–35)	Very beautiful things can sometimes turn out to be dangerous.
Four round stones in my pocket I carry back the ocean/Thirty thousand years ago to suck and taste. ("Prayer to the Pacific," lines 15–16)	The ocean is very old and carries with it many mysteries.
Here, roots, ire, origins exposed / across this twig-strewn, leaf-strewn road they lie,/mute, and ashamed, and through. ("Tornado at Tallageda," lines 11–13)	Nature is powerful and can quickly demolish even a mighty tree.

Background Nature has been an inspiration to poets and writers for thousands of years. Whether it's the soothing view of a sunset over the ocean or the startling sound of thunder in a rainstorm, nature can excite the senses and the imaginations of all people. The following three poems present different views on three aspects of nature.

Poems About Nature

Problems with Hurricanes . . . . Victor Hernández Cruz
Prayer to the Pacific . . . . Leslie Marmon Silko
Tornado at Talladega. . . . . Gwendolyn Brooks

Victor Hernández Cruz was born in Puerto Rico in 1949. When he was five, his family moved to New York City. He began writing at the age of 15. His lively, often humorous poems reflect his bilingual and bicultural heritage. Cruz is the author of numerous poetry collections and the recipient of many awards.

Leslie Marmon Silko was born in Albuquerque, New Mexico, in 1948. She grew up on the Laguna Pueblo reservation. Her mixed ancestry (Laguna Pueblo, Mexican, and Caucasian) caused her a lot of pain, as she faced discriminatation from both the Native American and white communities. She would go on to write stories that explore how differences can be reconciled.

Gwendolyn Brooks was born in Kansas in 1917, but grew up in Chicago. She published her first poem when she was 14 years old. By the time she was 17, over one hundred of her poems were published in a poetry column in the Chicago Defender. She went on to become the first African American author to win the Pulitzer Prize.

55

1. **READ** ▶ As you read "Problems with Hurricanes," collect and cite textual evidence.

- In the first stanza, underline what the campesino says to worry about.
- Circle words the campesino uses to assess various ways of dying. In the margin, note the distinction he makes.
- In the margin, write why the campesino warns of "beautiful sweet things" (lines 34–35).

Problems with Hurricanes
by Victor Hernández Cruz

A campesino¹ looked at the air
And told me:
With hurricanes it's not the wind
or the noise or the water.
5   I'll tell you he said:
it's the mangoes, avocados
Green plantains and bananas
flying into town like **projectiles**.

projectile:
object thrown with great force

A How would your family
10   feel if they had to tell
The generations that you
got killed by a flying
Banana.

The campesino says that being killed by the water or wind is honorable but being killed by a flying fruit would be shameful.

Death by drowning has honor
15   If the wind picked you up
and slammed you
Against a mountain boulder
This would not carry shame
But
20   to suffer a mango smashing
Your skull
or a plantain hitting your
Temple at 70 miles per hour
is the ultimate disgrace.

¹ **campesino** (käm-pĭ-sē´-nō): a farm worker.

56

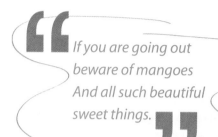

> *If you are going out*
> *beware of mangoes*
> *And all such beautiful*
> *sweet things.*

B 25   The campesino takes off his hat—
As a sign of respect
toward the fury of the wind
And says:
Don't worry about the noise
30   Don't worry about the water
Don't worry about the wind—
If you are going out
beware of mangoes
And all such beautiful
35   sweet things.

The campesino warns the narrator to watch out for appealing things that may seem harmless.

2. **◀ REREAD** Reread the poem. What does the speaker suggest about nature in lines 32–35? What broader message about life might he be conveying?

The speaker suggests that nature can turn something as harmless as a mango into a deadly object. The speaker may be conveying the message that it is easy to be mindful of obvious dangers, but we should also be wary of seemingly innocent things in our lives.

57

---

1. **READ AND CITE TEXT EVIDENCE**   The author tells readers that it would be shameful and disgraceful to die from being hit by a flying banana or mango.

A **ASK STUDENTS** whether or not they think the poet is trying to be funny in lines 9–13. Have them support their answer with evidence from the text. *Students might say that they know the author is trying to be funny because he uses a funny example: bananas. Also, the idea of someone's legacy being ruined because he or she was hit by a flying banana is funny as well.*

Critical Vocabulary: projectile (line 8) Have students share their definitions of *projectile*. Ask them to explain why they would not want to be hit by a projectile. *Students might say they don't want to be hit by a projectile because a projectile would be whizzing through the air and would probably hurt if it struck someone.*

2. **REREAD AND CITE TEXT EVIDENCE**   The poem talks about both the beauty and the unexpected power of nature.

B **ASK STUDENTS** how the campesino feels about nature and the power of storms. *The campesino respects nature and the power of storms. You can tell this because he takes off his hat as a sign of respect.*

CLOSE READ Notes

3. **READ** As you read "Prayer to the Pacific," continue to cite textual evidence.

- In the margin, explain what Silko means when she calls the ocean "Big as the myth of origin" (line 5).
- Underline examples of personification in the poem.
- Circle the lines that have large gaps between words.

Prayer to the Pacific
by Leslie Marmon Silko

The ocean has many mysteries that cannot be known. We have many stories that tell how the world started, but no one can be certain of the truth.

I traveled to the ocean
     distant
         from my southwest land of sandrock
        to the moving blue water
5   Big as the myth of origin.
Pale
 pale water in the yellow-white light of
     sun   floating west
       to China
10   where ocean herself was born.
Clouds that blow across the sand are wet.

Squat in the wet sand and speak to the Ocean:
    I return to you turquoise the red coral you sent us,
      sister spirit of Earth.
15   Four round stones in my pocket I carry back the ocean
Thirty thousand years ago to suck and to taste.
      Indians came riding across the ocean
      carried by giant sea turtles.
Waves were high that day
20   great sea turtles waded   slowly out
       from the gray sundown sea.
Grandfather Turtle rolled in the sand   four times
     and disappeared
       swimming into the sun.

CLOSE READ Notes

25 And so   from that time
    immemorial,
      as the old people say,
rain clouds drift from the west
      gift from the ocean.
30 Green leaves in the wind
Wet earth on my feet
    swallowing raindrops
      clear from China.

immemorial: ancient; centuries old

4. **REREAD** Reread the poem and note the lines you circled. What is the effect of separating words within a line? What does it contribute to the meaning of the poem? Support your answer with explicit textual evidence.

It creates a sense of long, drawn-out movement. The water of the ocean is "floating" along, it isn't rushed. A turtle wading out to sea or rolling in sand will do so slowly because turtles move slowly. Gaps like the one in line 25 also suggest movement by the waves.

58   59

---

3. **READ AND CITE TEXT EVIDENCE**

C **ASK STUDENTS** why the author might have chosen to use personification in the poem. Have them note the poem's title. *The poem is a "prayer," and as such, it is directed to someone.* How does the author personify the ocean? *as a woman ("ocean herself"; "sister spirit")* What other things are personified? *Earth (who has a sister spirit), Grandfather turtle, and the ground swallowing raindrops.*

FOR ELL STUDENTS Clarify the meaning of the verb *squat*. Explain that in this context, it means to lower your body close to the floor by bending your knees.

4. **REREAD AND CITE TEXT EVIDENCE**

D **ASK STUDENTS** to read the poem quietly to themselves, resting at the separations within sentences, and pausing before each indented line. How does reading the poem as it is written affect its meaning? *Students may suggest that the poem becomes more of a spoken "prayer," and the pauses intensify the meaning.* Ask what visual effect the structure of the poem has. *Students may notice that some of the lines are arranged in a formation that resembles a wave.*

Critical Vocabulary: immemorial (line 26) The text says that *immemorial* has something to do with time. Have students share examples of other things that human beings have been doing since time immemorial (for example, *creating art, making music, waging war*). Then, ask students to share their definitions of *immemorial*.

CLOSE READ
Notes

5. (READ ▶) As you read "Tornado At Talladega," continue to cite textual evidence.

    • Underline examples of personification in the poem.
    • Circle examples of repetition.

Tornado at Talladega
by Gwendolyn Brooks

Who is that <u>bird</u>
<u>reporting the storm?</u>—
Ⓔ after <u>What came through</u>
<u>to do some landscaping.</u>

5 (Certain) trees
stick across the road.
They are unimportant now.
Ⓕ They cannot sass (anymore)
Not a one of these, <u>the bewildered</u>,
10 can announce (anymore) "How fine I am!"
Here, roots, **ire**, origins exposed,
across this twig-strewn, leaf-strewn road they lie,
<u>mute</u>, and <u>ashamed</u>, and <u>through</u>.

It happened all of a sudden.

15 (Certain) women and men and children
come out to stare.

ire:
*rage; anger;
indignation*

6. (◀ REREAD AND DISCUSS) Reread the poem. In a small group, discuss the way personification affects your perception of the trees.

SHORT RESPONSE

Cite Text Evidence How does each poet present nature in these poems? Review your reading notes and **cite text evidence** in your response.

Nature is shown as a powerful force in many ways. The speaker in Cruz's poem states that nature can make weapons of any object. Silko says one cannot fully comprehend all of the ocean's mysteries. Brooks presents a powerful image of trees destroyed by a tornado.

60

TO CHALLENGE STUDENTS . . .

To deepen their understanding of poetry, have students research and find other poems that deal with nature. Then, have them choose three poems that they find particularly appealing.

ASK STUDENTS to describe how the poems they chose are alike or different from the three poems they have just studied. Remind students to cite specific passages from the poems to support each point in their analysis. For each poem, students should address:

• the author's tone, or how he or she feels about or treats the subject matter. Is the author's tone serious, respectful, humorous, flippant, or something else?

• the author's use of figurative language, such as metaphor, simile, and personification. How does this use of language add to the meaning of the poem?

• the author's use of sound, rhythm, and repetition for effect. Does the author's use of sound, rhythm, or purposeful repetition affect the poem's meaning? If so, how?

• how the author has structured the poem.

• the meaning of the poem and how it is similar to or different from the other poems they have read.

---

5. (READ AND CITE TEXT EVIDENCE)

Ⓔ **ASK STUDENTS** why the author describes the storm as something that "came through to do some landscaping." *The image conveys that the trees have been changed by the storm.*

6. (REREAD AND CITE TEXT EVIDENCE)

Ⓕ **ASK STUDENTS** to name some of the ways trees are affected by the storm. *They are "mute, and ashamed, and through."*

Critical Vocabulary: ire (line 11) Have students give examples of situations that would probably arouse their ire.

SHORT RESPONSE

(*Cite Text Evidence*) Students should:

• explain how each author presents nature.

• cite text evidence to support their answers.

DIG DEEPER

With the class, return to the Short Response question. Have students share their answers.

ASK STUDENTS what additional information they can give about how each author they have studied dealt with the topic of nature in his or her poetry. Remind students to cite evidence from the text to support each of their points. Students should:

- consider the author's tone, or his or her attitude toward the subject. *The tone of "Problems with Hurricanes" is humorous until the very end, when it becomes serious. The tone of "Prayer to the Pacific" is reverent and serious. The tone of "Tornado at Talladega" is at various points humorous, awestruck, and sad.*

- consider the author's use of figurative language, such as similes, metaphors, and personification to express feelings. *In "Problems with Hurricanes," the author uses a simile—flying into town like projectiles—to describe the flight of fruit during a hurricane. In "Prayer to the Pacific" the author uses a simile to describe the ocean—big as the myth, or origin. In "Tornado at Talladega" the author uses a metaphor—landscaping—to describe the effect of the tornado.*

- consider how the author structures the poem. Look at where lines break and the gaps between words. *In "Problems with Hurricanes" the author places the word "But," line 19, on its own separate line to emphasize the difference between a death with honor and dying because a mango smashed into your head. In "Prayer to the Pacific" the author places large gaps between words when she wants the reader to slow down and feel the slow passage of time. In "Tornado at Talladega" the author emphasizes the suddenness and swiftness of a tornado's destruction by setting "It happened all of a sudden," line 14, totally apart from the rest of the poem.*

ASK STUDENTS to return to their Short Response answer and revise it based on the class discussion.

CLOSE READING NOTES

Write a Memoir

COMMON
CORE

W 3a–e Write narratives.
W 4 Produce clear and coherent writing.
W 5 Develop and strengthen writing.
W 10 Write routinely.

In this collection, you read about the strong and emotional connections that people have with different elements of nature. In particular, consider the experience that Eddy Harris recounts in the excerpt from his memoir, *Mississippi Solo*. Then think about your own interactions with nature. Write a memoir about a natural setting that is meaningful to you.

A successful memoir

- begins with a captivating lead that clearly establishes the situation
- contains a well-structured event sequence that unfolds naturally and logically
- uses descriptive details that offer insight on significant events and feelings
- creates vivid images in the reader's mind through the use of sensory language
- provides a conclusion that follows from and reflects on the narrated experiences and events

> **PLAN**

Establish the Situation A memoir is a story that describes a memorable experience or time period in a person's life. Consider what made the sudden rainstorm on the Mississippi River memorable to Eddy Harris. Then think about memorable experiences you have had in a natural setting.

- Consider how the natural setting is important to you. Is it important now, or was it important in the past?
- Determine whether you have a story to tell about yourself and the setting.
- Identify the feelings you have about the setting.
- Think about how the experience with the natural setting changed your feelings or ideas.
- Specify the most important idea you want the reader to know.

myNotebook

Use the annotation tools in your eBook to mark up sensory language that you can use as inspiration later. Save each example to your notebook.

ACADEMIC VOCABULARY

As you share your experience, be sure to use the academic vocabulary words.

affect
element
ensure
participate
specify

WRITE A MEMOIR

COMMON CORE   W 3a-e, W 4, W 5, W 10

Introduce students to the Performance Task by reading the introductory paragraph with them and reviewing the criteria for what makes a good memoir. Remind students that a memoir is a kind of autobiographical writing in which a writer uses vivid details to describe important events in his or her life.

PLAN

ESTABLISH THE SITUATION

Explain to students that they should choose an experience to write about that had a profound effect on them. Have students ask themselves:

- What specific details do I remember about the experience?
- What does the experience reveal about me, someone else, or human nature in general?
- Why would reading about this experience be interesting to others?

PERFORMANCE TASK A

Organize Your Ideas In a memoir, you are the narrator, or the person telling the story. A graphic organizer, like the one shown, can help you to organize your ideas and describe the events in a logical way.

> Setting:
>
> Events:
>
> Sensory Details: | Emotions, Feelings, and Reactions:
>
> Conclusion:

Brainstorm Images In *Mississippi Solo*, Eddy Harris uses descriptive words to create vivid images that appeal to all five senses. Think about the images of your experience. Which aspects of those images were most significant for you? Describe these images using words and phrases that convey:

- vivid colors
- specific sounds
- scents, tastes, or tactile feelings

Consider Your Purpose and Audience Who will read or listen to your memoir? What do you want them to understand about your experience? Think about that audience as you prepare to write. Your wording and tone may be different for a group of classmates or friends than it would be for a group of adults.

PRODUCE

*my*WriteSmart

Write Your Memoir Review the information in your graphic organizer as you begin your draft.

- Begin with an introduction that clearly establishes the situation and grabs the attention of your audience.
- Use first-person point of view to present the events in a clear and logical sequence.
- Create a mental image of your experience, and write what you see, hear, smell, taste, and feel.

Write your rough draft in *my*WriteSmart. Focus on getting your ideas down, rather than perfecting your choice of language.

PRODUCE

WRITE YOUR MEMOIR

Explain to students that a memoir is written from the writer's point of view. Point out that they should use the pronouns *I, me,* and *my* when referring to themselves in the memoir. Remind students that first-person narrators know only their own thoughts and feelings, not those of others.

Discuss ways students might begin a memoir in a way that captivates and draws in an audience, reviewing suggestions such as the following:

- Include a funny or dramatic anecdote.
- Use vivid details and descriptions to paint a dramatic setting or first event.
- Use dramatic dialogue exchanged between the writer and another person in the memoir.

- Elaborate on your ideas, including descriptive details to capture your experience for readers.
- Bring your memoir to a conclusion by telling how the experience ended. Reflect on what made the experience significant for you by explaining what you learned from it or how it had an impact on your life.

REVISE

Review Your Draft Work with a partner to determine if you have described your experience clearly and have used vivid details that will interest readers. Be sure to consider the following points in each other's drafts:

- Examine the sequence of events. Delete any event that is not important to describing your experience. If necessary, add events that will help readers understand the experience.
- Check that you have made the order of events clear with transition words such as *next, finally,* or *a day later.*
- Look back to see if you have described your experience in a way that creates a vivid image for readers. Check that your descriptions include details that appeal to a variety of senses.
- Decide if dialogue would add interest to your experience.
- Check that it is clear why the experience you have described is significant for you. If necessary, add a sentence or two to show your thoughts and feelings about the experience.

my **WriteSmart**

Have your partner or a group of peers review your draft in *my*WriteSmart. Ask your reviewers to note any words or phrases that could be replaced with more descriptive language.

PRESENT

Create a Finished Copy Finalize your memoir and choose a way to share it with your audience. Consider these options:

- Present your memoir as a story that you recount aloud to your class.
- Post your memoir as a blog entry on a personal or school website.
- Dramatize your memoir in a one-person theater performance.

REVISE

REVIEW YOUR DRAFT

Explain to students that memoirs are engaging when they include descriptive details. Have students review their memoirs to see if they have used sensory details and vivid action words. Suggest that students use a thesaurus to replace vague and uninteresting words with ones that precisely describe actions, feelings, and thoughts.

PRESENT

CREATE A FINISHED COPY

Students can
- read aloud their memoirs to the class. Remind them to use different voices for characters and to modulate their tone
- post their memoirs as a blog entry on a personal or school website. Encourage students to respond to comments and questions from their readers
- dramatize their memoirs in a one-person performance. Have students work with a partner to discuss how to make their memoirs work as a dramatic monologue

LANGUAGE

Have students look at the chart and identify how they did on the Performance Task in each of the three main categories. In particular, have students discuss how effectively they used vivid sensory language to describe people, places, and events. Ask students to name one way in which they could improve their writing in each category. You can provide models that demonstrate good examples for each of the categories.

COLLECTION 3 TASK A
MEMOIR

	Ideas and Evidence	Organization	Language
ADVANCED	• The introduction engagingly and clearly establishes the natural setting and identifies the writer's experience in nature. • Descriptive details, realistic dialogue, and reflection strongly re-create the experience. • The conclusion summarizes the significance of the experience and leaves readers with an interesting thought.	• The organization is effective; ideas are arranged logically, and events are organized chronologically. • The pace is effective. • Transitions successfully connect ideas and show a naturally flowing sequence of events.	• The first-person point of view is used creatively and consistently. • Sensory language vividly describes people, places, and events. • Sentence beginnings, lengths, and structures vary and have a rhythmic flow. • Spelling, capitalization, and punctuation are correct. • Grammar and usage are correct.
COMPETENT	• The introduction identifies the experience but could do more to present the natural setting and engage the reader. • Descriptive details and dialogue generally re-create the experience. • The conclusion summarizes most of the writer's ideas and feelings about the experience.	• The organization of ideas is generally logical; the sequence of events is occasionally confusing. • At times, the pace is uneven. • A few more transitions are needed to clarify the sequence of events and give it a more natural flow.	• The narrative occasionally shifts from the first-person point of view. • Sensory language describes people, places, and events but could be used more effectively. • Sentence beginnings, lengths, and structures vary somewhat. • Few spelling, capitalization, and punctuation errors occur. • Some grammatical and usage errors are repeated in the narrative.
LIMITED	• The introduction is ordinary; it mentions an experience in nature and hints at the setting. • A few descriptive details create lively scenes, but most details are ordinary; dialogue is lacking. • The conclusion only hints at the significance of the experience.	• The organization of ideas often doesn't follow a pattern, and the sequence of events is confusing in several places. • The pace overall is either too slow or too fast. • More transitions are needed throughout to clarify the sequence of events.	• The narrative frequently shifts from the first-person point of view. • The narrative lacks sensory language in several key parts. • Sentence structures barely vary, with some fragments or run-on sentences. • Spelling, capitalization, and punctuation are often incorrect. • Grammar and usage are incorrect in several places.
EMERGING	• The introduction does not focus on an experience or establish a setting. • Descriptive details and dialogue are unrelated or missing. • The narrative lacks a conclusion.	• The narrative is not organized; information and details are presented randomly. • The pace is ineffective. • Transitions are not used, making the narrative difficult to understand.	• The narrative lacks a consistent point of view. • Sensory language is not used. • Repetitive sentence structure, fragments, and run-on sentences make the writing confusing. • Spelling, capitalization, and punctuation are incorrect throughout. • Several grammatical and usage errors change the meaning of the writer's ideas.

Write a Poetry Analysis

"Ode to enchanted light" and "Sleeping in the Forest" are lyric poems that convey an appreciation of different aspects of nature. In this activity, you will analyze each poet's style by comparing and contrasting elements such as form, structure, and use of figurative language.

A successful poetry analysis

- begins with an engaging introduction that establishes a clear point or controlling idea

- uses an effective organizational structure and transitions to connect ideas

- analyzes ideas and elements of the text and provides supporting textual evidence

- clearly explains how the poets use figurative language to convey meaning

- provides a conclusion that follows from the explanation, summarizes main points, and offers an insight

COMMON CORE

RL 1 Cite textual evidence.
RL 4 Determine the meanings of words and phrases.
RL 5 Analyze a poem's form.
W 2a–e Write informative/explanatory texts.
W 4 Produce clear and coherent writing.
W 5 Develop and strengthen writing.
W 9 Draw evidence from literary or informational texts.
W10 Write routinely.

PLAN

Identify Stylistic Elements Every poet has his or her own style, or way of making his or her writing recognizable through form, structure, and use of figurative language. Reread each poem. Jot down stylistic elements of each poem as you read.

- Consider each poem's subject. What is your initial impression? What does the title tell you about the subject? What is the poet's attitude toward the subject?

- Study the form and structure of each poem. Note how the lines are organized and grouped. Think about the sound and rhythm. What effects do they create in the poem?

- Examine word choice. Are the words concrete or abstract? Do the word choices make the poem seem happy? sad? funny?

- Identify figurative language, and explain what it means. What images does it evoke? How does it affect emotions?

*my*Notebook

Use the annotation tools in your eBook to find evidence to support your ideas. Save each piece of evidence to your notebook.

ACADEMIC VOCABULARY

As you share your ideas, be sure to use the academic vocabulary words.

affect
element
ensure
participate
specify

WRITE A POETRY ANALYSIS

COMMON CORE
RL 1, RL 4,
RL 5, W 2a-e,
W 4, W 5,
W 9, W 10

Introduce students to the Performance Task by reading the introductory paragraph with them and reviewing the criteria for what makes a good poetry analysis. Remind students that when you analyze a poem, you look at its different parts to understand the poem's meaning and to appreciate the poet's craft.

PLAN

IDENTIFY STYLISTIC ELEMENTS

Suggest that students think about how to organize their analyses. Have students consider using

- a poem-by-poem organization that presents all the points about one poem and then all the points about the other

- a point-by-point organization that discusses each point and how it applies to both poems

Organize Your Ideas A graphic organizer can help you to organize and compare your ideas. Use a Venn diagram to compare and contrast elements of each poet's style.

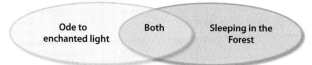

Then think about how you can present your ideas to make your analysis clear.

- Use a compare/contrast structure, and arrange your ideas in order of importance.
- Support your ideas with evidence, including details and quotations from the poems.

Develop Your Controlling Idea A controlling idea identifies the main points of your analysis. It states what you want to say about the topic. A good controlling idea engages the reader's curiosity or gets the reader to ask a question such as *How? In what way?* or *What does that mean?*

Consider Your Purpose and Audience Think about the audience as you prepare to write. It may include readers who have read these poems or others by the poets, as well as readers who haven't read the poems. Your purpose is to share ideas about the effects of each poet's stylistic elements. How will you support your ideas so they appeal to readers who might have different views? What will people who haven't read the poems need to know?

PRODUCE

my WriteSmart

Write your rough draft in *my*WriteSmart. Focus on getting your ideas down, rather than perfecting your choice of language.

Write Your Analysis Review the information in your Venn diagram as you begin your draft.

- Start with an introduction that engages the reader and clearly identifies your topic and controlling idea.
- Arrange your information clearly and logically. If you use a compare/contrast structure, you might want to discuss the differences and similarities of each stylistic element. For example, start with an analysis of the two poems' forms, then word choice and figurative language, and, finally, the structure of each poem.

PRODUCE

WRITE YOUR ANALYSIS

Suggest to students that they use their graphic organizers as a guide for writing the drafts of their analyses. Remind students to use separate paragraphs for each of their main points to make their analyses easier to understand. Point out that students can also add new ideas as they write.

- Organize your main points in order of importance.
- Include relevant evidence from the poems to support your ideas.
- Maintain a formal style and use transitions to connect ideas.
- Conclude by summarizing your main points and offering an overall insight about each poet's style and its effects.

REVISE

Review Your Draft Work with a partner or a group of peers to determine whether your analysis is effective. Be sure to consider the following points in each other's drafts:

my **WriteSmart**

Have your partner or a group of peers review your draft in *my*WriteSmart. Ask your reviewers to note whether the evidence you provide supports your main points.

- Check that your introduction engages the reader and clearly states your topic and controlling idea.
- Examine the structure. Check that stylistic elements are compared and contrasted clearly and that your points are presented in order of importance.
- Look back to ensure that each point is supported by relevant evidence from the texts. Quotations from the poems can be very effective in illustrating your points.
- Be sure that you use transition words and phrases such as *like*, *similarly*, or *in contrast* to show relationships between ideas.
- Check that the conclusion summarizes your ideas and provides an insight about the effects of each poet's style.

PRESENT

Create a Finished Copy Finalize your analysis and choose a way to share it with your audience. Consider these options:

- In a small group, take turns reading your analyses aloud. Then discuss the most interesting insights each analysis offers.
- Post your analysis as a blog on a personal or school website.
- Send your analysis to a magazine or newspaper that publishes literary reviews.

REVISE

REVIEW YOUR DRAFT

Remind students that they don't have to worry about every little grammatical detail as they begin to revise. Suggest that they first focus on improving the content, organization, and style of their analyses. Point out that they can correct grammar, spelling, and punctuation as they prepare the final version of their analyses.

PRESENT

CREATE A FINISHED COPY

Students can

- read aloud their analyses in small groups. Then they can compare and contrast their analyses
- post their analyses as a blog on a personal or school website. Encourage readers to post comments for the authors to respond to
- send their analyses to a magazine or newspaper. Have students research the names of publications that publish literary reviews

PERFORMANCE TASK B

ORGANIZATION

Have students look at the chart and identify how they did on the Performance Task in each of the three main categories. Partners can exchange their poetry analyses and critique them for each other. Encourage students to focus on the organization of each analysis and how effective it was in communicating their points.

COLLECTION 3 TASK B
POETRY ANALYSIS

	Ideas and Evidence	Organization	Language
ADVANCED	• The introduction is interesting; the controlling idea identifies the two poems and sets up a number of literary elements for comparison and contrast. • Specific, well-chosen quotations from the poems support the key points. • A satisfying concluding section summarizes the analysis and offers an original thought about the two poems.	• Key points and supporting text evidence are organized effectively and logically throughout the literary analysis. • The compare/contrast structure is clearly followed. • Transitions successfully show the relationships between ideas.	• The analysis has an appropriately formal style with precise language. • Sentence beginnings, lengths, and structures vary and flow well. • Spelling, capitalization, and punctuation are correct. • Grammar and usage are correct.
COMPETENT	• The introduction could be more engaging; the controlling idea sets up a few elements for analysis. • A few more relevant quotations from the poems are needed to support key points. • The concluding section summarizes most of the analysis but doesn't leave the reader with a new idea to think about.	• The organization of key points and supporting text evidence is confusing in a few places. • The compare/contrast structure is not followed in some places. • A few more transitions could clarify the relationships between ideas.	• The style becomes informal in a few places, with some imprecise language. • Sentence beginnings, lengths, and structures vary somewhat. • Few spelling, capitalization, and punctuation mistakes occur. • Some grammatical and usage errors are repeated.
LIMITED	• The introduction is ordinary; the controlling idea only hints at the main comparisons and contrasting points of the analysis. • Quotations from the poems support some key points but are unclear or poorly chosen. • The concluding section restates the controlling idea but gives an incomplete summary of the analysis.	• Most key points are organized logically, but much of the supporting text evidence is out of place or used in a confusing manner. • There are many places where the compare/contrast structure is absent. • More transitions are needed throughout the literary analysis to connect ideas.	• The style is informal in many places, with too much vague and repetitive language. • Sentence structures barely vary, with some fragments or run-on sentences. • Spelling, capitalization, and punctuation are often incorrect. • Grammar and usage are incorrect in several places.
EMERGING	• The introduction is missing. • Examples and quotations from the poems are either irrelevant or missing. • The literary analysis lacks a concluding section.	• A logical organization is not apparent; ideas are presented randomly. • There is no sense of comparing and contrasting ideas. • Transitions are not used, making the literary analysis difficult to understand.	• The style is inappropriate, and the language is inaccurate, repetitive, and too general. • Repetitive sentence structures, fragments, and run-on sentences make the writing confusing. • Spelling, capitalization, and punctuation are incorrect throughout. • Several grammatical and usage errors change the meaning of the writer's ideas.

©PhotoSpin, Inc/Alamy; (bg) ©Corbis

CONNECTING WORD AND IMAGE

ASK STUDENTS to discuss how the collection opener image and the collection quotation work together to create a connection.

PERFORMANCE TASK PREVIEW

Point out to students that they will complete one performance task at the end of the collection. The performance task will require them to further analyze the selections in the collection and to synthesize ideas about these analyses. Students will present their findings in a variety of products.

ACADEMIC VOCABULARY

View It!
Professional Development Podcast:
Academic Vocabulary

Students can acquire facility with the academic vocabulary words through frequent, repeated exposure as they analyze and discuss the selections in the collection. Academic vocabulary can be used in the instructional contexts shown below. This will enable students to incorporate the academic vocabulary words into their working vocabulary.

- Collaborative Discussion at the end of each selection
- Analyzing the Text questions for each selection
- Selection-level performance task
- Vocabulary instruction (for Critical Vocabulary and/or for Vocabulary Strategy)
- Language Conventions
- End-of-collection performance task for all selections in the collection

ASK STUDENTS to review the Academic Vocabulary word list for this collection. You may wish to pronounce each word aloud so students hear the correct pronunciation. Then, discuss the definitions and the related forms for each word. Remind students that they will encounter these five academic vocabulary words throughout the collection.

COLLECTION 4

Risk and Exploration

In this collection, you will encounter individuals who must confront a compelling question: How far is too far?

hmhfyi.com

COLLECTION
PERFORMANCE TASK Preview

After reading the selections in this collection, you will consider the risks of exploration in extreme conditions and write a persuasive speech on whether it is worth the costs.

ACADEMIC VOCABULARY

Study the words and their definitions in the chart below. You will use these words as you discuss and write about the texts in this collection.

Word	Definition	Related Forms
complex (kŏm´plĕks´) *adj.*	consisting of many interwoven parts that make something difficult to understand	complex number, complexity, complicate, complicated
potential (pə-tĕn´shəl) *adj.*	capable of doing or being something; having possibility	potent, potentiality, potential energy
rely (rĭ-lī´) *v.*	to depend on something or someone for support, help, or supply	reliable, reliability, reliance, reliant
stress (strĕs) *v.*	to put emphasis on something	stress fracture, stressed, stressed-out, unstressed, stressful
valid (văl´ĭd) *adj.*	convincing or having a sound reason for something	invalid, invalidation, validate, validation

USING COLLECTIONS YOUR WAY

Use the following information, along with the charts on the following pages, to help you decide how you want to introduce the collection. Based on your teaching style, your students' interests, or your instructional goals, you may want to structure this collection in various ways. You may choose different entry points each time you teach the collection.

"I require my students to do a lot of research."

Students will follow their reading of Philippe Cousteau's commentary with a performance task that asks them to research additional information related to ocean exploration.

Background Today, concerns over the ocean environment and potential economic and technological benefits are spurring greater interest in deep-sea exploration. **Philippe Cousteau** (b. 1980) is the grandson of Jacques Cousteau, the explorer whose 1960s television show revealed undersea wonders. Philippe Cousteau shares his grandfather's passion for ocean conservation, and he reports regularly on environmental and humanitarian stories from around the world.

Why Exploring the Ocean Is Mankind's Next Giant Leap

Commentary by Philippe Cousteau

SETTING A PURPOSE As you read, consider whether Philippe Cousteau's reasons for further ocean exploration are valid. Write down any questions you may have while reading.

"Space . . . the final frontier." Not only has this classic phrase dazzled the many millions of fans of the Star Trek franchise, some could argue it has defined a big part of the American ideal for the last 50 years. The 1960s were dominated by the race to the moon and Americans were rightfully proud to be the first nation to make it there.

However, another incredible feat happened in 1960 that is largely forgotten today. For the first time in history, on January 23, 1960, two men, Lt. Don Walsh and Jacques Picard, descended to the deepest part of the ocean, the bottom of the Challenger Deep in the Mariana Trench located in the western Pacific Ocean. While this feat made international news, the race to the depths of this planet was quickly overshadowed by the race to the moon—and no one has ever gone that deep since.

Why Exploring the Ocean Is Mankind's Next Giant Leap   193

Background In 1957, the country then known as the Soviet Union launched the first satellite to orbit Earth. The Soviet Union and the United States were bitter enemies at the time. After becoming the 35th president of the United States in 1961, **John F. Kennedy** was determined to equal the Soviet's knowledge of space. Well known for many accomplishments as president, Kennedy is also remembered as an inspirational speaker. He gave this speech the day before his assassination in November 1963.

Remarks at the Dedication of the Aerospace Medical Health Center

Speech by John F. Kennedy

SETTING A PURPOSE As you read, pay attention to the points President Kennedy is making. Why does he think the United States should be involved with space research?

Mr. Secretary, Governor, Mr. Vice President, Senator, Members of the Congress, members of the military, ladies and gentlemen:

For more than 3 years I have spoken about the New Frontier.[1] This is not a partisan term, and it is not the exclusive property of Republicans or Democrats. It refers, instead, to this Nation's place in history, to the fact that we do stand on the edge of a great new era, filled with both crisis and opportunity, an era to be characterized by achievement and by challenge. It is an era which calls for action and for the best efforts of all those who would test the unknown and the

[1] **New Frontier:** term Kennedy used in his presidential campaign.

Remarks at the Dedication of the Aerospace Medical Health Center   185

"I want to concentrate on standards coverage."

This 1961 speech by President John F. Kennedy, arguing persuasively in favor of America's continued exploration of space, requires students to analyze argument, text structure, the organization of ideas, and the use of rhetorical devices.

"I emphasize building vocabulary."

This science article about deep ocean habitats provides numerous opportunities for students to expand both technical and non-technical vocabulary.

Background For many years, it was nearly impossible to study life at the bottom of our oceans. Therefore, very little was known about deep-sea habitats. But recent 20th-century technological advances have allowed scientists to begin to discover surprising forms of life in the ocean depths. In her writing, **Cheryl Bardoe** likes to draw back the curtain to reveal how scientists explore the unknown. She presently lives in Chicago, Illinois, where she once worked at the city's famous Field Museum of Natural History.

from Living in the Dark

Science Article by Cheryl Bardoe

SETTING A PURPOSE As you read, notice how scientific study has altered past beliefs about Earth's oceans. Write down any questions you have while reading.

When a Whale Falls

Imagine the moment when a great blue whale, undernourished and exhausted from migrating, grunts out its last breath somewhere in the Pacific Ocean.

Then, as the pressure of the surrounding water squeezes the last air reserves from the whale's lungs, this massive creature begins to sink.

It plunges 700 feet (200 meters) through the ocean's top layer, the warm "sunlight zone" where algae kick-start life's food chain with photosynthesis. It drops another 2,600 feet (800 meters) through the cold twilight zone, where no plants live and fish have extra-large eyes to catch the faintest glimmers of sun. It descends down, down, down through 3,300 feet (1 kilometer) or more of the midnight zone. Here, temperatures hover close to freezing; deep-sea creatures must

from Living in the Dark   201

mySmartPlanner | **eBook** | *my*Notebook | **WriteSmart** | **fyi** hmhfyi.com

Collection 4 Lessons	Media	Teach and Practice
Student Edition | eBook	▶ Video HISTORY A+E	**Close Reading and Evidence Tracking**
ANCHOR TEXT Speech by John F. Kennedy **"Remarks at the Dedication of the Aerospace Medical Health Center"**	▶ **Video HISTORY** *JFK's New Frontier* ◀ **Audio** "Remarks at the Dedication of the Aerospace Medical Health Center"	**Close Read Screencasts** • Modeled Discussion 1 (lines 4–13) • Modeled Discussion 2 (lines 31–42) • Close Read application PDF (lines 112–119)	**Strategies for Annotation** • Trace and Evaluate an Argument • Using Context Clues
CLOSE READER Online Essay by Joan Vernikos **"Is Space Exploration Worth the Cost?"**	◀ **Audio** "Is Space Exploration Worth the Cost?"		
Commentary by Philippe Cousteau **"Why Exploring the Ocean Is Mankind's Next Giant Leap"**	◀ **Audio** "Why Exploring the Ocean Is Mankind's Next Giant Leap"	**Strategies for Annotation** • Determine Meanings • Analyze Structure: Sound Reasoning • Vocabulary Strategy: Prefixes
Science Article by Cheryl Bardoe **from "Living in the Dark"**	◀ **Audio** from "Living in the Dark"	**Strategies for Annotation** • Determine Central Ideas and Details • Analyze Structure • Vocabulary Strategy: Greek Roots
CLOSE READER Science Article by Elisabeth Rosenthal **"Stinging Tentacles Offer Hint to Oceans' Decline"**	◀ **Audio** "Stinging Tentacles Offer Hint to Oceans' Decline"	
Poem by Georgia Douglas Johnson **"Your World"**	◀ **Audio** "Your World"	**Strategies for Annotation** • Determine Meanings
Collection 4 Performance Tasks: **A** Give a Persuasive Speech	**fyi** hmhfyi.com	**Interactive Lessons** **A** Writing Arguments **A** Writing as a Process **A** Using Textual Evidence

For Systematic Coverage of Writing and Speaking & Listening Standards	**Interactive Lessons** Using Textual Evidence Using Media in a Presentation

Assess		Extend	Reteach
Performance Task	**Online Assessment**	**Teacher eBook**	**Teacher eBook**
Writing Activity: Research Report	Selection Test	**Compare and Contrast Two Versions of a Speech > Interactive Lesson >** Analyzing and Evaluating Presentations	**Trace and Evaluate an Argument > Level Up Tutorial >** Elements of an Argument
Speaking Activity: Informal Debate	Selection Test	**Hold an Informal Debate**	**Determine Meanings > Level Up Tutorial >** Tone
Writing Activity: Persuasive Essay	Selection Test	**Analyze Technical Meanings**	**Analyze Structure: Cause-and-Effect Relationships > Level Up Tutorial >** Cause-and-Effect Organization **> Interactive Graphic Organizer >** Cause-and-Effect Chain
Writing Activity: Analysis	Selection Test	**Determine Meanings: Metaphor Cite Evidence Form in Poetry > Interactive Whiteboard Lesson >** Form in Poetry	**Determine Meanings: Imagery > Level Up Tutorial >** Imagery
Present an Argument in a Speech	Collection Test		

Lesson Assessments
Using Textual Evidence
Using Media in a Presentation

Collection 4 Lessons	Key Learning Objective	Performance Task
ANCHOR TEXT **Speech by John F. Kennedy "Remarks at the Dedication of the Aerospace Medical Health Center," p. 185A** Lexile 1380L	**The student will be able to . . .** trace and evaluate an argument.	Writing Activity: Research Report
Commentary by Philippe Cousteau "Why Exploring the Ocean Is Mankind's Next Giant Leap," p. 193A Lexile 1360L	**The student will be able to . . .** identify tone and evaluate the reasoning used to support a claim.	Speaking Activity: Informal Debate
Science Article by Cheryl Bardoe from "Living in the Dark," p. 201A Lexile 1200L	**The student will be able to . . .** analyze the structure of an informational text and paraphrase central ideas and details.	Writing Activity: Persuasive Essa
Poem by Georgia Douglas Johnson "Your World," p. 213A	**The student will be able to . . .** identify and analyze how imagery and extended metaphor can express a particular message or idea.	Writing Activity: Analysis

Collection 4 Performance Task
A Give a Persuasive Speech

Vocabulary Strategy	Language and Style	Student Instructional Support	CLOSE READER Selection
Using Context Clues	Capitalization	**Scaffolding for ELL Students:** Analyze Language **When Students Struggle:** Analyze Language	Online Essay by Joan Vernikos "Is Space Exploration Worth the Cost?" p. 192b **Lexile 1130L**
Prefixes	Adjective Clauses	**Scaffolding for ELL Students:** Analyze Structure **When Students Struggle:** Trace an Argument **To Challenge Students:** Compare Two Arguments	
Greek Roots	Verbal Phrases	**Scaffolding for ELL Students:** Analyze Language **When Students Struggle:** Track Causes and Effects **To Challenge Students:** Make Connections	Science Article by Elisabeth Rosenthal "Stinging Tentacles Offer Hint to Oceans' Decline," p. 212b **Lexile 1370L**
		Scaffolding for ELL Students: Determine Meanings	

mySmartPlanner Create lesson plans and access resources online.

ANCHOR TEXT

Remarks at the Dedication of the Aerospace Medical Health Center

Speech by John F. Kennedy

Why This Text?

Students regularly encounter formal and informal arguments in media, in conversations, and in text materials. This lesson explores the argument developed in Kennedy's speech about the value of the space program.

▶ View It!

Professional Development Podcast:

Teaching Argument

Key Learning Objective: The student will be able to trace and evaluate an argument.

For practice and application:

Is Space Exploration Worth the Cost?

Close Reader selection
"Is Space Exploration Worth the Cost?"
Online Essay by Joan Vernikos

COMMON CORE — Common Core Standards

RI 1 Cite text evidence.
RI 4 Analyze the impact of word choice on meaning and tone.
RI 5 Analyze the structure an author uses to organize a text.
RI 6 Determine an author's purpose.
RI 7 Compare and contrast a text to an audio, video, or multimedia version of the text.
RI 8 Trace and evaluate an argument.
SL 1 Engage effectively in a range of collaborative discussions.
SL 3 Delineate a speaker's argument and specific claims, evaluating the soundness of the reasoning and the relevance of the evidence.
W 2 Write informative/explanatory texts.
W 7 Conduct short research projects.
W 8 Gather relevant information.
L 4 Determine the meaning of unknown words and phrases.
L 4a Use context as a clue to the meaning of a word or phrase.
L 4c Consult general reference materials.
L 4d Verify the preliminary determination of the meaning of a word or phrase.

▲ Text Complexity Rubric

	Remarks at the Dedication of the Aerospace Medical Health Center
Quantitative Measures	Lexile: 1380L

Levels of Meaning/Purpose

●—●—●—●—→

more than one purpose; implied, easily identified from context

Structure

●—●—●—●—→

organization of main ideas and details complex; but clearly stated and generally sequential

Qualitative Measures

Language Conventionality and Clarity

●—●—●—●—→

some unfamiliar, academic, or domain-specific words

Knowledge Demands

●—●—●—●—→

specialized knowledge required

Reader/Task Considerations	Teacher determined Vary by individual reader and type of text

CLOSE READ

Background Have students read the background and information about the author. Tell students that President Kennedy was known for giving memorable, powerful speeches. On the day of his inauguration in 1961, he famously stated, "Ask not what your country can do for you—ask what you can do for your country." In 1961, two years before this speech, Kennedy went before Congress and called for plans to send astronauts to the moon.

SETTING A PURPOSE Direct students to use the Setting a Purpose question to focus their reading. Remind students to generate questions as they read.

Determine Author's Purpose (LINES 1–13)

COMMON CORE RI 1, RI 6

Explain to students that Kennedy prepared this speech for a specific **audience**—the group of people who listen to a speech or watch a performance. By identifying his audience, the speaker can select specific language and ideas that will appeal to the audience to achieve his **purpose,** or the reason he is giving the speech.

 CITE TEXT EVIDENCE Have students reread lines 1–13 and identify Kennedy's audience. What is Kennedy's likely purpose, and which words hint at this purpose? *(Kennedy is speaking to the Secretary, Governor, Vice President, Senator, members of Congress, members of the military, and assorted ladies and gentlemen. His purpose seems to be a call to action to do something new and pioneering. Phrases such as "It is an era that calls for action," "test the unknown and the uncertain," and "It is a time for pathfinders and pioneers" suggest this.)*

Background *In 1957, the country then known as the Soviet Union launched the first satellite to orbit Earth. The Soviet Union and the United States were bitter enemies at the time. After becoming the 35th president of the United States in 1961,* **John F. Kennedy** *was determined to equal the Soviet's knowledge of space. Well known for many accomplishments as president, Kennedy is also remembered as an inspirational speaker. He gave this speech the day before his assassination in November 1963.*

Remarks at the Dedication of the Aerospace Medical Health Center

Speech by John F. Kennedy

SETTING A PURPOSE As you read, pay attention to the points President Kennedy is making. Why does he think the United States should be involved with space research?

Mr. Secretary, Governor, Mr. Vice President, Senator, Members of the Congress, members of the military, ladies and gentlemen:

For more than 3 years I have spoken about the New Frontier.[1] This is not a partisan term, and it is not the exclusive property of Republicans or Democrats. It refers, instead, to this Nation's place in history, to the fact that we do stand on the edge of a great new era, filled with both crisis and opportunity, an era to be characterized by achievement
10 and by challenge. It is an era which calls for action and for the best efforts of all those who would test the unknown and the

---

[1] **New Frontier:** term Kennedy used in his presidential campaign.

(t) ©John F. Kennedy Library; (b) ©HoughtonMifflinHarcourt; (bg) ©Corbis

---

Close Read Screencasts ▶ View It!

Modeled Discussions

Have students click the *Close Read* icons in their eBooks to access two screencasts in which readers discuss and annotate the following key passages:

- For more than 3 years . . . (lines 4–13)
- Many Americans make the mistake . . . (lines 31–42)

As a class, view and discuss at least one of these videos. Then, have students work in pairs to do an independent close read of an additional passage—Kennedy's call to action and conclusion (lines 112–119).

For more context and historical background, students can view the video "JFK Sets Goal for Man on Moon" in their eBooks.

Trace and Evaluate an Argument (LINES 31–42, 43–55)

 COMMON CORE RI 1, RI 5, RI 8

Explain that in an **argument** the speaker or writer states a claim supported by reasons and evidence.

B **CITE TEXT EVIDENCE** Ask students to reread lines 31–42 and cite the lines in which Kennedy states his claim. *(Lines 40–42)* Ask students to restate that claim in their own words. *(The study of medicine in space will make everyone's lives healthier and happier.)*

Tell students that to organize a text around a claim, a writer or speaker provides reasons and evidence that support the claim. **Reasons** explain a person's beliefs or actions. **Evidence** includes the facts, statistics, quotations, or anecdotes that support each reason.

C **CITE TEXT EVIDENCE** Ask students to reread lines 43–55, identify the first reason Kennedy uses to prove his claim, and cite the evidence he provides for support. *(Reason: Medical space research may open up new understanding of man's relation to his environment. Evidence: (1) Examinations of the astronaut's physical, mental, and emotional reactions can teach us more about the differences between normal and abnormal, about disorientation, and about changes in metabolism which could result in extending life span. (2) When you study the effects of exhaust gases on our astronauts, and you seek ways to reduce their toxicity, you are working on problems similar to those we face in our polluted urban centers.)*

CRITICAL VOCABULARY

metabolism: Kennedy believes that medical space research will teach us about "changes in metabolism" that happen during space travel.

ASK STUDENTS what system of an astronaut's metabolism does Kennedy imply might be affected by space exploration. *(the pulmonary system, or lungs)*

---

uncertain in every phase of human endeavor. It is a time for pathfinders and pioneers.

I have come to Texas today to salute an outstanding group of pioneers, the men who man the Brooks Air Force Base School of Aerospace Medicine and the Aerospace Medical Center. It is fitting that San Antonio should be the site of this center and this school as we gather to dedicate this complex of buildings. For this city has long been the home of the pioneers
20 in the air. It was here that Sidney Brooks, whose memory we honor today, was born and raised. It was here that Charles Lindbergh and Claire Chennault,[2] and a host of others, who, in World War I and World War II and Korea, and even today have helped demonstrate American mastery of the skies, trained at Kelly Field and Randolph Field,[3] which form a major part of aviation history. And in the new frontier of outer space, while headlines may be made by others in other places, history is being made every day by the men and women of the Aerospace Medical Center, without whom there
30 could be no history.

B Many Americans make the mistake of assuming that space research has no values here on earth. Nothing could be further from the truth. Just as the wartime development of radar gave us the transistor, and all that it made possible, so research in space medicine holds the promise of substantial benefit for those of us who are earthbound. For our effort in space is not, as some have suggested, a competitor for the natural resources that we need to develop the earth. It is a working partner and a coproducer of these resources. And
40 nothing makes this clearer than the fact that medicine in space is going to make our lives healthier and happier here on earth.

C I give you three examples: first, medical space research may open up new understanding of man's relation to his environment. Examinations of the astronaut's physical, and mental, and emotional reactions can teach us more about the differences between normal and abnormal, about the causes and effects of disorientation, about changes in **metabolism**

metabolism
(mĭ-tăb´ə-lĭz´əm) *n.* The *metabolism* of a living thing is all the processes that allow for growth and life.

---

[2] **Sidney Brooks . . . Charles Lindbergh . . . Claire Chennault** (shən´ôlt): Sidney Brooks was a young flyer killed in a training accident. Charles Lindbergh was the first transatlantic solo pilot, and Claire Chennault was an important figure in the development of air-war theories.

[3] **Kelly Field and Randolph Field:** airfields in the San Antonio area where many military pilots were trained.

186 Collection 4

SCAFFOLDING FOR ELL STUDENTS

Analyze Language Using a whiteboard, project the introduction to Kennedy's speech. Invite volunteers to mark up lines 3–13. Have students highlight in green any repeated words and underline the words used to describe the era.

ASK STUDENTS what Kennedy is trying to emphasize about this era. *(It is a time of challenge, but a time of achievement and opportunity, requiring action.)*

do stand on the edge of a great new era, filled with both crisis and

opportunity, an era to be characterized by achievement

and by challenge. It is an era which calls for action and for the

which could result in extending the life span. When you study the effects on our astronauts of exhaust gases which can contaminate their environment, and you seek ways to alter these gases so as to reduce their toxicity, you are working on problems similar to those we face in our great urban centers which themselves are being corrupted by gases and which must be clear.

And second, medical space research may revolutionize the technology and the techniques of modern medicine. Whatever new devices are created, for example, to monitor our astronauts, to measure their heart activity, their breathing, their brain waves, their eye motion, at great distances and under difficult conditions, will also represent a major advance in general medical instrumentation. Heart patients may even be able to wear a light monitor which will sound a warning if their activity exceeds certain limits. An instrument recently developed to record automatically the impact of acceleration upon an astronaut's eyes will also be of help to small children who are suffering miserably from eye defects, but are unable to describe their **impairment**. And also by the use of instruments similar to those used in Project Mercury, this Nation's private as well as public nursing services are being improved, enabling one nurse now to give more critically ill patients greater attention than they ever could in the past.

And third, medical space research may lead to new safeguards against hazards common to many environments. Specifically, our astronauts will need fundamentally new devices to protect them from the ill effects of radiation which can have a profound influence upon medicine and man's relations to our present environment.

Here at this center we have the laboratories, the talent, the resources to give new **impetus** to vital research in the life centers. I am not suggesting that the entire space program is justified alone by what is done in medicine. The space program stands on its own as a contribution to national strength. And last Saturday at Cape Canaveral I saw our new Saturn C-1 rocket booster,[4] which, with its payload,[5] when it rises in December of this year, will be, for the first time, the largest booster in the world, carrying into space the largest payload that any country in the world has ever sent into space.

impairment
(ĭm-pâr´mənt) n. An impairment is an injury or weakness.

impetus
(ĭm´pĭ-təs) n. The impetus is the driving force or motivation behind an action.

---

[4] **booster:** a rocket used to launch a spacecraft.
[5] **payload:** the load carried by a rocket or other vehicle.

Remarks at the Dedication of the Aerospace Medical Health Center **187**

APPLYING ACADEMIC VOCABULARY

stress	valid

As you discuss the Kennedy speech, incorporate the following Collection 4 academic vocabulary words: *stress* and *valid*. To probe Kennedy's argument, ask students to indicate what Kennedy **stresses** to support his claim. As you evaluate the effectiveness of the argument, ask students to explain if Kennedy provides **valid** evidence to support his reasons.

COMMON CORE RI 1, RI 5, RI 8

Trace and Evaluate an Argument (LINES 56–72, 79–88)

Explain that to prove a claim a writer or speaker must provide sufficient and credible reasons and evidence that clearly relate to the claim.

D **ASK STUDENTS** to reread lines 56–72 and explain how the second reason differs from the first reason. (*The second reason focuses on medical technology and techniques, while the first focuses on how medical research in space might open up new understandings of our relationship to our environment on Earth.*)

Explain that strong arguments include statements called counterarguments that address opposing viewpoints. Counterarguments show that the speaker or writer can disprove other viewpoints.

E **CITE TEXT EVIDENCE** Have students reread lines 79–88 and cite evidence of a counterargument. (*Kennedy anticipates the opposing view that medical research in space doesn't justify the entire program. He counters by stating that "the space program stands on its own as a contribution to national strength."*)

CRITICAL VOCABULARY

impairment: Kennedy explains that medical space research has led to new inventions that automatically record physical reactions.

ASK STUDENTS how automatic monitoring of physical responses would benefit the children who can't describe their impairments. (*Adults can't fix or minimize the impairment until they can identify what the problem is.*)

impetus: Kennedy wants to convince his audience that the Aerospace Medical Health Center can provide the "impetus to vital research."

ASK STUDENTS why a new medical center might serve as an impetus for such a purpose. (*A new medical center would gather intelligent researchers and modern equipment, which are necessary for research projects.*)

Trace and Evaluate an Argument (LINES 89–96)

COMMON CORE RI 1, RI 5, RI 8

Tell students that complex arguments can include more than one claim.

F **CITE TEXT EVIDENCE** Have students reread lines 89–96 and cite evidence of Kennedy's second claim. *(Claim: Despite "pressures in this country" to stop space exploration, the "space effort must go on.")* Then, ask students to determine the reason and evidence Kennedy offers to support this claim. *(Reason: The United States should be a leader. Evidence: "And in December" with the launch of the largest booster in the world— "the United States will be ahead.")*

CRITICAL VOCABULARY

tedious: Kennedy knows that there is hard work ahead in the U.S. space effort.

ASK STUDENTS to explain how the medical research that Kennedy proposes could be tedious. *(Medical research entails a good deal of detailed work, extreme precision, and dead ends.)*

COLLABORATIVE DISCUSSION Have students pair up and discuss specific language and techniques that Kennedy uses that would be inspirational to his specific audience. Ask students to consider and discuss the validity of Kennedy's points, explaining their reasons for their opinions. Then, have students share their conclusions with the class as a whole.

ASK STUDENTS to share any questions they generated in the course of reading and discussing the selection.

WHEN STUDENTS STRUGGLE

To guide students' comprehension of the reasons that Kennedy has cited to support his claim, have students work in pairs to fill out a chart like the one shown. For additional help, suggest that they look for signal words like *first*, *second*, and *third* to identify the reasons Kennedy uses in his argument.

F 90   I think the United States should be a leader. A country as rich and powerful as this which bears so many burdens and responsibilities, which has so many opportunities, should be second to none. And in December, while I do not regard our mastery of space as anywhere near complete, while I recognize that there are still areas where we are behind—at least in one area, the size of the booster—this year I hope the United States will be ahead. And I am for it. We have a long way to go. Many weeks and months and years of long, **tedious** work lie ahead. There will be setbacks and frustrations and disappointments. There will be, as there always are, pressures in this country

100 to do less in this area as in so many others, and temptations to do something else that is perhaps easier. But this research here must go on. This space effort must go on. The conquest of space must and will go ahead. That much we know. That much we can say with confidence and conviction.

    Frank O'Connor, the Irish writer, tells in one of his books how, as a boy, he and his friends would make their way across the countryside, and when they came to an orchard wall that seemed too high and too doubtful to try and too difficult to permit their voyage to continue, they took off their hats and

110 tossed them over the wall—and then they had no choice but to follow them.

    This Nation has tossed its cap over the wall of space, and we have no choice but to follow it. Whatever the difficulties, they will be overcome. Whatever the hazards, they must be guarded against. With the vital help of this Aerospace Medical Center, with the help of all those who labor in the space endeavor, with the help and support of all Americans, we will climb this wall with safety and with speed—and we shall then explore the wonders on the other side.

120   Thank you.

tedious
(tē´dē-əs) *adj.*
Something that is *tedious* is boring.

COLLABORATIVE DISCUSSION Kennedy makes several points about why he thinks the United States should be involved with space research. Do you think the points he makes are valid? Does his speech inspire you to support space research? Discuss your ideas with a partner.

188 Collection 4

Claim: Medicine in space will make people's lives better.
SUPPORT:
Reason 1: understand man's relationship to his environment
Reason 2: revolutionize modern medicine
Reason 3: reduce environmental hazards

Trace and Evaluate an Argument

COMMON CORE RI 5, RI 8

The speech you've just read is an **argument,** in which the speaker states a claim supported by reasons and evidence. A **claim** is the speaker's position on a problem or an issue. The strength of an argument relies not on the claim but on the support. **Support** consists of reasons and evidence used to prove the claim. **Reasons** are declarations made to explain an action or belief. **Evidence** includes specific facts, statistics, or examples.

To **trace,** or follow the reasoning of, an argument:

- Identify the claim, which may be stated directly or implied.
- Look for reasons and evidence that support the claim.
- Pay attention to the way the author connects the claim, reasons, and evidence.
- Identify **counterarguments,** which are statements that address opposing viewpoints. A good argument anticipates opposing viewpoints and provides counterarguments to disprove the opposing views.

Some arguments have more than one claim, which might only be determined after careful examination of the text. To trace the argument in Kennedy's speech:

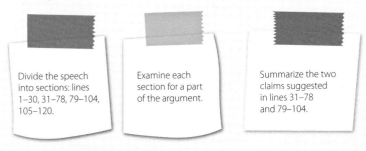

Divide the speech into sections: lines 1–30, 31–78, 79–104, 105–120.

Examine each section for a part of the argument.

Summarize the two claims suggested in lines 31–78 and 79–104.

To **evaluate** an argument, or decide whether it makes sense and is convincing:

- Consider whether the evidence logically supports the claim.
- Examine the logic to ensure the ideas make sense and are in a proper order.
- Consider whether the opposing view has been adequately addressed.
- Identify persuasive techniques such as appeals to emotion.

CLOSE READ

Trace and Evaluate an Argument

COMMON CORE RI 5, RI 8

Help students understand the terms and divide the speech into sections. Once students have examined the sections, have them summarize the claims. *(In lines 31–78, Kennedy gives examples to support his claim that medical space research makes life on Earth better. In lines 79–104, Kennedy gives examples that support his claim that space research increases our national strength.)*

To help students evaluate an argument, make sure they understand how to judge logical relationships between ideas:

- Explain that there must be a clear and reasonable connection between the claim and its support.
- Explain that writers and speakers can use different organizational patterns to make their arguments clear and coherent. For example, they can use order of importance, going from the least to the most important reason (or the reverse), or cause-and-effect relationships, showing how one event or action either leads to or results from another.

Strategies for Annotation 🖉 📋 *Annotate it!*

Trace and Evaluate an Argument

COMMON CORE RI 1, RI 5, RI 8

Share these strategies for guided or independent analysis:

- Highlight in yellow the claims that Kennedy makes.
- Underline each reason and the evidence that supports it. On a note, list the types of evidence that Kennedy relies on.
- Highlight in blue opposing claims Kennedy anticipates. Summarize his counterarguments in a note.
- On a note, record words or phrases that express an inspiring tone.

Many Americans make the mistake of assuming that space research has no values here on earth. Nothing could further from the truth. Just as the wartime development of radar gave us the transistor, and all that it made possible, so research in space medicine holds the promise of substantial benefit for those of us who are earthbound. For our effort

Research in space medicine may benefit people on Earth.

Analyzing the Text
COMMON CORE RI 1, RI 4, RI 5, RI 8

Possible answers:

1. These words support his position that the United States needs to be a pioneer in space research and that the members of his audience are the pioneers in that field. He compliments them by associating them with leaders in their field and implies that they are making history.

2. **Opposing Viewpoints:** (1) Space research has no value on Earth. (2) Research in space medicine competes for natural resources that are needed to develop Earth.
   Kennedy's Counterarguments: (1) Research holds the promise of substantial benefit. The wartime development of radar spurred the development of the transistor. (2) Space is a partner and coproducer of resources, and space medicine is going to make people's lives healthier and happier.

3. Kennedy speaks of "small children who are suffering miserably from eye defects." This language elicits sympathy from his listeners, which may lead them to accept his argument.

4. The focus has shifted from the ways in which medical space research improves life on Earth to the way the space program contributes to national strength. Lines 87–90 state the new focus. Kennedy has shifted his focus in order to make another claim and to appeal to national pride.

5. Kennedy repeats words "Whatever the" at the beginning of sentences in lines 113–115. In lines 115–117, he repeats phrases "with the help of." The repetition reinforces a belief in success, no matter how difficult the task may be, if we stay committed to the program.

6. Kennedy establishes an effective, coherent, and logical argument. His claim about the need for medical space research is clearly supported with three reasons, each of which is supported by relevant evidence. The second claim about continuing the space program is also supported by a clear reason (the American leadership role) and evidence (the U.S. is rich and powerful.)

Speaking and Listening
COMMON CORE RI 7, SL 3

Have students listen to and analyze an audio version of Kennedy's speech while they reread the text of the speech. The audio speech can be found in their eBook. See Enhancing Student Learning at the end of this selection for further instruction on comparing two versions of a speech.

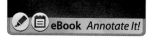
eBook *Annotate It!*

Analyzing the Text
COMMON CORE RI 1, RI 4, RI 5, RI 7, RI 8, W 2, W 7, W 8, SL 3

Cite Text Evidence   Support your responses with evidence from the text.

1. **Interpret** Kennedy refers to his audience as *pathfinders* and *pioneers* and mentions the *New Frontier*. Why might Kennedy use these words?

2. **Cite Evidence** Using a chart like the one shown, identify two opposing viewpoints that Kennedy anticipates in lines 31–42 and cite Kennedy's counterarguments to those viewpoints.

Opposing Viewpoints	Kennedy's Counterarguments

3. **Draw Conclusions** Reread lines 64–68. How does Kennedy describe the children who might benefit from medical space technology? What might Kennedy be trying to accomplish through his choice of language?

4. **Draw Conclusions** Examine lines 79–88. Describe Kennedy's shift in focus. Why might Kennedy make this shift in his argument?

5. **Cite Evidence** Examine lines 112–119. Identify phrases that Kennedy repeats. What ideas is he emphasizing with this repetition?

6. **Evaluate** Considering the audience and purpose of Kennedy's speech, is his argument convincing? Do his conclusions arise logically from the reasons and evidence he has cited?

Speaking and Listening

Listen to an audio version of President Kennedy delivering the speech you have just read. How is hearing the speech different from reading it? With a partner or small group, choose two sections of the speech and discuss how the delivery of the speech conveys the meaning of the words.

PERFORMANCE TASK

Writing Activity: Research Report Research a recent or planned space mission for medical research by NASA (National Aeronautics and Space Administration).

- Identify one mission and write a brief description of its purpose and outcome.
- Explain whether or not it is in keeping with Kennedy's views about space research.
- Share your findings with the class.

Assign this performance task.

PERFORMANCE TASK
COMMON CORE W 2, W 7, W 8

Writing Activity: Research Report Have students work in pairs or small groups.

- Direct students to reread the speech to review Kennedy's position on medical space research.
- Have students review how to use search terms to gather information effectively.

Critical Vocabulary

COMMON CORE L 4a, L 4c, L 4d

| metabolism | impairment | impetus | tedious |

Practice and Apply Choose the response that best answers each question. Then discuss with a partner why the other choices are incorrect.

1. If a person's **metabolism** were not functioning properly, what symptom might be present?
   a. toned muscles
   b. labored breathing
   c. tanned skin
   d. shiny hair

2. Which condition would be considered an **impairment?**
   a. sensitive taste buds
   b. a slight limp
   c. 20/20 vision
   d. a photographic memory

3. Which would NOT serve as an **impetus** to study harder?
   a. a chance to play on a team
   b. a mention on the honor roll
   c. a reward from a parent
   d. a speech on physical fitness

4. Which task might be the most **tedious?**
   a. walking your dog
   b. redecorating your room
   c. shopping for groceries
   d. planning a party

Vocabulary Strategy: Using Context Clues

When you encounter an unfamiliar word, look at its **context**—or the surrounding words, phrases, or sentences—to try to understand its meaning. Look at the following example:

> We have a long way to go. Many weeks and months and years of long, *tedious* work lie ahead.

The work described as "tedious" is also described as "long" and lasting for "many weeks and months and years." Work that lasts a very long time has the potential to be difficult, boring, or tiring. Checking the word's meaning in the dictionary confirms that *tedious* means "tiresome" or "boring."

Practice and Apply Reread Kennedy's speech and find the following words: *host, substantial, impairment, profound*. Look at the surrounding sentences for clues to each word's meaning. Then fill out a chart like the one shown.

Word	Context Clues	Guessed Definitions	Dictionary Definition
host (lines 21–24)			
substantial (lines 31–36)			
impairment (lines 64–68)			
profound (lines 73–78)			

PRACTICE & APPLY

Critical Vocabulary

COMMON CORE L 4a, L 4c, L 4d

Answers: 1. *b;* **2.** *b;* **3.** *d;* **4.** *c*

Vocabulary Strategy: Using Context Clues

Word	Context Clues	Guessed Definitions	Dictionary Definition
host	follows a list of names; followed by "of others"	a lot; many	a great number
substantial	modifies benefit, something Kennedy wants to emphasize	great; significant	considerable in importance
impairment	children unable to describe impairment are suffering from "eye defects."	injury; damage	condition of being damaged or injured
profound	modifies influence, something Kennedy wants to emphasize	great	deep or far-reaching

---

Strategies for Annotation 🖊 📗 *Annotate it!*

Using Context Clues

COMMON CORE L 4a

Have students locate the sentences containing *host, substantial, impairment,* and *profound* in Kennedy's speech. Encourage students to use their eBook annotation tools to do the following:

- Highlight each word.
- Reread the surrounding sentences, looking for clues to the word's meaning. Underline any clues you find, such as examples, synonyms, or antonyms.
- Review your annotations and try to infer the word's meaning.

space research has no values here on earth. Nothing co[ld be] further from the truth. Just as the wartime developmen[t of] radar gave us the transistor, and 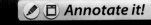all that it made possible, so research in space medicine holds the promise of substantial benefit for those of us who are earthbound. For our effort

> substantial: "great" or "significant"?

PRACTICE & APPLY

Language Conventions: Capitalization

COMMON CORE L2, L3

Tell students that the examples in the chart are just a few of the types of proper nouns that need capitalization. Invite volunteers to supply other organizations, events, and/or documents as examples. *(Possible answers: Library of Congress, Boy Scouts of America, Memorial Day, Fourth of July, United States Constitution)*

Answers:

1. *the State of the Union*

2. *Martin Luther King Jr. Day*

3. *Apollo 11 Flight Plan*

4. *NASA; National Aeronautics and Space Administration*

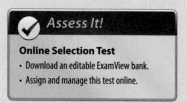

✓ Assess It!

Online Selection Test
- Download an editable ExamView bank.
- Assign and manage this test online.

Language Conventions: Capitalization

COMMON CORE L4

In your writing, you will need to apply the rules of capitalization to **proper nouns**—the names of specific people, places, and things—including organizations, historical documents, and events. In the following example, note which proper nouns are capitalized.

> In "Remarks at the Dedication of the Aerospace Medical Health Center," President Kennedy honored the Brooks Air Force Base School of Aerospace Medicine. He also mentioned that Americans demonstrated "mastery of the skies" in World War I, World War II, and the Korean War.

Note that when writing a title, the articles *and* and *the* remain lowercase, as do the prepositions *at* and *of*. The chart below shows three types of proper nouns that require capitalization. When events or organizations are abbreviated, their abbreviations are also capitalized.

Capitalization of Proper Nouns		Abbreviations
Organizations	American Library Association	ALA
	World Health Organization	WHO
Events	World War II	WW II
	Presidents' Day	
Documents	Bill of Rights	
	Declaration of Independence	

Practice and Apply These sentences include proper nouns that lack correct capitalization. In each sentence, indicate which proper nouns should be capitalized. Consult reference materials for terms or titles that are unfamiliar to you.

1. Each January, the President of the United States delivers a speech called the state of the union.

2. Once a year, we observe Martin Luther King Jr. day to celebrate the great civil rights leader.

3. In 1969, Apollo 11 was the first manned space mission to land on the Moon. The details of the mission are preserved in a document called the Apollo 11 flight plan.

4. In 2011, five top scientists were selected by nasa, the national aeronautics and space administration, to investigate discoveries on the planet Mars.

Compare and Contrast Two Versions of a Speech

COMMON CORE

RI 7,
SL 1,
SL 3

TEACH

Point out that the sound of a speaker's voice can be a powerful tool of persuasion. The delivery of a speech can affect how the ideas are received. Have students listen to the audio version of Kennedy's speech and ask them to note the following:

- **Tone** is the attitude a writer or speaker has toward a subject. In speaking, tone can be conveyed by the sound of the voice. For example, a speaker might state a phrase in a manner that is playful, casual, mournful, or insistent, indicating the tone.

- **Emphasis** is the stress a speaker places on certain words or main points of an argument. A raised voice or a lowered voice creates emphasis. Gestures, such as a loud clap of hands, can be used as well, often indicating a speaker's strong emotion.

- **Pace** is the speed at which someone delivers a speech. It can create a certain rhythm, captivating listeners to follow the flow of ideas.

PRACTICE AND APPLY

Audio Clip: 10 minutes

Suggest students listen to the speech more than once, pausing when necessary to determine what vocal techniques help to support Kennedy's argument and recording them in a chart like the one shown below.

Technique	Evidence from Speech
Tone	
Emphasis	
Pace	

After students listen to the speech, have them hold a discussion to compare and contrast the print and audio texts of the speech. Ask students to explain how hearing the speech is different from reading it and how the delivery of the speech conveys the meaning of the words, citing passages from the speech to support their answers. *(Accept all reasonable responses.)*

 INTERACTIVE LESSON Have students complete the tutorial in this lesson: **Analyzing and Evaluating Presentations**

Trace and Evaluate an Argument

COMMON CORE

RI 5,
RI 8

RETEACH

Review the terms *claim, reasons, evidence, opposing claims,* and *counterargument.* Then, give an example of a claim, such as "Animal dissection in middle schools should be banned."

- Ask students to provide examples of types of reasons and evidence that might be used to support the claim. *(Sample Reason: The practice can have a negative impact on students performing the dissections.)*

- Provide the following opposing claim: "Animal dissection is an important way for students to learn about biology." Ask: How could you counter this viewpoint? *(Sample Answer: Save dissections for college students majoring in biology or medical school students.)*

 LEVEL UP TUTORIALS Assign the following *Level Up* tutorial: **Elements of an Argument**

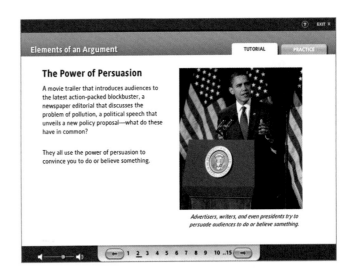

CLOSE READING APPLICATION

Students can apply the skill to a current magazine or newspaper editorial. Have students work independently to outline the claim, support, opposing claim, and counterargument. Ask: Does the writer include enough support to prove the claim? Does he or she do an adequate job of anticipating possible objections?

Is Space Exploration Worth the Cost?

Online Essay by Joan Vernikos

Why This Text

Students often finish reading the text of an argument without a complete grasp of the author's ideas and evidence. Arguments like this one by Joan Vernikos may have difficult language or complex reasoning that becomes clear only with careful study. With the help of the close-reading questions, students will trace and evaluate her argument on the risks and rewards of space exploration. This close reading will lead students to develop a coherent understanding of Vernikos's argument.

Background Have students read the background and information about the author. Introduce the selection by telling students that Dr. Joan Vernikos strongly believes that knowledge gained from space exploration can greatly benefit humans here on Earth. An expert on stress and healthy aging, she wrote one of her most popular books—*Sitting Kills, Moving Heals*—using information gained from astronauts' experiences in space to remedy sedentary earthbound lifestyles.

SETTING A PURPOSE Ask students to pay attention to the reasons Vernikos uses to support her position. How soon into the essay can they begin to identify her position?

 COMMON CORE

Common Core Support

- cite several pieces of textual evidence
- determine central ideas in a text
- trace and evaluate an argument
- assess an author's claims and reasoning

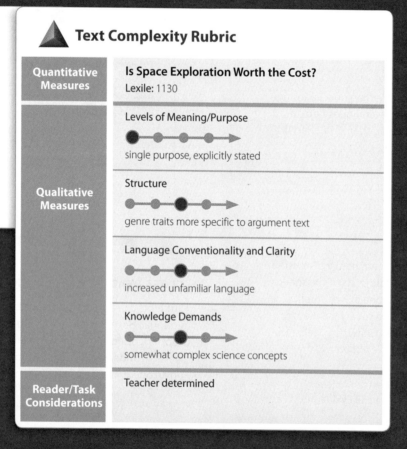

Text Complexity Rubric

Quantitative Measures	**Is Space Exploration Worth the Cost?** Lexile: 1130
Qualitative Measures	**Levels of Meaning/Purpose** single purpose, explicitly stated
	Structure genre traits more specific to argument text
	Language Conventionality and Clarity increased unfamiliar language
	Knowledge Demands somewhat complex science concepts
Reader/Task Considerations	Teacher determined

Strategies for CLOSE READING

Trace and Evaluate an Argument

Students should read this argument carefully all the way through. Close-reading questions at the bottom of the page will help them focus on a thorough analysis of the argument. As they read, students should jot down comments or questions about the text in the side margins.

WHEN STUDENTS STRUGGLE . . .

To help students follow the reasons Vernikos cites to support her claim, have students work in small groups to fill out a chart like the one shown as they analyze the essay.

CITE TEXT EVIDENCE For practice in tracing an argument, ask students to cite the evidence Vernikos uses to support each reason.

CLAIM: Human space exploration is worth the cost.

SUPPORT:

Reason 1: Humans may need to populate other planets in the future, and only trained astronauts can adequately prepare for this.

Reason 2: Knowledge gained from human space exploration greatly benefits many aspects of life on Earth.

Reason 3: Monetary returns on space investments far outweigh the costs.

Reason 4: The creativity of our nation's youth in fields such as science and engineering must propel the U.S. into a leadership role in space exploration.

Background *Beginning in 1981, NASA launched American astronauts into outer space through the Space Shuttle Program. However, budget cuts forced NASA to discontinue the shuttle program in 2011. For years, scientists and economists have debated whether NASA should carry out human space travel in the future. As Director of NASA's Life Sciences Division,* **Dr. Joan Vernikos** *studied the harmful effects of weightlessness on astronauts.*

Is Space Exploration Worth the Cost?

Online Essay by Joan Vernikos

CLOSE READ
Notes

1. **READ ▶** As you read lines 1–31, begin to collect and cite evidence.
   - Circle the question at the beginning of the essay.
   - In the margin, explain what Vernikos says about the human spirit in lines 5–7.
   - Then, underline the main idea in each of the next two paragraphs.

(A) Why explore? Asked why he kept trying to climb Everest, English mountaineer George Mallory reputedly replied, "Because it was there." Exploration is intrinsic to our nature. It is the contest between man and nature mixed with the primal desire to conquer. It fuels curiosity, inspiration and creativity. The human spirit seeks to discover the unknown, and in the process explore the physical and psychological potential of human **endurance**.

There have always been the few risk-takers who ventured for the rest of us to follow. Because of earlier pioneers, air travel is now
10 commonplace, and space travel for all is just around the corner. Economic and societal benefits are not immediately evident, but they always follow, as does our understanding of human potential to overcome challenges. Fifty years after Sputnik,[1] space remains the next frontier.

Humans seek to test their limits and explore the mysterious.

endurance: *ability to withstand difficulties over time*

[1] **Sputnik:** the world's first artificial satellite was put into orbit around Earth by the Soviet Union on October 4, 1957. Its launch marked the start of the space age.

63

---

1. **READ AND CITE TEXT EVIDENCE** Students' goals in reading lines 1–31 are to begin to grasp Vernikos's position on space exploration and to identify her main ideas.

(A) ASK STUDENTS to infer Vernikos's answer to the title's question based on the information she introduces in the first and second paragraphs. *Students may point to her positive discussion of humans' enduring and "intrinsic" need to explore, as well as her references to specific "economic and societal benefits" of space exploration to infer that Vernikos supports the idea that space exploration is worth the cost.*

Critical Vocabulary: endurance (line 7) Ask students to share their definitions of *endurance*. Ask how endurance fits into Vernikos's discussion of exploration. *Vernikos believes that exploration of the unknown tests the limits of humans' physical and mental abilities.*

CLOSE READ
Notes

B   Without risking (human) lives, robotic technology such as unmanned missions, probes, observatories, and landers enables space exploration. It lays the groundwork, and does the scouting. But as I heard former astronaut Thomas Jones often say, "only a (human) can experience what being in space feels like, and only a (human) can
20 communicate this to others." It is (humans) who repair the Hubble telescope.[2] It is (humans) who service the International Space Station (ISS). Mercury astronauts were the first to photograph Earth from space with hand-held cameras. Earth scientists in orbit on the ISS may view aspects of global change that only a trained eye can see. In addition, studying astronauts in the microgravity of space has been the only means of understanding how gravity affects (human) development and health here on Earth. It is highly probable that, in this century, (humans) will settle on other planets. Our ability to explore and sustain (human) presence there will not only expand
30 Earth's access to mineral resources but, should the need arise, provide alternative habitats for humanity's survival.
    (At what cost?) (Is there a price to inspiration and creativity?)
C Economic, scientific and technological returns of space exploration have far exceeded the investment. Globally, 43 countries now have

> [2] **Hubble telescope:** a space telescope launched in April of 1990 by the United States, the Hubble telescope orbits Earth and provides clear pictures for astronomical study. It was named for the astronomer Edwin Powell Hubble.

---

2. ◀ REREAD Reread lines 15–31. Circle every use of the word *human* in this paragraph. What idea is Vernikos emphasizing by repeating this word? What opposing viewpoint does she refute?

> *It is not enough to send unmanned missions into space. Humans must actually go into space if we are to keep expanding our knowledge. She is addressing the opposing viewpoint that it is cheaper and safer to explore space with robotic technology.*

3. READ ▶ As you read lines 32–55, continue to cite text evidence.
- Circle the questions at the beginning of the first paragraph.
- Underline the claim Vernikos makes about the benefits of space exploration in lines 32–47.
- Underline the claim in lines 48–55 and paraphrase it in the margin.

64

CLOSE READ
Notes

Astronaut Susan L. Still in the Spacelab Module during a mission aboard the Space Shuttle Columbia.

their own observing or communication satellites in Earth orbit. Observing Earth has provided G.P.S.,[3] meteorological forecasts, predictions and management of hurricanes and other natural disasters, and global monitoring of the environment, as well as **surveillance** and intelligence. Satellite communications have changed
40 life and business practices with computer operations, cell phones, global banking, and TV. Studying humans living in the microgravity[4] of space has expanded our understanding of osteoporosis and balance disorders, and has led to new treatments. Wealth-generating medical devices and instrumentation such as digital mammography and outpatient breast biopsy procedures and the application of telemedicine to emergency care are but a few of the social and economic benefits of manned exploration that we take for granted.

D   Space exploration is not a drain on the economy; it generates infinitely more wealth than it spends. Royalties on NASA patents and
50 licenses currently go directly to the U.S. Treasury, not back to NASA. I firmly believe that the Life Sciences Research Program would be self-supporting if permitted to receive the return on its investment. NASA has done so much with so little that it has generally been assumed to have had a huge budget. In fact, the 2007 NASA budget of $16.3 billion is a minute fraction of the $13 trillion total G.D.P.[5]

> [3] **G.P.S.:** an abbreviation for Global Positioning System, a system for determining one's position on Earth by comparing radio signals received from different satellites placed into orbit by the United States Department of Defense (DOD).
> [4] **microgravity:** also called *zero gravity* or *weightlessness*, microgravity is the near absence of gravity.
> [5] **G.D.P.:** an abbreviation for Gross Domestic Product, the total market value of all the goods and services that are produced inside a country during a specified period.

surveillance:
close observation

New technology developed by NASA has made much more money than it has cost the government.

4. ◀ REREAD AND DISCUSS With a small group, discuss whether the evidence Vernikos cites to defend the cost of space exploration is sufficient (lines 48–55). Cite text evidence in your discussion.

5. READ ▶ Read lines 56–67. Underline the opposing viewpoint Vernikos references, and restate it in the margin.

65

---

2. **REREAD AND CITE TEXT EVIDENCE**

B **ASK STUDENTS** to evaluate the effectiveness of the repetition of "human." *The repetition emphasizes the role humans play and refutes the idea that robotic space exploration is adequate.*

FOR ELL STUDENTS Explain that the prefix *un* in *unmanned* means "not." The mission does not include humans but rather robots or mechanical beings.

ASK STUDENTS to look for other uses of the prefix *un* and cite them in the margin.

3. **READ AND CITE TEXT EVIDENCE** Vernikos claims that the "social and economic benefits" of manned exploration outweigh the costs.

C **ASK STUDENTS** to find and cite specific examples of these benefits in the text and in their margin notes. *Students should cite examples in lines 34–47.*

4. **REREAD AND DISCUSS USING TEXT EVIDENCE**

D **ASK STUDENTS** to appoint a reporter for each group to cite specific text evidence and line numbers to support their position about the sufficiency of Vernikos's evidence. *Students should cite evidence from lines 48–50 and 54–55.*

5. **READ AND CITE TEXT EVIDENCE**

ASK STUDENTS to read their margin notes to a partner and then create one response that best states the opposing viewpoints in lines 56–67 and uses specific textual evidence. *Students should emphasize that NASA generates "more wealth than it spends."*

Critical Vocabulary: surveillance (line 39) Ask students what examples of surveillance they can associate with cell phones. *Students should be able to point to apps that enable them to locate their lost phones.*

CLOSE READ Notes

legitimate:
logical

Some say
there are
more
important
things than
space
exploration.

Education is
the most
important
aspect.

E "What's the hurry?" is a **legitimate** question. As the late Senator William Proxmire said many years ago, "Mars isn't going anywhere." Why should we commit hard-pressed budgets for space exploration when there will always be competing interests? However, as Mercury, 60 Gemini and Apollo did 50 years ago, our future scientific and technological leadership depends on exciting creativity in the younger generations. Nothing does this better than manned space exploration. There is now a national urgency to direct the creative interests of our youth towards careers in science and engineering. We need to keep the flame of manned space exploration alive as China, Russia, India, and other countries forge ahead with substantial investments that challenge U.S. leadership in space.

6. ◀ REREAD Reread lines 56–67 and continue to cite text evidence.
- Underline the counterargument Vernikos addresses.
- Then circle the pieces of evidence you find most convincing.
- Make notes in the margin to justify your choices.

SHORT RESPONSE

Cite Text Evidence Explain whether or not Vernikos convinced you that space exploration is worth the cost. Review your reading notes, and evaluate the strength and reasonableness of the claims and evidence offered. Be sure to **cite text evidence** from the essay in your response.

Vernikos did convince me that space exploration is worth the cost. Her claim that what we learn from space exploration improves life for all of us on Earth was supported by strong evidence, including new medical treatments, faster and better communication, and better weather forecasting. Her claim that space exploration doesn't actually cost much is supported well by the minute fraction of the G.D.P. that is spent on it.

66

6. (REREAD AND CITE TEXT EVIDENCE)

E **ASK STUDENTS** to cite text evidence that shows how Vernikos appeals to the reader's patriotism. *By citing China, Russia, India, and other countries, she uses an emotional appeal of competitive and patriotic pride.*

Critical Vocabulary: legitimate (line 57) Ask students to explain *legitimate* as Vernikos uses it here. *She probably wants to appear fair-minded and open to considering all sides of an issue.*

SHORT RESPONSE

Cite Text Evidence Student responses will vary, but they should cite evidence from the text to support their positions. Students should:
- explain whether or not they agree with Vernikos's argument.
- cite specific evidence from the text to support their reasons.

TO CHALLENGE STUDENTS . . .

For more context and an additional expert opinion on the future of space travel, students can view the video *Buzz Aldrin on Future of Space Exploration* in their eBooks.

ASK STUDENTS what opinion Vernikos and Aldrin share and where Aldrin thinks U.S. space exploration should be headed in the future. *Students should recognize that both Vernikos and Aldrin believe that other nations, such as China, will leap ahead of the United States in exploring space. Aldrin believes that we should establish a space colony on Mars.*

DIG DEEPER

With the class, return to Question 4, Reread and Discuss. Have students share the results of their discussion.

ASK STUDENTS whether they were satisfied with the outcome of their small-group discussions. Have each group share what their majority opinion was. What compelling evidence did the group cite from the article to support this opinion?

- Encourage students to tell whether there was any compelling evidence cited by group members holding the minority opinion. If so, why didn't it sway the group's position?
- Have groups explain how they decided whether or not they had found sufficient evidence to support their opinion. Did everyone in the group agree as to what made the evidence sufficient? How did the group resolve any conflicts or disagreements?
- After students have shared the results of their group's discussion, ask whether another group shared any findings they wished they had brought to the table.

ASK STUDENTS to return to their Short Response answer and to revise it based on the class discussion.

mySmartPlanner Create lesson plans and access resources online.

Why Exploring the Ocean Is Mankind's Next Giant Leap

Commentary by Philippe Cousteau

Why This Text?

Students regularly encounter opinions and persuasive language in texts, speech, and media. This lesson guides students to evaluate the strength of an argument and focuses attention on language that reveals an author's attitude.

Key Learning Objective: The student will be able to evaluate the reasoning used to support a claim and identify tone.

COMMON CORE Common Core Standards

RI 1 Cite textual evidence.
RI 2 Determine central idea.
RI 4 Determine meanings of words and phrases.
RI 5 Analyze structure.
RI 6 Determine author's point of view or purpose.
RI 8 Assess argument and claims for sound reasoning.
W 7 Conduct short research projects.
W 8 Gather information from multiple print/ digital sources.
SL 1 Engage in collaborative discussions.
SL 3 Delineate a speaker's argument and specific claims.
SL 4 Present claims and findings in a focused, coherent manner.
L 1a Explain function of phrases and clauses.
L 4b Use Latin affixes as clues to meaning.
L 6 Acquire and use grade-appropriate academic vocabulary.

Text Complexity Rubric

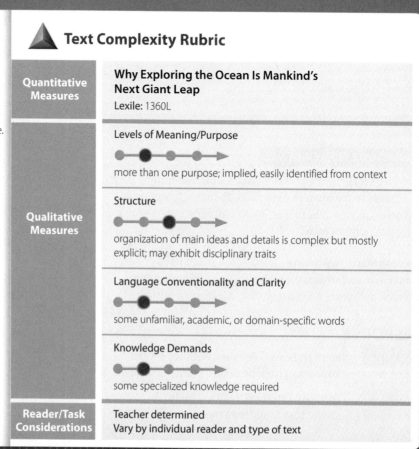

Quantitative Measures	**Why Exploring the Ocean Is Mankind's Next Giant Leap** Lexile: 1360L
Qualitative Measures	**Levels of Meaning/Purpose** more than one purpose; implied, easily identified from context
	Structure organization of main ideas and details is complex but mostly explicit; may exhibit disciplinary traits
	Language Conventionality and Clarity some unfamiliar, academic, or domain-specific words
	Knowledge Demands some specialized knowledge required
Reader/Task Considerations	Teacher determined Vary by individual reader and type of text

TEACH

Background Have students read the background and information about the author. Supplement the information by telling students that Philippe Cousteau Jr. is continuing the family tradition of environmental activism. Philippe's grandfather was Jacques-Yves Cousteau (1910–1997), a French naval officer who became an ocean explorer. He helped to invent diving equipment, underwater cameras, and other technologies for undersea exploration. His books and appearances in movies and on TV brought public awareness to the wonders of the oceans. He continued working with his son, the author's father, filmmaker and environmentalist Philippe Cousteau Sr. (1940–1979).

SETTING A PURPOSE Direct students to use the Setting a Purpose text to focus their reading. Remind them to generate questions as they read.

Analyze Structure: Sound Reasoning (LINES 1–15)

COMMON CORE RI 5, RI 8

Point out that the title includes a reference to Neil Armstrong's famous words, spoken as he became the first human to walk on the moon. Armstrong's words: "That's one small step for [a] man, one giant leap for mankind."

A **ASK STUDENTS** to reread the title and lines 1–15 and tell what the title and text reveals about Philippe Cousteau's **claim,** or position on an issue. *(Cousteau believes that space exploration has overshadowed ocean exploration, and it is time for that to change. The new "giant leap" will be the exploration of the ocean.)*

SCAFFOLDING FOR ELL STUDENTS

Analyze Structure As students read, have them identify words that signal contrasts *(however, while, but, not, despite)* and explain differences shown. They may use their eBook annotation tools to

- underline any words that signal contrasts
- highlight in two colors words that tell about two contrasting ideas

ASK STUDENTS why the author is pointing out this difference. *(To show that there is another important area of exploration besides space.)*

Background *Today, concerns over the ocean environment and potential economic and technological benefits are spurring greater interest in deep-sea exploration.* **Philippe Cousteau** *(b. 1980) is the grandson of Jacques Cousteau, the explorer whose 1960s television show revealed undersea wonders. Philippe Cousteau shares his grandfather's passion for ocean conservation, and he reports regularly on environmental and humanitarian stories from around the world.*

Why Exploring the Ocean Is Mankind's Next Giant Leap

Commentary by Philippe Cousteau

SETTING A PURPOSE As you read, consider whether Philippe Cousteau's reasons for further ocean exploration are valid. Write down any questions you may have while reading.

"Space . . . the final frontier." Not only has this classic phrase dazzled the many millions of fans of the Star Trek franchise, some could argue it has defined a big part of the American ideal for the last 50 years. The 1960s were dominated by the race to the moon and Americans were rightfully proud to be the first nation to make it there.

However, another incredible feat happened in 1960 that is largely forgotten today. For the first time in history, on January 23, 1960, two men, Lt. Don Walsh and Jacques Picard, 10 descended to the deepest part of the ocean, the bottom of the Challenger Deep in the Mariana Trench located in the western Pacific Ocean. While this feat made international news, the race to the depths of this planet was quickly overshadowed by the race to the moon—and no one has ever gone that deep since.

---

of the American ideal for the last 50 years. The 1960s were

dominated by the race to the moon and Americans were

rightfully proud to be the first nation to make it there.

However, another incredible feat happened in 1960 that

is largely forgotten today. For the first time in history, on

CLOSE READ

Analyze Structure: Sound Reasoning (LINES 41–56)

COMMON CORE RI 1, RI 8

Point out that Cousteau is making the claim that the end of the space shuttle program is an opportunity for a valuable ocean-exploration program. He supports this claim with **reasons,** logical statements given to support a claim.

B CITE TEXT EVIDENCE Tell students to reread lines 41–56 to name the two main reasons Cousteau gives to support his claim. *(We have (1) "a golden opportunity" and (2) "a pressing need" to explore the oceans.)*

Point out that a solid persuasive argument contains **evidence,** or facts, examples, quotations, experiences, and other pieces of information that support the claim.

C CITE TEXT EVIDENCE Ask students to reread lines 49–51 and identify a piece of evidence in this paragraph that supports one of Cousteau's reasons for ocean exploration. *(The reason that we have a "golden opportunity" is supported by the evidence of "critical medical advances," such as AZT derived from a reef sponge.)*

CRITICAL VOCABULARY

diplomat: The author says that the space shuttle program led to diplomatic firsts. The adjective *diplomatic* describes international relations.

ASK STUDENTS what diplomatic events occurred as a result of the space shuttle trips to the International Space Station. *(Astronauts from different countries worked together on the ISS.)*

sustain: Forms of energy that are sustainable can be used without harming the environment.

ASK STUDENTS how the author feels about sustainable forms of energy. *(He believes that sustainable energy sources are a worthwhile goal.)*

And for the last 50 years, we have largely continued to look up. But that trend may be changing.

In July 2011, the space shuttle program that had promised to revolutionize space travel by making it (relatively)
20 affordable and accessible came to an end after 30 years. Those three decades provided numerous technological, scientific and **diplomatic** firsts. With an estimated price tag of nearly $200 billion, the program had its champions and its detractors. It was, however, a source of pride for the United States, capturing the American spirit of innovation and leadership.

With the iconic space program ending, many people have asked, "What's next? What is the next giant leap in scientific and technological innovation?"

Today a possible answer to that question has been
30 announced. And it does not entail straining our necks to look skyward. Finally, there is a growing recognition that some of the most important discoveries and opportunities for innovation may lie beneath what covers more than 70 percent of our planet—the ocean.

You may think I'm doing my grandfather Jacques Yves-Cousteau and my father Philippe a disservice when I say we've only dipped our toes in the water when it comes to ocean exploration. After all, my grandfather co-invented the modern SCUBA system and "The Undersea World of
40 Jacques Cousteau" introduced generations to the wonders of the ocean. In the decades since, we've only explored about 10 percent of the ocean—an essential resource and complex environment that literally supports life as we know it, life on earth.

We now have a golden opportunity and a pressing need to recapture that pioneering spirit. A new era of ocean exploration can yield discoveries that will help inform everything from critical medical advances to **sustainable** forms of energy. Consider that AZT, an early treatment
50 for HIV, is derived from a Caribbean reef sponge, or that a great deal of energy—from offshore wind, to OTEC (ocean thermal energy conservation), to wind and wave energy—is yet untapped in our oceans. Like unopened presents under the tree, the ocean is a treasure trove of knowledge. In addition, such discoveries will have a tremendous impact on economic growth by creating jobs as well as technologies and goods.

diplomat
(dĭp´lə-măt´) *n.*
A *diplomat* is a person appointed by a government to interact with other governments.

sustain
(sə-stān´) *v.* If things *sustain*, they remain in existence.

WHEN STUDENTS STRUGGLE...

To help students follow Cousteau's argument more clearly, tell them to fill in an outline as they read to track the claim, reasons, and evidence. Have students work in pairs and use an outline with three sections labeled "Thesis," "Key Point," and "Support." In the section labeled "Thesis," have students write Cousteau's claim *(People should devote time and resources to ocean exploration)*. In the "Key Point" section, have students list reasons. In the "Support" section, have students list evidence that supports the key points.

A submersible, a craft designed for deep-sea research, glides just above the ocean floor.

In addition to new discoveries, we also have the opportunity to course correct when it comes to **stewardship** of our oceans. Research and exploration can go hand in glove[1] with resource management and conservation.

Over the last several decades, as the United States has been exploring space, we've **exploited** and polluted our oceans at an alarming rate without dedicating the needed time or resources to truly understand the critical role they play in the future of the planet. It is not trite to say that the oceans are the life support system of this planet, providing us with up to 70 percent of our oxygen, as well as a primary source of protein for billions of people, not to mention the regulation of our climate.

Despite this life-giving role, the world has fished, mined and trafficked the ocean's resources to a point where we are actually seeing dramatic changes that are seriously impacting today's generations. And that impact will continue as the world's population approaches 7 billion people, adding strain to the world's resources unlike any humanity has ever had to face before.

In the long term, destroying our ocean resources is bad business with devastating consequences for the global economy, and the health and sustainability of all

steward
(stōō′ərd) *n.* A *steward* is a person who supervises and manages something.

exploit
(ĕk′sploit′) *v.* If you *exploit* something, you use it selfishly.

---

[1] **hand in glove:** in close combination with something else.

© Ralph White/Corbis

CLOSE READ

Analyze Structure: Sound Reasoning (LINES 57–69)

COMMON CORE RI 1, RI 8

Cousteau presents another reason to support his claim that we should prioritize ocean exploration.

D **CITE TEXT EVIDENCE** Have students reread lines 57–69, identify the reason he gives, and cite evidence that supports his reason. *(Reason: Ocean exploration will help us "course correct" resource use and ocean conservation. Evidence: Oceans have become polluted. Oceans provide oxygen and food and regulate climate.)*

Determine Meanings

COMMON CORE RL 4

(LINE 70)

Tell students that authors of persuasive writing use words that appeal to the emotions.

E **ASK STUDENTS** what impact the words *life-giving role* (line 70) have. *(to show we owe our lives to oceans)*

CRITICAL VOCABULARY

steward: The author says we can correct the course we're taking regarding stewardship of our oceans.

ASK STUDENTS why the author wants us to care about ocean stewardship. *(Because we've harmed the oceans, we're responsible for taking care of them.)*

exploit: The author says we've exploited the ocean.

ASK STUDENTS how people exploit oceans. *(They fish from it, drill for oil from it, and ship goods on it.)*

Strategies for Annotation 🖉 🗐 *Annotate it!*

Determine Meanings

COMMON CORE RI 4

Share these strategies for guided or independent analysis:

- Select a segment to analyze, such as lines 70–76 shown here.
- Highlight in yellow words and phrases that indicate a tone and emotional quality.
- Make a note about the tone these words reveal.

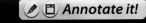

Despite this life-giving role, the world has fished, mined and trafficked the ocean's resources to a point where we are actually seeing dramatic changes that are seriously impacting today's generations. And that impact will continue as the world's population approaches 7 billion people, adding strain to the world's resources unlike any humanity has ever had to

Tone: alarmed, threatening, urgent

Determine Meanings

COMMON CORE RI 1, RI 4

(LINES 87–93)

Tell students that Cousteau uses words to convey a tone of thrilled optimism about future ocean exploration.

 CITE TEXT EVIDENCE Have students identify words and phrases in lines 87–93 that convey Cousteau's attitude. Ask what effect these words are intended to have on readers. *("next big leap"; "exciting and bold"; "'wow' factor"; "dazzling technological feats"; "mystery of the unknown"; "scientific muscle"; "entrepreneurial spirit." All of these words have emotional impact and could inspire people to share the author's viewpoint.)*

Analyze Structure: Sound Reasoning (LINES 94-96)

COMMON CORE RI 8

Tell students that readers of persuasive writing evaluate how convincing the author has been.

G **ASK STUDENTS** to reread the next-to-last paragraph (lines 94–96) and tell what the author implies will happen if people don't "take the plunge." *(He is suggesting that if we don't invest in exploring oceans, they won't "continue to provide life to future generations.")* Ask for ideas about how valid this suggestion is based on reasons and evidence in the commentary. *(Sample answer: This argument is very valid because it shows that our future is tied to the health of the world's oceans.)*

COLLABORATIVE DISCUSSION Have small groups review the text to note statements in which Cousteau tells what he believes should be done. Have students write the reasons and evidence he provides to support his claim, and why his argument is or is not convincing.

ASK STUDENTS to share any questions they generated in the course of reading and discussing the selection.

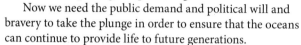

80 creatures—including humans. Marine spatial planning, marine sanctuaries, species conservation, sustainable fishing strategies, and more must be a part of any ocean exploration and conservation program to provide hope of restoring health to our oceans.

While there is still much to learn and discover through space exploration, we also need to pay attention to our unexplored world here on earth. Our next big leap into the unknown can be every bit as exciting and bold as our pioneering work in space. It possesses the same "wow" factor: 90 alien worlds, dazzling technological feats and the mystery of the unknown. The United States has the scientific muscle, the diplomatic know-how and the entrepreneurial[2] spirit to lead the world in exploring and protecting our ocean frontier.

Now we need the public demand and political will and bravery to take the plunge in order to ensure that the oceans can continue to provide life to future generations.

Today is a big step in that direction and hopefully it is just the beginning.

COLLABORATIVE DISCUSSION What does Philippe Cousteau want you to realize after reading this commentary? What does he want you to do? Is his evidence convincing? Talk about your ideas with other group members.

---

[2] **entrepreneurial** (ŏn´trə-prə-nŏŏr´ē-əl): business-starting.

TO CHALLENGE STUDENTS . . .

Compare Two Arguments Have students complete a comparison and contrast analysis of Philippe Cousteau's argument for ocean exploration and John F. Kennedy's argument for space exploration. Students should work independently at first to analyze the arguments. Then, have students work in small groups to discuss their analyses. Students should answer questions similar to those below:

- Which argument is more persuasive and why?
- Which argument follows a clearer, more logical organizational structure?
- Are there any instances of **logical fallacy** (an error in reasoning that starts with a false assumption or mistaken belief) in either of the arguments? Explain.
- How do the arguments appeal to audience emotion, and how effective is this?

Analyze Structure: Sound Reasoning

Strong arguments use sound reasoning and evidence to support any claims. A carefully constructed written argument includes the following elements:

- **claim:** the writer's position on an issue or problem
- **reasons:** logical statements that explain an action or belief
- **evidence:** facts, examples, quotations, experiences, and other pieces of information that support the claim
- **counterargument:** reasons and evidence given to disprove an opposing viewpoint

An argument may appear to be persuasive, but it may be based on faulty reasoning. A **logical fallacy** is an error in reasoning that often starts with a false assumption or mistaken beliefs. Here are a few logical fallacies:

Logical fallacy	Definition	Example
Circular reasoning	Repeating an idea rather than providing evidence.	I am too tied to my cell phone because I can't put it down.
Either/or fallacy	A statement that suggests there are only two choices available in a situation that really offers more than two options.	Either the city should provide recycling bins or throw out the Recycling Act.
Overgeneralization	A generalization that is too broad.	A ballet dancer would be a natural at gymnastics.

Assess the reasoning in an argument by determining whether

- the argument presents a clear claim
- the reasons make sense and are presented in a logical order
- the evidence is valid and adequately supports the claim
- there are no instances of logical fallacies or faulty reasoning

Determine Meanings

The **tone** of a written work expresses the author's attitude toward his or her subject. For example, the tone can be described as angry, sad, or humorous. An author's choice of words, phrases, and details signal the tone of the work.

This sentence from Philippe Cousteau's commentary includes words that reveal his attitude about ocean exploration:

> **We now have a golden opportunity and a pressing need to recapture that pioneering spirit.**

What words in this sentence show an enthusiastic tone?

TEACH

CLOSE READ

Analyze Structure: Sound Reasoning

After reviewing the elements of a well-constructed argument, have students state Cousteau's claim. *(We should invest in exploring and protecting the oceans.)*

After reviewing the logical fallacies in the chart:

- Have students look through the commentary to find the author's references to the space program.
- Have students decide if Cousteau's reasoning is sound or if it uses an either/or fallacy. *(An either/or choice between exploring the ocean or space is implied, when it's possible other options exist. However, there's no logical fallacy because he isn't focused on the choice. He's using comparisons to the space program to structure his argument.)*

Determine Meanings

Review that writing that is intended to persuade often has words that appeal to the emotions. Philippe Cousteau has strong feelings about his subject, which he shares with readers through his choice of words.

Have students identify words that convey an enthusiastic tone in the excerpted sentence. *("golden opportunity," "pressing need," "pioneering spirit")*

Strategies for Annotation   *Annotate it!*

Analyze Structure: Sound Reasoning

Use this excerpt from lines 46–53 and share these strategies for guided or independent analysis:

- Highlight in yellow the reason the author gives for why ocean exploration is important.
- Underline evidence that supports the reason.
- On a note, comment about how persuasive the argument seems.

exploration can yield discoveries that will help inform everything from critical medical advances to sustainable forms of energy. Consider that AZT, an early treatment for HIV, is derived from a Caribbean reef sponge, or that a great deal of energy—from offshore wind, to OTEC (ocean

> AZT point is good evidence; No specific evidence of energy production, just types of energy.

PRACTICE & APPLY

Analyzing the Text

 RI 1, RI 2, RI 4, RI 5, RI 8

Possible answers:

1. *The author compares space exploration with ocean exploration. He is making the point that the same pride, spirit, innovation, and leadership that Americans showed in space exploration can be shown in exploring the next frontier—the oceans.*

2. *The author states his claim in the last sentence. Ocean exploration will lead to discoveries and innovations.*

3. *Examples of support: medical advances such as AZT from marine life; untapped energy sources, such as offshore wind, ocean thermal energy conservation, and wind and wave energy, come from the ocean; discoveries in the ocean will lead to economic growth. The support seems plausible, but predictions are not the same as factual evidence.*

4. *The author's tone is urgent. He is warning about all that can go wrong if we don't act. Warning words include* exploited, polluted, alarming rate, critical role, life support system, strain to the world's resources unlike any humanity has ever had to face before, *and* devastating consequences.

5. *The author looks back to the space program and ahead to an ocean program to point out positive similarities: innovation, pioneering spirit, excitement, new technologies with far-reaching benefits. The author also looks back to the harm caused by our neglect of the oceans and ahead to a devastating future that would result if we continued our neglect.*

6. *The author acknowledges that others might want to continue to invest in the space program, but he argues that "we also need to pay attention to our unexplored world here on Earth." His whole commentary offers support for shifting attention to ocean exploration, though he doesn't directly address objections such as financial costs.*

eBook *Annotate It!*

Analyzing the Text

 RI 1, RI 2, RI 4, RI 5, RI 8, W 7, W 8, SL 1, SL 4

Cite Text Evidence   Support your responses with evidence from the text.

1. **Compare** What comparison does the author develop in the first five paragraphs, and what is his purpose?

2. **Interpret** Reread lines 26–34. Which sentence presents the author's claim? Assess the clearness of the claim by restating it in your own words.

3. **Assess Reasoning** Reread lines 45–56. Do the examples of support seem valid? Explain.

4. **Infer** Reread lines 61–84. What is the author's tone? Which words and phrases in the paragraphs reveal that tone?

5. **Analyze** How does the author describe both past events and future events to persuade readers to agree with him?

6. **Evaluate** Examine lines 85–93. How sound is the author's reasoning here? Explain your assessment.

PERFORMANCE TASK

Speaking Activity: Informal Debate Philippe Cousteau begins by mentioning the 1960 exploration of the Mariana Trench. Would further exploration of this deep-sea region be worthwhile? Divide your group into two teams to informally debate that question.

In an informal debate, speakers from each side take turns presenting and supporting valid claims and countering opposing claims. The whole group can decide on the rules to follow. You may want to use a moderator, for example, and have a time limit for each speaker.

- First, research the Mariana Trench and any attempts to explore it in recent years.
- Investigate the potential for benefits in exploring the region.
- Identify the potential risks involved. Find out if any issues or problems have been reported.
- Listen well to any opponent's points to help you prepare your responses.

PERFORMANCE TASK

COMMON CORE W 7, W 8, SL 1, SL 4

Assign this performance task.

Speaking Activity: Informal Debate Guide students to reliable sources of information about the Mariana Trench. Suggest that students prepare for the debate by

- taking notes in three categories: Facts, Benefits, Risks
- developing a proposition to debate, such as "Exploring the Mariana Trench is a worthwhile effort"
- deciding on a fair way to divide into teams

See the lesson Hold an Informal Debate in Extend and Reteach for additional instructional ideas on holding a debate.

Critical Vocabulary

diplomat	sustain	steward	exploit

Practice and Apply Choose the situation that is the better match with the meaning of the vocabulary word. Give your reasons.

1. **diplomat** **a.** Leaders discuss policy with leaders of other countries.
   b. Political leaders are chosen on Election Day.

2. **sustain** **a.** Laws limit the kinds of fish that can be caught.
   b. Fishing boats overfish local fishing stocks.

3. **steward** **a.** The city ignores its local fishing industry.
   b. Citizens rely on their city to clean up polluted areas.

4. **exploit** **a.** Young children attend school for six hours a day.
   b. Young children work long hours in factories.

Vocabulary Strategy: Prefixes

A **prefix** is a word part added before a word or a root. Readers can use their knowledge of prefixes to analyze words and find familiar parts and relationships. This chart shows two common prefixes.

Prefix	Meaning	Example Words
dis-	not, lack of, opposite of	dishonest, disgrace, disinfect, discourage, dispute, distract
ex-	not, lack of, opposite of	exchange, exhale, exclude, expose, extract, external

Notice the words with prefixes in this sentence from Cousteau's commentary:

> You may think I'm doing my grandfather Jacques Yves-Cousteau and my father Philippe a disservice when I say we've only dipped our toes in the water when it comes to ocean exploration.

You can see that *disservice* has the prefix *dis-*. A disservice is the opposite of a helpful service. The word *exploration* has the prefix *ex-* before a Latin root; the original meaning of the Latin word is "to search out."

Practice and Apply Complete each word with the prefix *dis-* or *ex-*. Check a print or digital dictionary to make sure the word makes sense.

1. People have always ___**ploited** natural resources.

2. Marine animals that are ___**posed** to pollutants may become ill.

3. Overfishing may cause some fish to become ___**tinct**.

4. There are ___**tinct** actions to take to protect oceans.

Critical Vocabulary

Answers: **1.** *a;* **2.** *a;* **3.** *b;* **4.** *b*

Vocabulary Strategy: Prefixes

1. *exploited*

2. *exposed*

3. *extinct*

4. *distinct*

Vocabulary Strategy: Prefixes

Have students use their eBook annotation tools to analyze words with *dis-* and *ex-* on page 196:

- Highlight the word.
- Underline the target prefix.
- On a note, give a meaning for the word that includes a meaning for the prefix.
- Check their ideas in a print or digital dictionary. Adjust the note as needed.

While there is still much to learn and discover through space exploration, we also need to pay attention to our unexplored world here on earth. Our next big leap into the unknown can be every bit as exciting and bold as our pioneering work in space. It possesses the same "wow" factor:

> discover: to reveal, as in "the opposite of cover"

PRACTICE & APPLY

Language Conventions: Adjective Clauses

 COMMON CORE L 1a

Use the example sentences in the instructional segments of the lesson to clarify that an adjective clause modifies a noun or a pronoun, just as a single adjective does:

- However, another incredible feat happened in 1960 that is largely forgotten today. (modifies the noun *feat*)
- Lt. Don Walsh and Jacques Piccard descended to Challenger Deep, which is the deepest part of the ocean. (modifies the proper noun *Challenger Deep*)
- Jacques Piccard, who was a Swiss engineer, developed underwater vehicles. (modifies the proper noun *Jacques Piccard*)
- More people know about the astronauts who traveled to the moon than about these two explorers. (modifies the noun *astronauts*)

Sample answers for Practice and Apply:

1. *Scientists who want to learn about weather patterns study the ocean.*

2. *Ocean exploration will be the next giant leap that will bring new technologies to everyone.*

3. *Discoveries about ocean life will affect everyone who lives on planet Earth.*

4. *Our pioneering spirit, which led us to the Moon, is still strong.*

 Assess It!

Online Selection Test
- Download an editable ExamView bank.
- Assign and manage this test online.

Language Conventions: Adjective Clauses

 COMMON CORE L 1a

An **adjective** is a part of speech that modifies a noun or a pronoun. It answers the question *What kind? Which?* or *How many?* A **clause** is a group of words that has a subject and a predicate—the two main parts of a complete sentence. An **adjective clause** acts like an adjective to modify a noun or pronoun in the rest of the sentence.

In an adjective clause, the subject is often a **relative pronoun**—a pronoun that relates, or connects, adjective clauses to the words they modify in a sentence. Relative pronouns include *who, whom, whose, which,* and *that.* Notice the relative pronoun in this sentence from "Why Exploring the Ocean Is Mankind's Next Giant Leap":

> However, another incredible feat happened in 1960 that is largely forgotten today.

The relative pronoun *that* introduces the adjective clause *that is largely forgotten today.* The clause modifies the noun *feat,* answering the question *What kind of feat?*

When you write, you can use adjective clauses to tell more about a noun or a pronoun in a sentence. The adjective clause is underlined in each of these sentences.

> Lt. Don Walsh and Jacques Piccard descended to Challenger Deep, which is the deepest part of the ocean. (The adjective clause tells more about *Challenger Deep.*)

> Jacques Piccard, who was a Swiss engineer, developed underwater vehicles. (The adjective clause tells more about *Jacques Piccard.*)

> More people know about the astronauts who traveled to the moon than about these two explorers. (The adjective clause tells more about *astronauts.*)

Practice and Apply Use the relative pronoun in parentheses to introduce an adjective clause that tells about the underlined noun or pronoun. Write the new sentence.

1. Scientists study the ocean. (who)

2. Ocean exploration will be the next giant leap. (that)

3. Discoveries about ocean life will affect everyone. (who)

4. Our pioneering spirit is still strong. (which)

Hold an Informal Debate

COMMON CORE SL 1, SL 3, SL 4

TEACH

To help students prepare for the Performance Task, offer information about debates. Display these terms and definitions:

- **proposition**: A positively worded statement, or claim, that can clearly be supported or opposed.
- **affirmative speaker**: A debater who supports the proposition.
- **negative speaker**: A debater who opposes the proposition.
- **case**: A group of arguments on either the affirmative or negative side.
- **rebuttal**: A speech that attacks the opponent's stated arguments and evidence.

Explain that to make a persuasive case debaters need to research the facts and learn about differing viewpoints on the issue. In planning their arguments, each team must prepare to rebut the arguments and evidence of the opposing side.

Explain that a formal debate has rules about the numbers of speakers and the content and sequence of speeches. Though an informal debate is organized more loosely, debaters still follow rules for speaking and listening. Display and discuss the following:

When speaking, remember to

- choose words that help you convey a confident, convincing tone
- speak loudly, calmly, and clearly
- avoid *ums*, *likes*, and *y'knows*
- rebut politely, without sarcasm or personal attacks

When listening, remember to

- take notes about the points made
- listen for reasons and evidence that can be disputed
- not interrupt

PRACTICE AND APPLY

Direct students to this sentence in line 23 of Cousteau's commentary, in which he notes opposing viewpoints about the space shuttle program:

> With an estimated price tag of nearly $200 billion, the program had its champions and its detractors.

Ask the group to come up with a proposition that would belong in a debate on this issue. *(Example: The space shuttle program was worth its $200 billion cost.)* Assign the role of a champion or a detractor to each student. Have students demonstrate making affirmative and negative statements that could belong in a debate.

Determine Meanings

COMMON CORE RI 4

RETEACH

Display a short descriptive sentence, such as "The door is shut." Have students read it using different tones of voice, such as annoyed, playful, worried, angry, hopeful, pleased. Explain that just as a tone of voice expresses feelings, written words express an author's feelings about a subject. Tell students that examples of tones in a written work include angry, humorous, admiring, annoyed, urgent, and enthusiastic.

Point out that an author chooses words carefully to convey just the right tone. Display these two sentences for students to compare. Prompt students to identify the words with emotional impact and name the tone in each.

- The dark, mysterious ocean holds hidden dangers. *(threatening, advising)*
- The ocean depths startle us with amazing things. *(surprised, intrigued)*

 LEVEL UP TUTORIALS Assign the following *Level Up* tutorial: **Tone**

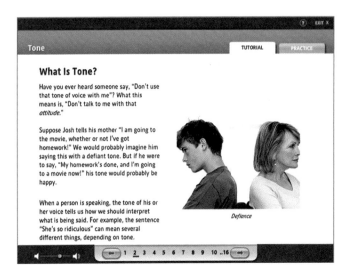

CLOSE READING APPLICATION

Show students typical persuasive texts, such as editorials, blogs, and advertisements. Have students identify words that appeal to emotion and use an adjective to describe the general tone.

Living in the Dark

Science Article by Cheryl Bardoe

Why This Text?

Nonfiction articles are a main way to learn about our world. Understanding how an author structures an article and learning to determine central ideas and details will help students critically analyze texts. This lesson examines text structure and asks students to identify and paraphrase central ideas and important details.

▶ **View It!**

Professional Development Podcast:

Informational Text

Key Learning Objective: The student will be able to analyze the structure of an informational text and paraphrase central ideas and details.

For practice and application:

Background *Elisabeth Rosenthal (born 1956) is a medical doctor and an award-winning journalist. Before Rosenthal was named science editor for the New York Times, she worked as a reporter in Beijing, China, where she broke landmark stories on health in China. In this article, she writes about swarms of jellyfish in the waters off the coast of Barcelona, Spain, and explores what their growing numbers tell us about the health of the world's oceans.*

Stinging Tentacles Offer Hint of Ocean's Decline
Newspaper Article by Elisabeth Rosenthal

Close Reader selection
"Stinging Tentacles Offer Hint to Oceans' Decline,"
Science Article by Elisabeth Rosenthal

COMMON CORE Common Core Standards

RI 1 Cite textual evidence.
RI 2 Determine central ideas in a text; provide an objective summary.
RI 3 Analyze interactions between individuals, events, and ideas.
RI 4 Determine technical meanings.
RI 5 Analyze the structure an author uses.
RI 6 Determine an author's purpose.
W 1 Write arguments to support claims.
W 4 Produce clear and coherent writing appropriate to purpose and audience.
W 8 Gather relevant information and paraphrase the data and conclusions.
W 10 Write routinely.
L 1a Explain the function of phrases.
L 4a Use context.
L 4b Use Greek roots.
L 4c Consult reference materials to clarify meaning.
L 6 Acquire and use academic and domain-specific words.

▲ Text Complexity Rubric

Quantitative Measures	**Living in the Dark** Lexile: 1200L
Qualitative Measures	**Levels of Meaning/Purpose** ●—●—●—●—●→ more than one purpose; implied
	Structure ●—●—●—●—●→ mostly implied cause-and-effect structure; simple graphics, supplementary to understanding
	Language Conventionality and Clarity ●—●—●—●—●→ fairly straightforward sentence structure; many unfamiliar domain-specific words
	Knowledge Demands ●—●—●—●—●→ complex science concepts
Reader/Task Considerations	Teacher determined Vary by individual reader and type of text

CLOSE READ

Background Have students read the background and information about the author. Tell students that even with early submarine technology scientists were able to travel only a limited distance into the oceans' depths. In the 1970s, however, new technologies set deep-sea exploration on a remarkable trajectory. Explain that scientists often have to re-evaluate their theories and beliefs based on new evidence. This article provides a good example of that process.

SETTING A PURPOSE Direct students to use the Setting a Purpose prompt to focus their reading. Remind them to write down their own questions as they read.

Analyze Structure

(HEADING ABOVE LINE 1)

Explain to students that authors often use text features such as **headings** to organize information. The heading that precedes a section of an article can give readers an idea of what the section is about. Suggest that students turn headings into questions to help figure out what information will follow.

Ⓐ ASK STUDENTS what they think this first section of the article will be about based on the heading. *(The heading suggests that the section will tell what happens when a whale "falls," or dies and drops to the bottom of the ocean.)*

Background *For many years, it was nearly impossible to study life at the bottom of our oceans. Therefore, very little was known about deep-sea habitats. But recent 20th-century technological advances have allowed scientists to begin to discover surprising forms of life in the ocean depths. In her writing,* **Cheryl Bardoe** *likes to draw back the curtain to reveal how scientists explore the unknown. She presently lives in Chicago, Illinois, where she once worked at the city's famous Field Museum of Natural History.*

from
Living in the Dark

Science Article by Cheryl Bardoe

SETTING A PURPOSE As you read, notice how scientific study has altered past beliefs about Earth's oceans. Write down any questions you have while reading.

When a Whale Falls

Imagine the moment when a great blue whale, undernourished and exhausted from migrating, grunts out its last breath somewhere in the Pacific Ocean.

Then, as the pressure of the surrounding water squeezes the last air reserves from the whale's lungs, this massive creature begins to sink.

It plunges 700 feet (200 meters) through the ocean's top layer, the warm "sunlight zone" where algae kick-start life's food chain with photosynthesis. It drops another 2,600 10 feet (800 meters) through the cold twilight zone, where no plants live and fish have extra-large eyes to catch the faintest glimmers of sun. It descends down, down, down through 3,300 feet (1 kilometer) or more of the midnight zone. Here, temperatures hover close to freezing; deep-sea creatures must

---

SCAFFOLDING FOR ELL STUDENTS

Analyze Language Using a whiteboard, project lines 7–9. Highlight the word *photosynthesis* and explain that it is the first of a number of science terms used in the article. Model using context and word parts to help students understand that photosynthesis is a process plants use to convert light energy from the sun into chemical energy. Discuss why photosynthesis occurs only in the ocean's top layer.

ASK STUDENTS to use this strategy to help them understand other science terms in the article, such as *habitat, bacteria,* and *ecosystem*. Explain that if students can't figure out the meaning from context and word parts, they can consult a dictionary or a science reference source.

Determine Central Ideas and Details (LINES 24–32)

 COMMON CORE RI 2, RI 3

Explain to students that **paraphrasing,** or restating information in your own words, is an effective strategy to help them understand complex ideas in a text.

B **ASK STUDENTS** to reread lines 24–32 and paraphrase the description of the whale fall. *(Sample answer: A variety of deep-sea creatures come to feed upon the fallen whale body. Some eat the outside flesh, and others eat the carcass from within. The whale fall becomes a habitat for all these diverse creatures.)*

CRITICAL VOCABULARY

cache: The author describes the whale carcass as a "cache of resources" for a variety of deep-sea creatures.

ASK STUDENTS what the author's use of this phrase suggests. *(The phrase conveys that the wealth of food provided by the whale carcass is hidden or inaccessible. It suggests a hidden or buried treasure.)*

geyser: The author chose to use the more familiar word *geyser* as a way to help readers understand hydrothermal vents.

ASK STUDENTS how a hydrothermal vent is like a geyser. *(It leaks natural gas into the ocean, the way a geyser shoots hot water and steam into the air.)*

---

flash their own lights to break the darkness; and the weight of the water feels like about 500 bowling balls pressing in on every square inch of the whale's carcass.

The tiny flecks of dead plankton that are called marine snow may drift for months before reaching the ocean floor. But this great blue whale plummets so quickly that scavengers barely get a nibble. Its 160-ton carcass thumps down nearly intact, depositing as many nutrients as several thousand years' worth of marine snow—all in one fell swoop.

B This **cache** of resources, called a whale fall, will become the center of a unique habitat. First, it attracts deep-sea scavengers. Hagfish—unsightly creatures also called slime eels—wriggle inside the carcass and begin to eat it from the inside out. Squat lobsters, sleeper sharks, and crabs tear at the whale's flesh and scatter crumbs into nearby sediments. Then mollusks colonize those sediments. Meanwhile, fantastical worms, slugs, and bacteria bore into the whale's bones to feast on fatty marrow.

Finally come bacteria that transform the chemicals leaking out of the decaying bones into food for themselves and others. Much as plants use energy from the sun to make their own nourishment, these "chemosynthetic" bacteria use energy from chemical reactions to create the basic building blocks of life. Within months this whale carcass may support more than 40,000 creatures; it might keep this chemosynthetic ecosystem going for up to a century.

The living things that take up residence on this whale fall are similar to those that live near undersea **geysers** (called hydrothermal vents) or cracks that leak natural gas into the ocean (called cold seeps). Together, these three habitats have completely changed how scientists think about the basic rules for life.

cache
(kăsh) *n.* A *cache* is an amount of something that has been hidden away.

geyser
(gī´zər) *n.* A *geyser* is a natural hot spring that shoots hot water and steam into the air.

Life Where Life Isn't Possible

For most of human history, the ocean's secrets have been beyond reach. Gazing across the water's rippling surface, who could have guessed what truly lay beneath? In the 1840s, British naturalist Edward Forbes dredged the Aegean Sea[1] 100 times to find out. The deeper his device went, the less it

---

[1] **Aegean Sea** (ĭ-jē´ən sē): an arm of the Mediterranean Sea between Greece and Turkey.

Strategies for Annotation 🖉 📘 Annotate it!

Determine Central Ideas and Details

COMMON CORE RI 2

Share these strategies for guided or independent analysis.

- As you read, highlight in yellow central ideas.
- Underline the details that support them.
- Use the text you've annotated to paraphrase, or restate the information in your own words.

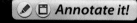

This cache of resources, called a whale fall, will become the center of a unique habitat. <u>First, it attracts deep-sea scavengers.</u> Hagfish— unsightly creatures also called slime eels—wriggle inside the carcass and begin to eat it from the inside out. . . . <u>Then mollusks colonize those sediments.</u> Meanwhile, fantastical worms, slugs, and bacteria <u>bore into the whale's bones</u> to feast on fatty marrow.

dragged up, and Forbes concluded that nothing at all lived below 1,600 feet (500 meters) deep. This theory fit perfectly with what others had observed on land. If the extreme climates of the Arctic and high mountain peaks snuffed out life, then the cold, dark, deep sea must be empty too.

> ❝ **Within months this whale carcass may support more than 40,000 creatures.** ❞

Over the next century, people challenged this theory. Corals were hauled up from 2,500 feet (750 meters) deep; starfish and oysters were gathered from 7,500 feet
60 (2,300 meters). One expedition collected 4,700 new species from as deep as 16,000 feet (5,000 meters)—that's more than three miles underwater! Because photosynthesis isn't possible at such depths, scientists decided that marine snow provided the base of the food chain for these animals. Sure, they acknowledged, life was possible in the deep sea. But scientists assumed that life forms living off such scraps would be **meager**. And so they continued to believe that life couldn't survive in the most extreme ocean-floor conditions.

Then everything changed.
70 In 1977, a team of geologists squeezed into the research mini-sub called *Alvin,* hoping to confirm whether geysers (like Old Faithful in Yellowstone National Park) existed on the ocean floor. The hydrothermal vents were there, all right. So was a "Garden of Eden,"[2] as the scientists called it, of mussels, anemones, and 7-foot (2-meter) worms with crimson, feather-like plumes. The stunned researchers gathered samples and called biologists at the Woods Hole Oceanographic Institute (WHOI) in Massachusetts.

meager
(mē´gər) *adj.* If something is *meager,* it is small or deficient in quantity.

---
[2] **Garden of Eden:** the garden that was the first home of Adam and Eve according to the Bible.

from Living in the Dark   **203**

TEACH

CLOSE READ

Analyze Structure

(LINES 62–68)

Explain that writers of science articles often use a **cause-and-effect** structure to show relationships between events and concepts. This helps readers understand how the first event, the **cause,** leads to one or more **effects. Signal words,** such as *because, since,* and *therefore,* help readers identify cause-and-effect relationships.

Ⓒ CITE TEXT EVIDENCE Have students reread lines 62–68. Ask students to explain the cause-and-effect relationship and to cite the words that signal it. *(Cause: Photosynthesis isn't possible at very great ocean depths. Effects: Scientists believed that marine snow [flecks of dead plankton] was the main source of food there. They also assumed that only "meager" life forms could survive. Signal words: "Because," "And so.")*

> **CRITICAL VOCABULARY**
>
> **meager:** The author uses the word *meager* to describe how few life forms scientists expected to find on the ocean floor.
>
> **ASK STUDENTS** why the scientists believed that life forms on the ocean floor would be meager. *(Scientists assumed that there wasn't enough food available to sustain a multitude of life forms.)*

ACADEMIC VOCABULARY

complex	rely

As you discuss the text, incorporate the following Collection 4 academic vocabulary words: *complex* and *rely.* Note that the author discusses a number of **complex** scientific processes, and suggest that paraphrasing is a way to help understand the concepts. Point out how interconnected the deep-sea environment is, and ask students to describe some of the ways the creatures **rely** on each other to survive.

Analyze Structure

COMMON CORE — RI 1, RI 3, RI 5

(LINES 79–86)

Remind students that a cause-and-effect pattern of organization shows the relationship between events or ideas.

D CITE TEXT EVIDENCE Have students reread lines 79–86. Ask students to cite the causes of scientists' ideas about life on Earth being "suddenly turned upside down." *("Scientists had found an ecosystem that didn't rely on the sun for energy"; creatures were "thriving in a place that would be toxic for any other known organisms.")*

CRITICAL VOCABULARY

tectonic: The author introduces a geological term, *tectonic plates*, to help explain what hydrothermal vents are and how they occur.

ASK STUDENTS what other kinds of geological events might result from the shifting of tectonic plates. *(earthquakes, volcanoes)*

On the sea floor, a spider crab, mussels, and worms are revealed by the light of a submersible vehicle.

 80 "It was predicted that vents would exist," explains Santiago Herrera, a biologist currently working at WHOI. "What wasn't predicted was that there would be anything living there." Scientists had found an ecosystem that didn't rely on the sun for energy. Not only that, but its inhabitants were thriving in a place that would be toxic for any other known organism. Ideas about the origins and requirements for life on Earth were suddenly turned upside down.

Hydrothermal Vents

You can often find undersea volcanic activity where Earth's **tectonic** plates are pulling apart. As the planet's crust stretches thin, molten rock breaks through to create new 90 crust. Meanwhile, water soaks into the crust through nearby cracks, dissolving rocks and heating up to temperatures of 660 degrees Fahrenheit (350 degrees Celsius) before rising again through a "chimney" on the ocean floor. When the mineral-rich, super-hot water from the geyser meets the oxygen-rich, frigid water of the deep sea, a chemical reaction is triggered that forms hydrogen sulfide. This smells like rotten eggs and looks like black smoke spewing into the ocean.

tectonic
(těk-tŏn´ĭk) *adj.*
If something is *tectonic*, it relates to the deformation of Earth's rocky crust.

©l. MacDonald/National Oceanic And Atmospheric Administration (NOAA)

204 Collection 4

WHEN STUDENTS STRUGGLE . . .

Help students understand the complex processes described in the text by using a graphic organizer like the one shown. Direct students to reread lines 87–93. Have students work in pairs to fill out the chart to show the chain of causes and effects that creates a hydrothermal vent. Explain that each new effect the author mentions becomes the cause of the next one. When they have finished, have students use the chart to paraphrase the process.

Scientists now know that some bacteria release energy by
breaking down these sulfides spewing from the geysers. These
100 same bacteria then harness that energy to turn carbon dioxide
and oxygen from the ocean water into sugars—that is, food
energy. Ta-da! Here's the foundation for an entire deep-sea
food chain.

These chemosynthetic bacteria may be food for other
creatures themselves, or may live in symbiosis[3] with other
deep-sea dwellers. The giant tube worms, for example, have no
mouths or stomachs, but get their food by hosting billions of
bacteria within their bodies. Many clams and mussels living
near these vents get their food the same way.

110 Hydrothermal vents have been a constant source of
surprises, ranging from the single-celled microbe that actually
lives *inside* a vent (and tolerates temperatures of 250 degrees
Fahrenheit, or 120 degrees Celsius) to the white crab with such
furry arms that it was dubbed the "yeti crab."

Cold Seeps

Scientists discovered a second type of deep-sea chemosynthetic
habitat in 1984. This time, bacteria were breaking down the
hydrogen sulfide and methane that oozed from cracks in
the ocean floor near Monterey Bay, California. Scientists
have since identified three sources for these "cold seep"
120 communities: large deposits of oil or natural gas beneath the
seabed; deep trenches created by one tectonic plate sinking
below another; and undersea landslides or erosion that expose
chemical deposits in the seabed.

Cold seep communities play a major role in shaping
Earth's climate, Herrera says. "If they did not exist, a lot of
methane would end up in the atmosphere." Without bacteria
breaking down methane from the ocean floor, this greenhouse
gas[4] would escape from the ocean and make Earth warmer.

Cold seep habitats develop like those at hydrothermal
130 vents do, but with different species. Chemosynthetic bacteria
arrive first, forming large white mats on the sea floor. Crabs
and shrimp come to scavenge dead bacteria, and mussels
arrive that live with symbiotic bacteria. Over time, the

---

[3] **symbiosis** (sĭm´bē-ō´sĭs): a relationship between two living things that benefits
both of them.

[4] **greenhouse gas:** a gas in the atmosphere that traps heat.

CLOSE READ

Determine Central Ideas and Details (LINES 98–103)

 COMMON CORE RI 2, RI 3

In lines 98–103, the author describes the key process
that creates the deep-sea food chain.

E **ASK STUDENTS** to reread lines 98–103 and
paraphrase the chemical process that creates the
deep-sea food chain. *(Possible answer: Bacteria around
the geysers break down sulfides. They use the energy this
releases to turn carbon dioxide and oxygen into sugars,
which form the basis of the food chain.)*

Analyze Structure

COMMON CORE RI 1, RI 3, RI 5

(LINES 129–138)

In the section "Cold Seeps," the author provides
a range of information about a deep-sea
chemosynthetic habitat discovered in 1984. She
organizes this information in a number of paragraphs
showing cause-and-effect relationships, in which one
event brings about, or causes, another.

F **CITE TEXT EVIDENCE** Have students reread
lines 129–138 and cite the cause-and-effect structure
of the paragraph. *(cause: chemosynthetic bacteria
arrive; effect: large white mats form on the sea floor;
effect: crabs and shrimp come to scavenge on dead
bacteria, and muscles arrive; effect: carbonate produced
by the bacteria gives tube worms a better grip; effect:
tube worms build up branches; effect: other organisms
live in the tube worm branches)*

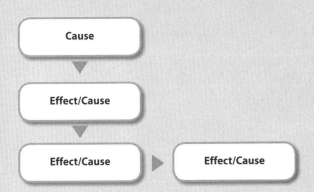

Cause

↓

Effect/Cause

↓

Effect/Cause ▶ Effect/Cause

Determine Central Ideas and Details

 COMMON CORE RI 2, RI 3

(HEADING; LINES 139–155)

Remind students that readers can use headings in a text to help identify central ideas.

 ASK STUDENTS to reread lines 139–155 under the heading "Whale Bones, Stepping Stones" and to paraphrase the explanation of how whale bones act as stepping stones. *(Some species travel long distances from one deep-sea habitat to another. Scientists think that they may use whale falls as "stepping stones," or stops along the way, on this journey.)*

Analyze Language

 COMMON CORE RI 4, L 4a

(LINES 152–153)

Point out that the scientist Craig Smith uses the word *specialists* in an unusual way. Explain that students can use context clues, or the words and phrases surrounding a word that provide hints, to determine the word's meaning.

ASK STUDENTS to reread lines 152–153 and to use context to determine what Smith means by "specialists." Ask how this differs from the ordinary use of the word. *(In this context,* specialists *refers to species that are particularly well suited for life in a certain type of habitat. The context clues "In each habitat" and "Some species" hint that the meaning has to do with animal species and not "human experts in a field," which is a more common meaning. The overall topic of the paragraph also hints at a discussion about animals and not human "specialists.")*

CRITICAL VOCABULARY

decompose: The author describes what happens to the fat found in whale bones.

ASK STUDENTS to describe what happens when the fats in the whale bones are decomposed. *(The bacteria that decompose the fat give off hydrogen sulfides, which attract species that live off the sulfides.)*

---

chemosynthetic bacteria produce a hard material called carbonate, which offers tube worms a firmer ground to grip than the muddy sea floor. Then tube worms build up their hard, protective branches, providing living space for even more organisms.

Whale Bones, Stepping Stones

140 So far, whales are the only animals we know of that can affect life on the ocean floor the same way shifting tectonic plates do. Besides their hefty size, whales are unique in that fats make up 60 percent of their bone weight. (For comparison, humans are born with almost no fat in their bones.) In life, this bone fat helps whales float and store energy. In death, these fats are **decomposed** by bacteria that give off hydrogen sulfide—sound familiar? Once the chemosynthetic community that lives off these sulfides is in full swing, whale falls host an average of 185 different species—the highest number yet observed in such deep-sea communities.

150 Whale falls might explain how species travel across vast ocean spaces from one hydrothermal vent or cold seep to the next. "There are specialists in each habitat, but there is also overlap," says Craig Smith, a professor at the University of Hawaii, who discovered the first whale fall in 1987. "Some species may use whale falls as stepping stones."

Smith says that seeing the same kinds of communities at hydrothermal vents, cold seeps, and whale falls shows us how connected the oceans really are. "The connectivity is across widespread spaces from seemingly isolated habitats."

At the Whims of the Waves

160 Thirty-five years have passed since the discovery of the first hydrothermal vent—but study of the deep sea has really just begun. The main obstacle is getting there.

Fieldwork in the ocean requires tremendous resources. For starters, scientists need a ship and a crew. Reaching a field site may take weeks at sea. Then scientists need high-tech equipment to open a window onto the watery world. Even if everything comes together, success is at the whims of weather and waves. Herrera remembers one expedition where an unmanned, remotely operated vehicle (called an ROV) drifted

170 into the wrong place at the wrong time and was destroyed

decompose
(dē´kəm-pōz´) *v.*
When things
decompose, they
decay and break
down into their basic
parts.

The *Alvin* submersible begins its descent under water.

by the ship's propellers. "Every time you put something overboard on a ship," he says, "it's basically a miracle that you get it back."

Under such conditions, scientists must balance the thrill of discovery with persistence and patience. Smith knows what that's like. His team discovered the first whale fall at the tail end of the last *Alvin* dive on a research trip. "Within ten minutes of *Alvin's* return, we knew what we had," he says, "but we had to wait a year to get back and investigate it."

180   Fortunately, improvements in technology are giving scientists more ocean access than ever. In 2010, Herrera sailed to the Coral Triangle, near Indonesia. This is the most diverse marine ecosystem on the planet, and scientists wonder if the deep-sea communities underlying the coral reefs there might be the reason. Herrera was one of only a few scientists on the ship, but video footage of his ROV dives was transmitted to Massachusetts, Maryland, and Washington, plus Canada

©Gavin Eppard/National Oceanic And Atmospheric Administration (NOAA)

CLOSE READ

Analyze Structure

COMMON CORE **RI 5**

(photo and caption above line 171)

Explain that visual elements such as photos, maps, or graphics can add to or clarify information in the text. Captions help to identify or explain the visual.

I ASK STUDENTS what the photo shows and why the author might have included it. *(It shows the submersible* Alvin *beginning its descent; it is included to clarify for readers what the submarine looks like and how small it is.)*

Cite Evidence (LINES 174–179)

COMMON CORE **RI 1**

Tell students that in lines 174–175 the author draws a **conclusion,** or makes a statement based on evidence and experience, about scientific exploration: "scientists must balance the thrill of discovery with persistence and patience."

J CITE TEXT EVIDENCE Have students reread lines 174–179 and cite text evidence in the paragraph that supports the author's conclusion. *(Smith was part of a team that discovered the first whale fall at the bottom of the ocean, but he had to wait a year before he could return and investigate.)*

CLOSE READ

Analyze Structure

COMMON CORE

RI 1,
RI 3,
RI 5

(LINES 190–200)

Explain to students that cause-and-effect patterns of organization are not always explicit, or clearly stated. Sometimes readers need to infer the relationship based on evidence in the text.

K **CITE TEXT EVIDENCE** Have students closely reread lines 190–200. Ask what cause-and-effect relationship they can infer and what evidence supports their inference. *(Because of the amazing discoveries made on this expedition, and because there is so much left to discover, scientists will return to study the area. Evidence: "The goal . . . was to identify places worth returning to"; "saw far more than they expected"; "We suspect this is one of the areas of highest biodiversity on Earth"; "Scientists will definitely be going back")*

COLLABORATIVE DISCUSSION Have groups of students discuss the recent discoveries about the ocean and scientists' reactions to them. Encourage students to write notes as they talk. Then, have each group share their ideas with the class.

ASK STUDENTS to share any questions they generated in the course of reading and discussing the selection.

---

and Indonesia. Dozens of scientists worldwide witnessed and discussed the dives as if they were all present on the ship.

190   The goal of this expedition was to explore unseen waters and identify places worth returning to for in-depth research. Scientists saw far more than they expected. Monitoring video from most exploratory dives means watching hours of flat and empty (which is to say, boring) seabed scroll by, hoping to spot something exciting. But on this expedition, Herrera says, "we were never bored because we were constantly seeing amazing species. We suspect this is one of the areas of highest biodiversity[5] on Earth." Scientists will definitely be going back—just as soon as they can find the money to fund

200 another expedition.

    To date, scientists have identified more than 1,300 species in deep-sea chemosynthetic habitats. These organisms have introduced us to completely new ways of life and expanded our view of how adaptable life can be. Yet they raise as many questions as they answer. Smith predicts that scientists will find life popping up in even more surprising locations: "We haven't exhausted the list of processes that create these kinds of ecosystems."

    The oceans cover 70 percent of Earth's surface, yet less

210 than 5 percent of this resource has been explored. "This is definitely worth investing your whole life to study," Herrera says.

COLLABORATIVE DISCUSSION The author tells how scientists react to evidence that challenges ideas they had long accepted as possibilities. How have scientists reacted to the discoveries of deep-sea habitats? Talk about your ideas with other group members.

---

[5] **biodiversity:** the range of living things within an environment.

TO CHALLENGE STUDENTS . . .

Make Connections The article "Living in the Dark" illustrates how scientists sometimes must change their beliefs and assumptions in the light of new evidence.

ASK STUDENTS to discuss in small groups other examples of scientists re-evaluating their beliefs, such as in the study of outer space or in medical research. Direct students to analyze the cause of each re-evaluation and what additional effects it might have. Suggest that students do some brief research to prepare for the discussion.

Analyze Structure

 COMMON CORE RI 3, RI 5

Science writing usually presents relationships between events or ideas. Events can show **cause-and-effect relationships,** in which one event brings about, or causes, the other. The event that happens first is the **cause;** the one that follows is the **effect.**

Readers of science writing can grasp cause-and-effect relationships by thinking about what happens and why. One of the main clues readers can look for are **signal words.** Words or phrases that signal causes are *due to, because of,* or *since.* Words or phrases that signal effects are *as a result, therefore,* and *led to.* Sometimes the cause-and-effect relationship is not obvious, and readers must look deeper for **implied** causes and effects. This involves making inferences based on clues in the text.

Organizing information into a chart can help you to connect causes and effects. This chart shows a cause-and-effect chain based on ideas in the section "Cold Seeps" of the excerpt from "Living in the Dark."

Cause	Effect	Effect	Effect
cold seep communities form	bacteria break down hydrogen sulfide and methane	methane can't escape from ocean floor	potential global warming is reduced

Reread lines 1–13 from the section "When a Whale Falls." Organize the information into a chart that shows a cause-and-effect chain.

Determine Central Ideas and Details

 COMMON CORE RI 2, RI 3

Paraphrasing is the restating of information in your own words. When you read science texts, you may encounter complex ideas and new vocabulary. To check your understanding, use paraphrasing to restate the language in the text. For example, reread lines 33–40 of the excerpt from "Living in the Dark." Then read this paraphrase of the sentence comparing green plants and deep-sea bacteria:

> **Plants make their own food using the sun's energy, but these "chemosynthetic" bacteria use chemical energy to make food.**

Look back at lines 33–40 again. Tell what a "chemosynthetic ecosystem" is in your own words.

TEACH

CLOSE READ

Analyze Structure

 COMMON CORE RI 3, RI 5

To help students understand how to identify cause-and-effect relationships, explain that it is sometimes easier to identify the effect first and then examine the text for the causes. Also point out that the cause is not always the first event mentioned in the text. To understand the cause-and-effect relationship, readers need to think about how the events are related.

Have students study the sample cause-and-effect chain. Then, direct them to reread lines 1–13 and create a similar chain to show the cause-and-effect relationship. *(cause: the whale becomes undernourished and exhausted from migration —> effect: the whale dies —> effect: water pressure squeezes the last air from the whale's lungs —> effect: the whale carcass begins to sink)*

Determine Central Ideas and Details

 COMMON CORE RI 2, RI 3

Remind students that they can paraphrase, or use their own words, to help them understand confusing or complex parts of a text. Have students study the sample paraphrase and compare it to the author's original text. Next, have students reread lines 33–40 and paraphrase the explanation of "chemosynthetic ecosystem."

(Possible answer: A chemosynthetic ecosystem is a community of life forms that depend directly and indirectly on the whale carcass for food.)

Strategies for Annotation   🖊 🗔 *Annotate it!*

Analyze Structure

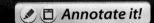 COMMON CORE RI 3, RI 5

Share these strategies for guided or independent analysis:

- Highlight in yellow the effects.
- Underline causes the author gives for those effects.
- Use your annotations to help you paraphrase the cause-and-effect relationships.

In life, this bone fat helps whales float and store energy. In death, these fats are decomposed by bacteria that give off hydrogen sulfide—sound familiar? Once the chemosynthetic community that lives off these sulfides is in full swing, whale falls host an average of 185 different species—the highest yet observed in such deep-sea communities.

Analyzing the Text

COMMON CORE RI 1, RI 2, RI 3, RI 5, RI 6

Possible answers:

1. *The carcass on the ocean bottom supports animals that feed on the whale's flesh. Bacteria give off hydrogen sulfide as they decompose the fats in the whale's bones. Hydrogen sulfide, in turn, powers a chemosynthetic community that can live for up to a century.*

2. *cause: water soaks into cracks in Earth's stretched crust —> effect: water dissolves rocks, becomes very hot, and rises through a chimney formation —> effect: minerals in hot water meet oxygen in frigid water —> effect: hydrogen sulfide forms*

3. *The three habitats are whale falls, hydrothermal vents, and cold seeps. All the habitats are on the ocean floor. All are sources of chemosynthetic ecosystems—varied life forms that don't depend on sunlight for food. At the bottom of each food chain in these habitats are bacteria that produce food from sulfides.*

4. *The bacteria that make food energy from sulfides may become food for other living things, or they may live inside the bodies of other living things and produce food there.*

5. *Until scientists found thriving communities around hydrothermal vents, they believed that life in the deep ocean would be meager. Scientists thought that photosynthesis was the basis for every food chain, and that deep-sea life would depend on marine snow for food. At the vents, they found an entirely new kind of food chain, built on chemicals, in an area that would be toxic to most organisms on Earth.*

6. *The author has quoted biologist Santiago Herrera throughout the article, so another quotation brings the article to a close. In addition, his comment captures the excitement that the author wants to convey about exploration of the deep sea.*

 eBook *Annotate It!*

Analyzing the Text

COMMON CORE RI 1, RI 2, RI 3, RI 5, RI 6, W 1, W 4, W 8, W 10

Cite Text Evidence Support your responses with evidence from the text.

1. **Cause-Effect** What are the major effects of a giant whale's death on ocean life?

2. **Cause-Effect** Reread lines 87–97. Note the cause-and-effect connections in that paragraph. Paraphrase the information in the form of a chart that shows the cause-and-effect chain. Label the first box as "Cause" and complete it with this entry:
Water soaks into cracks in Earth's stretched crust.

3. **Compare** What are the three types of habitats described in this article, and how are they alike?

4. **Interpret** Reread lines 104–109. How would you paraphrase the information in the first sentence of this paragraph?

5. **Cite Evidence** Reread lines 79–86 from the section "Life Where Life Isn't Possible." What ideas were "suddenly turned upside down," and why?

6. **Evaluate** Why might the author have decided to end the article using the scientist's quotation?

PERFORMANCE TASK

Writing: Persuasive Essay Think about Santiago Herrera's statement at the end of the excerpt from "Living in the Dark." Why does he have that opinion? Why might someone else have a different opinion? Do you agree with Herrera's statement? Use your answers to those questions to write a one- to three-paragraph persuasive essay.

- In your introduction, state your opinion, or claim, clearly.
- In the rest of the essay, present valid reasons for your opinion and support them with evidence from the text and other sources that you can rely on.
- Try to present and refute one counterargument to your claim.

PERFORMANCE TASK

COMMON CORE W 1, W 4, W 8, W 10

 Assign this performance task.

Writing Activity: Persuasive Essay Have students work independently to plan and write the essay.

- Direct students to reread Herrera's statement (lines 210–212) and the questions posed in the Performance Task.
- Have students decide on their opinion and take notes from the text to support it.

- If students have trouble coming up with a counterargument, suggest that they work with a partner, each arguing a different side of the question.

Critical Vocabulary

cache   geyser   meager   tectonic   decompose

Practice and Apply Complete each sentence to show that you understand the meaning of the vocabulary word.

1. It's wise to keep a **cache** of . . .

2. Scientists study **geysers** to learn . . .

3. If you ate a **meager** meal, you . . .

4. Everywhere on Earth, **tectonic** . . .

5. Bacteria will **decompose** . . .

Vocabulary Strategy: Greek Roots

A **root** is a word part that came into English from an older language. You can check a print or digital dictionary to learn about roots; the entry for a word often gives details about the word's origin. Roots from ancient Greek are often called **combining forms** because they are combined to form words, especially terms in science and technology.

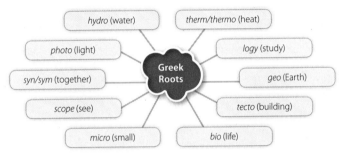

In the excerpt from "Living in the Dark," you read about Earth's tectonic plates. What do tectonic plates have to do with the meaning of the Greek root *tecto*, "building"? The movements of the plates are responsible for building continents, mountains, and oceans.

Practice and Apply Read each phrase and identify the word made from Greek combining forms. Refer to the chart for the root's meaning. Then define the phrase. Use a print or digital dictionary to check your ideas.

1. hydrothermal vents
2. photosynthesis in green plants
3. microscopic organisms
4. symbiotic bacteria
5. hydrogeological events

from Living in the Dark   **211**

Critical Vocabulary

Possible answers:

1. *It's wise to keep a* **cache** *of canned food in case the power goes out.*

2. *Scientists study* **geysers** *to learn about what is below Earth's surface.*

3. *If you ate a* **meager** *meal, you would still be hungry.*

4. *Everywhere on Earth,* **tectonic** *forces are moving continents.*

5. *Bacteria will* **decompose** *dead organic matter, such as fallen leaves.*

Vocabulary Strategy: Greek Roots

Possible answers:

1. **hydrothermal:** *hydrothermal vents are "heated water" openings in the sea floor.*

2. **photosynthesis:** *photosynthesis in green plants is the use of "light" to "put together" chemicals and make food.*

3. **microscopic:** *microscopic organisms are too "small" to "see" with the naked eye.*

4. **symbiotic:** *symbiotic bacteria live "together with other life forms" in an interdependent connection.*

5. **hydrogeological:** *hydrogeological events have to do with "water" and "earth," or the actions of groundwater.*

Strategies for Annotation 🖊 📖 *Annotate it!*

Vocabulary Strategy: Greek Roots

Have students locate words in the article that include Greek roots. Encourage them to use their eBook annotation tools to do the following:

- Highlight each word in yellow.
- Underline surrounding words or phrases that help in determining the meaning.
- In a note, explain the connection between the Greek roots and the surrounding text.

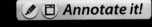

Much as plants use energy from the sun to make their own nourishment, these "chemosynthetic" bacteria use energy from chemical reactions to create the basic building bl[ock] of life. . . .

"Syn" means "together." The bacteria make food when chemicals come together.

from Living in the Dark   **211**

PRACTICE & APPLY

Language Conventions: Verbal Phrases

COMMON CORE L 1a

Tell students that we use verbal phrases frequently when we speak or write. Ask students to think about how often they use the word *to*. Often, they are using it as part of a verbal phrase: *I have to run to the store; You need to find that homework assignment.* Point out that verbal phrases can appear at any point in a sentence. For example, in the third sample sentence, *To breathe the air they need, whales come to the surface,* the order could be changed to *Whales come to the surface to breathe the air they need.*

Possible answers:

1. *Deep-sea scientists want to learn about communities on the sea floor.*

2. *To see in darkness, fish of the deep sea have extra-large eyes.*

3. *Crabs and shrimp come to the ocean floor to scavenge dead bacteria.*

4. *Scientists need equipment to detect undersea vents, seeps, and whale falls.*

5. *To explore new worlds is the goal of a deep-sea expedition.*

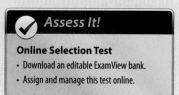

✓ Assess It!

Online Selection Test
- Download an editable ExamView bank.
- Assign and manage this test online.

Language Conventions: Verbal Phrases

COMMON CORE L 1a

A **verbal** is a verb form that is used as a noun, an adjective, or an adverb. An **infinitive** is a verbal that begins with *to* and has the base form of a verb. The infinitive is underlined in each of these sentences.

- Our plan is to sail. (The infinitive acts like a noun and tells what *our plan* is.)
- There may be whales to photograph. (The infinitive acts like an adjective to modify *whales* and tell *what kind*.)
- To breathe, whales come to the surface. (The infinitive acts like an adverb to modify *come* and tell *why*.)

A **verbal phrase** is made of a verbal and any other words that complete its meaning. The **infinitive phrase** is underlined in each of these sentences. The whole phrase in each sentence acts the same way as the infinitive alone.

- Our plan is to sail tomorrow.
- There may be whales to photograph from the boat.
- To breathe the air they need, whales come to the surface.

Note the infinitive phrase in this sentence from "Living in the Dark":

Meanwhile, fantastical worms, slugs, and bacteria bore into the whale's bones to feast on fatty marrow.

The infinitive phrase acts like an adverb to modify the verb **bore.** It tells why bacteria bore into the whale's bones.

Practice and Apply Read each group of words and the question in parentheses. Add an infinitive phrase to answer the question and complete a sentence using the words. Refer to the excerpt from "Living in the Dark" for ideas to include.

1. deep-sea scientists want (What do they want?)

2. fish of the deep sea have extra-large eyes (Why do they have such eyes?)

3. crabs and shrimp come to the ocean floor (Why do they come?)

4. scientists need equipment (What kind of equipment?)

5. the goal of a deep-sea expedition (What is the goal?)

Analyze Technical Meanings

COMMON CORE
RI 4, L 4a, L 4c, L 4d

TEACH

Informational texts often contain **technical language,** or language that has meaning specific to a technical field, such as oceanography or astrophysics. Provide students with the following strategies for determining the meaning of technical language:

- **Use context clues** in the surrounding text to help determine a word's meaning. For example, lines 35–37 of "Living in the Dark" state, "Much as plants use energy from the sun to make their own nourishment, these 'chemosynthetic' bacteria use energy from chemical reactions . . ." The writer provides clues to the meaning of "chemosynthetic" by comparing it to how plants use energy from the sun.

- **Use familiar word parts** For example, if you can identify a Greek or Latin root, such as "hydro" (water) or "bio" (life), in a term you don't know, it will give you an idea of what the term means.

- **Look it up in a dictionary** or science-specific resource. Use print or online dictionaries, encyclopedias, or glossaries to confirm your understanding of a technical term.

PRACTICE AND APPLY

Have students in small groups find and read a science article about a subject they are interested in. Direct them to record unfamiliar technical language in a chart like the one shown. Have students write what they think the word means in the middle column, look up the meaning in a reference source, and write that definition in the last column.

Unfamiliar Word	Your Definition	Reference Definition

Analyze Structure: Cause-and-Effect Relationships

COMMON CORE
RI 3, RI 5

RETEACH

Review with students that writers use a **cause-and-effect** pattern of organization to explain why something happened, what resulted from a specific action, or what relationship exists between events or ideas. Share these strategies with students:

- Look for headings that indicate cause and effect, such as "When a Whale Falls."
- To find effects, read to answer "What happened?" To find causes, read to answer "Why did it happen?"
- Look for signal words and phrases, such as *because, since, due to,* and *therefore.*
- Don't assume that the first event *caused* the second event.
- Use a graphic organizer to record cause-and-effect relationships as you read.

 LEVEL UP TUTORIALS Assign the following *Level Up* tutorial: **Cause-and-Effect Organization**

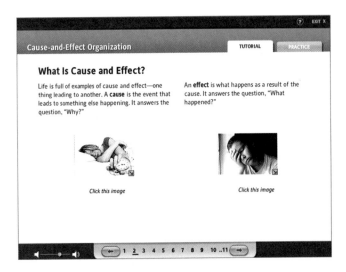

CLOSE READING APPLICATION

Students can apply the skill to another science article of their own choosing. Have them use a graphic organizer such as the Cause-and-Effect Chain to record cause-and-effect relationships as they read. Have small groups discuss the relationships they found.

 INTERACTIVE GRAPHIC ORGANIZER Have students complete the Cause-and-Effect Chain.

Stinging Tentacles Offer Hint of Oceans' Decline

Newspaper Article by Elisabeth Rosenthal

Why This Text

Students may have difficulty understanding long newspaper articles in which central ideas are developed over several pages. When an article includes unfamiliar scientific concepts, this problem may become acute. With the help of the close-reading questions, students will analyze the cause-and-effect relationships that the author uses to organize her writing. This close reading will lead students to understand the article's central ideas and how those ideas influence individuals featured in the article.

Background Have students read the background and information about the author and the article. Introduce the article by reminding students that oceans are vast—covering about 70 percent of Earth's surface—but fragile. Much industrial and consumer pollution ends up in oceans. No international body effectively controls the fishing industry, and overfishing is rampant. Oceans, which are key to the planet's climate system, are also sensitive to climate change.

SETTING A PURPOSE Ask students to pay attention to the cause-and-effect relationships in the article. How does the author use them to organize her writing?

Common Core Support

- cite several pieces of textual evidence
- determine central ideas in a text
- analyze interactions between individuals, events, and ideas
- determine the meaning of words and phrases
- analyze the structure an author uses to organize a text

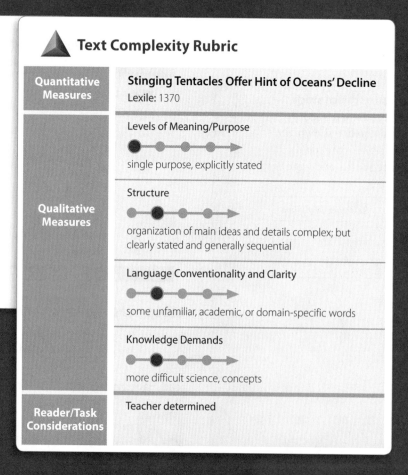

Text Complexity Rubric

Quantitative Measures

Stinging Tentacles Offer Hint of Oceans' Decline
Lexile: 1370

Qualitative Measures

Levels of Meaning/Purpose

single purpose, explicitly stated

Structure

organization of main ideas and details complex; but clearly stated and generally sequential

Language Conventionality and Clarity

some unfamiliar, academic, or domain-specific words

Knowledge Demands

more difficult science, concepts

Reader/Task Considerations

Teacher determined

Strategies for CLOSE READING

Analyze the Structure of a Newspaper Article

Students should read this article carefully all the way through. Close-reading questions at the bottom of the page will help them focus on a thorough analysis of the structure of the article. As they read, students should jot down comments or questions about the text in the margins.

WHEN STUDENTS STRUGGLE . . .

To help students analyze the structure of "Stinging Tentacles Offer Hint of Oceans' Decline," have them work in small groups to fill out a chart like the one shown below.

CITE TEXT EVIDENCE For practice in analyzing the structure of a newspaper article, ask students to cite text evidence for a cause-and-effect chain.

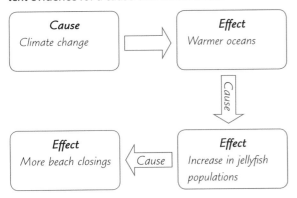

Cause — Climate change → Effect — Warmer oceans → (Cause) Effect — Increase in jellyfish populations → (Cause) Effect — More beach closings

---

Right side:

Background Elisabeth Rosenthal *(born 1956) is a medical doctor and an award-winning journalist. Before Rosenthal was named science editor for the* New York Times, *she worked as a reporter in Beijing, China, where she broke landmark stories on health in China. In this article, she writes about swarms of jellyfish in the waters off the coast of Barcelona, Spain, and explains what their growing numbers tell us about the health of the world's oceans.*

Stinging Tentacles Offer Hint of Ocean's Decline

Newspaper Article by Elisabeth Rosenthal

CLOSE READ
Notes

1. **READD** As you read lines 1–17, begin to collect and cite evidence.

• Circle the central idea in the third paragraph, and underline the details that support it.
• In the margin, restate the central idea of this paragraph.
• Circle the central idea in lines 15–17, and paraphrase the idea in the margin.

August 3, 2008

BARCELONA, Spain—Blue patrol boats crisscross the swimming areas of beaches here with their huge nets **skimming** the water's surface. The yellow flags that urge caution and the red flags that prohibit swimming because of risky currents are sometimes topped now with blue ones warning of a new danger: swarms of jellyfish.

In a period of hours during a day a couple of weeks ago, 300 people on Barcelona's bustling beaches were treated for stings, and 11 were taken to hospitals.

From Spain to New York, to Australia, Japan and Hawaii, jellyfish
10 are becoming more numerous and more widespread, and they are showing up in places where they have rarely been seen before, scientists say. The faceless marauders are stinging children blithely bathing on summer vacations, forcing beaches to close and clogging fishing nets.

skimming:
gliding across water

The jellyfish population is exploding. They show up where they were rarely seen before.

67

---

1. **READ AND CITE TEXT EVIDENCE** Explain to students that beach patrols often use flags to warn bathers of potential hazards, such as riptides and dangerous waves.

A ASK STUDENTS to discuss the cause-and-effect relationships described in the third paragraph. *Students should recognize that there are two causes—there are more jellyfish, and they are showing up where they were rarely seen before—and three effects—children are stung, beaches close, and fishing nets are clogged. Students may point out that in this paragraph the central idea is the cause of the supporting details.*

Critical Vocabulary: skimming (line 2) Have students model the gerund *skimming*, and ask volunteers to use the word in sentences with a marine context. *We saw pelicans skimming the waves.*

CLOSE READ
Notes

Jellyfish
invasions are a
sign of
unhealthy
oceans.

pronounced:
observable,
evident

But while jellyfish invasions are a nuisance to tourists and a hardship to fishermen, for scientists they are a source of more profound alarm, a signal of the declining health of the world's oceans.

"These jellyfish near shore are a message the sea is sending us saying, 'Look how badly you are treating me,'" said Dr. Josep-María

20 Gili, a leading jellyfish expert, who has studied them at the Institute of Marine Sciences of the Spanish National Research Council in Barcelona for more than 20 years.

The explosion of jellyfish populations, scientists say, reflects a combination of severe overfishing of natural predators, like tuna, sharks and swordfish; rising sea temperatures caused in part by global warming; and pollution that has depleted oxygen levels in coastal shallows.

These problems are **pronounced** in the Mediterranean, a sea bounded by more than a dozen countries that rely on it for business

30 and pleasure. Left unchecked in the Mediterranean and elsewhere, these problems could make the swarms of jellyfish menacing coastlines a grim vision of seas to come.

"The problem on the beach is a social problem," said Dr. Gili, who talks with admiration of the "beauty" of the globular jellyfish. "We need to take care of it for our tourism industry. But the big problem is not on the beach. It's what's happening in the seas."

---

2. ◀ REREAD   Reread lines 9–17. Review the central ideas in the two paragraphs and write a summary of the text so far. Include essential supporting details.

Jellyfish are all over beaches and appearing in places where they have never been seen before. They are stinging children, forcing beaches to close, and getting caught in fishing nets. Scientists think their invasion means that the oceans are not healthy.

3. READ ▶   As you read lines 18–59, analyze the cause-and-effect pattern of organization.

• Circle the causes of events and underline the effects of each cause.
• Record notes in the margin about how one or more events, or causes, bring about one or more other events, or effects.

68

Jellyfish, relatives of the sea anemone and coral that for the most part are relatively harmless, in fact are the cockroaches of the open waters, the ultimate maritime survivors who thrive in damaged

40 environments, and that is what they are doing.

Within the past year, there have been beach closings because of jellyfish swarms on the Côte d'Azur in France, the Great Barrier Reef of Australia, and at Waikiki in the United States.

In Australia, more than 30,000 people were treated for stings last year, double the number in 2005. The rare but deadly Irukandji jellyfish is expanding its range in Australia's warming waters, marine scientists say.

While no good global database exists on jellyfish populations, the increasing reports from around the world have convinced scientists

50 that the trend is real, serious and climate-related, although they caution that jellyfish populations in any one place undergo year-to-year variation.

"Human-caused stresses, including global warming and overfishing, are encouraging jellyfish surpluses in many tourist destinations and productive fisheries," according to the National Science Foundation, which is issuing a report on the phenomenon this fall and lists as problem areas Australia, the Gulf of Mexico, Hawaii, the Black Sea, Namibia, Britain, the Mediterranean, the Sea of Japan and the Yangtze estuary.

CLOSE READ
Notes

Causes:
overfishing,
rising sea
temperatures,
pollution
Effects:
business and
tourism
suffering,
beaches
closing,
jellyfish
stinging
people.

---

4. ◀ REREAD   Reread Dr. Gili's statements in lines 18–19 and 33–36. Paraphrase his comments in your own words.

Gili says that the jellyfish are close to the shore because the condition of the ocean is poor. He says that the big problem is not with tourism at the beach but in the declining quality of the ocean.

69

---

2. **REREAD AND CITE TEXT EVIDENCE**

Ⓑ **ASK STUDENTS** to discuss the cause-and-effect relationship identified in lines 16–17. How does this relationship connect to the ones you discussed in Question 1? *Students should recognize that the author identifies a primary cause—the declining health of the oceans—which leads to the proliferation of jellyfish, which leads to beach closings and clogged fishing nets.*

3. **READ AND CITE TEXT EVIDENCE**

Ⓒ **ASK STUDENTS** to discuss how the causes they circled in lines 23–27 relate to the cause-and-effect relationship they discussed in Question 2. *Students should understand that these are the causes of the declining health of the ocean.*

Critical Vocabulary: pronounced (line 28) Have students suggest synonyms of the adjective *pronounced. striking, marked, clear, noticeable*

4. **REREAD AND CITE TEXT EVIDENCE**

Ⓓ **ASK STUDENTS** what Dr. Gili's main argument is. *He thinks that the big problem is "what's happening in the seas"; that is, how the oceans are being badly treated by people.* How does Dr. Gili view the jellyfish problem? *He argues that increased jellyfish populations near shore send the message that we're damaging the oceans. So the jellyfish invasions are a symptom of the main problem. However, he recognizes that they also create social problems, like downturns in the tourism industry.*

FOR ELL STUDENTS Challenge your students by pointing out the words *relatives* and *relatively*. Have a volunteer explain their meaning and guess why they may share the same root.

CLOSE READ
Notes

> ❝ Though the stuff of horror B-movies, jellyfish are hardly aggressors. ❞

Boats check on jellyfish at sea. If jellyfish end up on the beaches they will be collected there.

lethal:
deadly

60   In Barcelona, one of Spain's most vibrant tourist destinations, city
E officials and the Catalan Water Agency have started fighting back,
trying desperately to ensure that it is safe for swimmers to go back in
the water.

F   Each morning, with the help of Dr. Gili's team, boats monitor
offshore jellyfish swarms, winds and currents to see if beaches are
threatened and if closings are needed. They also check if jellyfish
collection in the waters near the beaches is needed. Nearly 100 boats
stand ready to help in an emergency, said Xavier Duran of the water
agency. The constant squeal of Dr. Gili's cellphone reflected his de
70   facto role as Spain's jellyfish control and command center. Calls came
from all over.

Officials in Santander and the Basque country were concerned
about frequent sightings this year on the Atlantic coast of the
Portuguese man-of-war, a sometimes **lethal** warm-water species not
previously seen regularly in those regions.

Farther south, a fishing boat from the Murcia region called to
report an off-shore swarm of Pelagia noctiluca—an iridescent
purplish jellyfish that issues a nasty sting—more than a mile long. A

5. **READ** ▶ As you read lines 60–97, continue to cite evidence.
- In the margin, list the steps Dr. Gili takes to protect the beaches.
- Underline the dangers the jellyfish pose for humans.

70

---

chef, presumably trying to find some advantage in the declining
80   oceans, wanted to know if the local species were safe to eat if cooked.
Much is unknown about the jellyfish, and Dr. Gili was unsure.

In previous decades there were jellyfish problems for only a couple
of days every few years; now the threat of jellyfish is a daily headache
for local officials and is featured on the evening news. "In the past few
years the dynamic has changed completely—the temperature is a little
warmer," Dr. Gili said.

Though the stuff of horror B-movies, jellyfish are hardly
aggressors. They float haplessly with the currents. They discharge
their venom automatically when they bump into something warm—a
90   human body, for example—from poison-containing stingers on
mantles, arms or long, threadlike tendrils, which can grow to be yards
long.

Some, like the Portuguese man-of-war or the giant box jellyfish,
can be deadly on contact. Pelagia noctiluca, common in the
Mediterranean, delivers a painful sting producing a wound that lasts
weeks, months or years, depending on the person and the amount of
contact.

In the Mediterranean, overfishing of both large and small fish has
left jellyfish with little competition for plankton, their food, and fewer
100   predators. Unlike in Asia, where some jellyfish are eaten by people,
here they have no economic or **epicurean** value.

epicurean:
relating to the enjoyment of food

6. ◀ **REREAD AND DISCUSS** Reread lines 64–86. With a small group,
evaluate the efforts of Dr. Gili's team in the struggle to protect the
beaches. Is this a long-term solution or a short-term solution to the
problem? Cite text evidence in your discussion.

7. **READ** ▶ As you read lines 98–117, continue to cite text evidence.
- Circle the central ideas attributed to Purcell and Gili.
- Then in the margin, summarize what the two experts see as the major
  causes for the jellyfish invasion.

71

---

5. **READ AND CITE TEXT EVIDENCE**

E **ASK STUDENTS** to paraphrase how the Catalan Water
Agency is "fighting back" against jellyfish. *The agency works with
Dr. Gili's team to monitor jellyfish swarms, determine whether
beaches need to be closed, and collect jellyfish near beaches. These
measures are designed to make the sea safe for swimmers.*

Critical Vocabulary: lethal (line 74) Have students share their
definitions of *lethal*, and ask volunteers to use the adjective in
sentences about other sea animals. *Sharks can be dangerous, but
remarkably few shark-human encounters prove lethal.*

6. **REREAD AND DISCUSS USING TEXT EVIDENCE**

F **ASK STUDENTS** in each group to explain their reasoning.
*Students should realize that the team's efforts are short-term
solutions because they focus on the immediate problem—jellyfish
swarms—and not on the underlying cause of the problem—
declining ocean health.*

7. **READ AND CITE TEXT EVIDENCE**

G **ASK STUDENTS** to outline one of the cause-and-effect
relationships described by Dr. Purcell. *Global warming leads to
warmer seas, which allows jellyfish to breed "better and faster."*

Critical Vocabulary: epicurean (line 101) Have students give
the meaning of the base word *epicure. someone with refined
tastes in food* Have students give the meaning of the suffix
-an. characteristic of So what is the definition of *epicurean*?
characteristic of a person who has refined tastes in food

G The warmer seas and drier climate caused by global warming work to the jellyfish's advantage, since nearly all jellyfish breed better and faster in warmer waters, according to Dr. Jennifer Purcell, a jellyfish expert at the Shannon Point Marine Center of Western Washington University.

Global warming has also reduced rainfall in temperate zones, researchers say, allowing the jellyfish to better approach the beaches. Rain runoff from land would normally slightly decrease the salinity
110 of coastal waters, "creating a natural barrier that keeps the jellies from the coast," Dr. Gili said.

Then there is pollution, which reduces oxygen levels and visibility in coastal waters. While other fish die in or avoid waters with low oxygen levels, many jellyfish can thrive in them. And while most fish have to see to catch their food, jellyfish, which filter food passively from the water, can dine in total darkness, according to Dr. Purcell's research.

Global warming helps jellyfish breed faster. Reduced rainfall lets them get to the coast. Jellyfish can live in polluted water.

---

8. **READ** ▶ As you read lines 118–144, continue to cite text evidence.

- Underline what happens to Mirela Gómez after she is stung.
- Underline what Dr. Nogué says about the effect of the stings.
- Circle what Antonio López says about jellyfish.

72

Residents in Barcelona have forged a prickly coexistence with their new neighbors.

H 120 Last month, Mirela Gómez, 8, ran out of the water crying with her first jellyfish sting, clutching a leg that had suddenly become painful and itchy. Her grandparents rushed her to a nearby Red Cross stand. "I'm a little afraid to go back in the water," she said, displaying a row of angry red welts on her shin.

Francisco Antonio Padrós, a 77-year-old fisherman, swore mightily as he unloaded his catch one morning last weekend, pulling off dozens of jellyfish clinging to his nets and tossing them onto a dock. Removing a few shrimp, he said his nets were often "filled with more jellyfish than fish."

130 By the end of the exercise his calloused hands were bright red and swollen to twice their normal size. "Right now I can't tell if I have hands or not—they hurt, they're numb, they itch," he said.

Dr. Santiago Nogué, head of the **toxicology** unit at the largest hospital here, said that although 90 percent of stings healed in a week or two, many people's still hurt and itched for months. He said he was now seeing 20 patients a year whose symptoms did not respond to any treatment at all, sometimes requiring surgery to remove the affected area.

toxicology: the study of poisons

73

---

8. **READ AND CITE TEXT EVIDENCE**

H **ASK STUDENTS** to discuss the chain of events demonstrated by the experience of Mirela Gómez. *Students should note that the girl went to the beach with her grandparents, where she was stung by a jellyfish, which made her cry and run out of the water. The girl's distress convinced her grandparents to take her to a first-aid stand. Now Mirela is "a little afraid" to go back in the water.* Why might the author have included this anecdote in her article? *This story is a good example of how increasing jellyfish populations can hurt the tourism industry, which is one of the central ideas of the article.*

Critical Vocabulary: toxicology (line 133) Have students give the meaning of the base word *toxic. poisonous, or relating to poison* Have students give the meaning of the suffix *-logy. science* Explain that this suffix is usually preceded by a connective vowel, in this case *o*. So what is the definition of *toxicology*? *the science of poisons and their effects*

FOR ELL STUDENTS Challenge students to interpret the meaning of the adjective *angry* in the context of this text (line 124).

CLOSE READ
Notes

The sea, however, has long been central to life in Barcelona, and
140 that is unlikely to change. Recently when the beaches were closed,
children on a breakwater collected jellyfish in a bucket. The next day,
Antonio López, a diver, emerged from the water. "There are more
every year—we saw hundreds offshore today," he said. "You just have
to learn how to handle the stings."

9. **◀ REREAD** Reread lines 139–144. Restate what Antonio López says
in your own words.

*People will have to put up with jellyfish because more and more of
them are showing up in the ocean.*

SHORT RESPONSE

Cite Text Evidence Briefly summarize the growing problem of jellyfish as it is
presented in this article. Review your notes, and be sure to **cite text evidence**
as you explain the causes and effects of the growing population of jellyfish.

*Jellyfish are all over the beaches and appearing in places where they
have never been seen before. They are stinging children, forcing
beaches to close, and getting caught in fishing nets. Scientists think
that jellyfish invasions are a sign that oceans are not healthy. In the
past, jellyfish problems lasted for only a few days. Today, they are a
constant problem due to warmer waters, reduced rainfall, and
pollution—conditions that allow jellyfish to thrive. Since the jellyfish
seem to be here to stay, people will have to learn to live with them
and their stings.*

74

9. **REREAD AND CITE TEXT EVIDENCE**

ⓘ **ASK STUDENTS** why the author might have ended her
article with López's statement. *Students should recognize that the
diver's statement is one of resignation, or even pessimism. He doesn't
believe that society will address the underlying cause of the jellyfish
problem—declining ocean health. So his advice is simply to accept
the fact that there will be more and more jellyfish and to get used to
the stings. By ending the article with this quote, the author seems to
be saying that it is hard to disagree with Lopez's view.*

SHORT RESPONSE

Cite Text Evidence Students' responses should include text
evidence that supports their positions. They should:

- give examples of problems caused by growing jellyfish
  populations.
- explain what is causing the increase in jellyfish populations.
- describe possible responses to the problem.

TO CHALLENGE STUDENTS . . .

For greater understanding, students can research how increasing
jellyfish populations may affect the ocean's chemistry and
ecosystems.

ASK STUDENTS what some of the "feedback loops" are that
scientists believe exacerbate the jellyfish problem. *Students may
describe a feedback loop involving the climate system. Scientists
have discovered that ocean bacteria, which play a crucial role
in recycling the nutrients of dead organisms, have a hard time
with jellyfish. Instead of absorbing dead jellyfish's carbon, the
bacteria breathe it back out as carbon dioxide, thus increasing the
atmospheric concentrations of this greenhouse gas . . . leading to
greater climate change and more jellyfish. Alternatively, students
may describe a feedback loop involving the food chain. Jellyfish
consume large amounts of plankton, which means less food for
small fish. If populations of small fish decline, so will populations of
their predators, including many of the marine animals that prey on
jellyfish. So, the more jellyfish there are, the fewer jellyfish predators
will survive.*

DIG DEEPER

With the class, return to Question 3, Read. Have students share
their margin notes about causes and effects.

ASK STUDENTS to follow the cause-and-effect chains back as far
as they can.

- What is the primary cause of the jellyfish problem? *Students
  should understand that scientists have identified three main
  causes for surging jellyfish populations: climate change (warmer
  seas and less runoff), overfishing (of jellyfish predators), and
  pollution (which jellyfish can thrive in). Each of these factors,
  students should realize, is caused by humans.*
- What are the obstacles to long-term solutions to the jellyfish
  problem? *Since modern society is the source of the three main
  causes of increased jellyfish populations, the solutions would
  have to come from people. Governments would need to curb
  ocean pollution, crack down on overfishing, and enact measures
  to reduce greenhouse gas emissions. So the obstacles are
  political.*

ASK STUDENTS to return to their Short Response answer and
revise it based on the class discussion.

Your World

mySmartPlanner Create lesson plans and access resources online.

Poem by Georgia Douglas Johnson

Why This Text?

Poetry can open up the mind to new ideas and inspire readers to action. This lesson focuses on how poets use imagery and figurative language to convey an inspiring message.

Key Learning Objective: The student will be able to identify and analyze how imagery and extended metaphor can express a particular message or idea.

COMMON CORE Common Core Standards

RL 1 Cite textual evidence.
RL 2 Determine a theme or central idea.
RL 4 Determine the meaning of words and phrases.
W 2 Write informative/explanatory texts.
W 9a Draw evidence from literary texts.

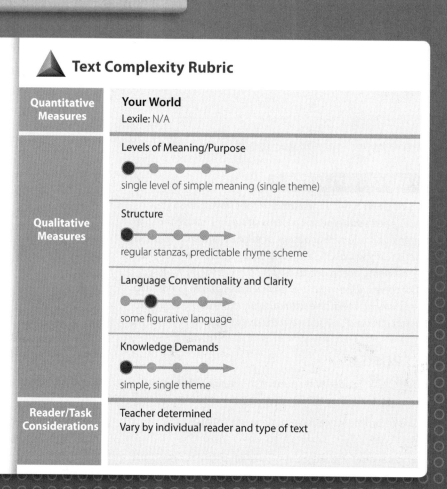

Text Complexity Rubric

Quantitative Measures

Your World
Lexile: N/A

Qualitative Measures

Levels of Meaning/Purpose

single level of simple meaning (single theme)

Structure

regular stanzas, predictable rhyme scheme

Language Conventionality and Clarity

some figurative language

Knowledge Demands

simple, single theme

Reader/Task Considerations

Teacher determined
Vary by individual reader and type of text

Background Have students read the information about the poet. Tell students that in the early 1900s the need for workers in Northern factories of the United States caused a mass migration of African Americans from the South. Many settled in Harlem, a neighborhood of New York City. There, writers, artists, and musicians worked to establish a proud cultural identity. The neighborhood was transformed from a deteriorating area to a thriving middle-class community. This movement was called the Harlem Renaissance.

SETTING A PURPOSE Direct students to use the Setting a Purpose prompt to focus their reading. Remind students to write down questions they have as they read.

Determine Meanings

COMMON CORE **RL 1, RL 4**

(LINES 1–4, 5–8)

Explain that **figurative language** communicates meanings beyond the literal meanings of words. Poets often use figurative language to compare things, emphasize ideas, or give an emotional effect. One type of figurative language is extended metaphor. An **extended metaphor** compares two essentially unlike things at some length and in several ways.

A **CITE TEXT EVIDENCE** Have a volunteer reread lines 1–4 aloud. Explain that these first few lines of the poem introduce an extended metaphor that unifies the entire poem. Have students cite details that reveal the metaphor and what it might represent. *("In the narrowest nest" is a clue to the extended metaphor. The poet may be using* nest *as a metaphor for the speaker's home.*)

Explain that another type of figurative language is **imagery**—the use of words and phrases that convey how things look, feel, smell, sound, and taste.

B **ASK STUDENTS** to reread lines 5–8 aloud. Have them describe what they imagine as they read the lines and identify words and phrases that appealed to their senses. *(Possible answer: The words "sighted the distant horizon" and "sky-line encircled the sea" create the visual image of the point where the sky meets the sea.)*

COLLABORATIVE DISCUSSION Have partners discuss their questions and what the poem teaches about risk taking. Have them share their ideas with the larger group.

Your World

Poem by Georgia Douglas Johnson

Georgia Douglas Johnson (1880–1966) *was one of the most famous African American women writers of the early 1900s. She is associated with the Harlem Renaissance—an African American literary and cultural movement of the 1920s and 1930s. Johnson wrote four volumes of poetry as well as plays and fiction.*

SETTING A PURPOSE Sometimes a poem contains a message designed to inspire. As you read, consider the poet's message and how it may inspire others to take risks.

Your world is as big as you make it
I know, for I used to abide
In the narrowest nest in a corner
My wings pressing close to my side.

5 But I sighted the distant horizon
Where the sky-line encircled the sea
And I throbbed with a burning desire
To travel this immensity.

I battered the cordons¹ around me
10 And cradled my wings on the breeze
Then soared to the uttermost reaches
With rapture, with power, with ease!

COLLABORATIVE DISCUSSION In what ways does this poem teach a lesson about risk-taking? Share your ideas with other group members.

---

¹ **cordons** (kôr´dnz): lines or borders stretched around an area, indicating that access is restricted.

©Ikon Images/SuperStock

SCAFFOLDING FOR ELL STUDENTS

Determine Meanings Display lines 1–4. Invite volunteers to highlight words and phrases that help them imagine a sight, feeling, smell, sound, or taste.

ASK STUDENTS to discuss how these details help them understand the meaning of the poem. Remind students to use this strategy as they continue reading the poem.

Determine Meanings COMMON CORE RL 4

Review the information about figurative language. Remind students that in this poem one of the things being compared in the metaphor is the speaker herself. Discuss the examples of imagery that give clues to this extended metaphor. Ask students to describe what they see, hear, feel, smell, or taste as they read the lines. Then, work with students to identify other examples of imagery that help develop the metaphor. *(Examples of imagery and clues to the metaphor include "narrowest nest," "My wings pressed close to my side," "cradled my wings," and "soared to the uttermost reaches.")* Discuss the impact each one has on meaning and emotion.

Analyzing the Text COMMON CORE RL 1, RL 2, RL 4

Possible answers:

1. *Words that appeal to the senses include "sky-line encircled the sea" (sight); "throbbed" (touch); "burning desire" (touch).*

2. *The speaker means that she broke through the barriers that were holding her back.*

3. *The poet makes a comparison between the speaker and a trapped bird.*

4. *The theme of "Your World" might be life is what you make of it. If you set your dreams high, you can reach them.*

 eBook *Annotate It!*

Determine Meanings COMMON CORE RL 4

In the poem "Your World," the poet conveys a comparison of two unlike things through the **speaker,** or the voice that "talks" to the reader. Because this figurative comparison is carried through the entire poem, it is called an **extended metaphor,** a figure of speech that compares two essentially unlike things at some length and in several ways.

The poet also uses **imagery,** words and phrases that appeal to the senses, to engage the reader and develop the extended metaphor. In these two lines, the descriptions encourage readers to use their senses:

> **line 6: Where the sky-line encircled the sea**
> **line 10: And cradled my wings on the breeze**

Look back at the poem. Find additional examples of imagery and lines that give clues about the extended metaphor.

Analyzing the Text  COMMON CORE RL 1, RL 2, RL 4, W 2, W 9a

Cite Text Evidence   Support your responses with evidence from the text.

1. **Interpret** What words in the second stanza appeal to the senses?

2. **Interpret** What does the speaker mean when she says, "I battered the cordons around me"?

3. **Compare** Through the extended metaphor, what comparison does the poet make?

4. **Draw Conclusions** A poem's **theme** is a message about life or human nature that the poet shares with the reader. What is the theme of "Your World"?

PERFORMANCE TASK

Writing Activity: Analysis Think about the extended metaphor in this poem. Write at least one paragraph analyzing the extended metaphor. These questions may help you organize your thoughts and writing:

- What words and phrases show the comparison throughout the poem?
- Why might the poet have chosen this comparison?
- What feelings are suggested by the comparison?

Assign this performance task.

PERFORMANCE TASK COMMON CORE W 2, W 9a

Writing Activity: Analysis Have students work independently. Direct them to

- create a chart listing text evidence that develops the metaphor
- use the chart to draft their paragraphs
- organize their ideas in a logical way
- conclude by restating their main ideas and insights

Determine Meanings: Metaphor

COMMON CORE
RL 4

TEACH

Review with students that **figurative language** is a way of using words to express ideas that are not literally true, and that poets often use figurative language to compare things, emphasize ideas, or give an emotional effect. Tell students that a **metaphor** is one common type of figurative language. Explain that a metaphor is a comparison of two things that are basically unlike but have some qualities in common, and that a metaphor does not use the words *like* or *as*.

Provide a simple example of a metaphor, prompting students with relevant questions:

That girl is a walking encyclopedia.

- What two things are being compared?
- What is the meaning of the metaphor?
- How is this comparison different from saying that the girl is smart?
- What effect does the metaphor have on the reader?

PRACTICE AND APPLY

Have students explore the use of metaphor in a poem of their choosing. Have students identify examples and explain the meaning and effect of each one.

Cite Evidence

COMMON CORE
RL 1

TEACH

Tell students that one way to better understand a poem is to paraphrase it. Explain that to **paraphrase** means to restate or express the poet's ideas in your own words without changing or adding to the poem's meaning.

Explain that stopping occasionally to paraphrase can help students to be sure that they understand the meaning of a poem.

Display the following lines from "Your World":

> **Your world is as big as you make it**
> **I know, for I used to abide**
> **In the narrowest nest in a corner**
> **My wings pressing close to my side.**

Work with students to paraphrase the lines.

- Identify the main idea, or what the poet is trying to say.
- Look up any unfamiliar words or phrases.
- Restate important ideas in their own words.

Point out how the paraphrase says the same thing as the line in the poem, only using different words.

> *Sample paraphrase:*
> *Everyone has the power to live a big life*
> *I know, because I use to live*
> *In a world that was like a tiny nest in the corner of a room*
> *It was so small, my arms were pinned to my sides.*

PRACTICE AND APPLY

Have students work in small groups to discuss the meaning of the remaining stanzas in the poem. Then, have students take turns paraphrasing each one.

INTERACTIVE WHITEBOARD LESSON
Form in Poetry

COMMON CORE

RL 5

TEACH

Explain to students that the **form** of a poem is the way in which the words and lines are arranged on the page.

- A **line** is the core unit of a poem.
- A **stanza** is a group of two or more lines. Often, each stanza in a poem contains a complete idea that contributes to the overall meaning of the poem.
- The place where a line ends is called a **line break.**

Explain that a line break does not always signal the end of a sentence or thought. A line break can occur in the middle of a sentence or phrase to create emphasis or a meaningful pause. Poets use a variety of line breaks to convey a wide range of effects, such as pace, mood, rhythm, and tone.

Provide the following definitions of each of these effects:

- **Pace** is how fast or slow a poem is read. Short sentences speed up the pace of a poem. Longer sentences slow down the pace.
- **Mood** is the feeling or atmosphere that the poet creates for the reader.
- **Rhythm** is a pattern of stressed and unstressed syllables in a line of poetry. Rhythm brings out the musical quality of language, emphasizes ideas, and creates mood.
- The **tone** of a poem expresses the speaker's attitude toward his or her subject.

PRACTICE AND APPLY

Display "Your World" on the board or on a device. Work with students to analyze its form. Have students

- tell how many lines and stanzas the poem has
- describe how each thought begins and ends
- explain the effects that are created by the poem's line breaks

INTERACTIVE WHITEBOARD LESSON
Determine Meanings: Imagery

COMMON CORE

RL 4

RETEACH

Review that figurative language is a way of using words to express ideas that are not literally true, and that **imagery** is a type of figurative language that consists of words and phrases writers use to create pictures in the reader's mind. Imagery draws on **sensory details,** or words and phrases that appeal to the reader's senses of sight, hearing, smell, taste, and touch.

Have volunteers suggest sensory words for each sense, such as *dazzling, luminous,* and *vivid* for sight. List the words on the board, and discuss how each word appeals to that sense.

Then, work with students to analyze the imagery in "Your World." Have students reread the poem. Then, have students identify words and phrases that appeal to their senses. Ask:

- How did you feel?
- What did you imagine as you read?
- How does this imagery affect meaning?

LEVEL UP TUTORIALS Assign the following *Level Up* tutorial: **Imagery**

CLOSE READING APPLICATION

Individual students or partners can apply the skill to another poem they have read. Have students identify specific words and phrases that appeal to the senses and describe how these details appeal to the senses.

Interactive Lessons

If you need help . . .
• **Writing Arguments**
• **Writing as a Process**
• **Using Textual Evidence**

Give a Persuasive Speech

Persuasive speeches such as John F. Kennedy's "Remarks at the Dedication of the Aerospace Medical Health Center" can inspire listeners to rise to great challenges. In the following activity, you will draw from Kennedy's speech and other texts in the collection to prepare and give a persuasive speech. You will try to persuade others whether major exploration is worth the risk.

A successful persuasive speech

- contains an engaging introduction that clearly establishes the claim being made
- supports key points with reasoning and relevant evidence pulled from a variety of solid, credible sources
- uses language that effectively conveys ideas and adds interest
- concludes by leaving the audience with a lasting impression

COMMON CORE

W 1a–e Write arguments.
W 4 Produce clear and coherent writing.
W 5 Develop and strengthen writing.
W 7 Conduct short research projects.
W 8 Gather relevant information.
SL 4 Present claims and findings.
SL 5 Include multimedia components and visual displays.
SL 6 Adapt speech to a variety of contexts and tasks.

PLAN

Choose Your Position Think about the texts you read in this collection and the various points made by each of the writers concerning risk and exploration. Then choose a position either for or against major exploration based on the risks involved, and write out your claim in a statement.

Gather Information Focus on the selection(s) that have information you can cite to support your position. Jot down important details that provide reasons and evidence that support your claim. Consider the following:

- What are your reasons for taking the position you took?
- Which statements from the selections can you use as quotes to provide facts and examples to support your claim?
- What might others say to oppose your claim? How would you try to convince them to agree with you?
- What do you want your audience to understand about your position?

myNotebook

Use the annotation tools in your eBook to find evidence that supports your claim. Save each piece of evidence to your notebook.

ACADEMIC VOCABULARY

As you plan and present your speech, be sure to use the academic vocabulary words.

complex
potential
rely
stress
valid

PERFORMANCE TASK

GIVE A PERSUASIVE SPEECH

COMMON CORE W 1a-e, W 4, W5, W 7, W 8, SL 4, SL 5, SL 6

Introduce students to the Performance Task by reading the introductory paragraph with them and reviewing the criteria for what makes a good persuasive speech. Remind students that a speech needs to be written well, in the same way that an essay does, but that the delivery of the speech is of equal importance.

PLAN

GATHER INFORMATION

Remind students that organizing information as they research will make it easier for them to write their speeches. Point out that students can arrange all the evidence for a particular reason together in a file, or they can color code the information within their notes to support a particular reason.

Do Further Research Research additional print and digital sources to find solid, credible evidence for your argument.

- Search for facts, quotes, and statistics that support your claims.
- Try to find sources that don't agree with you. Develop counterclaims against their arguments.
- Identify any visuals, such as charts, graphs, or pictures, that illustrate your ideas.

Organize Your Ideas Think about how you will organize your speech. A graphic organizer, such as a hierarchy chart, can help you to present your ideas logically.

Place your claim in the top box, your reasons in the next row of boxes, and your evidence in the final row.

Consider Your Purpose and Audience Who will listen to your speech? What specific ideas will be most convincing to them? Think about that audience as you prepare to write. Your tone and word choices should be appealing and targeted toward them. Speaking to a group of classmates or friends would be different than speaking to a group of adults.

PRODUCE

DRAFT YOUR SPEECH

Remind students that they should keep their audience in mind as they write and that they should try to be persuasive. Point out that as they write students should hear their arguments in their head to make sure they are sounding both logical and convincing to the people they will be addressing.

PRODUCE

Draft Your Speech Use the information in your graphic organizer to help you write your speech.

- Introduce your claim to your audience. Begin with an attention-grabbing comment or an unusual or funny quote, statistic, or story.
- Organize your reasons and evidence logically. For example, will it work better to start with your weakest or strongest argument? What words and phrases will best appeal to your audience?

my **WriteSmart**

Write your rough draft in *my*WriteSmart. Focus on getting your ideas down, rather than perfecting your choice of language.

- Be sure to include quotes and other data from your sources. Feel free to paraphrase this data, or put it into your own words.

- Use words and phrases such as *because, therefore,* and *for that reason* to make your argument clearer and more coherent.

- Bring your speech to a conclusion. Summarize your main points in a concluding statement, and connect them to your introduction. Tell your audience what you want them to believe or inspire them to do.

Prepare Visuals Select multimedia resources to create charts, graphs, or pictures that clarify and strengthen your claims. Make sure that all visuals are large and clear enough that everyone in the audience can read them.

REVISE

Practice Your Speech Present your speech aloud. Try speaking in front of a mirror, or make a recording of your speech and listen to it. Then practice your speech with a partner.

- Use your voice effectively. Speak loudly, varying your pitch and tone.

- Maintain eye contact. Look directly at individuals in your audience.

- Use gestures and facial expressions that allow your audience to see how you feel.

Evaluate Your Speech Work with your partner to determine whether your speech is effective.

- Check that your claim is clear and logically supported with reasons and evidence.

- Examine your evidence to make sure it is relevant and based on accurate, credible sources.

- Check that your speech keeps your audience's attention and concludes with a statement that sums up your argument.

PRESENT

Deliver Your Speech Finalize your persuasive speech and present it to the class.

*my*WriteSmart

Have your partner or a group of peers review your draft in *my*WriteSmart. Ask your reviewers to note any reasons that do not support the claim or lack sufficient evidence.

PERFORMANCE TASK

REVISE

PRACTICE YOUR SPEECH

Suggest to students that they complete their drafts a day ahead of their scheduled speech so they have time for revision. Whether they practice in front of a mirror or with a partner, students should evaluate both content and delivery. Talk with students about a well-organized speech that is mumbled or delivered hesitantly as opposed to a well-delivered speech that is based on bad reasoning or weak evidence. Help students to recognize the importance of both parts of the task.

PRESENT

DELIVER YOUR SPEECH

Students may present their speeches in a number of ways:

- Present it directly to the class. Remind students to use appropriate eye contact, adequate volume, and clear pronunciation.

- Videotape themselves delivering the speech and play it for the class or post it on a school or class website. Videotaping will allow them to critique themselves on their performance as well as to create an artifact for a portfolio.

- Create a multimedia presentation on their topic, using photographic and video images, with a recording of the speech as background narration. Students may also want to use music to accompany their presentations.

- Post the text of the speech on a school or class website, and ask other students to prepare readings of the text.

PERFORMANCE TASK

IDEAS AND EVIDENCE

Have students look at the chart and identify how they did on the Performance Task in each of the three main categories. In particular, ask students to discuss how effectively they anticipated and addressed opposing claims. Ask students to set goals for the next time they might write another persuasive speech or essay. Encourage students to name the areas they will work on.

	Ideas and Evidence	Organization	Language
ADVANCED	• The introduction grabs the audience's attention; the claim clearly states the speaker's position on an issue. • Logical reasons and relevant evidence support the speaker's claim. • Opposing claims are anticipated and effectively addressed. • The concluding section effectively summarizes the claim.	• The reasons and evidence are organized logically and consistently throughout the speech. • Transitions logically connect reasons and evidence to the speaker's claim.	• The speech reflects a formal style. • Sentence beginnings, lengths, and structures vary and have a rhythmic flow. • Grammar, usage, and mechanics are correct.
COMPETENT	• The introduction could do more to grab the audience's attention; the speaker's claim states a position on an issue. • Most reasons and evidence support the speaker's claim, but they could be more convincing. • Opposing claims are anticipated, but the responses need to be developed more. • The concluding section restates the claim.	• The organization of key reasons and supporting evidence is logical in some places. • A few more transitions are needed to clarify the relationships between ideas.	• The style becomes informal in a few places. • Sentence beginnings, lengths, and structures vary somewhat. • Some grammatical and usage errors are present.
LIMITED	• The introduction does not grab the audience's attention; the speaker's claim identifies an issue, but the position is not clearly stated. • The reasons and evidence are not always logical or relevant. • Opposing claims are anticipated but not addressed logically. • The concluding section includes an incomplete summary of the claim.	• The organization of reasons and evidence is confusing in some places, and it often doesn't follow a pattern. • Several more transitions are needed to connect reasons and evidence to the speaker's claim.	• The style becomes informal in several places. • Sentence structures rarely vary, and some fragments or run-on sentences are present. • Grammar and usage are incorrect in several places, but the speaker's ideas are still clear.
EMERGING	• The introduction is confusing. • Supporting reasons and evidence are missing. • Opposing claims are neither anticipated nor addressed. • The concluding section is missing.	• A logical organization is not used; reasons and evidence are presented randomly. • Transitions are not used, making the speech difficult to understand.	• The style is inappropriate for the speech. • Repetitive sentence structure, fragments, and run-on sentences make the speech hard to follow. • Several grammatical and usage errors change the meaning of ideas.

The Stuff of Consumer Culture

"We live much of our lives in a realm I call the *buyosphere*."

—Thomas Hine

CONNECTING WORD AND IMAGE

ASK STUDENTS to discuss how the collection opener image and the collection quotation work together to create a connection.

PERFORMANCE TASK PREVIEW

Point out to students that they will complete one performance task at the end of the collection. The performance task will require them to further analyze the selections in the collection and to synthesize ideas about these analyses. They will present their findings in a variety of products.

ACADEMIC VOCABULARY

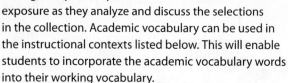

View It!

Professional Development Podcast:
Academic Vocabulary

Students can acquire facility with the academic vocabulary words through frequent, repeated exposure as they analyze and discuss the selections in the collection. Academic vocabulary can be used in the instructional contexts listed below. This will enable students to incorporate the academic vocabulary words into their working vocabulary.

- Collaborative Discussion at the end of each selection
- Analyzing the Text questions for each selection
- Selection-level Performance Task
- Vocabulary instruction (for Critical Vocabulary and/or for Vocabulary Strategy)
- Language Conventions
- End-of-collection Performance Task for all selections in the collection

ASK STUDENTS to review the Academic Vocabulary word list for this collection. You may wish to pronounce each word aloud so students hear the correct pronunciation. Then, discuss the definitions and the related forms for each word. Remind students that they will encounter these five academic vocabulary words throughout the collection.

COLLECTION 5
The Stuff of Consumer Culture

In this collection, you will take a look at our consumer culture and consider the question: How much is enough?

hmhfyi.com

COLLECTION
PERFORMANCE TASK Preview

At the end of this collection, you will research and write an informative essay about consumerism, using information from the selections in the collection as your starting point. Then you will create a multimedia presentation of your essay to share with others.

ACADEMIC VOCABULARY

Study the words and their definitions in the chart below. You will use these words as you discuss and write about the texts in this collection.

Word	Definition	Related Forms
attitude (ăt′ĭ-tōōd′) n.	a way of thinking or feeling about something or someone	attitudes, attitudinal, attitudinize
consume (kən-sōōm′) v.	to buy things for your own use or ownership	consumed, consumer, consumer good, consuming, consumption
goal (gōl) n.	the object toward which your work and planning is directed; a purpose	goals
purchase (pûr′chĭs) v.	to buy	purchasable, purchaser, purchasing, purchasing power
technology (tĕk-nŏl′ə-jē) n.	the application of science and engineering as part of a commercial or industrial undertaking	technologic, technological, technologist

220

USING COLLECTIONS YOUR WAY

Use the following information, along with the charts on the following pages, to help you decide how you want to introduce the collection. Based on your teaching style, your students' interests, or your instructional goals, you may want to structure this collection in various ways. You may choose different entry points each time you teach the collection.

"I require my students to do a lot of research."

While exploring this statistics-laden analysis of Americans' relationship with the television, students will encounter other opportunities to research popular technologies and their impact on society.

Background It's hard to imagine, but less than 100 years ago, television as we know it didn't exist. Then in 1927, Philo T. Farnsworth successfully transmitted an image onto a remote screen. By the early 1950s, TV purchases skyrocketed. Today almost every home in the United States has at least one. This excerpt from Life at Home in the Twenty-First Century describes what a team of archaeologists uncovered about TVs when they examined the daily lives of 32 California families.

from

LIFE at HOME in the TWENTY-FIRST CENTURY

Informational Text by Jeanne E. Arnold

SETTING A PURPOSE Perhaps no other technology is more widely shared as the television. As you read, keep track of how the popularity of this consumer good has changed over time. How will archaeologists of the future track its significance? Write down any questions you have while reading.

Television and Daily Life

In North America, and in as few as three generations, mass media broadcast by analog and digital signal has all but replaced oral history and become the primary conveyor of culturally shared ideas. Broadcast communication, particularly television-streamed content, figures so prominently in economic decisions, political outcomes, and moral reasoning that even at the height of the last U.S. recession, TV advertising expenditures exceeded $50 billion.

Television is now so intricately woven into the fabric of the American family experience that few children born during the last two decades will be able to imagine a social world that

Life at Home in the Twenty-First Century 221

"I like to teach by comparing texts."

Poets Gary Soto and X. J. Kennedy offer two very different takes on America's consumer culture.

COMPARE TEXTS

Background Writers and poets alike often use their writing to make statements about important topics like consumerism. X. J. Kennedy and Gary Soto each examine our consumer society in their respective poems "Dump" and "How Things Work."

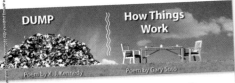

DUMP

Poem by X. J. Kennedy

How Things Work

Poem by Gary Soto

X. J. Kennedy (b. 1929) has won many awards for his poetry collections, including the Robert Frost Medal. Kennedy has published numerous books for young people, including collections of poetry and novels. Traditional in form, Kennedy's poems often include narrative, wit, and humor, but he also explores themes about serious topics, such as growing up and loss.

Gary Soto (b. 1952) never dreamed about writing as a child. But after reading a book of poetry in college, he began to write his own poems and dedicated himself to the craft. While Soto has written poetry and novels for adults, he is probably best known as a writer for young adults and children. From his point of view, he is writing about the feelings and experiences of most American kids.

SETTING A PURPOSE As you read, think about what each poet is saying about our consumer society and how that society works.

Compare Texts 241

"I emphasize informational texts."

Culture writer Thomas Hine offers an artful—and sometimes arch—take on what drives human beings to shop, perpetually and endlessly wanting more of the material things we already have plenty of.

Background A writer on history, culture, and design, Thomas Hine coined the word populux as the title of his first book. The word has become commonly used to describe the enthusiasms of post-World War II America. Hine was born in a small New England town near Boston. He lived in a house that was built in 1770, a very different setting from the modern world he writes about now.

Always Wanting More
from I WANT THAT!

Informational Text by Thomas Hine

SETTING A PURPOSE What keeps people in our consumer society always wanting more? And when is having more enough? As you read, consider how Thomas Hine answers these questions.

Throughout most of history, few people had more than a couple of possessions, and as a consequence, people were very aware of each object. Life was austere. The ability to be bored by a material surfeit[1] was a rare privilege. There are many stories of kings and emperors who sought a simpler life, if only briefly. Now, that emotion has become widespread, and those who wish to simplify are identified as a distinct market segment. Whole lines of "authentic" products have been created to serve this market, and magazines are published to tell people what they need to buy to achieve a simpler life. In our age of careless abundance, austerity is a luxury, available

[1] **surfeit** (sûr′fĭt): an excessive amount.

Always Wanting More from I Want That! 233

mySmartPlanner | **eBook** | **myNotebook** | **my WriteSmart** | **fyi** hmhfyi.com

Collection 5 Lessons	Media	Teach and Practice
Student Edition | eBook	▶ **Video Links** HISTORY A&E	**Close Reading and Evidence Tracking**
ANCHOR TEXT **Informational Text by Jeanne E. Arnold** from *Life at Home in the Twenty-First Century*	🔊 **Audio** from *Life at Home in the Twenty-First Century*	**Close Read Screencasts** • Modeled Discussion 1 (lines 23–1) • Modeled Discussion 2 (lines 134–142) • Close Read application PDF (lines 173–183)	**Strategies for Annotation** • Analyze Structure: Cause and Effect • Cite Evidence • Domain-Specific Words
CLOSE READER **Essay by Andres Padilla-Lopez** "Teenagers and New Technology"	🔊 **Audio** "Teenagers and New Technology"		
Informational Text by Thomas Hine "Always Wanting More" from *I Want That*	🔊 **Audio** "Always Wanting More" from *I Want That*		**Strategies for Annotation** • Make Inferences • Determine Meaning • Synonyms and Antonyms
CLOSE READER **Essay by Lourdes Barranco** "Labels and Illusions"	🔊 **Audio** "Labels and Illusions"		
Poem by X. J. Kennedy "Dump" **Poem by Gary Soto** "How Things Work"	🔊 **Audio** "Dump" 🔊 **Audio** "How Things Work"		**Strategies for Annotation** • Analyze Poetry: Form • Determine Theme
Short Story by Charles Yu "Earth (A Gift Shop)"	🔊 **Audio** "Earth (A Gift Shop)"		**Strategies for Annotation** • Determine Theme • Analyze Stories: Science Fiction • Verifying Meaning
CLOSE READER **Short Story by Shinichi Hoshi** "He-y Come On Ou-t!"	🔊 **Audio** "He-y Come On Ou-t!"		
Collection 5 Performance Tasks: **A** Create a Multimedia Presentation	**fyi** hmhfyi.com	**Interactive Lessons** **A** Writing Informative Texts **A** Giving a Presentation Using Media in a Presentation

	For Systematic Coverage of Writing and Speaking & Listening Standards	**Interactive Lessons** Writing a Narrative Producing and Publishing with Technology

Assess		Extend	Reteach
Performance Task	**Online Assessment**	**Teacher eBook**	**Teacher eBook**
Writing Activity: Essay	Selection Test	**Cite Evidence: Understanding Statistics**	**Cite Evidence > Level Up Tutorial >** Reading Graphic Aids
Speaking Activity: Discussion	Selection Test	**Determine Central Ideas and Details > Interactive Whiteboard Lesson >** Main/ Central Ideas and Details	**Determine Meaning > Level Up Tutorial >** Author's Style
Writing Activity: Analysis	Selection Test		**Determine Theme > Level Up Tutorial >** Theme **Compare Forms in Poetry > Level Up Tutorial >** Elements of Poetry
Writing Activity: Short Story	Selection Test	**Analyze Stories: Setting > Interactive Whiteboard Lesson >** Setting	**Analyze Stories: Science Fiction**
Create a Multimedia Presentation	Collection Test		

Lesson Assessments
Writing a Narrative
Producing and Publishing with
Technology

COLLECTION 5 INSTRUCTIONAL OVERVIEW

Collection 5 Lessons	Key Learning Objective	Performance Task
ANCHOR TEXT **Informational Text by Jeanne E. Arnold** **Lexile 1640L** from _Life at Home in the Twenty-First Century_, **p. 221A**	**The student will be able to . . .** identify cause-and-effect patterns of organization in an informational text and draw conclusions from the text and graphs.	Domain-Specific Words
Informational Text by Thomas Hine **Lexile 1240L** "Always Wanting More" from _I Want That_ **p. 233A**	**The student will be able to . . .** identify features of an author's style and make inferences using textual details and their own knowledge.	Speaking Activity: Discussion
Poem by X. J. Kennedy "Dump," **p. 241A** **Poem by Gary Soto** "How Things Work," **p. 241A**	**The student will be able to . . .** analyze a poem's form and identify theme and irony.	Writing Activity: Analysis
Short Story by Charles Yu "Earth (A Gift Shop)" **p. 249A** **Lexile 1010L**	**The student will be able to . . .** identify elements of science fiction and analyze a story to determine its theme.	Writing Activity: Short Story

Collection 5 Performance Tasks:
A Create a Multimedia Presentation

Vocabulary Strategy	Language and Style	Student Instructional Support	CLOSE READER Selection
Domain-Specific Words	Eliminate Redundancy	**Scaffolding for ELL Students:** Determine Meaning **When Students Struggle:** Conclusions and Statistics **To Challenge Students:** Group Discussion	Essay by Andres Padilla-Lopez "Teenagers and New Technology," p. 232b **Lexile 1040L**
Synonyms and Antonyms	Noun Clauses	**Scaffolding for ELL Students:** Determine Meaning	Essay by Lourdes Barranco "Labels and Illusions," p. 240b **Lexile 1030L**
		Scaffolding for ELL Students: Analyze Language: Imagery **When Students Struggle:** • Analyze Structure • Analyze Poetry: Form	
Verifying Meaning	Spelling	**Scaffolding for ELL Students**: Analyze Language **When Students Struggle:** Informal Debate	Short Story by Shinichi Hoshi "He-y Come On Ou-t!" p. 258b **Lexile 860L**

ANCHOR TEXT

from Life at Home in the Twenty-First Century

Informational Text by Jeanne E. Arnold

*my***SmartPlanner** Create lesson plans and access resources online.

Why This Text?

In the social sciences, researchers gather and analyze data and present their findings. As students read more academic texts, they can build their understanding of how research is documented. In this lesson, students analyze organization and draw conclusions from it.

▶ View It!

Professional Development Podcast:

Text Complexity

Key Learning Objective: The student will be able to identify cause-and-effect patterns of organization in an informational text and draw conclusions from the text and graphs.

For practice and application:

Teenagers and New Technology

Magazine Article by Andres Padilla-Lopez

Close Reader selection
"Teenagers and New Technology"
Essay by Andres Padilla-Lopez

COMMON CORE

Common Core Standards

RI 1 Cite text evidence.

RI 2 Determine central ideas.

RI 3 Analyze interactions between ideas in a text.

RI 4 Determine meanings of words and phrases; determine technical meanings.

RI 5 Analyze organizational structure.

W 1b Support claims with logical reasoning and relevant evidence.

W 6 Use technology to produce and publish writing and link to and cite sources.

L 3a Eliminate redundancy.

L 4a Use context as a clue to the meaning of a word or phrase.

L 6 Acquire and use accurately grade-appropriate words.

▲ Text Complexity Rubric

Quantitative Measures

from **Life at Home in the Twenty-First Century**
Lexile: 1640L

Qualitative Measures

Levels of Meaning/Purpose

more than one purpose; implied, easily identified from context

Structure

sophisticated graphics, essential to understanding the text; may also provide information not otherwise conveyed in the text

Language Conventionality and Clarity

increased unfamiliar, academic, or domain-specific words

Knowledge Demands

complex social sciences and statistical concepts

Reader/Task Considerations

Teacher determined
Vary by individual reader and type of text

TEACH

CLOSE READ

Background After students read the background information, offer supplementary details:

- Although archaeologists study what is left behind by past cultures, the archaeological study cited in this text is of 32 families in present-day Los Angeles, California.

- The abbreviation *CRT* stands for "cathode ray tube," a kind of vacuum tube used in electronic devices. CRTs were in heavy, bulky monitors used for TV sets and computers.

SETTING A PURPOSE Direct students to use the Setting a Purpose prompt to focus their reading. Remind students to generate questions as they read.

Analyze Structure: Cause and Effect (LINES 1–8)

COMMON CORE RI 1, RI 5

Tell students that the **structure** of an informational text is the way the text is put together to organize the author's ideas. Explain that one **pattern of organization,** or particular arrangement of ideas and information, in this informational text is **cause and effect.** Using this pattern, the author tells about the big changes in American life that have been caused by the television.

A **CITE TEXT EVIDENCE** Have students reread lines 1–8 and cite three major areas affected by broadcast communication. *("economic decisions, political outcomes, and moral reasoning")* Have students use familiar examples of TV programs and advertisements to tell about the impact in the three areas cited. *(Student responses should clearly show how present-day television programming has impacted society in these three areas, such as advertisements impacting buying habits, news commentary affecting elections, and the behavior of characters in popular fictional programs [and real life personalities in "reality TV"] impacting morality.)*

Background *It's hard to imagine, but less than 100 years ago, television as we know it didn't exist. Then in 1927, Philo T. Farnsworth successfully transmitted an image onto a remote screen. By the early 1950s, TV purchases skyrocketed. Today almost every home in the United States has at least one. This excerpt from Life at Home in the Twenty-First Century describes what a team of archaeologists uncovered about TVs when they examined the daily lives of 32 California families.*

from

LIFE at HOME in the TWENTY-FIRST CENTURY

Informational Text by Jeanne E. Arnold

SETTING A PURPOSE Perhaps no other technology is more widely shared as the television. As you read, keep track of how the popularity of this consumer good has changed over time. How will archaeologists of the future track its significance? Write down any questions you have while reading.

Television and Daily Life

In North America, and in as few as three generations, mass media broadcast by analog and digital signal has all but replaced oral history and become the primary conveyor of culturally shared ideas. Broadcast communication, particularly television-streamed content, figures so prominently in economic decisions, political outcomes, and moral reasoning that even at the height of the last U.S. recession, TV advertising expenditures exceeded $50 billion.

Television is now so intricately woven into the fabric of the
10 American family experience that few children born during the last two decades will be able to imagine a social world that

---

Close Read Screencasts ▶ View It!

Modeled Discussions

Have students click the *Close Read* icons in their eBooks to access two screencasts in which readers discuss and annotate the following key passages:

- "One set is typically located . . . how we orient our bodies" (lines 23–31).
- "Archaeologists rely on seriation . . . determines the relative age of each layer" (lines 134–142).

As a class, view and discuss at least one of these videos. Then, have students work in pairs to do an independent close read of an additional passage—"In the complex story . . . CRT use plummeted" (lines 173–183).

Determine Central Ideas (LINES 24–28)

COMMON CORE RI 2

Tell students that archaeologists study the roles that objects play in people's lives. In this study of how families use TV sets, the author points out that a TV set plays a significant role in daily social life.

B ASK STUDENTS to reread the sentence that begins with the words *The set used by the collective* in lines 24–28. Discuss the author's main idea—that TV is "an agentive participant." Ask students to restate that idea in their own words. (*The TV set is more than an object made by people; it changes how people live with one another.*)

Cite Evidence (LINES 32–38)

COMMON CORE RI 1, RI 2

Point out that the paragraph running from lines 32 to 49 tells about living spaces that include TV sets.

C CITE TEXT EVIDENCE Have students reread lines 32–38 and cite text that describes what photographs of living rooms reveal. (*The photos "repeatedly reveal spaces organized around televisions."*) Ask what point the author is making. (*When people gather in their living room, they don't look at one another when talking. Their attention is on the TV set.*)

SCAFFOLDING FOR ELL STUDENTS

Determine Meaning Offer support for challenging sentence structures, idioms, and domain-specific terminology. Have students use their eBook annotation tools to underline and highlight the words that match your paraphrases. These are possible paraphrases for the sample shown, from lines 13–19:

- Children are born near TV sets.
- A TV set seems to be watching the close connection between mother and newborn.
- That shows how important TV is in American life.

---

has not been partly shaped by the imagery, discourse, and ideas originating from television programming. In fact, many twenty-first century children are born in the physical presence of a TV: most labor, delivery, and recovery rooms in the U.S. now feature large, wall-mounted flat-panel sets. That TVs are witness to such intimate and emotionally bonding experiences speaks volumes about televisions and the American way of being.

20   Currently, 99 percent of U.S. households own a TV, and more than 50 percent own three or more. All of the families in our study have at least one TV, and most have two or more. One set is typically located in a large space used by all family members, such as the living room, family room, or den. The set used by the collective is a compelling example of an object that is not merely a tangible product of otherwise invisible cultural forces but rather an agentive[1] participant in the daily production of social lives. The introduction of a new TV to a living room, for example, shapes the decisions underlying

30 where we locate our furniture, where we direct our gaze, and how we orient our bodies.

At some deeper cognitive level, our relationship to the TV—which includes a relationship to the object itself but also our personal experiences centering on TV media— even shapes the ways that we relate to our built spaces. Our photographs of living room assemblages[2] repeatedly reveal spaces organized around televisions rather than spaces with other primary affordances, such as face-to-face conversation. For all of its influence on the design and organization of

40 space, the TV may as well be a hearth,[3] which until quite recently in human history exerted the most influence on the spatial distribution of social interactions and activities inside homes. Indeed, families often locate the TV immediately adjacent to a wood-burning stove or fireplace, and new homes feature recessed fireplace-like nooks designed for television sets. The TV has ascended to the rank of essential major appliance (alongside the refrigerator, clothes washer, and dryer) around which builders and architects imagine the designs of residential spaces.

---

[1] **agentive:** having the power to cause an effect.
[2] **assemblages:** collections of people or things.
[3] **hearth:** the brick or cement floor of a fireplace that extends into a room.

---

ideas originating from television programming. In fact, many twenty-first century <u>children are born in the physical presence of a TV</u>: most labor, delivery, and recovery rooms in the U.S. now feature large, wall-mounted flat-panel sets. That TVs are witness to such intimate and emotionally bonding experiences speaks volumes about televisions and the American way of being.

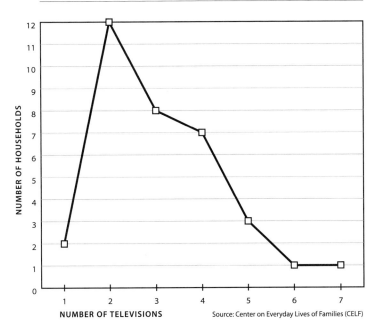

LOS ANGELES HOUSEHOLDS AND TV OWNERSHIP

NUMBER OF HOUSEHOLDS

NUMBER OF TELEVISIONS

Source: Center on Everyday Lives of Families (CELF)

This graph is based on data about TV ownership among 32 California families. The data was gathered by researchers from the University of California, Los Angeles (UCLA), and Connecticut College.

Families now also routinely equip various bedrooms with televisions. Fully 25 of the 32 CELF[4] families (78 percent) have a TV in the parents' bedroom, and 14 families (47 percent) place a TV in one or more of the bedrooms used by children. Researchers at the Kaiser Family Foundation surveyed 1,051 U.S. households with young children and found that 43 percent place a TV in at least one child's bedroom.

The same Kaiser-funded project reveals that 87 percent of children age four to six years are able to turn on the TV without assistance. Most two- and three-year-olds can do the

_____

[4] **CELF:** the Center on the Everyday Lives of Families at the University of California at Los Angeles, which studies how families approach the challenges of everyday life.

WHEN STUDENTS STRUGGLE . . .

Students may struggle with the statistical figures that the author uses to support his conclusions. Suggest that students track the statistics and conclusions by filling in a graphic organizer as shown here. Students can also use the chart to track conclusions to figures presented in the graphs in this selection.

Conclusion	Statistics
Our relationship to TVs shape how we arrange our living spaces.	*• 25 of 32 families: TVs in parents' bedroom* *• 14 of 32 families: TVs in children's bedrooms*

CLOSE READ

For more context and historical background, students can view the video "America The Story of Us: The Rise of Television" in their eBooks.

HISTORY

Cite Evidence (GRAPH)

COMMON CORE RI 1, RI 2

Explain that **graphic aids** are diagrams, graphs, maps, and other visual tools that are printed, handwritten, or drawn in a text. Explain that line graphs such as the one on this page can indicate trends. Point out that the **horizontal axis** of the graph shows the increasing number of TV sets, left to right, and the **vertical axis** shows the increasing number, or frequency, of households, bottom to top.

 ASK STUDENTS to reread the information in the line graph and explain the patterns the line graph reveals about the 32 households studied. *(Every household had at least one TV. Only two households had just one TV set. At the other extreme, two households had six or seven TV sets.)*

Analyze Structure: Cause and Effect (LINES 50–65)

COMMON CORE RI 1, RI 3, RI 5

Tell students that the researchers gathered data about the number of TV sets per household, the locations of those sets, and the TV-related activities of young children.

CITE TEXT EVIDENCE Have students reread lines 50–65 and cite text evidence that explains what societal phenomenon has resulted in thousands of studies of the effects of TV on children. *(More than 40 percent of families place a TV "in at least one child's bedroom," and "American children learn how to operate and engage with the TV at a very young age." As a result, TV has an impact on children's lives. The studies are designed to find out more about that impact.)*

TEACH

CLOSE READ

Analyze Structure: Cause and Effect (LINES 66–98)

COMMON CORE RI 1, RI 3, RI 5

Point out that the researchers took notes on the activities of individual family members and also videotaped families they were studying. They then examined the videos to code the behaviors they saw. They were looking for evidence of the impacts of television viewing, which have been debated.

G CITE TEXT EVIDENCE Have students reread lines 66–98, cite examples of what has been debated, and explain what the researchers discovered to support both sides of the debate. *(The debate asks whether TV viewing leads to "reduced social interaction" or whether families use TV time "as a platform for togetherness." Researchers found that, on weekdays, an "average daily total of just 46 minutes" is spent on "attentive, focused TV viewing"—which is less than predicted. They also found that when family members watch together, it's "usually a social experience." However, they also found that "kids view solo" more than adults, and "children in families that have TVs in one or more bedroom spaces are more likely to watch TV alone.")*

CRITICAL VOCABULARY

observation: Tell students that when scientists make observations they use a coding system so that they can gather data in a systematic way.

ASK STUDENTS what kinds of coding might have been used for the video observations. *(There may have been a list of activities, and researchers checked off the ones they observed families engage in.)*

---

60 same (82 percent), and the majority of children belonging to both age groups are capable of changing the channel. Suffice it to say that American children learn how to operate and engage with the TV at a very young age, a fact that has motivated more than 4,000 studies addressing the impacts of TV on children, education, and the social lives of families.

These impacts, however, are debated. Some researchers associate TV viewing with reduced social interaction, while others report the opposite and even see evidence for families' use of TV time as a platform for togetherness. Research based

70 on our unique observational data sets is new to the discussion and actually lends support to both generalizations, reflecting the complex relationship Americans have with television. For example, our study shows that families are not actively engaging with TV as much as we might otherwise predict. Attentive, focused TV viewing accounts for only 11 percent of all primary person-centered scan sampling **observations**, and the careful coding of 380 hours of videotape (derived from our observational videography) reveals that families engage with TV media on weekday afternoons and evenings for an

80 average daily total of just 46 minutes (although the TV may be turned on for much longer periods). Furthermore, families' viewing is usually a social experience: during about two-thirds of observations where a child or adult watches TV, at least one other family member is present.

However, children are slightly more likely than their parents to watch TV alone. Kids view solo in about 17 percent of the cases where we record TV viewing as the primary activity, mothers and fathers watch alone in only 6 percent and 13 percent of the cases, respectively. We also found that

90 children much more frequently watch TV in a bedroom (34 percent of primary TV observations, alone or with others) than either of their parents (9 percent for mothers and 10 percent for fathers). Indeed, the socially isolating potential of TV appears higher among families that have more than one TV set in the home. Children in families that have TVs in one or more bedroom spaces are more likely to watch TV alone than children in families that do not have a TV in a child's or parents' bedroom.

observation
(ŏb´zər-vā´shən) *n.*
An *observation* is the act of watching something.

Strategies for Annotation 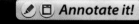 Annotate it!

Analyze Structure

COMMON CORE RI 1, RI 2, RI 5

Have students use their eBook annotation tools to cite information about the effects of television in the paragraphs that begin "These impacts, however, are debated" (lines 66–98).

- Highlight in yellow references to *less social interaction* as a result of TV use.
- Highlight in green references to *more social interaction* as a result of TV use.
- Underline the researchers' summarizing statements about both effects.

These impacts, however, are debated. Some researchers associate TV viewing with reduced social interaction, while others report the opposite and even see evidence for families' use of TV time as a platform for togetherness. Research based on our unique observational data sets is new to the discussion and actually lends support to both generalizations, reflecting the complex relationship Americans have with television.

> ## *Some researchers associate TV viewing with reduced social interaction.*

The Material Legacy of TV

The **proliferation** of video media technology since the debut
100 of network television in 1946 has had a profound influence
on American lifestyles. Indeed, few Americans can imagine
everyday life without access to TV. Television is so entrenched
in popular culture that we are surprised when we meet people
who do not have at least one set. In 1947, U.S. households
owned 44,000 TVs, just one set per 3,275 people. During
the early 2000s, people purchased about 31 million TVs
annually in the U.S., or one new TV for every nine Americans
each year.

Of course, sales figures do not reflect the number of
110 sets already found in what archaeologists regard as systemic
context (here, the home): the behavioral system in which
artifacts[5] participate in everyday life. The full inventory of
TVs emerges only when the count includes the sets purchased
in years past and still in the house. Only some older TVs
are replaced. As is true for most artifacts, the life history of
each individual television is entangled in the changing ways
that families use them, the availability of similar artifacts
in the home, and the desire for newer forms of visual
media technologies.

120 Eventually the life history of a TV, or at least the portion
of the life history that overlaps with family use, comes to an
end. At that point, the artifact exits the systemic context and
enters an archaeological context, a state in which interaction
is primarily with the natural environment, such as the city
dump. The Environmental Protection Agency estimates that

proliferation
(prə-lĭf´ər-rā´shən) *n.*
A *proliferation* is
the fast growth of
something.

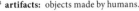

[5] **artifacts:** objects made by humans.

APPLYING ACADEMIC VOCABULARY

| technology | purchase |

As you discuss the information and concepts in this text, incorporate the
following Collection 5 academic vocabulary words: *technology* and *purchase*.
Talk about the influence of **technology** on family life and the reasons that
families **purchase** new **technologies**.

Analyze Structure: Cause and Effect (LINES 115–119)

  COMMON CORE RI 1, RI 3, RI 5

Tell students that when archaeologists study artifacts
they look for evidence about how the objects made
their way into a particular location and how and why
people used them.

H **CITE TEXT EVIDENCE** Tell students to reread
lines 115–119 and cite one of the reasons that
consumers get rid of older TV sets. *(People may replace
older TV sets because of "the desire for newer forms of
visual media technologies." For example, a family might
replace an older model with an Internet TV or a 3D TV
because they want more viewing options.)*

Determine Meanings

  COMMON CORE RI 4

(LINES 120–125)

Tell students that the author uses the technical terms
systemic context and *archaeological context*.

I **ASK STUDENTS** to reread lines 120–124 and
explain the difference between both contexts. *(The
systemic context is how and where the artifact is used;
the archaeological context is where it goes after it is
thrown out.)*

CRITICAL VOCABULARY

proliferation: There has been a proliferation of
video media technology ever since Americans
were first exposed to TV programs.

ASK STUDENTS why the proliferation of this
technology has had a "profound influence on
American lifestyles." *(With ever-growing numbers of
TV sets in their homes, Americans watch more TV and
make it an important part of their daily lives.)*

Analyze Structure: Cause and Effect (LINES 130–142)

COMMON CORE · RI 3, RI 5

Point out and read aloud the sentence in lines 141–142: *Frequency seriation thus determines the relative age of each layer.*

 ASK STUDENTS to reread lines 130–142 and include the word *because* in an explanation of what that sentence in lines 141–142 means. *(Because styles of artifacts change over time, archaeologists look at layers of buried trash to see which layers have shared styles of artifacts. They can use changing styles to tell which layers are older or younger than others.)*

Cite Evidence (LINES 143–150)

COMMON CORE · RI 1, RI 2

Explain that students can make judgments based on evidence and reasoning, or **draw conclusions,** as they read informational text like this. Point out that text evidence about archaeologists digging in landfills today and in the future can help them draw conclusions about evidence of TV use.

(K) CITE TEXT EVIDENCE Have students reread lines 143–150 and draw a conclusion about TV owners' preferences based on evidence in garbage layers forming today. *(People preferred color CRT TV sets through the 1980s, but people today prefer flat-screen TVs. The evidence that supports this is that today's landfills will have few black-and-white sets and significantly more color CRT sets. The increasing number of flat screens will show that their popularity has just taken off.)*

CRITICAL VOCABULARY

municipal: Trash may be dumped in municipal landfills.

ASK STUDENTS what landfills have to do with municipal services. *(Sanitation is one of the responsibilities of city and town governments.)*

---

during the mid-2000s, Americans discarded an average of 1.5 billion pounds of TVs each year, in the range of 25 to 27 million sets annually, of which only 4 to 4.5 million were collected for domestic recycling.

An Archaeology of TVs

130 The rate at which TV technology evolves and the sheer volume of television sets people discard both suggest that this artifact will be particularly useful for teasing out discrete generations of household refuse from the materially complex and jumbled strata[6] that constitute our **municipal** landfills. Archaeologists rely on seriation—the sequencing of functionally similar artifacts based on stylistic differences—as a method for ascertaining relative chronology[7] at archaeological sites. Although seriation cannot be used to pinpoint a specific date, it places older and younger materials in order based 140 on the simple assumption that object styles change over time. Frequency seriation thus determines the relative age of each layer.

We expect 1980s-era landfill strata to contain high proportions of black-and-white TVs and color CRT TV sets, but very low proportions of rear-projection TVs and no flat panels. Garbage layers forming today will contain few black-and-white sets, numerous color CRT sets, and (assuming a continued low rate of recycling) an increasing number of flat panels, assuming that household disposal of any particular 150 TV may postdate its purchase by a decade or more.

Archaeologists often use battleship curves to depict frequency seriation patterns. These graphs are particularly useful for showing changes in the proportion of different technological styles of artifacts over time. Interpretation of the curves is straightforward: the width of a horizontal bar for each year represents a percentage of a total count (see right axis opposite). In 1990, for example, 22.6 million TVs were purchased in the U.S. Only 6 percent were black-and-white sets, whereas 46 percent were color CRT models 160 less than 19 inches in size and another 46 percent were large color CRT models. Just 2 percent were the new rear-projection models, and flat panels had not yet debuted.

---

[6] **strata:** layers.
[7] **chronology** (krə-nŏl´ə-jē): the order of events in time.

municipal
(myo͞o-nĭs´ə-pəl) *adj.*
If something is *municipal*, it relates to a city or town.

DISPOSAL RATE OF TELEVISIONS

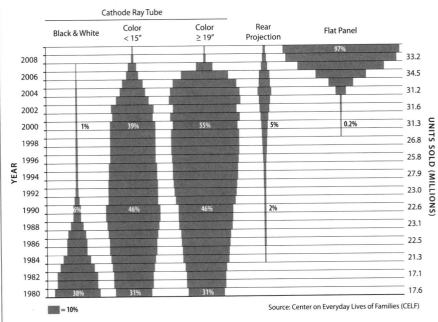

This battleship curve is a graphic aid used by archaeologists to record an artifact's patterns of use across a period of time. Here, the battleship curve indicates periods of popularity and fading use of different styles of TVs.

The shape of each battleship curve is particularly telling, providing an at-a-glance account of changes in the popularity of an artifact style or type over the course of its history. After the artifact's introduction, curves typically become gradually wider as the artifact style becomes more popular. As newer styles enter the material system, the first curve **tapers** and eventually terminates altogether. The maximum widths and rates of tapering (in both directions) summarize the popularity, rapidity of change in preference or supply, and persistence through time.

170

In the complex story of U.S. television consumption, several well-defined patterns emerge. Black-and-white TV sets persisted until the early 2000s, long after color CRT sets began dominating household assemblages, and rear-projection units enjoyed a long lifespan but never gained popularity. When

taper
(tā´pər) *v.* When things *taper*, they gradually get thinner.

CLOSE READ

Cite Evidence

COMMON CORE RI 1, RI 2, RI 3

(LINES 151–172; GRAPH)

Tell students that the author helps readers understand how to interpret this graph of "battleship curves," so named because the step-like shapes, or curves, resemble the head-on profiles of battleships. Explain that the text that accompanies a graph, the title and caption, and the label for each vertical axis enable readers to understand the information shown.

L CITE TEXT EVIDENCE Have students study the graph and reread lines 151–172. Have students cite data in the text or graph as they answer the following:

- What does the width of a horizontal bar represent? (*Its width "represents a percentage of a total count" of TVs purchased for a particular year.*)

- The text says that in 1990, "46 percent were color CRT models less than 19 inches in size." Where is that data on the graph? (*In the second battleship, between four and five squares make up the width of the bar for 1990.*)

- In the period shown, what was the most popular and longest-lasting TV set purchased? (*Color CRT TV sets that were equal to or greater than 19 inches were popular from the 1980s into the mid-2000s.*)

- Why is the battleship for Rear Projection sets so thin? (*Fewer were sold than other kinds of TV sets.*)

CRITICAL VOCABULARY

taper: As newer styles of TVs become available, the battleship curves of older styles taper.

ASK STUDENTS what a tapering curve indicates in the graph. (*That style of TV is less popular.*)

Strategies for Annotation 🖉 📄 *Annotate it!*

Cite Evidence

COMMON CORE RI 1, RI 2, RI 3

Have students use their eBook annotation tools to cite text evidence that connects data from the graph to the text. For example, in lines 173–177:

- Highlight in yellow the text that interprets data from the Black & White column of the graph from 1980–2001.

- Highlight in green information that reflects the percentages of 39% and 55% in 2000. Highlight in blue text that summarizes data showing usage no greater than 10%.

- Add a note showing data from the graph that indicates the persistence of black-and-white TV sets.

In the complex story of U.S. television consumption, several well-defined patterns emerge. Black-and-white TV sets persisted until the early 2000s, long after color CRT sets began dominating household assemblages, and rear-projection units enjoyed a long lifespan but never gained popularity. When

1990–2008, B&W TVs account for between 6% and about 1% of sets in landfills

Cite Evidence (LINES 173–183) (COMMON CORE) RI 1, RI 3

Point out that in the last paragraph of this excerpt the author sums up the patterns shown in the battleship curve.

 CITE TEXT EVIDENCE Have students tell what is significant about the adoption rate of flat-panel sets and cite evidence from the battleship graph that supports their conclusion. *(The rate is "unprecedented in the domain of television technology." In the graph, between 1999 and 2008 (less than 10 years), flat-screens in landfills soared from less than 1% to nearly 100% (97%). That means flat-panel sets replaced earlier models faster than replacements had ever occurred before.)*

CRITICAL VOCABULARY

precipitous: Sales of color CRT models declined precipitously.

ASK STUDENTS to show on the graph where the precipitous decline began. *(Sudden tapering of the second and third battleships starts in 2006.)*

COLLABORATIVE DISCUSSION Have students work in small groups to discuss the clues that TV sets in landfills will provide archaeologists and the conclusions archaeologists are likely to draw from these clues. Suggest that students find evidence in the text about what happens to TV sets after they are no longer used and what "frequency seriation" is.

ASK STUDENTS to share any questions they generated in the course of reading and discussing the selection.

---

significantly better TV technology emerged in the form of flat-panel models, color CRT models declined **precipitously**,
180 producing the narrow profiles at the tops of the CRT battleships. The adoption rate of flat-panel sets has been steep and unprecedented in the domain of television technology, expanding as CRT use plummeted.

precipitous
(prĭ-sĭp´ĭ-təs) *adj.*
When something is *precipitous*, it is very steep, like a cliff.

COLLABORATIVE DISCUSSION When future archaeologists study life in the past—the early twenty-first century—what clues will TV sets provide? Talk about your ideas with other group members.

TO CHALLENGE STUDENTS . . .

Group Discussion In lines 50–99, the author points out that research has caused some debate about TV's impact on the family, with some researchers concluding that TV isolates family members from each other, while other researchers conclude that TV actually brings families together. Have students work in small groups to discuss the implications of these findings. How is TV shaping family life? What are the qualitative costs and benefits of TV use for families? Have students cite evidence from the selection to support their claims and conclusions.

Analyze Structure: Cause and Effect RI 2, RI 5

The **structure** of a text is the way it is put together. Authors of informational texts organize their central ideas in paragraphs, and may organize the paragraphs in sections with **headings.** Within the sections, you can identify **patterns of organization,** a particular arrangement of ideas and information. For example, a **cause-and-effect** pattern of organization shows one or more events (causes) leading to one or more other events (effects).

This chart shows a single cause leading to multiple effects, based on details in the first four paragraphs of the section "Television and Daily Life" in the informational text you've just read.

> **CAUSE:** There is at least one TV in 99 percent of U.S. households.
>
> **EFFECT:** Media broadcast is the main conveyor of culturally shared ideas.
>
> **EFFECT:** Living spaces are organized and designed around a TV set.
>
> **EFFECT:** Oral history and face-to-face conversation are reduced.

Restate one of these cause-and-effect connections, using the phrase *as a result.*

Cite Evidence RI 1, RI 2

Graphic aids are diagrams, graphs, maps, and other visual tools that are printed, handwritten, or drawn. In informational texts, graphic aids organize, simplify, and summarize information. Here are a few types of graphic aids:

- Line graphs show numerical quantities across time and can indicate trends. The **vertical axis** of a graph indicates frequency. The **horizontal axis** shows the categories being considered.
- Bar graphs use horizontal and vertical bars to show or compare categories of information.
- Picture graphs convey information through symbols instead of lines and bars.

As you read, you can use evidence from both the text and the graphic aids to **draw a conclusion**—make a judgment based on evidence and reasoning.

Reread lines 157–162. Examine the graph on page 227. What conclusion can you draw from the text and the graph about flat-panel TV sets?

Life at Home in the Twenty-First Century **229**

CLOSE READ

Analyze Structure: Cause and Effect RI 2, RI 5

Tell students that science texts are often organized in cause-and-effect patterns because scientists look for answers to the question *Why?* Answers to *why* questions are causes. A cause can lead to one effect or many effects or be part of a cause-and-effect chain, in which one effect becomes the cause of another effect. *(Sample responses: At least one TV is found in almost every household; as a result, American culture is spread by media broadcast. Living spaces are organized and designed around TV sets as a result of the presence of at least one TV in 99 percent of households. Oral history and face-to-face conversation are reduced as a result.)*

Cite Evidence RI 1, RI 2

Review different types of graphic aids with students. Explain that each time students encounter a graphic aid they should look for its title, read any captions to determine what information is being presented, and examine any labels on the axes. Point out that the axes do not always show the same things and can vary not only between types of graphs, but also between different applications of the same type of graph. *(Sample answer: For the first few years that flat-panel TVs were available, not many people bought them. But they then became popular faster than any previous types of TVs.)*

Analyze Structure: Cause and Effect RI 2, RI 5

Using lines 93–98 as an example, share these strategies for guided or independent analysis:

- Highlight in yellow information about causes.
- Highlight in green information about effects.
- In a note, summarize the cause-and-effect connection.

10 percent for fathers). Indeed, the socially isolating potential of TV appears higher among families that have more than one TV set in the home. Children in families that have TVs in one or more bedroom spaces are more likely to watch TV alone than children in families that do not have a TV in a child's or parents' bedroom.

> One possible effect of a TV in a child's bedroom is greater social isolation.

Analyzing the Text

 COMMON CORE RI 1, RI 2, RI 5

Possible answers:

1. *Because consumers depend so much on television-streamed content to make decisions, advertisers spend tens of billions of dollars to influence these viewers.*

2. *The authors have studied families to observe the influences of TV in the home. As scientists, they want to gather numerical data about how people actually behave around their TV sets.*

3. *Through most of human history, the hearth was the place where families gathered for warmth, food, and social activity. A modern TV set is like a hearth because it has become a central spot in the home for family activities.*

4. *The most important findings have to do with the complex relationship that Americans have with television. The authors found support for opposing views: TV is a way for families to be together, and TV is a way for children to be alone. They also discovered that people are actively watching TV for less time than one might predict.*

5. *The details in this section show that in the early 2000s people purchased about "31 million TVs annually in the U.S." The data also suggests that American consumers at this time did not exhibit good recycling habits when it came to discarding TVs.*

6. *Twelve households owned only two TVs. This is notable because it is the largest number of households of the 32 represented in the graph. It suggests that most homes own two TVs only.*

7. *Flat-panel TVs will continue to be most popular, with wide bands extending up through several years. Then, a new TV technology will likely be introduced. As it grows in popularity, its bands will widen as the bands for flat panels narrow.*

8. *Archaeologists look for how artifacts are arranged when buried. By counting the discarded objects and measuring where they lie in an ancient trash mound or a more recent landfill, archaeologists can tell how popular the objects were and how long ago they were used. TVs are artifacts because they are objects that reveal the culture of the people who used them.*

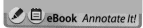
eBook *Annotate It!*

Analyzing the Text

 COMMON CORE RI 1, RI 2, RI 5, W 1b, W6

Cite Text Evidence Support your responses with evidence from the text.

1. **Cite Evidence** Reread the first paragraph. What causes more than $50 billion of TV advertising expenditures?

2. **Infer** What information about American families were the archaeologists gathering?

3. **Compare** Reread lines 39–46. According to the author, in what ways is a TV like a hearth?

4. **Summarize** Reread lines 66–99. What are the most important findings in this study of the impacts of TV?

5. **Infer** According to the details in "The Material Legacy of TV" section, during the mid-2000s, 25–27 million American-owned sets were discarded, but only 4–4.5 million were collected in domestic recycling. What might these figures suggest about the purchasing habits of American consumers?

6. **Analyzing Graphics** Of the 32 households represented in the graph on page 223, what number of households own only two TVs? What makes that figure worth noting?

7. **Predict** Look at the graph of battleship curves. How do you think the graph might change in the years ahead?

8. **Draw Conclusions** What do archaeologists look for as they study artifacts, and what does TV have to do with artifacts?

PERFORMANCE TASK

Writing Activity: Essay You've just read that a number of different types of televisions have been available through the years. Find out about a new development in TV technology and write about it in a brief informational essay.

- Use digital or print sources about consumer electronics to research your topic.
- Take notes as you try to answer questions like: Who invented this technology and when? How does it work? How could it change how people watch TVs? Why would consumers want to purchase it?
- Use your notes to create an outline of your ideas.
- Share your completed essay with a partner or group that has written about other new features of TVs. Discuss the different features and consumers' attitudes toward them.

Assign this performance task.

PERFORMANCE TASK

COMMON CORE W 1b, W 7

Writing Activity: Essay Have students do preliminary research by scanning sources about consumer electronics to find information about recent TV types.

- Students may jot down questions based on the products described.
- They then review questions for one or two that can lead to more research.
- Have them pick a topic that has enough information for an essay.

Critical Vocabulary

observation	proliferation	municipal
taper	precipitous	

Practice and Apply Complete each sentence to show that you understand the meaning of the bold word.

1. The scientist counted each **observation** of . . .

2. We've recently had a **proliferation** of . . .

3. An example of a **municipal** service is . . .

4. To draw lines that **taper,** you . . .

5. A change that occurs in a **precipitous** way is . . .

Vocabulary Strategy: Domain-Specific Words

The subject areas of *Life at Home in the Twenty-First Century* are sociology and archaeology. Sociology is the study of human societies. Archaeology is the study of the things left behind by past societies. When you read about any area of study, you will encounter **technical language,** terms and phrases used by specialists in a certain field or domain. Note the term *social interactions* in this quotation:

> For all of its influence on the design and organization of space, the TV may as well be a hearth, which until quite recently in human history exerted the most influence on the spatial distribution of *social interactions* and activities inside homes.

One way to figure out the meaning is by looking at its two parts: *social* has something to do with living with other people; *interactions* are the ways people communicate with each other. But often with technical language, you need to use a print or digital dictionary to confirm the meaning. For more highly specialized terms, you might have to use resources specific to the field, such as a manual of nautical terms for language about sailing.

Practice and Apply Compare your ideas with other group members as you find and define these terms: *observational data sets* (line 70); *observations* (line 76); *systemic context* (lines 110–111).

PRACTICE & APPLY

Critical Vocabulary

COMMON CORE L 6

Possible Answers:

1. *The scientist counted each observation of a family member turning on a TV.*

2. *We've recently had a proliferation of cicadas, which seem to be in every tree.*

3. *An example of a municipal service is trash collection.*

4. *To draw lines that taper, you start with a thick marker and switch to a thin one.*

5. *A change that occurs in a precipitous way is so sudden that people are unprepared for it.*

Vocabulary Strategy: Domain-Specific Words

Possible Answers:

Observational data sets *are the sets of numbers that researchers recorded as they observed family members interacting with their TV sets.* Observations *are acts of watching something, such as animal behavior, and making a record of the information that is observed.* Systemic context *refers to the place—the context—and the ways in which an object is used. Archaeologists are interested in the systemic context because they want to understand how an artifact was used in everyday life.*

Strategies for Annotation 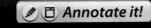 Annotate it!

Vocabulary Strategy: Domain-Specific Words

 COMMON CORE RI 4, L 4a, L 6

Have students use their eBook annotation tools to examine the context for domain-specific terms. Ask students to do the following:

- Highlight in yellow the target term.
- Highlight in green context clues.
- Note a likely meaning.
- See if the meaning makes sense in context; adjust note as needed.
- Consult a specialized dictionary, if needed.

> Of course, sales figures do not reflect the number of sets already found in what archaeologists regard as systemic context (here, the home): the behavioral system in which artifacts participate in everyday life. The full

> Likely: The way in which an artifact is actually used.
> Actual: The living society that artifacts were once a part of.

PRACTICE & APPLY

Language Conventions: Eliminate Redundancy

Review the common redundancies shown in the chart by having students tell why the underlined words are unnecessary. Offer support as needed for Practice and Apply by directing students to identify words that repeat the same meaning.

Possible Answers:

1. *Television sets are now essential appliances in our homes, like refrigerators and stoves.*

2. *Most American toddlers can turn on the TV and change a channel without assistance.*

3. *Although many people believe that watching TV is a solitary activity, some researchers have evidence that families use TV to spend time together.*

4. *The enormous number of TV sets that we discard will provide future archaeologists with clues about how we lived.*

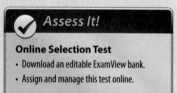

Assess It!

Online Selection Test
- Download an editable ExamView bank.
- Assign and manage this test online.

Language Conventions: Eliminate Redundancy

When you write to inform and explain, your goal is to be clear and concise. Watch out for **redundancy,** the use of unnecessary words. Reread your sentences to make sure that every word has a purpose.

This list shows common redundancies; the unnecessary words are underlined.

- each <u>and every</u> person
- never before <u>in the past</u>
- the <u>true</u> facts
- may <u>possibly</u> exist
- big <u>in size</u>
- prepared <u>in advance</u>
- <u>entirely</u> complete
- connect <u>together</u>

Avoid using words that repeat what you've already said. Compare these two sentences:

> Television has an impact on our behaviors and actions, affecting everything from what we purchase to what we talk about in our conversations.

> Television has an impact on our behaviors, from what we purchase to what we talk about.

You can tell that the second sentence is stronger because it makes its point in fewer words. In the first sentence, *behaviors* and *actions* are synonyms; *impact* and *affecting* express the same meaning; and *in our conversations* repeats the meaning of *what we talk about*.

Practice and Apply Rewrite each sentence to eliminate the redundancy.

1. Television sets are now essential items in our homes, as basic to our living spaces as refrigerators, stoves, and other necessary appliances.

2. Most American toddlers can turn on the TV without assistance or help from an adult and are also capable of changing a channel from one to another.

3. Although many people hold the belief and opinion that watching TV is a solitary activity, some researchers have evidence that families use the time in front of a TV as a way of spending time together.

4. The TV sets that we discard are enormous in number and will surely provide clues about how we live to archaeologists of the future looking back into the past.

Cite Evidence: Understanding Statistics

COMMON CORE

RI 1,
RI 2,
RI 3

TEACH

Tell students that because scientific research involves collecting, organizing, and interpreting data, researchers provide **statistics,** or numerical information, in their reports. Together, reread lines 86–93 of the excerpt from *Life at Home in the Twenty-First Century* to identify the statistics and discuss the comparisons the researchers are pointing out.

> **Kids view solo in about 17 percent of the cases where we record TV viewing as the primary activity, mothers and fathers watch alone in only 6 percent and 13 percent of the cases, respectively. We also found that children much more frequently watch TV in a bedroom (34 percent of primary TV observations, alone or with others) than either of their parents (9 percent for mothers and 10 percent for fathers).**

Explain that the term *statistics* also refers to the methods that researchers use to collect and analyze data. Remind students that these researchers' observations were made based on 32 families. Ask whether the conclusions drawn about those families could be applied to most American families. During the discussion, make these points about statistics:

- For studies about large populations, researchers choose a **sample** of a population to study. The sample must be chosen so that it is representative of the larger population.
- If the researchers choose a **random sample,** they choose in a way that all possible samples have an equal **probability,** or chance, of being selected. A random sample reduces the likelihood of bias.
- When studying causes and effects, researchers use statistical methods to determine the probability that a particular outcome would have occurred by chance and does not have the cause under study.

PRACTICE AND APPLY

Have students examine the numerical data in another segment of this informational text or in another informational text. Tell students to explain the pattern by writing a summarizing sentence or drawing a graphic. Direct students to write two thoughtful questions about how the statistics were gathered and analyzed.

Cite Evidence

COMMON CORE

RI 1,
RI 2

RETEACH

Review that **graphic aids** are visual tools that accompany text. Review the following graphic aids:

- **diagram:** a kind of drawing that shows the parts of an object or the steps in a process
- **map:** a kind of drawing showing part of the surface of Earth
- **graph:** a kind of drawing that shows numerical relationships

Review common kinds of graphs:

- **circle graph, or pie chart:** a graph that shows percentages
- **line graph:** a graph that shows changes over time
- **bar graph:** a graph that compares size or number
- **pictograph:** a graph in which icons stand for quantities

Use either of the graphs in the excerpt from *Life at Home in the Twenty-First Century* to review strategies for understanding graphs:

- Read the **title** to see what the graph shows.
- Look at the **labels** on the **horizontal** and **vertical axes.**
- Read any **captions.**
- Draw conclusions about the patterns shown.

 LEVEL UP TUTORIALS Assign the following *Level Up* tutorial: **Reading Graphic Aids**

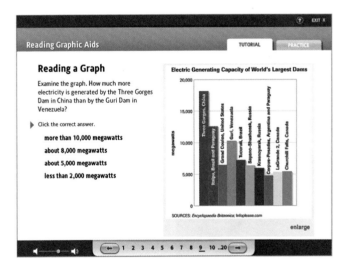

CLOSE READING APPLICATION

Guide students to informational texts that contain graphs. Have partners choose a graph to examine. Ask students to write two or more observations about details or patterns in the graph.

Teenagers and New Technology

Magazine Article by Andres Padilla-Lopez

Why This Text

Students may be overwhelmed by magazine articles with complex, multi-part structures. If the article includes an array of supporting evidence—personal anecdotes, numerical data, and graphs—students may find themselves even more at a loss. With the help of the close-reading questions, students will analyze the evidence presented in the article. This close reading will lead students to understand the structure of the article, including the cause-and-effect relationships used to organize its sections.

Background Have students read the background and information about the article. Introduce the article by pointing out that communication technologies have, from time to time, upset the social order. In 1946, for example, U.S. households owned about 40 million radios—and only 50,000 televisions. Within a few years, television would supplant radio in the American household, and everyone would have something to say about the social and cultural consequences.

SETTING A PURPOSE Ask students to pay attention to the cause-and-effect relationships in many paragraphs. How does the author use them to organize his writing?

Common Core Support

- cite multiple pieces of text evidence
- determine central ideas in a text
- determine the meaning of words
- analyze the structure used to organize a text
- determine an author's point of view

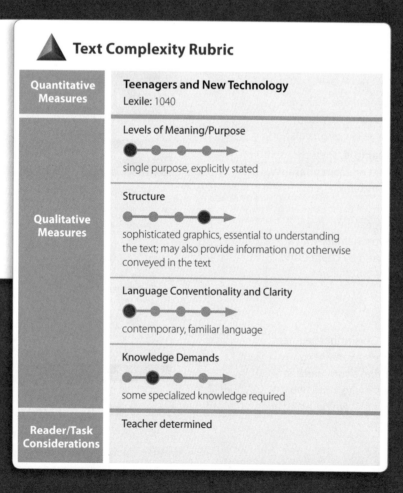

▲ Text Complexity Rubric

Quantitative Measures	**Teenagers and New Technology** Lexile: 1040
Qualitative Measures	**Levels of Meaning/Purpose** single purpose, explicitly stated
	Structure sophisticated graphics, essential to understanding the text; may also provide information not otherwise conveyed in the text
	Language Conventionality and Clarity contemporary, familiar language
	Knowledge Demands some specialized knowledge required
Reader/Task Considerations	Teacher determined

Strategies for CLOSE READING

Analyze the Structure of a Magazine Article

Students should read this article carefully all the way through. Close-reading questions at the bottom of the page will help them focus on a thorough analysis of the structure. As they read, students should jot down comments or questions about the text in the margins.

WHEN STUDENTS STRUGGLE . . .

To help students analyze the structure of "Teenagers and New Technology," have them work in small groups to fill out a chart like the one shown below.

CITE TEXT EVIDENCE For practice in analyzing the structure of a magazine article, ask students to cite text evidence for some of the cause-and-effect relationships.

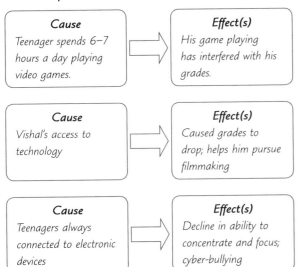

Cause	Effect(s)
Teenager spends 6–7 hours a day playing video games.	His game playing has interfered with his grades.

Cause	Effect(s)
Vishal's access to technology	Caused grades to drop; helps him pursue filmmaking

Cause	Effect(s)
Teenagers always connected to electronic devices	Decline in ability to concentrate and focus; cyber-bullying

---

Background *The world's first text message was sent on December 3, 1992. Neil Papworth sent the message "Merry Christmas" from his personal computer to the phone of Richard Jarvis. Technology has come quite a long way since then. The social networking site Facebook has over one billion active users; 2.4 billion people around the world use text messaging as a means of communication; and 30.2 percent of the world's population now use the Internet. Maybe it's important to ask: What are the effects of our obsession with new technology?*

Teenagers and New Technology

Magazine Article by Andres Padilla-Lopez

CLOSE READ
Notes

1. **READ ▷** As you read lines 1–23, begin to collect and cite text evidence.

   - Underline examples of technology overuse.
   - In the margin, summarize the cause-and-effect relationship found in lines 6–10.
   - In the margin, write what the author is seeking to determine by asking questions (lines 16–23).

Teenage Use of Electronic Devices

B Allison, a fifteen-year-old teenager from Redwood City, California, receives more than 27,000 text messages a month. This averages out to about 900 texts per day. Allison explains, "I text while I'm doing like *everything*. . . . I *need* to answer that text. I need to know who's talking to me, to know what they're going to say."

Another teenager, also from Redwood City, spends six to seven hours a day playing video games. He admits that his game playing has **A** interfered with his grades. But, he argues that video games "give me a shot of energy" and "playing just makes me happy . . . I can't stop
10 playing them. I don't want to stop playing them."

In an interview with a British reporter, one teenager said with feeling, "I'd rather give up a kidney than my phone." Another told the same reporter that she spends over an hour on school days and about

Because the teenager spends so many hours a day playing video games, his grades have suffered.

77

---

1. **READ AND CITE TEXT EVIDENCE** Tell students that this magazine article, like many, is organized in sections with subheadings. The subheadings tell you what a particular section is about and may be important clues about the article's overall structure.

A **ASK STUDENTS** to further explore the cause-and-effect relationship described for the Redwood City teenager. What causes him to spend so many hours playing video games each day? *Students should note that playing video games makes him happy and gives him "a shot of energy" (lines 8–9). So, students can now describe a causal chain: playing video games makes teenager happy* ➞ *he plays the games 6–7 hours each day* ➞ *his grades have suffered.*

CLOSE READ
Notes

The author is
asking the
reader to
examine the
benefits of
technology.

double that time on weekends hanging out with some 450 Facebook
friends.

So, how do *you* use electronic devices? Are your Facebook friends
the same as your real-life friends, or do they include people you've
never met? Are the friends you've never met more interesting than
your real-life friends? Do you feel lost without your cell phone? Must
20 you answer every text message immediately? Are you itching to get
out of class to play video games? Or perhaps you worry about the
amount of time you spend on your electronic devices. Maybe you
think that texting and Facebook are a waste of time.

Facts and Figures

The numerical
data is more
specific than
the
generalizations.

Recent studies estimate that 93 percent of teenagers between the
ages of 12 and 17 years of age regularly go online to use the Internet.
Studies also show that 75 percent of all teenagers own cell phones.
Half of that 75 percent sends fifty or more texts a day. One in three
sends 100 or more texts per day. Some teenage cellphone users don't
even use their phones to make actual phone calls—except to their

Teenagers and the Internet

- 74% have their own computer
- 63% of Internet users go online daily
- 27% use phones to go online
- 73% are on a social network

Contact with Friends Every Day

- 54% text message
- 38% call on a cell phone
- 30% talk on a landline phone
- 24% instant message
- 11% e-mail
- 25% use a social network site

Note that if you add up the percents, you find that many teenagers must use
various methods of contacting friends daily.

Landline
phones are
being
surpassed in
popularity by
cell phones.

2. **◀ REREAD** Reread lines 1–15. What are the similarities of the
structure of each of the first three paragraphs? Support your
response with explicit textual evidence.

Each paragraph begins with the introduction of a teenager and then
follows up with an explanation of how each teen is addicted to
technology—"a fifteen-year-old teenager" who receives "about
900 texts per day" is followed by "another teenager, also from
Redwood City" who plays video games "six to seven hours a day."

3. **READ ▶** As you read lines 24–35 and study the bar graphs,
continue to cite evidence.

- Underline text that contains numerical data, and circle text that makes
  a generalization. In the margin, note a difference between these two
  kinds of information.
- What conclusion can you draw about landline phones from the
  information in the graphs? Note your conclusion in the margin.
- In the margin, make an inference about the reason teenagers may
  make "actual phone calls" to their parents.

4. **◀ REREAD** Review the graphs. What conclusion can you draw
about why significantly more teenagers use text messaging than
e-mail to communicate with their friends? Support your answer with
explicit evidence from the graphs.

More teenagers probably use text messaging to communicate with
their friends because it can be done on a phone, instead of being
done at a computer. Only 27 percent of teenagers use their phone to
go online. Since e-mail requires the user to be online, we might be
able to assume that the 54 percent of teens who communicate via
text message have easier access to their phones than their
computers.

78

79

2. **REREAD AND CITE TEXT EVIDENCE**

Ⓑ **ASK STUDENTS** to summarize each of the first three
paragraphs. *Cause-and-effect relationships define the teenagers'
experiences. Allison gets more than 27,000 texts a month and needs
to answer each one. A teenager plays video games 6 to 7 hours a day
because they make him happy. Another has over 450 Facebook
friends and spends hours each weekend hanging out with them.*

3. **READ AND CITE TEXT EVIDENCE**

Ⓒ **ASK STUDENTS** to discuss the first bar graph. What
conclusion can you draw about phones from this graph? *Students
should understand that only about a quarter of teenagers use
phones to go online.* What kind of phones are these teenagers
using? *Students should realize that people use cell phones or smart
phones to connect to the Internet.*

FOR ELL STUDENTS Explain that in this context, *itching* means
"having a restless desire" rather than "having a skin irritation."

4. **REREAD AND CITE TEXT EVIDENCE**

Ⓓ **ASK STUDENTS** to discuss whether the first bar graph gives
evidence about why more teenagers communicate with friends
by text message than by e-mail. *Students should realize that text
messaging is done by phone, while e-mail is done (online) by
computer or phone. The first bar graph shows that few teenagers use
their phones to go online, but 74 percent of them own a computer. It
also shows that 63 percent of teenage Internet users go online each
day. The graph doesn't say how many teenagers are Internet users,
but it does say that 73 percent of teenagers belong to a social
network. So, the first graph would seem to indicate that plenty of
teenagers have computers, use the Internet, and go online daily to
communicate by e-mail if they wish to. The reason(s) for their
preference for text messaging must lie elsewhere.*

CLOSE READ Notes

> **" Scientists wonder about the long-term effects on a teenager's still-developing brain. "**

Parents may not know how to send text messages.

30 parents. Instead, they use texting to communicate. And, as all cell phone owners know, today's phones enable you to do much more than just texting. They allow users to take and share pictures, play games, listen to music, swap videos, and access the Internet and social networking sites such as Facebook and Twitter. The average teenager has 201 Facebook friends!

The Pros and the Cons

aptly:
appropriately

One high school student from California **aptly** sums up the conflicting attitudes held by both adults and teenagers about the use of digital devices. Vishal is a bright seventeen-year old with a passionate interest in filmmaking. As he puts it, technology is "bad
40 for me as a student" because it has caused his grades to go down. On the other hand, he says, it is "good for me as a learner." Vishal's access to technology has distracted him and made it difficult for him to concentrate on his assigned schoolwork, but it has also helped him to pursue in depth his interest in filmmaking.

Currently educators, scientists, parents, and even some teenagers themselves worry about the long-term effects of always being

---

5. **READ** ▶ As you read lines 36–57, continue to cite textual evidence.
- Underline negative effects of using digital devices.
- Circle positive effects of using digital devices.
- In the margin, explain what positions, pro or con, the author seems to emphasize.

80

---

connected to electronic devices. Educators notice a decline in students' ability to concentrate on any one thing for an extended period of time. Scientists wonder about the long-term effects on a
50 teenager's still-developing brain. What do the instant **gratification** and rapid stimulation offered by electronic media do to a teenager's brain? Scientists also fear that yielding to one distraction after another develops an inability to focus. Parents worry about the presence of predators on social networking sites. They are also alarmed by the threat of cyber-bullying. Teenagers, like Vishal and Allison, ask themselves if their slipping grades and inability to concentrate on school tasks are worth it.

On the other hand, supporters argue that today's powerful cell phones offer teenagers new worlds of opportunity. They stress that
60 understanding new technology is essential to future success. They recognize that tools, such as texting and Facebook, meet needs common to all teenagers, such as defining their personal identity and establishing their independence. These technologies provide new avenues for teenagers to do the things teenagers have always wanted to do: flirt, boast, gossip, complain, tease, and get news. Some educators see new technologies as an exciting way of connecting with students. Others view them as a tool for personalizing education and encouraging individual students' interests.

gratification:
reward

The information is mostly against the overuse of technology.

These statements support the use of technology.

---

6. **REREAD** Reread lines 36–57. Explain how the cause-and-effect pattern of organization is used in this section to connect ideas. Support your answer with explicit textual evidence.

The author explicitly lists the effects of technology. An "inability to focus" and a "decline in students' ability to concentrate on any one thing for an extended period of time" are both directly attributed to "the use of digital devices." Vishal's access to technology—a cause—has "distracted him and made it difficult for him to concentrate"—an effect.

---

7. **READ** ▶ As you read lines 58–71, continue to cite textual evidence.
- Circle positive effects of using digital devices.
- In the margin, explain which position, pro or con, the author emphasizes now.

81

---

5. **READ AND CITE TEXT EVIDENCE**

🅔 **ASK STUDENTS** to weigh the negative and positive effects of using digital devices. *On the negative side, students should cite Vishal's admission that technology distracts him and makes it hard for him to concentrate on schoolwork; educators' observation that students' ability to concentrate is declining; scientists' fear that technology causes an "inability to focus"; and parents' worries about online predators and cyber-bullies. On the positive side, there are only Vishal's assertions that technology is good for him "as a learner" and that it has helped him pursue filmmaking.*

Critical Vocabulary: aptly (line 36) Have students give the definition of the base word *apt*. *"well suited or intelligent"* Have them give the definition of the suffix *-ly*. *"in a certain manner"* So what is the meaning of *aptly*? *"in a suitable or intelligent manner"*

6. **REREAD AND CITE TEXT EVIDENCE**

🅕 **ASK STUDENTS** to describe the general cause-and-effect pattern. *There is only one cause—technology, or more precisely, the overuse of electronic devices—and several effects. However, the author implies some causal chains. For example, electronic devices give users "instant gratification and rapid stimulation," which may affect teenagers' brains in the long term (lines 50–51).*

7. **READ AND CITE TEXT EVIDENCE**

🅖 **ASK STUDENTS** to paraphrase the positive effects of using digital devices. *Technology lets teenagers define their identities and establish their independence. It gives teenagers a new way to socialize. It gives teachers a way to connect with students, personalize lessons, and encourage students.*

Critical Vocabulary: gratification (line 50) Have students suggest synonyms of *gratification* that would work in this context. *fulfillment, pleasure, enjoyment*

CLOSE READ
Notes

Wherever you stand on the various issues raised, there is no doubt
70 that electronic devices are here to stay. How we use these devices,
whether we choose to have them work for us or against us, is up to us.

8. ◀ REREAD AND DISCUSS Reread lines 58–71. With a small group,
draw several conclusions about the ways that teens can use
technological devices to work for them instead of against them. Cite
explicit textual evidence in your discussion.

SHORT RESPONSE

Cite Text Evidence What types of information does the author include to
show the ways in which teens use technological devices? What overall insight
does the reader gain on the use of these devices? Review your reading notes,
and be sure to **cite evidence from the text** in your response.

> The article presents a variety of information to show the ways that
> teens use or misuse technology. The article quotes examples of the
> negative effects of technology overuse: "Allison, a fifteen-year old
> teenager from Redwood City, California," who "receives more than
> 27,000 text messages a month." Statistics provide insight into the
> cause of the problem: "75 percent of all teenagers own cell phones."
> The author also uses bar graphs to illuminate the various ways in which
> teens use technology—e-mail, instant message, and social network
> sites. The reader gains insight into "how we use these devices" and
> "whether we choose to have them work for us or against us."

82

TO CHALLENGE STUDENTS . . .

For deeper understanding, students can research negative and
positive effects of using electronic devices in cars.

ASK STUDENTS to discuss some of the negative effects of using
electronic devices in cars. *Students should understand that talking
on a cell phone while driving is dangerous. The driver, distracted, is at
risk of not seeing other cars, traffic lights, or pedestrians until it is too
late to avoid crashing. Researchers have compiled statistics showing
that driving while talking on a cell phone is about as dangerous as
driving while drunk. Interestingly, the effect is the same for hands-
free phones as for handheld phones. The problem, scientists say, is
not that we're holding a cell phone but that our brains are focused
on the conversation, not the road.*

Have students discuss some of the positive effects of new
technology in cars. *Students should recognize that cell phones are
useful in case of breakdowns or emergencies. People can summon
assistance immediately, and lives might be saved. Many smart
phones have GPS, which helps drivers get places without becoming
lost. Cell phones and other electronic devices are also a way to keep
children occupied during long drives, which means fewer distractions
for the driver.*

---

8. **REREAD AND DISCUSS USING TEXT EVIDENCE**

H **ASK STUDENTS** in each group to start by considering their
responses to Question 7. How can teens use digital devices to
achieve each of these positive outcomes? *Students may note, for
example, that by texting and using Facebook, teens are able to define
their identities. Students could also mention that by flirting and
gossiping online, teens can socialize much as their parents did, but
with new technology. Finally, students may say that computers,
smart phones, and tablets let them pursue their interests, further
their education, and connect with teachers.*

SHORT RESPONSE

Cite Text Evidence Students should:

- describe the types of information included in the article.
- give examples of evidence from anecdotes, statistics, and bar
  graphs.
- explain what insight they gained from the article.

DIG DEEPER

1. With the class, return to Question 1, Read. Have students share their underlined examples.

ASK STUDENTS to discuss the term *technology overuse.*

- What is the nature of the problem this article explores? *Students should realize that the author examines the consequences of teenagers' overuse of electronic devices. The new technology isn't a problem if teenagers don't dedicate excessive amounts of time to it.*

- What evidence—explicit or implied—does the author present of "technology overuse"? *Students should note that receiving 900 text messages a day will necessarily consume a large part of Allison's waking hours. On average, she will "need" to answer a text almost every minute. Similarly, students will probably deem six to seven hours of daily video games as "overuse," especially since the Redwood City teenager says that he can't stop playing them. However, students may feel that the third teenager is not overusing her devices. She has a large number of Facebook friends but spends only one to two hours online with them each day.*

2. With the class, return to Question 3, Read. Have students share their responses to the question.

ASK STUDENTS to discuss the data presented here.

- Have students analyze the numerical data and the generalizations presented in lines 24–35. *Students should recognize that the generalizations are supported by logic and experience. We all know people who use their phones mainly or exclusively to text, and of course it is true that smart phones can take pictures, play games, and listen to music. The numerical data, on the other hand, comes from "studies" that, although not cited, carry greater authority. The author implies that the studies are reputable, so readers should consider the data seriously.*

ASK STUDENTS to return to their Short Response answer and revise it based on the class discussion.

CLOSE READING NOTES

mySmartPlanner Create lesson plans and access resources online.

Always Wanting More
from I Want That!

Informational Text by Thomas Hine

Why This Text?

This nonfiction text presents a familiar economic topic—shopping. The text lets students examine how an author combines facts and reflection. This lesson focuses on the language an author uses to express ideas and viewpoints and on inferences readers can make.

► View It!

Professional Development Podcast:

Informational Text

Key Learning Objective: The student will be able to identify features of an author's style and make inferences using textual details and prior knowledge.

For practice and application:

Labels and Illusions

Close Reader selection
"Labels and Illusions"
Essay by Lourdes Barranco

COMMON CORE — Common Core Standards

RI 1 Cite text evidence.
RI 2 Determine central idea.
RI 4 Determine meanings of words and phrases.
RI 5 Analyze the structure an author uses to organize a text.
RI 8 Evaluate specific claims in a text.
SL 1 Engage in collaborative discussions.
L 1a Explain the function of phrases and clauses.
L 4d Verify the preliminary determination of the meaning of a word or phrase.
L 5b Use synonym/antonym relationships to understand words.
L 6 Acquire and use grade-appropriate academic vocabulary.

▲ Text Complexity Rubric

Quantitative Measures	**Always Wanting More *from* I Want That!** Lexile: 1240L
Qualitative Measures	**Levels of Meaning/Purpose**  more than one purpose; implied, easily identified from context
	Structure organization of main ideas and details is complex, but clearly stated and generally sequential
	Language Conventionality and Clarity increased unfamiliar language
	Knowledge Demands somewhat complex social science, social studies concepts
Reader/Task Considerations	Teacher determined Vary by individual reader and type of text

Background Have students read the information about the author. Share that this excerpt comes from the book *I Want That! How We All Became Shoppers*. In the book, Hine traces the history of shopping back to before shopping existed, in prehistoric times, to show that human beings have always been motivated to acquire things. He has said his style of writing in the book is intended to replicate the experience of shopping as if the reader is shopping in his store of ideas. Hine invites his readers to look out for surprises in his books in the way that a shopper might find surprises while perusing the aisles in a store.

SETTING A PURPOSE Direct students to use the Setting a Purpose questions to focus their reading. Remind students to generate questions as they read.

Determine Meaning
COMMON CORE RI 1, RI 4

(LINES 1–13)

Tell students that an author's **style** of writing involves *how* something is said rather than *what* is said. An author's **word choices** reveal how the author feels about the topic. This attitude is called **tone.**

(A) CITE TEXT EVIDENCE Have students cite words and phrases in lines 1–13 that reveal an amused, even ironic tone. *(People who seek a simpler life are "a distinct market segment." He uses quotation marks around the word* authentic *to show that the products designed for this market are not real at all. It's ironic that people are told "what they need to buy" to "achieve a simpler life." He makes a humorous grouping: "multimillionaires, the occasional monk, and the really smart shopper.")*

Make Inferences (LINES 1–13)
COMMON CORE RI 1

Tell students that when readers make an **inference** they use what the author says along with what they know to make a logical guess about what is not directly stated.

(B) ASK STUDENTS to reread the first paragraph and tell what they can infer about the reasons people of the past and present seek a simpler life. *(In the past, wealthy rulers sought a simpler life because they felt bored by their many possessions. Many people today face the same issue—they have many possessions, but nothing pleases them. Some believe a simpler life will bring satisfaction and meaning.)*

Background *A writer on history, culture, and design,* **Thomas Hine** *coined the word* populux *as the title of his first book. The word has become commonly used to describe the enthusiasms of post-World War II America. Hine was born in a small New England town near Boston. He lived in a house that was built in 1770, a very different setting from the modern world he writes about now.*

Always Wanting More
from I WANT THAT!

Informational Text by Thomas Hine

SETTING A PURPOSE What keeps people in our consumer society always wanting more? And when is having more enough? As you read, consider how Thomas Hine answers these questions.

(A)
(B)

Throughout most of history, few people had more than a couple of possessions, and as a consequence, people were very aware of each object. Life was austere. The ability to be bored by a material surfeit[1] was a rare privilege. There are many stories of kings and emperors who sought a simpler life, if only briefly. Now, that emotion has become widespread, and those who wish to simplify are identified as a distinct market segment. Whole lines of "authentic" products have been created to serve this market, and magazines are published to

10 tell people what they need to buy to achieve a simpler life. In our age of careless abundance, austerity is a luxury, available

---

[1] **surfeit** (sûr´fĭt): an excessive amount.

SCAFFOLDING FOR ELL STUDENTS

Determine Meaning Offer support for challenging vocabulary and sentence structures by prompting students to identify units of ideas. These questions, for example, may help students build meaning of the sentence shown (lines 38–41):

- What is comfort? What is modernity? Why do we wish for them?
- What is a standard? Why do standards change?
- The author says that buying can never stop. Why not?

> We aspire instead to such intangibles as comfort and modernity, qualities for which standards change so rapidly that the buying can never stop.

TEACH

CLOSE READ

Make Inferences

COMMON CORE RI 1

(LINES 20–22)

Tell students that an important idea in economics is the difference between needs and wants. Needs are the basic things that everyone requires to live. Wants are the things that people desire.

C **ASK STUDENTS** what the sentence in lines 20–22 seems to say about human nature in societies with a high standard of living. *(People are never satisfied with just meeting their needs, and no matter how many wants are met, they can still come up with new ones.)*

CRITICAL VOCABULARY

superfluity: The author points out that superfluity might be a sign of a high standard of living.
ASK STUDENTS why superfluity makes some people uneasy. *(It seems wasteful to have more stuff than you need.)*

intangible: People enjoy owning objects, but they often seek satisfaction from intangibles too.
ASK STUDENTS what examples of intangibles are given in the text, and why they are called intangibles. Have students suggest other intangibles people value. *(The examples are comfort and modernity. They're intangibles because they're qualities or ideas—you can't see or touch them. Other intangibles are learning, friendship, progress, and beauty.)*

---

only to multimillionaires, the occasional monk, and the really smart shopper.

"The standard of life is determined not so much by what a man has to enjoy, as by the rapidity with which he tires of any one pleasure," wrote Simon Patten, the pioneering economist-philosopher of consumption, in 1889. "To have a high standard of life means to enjoy a pleasure intensely and tire of it quickly." Patten's definition of the standard of life was based

20 on **superfluity**: He expected that people would always have more than they need and would never have all they might want. That was a novel idea in Patten's time, and it is one that still makes many people uneasy. In material terms, it seems terribly wasteful, a misuse of the resources of a finite world. And in psychological terms, it seems to trap us in a cycle of false hope and inevitable disappointment. We work in order to consume, and we consume in order to somehow compensate for the emptiness of our lives, including our work. Indeed, there is some evidence that people who feel least fulfilled

30 by their work are the most avid shoppers, while those who love their work find shopping a burden, though they don't necessarily buy less.

Our materialism is oddly abstract, a path toward an ideal. The things we acquire are less important than the act of acquiring, the freedom to choose, and the ability to forget what we have and to keep on choosing. We don't aspire, as people in China did during the 1970s, to "Four Musts": a bicycle, a radio, a watch, and a sewing machine. We aspire instead to such **intangibles** as comfort and modernity,

40 qualities for which standards change so rapidly that the buying can never stop. "Progress is our most important product," Ronald Reagan used to say during his tenure as spokesman for General Electric. And in 1989, after the Berlin Wall fell, multitudes throughout Eastern Europe disappointed intellectuals in the West by behaving as if freedom was the same thing as going shopping. Even China moved on in the 1980s to the "Eight Bigs": a color television, an electric fan, a refrigerator, an audio system, camera, a motorcycle, a furniture suite, and a washing machine. Now China is moving

50 beyond the specific "Bigs" and aspires to more, a quest that will never end. A large super-store chain is opening stores there.

superfluity
(sōō′pər-flōō′ĭ-tē) *n.*
Superfluity is
overabundance or
excess.

intangible
(ĭn-tăn′jə-bəl) *n.*
An *intangible* is
something that is
hard to describe
because it cannot
be perceived by the
senses.

234 Collection 5

Strategies for Annotation ✎ ▭ Annotate it!

Make Inferences

COMMON CORE RI 1

Have students reread lines 33–52 to think about what is directly stated and what can be inferred. Encourage students to use their eBook annotation tools to do the following:

- Highlight in yellow the author's statements about China's future.
- Underline statements that help you infer why that future is predicted.
- On a note, write an inference about why the author is telling about China.

234 Collection 5

same thing as going shopping. <u>Even China moved on in the 1980s to the "Eight Bigs":</u> a color television, an electric fan, a refrigerator, an audio system, camera, a motorcycle, a furniture suite, and a washing machine. Now China is moving beyond the specific "Bigs" and aspires to more, a quest that will never end. <u>A large super-store chain is opening stores there.</u>

The author wants to show that China is becoming more like the U.S.

It is amazing to think that from the dawn of time until the time of Adam Smith,[2] a bit more than two centuries ago, people believed that wanting and having things was a drain on wealth, rather than one of its sources. That doesn't mean, however, that they didn't want things or that they didn't, at times, go to great lengths to attain them.

Now, as I move, mildly entranced, behind my cart at a 60 super store, grabbing items I feel for a moment that I need, I am assumed to be increasing the prosperity not merely of my own country, but of the entire world. Indeed, in the wake of the World Trade Center attacks, Americans were **exhorted** not to sacrifice, as is usual in wartime, but to consume.

There are those who disagree. Can the massive deficit that the United States runs with other countries, which is driven by our hunger for ever more low-priced goods, be sustained indefinitely? Does our appetite for inexpensive goods from overseas exploit the low-wage workers who make them, or 70 does it give them new opportunities? And more profoundly, are there enough resources in the world to provide everyone with this kind of living standard and still have enough clean air and clean water? How many super-store shoppers can one planet sustain?

exhort
(ĭg-zôrt´) *v.* If you *exhort*, you make an urgent appeal to others.

[2] **Adam Smith:** a Scottish economist who lived in the 18th century.

Always Wanting More *from* I Want That! **235**

APPLYING ACADEMIC VOCABULARY

attitude	consume	goal

As you discuss the information and concepts in this text, incorporate the following Collection 5 academic vocabulary words: *attitude, consume,* and *goal.* Talk about the **attitudes** of **consumers** that make consumption—always wanting more—an important **goal** in life.

CLOSE READ

Determine Meaning

COMMON CORE RI 4

(LINES 53–64)

Tell students that the term **voice** refers to an author's unique style of expression. The personality of this author is revealed through his voice.

D CITE TEXT EVIDENCE Have students reread lines 53–64 and cite evidence of the author's voice. *(He says, "It is amazing to think" to express his own surprise at how ideas about wealth have changed only in the last two hundred years. Then, he inserts himself into the scene with the pronoun I. He tells about his own experience at a superstore: He is "mildly entranced" and "grabbing items I feel for a moment that I need.")* What does this reveal about the author's personality? *(He is playful, humorous, and sometimes sarcastic when explaining things that amaze or confound him.)*

Determine Central Idea

COMMON CORE RI 2

(LINES 65–74)

Tell students that on this page the author explores contrasting ideas about prosperity and consumption.

E ASK STUDENTS to reread lines 65–74 and tell what point the author is making. *(The author raises questions about whether spending money on things as a way to increase wealth and prosperity is valid. The questions ask whether a high standard of living can really last for Americans and for the rest of the planet.)*

exhort: After an attack on the United States, Americans were exhorted to shop.

ASK STUDENTS why Americans were exhorted to shop. *(The government encouraged them to consume to keep the economy prosperous in spite of war.)*

CLOSE READ

Determine Meaning

COMMON CORE · RI 1, RI 4

(LINES 78–81)

Point out that the word *buyosphere* in line 80 has been invented by the author.

 CITE TEXT EVIDENCE Have students reread lines 78–81 and name examples of places in the buyosphere. Ask for ideas about what the word suggests to readers and why the author made this word choice. *(The buyosphere is made of "big box stores, boutiques, malls, Main streets, Web sites, and other retailers." The author chose this word to be both comical and startling, suggesting a scientific concept, like the biosphere or atmosphere, that defines the sphere in which we live as defined by the buying of things.)*

Make Inferences

COMMON CORE · RI 1

(LINES 86–89)

Tell students that the author is reflecting on what he has observed in superstores.

G **ASK STUDENTS** to reread lines 86–89. Have students discuss why the author uses the phrase "perverse tribute." *(We live in a world of plenty, but instead of showing gratitude, we're bored. We lack emotional connections to the things we own.)*

> **CRITICAL VOCABULARY**
>
> **apathy**: The author says that a superstore provokes apathy rather than amazement.
>
> **ASK STUDENTS** why the author contrasts apathy with amazement. *(to point out that we should be amazed by a superstore rather than indifferent to it)*

COLLABORATIVE DISCUSSION Have students form small groups to review the text for references to the past, present, and future. Suggest that they think about how modern consumers are like and different from those in past ages. In what ways may future consumers change, and why?

ASK STUDENTS to share any questions they generated in the course of reading and discussing the selection.

These are serious questions that need to be addressed, but those who raise such issues have rarely considered the power of objects and the fundamental role that acquiring and using objects has played since prehistoric times. In this story, the

F

80 big box stores, boutiques, malls, Main Streets, Web sites, and other retailers that constitute the buyosphere[3] represent the fulfillment of an ancient dream. The local super store is a wonder of the world. Never before have so many goods come together from so many places at such low cost. And never before have so many people been able to buy so many things.

Nevertheless, we yawn at a super store rather than marvel at it. That such a store could provoke **apathy** instead of amazement is a perverse tribute to the plenitude of our consumer society and the weakness of the emotional ties that bind us to the many objects in our lives. Never before has so

G

90 much seemed so dull.

And even if a super store is not the noblest expression of personal liberty or the highest achievement of democracy, we should consider that it does provide a setting for exercising a kind of freedom that has threatened tyrants and autocrats for thousands of years. We go to a super store to acquire things that prove our own power. It is a place where people really do get to choose.

apathy
(ăp´ə-thē) *n.* Apathy is indifference or the lack of interest or concern.

COLLABORATIVE DISCUSSION The author presents ideas about wanting and having things in the past, the present, and the future. What does he say about how wanting and having things change over time? Talk about your ideas with other group members.

---

[3] **buyosphere:** a term the author uses to describe all the places that modern consumers buy things.

Determine Meaning

Often, a written work is a reflection of an author's **style**, a manner of writing that involves how something is said rather than what is said. An author can share ideas or express viewpoints by using stylistic elements like these:

- **Word choice** is an author's use of words. Well-chosen words help an author to express ideas precisely and artistically. Word choice is part of **diction**, which involves the use of vocabulary and word order. An author's word choice can be formal or informal, serious or humorous.
- **Tone** is the author's attitude toward a subject. Like word choice, a tone can convey different feelings. The tone of a work can often be described in one word, such as *playful, serious,* or *determined.*
- **Voice** is an author's unique style of expression. The use of voice can reveal an author's personality, beliefs, or attitudes.

Consider the word choices in this sentence from "Always Wanting More," which describes the author's feelings about being part of a consumer culture:

> **Now, as I move, mildly entranced, behind my cart at a super store, grabbing items I feel for a moment that I need, I am assumed to be increasing the prosperity not merely of my own country, but of the entire world.**

The tone in this sentence could be described as self-mocking, meaning the author is making fun of himself. What word choices are examples of this?

Make Inferences

COMMON CORE RI 1

To grasp an implied or unstated idea in a text, readers can make an **inference**—a logical guess based on facts and a person's own knowledge. The chart shows an inference made from a section of the text you've just read.

Textual Detail	Knowledge	Inference
"And in 1989, after the Berlin Wall fell, multitudes throughout Eastern Europe disappointed intellectuals in the West by behaving as if freedom was the same thing as going shopping."	The Berlin Wall separated East Germany, which was under Communist control, from West Germany, which had a democratic form of government and greater freedom.	The fall of the Berlin Wall signaled freedom for East Germans. They focused on purchasing things that they had not been able to get before.

What inference can you make about the reason "intellectuals in the West" were disappointed?

Always Wanting More *from* I Want That! **237**

TEACH

CLOSE READ

Determine Meaning

COMMON CORE RI 4

Explain that readers can deepen their appreciation of a text's sytle by observing how the author uses sentence fragments or long sentences, for example, or precise adjectives and vivid verbs. Explain that every writer has a different *voice* because every writer uses language in his or her own way. Voice is what allows a reader to "hear" a personality in a selection.

After students read the boldfaced sentence, have them find words that convey a self-mocking tone and explain why the author has this attitude. *(Possible answers: The phrases "mildly entranced" and "grabbing items I feel for a moment that I need" show that the author behaves like every other unthinking shopper, under the influence of an ancient urge to acquire.)*

Make Inferences

COMMON CORE RI 1

Review that readers use what is directly stated in text to draw conclusions. After students read the example in the chart, ask them what it means to "make an inference."

To help students answer the question below the chart, discuss what is directly stated in the text and what students know about "intellectuals in the West." *(Possible answer: Intellectuals in the West had hoped that East Germans would express their new freedom in a "high" way, such as expressing political and personal freedoms. The intellectuals were disappointed when the East Germans focused on the "low" activity of shopping.)*

Strategies for Annotation ✎ 🖥 *Annotate it!*

Determine Meaning

COMMON CORE RI 4

Share these strategies for guided or independent analysis:

- Highlight in yellow words and phrases that help you hear the author's voice.
- On a note, write words that seem to describe the author.

Now, as I move, mildly entranced, behind my cart at a super store, grabbing items I feel for a moment that I need, I am assumed to be increasing the prosperity not m own country, but of the entire world. Indeed, in th

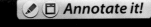

witty, honest, playful, doesn't act superior or take himself too seriously

Always Wanting More *from* I Want That! **237**

Analyzing the Text

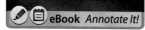

COMMON CORE RI 1, RI 2, RI 4, RI 5

Possible answers:

1. The statements "those who wish to simplify are identified as a distinct market segment" and "tell people what they need to buy to achieve a simpler life" are ironic because the point of simplifying is to remove oneself from the market; the word *authentic* is in quotation marks to show that the author means the opposite; the contradiction "austerity is a luxury" and the list "multimillionaires, the occasional monk, and the really smart shopper" point out how absurd the simplifying trend is.

2. The author's tone might be described as serious. Words such as "trap us in a cycle of false hope and inevitable disappointment" and "emptiness of our lives" suggest an earnest, serious attitude about the issue of shopping.

3. The serious questions have to do with the negative effects of Americans' desire to consume: the continuation of the U.S. trade deficit because of imported, low-priced goods; the effects of low wages on overseas workers; and the misuse of natural resources.

4. The author is making the point that we are so accustomed to abundance that we don't realize how amazing a superstore is; we are so accustomed that we find superstores boring.

5. The first paragraph introduces the idea that through most of history only kings and emperors had the "rare privilege" of owning more things than they needed. The last paragraph points out that now most people have as much economic power as "tyrants and autocrats."

6. Thomas Hine's style of writing includes vocabulary that is somewhat formal or academic: *material surfeit, misuse of the resources of a finite world, such intangibles as comfort and modernity.* But he incorporates his own personal experiences in an informal, friendly way. His tone is occasionally serious, but mostly playful, as he points out the absurdities of consumer culture. It's human nature to acquire things, he says, so we can't help ourselves. We have to shop, but no matter how much we buy, we'll never be satisfied.

Analyzing the Text

COMMON CORE RI 1, RI 2, RI 4, RI 5, RI 8, SL 1

Cite Text Evidence Support your responses with evidence from the text.

1. **Interpret** A contrast between what is expected and what actually happens is called **irony.** Authors who use irony are often adding a humorous touch in expressing their ideas. In the first paragraph, what words and phrases does the author use to show an ironic tone?

2. **Analyze** An author may express more than one kind of tone in a piece of writing. Reread lines 26–32. What word would you use to describe the author's tone here? What words or phrases contribute to this tone?

3. **Summarize** Reread lines 65–78. How would you summarize the "serious questions" that the author refers to?

4. **Infer** Reread lines 85–90. What point is the author making when he says that we "yawn at a superstore"?

5. **Compare** Reread to compare the ideas in lines 1–13 with the ideas expressed in lines 91–97. What does an ordinary person in modern times now have in common with the kings and emperors of the past?

6. **Analyze** Based on this informational text, what are your impressions of the writing style of Thomas Hine? Explain how the author's word choice, tone, and voice support his style and express his ideas about consumerism.

PERFORMANCE TASK

Speaking Activity: Discussion
In small groups, prepare for a class discussion about the claims, or positions, that Thomas Hine shares about our consumer culture.

- First, identify a list of the claims.
- Consider the following questions: How well does the author support his claims? Are there any I would challenge? How does my own experience as a consumer connect to these claims?

- With your other group members, discuss responses to the questions.
- Participants who disagree with Hine's ideas can present their own views. Be sure to support points with evidence.
- For the class discussion, each small group might choose a reporter to present your responses to the questions.

Assign this performance task.

PERFORMANCE TASK

COMMON CORE RI 8, SL 1

Speaking Activity: Discussion Before students divide into small groups, you may want to guide the whole group in identifying the author's claims by

- asking students to note the author's beliefs about the reasons for and results of shopping
- emphasizing that a belief may be supported by facts and reasons, but it may also be disputed

Critical Vocabulary

COMMON CORE L 4d, L 5b, L 6

superfluity   intangible   exhort   apathy

Practice and Apply Answer each question with *yes* or *no*. With your group, use examples and reasons to explain your answer.

1. Would you want a **superfluity** of luck?

2. Do **intangibles** bring success?

3. Can advertising **exhort**?

4. Is **apathy** like sympathy?

Vocabulary Strategy: Synonyms and Antonyms

Synonyms are words with similar meanings, such as *chilly* and *cool*. **Antonyms** are words with opposite meanings, such as *chilly* and *warm*. Identifying synonyms and antonyms can help readers understand the meanings of unfamiliar words. Note the synonyms in this sentence from "Always Wanting More":

> We aspire instead to such *intangibles* as comfort and modernity, *qualities* for which standards change so rapidly that the buying can never stop.

Intangibles are like qualities—both are things that cannot be seen or touched, but still have value.

Note the antonyms in this quotation:

> That such a store could provoke *apathy* instead of *amazement* is a perverse tribute to the plenitude of our consumer society . . .

Apathy is the opposite of amazement—apathy is a lack of interest.

Practice and Apply Identify the synonym or antonym for the bold word in each sentence. Use it to make a logical guess about the meaning of the bold word. Verify the meaning in a print or digital dictionary.

1. We live in a **finite** world where resources are limited.

2. The abundance of products makes us forget that we didn't always have such **plenitude.**

3. It is ironic that **austerity** should seem like luxury to wealthy consumers.

4. We were told not to **sacrifice,** as is usual in wartime, but to consume.

5. Individual freedoms have always threatened tyrants and **autocrats.**

PRACTICE & APPLY

Critical Vocabulary

COMMON CORE L 4d, L 5b, L 6

Possible Answers:

1. *Yes, if I had a superfluity of luck, I'd be extremely lucky.*

2. *Yes, intangibles like good health and intelligence can help a person achieve goals.*

3. *Yes, the purpose of advertising is to exhort consumers to buy.*

4. *No, apathy is not having any feelings about someone, and sympathy is having kind, caring feelings for someone. Yes, because apathy and sympathy are both ways of reacting to others.*

Vocabulary Strategy: Synonyms and Antonyms

1. finite *and* limited *are synonyms; a finite world has limits.*

2. abundance *and* plenitude *are synonyms; plenitude is the condition of having plenty.*

3. austerity *and* luxury *are antonyms; austerity is the condition of living with less.*

4. sacrifice *and* consume *are antonyms; to sacrifice is to give up something.*

5. tyrants *and* autocrats *are synonyms; autocrats control the people they rule.*

 INTERACTIVE VOCABULARY TUTOR
WordSharp Context Clues: Synonym and Restatement
WordSharp Context Clues: Antonym and Contrast

Strategies for Annotation   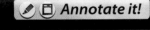 *Annotate it!*

Vocabulary Strategy: Synonyms and Antonyms

COMMON CORE L 4d, L 5b, L 6

Have students use their eBook annotation tools to identify synonyms and antonyms in lines 33–34:

- Underline the word *abstract*.

- Highlight in yellow a synonym for *abstract*.

- Highlight in green a word part that is an antonym for *abstract*.

- Note the meaning for *abstract*. Check your idea in a print or digital dictionary. Adjust the note as needed.

> Our materialism is oddly <u>abstract</u>, a path toward an ideal. The things we acquire are less important than the

abstract: not concrete or not material

PRACTICE & APPLY

Language Conventions: Noun Clauses COMMON CORE L 1a

Use the example sentences in the chart on this page to clarify the varied functions of a noun:

- The noun *choices* is the simple subject because it tells what the sentence is about.
- A noun that is a direct object receives the action of a transitive verb. The noun *things* receives the action of the verb *purchase*.
- The noun *Mom* is the object of the preposition *for*.
- A predicate noun follows an intransitive verb. Intransitive verbs include all forms of *to be*. The noun *superstore* follows the verb *is*.

Have students offer similar explanations for the functions of the listed noun clauses.

After students read the strategy for distinguishing noun clauses from other subordinate clauses, have them apply the strategy—replacing the whole clause with the pronoun *someone* or *something*—to each noun clause in the chart.

Possible Answers to Practice and Apply:

1. *"Why we always want more things"* functions as the subject of the sentence.

2. *"how we live today"* functions as a predicate noun.

3. *"what we already have"* functions as the object of the preposition *of*.

4. *"that more is better"* functions as the direct object of the verb *believe*.

5. *"where all this shopping is leading us"* functions as the object of the preposition *about*.

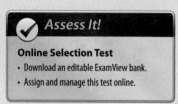

✓ Assess It!

Online Selection Test
- Download an editable ExamView bank.
- Assign and manage this test online.

Language Conventions: Noun Clauses COMMON CORE L 1a

A **clause** is a group of words that has a subject and a predicate—the two main parts of a sentence. A **noun clause** is a subordinate clause that is used as a noun; it cannot stand alone and make sense. As the chart shows, the function of noun clauses can vary depending on the specific sentence.

Function	Noun	Noun Clause
subject	Shoppers' <u>choices</u> are amazing.	<u>That shoppers have so many choices</u> is amazing.
direct object	We purchase <u>things</u>.	We purchase <u>whatever we want</u>.
object of preposition	Buy the dress for <u>Mom</u>.	Buy the dress for <u>whoever can wear it</u>.
predicate noun	This place is a <u>superstore</u>.	This place is <u>where we shop</u>.

These pronouns may introduce noun clauses: *that, what, who, whoever, which, whose*. These conjunctions may introduce noun clauses: *how, when, where, why, whether*.

The listed pronouns and conjunctions also introduce other kinds of subordinate clauses. To identify a noun clause, think about how the clause functions in the sentence. Ask: Can I replace the whole clause with a noun or the pronoun *someone* or *something*? If the substituted word fits, you've identified a noun clause.

The noun clause is underlined in this quotation from "Always Wanting More":

> He expected <u>**that people would always have more than they need and would never have all they might want.**</u>

The noun clause functions as a direct object of the verb *expected*. The pronoun *something* could replace the clause and fit in the sentence: "He expected something."

Practice and Apply Identify the noun clause in each sentence. Tell how you know it is a noun clause.

1. Why we always want more things is an interesting question.

2. We see new products and buy them; this is how we live today.

3. Sometimes we buy more of what we already have.

4. Perhaps we believe that more is better, but we're never content.

5. It's time to step back and think about where all this shopping is leading us.

INTERACTIVE WHITEBOARD LESSON
Determine Central Ideas and Details

COMMON CORE

RI 1,
RI 2,
RI 5

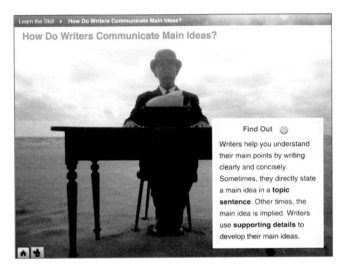

Learn the Skill ▸ How Do Writers Communicate Main Ideas?

How Do Writers Communicate Main Ideas?

Find Out

Writers help you understand their main points by writing clearly and concisely. Sometimes, they directly state a main idea in a **topic sentence**. Other times, the main idea is implied. Writers use **supporting details** to develop their main ideas.

TEACH

Tell students that to understand an informational text readers look at its **structure.** Informational texts are often organized in paragraphs that present **main ideas** and **supporting details.**

With students, reread lines 14–32 of the selection. Then, ask these questions to help them identify the topic and supporting details:

- What is the topic of this paragraph—a few words that tell what it is about? *(consumption; a high standard of life)*
- What is a problem with superfluity "in material terms"? *(It's wasteful and "a misuse of the resources of a finite world.")*
- What is wrong with superfluity "in psychological terms"? *(It's a trap. "We work . . . to consume . . . we consume to compensate for the emptiness of our lives, including . . . work.")*

Consider the details and state a main-idea sentence that sums up the author's point about the topic. *(A high standard of life brings problems because people have too much but are never satisfied.)*

PRACTICE AND APPLY

Have students reread the third paragraph of "Always Wanting More," which begins on line 33. Have them work in pairs to write a topic, note supporting details, and state the main idea. *(Main idea: The act of acquiring, the freedom to choose, and the ability to forget what we have are more important than the actual things we buy. Details: China once only aspired to "Four Musts." That changed to "Eight Bigs" as it grew. Now, a super-store chain is opening there. When the Berlin Wall fell, people expressed "freedom" by shopping.)*

Determine Meaning

COMMON CORE

RI 1,
RI 4

RETEACH

Review the concept of *style* by displaying these two sentences and asking how they are alike and how they differ:

- Americans sure seem to love their gadgets, and they're willing to spend, spend, spend to own them.
- U.S. household expenditures on electronic devices have shown steady annual increases.

Point out that although the sentences' meanings are similar the **style**—how each is written—differs. Help students to identify differences in **word choices.** Point out that the **voice** of the author is what the reader "hears." The voice in the first sentence is chatty and casual. In the second, the voice is more formal.

Tell students that a related feature of style is **tone.** The tone of a text reveals the author's attitude toward the topic and may be described with just one word, such as *concerned* or *lighthearted.*

Ask students for a word to describe the author's tone in this selection. *(Samples: enthusiastic, pleased, awed, appreciative)*

LEVEL UP TUTORIALS Assign the following *Level Up* tutorial: **Author's Style**

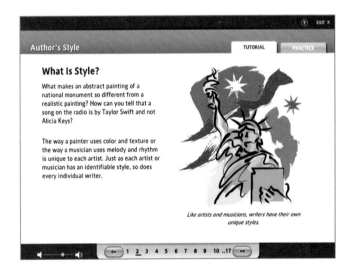

Author's Style — TUTORIAL — PRACTICE

What Is Style?

What makes an abstract painting of a national monument so different from a realistic painting? How can you tell that a song on the radio is by Taylor Swift and not Alicia Keys?

The way a painter uses color and texture or the way a musician uses melody and rhythm is unique to each artist. Just as each artist or musician has an identifiable style, so does every individual writer.

Like artists and musicians, writers have their own unique styles.

CLOSE READING APPLICATION

Provide another informational text in which the author's voice comes through. After reading, ask small groups to write one or two sentences about the author's style. Have students discuss supporting evidence and reasons for their statements.

Labels and Illusions

Essay by Lourdes Barranco

Why This Text

Students often have difficulty with a text that requires them to make inferences and identify and interpret elements of a writer's style. This essay is such a text. With the help of the close-reading questions, students will interpret irony, make inferences based on text evidence, and analyze the author's word choice and tone. The results of their close reading will help students develop a thorough understanding of what the text says both explicitly and implicitly.

Background Have students read the background information describing the obesity problem in the United States. Tell them that this article examines how marketing strategies, especially deceptive labeling, have contributed to the problem. Encourage students to share their own examples of deceptive labeling.

SETTING A PURPOSE Tell students to pay close attention to what the author suggests or implies as well as what she says directly.

 Common Core Support

- cite multiple pieces of textual evidence
- make inferences
- determine the central idea of a text
- determine the meanings of words and phrases as they are used in the text
- analyze the impact of a specific word choice on meaning and tone

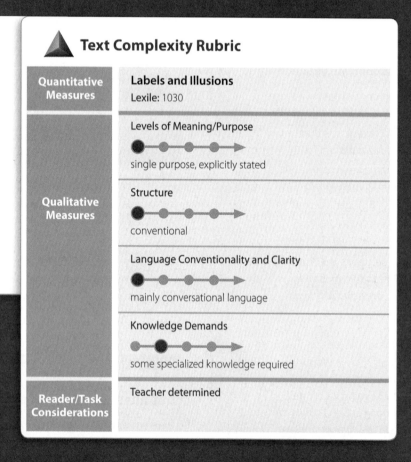

Text Complexity Rubric

Quantitative Measures

Labels and Illusions
Lexile: 1030

Qualitative Measures

Levels of Meaning/Purpose
single purpose, explicitly stated

Structure
conventional

Language Conventionality and Clarity
mainly conversational language

Knowledge Demands
some specialized knowledge required

Reader/Task Considerations
Teacher determined

Strategies for CLOSE READING

Make Inferences

Students should read the essay carefully, thinking about what the author is implying as well as what she says directly. Close-reading questions will help students collect and cite text evidence to support their inferences. As they read, students should summarize their inferences in the margin.

WHEN STUDENTS STRUGGLE . . .

To help students make inferences, have them work in small groups to fill out a chart like the one shown below.

CITE TEXT EVIDENCE For practice making inferences, ask students to make inferences based on the text evidence below.

Text from the Article	Inferences
"The labeling of these food and drink items seems whimsical, if not completely inaccurate." (lines 16–17)	"Whimsical" implies that the labels are not serious, let alone accurate.
"To make the problem worse, marketers working in the clothing industry have created strategies for making us think we are thinner than we are." (lines 37–39)	Marketers are more interested in selling products than in labeling them accurately.

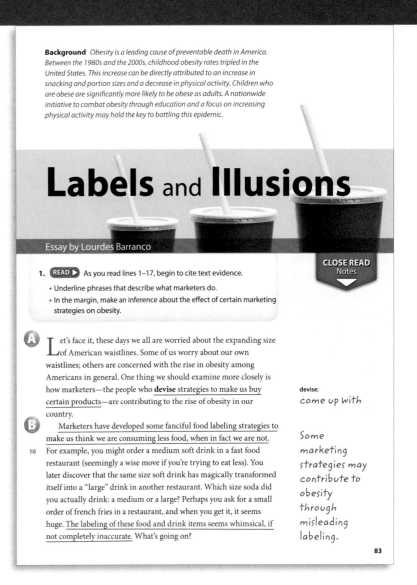

Background *Obesity is a leading cause of preventable death in America. Between the 1980s and the 2000s, childhood obesity rates tripled in the United States. This increase can be directly attributed to an increase in snacking and portion sizes and a decrease in physical activity. Children who are obese are significantly more likely to be obese as adults. A nationwide initiative to combat obesity through education and a focus on increasing physical activity may hold the key to battling this epidemic.*

Labels and Illusions

Essay by Lourdes Barranco

CLOSE READ
Notes

1. **READ ▶** As you read lines 1–17, begin to cite text evidence.
   • Underline phrases that describe what marketers do.
   • In the margin, make an inference about the effect of certain marketing strategies on obesity.

A Let's face it, these days we all are worried about the expanding size of American waistlines. Some of us worry about our own waistlines; others are concerned with the rise in obesity among Americans in general. One thing we should examine more closely is how marketers—the people who **devise** strategies to make us buy certain products—are contributing to the rise of obesity in our country.

B Marketers have developed some fanciful food labeling strategies to make us think we are consuming less food, when in fact we are not. For example, you might order a medium soft drink in a fast food restaurant (seemingly a wise move if you're trying to eat less). You later discover that the same size soft drink has magically transformed itself into a "large" drink in another restaurant. Which size soda did you actually drink: a medium or a large? Perhaps you ask for a small order of french fries in a restaurant, and when you get it, it seems huge. The labeling of these food and drink items seems whimsical, if not completely inaccurate. What's going on?

devise:
come up with

Some marketing strategies may contribute to obesity through misleading labeling.

83

1. **READ AND CITE TEXT EVIDENCE** Remind students that they have underlined phrases that describe what marketers do.

A **ASK STUDENTS** to use details and phrases in lines 1–17 to infer the effects of some marketing strategies. *Possible response: Marketing strategies contribute to obesity by making us think we are eating less than we actually are.*

Critical Vocabulary: devise (line 5) Have students share their definitions of *devise*. Ask them when they have devised a plan or a solution to a problem. *Answers will vary. Possible response: getting a friend to a surprise birthday party.*

For those of us trying to eat reasonable portions, an additional problem can arise from our own inability to judge the size of our meals. Consider the following optical illusion, first documented in 1875: the Delboeuf [del bœf] effect. Start with two dots of equal size. Then surround one dot with a large circle and the other with a small circle. Guess what happens—suddenly the second dot, the one surrounded by the small circle, looks much larger than the first dot, even though they are the same size.

What does this have to do with the amount of food we eat? Koert van Ittersum, a professor of marketing at Georgia Tech, and Brian Wansink, director of the Food and Brand Lab at Cornell, found out. They performed a series of experiments to measure the effect of the Delboeuf illusion on people's perception of portion size. They served two groups of people the same size portion but on different-size plates. People who were served on larger plates thought that they had been served a small portion. People served on smaller plates thought that they had been served a large portion. The research showed that

Both studies show that the size of the surrounding circle affects the perception of the size of what is in it.

our eyes can deceive us about the amount of food we're actually eating.

To make the problem worse, marketers working in the clothing industry have created strategies for making us think that we are thinner than we actually are. A common dilemma faced by people of all ages is trying to determine which size of an article of clothing fits them. Their confusion is understandable. Depending on the store, a pair of slacks labeled size 8, 6, or 4 might fit the same woman. A sweater labeled extra large or medium might fit a large man.

What causes these differences? The answer is "vanity sizing," the practice of labeling clothes as smaller sizes than they really are. In other words, a dress that is really a size 8 may be labeled a size 2. By using vanity sizing, clothing manufacturers flatter people into thinking that they are not as large as they may actually be. Apparently, this encourages people to purchase the items of clothing. Remember, the marketers who devise these labels are people who want you to buy their company's products.

2. ◀ REREAD Reread lines 8–17. A contrast between what is expected and what actually occurs is called *irony*. The use of irony can create strong effects, including humor. What words and phrases add an ironic tone to this paragraph?

The words "fanciful" and "whimsical" and the phrase "magically transformed itself" add an ironic tone to the paragraph. The words "fanciful" and "whimsical" add a slightly humorous tone to the paragraph because food labels aren't usually thought of as having a personality. When we realize how many "strategies" have been put into these simple labels and the harmful effects they have, these labels are no longer "fanciful."

3. READ ▶ As you read lines 18–36, continue to cite textual evidence.
- Underline the results of each experiment.
- In the margin, explain how the results of the Delboeuf effect compare to those of the van Ittersum/Wansink experiment.

4. ◀ REREAD Reread lines 18–36. State the main idea of this section and explain how both experiments support it.

The Delboeuf effect provides insight into why people in the van Ittersum/Wansink experiment were deceived into thinking they had more or less food, depending on the size of the plate. Both the Delboeuf effect and the van Ittersum/Wansink experiment support the main idea of this section, "The research showed that our eyes can deceive us about the amount of food we're actually eating."

5. READ ▶ As you read lines 37–58, continue to cite textual evidence.
- Underline phrases that suggest that "vanity sizing" makes people feel good.
- Circle the conclusion that sums up the central idea of this essay.
- In the margin, restate what consumers can do to counteract the influence of marketers.

84

85

2. REREAD AND CITE TEXT EVIDENCE   Remind students that irony occurs when the author's meaning is the opposite of what he or she actually says.

🅑 **ASK STUDENTS** to find a phrase in lines 8–17 in which the author means the opposite of what she actually says. *magically transformed (line 12)*

3. READ AND CITE TEXT EVIDENCE

🅒 **ASK STUDENTS** to explain how the results of the van Ittersum/Wansink experiment show that the Delboeuf effect does influence people's perception of how much they are eating. *Possible response: The van Ittersum/Wansink experiment proves that the way food is presented affects our perception of how much we are eating.*

FOR ELL STUDENTS Explain that the word *reasonable* can mean "capable of thinking clearly," but in this context it means "conforming with common sense."

4. REREAD AND CITE TEXT EVIDENCE   Encourage students to describe the Delboeuf effect and to compare that description with the results of the van Ittersum/Wansink experiment.

🅓 **ASK STUDENTS** to state the main idea of each paragraph on page 84. *The Delboeuf effect shows that factors affect how people perceive the size of their meals. The van Ittersum/Wansink experiment supported this claim.*

5. READ AND CITE TEXT EVIDENCE   Have students identify any phrases that help them understand what *vanity sizing* means.

🅔 **ASK STUDENTS** to explain the concept of "vanity sizing" and why it might be useful to clothing manufacturers. *Vanity sizing is the practice of labeling larger articles of clothing with smaller sizes. It flatters people by making them think that they are not as large as they really are and, thereby, increases sales.*

CLOSE READ
Notes

Consumers should be suspicious of labels and use common sense.

F   What can consumers do? First, we should ignore the labels "small," "medium," and "large" as they apply to food and drink. We're probably buying a lot more than we need. We should also be skeptical of clothing labels. We may not be as trim and physically fit as the label would lead us to believe. To stay healthy and avoid obesity, we must rely on our own good sense and on our knowledge of what characterizes a healthy person.

6. **◀ REREAD** Reread lines 52–58. An author may use more than one kind of tone in an essay. What word would you use to describe the author's tone in this paragraph? What words and phrases reflect this tone?

The author's tone in this paragraph is serious. She tells readers to be "skeptical" or even to "ignore" labels, and recommends that readers rely on their "knowledge" of what being healthy means and their "own good sense" instead of being misled by labels.

SHORT RESPONSE

Cite Text Evidence   Summarize the central idea of this essay and the most effective information the author includes to support it. **Cite text evidence** and relevant reading notes in your response.

The author gives factual information to support her position that marketers "devise strategies to make us buy certain products." By showing us the way the Delboeuf effect works and how easily "our eyes can deceive us about the amount of food we're actually eating," it's easy to see how easily consumers are manipulated. By using phrases such as "devise strategies" to describe what marketers do, and "flattered" and "fooled" to describe how consumers are manipulated, the argument that obesity and marketing are linked is quite persuasive.

86

6. **REREAD AND CITE TEXT EVIDENCE** Tell students that some adjectives that may describe tone are *playful, sarcastic, serious, cheerful,* and *reverent.*

F **ASK STUDENTS** to find words or phrases that suggest the author's tone. *Possible responses:* should ignore, be skeptical, to stay healthy, we must, our own good sense.

FOR ELL STUDENTS Point out to Spanish-speaking students that *skeptical* has a cognate, *escéptico.*

SHORT RESPONSE

Cite Text Evidence   Students' responses will vary, but they should cite evidence from the text to support their answers. They should:

- summarize the central idea of the essay.
- cite the author's most convincing information.
- cite specific evidence from the text to support their ideas.

TO CHALLENGE STUDENTS . . .

To extend students' understanding of this essay, have them research the practice of vanity sizing.

ASK STUDENTS to research at least five articles on the subject and summarize their findings in an essay. Encourage them to include charts, graphs, and other visual representations. Their essays should address:

- what vanity sizing is.
- the purpose of vanity sizing.
- why vanity sizing is appealing to some people.
- the extent to which markets target vanity sizing to specific groups.
- why some retailers and dress designers argue that vanity sizing is a myth.
- why vanity sizing is or is not an effective marketing strategy.

DIG DEEPER

With the class, return to the Short Response question. Have students share and discuss their answers.

ASK STUDENTS to note how their responses are alike and how they are different.

- Have students discuss in more depth how inaccurate labeling is linked to the problem of obesity in the United States.
- Summarize the strategies marketers use to make us think that we are eating less than we actually are.
- Ask students to give personal examples that illustrate their experience of faulty labeling or labeling inconsistencies.
- Have students discuss what they can infer the author thinks of marketers who use these strategies and of us if we fall for these strategies.

ASK STUDENTS to return to their response to the Short Response question and revise it based on their discussion.

Dump

How Things Work

Poem by X. J. Kennedy

Poem by Gary Soto

Why These Texts?

An understanding of and appreciation for poetry can enhance students' experiences with other related forms, including the lyrics in popular music. This lesson focuses on the poetic form in two poems and how theme and irony contribute to a poem's meaning.

▶ **View It!**

Professional Development Podcast:

Text-Dependant Analysis

Key Learning Objective: The student will be able to analyze a poem's form and how to identify theme and irony.

COMMON CORE Common Core Standards

RL 1 Cite textual evidence.

RL 2 Determine theme.

RL 4 Determine the meanings of words and phrases.

RL 4 Analyze the impact of rhymes and other repetitions of sounds on a verse or stanza of a poem.

RL 5 Analyze how a poem's form contributes to its meaning.

W 2 Write informative/explanatory texts.

W 4 Produce clear and coherent writing.

W 10 Write routinely over extended time frames.

▲ Text Complexity Rubric

	Dump Lexile: N/A	How Things Work Lexile: N/A
Quantitative Measures		
Qualitative Measures	Levels of Meaning/Purpose single level of complex meaning	Levels of Meaning/Purpose single level of complex meaning
	Structure regular stanzas with some liberties taken	Structure free verse, no particular patterns
	Language Conventionality and Clarity some figurative language	Language Conventionality and Clarity contextual ambiguous language
	Knowledge Demands moderately complex theme	Knowledge Demands moderately complex theme
Reader/Task Considerations	Teacher determined Vary by individual reader and type of text	Teacher determined Vary by individual reader and type of text

TEACH

CLOSE READ

Background Have students read the background and information about the poets. Explain that students are going to read two poems that reflect on people's everyday experiences and relationships with material things. The first poem commemorates the dump, a place where people discard old, used, broken, or unwanted items. The second poem shares a perception about people's everyday spending and its effects on others' ability to spend.

SETTING A PURPOSE Direct students to use the Setting a Purpose prompt about our consumer society to focus their reading. Remind students to write down questions they have as they read.

SCAFFOLDING FOR ELL STUDENTS

Analyze Language: Imagery Explain to students that poets often use imagery to help a reader imagine how things look, feel, smell, sound, and taste. Tell students that **imagery** consists of words and phrases that appeal to these five senses. Display lines 21–24 of "Dump." Have students read the lines aloud with you. Highlight the phrase "acrid smell of trash / Arises like perfume." Remind students that this poem is set in a dump, reviewing what a dump is.

Background *Writers and poets alike often use their writing to make statements about important topics like consumerism. X. J. Kennedy and Gary Soto each examine our consumer society in their respective poems "Dump" and "How Things Work."*

DUMP

Poem by X. J. Kennedy

How Things Work

Poem by Gary Soto

X. J. Kennedy (b. 1929) *has won many awards for his poetry collections, including the Robert Frost Medal. Kennedy has published numerous books for young people, including collections of poetry and novels. Traditional in form, Kennedy's poems often include narrative, wit, and humor, but he also explores themes about serious topics, such as growing up and loss.*

Gary Soto (b. 1952) *never dreamed about writing as a child. But after reading a book of poetry in college, he began to write his own poems and dedicated himself to the craft. While Soto has written poetry and novels for adults, he is probably best known as a writer for young adults and children. From his point of view, he is writing about the feelings and experiences of most American kids.*

SETTING A PURPOSE As you read, think about what each poet is saying about our consumer society and how that society works.

(bg) ©Don Farrall/Getty Images; (tl) ©Ulrich Mueller/Shutterstock; (tr) ©archideaphoto/Shutterstock; (tc) ©canikligil/Shutterstock; (b) ©vX.J. Kennedy; (b) ©The Associated Press/AP Images

ASK STUDENTS to name the objects they would likely find in a dump. Then, ask students to name words that would describe how a dump looks, smells, sounds, and feels. Point out that the word *acrid* is a word that relates to the sense of smell, as does the word *perfume*. Ask students what an "acrid perfume" might smell like, and discuss how the author is playing with the words to appeal to the readers' senses.

> As we turn now to return
>
> To our lightened living room,
>
> The acrid smell of trash
>
> Arises like perfume.

Analyze Poetry: Form (LINES 1–20)

COMMON CORE · RL 1, RL 4, RL 5

Explain to students that the **form** of a poem is its arrangement of words and lines on the page. A poem's form gives it rhythm and emphasizes meaning. Explain that **traditional** forms of poetry have a fixed set of rules for:

- the number of lines the poem has
- how the lines are divided into **stanzas,** or groups
- the pattern of end rhymes, called **rhyme scheme**
- the pattern of stressed and unstressed syllables, called **meter,** with each unit of meter called a **foot**

 CITE TEXT EVIDENCE Have students reread lines 1–20 aloud. Ask students to cite evidence that reveals whether or not the poem has a traditional form. *(The poem has a traditional form. It has a fixed rhyme scheme, such as the end rhyming words* pour / store *and* find / mind, *in the first stanza. Each stanza has a fixed number of four lines. In general, it has a fairly regular meter, with the second syllable in each foot being stressed: Here **lies** dis**card**ed **hopes.** The word* over *is likely pronounced as one syllable: ov'r.)*

Determine the Meanings of Words and Phrases

COMMON CORE · RL 4

(LINES 13–16)

Explain to students that poets often use irony as a way to express disapproval of something or to emphasize a point. **Irony** is a contrast, or difference, between what is expected to happen and what actually happens.

B **CITE TEXT EVIDENCE** Ask students to reread lines 13–16 and identify evidence of the irony in these lines. How is this an example of irony? *("Roof shingles bought on sale / That rotted on their roof" is ironic because the speaker probably thought he or she was saving money but then lost that money when the shingles rotted and had to be thrown out.)*

Dump
by X. J. Kennedy

A The brink over which we pour
Odd items we can't find
Enough cubic inches to store
In house, in mind,

5 Is come to by a clamber
Up steep unsteady heights
Of beds without a dreamer
And lamps that no hand lights.

Here lie discarded hopes
10 That hard facts had to rout:
Umbrellas—naked spokes
By wind jerked inside-out,

Roof shingles bought on sale
That rotted on their roof, **B**
15 Paintings eternally stale
That, hung, remained aloof,

Pink dolls with foreheads crushed,
Eyes petrified in sleep.
We cast off with a crash
20 What gives us pain to keep.

©Ulrich Mueller/Shutterstock

APPLYING ACADEMIC VOCABULARY

attitude	consume

As you discuss the two poems, incorporate the following Collection 5 academic vocabulary words: *attitude* and *consume*. Have students describe the speakers' **attitudes** in each poem about how people **consume** things.

As we turn now to return
To our lightened living room,
The acrid smell of trash
Arises like perfume.

25 Maneuvering steep stairs
Of bedsprings to our car,
We stumble on homecanned pears
Grown poisonous in their jar

And nearly gash an ankle
30 Against a shard of glass.
Our emptiness may rankle,[1]
But soon it too will pass.

---

[1] **rankle:** to cause constant irritation.

WHEN STUDENTS STRUGGLE ...

Guide students in understanding the rhythmic pattern, or meter, of the poem by reading the poem aloud, clapping on the stressed syllables. (Note that in the first line, *over* is likely pronounced as one complete unstressed syllable, as "ov'r.")

The **brink** over **which** we **pour**
Odd items **we** can't **find**

Read aloud each stanza, clapping out the beat. Note the sections such as "homecanned peaches" where the rhythm temporarily changes.

ASK STUDENTS to reread a stanza on their own, clapping out the beats to identify the rhythm.

CLOSE READ

Analyze Poetry: Form (LINES 25–28)

COMMON CORE RL 1, RL 5

Explain to students that within traditional poems, such as this one, each metrical foot is called an iamb—an unstressed syllable followed by a stressed syllable. This creates the rhythm of duh-DAH, duh-DAH, duh-DAH. However, within this pattern poets can vary the rhythm slightly to stress ideas by interrupting the familiar pattern.

C **CITE TEXT EVIDENCE** Ask students to reread lines 25–28 and cite an example of a break in the regular singsong iambic rhythm and to explain how it impacts the meaning of the poem. *(Lines 27 and 28 do not end with iambs. The rhythm of "homecanned pears" and "in their jars" calls for each syllable to be stressed. This breaks the pattern and draws attention to the idea of "poisonous pears," emphasizing how familiar, comforting items made at "home" have now grown toxic.)*

Determine Meanings of Words and Phrases
(LINES 29–32)

COMMON CORE RL 1, RL 4

Explain to students that the **tone** of a poem expresses the speaker's attitude, or how he or she feels toward a subject. Tell students that the tone of a poem can have a powerful impact on meaning. The words and phrases that a poet uses reveal the speaker's personality.

D **CITE TEXT EVIDENCE** Ask students to reread the last stanza, lines 29–32. Have students identify words and phrases that help the reader understand how the speaker feels. *(The lines "Our emptiness may rankle, / But soon it too will pass" convey a feeling of sarcasm about how quickly our feelings of loss of material things passes, implying that we move on to consume more stuff that we'll end up throwing away, too.)*

Analyze Poetry: Form COMMON CORE RL 5

Review the features of a traditional poem. Have students describe the rhyme scheme and meter of "Dump." Discuss how these contribute to the rhythm, meaning, and mood of the poem. (*The iambic meter creates a singsong rhythm, giving the poem a familiar nursery-rhyme feeling, which contrasts with the sad images of "discarded hopes" and "Eyes petrified in sleep." This creates an ironic, biting tone that shows that the poet regrets the way we toss out so much of the things that are supposed to give life meaning.*)

Analyzing the Text COMMON CORE RL 1, RL 4, RL 5

Possible answers:

1. *There are eight stanzas with four lines each. This form gives the poem a quick pace and regular chanting rhythm, thus creating a light contrast to the darker ideas of loss and emptiness throughout the poem.*

2.
   ´ ŭ ŭ ´   ŭ ´
   Roof shingles bought on sale
   ŭ ´ ŭ ´ ŭ ´
   That rotted on their roof,
   ´   ŭ   ŭ ´ ŭ   ´
   Paintings eternally stale
   ŭ   ´   ŭ ´   ŭ ´
   That, hung, remained aloof,

3. *Stanzas 2, 4, and 6 break from the* abab *rhyme scheme, disrupting the reader and creating a feeling that a visit to the dump can be unsettling and jarring.*

4. *The poem's form creates its rhythm and emphasizes the meaning of certain words, contributing to the irony that familiar items of consumer comfort have turned dangerous and toxic in the dump.*

 eBook *Annotate It!*

Analyze Poetry: Form COMMON CORE RL 5

The **form** of a poem is its structure, including the arrangement of words and lines. The poem "Dump" has a **fixed,** or **traditional, form** because it follows fixed rules:

- The poem is divided into **stanzas** that include the same number of lines.
- The poem has a pattern of end rhymes, called a **rhyme scheme.** A rhyme scheme is noted by assigning a letter of the alphabet, beginning with *a*, to each line. Lines that rhyme are given the same letter. For example, in the first stanza, the end words are *pour, find, store,* and *mind.* The stanza's rhyme scheme is *abab.*

The **meter** of a poem is the regular pattern of stressed and unstressed syllables. Each **foot,** or unit of meter, includes one stressed syllable. "Dump" has these characteristics of meter:

- Most lines have the same number of feet.
- Each metrical foot is the kind called an iamb—an unstressed syllable followed by a stressed syllable: duh-DAH, duh-DAH.

Because a meter that follows a rigid pattern can sound as singsong as a nursery rhyme, poets often choose to work more loosely with meter. Listen for the meter in stanza 3:

> Here lie discarded hopes
> That hard facts had to rout:
> Umbrellas—naked spokes
> By wind jerked inside-out,

Analyzing the Text COMMON CORE RL 1, RL 4, RL 5

Cite Text Evidence   Support your responses with evidence from the text.

1. **Identify Patterns** How many stanzas does the poem have? How many lines are in each stanza? Why might the poet have chosen to organize the poem this way?

2. **Identify Patterns** Choose and copy a stanza from the poem. Use stress marks to identify the stressed syllables in each line of the stanza.

3. **Analyze** Which stanzas vary from the *abab* rhyme scheme? What impact does this variation have on the poem's meaning?

4. **Analyze** How does the poem's form contribute to its meaning?

Strategies for Annotation  *Annotate it!*

Analyze Poetry: Form COMMON CORE RL 1, RL 5

Have students use their eBook annotation tools to identify the rhyme scheme in "Dump." Ask students to do the following:

- Highlight the words at the end of each line to show the rhyme scheme, using a different color for each rhyming pair.
- Review your highlights. On a note, use the letters *a* and *b* to indicate the rhyme scheme.
- Continue in the same way for the remaining stanzas.

The brink over which we pour

Odd items we can't find

Enough cubic inches to store

In house, in mind,

(lines 1–4)

Rhyme scheme, first stanza: *abab*

Analyze Poetry:

Form (Lines 1–9)

COMMON CORE   RL 1, RL 5

Review with students that the form of a poem is the way in which the words and lines are arranged on the page, and that traditional forms follow fixed rules for number of lines, rhyme scheme, and meter. Then, explain that other forms of poems do not have these rules. These poems are called **free verse.** Free verse often sounds like everyday conversational speech. Remind students that analyzing the lines of a poem can help them identify its form.

 CITE TEXT EVIDENCE Ask students to reread lines 1–9 and cite examples from the text that show it is written in free verse. (*The lines of the poem are different lengths, and there is no rhyme scheme. None of the end words in any of the lines rhyme, and sentences often end in mid-line. For example,* Today it's going to cost us twenty dollars / To live. Five for a softball. Four for a book.) Ask students to point to examples of incomplete sentences—or fragments—and explain how these affect the poem. (*Sentence fragments such as "Five for a softball" and "Four for a book" give the poem a conversational tone. When people speak to each other, they often speak in fragments as ideas come to mind.*)

COLLABORATIVE DISCUSSION Have students work initially with a partner to analyze the poems and answer the questions. Then, have pairs join the larger group to discuss their ideas.

ASK STUDENTS to share any questions they generated in the course of reading and discussing the poems.

How Things Work
by Gary Soto

  Today it's going to cost us twenty dollars
To live. Five for a softball. Four for a book,
A handful of ones for coffee and two sweet rolls,
Bus fare, rosin[1] for your mother's violin.
5   We're completing our task. The tip I left
For the waitress filters down
Like rain, wetting the new roots of a child
Perhaps, a belligerent cat that won't let go
Of a balled sock until there's chicken to eat.
10   As far as I can tell, daughter, it works like this:
You buy bread from a grocery, a bag of apples
From a fruit stand, and what coins
Are passed on helps others buy pencils, glue,
Tickets to a movie in which laughter
15   Is thrown into their faces.
If we buy a goldfish, someone tries on a hat.
If we buy crayons, someone walks home with a broom.
A tip, a small purchase here and there,
And things just keep going. I guess.

COLLABORATIVE DISCUSSION Both poems have speakers who share thoughts about their surroundings or situations. Which speaker expresses stronger reactions to the situation? What degree of control does either speaker appear to have over what they describe? Discuss your responses with other group members.

---

[1] **rosin** (rŏz´ĭn): a sticky substance that comes from tree sap and is used to increase sliding friction on certain stringed instruments' bows.

WHEN STUDENTS STRUGGLE . . .

Point out that "How Things Work" has a much different form than "Dump." Reread the first eight lines of each poem aloud with students. Emphasize the predictable rhythm and rhyme scheme of "Dump" and the unpredictable, almost stop-and-go flow of ideas in "How Things Work." Then, have students work with partners to take turns rereading the sections of each poem to each other.

ASK STUDENTS to describe how they feel after reading and listening to each poem.

Analyze Poetry: Form

 COMMON CORE RL 5

Review the information about free verse, and have students discuss their answers to the questions.

(Possible answers:

- *The poet expresses the idea that one person's spending allows another to spend. Free verse allows him to explain this in a simple, clear way.*
- *The varying line lengths, sentence fragments, and random punctuation give the poem its form. This seems more like regular conversation.)*

Analyzing the Text

COMMON CORE RL 1, RL 4, RL 5

Possible answers:

1. *The reader would pause after the first line and then emphasize "To live," as if the speaker is startled by the realization that money is a requirement "to live."*

2. *The tip for the waitress is compared to rain; it "filters down like rain, wetting the new roots of a child." The figurative comparison suggests that the waitress will use the money for things her child needs and that money "passed on" nourishes other things.*

3. *The reader should pause briefly after each comma, a bit longer after the period, and then stress "I guess" to show the speaker's doubt about "how things work."*

4. *The lines are different lengths, containing many phrases to give it rhythm and emphasize the meaning that one person's spending enables another to spend.*

5. *The form creates a feeling of thoughts tumbling out of the speaker's mind, as if the speaker is figuring out "how things work" and explaining it at the same time.*

---

 eBook *Annotate It!*

Analyze Poetry: Form

COMMON CORE RL 5

A poem's **form** is its structure and the way its words and lines are arranged. Some forms are also defined by poetic devices, such as rhyme, rhythm, and meter. A poem's form is closely linked to its meaning, which makes the poem's form important to its message.

The poem "How Things Work" is written in a form called **free verse,** which has natural rhythms rather than regular patterns of rhyme, rhythm, meter, or line length. A poet may choose free verse to make the language similar to natural speech.

Still, the sounds of words and the rhythms within lines matter in free verse. The poet has made choices about where to break lines, how to punctuate each line, and which words and phrases will best convey particular sound-meaning connections.

To analyze free verse, ask questions such as the following:

- What ideas is the poet expressing? How does the use of free verse support those ideas?
- What rhythms do the line lengths and the punctuation in the poem create? How do these poetic devices add to my understanding of the poem?

Analyzing the Text

COMMON CORE RL 1, RL 4, RL 5

Cite Text Evidence Support your responses with evidence from the text.

1. **Interpret** Reread the first sentence of the poem in lines 1–2. Where would you pause, and what words would you stress to give that sentence meaning and feeling?

2. **Interpret** In lines 5–7, what does the speaker compare to rain, and what does that comparison help readers picture?

3. **Interpret** Reread the last two lines of "How Things Work." Where might be the best places to pause? What words should you stress to help convey the poem's meaning?

4. **Analyze** Review lines 14–19 and examine how the poet arranges the words and lines. Describe the variations in line lengths. What is the poet trying to explain, and how does the form support those ideas?

5. **Analyze** How does the poem's form contribute to its meaning?

Strategies for Annotation   *Annotate it!*

Analyze Poetry: Form

COMMON CORE RL 1, RL 5

Share these strategies for guided or independent analysis:

- Highlight in yellow words that are emphasized in each line.
- On a note, write how the emphasis on these words affects rhythm and meaning.

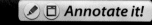

Today it's going to cost us twenty dollars To live. Five for a softball.

Four for a book, A handful of ones for c[...]

Bus fare, rosin for your mother's violin.

Rhythm stops and starts like real thoughts. The emphasized words show the speaker is surprised and maybe appalled by how much life costs.

Determine Theme

Poems like "Dump" and "How Things Work" often have a **theme,** or a lesson about life or human nature that the poet shares with the reader. A theme usually is developed over the course of a poem, rather than stated directly at the beginning or end. Readers can infer a poem's theme by thinking about the title, the imagery, the form, and the language the poet uses to describe the subject.

Poets might give clues about the poem's theme through the **tone,** or the speaker's attitude toward the subject. One way they may convey the tone is through the use of **irony,** or the use of language to say the opposite of what is meant.

How can you tell that the speaker in "Dump" is using an ironic tone in these lines?

> The acrid smell of trash
> Arises like perfume.

Pay attention to text details as you dig deeper into the poems. Use text clues to determine the themes in each poem and to analyze how those themes are developed through the tones.

Compare Forms in Poetry

You have read two poems on a shared subject—the things we own. Each poet describes an everyday activity and reflects on it in a unique way. The poem's form is the way the poet organizes ideas, including the arrangement of words and lines.

To compare the forms of these poems, analyze the structure that each poet uses. Use a chart like this to help you make comparisons between the two poems.

Elements to Think About	"Dump"	"How Things Work"
form of poem		
setting		
lines and stanzas		
sensory and figurative language		
tone		
theme		

PRACTICE & APPLY

Determine Theme

Review the information about theme and how a poet can convey a theme through tone and irony. Then, have students answer the question. *(Possible answers: Saying that an "acrid smell" is like "perfume" is ironic because this is the opposite of what the speaker means. The acrid smell of trash isn't like perfume—it stinks.)*

Compare Forms in Poetry

Have partners work together to analyze the structure of each poem and fill in the chart. As a group, discuss how the differences in form affect the meaning of each poem.

Sample answers:

Elements to Think About	"Dump"	"How Things Work"
form of poem	traditional	free verse
setting	the dump	a walk in town or the city, after having a coffee and rolls at a restaurant
lines and stanzas	8 stanzas; 4 lines each	no stanzas; 19 lines
sensory and figurative language	"by a clamber," "steep unsteady heights"	"Like rain wetting the new roots of a child"
tone	light rhythm but dark images; ironic	frustrated but resigned
theme	We are part of the toxic cycle of acquiring and discarding things.	Life is unfortunately a chain of events linked by money.

Strategies for Annotation  Annotate it!

Determine Theme

Share these strategies for guided or independent analysis:

- Highlight in yellow examples of ironic tone.
- Highlight in blue text clues that convey theme.
- Use a note to explain the theme of the poem.

As far as I can tell, daughter, it works like this:
You buy bread from a grocery, a bag of apples
From a fruit stand, and what coins
Are passed on helps others buy pencils, glue,
Tickets to a movie in which laughter
Is thrown into their faces.

> Theme: It's sad that life is a chain of money.

PRACTICE & APPLY

Analyzing the Text

COMMON CORE RL 1, RL 2, RL 4, RL 5

Possible answers:

1. The theme is that the value people put on material things lasts for only a short time.

2. It's sort of sad that money makes things work.

3. Both poems address the same subject: how the things we buy and own are such important parts of our lives. The speaker in each poem describes personal reactions to experiences with things that are purchased.

4. The tone in both poems is somewhat ironic. "Dump" is ironic because the speaker seems disgusted by all the junk at the dump but will continue to buy more stuff that will become junk. The tone in the lines "Tickets to a movie in which laughter / Is thrown into their faces" of "How Things Work" also has irony because the speaker is saying the opposite of what he means: Laughter suggests pleasure and fun, but not if it's "thrown" into your face.

5. In both poems, the speakers are summing up what they have observed about consumerism—using an ironic tone that seems to cast some doubt on the subject. The last two lines of "Dump" tell that people dislike the feeling of "emptiness" that occurs when they have fewer things, but the feeling soon passes as they refill empty spaces with new stuff—our lives have become an endless cycle of acquiring and discarding. The last two lines of "How Things Work" create a similar message that money connects us all in a possibly unfortunate, endless cycle.

6. The repetitious rhythms and end rhymes in "Dump" suggest lighthearted, playful feelings, which contrast with the negative descriptions and serious message of the poem. This contrast is disturbing to the reader or listener, which might be why the poet chose this form. The speaker in "How Things Work" is talking to his daughter. The poet may have chosen the form of free verse because its natural rhythms suggest an everyday conversation. It's a sweet, natural conversation with a child about a serious, grownup subject.

7. Students can develop understanding of both forms by taking the words and ideas in "Dump" and restating them to imitate the free verse in "How Things Work":
    Sample:
    At the dump, we clamber up
    steep unsteady heights
    to the brink.
    Beds without a dreamer.
    Lamps that no hand lights.
    We can't find enough cubic inches
    in our house, our mind
    to store odd items.

248 Collection 5

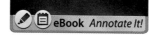

Analyzing the Text

COMMON CORE RL 1, RL 2, RL 4, RL 5, W 2, W 4, W 10

Cite Text Evidence Support your responses with evidence from the poems.

1. **Draw Conclusions** What is the theme of "Dump"?

2. **Draw Conclusions** What is the theme of "How Things Work"?

3. **Compare** In what ways do the poems "Dump" and "How Things Work" seem most alike?

4. **Compare** Reread lines 14–15 of "How Things Work." In what way is the tone similar to the tone in "Dump"?

5. **Compare** Reread the last two lines of each poem. How are the speakers' statements alike, and what message, or theme, do they leave the reader with?

6. **Evaluate** Why might the poet have chosen regular meter and rhyme to express the ideas in "Dump"? Why might the poet have chosen free verse for "How Things Work"?

7. **Connect** Reread lines 1–8 of "Dump." How might those ideas be expressed in language like that in "How Things Work"?

PERFORMANCE TASK

Writing Activity: Analysis Write a one-page analysis of the poems "Dump" and "How Things Work." In your analysis, compare and contrast the views and experiences of consuming expressed in each poem.

- Complete the graphic organizer from the Compare Forms in Poetry section. Use the completed chart to organize your ideas.

- Include words and lines from the poems to support the key points and ideas in your analysis.
- Organize your analysis clearly, using a compare-contrast structure.
- Sum up each speaker's central idea, or theme, and the tone, or attitude toward the subject.

248 Collection 5

Assign this performance task.

PERFORMANCE TASK

COMMON CORE W 2, W 4, W 10

Writing Activity: Analysis Have students work independently. Direct them to
- use the chart to draft their analysis
- organize their ideas in a logical way
- conclude by restating their main idea and insights

Determine Theme

COMMON CORE
RL 2

RETEACH

Explain that the **theme** of a poem is the message a poet communicates. Discuss the topic and theme of the poem "Dump." Explain that while the topic is a look at the things left at a dump the theme is a message about that topic: how we participate in an endless cycle of acquiring things that temporarily give us meaning, which we eventually throw away.

Point out that the theme is often implied rather than directly stated. Readers can identify the theme by paying attention to the words and details in a poem and by asking themselves, "What big message about life is the poet trying to tell me?"

Review the following steps for identifying the theme:

1. Examine clues in the text. What does the title tell you? How does the poet use words and details to convey a message?
2. Use the clues to figure out the message.

Together, consider the details and state a main-idea sentence that sums up the author's message. *(A high standard of life brings problems because people have too much but are never satisfied.)*

 LEVEL UP TUTORIALS Assign the following *Level Up* tutorial: **Theme**

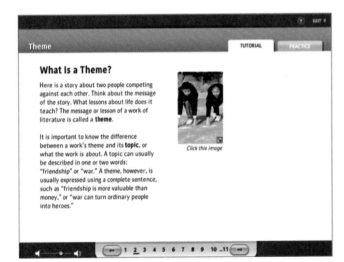

PRACTICE AND APPLY

Have students work with a partner to apply the steps to another poem of their choosing. After their analysis, have students share their ideas about theme with other pairs of students in the class.

Compare Forms in Poetry

COMMON CORE
RL 2

RETEACH

Review that the **form,** or structure, of a poem is the arrangement of the words and lines on the page. Remind students that **traditional** forms follow a set of rules that apply to their rhythmic pattern, line length, or rhyme scheme, while in **free verse** the poet decides on the form. Poets choose a form of poetry that works best for the thoughts and ideas they want to express.

Review these steps for comparing form:

1. Examine the line lengths and stanzas. Compare the number of lines per stanza and how the stanzas are organized. Note the emphasis created by the line breaks in each form.
2. Look for patterns of rhythm. Analyze line length and rhyming words, and identify any patterns of stressed and unstressed syllables (meter).
3. Compare the effects each form has on the poem's meaning.

 LEVEL UP TUTORIALS Assign the following *Level Up* tutorial: **Elements of Poetry**

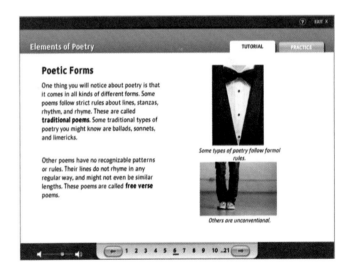

CLOSE READING APPLICATION

Have partners apply the steps to another pair of poems of their choosing. Encourage students to find examples of both traditional and free verse poetry. Suggest they fill out a Compare and Contrast graphic organizer as they do their analyses. Have pairs read their poetry choices aloud to a group and explain their analyses in a group discussion.

*my*SmartPlanner   Create lesson plans and access resources online.

Earth (A Gift Shop)

Short Story by Charles Yu

Why This Text?

Science fiction offers readers opportunities to explore how works of imagination can draw attention to social issues and provoke thought and debate. This lesson leads students to analyze a science fiction story and think about the big ideas in it.

Key Learning Objective: The student will be able to identify elements of science fiction and analyze a story to determine its theme.

For practice and application:

Close Reader selection
"He-y Come On Ou-t!"
Short Story by Shinichi Hoshi

COMMON CORE
Common Core Standards

RL 1 Cite textual evidence.
RL 2 Determine theme.
RL 3 Analyze story elements.
RL 4 Determine the meanings of words and phrases.
W 3 Write narratives to develop imagined experiences or events.
W 4 Produce clear and coherent writing.
W 10 Write routinely over extended time frames.
L 2b Spell correctly.
L 4d Verify the preliminary determination of word meaning by checking the context and a dictionary.
L 6 Acquire and use accurately grade-appropriate words.

▲ Text Complexity Rubric

Quantitative Measures	**Earth (A Gift Shop)** Lexile: 1010L
Qualitative Measures	**Levels of Meaning/Purpose** single level of complex meaning
	Structure less familiar story concepts
	Language Conventionality and Clarity contemporary, familiar language
	Knowledge Demands clearly fantastical perspective
Reader/Task Considerations	Teacher determined Vary by individual reader and type of text

TEACH

CLOSE READ

Charles Yu Have students read the information about the author. Supplement the information by telling students that in his writing Yu likes to play with ideas about science fiction itself and the blurry boundary between science fiction and real life. He uses humor to explore the question "Are we real?"

SETTING A PURPOSE Direct students to use the Setting a Purpose prompt to focus their reading. Remind them to generate questions as they read.

Analyze Stories: Science Fiction (LINES 9–11)
COMMON CORE **RL 1, RL 3**

Tell students that **science fiction** is a subcategory of fiction, in which an author uses scientific ideas and imagination to explore unexpected possibilities of the past or future.

A **CITE TEXT EVIDENCE** Have students reread lines 9–11 and cite text evidence that indicates this story is set in the future. (*The author is describing planet Earth at a time after "the fossil fuels ran out and all of the nation-states collapsed and a lucky few escaped Earth and went out in search of new worlds to colonize."*)

Determine the Meanings of Words and Phrases (LINES 14–15)
COMMON CORE **RL 1, RL 4**

Tell students that **style** is *how* an author writes rather than *what* an author writes. Point out that this author's style includes sentence fragments and informal word choices.

B **CITE TEXT EVIDENCE** Direct students to reread lines 14–15 and give ideas about why the author chose to write in this style, citing examples of the author's choices that reveal his style. (*The phrases "pretty long" and "really long" and the sentence fragments "Followed by another pretty long time" and "Which was then followed by a really long time" convey an informal, humorous tone and help readers hear the narrator's conversational voice.*)

Charles Yu (b. 1976) *wrote his first short story in college, but he didn't write another one until years later after he graduated from law school. During the day, he works as a lawyer for a visual effects company in southern California. He does most of his writing at night, after he has spent time with his family and his children have gone to bed. Yu has written two short story collections and a novel.*

Earth (A Gift Shop)

Short Story by Charles Yu

SETTING A PURPOSE As you read this science fiction story, think about the author's portrayal of Earth's future and how he creates this portrayal.

Come to Earth! Yes, that Earth. A lot of people think we're closed during construction, but we are not! We're still open for business.

Admittedly, it's a little confusing.

First, we were Earth: The Planet. Then life formed, and that was a great and good time.

And then, for a little while, we were Earth: A Bunch of Civilizations!

10 Until the fossil fuels ran out and all of the nation-states collapsed and a lucky few escaped Earth and went out in search of new worlds to colonize. **A**

Then, for what seemed like forever, we were Earth: Not Much Going On Here Anymore.

And that lasted for a long time. Followed by another pretty long time. Which was then followed by a really long time. **B**

Earth (A Gift Shop) **249**

SCAFFOLDING FOR ELL STUDENTS

Analyze Language Offer support as needed in interpreting the casual, idiomatic speech of the narrator. Have students reread lines 28–30. Use prompts such as the following and have students provide paraphrases:

- When people *pool their resources*, everyone brings something to share. What is another way of saying the first sentence? (*We brought things and put them together.*)
- People say "to be sure" to mean "it's true" or "certainly." People say "a whole lot of good stuff " to mean "valuable things." What is the most important idea in the second sentence? (*After the end of civilization on Earth, few valuable things were left.*)

Analyze Stories: Science Fiction (LINES 28–41)

 COMMON CORE **RL 3**

Point out that the author imagines a future Earth that has been turned into a museum.

 ASK STUDENTS to reread lines 28–41 and tell what the objects in the museum reveal about future Earth. *(After the collapse of civilizations, people are uneducated and can't recognize or appreciate art. They mix opera with a TV talk show and know nothing about a painting except that it was important.)*

Determine Theme

COMMON CORE **RL 1, RL 2**

(LINES 51–60)

Tell students that a **theme** is a message about life or human nature that the author shares with the reader. Explain that in this segment of the story the narrator is describing what human beings value.

 CITE TEXT EVIDENCE Have students reread lines 51–60 to note the words that reveal what is most important to humans at this time in the future. Ask what point the author might be making. *(After only five years of schooling, kids "join the leisure force as full-time professional consumers." Humans who visit Earth still want "credit accounts" and "lifelong loyalty rewards programs." The author is pointing out that to be human is to buy things.)*

CRITICAL VOCABULARY

enterprising: The narrator says that human beings are an enterprising species. **ASK STUDENTS** what they would expect enterprising people to do. *(open a business, invent a product, make money)*

mandatory: The narrator says that five years of schooling are mandatory. **ASK STUDENTS** how education in the future has changed, according to the narrator. *(In the future, students don't have to attend school beyond fourth or fifth grade.)*

Then, after a while, humans, having semi-successfully established colonies on other planets, started to come back to Earth on vacation. Parents brought their kids, teachers brought their classes on field trips, retirees came in groups of twenty or thirty. They wanted to see where their ancestors had come from. But there was nothing here. Kids and parents and teachers left, disappointed. *That's it?* they would say, or some would even say, *It was okay I guess, but I thought there would be more.*

So, being an **enterprising** species and all, some of us got together and reinvented ourselves as Earth: The Museum, which we thought was a great idea.

We pooled our resources and assembled what we could find. To be sure, there was not a whole lot of good stuff left after the collapse of Earth: A Bunch of Civilizations! One of us had a recording of Maria Callas singing the Violetta aria in *La Traviata*.[1] We all thought it sounded very pretty, so we had that playing in a room in the museum. And I think maybe we had a television playing episodes of *The Tonight Show Starring Johnny Carson*. The main attraction of the museum was the painting we had by some guy of some flowers. No one could remember the name of the guy or the painting, or even the flowers, but we were all pretty sure it was an important painting at some point in the history of paintings and also the history of people, so we put that in the biggest room in the center of everything.

But parents and teachers, being humans (and especially being descendants of the same humans who messed everything up in the first place) thought the whole museum was quite boring, or even *very* boring, and they would say as much, even while we were still within earshot, and we could hear them saying that to each other, about how bored they were. That hurt to hear, but more than that what was hurtful was that no one was coming to Earth anymore, now that it was a small and somewhat eclectic museum. And who could blame them? After the collapse of civilization, school just has never been the same. By the time kids are done with their five years of **mandatory** schooling, they are eight or even nine years old and more than ready to join the leisure force as full-time professional consumers. Humans who went

enterprising
(ĕn'tər-prī'zĭng) *adj.*
An *enterprising* person is someone who accepts challenges and takes initiative.

mandatory
(măn'də-tôr'ē) *adj.*
If something is *mandatory*, it is required.

---

[1] **Violetta aria in *La Traviata*:** a song from the famous opera by Giuseppe Verdi in which the character Violetta sings joyfully about love.

> ## After the collapse of civilization, school just has never been the same.

elsewhere have carried on that tradition from their days on Earth. They are ready to have their credit accounts opened, for their spending to be tracked, to get started in their lifelong loyalty rewards programs. Especially those humans who are
60 rich enough to be tourists coming back here to Earth.

Eventually one of us realized that the most popular part of the museum was the escalator ride. Although you would think interstellar[2] travel would have sort of raised the bar on what was needed to impress people, there was just something about moving diagonally that seemed to amuse the tourists, both kids and adults, and then one of us finally woke up and said, well, why not give them what they want?

So we did some research, in the few books we had left, and on the computer, and the research confirmed our **hypothesis:**
70 Humans love rides.

So Earth: The Museum was shuttered for several years while we reinvented ourselves and developed merchandise and attractions, all of the things we were naturally good at, and after another good long while, we finally were able to reopen as Earth: The Theme Park and Gift Shop, which did okay but it was not too long before we realized the theme park part of it was expensive to operate and kind of a hassle, really, as our engineering was not so good and we kept making people sick or, in a few cases, really **misjudging** g-forces,[3] and word got
80 out among the travel agencies that Earth: The Theme Park and Gift Shop was not so fun and actually quite dangerous, so we really had no choice but to drop the theme park part and that is how we became Earth: The Gift Shop.

Which was all anyone ever wanted anyway. To get a souvenir to take home.

We do have some great souvenirs.

hypothesis
(hī-pŏth´ĭ-sĭs) *n.*
A *hypothesis* is an explanation or theory for something that can be tested for validity.

misjudge
(mĭs-jŭj´) *v.* If you *misjudge* something, you form an incorrect opinion about it.

___

[2] **interstellar:** between stars.

[3] **g-forces:** the amount of force someone experiences when he or she accelerates at the same rate as every unit of his or her mass.

Earth (A Gift Shop) **251**

CLOSE READ

Determine Theme

COMMON CORE **RL 2**

(LINES 71–83)

Tell students that the narrator's description of how Earth is reinvented shows what human beings value.

E **ASK STUDENTS** to reread lines 71–83 to sum up what readers learn about Earth's transformations. *(After Earth: The Museum was closed because it was too boring, humans on Earth developed merchandise and attractions in Earth: The Theme Park and Gift Shop. But because they no longer had engineering skills, the rides were too dangerous. Earth became just a gift shop instead.)* What theme do these details suggest? *(The details suggest that of all the money-making ventures that people in the future have made of Earth, the best was to make it solely a place to buy things instead of experiences.)*

CRITICAL VOCABULARY

hypothesis: The narrator says that research confirmed the hypothesis that people love rides. **ASK STUDENTS** what is ridiculous about using the word *hypothesis* here. *(The narrator is suggesting that their research was scientific, but their knowledge of science was limited.)*

misjudge: The author says that the ride designers misjudged g-forces. **ASK STUDENTS** why misjudging g-forces would be a problem. *(People would be thrown off the rides or injured because of poor planning.)*

Strategies for Annotation

🖉 🗐 *Annotate it!*

Determine Theme

COMMON CORE **RL 2**

Have students use their eBook annotation tools to note clues to a theme about human activities today in lines 57–60.

- Highlight words, phrases, and sentences that tell about today's economic activities.
- Add a note to sum up the author's point.

Earth. They are ready to have their credit accounts opened,

for their spending to be tracked, to get started in their lifelong

loyalty rewards programs. Especially those huma~~

enough to be tourists coming back here to Earth

In the future, credit and spending will be even more important than today.

TEACH

CLOSE READ

Determine Theme
COMMON CORE RL 2

(LINES 88–92)

Tell students that an idea about human values presented earlier is repeated in the first catalog item in lines 88–92.

 ASK STUDENTS to reread the description after number 1 (lines 88–92) and tell what point is being made about human "progress." *(Humans moved past the Age of Learning, later seen as boring, into the Age After the Age of Learning, in which learning was no longer valued—people preferred ignorance.)*

Analyze Stories: Science Fiction
COMMON CORE RL 1, RL 3

(LINES 87–113)

Tell students that future worlds depicted in science fiction have many similarities with the world of the present.

 CITE TEXT EVIDENCE Have students reread lines 87–113 and note details that are really about our world today, not the future. Ask for ideas about the author's purpose in listing these "top-selling items." *(The distant future is unlikely to still have karaoke, DVDs, and video games. The author is poking fun at what we purchase today and our shallowness, making the point that today's consumer society is just as likely to be thriving centuries into the future. Saying that a "beautiful painting of a nature scene" is "almost like a photograph" points out that we've lost our appreciation of both nature and art.)*

Our top-selling items for the month of October:

1. *History: The Poster!* A 36" × 24" color poster showing all of the major phases of human history. From the Age Before
90 Tools, through the short-lived but exciting Age of Tools, to the (yawn) Age of Learning, and into our current age, the Age After the Age of Learning.

2. *War: The Soundtrack.* A three-minute musical interpretation of the experience of war, with solos for guitar and drums. Comes in an instrumental version (for karaoke lovers).

3. *Art: The Poster!* Beautiful painting of a nature scene. Very realistic-looking, almost like a photograph. Twenty percent off if purchased with History: The Poster!

100 4. *God, the Oneness: A Mystical 3-D Journey.* 22-minute DVD. Never-before-seen footage. Comes with special glasses for viewing.

5. *Science: The Video Game.* All the science you ever need to bother with! Almost nothing to learn. So easy you really don't have to pay attention. For ages three to ninety-three.

6. *Summer in a Bottle.* Sure, no one can go outside on Earth anymore because it's 170 degrees Fahrenheit, but who needs outside when they have laboratory-synthesized Summer

252 Collection 5

Guy Jarvis/Houghton, Mifflin, Harcourt and NASA Goddard Space Flight Center

APPLYING ACADEMIC VOCABULARY

attitude	consume	purchase

As students explore the theme in this story, incorporate the following Collection 5 academic vocabulary words: *attitude, consume,* and *purchase.* Talk about the narrator's **attitude** toward the tourists who visit Earth to **purchase** things. Discuss what the story seems to say about the human drive to **consume.**

in a Bottle? Now comes in two odors: "Mist of Nostalgia" or
"Lemony Fresh."

7. *Happiness: A Skin Lotion.* At last you can be content and
moisturized, at the same time. From the makers of Adventure:
A Body Spray.

Other strong sellers for the month include Psychologically
Comforting Teddy Bear and Shakespeare: The Fortune
Cookie. All of the items above also come in ring tones,
T-shirts, cups, and key chains.

And coming for the holidays, get ready for the latest
installment of Earth's greatest artistic work of the last century:
Hero Story: A Hero's Redemption (and Sweet Revenge), a
computer-generated script based on all the key points of the
archetypal[4] story arc that we humans are.

Which brings us back to our original point. What was our
original point? Oh yeah, Earth: The Gift Shop is still here. Not
just here, but doing great! Okay, maybe not great, but okay,
we're okay. We would be better if you came by and shopped
here. Which is why we sent you this audio catalog, which we
hope you are reading (otherwise we are talking to ourselves).
Earth: The Gift Shop: The Brochure. Some people have said
the name, Earth: The Gift Shop, is a bit confusing because it
makes it seem like this is the official gift shop of some other
attraction here on Earth, when really the attraction is the
gift shop itself. So we are considering changing our name to
Earth (A Gift Shop), which sounds less official but is probably
more accurate. Although if we are going down that road, it
should be pointed out that the most accurate name would
be Earth = A Gift Shop, or even Earth = Merchandise, since
basically, if we are being honest with ourselves, we are a theme
park without the park part, which is to say we are basically
just a theme, whatever that means, although Earth, an Empty
Theme Park would be an even worse name than Earth = A
Gift Shop, so for now we're just going to stick with what we've
got, until something better comes along.

So, again, we say: Come to Earth! We get millions of
visitors a year, from near and far. Some of you come by
accident. No shame in that! We don't care if you are just
stopping to refuel, or if you lost your way, or even if you just

---

[4] **archetypal:** having the qualities of an original model or prototype. Common
archetypes include the hero, the trickster, the wise old man, and the Earth
mother.

CLOSE READ

Analyze Stories: Science Fiction (LINES 118–122)

COMMON CORE   RL 3

Point out that the narrator describes the greatest
artistic work of the previous century in this imagined
future Earth.

 ASK STUDENTS to reread lines 118–122 and give
their own ideas about whether this work deserves
to be called artistic. *(The "greatest artistic work" is a
script about the "archetypal story arc that we humans
are," generated by a computer using "key data points."
Literature developed by computers might be called
artistic, but there's no real human creativity involved.)*

Determine Theme

COMMON CORE   RL 1, RL 2

(LINES 123–143)

Tell students that the narrator offers different names
for Earth and even tells what the theme of Earth is.

 CITE TEXT EVIDENCE Have students reread
the paragraph that begins on line 123 and cite the
different names for Earth. Ask them what the narrator
points out about a theme and how that idea is
connected to the theme of this story. (Earth: The
Gift Shop *which might change to* Earth (A Gift Shop) *or*
Earth = A Gift Shop *or* Earth = Merchandise. *The
narrator says that "we are a theme park without the
park part, which is to say we are basically just a theme."
The theme of the story has to do with our planet
becoming a place to shop.)*

Analyze Stories: Science Fiction (LINES 155–162)

COMMON CORE RL 3

Tell students that the narrator's "audio catalog" is coming to a close, with a final attempt to appeal to the emotions of potential tourists.

 ASK STUDENTS to reread the sentences in which the narrator repeats the word *home*, beginning on line 155, and tell how effective the narrator seems to be. *(The narrator is advertising planet Earth as home to humans, though he or she can't help mentioning that it might not be home anymore, because humans left it thousands of years ago. The narrator is not very effective here in selling the idea of visiting Earth to people of the future. He is effective in showing the irony of the fate of Earth as he presents it in this science fiction.)*

Determine Theme

COMMON CORE RL 1, RL 2

(LINES 161–162)

Review that the theme of a story is the "big idea" about life or human nature that the author wants to leave the reader with.

CITE TEXT EVIDENCE Have students identify the two sentences that best point to the theme of this story. *("I was a human on Earth. Even if all I did was shop there.")* Ask how students would recast that theme in their own words. *(In the end, the future Earth will be nothing more than a place for human beings to shop.)*

COLLABORATIVE DISCUSSION Have students work in small groups to talk about answers to the questions. Suggest that they contrast *what* the author wants to point out and *how* he points it out.

ASK STUDENTS to share any questions they generated in the course of reading and discussing the selection.

---

want to rest for a moment and eat a sandwich and drink a cold bottle of beer. We still have beer! Of course, we prefer if you come here intentionally. Many of you do. Many of you read about this place in a guidebook, and some of you even go out of your way and take a detour from your travels to swing by the gift shop. Maybe you are coming because you just want to look, or to say you were here. Maybe you are coming to have a story to tell when you get back. Maybe you just want to be able to say: I went home. Even if it isn't home, was never your home, is not anyone's home anymore, maybe you just want to say, I touched the ground there, breathed the air, looked at the moon the way people must have done nine or ten or a hundred thousand years ago. So you can say to your friends, if only for a moment or two: I was a human on Earth. Even if all I did was shop there.

COLLABORATIVE DISCUSSION In what ways is this a serious story? In what ways is it not at all serious, and why did the author choose to do both with his portrayal of Earth's future? Talk about your ideas with other group members.

TO CHALLENGE STUDENTS ...

Analyze Theme Suggest that students consider the central idea in the selection "Always Wanting More" from earlier in Collection 5 and compare those ideas to the theme of "Earth (A Gift Shop)." Have small groups hold an informal debate to explain how each author makes his point or develops his theme, and make a case about which author's approach is more effective. Make sure that students cite evidence from both texts to make their cases.

Analyze Stories: Science Fiction

Written works that come from an author's imagination fall in the broad category called fiction. In **science fiction,** an author explores unexpected possibilities of the past or the future. The author combines knowledge of science and technology with a creative imagination to present a new world. "Earth (A Gift Shop)" has elements found in other science fiction stories:

Elements of Science Fiction

- descriptions of how humankind's technologies have altered planet Earth
- colonization of other planets
- impossible events and settings like those in a fantasy story
- a future world with many features and issues common in today's world

Science fiction writers create fantasy worlds, but they often include familiar elements to make these worlds seem believable. Characters usually speak and behave the way real people do. They often have the same goals and motivations as real people, but they pursue them in fantasy worlds set in the future, the past, or a time completely separate from history.

Choose one of the elements in the list and tell how it is shown in "Earth (A Gift Shop)."

Determine Theme

A **theme** is a message about life or human nature that the author shares with the reader. In works of fiction, themes are the "big ideas" that readers can infer based on the story the author tells.

While the topic of a science fiction story might be time travel, its theme might be about humans' responsibility for future generations. The following are examples of themes found in science fiction:

Themes in Science Fiction

- Technological advances will make us smarter and happier.
- Technological advances will cause us to lose control over our lives.
- Tampering with biological systems brings ruin.
- Humanity will survive only if we conquer our urge for war.

To identify the theme in a science fiction text, look at the details the author presents. Do certain characters make significant statements about science and technology? Is technology presented as a positive force that benefits mankind, or is it shown as a potentially threatening force? Consider these questions in the context of "Earth (A Gift Shop)."

TEACH

CLOSE READ

Analyze Stories: Science Fiction

Discuss what is meant by the phrase "unexpected possibilities of the past or future." Then, review how science fiction is like and different from fantasy stories: Impossible events and imaginary characters are in both kinds of fiction, but science fiction often explores the effects of science and technology.

After students read the list of elements of science fiction, have them review "Earth (A Gift Shop)" to find an example of each element. *(Sample answers: Humankind's technologies have altered planet Earth to make it unlivable—the temperature outside is 170 degrees Fahrenheit. Wealthy human beings left Earth to colonize other planets, though some come back as tourists. The main impossible event is that the whole planet can be turned into a museum, theme park, or gift shop. The author is exaggerating today's consumer culture by imagining a future Earth that exists solely for the purpose of shopping.)*

Determine Theme

Use the examples of themes in science fiction to emphasize that the theme of a story is not the same as its topic. Remind students that in "Earth (A Gift Shop)" the human drive to make technology has turned the setting—planet Earth—into a place filled with not much more than things to purchase. Encourage students to keep this in mind as they share ideas about the theme of "Earth (A Gift Shop)."

Strategies for Annotation 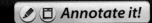 *Annotate it!*

Analyze Stories: Science Fiction

Share these strategies for guided or independent analysis:

- Highlight in yellow details showing an element of science fiction stories.
- Add a note to tell about the element.

could blame them? After the collapse of civilization, school just has never been the same. By the time kids are done with their five years of mandatory schooling, they are eight or even nine years old and more than ready to join the leisure force as full-time professional consumers. Humans . . . (lines 51–55).

> a future world where buying things is more important than learning— like today's world?

PRACTICE & APPLY

Analyzing the Text COMMON CORE RL 1, RL 2, RL 3, RL 4

Possible answers:

1. *"Earth (A Gift Shop)" is science fiction because the author imagines a future world with issues that are similar to those on Earth today. Technologies have altered planet Earth, causing fossil fuels to run out and nation-states to collapse. Some humans are able to leave to colonize other planets, so interplanetary travel is common.*

2. *The narrator uses* we *and* us *to refer to the people left behind on Earth, and* all of us *to refer to those who live on Earth now.*

3. *Descriptions that convey ideas about today's consumer culture include language familiar in ads: "Never-before-seen footage," "For ages three to ninety-three," "be content and moisturized." Things commonly offered today—"ring tones, T-shirts, cups, and key chains"—are still offered. There's an unrealistic, comical suggestion that many basic consumer technologies have not advanced at all in the far-distant future.*

4. *The sequence of names is "Earth: The Planet"; "Earth: A Bunch of Civilizations!" "Earth: Not Much Going On Here Anymore"; "Earth: The Museum"; "Earth: The Theme Park and Gift Shop"; "Earth: The Gift Shop." Future names could be "Earth (A Gift Shop)" or "Earth = A Gift Shop" or "Earth = Merchandise." The author uses the name changes to suggest that the whole planet has been just a brand for centuries. The name changes show how widespread marketing and merchandising are on Earth—in the future and now.*

5. *Our preoccupation with consuming and with merchandise is destroying our civilization and replacing deep values with superficial ones.*

6. *The author uses humor to show that he disapproves of modern consumer culture. His language has an ironic, disrespectful tone. For example, to point out the loss of knowledge, the narrator uses the ridiculous example that the main attraction of the museum was "the painting we had by some guy of some flowers."*

 eBook *Annotate It!*

Analyzing the Text  COMMON CORE RL 1, RL 2, RL 3, RL 4, W 3, W 4, W 10

Cite Text Evidence Support your responses with evidence from the text.

1. **Identify** What elements of science fiction does the story "Earth (A Gift Shop)" have?

2. **Infer** To whom might the narrator be referring when using the pronoun *we* throughout the story?

3. **Cite Evidence** In the list of "top-selling items," what are some descriptions that convey ideas about today's consumer culture?

4. **Draw Conclusions** The narrator tells how "Earth: The Planet" has undergone several name changes. What point might the author be making?

5. **Draw Conclusions** What is the theme of this story?

6. **Analyze** How does the narrator's use of language reveal the author's attitude toward the story topic?

PERFORMANCE TASK  my WriteSmart

Writing Activity: Short Story In the science fiction world of "Earth (A Gift Shop)," humans no longer live on Earth. What would it be like to vacation in that world? How and why might someone have had to escape Earth to find a home on another planet? Pick a part of that plot to expand into a short story of your own.

- Create an outline of your story, including the narrator, characters, setting, and plot events with a conflict and resolution.
- List the gadgets or technologies that the characters will encounter.
- Include a theme that leaves readers with a message about technology.
- Use your plan to draft and then revise a 2–3-page short story.

PERFORMANCE TASK COMMON CORE W 3, W 4, W 10

Assign this performance task.

Writing Activity: Short Story Help students develop a plan for a story in a brief form, such as "flash fiction" or a "short short." Have students

- freewrite or brainstorm to answer the questions *who? Where and when? What if . . . ?*
- imagine the problem or conflict that characters face
- list possible main events that will lead from the conflict to the climax to the resolution

See the lessons in Extend and Reteach for ideas for additional instruction in plot and setting.

Critical Vocabulary

COMMON CORE L 4d, L 6

enterprising   mandatory   hypothesis   misjudge

Practice and Apply Use your own knowledge and experiences to answer each question.

1. Who is an **enterprising** person you know? What makes him or her enterprising?

2. What is **mandatory** at your school? Why?

3. What **hypothesis** can you make about human nature? Why is it a hypothesis?

4. When have you **misjudged** someone or something? How did you find out the truth?

Vocabulary Strategy: Verifying Meaning

When you come across an unfamiliar word in a text, there are a number of steps you can take to verify the word's correct meaning.

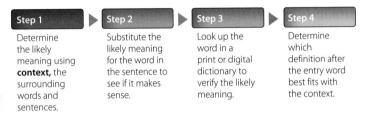

Step 1	Step 2	Step 3	Step 4
Determine the likely meaning using **context,** the surrounding words and sentences.	Substitute the likely meaning for the word in the sentence to see if it makes sense.	Look up the word in a print or digital dictionary to verify the likely meaning.	Determine which definition after the entry word best fits with the context.

Use the steps to consider and verify the meaning of *enterprising* in this sentence from "Earth (A Gift Shop)":

> So, being an *enterprising* species and all, some of us got together and reinvented ourselves as Earth: The Museum, which we thought was a great idea.

The context shows that being enterprising has to do with a great idea and inventing something again, so it might mean "creative" or "cooperative." Both of those meanings make sense in the sentence. The dictionary offers this definition: "Showing initiative and willingness to take on new projects." To be enterprising is to be willing to take on the project Earth: The Museum.

Practice and Apply Find the sentence with the word *eclectic* in line 50 of "Earth (A Gift Shop)." Complete the four steps in the chart to verify the meaning for this context. Then restate the sentence using the dictionary meaning you have identified.

Earth (A Gift Shop) **257**

PRACTICE & APPLY

Critical Vocabulary

COMMON CORE L 4d, L 6

Possible answers:

1. *My uncle is enterprising because he came to this country as a teenager, and within ten years he had his own business.*

2. *Attendance is mandatory. Students are not allowed to move to the next grade unless they have come to school for a certain number of days each year.*

3. *Based on my personal experiences, I have the hypothesis that most people cannot keep secrets. It's a hypothesis because I haven't done the research yet to prove it.*

4. *I misjudged the distance from the high diving board to the pool. When I got up there, I turned around and came down.*

Vocabulary Strategy: Verifying Meaning

Sample restatement of sentence with eclectic:

That hurt to hear, but more than that, what was hurtful was that no one was coming to Earth anymore, now that it was a small museum with items from various sources.

Strategies for Annotation 🖊 📖 *Annotate it!*

Vocabulary Strategy: Verifying Meaning

COMMON CORE L 4d, L 6

Have students use their eBook annotation tools and the steps for verifying meaning to do the following:

- Highlight in yellow the word *eclectic.*
- Highlight In green clues to meaning in the surrounding words and sentences.
- Note one or more likely meanings.
- Decide which meaning makes sense in the context.

the whole museum was quite boring, or even *very* boring, and they would say as much, even while we were still within earshot, and we could hear them saying . . . how bored they were. . . . now that it was a small and somewhat eclectic m

> eclectic
> Possible meaning from context: "boring" Dictionary definition: "Made up of elements from a variety of sources." This makes more sense in the context of the paragraph before this one.

Earth (A Gift Shop) **257**

PRACTICE & APPLY

Language Conventions: Spelling

   COMMON CORE L 2b

Review that homophones are words that sound alike but have different spellings and meanings. If students find that they often misspell particular homophones, suggest that they keep a list with a meaning clue beside each.

Answers:

1. *It's, their*

2. *effect, capitals*

3. *peace, principal*

4. *aisles, scents*

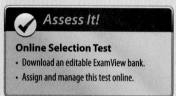

Language Conventions: Spelling

  COMMON CORE L 2b

When you proofread your writing for accuracy, always check that every word is spelled correctly. If you are using a computer, the spellcheck feature catches most misspellings—but not all. Be especially attentive to **homophones,** words that sound alike but have different meanings and spellings. These descriptions of souvenir items come from "Earth (A Gift Shop)":

> **painting of a nature scene**
> **never-before-seen footage**

The words *scene* ("something to view") and *seen* (a form of the verb *to see*) are homophones. Knowing that a word has one or more homophones helps you check for correct meaning-spelling matches. You can verify the spelling and meaning of a homophone in a digital or print dictionary.

Some commonly misspelled homophones are *threw/through, right/write/rite, their/there/they're,* and *your/you're.*

This chart shows other commonly misspelled homophones.

affect (to cause a change) **effect** (result)	**cents** (pennies) **scents** (smells) **sense** (feeling; intelligence)	**peace** (calm state) **piece** (part)
aisle (pathway) **I'll** (I will) **isle** (island)	**cereal** (of grain) **serial** (in a series)	**principal** (chief) **principle** (standard; belief)
capital (city; money) **capitol** (lawmakers' building)	**currant** (small raisin) **current** (present time; flow of water)	**rain** (precipitation) **reign** (period of control) **rein** (strap for horse)
cite (quote; summon to court) **sight** (what is seen) **site** (location)	**it's** (it is) **its** (belonging to it)	**wait** (stay) **weight** (heaviness)

Practice and Apply Correct one or more spelling errors in each sentence.

1. Its time for tourists to visit there old planet, Earth.

2. One affect of the collapse of civilizations was the end of national capitols, such as Paris and Washington, D.C.

3. Earth is at piece now, and our principle activity is selling things.

4. Walk through the isles of the gift shop and sniff the sense "Mist of Nostalgia" and "Lemony Fresh."

INTERACTIVE WHITEBOARD LESSON

Analyze Stories: Setting

COMMON CORE

RL 3

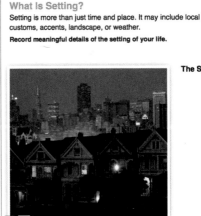

Share What You Know ▶ What Is Setting?

What Is Setting?
Setting is more than just time and place. It may include local customs, accents, landscape, or weather.
Record meaningful details of the setting of your life.

The Setting of Your Life

TEACH

Prepare students for the Performance Task by focusing attention on the setting of their stories. Review that the **setting** is the time and place of the story action.

Explain that writers include details of the setting, showing features such as the landscape, weather, season, time of day or night, living conditions, and the way that people dress and talk. Emphasize that in a science fiction story the setting is especially significant. The writer provides details to help readers know that the characters are not on Earth, for example, or that events are taking place in a future time.

Display the following influences of settings in fiction. For each one, ask students to name stories in which setting plays that role.

- affects how characters act and feel
- creates the story conflict
- conveys a mood, such as peacefulness or fear
- suggests a theme or has symbolism

COLLABORATIVE DISCUSSION

Encourage students to visualize a setting they might use in their story. Have students write two or three sentences to describe it. Each writer may find ideas for clarifying or enhancing the sentences by reading them aloud and listening as other group members tell what they picture.

Analyze Stories: Science Fiction

COMMON CORE

RL 3, W 3

TEACH

Remind students that any story that comes from the author's imagination is called fiction. Explain that within the broad category of fiction are varied kinds of stories, including science fiction. As you make the following points about **science fiction,** encourage students to give examples from stories they have read or viewed:

- The story may be set in the future.
- The characters may not all be human.
- The plot may involve actual recent technologies and scientific discoveries.
- The story may deal with the effects of technology on individuals, societies, and planet Earth.
- The story may deal with humans' place in the universe.

Tell students that science fiction is most like another kind of fiction, fantasy, because both often involve imaginary worlds and impossible events. Explain that the main difference is the connection to science and technology in science fiction. Offer these descriptions of stories, and have students tell which ones are science fiction, and why:

- A group of human astronauts sets up permanent settlements on Mars. *(science fiction)*
- Human civilizations vanish as Earth's resources are used up. *(science fiction)*
- Mice that talk and act like people live in an underground city. *(fantasy)*
- A killer virus is released by a laboratory worker seeking revenge against a boss. *(science fiction)*
- A brother and sister discover their supernatural ability to read people's minds. *(fantasy)*
- A robot programmed to protect a house refuses to let anyone leave. *(science fiction)*

PRACTICE AND APPLY

Have students look through "Earth (A Gift Shop)" for elements it shares with other science fiction. Tell students to complete each of these sentences with information from the story:

- *The setting for the story "Earth (A Gift Shop)" is . . .*
- *The narrator tells how planet Earth . . .*
- *Human beings who colonized other planets may . . .*

He—y, Come On Ou—t!

Short Story by Shinichi Hoshi

Why This Text

Some stories are so complex the theme must be inferred from details in the text. Other stories are relatively simple in their structure and plot, with a message that is directly stated. "He—y, Come On Ou—t!" is an uncomplicated tale with the feel of an allegory, and although the message is clear, students may have difficulty seeing how it points to a greater truth, one that is not limited to the scope of the story. With the help of the close-reading questions, students will understand what the author is saying about preserving not only the earth but also the truth for future generations.

Background Have students read the background and information about the author. Explain that the name Hoshi means "star" in Japanese, and it is not the pseudonym readers may assume it is given his favorite setting, outer space. But Hoshi's stories are not simply "science fiction": they defy category, blending together dystopic visions of the future with elements of folklore, fantasy, social criticism, and humor. Hoshi's universal themes have earned him a worldwide audience, and his stories have been translated into more than 20 languages. Today his cautionary tales seem more relevant than ever.

SETTING A PURPOSE Ask students to pay attention to the way the author uses details of setting, plot, character, and dialogue to convey the story's theme.

Common Core Support

- cite textual evidence
- determine a theme or central idea in a text
- analyze how particular elements of a story interact
- determine the meanings of words and phrases as they are used in text

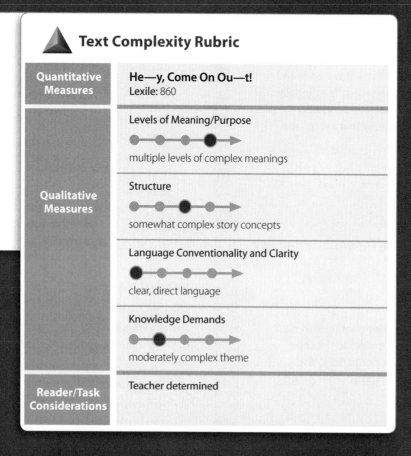

Text Complexity Rubric

Quantitative Measures

He—y, Come On Ou—t!
Lexile: 860

Qualitative Measures

Levels of Meaning/Purpose
multiple levels of complex meanings

Structure
somewhat complex story concepts

Language Conventionality and Clarity
clear, direct language

Knowledge Demands
moderately complex theme

Reader/Task Considerations
Teacher determined

Strategies for CLOSE READING

Determine Theme

Students should read this story carefully all the way through. Close-reading questions at the bottom of the page will help them use details in the text to determine the story's "message," or theme. As they read, students should jot down comments or questions about the text in the margins.

WHEN STUDENTS STRUGGLE . . .

To help students determine theme in "He—y, Come On Ou—t!," have them work in small groups to fill out a chart like the one shown below.

CITE TEXT EVIDENCE For practice in using details in the text to make inferences about the theme, have students analyze each of the following details from the story.

Detail	What It Reveals
". . . a small shrine had been swept away by a landslide." (lines 3–4)	This image of destruction provides an intriguing setting for the story.
"You might bring down a curse on us. Lay off." (line 24)	This dialogue shows that some people are afraid of acting on a situation without a full understanding of it.
"the scientist . . . [s]uggesting the thing had a perfectly plausible explanation, said simply, 'Fill it in.'" (lines 54–57)	Scientists may "cover up" the truth because they don't want to lose face.
"The concessionaire had his cohorts mount a loud campaign . . . 'Perfect for the disposal of such things as waste from nuclear reactors.'" (lines 81–84)	People out to make a profit may not consider the consequences of some of their actions.
"Young girls whose betrothals had been arranged discarded old diaries in the hole." (lines 114–115)	Memories and experiences are equated with toxic waste.

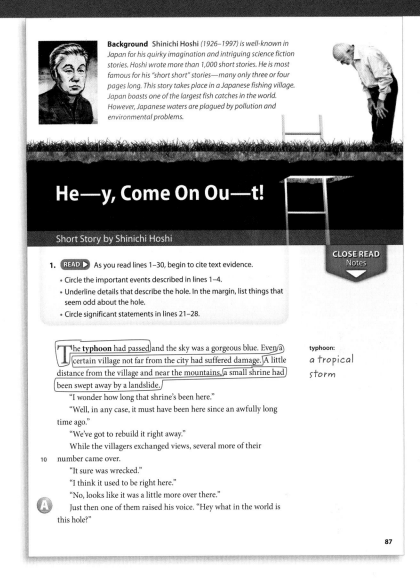

Background Shinichi Hoshi *(1926–1997) is well-known in Japan for his quirky imagination and intriguing science fiction stories. Hoshi wrote more than 1,000 short stories. He is most famous for his "short short" stories—many only three or four pages long. This story takes place in a Japanese fishing village. Japan boasts one of the largest fish catches in the world. However, Japanese waters are plagued by pollution and environmental problems.*

He—y, Come On Ou—t!

Short Story by Shinichi Hoshi

CLOSE READ
Notes

1. **READ ▶** As you read lines 1–30, begin to cite text evidence.

   • Circle the important events described in lines 1–4.
   • Underline details that describe the hole. In the margin, list things that seem odd about the hole.
   • Circle significant statements in lines 21–28.

The **typhoon** had passed and the sky was a gorgeous blue. Even a certain village not far from the city had suffered damage. A little distance from the village and near the mountains, a small shrine had been swept away by a landslide.

    "I wonder how long that shrine's been here."

    "Well, in any case, it must have been here since an awfully long time ago."

    "We've got to rebuild it right away."

    While the villagers exchanged views, several more of their
10 number came over.

    "It sure was wrecked."

    "I think it used to be right here."

    "No, looks like it was a little more over there."

A   Just then one of them raised his voice. "Hey what in the world is this hole?"

typhoon:
a tropical storm

87

1. **READ AND CITE TEXT EVIDENCE** In line 14, one of the villagers discovers a hole in the ground.

   A ASK STUDENTS about the reaction of the other villagers to the hole. Why do they gather around it? *They are curious about it because it seems odd.* What explanation is suggested in line 20? *Someone wonders if it's a fox's hole.*

   Critical Vocabulary: typhoon (line 1) Have students explain the meaning of *typhoon.* What can they infer about the severity of the typhoon from the first paragraph? *It was a bad storm with a wide reach.*

CLOSE READ
Notes

It is totally
dark.
It is very deep.

It doesn't
produce
an echo.

There is no
indication
where it
came from.

B Where they had all gathered there was a hole about a meter in diameter. They peered in, but it was so dark nothing could be seen. However, it gave one the feeling that it was so deep it went clear through to the center of the earth.

20   There was even one person who said, "I wonder if it's a fox's hole."

"He—y, come on ou—t!" shouted a young man into the hole. There was no echo from the bottom. Next he picked up a pebble and was about to throw it in.

"You might bring down a curse on us. Lay off," warned an old man, but the younger one energetically threw the pebble in. As before, however, there was no answering response from the bottom. The villagers cut down some trees, tied them with rope and made a fence which they put around the hole. Then they repaired to the village.

"What do you suppose we ought to do?"

30   "Shouldn't we build the shrine up just as it was over the hole?"

A day passed with no agreement. The news traveled fast, and a car from the newspaper company rushed over. In no time a scientist came out, and with an all-knowing expression on his face he went over to the hole. Next, a bunch of gawking curiosity seekers showed up; one could also pick out here and there men of shifty glances who appeared to be **concessionaires**. Concerned that someone might fall into the hole, a policeman from the local substation kept a careful watch.

One newspaper reporter tied a weight to the end of a long cord and lowered it into the hole. A long way down it went. The cord ran
40   out, however, and he tried to pull it out, but it would not come back up. Two or three people helped out, but when they all pulled too hard, the cord parted at the edge of the hole. Another reporter, a camera in

concessionaire:
businessperson

---

2. **◀ REREAD** Reread lines 1–30. Which details about the setting seem realistic? Which details suggest an otherworldly setting?

Typhoons and landslides may occur and buildings may be damaged during an actual natural disaster. However, the creation of a hole with "no echo from the bottom" suggests an otherworldly setting.

3. **READ ▶** As you read lines 31–74, continue to cite text evidence.
- Circle the sentences that show the scientist's thoughts.
- In the margin, paraphrase the significant statement in line 58.
- Underline the concessionaire's offers to the mayor in lines 59–68.

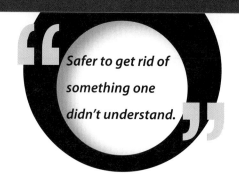

Safer to get rid of something one didn't understand.

hand, who had been watching all of this, quietly untied a stout rope that had been wound around his waist.

C The scientist contacted people at his laboratory and had them bring out a high-powered bull horn, with which he was going to check out the echo from the hole's bottom. He tried switching through various sounds, but there was no echo. The scientist was puzzled, but
50   he could not very well give up with everyone watching him so intently. He put the bull horn right up to the hole, turned it to its highest volume, and let it sound continuously for a long time. It was a noise that would have carried several dozen kilometers above ground. But the hole just calmly swallowed up the sound.

In his own mind the scientist was at a loss, but with a look of apparent **composure** he cut off the sound and, in a manner suggesting that the whole thing had a perfectly plausible explanation, said simply, "Fill it in."

D Safer to get rid of something one didn't understand.

The onlookers, disappointed that this was all that was going to
60   happen, prepared to disperse. Just then one of the concessionaires, having broken through the throng and come forward, made a proposal.

"Let me have that hole. I'll fill it in for you."

"We'd be grateful to you for filling it in," replied the mayor of the village, "but we can't very well give you the hole. We have to build a shrine there."

"If it's a shrine you want, I'll build you a fine one later. Shall I make it with an attached meeting hall?"

Before the mayor could answer, the people of the village all
70   shouted out.

composure:
being calm
and in control
of yourself

It is better to
take attention
away from
something
than it is to
admit it is
beyond com-
prehension.

CLOSE READ
Notes

---

2. **REREAD AND CITE TEXT EVIDENCE** Point out that the setting of the story starts to change in lines 16–19.

B **ASK STUDENTS** to cite the line that signals a shift from a realistic setting to a more otherworldly setting. *Students may cite "However, it gave one the feeling that it was so deep it went clear through to the center of the earth."*

3. **READ AND CITE TEXT EVIDENCE** Explain that in lines 45–51 the scientist does a series of things in the hope of getting some answers.

C **ASK STUDENTS** to name the scientist's actions in the correct sequence. *The scientist contacts people at his lab; he instructs them to bring out a high-powered bull horn; he switches through various sounds; he turns it up to its highest volume; he sounds it continuously for a long time.* What is he hoping to find? *He is hoping to find an echo.*

Critical Vocabulary: concessionaire (line 36) Have students compare their definitions for *concessionaire*.

Critical Vocabulary: composure (line 55) Have students explain the meaning of *composure*. What is behind the scientist's "apparent composure"? What is he unwilling to show the others? *He doesn't want to show that he has failed to find an explanation. He is trying to appear confident.*

FOR ELL STUDENTS Encourage students to guess the meaning of *bull horn*. Have a volunteer identify the meaning of each of the words. Then have another volunteer guess the meaning of *bull horn* and why it is called that.

"Really? Well, in that case, we ought to have it closer to the village."

"It's just an old hole. We'll give it to you!"

So it was settled. And the mayor, of course, had no objection.

 The concessionaire was true to his promise. It was small, but closer to the village he did build for them a shrine with an attached meeting hall.

About the time the autumn festival was held at the new shrine, the hole-filling company established by the concessionaire hung out
80 its small shingle at a shack near the hole.

The concessionaire had his cohorts mount a loud campaign in the city. "We've got a fabulously deep hole! Scientists say it's at least five thousand meters deep! Perfect for the disposal of such things as waste from nuclear reactors."

Government authorities granted permission. Nuclear power plants fought for contracts. The people of the village were a bit worried about this, but they **consented** when it was explained that there would be absolutely no above-ground contamination for several thousand years and that they would share in the profits. Into the
90 bargain, very shortly a magnificent road was built from the city to the village.

Trucks rolled in over the road, transporting lead boxes. Above the hole the lids were opened, and the wastes from nuclear reactors tumbled away into the hole.

consent:
agree

4. **REREAD** Certain statements in a story will hint at a theme. What theme is suggested by the statement you paraphrased in line 58?

The statement suggests that it is not wise to make decisions without a full understanding of what is involved.

5. **READ** As you read lines 75–136, continue to cite textual evidence.
- Underline all the things that people throw into the hole.
- Make notes in the margin about how the hole is affecting people's behavior.
- Circle details in lines 126–136 that recall an episode earlier in the story.

90

The hole showed no signs of filling up.

From the Foreign Ministry and the Defense Agency boxes of unnecessary classified documents were brought for disposal. Officials who came to supervise the disposal held discussions on golf. The lesser functionaries, as they threw in the papers, chatted about pinball.
100 The hole showed no signs of filling up. It was awfully deep, thought some; or else it might be very spacious at the bottom. Little by little the hole-filling company expanded its business.

Bodies of animals used in contagious disease experiments at the universities were brought out, and to these were added the unclaimed corpses of vagrants. Better than dumping all of its garbage in the ocean, went the thinking in the city, and plans were made for a long pipe to carry it to the hole.

The hole gave peace of mind to the dwellers of the city. They concentrated solely on producing one thing after another. Everyone
110 disliked thinking about the eventual consequences. People wanted only to work for production companies and sales corporations; they had no interest in becoming junk dealers. But, it was thought, these problems too would gradually be resolved by the hole.

Young girls whose betrothals had been arranged discarded old diaries in the hole. There were also those who were inaugurating new love affairs and threw into the hole old photographs of themselves taken with former sweethearts. The police felt comforted as they used the hole to get rid of accumulations of expertly done **counterfeit** bills. Criminals breathed easier after throwing material evidence into the
120 hole.

Whatever one wished to discard, the hole accepted it all. The hole cleansed the city of its filth; the sea and sky seemed to have become a bit clearer than before.

The hole lets people get rid of anything.

It gives people peace of mind.

People don't need to think about trash or waste.

People don't need to think of the consequences of their actions.

counterfeit:
fake

91

4. **REREAD AND CITE TEXT EVIDENCE** Have students note the unusual structure, style, and word choice in line 58.

D **ASK STUDENTS** to analyze why the phrase stands out. *It is in a paragraph of its own; it uses the pronoun* one, *which makes it seem like a general rule.* Why might the author want to call attention to this line? *It might be an important part of the story.*

5. **READ AND CITE TEXT EVIDENCE** Explain that in this section, people get rid of waste materials by throwing them into the hole.

E **ASK STUDENTS** to name a kind of waste that could pose a public health hazard. *Students may suggest nuclear waste, dead animals, or corpses of vagrants.*

Critical Vocabulary: consent (line 87) Have students explain the meaning of *consent.* What was offered to the villagers to get them to consent to the building of a nuclear plant? *Students may suggest official assurances of safety and a share of the profits.*

Critical Vocabulary: counterfeit (line 118) Have students explain the meaning of *counterfeit.* Why would counterfeit bills be something people would want to get rid of? *They are illegal to print; if large caches are found, there can be serious penalties.*

FOR ELL STUDENTS Explain that a betrothal is the act of getting engaged to marry someone. Then encourage students to guess why girls with arranged betrothals would throw their diaries into the hole.

CLOSE READ
Notes

Aiming at the heavens, new buildings went on being constructed one after the other.

One day, atop the high steel frame of a new building under construction, a workman was taking a break. Above his head he heard a voice shout:

"He—y, come on ou—t!"

130   But, in the sky to which he lifted his gaze there was nothing at all. A clear blue sky merely spread over all. He thought it must be his imagination. Then, as he resumed his former position, from the direction where the voice had come, a small pebble skimmed by him and fell on past.

F   The man, however, was gazing in idle reverie at the city's skyline growing ever more beautiful, and he failed to notice.

6. ◀ **REREAD AND DISCUSS** Reread lines 126–136. With a small group, discuss your interpretation of the story's ending. Review your reading notes and cite text evidence in your discussion.

SHORT RESPONSE

Cite Text Evidence   A story's theme is the central idea about life that the writer conveys. What is the theme of "He—y, Come On Ou—t!"? Review your reading notes and **cite text evidence** in your response.

The theme of the story is that humans will face consequences if they behave foolishly. In spite of a warning, a young man tosses a pebble into a hole that appears mysteriously. More people gather around the hole, but no one has figured out quite what it is. However, it is decided that the hole should be filled and a shrine should be built over it because it is "safer to get rid of something one didn't understand." Characters carelessly fill the hole with all sorts of garbage, and the village seems to prosper as a result. However, the incident at the conclusion of the story suggests that all of the garbage they have disposed of is about to come back upon them.

92

---

6. (REREAD AND DISCUSS USING TEXT EVIDENCE)

F **ASK STUDENTS** to discuss details in the final sentence (lines 135–136). Who is the man? What is he doing? *He is a construction worker; he is looking up at the city's beautiful skyline.* What doesn't he see? *He doesn't see a small pebble falling past him.* Where have students encountered the same image? *At the beginning of the story a young man throws a pebble in the hole (lines 24–25).*

SHORT RESPONSE

Cite Text Evidence   Students should:

- draw conclusions about the theme from details in the text.
- identify plot elements that contribute to the story's message.
- analyze the impact of images, word choice, and dialogue on meaning.
- interpret the conclusion and what it reveals about the author's attitude toward the subject.

TO CHALLENGE STUDENTS . . .

Tell students that in this story Shinichi Hoshi presents a bleak picture of a world where people are eager to "bury" unpleasant things—including cadavers and nuclear waste—without thinking about the consequences of their actions, or their legacy for future generations.

ASK STUDENTS to work with a partner or small group to list the items people throw into the hole and tell who benefits and who is hurt as a result. Point out that there can be immediate and long-term effects: for instance, the act of throwing away a diary can immediately benefit the diarist who has something to hide. On the other hand, if nothing of the truth remains, future generations will have nothing to learn from.

- Point out that throwing away some things may serve the immediate interests of a few but in the process may damage the lives of many. For instance, the practice of burying nuclear waste and other toxic substances can have deleterious effects on the population at large for a very long time.

- Have groups research the issue of nuclear waste. They can explore storage and disposal in the United States and other countries, health effects, and what to do in the event of contamination.

- Students can research the meltdown at Japan's Fukushima nuclear reactor in 2011—one of the worst nuclear disasters of all time—and compare it with the incidents at Three Mile Island (1979) and Chernobyl (1986).

- Students may want to speculate about what Hoshi, who died in 1997, might have thought about the disaster that did so much damage to his home country.

DIG DEEPER

1. With the class, return to Question 3, Read. Have students share their responses.

ASK STUDENTS to think about the way the author uses each of the characters to exemplify a particular kind of self-interest.

- Have students describe the actions of the scientist, the curiosity-seekers, the newspaper reporters, the concessionaires, the police, and the mayor. How does each one react to the hole? What do they want to do with it?
- Have students draw conclusions about their motives. What might each stand to gain from the situation?
- Have students share ideas about who wields the most influence in the village. How do the businessmen get people to agree to their plans? How does the author reveal his attitude toward them?
- Have students share ideas about the scientist's role. How does he get people to believe in what he is saying? What is the author's attitude toward the scientist?

2. With the class, return to Question 6, Reread and Discuss. Have students share their responses.

ASK STUDENTS to share their interpretations of the end of the story.

- Have students discuss the significance of the line "He—y, come on ou—t!" (line 129). Who is speaking these words? Where else in the text have they seen them? Why did the author choose this as the title of the story?
- Have students draw conclusions about the pebble. Was it the same pebble that was thrown into the hole by the young man in line 25? Where did it come from?
- Have students describe the workman's attitude toward the pebble. Why did he "fail to notice" it as it fell? What was he looking at instead?
- Have students discuss the author's vision of the future. How does he see our present mistakes backfiring on us?

ASK STUDENTS to return to their Short Response answer and revise it based on the class discussion.

CLOSE READING NOTES

PERFORMANCE TASK

Create a Multimedia Presentation

This collection focuses on the proliferation of consumerism and how it has affected American culture and our environment. In this activity, you will research a topic related to consumerism. You will draw from *Life at Home in the Twenty-First Century,* other texts in the collection, and your research findings to write an informative essay about the topic you chose. Then you will prepare and give a multimedia presentation on that topic.

A successful multimedia presentation

- provides an attention-grabbing introduction that clearly establishes the topic
- organizes ideas logically in a way that is interesting and appropriate to purpose and audience
- includes facts, definitions, and examples that support main ideas
- integrates graphics, text, video, music, and/or sound to emphasize salient points
- concludes by leaving the audience with a lasting impression

COMMON CORE

W 2a–f Write informative/ explanatory texts.
W 4 Produce clear and coherent writing.
W 5 Develop and strengthen writing.
W 6 Use technology to produce and publish writing.
W 7 Conduct short research projects.
W 8 Gather relevant information.
W 10 Write routinely.
SL 4 Present claims and findings.
SL 5 Include multimedia components in presentations.
SL 6 Adapt speech to a variety of contexts and tasks.

Interactive Lessons
If you need help . . .
- **Writing Informative Texts**
- **Giving a Presentation**
- **Using Media in a Presentation**

PLAN

Determine Your Topic Review the texts in the collection. Think about the points each author makes about consumerism. Brainstorm a list of possible topics, such as how TV ads influence consumers or how purchasing behavior in reality TV might affect consumerism. Choose a topic that will interest you and others.

- Transform your topic into a research question you want to answer, such as *What kinds of TV ads influence teenage consumers?* or *How does reality TV change people's attitudes toward and increase consumerism?*
- Make sure your question is open-ended and cannot be answered in a single word.
- Generate further questions that will help you find evidence.

*my*Notebook

Use the annotation tools in your eBook to find evidence that supports your points. Save each piece of evidence to your notebook.

ACADEMIC VOCABULARY

As you plan and present your presentation, be sure to use the academic vocabulary words.

attitude
consume
goal
purchase
technology

COMMON CORE
W 2a–f, W 4,
W 5, W 6,
W 7, W 8,
W 10, SL 4,
SL 5, SL 6

CREATE A MULTIMEDIA PRESENTATION

Introduce students to the Performance Task by reading the introductory paragraph with them and reviewing the criteria for what makes a good multimedia presentation. Remind students that a good multimedia presentation needs to combine strong information and well-organized multimedia to support that information.

View It!

Professional Development Podcast:
Performance Tasks

PLAN

GATHER INFORMATION

Share with students that when they take notes during research they can write information on individual file cards or color code information in their notebooks. Information about the same ideas can then easily be organized to include in their outlines.

Gather Information In the collection's texts, look for information related to the topic you chose. Take notes on key points, observations, and events that will help you understand your topic, answer your questions, and support your ideas.

Do Research Use print and digital resources to find additional information that addresses your research question.

- Search for credible sources. Use keywords or subject searching in the library to find books related to your topic. Use a search engine to find Internet sources.
- Take notes on facts, details, and examples that explain and support your main points.
- Identify multimedia components, such as graphics, maps, videos, or sound that could emphasize your main points.

Organize Your Ideas Think about how you will organize your information. Create an outline showing the information you will present in each paragraph. Make sure each idea follows from the previous idea and leads into the next idea.

> **I.** Use Roman numerals for main topics.
>   A. Indent and use capital letters for subtopics.
>   1. Indent and use numbers for supporting facts and details.
>   2. Indent and use numbers for supporting facts and details.
> **II.** Use Roman numerals for main topics.
>   B. Indent and use capital letters for subtopics.
>   1. Indent and use numbers for supporting facts and details.

Consider Your Purpose and Audience Think about your audience as you prepare your presentation. Your goal is to use multimedia to get your points across most effectively to this particular audience.

PRODUCE

DESIGN AND DRAFT YOUR PRESENTATION

Explain to students that the text and multimedia need to work together to present information to viewers. Remind students that all multimedia should support the points they want to make in their presentations. Suggest that students choose only the best examples to include so as to avoid overwhelming their audience.

PRODUCE

my **WriteSmart**

Write your rough draft in *my*WriteSmart. Focus on getting your ideas down, rather than on perfecting your choice of language.

Draft an Informative Essay Use your notes and your outline to draft an informative essay that you can use to create your presentation.

- Begin with an attention-grabbing introduction that defines your topic. Include an unusual comment, fact, quote, or story.
- Organize your information into paragraphs of related ideas.

- Include supporting facts, details, and examples.
- Make sure your ideas transition logically.
- Write a conclusion that follows from and supports your main ideas and leaves the reader with a lasting impression.

Design and Draft Your Presentation Think about what you want your presentation to look like. Choose a presentation tool to create a slideshow.

- Use text from your essay that explains each topic and subtopic. Revise the text to keep your presentation brief and clear.
- Integrate multimedia components that emphasize your main points. Each component should have a clear purpose.
- Check that all text and visuals are large and clear enough that everyone in the audience can see them.

REVISE

_my_WriteSmart

Have a group of peers review your draft and your multimedia elements in _my_WriteSmart. Ask your reviewers to note any ideas or visuals that are unclear or not in a logical sequence.

Practice Your Presentation Try speaking in front of a mirror, or make a recording of your presentation and listen to it. Then practice your presentation with a partner.

- Speak clearly and loudly.
- Maintain eye contact. Look directly at your audience.
- Use gestures and facial expressions to emphasize ideas.

Evaluate Your Presentation Use the chart on the following page to determine whether your presentation is effective.

- Check that your ideas are clearly and logically presented.
- Verify that your text includes specific and accurate information.
- Examine your audio and visual components to make sure they are relevant and well integrated.

PRESENT

Deliver Your Presentation Finalize your multimedia presentation. Then choose a way to share it with your audience. Consider these options:

- Use your presentation to give a news report about your topic.
- Create and share a video recording of your presentation.

Collection Performance Task **261**

REVISE

PRACTICE YOUR PRESENTATION

Suggest that partners work together to critique each other's multimedia presentations. Point out that students should not only evaluate the information in the essay but also the multimedia that accompanies it. Partners should offer suggestions to each other for how they can make their presentations work more smoothly.

PRESENT

DELIVER YOUR PRESENTATION

Students can
- use their presentations to make news reports about their topics. Remind students to include information in the news reports that answers these questions: _who, when, what, where, why,_ and _how._
- make video recordings of their presentations. The videos can be presented to the class or uploaded onto a school website for others to watch.

PERFORMANCE TASK

ORGANIZATION

Have students look at the chart and identify how they did on the Performance Task in each of the three main categories. In particular, ask students to discuss how effectively they integrated text, sound, and visuals to create a complete and compelling presentation. If students made a video recording of their presentation, they can view and critique it. Ask students to tell how they would improve their presentations and what goals they would set for themselves the next time they create a multimedia presentation.

MULTIMEDIA PRESENTATION

	Ideas and Evidence	Organization	Language
ADVANCED	• The introduction is appealing and informative. • The topic is well developed with relevant facts, concrete details, interesting quotations, and examples from reliable sources. • The conclusion capably summarizes the information presented.	• The organization is effective and logical throughout the essay. • Text, visuals, and sound are combined in a coherent manner. • Transitions successfully connect related ideas.	• The language reflects a formal style. • Sentence beginnings, lengths, and structures vary and have a rhythmic flow. • Grammar, usage, and mechanics are correct.
COMPETENT	• The introduction could do more to grab the reader's attention; the introduction states the topic. • One or two key points could use more support in the form of relevant facts, concrete details, quotations, and examples from reliable sources. • The concluding section summarizes the information presented.	• The organization is confusing in a few places. • Text, visuals, and sound are mostly combined in a coherent manner. • A few more transitions are needed to connect related ideas.	• The style becomes informal in a few places. • Sentence beginnings, lengths, and structures vary somewhat. • Some grammatical and usage errors are repeated in the presentation.
LIMITED	• The introduction is only partly informative; the topic and purpose are unclear. • Most key points need more support in the form of relevant facts, concrete details, quotations, and examples from reliable sources. • The concluding section partially summarizes the information presented.	• The organization is logical in some places but often doesn't follow a pattern. • Text, visuals, and sound are combined in a disorganized way. • More transitions are needed throughout to connect related ideas.	• The style becomes informal in several places. • Sentence structures barely vary, and some fragments or run-on sentences are present. • Grammar and usage are incorrect in several places, but the speaker's ideas are still somewhat clear.
EMERGING	• The introduction is missing. • Facts, details, quotations, and examples are from unreliable sources or are missing. • The conclusion is missing.	• A logical organization is not used; information is presented randomly. • Text, visuals, and sound are missing. • Transitions are not used, making the presentation difficult to understand.	• The style is inappropriate for the presentation. • Repetitive sentence structure, fragments, and run-on sentences make the presentation hard to follow. • Several grammatical and usage errors change the meaning of ideas.

Guided by a Cause

"The fullness of our heart comes in our actions."

—Mother Teresa

CONNECTING WORD AND IMAGE

ASK STUDENTS to discuss how the collection opener image and the collection quotation work together to create a connection.

PERFORMANCE TASK PREVIEW

Point out to students that they will complete two performance tasks at the end of the collection. The performance tasks will require them to further analyze the selections in the collection and to synthesize ideas about these analyses. Students will present their findings in a variety of products.

ACADEMIC VOCABULARY

View It!

Professional Development Podcast:
Academic Vocabulary

Students can acquire facility with the academic vocabulary words through frequent, repeated exposure as they analyze and discuss the selections in the collection. Academic vocabulary can be used in the instructional contexts listed below. This will enable students to incorporate the academic vocabulary words into their working vocabulary.

- Collaborative Discussion at the end of each selection
- Analyzing the Text questions for each selection
- Selection-level Performance Task
- Vocabulary instruction (for Critical Vocabulary and/or for Vocabulary Strategy)
- Language Conventions
- End-of-collection Performance Task for all selections in the collection

ASK STUDENTS to review the Academic Vocabulary word list for this collection. You may wish to pronounce each word aloud, so students hear the correct pronunciation. Then, discuss the definitions and the related forms for each word. Remind students that they will encounter these five academic vocabulary words throughout the collection.

COLLECTION 6
Guided by a Cause

In this collection, you will consider the question: What inspires people to take action to improve their world?

hmhfyi.com

COLLECTION
PERFORMANCE TASK Preview

At the end of this collection, you will have the opportunity to:

- research and write an expository essay about a dramatic and deadly fire that destroyed a New York City factory in 1911
- write a personal essay about a cause that is important to you, in a similar way that the cause of child labor is important to one of the authors in this collection

ACADEMIC VOCABULARY

Study the words and their definitions in the chart below. You will use these words as you discuss and write about the texts in this collection.

Word	Definition	Related Forms
contrast (kən-trăst´) v.	to show differences between two or more things that are being compared	contrasted, contrasting, contrastive
despite (dĭ-spīt´) prep.	in spite of; even though	despiteful
error (ĕr´ər) n.	a mistake	erroneous, erroneously, errorless
inadequate (ĭn-ăd´ĭ-kwĭt) adj.	not enough or sufficient to fulfill a need or meet a requirement	adequate, adequately, inadequacy, inadequately
interact (ĭn´tər-ăkt´) v.	to act upon each other	interaction, interacting, interactive, interactively

USING COLLECTIONS YOUR WAY

Use the following information, along with the charts on the following pages, to help you decide how you want to introduce the collection. Based on your teaching style, your students' interests, or your instructional goals, you may want to structure this collection in various ways. You may choose different entry points each time you teach the collection.

"I like to use digital products as a starting point."

This film clip from the documentary "It Takes a Child" introduces students to the twelve-year-old Canadian activist Craig Kielburger and his efforts to investigate child labor practices around the world.

Background *When child activist Craig Kielburger was twelve years old, he became interested in the plight of child laborers. Inspired by the story of twelve-year-old Iqbal, a child labor activist who had been murdered in South Asia, Kielburger realized that a child could make a difference in the world. Kielburger then traveled to South Asia to see child labor first hand. With the help of a film crew, he documented his journey so that the world could see what he himself had witnessed.*

MEDIA ANALYSIS

from
It Takes a Child
Documentary directed by Judy Jackson

SETTING A PURPOSE The documentary you are about to view features some of the adults and children Craig Kielburger spoke with during his trip to South Asia. It also shows workplaces he visited and what he observed there.

As you view the film clip, think about why Kielburger decided to make this journey and what he wanted to find out. Notice the ways that filmmaking and news reporting come together to help you understand Kielburger's reasons for traveling to South Asia. Write down any questions you have during viewing.

It Takes a Child **317**

Margaret Peterson Haddix (b. 1964) *grew up on a farm in Ohio. While her father was a farmer and her mother a nurse, Haddix always wanted to be a writer. Her inspiration was her father, who was always telling her stories. Haddix has now written more than a dozen books for young adults. Asked why she likes writing for young audiences, Haddix replies that teenagers are naturally great characters in books—often more interesting than adults.*

from **Uprising**
Historical Novel by Margaret Peterson Haddix

SETTING A PURPOSE This fiction excerpt is based on the real-life event of the Triangle Factory Fire. As you read, think about how the author has used facts and her own imagination to make the events of the fire come to life.

Yetta

Yetta was listening for the bell on the time clock, waiting to finish her day. It was a Saturday afternoon in March, and the spring breezes were back. She'd heard them rattling the windows when the machines were shut down for lunch; she knew that as soon as she stepped outside, they'd tease at her hair and tug at her hat. This year, the breezes seemed to carry a slightly different message: *Another year past and what do you have to show for yourself? So you can read English a little bit better, so you handed out a few suffrage[1] flyers—do you think that that's enough?*

What would ever be enough for Yetta?

[1] **suffrage:** the right or privilege of voting.

Uprising **283**

"I like to connect literature to history."

This excerpt from a historical novel uses the art of storytelling to bring to life the events of the Triangle Factory Fire in 1911, allowing students to make connections to two pieces of nonfiction history writing on the same event.

Nikki Giovanni (b. 1943) *has been one of the best-known American poets since publishing her first book of poetry in 1968. Giovanni grew up in the racially segregated South. When Giovanni attended college, she became a part of a movement of African American writers who were finding new ways to express pride in their distinct culture. In addition to her poetry collections, Giovanni is also an award-winning children's author.*

A Poem for My Librarian, Mrs. Long
(YOU NEVER KNOW WHAT TROUBLED LITTLE GIRL NEEDS A BOOK)
Poem by Nikki Giovanni

AS YOU READ In the poem, Nikki Giovanni looks back at her childhood and the people who most influenced her. As you read, think about how Giovanni's childhood experiences shaped her dreams and her writing.

At a time when there was no tv before 3:00 P.M.
And on Sunday none until 5:00
We sat on front porches watching
The jfg[1] sign go on and off greeting
The neighbors, discussing the political
Situation congratulating the preacher
On his sermon

[1] **jfg:** a brand of coffee that was popular in Knoxville . . . ., an old . . . . the coffee is a famous landmark in Knoxville, Tennessee.

A Poem for My Librarian, Mrs. Long **321**

"I stress the importance of language and style."

All of Nikki Giovanni's gifts for language, rhythm, and style poetically celebrate the memory of a childhood mentor who nurtured her deep love for books.

| mySmartPlanner | eBook | myNotebook | myWriteSmart | fyi hmhfyi.com |

Collection 6 Lessons	Media	Teach and Practice
Student Edition | eBook	▶ **Video Links**	**Close Reading and Evidence Tracking**

Collection 6 Lessons

ANCHOR TEXT

History Writing by Albert Marrin
from *Flesh & Blood So Cheap: The Triangle Factory Fire and Its Legacy*

History Writing by Zachary Kent
from *The Story of the Triangle Factory Fire*

CLOSE READER

History Writing by Lynne Olsen
"The Most Daring of Our Leaders"

Speech by John Lewis
"Speech to the Democratic National Convention"

Historical Novel by Margaret Peterson Haddix
from *Uprising*

CLOSE READER

Short Story by ZZ Packer
from "Doris Is Leaving"

ANCHOR TEXT

Personal Essay by Craig Kielburger
"Craig Kielburger Reflects on Working Toward Peace"

CLOSE READER

Online Article by David Karas
"Difference Maker: John Bergman and Popcorn Park"

Documentary directed by Judy Jackson
"It Takes a Child"

EXEMPLAR

Poem by Nikki Giovanni
"A Poem for My Librarian, Mrs. Long"

Short Story by D'Arcy McNickle
"Train Time"

Collection 6 Performance Tasks:
A Write an Expository Essay
B Write a Personal Essay

Media

🔊 Video HISTORY *America The Story of Us: The Triangle Shirtwaist Fire*
🔊 Audio from *Flesh & Blood So Cheap*
🔊 Audio from *The Story of the Triangle Factory Fire*

🔊 Audio "The Most Daring of Our Leaders"
🔊 Audio "Speech to the Democratic National Convention"

🔊 Audio from *Uprising*

🔊 Audio from "Doris Is Leaving"

🔊 Audio "Craig Kielburger Reflects on Working Toward Peace"

🔊 Audio "Difference Maker: John Bergman and Popcorn Park"

🔊 Aud io "A Poem for My Librarian, Mrs. Long"

🔊 Audio "Train Time"

fyi hmhfyi.com **hmhfyi.com**

Teach and Practice

Close Read Screencasts
- Modeled Discussion 1
  Flesh & Blood So Cheap
  (lines 45–55)
- Modeled Discussion 2
  The Story of the Triangle Factory Fire, (lines 20–28)
- Close Read application PDF
  Flesh & Blood So Cheap, (lines 197–206)
  The Story of the Triangle Factory Fire, (lines 33–41)

Strategies for Annotation
- Determine Central Idea and Details
- Analyze Structure: Chronological Order
- Analyze Presentations of Information
- Latin Roots

Strategies for Annotation
- Analyze Point of View
- Compare and Contrast: Genres
- Analogies

Close Read Screencasts
- Modeled Discussion (lines 7–14)
- Close Read application PDF
  (lines 138–145)

Strategies for Annotation
- Analyze Text: Personal Essay
- Multiple Meanings

Strategies for Annotation
- Determine Meaning: Style

Strategies for Annotation
- Analyze Stories: Character Development
- Using a Dictionary

Interactive Lessons
A Writing Informative Texts
A Conducting Research
A Producing and Publishing with Technology

B Writing Informative Texts
B Producing and Publishing with Technology

For Systematic Coverage of Writing and Speaking & Listening Standards

Interactive Lessons
Writing Informative Texts
Giving a Presentation

Assess		Extend	Reteach
Performance Task	**Online Assessment**	**Teacher eBook**	**Teacher eBook**
Speaking Activity: Oral Presentation	Selection Test	**Primary and Secondary Sources > Interactive Whiteboard Lesson >** Primary and Secondary Sources	**Analyze Presentations of Information**
Writing Activity: New Chapter	Selection Test		**Analyze Point of View > Level Up Tutorial >** Third-Person Point of View **Compare and Contrast: Genres > Level Up Tutorial >** Prose Forms
Writing Activity: Critique	Selection Test	**Trace an Argument > Interactive Whiteboard Lesson >** Elements of an Argument	**Analyze Text: Personal Essay**
Media Activity: Photo Documentary	Selection Test	**Camera Shots and Shot Selection**	**Elements of a Documentary**
Writing Activity: Poem	Selection Test	**Determine the Meanings of Words and Phrases**	**Determine Meaning: Style > Level Up Tutorial >** Author's Style
Writing Activity: Character Analysis	Selection Test	**Analyze Story Elements: Plot > Interactive Whiteboard Lesson >** Plot and Conflict **Analyze Story Elements: Setting > Interactive Whiteboard Lesson >** Setting **Analyze Story Elements: Mood**	**Analyze Stories: Characterization > Level Up Tutorial >** Methods of Characterization
A Write an Expository Essay **B** Write a Personal Essay	Collection Test		

Lesson Assessments
Writing Informative Texts
Giving a Presentation

Collection 6 Lessons	Key Learning Objective	Performance Task
ANCHOR TEXT **History Writing by Albert Marrin** **Lexile 900L** from *Flesh & Blood So Cheap: The Triangle Factory Fire and Its Legacy*, p. 265A **History Writing by Zachary Kent** **Lexile 1110L** from *The Story of the Triangle Factory Fire*, p. 265A	**The student will be able to . . .** determine central ideas and details analyze chronological order, and analyze authors' writings on the same topic.	Speaking Activity: Oral Presentation
Historical Novel by Margaret Peterson Haddix **Lexile 800L** from *Uprising*, p. 283A	**The student will be able to . . .** analyze points of view in a text and compare and contrast different genres.	Writing Activity: New Chapter
ANCHOR TEXT **Personal Essay by Craig Kielburger** **Lexile 1080L** **"Craig Kielburger Reflects on Working Toward Peace,"** p. 307A	**The student will be able to . . .** identify and analyze elements of a personal essay and determine an author's point of view.	Writing Activity: Critique
Documentary directed by Judy Jackson **"It Takes a Child,"** p. 317A	**The student will be able to . . .** analyze the purpose of a documentary and understand the features used in it.	Media Activity: Photo Documentary
EXEMPLAR **Poem by Nikki Giovanni** **"A Poem for My Librarian, Mrs. Long,"** p. 321A	**The student will be able to . . .** aanalyze a poet's style and determine a theme.	Writing Activity: Poem
Short Story by D'Arcy McNickle **Lexile 670L** **"Train Time,"** p. 327A	**The student will be able to . . .** analyze methods of characterization and flashback in a short story.	Writing Activity: Character Analysis

Collection 6 Performance Tasks:
A Write an Expository Essay
B Write a Personal Essay

Vocabulary Strategy	Language and Style	Student Instructional Support	CLOSE READER Selection
Latin Roots	Capitalization	**Scaffolding for ELL Students:** • Analyze Language • Determine Meaning **When Students Struggle:** Restate Main Ideas	History Writing by Lynne Olsen "The Most Daring of Our Leaders," p. 282b **Lexile 1190L**
Analogies	Phrases	**Scaffolding for ELL Students:** Characters' Thoughts **When Students Struggle:** • Track Causes and Effects • Obstacles in Plot **To Challenge Students:** Discuss the Role of Women	Speech by John Lewis "Speech to the Democratic National Convention," p. 282b **Lexile 890L**
Multiple Meanings	Dangling Modifiers	**Scaffolding for ELL Students:** Analyze Language **When Students Struggle:** Track Elements of Personal Essays	Short Story by ZZ Packer from *Doris Is Coming,* p. 306b **Lexile 880L**
		Scaffolding for ELL Students: Language Support	Online Article by David Karas "Difference Maker: John Bergman and Popcorn Park," p.320b **Lexile 1130L**
	Combining Sentences with Phrases	**Scaffolding for ELL Students**: Analyze Language: Punctuation and Print Cues **When Students Struggle:** Determine Meaning: Style	
Using a Dictionary	Misplaced Modifiers	**Scaffolding for ELL Students**: Analyze Language **When Students Struggle:** Characterization **To Challenge Students:** Character's Point of View	

from Flesh & Blood So Cheap: The Triangle Fire and Its Legacy

from The Story of the Triangle Factory Fire

*my*SmartPlanner Create lesson plans and access resources online.

History Writing by Albert Marrin

History Writing by Zachary Kent

Why These Texts?

This lesson guides students to compare two examples of history writing on the same topic and to understand how an author's perspective shapes his or her presentation of history.

▶ **View It!**

Professional Development Podcast:

Informational Text

Key Learning Objective: The student will be able to determine central ideas and details, analyze chronological order, and analyze authors' writings on the same topic.

For practice and application:

Close Reader selections
"The Most Daring of Our Leaders"
History Writing by Lynne Olsen

"Speech from the Democratic National Convention"
Speech by John Lewis

Common Core Standards

RI 1   Cite text evidence.
RI 2   Determine central ideas.
RI 3   Analyze interactions between individuals, events, and ideas.
RI 5   Analyze structure.
RI 6   Determine author's point of view or purpose.
RI 9   Analyze how authors shape presentations.
W 1b Support claims with reasoning and evidence.
W 6   Use technology to cite sources.
SL 4   Present claims and findings.
SL 6   Adapt speech to contexts and tasks.
L 2   Demonstrate command of the conventions of capitalization.
L 4b   Use Latin affixes and roots as clues to meaning.
L 4d   Verify the meaning of a word or phrase.

▲ Text Complexity Rubric

	from Flesh & Blood So Cheap Lexile: 900L	*from* The Story of the Triangle Factory Fire Lexile: 1110L
Quantitative Measures		
Qualitative Measures	**Levels of Meaning/Purpose** single purpose and topic	**Levels of Meaning/Purpose** single purpose and topic
	Structure conventional organization of main ideas and details; traits common to informational texts	**Structure** organization somewhat complex but generally sequential
	Language Conventionality and Clarity clear and direct, but some unfamiliar academic language and longer descriptions	**Language Conventionality and Clarity** less straightforward sentence structure; some unfamiliar academic language
	Knowledge Demands some simple historical concepts	**Knowledge Demands** some simple historical concepts
Reader/Task Considerations	Teacher determined Vary by individual reader and type of text	Teacher determined Vary by individual reader and type of text

CLOSE READ

Background Have students read the background and information about the authors. Offer additional information about the allusion in the title of Albert Marrin's book:

- The quotation "flesh and blood so cheap" comes from a poem of social protest "The Song of the Shirt" by the English poet Thomas Hood (1799–1845).

- The first stanza of the poem has the lines "With fingers weary and worn, / With eyelids heavy and red, / A woman sat in unwomanly rags / Plying her needle and thread— / Stitch! stitch! stitch! / In poverty, hunger, and dirt."

- The fifth stanza includes the lines, "O God! that bread should be so dear, / And flesh and blood so cheap!"

SETTING A PURPOSE Direct students to use the Setting a Purpose questions to focus their reading. Remind students to generate questions as they read.

COMPARE ANCHOR TEXTS

Background *An event can be so dramatic and so haunting that it compels the generations that follow it to dissect its details and to trace its impact. A deadly disaster occurred in New York City in 1911 at a company in the ten-story Asch Building. Known today as the Brown Building, it is now a National Historic Landmark. These history writings are detailed accounts of what happened and the long-term effects.*

The Triangle Factory Fire

(l) ©Photodisc/Getty Images; (r) ©Underwood & Underwood/Corbis

from **Flesh & Blood So Cheap: The Triangle Fire and Its Legacy**
History Writing by Albert Marrin

Albert Marrin (b. 1936) *taught social studies in a junior high school and then became a college teacher. But he realized that he missed telling stories as he had as a teacher. That's when Marrin decided to write history for young adults. He has now produced more than thirty nonfiction books, for which he has won numerous awards.*

from **The Story of the Triangle Factory Fire**
History Writing by Zachary Kent

Zachary Kent *is the author of over fifty books for young readers. He writes primarily about history and has written biographies of various noted figures, including Abraham Lincoln and Charles Lindbergh.*

SETTING A PURPOSE As you read, think about how each writer presents information on the same event. How are the pieces similar? How are they different? Write down any questions you have while reading.

Flesh & Blood So Cheap **265**

Close Read Screencasts

Modeled Discussions

Have students click the *Close Read* icons in their eBooks to access two screencasts in which readers discuss and annotate the following key passages:

- *Flesh & Blood So Cheap*, lines 45–55
- *The Story of the Triangle Factory Fire*, lines 20–28

As a class, view and discuss the videos. Then, have students work in pairs to do an independent close read of two additional passages:

- *Flesh & Blood So Cheap*, lines 197–206
- *The Story of the Triangle Factory Fire*, lines 33–41

Determine Central Idea and Details (LINES 1–30)

COMMON CORE RI 1, RI 2

Tell students that lines 1–30 present facts and information, or **details,** about the type of work being done and the materials used on each of the top three floors of the building. The author is preparing readers to visualize the setting and understand the dangers to come.

 CITE TEXT EVIDENCE Have students identify the main activity on each of the three floors, including details that reveal the danger of fire. *(On the eighth floor, the cutters cut lightweight cotton fabric called lawn, which "burned as easily as gasoline." On the ninth floor, workers sewed the fabric using machines on tables so close together that there was "only a narrow aisle" between rows. On the tenth floor, the shirtwaists were inspected, packed, and shipped. The tenth floor "also held the showroom and owners' offices.")*

CRITICAL VOCABULARY

flammable: The cotton fabric called lawn and the tissue paper that separated the fabric layers were both flammable.

ASK STUDENTS why the author is pointing out that these things were flammable. *(They will catch fire and burn easily, contributing to the spread of the fire.)*

SCAFFOLDING FOR ELL STUDENTS

Analyze Language Help students to clarify the meanings of words important to this text by putting them in categories, such as "Fabric Words," "Fire Words," and "Safety Words." To demonstrate, display lines 45–50 and highlight in yellow words related to fire.

ASK STUDENTS how these words are alike. Suggest that they use their eBook annotation tools to highlight each category of words in a different color.

---

from **Flesh & Blood So Cheap**
by Albert Marrin

The Triangle Waist Company occupied the top three floors of the Asch Building. On the eighth floor, forty cutters,[1] all men, worked at long wooden tables. Nearby, about a hundred women did basting[2] and other tasks. Paper patterns hung from lines of string over the tables. Although cutters wasted as little fabric as possible, there were always scraps, which they threw into bins under the tables. Every two months or so, a rag dealer took away about a ton of scraps, paying about seven cents a pound. He then sold them back
10 to cotton mills to remake into new cloth. The last pickup was in January.

On March 25, the cutters prepared for their next day's work. Since it was Saturday, everyone would leave early, at 4:45 P.M. Workers from other firms had already left; Triangle employees had to stay longer to fill back orders. Carefully, cutters spread "lawn" (from the French word *lingerie*) on their tables 120 layers thick. Lawn was not just *any* cotton fabric. Sheer and lightweight, it was beautiful and comfortable—and burned as easily as gasoline. Each layer was separated from the
20 others by a sheet of equally **flammable** tissue paper.

After cutting, the various pieces would go by freight elevator to the ninth floor for sewing and finishing. There, eight rows of sewing machine tables, holding 288 machines in all, occupied the entire width of the room. Only a narrow aisle separated one row from another; the tables were so close together that chairs touched back to back between the rows. From time to time, workers would take the finished shirtwaists[3] to the tenth floor for inspection, packing, and shipping. This floor also held the showroom and
30 owners' offices.

By 4:40 P.M., the cutters had finished their work. With five minutes to go, they stood around, talking until the quitting bell rang. Although it was against the rules, some lit cigarettes, hiding the smoke by blowing it up their jacket sleeves. On the floor above, workers had begun to walk toward the lockers to

---

[1] **cutters:** people who cut cloth in a clothing factory.
[2] **basting:** stitching.
[3] **shirtwaists:** women's blouses that resemble men's shirts.

flammable
(flămˊə-bəl) *adj.*
If something is *flammable*, it is easy for it to catch on fire and burn.

©Photodisc/Getty Images

Cutters flung buckets of water at the smoking spot, without effect. Flames shot up, igniting the line of hanging paper patterns. "They began to fall on the layers of thin goods underneath them," recalled cutter Max Rothen. "Every time another piece dropped, light scraps of burning fabric began to

get their coats and hats. They looked forward to Sunday and family visits, boyfriends, dances, and nickelodeons.[4] Although they had no inkling of what was about to happen, many had only minutes to live.

We will never know for sure what started the Triangle Fire. Most likely, a cutter flicked a hot ash or tossed a live cigarette butt into a scrap bin. Whatever the cause, survivors said the first sign of trouble was smoke pouring from beneath a cutting table.

Cutters flung buckets of water at the smoking spot, without effect. Flames shot up, igniting the line of hanging paper patterns. "They began to fall on the layers of thin goods underneath them," recalled cutter Max Rothen. "Every time another piece dropped, light scraps of burning fabric began to fly around the room. They came down on the other tables and they fell on the machines. Then the line broke and the whole string of burning patterns fell down." A foreman ran for the hose on the stairway wall. Nothing! No water came. The hose had not been connected to the standpipe.[5] Seconds later, the fire leaped out of control.

Yet help was already on the way. At exactly 4:45 P.M., someone pulled the eighth-floor fire alarm. In less than two minutes, the horse-drawn vehicles of Engine Company 72 arrived from a firehouse six blocks away. The moment they arrived, the firefighters unloaded their equipment and prepared to swing into action. As they did, the area pumping station raised water pressure in the hydrants near the Asch Building. Other units soon arrived from across the Lower East Side with more equipment.

Meanwhile, workers on the eighth floor rang furiously for the two passenger elevators. Safety experts have always advised against using elevators in a fire. Heat can easily damage their machinery, leaving trapped passengers dangling in space, to burn or suffocate. Despite the danger, the operators made several trips, saving scores of workers before heat bent the elevators' tracks and put them out of action.

Those who could not board elevators rushed the stairway door. They caused a pileup, so that those in front could not open the door. Whenever someone tried to get it open, the crowd pinned her against it. "All the girls were falling on me

---
[4] **nickelodeons:** early movie theaters that charged five cents for admission.
[5] **standpipe:** a large pipe into which water is pumped.

TEACH

CLOSE READ

For more context and historical background, students can view the video *America The Story of Us: The Triangle Shirtwaist Fire* in their eBooks.

Analyze Presentations of Information (LINES 40–44)

COMMON CORE RI 1, RI 6

Point out that history writers offer their interpretations along with factual information.

B CITE TEXT EVIDENCE Have students closely reread lines 40–44 and cite details in which the author interprets his research. *("We will never know for sure what started the Triangle Fire." He describes the "most likely" cause based on survivors' reports.)*

Determine Central Idea and Details (LINES 45–71)

COMMON CORE RI 2

Tell students that **central ideas,** or main ideas, are the most important ideas in a text. To identify the main idea in a paragraph, readers should pay attention to what all the sentences tell about.

C ASK STUDENTS to reread lines 45–71. Have students summarize this section by stating the main idea of each paragraph in a sentence. *(Cloth and paper burst into flames that were out of control in seconds. Firefighters quickly arrived at the building. Scores of workers managed to escape in two passenger elevators before heat destroyed the tracks.)*

Analyze Presentations of Information RI 6
(LINES 89–96)

Explain that a history author's **point of view** may be **subjective** at times, revealing the author's opinions and beliefs. This may be done through the author's word choice and through the details the author emphasizes.

D CITE TEXT EVIDENCE Have students reread lines 89–96. Ask students to cite especially vivid descriptive details and explain why the author includes those details. (*"Wind gusts made eerie sounds, like the howling of great beasts in pain." The author believes the event was horrifying and wants readers to share the terror and panic experienced by the victims.*)

Determine Central Idea and Details RI 2
(LINES 100–104)

Point out that the author is using quotations from survivors to support his main ideas.

E ASK STUDENTS what Mary Bucelli's words, in lines 100–104, reveal about the situation. (*Her words support the idea that there was no plan for escaping a fire, and no one knew what to do. The workers panicked and thought only of saving themselves.*)

> **CRITICAL VOCABULARY**
>
> **reign:** The author says that confusion reigned.
>
> **ASK STUDENTS** what caused confusion to reign. (*The workers had not had fire drills, so they didn't know what to do. Confusion took control.*)

and they squeezed me to the door," Ida Willensky recalled. "Three times I said to the girls, 'Please, girls, let me open the door. Please!' But they would not listen to me." Finally, cutter Louis Brown barged through the crowd and forced the
80 door open.

Workers, shouting, crying, and gasping for air, slowly made their way downstairs. There were no lights in the stairway, so they had to grope their way in darkness. A girl fell; others fell on top of her, blocking the stairs until firefighters arrived moments later. Yet everyone who took the strairway from the eighth floor got out alive, exiting through the Washington Place doors. Those on the ninth floor were not so lucky.

D 90 New Yorkers say that March comes in like a lion (with cold wind) and leaves like a lamb (with April's warm showers). Now, as fire raged on the eighth floor, the elevator shafts became wind tunnels. Wind gusts made eerie sounds, like the howling of great beasts in pain, while sucking flaming embers upward. On the ninth floor, embers landed on piles of finished shirtwaists and cans of oil used to make the sewing machines run smoothly. Instantly, the air itself seemed to catch fire.

Had there been fire drills, surely more would have survived. Unfortunately, confusion **reigned**. Workers had to make life-and-death decisions in split seconds amid fire,
E 100 smoke, and panic. It was everyone for themselves. "I was throwing them out of the way," Mary Bucelli said of the women near her. "No matter whether they were in front of me or coming from in back of me, I was pushing them down. I was only looking out for my own life." Mary joined others who ran to the Greene Street stairway. They made it down to the street or up to the tenth floor and the roof, before flames blocked this escape route.

Others headed for the elevators and stairway on the Washington Place side of the building. Forcing open the
110 doors to the elevator shaft, they looked down and saw an elevator starting what would be its last trip from the eighth floor. "I reached out and grabbed the cables, wrapped my legs around them, and started to slide down," recalled Samuel Levine, a sewing machine operator. "While on my way down, as slow as I could let myself drop, the bodies of six girls went falling past me. One of them struck me, and I fell on top of the elevator. I fell on the dead body of a girl. Finally I heard

reign
(rān) *v.* If some things *reign* over something else, it means they dominate it.

Firefighters in a horse-drawn fire engine race to the respond to the fire at the Triangle Waist Company.

the firemen cutting their way into the elevator shaft, and they came and let me out."

120   Those who reached the ninth-floor stairway door found it locked. This was not unusual, as employers often locked doors to discourage latecomers and keep out union organizers. "My God, I am lost!" cried Margaret Schwartz as her hair caught fire. Nobody who went to that door survived, nor any who reached the windows.

    With a wave of fire rolling across the room, workers rushed to the windows, only to meet more fire. Hot air expands. Unless it escapes, pressure will keep building, eventually blowing a hole even in a heavy iron container

130 like a boiler. Heat and pressure blew out the eighth-floor windows. Firefighters call the result "lapping in"—that is, sucking flames into open windows above. That is why you see black scorch marks on the wall above the window of a burnt-out room.

    With fire advancing from behind and flames rising before them, people knew they were doomed. Whatever they did meant certain death. By remaining in the room, they chose death by fire or suffocation. Jumping ninety-five feet to the ground meant death on the sidewalk. We cannot know what

140 passed through the minds of those who decided to jump. Yet

Flesh & Blood So Cheap **269**

Analyze Presentations of Information (LINES 120–125)

Tell students that an **author's perspective** is the combination of ideas, feelings, values, and beliefs that influence the way the author presents information.

F **CITE TEXT EVIDENCE** Have students reread lines 120–125 and cite the reason that the ninth-floor stairway door was locked. *("This was not unusual, as employers often locked doors to discourage latecomers and keep out union organizers.")* Ask students why the author might have included this detail. *(He wants to show how little power workers had at that time.)*

Determine Central Idea and Details (LINES 130–132)

Point out that the author is continuing to describe events on the ninth floor.

G **ASK STUDENTS** to reread the information about "lapping in" in lines 130–132 and to explain what this detail helps readers understand. *(Because flames were sucked into the open windows above the eighth floor, the fire on the ninth floor grew stronger.)*

APPLYING ACADEMIC VOCABULARY

contrast	despite	inadequate

As you discuss the events recounted in this text, incorporate the following Collection 6 academic vocabulary words: *contrast, despite,* and *inadequate.* Have students find reasons why so many people died **despite** firefighters' efforts. Discuss the effects of **inadequate** safety measures. Prompt students to **contrast** the situations on the different floors of the building.

CLOSE READ

Determine Central Idea and Details (LINES 152–177)

 COMMON CORE RI 2

Point out that the two paragraphs in lines 152–177 tell about the work of firefighters.

(H) ASK STUDENTS to closely reread lines 152–177, determine what each paragraph is mainly about, and state each main idea in a sentence. *(Firefighters brought water, but they couldn't use it on the windows with people near them. Firefighters brought life nets, but these failed due to the tremendous force of the falling bodies.)*

CRITICAL VOCABULARY

portable: Water streamed from portable towers.

ASK STUDENTS why the towers had to be portable. *(so that they could be carried on the fire wagons)*

---

their thinking, in those last moments of life, may have gone like this: If I jump, my family will have a body to identify and bury, but if I stay in this room, there will be nothing left.

A girl clung to a window frame until flames from the eighth floor lapped in, burning her face and setting fire to her hair and clothing. She let go. Just then, Frances Perkins reached the scene from her friend's town house on the north side of Washington Square. "Here they come," onlookers shouted as Engine Company 72 reined in their horses. "Don't
150 jump; stay there." Seconds later, Hook and Ladder Company 20 arrived.

Firefighters charged into the building, stretching a hose up the stairways as they went. At the sixth-floor landing, they connected it to the standpipe. Reaching the eighth floor, they crawled into the inferno on their bellies, under the rising smoke, with their hose. Yet nothing they did could save those at the windows. Photos of the **portable** towers show streams of water playing on the three top floors. (A modern high-pressure pumper can send water as high as one thousand feet.)
160 Plenty of water got through the windows, but not those with people standing in them. A burst of water under high pressure would have hurled them backward, into the flames.

Hoping to catch jumpers before they hit the ground, firefighters held up life nets, sturdy ten-foot-square nets made of rope. It was useless. A person falling from the ninth floor struck with a force equal to eleven thousand pounds. Some jumpers bounced off nets, dying when they hit the ground; others tore the nets, crashing through to the pavement. "The force was so great it took men off their feet," said Captain
170 Howard Ruch of Engine Company 18. "Trying to hold the nets, the men turned somersaults. The men's hands were bleeding, the nets were torn and some caught fire" from burning clothing. Officers, fearing their men would be struck by falling bodies, ordered the nets removed. The aerial ladders failed, too, reaching only to the sixth floor. Desperate jumpers tried to grab hold of a rung on the way down, missed, and landed on the sidewalk.

People began to jump singly or in groups of two or three, holding hands as they stepped out the windows.
180 William G. Shepherd, a reporter for United Press, watched the "shower of bodies" in horror.

portable
(pôr′tə-bəl) *adj.*
If something is *portable*, it can be carried or moved easily.

WHEN STUDENTS STRUGGLE . . .

To help students develop statements of main ideas, guide them in following these steps:

- Reread one paragraph.
- Think of a good title for the paragraph. It should name the paragraph topic—what most or all of the sentences tell about.
- Think about the details in the paragraph. Ask: What is most important to know about the paragraph topic?
- Write a sentence that answers that question.
- Use a graphic organizer like the one shown to record topics and main ideas.

I saw every feature of the tragedy visible from outside the building. I learned a new sound—a more horrible sound than any description can picture. It was the sound of a speeding, living body on a stone sidewalk.

Thud—dead, thud—dead, thud—dead, thud—dead. Sixty-two thud—dead. I call them that, because the sound and the thought of death came to me each time, at the same instant. . . . Down came the bodies in a shower, burning,
190 *smoking—flaming bodies, with the disheveled hair trailing upward. . . .*

On the sidewalk lay heaps of broken bodies. A policeman later went about with tags, which he fastened with wires to the wrists of the dead girls. . . . The floods of water from the firemen's hose that ran into the gutter was actually stained red with blood.

Onlookers saw many dreadful sights, none more so than the end of a love affair. A young man appeared at a window. Gently, he helped a young woman step onto the windowsill,
200 held her away from the building—and let go. He helped another young woman onto the windowsill. "Those of us who were looking saw her put her arms around him and kiss him," Shepherd wrote. "Then he held her out into space and dropped her. But quick as a flash he was on the windowsill himself. . . . He was brave enough to help the girl he loved to a quicker death, after she had given him a goodbye kiss."

Meanwhile, others managed to reach the fire escape. It had not been designed for a quick exit. FDNY[6] experts later declared that those on the three top floors of the Asch
210 Building could not have made it to the ground in under three hours. In reality, they had only minutes.

People crowded onto the fire escape. As they walked single file, flames lapped at them through broken windows. Worse, the human load became too heavy for the device to bear. Bolts that fastened it to the building became loose. It began to sway, then collapsed at the eighth floor, tumbling dozens into the courtyard. "As the fire-crazed victims were thrown by the collapse of the fire escape, several struck the sharp-tipped palings,"[7] the New York *Herald* reported. "The
220 body of one woman was found with several iron spikes driven

---

[6] **FDNY:** the Fire Department of New York City.
[7] **palings:** fences with stakes.

CLOSE READ

Analyze Presentations of Information (LINES 182–196)

COMMON CORE RI 5

Tell students that history researchers use **primary sources,** firsthand accounts by people who witnessed or took part in an event. In lines 182–196, this author includes an excerpt from an eyewitness account, an example of a primary source.

ASK STUDENTS to reread lines 182–196 and explain why the author included this excerpt. *(It is a vivid description of the horror of that day, and it helps put the reader in the scene.)*

Determine Central Idea and Details (LINES 207–219)

COMMON CORE RI 2

Clarify that a fire escape is a metal stairway on the exterior of a building, accessible from windows.

ASK STUDENTS to reread lines 207–219 and summarize the most important information about the fire escape. *(The fire escape collapsed under the weight of the people, but its design would not have allowed people to reach the ground in time anyway.)*

Paragraph Title (Topic)	Main Idea
Life Nets	*The firefighters' rope nets were not strong enough to hold the falling bodies.*

This is a photograph of the gutted tenth floor of the Asch Building that was taken in the aftermath of the fire.

Determine Central Idea and Details (LINES 223–239)

COMMON CORE RI 1, RI 2

Remind students that the author has previously described events on the eighth and ninth floors. Beginning on line 223, he begins describing what happened on the tenth floor.

K **CITE TEXT EVIDENCE** Have students reread lines 223–239 and cite a sentence that states the main idea. (*"The tenth floor was the best place to be."*) Ask students to cite details that support that idea. (*People there "survived by dashing up the stairs to the roof." In the next building, "students lowered the ladders, climbed down, and led the survivors to safety." "Only one person from the tenth floor died."*)

CRITICAL VOCABULARY

inspection: Fire Chief Croker made an inspection of the building.

ASK STUDENTS what he was probably doing to make his inspection. (*looking at the burned-out rooms, studying the fire escape and stairwells, examining the site for evidence of how the fire started*)

---

entirely through it." Others crashed through the skylight into the room below, where they died on the cement floor.

The tenth floor was the best place to be. Those who worked there, or reached it from the floor below, survived by dashing up the stairs to the roof. When they arrived, they found the roof fifteen feet lower than its Washington Place neighbor's, a building shared by New York University and the American Book Company.

230 Luckily, Professor Frank Sommer was teaching his law class in a room that overlooked the Asch Building. When Sommer realized what was happening, he led his class to the roof of their building. There they found two ladders left by painters during the week. Students lowered the ladders, climbed down, and helped survivors to safety. For some women, said Sommer, "it was necessary to beat out the flames that had caught their clothing, and many of them had blackened faces and singed hair and eyebrows." Yet only one person from the tenth floor died. Seeing flames licking up from the ninth floor, she panicked and jumped out a window.

240 By 5:15 P.M., exactly thirty-five minutes after flames burst from beneath a cutting table, firefighters had brought the blaze under control. An hour later, Chief Croker made his **inspection**. He found that the Asch Building had no damage

inspection
(ĭn-spĕk´shən) *n.*
An *inspection* is an official examination or review.

©Bettmann/Corbis

Strategies for Annotation 🖉 📋 *Annotate it!*

Determine Central Idea and Details

COMMON CORE RI 2

Have students use their eBook annotation tools to annotate lines 223–239.

- Highlight the sentence that states the main idea.
- Underline details that support that main idea.

The tenth floor was the best place to be. Those who worked there, or reached it from the floor below, survived by dashing up the stairs to the roof. When they arrived, they

to its structure. Its walls were in good shape; so were the floors. It had passed the test. It was fireproof.

The woodwork, furniture, cotton goods, and people who worked in it were not. Of the 500 Triangle employees who reported for work that day, 146 died. Of these, sixteen men were identified. The rest were women or bodies and body
250 parts listed as "unidentified." The Triangle Fire was New York's worst workplace disaster up to that time. Only the September 11, 2001, terrorist attacks on the twin towers of the World Trade Center took more (about 2,500) lives.

Chief Croker was no softie; he was used to the horrors that came with his job. But this was different. As he explored the top three floors of the Asch Building, he saw sights "that utterly staggered him," the New York *World* reported. "In the drifting smoke, he had seen bodies burned to bare bones, skeletons bending over sewing machines." Those sights sent
260 him down to the street with quivering lips.

Next morning, March 26, Chief Croker returned for another look. The only creatures he found alive were some half-drowned mice. He picked one up, stroked it gently, and put it in his pocket. The chief would take it home, he said. "It's alive. At least it's alive."

CLOSE READ

Analyze Presentations of Information (LINES 254–265)

COMMON CORE RI 1, RI 6

Tell students that a history author uses **portrayals,** descriptions of historical figures, to reveal their perspective on events.

L **CITE TEXT EVIDENCE** Have students cite details about Chief Croker and explain why the author includes them. *("Chief Croker was no softie; he was used to the horrors that came with his job." The author quotes a newspaper report that said Croker was "utterly staggered." The author says, "Those sights sent him down to the street with quivering lips," and describes Croker gently stroking a half-drowned mouse. The author wants to show that even a hardened professional had difficulty coping with the enormity of this disaster.)*

PRACTICE & APPLY

Determine Central Idea and Details COMMON CORE RI 2

Guide students to review the text to find details that support the main idea shown in the partial outline. (Possible details: no-smoking rules were not enforced; aisles were too narrow; water hose was not connected to standpipe; doors to stairwells were locked; fire drills had never been held; fire escape was unsound)

Analyzing the Text COMMON CORE RI 1, RI 6

Possible answers:

1. *The fire began on the eighth floor where most of the workers escaped by elevators or stairs. On the ninth floor, some used a stairway to escape, but the other stairway was locked. These workers jumped to their death or died in the fire. On the tenth floor, workers climbed the stairs to the roof and found safety.*

2. *The author is giving a reason for the disorder and panic that led to so much loss of life. The lack of fire drills meant that workers had no idea what to do.*

3. *The author suggests that people jumped from windows so that their bodies would be identified.*

4. *The author believes the firefighters did what they could and acted heroically but that their equipment was not sufficient and the situation was hopeless.*

5. *It is most important to understand that this disaster could have been prevented.*

6. *The story is still told because of the lessons learned as a result of that disaster.*

 eBook *Annotate It!*

Determine Central Idea and Details COMMON CORE RI 2

The **central idea,** or main idea, in a piece of history writing is the most important idea about the topic. It may be stated explicitly in a sentence, or it may be implied. The main idea is often suggested by smaller key ideas, each developed in a paragraph or a longer section of the work.

Main ideas are supported by **details,** facts and other pieces of information that build upon or clarify the main ideas. When you read history writing, notice the details that answer basic questions, such as, *When and where does the event take place? Who is involved? What are the causes and the immediate and long-term effects?*

As you read, you can keep track of key ideas and details by taking notes in outline form. Restate the main ideas of paragraphs or sections, numbered in Roman numerals. Below each idea, list the supporting details.

> The Triangle Waist Company Fire
> I. The Triangle factory was a dangerous firetrap.
>   A. Paper scraps hung from the rafters.
>   B. There were always scraps under the tables.
>   C.

Once you have completed an outline for the entire text, look to see how all the main ideas and details help to develop the main idea of the entire text. What other details from *Flesh & Blood So Cheap* could you add to this outline?

Analyzing the Text COMMON CORE RI 1, RI 6

Cite Text Evidence Support your responses with evidence from the text.

1. **Summarize** Review the text to find details about the different floors of the building. What is important to understand about these locations?

2. **Cause/Effect** Reread lines 97–100. Why does the author give a detail about fire drills?

3. **Draw Conclusions** According to the author, why might workers have jumped from the windows?

4. **Cite Evidence** What does the author seem to think of the firefighters' efforts during this disaster?

5. **Evaluate** What is most important to understand about this event?

6. **Connect** Why is the story of the Triangle Fire still being told?

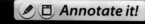 **Strategies for Annotation** *Annotate it!*

Determine Central Idea and Details COMMON CORE RI 2

Have students locate lines 127–132. Share these strategies for guided or independent analysis:

- Select a paragraph or section.
- Highlight the stated main idea.
- Underline details that support that main idea

rushed to the windows, only to meet more fire. Hot air expands. Unless it escapes, pressure will keep building, eventually blowing a hole even in a heavy iron container like a boiler. Heat and pressure blew out the eighth-floor windows. Firefighters call the result "lapping in"—that is, sucking flames into open windows above. That is why you

from **The Story of the Triangle Factory Fire**
by Zachary Kent

A In the days following the fire, city officials sifted through the charred rubble at the Asch Building and tried to fix the fault for the tragedy. Fire Chief Croker angrily stated, "There wasn't a fire escape anywhere fronting on the street by which these unfortunate girls could escape." Doors that opened inward instead of outward, overcrowding in work areas, and blocked exits also were to blame. Fire Marshal William Beers stunned New Yorkers by soon declaring, "I can show you 150 loft buildings far worse than this one."
10 Lillian D. Wald of the Joint Board of Sanitary Control also reported on the general situation. "The conditions as they now exist are hideous. . . . Our investigators have shown that there are hundreds of buildings which invite disaster just as much as did the Asch structure."

B Accused of ignoring their employees' safety, Triangle owners Blanck and Harris were charged with manslaughter. During the three week trial angry citizens packed the courtroom. Outside, in the **corridors**, women screamed, "Murderers! Murderers! Make them suffer for
20 killing our children!" Lawyers argued that Blanck and Harris kept all of the Triangle doors locked during the workday, therefore causing many of the deaths. Weighing the evidence, however, the jury returned a verdict of not guilty. "I cannot see that anyone was responsible for the disaster," explained juror H. Houston Hierst. "It seems to me to have been an act of the Almighty.[1]" The New York *Call* viewed the matter differently. "Capital can commit no crime," it angrily declared, "when it is in pursuit of profits."
Furious New Yorkers refused to let the issue rest.
30 In October 1911 the city established a Bureau of Fire Prevention to inspect safety standards in other buildings. Five months earlier the New York State legislature created a special Factory Investigating Commission. Through the

corridor
(kôr´ĭ-dər) *n.*
A *corridor* is a narrow hallway or passageway.

---

[1] **an act of the Almighty:** a term that refers to events or actions that are beyond the control of human beings.

©Photodisc/Getty Images

The Story of the Triangle Factory Fire **275**

TEACH

CLOSE READ

Analyze Structure: Chronological Order
COMMON CORE RI 1, RI 5

(LINES 1–14)

Explain that history writers often use **chronological order,** presenting events in the order they occurred. Dates and words can signal chronological order.

A CITE TEXT EVIDENCE Have students find words that signal chronology in lines 1–14. *("soon"; "'now'"; "the days following")* Have them summarize events in chronological order. *(Officials investigated the tragedy's cause. They found many issues with the building. Others claimed there were many other unsafe buildings.)*

Analyze Presentations of Information (LINES 15–28)
COMMON CORE RI 6

Tell students that when an author's point of view is **subjective,** he or she reveals personal feelings. When an author is **objective,** he or she sticks to the facts.

B ASK STUDENTS to reread lines 15–28, determine whether the point of view is subjective or objective, and explain why. *(It's mostly objective because Kent reports the facts of the trial and quotes people with opposing viewpoints. But it's also subjective because he uses quotations that are emotional and powerful, such as quotations calling the owners "murderers".)*

CRITICAL VOCABULARY

corridor: Women gathered in the corridors.

ASK STUDENTS what they visualize in the corridors. *(crowds of angry women in long hallways)*

SCAFFOLDING FOR ELL STUDENTS

Determine Meaning Guide students to understand the author's use of quotations from various participants in the event.

- Display a segment of text that includes multiple quotations, such as lines 3–9.
- Use the same color to highlight the name of the speaker and the spoken words.
- Together, read aloud the spoken words. Prompt students to paraphrase the quotation in a note.

the fault for the tragedy. Fire Chief Croker angrily stated,

"There wasn't a fire escape anywhere fronting on the street

by which these unfortunate girls could escape." . . .

areas, and blocked exits also were to blame. Fire Marshal

William Beers stunned New Yorkers by soon declaring,

"I can show you 150 loft buildings far worse than this one."

Because there wasn't a fire escape to the street, many women died.

Analyze Structure: Chronological Order

  RI 5

(LINES 39–41)

Point out that the author is describing what happened after the fire, which occurred on March 25, 1911.

C **ASK STUDENTS** to reread lines 39–41 and tell how long it took New York State lawmakers to pass safety laws for workers. (*Laws were passed within three years after the fire.*)

Analyze Presentations of Information (LINES 41–42)

  RI 1, RI 6

Review that an **author's perspective** is the combination of ideas, feelings, values, and beliefs that influence the way the author presents information.

D **CITE TEXT EVIDENCE** Have students reread lines 41–42 and cite evidence that reveals what the author values. (*"New York State's Industrial Code, the finest in the nation."*) Ask if the statement reveals an objective or subjective point of view. (*subjective, because it is the author's opinion*)

New York City garment workers take part in a May Day parade in 1916.

next four years Commission investigators crawled and pried through the rooms and cellars of factories and tenement houses[2] all across the state. They examined workers' filthy living conditions and witnessed the dangers of crippling machinery and long work hours in dusty, dirty firetraps.

  As a result of the Commission's shocking findings,
40 New York State quickly passed thirty-three new labor laws by 1914. These laws formed the foundation of New York

---

[2] **tenement houses:** very run-down city apartments where the poor and immigrants often live.

State's Industrial Code, the finest in the nation. Soon other states followed New York's example and **enacted** protective labor laws.

One Factory Commission investigator had witnessed the fateful Triangle fire. Frances Perkins said, "We heard the fire engines and rushed . . . to see what was going on. . . . We got there just as they started to jump. I shall never forget the frozen horror which came over us as we stood with our hands on our throats watching that horrible sight, knowing that there was no help."

In 1933 President Franklin Roosevelt named Frances Perkins secretary of labor. She and other social reformers dedicated their lives to insuring worker safety throughout the country. "They did not die in vain and we will never forget them," vowed Perkins. From the ashes of the tragic Triangle factory fire came help for millions of United States laborers today.

COLLABORATIVE DISCUSSION You've now read two accounts of a disaster that occurred a century ago. If a similar fire were to start in a garment factory of today, how might the events be the same or different? Talk about your thoughts with other group members.

enact
(ĕn-ăkt´) *v.* If you *enact* something, you make it into a law.

CLOSE READ

Analyze Structure: Chronological Order

 COMMON CORE RI 5

(LINES 45–51)

Tell students that history texts may sometimes refer back in time to earlier events. Readers must pay close attention to determine the time period being referenced.

E **ASK STUDENTS** to closely reread lines 45–51 and determine when Frances Perkins made the comments that are quoted and what those comments refer to. *(When she was working on the Factory Commission, sometime in the years after the fire, Perkins recalled what she had seen on that day.)*

> #### CRITICAL VOCABULARY
>
> **enact**: States enacted protective labor laws.
>
> **ASK STUDENTS** what happens before a law is enacted. *(Lawmakers debate it and then vote on it.)*

COLLABORATIVE DISCUSSION Have students work in groups to discuss the question. Remind students to cite evidence from both texts about the effects of the Triangle Factory Fire.

ASK STUDENTS to share any questions they generated in the course of reading and discussing the selection.

PRACTICE & APPLY

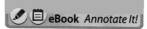
Analyze Structure: Chronological Order

 COMMON CORE RI 5

Help students understand the terms. Review the types of text clues that signal sequence, and discuss how these can help readers track events in a piece of history writing. Clues to chronological order in the lesson excerpt are *"October 1911," "Five months earlier,"* and *"Through the next four years."*

Analyzing the Text

 COMMON CORE RI 1, RI 2, RI 5

Possible answers:

1. *Before the Triangle Factory Fire, factories in New York City were dirty, overcrowded firetraps. Exits were blocked, and fire escapes didn't exist or didn't work. The workers had no legal protections for their safety.*

2. *Citizens pushed lawmakers to make buildings safer. New York City established a bureau to inspect safety standards. New York State had investigators report on safety conditions in factories and tenements. As a result, the state passed thirty-three new labor laws to make working conditions safer.*

3. *Angry citizens wanted the factory owners to be punished. Jurors believed the fire was not the fault of the owners. The jurors might have found no legal proof of responsibility, or they might have been swayed by the power of the business owners, as suggested by the newspaper the* New York Call.

4. *The author is making the point that a disaster can have a positive result. Although the Triangle Factory Fire was a great tragedy, it led to some beneficial changes in labor and safety laws.*

Analyze Structure: Chronological Order

COMMON CORE RI 5

A **pattern of organization** is the particular arrangement of ideas and information. Authors of history texts often use the **chronological order** organization to arrange events by their order of occurrence—what happens first, next, then, and finally. When reading history texts, pay attention to dates, times, and words and phrases that signal sequence, such as *before, meanwhile, later,* and *after that.*

Identify the clues to the chronological organization in this paragraph from *The Story of the Triangle Factory Fire:*

> Furious New Yorkers refused to let the issue rest. In October 1911, the city established a Bureau of Fire Prevention to inspect safety standards in other buildings. Five months earlier the New York State legislature created a special Factory Investigating Commission. Through the next four years Commission investigators crawled and pried through the rooms and cellars of factories and tenement houses all across the state.

Analyzing the Text

 COMMON CORE RI 1, RI 2, RI 5

Cite Text Evidence Support your responses with evidence from the selection.

1. **Infer** What was true of factories in New York City before the Triangle Fire?

2. **Summarize** What changes occurred in the aftermath of the tragedy? Within what time period did the changes happen?

3. **Compare** Reread lines 15–28. How and why did the jurors' viewpoint differ from that of angry citizens?

4. **Infer** Reread the last sentence. Despite the horror and loss of life caused by the fire, how might it have been a useful experience, according to the author?

Strategies for Annotation  *Annotate it!*

Analyze Structure: Chronological Order

COMMON CORE RI 5

Have students locate lines 29–33. Share these strategies for guided or independent analysis:

- Highlight in yellow words and phrases that signal chronological order.
- Underline the event that happened first.

> Furious New Yorkers refused to let the issue rest. In October 1911 the city established a Bureau of Fire Prevention to inspect safety standards in other buildings. Five months earlier the New York State legislature created a special Factory Investigating Commission. Through the next four years Commission investigators crawled and pried

Analyze Presentations of Information

COMMON CORE RI 3, RI 6, RI 9

History writing is nonfiction that presents events and people of the past. What makes this type of writing interesting is how it presents interactions between people and events. History writing often combines features of a narrative text (a true story with a setting, characters, and a plot) and an informational text (paragraphs of main ideas and factual details).

History writers base their work on factual research. However, two history writers might write about the same event in different ways. How writers shape their presentations of key information can depend on individual points of view. **Author's perspective** is the unique combination of ideas, values, feelings, and beliefs that influence the way a writer looks at a topic.

In comparing the perspectives of two or more authors writing about the same event, look for clues like these in the texts:

Tone	**Tone** is the author's attitude toward his or her subject. Would you describe the writing as serious? Lively? Angry? Notice any emotions the writer expresses while presenting the facts and how the emotions contribute to the overall effect of the writing.
Point of view	Analyze the author's presentation of information to determine his or her point of view. When writing from a **subjective** point of view, an author includes personal opinions, feelings, and beliefs. When writing from an **objective** point of view, the author focuses on factual information and leaves out personal opinions.
Direct statements	Be aware of any statements or comments that seem to come directly from the author. In particular, watch for ideas that may be repeated or restated. What light do these statements shed on the writer's interpretation of facts?
Emphasis	Determine how each author presents his or her ideas about the topic. Do the writers emphasize different evidence? Do they put forth different interpretations of facts?
Portrayals	Pay attention to how the historical figures are portrayed. Think about why that person is included and what makes him or her memorable.

In the excerpt from *Flesh & Blood So Cheap*, read how author Albert Marrin describes Chief Croker (lines 261–265). Next, read the description of Croker by author Zachary Kent in lines 1–7 from *The Story of the Triangle Factory Fire*. Then, compare these two passages. What similarities and differences do you notice in the history writers' descriptions? What do these details reveal about each author's perspective?

TEACH

CLOSE READ

Analyze Presentations of Information

COMMON CORE RI 3, RI 6, RI 9

Review the definition of *author's perspective* and the elements shown in the chart. After students have studied the chart, discuss why interpretation is such an important part of a history writer's work and why readers should be sensitive to an author's perspective.

(Possible answers to the questions about the two presentations of Chief Croker: Both passages tell about the aftermath of the fire and the reaction of Fire Chief Croker. Both include quotations from the chief. Albert Marrin describes Chief Croker picking up a half-drowned mouse, stroking it gently, and taking it home because "At least it's alive." Marrin chooses this episode to show that the fire was so terrible, even the hardened chief was overcome with emotion. Marrin presents a more subjective, emotional perspective than Zachary Kent does. Kent shows the fire chief as angry at the lack of safety in the building. Kent displays a more objective point of view, choosing to focus on the chief's professionalism and the causes and effects of the fire.)

Strategies for Annotation ✐ 🖥 *Annotate it!*

Analyze Presentations of Information

COMMON CORE RI 3, RI 6

Share these strategies for guided or independent analysis using lines 97–101 from *Flesh & Blood So Cheap*:

- Highlight in yellow text that reveals the author's interpretation of facts.
- Underline words with emotional impact.
- In a note, write a word that labels the tone.

Had there been fire drills, surely more would have survived. Unfortunately, confusion reigned. Workers h[ad] to make <u>life-and-death decisions in split seconds</u> amid [smoke], and <u>panic</u>. It was everyone for themselves. "<u>I was throwing them out of the way</u>," Mary Bucelli said of the

> urgent, serious, grim

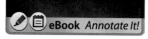

PRACTICE & APPLY

Analyzing the Text

COMMON CORE RI 1, RI 2, RI 3, RI 6, RI 9

Possible answers:

1. *The Story of the Triangle Factory Fire would be a better source for research on the effects because it covers the short-term and long-term effects of the fire.*

2. *Frances Perkins witnessed the Triangle Factory Fire and was horrified by it. She never forgot that unsafe working conditions led to the tragedy, and she used that knowledge when she became secretary of labor under President Franklin Roosevelt.*

3. *Both authors used primary sources, information published at the time of the event. They quoted from eyewitness accounts, news reports, and editorials.*

4. *These lines are an example of Marrin's perspective. The author's description is evidence of a dramatic tone ("a wave of fire rolling across the room"). The point of view is objective, giving factual information about the action of heat.*

5. *The phrases "filthy living conditions," "dangers of crippling machinery," "long work hours in dusty, and dirty firetraps" all reveal the author's feelings of disgust at the conditions.*

6. *Both authors emphasize the importance of safe working conditions. Today, we have fire drills, and our buildings have smoke alarms and fire and safety inspections. These regulations are the result of laws designed to prevent tragedies like the Triangle Factory Fire.*

7. *The emphasis in the excerpt from* Flesh & Blood So Cheap *is on the causes of the fire and the events during the fire. The author includes graphic details to convey the panic and horror. In the excerpt from* The Story of the Triangle Factory Fire, *the author focuses on the aftermath of the tragedy and on the effects it had on safety regulations in workplaces.*

Analyzing the Text

COMMON CORE RI 1, RI 2, RI 3, RI 6, RI 9, W 1b, W 6, SL 4, SL 6

Cite Text Evidence   Support your responses with evidence from the texts.

1. **Cause/Effect** Which of the two texts would you use to research the effects of the Triangle Fire? Why?

2. **Compare** Look back at both texts to find mention of Frances Perkins. Why is she an important person to know about?

3. **Infer** What kinds of sources did both authors use in researching this topic?

4. **Analyze History Writing** Read lines 126–130 from *Flesh & Blood So Cheap.* Are these lines an example of author Albert Marrin's perspective? Explain why or why not.

5. **Analyze Tone** Read lines 36–38 from *The Story of the Triangle Factory Fire.* What clues do you see in these lines to Zachary Kent's attitude about the conditions that are described?

6. **Connect** What idea presented by both authors is most relevant to us today? Why?

7. **Analyze Key Information** The two historical writings cover different aspects of the same event. Briefly review each text for its key details. Then tell what each selection emphasizes.

PERFORMANCE TASK

Speaking Activity: Oral Presentation
The Triangle Factory Fire raised issues about inadequate workplace safety, labor rights, and factory jobs. Despite great progress in improving working conditions since 1911, these issues are still in the news. Make an oral presentation about a current event that shares features with the Triangle Factory Fire.

- Use online and print resources to learn about a recent event.

- Use several sources to get varied viewpoints and interpretations of the event.

- Prepare a talk to tell about the event, the people, and the issues.

- End your talk by telling how this event is similar to and different from the Triangle Factory Fire.

- After rehearsing, deliver your talk to classmates.

PERFORMANCE TASK

COMMON CORE W 2, W 6, SL 4, SL 6

Assign this performance task.

Speaking Activity: Oral Presentation Guide students to reliable sources of current events, and suggest that they not limit themselves to events in the United States. Students' oral presentations should include:

- a summary of the event with answers to the questions *what, where, when, who,* and *how*

- examples of causes, immediate effects, and future effects

- comparisons and contrasts with the Triangle Factory Fire

INTERACTIVE LESSON Have students complete the tutorials in this lesson: **Giving a Presentation**

Critical Vocabulary

flammable	reign	portable
inspection	corridor	enact

Practice and Apply Complete each sentence to show that you understand the meaning of the bold word.

1. If a cleaning fluid is **flammable,** you should . . .

2. Fear and worry **reign** when . . .

3. A **portable** desk is one that . . .

4. An **inspection** of a restaurant is done to . . .

5. A **corridor** is the same as . . .

6. If a rule is **enacted,** it . . .

Vocabulary Strategy: Latin Roots

A **root** is a word part that came into English from an older language. Roots from the ancient language of Latin appear in many English words. This chart shows three common Latin roots:

Latin Root	Meaning	Example Words
spec	"to look at"	inspect, spectacle, aspect
struct	"to build"	construct, destructive, instruction
dic	"to say or tell"	dictate, predict, contradiction

Note the words with Latin roots in this sentence from *Flesh & Blood So Cheap*:

> An hour later, Chief Croker made his inspection. He found that the Asch Building had no damage to its structure.

The root meaning of *spec*, "to look at," is in the word *inspection*, "the act of looking closely." The root meaning of *struct*, "to build," is in the word *structure*, "something that is built." Finding a Latin root in an unfamiliar word can help to unlock the word's meaning. A print or digital dictionary can help confirm the meaning.

Practice and Apply Find the words with Latin roots in each sentence. Give a meaning for the word that includes the meaning of the Latin root.

1. Fire obstructed the doorways, so there was no prospect of escape.

2. Nobody could have predicted the destruction caused by the fire.

3. From the perspective of the jurors, their verdict was fair.

PRACTICE & APPLY

Critical Vocabulary

Possible answers:

1. *If a cleaning fluid is flammable, you should never use it near heat or a spark.*

2. *Fear and worry reign when people learn that a war is about to begin.*

3. *A portable desk is one that is small and light enough to carry around with you.*

4. *An inspection of a restaurant is done to make sure that food is being prepared safely.*

5. *A corridor is the same as a hallway.*

6. *If a rule is enacted, it is put into effect, and people must follow it.*

Vocabulary Strategy: Latin Roots

Possible Answers:

1. obstructed *means "blocked, or built against something";* prospect *means "what you can expect, or look toward in the future."*

2. predicted *means "told about ahead of time";* destruction *means "the opposite of building."*

3. perspective *means "viewpoint, or the way you look at something";* verdict *means "the jury's decision, or what the jury says."*

 INTERACTIVE VOCABULARY TUTOR WordSharp **Word Structure: Latin Roots**

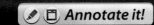
Strategies for Annotation ✎ 🖉 *Annotate it!*

Vocabulary Strategy: Latin Roots COMMON CORE L 4b, L 4d

Have students use their eBook annotation tools to identify a word with a Latin root in the sentence that begins in line 30 of *The Story of the Triangle Factory Fire*.

- Highlight in yellow a word with a Latin root listed in the Vocabulary Strategy chart.
- Underline the root.
- In a note, write a meaning for the word that is connected to the meaning of the root.
- Check the meaning in a print or digital dictionary.

In October 1911 the city established a Bureau of Fire Prevention to inspect safety standards in other buildings. Five months earlier the New York State legislature created

"to look into"

Language Conventions: Capitalization

Review the examples in the chart. Before assigning Practice and Apply, ask students to offer additional examples.

Answers:

1. *capitalize* Waist Company, Italian

2. *capitalize* Engine Company, *lowercase* firehouse

3. *lowercase* operator, *capitalize* Finally, *lowercase* firemen

4. *capitalize* On, March, *lowercase* professor, *capitalize* Building

5. *capitalize* New, World, Chief

 GRAMMAR NOTES: Level One
Lesson 14: Using Capital Letters

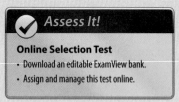

Assess It!

Online Selection Test
· Download an editable ExamView bank.
· Assign and manage this test online.

Language Conventions: Capitalization

When you proofread your writing, check to see that you have used capital and lowercase letters correctly. This chart shows general rules.

Capitalize	Examples
First words of sentences and quotations	A fire started. One man called, "Everyone out now!"
People and titles	Mayor Sanchez, General Robert E. Lee, Fire Chief Croker
Geographical names such as cities, continents, regions, streets, roads	New York, East River, Fifth Avenue
Organizations and buildings	League of Women Voters, International Monetary Fund, Empire State Building, Eiffel Tower
Time periods such as days, months, holidays, events, and eras (but not seasons)	Friday, May 3; the Fourth of July; the Triangle Factory Fire; the Jurassic Period
Documents and publications	Declaration of Independence, *Harper's Weekly, The Boston Globe*
Adjectives formed from proper nouns	North American cities, Japanese food, Mexican folklore

When you're unsure of which capitalization rule applies, a digital or print manual for usage and style can come in very handy to jog your memory of these rules.

Practice and Apply Some capital letters should be lowercase, and some lowercase letters should be capitalized. Find and fix the errors.

1. Most of the workers at the Triangle waist company were young women, including many italian immigrants.

2. The horse-drawn vehicles of engine company 72 arrived from a Firehouse six blocks away.

3. Sewing machine Operator Samuel Levine recalled, "finally I heard the Firemen cutting their way into the elevator shaft, and they came and let me out."

4. on that Saturday in march, Frank Sommer, a Professor of law, was teaching his class in a room that overlooked the Asch building.

5. The new York *world* reported on chief Croker's reaction to viewing the horrible scene.

INTERACTIVE WHITEBOARD LESSON
Primary and Secondary Sources

RI 5,
RI 6

COMMON
CORE

Learn the Skill ▸ What Are Primary and Secondary Sources?

What Are Primary and Secondary Sources?

Find Out

• A **primary source** is written or created by someone who took part in or witnessed an event.

• A **secondary source** is written or created by someone who was not directly involved in or present at the event.

TEACH

Tell students that the two selections about the Triangle Factory Fire are secondary sources and that each includes quotations from primary sources. Offer these definitions and examples:

- A **primary source** is created by someone who took part in or witnessed an event. Examples include eyewitness accounts, speeches, diaries, autobiographies, photos, and video footage.
- A **secondary source** is created by someone not directly involved in or present at the event. Examples include informational books, textbooks, encyclopedia articles, and essays and articles written after the event.

Point out that when students do research for their oral presentations for the Performance Task they will be doing what authors Albert Marrin and Zachary Kent did: reviewing multiple sources, both primary and secondary. Discuss the main purposes of each kind of source:

- Primary sources provide personal, subjective views of the event and a sense of time and place.
- Secondary sources provide an overview and factual details. The points of view are often both subjective and objective.

COLLABORATIVE DISCUSSION

Help students locate either author's book or another secondary source on the Triangle Factory Fire. Have students find references to primary sources that were consulted and discuss how and why the author incorporated the primary source material into the text.

Analyze Presentations of Information

RI 6,
RI 9

COMMON
CORE

RETEACH

Review that the term **author's perspective** refers to beliefs, opinions, and ideas that affect how an author presents information. Explain that paying attention to clues about an author's perspective helps readers make thoughtful judgments about the information in the text.

Display the two sentences shown below, and ask students to compare and contrast them. During discussion, guide students to note that each author has a different perspective. Discuss the **tone** (author's attitude toward the topic); **word choices** (including connotations), and **emphasis** (what details are given importance) in each sentence.

- If workers at the Triangle Factory had practiced fire drills, they would not have become panic-stricken victims of this horrific disaster.
- The Triangle Factory Fire happened so quickly that many workers never had a chance to escape.

PRACTICE AND APPLY

Have students locate each of the passages listed below in their text. Ask: What is each author's perspective in the passage? How do the passages differ in tone, word choice, and emphasis?

- Lines 120–125, from *Flesh & Blood So Cheap*
- Lines 20–22, from *The Story of the Triangle Factory Fire*

from "The Most Daring of [Our] Leaders"

By Lynne Olson

Why These Texts

Students may be surprised when they read about the many changes that have occurred in recent U.S. history. Over the last few decades, much has changed in the United States for African Americans. With the help of the close-reading questions, students will analyze how two texts present information about key events in the civil rights movement. This close reading will lead students to compare and contrast the two presentations.

Speech from the Democratic National Convention

By John Lewis

Background Have students read the background and author information. Point out that in 1865 the Thirteenth Amendment abolished slavery, but not racial prejudice. Throughout the United States, politicians devised legal structures to segregate blacks from whites, maintain white privileges, and prevent blacks from making political and economic gains.

SETTING A PURPOSE Ask students to pay attention to the presentation of information in the two texts. How are they similar and how are they different?

Common Core Support

- cite multiple pieces of text evidence
- determine central ideas in a text
- analyze interactions between individuals, events, and ideas
- determine the meaning of words
- analyze the structure of a text
- determine an author's purpose
- analyze how two authors write about history

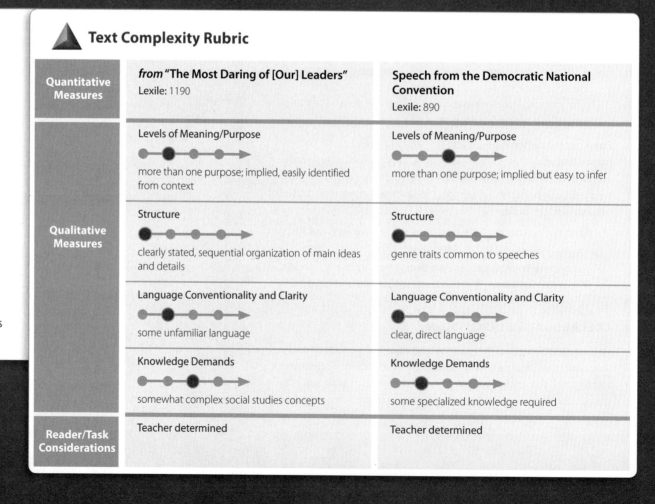

Text Complexity Rubric

	from "The Most Daring of [Our] Leaders"	Speech from the Democratic National Convention
Quantitative Measures	Lexile: 1190	Lexile: 890
Qualitative Measures	Levels of Meaning/Purpose more than one purpose; implied, easily identified from context	Levels of Meaning/Purpose more than one purpose; implied but easy to infer
	Structure clearly stated, sequential organization of main ideas and details	Structure genre traits common to speeches
	Language Conventionality and Clarity some unfamiliar language	Language Conventionality and Clarity clear, direct language
	Knowledge Demands somewhat complex social studies concepts	Knowledge Demands some specialized knowledge required
Reader/Task Considerations	Teacher determined	Teacher determined

Strategies for CLOSE READING

Analyze Presentations of Information

Students should read both texts carefully all the way through. Close-reading questions at the bottom of the page will help them focus on a thorough analysis of the presentation of information. As they read, students should jot down comments or questions about the text in the margins.

WHEN STUDENTS STRUGGLE . . .

To help students analyze how the authors present information, have them work in small groups to fill out a chart like the one shown below.

CITE TEXT EVIDENCE For practice in analyzing the presentation of information, ask students to cite text evidence for the first two rows of the chart and then write their impressions for the last row.

from "The Most Daring of [Our] Leaders"	Speech from the Democratic National Convention
Point of View	Point of View
Third-person: ". . .the students . . . formed a central committee . . ." (lines 50–51)	First-person: ". . . when my seatmate, Albert Bigelow, and I tried to enter . . ." (lines 10–11)
Author's purpose	Author's purpose
To document how Diane Nash and other Fisk students organized sit-ins at lunch counters and restaurants of Nashville's downtown stores	To attest that the U.S. has made great progress since the author's 1961 "Freedom Ride" but that people still need to vote and "speak out"
Effect on reader	Effect on reader
This text gives a clear, chronological account of what happened. It's a good presentation of history.	This speech is stirring and hopeful. It convinces you to keep fighting, to "stand up."

Background From the 1880s until the 1960s, "Jim Crow" laws in many American states enforced segregation between white people and black people. When the U.S. Supreme Court overturned the "separate but equal" doctrine in 1954, it was the beginning of a period of upheaval and marked the beginning of the civil rights movement. Civil rights activists participated in nonviolent forms of protest, such as sit-ins at lunch counters, and engaged in acts of civil disobedience, such as riding buses into the Deep South to challenging segregation at interstate terminals.

from "The Most Daring of [Our] Leaders" By Lynne Olson

Speech from the Democratic National Convention By John Lewis

Lynne Olson writes books of nonfiction. Before she started writing books full-time, she worked as a journalist for the Associated Press and as the White House correspondent for the Baltimore Sun. Her book Freedom's Daughters was the first book to take an in-depth look at women's roles in the civil rights movement. The portion of Freedom's Daughters that you will read here tells of the experiences of Diane Nash, a young woman from Chicago who attended Fisk University in Nashville, Tennessee, in 1959. In Nashville, both Diane Nash and John Lewis were influenced by Reverend James Lawson's teachings on the philosophy of nonviolence.

John Lewis was born in Alabama in 1940. He was a student at Fisk University when the civil rights movement gained momentum. As a college student, he studied the philosophy of nonviolence. In 1960, he helped plan a lunch counter sit-in in Nashville that went on peacefully for a month and then ended in the beating and arrest of the protesters. Eventually these protests were successful, and Nashville became the first major city in the South to desegregate its lunch counters. Lewis has served as the U.S. Representative of Georgia's Fifth Congressional District since his election to Congress in 1986. In his Speech to the Democratic National Convention, delivered in Charlotte, North Carolina, in 2012, Lewis talks about the progress America has made since he made an earlier trip to Charlotte in 1961.

95

1. **READ** ▶ As you read lines 1–55, begin to collect and cite text evidence.

- Underline Nash's and the Fisk students' reactions to segregation. Explain in the margin how the other students' reactions influenced Nash.
- In the margin, note the central idea of the section. Circle three details that support the main idea.

epiphany:
discovery

from "The Most Daring of [Our] Leaders"
History Writing by Lynne Olson

Nash's moment of **epiphany** came at the Tennessee State Fair in 1959. She had gone to the fair on a date, and wanted to use the ladies' room. She found two—one marked WHITE WOMEN, the other COLORED WOMEN—and for the first time in her life suffered the degradation of Jim Crow. This was no longer an intellectual exercise: She was being told in the most searing way imaginable that *she* was beyond the pale, unfit to use the same facilities as white

(A) women. Outraged by the experience, she was even more upset that her date, a Southerner, did not share her fury. Neither did most of her

10 fellow Fisk students. They did not seem to care that they could shop at downtown stores but not eat at the stores' lunch counters, or that they had to sit in the balcony to see a movie. The more Nash found out about segregation in Nashville, the more she felt "stifled and boxed in." In the rest of the country, Nashville had the reputation of being more racially progressive than most Southern cities. Blacks could vote in Nashville. The city's schools and buses were integrated. Blacks served on the police force, fire department, City Council, and Board of Education. But segregation still firmly ruled in theaters, restaurants, hotels, and libraries, and Diane Nash, a deep-dyed

20 moralist, decided then and there that Nashville was in a "stage of sin." She couldn't believe that "the children of my classmates would have to be born into a society where they had to believe that they were inferior." Above all, she could not believe that her classmates were willing to let that happen.

Since they did not seem to share her anger, she looked elsewhere for support. Paul LaPrad, a white exchange student at Fisk, told her about a black minister named James Lawson, who was training college students in the use of nonviolence as the framework for an all-out attack on segregation. For Lawson, who had spent three years

30 in India studying the principles of Gandhi, nonviolence was more than just a protest technique: It was the means by which he ordered his life. The young minister talked about the power of nonviolent confrontation with evil, about overcoming the forces of hate and transforming society through love and forgiveness. At first, Nash was skeptical. How could such high-flown idealism be harnessed as a weapon against gun-toting sheriffs and club-swinging racists? Even after attending several of Lawson's workshops, she still was sure "this stuff is never going to work." But since, as she said, it was "the only game in town," she kept going back, and after weeks of studying

40 theology and philosophy, of reading Thoreau and other advocates of passive resistance, of discussion and arguments with the workshop's other participants, the intense young woman from Chicago was finally captured by Lawson's vision. She was particularly drawn to his

(B) belief that to be effective, these young would-be activists would have to transcend self-hatred and a sense of inferiority, that they would have to learn to love themselves. Having been raised in a **milieu** that downplayed her blackness, she now found herself part of a group "suddenly proud to be called 'black.'" Within the movement . . . we came to a realization of our own worth . . ."

50 In the late fall of 1959, the students at Lawson's workshops formed a central committee to act as the decision-making body for the group. Nash, who had impressed everyone with her clear-eyed thinking and the intensity of her developing commitment to nonviolence, was named to the committee. More and more, the students were turning to her as one of their main leaders.

2. **◀ REREAD** Reread lines 26–49. Why was Nash drawn to the idea of the activists learning "to love themselves"? Support your answer with explicit textual evidence.

In the past, Nash had "downplayed her blackness," so the idea of African Americans recognizing their "own worth" and learning to be "proud to be called 'black'" was an important idea for her.

Nash is upset by their indifference, and inspired to take action. Their apathy led Nash to like-minded people.

Upset with Nashville's segregation laws, Nash becomes involved in nonviolent practices.

milieu:
environment

---

1. **READ AND CITE TEXT EVIDENCE** Explain to students that segregation had been part of southern life for many generations. People took it for granted.

(A) **ASK STUDENTS** to compare and contrast Nash's opinion of segregation with that of her fellow students at Fisk University. *Students should understand that Nash, who was from the northern city of Chicago, where segregation was not as severe, was "outraged" by the experience of being relegated to second-class citizenship. On the other hand, her classmates were used to segregation, "did not seem to care," and basically just went about with their lives.* What did Nash think of her classmates' reaction? *She found it even more upsetting than the segregation itself.*

Critical Vocabulary: epiphany (line 1) Have students share their definitions of *epiphany*. What made Nash's moment at the state fair an epiphany? *It was an epiphany because she experienced something that made her realize the true meaning of segregation.*

2. **REREAD AND CITE TEXT EVIDENCE**

(B) **ASK STUDENTS** why black Americans raised in the South might have a "sense of inferiority." *Students should realize that southern blacks encountered segregation every day of their lives. To survive, they might adapt, unconsciously accepting their position as second-class citizens.* Why might Nash also have had a "sense of inferiority"? *She was raised in Chicago, where segregation wasn't so bad, but it was an environment that "downplayed her blackness."* What mental change did Nash and other activists have to accomplish? *They had to learn to be proud of their blackness instead of downplaying it or hating themselves.*

Critical Vocabulary: milieu (line 46) Have students suggest synonyms of the noun *milieu*. *setting, background, location*

FOR ELL STUDENTS Ask students to try to infer the meaning of the idiomatic phrase *clear-eyed thinking* (line 52). *The phrase means "perceptive thinking," "smart thinking," or "thinking that is not muddled."*

CLOSE READ
Notes

> *What am I doing? And how is this little group of students my age going to stand up to these powerful people?*

The committee had chosen the lunch counters and restaurants of Nashville's downtown stores as the target of the students' first protest, scheduled for February 1960. For the next several months, the students underwent rigorous training to prepare for the upcoming
60 sit-ins, and on February 13, 124 students left a Nashville church and made their way to the lunch counters of several downtown stores. There, they took their seats and asked for service. The men wore suits and ties, the women, dresses, stockings, and high heels. They were poised and polite and gave little outward sign of the fear many of them felt. Diane Nash, for one, was terrified—a terror that would never leave her, no matter how many sit-ins and protests she would participate in afterward.

As frightened as the students were during that first sit-in, however, they had to struggle to keep from laughing at the stunned, panicky
70 reactions of white store workers and **patrons**, who acted, Nash recalled, as if these well-dressed young people were "some dreadful monster . . . about to devour them all." Waitresses dropped dishes, cashiers broke down in tears, an elderly white woman almost had a seizure when she opened the door of a store's "white" ladies' room and found two young black women inside.

patron:
customer

There were no arrests and no violence. After a couple of hours, the students left the stores, jubilant that their first foray had gone without a hitch. A second sit-in was planned for the following week. In the meantime, several members of the students' Central Committee came
80 to Nash and asked her to head the group. She was hardworking and outwardly fearless, and she did not seem to have the ego problems that a lot of the men had. "Because she was a woman and not a man, I think Diane never had to go around and do any posturing," said Bernard Lafayette, an American Baptist College student and one of the Nashville movement's leaders. But Nash had no desire to become the recognized head of this movement. Like most young women of that time, she had been raised to stay in the background. The men pressured her into accepting, however, and when she returned to her dorm room, she was so frightened by what she had done that she
90 could hardly keep her legs from collapsing under her. "This is Tennessee," she told herself. "We are going to be coming up against . . . white Southern men who are forty and fifty and sixty years old, who are politicians and judges and owners of businesses, and I am twenty-two years old. What am I *doing*? And how is this little group of students my age going to stand up to these powerful people?"

Once again, she managed to damp down her fear. She joined the other students in the second sit-in, which was as quietly successful as the first. Nevertheless, the city was losing its patience. Nashville
100 officials, deluged by complaints from store owners that the sit-ins were causing whites to stay away from downtown, warned the students not to continue. If the warning wasn't heeded, they made clear, the kids could forget about being treated with kid gloves any longer. Worried about the possibility of violence and arrests, the ministers connected with the movement urged the students to reconsider their plans for another demonstration on February 27.

She was "hardworking," "fearless," and without ego. Committee members pressured her into accepting.

This section is organized chronologically: planning the protests; the first sit-in; the second sit-in; Nash becoming a leader.

3. **READ ▶** As you read lines 56–106, continue to cite textual evidence.

• Underline activists' preparations and actions in the sit-ins.
• Circle how white store workers, patrons, and the city reacted to the sit-ins.
• In the margin, summarize why Nash was made the head of the committee.
• In the margin, explain how this section is organized.

4. **◀ REREAD AND DISCUSS** Reread lines 56–67. In a small group, discuss why the students prepared so intensely for the sit-ins, and why they dressed up for the first protest.

5. **READ ▶** As you read lines 107–123, continue to cite textual evidence. Underline police actions in the February 27 demonstration.

---

3. **READ AND CITE TEXT EVIDENCE**

C **ASK STUDENTS** to find and summarize text evidence of how the activists prepared for and carried out the two sit-ins. *Students should mention the following: the committee chose their first targets (lines 56–57); students underwent training (lines 59–60); students, "poised and polite," undertook the first sit-in (lines 62–64); students left the stores (lines 76–77); the second sit-in was planned (line 78); and Nash and other students successfully carried out the second sit-in (lines 97–99).*

Critical Vocabulary: patron (line 70) Have students share their definitions of *patron*, and ask volunteers to use the noun in sentences. *Example: White patrons were astonished to see blacks seating themselves at the lunch counter.*

4. **REREAD AND DISCUSS USING TEXT EVIDENCE**

D **ASK STUDENTS** to infer reasons for the "rigorous training." *Students should recognize that the sit-in students would possibly be met with violence from customers, store employees, or the Nashville police. Earlier, Nash wondered how nonviolence could work against "gun-toting sheriffs and club-swinging racists" (lines 35–36). For the sit-in to succeed, students would need training in nonviolent methods of demonstration.*

5. **READ AND CITE TEXT EVIDENCE**

E **ASK STUDENTS** to find and summarize evidence for the police's role during the Woolworth's sit-in. *Students should note the following: the police were absent when the students were being beat up (line 115); when the police arrived, they left the attackers alone and instead told the students to leave the lunch counter (lines 116–119); the police arrested the students who were practicing nonviolence for "disorderly conduct" (120–122).*

from "The Most Daring of [Our] Leaders" / Speech from the Democratic National Convention **282e**

CLOSE READ
Notes

With their numbers swelling, the young people refused. In the middle of another snowstorm, more than three hundred of them poured into downtown Nashville. No sooner had some of them sat down at the Woolworth's lunch counter than the ministers' fears proved justified. The demonstrators were met by an opposing force of cursing young white toughs, who yanked them from their stools and threw them to the floor, beat them with fists and clubs, kicked them, spat on them, extinguished lighted cigarettes on their backs and in their hair. The police were nowhere in sight, and when they finally arrived, they approached not the white attackers, but the bruised and shaken demonstrators, who were spattered with mustard and ketchup, spit and blood. "Okay, get up from the lunch counter or we're going to arrest you," one of the cops barked. When no one obeyed, the students were ordered to their feet, arrested for disorderly conduct, and marched out, through a gauntlet of hostile whites, to police paddy wagons. When they looked over their shoulders at the lunch counter, they saw a new wave of students quietly moving in to take their place.

110

120

E

F

---

6. **REREAD** Reread lines 107–123. Explain why the "ministers' fears proved justified" during the sit-in at the Woolworth's lunch counter. In what respect could this sit-in be regarded as a victory? Support your response with explicit textual evidence.

This time the young people were cursed at, beaten, and kicked. The police arrested the demonstrators, not their attackers. Despite the violence and lack of police support, the students didn't give up: "they saw a new wave of students quietly moving in to take their place."

100

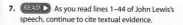

7. **READ** As you read lines 1–44 of John Lewis's speech, continue to cite textual evidence.

• Underline what happened when the Freedom Riders got off the buses, and note in the margin what you can infer about their journey (lines 1–16).

• In the margin, explain the parallels between the Freedom Riders and voting.

Speech from the Democratic National Convention
Speech by John Lewis

I first came to this city in 1961, the year Barack Obama was born. I was one of the 13 original "Freedom Riders." We were on a bus ride from Washington to New Orleans trying to test a recent Supreme Court ruling that banned racial discrimination on buses crossing state lines and in the stations that served them. Here in Charlotte, a young African-American rider got off the bus and tried to get a shoe shine in a so-called white waiting room. He was arrested and taken to jail.

On that same day, we continued on to Rock Hill, South Carolina, about 25 miles. From here, when my seatmate, Albert Bigelow, and I tried to enter a white waiting room, we were met by an angry mob that beat us and left us lying in a pool of blood. Some police officers came up and asked us whether we wanted to press charges. We said, "No, we come in peace, love and nonviolence." We said our struggle was not against individuals, but against unjust laws and customs. Our goal was true freedom for every American.

Since then, America has made a lot of progress. We are a different society than we were in 1961. And in 2008, we showed the world the true promise of America when we elected President Barack Obama. A few years ago, a man from Rock Hill, inspired by President Obama's election, decided to come forward. He came to my office in Washington and said, "I am one of the people who beat you. I want to apologize. Will you forgive me?" I said, "I accept your apology." He started crying. He gave me a hug. I hugged him back, and we both started crying. This man and I don't want to go back; we want to move forward.

10

G

20

H

As the Freedom Riders got closer to New Orleans, they were in more danger.

101

---

6. **REREAD AND CITE TEXT EVIDENCE**

F **ASK STUDENTS** to discuss how the participants in the Woolworth's sit-in might have perceived the day's events. *Students should understand that the sit-in students probably didn't feel like they had won a decisive or even symbolic victory. They had been beat up; the police hadn't helped them or even apprehended their attackers; instead, the police had arrested the protesters themselves, who were the victims of violence. Still, the students could possibly see cause for hope—the nonviolence movement was gaining adherents and it was putting intense public attention on segregation.*

FOR ELL STUDENTS Explain that the word *swelling* (line 107) refers to numbers—the numbers got greater.

7. **READ AND CITE TEXT EVIDENCE**

G **ASK STUDENTS** to make and support inferences about the journey of the Freedom Riders. *Students can infer that at least some southern police wanted to enforce the law or even sympathized with the Freedom Riders. Several officers asked Lewis and his companion if they wanted to press charges against their attackers. Students can also infer that as the Freedom Ride continued south and gained media attention, the response of whites grew more violent. A Freedom Rider was arrested in Charlotte; Lewis and Bigelow were beat up in Rock Hill.*

CLOSE READ
Notes

The Riders were engaged in nonviolent protest to achieve equality, leading to the freedom to vote without restrictions.

Brothers and sisters, do you want to go back? Or do you want to keep America moving forward? My dear friends, your vote is precious, almost sacred. It is the most powerful, nonviolent tool we
30 have to create a more perfect union. Not too long ago, people stood in unmovable lines. They had to pass a so-called literacy test, pay a poll tax. On one occasion, a man was asked to count the number of bubbles in a bar of soap. On another occasion, one was asked to count the jelly beans in a jar—all to keep them from casting their ballots.

Today it is unbelievable that there are officials still trying to stop some people from voting. They are changing the rules, cutting polling hours and imposing requirements intended to suppress the vote.

I've seen this before. I've lived this before. Too many people struggled, suffered and died to make it possible for every American to
40 exercise their right to vote.

And we have come too far together to ever turn back. So we must not be silent. We must stand up, speak up and speak out. We must march to the polls like never before. We must come together and exercise our sacred right.

---

8. **◀ REREAD AND DISCUSS** Reread lines 17–26. With a small group, discuss the anecdote Lewis relates about the man from Rock Hill. In what way did this incident allow both men "to move forward"? Cite text evidence in your discussion.

SHORT RESPONSE

Cite Text Evidence Compare and contrast the texts by Olson and Lewis. What is similar and different in the two accounts? Review your reading notes and be sure to **cite text evidence** in your response.

Olson writes about Nash's experiences so that readers understand the historical importance of her actions. Lewis shares his thoughts and feelings about his experiences to emphasize that people should learn from the past and guard against repeating similar injustices today.

102

---

8. **REREAD AND DISCUSS USING TEXT EVIDENCE**

🅗 **ASK STUDENTS** to compare and contrast the encounters between the two men, from the original beating in Rock Hill to the hug in Washington. *Students should note that the Rock Hill man took part in a violent crime. He must have come to realize how wrong his actions were, for he was "inspired" by the election of the first black President to pay Lewis a visit. He must have felt a lot of guilt over the years. Lewis, although he believed in the nonviolence movement, surely felt some resentment and anger at his attackers. So, to move forward, the man needed forgiveness, while Lewis needed to hear and accept the man's apology.*

SHORT RESPONSE

Cite Text Evidence Students' responses should include text evidence that supports their positions. They should:

- explain how the texts are similar and different.
- give examples of differences of perspective.
- give examples of differences of purpose.

TO CHALLENGE STUDENTS . . .

For greater understanding, students can view the video, *Separate But Not Equal*, in their eBooks.

ASK STUDENTS what had been the legal basis for segregation, despite the Fourteenth Amendment. *The legal doctrine of "separate but equal" allowed government institutions to provide different—but supposedly equivalent—services to white and black citizens.* How did a Supreme Court decision help the civil rights movement? *In 1954, the Supreme Court in the case Brown v. Board of Education unanimously declared that separate was "inherently unequal" and therefore unconstitutional. With its legal justification destroyed, segregation became a major focus of the civil rights movement.*

DIG DEEPER

With the class, return to Question 3, Read. Have students share their underlined texts about the activists' preparations.

ASK STUDENTS to discuss the activists' clothing and demeanor during the sit-in.

- What was the importance of the men's "suits and ties" and the women's "dresses, stockings, and high heels"? *Students should recognize that the protesters wanted to send a message to white owners, employees, and customers. Segregation essentially told blacks that they were "inferior" and thus "unfit to use the same facilities" as whites. By dressing their best, the students were countering with their own message: they were equal and deserved equal treatment.*

- Why was it important for the students to be "poised and polite?" *Again, the students wanted to send a message. By behaving politely in a dangerous situation, they showed that they were equal, not inferior, to white patrons. Also, they were practicing nonviolence, so poise and politeness were probably parts of their strategy.*

ASK STUDENTS to return to their Short Response answer and revise it based on the class discussion.

my SmartPlanner Create lesson plans and access resources online.

from Uprising

Historical Novel by Margaret Peterson Haddix

Why This Text?

Students will often encounter works of historical fiction in their personal reading or in their reading at school. Understanding how an author uses elements of storytelling to bring a historical event to life will help students become more astute readers. This lesson also asks students to compare historical fiction and nonfiction texts to understand the important differences between the genres.

Key Learning Objective: The student will be able to analyze points of view in a text and compare and contrast different genres.

For practice and application:

Close Reader selection
from Doris Is Coming
Short Story by ZZ Packer

COMMON CORE Common Core Standards

RL 1 Cite textual evidence.

RL 2 Provide an objective summary.

RL 3 Analyze story elements.

RL 4 Determine the meaning of words and phrases.

RL 6 Analyze point of view.

RL 9 Compare and contrast fictional and historical accounts of the same event.

W 3 Write a narrative based on a historical event.

W 4 Produce clear and organized writing.

W 5 Revise, edit, and rewrite to strengthen writing.

W 9 Draw evidence from literary and historical texts to support analysis, reflection, and research.

W 10 Write routinely for longer/shorter time frames.

L 1a Explain the function of phrases and clauses.

L 5 Demonstrate understanding of figurative language.

L 5b Use an analogy to better understand words.

▲ Text Complexity Rubric

Quantitative Measures	*from* Uprising Lexile: 800L
Qualitative Measures	**Levels of Meaning/Purpose** ●—●—●—●—▶ single level of simple meaning (single theme)
	Structure ●—●—●—●—▶ some unconventional story structure elements
	Language Conventionality and Clarity ●—●—●—●—▶ increased, clearly assigned dialogue
	Knowledge Demands ●—●—●—●—▶ unfamiliar, multiple perspectives
Reader/Task Considerations	Teacher determined Vary by individual reader and type of text

Margaret Peterson Haddix Have students read the information about the author. Tell students that nearly a decade before the Triangle fire, the Iroquois Theater in Chicago went up in flames and killed over 500 people because they couldn't get out of the building. Across the country, building codes for public spaces were changed in response to the tragedy in Chicago. Despite the tragedy of the Triangle fire, there were positive and lasting reforms made in the areas of worker safety. When details of the fire and the working conditions in the Asch Building became public, people in New York and across the country protested on behalf of safer working conditions. Some of the reforms made after the Triangle fire are still followed in today's workplace buildings.

SETTING A PURPOSE Direct students to use the Setting a Purpose prompt to focus their reading. Remind students to generate questions as they read.

Analyze Point of View

 COMMON CORE RL 6

(LINES 7–10)

Explain to students that in fiction the **narrator** is the voice that tells the story. The author's choice of a narrator is called the **point of view,** which gives readers a specific perspective on the story. In *Uprising*, the author uses **third-person limited,** which has the following characteristics:

- The narrator is not a character and is outside the story.
- The narrator uses third-person pronouns, such as *he, she, him, her, their.*
- The reader sees the story events and other characters through the eyes of one character, who is often the main character of the story.

Explain that lines 7–10 are italicized to indicate internal dialogue, meaning this is what the character Yetta is thinking to herself.

A ASK STUDENTS what the internal dialogue in lines 7–10 reveals about Yetta. *(Possible answer: It reveals that Yetta is hard on herself and expects more than what she has recently accomplished.)*

Margaret Peterson Haddix (b. 1964) *grew up on a farm in Ohio. While her father was a farmer and her mother a nurse, Haddix always wanted to be a writer. Her inspiration was her father, who was always telling her stories. Haddix has now written more than a dozen books for young adults. Asked why she likes writing for young audiences, Haddix replies that teenagers are naturally great characters in books—often more interesting than adults.*

from
Uprising

Historical Novel by Margaret Peterson Haddix

SETTING A PURPOSE This fiction excerpt is based on the real-life event of the Triangle Factory Fire. As you read, think about how the author has used facts and her own imagination to make the events of the fire come to life.

Yetta

Yetta was listening for the bell on the time clock, waiting to finish her day. It was a Saturday afternoon in March, and the spring breezes were back. She'd heard them rattling the windows when the machines were shut down for lunch; she knew that as soon as she stepped outside, they'd tease at her hair and tug at her hat. This year, the breezes seemed to carry a slightly different message: *Another year past and what do you have to show for yourself? So you can read English a little bit better, so you handed out a few suffrage[1] flyers—do you*
10 *think that that's enough?*

What would ever be enough for Yetta?

---

[1] **suffrage:** the right or privilege of voting.

Uprising **283**

SCAFFOLDING FOR ELL STUDENTS

Characters' Thoughts Explain to students that the author tells this fiction story in three parts and that each part tells how one character experiences the events of the Triangle Factory Fire. Have students reread lines 1–10 with you. Point out that this paragraph introduces one of the three characters, named Yetta. Point out the words in italic type and explain that these are words that show what Yetta is thinking. Continue on in the selection to an example of dialogue that Yetta is speaking. Have students reread the dialogue and discuss the differences between the internal dialogue and dialogue spoken aloud. Explain that as they read students can look for other examples of italicized text that shows each character's thoughts.

ASK STUDENTS why they think the author uses a different type of text to show what a character is thinking.

(t) ©The Backstage Studio/Adams Literary; (l) ©SuperStock/SuperStock; (r) ©Lewis Hine/Kheel Center/Cornell University

Compare and Contrast: Genres (LINES 23–26)

COMMON CORE RL 1, RL 3, RL 9

Explain to students that **historical fiction** is a type of story that is set in the past and includes real places and events. Authors base the stories on facts and research, but they use their imaginations to create scenes, dialogue, and sometimes even characters to tell the story.

B CITE TEXT EVIDENCE Have students reread lines 23–26. What does the author's description of the characters' actions reveal about the real-life working conditions at the factory? *(Yetta and Jennie both stand up and stretch "cramped muscles," unhunch "rounded shoulders," and stamp their feet to wake up "feet that had gone numb on the sewing machine pedal." This suggests that the work the women did was physically demanding and potentially damaging to their bodies.)* Have students reread lines 21–30 of the excerpt from *Flesh & Blood So Cheap* and note how that description of the working conditions compares to this description. *(The description in the informational text does not describe the effect the conditions have on the workers' bodies, as does the historical fiction, but it allows readers to visualize the working conditions that make Yetta and Jennie feel the way they do.)*

CRITICAL VOCABULARY

mischievous: The author describes the little dance Jennie does as mischievous.

ASK STUDENTS why Jennie's dance might be considered mischievous. *(because dancing in the factory might not be allowed; because Jennie is teasing Yetta about Jacob, who had asked Yetta to go dancing with him)*

"I think they set the clocks back again," the girl beside her muttered. "It's got to be past quitting time!"

"And that's why we need a strong union, why we need a closed shop," Yetta muttered back.

The girl rolled her eyes at Yetta.

"Don't you ever give up?" she asked over the clatter of the machine.

20 "No," Yetta said, but she grinned at the girl, and the girl grinned back, and Yetta thought maybe, just maybe, they'd inched just a little closer to the solidarity[2] Yetta longed for. This girl's name was Jennie, and she was new.

The bell finally rang, and Yetta and Jennie both stood up and stretched, reviving cramped muscles, unhunching rounded shoulders, stamping feet that had gone numb on the sewing machine pedal.

"I'm going dancing tonight," Jennie said, **mischievously** tapping out a rhythm on the floor. "What are you doing?"

"Um . . . I don't know," Yetta said. "I haven't decided yet."

30 Bella and Jane had been nagging her to go visit Rahel and the new baby, a little boy they'd named Benjamin. Bella and Jane had already gone once, but Yetta had had a cold then and only sent her regrets.

Well, really, I wouldn't want the baby getting sick because of me, Yetta told herself. *Maybe I'm not well enough, even yet. . . .*

"I bet that cutter who watches you all the time would take you dancing," Jennie said. "All you have to do is just . . ." She pantomimed cozying up to an invisible man, gazing up adoringly at the invisible man's face, fluttering her eyelashes.

40 Yetta blushed.

"There's not a cutter who watches me all the time," she said, but she couldn't help glancing toward Jacob's table. Jacob hadn't said a word to her about dancing since she'd turned down his invitation, all those months ago. But he did seem to find lots of reasons to walk past her sewing machine, to ride in the same elevator with her, morning and evening. Even halfway across the room, she could instantly pick out his figure in the cluster of cutters standing around laughing and talking and smoking. Jacob was bent over the table, smoothing

50 out the layers of lawn fabric ready to be cut first thing Monday morning. There had to be at least a hundred and twenty layers

mischievous (mǐs´chə-vəs) *adj.* If someone is *mischievous*, the person is naughty.

---

[2] **solidarity:** unity, especially in the case of workers joining together in a union.

WHEN STUDENTS STRUGGLE ...

To be sure students understand the series of events in a rapidly developing plot, it can help to break down each action in the series. In lines 69–86, the author describes the quick spread of the fire and Yetta's realization of the danger.

Have students reread lines 69–86. In pairs, have them fill out a cause-and-effect chain like the one shown. Explain that the chain will help them clearly understand what is happening in this part of the story leading to Yetta's realization. When they are finished, have students paraphrase what happened in their own words. Encourage students to continue with this strategy as they read or reread the selection.

of the gauzy fabric spread across the table, each one separated
from the others by sheer tissue paper. Jacob handled it all
so gently, almost lovingly. Above his head, the tissue-paper
patterns dangled from wires, so when he stood up it was like
watching someone across a forest, half hidden by hanging
moss and low branches.

Suddenly Jacob and the other cutters jumped back. One
of the men sprinted over to a shelf on the wall and seized a
60 red fire pail. Jerkily, he raced back and threw the pail of water
under one of the tables, at the huge bin of fabric scraps left
over from days and days of cutting out shirtwaists.

"Not again! Those cutters and their cigarettes," Yetta said
scornfully. It was clear what had happened: One of them had
dropped a match or a cigarette butt or a still-burning ember
into the scrap bin. At least someone was smart enough to keep
buckets of water around, if the cutters couldn't be stopped
from smoking.

But then there was a flash, and Yetta saw the flame jump,
70 from under the table to the top of it. More men grabbed
buckets, desperately pouring water onto the flames, but
there'd been only three buckets on that shelf, so they had to
run across the room for more.

The water was nothing to the fire. The flames raced
the length of the lawn fabric; they sprang up to the
dangling paper patterns and danced from one to the next,
the patterns writhing[3] down to ash and spitting off more
flames. In seconds the fire had gone from being something
to scoff at under a table to a voracious beast ready to engulf
80 the entire room.

Beside Yetta, Jennie began to scream.

"Stop it! This is a fireproof building!" Yetta yelled at
Jennie.

But we're tinder,[4] she remembered.

Yetta slammed her hands against Jennie's shoulders and
screamed, "Go!"

The aisle between the sewing machine tables was narrow,
and the wicker baskets where they stacked the shirtwaists kept
snagging their skirts. And other girls were blocking the aisle,
90 some screaming and hysterical like Jennie'd been. One girl

scorn
(skôrn) *n.* Scorn is
disrespect or disdain.

---
[3] **writhing:** twisting.
[4] **tinder:** material that burns easily.

Uprising **285**

CLOSE READ

Compare and Contrast: Genres (LINES 63–68)

 COMMON CORE RL 1, RL 9

Remind students that this is a fictionalized account
of the Triangle Factory Fire that they read about
earlier in Collection 6. Point out that lines 31–44 of
the excerpt from *Flesh & Blood So Cheap* describe how
the fire started. In lines 63–68 of *Uprising*, the author
depicts the same event.

C **CITE TEXT EVIDENCE** Have students reread
lines 31–44 of *Flesh & Blood So Cheap* and then reread
lines 63–68 of *Uprising*. Ask students to cite evidence
of the similarities between the two accounts and
how the author's description of the scene in *Uprising*
reveals it to be historical fiction. *(The cutters are
smoking in each account, and the fire starts beneath
a cutting table; in Uprising, Yetta is commenting on
the cutters and what their smoking caused, as well as
the fact that some of them had sense enough to keep
water nearby.)*

CRITICAL VOCABULARY

scorn: The author uses the word *scornfully* to
convey how disgusted Yetta is about the cutters
and their smoking in the factory.

ASK STUDENTS why Yetta feels such disdain at the
cutters starting a small fire that she looks at them
scornfully. *(because it's dangerous and seems like it's
something the cutters do too often)*

Cause	Effect	Effect	Effect
fire spreads to table top	water won't put out fire	fire burns up fabric and spreads quickly	Jennie screams, but Yetta tells her not to worry.

CLOSE READ

Analyze Story Elements

COMMON CORE **RL 3**

(LINES 91–103)

Explain to students that authors reveal information about characters through text details such as dialogue (what the characters say out loud), actions, internal thoughts, and interactions with other characters. In this section, the author depicts two different sides of Yetta's character.

 ASK STUDENTS to reread lines 91–103 and describe what change in Yetta's character is depicted. *(At first she's trying to help others escape, but when she sees the woman fall out of the eighth-story window, she panics and freezes, realizing she might die.)*

---

 fainted right at Yetta's feet. Yetta reached down and slapped her, jerked her up.

"No time for that!" Yetta screamed. "You'll die!"

Across the room, Yetta saw a spark land in a woman's hair. In seconds, the woman's whole pompadour[5] was aflame. Everyone was screaming, but Yetta thought she could hear this woman's screams above all the others. The woman lurched across the room, slammed into one of the windows. No— slammed through. She'd thrown herself out the window.

100 *We're on the eighth floor,* Yetta thought numbly, and now it was her turn to freeze in panic and fear. Sparks were flying throughout the room now, landing everywhere. Anyone could be next.

Hands grabbed Yetta from behind.

"Yetta, come on!"

It was Jacob.

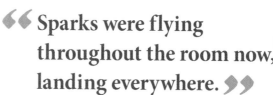 

> ❝ **Sparks were flying throughout the room now, landing everywhere.** ❞

Jacob and Yetta shoved forward, toward the Washington Place stairs, pulling along Jennie and the girl who'd fainted. Yetta glanced back once more and was relieved to see that
110 Mr. Bernstein, the factory manager, had had some of the men pull a fire hose out of the Greene Street stairwell. He stood over the worst of the flames, pointing the hose confidently.

No water came out.

"Turn it on! Turn it on!" Mr. Bernstein was screaming. Yetta wasn't sure if she could hear him or if she was just reading his lips. "Where is the water?" he screamed again.

Not a drop. He flung down the hose and ran.

---

[5] **pompadour:** a woman's hairstyle.

APPLYING ACADEMIC VOCABULARY

despite	inadequate	interact

As you discuss the text, incorporate the following Collection 6 academic vocabulary words: *despite, inadequate,* and *interact*. Discuss how **inadequate** the safety measures at the factory were in case of a major fire. Discuss how the fire and the various characters **interact** throughout the story and how, **despite** the terrifying obstacles, the characters continue with their efforts to escape.

Now Mr. Bernstein was rushing through the crowds
of girls, some still heading toward the cloakroom[6] to get
120 their hats.

"Don't worry about your hats!" he screamed. "Just get out!"

He was slapping and punching the girls, beating them
as though he blamed them for the fire. No—he was goading
them toward the doors, toward the elevators and the fire
escape. He was only slapping the hysterical girls, like Yetta
had done with the girl who'd fainted. He was trying to save
their lives.

We are on the same side now, Mr. Bernstein and me,
Yetta **marveled**.

130 She shoved against a girl who'd dropped her purse, who'd
seen her coins roll under the table.

"Don't stop for that!" Yetta screamed. "It's not worth it!
Save your life!"

She and Jacob together pulled the girl up, lifting her past
the table, toward the door. There were already dozens of
other girls crowded around the door, screaming in Yiddish
and English and what Yetta now recognized as Italian. "Open
it! Open it!" "Oh, please, for the love of God!" "*Madonna
mia, aiutami!*"

140 But it was locked.

Some of the girls were pounding on the elevator door,
too, screaming for the elevator operator to come to them.
Miraculously, the elevator door opened, and the crowd surged
forward, sobbing and praying and screaming.

"Just wait—just wait—I'll come right back!" the operator
hollered.

The doors were closing, but Yetta shoved Jennie forward,
shoving her on top of the girls already in the elevator. Saving
her, at least.

150 "*Will* he come back?" Yetta asked Jacob, and Jacob
shrugged.

Yetta couldn't just stand there and wait. She wasn't going
to stand still while the flames raced toward her, while others
pressed their faces against a door that might never open. She
grabbed Jacob's hand and pulled him along, circling around
the fire. She looked back once and saw that someone had
managed to open the door to the Washington Place stairs;

---

[6] **cloakroom:** a room where coats are hung up.

marvel
(märˊvəl) *v.* If you
marvel at something,
you are surprised or
astonished by it.

CLOSE READ

Analyze Point of View

COMMON CORE RL 1, RL 6

(LINES 118–129)

The author describes the actions of one of the
managers of the factory from Yetta's perspective.

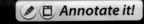 **CITE TEXT EVIDENCE** Have students reread
lines 118–129, and ask them to identify why Yetta
thinks she and Mr. Bernstein were on the same side.
*(Possible answer: He slapped and punched some of the
hysterical girls to make them keep moving toward the
doors, which is similar to what Yetta did to a couple of
the women who were panicking.)*

> **CRITICAL VOCABULARY**
>
> **marvel:** The author uses the word *marveled* to
> described Yetta's reaction to what Mr. Bernstein
> was doing.
>
> **ASK STUDENTS** how Yetta feels about her
> realization that she and Mr. Bernstein are "on the
> same side now"? *(Yetta is a union organizer, and Mr.
> Bernstein probably fought against her efforts to start
> a union. When lives are on the line, she is surprised to
> see that they can work together for the same goal.)*

Strategies for Annotation   **Annotate it!**

Analyze Point of View

COMMON CORE RL 6

Share these strategies for identifying point of view:

- Highlight in blue the phrases that reveal Yetta's point of view.
- Highlight in yellow the actions Yetta takes.
- Add a note that describes Yetta's perspective on the actions of the
  other women.

Yetta couldn't just stand there and wait. She wasn't going
to stand still while the flames raced toward her, whi[
pressed their faces against a door that might never o[
grabbed Jacob's hand and pulled him along, circling
the fire. She looked back once and saw that someone had
managed to open the Washington Place stairs;

Yetta sees that
what the others are
doing isn't going to
be effective.

Compare and Contrast: Genres (LINES 161–165)

COMMON CORE RL 1, RL 9

Remind students that *Uprising* is based on factual details of the Triangle Factory Fire.

 CITE TEXT EVIDENCE Have students read lines 91–96 of the excerpt from *Flesh & Blood So Cheap* and then reread lines 161–165 of *Uprising*. Ask students to cite details that are similar in each account of the spreading fire. *("cans of oil," "the oiled floor," "finished shirtwaists," "fabric scraps," "the air itself seemed to catch fire," and "the air itself seemed to be on fire.")* Point out the similar detail in both accounts of the air seeming to be on fire. Ask students what would likely be the source of this detail that makes it a fact and not an image from the author's imagination. *(The image that the air "seemed to be on fire" likely came from an interview or account of someone who was on the ninth floor and survived the fire.)*

CRITICAL VOCABULARY

singe: The author describes what happens when a spark of flame lands on Yetta's arm.

ASK STUDENTS to describe why Yetta was horrified when the spark singed her arm. *(Sample answer: She'd watched the fabrics in the factory go up in flames so quickly she feared the spark was going to light her clothes ablaze.)*

---

the door opened in, toward the crowd. Maybe it hadn't been locked after all. Maybe it was just the weight of the crowd
160 pushing forward, pinning it shut.

But it was too late to go back now. Flames were shooting across the path they'd just crossed, speeding across the oiled floor, licking up shirtwaists and fabric scraps and wicker baskets. The air itself seemed to be on fire, the flames living on fabric dust.

"Fire escape," Yetta moaned to Jacob, and it was so hot now that her words felt like flames themselves, painful on her tongue.

"No good," Jacob mumbled back. "Doesn't go all the way
170 to the ground."

So they didn't head for the window near the airshaft, where people were climbing out one at a time, onto the rickety metal railing. What was left?

"Greene Street stairs," Jacob whispered.

Those were back by the table where the fire had started, where it now burned the fiercest. But there was a partition wall blocking off the stairs and the elevator from the rest of the room. On a normal workday that was where the guard sat, inspecting purses and glaring at the girls as if he thought they
180 were all thieves. Today, maybe that partition was enough to keep the fire away from the stairs.

Yetta and Jacob raced on, skirting the flames, still pulling along hysterical, senseless workers who didn't seem to know where to go. They passed a desk where the bookkeeper, Miss Lipshutz, was shouting into the mouthpiece of a telephone, "Please! Somebody listen! Somebody's got to tell the ninth floor! Hello? Somebody—please!"

A spark landed on the sleeve of Yetta's shirtwaist, and she watched in horror as it sputtered and shimmered and burned
190 straight through. She could feel it **singeing** her skin.

Jacob slapped his bare hand onto Yetta's sleeve, starving the flame.

"*A dank,*[7]" Yetta whispered, but there was no time for him to say, "You're welcome," because they were at the doorway to the partition now, shoving their way behind it.

No flames here.

singe
(sĭnj) *v.* If you *singe* something, you slightly burn it.

---

[7] **a dank** (ă dănk): "thank you" in the Yiddish language.

Girls were still standing by the freight elevator door, the only elevator they were normally allowed to use. They were pounding on the closed door like they thought that was their
200 only chance. It was so hot behind the partition that Yetta could barely breathe.

Can people melt? she wondered. In her mind she saw wax dripping down from Sabbath[8] candles. *My life, melting away . . .*

"Stairs!" Jacob screamed at the girls by the elevator door.

He jerked open the stairway door and it opened out, making another obstacle in the tiny vestibule. Yetta and Jacob shoved the girls through the doorway and scrambled in behind them. The stairway was airless and close and still
210 hot, but there were no sparks flying through the air. Through the window in the stairwell, Yetta could see the workers scrambling down the fire escape, teetering precariously on the metal railings, struggling past the metal shutters.

"Hurry!" Yetta screamed at the girls around her. They were sobbing hysterically, clutching the railing, clutching each other. They were yammering away in some language Yetta didn't recognize, or maybe it wasn't a language at all, just witless jabbering.

> ## **They were sobbing hysterically, clutching the railing, clutching each other.**

"The fire!" one of them managed to say. "What if it's
220 everywhere?"

"There's no smoke coming from down there!" Yetta screamed at them, pointing at the landings below them. "Go down to the ground! You'll be safe! The flames are going up, not down!"

Up.

---

[8] **Sabbath:** the day of worship in the Jewish and other religions.

CLOSE READ

Analyze Figurative Language (LINES 202–204)

COMMON CORE · RL 4, L 5

Remind students that a **metaphor** is a form of analogy comparing two unlike objects or ideas. Have students reread lines 202–204, in which the author employs a candle metaphor.

H **ASK STUDENTS** why the author chose to use a candle metaphor for Yetta's life at this point in the story. *(Possible answer: The author uses the candle metaphor because Yetta is caught in a fire, picturing in her mind religious candles melting. She had seemed afraid about the direction of her own life earlier in the story. Now, she is afraid that her life will actually melt away like the wax in a candle.)*

Compare and Contrast: Genres (LINES 205–213)

COMMON CORE · RL 1, RL 9

Point out that the author of *Uprising* is describing details that were also recounted in lines 5–7 of the history writing in the excerpt from *The Story of the Triangle Factory Fire* by Zachary Kent.

I **CITE TEXT EVIDENCE** Have students reread lines 5–7 of the history writing and lines 205–213 of the historical fiction text. Ask students to cite examples of how the author of *Uprising* took these details and expanded them into fiction. *(In the history writing, there is the brief mention of this detail: "Doors that opened inward instead of outward, overcrowding in work areas, and blocked exits also were to blame." In Uprising, the author has added details that expand on these details to make the story come to life: Jacob "jerked open the stairway door and it opened out, making another obstacle in the tiny vestibule." Additional details, such as Jacob shoving the girls through the doorway, where the stairway was "airless and still hot," show that, for a second, the women and Jacob are safe.)*

Analyze Point of View **RL 6**

(LINES 237–243)

Explain to students that the author often uses italicized text to indicate what the character is thinking. Because the author is using third-person limited point of view, readers are only allowed to see the interior thoughts of the primary character the author has chosen.

J **ASK STUDENTS** to reread lines 237–243 and ask them why Yetta feels compelled to warn the workers on the ninth floor. (*Sample answer: Her friend Bella is on the ninth floor, but Yetta also feels responsible for her fellow workers because she is a union organizer.*)

Yetta glanced up to the landing above her, remembering what the bookkeeper had been screaming into the phone: *Somebody listen! Somebody's got to tell the ninth floor!*

They didn't know. One flight up, on the ninth floor, where
230 two hundred and fifty girls worked, where Yetta had worked before the strike, where Bella worked now—up there, they had no idea there was an inferno raging beneath them, eating up the air, climbing higher and higher and higher.

Almost on their own, Yetta's feet had already started slapping down the stairs, once she finally got the jabbering girls moving. But now she stopped.

Bella, she thought. My other friends. *My sisters. My comrades. My unio*n.

"What are you doing?" Jacob screamed, already three
240 steps down.

"Somebody has to tell the ninth floor!" she screamed back. "I have to!"

She turned around and began clattering up the stairs.

Strategies for Annotation

Compare and Contrast: Genres **RL 9**

Share these strategies for guided or independent analysis:

- Historical fiction authors base their stories on the facts of an event.
- In the excerpt, highlight in yellow the information that likely can be verified by researching the facts of the Triangle Factory Fire.
- Underline the text that appears to be fiction.

Yetta glanced up to the landing above her, remembering what the bookkeeper had been screaming into the phone: *Somebody listen! Somebody's got to tell the ninth floor!*

They didn't know. One flight up, on the ninth floor, where two hundred and fifty girls worked, where Yetta had worked

Jane

"Papa's taking us shopping! Papa's taking us shopping!" Harriet chanted, bouncing up and down joyously in the elevator on the way to Mr. Blanck's office at the Triangle factory.

"Hush. Everybody knows that," Millicent said scornfully.

250 "She's just excited," Jane said mildly. She patted Harriet's shoulder, trying to calm her down, and gave Millicent and the elevator operator a sympathetic smile. Harriet's chanting was a bit maddening. But, as always, it was hard to know the best way to handle the girls. Miss Milhouse would have scolded Harriet soundly; she would have taken it as her personal mission to **stifle** the little girl's exuberant personality. And she would have praised Millicent to the skies for her tidiness, her aversion to noise and mess, her ability to sit or stand still practically forever without squirming or exclaiming.

Personally, Jane thought Millicent was in danger of
260 becoming a priggish bore. And she worried that someday somebody *would* stifle Harriet's exuberance.

"Make it be like a stream," Bella had advised her, when Jane had asked for help. "You don't want to chop her off—*bam!*" She'd slammed the side of her right hand against her left palm. "But make it go a good way."

"You mean, I should try to channel her enthusiasm into positive outlets?" Jane asked.

After Jane explained what "channel," "enthusiasm," "positive," and "outlets" meant, Bella grinned and nodded:
270 "Yes, yes, exactly! You say what is in my heart for that girl!"

Now, as the elevator zoomed upward, Harriet began tugging on the elevator operator's jacket.

"Mister, you didn't know we were going shopping, did you? Papa's taking us as a treat, because our mama went to Florida for the—what's it called?—social season. And she took the car with her, on the train, so we had to take a taxi cab to get here, and the taxi cab's still waiting outside, for us to come back. Except Madam'selle Michaud's not going shopping with us, just Papa, and—"
280 "Harriet," Jane said warningly.

"She's okay," the elevator operator said. "You're the Blanck girls, right? The boss's daughters?"

stifle
(stī´fəl) *v.* If you *stifle* something, you hold it back.

CLOSE READ

Analyze Point of View
(LINES 248–261)

COMMON CORE RL 1, RL 6

Point out to students that this section, titled "Jane," is told from the point of view of the governess for the children of one of the Triangle factory owners, Mr. Blanck. Explain that a governess is a woman who is hired by families to educate and train the children. Point out that shifting points of view from one character to another allows an author to explore more deeply a character who might have been mentioned only in passing in an earlier part of the story. It also tells the same story from another perspective.

K **CITE TEXT EVIDENCE** Have students reread lines 248–261 and cite evidence of Jane's relationship with her boss at the Blanck household. What does this evidence reveal about Jane's job? *(Here, the author is noting how Miss Milhouse usually reacts to the two Blanck girls. The details are not in italicized print, so they are not shared as Jane's actual thoughts. The author as narrator is telling them to the reader. The author notes that Miss Milhouse would have scolded Harriet and praised Millicent. It's clear, however, that Jane likes "Harriet's exuberance" and thinks Millicent is "in danger of becoming a priggish bore." This suggests that Jane and her boss do not see eye to eye when it comes to dealing with the children, which might make Jane's job difficult for her.)*

CRITICAL VOCABULARY

stifle: The author describes Miss Milhouse's actions as holding back young Harriet's lively personality.

ASK STUDENTS why Jane might be concerned about Harriet being stifled. *(Jane might be afraid that with too much negative feedback from Miss Milhouse Harriet will stop being such an energetic and curious child.)*

Analyze Story Elements

COMMON CORE · RL 1, RL 3

(LINES 293–315)

Explain to students that authors use **dialogue,** written conversations between two or more characters, to bring characters to life and give the reader some insight into the character's personality.

🄛 **CITE TEXT EVIDENCE** Have students reread lines 293–315. What is Jane's attitude toward Harriet's questions? Ask students to cite specific evidence in the passage to support their answer. *(Jane tries to answer Harriet's questions directly and logically, saying "There are scientific reasons" that the elevator would not go through the roof. Then, when Harriet keeps asking more questions, Jane realizes she doesn't have the answers and says they'll have to research the answer at a bookstore. This suggests Jane does not want to just dismiss or mislead Harriet like Millicent does.)*

> #### CRITICAL VOCABULARY
>
> **reprove:** The author says Jane gives Millicent a reproving look, suggesting Jane doesn't like what the girl has said.
>
> **ASK STUDENTS** for examples when a student might receive a reproving look from an adult or an authority figure. *(Sample answers: when someone says something that embarrasses a parent; when someone treats a sibling poorly)*

"Our papa and Uncle Isaac own the whole factory," Millicent bragged. "They employ more than seven hundred people."

"Millicent!" Jane shot the girl a **reproving** look. *Remember what I've told you about bragging?* she wanted to scold. But she'd always hated Miss Milhouse correcting her in front of other people, so she'd vowed not to do that to Millicent or
290 Harriet. It was just really tempting at times like this. *First thing Monday morning, I need to have a little talk with both girls . . . .*

The elevator was gathering speed. Harriet clutched Jane's hand.

"What if the elevator goes all the way through the roof?" she asked.

"Silly, that would never happen," Millicent scoffed.

"Why not?"

"Because—because it wouldn't be proper," Millicent said.
300 She lowered her voice, as if that would keep the elevator operator from hearing. "If we went through the roof, the people below us could see up our skirts."

The elevator operator's face turned red, he was trying so hard not to laugh.

Jane sighed.

"There are scientific reasons the elevator would never go through the roof," she said. "Because of how the elevator's made, how it works."

"How does it work?" Harriet asked.
310 Oops. Jane had been afraid she'd ask that. Somehow elevator mechanics had not been in the curriculum at Jane's finishing school.

"Next week we can go to the bookstore and find a book that explains it all," Jane said. "Or maybe you can find one with your papa."

"The elevator runs on a cable," the operator said. "The cable goes up to gears, and those are on the roof. Maybe sometime you can ask your papa to show you the gearbox. But if you want to go to the roof, you have to use the Greene Street
320 stairs. That's the only way to get there."

"Thank you," Jane said, smiling gratefully at the operator. He was a pimply boy, maybe a little younger than her. A year ago, he would have been completely invisible to her, but now she wondered about his life. Which country had he come

reprove
(rĭ-prōōv´) *v.* If you *reprove* someone, you express disapproval.

from? Did he bring his family with him, or was he all alone? Was he supporting a widowed mother and a younger brother and sister or two on his salary as an elevator operator? Did Mr. Blanck and Mr. Harris pay him more or less than they paid their sewing machine operators?

330   "Tenth floor," the operator announced, bringing the elevator to a halt and sweeping open the barred door. "Where your papa the boss works."

    He had the slightest hint of mockery in his voice, just enough for Jane to hear. He even gave her a conspiratorial wink, which was much too forward, but somehow Jane didn't mind. She winked back, and stepped out onto the polished wood floor of a spacious reception area.

    "Miss Mary! Miss Mary!" Harriet cried, running over to one of the desks.

340   "Oh, sweetie, Miss Mary's busy right now," said the short, frazzled-looking woman behind the desk. "The switchboard operator didn't come in today, so Miss Mary has to do all her typing *and* connect every call that comes in. The eighth floor can't even call the ninth floor without my help."

    Harriet inspected the telephone switchboard behind the woman's desk, the wires hanging slack.

    "So if you plug in this wire here, then—"

    "Oh, sweetie, don't touch," Miss Mary said, gently pushing Harriet's hand away. "I really don't have time—I'll explain

350 it to you some other day." She looked up at Jane. "You're the governess, right? You can just take them into Mr. Blanck's office, and then go tell him they're here."

    "Where is Mr. Blanck?" Jane asked.

    "Oh, he was just down on the ninth floor—no, wait, back in the storeroom? I'm sorry, I'd look for him myself, but—" The harried secretary gestured at the papers strewn across her desk, the bill poking out from her typewriter.

    A contraption beside the typewriter buzzed, and Miss Mary looked over at it expectantly.

360   "What's that?" Harriet whispered.

    "Oh, it's the new telautograph," Miss Mary said. "'The latest in business machinery,' is how it's advertised. Looks like there's a message coming from the eighth floor. They write something on a pad of paper downstairs, and this pen is supposed to write the same thing on this pad right here."

    "Like magic," Harriet breathed.

CLOSE READ

Analyze Point of View   COMMON CORE   RL 6
(LINES 333–337)

The author describes this silent exchange between Jane and the elevator operator strictly from Jane's point of view.

M   **ASK STUDENTS** to reread lines 333–337 and explain why Jane gladly returns the elevator operator's wink. *(Even though Jane works for a wealthy family, she feels she has more in common with the elevator operator, and this is a way to let him know that she is more like him than the boss's daughters.)*

WHEN STUDENTS STRUGGLE...

Though there is a lot of plot activity and dialogue in this section, the author reveals some important factual information about what was happening on the tenth floor as the fire was burning two floors below.

Have students reread lines 338–366. Ask them to look for information that indicates why there was a lack of communication between the eighth, ninth, and tenth floors when the fire started. Have students record the information in a simple chart like the one shown.

ASK STUDENTS who or what is to blame for the communication problems. *(Possible answers: the phones and telautograph didn't work right; Miss Mary didn't keep up with her switchboard duties; the fire burned up the phone and telautograph lines.)*

Communication Problems
"The eighth floor can't even call the ninth floor without my help."
"Looks like there's a message coming from the eighth floor."
"The pen didn't move."
"It'd be magic if it ever worked right."

Compare and Contrast: Genres (LINES 388–400)

COMMON CORE RL 1, RL 9

Remind students that historical fiction has the advantage of allowing the author to take factual information and embellish the story to make it more engaging to the reader.

(N) CITE TEXT EVIDENCE Have students reread lines 21–27 from the history writing *Flesh & Blood So Cheap* and then read lines 388–400 of *Uprising*. How does the author's description of the ninth floor in *Uprising* make the facts presented in *Flesh & Blood So Cheap* more compelling? *(The* Uprising *author makes the packed room seem even more difficult to work in with hot irons and dangerous gas tubes overhead. The author also describes the workers as looking weary.)*

The pen didn't move.

"It'd be magic if it ever worked right," Miss Mary snorted. "Probably isn't anything anyhow, just the girls downstairs
370 playing with it on their way out the door."

Miss Mary turned back to her typing, and Jane shooed the girls toward Mr. Blanck's office.

"I want to go see the showroom!" Harriet said, skipping down the hall. "Madam'selle Michaud, you'll love it! You can see all the latest fashions before Paris!"

"That's because even Paris doesn't know as much about fashion as our papa," Millicent said, agreeing with her younger sister for once.

"Some other time," Jane said. "Miss Mary said to wait in
380 his office, remember?"

They turned in at a doorway, but the sign on the door said ISAAC HARRIS, not MAX BLANCK.

"Uncle Isaac!" Harriet called.

A man behind a desk waved, but there was another man with him, a dapper-looking gentleman holding up samples of delicate embroidery.[9] Jane flashed an apologetic look at Mr. Harris and pulled the girls away.

"Look, you can see into the pressing department from here," Harriet said, pointing past a break in the wall into
390 a vast open space, where rows and rows of weary-looking workers stood over ironing boards. Each one of the irons was connected to the ceiling by an odd array of tubes.

"Is Papa afraid those workers are going to steal his irons?" Harriet asked. "Is that why the irons are tied up?"

Jane didn't have the slightest idea, so she was glad that Millicent answered first.

"No, silly. The gas comes down those tubes and heats the irons," Millicent said. "Papa says we must never ever go in there, because one of those irons could blister our skin in
400 an instant."

And does he care at all about the workers operating the irons? Jane wondered bitterly. *Some of them look no older than Millicent!*

"Quick, now," she told the girls. "Into the office. Wait right there."

---

[9] **embroidery:** decorative needlework in cloth.

> ❝ **Papa says we must never ever go in there, because one of those irons could blister our skin in an instant.** ❞

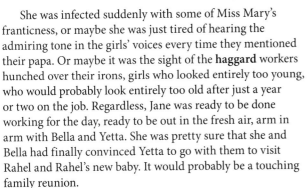

She was infected suddenly with some of Miss Mary's franticness, or maybe she was just tired of hearing the admiring tone in the girls' voices every time they mentioned their papa. Or maybe it was the sight of the **haggard** workers
410 hunched over their irons, girls who looked entirely too young, who would probably look entirely too old after just a year or two on the job. Regardless, Jane was ready to be done working for the day, ready to be out in the fresh air, arm in arm with Bella and Yetta. She was pretty sure that she and Bella had finally convinced Yetta to go with them to visit Rahel and Rahel's new baby. It would probably be a touching family reunion.

Yes, Yetta will be so much happier if she'll just forgive her sister for getting married, Jane thought. *My father and I, on the*
420 *other hand . . .*

She hadn't forgotten her promise to Mr. Corrigan to write her father a letter. She'd written him many, many letters, actually—she'd just torn them all up.

What is there to say?

Jane pulled the door shut on Millicent and Harriet, catching barely a glimpse of Mr. Blanck's imposing mahogany desk, of the lovely arched windows behind the desk. Harriet was scrambling into the huge leather chair.

"Harriet! A young lady would never put her feet up on the
430 desk!" she heard Millicent cry out, in scandalized horror.

Jane decided to let Millicent wage that battle on her own. Secretly, she was thinking, *Oh, Harriet, maybe you should go on being the kind of girl who puts her feet on desks. Better that, than hiding under them . . .*

She scurried down the hall, back to the double elevator doors. She decided to look for Mr. Blanck on the ninth floor first. She knew that was where Bella worked, and it'd be good

haggard
(hăg´ərd) *adj.* If you're *haggard*, you are worn out and exhausted.

(r) ©Photodisc/Getty Images

Uprising **295**

Analyze Point of View COMMON CORE RL 6

(LINES 406–414)

Explain that third-person limited point of view allows the author to explore the character's thoughts and dreams without putting them into dialogue form with another character. In this section, the author is limited to doing this for Jane only.

ASK STUDENTS to reread lines 406–414 and explain why the sight of the workers hunched over their irons agitated Jane and made her want to leave quickly. *(Jane identified with the factory workers and had good friends who worked in the factory, so the sight of the workers reminded her that she is still like them even though she works for the wealthy owner of the factory. She wants to leave quickly because the weekend means free time to do what workers want with their friends and families.)*

CRITICAL VOCABULARY

haggard: This is the second time Jane has observed the worn-out workers and wondered how young they were.

ASK STUDENTS why Jane is concerned with the age of the haggard-looking workers. *(because some of them are about the same age as Millicent, the boss's daughter, who has a much easier life and will not be ground down by work at such a young age)*

Analyze Story Elements

COMMON CORE RL 1, RL 3

(LINES 468–470)

Remind students that authors often include details that reveal traits or qualities about a character without directly stating the traits or qualities. Students can use these details to **infer,** or make good guesses, about the characters.

P **CITE TEXT EVIDENCE** Have students reread lines 468–470 and make an inference about Jane's relationship with Bella. Ask students to cite evidence to support their inferences. *(The author shows Jane's thoughts about Bella: "No wonder Bella felt so overwhelmed, coming here from her tiny little village in Italy." This suggests that Jane is empathetic to her friend and can relate to Bella's feelings about the factory.)*

---

if she could warn Bella that she'd be a few minutes late getting out to the street, especially if it took her a long time to find Mr. Blanck.

Passing Miss Mary's desk, Jane was surprised to notice that the woman had vanished, leaving the telephone receiver hanging off the hook.

That's odd. She seemed like such a conscientious sort . . . .

A different elevator operator came up this time, a swarthily handsome Italian man.

If Bella's precious Pietro looks anything like that, no wonder she can't forget him! Jane thought. Then she had to hide her face so he didn't see her giggling at her own wickedness.

450   The elevator buzzed annoyingly. Again and again and again.

"Eighth floor's going crazy," the elevator operator growled. He scowled at the panel of lights that kept flashing at him as he shut the door behind Jane and the elevator began its descent. "Hold on a minute! I'm coming! I'm coming!"

"They've probably all got spring fever," Jane said. "And it's Saturday."

"Yeah, yeah," the operator grumbled, letting her out on the ninth floor. "But do they gotta take it out on me?"

460   The ninth floor was not what Jane expected. After the cleanliness and elegance of the tenth floor, she wasn't prepared for this dim, dirty space with the tables and the machines and the girls packed in so tightly together. The room was huge, but the tables stretched from one side of the building to the other. By the windows, there wasn't even space to walk around the tables. And shirtwaists and shirtwaist parts were piled everywhere, mountains of fabric by each machine.

P   *No wonder Bella felt so overwhelmed, coming here from her tiny little village in Italy,* Jane thought.

470   Jane herself felt a little overwhelmed.

"Excuse me. Do you know where I could find Mr. Blanck or Bella Rossetti?" she asked the girl at the nearest sewing machine.

The girl looked up blankly, and said something that might have been "I don't speak English" in some other language. Just then a bell sounded, and the machines stopped and hundreds of girls sprang up from their machines all at once. It spooked Jane a little, the darkness of the room and the foreign jabbering and the girls moving like machines, themselves. But

---

Strategies for Annotation 🖉 🗐 *Annotate it!*

Compare and Contrast: Genres

COMMON CORE RL 9

Share these strategies for comparing nonfiction and historical fiction texts:

- Reread the paragraph.
- Highlight in yellow details that might have come from a nonfiction article source like *Flesh & Blood So Cheap.*
- Add a note offering your opinion about whether *Uprising* uses the facts of the Triangle Factory Fire fairly or unfairly.

The historical accounts say that the working conditions at the factory were hideous. Adding fiction details to show this seems very fair.

The ninth floor was not what Jane expecte

cleanliness and elegance of the tenth floor, she

for this dim, dirty space with the tables and machines and

the girls packed in so tightly together. The room was huge,

but the tables stretched from one side of the building to the

other. By the windows, there wasn't even space to walk around

480 then one of the girls stepping out of the cloakroom began to sing, "Ev'ry little movement has a meaning of its own"—one of those popular songs that you heard everywhere, nowadays. Some of the other girls joined in, and they all seemed so light-hearted suddenly. Saturday afternoon and the sun was shining and work was over; these girls looked happier than anyone Jane had ever seen at a formal ball.

Then, two tables away, Jane spotted Bella heading down the aisle between the tables and laughing and talking to the girls around her.

490 "Jane! What are you doing here?" Bella shouted over to her.

> ❝ **Just then a bell sounded, and the machines stopped and hundreds of girls sprang up from their machines all at once.** ❞

"Looking for you and Mr. Blanck," Jane said.

"Well, we wouldn't be together!" Bella called back merrily.

Jane worked her way through the crowd toward her friend. She explained about Millicent and Harriet and the shopping, and how long it would take her to get down to the sidewalk. Then Bella said, "Oh, wait, you have to meet my friends—this is Annie and Dora and Josie and Essie and Ida. And come here—" She pulled her back down the aisle between the tables.

500 "This is my boss, Signor Carlotti. This is my friend, Jane Wellington, Signor Carlotti, and she knows proper Italian *and* proper English."

"Hello," Signor Carlotti said.

"I am a factory inspector," Jane said, suddenly inspired to lie. "If I were to interview the girls in this factory, would they tell me that you treat them with respect? Are you fair to all your workers?"

Uprising **297**

CLOSE READ

Compare and Contrast: Genres (LINES 480–486)

Explain that authors of historical fiction often use a wide range of sources when they write a story. Point out that authors often add historical details not only about the specific event that they are writing about, but also about the time period in which the event is set. They use these details to give a broader view into the popular culture and society of the time.

Q **CITE TEXT EVIDENCE** Ask students to reread lines 480–486 and to cite an example of a cultural detail that likely came from sources about the time period rather than about the Triangle Factory Fire itself. Have students describe how the addition of this detail enhances the story. (*The author includes the detail of the singing of the popular song that begins with the line "Ev'ry little movement has a meaning of its own" and explains through Jane's perspective that it was "one of those popular songs that you heard everywhere, nowadays." This shows that popular music seemed as important and influential to young people of this time period as it is today. This makes it easier to relate to and sympathize with the young women in the factory.*)

Analyze Story Elements (LINES 504–507)

Remind students that we know Jane is very fond of Bella and is looking forward to spending time having fun with her friends.

R **ASK STUDENTS** to reread lines 504–507. Why might Jane decide to lie to Bella's boss? (*Jane is in a good mood and is happy to see her friend, so she may have decided to lie to Bella's boss in a playful way to not only poke fun at him but also to make a point about treating her friend fairly.*)

Analyze Point of View

COMMON CORE **RL 3, RL 6**

(LINES 516–521)

Explain to students that **dramatic irony** occurs when the reader knows something that a character in a story does not know. Because third-person limited point of view only permits the author to reveal one character's thoughts and perspective, it allows the author to create situations of dramatic irony.

(S) ASK STUDENTS how lines 516–521 create dramatic irony in the story. *(Jane thinks she hears Yetta calling out to convince the girls to form a union—"her dearest wish"—but the reader knows that Yetta is trying to save the girls from the fire on the eighth floor—again, Yetta's "dearest wish" at the time.)*

CRITICAL VOCABULARY

wistful: The author uses the word *wistful* to describe Bella's response to Jane's comment.

ASK STUDENTS why Bella might feel wistful about her boss treating her better. *(because Bella's boss probably doesn't treat her or the other girls all that well, and a change in his attitude is something Bella may have hoped for since she started working there)*

At the first word out of her mouth, Signor Carlotti's face changed—first, to awe at her upper-class accent, then to fear.

510   "Oh, er—yes! Yes! Of course!" Signor Carlotti exclaimed.

It was all Jane and Bella could do, not to double over giggling as they walked away.

"Maybe he really will change how he treats you, Monday morning!" Jane whispered.

"Oh, do you think so?" Bella asked **wistfully**.

(S) Across the room, strangely, Jane heard Yetta's voice now. She couldn't make out the words, but Yetta seemed to be calling out in great excitement, from the midst of the crowd of girls getting ready to leave. Maybe she was talking them

520   into another strike. Maybe this one would work—maybe Yetta would get her dearest wish.

"Doesn't Yetta work on the eighth floor?" Jane asked.

Before Bella could answer, screams came suddenly from the back of the room. Screams—and a great burst of light.

wistful
(wĭst′fəl) *adj.* If you're *wistful*, you are thoughtful and longing for something.

Bella

Bella couldn't tell what had happened. It was just like her first day of work, when everyone else was yelling and running and knocking over baskets and trampling shirtwaists they didn't bother to stop and pick up. And, for a moment, just like on that first day, Bella couldn't understand the words everyone
530 else kept saying. The English part of her brain shut off, the Yiddish words in her brain evaporated, even the Italian she heard around her sounded garbled and foreign.

Then she smelled smoke, and the words made sense.

"Fire!"

"*S'brent!*"

"*Fuoco!*"

Jane clutched her shoulders.

"Where do we go? What do we do?" Jane asked. "We always had fire drills at school—where have they told you to
540 go in the event of a fire?"

Bella didn't know what a fire drill was. People were crowded in all around her, shoving and pushing from behind, blocking the way in front of her. The tables on either side of the aisle seemed to be closing in on her. She was penned in, just like a goat or a pig.

No better than an animal, Bella thought, and somehow this seemed all of piece with not being able to read and wanting only food and Signor Carlotti spitting on her and Signor Luciano cheating her. *I bet back home your family*
550 *slept with goats and chickens in the house,* Signora Luciano had sneered at her once, and Bella hadn't even understood that that was an insult. But now she'd seen how other people lived; she'd seen what Jane and Yetta expected out of life. She refused to think of herself as a hog in a pen waiting to be slaughtered.

"This way!" she said, grabbing Jane's hand and scrambling up on top of the nearest table.

From there, she could see the fire. It was blowing in the back window, one huge ball of flame rolling across the
560 examining tables stacked with shirtwaists. The flames kept dividing, devouring stack after stack of shirtwaists, racing each other down the tables.

Where are they trying to get to? Bella wondered.

CLOSE READ

Analyze Figurative Language (LINES 544–555)

COMMON CORE RL 1, RL 4, L 5

Remind students that a **simile** compares two unlike things using the word *like* or *as*. Authors use similes to provide information or insight about their characters.

T **CITE TEXT EVIDENCE** Ask students to reread lines 544–545 and cite evidence of a simile. (*The simile is "She was penned in, just like a goat or a pig."*) Ask students to describe the effect of this simile on the story events. (*Pigs and goats are put in pens before they are slaughtered, and Bella feels penned in like an animal waiting to die in the fire.*)

Ask students to reread further into the paragraph (lines 546–555) to find details that reinforce this interpretation of the image created by the simile. (*The paragraph ends with Bella's thought that she "refused to think of herself as a hog in a pen waiting to be slaughtered."*)

Strategies for Annotation

🖊 📄 *Annotate it!*

Analyze Point of View

COMMON CORE RL 6

Tell students that this passage depicts what Bella is thinking as she tries to navigate through the fire. Her thinking is based on her fear of dying like an animal, stated in lines 544–545.

- Highlight in blue the animal comparisons Bella makes.
- Make a note about why an immigrant like Bella might think of herself as an animal.

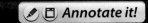

No better than an animal, Bella thought, and som this seemed to all of piece with not being able to read wanting only food and Signor Carlotti spitting on her Signor Luciano cheating her. *I bet back home your family slept with goats and chickens* in the house, Signora Luciano

> Immigrants at this time were probably treated cruelly, in the same way that animals are treated.

Compare and Contrast: Genres (LINES 568–570)

COMMON CORE — RL 1, RL 3, RL 9

The author's dramatic depiction of Bella and Yetta trying to escape the fire both brings the horrible real-life event to life and adds a human element to the facts of the tragedy.

Ⓤ CITE TEXT EVIDENCE Have students reread lines 568–570. Then, direct them back to the historical account *Flesh & Blood So Cheap* to look for nonfiction evidence of what is described here in *Uprising*. *(Lines 72–75 from* Flesh & Blood So Cheap *depict workers piled up at the doors.)*

Ask students to cite details that were added by the author of *Uprising* that bring this part of the story to life and to describe the impact of these details. *(The author adds that Bella "looked around frantically," which is probably how everyone on this floor is acting at this moment—frantic. These details heighten the suspense, adding a sense of true desperation felt by the characters in the fictional account.)*

The first flame leaped from the examining table to the first row of sewing tables.

"It's coming toward us!" Jane screamed behind her. "Where do we go?"

Ⓤ Bella looked around frantically. Girls were packed in around the doors and elevators. Only a handful seemed to
570 remember that there was another way out.

"The fire escape!" Bella screamed back, grateful for that day so long ago, before the strike, when she'd actually seen where the fire escape was.

The aisles were still crowded. Bella leaped from one table to the next, and somehow Jane managed to follow. Bella leaped again, suddenly surefooted. Except for the smoke burning her eyes and throat, she could have been back in the mountains near Calia, jumping from rock to rock.

"I've got to—make sure—Harriet and Millicent—are—
580 all—right," Jane panted behind her, as they cleared another table. She began coughing, choking on the smoke.

Bella bent down and snatched up a pile of shirtwaist sleeves. She held two over her mouth and handed the others to Jane.

"Here. So you can breathe."

They kept racing across the tables. And it really was a race, because the flames were speeding toward the fire escape window too. Through the smoke, Bella could barely make out the progress of the fire. *The flames are going to get there first—*
590 *no, we are!—no, look how fast the fire's moving . . . .*

They reached the end of the tables and jumped down to the floor. The flames were reaching for Bella's skirt, so she lifted it up as she ran for the fire escape. She had one leg out the window, balanced on the metal railing, when Jane grabbed for her arm.

"Wait—is that safe?" Jane asked.

She'd actually stopped to peer down at the rickety stairs, at the flames shooting out the eighth-floor window, at the eighth-floor shutters that seemed to be blocking the path of all
600 the other girls already easing their way down.

"Safe?" Bella repeated numbly. Anything seemed safer than where they were now. But she pulled back a little, reconsidering. She shifted her weight back from the foot that was on the fire escape to the knee perched on the windowsill. And in that moment, the fire escape just . . . fell away.

> ## " She'd actually stopped to peer down at the rickety stairs, at the flames shooting out "

"*Madonna mia!*" Bella cried. Jane grabbed her, pulling her back in through the window. "The other girls—"

Jane shook her head, maybe meaning, *Don't ask,* maybe meaning, *I saw it all, them falling, I can't even begin to tell*
610 *you how awful it was* . . . . Bella tried to remember who'd been ahead of her on the fire escape—Dora? Essie? Ida? All of them? The boot of the girl immediately in front of Bella had had a fancy silver buckle, the kind of thing a girl would have been proud of, the kind of thing she would have gone around showing off, making sure her skirt flounced up to display it as much as possible. Had Bella seen that buckle before?

"Bella! Where's another exit?" Jane cried out.

But Bella couldn't think about anything but a fancy silver buckle.

620   Suddenly Yetta was there.

"Greene Street stairs!" Yetta was screaming. "Go!"

Bella grabbed her friends' hands and took off running again. But Yetta pulled her hand back.

"You go on!" she screamed. "I still have to—"

The rest of Yetta's words were lost in the crackle of advancing flames.

The smoke rose and fell and shifted. One minute, Bella could see ahead of her, a straight path to the partition by the door. The next minute, she was groping blindly forward,
630 tripping over people who had fallen. She'd dropped the shirtwaist sleeves she'd been using to cover her mouth and nose. She grabbed up another stack, but just before she pressed it to her face she noticed that these shirtwaist sleeves were already burning. She dropped them to the floor, and began to sag toward the floor herself.

But she was still holding Jane's hand. Jane yanked her back up.

Uprising **301**

TO CHALLENGE STUDENTS . . .

Discuss the Role of Women Remind students that *Uprising* is told through the eyes of three different women. Point out that most of the employees of the Triangle Shirtwaist Factory were women. Ask students to work in a small group to discuss what the details in *Uprising* might reveal about the role of women in America in the early 1900s. Ask students to cite details from the story that reveal the women characters' attitudes toward work, colleagues, and their personal lives. Ask groups to consider and discuss how attitudes and roles have changed since this time.

TEACH

CLOSE READ

Compare and Contrast: Genres (LINES 606–616)
COMMON CORE RL 9

Have students reread lines 212–223 of the selection *Flesh & Blood So Cheap.*

V ASK STUDENTS to reread lines 606–616 of this story and to tell how the fire escape collapse might have been depicted differently if the author were telling the story from Jane's perspective looking out the window. *(Sample answer: Because Jane was at the window and saw the fire escape fall, the author could have described some of the brutal deaths depicted in the nonfiction account.)*

Analyze Story Elements
COMMON CORE **RL 1, RL 3**

(LINES 659–671)

The author depicts a dilemma for Bella: does she save her friend Jane or does she save herself?

(W) **CITE TEXT EVIDENCE** Ask students to reread lines 659–671 and cite who Bella saves. Ask students to go back through this section of the story (the entire section titled "Bella") and look for evidence to support their answers. *(Bella saves herself because earlier in the section she says she refuses to die like an animal in the fire.)*

COLLABORATIVE DISCUSSION Have groups of students discuss the depictions of the Triangle Factory Fire in *Uprising* and the history writing pieces *Flesh & Blood So Cheap* and *The Story of the Triangle Factory Fire* read earlier in the collection to identify different examples of where the author of *Uprising* combines fact and fiction. Ask students to consider and discuss how the combination of fact and fiction gives the reader a new dimension of understanding about the real-life event. Encourage students to write notes as they talk. Then, have students share their thoughts with the class.

ASK STUDENTS to share any questions they generated in the course of reading and discussing the selection.

"The stairs—" Jane gasped.

They stumbled forward. Bella pulled her wool skirt
640 up over her head, blocking out the smoke and the flames. *Immodest*, she thought, an English word she'd just learned. She didn't care.

Jane grabbed a bucket of water from a nearby shelf and flung it toward the fire, and some of it splashed back onto Bella. None of it seemed to reach the fire. Or, if it did, it didn't make any difference. The flames kept shooting forward. There were no more buckets left on the shelf, only some tipped over empty on the floor.

"The girls will be so scared," Jane breathed, and Bella
650 knew she meant Harriet and Millicent, waiting in their father's office upstairs. "I've got to—"

She stopped, looking down.

"My skirt," she said.

A ring of flames was dancing along the bottom of her skirt. She stepped forward and the flames flared.

"We'll put it out," Bella said.

Jane began rushing toward a vat by the stairs.

"Water—"

(W) "No, no! That's machine oil, sewing machine oil!" Bella
660 screamed, pulling her back. The dark oil was bubbling over, running down the sides of the vat. The fire was beginning to race along the streams of oil. Bella had to jump past it. And then Jane was on one side of the flames, Bella on the other.

"Jane!" Bella screamed.

"Go on!" Jane screamed back. "Go get the girls! Make sure they're safe up there!"

"But you—"

"I'll go another way!" Jane said. "I'll meet you later!"

Bella whirled around. The pathway to the stairs was
670 closing in. In a second it would be gone.

Bella ran forward.

COLLABORATIVE DISCUSSION How has the author combined fact and fiction in this novel excerpt? Talk about your ideas with other group members.

Analyze Point of View

COMMON CORE RL 3, RL 6

In a work of fiction, the **narrator** is the voice that tells the story. The author's choice of narrator is called the **point of view**. Authors deliberately choose a point of view in order to give readers a certain perspective on the story. The three types of point of view are shown in this chart.

Point of View in Narratives		
First Person	**Third-Person Limited**	**Third-Person Omniscient ("All-Knowing")**
• Narrator is a story character. • Narrator uses first-person pronouns such as *I, me, mine, we, our.* • Reader sees events and characters through narrator's eyes.	• Narrator is not a character and is outside the story. • Narrator uses third-person pronouns such as *he, she, him, her, their.* • Reader sees events and characters through one character's eyes.	• Narrator is not a character and is outside the story. • Narrator uses third-person pronouns such as *he, she, him, her, their.* • Reader is shown different characters' thoughts and feelings.

In the novel excerpt you've just read, the author has made an unusual choice in point of view. By presenting events through the eyes of multiple characters, the author:

- shows what the characters think of one another as they interact
- shows characters in different places at the same time
- builds suspense by shifting back in time when the reader already knows about the danger to come

Which point of view has the author chosen, and what impact does this have on how the reader experiences the story?

Compare and Contrast: Genres

COMMON CORE RL 9

Historical fiction is set in the past and includes real places and events. The author researches the topic as a nonfiction author does, but uses imagination as well as facts to create imaginary scenes and dialogue between characters. Sometimes the fictional story will depict real people and imaginary characters interacting and experiencing real historical events.

To compare and contrast two forms of writing, notice how the details of real events appear in the fictional story. For example, read lines 15–20 from the nonfiction excerpt *Flesh & Blood So Cheap*. Then read lines 51–57 from the novel *Uprising*. How has the author of the fictional story used factual details differently from the author of the nonfiction selection?

TEACH

CLOSE READ

Analyze Point of View

COMMON CORE RL 3, RL 6

Help students understand the different points of view that authors use. Have students reread lines 221–228. Ask them how this is an example of third-person limited narration. *(This part of the story is told from Yetta's perspective. We are able to see her thoughts and the events through her eyes. The author also uses the third-person pronoun her.)* Discuss answers to the questions. *(Possible answers: The author has chosen to tell the story through the eyes of three different characters experiencing the same event. In each section, the author uses third-person limited to give us a unique look into one character's experience.)*

Compare and Contrast: Genres

COMMON CORE RL 9

Explain to students that one of the reasons historical fiction is such a popular genre is that it combines facts about an event with the art of storytelling. To compare and contrast a historical account and a fictional account of the same event, have students reread the lines from the two selections. Discuss which passage engaged students more and what they think are the pros and cons of the two genres. Then, discuss students' answers to the final question in the lesson. *(The author of* Uprising *has provided the same information about the cotton fabrics being separated by sheer tissue paper. She has added a character, Jacob, who is working with the fabric and has added a figurative description of tissue paper patterns like "hanging moss and low branches.")*

Strategies for Annotation 🖉 📄 *Annotate it!*

Analyze Point of View

COMMON CORE RL 6

Have student locate lines 571–578. Share these strategies for guided or independent analysis:

- Highlight in yellow words and phrases that reveal the author's use of point of view.
- Underline any pronouns that are also clues to the point of view.
- Write a note identifying the type of point of view and through whose eyes the passage is being told.

The aisles were still crowded. Bella leaped from one table to the next, and somehow Jane managed to follow. Bella leaped again, suddenly surefooted. Except for the smoke burning <u>her</u> eyes and throat, <u>she</u> could have been back in the mountains near Calia, jumping from rock to rock.

> 3rd-person limited; seeing events through Bella's eyes and thoughts

Analyzing the Text

COMMON CORE RL 2, RL 3, RL 6, RL 9

Possible answers:

1. At the end of the excerpt, Yetta, Jane, and Bella are all trying to escape from the fire on the ninth floor. Bella makes it toward the Greene Street stairs, but Jane is cut off by the fire and must find another way. After pointing her friends toward that exit, Yetta has held back for some reason not yet known.

2. During each account, we find out something about each character's background and goals. This makes the characters come alive to the reader and seem more sympathetic. Yetta is Jewish, a union organizer who believes in fair treatment of workers. Jane was educated at a finishing school, works as a governess, and her friendship with Yetta and Bella is helping her to understand class differences. Bella is an Italian immigrant and has struggled with prejudice; she has a boyfriend named Pietro. The girls all seem like real people, and although they come from different backgrounds, they have hopes and dreams for the future—boyfriends, better jobs, fairer treatment. But now none of that matters; they all have one common goal—to escape with their lives.

3. Jane brings her charges to the tenth floor, with its big offices and fancy desks. Mr. Blanck's daughters have a governess and a mother who travels to Florida for the social season. Jane is overwhelmed by the contrast with the "dim, dirty space" on the ninth floor and the packed working conditions the girls must endure. We hear her thoughts such as "No wonder Bella felt so overwhelmed . . ." that show she is not happy seeing the difficult working conditions.

4. Although the nonfiction account shows that the fire escape's collapse was part of the real-life event, the image of the fancy silver buckle is from the author's imagination. It shocks the reader, just as it shocks the character Bella. The author uses details like this to bring readers into the scene and into the minds of the characters.

5. On the tenth floor, Harriet points out the pressing department through a "break in the wall into a vast open space, where rows and rows of weary-looking workers stood over ironing boards." The author then uses dialogue between Harriet and Millicent to describe the irons and the gas heating system. This is a natural way to work information into any story.

6. The dialogue in historical fiction has two purposes: to move the narrative along, as in any fiction story, and to provide factual information. The dialogue in the excerpt from Uprising is like natural conversation. The quotations in the nonfiction work stand alone and provide supporting evidence for the author's main ideas.

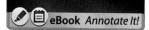

Analyzing the Text

COMMON CORE RL 2, RL 3, RL 6, RL 9, W 3, W 4, W 5, W 9, W 10

Cite Text Evidence　Support your responses with evidence from the text.

1. **Summarize** At the end of this novel excerpt, where is each character going and why?

2. **Compare** How does the shifting point of view help you understand the similarities and differences among the three characters?

3. **Cite Evidence** How does the author use the chapter entitled "Jane" to show contrasts between the business owners and the workers?

4. **Analyze** Reread lines 590–618. Then look back to lines 212–222 of the excerpt from *Flesh & Blood So Cheap*. Why might the author of *Uprising* have introduced the fancy silver buckle?

5. **Evaluate** Find a passage in which the author provides facts about the setting. How effectively does the author make this information seem part of a fictional work? Explain.

6. **Synthesize** How is dialogue in this historical novel different from the quotations in the nonfiction excerpt from *The Story of the Triangle Factory Fire*?

PERFORMANCE TASK

Writing Activity: New Chapter
Suppose that a short chapter follows the three that you have read. In this chapter, the point of view remains third-person limited, but events are seen through the eyes of a different character. Write that new chapter.

- Choose a character already introduced, such as Jacob or Harriet.
- Read closely to learn about the character's likely goals, experiences, and interactions with other characters.

- Reread the nonfiction excerpts about the Triangle Fire to gather more factual details.
- Write a draft of your chapter.
- Read it aloud to a partner, and make revisions based on your listener's suggestions.

Assign this performance task.

PERFORMANCE TASK

COMMON CORE W3, W4, W5, W9, W10

Writing Activity: New Chapter Have students work independently to write a new chapter. Direct students to choose a character to serve as narrator. Have them make notes on the character's actions, dialogue he or she may have, and any other details that will help shape the narrative. Remind students to reread the nonfiction accounts of the event and make notes on usable details. Have students revise and edit their drafts based on feedback from a partner.

Critical Vocabulary

COMMON CORE L 5b

| mischievous | scorn | marvel | singe |
| stifle | reprove | haggard | wistful |

Practice and Apply Use each bold word in your answer to the question. Explain your reasoning.

1. Would someone smile with **scorn** or have or a **wistful** smile while thinking about an unreachable goal?

2. Would someone have a **haggard** expression while behaving in a **mischievous** way?

3. What might a **reproving** look **stifle**?

4. Would you rather **marvel** at a campfire or have it **singe** you?

Vocabulary Strategy: Analogies

Verbal analogies are comparisons between two pairs of words. The relationship between the first pair of words is the same as the relationship between the second pair. For example, if the first pair of words is *big* and *little*, the second pair might be *tall* and *short*, because both words in each pair are antonyms. The analogy is stated, "*Big* is to *little* as *tall* is to *short*." It is written with colons in this pattern: **big : little :: tall : short**. This chart shows common relationships in verbal analogies.

Relationship	Example
Word : Antonym	heavy : weightless :: troubled : joyful
Word : Synonym	rush : haste :: mistake : error
Part : Whole	finger : hand :: branch : tree
Object : Description	blanket : warm :: sun : bright
Object : Action or Use	ruler : measure :: hammer : pound

Practice and Apply Choose the word that best completes each analogy. Give the reason for your choice.

1. obstacle : barrier :: goal : (achieve, difficulty, destination)

2. basket : wicker :: sweater : (wool, container, jacket)

3. partition : separate :: doorway : (build, enter, elevator)

4. flame : inferno :: snowflake : (fire, blizzard, cooling)

5. respectfully : scornfully :: generously : (selfishly, admiringly, humorously)

PRACTICE & APPLY

Critical Vocabulary

COMMON CORE L 5b

Possible answers:

1. *Someone would have a wistful smile while thinking about an unreachable goal. Smiling wistfully suggests the thought "I wish I could have that but I can't." A scornful smile suggests the thought "That isn't worth having."*

2. *Someone behaving in a mischievous way is having fun and probably has a lively expression, not a haggard one. A haggard expression shows tired, worn-out feelings.*

3. *A reproving look is one that shows disapproval, so it might stifle misbehavior.*

4. *I'd rather marvel at a campfire, enjoying its amazing warmth and color. I wouldn't want it to singe me by burning my skin.*

Vocabulary Strategy: Analogies

Possible answers:

1. *obstacle : barrier :: goal : destination; it's a synonym for goal, just as barrier is a synonym for obstacle.*

2. *basket : wicker :: sweater : wool; a sweater is made of wool, just as a basket is made of wicker.*

3. *partition : separate :: doorway : enter; you enter a space through a doorway, just as you separate a space with a partition.*

4. *flame : inferno :: snowflake : blizzard; a snowflake is part of a blizzard, just as a flame is part of an inferno.*

5. *respectfully : scornfully :: generously : selfishly; selfishly is an antonym for generously, just as scornfully is an antonym for respectfully.*

Strategies for Annotation  *Annotate it!*

Vocabulary Strategy: Analogies
COMMON CORE L 5b

Have students locate analogies in the selection. Remind students that elements of figurative language such as metaphors and similes are types of analogies. Encourage students to use their eBook annotation tools to do the following:

- Highlight each analogy they find.
- Look for and underline the specific things that are being compared.

so gently, almost lovingly. Above his head, the tissue-paper patterns dangled from wires, so when he stood up it was like watching someone across a forest, half hidden by hanging moss and low branches.

PRACTICE & APPLY

Language Conventions: Phrases

COMMON CORE L 1a

Tell students that participial phrases and gerunds can help make writing compelling to read. They can enhance descriptions and provide vivid action. Writers and storytellers rely on such evocative use of language to draw in readers and listeners. Use the following as a comparative example:

The programmers worked long hours to finish the beta version of the software.

This conveys information about what the programmers were doing, but the writing is dull.

Glued to their keyboards and typing frantically, the programmers logged endless hours to finish the beta version of the software.

By adding participial and gerund phrases, the second sentence pops off the page and engages the reader.

Possible answers:

1. *"Pouring water onto the flames" is a gerund phrase because it functions as a noun, naming what was started. (The phrase is the direct object of the verb* started.*)*

2. *"Blinded by the smoke" is a participial phrase because it functions as an adjective, modifying* workers.

3. *"Attacking everything in its path" is a participial phrase because it functions as an adjective, modifying* beast.

4. *"Leaping out a window" is a gerund phrase because it functions as a noun, naming what was done. (The phrase is the object of the preposition* by.*)*

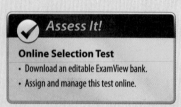

✓ Assess It!

Online Selection Test
- Download an editable ExamView bank.
- Assign and manage this test online.

Language Conventions: Phrases

COMMON CORE L 1a

A **verbal** is a verb form used as a noun, an adjective, or an adverb. A **participle** is a verbal that functions as an adjective to modify a noun or pronoun.

Verb	Present Participle	Past Participle	Adjective Use
hurry	(is) hurrying	(has) hurried	a hurrying crowd; a hurried job
pay	(is) paying	(has) paid	the paying viewers; a paid bill;
sing	(is) singing	(has) sung	all of us singing; the sung tunes

A **participial phrase** is made of a participle and any other words that complete its meaning. The participial phrase is underlined in each of these sentences. The whole phrase functions as an adjective.

> Yetta listened for the bell <u>signaling the end of work</u>. (participial phrase modifies the noun *bell*)

> <u>Hunched over their machines</u>, the workers grew tired. (participial phrase modifies the noun *workers*)

> <u>Reading this historical novel</u>, we learned about a tragic fire. (participial phrase modifies the pronoun *we*)

A **gerund** is another verbal. It is formed from the present participle of a verb, the form with the ending *-ing*. A gerund functions as a noun in a sentence.

Verb	Gerund	Noun Use
hurry	hurrying	I don't like hurrying.
pay	paying	Take a ticket after paying.
sing	singing	Singing lifts the spirits.

A **gerund phrase** is made of a gerund and any other words that complete its meaning. The gerund phrases are underlined in this sentence. Each whole phrase functions as a noun.

> The factory workers began <u>screaming in fear</u> and <u>running for their lives</u>, but <u>escaping the flames</u> was not possible.

Practice and Apply Identify the verbal phrase in each sentence. Tell how you know it is a gerund phrase or a participial phrase.

1. Men grabbed buckets and started pouring water onto the flames.

2. Blinded by the smoke, workers could not find their way.

3. The fire was like a wild beast, attacking everything in its path.

4. Some people met their death by leaping out a window.

Analyze Point of View

COMMON CORE

RL 6

RETEACH

The author of *Uprising* tells a fictionalized story of the Triangle Factory Fire through the eyes of three characters—Yetta, Jane, and Bella—each with her own unique perspective on the events. The author tells each character's story using the same point of view: third-person limited.

An author may employ multiple points of view for a number of reasons. He or she may want to show how the events affect characters in different ways. Another reason may be to give the reader a diverse perspective on the story's events. Others may want to explore a unique way of telling a complex story.

 LEVEL UP TUTORIALS Assign the following *LevelUp* tutorial: **Third-Person Point of View**

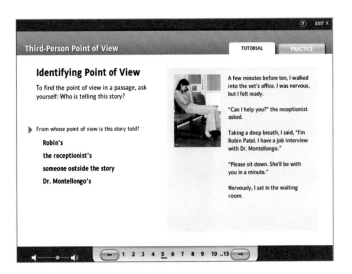

CLOSE READING APPLICATION

To explore the effect of using multiple points of view, have students fill in a comparison-and-contrast chart like the one shown below. What did each character uniquely think, see, and feel as the fire raged? What did all three characters experience that was similar? When they're done, have students meet in a small group to share their observations.

Yetta	Jane	Bella

Compare and Contrast: Genres

COMMON CORE

RL 9

RETEACH

Review **historical fiction** with students. Remind them that historical fiction authors base their stories on research and facts. Authors use their imaginations and storytelling tools to create the narrative, inventing characters and dialogue that could reasonably make sense based on the facts. Point out that historical fiction should never be considered an authoritative source—it is intended primarily to be a compelling read.

Point out that although historical fiction is based on information that might be found in informational texts historical fiction shares common elements with other types of fiction, including character, plot, setting, conflict, and a theme.

 LEVEL UP TUTORIALS Assign the following *LevelUp* tutorial: **Prose Forms**

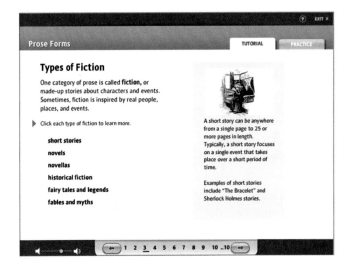

CLOSE READING APPLICATION

Have students find another example of historical fiction and a corresponding informational text about the same event. Direct students to look for specific factual information found in the nonfiction selection that appears or is somehow referenced in the fiction piece. Have students consider the following questions:

- Does the author of the historical fiction piece remain true to the facts?
- Are there instances during which the author of the fiction piece takes too much liberty with the facts?

Have students present their observations to the class.

Doris Is Coming

Short Story by ZZ Packer

Why This Text

"Doris Is Coming" is a short story about an African American girl who goes to a local lunch counter to order lunch. Students may not think this is a particularly exceptional undertaking unless they know that the story is set in the South in the 1960s, when groups of young black people risked their lives sitting at White-Only lunch counters in order to challenge racial segregation. Studying a fictional character from the same period and in the same setting will help students understand the thoughts and feelings of people who went through the experience in real life.

Background Have students read the background and information about ZZ Packer. Explain that in a sit-in, a group of students would go to a lunch counter and ask to be served; if they were not, they would refuse to move until they were. If they were arrested, a new group would take their place. Although the students were always nonviolent and respectful, they were often brutalized by local law officials and violent segregationists.

SETTING A PURPOSE Ask students to pay attention to the way the author uses story elements such as setting to convey the story's theme.

Common Core Support

- cite textual evidence
- analyze how particular elements of a story interact
- compare and contrast a fictional portrayal and a historical account of the same period

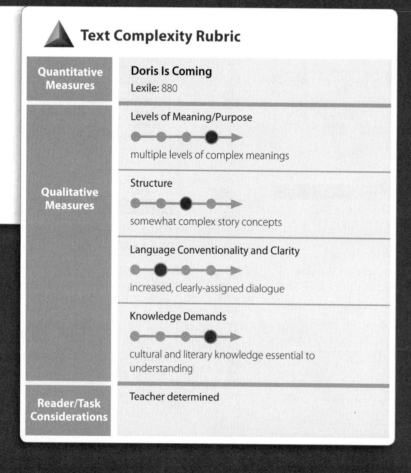

Text Complexity Rubric

Quantitative Measures	**Doris Is Coming** Lexile: 880
Qualitative Measures	Levels of Meaning/Purpose multiple levels of complex meanings
	Structure somewhat complex story concepts
	Language Conventionality and Clarity increased, clearly-assigned dialogue
	Knowledge Demands cultural and literary knowledge essential to understanding
Reader/Task Considerations	Teacher determined

Strategies for CLOSE READING

Compare and Contrast Genres

Students should read this story carefully all the way through. Close-reading questions at the bottom of the page will help them use details in the text that will help them to understand the story in its historical context. As they read, students should jot down comments or questions about the text in the margins.

WHEN STUDENTS STRUGGLE . . .

To help students compare "Doris Is Coming" with nonfiction works on the same subject, have them work in small groups to fill out a chart like the one below.

CITE TEXT EVIDENCE For practice in comparing and contrasting genres have students find examples in "Doris Is Coming" that correspond to the nonfiction examples in "The Most Daring Of [Our] Leaders."

The Most Daring of [Our] Leaders	Doris Is Coming
"This was no longer an intellectual exercise: She was being told in the most searing way imaginable that she was beyond the pale, unfit to use the same facilities as white women." (lines 5–8)	"Without looking up she said, 'Sorry. We don't serve colored people.'" (line 17)
"But segregation still firmly ruled in theaters, restaurants, hotels, and libraries . . ." (lines 18–19)	"The waitress frowned, confused, but when she finally got it, she laughed. 'Seriously though,' the waitress said, turning solemn. 'I can't serve you.'" (lines 21–23)
"She was particularly drawn to his belief that to be effective, these young would-be activists would have to transcend self-hatred and a sense of inferiority, that they would have to learn to love themselves." (lines 43–46)	"When Doris closed her book, about to leave, she said, 'I just want you to know I'm leaving now. Not because you're making me or because I feel intimidated or anything . . . Next time I'll want some food, all right?'" (lines 60–64)

Background ZZ Packer *(born 1973) is an award-winning writer of short fiction. She nicknamed herself ZZ because her given name, Zuwena (Swahili for "good"), was hard for teachers to pronounce. Recognized as a talent at an early age, Packer's first significant publication was in Seventeen magazine, when she was 19. "Doris Is Coming" is a short story about a young African American girl growing up Louisville, Kentucky, in the early 1960s.*

Doris Is Coming

Short Story by ZZ Packer

CLOSE READ Notes

1. **READ ▶** As you read lines 1–23, begin to collect and cite text evidence.
   - Underline parts of the text that describe the setting.
   - In the margin, summarize what the main character is doing in lines 1–14.
   - In the margin, note the conflict that arises in lines 15–23.

A She walked from Stutz's and up along Fourth Street. When she got to Claremont, the street where she lived, she kept going, past Walnut and Chestnut and all the other streets named after trees. She hit the little business district, which was still lit for New Year's, the big incandescent bulbs on wires like buds growing from vines, entwining the trees and lighting the shop facades. When she walked farther, she felt, for the first time, some purpose other than solitude motivating her. She rushed, and did not know why, until she found it, Clovee's Five and Dime. As soon as she saw it, she knew what she was doing.

10 It was warm inside, and she made her way to the soda fountain, even warmer from the grill's heat. A white man stood at the ice cream machine and whirred a shake. Two white men sat at the counter and talked in low, serious tones, occasionally sucking up clots of shake through a straw.

She walks past the street where she lives to the business district and goes into Clovee's to the soda fountain, where there are several white men.

103

1. **READ AND CITE TEXT EVIDENCE** In lines 1–14 the girl is rushing toward a destination.

A **ASK STUDENTS** to cite evidence marking her route. What is her starting point? Where does she end up? What familiar streets does she pass along the way? *She starts out at Stutz's and walks along Fourth Street. She passes Claremont and hits the business district. She ends up at Clovee's Five and Dime.*

FOR ELL STUDENTS Many students may not know what a *Five and Dime* was. Explain that it was a large store selling a variety of inexpensive items—originally for five cents or a dime.

CLOSE READ Notes

There was one waitress, hip propped against the side of the counter, wiping the countertop with a rag that had seen cleaner days. Without looking up she said. "Sorry. We don't serve colored people."

B "Good." Doris said. "I don't eat them." She remembered Helen telling her that this was the line someone used during a sit-in, and

20 Doris was glad to have a chance to use it.

The waitress frowned, confused, but when she finally got it, she laughed. "Seriously though," the waitress said, turning solemn. "I can't serve you."

The two men talking looked over at her and shook their heads. They began talking again, occasionally looking over at Doris to see if she'd left.

"What if I stay?"

C The waitress looked to the man making the shake, eyes pleading for help. "I don't know. I don't know. I just don't make the rules and I

30 feel sorry for you, but I don't make 'em."

The man walked over with a shake and gave it to the waitress, who bent the straw toward herself and began to drink it. "Look," the man said to Doris, "I wouldn't sit here. I wouldn't do that.

"You wouldn't?"

"I wouldn't if I were you."

She sat. Shaking, she brought out her World History book. She'd made a book cover for it with a paper bag, and she was glad she'd done it because she was sweating so much it would have slipped from her hands otherwise. She set it on the counter, opened it, as if she did

40 this everyday at this very shop, and tried to read about the Hapsburgs, but couldn't.

It occurred to her that other students who did sit-ins were all smarter than she; they'd banded together, and had surely told others

The waitress says that she can't serve Doris.

Doris is in a place where she's not welcome; she tries to overcome her fears by acting braver than she feels.

2. ◀ **REREAD AND DISCUSS** With a small group, discuss Doris's "joke"— what it means, what it tells you about Doris, and how it advances the plot (lines 15–20).

3. **READ** ▶ As you read lines 24–47, continue to cite textual evidence.
- Circle the actions that reveal Doris's feelings.
- Underline what the waitress and the man say to Doris.
- In the margin, summarize the developing situation.

104

---

of their whereabouts, whereas she had foolishly come to Clovee's all

D by herself. She stared at her book and didn't dare look up, but from the corner of her eye she noticed when the two men who'd been talking got up and left.

The man at the ice cream machine made himself some coffee and beckoned the waitress to him. When he whispered something to her,

50 she swatted him with the rag, laughing.

Once Doris felt the numbness settle in her, she felt she could do it. She tried at the Hapsburgs again.

The waitress said, "Student? High School?"

"Yes, Ma'am. Central."

"My daughter's over at Iroquois."

E "We played them last Friday." Doris didn't know what the scores were, didn't care, but had heard about the game over the intercom.

"Well." The waitress started wiping the counter again. Going over the same spots.

60 When Doris closed her book, about to leave, she said, "I just want you to know I'm leaving now. Not because you're making me or because I feel **intimidated** or anything. I just have to go home now."

The waitress looked at her.

"Next time I'll want some food, all right?"

"We can't do that, but here's half my shake. You can have it. I'm done."

The shake she handed over had a lipstick ring around the straw, and a little spittle. Doris knew she wouldn't drink it, but she took it anyway. "Thanks, ma'am."

The waitress looks at Doris and thinks of her own daughter, who is about the same age.

intimidate: *threaten; frighten*

4. **REREAD** Reread lines 42–47. What mistake does Doris see she's made? Cite text evidence in your answer.

She'd put herself in harm's way by thinking she could go it alone. Others had "banded together, and had surely told others of their whereabouts, whereas she had foolishly come" on her own.

5. **READ** ▶ As you read lines 48–79, continue to cite textual evidence.
- In the margin, explain the connection the waitress makes with Doris.
- Circle details that show Doris is in control of her actions and emotions.
- In the margin, make an inference about how Doris feels about her experience (lines 70–79).

105

---

2. **REREAD AND DISCUSS USING TEXT EVIDENCE** Explain that in line 18 Doris uses the line "I don't eat them" to respond to the waitress's comment about serving "colored" people.

B **ASK STUDENTS** to discuss evidence showing that Doris was prepared to say this. *Doris was "glad to have a chance to use it."* What was the joke intended to do? *It was intended to lighten the mood and to catch the workers off-guard.* What inference can be made from the fact that the joke had been used before? *There was always the possibility of violence at a lunch counter sit-in.*

3. **READ AND CITE TEXT EVIDENCE** Point out that the waitress seems uncomfortable with the store's policy.

C **ASK STUDENTS** what she says and does in lines 28–30 that reveals her attitude. *She looks at the man making the shake with "eyes pleading for help"; she tells Doris that "I just don't make the rules and I feel sorry for you . . ."*

4. **REREAD AND CITE TEXT EVIDENCE** In lines 45–47 Doris "stared at her book and didn't dare look up."

D **ASK STUDENTS** to make an inference about how she feels based on this behavior. *Students may say she feels threatened and vulnerable; the two men who leave seem menacing.*

5. **READ AND CITE TEXT EVIDENCE** In this section, Doris has a conversation with the waitress.

E **ASK STUDENTS** to think about the fact that Doris "didn't care" what the scores were. Why not? *She was too excited by the fact that they were having a real conversation; the scores were inconsequential.*

Critical Vocabulary: intimidate (line 62) Have students explain the meaning of *intimidate*. What situations might make someone feel intimidated? *Students may suggest being the new kid in school or talking to a celebrity.*

CLOSE READ
Notes

Doris seems to be a bit numb, as though she can't believe what she's just done. She also seems happy and relaxed, thinking about her family at home.

F 70　　Outside Clovee's Five and Dime, the world was cold around her, moving toward dark, but not dark yet, as if the darkness were being adjusted with a volume dial. Whoever was adjusting the dial was doing it slowly, consistently, with infinite patience. She walked back home and knew it would be too late for dinner, and the boys would be screaming and her father wanting his daily beer, and her mother worried sick. She knew that she should hurry, but she couldn't. She had to stop and look. The sky had just turned her favorite shade of barely lit blue, the kind that came to windows when you couldn't get back to sleep but couldn't quite pry yourself awake.

6. **◀ REREAD** Reread lines 51–79. How have the characters' perspectives changed? Cite explicit textual evidence in your response.

At first, the waitress tried to get Doris to leave. Then they actually have a conversation, which is courageous under the circumstances. The waitress offers Doris her shake, and Doris thanks her.

SHORT RESPONSE

Cite Text Evidence　Think about the texts in this Collection that describe the real experiences of Diane Nash and John Lewis during sit-ins in the 1960s. What references to historical details do you find in the story? In what ways are Doris's fictional experiences different from the real experiences of Nash and Lewis? **Cite text evidence** in your response.

Although Doris experienced resistance when she sat at the lunch counter, it was not as violent as the response Nash and Lewis faced. The fact that Doris was refused service at the lunch counter was based on historical accounts of similar events. While some people may have sympathized with Nash and Lewis, the behavior of the waitress is most likely fictional. It is also unlikely that the actual nonviolent protesters would have attempted a sit-in alone.

106

6. **REREAD AND CITE TEXT EVIDENCE**　Have students think about Doris's sense of euphoria in lines 70–79.

F **ASK STUDENTS** to explain why she feels so happy. How did the conversation with the waitress help change her mood? *The waitress made an effort to connect with Doris, and Doris found the strength to stand up for herself.*

SHORT RESPONSE

Cite Text Evidence　Students should support their positions with text evidence from this selection and two nonfiction selections describing the real experiences of Diane Nash and John Lewis. They should:

- compare and contrast the fiction and nonfiction stories with respect to character, setting, and point of view.
- examine how the author uses historical details to tell a story.
- determine which story details are fact-based and which are made-up.

TO CHALLENGE STUDENTS . . .

Tell students that the lunch counter sit-ins of the 1960s began in Greensboro, North Carolina, when a non-violent sit-in at a segregated lunch counter sparked a movement that spread throughout the region, forcing many establishments to change their segregationist policies.

ASK STUDENTS to research this important part of civil rights history through photography, videos, and articles. They can find online exhibits of photos and interviews with important participants in the events. Have students prepare short presentations about facts that they have discovered.

DIG DEEPER

With the class, return to Question 6, Reread. Have students share their responses.

ASK STUDENTS to think about how the perspectives of Doris and the waitress change at the end of the story.

- Why does the waitress start a conversation with Doris? *She may be aware that segregation is unjust; in telling Doris that she "doesn't make the rules" she shows she is conflicted about Clovee's policy. Students may also point out that the waitress seems to wait for the two men to leave before she can talk to Doris, suggesting she may feel intimidated by their presence.*

- Why does this change the dynamic between the two characters? How does this lead to a change in their perspectives? *The waitress asks Doris a friendly question, to which Doris gives a brief but polite reply; this gives the waitress the opportunity to take the next step ("My daughter's over at Iroquois"), which creates a connection between herself and Doris, resulting in a real conversation between two equals—an event neither one of them is likely to forget. Their brief exchange made it possible for them to imagine a different kind of world.*

ASK STUDENTS to return to their Short Response answer and revise it based on the class discussion.

ANCHOR TEXT

Craig Kielburger Reflects on Working Toward Peace

 **mySmartPlanner** Create lesson plans and access resources online.

Personal Essay by Craig Kielburger

Why This Text?

Students regularly read personal essay writing in print and digital media on their own and at school. Recognizing elements of personal essays helps students focus on an author's reasons for writing, giving them a deeper understanding of the topic. This lesson guides students to identify and analyze elements of personal essays and to determine an author's perspective.

Key Learning Objective: The student will be able to identify and analyze elements of a personal essay and determine an author's point of view.

For practice and application:

Difference Maker: John Bergmann and Popcorn Park
Newspaper Article By David Karas

Close Reader selection
"Difference Maker: John Bergman and Popcorn Park,"
Online Article by David Karas

COMMON CORE Common Core Standards

RI 1 Cite textual evidence.
RI 2 Determine central ideas.
RI 3 Analyze interactions between ideas.
RI 4 Determine the meaning of words and phrases.
RI 5 Analyze structure.
RI 6 Determine author's point of view.
RI 8 Trace and evaluate an argument.
W 1 Write arguments.
W 4 Produce clear and coherent writing.
W 9b Apply grade 7 Reading standards.
W 10 Write routinely over extended time frames.
L 1c Correct dangling modifiers.
L 4 Determine the meaning of multiple-meaning words.
L 4c Consult a dictionary to clarify the precise meaning of a word.
L 6 Acquire and use grade-appropriate general academic vocabulary.

▲ Text Complexity Rubric

Quantitative Measures	**Craig Kielburger Reflects on Working Toward Peace** Lexile: 1080L
Qualitative Measures	**Levels of Meaning/Purpose** single purpose, explicitly stated
	Structure clearly stated, sequential organization of main ideas and details
	Language Conventionality and Clarity clear, direct language
	Knowledge Demands everyday knowledge required
Reader/Task Considerations	Teacher determined Vary by individual reader and type of text

Craig Kielburger Reflects on Working Toward Peace.

Background Have students read the background information about Craig Kielburger and his founding of the organization Free the Children. Explain that along with his brother Marc, Kielburger has started other organizations and efforts to bring positive change to the world. Me to We aims to help people from all over become "world changers." An event called We Day ties to a yearlong activism effort called We Act.

SETTING A PURPOSE Direct students to use the Setting a Purpose prompt to focus their reading. Remind them to write down questions as they read.

Analyze Text:
Personal Essay (LINES 1–6)

COMMON CORE RI 1, RI 5

Tell students that a **personal essay** is a short work of nonfiction that reflects the writer's experiences, feelings, and personality. Explain that using first-person point of view and casual, informal language are two common elements of a personal essay.

Ⓐ **CITE TEXT EVIDENCE** Have students reread lines 1–6, and ask them how they know the essay is written using first-person point of view. *(The use of the pronouns* I, our, *and* my *indicate first-person point of view.)* Then, ask them to point out language the author uses that sounds informal and conversational. *(Possible responses: "I dreamed of being Superman"; "snatch up all of the bad people"; "I would spend hours flying across the park")*

Background *In 1995, when* **Craig Kielburger** *(b. 1982) was only twelve years old, he founded Free the Children, an international organization whose goal is to help young people achieve their fullest potential. Almost two million youths are now involved in education and development programs in 45 countries. Kielburger has received wide recognition, recently becoming one of the youngest recipients of the Order of Canada.*

Craig Kielburger Reflects on Working Toward Peace

Personal Essay by Craig Kielburger

SETTING A PURPOSE In this essay, Kielburger calls for a fairer, more just world. As you read, pay attention to how he describes his experiences as a young activist.

Ⓐ

When I was very young I dreamed of being Superman, soaring high above the clouds and swooping down to snatch up all of the bad people seeking to destroy our planet. I would spend hours flying across the park, stopping momentarily to kick a soccer ball in my path or to pat my dog, Muffin, who ran faithfully at my heels.

One day, when I was twelve years old and getting ready for school, I reached for the newspaper comics. On the front page was a picture of another twelve-year-old boy from Pakistan,
10 with a bright red vest and his fist held high. According to the article, he had been sold into bondage[1] as a weaver and forced to work twelve hours a day tying tiny knots to make carpets. He had lost his freedom to laugh and to play. He had lost his

---

[1] **bondage:** the state of being held as a slave.

Close Read Screencasts   ► *View It!*

Modeled Discussions

Have students click the *Close Read* icon in their eBook to access a screencast in which readers discuss and annotate lines 7–14, a key passage that discusses an important moment of discovery in the author's life.

As a class, view and discuss the videos. Then, have students work in pairs to do an independent close read of an additional passage—the author's conclusion (lines 138–145).

(t) ©David Livingston/Getty Images; (bl) ©Katrina Brown/Shutterstock; (br)

CLOSE READ

Analyze Text: Personal Essay (LINES 15–31)

COMMON CORE RI 3, RI 5

Explain to students that in a personal essay the author shares insights that have come from his or her life experiences. Often, the author wants others to become aware of an important issue or topic.

 ASK STUDENTS to review lines 15–31. Point out that Kielburger says the newspaper article about the boy murdered in Pakistan "changed my life forever." Ask students to summarize the issues that galvanized him to start Free the Children. (*He became deeply concerned about child labor in poverty-stricken areas of the world.*)

Determine Author's Point of View (LINES 36–48)

COMMON CORE RI 1, RI 6

Explain to students that an author's **perspective** is the unique combination of ideas, values, feelings, and beliefs that influences the way the writer looks at a topic. Point out that identifying words and descriptions that have emotional impact can help readers determine an author's perspective.

 CITE TEXT EVIDENCE Ask students to review lines 36–48 to identify statements with a strong emotional impact and explain what they tell about Kielburger's values. (*Statements like "I dream of a day when . . . children do not have to die," "This is less money than Americans spend on cosmetics," and "it is less than Europeans spend on ice cream" show that Kielburger feels that people who can spend money on things like cosmetics and ice cream could use that money to help the less fortunate.*)

CRITICAL VOCABULARY

syringe: A young girl spends her days pulling apart used syringes she collects from hospitals.

ASK STUDENTS to tell why separating used syringes might be dangerous. (*They have sharp needles; they might contain hazardous substances or bacteria.*)

---

freedom to go to school. Then, when he was twelve years old, the same age as me, he was murdered.

I had never heard of child labor and wasn't certain where Pakistan was—but that day changed my life forever. I gathered a group of friends to form an organization called Free the Children.

20 Over the past four years, in my travels for Free the Children, I have had the opportunity to meet many children around the world—children like Jeffrey, who spends his days in a Manila garbage dump, alongside rats and maggots, where he sifts through decaying food and trash, trying to salvage a few valuable items to help his family survive. He dreams of leaving the garbage dump one day.

I have met children like eight-year-old Muniannal, in India, with a pretty ribbon in her hair, but no shoes or gloves, who squats on the floor every day separating used **syringes** gathered from hospitals and the streets for their plastics.
30 When she pricks herself, she dips her hand into a bucket of dirty water. She dreams of being a teacher.

I have met children in the sugarcane fields of Brazil who wield huge machetes close to their small limbs. The cane they cut sweetens the cereal on our kitchen tables each morning. They dream of easing the hunger pains in their stomachs.

Poverty is the biggest killer of children. More than 1.3 billion people—one-quarter of the world's population— live in absolute poverty, struggling to survive on less than one dollar a day. Seventy percent of them are women and
40 children. I dream of a day when people learn how to share, so that children do not have to die.

Every year, the world spends $800 billion on the military, $400 billion on cigarettes, $160 billion on beer, and $40 billion playing golf. It would only cost an extra $7 billion a year to put every child in school by the year 2010, giving them hope for a better life. This is less money than Americans spend on cosmetics in one year; it is less than Europeans spend on ice cream. People say, "We can't end world poverty; it just can't be done." The 1997 United Nations Development Report carries
50 a clear message that poverty can be ended, if we make it our goal. The document states that the world has the materials and natural resources, the know-how, and the people to make a poverty-free world a reality in less than one generation.

syringe
(sə-rĭnj´) *n.* A *syringe* is a medical instrument used to inject fluids into the body.

SCAFFOLDING FOR ELL STUDENTS

Analyze Language Explain that the author often presents an example and ends with an important statement. Have students reread lines 19–25 and restate key information about Jeffrey's life. Invite volunteers to tell what Jeffery dreams about.

ASK STUDENTS to review more paragraphs on the page and identify how the author presents an example and ends with an important idea.

Gandhi[2] once said that if there is to be peace in the world it must begin with children. I have learned my best lessons from other children—children like the girls I encountered in India who carried their friend from place to place because she had no legs—and children like José.

I met José in the streets of San Salvador, Brazil, where
60 he lived with a group of street children between the ages of eight and fourteen. José and his friends showed me the old abandoned bus shelter where they slept under cardboard boxes. They had to be careful, he said, because the police might beat or shoot them if they found their secret hideout. I spent the day playing soccer on the streets with José and his friends—soccer with an old plastic bottle they had found in the garbage. They were too poor to own a real soccer ball.

> # "Gandhi once said that if there is to be peace in the world it must begin with children."

We had great fun, until one of the children fell on the bottle and broke it into several pieces, thus ending the game.
70 It was getting late and time for me to leave. José knew I was returning to Canada and wanted to give me a gift to remember him by. But he had nothing—no home, no food, no toys, no **possessions**. So he took the shirt off his back and handed it to me. José didn't stop to think that he had no other shirt to wear or that he would be cold that night. He gave me the most precious thing he owned: the jersey of his favorite soccer team. Of course, I told José that I could never accept his shirt, but he insisted. So I removed the plain white T-shirt I was wearing and gave it to him. Although José's shirt was
80 dirty and had a few small holes, it was a colorful soccer shirt

possession
(pə-zĕsh′ən) *n.*
A *possession* is something you own.

---
[2] **Gandhi:** Mohandas Karamchand Gandhi (more commonly called Mahatma Gandhi), an Indian leader whose belief in justice inspired many people around the world.

Determine Author's Point of View (LINES 59–77)

COMMON CORE RI 1, RI 6

Explain to students that one way readers can recognize an author's perspective is by paying attention to details and examples the author chooses to share from his or her experiences.

D CITE TEXT EVIDENCE Ask students to review lines 59–77 and explain how they can identify how the author feels about the experience he had with José and a group of street children in Brazil. *(Describing the game of soccer as "great fun" and pointing out that José gave Kielburger "the most precious thing he owned" show that the author feels warmly toward José and the other children and was deeply impressed by the experience.)*

CRITICAL VOCABULARY

possession: The author tells how a poor boy in Brazil gave him a T-shirt, the boy's favorite possession.

ASK STUDENTS to tell what it shows when someone like José, who has very little, is willing to give a new friend one of his few possessions. *(It shows that he thinks sharing is more important than owning things.)*

APPLYING ACADEMIC VOCABULARY

inadequate	interact

As you discuss "Craig Kielburger Reflects on Working Toward Peace," incorporate the following Collection 6 academic vocabulary words: *inadequate* and *interact*. Ask students to tell whether they think the author presents **adequate** evidence to support his ideas. Have students describe what they think about the author's **interactions** with children in areas of poverty and what people might learn from **interacting** with others who live very different lives.

CLOSE READ

Analyze Graphics

COMMON CORE · RI 2, RI 5

(PHOTOGRAPH)

Remind students that a **graphic aid** is a visual tool, such as a chart, diagram, graph, or photograph. Explain that graphic aids present readers with information in a visual way.

E **ASK STUDENTS** to examine the photograph and point out what they can tell from the image about Craig Kielburger's appearance and personality. *(Possible answer: He appears to be young; his facial expression makes him seem friendly and relaxed; he is dressed casually, so he doesn't seem to be too concerned about wanting to appear businesslike or professional.)* Then, ask students to describe what the image tells them about what Kielburger is doing. *(Possible answer: The podium and microphone indicate that he is giving a speech or talk to an audience and perhaps interacting with them; the projected images suggest that he is speaking about an effort that young people are working on together.)dcccccccc*

©Arthur Mola/AP Images

WHEN STUDENTS STRUGGLE...

To guide comprehension about elements of personal essays, have students work independently or with a partner to complete a chart like the one shown to identify ideas the author shares. Then have students share their charts with a larger group.

and certainly much nicer than mine. José grinned from ear to ear when I put it on.

I will never forget José, because he taught me more about sharing that day than anyone I have ever known. He may have been a poor street child, but I saw more goodness in him than all of the world leaders I have ever met. If more people had the heart of a street child, like José, and were willing to share, there would be no more poverty and a lot less suffering in this world. Sometimes young people find life today too depressing. It all seems so hopeless. They would rather escape, go dancing or listen to their favorite music, play video games or hang out with their friends. They dream of true love, a home of their own, or having a good time at the next party. At sixteen, I also like to dance, have fun, and dream for the future. But I have discovered that it takes more than material things to find real happiness and meaning in life.

One day I was the guest on a popular television talk show in Canada. I shared the interview with another young person involved in cancer research. Several times during the program this young man, who was twenty years old, told the host that he was "gifted," as indicated by a test he had taken in third grade. Turning my way, the host **inquired** whether I, too, was gifted. Never having been tested for the gifted program, I answered that I was not.

When I returned home my mother asked me, "Are you certain you aren't gifted?" I realized that I had given the wrong answer. I was gifted, and the more I reflected, the more I concluded that I had never met a person who was not special or talented in some way.

Some people are gifted with their hands and can produce marvelous creations in their **capacity** as carpenters, artists, or builders. Others have a kind heart, are compassionate, understanding, or are special peacemakers; others, again, are humorous and bring joy into our lives. We have all met individuals who are gifted in science or sports, have great organizational skills or a healing touch. And, of course, some people are very talented at making money. Indeed, even the most physically or mentally challenged person teaches all of us about the value and worth of human life.

inquire
(ĭn-kwīr´) v. If you *inquire* about something, you ask about it.

capacity
(kə-păs´ĭ-tē) n. A person's *capacity* is his or her role or position.

Thoughts the author shares	What he wants others to understand
José, who had nothing, taught him about sharing.	Life would be better for everyone if we all learned to share.
Many young people see life as depressing.	

CLOSE READ

Analyze Text: Personal Essay (LINES 94–107; 116–130)

COMMON CORE RI 3, RI 5

Remind students that in a personal essay an author often shares personal experiences from which he or she gained insight or learned a lesson.

F ASK STUDENTS to review lines 94–107 and explain how Kielburger learned an important lesson from his experiences with José in Brazil. *(Possible answer: From spending time with Jose and being so impressed with the boy's generosity, Kielburger learns that happiness and meaning in life do not come from material possessions.)*

Point out to students that a personal essay may be a blend of storytelling, facts, and wisdom.

G CITE TEXT EVIDENCE Ask students to reread lines 116–130 and identify elements of storytelling, facts, and wisdom. *(In lines 116–120, Kielburger concludes a story about being on a talk show and then presents the wise statement that he "had never met a person who was not special or talented in some way." He follows this up with facts that describe particular talents that people might have.)*

CRITICAL VOCABULARY

inquire: The author tells how a talk show host inquired about whether Kielburger was gifted.

capacity: The author uses capacities to discuss different roles or positions people have.

ASK STUDENTS to tell what questions the talk show host might have inquired of the author in his capacity as the founder of Free the Children. *(He might have asked how Kielburger got the idea, what inspired him, or what the organization has done.)*

Determine Author's Point of View (LINES 131–137) COMMON CORE RI 6

Explain that to determine an author's perspective students can look for **opinions,** or ideas that cannot be proved, that the author shares and examine the author's **tone,** or attitude toward a subject.

H ASK STUDENTS to reread lines 131–133 and note the author's opinion that God "gave each and every person special talents or gifts, but he made no one gifted in all areas." Have students reread lines 134–137 and tell what these lines reveal about the author's perspective. (*Possible answer: His perspective is that we have to pool our talents to bring about happiness.*)

Analyze the Meanings of Words and Phrases COMMON CORE RI 1, RI 4

(LINES 138–145)

Explain that an author's perspective can also be determined by examining the tone, or attitude toward a subject, that the author uses.

I CITE TEXT EVIDENCE Have students reread lines 138–145, cite details that reveal the author's tone, and explain the tone. (*"each of us has the power to be Superman," "I dream of the day," and "when all children … are free to be children" show that the tone is optimistic.*)

> **CRITICAL VOCABULARY**
>
> **exploitation:** The author uses the word *exploitation* to describe one of the world's "worst evils."
>
> **ASK STUDENTS** to identify examples the author provides to show how children are exploited. (*José has to sift through a garbage dump; Muniannal has to separate dangerous used syringes.*)

COLLABORATIVE DISCUSSION Have partners take notes on the children Kielburger describes and why he tells about them, citing evidence from the text.

ASK STUDENTS to share any questions they generated in the course of reading and discussing the selection.

I think that God, in fact, played a trick on us. He gave each and every person special talents or gifts, but he made no one gifted in all areas.

H Collectively, we have all it takes to create a just and peaceful world, but we must work together and share our talents. We all need one another to find happiness within ourselves and within the world.

140 I realize, now, that each of us has the power to be Superman and to help rid the world of its worst evils— poverty, loneliness, and **exploitation**. I dream of the day when Jeffrey leaves the garbage dump, when Muniannal no longer has to separate used syringes and can go to school, and when all children, regardless of place of birth or economic circumstance, are free to be children. I dream of the day when we all have José's courage to share.

exploitation
(ĕk´sploi-tā´shən) *n.*
Exploitation is the unfair treatment or use of something or someone for selfish reasons.

COLLABORATIVE DISCUSSION What is Craig Kielburger's purpose in describing the particular children he has met? Talk about your ideas with other group members.

Analyze Text: Personal Essay

 COMMON CORE RI 3, RI 5

A **personal essay**, like "Craig Kielburger Reflects on Working Toward Peace," is a nonfiction essay in which an author expresses an opinion or provides some insight based on personal experiences. Authors have different purposes for writing a personal essay. Often it is to make others aware of an important issue or topic by connecting the topic to the author's own life.

Personal essays often include the following elements:
- descriptions of personal experiences in which the author gained significant insight or learned a lesson
- first-person point of view, using the pronouns *I* and *we*
- a mixture of storytelling, personality, facts, and wisdom
- casual language that seems like a conversation with the reader

Review Kielburger's personal essay, and find an example of each element.

Determine Author's Point of View

 COMMON CORE RI 6

The author of a personal essay has a **perspective,** the unique combination of ideas, values, feelings, and beliefs that influence the way he or she looks at a topic. In his essay, Kielburger shows how he looks at himself, others, and his role in the world. To understand an author's perspective, note these features in the essay:
- statements of the author's **opinions**—personal ideas that cannot be proven true
- details and examples from the author's experiences
- words and descriptions that have emotional impact
- the writer's **tone,** or attitude toward a subject, such as humorous or serious

As you read personal essays, you can figure out the author's perspective by completing a chart such as this one.

Statement, Detail, or Tone	What It Reveals About Kielburger
"that day changed my life forever" (line 17)	He is affected by the stories and hardships of others.

Reread lines 20–41. What does the last sentence of each paragraph reveal about Kielburger's perspective?

CLOSE READ

Analyze Text: Personal Essay

 COMMON CORE RI 3, RI 5

Help students understand what a personal essay is. Discuss each part of the definition: it is nonfiction, it is an essay, and it shares an opinion or an insight that comes from the author's personal experiences.

Discuss the elements often included in personal essays. Have students point out examples of each element from the selection. *(Examples: Kielburger retells his personal experience of reading about a Pakistani child laborer and how it changed his life. Throughout, Kielburger uses the first-person pronoun I. Kielburger tells stories, such as his exchange of T-shirts with José. He interjects his own personality by sharing his amazed reaction to José's generosity. He includes facts and figures about the toll of poverty throughout the world ["more than 1.3 billion people . . . live in absolute poverty"]. He shares his wisdom in his insight that all people are "gifted." He begins with a casual description of his childhood fascination with Superman.)*

Determine Author's Point of View

 COMMON CORE RI 6

Discuss the author's perspective as a blend of his ideas, values, feelings, and beliefs. Have students explain what the text reveals about him. *(Possible answer: Each paragraph ends with a reference to a child's dream. Kielburger concludes with a dream of his own, showing that like all children he dreams of a better future.)*

Strategies for Annotation 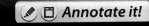 Annotate it!

Analyze Text: Personal Essay

 COMMON CORE RI 3, RI 5

Share these strategies for guided or independent analysis:
- Highlight in yellow a personal insight the author shares.
- Highlight in green first-person pronouns.
- Indicate where the author shares a personal experience by highlighting the beginning in pink.
- Underline words and phrases that are conversational and casual.

I have learned <u>my best lessons</u> from other children—children like the girls I encountered in India who carried their friend from place to place because she had no legs—and children like José.

<u>I met José in the streets of</u> San Salvador, Brazil, where he lived with a group of street children between the ages of eight

Analyzing the Text

RI 1, RI 2,
RI 3, RI 5,
RI 6

Possible answers:

1. *Kielburger was the same age as the murdered Pakistani boy, who had lived as a slave. The sudden awareness of injustice against a boy like him caused Kielburger to act like his hero, Superman, and try to save the world.*

2. *Kielburger is compassionate because he cares about children who are struggling and suffering. He is hopeful because he believes that poor people's lives can improve. He is motivated because he started his own organization and became an activist.*

3. *Kielburger gives facts and figures to support his claim that poverty can be ended. He probably hopes that readers will consider spending money on poor people instead of on luxury items like cosmetics and ice cream to help end world poverty.*

4. *Kielburger says that he—and everyone else in the world—is gifted. The gifts are unique talents that people can share with one another, such as the ability to build things, play sports, heal others, or make money. His purpose is to emphasize the great potential of every person and the connectedness of everyone in the world.*

5. *The essay introduction and conclusion both refer to Superman. In the introduction, Kielburger presents Superman as a child's fantasy hero. In the conclusion, he says that everyone has the power to be a real "Superman" and end real evils in the world.*

6. *It is valid because if people behaved less selfishly and shared what they had the world would be a better place. Selfishness about things, land, and beliefs are what cause fights, wars, and injustice. It's not valid because world suffering can't be reduced by people acting like street children and sharing what they have; that's too simple a view of how economies work in the real world.*

 eBook *Annotate It!*

Analyzing the Text

 RI 1, RI 2, RI 3, RI 5, RI 6, RI 8, W 1, W 4, W 9b, W 10

Cite Text Evidence   Support your responses with evidence from the text.

1. **Cause/Effect** Why did the story about the murdered boy have such a strong impact on Kielburger?

2. **Infer** What words would you use to describe Kielburger, and why are those descriptions fitting?

3. **Analyze** Reread lines 37–54. Why does Kielburger provide this information? What effect might he hope this section has on the reader?

4. **Draw Conclusions** What is Kielburger's purpose in saying that he is gifted?

5. **Analyze** How does Kielburger connect the introduction and conclusion of his essay?

6. **Evaluate** Reread lines 94–108. Is Kielburger's statement about "the heart of a street child" valid? Why do you think that?

PERFORMANCE TASK

Writing Activity: Critique Has this essay persuaded you that global poverty can be ended? Why or why not? Write a two to three paragraph essay offering your opinion of Craig Kielburger's essay.

- Consider questions such as, *Does Kielburger do enough to convince you? Does his choice of evidence effectively support his point of view? If not, why is it inadequate and what additional evidence might he have included?*

- Take notes on the evidence that Kielburger uses to support his claim about ending poverty.

- In your essay, be sure to include an interesting introduction that clearly states your claim.

- Use the evidence you found in the text to support your claim.

- Include a conclusion that summarizes your opinion.

Assign this performance task. my WriteSmart

PERFORMANCE TASK

COMMON CORE
RI 1, RI 8,
W 1, W 4,
W 9b, W 10

Writing Activity: Critique Have students work independently. Direct them to

- organize their critique in a logical way
- be sure they have clearly stated their claim
- include reasons and evidence from the text that support their ideas

Critical Vocabulary

COMMON CORE L 4, L 4c, L 6

syringe	possession	inquire
capacity	exploitation	

Practice and Apply Identify the vocabulary word that is tied in meaning to the italicized word in each question. Give your reasons.

1. Which word goes with *needle*?

2. Which word goes with *answer*?

3. Which word goes with *underpaid*?

4. Which word goes with *ownership*?

5. Which word goes with *skill*?

Vocabulary Strategy: Multiple Meanings

The definition of a word often depends on its **context**, the words and sentences that surround it. Note the word *capacity* in these two sentences:

> A. The only tickets left were "Standing Room Only" because the theater was filled to capacity.

> B. Some people are gifted with their hands and can produce marvelous creations in their capacity as carpenters, artists, or builders.

To figure out the meaning in each sentence, first use context to make a logical guess. Then you can use a print or digital dictionary to look up and choose the appropriate definition.

The word *capacity* has many meanings. The context helps you make a logical guess about which one fits in each sentence. In sentence A, *capacity* means "a maximum number." In sentence B, from Kielburger's essay, *capacity* means "a position or role." These meanings can be confirmed in a dictionary.

Practice and Apply Use context to give a likely meaning for the italicized word in each sentence. Check your idea in a print or digital dictionary.

1. A. Kielburger read an *article* in the newspaper.
   B. Remember to put the correct *article* before a noun.

2. A. Kielburger met children at work in fields of *cane*.
   B. The man tapped the *cane* on the sidewalk as he walked.

3. A. The United Nations published a *document* about ending poverty.
   B. Students learn to *document* their sources when doing research.

Critical Vocabulary

COMMON CORE L 4, L 4a, L 4c, L 4d, L 6

Possible answers:

1. syringe: *A needle is part of a syringe, which is a medical instrument that injects or draws out fluids.*

2. inquire: *When you inquire, or ask, you get an answer.*

3. exploitation: *Workers who are underpaid are being used unfairly, which is an example of exploitation.*

4. possession: *Something that you own, or possess, is a possession.*

5. capacity: *If you have the capacity to do something, you have the skill to do it.*

Vocabulary Strategy: Multiple Meanings

1. A. *a written account*
   B. *the word* the, a, *or an*

2. A. *sugarcane*
   B. *a walking stick*

3. A. *a published report*
   B. *to cite the source of a quotation or piece of information and to make a bibliography of sources used in research*

Strategies for Annotation 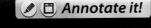 *Annotate it!*

Multiple Meanings

COMMON CORE L 4, L 4a, L 4d, L 6

Have students review lines 101–107 from the selection to identify which meaning of the word *material* the author intends. Encourage them to use their eBook annotation tools to do the following:

- Highlight the word *material* in yellow.
- Reread the surrounding words and sentences, looking for clues to the word's meaning. Underline the clues.
- Review your annotations and try to infer the word's meaning as it is used in the sentence.
- Use a print or digital dictionary to confirm which meaning the author intends, and make a note of that meaning.

They would rather escape, go dancing or listen to th[e] music, play video games or hang out with their frien[ds] of true love, a home of their own, or having a good ti[me] party. At sixteen, I also like to dance, have fun, and dream for the future. But I have discovered that it takes more than material things to find real happiness and meaning in life.

> material: *adj.* Of or concerned with the physical as opposed to the spiritual or intellectual.

PRACTICE & APPLY

Language Conventions: Dangling Modifiers

Discuss the terms and guide students to recognize how a dangling modifier does not connect to a specific word in a sentence. As you examine each example of a dangling modifier, point out that the modifier is intended to connect to a word that follows it but that no such word is present in the sentence.

Answers:

1. *Correct*

2. *Possible answer: To bring attention to child poverty, Kielburger took the first step of forming an organization.*

3. *Correct*

4. *Possible answer: Separating used syringes for plastic parts, the little girl is likely to harm her health.*

5. *Possible answer: Sharing their few possessions, the poor have generous hearts.*

6. *Possible answer: Finding poverty everywhere in the world, we cannot imagine ending the problem.*

 Assess It!

Online Selection Test
- Download an editable ExamView bank.
- Assign and manage this test online.

 COMMON CORE L 1c

Language Conventions: Dangling Modifiers

A **modifier** is a word or a group of words that changes, or modifies, the meaning of another word in a sentence. Some modifiers are phrases used as adjectives and adverbs to describe or give more detail. A **dangling modifier** is a modifier that modifies a word not clearly stated in the sentence. It often appears at the start of a sentence.

In the following examples, take note of the sentences with a dangling modifier and their corrected versions.

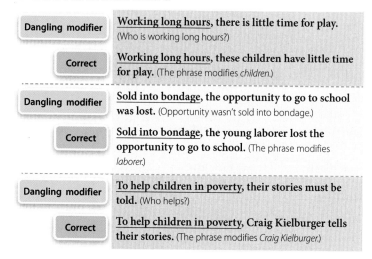

Dangling modifier	Working long hours, there is little time for play. (Who is working long hours?)
Correct	Working long hours, these children have little time for play. (The phrase modifies *children*.)
Dangling modifier	Sold into bondage, the opportunity to go to school was lost. (Opportunity wasn't sold into bondage.)
Correct	Sold into bondage, the young laborer lost the opportunity to go to school. (The phrase modifies *laborer*.)
Dangling modifier	To help children in poverty, their stories must be told. (Who helps?)
Correct	To help children in poverty, Craig Kielburger tells their stories. (The phrase modifies *Craig Kielburger*.)

Practice and Apply Identify the correctly written sentences. Fix the sentences with dangling modifiers.

1. Shocked by the article about a murdered child weaver, Kielburger felt a strong desire to make a change.

2. To bring attention to child poverty, the first step was forming an organization.

3. To support his family, one boy hunts for items in a garbage dump.

4. Separating used syringes for plastic parts, harm to the little girl's health is likely.

5. Sharing their few possessions, generous hearts are found among the poor.

6. Finding poverty everywhere in the world, it's hard to imagine ending the problem.

Trace an Argument

COMMON CORE

RI 2,
RI 8

TEACH

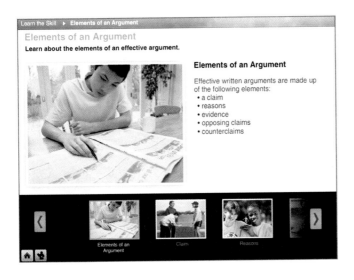

Explain to students that an argument is speaking or writing that expresses a position on a problem and supports it with reasons and evidence.

Use the Interactive Whiteboard Lesson "Elements of an Argument" to build background for and teach the skill. Guide students through the following sections:

1. Share What You Know
2. Learn the Skill
3. Reading an Argument
4. Elements of an Argument
5. Argument Machine
6. How to Read an Argument
7. Tips for Reading an Argument

PRACTICE AND APPLY

After completing the Practice and Apply screens of the IWB lesson, have partners review "Craig Kielburger Reflects on Working Toward Peace" and identify examples of claims the author presents and evidence he uses to support each claim.

Analyze Text:
Personal Essay

COMMON CORE

RI 3,
RI 5

RETEACH

Review with students that in a personal essay the author expresses an opinion or shares an insight based on his or her personal experiences. Often the author's purpose for writing a personal essay is to make others aware of an important issue or topic.

Use a graphic organizer like the one shown to discuss elements of personal essays. Guide students to add examples of each element from "Craig Kielburger Reflects."

Element	Example from text
• includes descriptions of personal experiences that resulted in a lesson or insight for the author	Craig's story about his television appearance that leads to his realization about people being "gifted"
• uses first-person point of view	"One day I was a guest"; "I shared"; "Turning my way"; "my mother asked me"
• presents a mix of storytelling, personality, facts, wisdom	His recounting of his realization shows his hopeful, optimistic personality.
• uses casual, conversational language	

You may wish to have students focus on a particular section of text, such as lines 108–137. Have students work independently or in pairs. When they are done, have students discuss their responses with a larger group.

CLOSE READING APPLICATION

Students can use the organizer to identify examples of each element from another personal essay they may have read or are reading on their own. Invite students to share their ideas about elements of a personal essay with the class.

mySmartPlanner   Create lesson plans and access resources online.

It Takes a Child

Documentary

Why This Media?

Students regularly encounter documentaries on television, online, and in classrooms. By learning to identify and analyze the different features in documentaries, students will become critical viewers—better able to understand the purposes of documentaries and how they convey information.

Key Learning Objective: The student will be able to analyze the purpose of a documentary and understand the features used in it.

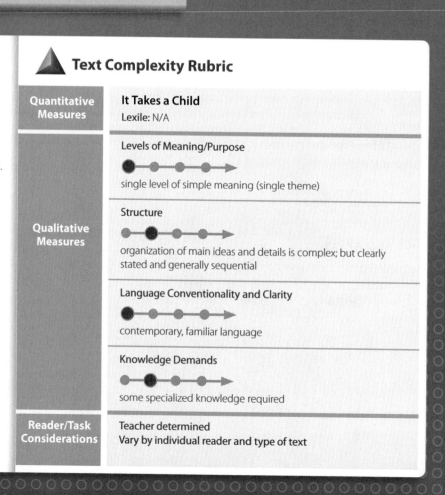

COMMON CORE Common Core Standards

RI 6   Determine point of view or purpose.
RI 7   Compare and contrast a text to an audio, video, or multimedia version.
SL 2   Analyze the main ideas and supporting details presented in diverse media.
SL 3   Delineate a speaker's argument and claims.
SL 4   Present claims and findings.
SL 5   Include multimedia and visuals in presentations.

Text Complexity Rubric

Quantitative Measures

It Takes a Child
Lexile: N/A

Qualitative Measures

Levels of Meaning/Purpose

single level of simple meaning (single theme)

Structure

organization of main ideas and details is complex; but clearly stated and generally sequential

Language Conventionality and Clarity

contemporary, familiar language

Knowledge Demands

some specialized knowledge required

Reader/Task Considerations

Teacher determined
Vary by individual reader and type of text

TEACH

CLOSE READ

Background Have students read the background information about *It Takes a Child*. Remind students that when Craig Kielburger was only twelve years old he founded Free the Children, an organization whose goal is to help young people achieve their fullest potential. Point out that Kielburger became interested in the plight of children after reading about a 12-year-old boy in Pakistan who had been sold into bondage. Explain that although many countries have laws forbidding the use of children as laborers other countries do not have these laws or are very lax in the enforcement of these laws. Discovering this, young Craig was inspired to show the world the sad realities of child labor in some parts of the world. This documentary tells about the trip he made to South Asia to view child labor up close.

SETTING A PURPOSE Direct students to use the Setting a Purpose information and prompt to focus their viewing. Remind students to generate questions as they read and view.

Background *When child activist Craig Kielburger was twelve years old, he became interested in the plight of child laborers. Inspired by the story of twelve-year-old Iqbal, a child labor activist who had been murdered in South Asia, Kielburger realized that a child could make a difference in the world. Kielburger then traveled to South Asia to see child labor first hand. With the help of a film crew, he documented his journey so that the world could see what he himself had witnessed.*

MEDIA ANALYSIS

from
It Takes a Child

Documentary directed by Judy Jackson

©Bullfrog Films

SETTING A PURPOSE The documentary you are about to view features some of the adults and children Craig Kielburger spoke with during his trip to South Asia. It also shows workplaces he visited and what he observed there.

As you view the film clip, think about why Kielburger decided to make this journey and what he wanted to find out. Notice the ways that filmmaking and news reporting come together to help you understand Kielburger's reasons for traveling to South Asia. Write down any questions you have during viewing.

SCAFFOLDING FOR ELL STUDENTS

Language Support Explain to students that the documentary contains both formal speech patterns and conversational speech patterns. For example, Kielburger speaks in an informal tone with a lot of phrases, whereas the narrator uses a formal tone and only complete sentences. Have mixed-ability groups watch the documentary together and compare the formal narration with the conversational interviews. Ask students to summarize the information included in both types of features.

TEACH

CLOSE READ

AS YOU VIEW Tell students that they will be watching a documentary. A **documentary** is a nonfiction film that gives information about important or noteworthy people, places, or events. Explain that documentary filmmakers use special kinds of filmmaking techniques in order to present information in a way that will have an impact on viewers. Point out that some of these techniques include the following:

- **interviews,** or the spoken words of people in the documentary
- **footage,** or sections of film that give specific information about the subject
- **voice-over narration,** or the spoken words of an unseen narrator who tells about the subject

Have students read the As You View paragraphs to help them focus their viewing and to understand how a documentary filmmaker makes choices about which techniques to use. Then, as students watch the video clip, have them keep track of examples of the documentary filmmaker's techniques, note how each is used in this film, and note the impact each technique has on the viewer.

COLLABORATIVE DISCUSSION Have students work with a partner to list the interviews and images that the filmmaker presents. Then, have students discuss each one and the impact it had on them as they watched the film clip. Students can tell which technique had the most impact on them and give reasons for their thinking.

ASK STUDENTS to share any questions they generated in the course of viewing and discussing the documentary.

Format: Documentary

Running Time: 2:54 minutes

AS YOU VIEW Documentary filmmakers gather factual material about their subjects, much like news reporters do, and use film to tell a true story about their subjects. The filmmakers then use various techniques to convey the information in a way that will have an impact on the viewers.

As you view the documentary clip, consider how the director's choice of scenes affects the impact of the words spoken in the interviews. As needed, pause the video and write notes about what impresses you and about ideas you might want to talk about later. Replay or rewind the video so that you can clarify anything you do not understand.

COLLABORATIVE DISCUSSION With a partner, discuss how the film presents an inside view into child labor conditions. Which of the interviews and images had the most impact? Why? Discuss the concepts the film conveys and how it conveys them. Cite specific evidence from the documentary to support your ideas.

©Bullfrog Films

APPLYING ACADEMIC VOCABULARY

contrast	interact

As you discuss the video, incorporate the following Collection 6 academic vocabulary words: *contrast* and *interact*. Ask students to describe how Kielburger and the children in the documentary **interact.** Then, ask students to **contrast** their lives to the lives of the children in the documentary.

Analyze Media

A **documentary** is a nonfiction film that gives viewers information about important people, major events, significant discoveries, or historical places. Documentaries use features to help viewers understand the information.

Features of a Documentary	Strategies for Viewing
Interviews are usually filmed specifically for a documentary. Filmmakers may interview: • experts on the subject • people who knew the person • people who were involved in an event	Think about why the filmmaker chose this person for an interview. Does the person: • have special knowledge about the subject? • present another side of the story?
Footage is filmed material that gives information about a subject. Documentary filmmakers combine different types of footage to tell their subject's story. Footage can include film clips, news reports, photographs, and interviews about a subject.	Think about why the particular footage was chosen. Does it: • show details of a historical time? • create an emotional response? • reveal the filmmaker's perspective or point of view?
Voice-over narration is the voice of an unseen speaker that is heard on a documentary. The voice-over can provide important facts about the subject. It can also help explain the footage.	Listen to the voice-over narration for additional information about the footage. Does the voice-over change from one speaker to another? What points made by voice-overs seem most important to the subject?
Sounds effects can be used for a variety of purposes.	Follow the music cues. Do they signal a change in the documentary's setting or mood? Listen for sound effects, such as screeching tires or bombs exploding. Do they help you better understand what is happening? Listen to the dialogue. Does it help you better understand the subjects?

Think about how these features interact with each other in the clip from *It Takes a Child* to tell the story of Craig Kielburger's commitment to the cause of exposing the injustices of child labor.

Analyze Media

 COMMON CORE SL 2

Help students understand the different kinds of features, or techniques, used by documentary filmmakers to convey information.

- Discuss the strategies for viewing for each kind of feature. Have students name one example of each type of feature from the documentary. *(Possible answers: Kielburger interviews a man who supervises a girl worker. There is film clip footage of Kielburger sitting with a group of children, asking them questions and clearly connecting with them on a personal level. A woman narrates the documentary, although the narration also includes sections of 15-year-old Craig talking about his trip. There is music from some of the places where Kielburger travels.)*

- Have students answer the corresponding questions about the strategies for viewing. *(Possible answers: The interview with the supervisor gives viewers knowledge about the work conditions of the girl with the syringes. The film clip of Kielburger shows the setting where he traveled and how close he became with the children he was interviewing. The music gives viewers a sense of the foreign cultures where Kielburger traveled.)*

- Point out that after filmmakers shoot the scenes and record the sounds, they assemble and edit the scenes and sounds to help convey the documentary's message. Explain that part of that editing process is deciding which techniques work best. Ask students how effectively the filmmakers of Craig Kielburger's trip wove the techniques together to tell Craig's story. How easy was it for students to understand the message of the documentary?

Analyzing the Media

COMMON CORE RI 6, RI 7, SL 2, SL 3

Possible answers:

1. The central idea of the documentary is that children in some parts of the world are forced to do hard work and that this practice is unjust. The documentary shows several scenes of actual children doing child labor, such as the little girl who is sorting through used medical syringes.

2. The filmmaker's purpose is to inform and to persuade the viewer that the practices of child labor are unjust. The footage and interviews about the girl with the syringes seem startling and sad. The interview with the man about the girl makes the example more startling because he seems so uninformed as to the dangers of her task.

3. **Interview:** Kielburger's interview with the man about the girl with the syringes shows how indifferent people in these countries are to the dangers of this type of child labor. **Footage:** Footage of Kielburger observing child laborers shows how closely he was able to research the subject. **Voice-over:** A female narrator's voice tells details about Kielburger's trip, and Kielburger's voice, as a fifteen-year-old, describes what he wanted to do and his reactions. **Sound effects:** We hear music from India stopping at important points to emphasize the seriousness of the content. Then, it softly and dramatically starts up again.

4. The opening footage, with scenes and music from some of the places Kielburger visits, gives viewers a sense of the cultures in these places.

5. The woman's and Craig's voice-overs contribute details about why and how Craig traveled to India, including Craig's feelings about the trip. The interviews with the little girl with the syringes and the man provide specific details about that situation and show the man's indifference to or ignorance of the dangers the girl faces.

6. In his essay, Craig shares additional details about the girl who was sorting syringes. We learn that she was eight years old when he met her and that she, like Craig and the other children he met, had a dream. Her dream was to be a teacher. The film clip shows the reality of the awful conditions she works in. It also shows twelve-year-old Craig's sad reaction when he talks to the man about the little girl's work and its dangers. Together, the documentary and the essay show that Craig not only investigated the issues in person, but that he followed up by sharing his findings and experiences. He was guided by a cause not only to investigate unfair child labor, but also to try to convince others of the need for action.

Analyzing the Media

COMMON CORE RI 6, RI 7, SL 2, SL 3, SL 4, SL 5

Cite Text Evidence   Support your responses with evidence from the media.

1. **Infer and Summarize** What is the **central idea,** or most important idea about a topic, that the documentary presents? Describe the scenes that take place in the film and how those scenes support the central idea.

2. **Analyze** Identify the filmmaker's purpose or purposes in making the documentary. What key parts of the film convey the purpose or purposes?

3. **Infer** Think about the features the filmmaker uses in the documentary. Fill out a chart like this one and tell how they clarify the issues presented.

Feature	How It Clarifies Issues

4. **Analyze** How does the opening introduce the setting? What combination of features work together in the opening to present a sense of the place Kielburger is visiting and to help you understand the setting?

5. **Compare** Compare and contrast the information in the narrator voice-over and in the interviews. What information does each feature contribute?

6. **Evaluate** Think about your reading of the personal essay by Craig Kielburger in this collection. How do the ideas presented in the documentary help clarify the points made in the essay and how do both relate to the collection topic, "Guided by a Cause"?

PERFORMANCE TASK

Media Activity: Photo Documentary
What does it take to be committed to a cause despite great obstacles? Let people know about a person in your school or community who works on an important social cause. Create a photo documentary to tell that person's story.

- Take photos of the person involved in his or her work, or use photos that already exist.

- Choose some of the documentary features you learned about to help you create your documentary.

- Interview your subject and include quotations in your documentary or record a soundtrack of the interview with music.

- Present your documentary to a group of classmates. Then discuss their reactions to it.

Assign this performance task.

PERFORMANCE TASK

COMMON CORE SL 4, SL 5

Media Activity: Photo Documentary Have students develop their documentaries about a school or community worker. Students should:

- choose the worker and gather or take photos of that person at work
- create a set of questions that will reveal his or her social cause
- record the interview or use quotations
- decide whether to add music and sound effects
- present the documentary to the class

Camera Shots and Shot Selection

COMMON CORE

SL 2

TEACH

Explain to students that filmmakers use different kinds of camera shots in their documentaries. A **camera shot** is a single continuous view taken by a camera. Each camera shot is chosen by a filmmaker to create a specific effect on viewers. When all the camera shots are completed, the filmmaker reviews them all and decides which ones to put together to create the entire film. Putting together a variety of camera shots allows the filmmaker to emphasize different ideas. It also adds variety to the film, making it more interesting to watch.

Discuss the following camera shots with students:

- An **establishing shot** introduces viewers to the location of the scene, usually by presenting a wide view of an area. A filmmaker will choose this kind of shot to establish the setting. In the Kielburger documentary, the first footage establishes the setting in a city in India, with evidence of poverty and more traditional forms of transportation.
- A **close-up** shot shows a close view of a person or object. A filmmaker will use this kind of shot to make viewers feel like they know the character. The filmmakers of *It Takes a Child* show close-ups of children's smiling faces, showing how young and innocent they are.
- A **long shot** gives a wide view of a scene, showing a person and his or her surroundings. A filmmaker uses this kind of shot to allow viewers to see the "big picture" and to show the relationship between the characters and the environment. The long shot of the boat on the river shows one of the common forms of transportation in this part of India.
- A **point-of-view** shot shows what a character sees through his or her eyes. A filmmaker uses this kind of a shot to help viewers identify with a character. Point-of-view shots of the syringes show the dangerous reality of the job done by the little girl.

PRACTICE AND APPLY

Have students view *It Takes a Child* again. Ask them to identify other examples of these camera shots and to tell their effects on viewers. Have students discuss how each shot makes the documentary more interesting and effective.

Elements of a Documentary

COMMON CORE

SL 2

RETEACH

Remind students that documentary filmmakers use different kinds of techniques to help viewers understand the information they want to convey. Review the following techniques with students:

- **Interviews** are question-and-answer sessions that are usually filmed specifically for a documentary. Filmmakers may interview experts on a subject, the people involved in an event or situation, or others who are close to those people.
- **Footage** is filmed material that gives information about a subject. Footage can include film clips, news reports, photographs, and interviews about a subject.
- **Voice-over narration** is the voice of an unseen speaker that is heard over a documentary. The voice-over can provide important facts about the subject or help explain the footage.
- **Sound effects** can be used for various purposes. Music can be used to create a mood or to give clues about the setting. Sound effects like cars driving give a sense of the setting. Dialogue can give viewers a better sense of the people in a documentary.

CLOSE VIEWING APPLICATION

Have students view another documentary and name the kinds of techniques the filmmaker uses. Have students discuss the purpose of these techniques and their effects on viewers.

Difference Maker: John Bergmann and Popcorn Park

Newspaper Article by David Karas

Why This Text

Students may have difficulty discerning the author's purpose and point of view in a newspaper article. When the article profiles a noteworthy character with a compelling story, figuring out the author's perspective becomes more challenging. With the help of the close-reading questions, students will analyze the author's statements, examples, and descriptions of the subject. This close reading will lead students to understand the author's purpose, as well as the remarkable subject.

Background Have students read the background and information about the article and John Bergmann. Introduce the article by reviewing the life histories of different kinds of domestic animals. Pets like cats, dogs, and canaries can hope to live out their lives in the homes of their owners. But other domestic animals—cast-offs from circuses, zoos, theme parks, and laboratories—face an uncertain future.

SETTING A PURPOSE Ask students to pay attention to the author's statements about—and descriptions of—Bergmann. What do they reveal about the author's purpose and point of view?

Common Core Support

- cite multiple pieces of text evidence
- determine central ideas in a text
- analyze individuals, events, and ideas
- determine the meaning of words
- determine an author's purpose or point of view

Text Complexity Rubric

	Difference Maker: John Bergmann and Popcorn Park
Quantitative Measures	Lexile: 1130
Qualitative Measures	**Levels of Meaning/Purpose** single topic
	Structure genre traits common to informational text
	Language Conventionality and Clarity literal, accessible language
	Knowledge Demands everyday knowledge required
Reader/Task Considerations	Teacher determined

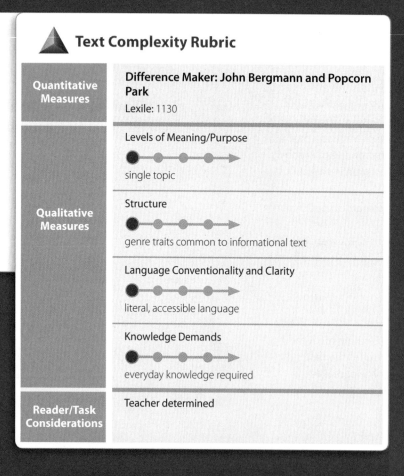

Strategies for CLOSE READING

Determine Author's Purpose and Point of View

Students should read this article carefully all the way through. Close-reading questions at the bottom of the page will help them focus on a thorough analysis of the author's purpose. As they read, students should jot down comments or questions about the text in the margins.

WHEN STUDENTS STRUGGLE . . .

To help students determine the author's purpose in "Difference Maker," have them work in small groups to fill out a chart like the one shown below.

CITE TEXT EVIDENCE For practice in determining an author's purpose, ask students to cite text evidence for each cell in the left column of the chart and then interpret the evidence in the adjoining cell of the right column.

Statement of opinion	What it reveals
Bergmann "seems to have found his dream job" (line 98)	The author understands how lucky Bergmann is; maybe the author is a little envious.
Bergmann "chuckles as he lifts up the towels that cover the papers in his office—which is in a barn." (lines 2–3)	The author thinks Bergmann is a kind, unassuming man.
Animals "treat Bergmann like a rock star." (lines 24–25)	The author has a sense of humor and uses it to make a point.
"It took many nights of comfort and coaxing to help him become comfortable" (lines 54–55)	The author admires Bergmann's compassionate attitude toward animals.

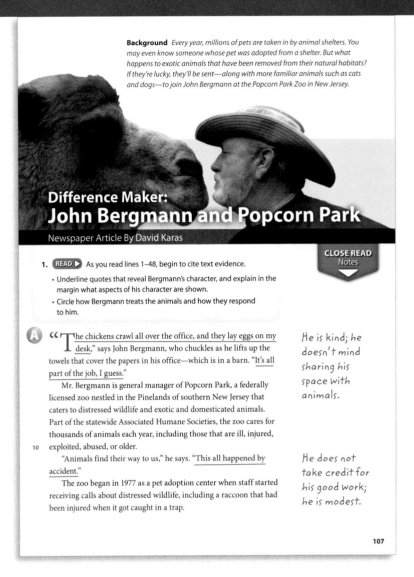

Background *Every year, millions of pets are taken in by animal shelters. You may even know someone whose pet was adopted from a shelter. But what happens to exotic animals that have been removed from their natural habitats? If they're lucky, they'll be sent—along with more familiar animals such as cats and dogs—to join John Bergmann at the Popcorn Park Zoo in New Jersey.*

Difference Maker:
John Bergmann and Popcorn Park
Newspaper Article By David Karas

CLOSE READ
Notes

1. **READ** ▶ As you read lines 1–48, begin to cite text evidence.
   • Underline quotes that reveal Bergmann's character, and explain in the margin what aspects of his character are shown.
   • Circle how Bergmann treats the animals and how they respond to him.

A "The chickens crawl all over the office, and they lay eggs on my desk," says John Bergmann, who chuckles as he lifts up the towels that cover the papers in his office—which is in a barn. "It's all part of the job, I guess."

Mr. Bergmann is general manager of Popcorn Park, a federally licensed zoo nestled in the Pinelands of southern New Jersey that caters to distressed wildlife and exotic and domesticated animals. Part of the statewide Associated Humane Societies, the zoo cares for thousands of animals each year, including those that are ill, injured,
10 exploited, abused, or older.

"Animals find their way to us," he says. "This all happened by accident."

The zoo began in 1977 as a pet adoption center when staff started receiving calls about distressed wildlife, including a raccoon that had been injured when it got caught in a trap.

He is kind; he doesn't mind sharing his space with animals.

He does not take credit for his good work; he is modest.

107

1. **READ AND CITE TEXT EVIDENCE** Explain to students that the article contains numerous quotes from Bergmann, and that such quotes can be informative at more than one level.

A ASK STUDENTS to find and cite quotes that tell the reader something about Bergmann. *Students should mention the article's opening sentence, "The chickens crawl all over the office.* What does this quote tell us about the chickens? *They have free run of Bergmann's office and do what chickens do—walk around and lay eggs.* What does the quote tell us about Bergmann? *It shows that he is the kind of person who welcomes animals into his life. He doesn't care if they mess up his office or lay eggs on his desk.*

CLOSE READ
Notes

CLOSE READ
Notes

As new animals came in, more cages were built, and piece by piece the zoo was born.

Today, more than 200 animals call the zoo home—including African lions, tigers, mountain lions, a camel, emus, wallabies, 20 monkeys, bears, and, of course, the peacocks that roam the property and greet the more than 75,000 annual visitors in the parking lot.

On a recent morning, Bergmann made his rounds to the different cages, greeting the animals individually and calling them by name.

The routine is a familiar one for the animal residents, who treat Bergmann like a rock star. Chickens hitch a ride on the back of his golf cart, and tigers twice his size rise to greet him and gain his attention.

"You are around [the animals] a lot," he says of his occupation. "I guess there is some realization [by them] that you have done 30 something for them."

B **C** Bergmann has bonded with each of the animals in his care, but Bengali is a special case. The Bengal tiger came to the zoo from Texas, where he had been rescued from an abusive, neglectful environment.

"He was **emaciated** . . . you could see all his ribs and bones," Bergmann recalls. "The way he looked, it was like he didn't have a will to live."

The staff slowly nursed Bengali back to health. He underwent surgeries to repair broken teeth and other ailments. His largest challenge, though, was getting back up to his proper weight—400 40 pounds—from 180 pounds.

It was when Bengali met an old lioness in the shelter next to his, Bergmann says, that he truly began to come alive. Each day, Bengali

He is humble. He does not say that the animals love him.

emaciated:
extremely thin

walked the fence to catch a glimpse of his new friend, until he finally built up the energy to walk his entire habitat.

"When he went out, he saw her, and he just got so excited," Bergmann said, smiling.

Today, when Bergmann visits, the massive tiger **chuffs** at him—a greeting—and rubs against the fence.

But helping animals recover from conditions like this isn't 50 achieved by sticking to an eight-hour workday.

"It is sometimes a 24/7 job," Bergmann says. "Dante [a tiger] is feeling uncomfortable, [so] you stay here through the night."

Dante, much the opposite of Bengali, became afraid of a lioness in a neighboring cage after his companion died. It took many nights of comfort and coaxing to help him again become comfortable with his enclosure.

D Bergmann credits his family with accommodating his unpredictable schedule – and his habit of occasionally bringing animals home with him to give them a little extra care and attention.

chuff:
make a sharp puffing sound

Staying up with Dante is similar to how parents sit through the night with a child who has nightmares.

2. ◀ REREAD Reread lines 31–46. Why does Karas include the story of Bengali? Support your answer with explicit textual evidence.

The story reveals Bergmann's connection to the animals. Bergmann nursed Bengali back to health, which made him very happy. Bengali returns Bergmann's affection—he "chuffs" when he sees Bergmann.

3. READ ▶ As you read lines 49–90, continue to cite textual evidence.

- Write two examples in the margin of how the zoo resembles a family, and underline sentences that support your answer.
- Circle how animals become residents of Popcorn Park.

Critical Vocabulary: emaciated (line 34) Have students share their definitions of *emaciated*. Explain whether you would describe an animal that should weigh 400 pounds but weighs only 180 pounds as emaciated. *An animal that is severely underweight must be described as emaciated.*

FOR ELL STUDENTS Explain to students that the phrase *made his rounds* means "went from place to place (as part of work)." Ask volunteers to name some jobs that involve making rounds. *Hospital doctors make daily rounds; delivery trucks make rounds.*

2. **REREAD AND CITE TEXT EVIDENCE**

B **ASK STUDENTS** to tell the story of Bengali in their own words. *He came from a place where he had been abused and neglected. Bergmann and his staff worked hard to make Bengali healthy. Bengali wasn't happy until he became friends with an old lioness. Bengali and Bergmann are glad when they see each other.*

3. **READ AND CITE TEXT EVIDENCE**

C **ASK STUDENTS** to find and cite passages about the zoo that remind them of family situations. *Students should note Bergmann's staying up all night with Dante (lines 51–56), his working seven days a week and not realizing it (lines 64–66), his comparison of the zoo to a retirement home (lines 74–75), and the home cooking for one of the animals (lines 85–87).*

Critical Vocabulary: chuff (line 47) Have students share their definitions of *chuff*, and ask volunteers to use the verb in sentences.

60 "My whole family has grown up with this," he says. His son, a veterinarian, works at the zoo, and his daughter, a teacher, uses animal themes in her lesson plans.

At the end of the day, Bergmann considers himself lucky.

"A lot of times you work seven days a week, and you don't even know it," he says. "You are doing what you love. You enjoy helping the animals out."

The staff has seen a wide range of animals find their way to Popcorn Park.

Porthos, a lion, was found in a converted horse stall with the floor
70 caked with excrement. Doe, a deer, is so old she has gray eyelashes. And Princess, a camel, has a talent for picking the winner of sporting events.

"We take them when no one else wants them," Bergmann says, admitting that the zoo can sometimes resemble a retirement home for older creatures living out their senior years in peace.

The zoo also has a large kennel, which has high adoption rates for the household pets there. Many come from states with severely overcrowded animal shelters, where animals would not be held long before being put down.

80 The zoo runs primarily on donations, Bergmann says, which help offset the cost of its 42 staff members, including veterinarians and animal control officers, who provide constant care for the animals.

And that doesn't include supplies and specialty food items needed to accommodate the picky eaters among the menagerie.

On a recent afternoon, the aroma of homemade mashed potatoes filled the zoo's kitchen. The meal was for one of the animals that enjoyed variety at lunchtime.

And, honoring the zoo's namesake, visitors can purchase air-popped popcorn to share with some of the farm and domesticated
90 animals that have less-rigid diets.

The animals are treated like family, including when it comes to their food preferences.

4. **REREAD AND DISCUSS** Reread lines 57–90. In a small group, discuss the ways Popcorn Park is different from other zoos.

5. **READ** As you read lines 91–119, continue to cite textual evidence.

- Underline what Bergmann wants people to learn from the zoo.
- Circle examples of Bergmann's compassionate character.

110

"He didn't belong here. . . . All we did was keep him company when he was here."

E Beyond helping animals in need, Bergmann says that the zoo has a larger mission.

"I always hope, and I always think, [that visitors] walk out of here with more compassion for animals than they walked in here with," he says. "I always thought that was a [large part] of our mission, that we would change the minds of people to have more compassion for animals."

While he seems to have found his dream job, Bergmann says he has trouble with one aspect of his work: saying goodbye to the
100 animals that die.

Sonny, an elephant, had been brought to the United States from Zimbabwe to be trained for circus work. After he resisted his training, he was sent to a New Mexico zoo, from which he escaped several times.

Rather than putting him down, in 1989 the zoo sent a letter to other facilities across the country to see if anyone might give a new home to the troubled creature.

"We were the only one that raised our hand," Bergmann says.

It took extensive care and much training, but Sonny finally
110 adapted to his new surroundings at Popcorn Park and lived there a dozen more years, dying in 2001.

A local funeral home donated its services to host a ceremony for Sonny, and Bergmann delivered a eulogy.

"He didn't belong here," he said, remembering his friend. "All we did was keep him company when he was here."

111

4. **REREAD AND DISCUSS USING TEXT EVIDENCE**

D **ASK STUDENTS** in each group to present the differences they found. *Students should mention the following differences: Popcorn Park is very much a family operation (lines 57–60), working at Popcorn Park is "doing what you love" (lines 64–66), Popcorn Park takes old and unwanted animals (lines 73–75), Popcorn Park has a kennel from which visitors can adopt household pets (lines 76–77), Popcorn Park's budget mainly comes from donations (line 80), and visitors can feed some of the animals at Popcorn Park (lines 88–90).*

5. **READ AND CITE TEXT EVIDENCE**

E **ASK STUDENTS** what Bergmann says about the zoo's "larger mission." *He hopes to "change the minds of" visitors when they go to the park and leave with "more compassion for animals" (lines 95–97).*

FOR ELL STUDENTS Spanish speakers will probably recognize a cognate for *eulogy (line 113): elogio*, meaning "a statement of praise." Point out that the English word *eulogy* often refers to a statement of praise given at a funeral.

CLOSE READ
Notes

For Bergmann, it was bittersweet to see Sonny leave Popcorn Park. "It is very sad that he is not with us any longer," Bergmann says, holding back tears as he adds a comforting thought. "But he is with his herd again."

F

6. **◀ REREAD** Reread lines 116–119. What does Bergmann mean when he says that Sonny is "with his herd again"?

He means that Sonny has joined all of the other elephants who have died. He also is inferring that being in a zoo didn't make Sonny any less of an elephant than those in the wild.

SHORT RESPONSE

Cite Text Evidence What is the author's purpose in writing this newspaper article? How does Karas portray Bergmann? Review your reading notes, and be sure to **cite text evidence** in your response.

Karas shows how one man's efforts can be the difference between life and death for many animals—those that are "ill, injured, exploited, abused, or older." He shows that the animals are well cared for at Popcorn Park: "Many come from states with severely overcrowded animal shelters, where animals would not be held long before being put down." Karas portrays Bergmann as a sensitive, humble and kind man—he does this in part by using Bergmann's own words: "You are doing what you love." He writes that the animals greet Bergmann like a "rock star," showing that the animals feel as strongly for him as he does for them.

112

TO CHALLENGE STUDENTS . . .

For more context, students can research zoos in the United States.

ASK STUDENTS how the mission of zoos has changed over the last hundred years. *Students should recognize that a century ago zoos were designed to showcase exotic animals to the public. Zoos were a spectacle. Scientists—and wealthy hunters and collectors—used to travel the world in search of new species and biological wonders. Many of the animals encountered by these expeditions were shot and preserved, their skins becoming parts of museum collections. Others, however, were captured, cared for, and transported back to major U.S. cities, where they were incorporated into zoological parks. The public flocked to see such incredible beasts as gorillas, yaks, and kangaroos.*

In recent decades, many animal species have become endangered in their native habitats. Zoos have responded by transforming themselves into conservation centers. Instead of simply showcasing exotic animals, they now work together to establish and maintain breeding populations of threatened species. Some zoos even fund conservation efforts in other countries. The goal of many modern zoos is to re-introduce species to their native habitats.

6. **REREAD AND CITE TEXT EVIDENCE**

F **ASK STUDENTS** how elephants live in the wild. *Students should understand that elephants are intelligent, long-living, social animals that live in large family groups, or herds, that roam vast distances.* How do elephants live in zoos? *They might live in small groups of two or three. Their enclosures are rarely more than a few acres.*

SHORT RESPONSE

Cite Text Evidence Students' responses should include text evidence that supports their positions. They should:

- describe Karas's purpose(s) in writing the article.
- give examples that show the author's purpose.
- describe Karas's portrayal of Bergmann.

DIG DEEPER

1. With the class, return to Question 1, Read. Have students share what they have circled.

ASK STUDENTS to discuss what Bergmann's relationship with the animals reveals about his character.

- Can we learn anything about Bergmann from how he treats the animals at the zoo? If so, what? *Bergmann greets each animal "by name," which shows that in his eyes they are individuals. This aspect of his character is reinforced by the author's observation that Bergmann "has bonded" with each of the zoo's animals. He knows each animal's history, problems, and personality.*

- Can we learn anything about Bergmann from how the animals treat him? If so, what? *The animals really seem to like Bergmann. They treat him "like a rock star." The chickens ride with him on his golf cart. Tigers rise to greet him and get his attention. So the animals trust Bergmann, which indicates that his affection is genuine—his kind words are backed up by real actions.*

2. With the class, return to Question 5, Read. Have students share what they have circled.

ASK STUDENTS to discuss how the story of Sonny reveals Bergmann's compassionate character.

- Why didn't other zoos want to take the elephant? *Sonny was a "troubled creature," unhappy and unruly, perhaps because he wasn't reared in captivity. He was brought from Zimbabwe to the United States to do "circus work," but he must have failed at that because he ended up at a zoo in New Mexico. He didn't like life at the zoo either, for he "resisted his training" and tried to escape several times.*

- How would you characterize Bergmann's relationship with Sonny? *Bergmann was realistic, for he knew that Sonny belonged back in Africa: "He didn't belong here." But Bergmann and his staff gave Sonny the care and training he needed, and eventually Sonny became a "friend," another member of the Popcorn Park family.*

ASK STUDENTS to return to their Short Response answer and revise it based on the class discussion.

CLOSE READING NOTES

*my*SmartPlanner Create lesson plans and access resources online.

EXEMPLAR

A Poem for My Librarian, Mrs. Long

Poem by Nikki Giovanni

Why This Text?

Poetry often reflects on the personal experiences of the writer. Analyzing a poet's style deepens the readers' understanding of those experiences. This lesson focuses on how poets use stylistic techniques to express a central idea.

Key Learning Objective: The student will be able to analyze a poet's style and to determine a theme.

COMMON CORE Common Core Standards

RL 1 Cite textual evidence.
RL 2 Determine theme.
RL 4 Determine the meanings of words and phrases.
RL 5 Analyze how a poem's form contributes to its meaning.
W 3 Write narratives.
W 4 Produce clear and coherent writing.
W 10 Write routinely over extended time frames.
L 1a Explain the function of phrases and clauses.
L 1c Place phrases and clauses within a sentence.

▲ Text Complexity Rubric

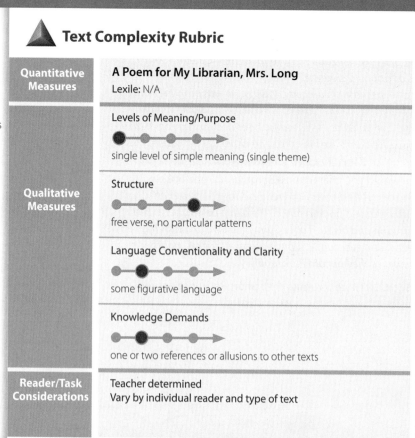

Quantitative Measures	**A Poem for My Librarian, Mrs. Long** Lexile: N/A
Qualitative Measures	**Levels of Meaning/Purpose** single level of simple meaning (single theme)
	Structure free verse, no particular patterns
	Language Conventionality and Clarity some figurative language
	Knowledge Demands one or two references or allusions to other texts
Reader/Task Considerations	Teacher determined Vary by individual reader and type of text

CLOSE READ

Background Have students read the information about the poet. Tell them that when Nikki Giovanni was growing up in the 1940s and early 1950s life for African Americans was very different than it is today. There were many laws that required the separation of blacks and whites. During the time of the Civil Rights Movement, Giovanni became inspired to begin writing poetry.

SETTING A PURPOSE Direct students to use the Setting a Purpose prompt to focus their reading.

Determine Theme (TITLE) RL 2

Tell students that the theme of a poem is a message about life or human nature that the poet wants to convey. Often, readers must infer, or make a good guess about, the theme from evidence in the text. Explain that authors sometimes reveal the theme in the poem's title.

Ⓐ ASK STUDENTS to reread the title and explain how it might reveal the poem's theme. *(Possible answer: The poet is writing about her childhood memories of Mrs. Long, her local or school librarian, who must have helped her find books to borrow when the poet was a troubled little girl. The theme might have to do with the power of books—and people who love books—to change the lives of young people.)*

Determine Meaning: Style (LINES 1–7) RL 4, RL 5

Explain to students that a poem usually has a particular **style,** or manner of writing. Style involves *how* something is said rather than *what* is said. Discuss with students literary elements that contribute to a poet's style:

- **structure:** line lengths, breaks, rhyme scheme, punctuation
- **figurative language:** using words and phrases to express ideas in an imaginative way
- **sound devices:** ways of using words for the sound qualities they create

Ⓑ CITE TEXT EVIDENCE Have students reread lines 1–7 aloud with you and identify elements of style. *(The line structure gives the poem a conversational feel; the repeating sound of words ending in -ing gives the poem rhythm. There is little punctuation, making it feel fluid.)*

Nikki Giovanni (b. 1943) *has been one of the best-known American poets since publishing her first book of poetry in 1968. Giovanni grew up in the racially segregated South. When Giovanni attended college, she became a part of a movement of African American writers who were finding new ways to express pride in their distinct culture. In addition to her poetry collections, Giovanni is also an award-winning children's author.*

Ⓐ A Poem for My Librarian, Mrs. Long

(YOU NEVER KNOW WHAT TROUBLED LITTLE GIRL NEEDS A BOOK)

Poem by Nikki Giovanni

AS YOU READ In the poem, Nikki Giovanni looks back at her childhood and the people who most influenced her. As you read, think about how Giovanni's childhood experiences shaped her dreams and her writing.

> At a time when there was no tv before 3:00 P.M.
> And on Sunday none until 5:00
> We sat on front porches watching
> The jfg[1] sign go on and off greeting
> 5 The neighbors, discussing the political
> Situation congratulating the preacher
> On his sermon   Ⓑ

[1] **jfg:** a brand of coffee that was popular in Knoxville, Tennessee; an old electrically lit sign for the coffee is a famous landmark in Knoxville, Tennessee.

(t) ©Monica Morgan/WireImage/Getty Images; (b) Terry Vine/Stone/Getty Images

SCAFFOLDING FOR ELL STUDENTS

Analyze Language: Punctuation and Print Cues Explain to students that some poets use punctuation in their poems differently than the way fiction authors might use punctuation in a story. Poets often use punctuation at the end of lines or within lines to signal pauses and changes in ideas that they want the reader to experience. Explain that if there is no punctuation in a line the poet might want the reader to barely pause just at the end of the line. If there is a period at the end of a line, the poet likely wants the reader to come to a full stop. Reread lines 1–7 aloud with students.

ASK STUDENTS to tell how not having much punctuation makes this poem sound different from a story.

Determine the Meanings of Words and Phrases

 COMMON CORE **RL 4**

(LINES 8–17)

Explain that in lines 8–17 Giovanni makes **allusions,** or references, to a number of jazz musicians who were popular at the time: Nat King Cole, Matt Dennis, Ella Fitzgerald, and Sarah Vaughn. In particular, she alludes to a hit song sung by Vaughn called "Black Coffee."

C **ASK STUDENTS** to reread lines 8–17 and explain what the allusions reveal about the young Nikki Giovanni. *(These allusions reveal that she loved music. The rhythms of jazz and the words in popular songs may have inspired her love for rhythm and words, which she later shared in her poetry.)*

Determine Meaning:

 COMMON CORE **RL 1, RL 4**

Style (LINES 28–33)

Point out that Giovanni's style includes frequent use of figurative language. One example is her use of an **idiom,** or an expression that has a meaning different from the meaning of its individual words.

D **CITE TEXT EVIDENCE** Ask students to reread lines 28–33 and identify the idiom. Have students explain its meaning in the poem. *(The phrase "hat in hand" is an idiom. It suggests begging and showing respect for someone more powerful. This reveals the powerless position that African Americans had in the southern United States at this time. It shows the speaker's appreciation for Mrs. Long for going to a library in a white neighborhood to borrow the books the girl wanted.)*

Determine Theme

 COMMON CORE **RL 2, RL 4**

(LINES 34–40)

Tell students that they can infer the theme of a poem by analyzing the words and actions of the speaker.

E **ASK STUDENTS** to reread lines 34–40. Ask them what these lines reveal about the poem's theme. *(The speaker tells that because of Mrs. Long she was able to get access to the books she wanted. This supports the idea that the girl is giving thanks to Mrs. Long.)*

There was always radio which brought us
Songs from wlac in nashville and what we would now call
10　Easy listening or smooth jazz but when I listened
Late at night with my portable (that I was so proud of)
Tucked under my pillow
I heard nat king cole and matt dennis, june christy and
　　ella fitzgerald
15　And sometimes sarah vaughan sing black coffee
Which I now drink
It was just called music

There was a bookstore uptown on gay street
Which I visited and inhaled that wonderful odor
20　Of new books
Even today I read hardcover as a preference paperback only
As a last resort

And up the hill on vine street
(The main black corridor) sat our carnegie library[2]
25　Mrs. Long always glad to see you
The stereoscope[3] always ready to show you faraway
Places to dream about

Mrs. Long asking what are you looking for today
When I wanted *Leaves of Grass* or alfred north whitehead
30　She would go to the big library uptown and I now know
Hat in hand to ask to borrow so that I might borrow
Probably they said something humiliating since southern
Whites like to humiliate southern blacks

But she nonetheless brought the books
35　Back and I held them to my chest
Close to my heart
And happily skipped back to grandmother's house
Where I would sit on the front porch
In a gray glider and dream of a world
40　Far away

---

[2] **carnegie library:** a library built with money donated by the businessman Andrew Carnegie.

[3] **stereoscope:** an optical instrument with two eyepieces used to create a three-dimensional effect when looking at two photographs of the same scene.

APPLYING ACADEMIC VOCABULARY

despite	interact

As you discuss the poem, incorporate the following Collection 6 academic vocabulary words: *despite* and *interact*. Have students tell why they think Mrs. Long went uptown to get books **despite** the negative **interactions** she most likely would encounter.

I love the world where I was
I was safe and warm and grandmother gave me neck kisses
When I was on my way to bed

But there was a world
45 Somewhere
Out there
And Mrs. Long opened that wardrobe
But no lions or witches⁴ scared me
I went through
50 Knowing there would be
Spring **G**

COLLABORATIVE DISCUSSION Notice how the poet talks about
familiar and faraway places. How does the poem itself travel
to a faraway place? How does it keep the reader grounded in
familiarity? Talk about your ideas with other group members.

⁴ **wardrobe . . . lions or witches:** refers to *The Lion, the Witch, and the Wardrobe*
by C. S. Lewis; in the book, the characters visit a make-believe land, called
Narnia, via the wardrobe, or closet, in a spare room.

WHEN STUDENTS STRUGGLE . . .

Display the poem for students. Have students use a chart such as the one
shown to guide them as they analyze stylistic techniques.

Technique	Example from the Poem
structure	varying line lengths; unconventional punctuation
figurative language	idiom: line 31
sound devices	repeating sounds: lines 3–6

CLOSE READ

Determine Meaning: Style (LINES 41–51)

COMMON CORE RL 4, RL 5

Tell students that another element that contributes
to Giovanni's style is the structure of the lines and
stanzas. Explain that Giovanni uses varying line
lengths and stanzas to create a rhythm that sounds
like everyday speech. Reread lines 41–51 aloud.

F ASK STUDENTS to tell how the line lengths and
stanzas contribute to the poem's meaning. *(Shorter
to longer line lengths help build ideas and link them
together. Different stanzas show movement from
one idea or event to another. The rhythm of the lines
captures the emotions of the speaker.)*

Determine Theme
(LINES 44–51)

COMMON CORE RL 1, RL 2

Point out that Giovanni concludes with a final symbol
that contributes to the poem's theme. Explain that a
symbol is a person, a place, an object, or an activity
that stands for something beyond itself. For example,
an olive branch is often seen as a symbol of peace.

G ASK STUDENTS to reread lines 44–51. Have
students analyze the lines, identify the symbol, and
explain what it means. *(Spring is a symbol for new
beginnings. In these lines, it means moving into the
future or bigger world with optimism.)*

COLLABORATIVE DISCUSSION Have students work
with a partner to identify the way the poet creates both
faraway and familiar places. Then, have partners join the
group and share their ideas in a broader discussion.

ASK STUDENTS to share any questions they generated
in the course of reading and discussing this selection.

TEACH

CLOSE READ

Determine Meaning: Style RL 4, RL 5

Discuss the definition of *style* and the ways in which a poet or author's style can be described. Explain that analyzing the words and phrases in a poem can help readers identify a poet's style.

Review the definitions of stylistic techniques listed in the chart, discussing how Nikki Giovanni uses these techniques in "A Poem for My Librarian, Mrs. Long." Ask students to explain what those uses reveal about her style.

Then, have students identify the stylistic technique in lines 8–17. *(Possible answers: The first word in each line is capitalized, and most proper nouns are lowercase. There is no end punctuation and only a few internal commas. As a result, the poem looks informal and suggests speed—as if we are seeing the poet's rush of thoughts and memories.)*

Determine Theme RL 2

Review the definition of *theme*. Emphasize that the theme of a poem is not always directly stated. Discuss how the theme is conveyed in "A Poem for My Librarian, Mrs. Long." Then, have students reread the poem and answer the question.

(Possible response: As a child, the poet was a "troubled little girl" who found help and dreams at the local public library. There, Mrs. Long, the librarian, welcomed the girl, was always glad to see her, and encouraged her reading. Mrs. Long gave the girl what she needed—support as well as books. Mrs. Long opened "that wardrobe" so that the girl could enter another world.)

Determine Meaning: Style RL 4, RL 5

Style is the particular way in which a poet or author writes—not *what* is said but *how* it is said. It is made up of many elements, including word choice, stanza and line length, figurative language, sound devices, and form. Style can be described with words such as *formal, whimsical, flowery,* and *plain.*

By making careful use of word choices and techniques, a poet can craft poetry with a signature style. For example, "A Poem for My Librarian, Mrs. Long," written by Nikki Giovanni in the form of **free verse**, presents irregular rhythm and rhyme and language that flows like everyday speech. The poet conveys meaning through a variety of stylistic techniques, including:

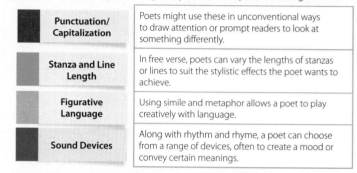

Punctuation/ Capitalization	Poets might use these in unconventional ways to draw attention or prompt readers to look at something differently.
Stanza and Line Length	In free verse, poets can vary the lengths of stanzas or lines to suit the stylistic effects the poet wants to achieve.
Figurative Language	Using simile and metaphor allows a poet to play creatively with language.
Sound Devices	Along with rhythm and rhyme, a poet can choose from a range of devices, often to create a mood or convey certain meanings.

Read lines 8–17 of "A Poem for My Librarian, Mrs. Long." Identify the stylistic technique you see.

Determine Theme RL 2

A **theme** is a message about life or human nature that a writer or poet shares with the reader. In poetry, themes are not always stated directly. The reader of a poem can infer a theme by thinking about the poem as a whole and looking at what is said, what is suggested, and how the words, sounds, and ideas come together.

In the poem you've just read, the poet is also the speaker, reflecting on her childhood experiences. After giving details about everyday activities, she turns her attention to her love of books. The poem is dedicated to Mrs. Long, the librarian who likely endured adversity so that the young girl could have access to the books she wanted.

What seems most important to understand about the poet's relationship with Mrs. Long?

Strategies for Annotation 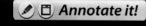 Annotate it!

Determine Meaning RL 1, RL 4

Share these strategies for guided or independent analysis:

- Highlight in yellow examples of figurative language.
- Highlight in blue examples of sound devices.

But there was a world

Somewhere

Out there

And Mrs. Long opened that wardrobe

But no lions or witches scared me

Analyzing the Text

Cite Text Evidence Support your responses with evidence from the text.

1. **Cite Evidence** What words would you use to describe the poet as a child? Why would those words fit?

2. **Infer** Reread lines 28–33. What does the poet now understand about Mrs. Long?

3. **Interpret** An **allusion** is a reference to a famous person, place, event, or work of literature. The final stanza of this poem makes an allusion to C. S. Lewis' famous fantasy novel *The Lion, the Witch, and the Wardrobe*, in which young characters help end a witch's curse of endless winter. Why might the poet have ended the poem with this allusion?

4. **Analyze** How does the poet's use of punctuation and capitalization contribute to the poem's meaning?

5. **Evaluate** The **tone** of a poem expresses the poet's attitude toward a subject. These are some words that can be used to describe tone: *awed, ironic, thoughtful, grateful, hopeful, angry*. Do any of those words seem to fit this poem? Choose one word, or think of another, that describes the poem's tone, and tell why that word fits the poem.

6. **Analyze** How would you describe Nikki Giovanni's style based on the stylistic techniques she employs in "A Poem for My Librarian, Mrs. Long"?

7. **Draw Conclusions** What could be the theme of this poem?

PERFORMANCE TASK

Writing Activity: Poem Mrs. Long acted generously to a child, and that child never forgot it. Think back to an experience or a connection with someone who acted generously to you. Free-write about your memory—noting phrases, sentences, quotations, and anything else that comes to mind.

Use your written ideas to write a poem in free verse form. Look back at the poem you've just read for ideas about how to:

- convey the sights, sounds, and smells you remember
- portray the person you remember
- tell about your feelings then and now

Analyzing the Text

Possible answers:

1. *Words to describe the poet as a child might be* imaginative, intelligent, loving, *and* hopeful. *She was imaginative because she liked to dream of faraway places. She was intelligent because she read challenging books, like Walt Whitman's* Leaves of Grass *and the philosopher Alfred North Whitehead. She was loving because of her affectionate relationship with her grandmother. She was hopeful because she knew that somewhere out in the world she would find "spring."*

2. *As an adult, the poet realizes the humiliation Mrs. Long went through to bring a child books that were available only in "the big library uptown." Mrs. Long had to ask to borrow the books "hat in hand"—acting deferential and probably enduring humiliation from the white librarians.*

3. *Because the poem deals with the importance of books in childhood, it ends fittingly with an allusion to a popular children's book. The poet might have included this particular book because it's about children who find a magical world behind a wardrobe, which the poet compares to the world made available by Mrs. Long.*

4. *The punctuation and capitalization are used in unconventional ways, and most times not used at all, to draw attention to certain words and phrases and to emphasize ideas.*

5. *The tone of the poem seems dreamy, as the poet moves from memory to memory, as if thinking aloud.*

6. *The poet's style is whimsical yet thoughtful.*

7. *Childhood experiences with loving adults shape a person and are never forgotten.*

Assign this performance task.

PERFORMANCE TASK

Writing Activity: Poem Have students work independently. Tell students to

- choose a person and an experience to write about
- decide on the main message they want to convey
- choose their words carefully, using only words that are necessary and that enhance meaning

Language Conventions: Combining Sentences with Phrases

COMMON CORE L 1a, L 1c

Review the definitions of types of phrases. Then, display the following sentences:

Mrs. Long wanted to help young Nikki. Mrs. Long would go to the big library uptown.

Read aloud the sentences and discuss the related ideas in them. Explain that students can combine these two sentences using a participial phrase to show a stronger connection between the ideas and to give the sentence a smoother, less choppy rhythm.

Wanting to help young Nikki, Mrs. Long would go to the big library uptown.

Discuss how the combined sentence connects the two ideas more closely. Then, use the examples in the chart to help students understand how to combine two sentences using different types of phrases.

Possible answers:

1. *Sitting on their front porches, families greeted their neighbors. Families sat on their front porches, greeting their neighbors.*

2. *To the young girl visiting the bookstore, new books smelled wonderful. The new books at the bookstore smelled wonderful to the young girl.*

3. *The library was located on Vine Street in the black neighborhood. The library was located in the black neighborhood, on Vine Street.*

4. *Because of her love of poetry, the girl asked the librarian for* Leaves of Grass. *Loving poetry, the girl asked the librarian for* Leaves of Grass.

5. *Mrs. Long borrowed the book from the uptown library, probably facing prejudice there. To borrow the book from the uptown library, Mrs. Long probably faced prejudice.*

6. *The poet says that Mrs. Long opened a wardrobe to help a child find a new world. The poet says that, by opening a wardrobe, Mrs. Long helped a child enter a new world.*

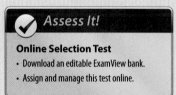

Assess It!

Online Selection Test
- Download an editable ExamView bank.
- Assign and manage this test online.

Language Conventions: Combining Sentences with Phrases

COMMON CORE L 1a, L 1c

By using phrases to combine sentences, you can vary the length of your sentences and make your writing sound mature. The following are types of phrases you can use to combine sentences.

- A **prepositional phrase** begins with a preposition, such as *at, about, for, from, in,* or *of.*
- An **infinitive phrase** begins with an infinitive verb (*to* + verb).
- A **participial phrase** begins with the past or present participle of a verb, such as *walked* or *walking.*
- A **gerund phrase** begins with a gerund, or *-ing* word. A gerund phrase always functions as a noun, rather than an adjective or an adverb.

The chart below provides an example for how to use each phrase type to combine sentences.

Phrase Type	Two Sentences	Combined Sentence
Prepositional phrase	The poet remembers her childhood. She has vivid memories.	The poet has vivid memories of her childhood.
Infinitive phrase	The stereoscope showed pictures of faraway places. The girl dreamed about the places.	The stereoscope showed the girl pictures of faraway places to dream about.
Participial phrase	The girl held borrowed books close to her heart. She skipped home with them.	Holding her borrowed books close to her heart, the girl skipped home.
Gerund phrase	The poet remembers her librarian. She feels grateful for the librarian's help.	Remembering her librarian's help makes the poet feel grateful.

Practice and Apply Combine the two sentences with a phrase of your choice.

1. Families sat on their front porches. They greeted their neighbors.

2. The young girl visited the bookstore. New books smelled wonderful.

3. The library was located in the black neighborhood. It was on Vine Street.

4. The girl loved poetry. She asked the librarian for *Leaves of Grass.*

5. Mrs. Long borrowed the book from the uptown library. She probably faced prejudice there.

6. The poet says that Mrs. Long opened a wardrobe. Mrs. Long helped a child enter a new world.

Determine the Meanings of Words and Phrases

COMMON CORE

RL 4

TEACH

Explain that an **allusion** is a reference to a famous person, place, event, or other work of literature. Then, discuss the following points:

- Poets use allusions to help them convey meaning in a single word or two.
- In order to understand an allusion, the reader must understand the meaning of the reference.
- No reader can recognize every allusion. It is sometimes necessary to do research in order to understand the reference.

Guide students to interpret examples such as the following:

- My mom is no Scrooge, but she almost never buys things she doesn't need. *(Scrooge is a character from* A Christmas Carol, *by Charles Dickens, who is stingy and mean. A Scrooge refers to a person who is miserly.)*
- That girl has a Mona Lisa smile. *(Leonardo Da Vinci's* Mona Lisa *is a painting of a woman that is known for her mysterious smile. A Mona Lisa smile is one that is very hard to understand.)*

PRACTICE AND APPLY

Students can apply the skill to identify and analyze some of the allusions in "A Poem for My Librarian, Mrs. Long" that they have not already explored. Have students answer the following questions about each allusion:

- What does the allusion refer to?
- What do you need to know about the allusion to understand its meaning in the poem?

Have students record their responses in a three-column chart like the one shown.

Allusion	What It References	Meaning in Poem
jfg		
gay street		
vine street		
wardrobe		

Determine Meaning: Style

COMMON CORE

RL 4,
RL 5

RETEACH

Discuss with students of their favorite types of music. Have students name different recording artists and discuss how each artist has a unique sound. Point out that this unique sound is the singer's or musician's own style—the way that the artist sings or plays music.

Review that in literature **style** is an author's unique way of writing; it is *how* something is written rather than *what* is written. Remind students that the following literary elements are part of an author's style:

- **punctuation/capitalization:** using unconventional ways to draw attention or prompt readers to look at something differently
- **stanza and line length:** varying lengths of lines and stanzas to create different effects
- **figurative language:** using simile and metaphor to play creatively with language
- **sound devices:** using different techniques to create mood or convey meaning

Reread the poem aloud. Work with students to identify elements of style in the poem.

LEVEL UP TUTORIALS Assign the following *Level Up* tutorial: **Author's Style**

CLOSE READING APPLICATION

Individual students can apply these skills to analyze another poem of their choosing. After their analysis, have students discuss the styles of other poets with a partner or small group.

Train Time

mySmartPlanner Create lesson plans and access resources online.

Short Story by D'Arcy McNickle

Why This Text?

This short story offers students an opportunity to analyze in depth a character with complex motivations as well as a moral dilemma set in an often-overlooked episode in our country's history. The story's sophisticated structure includes the use of flashback, and the lesson guides students to understand and analyze this literary technique.

Key Learning Objective: The student will be able to analyze methods of characterization and flashback in a short story.

Common Core Standards

RL 1 Cite text evidence.
RL 2 Determine theme or central idea.
RL 3 Analyze how elements of a story interact.
RL 4 Determine the meaning of words and phrases.
RL 6 Analyze points of view of different characters or narrators.
W 1 Write arguments to support claims.
W 4 Produce clear and coherent writing.
W 9a Apply *Grade 7* Reading standards to literature.
W 10 Write routinely for a range of tasks, purposes, and audiences.
L 1c Place phrases and clauses within a sentence, correcting misplaced modifiers.
L 4c Consult reference materials to determine or clarify meaning.
L 6 Acquire and use general academic words and phrases.

Text Complexity Rubric

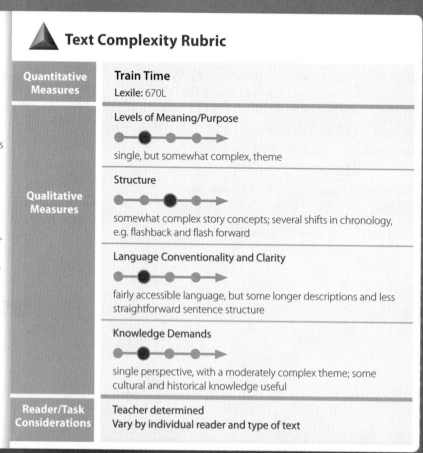

Quantitative Measures	**Train Time** Lexile: 670L
	Levels of Meaning/Purpose single, but somewhat complex, theme
Qualitative Measures	**Structure** somewhat complex story concepts; several shifts in chronology, e.g. flashback and flash forward
	Language Conventionality and Clarity fairly accessible language, but some longer descriptions and less straightforward sentence structure
	Knowledge Demands single perspective, with a moderately complex theme; some cultural and historical knowledge useful
Reader/Task Considerations	**Teacher determined** Vary by individual reader and type of text

CLOSE READ

Background Have students read the background and information about the author. Tell students that in addition to his writing D'Arcy McNickle was respected as a scholar and activist. He was the first director of the Chicago Newberry Library's Center for the History of the American Indian, which now is named after him. McNickle was an administrator in the U.S. Bureau of Indian Affairs and a founding member of the National Congress of American Indians. Although he sold his allotment of reservation land to finance his education at Oxford, McNickle remained a strong voice in support of Native American rights and culture.

SETTING A PURPOSE Direct students to use the Setting a Purpose question to focus their reading. Remind students to generate their own questions as they read.

Analyze Story Elements: Mood (LINES 1–16)

COMMON CORE RL 1, RL 4

Tell students that the **mood** is the feeling or atmosphere that a writer creates for the reader. Descriptive words, imagery, and dialogue can all help to establish the mood.

A **CITE TEXT EVIDENCE** Ask students to reread lines 1–16 and describe the mood the author establishes at the beginning of the story. Have students cite supporting evidence in the text. *(The mood is one of expectancy: "everybody stood waiting, listening"; "all stood waiting and gazing eastward"; "boys pushed forward to the edge of the platform." There is also a sense of confusion, as shown by the dialogue about whether anyone had heard the train whistle.)*

SCAFFOLDING FOR ELL STUDENTS

Analyze Language Using a whiteboard, project lines 1–4. Explain to students that if they encounter unfamiliar words in the story, they should try rereading the surrounding text for clues to meaning.

- Highlight the word *depot*.
- Underline clues to the meaning of the word, and model how to determine that it means a place where people wait for trains.

ASK STUDENTS to reread lines 13–16 and use context to figure out the meaning of *doubter*. Point out that students can use a dictionary to confirm meaning.

Background *In the late 1800s, social reformers in the United States believed they could help move Native Americans into mainstream society by re-educating Native American children away from their families. Author D'Arcy McNickle (1904–1977) was forced to go to a boarding school. McNickle went on to college where he became interested in literature and writing. In his stories, he gained a reputation for vivid descriptions of how the larger mainstream culture affected traditional Native American ways.*

Train Time

Short Story by D'Arcy McNickle

SETTING A PURPOSE As you read, think about the moral problem that the main character is faced with. What is that problem, and how does he deal with it?

A

On the depot platform everybody stood waiting, listening. The train has just whistled, somebody said. They stood listening and gazing eastward, where railroad tracks and creek emerged together from a tree-choked canyon.

Twenty-five boys, five girls, Major Miles—all stood waiting and gazing eastward. Was it true that the train had whistled?

"That was no train!" a boy's voice explained.

"It was a steer bellowing."

10 "It was the train!"

Girls crowded backward against the station building, heads hanging, tears starting; boys pushed forward to the edge of the platform. An older boy with a voice already turning heavy stepped off the weather-shredded boardwalk and stood wide-legged in the middle of the track. He was the doubter. He had heard no train.

©Flirt/SuperStock

On the depot platform everybody stood waiting, listening.

The train has just whistled, somebody said. They stood

listening and gazing eastward, where railroad tracks and creek

emerged together from a tree-choked canyon.

Analyze Stories: Character Development (LINES 28–36)

COMMON CORE RL 1, RL 3

Tell students that authors make characters seem real through **characterization,** methods of revealing the characters' **traits,** or qualities. One method of characterization is through comments made by the narrator. Another is through the character's own words, actions, and thoughts.

B CITE TEXT EVIDENCE Ask students to reread lines 28–36 and to cite what the narrator tells us directly about the Major. Then, ask what we can infer about the Major from his own actions and thoughts. *(The narrator tells us that the Major is a "man of conscience" and does everything "earnestly." From the Major's "soldier bearing," we learn that he is proud and intent on doing his duty. From the "words [that] tumbled about in his mind," we learn that he believes firmly in the importance of what he is doing for the children and is frustrated that they don't realize it.)*

CRITICAL VOCABULARY

exasperate: The author tells us that the Major was exasperated.

ASK STUDENTS to explain why the Major feels that way. *(The Major feels exasperated because he has been working hard to accomplish what he thinks is a worthy goal—sending the Indian children to boarding school. But instead of appreciating his efforts, the children resist.)*

conscience: Major Miles is described as a "man of conscience."

ASK STUDENTS what they would expect from a person of conscience. *(Possible answer: I would expect such a person to have strong ideas about what is right and to live up to them.)*

Major Miles boomed, "You! What's your name? Get back here! Want to get killed! All of you, stand back!"

The Major strode about, soldierlike, and waved
20 commands. He was **exasperated**. He was tired. A man driving cattle through timber had it easy, he was thinking. An animal trainer had no idea of trouble. Let anyone try corralling twenty to thirty Indian kids, dragging them out of hiding places, getting them away from relatives and together in one place, then holding them, without tying them, until train time! Even now, at the last moment, when his worries were almost over, they were trying to get themselves killed!

Major Miles was a man of **conscience**. Whatever he did, he did earnestly. On this hot end-of-summer day he perspired
30 and frowned and wore his soldier bearing. He removed his hat from his wet brow and thoughtfully passed his hand from the hair line backward. Words tumbled about in his mind. Somehow, he realized, he had to vivify[1] the moment. These children were about to go out from the Reservation and get a new start. Life would change. They ought to realize it, somehow—

"Boys—and girls—" there were five girls he remembered. He had got them all lined up against the building, safely away from the edge of the platform. The air was stifling with end-
40 of-summer heat. It was time to say something, never mind the heat. Yes, he would have to make the moment real. He stood soldierlike and thought that.

"Boys and girls—" The train whistled, dully, but unmistakably. Then it repeated more clearly. The rails came to life, something was running through them and making them sing.

Just then the Major's eye fell upon little Eneas and his sure voice faltered. He knew about little Eneas. Most of the boys and girls were mere names; he had seen them around
50 the Agency with their parents, or had caught sight of them scurrying behind tipis and barns when he visited their homes. But little Eneas he knew. With him before his eyes, he paused.

He remembered so clearly the winter day, six months ago, when he first saw Eneas. It was the boy's grandfather, Michel Lamartine, he had gone to see. Michel had contracted to cut wood for the Agency but had not started work. The Major had gone to discover why not.

exasperate
(ĭg-zăs′pə-rāt′) *v.*
If you *exasperate* someone, you make the person very angry.

conscience
(kŏn′shəns) *n.*
Conscience is the conforming to or living up to one's own sense of what is right.

---

[1] **vivify:** to make more lively.

WHEN STUDENTS STRUGGLE...

To guide students in understanding the author's use of characterization, have them work in pairs to fill out a chart like the one shown. Explain that from supporting evidence in the text they can make inferences about the Major's character traits. Supporting evidence can include what the narrator tells us as well as what the Major himself says, does, and thinks.

Model how to begin filling out the chart, and have students continue as they read the rest of the story.

It was the coldest day of the winter, late in February, and the cabin, sheltered as it was among the pine and cottonwood
60 of a creek bottom, was shot through by frosty drafts. There was wood all about them. Lamartine was a woodcutter besides, yet there was no wood in the house. The fire in the flat-topped cast-iron stove burned weakly. The reason was apparent. The Major had but to look at the bed where Lamartine lay, twisted and shrunken by rheumatism.[2] Only his black eyes burned with life. He tried to wave a hand as the Major entered.

"You see how I am!" the gesture indicated. Then a nerve-strung voice faltered. "We have it bad here. My old woman,
70 she's not much good."

Clearly she wasn't, not for wood-chopping. She sat close by the fire, trying with a good-natured grin to lift her **ponderous** body from a low seated rocking chair. The Major had to motion her back to her ease. She breathed with an asthmatic[3] roar. Wood-chopping was not within her range. With only a squaw's hatchet[4] to work with, she could scarcely have come within striking distance of a stick of wood. Two blows, if she had struck them, might have put a stop to her laboring heart.

"You see how it is," Lamartine's eyes flashed.

80 The Major saw clearly. Sitting there in the frosty cabin, he pondered their plight and at the same time wondered if he would get away without coming down with pneumonia.[5] A stream of wind seemed to be hitting him in the back of the neck. Of course, there was nothing to do. One saw too many such situations. If one undertook to provide **sustenance** out of one's own pocket there would be no end to the demands. Government salaries were small, resources were limited. He could do no more than shake his head sadly, offer some vague hope, some small sympathy. He would have to get away
90 at once.

Then a hand fumbled at the door; it opened. After a moment's struggle, little Eneas appeared, staggering under a full armload of pine limbs hacked into short lengths. The boy was no taller than an ax handle, his nose was running, and

---

ponderous
(pŏn´dər-əs) *adj.*
If something is *ponderous*, it is very heavy.

sustenance
(sŭs´tə-nəns) *n.*
Sustenance is the food needed to live.

---

[2] **rheumatism** (ro͞o´mə-tĭz´əm): a disease causing stiffness in the joints and muscles.

[3] **asthmatic** (ăz´măt´ĭk): characterized by labored breathing and coughing.

[4] **squaw's hatchet:** a small hand ax used by Native American women to cut small things.

[5] **pneumonia** (no͞o-mōn´yə): a disease causing inflammation of the lungs.

Train Time **329**

Character Traits	Supporting Evidence
wants to do the right thing	*"man of conscience"*
proud	*"soldier bearing"*
dutiful; sense of own importance	*"he had to vivify the moment"; "he would have to make the moment real"*

CLOSE READ

Analyze Stories:
Flashback (LINES 47–57)

 COMMON CORE RL 3

Explain to students that the author interrupts the scene at the depot with a **flashback,** a description of events that took place at an earlier time. A flashback can give the reader insight into the characters' current situation.

C **ASK STUDENTS** to reread lines 47–57. Ask what time period the flashback refers to and why the author includes it. (*It refers to a winter day six months ago when the Major first saw Eneas. It explains how the Major knew Eneas and why he feels differently about Eneas than he feels about the other children.*)

Tell students to pay attention to what other insights the rest of the flashback (lines 58–166) gives into the scene at the depot.

CRITICAL VOCABULARY

ponderous: The author describes the old woman's body as "ponderous."

ASK STUDENTS why he might have chosen this word instead of heavy or huge. (*Ponderous conveys how hard it was for the woman to move, not just that she was large.*)

sustenance: The Major felt that there was nothing he could do to provide sustenance for the Lamartine family.

ASK STUDENTS why it might not have been wise for the Major to provide sustenance. (*There were so many poor families in need of food that he could never provide for them all.*)

CLOSE READ

Analyze Stories: Character Development (LINES 99–118)

 COMMON CORE RL 1

Remind students that authors often provide clues to a character's traits through the character's own words and actions.

D CITE TEXT EVIDENCE Have students reread lines 99–118. Ask what we learn about the Major from this portion of the text and why the Major acted "against his own principles" in helping the family. *(This text provides further evidence that the Major is a "man of conscience" who wants to do the right thing. He is also capable of being touched by the devotion and loyalty that Eneas displays: "Something about the boy made the Major forget his determination to depart." This causes him to go against his principles, which oppose paying out of his own pocket to provide sustenance for the Indian families.)*

Analyze Stories: Flashback (LINES 124–133)

COMMON CORE RL 1, RL 3

Remind students that the author interrupted the scene at the depot with a flashback to the previous winter. Point out that while the flashback scene continues, in line 124 the action flashes forward in time.

E CITE TEXT EVIDENCE Ask students to reread lines 124–133 and to identify the evidence that signals the shift in time. Ask what has happened to the Major during that time. *(Evidence: "some weeks later." During those weeks, the Major has figured out a plan for helping Eneas and his family.)*

> **CRITICAL VOCABULARY**
>
> **inexplicable:** The Major inexplicably changed his mind about helping Eneas's family.
>
> **ASK STUDENTS** what might cause a person to behave inexplicably. *(an experience or event that has a strong impact and causes the person to change long-held beliefs, such as the impact that meeting Eneas had on the Major)*

he had a croupy cough.[6] He dropped the wood into the empty box near the old woman's chair, then straightened himself.

A soft chuckling came from the bed. Lamartine was full of pride. "A good boy, that. He keeps the old folks warm."

D 100 Something about the boy made the Major forget his determination to depart. Perhaps it was his wordlessness, his uncomplaining wordlessness. Or possibly it was his loyalty to the old people. Something drew his eyes to the boy and set him to thinking. Eneas was handing sticks of wood to the old woman and she was feeding them into the stove. When the firebox was full a good part of the boy's armload was gone. He would have to cut more, and more, to keep the old people warm.

The Major heard himself saying suddenly: "Sonny, show me your woodpile. Let's cut a lot of wood for the old folks."

110 It happened just like that, **inexplicably**. He went even farther. Not only did he cut enough wood to last through several days, but when he had finished he put the boy in the Agency car and drove him to town, five miles there and back. Against his own principles, he bought a week's store of groceries, and excused himself by telling the boy, as they drove homeward, "Your grandfather won't be able to get to town for a few days yet. Tell him to come see me when he gets well."

That was the beginning of the Major's interest in Eneas.
120 He had decided that day that he would help the boy in any way possible, because he was a boy of quality. You would be shirking your duty if you failed to recognize and to help a boy of his sort. The only question was, how to help?

E When he saw the boy again, some weeks later, his mind saw the problem clearly. "Eneas," he said, "I'm going to help you. I'll see that the old folks are taken care of, so you won't have to think about them. Maybe the old man won't have rheumatism next year, anyhow. If he does, I'll find a family where he and the old lady can move in and be looked after.
130 Don't worry about them. Just think about yourself and what I'm going to do for you. Eneas, when it comes school time, I'm going to send you away. How do you like that?" The Major smiled at his own happy idea.

inexplicable
(ĭn-ĕk´splĭ-kə-bəl) *adj.* If something is *inexplicable,* it is difficult to understand.

---

[6] **croupy cough:** an illness that causes a loud barking cough.

APPLYING ACADEMIC VOCABULARY

contrast	despite	error

As you discuss the short story, incorporate the following Collection 6 academic vocabulary words: *contrast, despite,* and *error.* Ask students to **contrast** the Major's point of view with that of the families on the Reservation. Discuss why he felt certain that he was right **despite** the attitudes of the families. Do students think that the Major made an **error** in judgment? Why or why not?

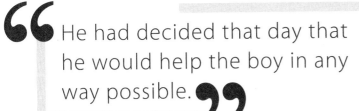

> He had decided that day that he would help the boy in any way possible.

There was silence. No shy smiling, no look of gratitude, only silence. Probably he had not understood.

"You understand, Eneas? Your grandparents will be taken care of. You'll go away and learn things. You'll go on a train."

The boy looked here and there and scratched at the ground with his foot. "Why do I have to go away?"

140 "You don't have to, Eneas. Nobody will make you. I thought you'd like to. I thought—" The Major paused, confused.

"You won't make me go away, will you?" There was fear in the voice, tears threatened.

"Why, no Eneas. If you don't want to go. I thought—"

The Major dropped the subject. He didn't see the boy again through spring and summer, but he thought of him. In fact, he couldn't forget the picture he had of him that first day. He couldn't forget either that he wanted to help him. Whether 150 the boy understood what was good for him or not, he meant to see to it that the right thing was done. And that was why, when he made up a quota[7] of children to be sent to the school in Oregon, the name of Eneas Lamartine was included. The Major did not discuss it with him again but he set the wheels in motion. The boy would go with the others. In time to come, he would understand. Possibly he would be grateful.

Thirty children were included in the quota, and of them all Eneas was the only one the Major had actual knowledge of, the only one in whom he was personally interested. With each 160 of them, it was true, he had had difficulties. None had wanted to go. They said they "liked it at home," or they were "afraid" to go away, or they would "get sick" in a strange country; and the parents were no help. They, too, were frightened and uneasy. It was a tiresome, hard kind of duty, but the Major knew what was required of him and never hesitated.

---

[7] **quota:** a predetermined, fixed amount of something or people.

CLOSE READ

Analyze Stories: Flashback (LINES 146–153)

 COMMON CORE RL 1, RL 2, RL 3

Explain that once again the action of the story flashes forward in time. Although we are still in the flashback scene, lines 146–153 bring us closer to the opening scene at the depot.

F **ASK STUDENTS** to reread lines 146–153. Have students identify the time shift and summarize what has occurred during that period. *(The time shift is signaled by "He didn't see the boy through spring and summer." During that time, the Major has decided that the best way to help Eneas is to include him in a group of children being sent away to school.)*

Analyze Stories: Character Development (LINES 149–165)

 COMMON CORE RL 1, RL 3

Point out that in lines 149–151 the Major thinks, "Whether the boy understood what was good for him or not, he meant to see to it that the right thing was done."

G **CITE TEXT EVIDENCE** Ask students what they can infer about the Major's character from this statement. *(He is stubborn. He is so certain that he is right, he is unable to see that others may hold different opinions.)* Ask students to continue rereading lines 151–165 and cite additional evidence to support their inference. *("The Major did not discuss it with him again but he set the wheels in motion"; "In time to come he would understand. Possibly he would be grateful"; "None had wanted to go"; ". . . the Major knew what was required of him and never hesitated.")*

Analyze Stories: Flashback (LINES 166–170)

 COMMON CORE RL 1, RL 2, RL 3

Explain that here, almost at the end of the story, the author ends the flashback and brings us back to the depot.

 CITE TEXT EVIDENCE Have students reread lines 166–170 and cite evidence that shows the end of the flashback. *("this moment of going away")* Ask them to summarize the insight the flashback gives into this scene. *(The flashback has given insight into why the Major feels that he is doing a good thing for Eneas and the other children, despite the contrast with their own feelings. It has also shown why the Major has taken such an interest in Eneas and believes that he is "a boy who, with the right help, would blossom and grow strong.")*

Determine Meanings of Words and Phrases

COMMON CORE RL 4

(LINES 181–188)

Explain that D'Arcy McNickle uses vivid **imagery,** or words that appeal to the senses, in his description of the approaching train.

 ASK STUDENTS to reread lines 181–188 and to identify examples of imagery. Ask what effect is created by the imagery. *(Examples: "pounding near"; "headlong flying locomotive"; "Whoo-oo, whoo-oo"; "roar of rolling steel." The imagery creates the effect of tremendous speed and of time passing too quickly.)*

> **CRITICAL VOCABULARY**
>
> **ignorance:** The Major believed that he was freeing the children from ignorance by sending them away.
>
> **ASK STUDENTS** to explain why he believed that. *(He believed they were ignorant of mainstream learning and culture. He was sending them to school to be educated.)*

COLLABORATIVE DISCUSSION Have small groups discuss the Major's successes and failures. Remind them to take notes as they talk and to cite evidence for their ideas. Have each group share their conclusions with the class.

The difference was, that in the cases of all these others, the problem was routine. He met it, and passed over it. But in the case of Eneas, he was bothered. He wanted to make clear what this moment of going away meant. It was a breaking
170 away from fear and doubt and **ignorance**. Here began the new. Mark it, remember it.

His eyes lingered on Eneas. There he stood, drooping, his nose running as on that first day, his stockings coming down, his jacket in need of buttons. But under that shabbiness, the Major knew, was real quality. There was a boy who, with the right help, would blossom and grow strong. It was important that he should not go away hurt and resentful.

The Major called back his straying thoughts and cleared his throat. The moment was important.
180 "Boys and girls—"

The train was pounding near. Already it had emerged from the canyon, and momentarily the headlong flying locomotive loomed blacker and larger. A white plume flew upward—*Whoo-oo, whoo-oo.*

The Major realized in sudden sharp remorse that he had waited too long. The vital moment had come, and he had paused, looked for words, and lost it. The roar of rolling steel was upon them.

Lifting his voice in desperate haste, his eyes fastened on
190 Eneas, he bellowed: "Boys and girls—be good—"

That was all anyone heard.

ignorance
(ĭg'nər-əns) *n.*
Ignorance is the condition of being uneducated or uninformed.

COLLABORATIVE DISCUSSION What has the Major succeeded in doing? What has he failed to do? Talk about your ideas with other group members.

TO CHALLENGE STUDENTS . . .

Character's Point of View In "Train Time," we learn a great deal about the Major's thoughts, beliefs, and motivations. But what about Eneas? What is he thinking as he stands on the platform waiting for the train? What would he like to say to the Major? to his grandparents?

ASK STUDENTS to discuss these questions in a group and to compose a brief monologue for Eneas. Remind students to review the story for evidence to support their ideas. Have volunteers deliver their monologues to the class.

Analyze Stories: Character Development

The **characters** in a work of fiction are the people, animals, or imaginary creatures who take part in the action. The way that the author creates and develops the characters is called **characterization**. Authors use four basic methods of characterization:

Methods of Characterization

- making direct comments about a character through the voice of the narrator
- describing the character's physical appearance
- presenting the character's speech, thoughts, and actions
- presenting information about the character through the thoughts, speech, and actions of other characters

With these methods, the author helps readers identify **character traits,** which are the qualities of appearance and personality that make a character seem real. Readers can infer character traits from the character's words, actions, thoughts, appearance, and interactions with other characters.

Reread lines 53–118 of "Train Time," the paragraphs in which the Major first meets Eneas. Tell how the author uses each of the four listed methods of characterization to show Eneas to readers and to develop his character.

Analyze Stories: Flashback

COMMON CORE RL 3

In a literary work, a **flashback** is an interruption of the action to show events that took place at an earlier time. A flashback provides information to help readers understand a character's current situation. To follow a narrative, readers pay attention to language that signals shifts in time. For example:

the author shifts back in time, using flashback	**"Stanley thought back to last month, when he first saw his new home."**
the author ends the flashback, shifting ahead to the present time of the story	**"Now, just one month later, Stanley felt as if he had never lived anywhere else."**

In which sentence of "Train Time" does the author first lead readers back in time?

TEACH

CLOSE READ

Analyze Stories: Character Development

COMMON CORE RL 2, RL 3

Review the term *characterization* and the four methods. Have students reread lines 53–118 of "Train Time" and identify examples of each method and what the examples reveal about Eneas. *(Possible answers: Narrator's direct comments: "Perhaps it was his wordlessness, his uncomplaining wordlessness. Or possibly it was his loyalty to the old people." These examples reveal that Eneas is loyal, kind, patient, and tolerant. Physical appearance: "The boy was no taller than an ax handle, his nose was running, and he had a croupy cough." Character's actions: " . . . staggering under a full armload of pine limbs . . . He dropped the wood into the empty box near the old woman's chair, then straightened himself. . . . Eneas was handing sticks of wood to the old woman." These reveal that Eneas is barely able to do the chores, but he is determined to help others. Thoughts, speech, and actions of other characters: "Lamartine was full of pride. 'A good boy, that. He keeps the old folks warm.'" This reveals Eneas's devotion to the older people.)*

Analyze Stories: Flashback

COMMON CORE RL 3

Review the term *flashback* and the examples. Point out that the flashback in "Train Time" begins in lines 53–54: "He remembered . . . when he first saw Eneas." Explain that students should think about why the author included the flashback and what it reveals.

Strategies for Annotation   Annotate it!

Analyze Stories: Character Development

COMMON CORE RL 2, RL 3

Share these strategies for guided or independent analysis:
- Highlight in yellow the narrator's comments about Eneas.
- Highlight in blue descriptions of Eneas's appearance.
- Highlight in pink descriptions of Eneas's actions.
- Highlight in green a character's speech, thoughts, or actions that reveal something about Eneas.

. . . little Eneas appeared, staggering under a full armload of pine limbs hacked into short lengths. The boy was no taller than an ax handle, his nose was running, and he had a croupy cough. He dropped the wood into the empty box near the old woman' s chair, then straightened himself. Lamartine was full of pride. "A good boy, that. He keeps the old folks warm."

PRACTICE & APPLY

Analyzing the Text

COMMON CORE RL 1, RL 2, RL 3, RL 6

Possible answers:

1. *They will be taken to a boarding school in Oregon, where they will learn to fit into mainstream culture.*

2. *From the Major's actions, we can tell that he is used to being obeyed. ("Major Miles boomed, 'You! What's your name? Get back here! Want to get killed! All of you, stand back!'" He "strode about, soldierlike, and waved commands.") From his thoughts, we can tell that he is somewhat blind to the feelings of others. (He had to drag the children out of hiding and get them away from their relatives, yet he felt that he was doing the right thing for them and they should be grateful.)*

3. *The Major's point of view is that he is helping the children by offering them the opportunity to go to school and get an education. However, the children feel that they are being sent away against their will, and they don't want to go. Their parents are "frightened and uneasy."*

4. *The flashback, which begins on line 53 and continues to line 156, takes the reader to a time six months before the opening scene during which the Major met Eneas and decided that the boy and his grandparents needed help. The author uses the flashback to develop the conflict between the Major and the Indians.*

5. *The Major feels that he is doing the right thing for the children and that their lives will be improved. The reader recognizes that the children's lives will change but not necessarily for the better. They are being taken from their homes, families, and culture.*

6. *The setting is an Indian reservation in the late 1800s. During this time, government officials believed that the best way to help Native American families was to send the children away to school. This helps the reader understand why the Major believed he was doing the right thing and why the children and their families were afraid.*

7. *In the end, the Major is not able to complete the speech he wanted to give about the importance of the moment. The author may have ended the story this way to show how pointless that message would have been.*

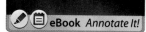 eBook *Annotate It!*

Analyzing the Text

COMMON CORE RL 1, RL 2, RL 3, RL 6, W 1, W 4, W 9a, W 10

Cite Text Evidence Support your responses with evidence from the text.

1. **Predict** What is going to happen to the children waiting for the train?

2. **Cite Evidence** Reread lines 17–27. What does this section tell you about Major Miles? What method(s) of characterization was used to convey that information?

3. **Infer** How does the Major's point of view differ from the other characters' points of view?

4. **Analyze** What section of the story is told as a flashback? What does the flashback reveal about the plot and characters?

5. **Analyze** What might the reader understand about the situation that the Major appears not to understand?

6. **Connect** How does the **setting**—the time and place of the action—affect the reader's understanding of the characters?

7. **Draw Conclusions** Why might the author have decided to end the story as he did?

 **WriteSmart**

PERFORMANCE TASK

Writing Activity: Character Analysis
In "Train Time," the Major does not think he is doing anything wrong—or does he? Write two or three paragraphs to describe the character of the Major.

- Answer these questions to help organize your ideas: What does the Major value? What actions does he take? How does the Major seem to feel about Reservation Indians?

- Include quotations from the story to support your ideas about the Major.

- Discuss the different ways the author reveals the Major's character traits.

Assign this performance task.  **WriteSmart**

PERFORMANCE TASK

COMMON CORE RL 1, RL 3, RL 6, W 1, W 4, W 9a, W 10

Writing Activity: Character Analysis Before students begin writing their character analyses, remind them of the different methods authors use to reveal character traits. Have students

- meet in groups to discuss the questions in the Performance Task
- work independently to write their analyses

Remind students to cite evidence from the text to support their ideas.

Critical Vocabulary

COMMON CORE L 4c, L 6

exasperate   conscience   ponderous

sustenance   inexplicable   ignorance

Practice and Apply Answer each question with *yes* or *no*. With your group, use examples and reasons to explain your answer.

1. If someone was **exasperated,** could you tell?

2. Should you trust a person of **conscience**?

3. Could an action be **ponderous**?

4. Is **sustenance** unnecessary?

5. Could a person behave in an **inexplicable** way?

6. Is **ignorance** the same as ignoring someone?

Vocabulary Strategy: Using a Dictionary

When you find an unknown word in a text, you can first use **context,** or the words and sentences around the word, to try to determine its meaning. Note the word *conscience* in this sentence from "Train Time": *Major Miles was a man of* conscience. There are no helpful context clues to the meaning of *conscience*. If you look it up in a dictionary, you might find these definitions:

> **1a.** An awareness of morality in regard to one's behavior; a sense of right and wrong that urges one to act morally: *Let your conscience be your guide.* **b.** A source of moral or ethical judgment or pronouncement: *a document that serves as the nation's conscience.* **c.** Conformity to one's own sense of right conduct: *a person of unflagging conscience.*

Definition **1c** best matches the meaning of *conscience* in the sentence.

A dictionary entry has additional information about a word, including a word's **pronunciation** and **part of speech**. The letters and symbols in parentheses show the word's pronunciation, followed by an italicized abbreviation of the part of speech. The pronunciation key in a dictionary can help you determine how to pronounce a word.

Practice and Apply Find these words in "Train Time": *bearing* (line 30), *tipis* (line 51), *gesture* (line 88). Use a print or digital dictionary to identify the definition that matches the context and the part of speech. Then use the pronunciation key to say the word.

Train Time **335**

PRACTICE & APPLY

Critical Vocabulary

COMMON CORE L4c, L6

Possible answers:

1. *Yes, because the exasperated person would be sighing, eye-rolling, and showing other signs of being annoyed.*

2. *Yes, because a person of conscience is principled and is likely to value honesty.*

3. *Yes, because a person could walk heavily, taking ponderous footsteps.*

4. *No, because sustenance, such as nourishment, is essential to life.*

5. *Yes, because people can do things for no apparent reason.*

6. *No, because ignorance is a lack of knowledge or education; ignoring someone means not paying attention.*

Vocabulary Strategy: Using a Dictionary

Possible answers:

bearing: n. (noun), *posture, how one carries oneself*

tipis: n. (noun), *tepees, dwellings made of a conical framework of poles covered with bark or skins*

gesture: n. (noun), *a motion of the limbs*

Strategies for Annotation 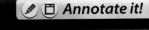 *Annotate it!*

Using a Dictionary

COMMON CORE L 4c, L 6

Have students locate the paragraph with the word *routine* (lines 166–171). Encourage them to use their eBook annotation tools to do the following:

- Highlight in yellow the word *routine*.
- Underline surrounding words and phrases that are likely clues to its meaning.
- Write a note that is a guess at the meaning based on the clues.
- Use a dictionary to confirm the meaning, writing the definition that best fits in this passage.

The difference was, that in the cases of all these others, the problem was routine. He met it, and passed over it. But in the case of Eneas, he was bothered. He wante[d] what this moment of going away meant.

routine
guess: ordinary
dictionary: having no special quality; ordinary

Train Time **335**

PRACTICE & APPLY

Language Conventions: Misplaced Modifiers

COMMON CORE L 1c

Review the definition of a modifier and the steps for correcting a misplaced modifier. Explain that a modifier can be a clause, as in the first example shown; a phrase, as in the second example; or a single word. Also point out that there can be more than one way to correct a misplaced modifier. For example, the second example could be rewritten as, *"The Major believed that, in the future, the children would thank him."*

Possible answers:

1. *Major Miles, fulfilling his duty, made a list of thirty children's names.*

2. *Of all the children, little Eneas was the only one the Major knew.*

3. *Major Miles was sure that the children leaving the reservation would have better lives.*

4. *The children who were leaving their families had tears and fearful faces.*

5. *At the school in Oregon, Eneas would give up the only culture he had known.*

6. *Coming down the tracks was the train that would change the children's lives forever.*

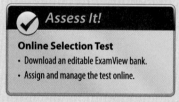

Assess It!

Online Selection Test
- Download an editable ExamView bank.
- Assign and manage the test online.

Language Conventions: Misplaced Modifiers

A **modifier** is a word or a group of words that changes, or modifies, the meaning of another word in a sentence. A **misplaced modifier** is in the wrong place in a sentence and can confuse a reader. As you review your writing, follow these steps to identify and fix misplaced modifiers.

- Find the modifier.
- Identify what word the modifier was intended to modify.
- Place the modifier as close as possible to the word, phrase, or clause it is supposed to describe.

In the following examples, note the underlined modifier and the word or phrase it was intended to modify.

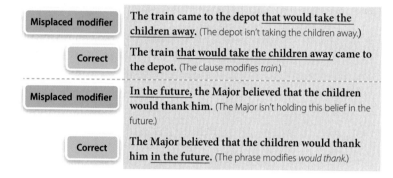

Misplaced modifier	The train came to the depot <u>that would take the children away</u>. (The depot isn't taking the children away.)
Correct	The train <u>that would take the children away</u> came to the depot. (The clause modifies *train*.)
Misplaced modifier	<u>In the future,</u> the Major believed that the children would thank him. (The Major isn't holding this belief in the future.)
Correct	The Major believed that the children would thank him <u>in the future</u>. (The phrase modifies *would thank*.)

Practice and Apply Each sentence has a misplaced modifier. Find and fix the error.

1. Major Miles made a list of thirty children's names fulfilling his duty.

2. Little Eneas was the only one of all the children the Major knew.

3. Leaving the Reservation, Major Miles was sure that the children would have better lives.

4. The children had tears and fearful faces who were leaving their families.

5. Eneas would give up the only culture he had known at the school in Oregon.

6. The train was coming down the tracks that would change the children's lives forever.

INTERACTIVE WHITEBOARD LESSON
Analyze Story Elements: Plot

COMMON CORE

RL 3

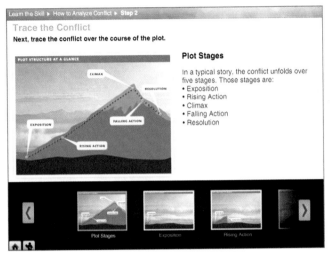

Learn the Skill ▶ How to Analyze Conflict ▶ Step 2

Trace the Conflict
Next, trace the conflict over the course of the plot.

PLOT STRUCTURE AT A GLANCE

CLIMAX
RESOLUTION
EXPOSITION
FALLING ACTION
RISING ACTION

Plot Stages

In a typical story, the conflict unfolds over five stages. Those stages are:
• Exposition
• Rising Action
• Climax
• Falling Action
• Resolution

Plot Stages   Exposition   Rising Action

TEACH

Explain to students that every good story is a series of events that center on the resolution of a struggle between opposing forces, called the **conflict.** Looking closely at the elements of the **plot,** or the series of events in a story, and seeing how conflicts develop over the five stages of the plot are key parts to analyzing a story and understanding why it captivates readers.

Use the plot diagram shown in the Interactive Whiteboard Lesson "Plot and Conflict" to introduce the five elements of **plot:**

- **Exposition** The exposition introduces the setting and characters and establishes the conflict.
- **Rising Action** In the rising action, the characters struggle to overcome obstacles that arise as they try to resolve the conflict. Suspense builds during the rising action.
- **Climax** The turning point of the story, the climax is the moment of greatest suspense where the outcome of the conflict becomes clear.
- **Falling Action** Here suspense eases as the characters resolve the conflict.
- **Resolution** Finally, the resolution reveals the final outcome and ties up any loose ends in the story.

Work with students to create a plot diagram for "Train Time." Note that the rising action occurs in a flashback to events of the previous winter.

CLOSE READING APPLICATION

Have students make a plot diagram for another short story. Have partners combine diagrams and retell the plot to the group.

INTERACTIVE WHITEBOARD LESSON
Analyze Story Elements: Setting

COMMON CORE

RL 3

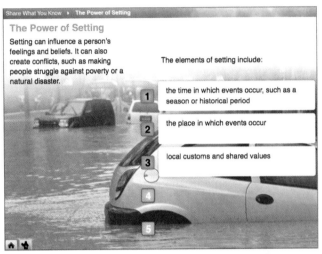

Share What You Know ▶ The Power of Setting

The Power of Setting
Setting can influence a person's feelings and beliefs. It can also create conflicts, such as making people struggle against poverty or a natural disaster.

The elements of setting include:

1 the time in which events occur, such as a season or historical period

2 the place in which events occur

3 local customs and shared values

4

5

TEACH

Explain that in addition to time and place, the **setting** of a story can include elements of culture, social class, weather, and landscape, thus transporting the reader into the world of the story.

Discuss how the setting can affect the plot of a story in a number of ways:

- The setting can influence characters by determining their living conditions and shaping their personalities, goals, and dreams.
- The setting can create obstacles to resolving the conflict, such as dangerous weather conditions or a difficult time period such as a war.
- Setting can also serve as a symbol. A **symbol** is a person, a place, an object, or an activity that stands for something beyond itself. A story's setting can represent an important idea, such as a garden standing for hope.
- Finally, the setting can affect the **theme** of the story. The theme is a message about life or human nature that the author wants to share with the reader.

Work with students to identify the setting of "Train Time" and analyze its effect on the plot. *(It contributes to the conflict between the Major and the families.)*

CLOSE READING APPLICATION

Students can apply the skill to another short story of their own choosing. Have them analyze the setting(s). Suggest that they use a chart to record ways in which the setting impacts the plot.

Analyze Story Elements: Mood

COMMON CORE
RL 3

TEACH

Point out to students that an author can use details as well as word choices to create the mood of a story. The **mood** is the feeling or atmosphere a writer creates in a story. Explain that whether the mood is lighthearted, somber, hopeful, or mysterious, it can affect the reader's emotional reaction to the characters and events.

Explain that mood can be created in a number of ways:

- **Descriptive words** Authors use specific words to create a mood. For example, in a mystery set in a haunted house, an author might use words such as *dark, dreary, eerie,* or *chilling* to create an ominous, foreboding mood.
- **Imagery** Authors often create mood with **imagery**— words and phrases that appeal to a reader's five senses. These sensory details help the reader to imagine how things look, feel, smell, sound, or taste. For example, the sentence "Flashes of lightning pierced the ink-black sky" appeals to the sense of sight, creating a mood of anticipation and tension.
- **Figurative language** Finally, the use of figurative language can create mood. Explain that figurative language is the use of words in imaginative ways to express ideas that are not literally true. In the sentence "The river was my constant companion, babbling away at me as I paddled," the river is compared to a chatty friend, creating a playful or whimsical mood.

PRACTICE AND APPLY

Have students reread "Train Time" to find details that create different moods. Have students list examples of descriptive words, imagery, and figurative language and explain how these details contribute to the mood. Tell students to be alert to sudden changes in mood, as the mood in a story can shift. Once students have compiled a list of examples, have them discuss their lists with a partner or small group of students who have also completed the activity. Encourage the group to use the details to compile a web of words to describe the mood or moods in different parts of the story.

Analyze Stories: Characterization

COMMON CORE
RL 3

RETEACH

Review the definition of *characterization* and the four basic methods authors use. Discuss examples of each method:

METHOD	EXAMPLE
direct comments through the voice of the narrator	Cinderella was always kind and patient, no matter how badly she was treated.
description of physical appearance	Her filthy rags and work-roughened hands could not disguise her delicate beauty.
the character's speech, thoughts, and actions	"I wish I could go to the ball, but there is so much cleaning to do!" she sighed.
other characters' speech, thoughts, and actions	"I must find her," the prince declared. "She is the sweetest, kindest woman I've ever met."

Discuss what inferences a reader can make about Cinderella from each example.

 LEVEL UP TUTORIALS Assign the following *Level Up* tutorial: **Methods of Characterization**

CLOSE READING APPLICATION

Students can apply the skill to another short story of their own choosing. Have students work independently to select a story and a character to analyze. Suggest that students use a chart to record each example of characterization and the inferences they can draw from it.

Interactive Lessons

If you need help...
• **Writing Informative Texts**
• **Conducting Research**
• **Producing and Publishing with Technology**

Write an Expository Essay

This collection focuses on important social causes and how people champion those causes. In the selections about the Triangle Factory Fire, you learned how a great tragedy led to public outcry for the causes of workplace safety and fair working conditions. In this activity, you will do additional research about a topic or person related to this fire. You will draw from the texts in the collection and your research findings to write an expository essay about the topic or person you chose.

COMMON CORE

W 2a–f Write informative/ explanatory texts.
W 4 Produce clear and coherent writing.
W 5 Develop and strengthen writing.
W 6 Use technology to produce and publish writing.
W 7 Conduct short research projects.
W 8 Gather relevant information.
W 10 Write routinely.

A successful expository essay

• provides an engaging introduction that clearly states the topic

• organizes ideas and concepts logically to make important connections and distinctions

• supports central ideas with details—facts, definitions, and examples—pulled from a variety of credible sources

• uses appropriate transitions to link ideas

• establishes and maintains a formal style

• provides a conclusion that follows from and supports the information presented

PLAN

Determine Your Topic Review the excerpts from *The Story of the Triangle Factory Fire, Flesh & Blood So Cheap,* and *Uprising*. Think about the major events and ideas in each selection. Brainstorm a list of possible topics or people to research, such as the trial following the fire, the new labor laws, Francis Perkins, or Fire Chief Croker. Choose the topic that most interests you.

• Transform your topic into a research question you want to answer, such as *How did the fire impact workplace safety, and what was Frances Perkins' role in that? Why were fire precautions so inadequate during that time?* or *What happened to the Asch Building after the fire, and how are the fire and its victims remembered?*

myNotebook

Use the annotation tools in your eBook to record details from the selections that support your topic. Save each detail to your notebook.

ACADEMIC VOCABULARY

As you plan and draft your essay, be sure to use the academic vocabulary words.

contrast

despite

error

inadequate

interact

WRITE AN EXPOSITORY ESSAY

COMMON CORE
W 2a–f, W 4,
W 5, W 6,
W 7, W 8,
W 10

Introduce students to the Performance Task by reading the introductory paragraph with them and reviewing the criteria for what makes a good expository essay. Remind students that a good expository essay includes evidence that supports the main points the writer makes.

PLAN

DETERMINE YOUR TOPIC

Remind students that their topic questions are likely to change as they do more research into their chosen topics. Explain that students should be open to adjusting their topics and questions as they find additional information that intrigues them or that takes them in a different direction. Point out that flexibility in planning is an important part of the planning phase for any writing task that involves research.

PERFORMANCE TASK A

PLAN

DO RESEARCH

Remind students that when researching on the Internet they will find websites with information that has not been checked. To evaluate a website, students should answer these questions:

- Who created the site?
- Why was the site created?
- Are there credits?
- Are there more reliable sources with information about the topic?

- Make sure your question is open-ended and cannot be answered in a single word.
- Generate further questions that will help you find specific evidence.

Gather Information Look for information in the selections that relates to your topic. Take notes on key points, observations, and events that will help you gain a better understanding of your topic, answer your questions, and support your main points.

Do Research Use print and digital sources to find additional information that addresses your research question.

- Search for credible and accurate sources. Use keywords or subject searching in the library to find print sources. Use a search engine or Internet directories to find credible digital sources.
- Take notes on facts, details, definitions, and examples that explain and support your main points.
- Check that the information you find is supported by the information you read in the collection.

Organize Your Ideas Think about how you will organize your essay. Create an outline showing the information you will present in each paragraph. Organize your ideas in a logical sequence, making sure each idea follows from the previous idea and leads into the next idea.

> **I.** Use Roman numerals for main topics.
>   A. Indent and use capital letters for subtopics.
>   1. Indent and use numbers for supporting facts and details.
>   2. Indent and use numbers for supporting facts and details.
> **II.** Use Roman numerals for main topics.
>   B. Indent and use capital letters for subtopics.
>   1. Indent and use numbers for supporting facts and details.

Consider Your Purpose and Audience Think about who will read or listen to your essay, and what you want them to understand. What does the audience already know? What background information will they need? Keep this in mind as you prepare to write.

PRODUCE

Write Your Essay Use your notes and your outline as you begin your draft.

*my*WriteSmart

Write your rough draft in *my*WriteSmart. Focus on getting your ideas down, rather than on perfecting your choice of language.

- Begin with an attention-grabbing introduction that defines your topic. Include an unusual comment, fact, quote, or story.
- Organize your information into paragraphs of related ideas.
- Include supporting facts, concrete details, definitions, and examples from the selections and other sources.
- Transition from one logical point to another, using words and phrases such as *because, despite, therefore,* and *as a result of.*
- Use a formal tone.
- Write a conclusion that follows from and supports your explanation.

PRODUCE

WRITE YOUR ESSAY

Remind students to use their outlines as a guide for their first draft. Point out that each main idea should be supported by the details and evidence included in their outlines. Suggest that students include only one main idea in each paragraph as they write.

REVISE

Evaluate Your Draft Use the chart on the following page to evaluate the substance and style of your essay.

*my*WriteSmart

Have a group of peers review your draft in *my*WriteSmart. Ask your reviewers to note any facts, details, or examples that do not support your main ideas.

- Check that your topic is clearly defined.
- Examine each paragraph to make sure each point is clearly stated and supported with facts, details, and examples.
- Be sure that the ideas are organized in a logical sequence. Check that transitions help the reader follow along and reinforce logic.
- Check that your conclusion supports the information presented.

REVISE

EVALUATE YOUR DRAFT

Have students work with a partner to help them revise their essays. Students can take turns listening to each other's essays and offering suggestions to make them more effective. After students revise their essays, partners can reread them and discuss whether they need further revisions.

PRESENT

Create a Finished Copy Finalize your essay and post it as a blog on a personal or school website. You might also want to use these additional formats to present it:

- Deliver your essay as a speech to the class.
- Organize a group discussion to share your ideas about your topic.
- Make a video recording of your essay, and share it on your class or school website.

PRESENT

CREATE A FINISHED COPY

To present their essays, students can:

- present their essays orally to the class. Remind students to speak loudly and clearly, look directly at the audience, and use gestures and facial expressions to emphasize ideas.
- organize a group discussion to share ideas about their topics. Remind students to take turns and listen attentively as others speak.
- produce a video of their essays. Suggest that students practice with partners to help them refine their performances before recording.

PERFORMANCE TASK A

LANGUAGE

Have students look at the chart and identify how they did on the Performance Task in each of the three main categories. In particular, ask students to discuss how effectively they used strong, precise language to create a formal style that was both clear and engaging for the reader. Ask students to think about how they could improve their writing when they next write an expository essay. You may want to provide some good models of expository writing and have students compare their essays to them.

COLLECTION 6 TASK A
EXPOSITORY ESSAY

	Ideas and Evidence	Organization	Language
ADVANCED	• The introduction is appealing and informative; a central idea clearly identifies the topic in an engaging way. • The topic is well developed with relevant examples, concrete details, and interesting facts from the selections and other credible sources. • The concluding section capably summarizes the information presented.	• The organization is effective and logical throughout the essay. • Transitions successfully connect related ideas.	• The writing reflects a formal style, with strong, precise language. • Sentence beginnings, lengths, and structures vary and have a rhythmic flow. • Spelling, capitalization, and punctuation are correct. • Grammar and usage are correct.
COMPETENT	• The introduction could do more to grab the reader's attention; the central idea identifies the topic. • One or two key points could be better supported with more relevant examples, concrete details, and facts from the selections and other credible sources. • The concluding section summarizes the information presented.	• The organization is confusing in a few places. • A few more transitions are needed to connect related ideas.	• The style is inconsistent in a few places. • Language is too general in some places. • Sentence beginnings, lengths, and structures vary somewhat. • A few spelling, capitalization, and punctuation mistakes occur. • Some grammatical and usage errors are repeated in the essay.
LIMITED	• The introduction is only partly informative; the central idea only hints at a topic. • Most key points need more support in the form of relevant examples, concrete details, and facts. • The concluding section partially summarizes the information presented.	• The organization is logical in some places but often doesn't follow a pattern. • More transitions are needed throughout to connect related ideas.	• The style becomes informal in several places. • Overly general language is used in several places. • Sentence structures barely vary, with some fragments or run-on sentences present. • Spelling, capitalization, and punctuation are often incorrect. • Grammar and usage are incorrect in several places.
EMERGING	• The introduction is missing. • Examples, details, and facts are missing. • The essay lacks a concluding section.	• A logical organization is not used; information is presented randomly. • Transitions are not used, making the essay difficult to understand.	• The style is inappropriate for the essay. • Language is too general to convey the information. • Repetitive sentence structure, fragments, and run-on sentences make the writing difficult to follow. • Spelling, capitalization, and punctuation are incorrect throughout. • Several grammatical and usage errors change the meaning of the writer's ideas.

COLLECTION 6
PERFORMANCE TASK B

Interactive Lessons
If you need help . . .
• **Writing Informative Texts**
• **Producing and Publishing with Technology**

Write a Personal Essay

In this collection, you read about problems in the world that inspire people to take action to solve those problems. For example, twelve-year-old Craig Kielburger was moved to expose the injustice of child labor practices around the world, as he described in "Craig Kielburger Reflects on Working Toward Peace." In this activity, you will draw from the selections you read and write a personal essay about a cause that is important to you.

COMMON CORE

W 2a–f Write informative/ explanatory texts.
W 4 Produce clear and coherent writing.
W 5 Develop and strengthen writing.
W 6 Use technology to produce and publish writing.
W 10 Write routinely.

A successful personal essay

- provides an engaging introduction that clearly states the topic
- organizes ideas and concepts logically to make important connections and distinctions
- supports central ideas with facts, details, and examples pulled from a variety of credible sources
- uses appropriate transitions to link ideas
- establishes and maintains a formal style
- provides a conclusion that follows from and supports the information presented

PLAN

Determine Your Topic A personal essay communicates the writer's thoughts or viewpoint. It can be written about a cause, or something that affects a person's life or the lives of others in a way that makes him or her want to do something about it. Consider the causes you read about in this collection. Think about what happened to influence each writer and how the writer took action. Then choose a cause that is important to you.

- Think about an experience that has affected you in a way that makes you want to inform others about it.
- Consider how the experience affected you and your beliefs.
- Identify a cause that is related to the experience.
- Record your ideas about what you have done or would like to do to support the cause.

myNotebook

Use the annotation tools in your eBook to record details that you might include. Save each detail to your notebook.

ACADEMIC VOCABULARY

As you plan and draft your essay, be sure to use the academic vocabulary words.

contrast
despite
error
inadequate
interact

WRITE A PERSONAL ESSAY

COMMON CORE W 2a–f, W 4, W 5, W 6, W 10

Introduce students to the Performance Task by reading the introductory paragraph with them and reviewing the criteria for what makes a good personal essay. Explain to students that a good personal essay presents a writer's thoughts or viewpoint about a cause that is important to him or her.

PLAN

DETERMINE YOUR TOPIC

Share with students that while brainstorming ideas for their personal essays they should think back over their lives. Have students list experiences that particularly affected them and think about which ones changed their lives in some way. Then, have students choose the single event that had the most profound effect on them.

Organize Your Ideas A graphic organizer like the one shown can help you to organize your ideas and explain your cause in a logical way.

Introduction:

Central Idea:

| Paragraph 1: | Paragraph 2: | Paragraph 3: |

Conclusion:

Consider Your Purpose and Audience Who will read or listen to your essay? What do you want them to understand about your cause? What does the audience already know? Keep this in mind as you prepare to write. Your wording and tone may be different for a group of classmates or friends than it would be for a group of adults.

PRODUCE

PRODUCE

WRITE YOUR ESSAY

Tell students to use their graphic organizers as they write their essay. Point out to students that a personal essay allows readers to see inside the mind of the writer. Remind students to let readers know what their thoughts and feelings were when they experienced the events. Students can also share their thoughts now about the past event, offering any insights about themselves or life in general that they took away from the event.

Write Your Essay Use your notes and your graphic organizer as you begin your draft.

- Begin with an attention-grabbing introduction that explains why the cause is important to you. In Craig Kielburger's essay, he draws the reader in with references to Superman. Connect your idea to ideas from the selections.

- Organize your ideas into paragraphs of related information.

- Include supporting facts, concrete details, and examples that emphasize your ideas.

- Make sure your ideas transition from one logical point to another.

- Use a formal tone.

- Conclude with a summary of your central idea, and offer your readers an insight about the importance of the cause.

my **WriteSmart**

Write your rough draft in *my*WriteSmart. Focus on getting your ideas down, rather than on perfecting your choice of language.

REVISE

Evaluate Your Draft Use the chart on the following page to work with a partner or a group of peers to evaluate the substance and style of one another's essays.

my WriteSmart

Have a partner or a group of peers review your draft in myWriteSmart. Ask your reviewers to note any information that isn't related to your cause.

- Check that your explanation about the importance of the cause is clear.
- Examine each paragraph to make sure each idea is clearly stated and supported with facts, details, and examples.
- Be sure that the ideas are organized in a logical sequence. Check that transitions help the reader follow along and reinforce logic.
- Check that your conclusion restates your main point and offers insight about the importance of the cause.

PRESENT

Create a Finished Copy Finalize your essay and present it as a podcast for other students to download and listen to. You might want to use these additional formats:

- Present your essay as a speech to the class.
- Organize a group discussion to share your ideas about your cause.
- Post your essay as a blog on a personal or school website.

REVISE

EVALUATE YOUR DRAFT

Remind students that the purpose of a personal essay is to persuade others to adopt a certain viewpoint. As students revise their essays, they should ask themselves:

- Have I provided a reasonable explanation?
- Is the relationship between my experiences and feelings clear?
- Do I sound logical and convincing?

PRESENT

CREATE A FINISHED COPY

To share their finished essays, students can:

- present their essays as speeches. Suggest that students videotape their speeches beforehand and then review the recordings to make sure they are speaking effectively.
- organize a group discussion to share their ideas. Remind students to speak clearly and loudly when they present their ideas.
- post their essays as a blog on a personal or school website. Encourage readers to post questions and comments for the writers to respond to.

PERFORMANCE TASK B

IDEAS AND EVIDENCE

Have students look at the chart and identify how they did on the Performance Task in each of the three main categories. In particular, ask students to discuss how effectively the introduction engages readers' interest and how capably the concluding section summarizes their main points. You may want to provide examples of essays that execute these aspects well. Have students compare their writing to the examples. Then, have students state goals for the next time they write a personal essay.

PERSONAL ESSAY

	Ideas and Evidence	Organization	Language
ADVANCED	• The introduction is appealing and informative; a central idea clearly identifies the topic in an engaging way. • The central idea is well developed with relevant facts and examples, concrete details, and interesting quotations. • The concluding section capably summarizes the idea presented.	• The organization is effective and logical throughout the essay. • Transitions successfully connect related ideas.	• The writing reflects a formal style, with strong, precise language. • Sentence beginnings, lengths, and structures vary and have a rhythmic flow. • Spelling, capitalization, and punctuation are correct. • Grammar and usage are correct.
COMPETENT	• The introduction could do more to grab the reader's attention; the central idea identifies the topic. • One or two key points could be better supported with more relevant facts and examples, concrete details, and quotations. • The concluding section summarizes the idea presented.	• The organization is confusing in a few places. • A few more transitions are needed to connect related ideas.	• The style is inconsistent in a few places. • Language is too general in some places. • Sentence beginnings, lengths, and structures vary somewhat. • A few spelling, capitalization, and punctuation mistakes occur. • Some grammatical and usage errors are repeated in the essay.
LIMITED	• The introduction is only partly informative; the central idea only hints at a topic. • Most key points need more support in the form of relevant facts and examples, concrete details, and quotations. • The concluding section partially summarizes the idea presented.	• The organization is logical in some places but often doesn't follow a pattern. • More transitions are needed throughout to connect related ideas.	• The style becomes informal in many places. • Overly general language is used in many places. • Sentence structures barely vary, with some fragments or run-on sentences present. • Spelling, capitalization, and punctuation are often incorrect. • Grammar and usage are incorrect in several places.
EMERGING	• The introduction is missing. • Facts, examples, details, and quotations from the selections and other credible sources are missing. • The essay lacks a concluding section.	• A logical organization is not used; information is presented randomly. • Transitions are not used, making the essay difficult to understand.	• The style is inappropriate for the essay. • Language is too general to convey the information. • Repetitive sentence structure, fragments, and run-on sentences make the writing monotonous and difficult to follow. • Spelling, capitalization, and punctuation are incorrect throughout. • Several grammatical and usage errors change the meaning of the writer's ideas.

TEACHER NOTE:
The page numbers to the left indicate pages in the Student Edition. Except for the two entries below, the page numbers in the Student Edition and Teacher's Edition correspond.

Writing an Argument

COMMON CORE W 1a-e, W 4

Many of the Performance Tasks in this book ask you to craft an argument in which you support your ideas with text evidence. Any argument you write should include the following sections and characteristics.

Introduction

Clearly state your **claim**—the point your argument makes. As needed, provide context or background information to help readers understand your position. Note the most common opposing views as a way to distinguish and clarify your ideas. From the very beginning, make it clear for readers why your claim is strong; consider providing an overview of your reasons or a quotation that emphasizes your view in your introduction.

EXAMPLES

vague claim: Dogs need places to play.

precise claim: The city should create a large designated dog park.

not distinguished from opposing view: There are plenty of people who are afraid of dogs.

distinguished from opposing view: While some people consider it dangerous for dogs to run free, the facts show that dog parks are safe.

confusing relationship of ideas: Bored dogs get sick. Dog parks have lots of space.

clear relationship of ideas: By providing a large, safe area for dogs to run off-leash and play, dog owners throughout the city would also benefit.

Development of Claims

The body of your argument must provide strong, logical reasons for your claim and must support those reasons with relevant evidence. A **reason** tells why your claim is valid; **evidence** provides specific examples that illustrate a reason. In the process of developing your claim you should also refute **counterclaims**, or opposing views, with equally strong reasons and evidence. To demonstrate that you have thoroughly considered your view, provide a well-rounded look at both the strengths and limitations of your claim and opposing claims. The goal is not to undercut your argument, but rather to answer your readers' potential objections to it. Be sure, too, to consider how much your audience may already know about your topic in order to avoid boring or confusing readers.

EXAMPLES

claim lacking reasons: A dog park would be a good thing because dogs would enjoy it and it would help the community.

claim developed by reasons: Among the benefits of a dog park are not only potentially healthier dogs and more well-adjusted pets, but also a stronger sense of community among dog owners.

omission of limitations: People who hate dogs and are opposed to this idea see no problems or safety issues, they just think the park is a waste of money.

fair discussion of limitations: We should not dismiss safety concerns. Planning for the park should include posted signs with rules of behavior, first aid facilities, and ongoing maintenance.

inattention to audience's knowledge: Socialization skills can't be taught in isolation, but issues of dominance are possible to teach with other dogs.

awareness of audience's knowledge: Readers unfamiliar with dog behavior may be surprised to learn that most injuries involving dogs happen in homes and on the street, not in well-planned dog parks.

Links Among Ideas

Even the strongest reasons and evidence will fail to sway readers if it is unclear how the reasons relate to the central claim of an argument. Make the connections clear for your readers, using not only transitional words and phrases, but also using clauses and even entire sentences as a bridge between ideas you have already discussed and ideas you are introducing.

EXAMPLES

transitional word linking claim and reason: The entire community will benefit from a dog park. First, dogs who are freed from always walking outside on leashes become better adjusted and better behaved, resulting in less aggressive behavior.

transitional phrase linking reason and evidence: A dog park must be large enough for dogs to run and not be crowded. In fact, evidence shows crowding can result in fights.

transitional clause linking claim and counterclaim: The benefits of the park are clear. Those opposed to the park plan, though, would say otherwise: They feel that there is too much potential for injuries to both people and pets.

Appropriate Style and Tone

An effective argument is most often written in a direct and formal style. The style and tone you choose in an argument should not be an afterthought—the way you express your argument can either drive home your ideas or detract from them. Even as you argue in favor of your viewpoint, take care to remain objective in tone—avoid using loaded language when discussing opposing claims.

EXAMPLES

informal style: The park will help dog owners all over the city, so the city should put out the cash.

formal style: Because the benefits of the park would reach dog owners throughout the city, it is logical for the city to provide the funding for the project.

continued

biased tone: It would be ridiculous to be against this plan.

objective tone: Arguments opposing the dog park plan have been refuted by statistics from reliable sources.

inattention to conventions: Let's make this park happen!

attention to conventions: This proposal, which will help provide humane treatment of pets at little cost, deserves City Council attention.

Conclusion

Your conclusion may range from a sentence to a full paragraph, but it must wrap up your argument in a satisfying way; a conclusion that sounds tacked-on helps your argument no more than providing no conclusion at all. A strong conclusion is a logical extension of the argument you have presented. It carries forth your ideas through an inference, question, quotation, or challenge.

EXAMPLES

inference: Humane treatment of dogs begins with community support.

question: Who doesn't want to live in community that cares for its dogs humanely?

quotation: As our city's animal control warden says, "Dogs who run freely and play companionably are far less likely to be aggressive and cause injury to themselves or others."

challenge: Facilities of this type make the difference between a city that treats its dogs humanely and a city that ignores dogs' needs.

Writing an Informative Essay

COMMON CORE W 2, W 4

Most of the Performance Tasks in this book ask you to write informational or explanatory texts in which you present a topic and examine it thoughtfully through a well-organized analysis of relevant content. Any informative or explanatory text that you create should include the following parts and features.

Introduction

Develop a strong **thesis statement.** That is, clearly state your **topic** and the **organizational framework** through which you will **connect** or **distinguish** elements of your topic. For example, you might state that your text will compare ideas, examine causes and effects, or explore a problem and its solutions.

EXAMPLE

Topic: street lighting		

Sample Thesis Statements		

Compare-contrast: To decide whether to install brighter street lamps or keep dimmer lights, consider the costs and the benefits of each type.

Cause-effect: While the causes of poor night-time visibility on city streets isn't difficult to guess, the effects can be many and devastating.

Problem-solution: Our town's poor nighttime visibility creates a growing problem with accidents, but through community action we can manage the issue.

Clarifying the organizational framework up front will help you organize the body of your text, suggest **headings** you can use to guide your readers, and help you identify **graphics** that you may need to clarify information. For example, if you compare and contrast the costs and benefits of installing brighter street lamps, you might create a chart like the one here to guide your writing. You could include the same chart in your paper as a graphic for readers. The row or column headings serve as natural paragraph headings.

	low lighting	bright lighting
Costs	Minimal maintenance of existing lights	Investment in all-new fixtures
Benefits	Old-fashioned charm	Increased visibility for motorists and pedestrians

Development of the Topic

In the body of your text, flesh out the organizational framework you established in your introduction with strong supporting paragraphs. Include only support directly relevant to your topic. Don't rely on a single source, and make sure the sources you do use are reputable and current. The table below illustrates types of support you might use to develop aspects of your topic. It also shows how transitions link text sections, create cohesion, and clarify the relationships among ideas.

Types of Support in Explanatory/ Informative Texts	Uses of Transitions in Explanatory/ Informative Texts
Facts and examples: One cause of poor lighting is inappropriate placement of lights; *for example, most pedestrian crosswalks currently have no extra lighting, increasing the risk to pedestrians from motor vehicles.*	*One cause* signals the shift from the introduction to the body text in a cause-and-effect essay. *For example* introduces the support for the cause being cited.

continued

Types of Support in Explanatory/ Informative Texts	Uses of Transitions in Explanatory/ Informative Texts
Concrete details: <u>On the other hand, if residents want to preserve the surrounding darkness of night, they may want to explore other sources of lighting for pedestrian safety.</u> *Hand-held flashlights, arm band lights, shoe reflectors, and strap-on head lighting are options.*	*On the other hand* transitions the reader from one point of comparison to another in a compare-contrast essay.
Statistics: <u>Turn to the city's accident statistics for evidence of pedestrian accidents that occur after dark: 54 accidents in the prior year.</u>	The entire transitional sentence introduces the part of a problem-solution essay that demonstrates the existence of a problem.

You can't always include all of the information you'd like to in a short essay, but you can plan to point readers directly to useful **multimedia links** either in the body of or at the end of your essay.

Style and Tone

Use formal English to establish your credibility as a source of information. To project authority, use the language of the domain, or field, that you are writing about. However, be sure to define unfamiliar terms to avoid using jargon your audience may not know. Provide extended definitions when your audience is likely to have limited knowledge of the topic.

Using quotations from reputable sources can also give your text authority; be sure to credit the source of quoted material. In general, keep the tone objective, avoiding slangy or biased expressions.

Informal, jargon-filled, biased language: People who think that navigating our city's streets as a pedestrian is a walk in the park obviously don't walk much. They have never had an SUV brush them off the crosswalk.

Extended definition in formal style and objective tone: Pedestrian safety refers to a variety of precautions. According to our city's official website, pedestrians can follow several tips for safe walking in low-light situations such as dusk, dawn, and night. Michael Keen, our city's safety expert, advises that as a pedestrian you should wear light clothing after dark, use a flashlight to light the walking path and to alert drivers, and never assume a car's driver will see you and stop for you, even if you have the Walk sign.

Conclusion

Wrap up your essay with a concluding statement or section that sums up or extends the information in your essay.

EXAMPLES

Articulate implications: Fifty-four pedestrian accidents in a year is an unacceptable number. If the city and its citizens can work together to provide necessary safety precautions and learn more about specific actions to encourage safety, we can significantly reduce the number of pedestrian accidents each year.

Emphasize significance: Pedestrian safety is everyone's responsibility. Safety islands, well-lit crosswalks, driver and pedestrian safety-awareness programs, and adequate street lighting are the city's responsibility. Pedestrians too have a responsibility—to dress so they are visible, to always look out for themselves, and to never assume a driver sees them. By working together toward awareness, we can significantly reduce pedestrian accidents in our city.

Writing a Narrative

COMMON CORE   W 3, W 4

When you are writing a fictional tale, an autobiographical incident, or a firsthand biography, you write in the narrative mode. That means telling a story with a beginning, a climax, and a conclusion. Though there are important differences between fictional and nonfiction narratives, you use similar processes to develop both kinds.

Identify a Problem, Situation, or Observation

For a nonfiction narrative, dig into your memory bank for a problem you dealt with or an observation you've made about your life. For fiction, try to invent a problem or situation that can unfold in interesting ways.

EXAMPLES

Problem (nonfiction)	Our family needed to train our newly chosen four-month-old West Highland White Terrier.
Situation (fiction)	One day, George, a nervous worrier, receives a mysterious gift in the mail.

Establish a Point of View

Decide who will tell your story. If you are writing a reflective essay about an important experience or person in your own life, you will be the narrator of the events you relate. If you are writing a work of fiction, you can choose to create a first-person narrator or to tell the story from the third-person point of view. The narrator can focus on one character or reveal the thoughts and feelings of all the characters. The examples below show the differences between a first- and third-person narrator.

First-person narrator (nonfiction)	Seven hundred fifty dollars: That's what it would cost me to go on the class trip to Washington, D.C. But it might as well have been a million dollars.

Third-person narrator (fiction)	Peter's fingers froze over the "What's new with you" prompt of his status page. The box was already filled out, waiting for him to press the Update key. "My mom found a new job!" said the box. Peter hadn't written those words. And, as far as he knew, his mother had stopped looking for work months ago.

Gather Details

To make real or imaginary experiences come alive on the page, you will need to use narrative techniques like description and dialogue. The questions in the left column in the chart below can help you search your memory or imagination for the details that will form the basis of your narrative. You don't have to respond in full sentences, but try to capture the sights, sounds, and feelings that bring your narrative to life.

Who, What, When, Where?	Narrative Techniques
People: Who are the people or characters involved in the experience? What did they look like? What did they do? What did they say?	**Description:** George, a friend I've known for as long as I can remember, is outgoing and loves being with people. But George has one quality that I find hard to understand. Even though he has no allergies, he is terribly afraid of certain foods and of getting sick from them. When we go out to eat together, he'll only eat fruit or a slice of meat. He'll never eat a sauce or any food like it. He'll say something like, "I don't know what's in their spaghetti sauce. It might not be good for me."

continued

Who, What, When, Where?	Narrative Techniques
Experience: What led up to or caused the event? What is the main event in the experience? What happened as a result of the event?	**Description:** The next morning my brother and I ventured outside with Maggie. It was February and freezing cold. Maggie didn't like the wind and snow. She balked, stopping with a jerk when we walked. An hour later, our fingers and toes numb, our noses red and raw, Maggie cooperated. She had learned something, and we did too—we had a stubborn dog to train.
Places: When and where did the events take place? What were the sights, sounds, and smells of this place?	**Description:** In December, the air crisp but not yet bitingly cold, I thought ahead to winter break delights—sledding swiftly down the steepest hill, the smell of peppermint cookies, the crunch of ice when we skated.

Sequence Events

Before you write, list key events of the experience or story in chronological, or time, order. Place a star next to the point of highest tension—for example, the point at which a key decision determines the outcome. In fiction, this point is called the climax, but a nonfiction narrative can also have a climactic event.

To build suspense—the uncertainty a reader feels about what will happen next—you'll want to think about the pacing or rhythm of your narrative. Consider disrupting the chronological order of events by beginning at the end, then starting over. Or interrupt the forward flow of events with a flashback, which takes the reader to an earlier point in the narrative.

Another way to build suspense is with multiple plot lines. For example, the story about George's fear of foods involves a second plot line in which the narrator's aunt discovers what happened to her holiday fruitcake. Both plot lines intersect when the narrator shovels snow for a week, and as a result raises money for the class trip.

Use Vivid Language

As you revise, make an effort to use vivid language. Use precise words and phrases to describe feelings and action. Use telling details to show, rather than directly state, what a character is like. Use sensory language that lets readers see, feel, hear, smell, and taste what you or your characters experienced.

First Draft	Revision
My aunt usually sends a fruitcake to us, and I can't stand fruitcake.	Suddenly I thought of my aunt's usual holiday present—the dreaded fruitcake. [telling details]
I remembered my friend George and his dislike for certain foods.	My friend George and his fear of foods with mixed ingredients came to mind. I began to concoct a delicious scheme. [precise words and phrases]
George was afraid when he opened the box and saw a weird-looking cake.	George felt the heavy box from the unknown sender and shrieked when he saw the sticky mixture of dried fruit. [sensory details]

Conclusion

At the conclusion of the narrative, you or your narrator will reflect on the meaning of the events. The conclusion should follow logically from the climactic moment of the narrative. The narrator of a personal narrative usually reflects on the significance of the experience—the lessons learned or the legacy left.

EXAMPLE

Puppy class and its grueling weekly sessions with 12 yipping puppies had ended long ago. Maggie's performance wasn't stellar—she'd had to repeat the whole class to pass. But as I remembered the chill of that first morning walk in sub-zero winds, and the feeling of my numbed fingers, I thought what a smart dog she was after all. After repeated efforts, many crunchy biscuit treats, and lots of warm hugs, Maggie was trained. I proudly stroked her fur as she looked up at me with her knowing eyes.

Performance Task Reference Guide   **R7**

Conducting Research

COMMON CORE W 7, W 8

The Performance Tasks in this book will require you to complete research projects related to the texts you've read in the collections. Whether the topic is stated in a Performance Task or is one you generate, the following information will guide you through your research project.

Focus Your Research and Formulate a Question

Some topics for a research project can be effectively covered in three pages; others require an entire book for a thorough treatment. Begin by developing a topic that is neither too narrow nor too broad for the time frame of the assignment. Also check your school and local libraries and databases to help you determine how to choose your topic. If there's too little information, you'll need to broaden your focus; if there's too much, you'll need to limit it.

With a topic in hand, formulate a research question; it will keep you on track as you conduct your research. A good research question cannot be answered in a single word. It should be open-ended. It should require investigation. You can also develop related research questions to explore your topic in more depth.

EXAMPLES

Possible topics	Sailing—too broad Navigating waves—too narrow Sailing—in fair and foul weather
Possible research question	What is involved in learning to sail in all kinds of weather?
Related questions	What sailing equipment and techniques are essential? What knowledge of weather patterns is critical?

Locate and Evaluate Sources

To find answers to your research question, you'll need to investigate primary and secondary sources, whether in print or digital formats. **Primary sources** contain original, firsthand information, such as diaries, autobiographies, interviews, speeches, and eyewitness accounts. **Secondary sources** provide other people's versions of primary sources in encyclopedias, newspaper and magazine articles, biographies, and documentaries.

Your search for sources begins at the library and on the World Wide Web. Use **advanced search features** to help you find things quickly. Add a minus sign (–) before a word that should not appear in your results. Use an asterisk (*) in place of unknown words. List the name and location of each possible source, adding comments about its potential usefulness. Assessing, or evaluating, your sources is an important step in the research process. Your goal is to use sources that are credible, or reliable and trustworthy.

Criteria for Assessing Sources	
Relevance: It covers the target aspect of my topic.	• How will the source be useful in answering my research question?
Accuracy: It includes information that can be verified by more than one authoritative source.	• Is the information up-to-date? Are the facts accurate? How can I verify them? • What qualifies the author to write about this topic? Is he or she an authority?
Objectivity: It presents multiple viewpoints on the topic.	• What, if any, biases can I detect? Does the writer favor one view of the topic?

Incorporate and Cite Source Material

When you draft your research project, you'll need to include material from your sources. This material can be **direct quotations, summaries,** or **paraphrases** of the original source material. Two well-known **style manuals** provide information on how to cite a range of print and digital sources: the *MLA Handbook for Writers of Research Papers* (published by the Modern Language Association) and Kate L. Turabian's *A Manual for Writers* (published by The University of Chicago Press). Both style manuals provide a wealth of information about conducting, formatting, drafting, and presenting your research, including guidelines for citing sources within the text (called parenthetical citations) and preparing the list of Works Cited, as well as correct use of the mechanics of writing. Your teacher will indicate which style manual you should use. The following examples use the format in the *MLA Handbook.*

Any material from sources must be completely documented, or you will commit **plagiarism,** the unauthorized use of someone else's words or ideas. Plagiarism is not honest. As you take notes for your research project, be sure to keep complete information about your sources so that you can cite them correctly in the body of your paper. This applies to all sources, whether print or digital. Having complete information will also enable you to prepare the list of Works Cited. The list of Works Cited, which concludes your research project, provides author, title, and publication information for both print and digital sources. The following pages show the *MLA Handbook's* Works Cited citation formats for a variety of sources.

EXAMPLES

Direct quotation
[The writer is citing a sailing manual.]

In high winds, you need to know how to tack into the wind. This is an essential skill. [Woods, 120]

Summary
[The writer is summarizing the experiences of a sailing expert.]

Johnson fought winds so stiff that if he hadn't had an expert sailor with him to assist with the boom, he would have definitely capsized. [Johnson, 94]

Paraphrase
[The writer is paraphrasing, or stating in her own words, material from page 48 of Gloria Schott's book.]

Learning key sailing terminology is essential. For example, as Schott explains, knowing what the preventer is and how to rig it can prevent the boom from swinging around and knocking someone overboard. [Schott, 48]

MLA Citation Guidelines

Today, you can find free websites that generate ready-made citations for research papers, using the information you provide. Such sites have some time-saving advantages when you're developing a Works Cited list. However, you should always check your citations carefully before you turn in your final paper. If you are following MLA style, use these guidelines to evaluate and finalize your work.

Books

One author

Lastname, Firstname. *Title of Book*. City of Publication: Publisher, Year of Publication. Medium of Publication.

Two authors or editors

Lastname, Firstname, and Firstname Lastname. *Title of Book*. City of Publication: Publisher, Year of Publication. Medium of Publication.

Three authors

Lastname, Firstname, Firstname Lastname, and Firstname Lastname. *Title of Book*. City of Publication: Publisher, Year of Publication. Medium of Publication.

Four or more authors

The abbreviation et al. means "and others." Use et al. instead of listing all the authors.

Lastname, Firstname, et al. *Title of Book*. City of Publication: Publisher, Year of Publication. Medium of Publication.

No author given

Title of Book. City of Publication: Publisher, Year of Publication. Medium of Publication.

An author and a translator

Lastname, Firstname. *Title of Book*. Trans. Firstname Lastname. City of Publication: Publisher, Year of Publication. Medium of Publication.

An author, a translator, and an editor

Lastname, Firstname. *Title of Book*. Trans. Firstname Lastname. Ed. Firstname Lastname. City of Publication: Publisher, Year of Publication. Medium of Publication.

Parts of Books

An introduction, a preface, a foreword, or an afterword written by someone other than the author(s) of a work

Lastname, Firstname. Part of Book. *Title of Book*. By Author of book's Firstname Lastname. City of Publication: Publisher, Year of Publication. Page span. Medium of Publication.

A poem, a short story, an essay, or a chapter in a collection of works by one author

Lastname, Firstname. "Title of Piece." *Title of Book*. Ed. Firstname Lastname. City of Publication: Publisher, Year of Publication. Page span. Medium of Publication.

A poem, a short story, an essay, or a chapter in an anthology of works by several authors

Lastname, Firstname. "Title of Piece." *Title of Book*. Ed. Firstname Lastname. City of Publication: Publisher, Year of Publication. Page range. Medium of Publication.

Magazines, Newspapers, and Encyclopedias

An article in a newspaper

Lastname, Firstname. "Title of Article." *Title of Book Periodical* Day Month Year: pages. Medium of Publication.

An article in a magazine

Lastname, Firstname. "Title of Article." *Title of Book Periodical* Day Month Year: pages. Medium of Publication.

An article in an encyclopedia

"Title of Article." *Title of Encyclopedia*. Year ed. Medium of Publication.

Miscellaneous Nonprint Sources

An interview

Lastname, Firstname. Personal interview. Day Month Year.

A video recording

Title of Recording. Producer, Year. Medium of Publication.

Electronic Publications

A CD-ROM

"Title of Piece." *Title of CD*. Year ed. City of Publication: Publisher, Year of Publication. CD-ROM.

A document from an Internet site

Entries for online source should contain as much information as available.

Lastname, Firstname. "*Title of Piece*." Information on what the site is. Year. Web. Day Month Year (when accessed)

Participating in a Collaborative Discussion

COMMON CORE SL 1a-d

Often, class activities, including the Performance Tasks in this book, will require you to work collaboratively with classmates. Whether your group will analyze a work of literature or try to solve a community problem, use the following guidelines to ensure a productive discussion.

Prepare for the Discussion

A productive discussion is one in which all the participants bring useful information and ideas to share. If your group will discuss a short story the class read, first re-read and annotate a copy of the story. Your annotations will help you quickly locate evidence to support your points. Participants in a discussion about an important issue should first research the issue and bring notes or information sources that will help guide the group. If you disagree with a point made by another group member, your case will be stronger if you back it up with specific evidence from your sources.

EXAMPLES

disagreeing without evidence: I don't think physical art is relevant today because nobody goes to museums.

providing evidence for disagreement: I disagree that physical art is relevant today because so few people go to museums. For example, every large museum, such as the Metropolitan Museum of Art in New York, the Art Institute of Chicago, and the San Francisco Museum of Modern Art, have websites where the public can view art online. Current exhibitions are shown and previous exhibitions are archived for viewing. Why would someone need to go to a dark museum when images are so easy to view online? Even artists such as Julian Beever, who creates physical public art, have websites for the public to view their art. We can clearly view and compare multiple images of Beever's chalk art by clicking on his online gallery.

Set Ground Rules

The rules your group needs will depend on what your group is expected to accomplish. A discussion of themes in a poem will be unlikely to produce a single consensus; however, a discussion aimed at developing a solution to a problem should result in one strong proposal that all group members support. Answer the following questions to set ground rules that fit your group's purpose:

- What will this group produce? A range of ideas, a single decision, a plan of action, or something else?
- How much time is available? How much of that time should be allotted to each part of our discussion (presenting ideas, summarizing or voting on final ideas, creating a product such as a written analysis or speech)?
- What roles need to be assigned within the group? Do we need a leader, a note-taker, a timekeeper, or other specific roles?
- What is the best way to synthesize our group's ideas? Should we take a vote, list group members as "for" or "against" in a chart, or use some other method to reach a consensus or sum up the results of the discussion?

Move the Discussion Forward

Everyone in the group should be actively involved in synthesizing ideas. To make sure this happens, ask questions that draw out ideas, especially from less-talkative members of the group. If an idea or statement is confusing, try to paraphrase it, or ask the speaker to explain more about it. If you disagree with a statement, say so politely and explain in detail why you disagree.

SAMPLE DISCUSSION

JACK: How about you, Ella? Do you think physical art is relevant to people today? The rest of us say it is.

Question draws out quiet member

ELLA: Well, I don't know. We took a field trip to an art museum once to learn about the importance of art and the time periods of art, but none of the people I know go to museums otherwise. We also read about art and artists, like Julian Beever, but we can see his art online too.

Response relates discussion to larger ideas

JOSHUA: But don't we have the option of going to see physical art? I mean, we can go to a public space that has public art or to a museum and experience the art in person, right?

Question challenges Ella's conclusion

ELLA: Sure, but think of the possibilities for comparing images online versus in person. Someone can view and compare images by the same artist that are displayed in different museums by clicking online. How could they do that in person?

Response elaborates on ideas

VIVIAN: So you mean that people can view and compare more art online and the experience and the quantity is significant and worthwhile? I can see that, but is it more worthwhile than being physically present to view the actual work of art? There are things we can see and experience by examining the real object—things like texture in a painting or drawing—that might not be seen as well in an on-screen image.

Paraphrases idea and challenges it further based on evidence

Respond to Ideas

In a diverse group, everyone may have a different perspective on the topic of discussion, and that's a good thing. Consider what everyone has to say, and don't resist changing your view if other group members provide convincing evidence for theirs. If, instead, you feel more strongly than ever about your view, don't hesitate to say so and provide reasons related to what those with opposing views have said. Before wrapping up the discussion, try to sum up the points on which your group agrees and disagrees.

SAMPLE DISCUSSION

VIVIAN: OK, we just have a few more minutes. Do we want to take a vote?

Vivian and Jack try to summarize points of agreement

JACK: Sure. I think the three positions are NO, YES, and YES, BUT. . . . Does that sound right?

JOSHUA: Yeah, let's make a chart of these. I still say YES, physical art is relevant today. No BUT about it, because physical elements and experience are at the core.

Joshua maintains his position

ELLA: And I say YES, BUT. You've convinced me that physical art offers some experiences and close viewing possibilities, but I still think that easy, quick, universal access to online images removes barriers for viewing art for a lot of people today.

Ella and Jack qualify their views based on what they have heard

JACK: That makes sense. I'm changing my position from solid YES to YES, BUT. I think quick and easy access is important, though not always more important than slow and careful scrutiny of physical art and actually being there—like walking alongside sidewalk art.

VIVIAN: I'm with Joshua. I think being able to move around a work of art literally adds a whole new dimension to understanding art.

Vivian supports her position by making a new connection

Debating an Issue

The selection and collection Performance Tasks in this text will direct you to engage in debates about issues relating to the selections you are reading. Use the guidelines that follow to have a productive and balanced argument about both sides of an issue.

The Structure of a Formal Debate

In a debate, two teams compete to win the support of the audience about an issue. In a **formal debate,** two teams, each with two members, present their arguments on a given proposition or policy statement. One team argues for the proposition or statement and the other team argues against it. Each debater must consider the proposition closely and must research both sides of it. To argue convincingly either for or against a proposition, a debater must be familiar with both sides of the issue.

Plan the Debate

The purpose of a debate is to allow participants and audience members to consider both sides of an issue. Use these planning suggestions to hold a balanced and productive debate:

- **Identify Debate Teams** Form groups of six members based on the issues that the Performance Tasks include. Three members of the team will argue for the affirmative side of the issue—that is, they support the issue. The other three members will argue for the negative side of the issue—that is, they do not support the issue.
- **Appoint a Moderator** The moderator will present the topic and goals of the debate, keep track of the time, and introduce and thank the participants.
- **Research and Prepare Notes** Search texts you've read as well as print and online sources for valid reasons and evidence to support your team's claim. As with argument, be sure to anticipate possible opposing claims and compile evidence to counter those claims. You will use notes from your research during the debate.

- **Assign Debate Roles** One team member will introduce the team's claim and supporting evidence. Another team member will respond to questions and opposing claims in an exchange with a member of the opposing team. The last member will present a strong closing argument.

Hold the Debate

A formal debate is not a shouting match—rather, a well-run debate is an excellent forum for participants to express their viewpoints, build on others' ideas, and have a thoughtful, well-reasoned exchange of ideas. The moderator will begin by stating the topic or issue and introducing the participants. Participants should follow the moderator's instructions concerning whose turn it is to speak and how much time each speaker has.

Formal Debate Format

Speaker	Role	Time
Affirmative Speaker 1	Present the claim and supporting evidence for the affirmative ("pro") side of the argument.	5 minutes
Negative Speaker 1	Ask probing questions that will prompt the other team to address flaws in the argument.	3 minutes
Affirmative Speaker 2	Respond to the questions posed by the opposing team and counter any concerns.	3 minutes

continued

Speaker	Role	Time
Negative Speaker 2	Present the claim and supporting evidence for the negative ("con") side of the argument.	5 minutes
Affirmative Speaker 3	Summarize the claim and evidence for the affirmative side and explain why your reasoning is more valid.	3 minutes
Negative Speaker 3	Summarize the claim and evidence for the negative side and explain why your reasoning is more valid.	3 minutes

Evaluate the Debate

Use the following guidelines to evaluate a team in a debate:

- Did the team prove that the issue is significant? How thorough was the analysis?
- How did the team members effectively argue that you should support their affirmative or negative side of the proposition or issue?
- How effectively did the team present reasons and evidence, including evidence from the texts, to support the proposition?
- How effectively did the team rebut, or respond to, arguments made by the opposing team?
- Did the speakers maintain eye contact and speak at an appropriate rate and volume?
- Did the speakers observe proper debate etiquette—that is, did they follow the moderator's instructions, stay within their allotted time limits, and treat their opponents respectfully?

Reading Informational Texts: Patterns of Organization

COMMON CORE RI 1, RI 2, RI 3, RI 4, RI 5, RI 10

Reading any type of writing is easier once you recognize how it is organized. Writers usually arrange ideas and information in ways that best help readers see how they are related. There are several common patterns of organization.

- main idea and supporting details
- chronological order
- cause-effect organization
- compare-and-contrast organization

1. Main Idea and Supporting Details

Main idea and supporting details is a basic pattern of organization in which a central idea about a topic is supported by details. The **main idea** is the most important idea about a topic that a particular text or paragraph conveys. **Supporting details** are words, phrases, or sentences that tell more about the main idea. The main idea may be directly stated at the beginning and then followed by supporting details, or it may be merely implied by the supporting details. It may also be stated after it has been implied by supporting details.

Sometimes you will come across a main idea that is a **factual claim**—a statement that can be verified by observation, a reliable source, or an expert's view. In some cases the main idea may be stated as a **commonplace assertion**—a statement that many people assume to be true, but is not necessarily so. In both cases, the details should support the statements.

Strategies for Reading

- To find a stated main idea in a paragraph, identify the paragraph's topic. The topic is what the paragraph is about and can usually be summed up in one or two words. The word, or synonyms of it, will usually appear throughout the paragraph. Headings and subheadings are also clues to the topics of paragraphs.
- Ask: What is the topic sentence? The topic sentence states the most important idea, message, or information the paragraph conveys about this topic. It is often the first sentence in a paragraph; however, it may appear at the end.
- To find an implied main idea, ask yourself: Whom or what did I just read about? What do the details suggest about the topic?
- Formulate a sentence stating this idea and add it to the paragraph. Does your sentence convey the main idea?

Notice how the main idea is expressed in each of the following models.

Model:
Main Idea as the First Sentence

> When the nomads of Africa began using camels around AD 300, trade across the Sahara became easier. **[Main idea]** The donkeys, horses, and oxen that had been used previously could not travel far without stopping for food and water. Camels, on the other hand, could cover 25 miles in a day and often go for two weeks without water. **[Supporting details]**

Model:
Main Idea as the Last Sentence

> The new trade routes passed through lands occupied by the Soninke people. These farming people referred to their chief as ghana. Soon the land came to be known as the kingdom of Ghana. The tribal chiefs taxed the goods that traveled across their territory. **[Supporting details]** By the eighth century, trade had made Ghana a rich kingdom. **[Main idea]**

Model:
Implied Main Idea

The West African savannas and forests south of the savanna were rich in gold. No salt was available there, though. In the Sahara, on the other hand, there was abundant salt but no gold. Traders brought salt south through the desert and traded it for gold mined from the forests.

> **Implied main idea:** Gold and salt were two important items that were traded in West Africa.

Practice and Apply

Read each paragraph, and then do the following:

1. Identify the main idea in the paragraph, using one of the strategies discussed on the previous page.
2. Identify whether the main idea is stated or implied in the paragraph.

Every day we are surrounded by technology and computerized devices. We sit at our computers for hours for all kinds of purposes—writing and researching topics for our assignments, watching movies, posting messages on our social network pages, listening to music, and more. We call friends on our mobile devices. We tweet. But what we do most frequently is text. E-mail used to be important for messages. Now, it's not fast enough to compete with texting.

When we view a news article or any other text, our eyes see the words, and we begin to read. The eye is the organ of vision, and its job is to send signals about visuals to the brain. Once the eyes transmit the words to the brain, the real actions involved in reading begin to happen. Many areas of the brain work together to decipher the written word, and signals travel with amazing speed to all those areas. We may think we read with our eyes, but really we read with our brains.

2. Chronological Order

Chronological order is the arrangement of events in the order in which they happen. This type of organization is used in short stories and novels, historical writing, biographies, and autobiographies. To show the order of events, writers use order words such as *before, after, next,* and *later* and time words and phrases that identify specific times of day, days of the week,

and dates, such as *the next morning, Tuesday,* and *on July 4, 1776.*

Strategies for Reading

- Look in the text for headings and subheadings that may indicate a chronological pattern of organization.
- Look for words and phrases that identify times, such as *in a year, three hours earlier, in 202 BC,* and *the next day.*
- Look for words that signal order, such as *first, afterward, then, during,* and *finally,* to see how events or steps are related.
- Note that a paragraph or passage in which ideas and information are arranged chronologically will have several words or phrases that indicate time order, not just one.
- Ask yourself: Are the events in the paragraph or passage presented in time order?

Notice the words and phrases that signal time order in the first two paragraphs of the following model.

Model

A Butterfly Gets Its Wings

How does a butterfly get its wings? During its life, the butterfly goes through different growth stages. There are four main stages altogether: 1) the egg, 2) the caterpillar, 3) the pupa, and 4) the adult. The ancient Greeks called this whole process *metamorphosis*, a word we still use today.

> **Events**

At first, the butterfly is a single slimy egg, no larger than a fingertip. The baby insect grows within the egg until it is ready to hatch. For most types of butterflies, this first stage lasts about ten days. When the egg cracks open, a caterpillar crawls out.

> **Order words and phrases**

> **Time words and phrases**

In the second stage, the caterpillar spends most of its time eating and growing. As the caterpillar becomes bigger, it sheds its spiky or fuzzy skin. This process is called *molting*. A caterpillar molts several times during its life. Once the caterpillar has shed its skin for the last time, it becomes a pupa.

COMMON CORE | RI 2, RI 3, RI 5

PRACTICE AND APPLY POSSIBLE ANSWERS

1. *First paragraph: Every day we are surrounded by technology and computerized devices.*
   Second paragraph: We may think we read with our eyes, but really we read with our brains.

2. *In the first paragraph, the main idea is stated. In the second paragraph, the main idea is implied.*

PRACTICE AND APPLY POSSIBLE ANSWERS

1. *"in the second stage"; "during its life"; "once"; "for the last time"; "in the third stage"; "immediately"; "then"; "after"; "finally"; "in a short time"*

2. *The four growth stages include the egg, the caterpillar, the pupa, and the adult.*

3. *A butterfly begins its life in the form of a single, slimy egg.*

In the third stage, the pupa immediately grows a hard shell called a *chrysalis*. Then, inside the chrysalis, the pupa goes through the changes that will make it a butterfly. The pupa's hormones turn its body into wings, antennas, and other butterfly parts. After all the changes are complete, the shell splits open. A butterfly is ready to make its entrance.

Finally, the adult butterfly breaks from the chrysalis. Its body, however, doesn't look quite right. It's all soft and wrinkly. As air and blood are pumped through the butterfly's body, it starts to look more like its usual self. In a short time, the butterfly is ready to try out its new wings. With a few flutters, it's off and away!

Practice and Apply

Refer to the preceding model to do the following:

1. List at least six words in the last three paragraphs that indicate time or order.
2. What does the writer call the four main parts in the life of a butterfly?
3. In what form does a butterfly begin its life?

3. Cause-Effect Organization

Cause-effect organization is a pattern of organization that shows causal relationships between events, ideas, and trends. Cause-effect relationships may be directly stated or merely implied by the order in which the information is presented. Writers often use the cause-effect pattern in historical and scientific writing. Cause-effect relationships may have several forms.

One cause with one effect

One cause with multiple effects

Multiple causes with a single effect

A chain of causes and effects

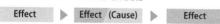

Strategies for Reading

- Look for headings and subheadings that indicate a cause-effect pattern of organization, such as "Effects of Food Allergies."
- To find the effect or effects, read to answer the question, What happened?
- To find the cause or causes, read to answer the question, Why did it happen?
- Look for words and phrases that help you identify specific relationships between events, such as *because, since, had the effect of, led to, as a result, resulted in, for that reason, due to, therefore, if . . . then,* and *consequently.*
- Look closely at each cause-effect relationship. Do not assume that because one event happened before another, the first event caused the second event.
- Use graphic organizers like the diagrams shown to record cause-effect relationships as you read.

Notice the words that signal causes and effects in the following model.

Model

How a Tsunami Forms

Tsunami is a word that brings fear to people who live near the sea. Also known in English as a tidal wave, a tsunami is a huge ocean wave caused by an underwater volcanic eruption or earthquake. | **Effect**

An earthquake or the explosion of a volcano on the ocean floor creates massive waves of energy. These energy waves spread out in widening circles, like waves from a pebble dropped into a pond.

Signal words

Cause

Cause

Effect

As the tsunami nears the shore, it begins to scrape along the ocean bottom. This friction causes the waves in the front to slow down. As a result, the waves traveling behind begin piling up and growing higher. This increase in height can happen very quickly—by as much as 90 feet in 10 or 15 minutes.

The effects of a tsunami can include the death of many people and the destruction of ships, buildings, and land along the shore. An especially dangerous situation may occur when the first part of a tsunami to hit the shore is the trough, or low point, rather than the crest of a wave. This trough sucks all the water away from the shore and may attract curious people on the beach. Within a few minutes, however, the crest of the wave will hit and may drown the onlookers. The most destructive tsunami ever recorded struck the Indonesian island of Sumatra, in 2004. It left more than 200,000 people dead.

Practice and Apply

1. Use the pattern of a chain of causes and effects, illustrated on page R18, to make a graphic organizer showing the causes and effects described in the text.
2. List three words that the writer uses to signal cause and effect in the last two paragraphs.

4. Compare-and-Contrast Organization

Compare-and-contrast organization is a pattern of organization that provides a way to look at similarities and differences in two or more subjects. A writer may use this pattern of organization to compare the important points or characteristics of two or more subjects. These points or characteristics are called **points of comparison.** The compare-and-contrast pattern of organization may be developed in either of two ways:

Point-by-point organization—The writer discusses one point of comparison for both subjects, then goes on to the next point.

Subject-by-subject organization—The writer covers all points of comparison for one subject and then all points of comparison for the next subject.

Strategies for Reading

- Look in the text for headings, subheadings, and sentences that may suggest a compare-and-contrast pattern of organization, such as "Plants Share Many Characteristics," to help you identify where similarities and differences are addressed.
- To find similarities, look for words and phrases such as *like, similarly, both, all, every, also,* and *in the same way.*
- To find differences, look for words and phrases such as *unlike, but, on the other hand, more, less, in contrast,* and *however.*
- Use a graphic organizer, such as a Venn diagram or a compare-and-contrast chart, to record points of comparison and similarities and differences.

COMMON CORE RI 2, RI 3, RI 5

PRACTICE AND APPLY POSSIBLE ANSWERS

1. *Students should create a graphic organizer that shows a chain of causes and effects.*

   cause: earthquake or volcano occurs in ocean; effect (cause): waves spread out; effect (cause): tsunami scrapes along shore bottom; effect (cause): friction slows down front waves; effect (cause): the back waves grow higher; effect: enormous wave crashes ashore

2. *causes, as a result, the effects*

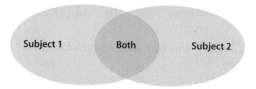

	Subject 1	Subject 2
Point 1		
Point 2		
Point 3		

Read the following models. As you read, use the signal words and phrases to identify the similarities and differences between the subjects and how the details are organized in each text.

Model 1

Living in Outer Space

Ten . . . nine . . . eight . . . The date is December 21, 1968.

Seven . . . six . . . five . . . alongside a launch gantry at cape Kennedy, Florida, a huge Saturn V rocket stands fueled and ready for blastoff, hydrogen vapor steaming from its rocket motors.

Four . . . three . . . two . . . at the top of the rocket sits the *Apollo 8* command module, the capsule that will ferry astronauts Frank Borman, James a. Lovell Jr., and William A. Anders to the moon and back.

One . . . zero . . . Liftoff! The Saturn's powerful engines roar to life, and another exciting chapter in the history of the United States space program begins.

Today, that same *Apollo 8* command module is one of the most popular attractions at the Henry Crown Space Center at the Museum of Science and Industry in Chicago. For six days in 1968, this cone-shaped capsule was home to the first humans to leave the security of earth's orbit and venture out to visit another heavenly body.

Museum visitors, especially young people accustomed to space travel in the shuttle era, are often amazed at the cramped quarters within the capsule, and they wonder just how three adults lived for six days in such a compact environment. Space travel has come a long way since those pioneering days of the 1960s. Some of the main similarities and differences relate to living quarters and food.

> **Comparison words and phrases**

Today's shuttle crews have both a flight deck and a lower crew-quarters deck in which to move around. The *Apollo* crews, however, were pretty much confined to their metal-and-fabric flight couches, although there was a little stretching room beneath the couches and around the hatch area that led to the lunar Excursion Module.

> **Contrast words and phrases**

> **Subjects**

Mealtime is a highlight of anyone's day, including every astronaut's. Early space travelers were limited to puréed foods squeezed out of toothpaste tubes and juices in plastic bags. Shuttle crews, on the other hand, enjoy a much more appetizing diet. It's still not exactly fine dining, but at least the food is served on trays, is eaten with utensils, and includes healthy snacks, like fresh fruit.

At the end of a working "day" in space, all astronauts are ready for some rest. In *Apollo*, the crew simply drifted off to sleep on their couches. Aboard the shuttle, crew members sleep in special sleep restraints. Some sleep horizontally, while others opt for a vertical snooze. In zero gravity, position doesn't matter!

The United States has continued to develop the space program. The lessons learned during the first three decades of space flight are making life in the alien environment beyond earth's atmosphere much more pleasant for a new generation of space explorers.

Model 2

To compare the two types of energy, we must first understand what energy is. Energy is the ability to do work. That doesn't just mean work as in homework or yard work. Energy comes in many forms, such as a rock falling off a cliff, a moving bicycle, or the stored energy in food. With all these forms, there are only two main types of energy, potential and kinetic. These are the energies of rest and motion.

Subjects

Potential energy is the energy an object has stored up based on how high up it is or how much it weighs. For instance, suppose two kids weigh the same and climb a tree. If they are on different branches, the kid on the higher branch has more potential energy than the kid on the lower branch. However, if one kid weighs more than the other, and they both sit at the same height, the heavier kid has more potential energy than the lighter kid.

Comparison words and phrases

Contrast words and phrases

If the kids jump out of the tree, their potential energy becomes kinetic energy. This kind comes from the motion of an object. Kinetic energy increases with the speed of an object. When the kids jump, their speed increases as they fall. They have more kinetic energy when they are falling faster than they do when they first jump and are falling more slowly. Also, the more mass an object has, the more kinetic energy it has. Even if both kids jump at the exact same time, the one with more mass will always have more kinetic energy.

These two kids probably knew they were using a lot of energy, but they would probably be surprised to know how much work they had been doing.

Practice and Apply

Refer to the preceding models to answer the following questions:

1. Which model is organized by subject? Which model is organized by points of comparison?
2. Identify two words or phrases in each model that signal a compare-and-contrast pattern of organization.
3. List two points that the writer of each model compares and contrasts.
4. Use a Venn diagram or a compare-and-contrast chart to identify two or more points of comparison and the similarities and differences shown in one of the two models.

5. Problem-Solution Order

Problem-solution order is a pattern of organization in which a problem is stated and analyzed and then one or more solutions are proposed and examined. This pattern of organization is often used in persuasive writing, such as editorials or proposals.

Strategies for Reading

- Look for an explanation of the problem in the first or second paragraph.
- Look for words, such as *problem* and *reason*, that may signal an explanation of the problem.
- To find the solution, ask: What suggestion does the writer offer to solve the problem?
- Look for words, such as *propose, conclude,* and *answer,* that may signal a solution.

COMMON CORE RI 2, RI 3, RI 5

PRACTICE AND APPLY POSSIBLE ANSWERS

1. *Model 1 is organized by points of comparison. Model 2 is organized by subject.*
2. *Possible answers: Model 1: "both," "although," "on the other hand," "while"; Model 2: "than," "both," "also," "same," "the larger of the two," "always"*
3. *Possible answers: Model 1: the size of the living quarters, the quality of the food, the shuttle's sleeping accommodations; Model 2: the relationship of height, weight, and speed to each type of energy*
4. *Students should create a Venn diagram or a compare-and-contrast chart. Possible answers:*
   Model 1: Apollo Crew (1968)—Living quarters: metal-and-fabric flight couches. Meals: pureed foods squeezed out of tubes and juice in plastic bags. Sleeping accommodations: slept on couches with no room to move or spread out. Shuttle crews (today)—Living quarters: separate flight deck and lower crew-quarters deck. Meals: food is served on trays, is eaten with utensils, and includes healthy snacks. Sleeping accommodations: use sleep restraints that allow crew to sleep horizontally or vertically.
   Model 2: Potential energy—based on height and weight; heavier objects have more potential energy. Kinetic energy—based on the motion of an object; energy increases with the speed of an object. Similarities—The heavier the object, the greater the energy.

PRACTICE AND APPLY POSSIBLE ANSWERS

1. *Fargo does not have a large enough population to financially support a major-league franchise.*

2. *The writer proposes that the town of Fargo and nearby towns such as Moorhead, Grand Forks, and Aberdeen combine to help finance and support a new baseball team. The words "here's my plan" provide a clue to the reader.*

Model

I love baseball, but I won't be going to any major-league games, and I won't be rooting for the local major-league team. The reason is simple. There is no local major-league team in North Dakota. There's none in South Dakota or in Montana or even in Wyoming. The closest major-league team is the Minnesota Twins, and that's over 240 miles away!

The problem is that getting a major-league team costs money. Any city that wants a team has to have enough money to build a stadium. The city also has to have a big enough population to support the team. Fargo is the biggest city in North Dakota, and it only has about 91,484 people. That's not enough to support a major-league franchise. Sports stadiums often hold more people than Fargo has!

Even though the towns around here aren't exactly huge, there are a lot of die-hard baseball fans like my friends and me. So here's my plan. Why couldn't a couple of towns get together to build a stadium and start a team? For example, Moorhead, Minnesota, is right next to Fargo. They already share the same airport, and the metropolitan area has about 174,367 people. That might be enough to support a team. If it's not, then maybe Grand Forks, or even Aberdeen, could join in too.

People might say that there would be a problem naming a team that is supported by cities in two or three different states. I think baseball fans would be so happy to have a team, they wouldn't really care what it was called.

If enough people wrote to the Fargo and Moorhead city governments, maybe the idea could be put on the ballot. Major-league baseball is supposed to be our national pastime. Shouldn't we be a part of it too?

Reread the model and then answer the following questions:

1. According to the model, what is the cause of the problem?
2. What solution does the writer offer? What words are a clue?

Reading Persuasive Texts

COMMON CORE RI 1, RI 3, RI 4, RI 5, RI 6, RI 8, RI 10

1. Analyzing an Argument

An **argument** expresses a position on an issue or problem and supports it with reasons and evidence. Being able to analyze and evaluate arguments will help you distinguish between claims you should accept and those you should not. A sound argument should appeal strictly to reason. However, arguments are often used in texts that also contain other types of persuasive devices. An argument includes the following elements:

- A **claim** is the writer's position on an issue or problem.
- **Support** is any material that serves to prove a claim. In an argument, support usually consists of reasons and evidence.
- **Reasons** are declarations made to justify an action, decision, or belief—for example, "My reason for thinking we will be late is that the drive takes longer than five minutes."
- **Evidence** can be the specific references, quotations, facts, examples, and opinions that support a claim. Evidence may also consist of statistics, reports of personal experience, or the views of experts.
- A **counterargument** is an argument made to oppose another argument. A good argument anticipates the opposition's objections and provides counterarguments to disprove or answer them.

Claim	I think I should be allowed more time online.
Reason	The Internet can provide opportunities for learning and enjoyment.
Evidence	The Internet can take you to faraway places and can bring art, music, and science right into your home.
Counter-argument	Some people think the Internet is bad for kids, but those people are looking at only the worst part of the Internet, not the best.

Practice and Apply

Read the following editorial and use a chart like the one shown to identify the claim, reason, evidence, and counterargument.

Important Hours by Gina Maraini

"The Golden Years." That is what some people call old age. They think it is a time of peace and relaxation. But many old people spend time alone. Some cannot get out of their homes because of illness. "What can I do?" you ask. You can do more than you think to make an important contribution to an older person's life. Even spending an hour a week can mean a lot to an older neighbor who lives alone.

Some kids might say that they can only do good for an older person if they have lots of time and lots of patience. It's easy to talk yourself out of volunteering your time by saying, "I only have an hour a week. What good would that do?" Never underestimate just how much good you can do even in a little bit of time.

Sometimes things happen that seem unimportant to a kid but can really be a problem to an old person. If a small object like a pen or pencil slides under furniture, an older person often is not able to stoop down and pick it up. But they feel embarrassed to ask for help. So, the pen stays there. Sometimes it gets forgotten about and becomes lost. You can help that older person find these things. and by helping, you are reminding that person that he or she is not forgotten about either.

Sometimes it is hard for an older person to reach up high. Putting things away, like groceries, becomes a problem. Often the older person gets tired and gives up. You can help to put groceries and other heavy objects away. And by doing that, you are helping that older person feel like he or she can still keep up with life's challenges.

One of the most important things you can do for a senior citizen who lives alone is to give that person someone to talk to. Old people, who have lived long lives and had many experiences, have stories to tell that you can learn a lot from. And it is important for you to say so, too. That way, you can show the older person that he or she is contributing to your life.

PRACTICE AND APPLY POSSIBLE ANSWERS

Students should create a chart similar to the one on page R23. The chart should include details similar to the ones below.

Claim: You can do more than you think to make an important contribution to an older person's life.

Reason: Even spending an hour a week can mean a lot to an older person.

Evidence: An older person may have trouble stooping down to pick up objects. You can help an older person find things. By helping, you are reminding the person that he or she is not forgotten.

Evidence: It can be hard for an older person to reach up high. By helping put away groceries and other heavy objects, you are helping the person feel that he or she can still keep up with life's challenges.

Evidence: Older people have lived a long life and have had many experiences. By listening to an older person's stories, you can show the person that he or she is contributing to your life.

Counterargument: It's easy to talk yourself out of volunteering your time by saying, "I only have an hour a week. What good would that do?" Never underestimate how much good you can do even in a little bit of time.

You can make a real contribution to an
older person's life. Even if you only have an
hour to spend, you can help an older person
feel cared about and important. Find ways
to reach out, whether through volunteer
organizations or just by being aware of who
is alone in your neighborhood. And always
remember: as much as you give, you get
back so much more, simply by knowing
the difference that you have made.

2. Recognizing Persuasive Techniques

Persuasive texts typically rely on more than
just the **logical appeal** of an argument to
be convincing. They also rely on ethical and
emotional appeals and other **persuasive
techniques**—devices that can convince you
to adopt a position or take an action.

Ethical appeals establish a writer's credibility
and trustworthiness with an audience. When a
writer links a claim to a widely accepted value,
the writer not only gains moral support for
that claim but also establishes a connection
with readers. For example, with the following
appeal, the writer reminds readers of a value
they should accept and links a claim to it: "Most
of us agree that we should protect our natural
resources, but we don't invest a lot of time or
money to preserve them."

The chart shown here explains several other
means by which a writer may attempt to sway
you to adopt his or her position. Learn to
recognize these techniques, and you are less
likely to be influenced by them.

Persuasive Technique	Example
Appeals by Association	
Bandwagon appeal Suggests that a person should believe or do something because "everyone else" does	Every day more buyers are enjoying the conveniences of Internet shopping.
Testimonial Relies on endorsements from well-known people or satisfied customers	Todd Marshall, star of stage and screen, buys his shoes at Fine Footwear. Shouldn't you?
Snob appeal Taps into people's desire to be special or part of an elite group	Be among the first to enjoy the upgraded facilities at Spring Lake Fitness Center.
Appeal to loyalty Relies on people's affiliation with a particular group	Say *Yes!* to your community— support the campaign to build a new library!
Emotional Appeals	
Appeals to pity, fear, or vanity Use strong feelings, rather than facts, to persuade	We need to keep the homeless shelter open— think how you would feel if you had no place to go.
Word Choice	
Glittering generality A generalization that includes a word or phrase with positive connotations, to promote a product, person, or idea.	Buying handmade jewelry from the Hang Up helps support small-town America.

Identify the persuasive techniques used in
this model.

Vote for Velazquez!

Whom do you want to represent you in
congress—a dinosaur who's stuck in the
past or someone who's courageously facing
the future? Why settle for Jill Jolsen, who
hasn't lifted a finger to help this community?
Don't let her slick ads fool you. Instead, join
the leaders in the community and many
of your neighbors who have already put
their support behind Victor Velazquez.
Local businesswoman Janice Wu is behind
Velazquez all the way—she says he will bring
new jobs and fresh ideas that will really work.
Don't miss this once-in-a-lifetime chance
to change this town. Vote for Velazquez!

3. Analyzing Logic and Reasoning

While persuasive techniques may sway you to side with a writer, they should not be enough to convince you that an argument is sound. To determine the soundness of an argument, you really need to examine the argument's claim and support and the logic or reasoning that links them. To do this, it is helpful to identify the writer's mode of reasoning.

The Inductive Mode of Reasoning

When a person uses specific evidence to arrive at a **general principle**, or generalization, that person is using **inductive reasoning.** Similarly, when a writer presents specific evidence first and then offers a generalization drawn from that evidence, the writer is making an **inductive argument.** Here is an example of inductive reasoning.

Specific Facts

Fact 1 Turtles are the only reptiles that have a shell.

Fact 2 The green turtle, a sea turtle, can swim almost 20 miles an hour.

Fact 3 Snapping turtles have powerful, sharp-edged jaws and are aggressive when attacked.

Generalization

Turtles have a variety of protective strategies.

There are several types of inductive reasoning.

- **argument by cause and effect:** In this type of argument, the writer or speaker attempts to persuade by showing the causes that would lead to a desired or an undesired effect. **Example:** *If we don't see the movie today, we won't be able to see it on the weekend because the theater will be too crowded.*
- **argument by analogy:** In this type of argument, the writer or speaker compares familiar events and things to those that are unfamiliar in an attempt to persuade the audience to accept the new situation. **Example:** *You'll like this new movie because it has a plot that is similar to others you've seen.*
- **argument by authority:** In this type of

argument, the writer or speaker attempts to persuade by using an authoritative and reliable source as evidence. **Example:** *The movie critic gave the new movie three stars, so we should go see it.*

Strategies for Determining the Soundness of Inductive Arguments

Ask yourself the following questions to evaluate an inductive argument:

- **Is the evidence valid and sufficient support for the conclusion?** Inaccurate facts lead to inaccurate conclusions.
- **Does the conclusion follow logically from the evidence?** From the facts listed above, the conclusion that *all* turtles have a wide variety of protective strategies would be too broad a generalization.
- **Is the evidence drawn from a large enough sample?** Even though there are only three facts listed above, the sample is large enough to support the claim. If you wanted to support the conclusion that only turtles have a variety of protective strategies, the sample is not large enough.

The Deductive Mode of Reasoning

When a person uses a **general principle,** or generalization, to form a conclusion about a particular situation or problem, that person is using **deductive reasoning.** For example,

Being exposed to loud noise over a long period will damage a person's hearing.	General principle or generalization
▼	
I listen to my stereo at its highest setting for hours every day.	The situation being observed or considered
▼	
I will have some hearing loss.	Conclusion (also considered a deduction)

Similarly, a writer is making a **deductive argument** when he or she begins the argument with a claim that is based on a general principle

Reading Persuasive Texts **R25**

COMMON CORE
RI 5,
RI 8

PRACTICE AND APPLY ANSWER

The paragraph uses inductive reasoning based on argument by cause and effect.

and then presents evidence to support the claim. For example, a writer might begin a deductive argument with the claim "Many people have some hearing loss."

Strategies for Determining the Soundness of Deductive Arguments

Ask yourself the following questions to evaluate a deductive argument.

- **Is the general principle actually stated, or is it implied?** Note that writers often use deductive reasoning in arguments without stating the general principles. They assume that readers will recognize and agree with the principles. Be sure to identify the general principle for yourself.

- **Is the general principle sound?** Don't just assume the general principle is sound. Ask yourself whether it is really true.

- **Is the conclusion valid?** To be valid, a conclusion in a deductive argument must follow logically from the general principle and the specific situation.

The following chart shows two conclusions drawn from the same general principle.

All seventh-graders are going to the zoo next week.	
Accurate Deduction	**Inaccurate Deduction**
Laura is in the seventh grade; therefore, Laura is going to the zoo next week.	Laura is going to the zoo next week; therefore, Laura is in the seventh grade.

Laura may be going to the zoo with her family or friends.

Practice and Apply

Identify whether inductive or deductive reasoning is used in the following paragraph. If the mode of reasoning used is inductive, tell whether the paragraph uses argument by cause and effect, analogy, or authority.

In science class, I learned what different substances do for the human body. Protein aids growth and repairs muscles. Fruits and vegetables provide critical vitamins, and calcium strengthens bones. Carbohydrates supply energy to the body. Clearly, a balanced diet is important for good health.

R26   Student Resources

R26   Student Resources

Identifying Faulty Reasoning

Sometimes an argument at first appears to make sense but isn't valid because it is based on a fallacy. A **rhetorical fallacy** is a false or misleading statement. Learn to recognize these rhetorical fallacies.

Type of Fallacy	Definition	Example
Circular reasoning	Supporting a statement by simply repeating it in different words	I'm tired because **I don't have any energy.**
Either/or fallacy	A statement that suggests that there are only two choices available in a situation that really offers more than two options	**Either** we raise taxes, **or** we close the parks.
Oversimplification	An explanation of a complex situation or problem as if it were much simpler than it is	Getting a good grade in Mrs. Raimi's class depends on **whether she likes you.**
Overgeneralization	A generalization that is too broad. You can often recognize overgeneralizations by the use of words such as *all, everyone, every time, anything, no one,* and *none.*	You **never** get me anything I want.
Hasty generalization	A conclusion drawn from too little evidence or from evidence that is biased	She left after fifteen minutes. **She must not like us.**
Stereotyping	A dangerous type of overgeneralization. Stereotypes are broad statements about people on the basis of their gender, ethnicity, race, or political, social, professional, or religious group	**All rock stars** are self-centered.
Ad hominem or attacking the person	An attempt to discredit an idea by attacking the person or group associated with it. Candidates often engage in name-calling during political campaigns.	The **narrow-minded** senator opposes recycling.
Evading the issue	Responding to an objection with arguments and evidence that do not address its central point	Yes, I broke my campaign promise not to raise taxes, **but higher taxes have led to increases in police patrols and paved highways.**
False cause	The mistake of assuming that because one event occurred after another event in time, the first event caused the second one to occur	John didn't get his homework done because he had to take the dog for a walk.

PRACTICE AND APPLY
POSSIBLE ANSWERS

Overgeneralization: "Nobody gets rid of his or her trash properly and everyone writes graffiti on the walls."
Explanation: The writer uses words such as nobody and everyone to make broad generalizations about people.

Hasty generalization: "If the school seemed more worth caring about, students would take better care of it."
Explanation: The statement presents a biased point of view based on one person's opinion.

False cause: "The halls are dark and the walls are dingy because the maintenance staff has been on strike for several weeks."
Explanation: The writer makes the assumption that one event (the strike) caused another (the condition of the building), but does not consider other possible causes.

Ad hominem or attacking the person: "old-fashioned school board"
Explanation: The writer uses negative language to discredit the board.

Either/or fallacy: "Either we build a new school, or it will be destroyed in three years."
Explanation: The statement does not take into account other alternatives.

Look for examples of logical fallacies in the following argument. Identify each one and explain why you identified it as such.

Dear Editors:

There has been a lot of talk about students' lack of concern for the appearance of our school. Nobody gets rid of his or her trash properly and everyone writes graffiti on the walls. But if the school seemed more worth caring about, students would take better care of it. Most of the school is very old. The halls are dark and the walls are dingy because the maintenance staff has been on strike for several weeks. The old-fashioned school board said that an entirely new building wasn't needed. So only a new gym was added. It is clean and bright because students have kept it that way. Either we build a new school, or it will be destroyed in three years.

4. Evaluating Persuasive Texts

Learning how to evaluate persuasive texts and identify bias will help you become more selective when doing research and also help you improve your own reasoning and arguing skills. **Bias** is an inclination for or against a particular opinion or viewpoint. A writer may reveal a strongly positive or negative bias on an issue by

- **presenting only one way** of looking at it
- **overlooking key information**
- **stacking more evidence on one side** of the argument than the other
- **using unfairly weighted evidence,** which is weak or unproven evidence that a writer treats as if it is more important than it really is
- **using loaded language,** which consists of words with strongly positive or negative connotations

EXAMPLE:

Barbara Larsen is the best choice for student council president because she has fresh ideas and fantastic people skills. (**Fresh** and **fantastic** have very positive connotations.)

Propaganda is any form of communication that is so distorted that it conveys false or misleading information. Some politicians create and distribute propaganda. Many logical fallacies, such as name-calling, the either/or fallacy, and false causes, are often used in propaganda. The following example shows an oversimplification. The writer uses one fact to support a particular point of view but does not reveal another fact that does not support that viewpoint.

EXAMPLE:

Since the new park opened, vandalism in the area has increased by 10 percent. Clearly, the park has had a negative impact on the area. (The writer does not include the fact that the vandalism was caused by people who were not drawn into the area by the park.)

Strategies for Assessing Evidence

It is important to have a set of standards by which you can evaluate persuasive texts. Use the questions below to help you assess the adequacy, accuracy, and appropriateness of facts and opinions that are presented as evidence.

- **Are the facts accurate?** Facts can be proved by eyewitness accounts, authoritative sources such as encyclopedias and experts, or research.

- **Are the opinions well informed?** Any opinions offered should be supported by facts, be based on research or eyewitness accounts, or come from experts on the topic.

- **Is the evidence sufficient?** Thorough, or sufficient, evidence leaves no reasonable question unanswered. If a choice is offered to the reader, enough evidence for making the choice should be given. If taking a side is called for, all sides of the issue should be presented.

- **Is the evidence biased?** Be alert to evidence that contains loaded language or other signs of bias.

- **Is the evidence relevant?** The evidence needs to apply to the topic and come from people, groups, or organizations that have important knowledge of, or credentials relating to, the topic.

- **Is it important that the evidence be current?** Where timeliness is crucial, as in the areas of medicine and technology, the evidence should reflect the latest developments in the areas.

Read the argument below. Identify the facts, opinion, and elements of bias.

Let your voice be heard. The students' league is hosting a demonstration against U.S. Representative Sharon Bullhorn on Saturday. Just last week, Representative Bullhorn voted against raising the minimum wage. Obviously Representative Bullhorn doesn't care about young people. If she did, she would have helped pass the much-needed minimum wage increase, so that preteens and teens could earn the money they deserve.

Strategies for Determining a Strong Argument

Make sure that all or most of the following statements are true:

- The argument presents a claim or thesis.
- The claim is connected to its support by a general principle that most readers would readily agree with. Valid general principle: *It is the job of a school to provide a well-rounded physical education program.* Invalid general principle: *It is the job of a school to produce healthy, physically fit people.*
- The reasons make sense.
- The reasons are presented in a logical and effective order.
- The claim and all reasons are adequately supported by sound evidence.
- The evidence is sufficient, accurate, and relevant.
- The logic is sound. There are no instances of faulty reasoning.
- The argument adequately anticipates and addresses reader concerns and counterclaims with counterarguments.

Use the preceding criteria to evaluate the strength of the following proposal.

Summary of Proposal

I propose that our school install video cameras in halls, lunchrooms, and other public areas to monitor students' activities.

Need

The halls and public areas of our school are not well supervised because of a shortage of security staff. Last month, three students were hurt in fights on school property.

Proposed Solution

Installing video monitors in the halls and public areas of the school will create a safe environment for students at a reasonable cost.

There is good evidence that video monitoring works. Westview school has monitored its students for over a year. In that time there has not been one incident of fighting or damage to property

People who are against video monitoring don't agree. They say that monitoring violates students' rights to privacy.

In my opinion, junior high students need to act like responsible adults. We need guidelines and monitoring to show us where the limits are and to help us learn to act responsibly on our own.

Not only does video monitoring work, but installing the equipment can lower supervisory costs in the long run. Only eight cameras would be needed, installed in the two main hallways, the lunchroom, and the auditorium. The total cost would be around $16,000. I believe the money can be found in the general school budget.

What idiot would not support video monitoring of students?

It would be a crime not to have video monitoring.

Most school officials only care about their jobs and not what's good for students. I say to those school officials who do care: Either install video cameras or wait for more students to be injured.

COMMON CORE RI 8

PRACTICE AND APPLY POSSIBLE ANSWERS

Facts: The Students' League is hosting a demonstration against Representative Sharon Bullhorn on Saturday. Last week, Representative Bullhorn voted against raising the minimum wage.
Opinion: "If she did [care], she would have helped pass the much-needed minimum wage increase, so that preteens and teens could earn the money they deserve."
Elements of bias: "Obviously Representative Bullhorn doesn't care about young people."

COMMON CORE RI 8

PRACTICE AND APPLY

Students' responses will vary, but they should evaluate the strength of the claim, the evidence supporting the claim, and the counterarguments.

POSSIBLE ANSWERS

The writer presents a clear thesis and offers a logical and effective solution to help maintain a safe learning environment. The evidence the writer provides in support of video monitoring is adequate, accurate, and appropriate. He or she also anticipates counterclaims and addresses concerns about maintaining students' privacy. For the most part, this person's argument is strong. However, the writer's proposal is undermined at the end by faulty reasoning; specifically, the use of name-calling, generalization, and false cause. Ad hominem statements weaken what would otherwise be a strong proposal.

Grammar

Writing that has a lot of mistakes can confuse or even annoy a reader. A business letter with a punctuation error might lead to a miscommunication and delay a reply. Or a sentence fragment might lower your grade on an essay. Paying attention to grammar, punctuation, and capitalization rules can make your writing clearer and easier to read.

Quick Reference: Parts of Speech

Part of Speech	Function	Examples
Noun	names a person, a place, a thing, an idea, a quality, or an action	
Common	serves as a general name, or a name common to an entire group	poet, novel, love, journey
Proper	names a specific, one-of-a-kind person, place, or thing	Jackson, Pleasant Street, Statue of Liberty
Singular	refers to a single person, place, thing, or idea	shark, planet, flower, truth
Plural	refers to more than one person, place, thing, or idea	sharks, planets, flowers, truths
Concrete	names something that can be perceived by the senses	snake, path, Philadelphia, damage
Abstract	names something that cannot be perceived by the senses	intelligence, fear, joy, loneliness
Compound	expresses a single idea through a combination of two or more words	girlfriend, father-in-law, Christmas Eve
Collective	refers to a group of people or things	army, flock, class, species
Possessive	shows who or what owns something	Strafford's, Bess's, children's, witnesses'
Pronoun	takes the place of a noun or another pronoun	
Personal	refers to the person making a statement, the person(s) being addressed, or the person(s) or thing(s) the statement is about	I, me, my, mine, we, us, our, ours, you, your, yours, she, he, it, her, him, hers, his, its, they, them, their, theirs
Reflexive	follows a verb or preposition and refers to a preceding noun or pronoun	myself, yourself, herself, himself, itself, ourselves, yourselves, themselves
Intensive	emphasizes a noun or another pronoun	(same as reflexives)
Demonstrative	points to one or more specific persons or things	this, that, these, those

continued

Part of Speech	Function	Examples
Interrogative	signals a question	who, whom, whose, which, what
Indefinite	refers to one or more persons or things not specifically mentioned	both, all, most, many, anyone, everybody, several, none, some
Relative	introduces an adjective clause by relating it to a word in the clause	who, whom, whose, which, that
Verb	expresses an action, a condition, or a state of being	
Action	tells what the subject does or did, physically or mentally	run, reaches, listened, consider, decides, dreamed
Linking	connects the subject to something that identifies or describes it	am, is, are, was, were, sound, taste, appear, feel, become, remain, seem
Auxiliary	precedes the main verb in a verb phrase	be, have, do, can, could, will, would, may, might
Transitive	directs the action toward someone or something; always has an object	The storm **sank** the ship.
Intransitive	does not direct the action toward someone or something; does not have an object	The ship **sank.**
Adjective	modifies a noun or pronoun	**strong** women, **two** epics, **enough** time
Adverb	modifies a verb, an adjective, or another adverb	walked **out, really** funny, **far** away
Preposition	relates one word to another word	at, by, for, from, in, of, on, to, with
Conjunction	joins words or word groups	
Coordinating	joins words or word groups used the same way	and, but, or, for, so, yet, nor
Correlative	used as a pair to join words or word groups used the same way	both . . . and, either . . . or, neither . . . nor
Subordinating	introduces a clause that cannot stand by itself as a complete sentence	although, after, as, before, because, since, when, if, unless
Interjection	expresses emotion	wow, ouch, hurrah

Quick Reference: The Sentence and Its Parts

The diagrams that follow will give you a brief review of the essentials of a sentence and some of its parts.

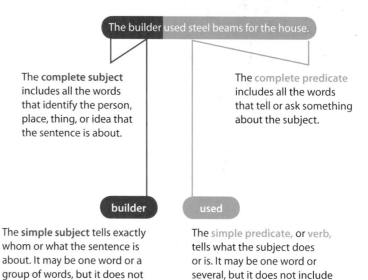

The builder used steel beams for the house.

The **complete subject** includes all the words that identify the person, place, thing, or idea that the sentence is about.

The complete predicate includes all the words that tell or ask something about the subject.

builder

used

The **simple subject** tells exactly whom or what the sentence is about. It may be one word or a group of words, but it does not include modifiers.

The simple predicate, or verb, tells what the subject does or is. It may be one word or several, but it does not include modifiers.

Every word in a sentence is part of a complete subject or a complete predicate.

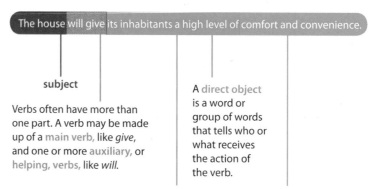

The house will give its inhabitants a high level of comfort and convenience.

subject

Verbs often have more than one part. A verb may be made up of a main verb, like *give*, and one or more auxiliary, or helping, verbs, like *will*.

A direct object is a word or group of words that tells who or what receives the action of the verb.

An indirect object is a word or group of words that tells to whom or for whom or to what or for what the verb's action is performed. A sentence can have an indirect object only if it has a direct object. The indirect object always comes before the direct object.

A prepositional phrase consists of a preposition, its object, and any modifiers of the object. In this phrase, *of* is the preposition and *comfort and convenience* is its object.

Quick Reference: Punctuation

Mark	Function	Examples
End Marks period, question mark, exclamation point	ends a sentence	We can start now**.** When would you like to leave**?** What a fantastic hit**!**
period	follows an initial or abbreviation	Mrs**.** Dorothy Parker C. P. Cavafy, P.M., A.D., lb., oz., Blvd., Dr.
	Exception: postal abbreviations of states	NE (Nebraska), NV (Nevada)

period	follows a number or letter in an outline	I. Volcanoes
		   A. Central-vent
		     1. Shield

Comma	separates part of a compound sentence	I had never disliked poetry, but now I really love it.
	separates items in a series	She is brave, loyal, and kind.
	separates adjectives of equal rank that modify the same noun	The slow, easy route is best.
	sets off a term of address	Maria, how can I help you? You must do something, soldier.
	sets off a parenthetical expression	Hard workers, as you know, don't quit. I'm not a quitter, believe me.
	sets off an introductory word, phrase, or dependent clause	Yes, I forgot my key. At the beginning of the day, I feel fresh. While she was out, I was here. Having finished my chores, I went out.
	sets off a nonessential phrase or clause	Ed Pawn, the captain of the chess team, won. Ed Pawn, who is the captain, won. The two leading runners, sprinting toward the finish line, finished in a tie.
	sets off parts of dates and addresses	Mail it by May 14, 2010, to the Hauptman Company, 321 Market Street, Memphis, Tennessee.
	follows the salutation and closing of a letter	Dear Jim, Sincerely yours,

continued

Mark	Function	Examples
	separates words to avoid confusion	By noon, time had run out. What the minister does, does matter. While cooking, Jim burned his hand.
Semicolon	separates items that contain commas in a series	We spent the first week of summer vacation in Chicago, Illinois; the second week in St. Louis, Missouri; and the third week in Albany, New York.
	separates parts of a compound sentence that are not joined by a coordinating conjunction	The last shall be first; the first shall be last. I read the Bible; however, I have not memorized it.
	separates parts of a compound sentence when the parts contain commas	After I ran out of money, I called my parents; but only my sister was home, unfortunately.
Colon	introduces a list	The names we wrote were the following: Dana, John, and Will.
	introduces a long quotation	Abraham Lincoln wrote: "Four score and seven years ago, our fathers brought forth on this continent a new nation. . . ."
	follows the salutation of a business letter	To Whom It May Concern: Dear Leonard Atole:
	separates certain numbers	1:28 P.M., Genesis 2:5
Dash	indicates an abrupt break in thought	I was thinking of my mother—who is arriving tomorrow—just as you walked in.
Parentheses	enclose less important material	It was so unlike him (John is always on time) that I began to worry. The last World Series game (did you see it?) was fun.

continued

Mark	Function	Examples
Hyphen	joins parts of a compound adjective before a noun	The not-so-rich taxpayer won't stand for this!
	joins parts of a compound with *all-*, *ex-*, *self-*, or *-elect*	The ex-firefighter helped rescue him. Our president-elect is self-conscious.
	joins parts of a compound number (to ninety-nine)	Today, I turned twenty-one.
	joins parts of a fraction	My cup is one-third full.
	joins a prefix to a word beginning with a capital letter	Which Pre-Raphaelite painter do you like best? It snowed in mid-October.
	indicates that a word is divided at the end of a line	How could you have any reason-able expectations of getting a new computer?
Apostrophe	used with *s* to form the possessive of a noun or an indefinite pronoun	my friend's book, my friends' books, anyone's guess, somebody else's problem
	replaces one or more omitted letters in a contraction or numbers in a date	don't (omitted *o*), he'd (omitted *woul*), the class of '99 (omitted *19*)
	used with *s* to form the plural of a letter	I had two A's on my report card.
Quotation Marks	set off a speaker's exact words	Sara said, "I'm finally ready." "I'm ready," Sara said, "finally." Did Sara say, "I'm ready"? Sara said, "I'm ready!"
	set off the title of a story, an article, a short poem, an essay, a song, or a chapter	I like Doctorow's "Another Place, Another Time" and Giovanni's "A Poem for My Librarian, Mrs. Long." I like Douglas Fox's essay "Big Rocks' Balancing Acts."
Ellipses	replace material omitted from a quotation	"When in the course of human events ... and to assume among the powers of the earth. ..."
Italics	indicate the title of a book, a play, a magazine, a long poem, an opera, a film, or a TV series, or the name of a ship	***Mississippi Solo, Sorry, Wrong Number, Newsweek,*** the ***Odyssey, Madame Butterfly, Gone with the Wind, Seinfeld, Titanic***
Brackets	indicate a word or phrase that has been added to a quotation to make it clearer	"Spreading awareness [of the hurricane's damage] is an important part of our work."

Quick Reference: Capitalization

Category	Examples
People and Titles	
Names and initials of people	Amy Tan, W. H. Auden
Titles used before a name	Professor Holmes, Senator Long
Deities and members of religious groups	Jesus, Allah, Buddha, Zeus, Baptists, Roman Catholics
Names of ethnic and national groups	Hispanics, Jews, African Americans
Geographical Names	
Cities, states, countries, continents	Philadelphia, Kansas, Japan, Europe
Regions, bodies of water, mountains	the South, Lake Baikal, Mount Everest
Geographic features, parks	Great Basin, Yellowstone National Park
Streets and roads, planets	318 East Sutton Drive, Charles Court, Jupiter, Pluto
Organizations, Events, Etc.	
Companies, organizations, teams	Ford Motor Company, Boy Scouts of America, St. Louis Cardinals
Buildings, bridges, monuments	Empire State Building, Eads Bridge, Washington Monument
Documents, awards	Declaration of Independence, Stanley Cup
Special named events	Mardi Gras, World Series
Government bodies, historical periods and events	U.S. Senate, House of Representatives, Middle Ages, Vietnam War
Days and months, holidays	Thursday, March, Thanksgiving, Labor Day
Specific cars, boats, trains, planes	Porsche, *Carpathia*, *Southwest Chief*, Concorde
Proper Adjectives	
Adjectives formed from proper nouns	French cooking, Spanish omelet, Edwardian age, Western movie
First Words and the Pronoun *I*	
First word in a sentence or quotation	This is it. He said, "Let's go."
First word of a sentence in parentheses that is not within another sentence	The spelling rules are covered in another section. (Consult that section for more information.)
First words in the salutation and closing of a letter	Dear Madam, Very truly yours,
First word, last word, and all important words in a title	*The Call of the Wild*, "Take Me Out to the Ball Game"

1 Nouns

A **noun** is a word used to name a person, a place, a thing, an idea, a quality, or an action. Nouns can be classified in several ways.

For more information on different types of nouns, see Quick Reference: Parts of Speech, page R30.

1.1 COMMON NOUNS

Common nouns are general names, common to entire groups.

1.2 PROPER NOUNS

Proper nouns name specific, one-of-a-kind people, places, and things.

Common	Proper
leader, park, forest, mountain	Sequoya, Sierra Nevada, Giant Forest, Mount Whitney

For more information, see Quick Reference: Capitalization, page R36.

1.3 SINGULAR AND PLURAL NOUNS

A noun may take a singular or a plural form, depending on whether it names a single person, place, thing, or idea or more than one. Make sure you use appropriate spellings when forming plurals.

Singular	Plural
tourist, city, mouse	tourists, cities, mice

For more information, see Forming Plural Nouns, page R61.

1.4 POSSESSIVE NOUNS

A **possessive noun** shows who or what owns something.

For more information, see Forming Possessives, page R62.

2 Pronouns

A **pronoun** is a word that is used in place of a noun or another pronoun. The word or word group to which the pronoun refers is called its **antecedent.**

2.1 PERSONAL PRONOUNS

Personal pronouns change their form to express person, number, gender, and case. The forms of these pronouns are shown in the following chart.

GRAMMAR PRACTICE ANSWERS

1. *Our class created a blog that tells about the books we've read.*

2. *When classmates write to us, we answer them.*

3. *If I find a comment from my teacher, I always answer him or her.*

4. *Every day there are more comments, and they are hard to ignore.*

5. *When you view the blog, you might enjoy the comments posted there.*

	Nominative	Objective	Possessive
Singular			
First person	I	me	my, mine
Second person	you	you	your, yours
Third person	she, he, it	her, him, it	her, hers, his, its
Plural			
First person	we	us	our, ours
Second person	you	you	your, yours
Third person	they	them	their, theirs

2.2 AGREEMENT WITH ANTECEDENT

Pronouns should agree with their antecedents in number, gender, and person.

If an antecedent is singular, use a singular pronoun.

> EXAMPLE: *Rachel wrote a **detective story**. **It** has a surprise ending.*

If an antecedent is plural, use a plural pronoun.

> EXAMPLES: ***The characters** have **their** motives for murder.*
> *Javier loves **mysteries** and reads **them** all the time.*

The gender of a pronoun must be the same as the gender of its antecedent.

> EXAMPLE: *The **man** has to use all **his** wits to stay alive and solve the crime.*

The person of the pronoun must be the same as the person of its antecedent. As

the chart in Section 2.1 shows, a pronoun can be in first-person, second-person, or third-person form.

> EXAMPLE: ***You** want a story to grab **your** attention.*

Grammar Practice

Rewrite each sentence so that the under-lined pronoun agrees with its antecedent.

1. Our class created a blog that tells about the books <u>they</u>'ve read.

2. When classmates write to us, we answer <u>him</u>.

3. If I find a comment from my teacher, I always answer <u>them</u>.

4. Every day there are more comments, and <u>it</u> is hard to ignore.

5. When you view the blog, <u>we</u> might enjoy the comments posted there.

2.3 PRONOUN FORMS

Personal pronouns change form to show how they function in sentences. The three forms are the subject form, the object form, and the possessive form. For examples of these pronouns, see the chart in Section 2.1.

A **subject pronoun** is used as a subject in a sentence.

> EXAMPLE: *All of my friends like our family dog. **He** is so friendly.*

Also use the subject form when the pronoun follows a linking verb.

> EXAMPLE: *The first puppy we chose was **he**.*

An **object pronoun** is used as a direct object, an indirect object, or the object of a preposition.

SUBJECT   OBJECT

He will lead them to us.

OBJECT OF PREPOSITION

A **possessive pronoun** shows ownership. The pronouns *mine, yours, hers, his, its, ours,* and *theirs* can be used in place of nouns.

EXAMPLE: *This money is mine.*

The pronouns *my, your, her, his, its, our,* and *their* are used before nouns.

EXAMPLE: *We thanked the neighbors for their help.*

WATCH OUT! Many spelling errors can be avoided if you watch out for *its* and *their.* Don't confuse the possessive pronoun *its* with the contraction *it's,* meaning "it is" or "it has." The homonyms *they're* (a contraction of *they are*) and *there* ("in that place" or an expletive) are often mistakenly used for *their.*

TIP To decide which pronoun to use in a comparison such as "He tells better tales than (*I* or *me*)," fill in the missing word(s): *He tells better tales than I tell.*

Grammar Practice

Write the correct pronoun form to complete each sentence.

1. William Butler Yeats wrote the poem "The Song of Wandering Aengus," and it was published when (he, him) was in his early 30s.
2. This poem of (him, his) was published in 1899 in the collection *The Wind Among the Reeds.*
3. This collection contains 37 poems. All of (they, them) are written in Yeats's early style.
4. Yeats wrote many other poems. All of (their, his) dates of publication can be found by searching reputable online sources.
5. Yeats won the Nobel Prize in Literature in 1923 for (his, its) literary contributions.

2.4 REFLEXIVE AND INTENSIVE PRONOUNS

These pronouns are formed by adding *-self* or *-selves* to certain personal pronouns. Their forms are the same, and they differ only in how they are used.

A **reflexive pronoun** follows a verb or preposition and reflects back on an earlier noun or pronoun.

EXAMPLES: *He likes himself too much. She is now herself again.*

Intensive pronouns intensify or emphasize the nouns or pronouns to which they refer.

EXAMPLES: *They themselves will educate their children. You did it yourself.*

WATCH OUT! Avoid using *hisself* or *theirselves.* Standard English does not include these forms.

NONSTANDARD: *Alex dedicated hisself to learning the magician's secrets.*

STANDARD: *Alex dedicated himself to learning the magician's secrets.*

2.5 DEMONSTRATIVE PRONOUNS

Demonstrative pronouns point out things and persons near and far.

	Singular	Plural
Near	this	these
Far	that	those

2.6 INDEFINITE PRONOUNS

Indefinite pronouns do not refer to specific persons or things and usually have no antecedents. The chart shows some commonly used indefinite pronouns.

Singular	Plural	Singular or Plural	
another	both	all	none
anybody	few	any	some
no one	many	more	most
neither			

 COMMON CORE L1

GRAMMAR PRACTICE ANSWERS

1. *he*
2. *his*
3. *them*
4. *their*
5. *his*

GRAMMAR PRACTICE ANSWERS

1. *Who has studied how brain works?*
2. *Individuals who study the brain understand more about how we learn and think.*
3. *Nobody knows everything he or she can about the brain.*
4. *Each person's brain develops and forms new connections, but he or she isn't aware of these changes.*
5. *Scientists themselves often can't tell how their own brains change over time.*

TIP Indefinite pronouns that end in *one, body,* or *thing* are always singular.

> INCORRECT: *Did everybody play their part well?*

If the indefinite pronoun might refer to either a male or a female, *his or her* may be used to refer to it, or the sentence may be rewritten.

> CORRECT: *Did everybody play his or her part well?*
> *Did all the students play their parts well?*

2.7 INTERROGATIVE PRONOUNS

An **interrogative pronoun** tells a reader or listener that a question is coming. The interrogative pronouns are *who, whom, whose, which,* and *what.*

> EXAMPLES: *Who is going to rehearse with you?*
> *From whom did you receive the script?*

TIP *Who* is used as a subject; *whom* is used as an object. To find out which pronoun you need to use in a question, change the question to a statement.

> QUESTION: *(Who/Whom) did you meet there?*

> STATEMENT: *You met (?) there.*

Since the verb has a subject (*you*), the needed word must be the object form, *whom.*

> EXAMPLE: *Whom did you meet there?*

WATCH OUT! A special problem arises when you use an interrupter, such as *do you think,* within a question.

> EXAMPLE: *(Who/Whom) do you think will win?*

If you eliminate the interrupter, it is clear that the word you need is *who.*

2.8 RELATIVE PRONOUNS

Relative pronouns relate, or connect, adjective clauses to the words they modify in sentences. The noun or pronoun that a relative clause modifies is the antecedent of the relative pronoun. Here are the relative pronouns and their uses.

	Subject	Object	Possessive
Person	who	whom	whose
Thing	which	which	whose
Thing/Person	that	that	whose

Often, short sentences with related ideas can be combined by using a relative pronoun to create a more effective sentence.

> SHORT SENTENCE: *Yeats wrote "The Song of Wandering Aengus."*

> RELATED SENTENCE: *"The Song of Wandering Aengus" is a well-known poem in literature.*

> COMBINED SENTENCE: *Yeats wrote "The Song of Wandering Aengus," which is a well-known poem in literature.*

Grammar Practice

Write the correct form of each incorrect pronoun.

1. Whom has read or studied how the brain works?
2. Individuals whom study the brain understand more about how we learn and think.
3. Nobody knows everything they can about the brain.
4. Each person's brain develops and forms new connections, but they aren't aware of these changes.
5. Scientists theyselves often can't tell how their own brains change over time.

2.9 PRONOUN REFERENCE PROBLEMS

The referent of a pronoun should always be clear. Avoid problems by rewriting sentences.

An **indefinite reference** occurs when the pronoun *it, you,* or *they* does not clearly refer to a specific antecedent.

> UNCLEAR: *My aunt hugged me in front of my friends, and it was embarrassing.*

> CLEAR: *My aunt hugged me in front of my friends, and I was embarrassed.*

A **general reference** occurs when the pronoun *it, this, that, which,* or *such* is used to refer to a general idea rather than a specific antecedent.

> UNCLEAR: *Jenna takes acting lessons. This has improved her chances of getting a part in the school play.*

> CLEAR: *Jenna takes acting lessons. The lessons have improved her chances of getting a part in the school play.*

Ambiguous means "having more than one possible meaning." An **ambiguous reference** occurs when a pronoun could refer to two or more antecedents.

> UNCLEAR: *Tony talked to Fred and said that he could meet us later.*

> CLEAR: *Tony talked to Fred and said that Fred could meet us later.*

Grammar Practice

Rewrite the following sentences to correct indefinite, ambiguous, and general pronoun references.

1. When computer networks were first developed in the late 1950s and early 1960s, they didn't know how it would change worldwide communications.
2. Early networks were created for special purposes, and airlines and the U.S. Department of Defense used it.
3. Today people all around the world can use the Internet. This makes immediate communication possible.
4. With the Internet and wireless access, it can connect almost anyone anywhere.

3 Verbs

A **verb** is a word that expresses an action, a condition, or a state of being.

For more information, see Quick Reference: Parts of Speech, page R30.

3.1 ACTION VERBS

Action verbs express mental or physical activity.

> EXAMPLE: *Mr. Cho slept with the window open.*

3.2 LINKING VERBS

Linking verbs join subjects with words or phrases that rename or describe them.

> EXAMPLE: *When he awoke the next morning, his bed was wet from the rain.*

3.3 PRINCIPAL PARTS

Action and linking verbs typically have four principal parts, which are used to form verb tenses. The principal parts are the **present,** the **present participle,** the **past,** and the **past participle.**

Action verbs and some linking verbs also fall into two categories: regular and irregular. A **regular verb** is a verb that forms its past and past participle by adding *-ed* or *-d* to the present form.

Present	Present Participle	Past	Past Participle
jump	(is) jumping	jumped	(has) jumped
solve	(is) solving	solved	(has) solved
grab	(is) grabbing	grabbed	(has) grabbed
carry	(is) carrying	carried	(has) carried

An **irregular verb** is a verb that forms its past and past participle in some other way than by adding *-ed* or *-d* to the present form.

Present	Present Participle	Past	Past Participle
begin	(is) beginning	began	(has) begun
break	(is) breaking	broke	(has) broken
go	(is) going	went	(has) gone

COMMON CORE L1

GRAMMAR PRACTICE ANSWERS

1. *When computer networks were first developed in the late 1950s and early 1960s, developers didn't know how it would change worldwide communications.*
2. *Early networks were created for special purposes. The airlines and the U.S. Department of Defense used the early networks.*
3. *Today people all around the world can use the Internet. The Internet makes immediate communication possible.*
4. *The Internet and wireless access can connect almost anyone anywhere.*

3.4 VERB TENSE

The **tense** of a verb indicates the time of the action or the state of being. An action or state of being can occur in the present, the past, or the future. There are six tenses, each expressing a different range of time.

The **present tense** expresses an action or state that is happening at the present time, occurs regularly, or is constant or generally true. Use the present part.

> NOW: *That snow looks deep.*
>
> REGULAR: *It snows every day.*
>
> GENERAL: *Snow falls.*

The **past tense** expresses an action that began and ended in the past. Use the past part.

> EXAMPLE: *The storyteller finished his tale.*

The **future tense** expresses an action or state that will occur. Use **shall** or **will** with the present part.

> EXAMPLE: *They will attend the next festival.*

The **present perfect** tense expresses an action or state that (1) was completed at an indefinite time in the past or (2) began in the past and continues into the present. Use **have** or **has** with the past participle.

> EXAMPLE: *Poetry has inspired many readers.*

The **past perfect tense** expresses an action in the past that came before another action in the past. Use **had** with the past participle.

> EXAMPLE: *He had built a fire before the dog ran away.*

The **future perfect tense** expresses an action in the future that will be completed before another action in the future. Use **shall have** or **will have** with the past participle.

> EXAMPLE: *They will have read the novel before they see the movie version of the tale.*

TIP A past-tense form of an irregular verb is not used with an auxiliary verb, but a past-participle main irregular verb is always used with an auxiliary verb.

INCORRECT: *I have saw her somewhere before.* (*Saw* is the past-tense form of an irregular verb and shouldn't be used with *have.*)

CORRECT: *I have seen her somewhere before.*

INCORRECT: *I seen her somewhere before.* (*Seen* is the past participle of an irregular verb and shouldn't be used without an auxiliary verb.)

3.5 PROGRESSIVE FORMS

The progressive forms of the six tenses show ongoing actions. Use forms of **be** with the present participles of verbs.

> PRESENT PROGRESSIVE: *She is rehearsing her lines.*
>
> PAST PROGRESSIVE: *She was rehearsing her lines.*
>
> FUTURE PROGRESSIVE: *She will be rehearsing her lines.*
>
> PRESENT PERFECT PROGRESSIVE: *She has been rehearsing her lines.*
>
> PAST PERFECT PROGRESSIVE: *She had been rehearsing her lines.*
>
> FUTURE PERFECT PROGRESSIVE: *She will have been rehearsing her lines.*

WATCH OUT! Do not shift from tense to tense needlessly. Watch out for the following special cases.

- In most compound sentences and in sentences with compound predicates, keep the tenses the same.

  INCORRECT: *His boots freeze, and he shook with cold.*

  CORRECT: *His boots freeze, and he shakes with cold.*

- If one past action happens before another, do shift tenses.

  INCORRECT: *They wished they started earlier.*

  CORRECT: *They wished they had started earlier.*

Grammar Practice

Rewrite each sentence using a form of the verb(s) in parentheses. Identify each form that you use.

1. Some medical developments (begin) with the space age—for example, laparoscopy and robotics.
2. Both of these areas (grow) and (advance) the field of surgery.
3. In the 1990s "robotic assistants" (help) in surgery.
4. People (come) to expect simpler procedures because of these new techniques.
5. Some day other procedures that avoid cutting into tissue (develop).

Rewrite each sentence to correct an error in tense.

1. I seen a movie about the cobra and its natural enemy, the mongoose.
2. Most snakes hide and avoided people.
3. The cobra raised its head when it seeks out its next victim.
4. Both the male and female protected their eggs and will attack an approaching intruder.
5. The venom of a cobra was deadly and kills a human being within a few hours.

3.6 ACTIVE AND PASSIVE VOICE

The voice of a verb tells whether its subject performs or receives the action expressed by the verb. When the subject performs the action, the verb is in the **active voice.** When the subject is the receiver of the action, the verb is in the **passive voice.**

Compare these two sentences:

ACTIVE: *Virginia Hamilton wrote "The People Could Fly."*

PASSIVE: *"The People Could Fly" was written by Virginia Hamilton.*

To form the passive voice, use a form of *be* with the past participle of the verb.

WATCH OUT! Use the passive voice sparingly. It can make writing awkward and less direct.

AWKWARD: *"The People Could Fly" is a folk tale that was written by Virginia Hamilton.*

BETTER: *Virginia Hamilton wrote the tale "The People Could Fly."*

There are occasions when you will choose to use the passive voice because:

- you want to emphasize the receiver: *The king was shot.*
- the doer is unknown: *My books were stolen.*
- the doer is unimportant: *French is spoken here.*

4 Modifiers

Modifiers are words or groups of words that change or limit the meanings of other words. Adjectives and adverbs are common modifiers.

4.1 ADJECTIVES

Adjectives modify nouns and pronouns by telling which one, what kind, how many, or how much.

WHICH ONE: *this, that, these, those*

EXAMPLE: *That bird is a scarlet ibis.*

WHAT KIND: *small, sick, courageous, black*

EXAMPLE: *The sick bird sways on the branch.*

HOW MANY: *some, few, ten, none, both, each*

EXAMPLE: *Both brothers stared at the bird.*

HOW MUCH: *more, less, enough*

EXAMPLE: *The bird did not have enough strength to remain perched.*

4.2 PREDICATE ADJECTIVES

Most adjectives come before the nouns they modify, as in the examples above. A **predicate adjective,** however, follows a linking verb and describes the subject.

EXAMPLE: *My friends are very intelligent.*

Be especially careful to use adjectives (not adverbs) after such linking verbs as *look, feel, grow, taste,* and *smell.*

EXAMPLE: *The bread smells wonderful.*

COMMON CORE **L 1**

GRAMMAR PRACTICE ANSWERS

1. *Some medical developments began with the space age—for example, laparoscopy and robotics. (past tense)*
2. *Both of these areas have grown and have advanced the field of surgery. (present perfect tense)*
3. *In the 1990s "robotic assistants" helped in surgery. (past tense)*
4. *People have come to expect simpler procedures because of these new techniques. (present perfect tense)*
5. *Some day other procedures that avoid cutting into tissue will be developed. (future tense)*

ANSWERS

1. *I saw a movie about the cobra and its natural enemy, the mongoose.*
2. *Most snakes hide and avoid people.*
3. *The cobra raises its head when it seeks out its next victim.*
4. *Both the male and female protect their eggs and will attack an approaching intruder.*
5. *The venom of a cobra is deadly and kills a human being within a few hours.*

4.3 ADVERBS

Adverbs modify verbs, adjectives, and other adverbs by telling where, when, how, or to what extent.

> WHERE: *The children played outside.*
>
> WHEN: *The author spoke yesterday.*
>
> HOW: *We walked slowly behind the leader.*
>
> TO WHAT EXTENT: *He worked very hard.*

Adverbs may occur in many places in sentences, both before and after the words they modify.

> EXAMPLES: *Suddenly the wind shifted.*
> *The wind suddenly shifted.*
> *The wind shifted suddenly.*

4.4 ADJECTIVE OR ADVERB?

Many adverbs are formed by adding **-ly** to adjectives.

> EXAMPLES: *sweet, sweetly; gentle, gently*

However, **-ly** added to a noun will usually yield an adjective.

> EXAMPLES: *friend, friendly; woman, womanly*

4.5 COMPARISON OF MODIFIERS

Modifiers can be used to compare two or more things. The form of a modifier shows the degree of comparison. Both adjectives and adverbs have **comparative** and **superlative** forms.

The **comparative form** is used to compare two things, groups, or actions.

> EXAMPLES: *His father's hands were stronger than his own.*
> *His father was more courageous than the other man.*

The **superlative form** is used to compare more than two things, groups, or actions.

> EXAMPLES: *His father's hands were the strongest in the family.*
> *His father was the most courageous of them all.*

4.6 REGULAR COMPARISONS

Most one-syllable and some two-syllable adjectives and adverbs form comparatives and superlatives by adding **-er** and **-est.** All three-syllable and most two-syllable modifiers have comparatives and superlatives formed with **more** or **most.**

Modifier	Comparative	Superlative
small	smaller	smallest
thin	thinner	thinnest
sleepy	sleepier	sleepiest
useless	more useless	most useless
precisely	more precisely	most precisely

WATCH OUT! Note that spelling changes must sometimes be made to form the comparatives and superlatives of modifiers.

> EXAMPLES: *friendly, friendlier* (Change *y* to *i* and add the ending.)
> *sad, sadder* (Double the final consonant and add the ending.)

4.7 IRREGULAR COMPARISONS

Some commonly used modifiers have irregular comparative and superlative forms. They are listed in the following chart. You may wish to memorize them.

Modifier	Comparative	Superlative
good	better	best
bad	worse	worst
far	farther *or* further	farthest *or* furthest
little	less *or* lesser	least
many	more	most
well	better	best
much	more	most

4.8 PROBLEMS WITH MODIFIERS

Study the tips that follow to avoid common mistakes.

Farther* and *Further Use *farther* for distances; use *further* for everything else.

Double Comparisons Make a comparison by using *-er/-est* or by using *more/most*. Using *-er* with *more* or using *-est* with *most* is incorrect.

> INCORRECT: *I like her more better than she likes me.*

> CORRECT: *I like her better than she likes me.*

Illogical Comparisons An illogical or confusing comparison results when two unrelated things are compared or when something is compared with itself. The word *other* or the word *else* should be used when comparing an individual member to the rest of a group.

> ILLOGICAL: *The narrator was more curious about the war than any student in his class.* (implies that the narrator isn't a student in the class)

> LOGICAL: *The narrator was more curious about the war than any other student in his class.* (identifies that the narrator is a student)

Bad vs. Badly *Bad,* always an adjective, is used before a noun or after a linking verb. *Badly,* always an adverb, never modifies a noun. Be sure to use the right form after a linking verb.

> INCORRECT: *Ed felt badly after his team lost.*

> CORRECT: *Ed felt bad after his team lost.*

Good vs. Well *Good* is always an adjective. It is used before a noun or after a linking verb. *Well* is often an adverb meaning "expertly" or "properly." *Well* can also be used as an adjective after a linking verb when it means "in good health."

> INCORRECT: *Helen writes very good.*

> CORRECT: *Helen writes very well.*

> CORRECT: *Yesterday I felt bad; today I feel well.*

Double Negatives If you add a negative word to a sentence that is already negative, the result will be an error known as a double negative. When using *not* or *-n't* with a verb, use *any-* words, such as *anybody* or *anything,* rather than *no-* words, such as *nobody* or *nothing,* later in the sentence.

> INCORRECT: *We haven't seen nobody.*

> CORRECT: *We haven't seen anybody.*

Using *hardly, barely,* or *scarcely* after a negative word is also incorrect.

> INCORRECT: *They couldn't barely see two feet ahead.*

> CORRECT: *They could barely see two feet ahead.*

Misplaced Modifiers Sometimes a modifier is placed so far away from the word it modifies that the intended meaning of the sentence is unclear. Prepositional phrases and participial phrases are often misplaced. Place modifiers as close as possible to the words they modify.

> MISPLACED: *We found the child in the park who was missing.*

> CLEARER: *We found the child who was missing in the park.* (The child was missing, not the park.)

Dangling Modifiers Sometimes a modifier doesn't appear to modify any word in a sentence. Most dangling modifiers are participial phrases or infinitive phrases.

> DANGLING: *Looking out the window, his brother was seen driving by.*

> CLEARER: *Looking out the window, Josh saw his brother driving by.*

Grammar Practice

Choose the correct word or words from each pair in parentheses.

1. When Ellis Island opened, it was the (larger, largest) port of entry to the United States.
2. In the 1980s, the facility underwent the (greatest, most greatest) restoration ever performed.
3. The restoration project (bad, badly) needed funds.
4. The project didn't have (no, any) funding until fundraising efforts began in 1982.
5. In 1990, the (grandly, grand) reopening was received (good, well).

COMMON CORE L1

GRAMMAR PRACTICE ANSWERS

1. *largest*
2. *greatest*
3. *badly*
4. *any*
5. *grand; well*

GRAMMAR PRACTICE ANSWERS

1. *correct*
2. *Possible answer: The mother bear growled as we drove by in our car.*
3. *Possible answer: We took pictures of the bears while we were inside the camper.*
4. *correct*
5. *Possible answer: We had lots of film to tape our adventures.*

Grammar Practice

Rewrite each sentence that contains a misplaced or dangling modifier. Write "correct" if the sentence is written correctly.

1. We traveled to Yellowstone Park with many tourists.
2. Driving our car, the mother bear growled.
3. We took pictures of the bears in the camper.
4. My brother and I went for a hike, but we got lost.
5. Taping our adventures, we had lots of film.

5 The Sentence and Its Parts

A **sentence** is a group of words used to express a complete thought. A complete sentence has a subject and a predicate.

For more information, see **Quick Reference: The Sentence and Its Parts,** page R32.

5.1 KINDS OF SENTENCES

There are four basic types of sentences.

Type	Definition	Example
Declarative	states a fact, a wish, an intent, or a feeling	Charles Yu understands science fiction.
Interrogative	asks a question	Did you read "Earth (A Gift Shop)"?
Imperative	gives a command or direction	Read the story.
Exclamatory	expresses strong feeling or excitement	The story is great!

5.2 COMPOUND SUBJECTS AND PREDICATES

A compound subject consists of two or more subjects that share the same verb. They are typically joined by the coordinating conjunction **and** or **or.**

EXAMPLE: *A short story or novel will keep you engaged.*

A compound predicate consists of two or more predicates that share the same subject. They too are usually joined by a coordinating conjunction such as **and, but,** or **or.**

EXAMPLE: *The class finished all the poetry but did not read the short stories.*

5.3 COMPLEMENTS

A **complement** is a word or group of words that completes the meaning of the sentence. Some sentences contain only a subject and a verb. Most sentences, however, require additional words placed after the verb to complete the meaning of the sentence. There are three kinds of complements: direct objects, indirect objects, and subject complements.

Direct objects are words or word groups that receive the action of action verbs. A direct object answers the question *what* or *whom.*

EXAMPLES: *The students asked many questions.* (Asked what?) *The teacher quickly answered the students.* (Answered whom?)

Indirect objects tell to whom or what or for whom or what the actions of verbs are performed. Indirect objects come before direct objects. In the examples that follow, the indirect objects are highlighted.

EXAMPLES: *My sister usually gave her friends good advice.* (Gave to whom?) *Her brother sent the store a heavy package.* (Sent to what?)

Subject complements come after linking verbs and identify or describe the subjects. A subject complement that names or identifies a subject is called a **predicate nominative.** Predicate nominatives include **predicate nouns** and **predicate pronouns.**

> EXAMPLES: *My friends are very hard workers.*
> *The best writer in the class is she.*

A subject complement that describes a subject is called a **predicate adjective.**

> EXAMPLE: *The pianist appeared very energetic.*

6 Phrases

A **phrase** is a group of related words that does not contain a subject and a predicate but functions in a sentence as a single part of speech.

6.1 PREPOSITIONAL PHRASES

A **prepositional phrase** is a phrase that consists of a preposition, its object, and any modifiers of the object. Prepositional phrases that modify nouns or pronouns are called **adjective phrases.** Prepositional phrases that modify verbs, adjectives, or adverbs are **adverb phrases.**

> ADJECTIVE PHRASE: *The central character of the story is a villain.*

> ADVERB PHRASE: *He reveals his nature in the first scene.*

6.2 APPOSITIVES AND APPOSITIVE PHRASES

An **appositive** is a noun or pronoun that identifies or renames another noun or pronoun. An **appositive phrase** includes an appositive and modifiers of it. An appositive usually follows the noun or pronoun it identifies.

An appositive can be either **essential** or **nonessential.** An **essential appositive** provides information that is needed to identify what is referred to by the preceding noun or pronoun.

> EXAMPLE: *The book is about the author Naomi Shihab Nye.*

A **nonessential appositive** adds extra information about a noun or pronoun whose meaning is already clear.

Nonessential appositives and appositive phrases are set off with commas.

> EXAMPLE: *The book, an autobiography, tells how she began writing.*

7 Verbals and Verbal Phrases

A **verbal** is a verb form that is used as a noun, an adjective, or an adverb. A **verbal phrase** consists of a verbal along with its modifiers and complements. There are three kinds of verbals: **infinitives, participles,** and **gerunds.**

7.1 INFINITIVES AND INFINITIVE PHRASES

An **infinitive** is a verb form that usually begins with *to* and functions as a noun, an adjective, or an adverb. An **infinitive phrase** consists of an infinitive plus its modifiers and complements.

> NOUN: *To know her is my only desire.* (subject)
> *I'm planning to walk with you.* (direct object)
> *Her goal was to promote women's rights.* (predicate nominative)

> ADJECTIVE: *We saw his need to be loved.* (adjective modifying *need*)

> ADVERB: *She wrote to voice her opinions.* (adverb modifying *wrote*)

Because *to,* the sign of the infinitive, precedes infinitives, it is usually easy to recognize them. However, sometimes *to* may be omitted.

> EXAMPLE: *Let no one dare [to] enter this shrine.*

7.2 PARTICIPLES AND PARTICIPIAL PHRASES

A **participle** is a verb form that functions as an adjective. Like adjectives, participles modify nouns and pronouns. Most participles are present-participle forms, ending in *-ing,* or past-participle forms ending in *-ed* or *-en.* In the examples below, the participles are highlighted.

> MODIFYING A NOUN: *The dying man had a smile on his face.*

GRAMMAR PRACTICE POSSIBLE ANSWERS

1. *I read Jackie Robinson's autobiography to learn more about segregation in baseball.*

2. *Researching Robinson, I found out about the first African American baseball player in the United States.*

3. *Robinson played his entire major-league career with the same team, the Dodgers.*

4. *By stealing bases, Robinson became one of the most popular Dodgers.*

5. *Robinson became famous worldwide, earning a place in the Baseball Hall of Fame.*

MODIFYING A PRONOUN: *Frustrated, everyone abandoned the cause.*

Participial phrases are participles with all their modifiers and complements.

MODIFYING A NOUN: *The dogs searching for survivors are well trained.*

MODIFYING A PRONOUN: *Having approved your proposal, we are ready to act.*

7.3 DANGLING AND MISPLACED PARTICIPLES

A participle or participial phrase should be placed as close as possible to the word that it modifies. Otherwise the meaning of the sentence may not be clear.

MISPLACED: *The boys were looking for squirrels searching the trees.*

CLEARER: *The boys searching the trees were looking for squirrels.*

A participle or participial phrase that does not clearly modify anything in a sentence is called a **dangling participle.** A dangling participle causes confusion because it appears to modify a word that it cannot sensibly modify. Correct a dangling participle by providing a word for the participle to modify.

DANGLING: *Running like the wind, my hat fell off.* (The hat wasn't running.)

CLEARER: *Running like the wind, I lost my hat.*

7.4 GERUNDS AND GERUND PHRASES

A **gerund** is a verb form ending in *-ing* that functions as a noun. Gerunds may perform any function nouns perform.

SUBJECT: *Running is my favorite pastime.*

DIRECT OBJECT: *I truly love running.*

INDIRECT OBJECT: *You should give running a try.*

SUBJECT COMPLEMENT: *My deepest passion is running.*

OBJECT OF PREPOSITION: *Her love of running keeps her strong.*

Gerund phrases are gerunds with all their modifiers and complements.

SUBJECT: *Wishing on a star never got me far.*

OBJECT OF PREPOSITION: *I will finish before leaving the office.*

APPOSITIVE: *Her avocation, flying airplanes, finally led to full-time employment.*

Grammar Practice

Rewrite each sentence, adding the type of phrase shown in parentheses.

1. I read Jackie Robinson's autobiography. (infinitive phrase)
2. Robinson was the first major league African American baseball player in the United States. (participial phrase)
3. Robinson played his entire major league career with the same team. (appositive phrase)
4. Robinson went on to become one of the most popular Dodger players. (gerund phrase)
5. Today Robinson is famous worldwide. (prepositional phrase)

8 Clauses

A **clause** is a group of words that contains a subject and a predicate. There are two kinds of clauses: independent, or main, clauses and subordinate clauses.

8.1 MAIN AND SUBORDINATE CLAUSES

A **main (independent) clause** can stand alone as a sentence.

MAIN CLAUSE: *I read "Train Time."*

A sentence may contain more than one main clause.

EXAMPLE: *I finished dinner, and I read the story.*

In the preceding example, the coordinating conjunction *and* joins two main clauses.

For more information, see **Coordinating Conjunction,** page R31.

A **subordinate (dependent) clause** cannot stand alone as a sentence. It is subordinate to, or dependent on, a main clause.

EXAMPLE: *After I finished dinner, I read "Train Time."*

The highlighted clause cannot stand by itself. Note that a comma is added to the end of a dependent clause when it comes before a main clause.

8.2 ADJECTIVE CLAUSES

An **adjective clause** is a subordinate clause used as an adjective. It usually follows the noun or pronoun it modifies.

EXAMPLE: *Antonio and I are the actors who play the lead characters in our school's play.*

Adjective clauses are typically introduced by the relative pronouns *who, whom, whose, which,* and *that.*

For more information, see **Relative Pronouns,** page R40.

EXAMPLE: *The production, which is our school's big theatrical event, will take place in May.*

An adjective clause can be either essential or nonessential. An **essential adjective clause** provides information that is necessary to identify the preceding noun or pronoun.

EXAMPLE: *The drama club had to make a decision that three performances would be sufficient.*

A **nonessential adjective clause** adds additional information about a noun or pronoun whose meaning is already clear. Nonessential clauses are set off with commas.

EXAMPLE: *The club members, who had been discussing it for a long time, needed to come to an agreement about performance times and dates.*

8.3 ADVERB CLAUSES

An **adverb clause** is a subordinate clause that is used to modify a verb, an adjective, or an adverb. It is introduced by a subordinating conjunction.

For examples of subordinating conjunctions, see **Noun Clauses,** page R49.

Adverb clauses typically occur at the beginning or end of sentences.

MODIFYING A VERB: *When we need you, we will call.*

MODIFYING AN ADVERB: *I'll stay here where there is shelter from the rain.*

MODIFYING AN ADJECTIVE: *Roman felt as good as he had ever felt.*

TIP An adverb clause should be followed by a comma when it comes before a main clause. When an adverb clause comes after a main clause, a comma may not be needed.

8.4 NOUN CLAUSES

A **noun clause** is a subordinate clause that is used as a noun. A noun clause may be used as a subject, a direct object, an indirect object, a predicate nominative, or the object of a preposition. Noun clauses are introduced either by pronouns, such as *that, what, who, whoever, which,* and *whose,* or by subordinating conjunctions, such as *how, when, where, why,* and *whether.*

For more subordinating conjunctions, see **Quick Reference: Parts of Speech,** page R30.

TIP Because the same words may introduce adjective and noun clauses, you need to consider how a clause functions within its sentence. To determine if a clause is a noun clause, try substituting *something* or *someone* for the clause. If you can do it, it is probably a noun clause.

EXAMPLE: *I know whose woods these are.* ("I know *something.*" The clause is a noun clause, a direct object of the verb *know.*) *Give a copy to whoever wants one.* ("Give a copy to *someone.*" The clause is a noun clause, an object of the preposition *to.*)

COMMON CORE **L 1a**

GRAMMAR PRACTICE POSSIBLE ANSWERS

1. *Students who want school credit volunteer at animal shelters.*

2. *They help take care of dogs and cats when the shelters are understaffed.*

3. *The veterinarian tries to explain to students how they should care for sick animals.*

4. *Many people appreciate the students who donate their time each week.*

5. *When soccer season ends, I plan to work at the shelter.*

Add descriptive details to each sentence by writing the type of clause indicated in parentheses.

1. Some students volunteer at animal shelters. (adjective clause)
2. They help take care of dogs and cats. (adverb clause)
3. The veterinarian tries to explain to the students. (noun clause)
4. Many people appreciate the students. (adjective clause)
5. I plan to work at the shelter. (adverb clause)

9 The Structure of Sentences

When classified by their structure, there are four kinds of sentences: simple, compound, complex, and compound-complex.

9.1 SIMPLE SENTENCES

A **simple sentence** is a sentence that has one main clause and no subordinate clauses.

> EXAMPLE: *Sam ran to the theater.*
> *Max waited in front of the theater.*

A simple sentence may contain a compound subject or a compound verb.

> EXAMPLE: *Sam and Max went to the movie.* (compound subject)
> *They clapped and cheered at their favorite parts.* (compound verb)

9.2 COMPOUND SENTENCES

A **compound sentence** consists of two or more main clauses. The clauses in compound sentences are joined with commas and coordinating conjunctions (*and, but, or, nor, yet, for, so*) or with semicolons. Like simple sentences, compound sentences do not contain any subordinate clauses.

> EXAMPLES: *Sam likes action movies, but Max prefers comedies.*
> *The actor jumped from one building to another; he barely made the final leap.*

WATCH OUT! Do not confuse compound sentences with simple sentences that have compound parts.

> EXAMPLE: *The actor knew all the lines but didn't play the part well.*
> (Here *but* joins parts of a compound predicate, not a compound sentence.)

9.3 COMPLEX SENTENCES

A **complex sentence** consists of one main clause and one or more subordinate clauses.

> EXAMPLE: *One should not complain unless one has a better solution.*
> *Mr. Neiman, who is an artist, sketched pictures until the sun went down.*

9.4 COMPOUND-COMPLEX SENTENCES

A **compound-complex sentence** contains two or more main clauses and one or more subordinate clauses. Compound-complex sentences are, simply, both compound and complex. If you start with a compound sentence, all you need to do to form a compound-complex sentence is add a subordinate clause.

> COMPOUND: *All the students knew the answer, yet they were too shy to volunteer.*

> COMPOUND-COMPLEX: *All the students knew the answer that their teacher expected, yet they were too shy to volunteer.*

9.5 PARALLEL STRUCTURE

When you write sentences, make sure that coordinate parts are equivalent, or **parallel,** in structure.

> NOT PARALLEL: *Erin loved basketball and to play hockey.* (*Basketball* is a noun; *to play hockey* is a phrase.)

> PARALLEL: *Erin loved basketball and hockey.* (*Basketball* and *hockey* are both nouns.)

> NOT PARALLEL: *He wanted to rent an apartment, a new car, and traveling around the country.* (*To rent* is an infinitive, *car* is a noun, and *traveling* is a gerund.)

PARALLEL: *He wanted to rent an apartment, to drive a new car, and to travel around the country.*
(*To rent, to drive,* and *to travel* are all infinitives.)

10 Writing Complete Sentences

Remember, a sentence is a group of words that expresses a complete thought. In writing that you wish to share with a reader, try to avoid both sentence fragments and run-on sentences.

10.1 CORRECTING FRAGMENTS

A **sentence fragment** is a group of words that is only part of a sentence. It does not express a complete thought and may be confusing to a reader or listener. A sentence fragment may be lacking a subject, a predicate, or both.

FRAGMENT: *Waited for the boat to arrive.* (no subject)

CORRECTED: *We waited for the boat to arrive.*

FRAGMENT: *People of various races, ages, and creeds.* (no predicate)

CORRECTED: *People of various races, ages, and creeds gathered together.*

FRAGMENT: *Near the old cottage.* (neither subject nor predicate)

CORRECTED: *The burial ground is near the old cottage.*

In your writing, fragments may be a result of haste or incorrect punctuation. Sometimes fixing a fragment is a matter of attaching it to a preceding or following sentence.

FRAGMENT: *We saw the two girls. Waiting for the bus to arrive.*

CORRECTED: *We saw the two girls waiting for the bus to arrive.*

10.2 CORRECTING RUN-ON SENTENCES

A **run-on sentence** is made up of two or more sentences written as though they were one. Some run-ons have no punctuation within them. Others may have only commas where conjunctions or stronger punctuation marks are necessary. Use your judgment in correcting run-on sentences, as you have choices. You can change a run-on to two sentences if the thoughts are not closely connected. If the thoughts are closely related, you can keep the run-on as one sentence by adding a semicolon or a conjunction.

RUN-ON: *We found a place for the picnic by a small pond it was three miles from the village.*

MAKE TWO SENTENCES: *We found a place for the picnic by a small pond. It was three miles from the village.*

RUN-ON: *We found a place for the picnic by a small pond it was perfect.*

USE A SEMICOLON: *We found a place for the picnic by a small pond; it was perfect.*

ADD A CONJUNCTION: *We found a place for the picnic by a small pond, and it was perfect.*

WATCH OUT! When you form compound sentences, make sure you use appropriate punctuation: a comma before a coordinating conjunction, a semicolon when there is no coordinating conjunction, and a semicolon before a conjunctive adverb and a comma after it. A very common mistake is to use a comma alone instead of a comma and a conjunction. This error is called a **comma splice.**

INCORRECT: *He finished the job, he left the village.*

CORRECT: *He finished the job, and he left the village.*

11 Subject-Verb Agreement

The subject and verb in a clause must agree in number. Agreement means that if the subject is singular, the verb is also singular, and if the subject is plural, the verb is also plural.

11.1 BASIC AGREEMENT

Fortunately, agreement between subjects and verbs in English is simple. Most verbs show the difference between singular and plural only in the third person of the present tense. In the present tense, the third-person singular form ends in **-s.**

Present-Tense Verb Forms	
Singular	**Plural**
I sleep	we sleep
you sleep	you sleep
she, he, it sleeps	they sleep

11.2 AGREEMENT WITH *BE*

The verb *be* presents special problems in agreement, because this verb does not follow the usual verb patterns.

Forms of *Be*			
Present Tense		**Past Tense**	
Singular	**Plural**	**Singular**	**Plural**
I am	we are	I was	we were
you are	you are	you were	you were
she, he, it is	they are	she, he, it was	they were

11.3 WORDS BETWEEN SUBJECT AND VERB

A verb agrees only with its subject. When a prepositional phrase or other words come between a subject and a verb, ignore them when considering proper agreement. Identify the subject, and make sure the verb agrees with it.

> EXAMPLES: *A story in the newspapers tells about the 1890s.*
> *Dad as well as Mom reads the paper daily.*

11.4 AGREEMENT WITH COMPOUND SUBJECTS

Use plural verbs with most compound subjects joined by the word *and.*

> EXAMPLE: *My father and his friends play chess every day.*

To confirm that you need a plural verb, you could substitute the plural pronoun *they* for *my father and his friends.*

If a compound subject is thought of as a unit, use a singular verb. Test this by substituting the singular pronoun *it.*

> EXAMPLE: *Peanut butter and jelly [it] is my brother's favorite sandwich.*

Use a singular verb with a compound subject that is preceded by *each, every,* or *many a.*

> EXAMPLE: *Each novel and short story seems grounded in personal experience.*

When the parts of a compound subject are joined by *or, nor,* or the correlative conjunctions *either . . . or* or *neither . . . nor,* make the verb agree with the noun or pronoun nearest the verb.

> EXAMPLES: *Cookies or ice cream is my favorite dessert.*
> *Either Cheryl or her friends are being invited.*
> *Neither ice storms nor snow is predicted today.*

11.5 PERSONAL PRONOUNS AS SUBJECTS

When using a personal pronoun as a subject, make sure to match it with the correct form of the verb *be.* (See the chart in Section 11.2.) Note especially that the pronoun *you* takes the forms *are* and *were,* regardless of whether it is singular or plural.

WATCH OUT! *You is* and *you was* are nonstandard forms and should be avoided in writing and speaking. *We was* and *they was* are also forms to be avoided.

> INCORRECT: *You was a good student.*

> CORRECT: *You were a good student.*

> INCORRECT: *They was starting a new school.*

> CORRECT: *They were starting a new school.*

11.6 INDEFINITE PRONOUNS AS SUBJECTS

Some indefinite pronouns are always singular; some are always plural.

Singular Indefinite Pronouns			
another	either	neither	one
anybody	everybody	nobody	somebody
anyone	everyone	no one	someone
anything	everything	nothing	something
each	much		

EXAMPLES: *Each of the writers was given an award.*
Somebody in the room upstairs is sleeping.

Plural Indefinite Pronouns			
both	few	many	several

EXAMPLES: *Many of the books in our library are not in circulation.*
Few have been returned recently.

Still other indefinite pronouns may be either singular or plural.

Singular or Plural Indefinite Pronouns		
all	more	none
any	most	some

The number of the indefinite pronoun *any* or *none* often depends on the intended meaning.

EXAMPLES: *Any of these topics has potential for a good article.* (any one topic)
Any of these topics have potential for good articles. (all of the many topics)

The indefinite pronouns *all, some, more, most,* and *none* are singular when they refer to quantities or parts of things. They are plural when they refer to numbers of individual things. Context will usually give a clue.

EXAMPLES: *All of the flour is gone.* (referring to a quantity)
All of the flowers are gone. (referring to individual items)

11.7 INVERTED SENTENCES

A sentence in which the subject follows the verb is called an **inverted sentence.** A subject can follow a verb or part of a verb phrase in a question; a sentence beginning with *here* or *there*; or a sentence in which an adjective, an adverb, or a phrase is placed first.

EXAMPLES: *There clearly are far too many cooks in this kitchen.*
What is the correct ingredient for this stew?
Far from the embroiled cooks stands the master chef.

TIP To check subject-verb agreement in some inverted sentences, place the subject before the verb. For example, change *There are many people* to *Many people are there.*

11.8 SENTENCES WITH PREDICATE NOMINATIVES

In a sentence containing a predicate noun (nominative), the verb should agree with the subject, not the predicate noun.

EXAMPLES: *The speeches of Martin Luther King Jr. are a landmark in American civil rights history.* (*Speeches* is the subject— not *landmark*—and it takes the plural verb *are.*)
One landmark in American civil rights history is the speeches of Martin Luther King Jr. (The subject is *landmark*—not *speeches*—and it takes the singular verb *is.*)

11.9 *DON'T* AND *DOESN'T* AS AUXILIARY VERBS

The auxiliary verb *doesn't* is used with singular subjects and with the personal pronouns *she, he,* and *it.* The auxiliary verb *don't* is used with plural subjects and with the personal pronouns *I, we, you,* and *they.*

SINGULAR: *She doesn't know Martin Luther King Jr.'s famous "I Have a Dream" speech. Doesn't the young woman read very much?*

COMMON CORE L1

GRAMMAR PRACTICE ANSWERS

1. *learn*
2. *offers*
3. *think*
4. *go; hang*
5. *go*
6. *has*
7. *want*
8. *are*
9. *are*
10. *leaves*

PLURAL: *We don't have the speech memorized.*
Don't speakers usually memorize their speeches?

11.10 COLLECTIVE NOUNS AS SUBJECTS

Collective nouns are singular nouns that name groups of persons or things. *Team,* for example, is the collective name of a group of individuals. A collective noun takes a singular verb when the group acts as a single unit. It takes a plural verb when the members of the group act separately

EXAMPLES: *Our team usually wins.* (The team as a whole wins.)
Our team vote differently on most issues. (The individual members vote.)

11.11 RELATIVE PRONOUNS AS SUBJECTS

When the relative pronoun *who, which,* or *that* is used as a subject in an adjective clause, the verb in the clause must agree in number with the antecedent of the pronoun.

SINGULAR: *I didn't read the **poem** about fireflies that was assigned.*

The antecedent of the relative pronoun *that* is the singular *poem*; therefore, *that* is singular and must take the singular verb *was.*

PLURAL: *Mary Oliver and Pat Moran, who are very different from each other, are both outstanding poets.*

The antecedent of the relative pronoun *who* is the plural compound subject *Mary Oliver and Pat Moran.* Therefore *who* is plural, and it takes the plural verb *are.*

Grammar Practice

Locate the subject of each verb in parentheses in the sentences below. Then choose the correct verb form.

1. In our school, students have a chance to (learn, learns) many techniques and media for making art.
2. Our art program (offer, offers) many different types of classes throughout the year.
3. Many of the students (think, thinks) that the summer is a good time for taking art class.
4. Some (go, goes) to camp, work part-time jobs, or take classes during the summer months, while others just (hang, hangs) around.
5. For those who (go, goes) to school for art class, the experience will be worth the time.
6. Everyone (has, have) a chance to try new techniques, such as printmaking or computer manipulation of photo-graphs and drawings.
7. Does anyone (want, wants) to discover creative ideas in art class?
8. Found objects, such as discarded wire or consumer by-products (is, are) useful for creating art with an environ-mental message.
9. There (is, are) many beautiful objects made from old things.
10. Each of the students (leave, leaves) art class having learned something special.

R54   Student Resources

Vocabulary and Spelling

COMMON CORE L 4a–d, L 5a–c, L 6

The key to becoming an independent reader is to develop a tool kit of vocabulary strategies. By learning and practicing the strategies, you'll know what to do when you encounter unfamiliar words while reading. You'll also know how to refine the words you use for different situations—personal, school, and work.

Being a good speller is important when communicating your ideas in writing. Learning basic spelling rules and checking your spelling in a dictionary will help you spell words that you may not use frequently.

1 Using Context Clues

The context of a word is made up of the punctuation marks, words, sentences, and paragraphs that surround the word. A word's context can give you important clues about its meaning.

1.1 GENERAL CONTEXT

Sometimes you need to determine the meaning of an unfamiliar word by reading all the information in a passage.

> *The sweater was of inferior quality. It was torn and had several buttons missing.*

You can figure out from the context that *inferior* means "poor or low."

1.2 SPECIFIC CONTEXT CLUES

Sometimes writers help you understand the meanings of words by providing specific clues such as those shown in the chart.

1.3 IDIOMS, SLANG, AND FIGURATIVE LANGUAGE

An **idiom** is an expression whose overall meaning is different from the meaning of the individual words. **Slang** is informal language in which madeup words and ordinary words are used to mean something different from their meanings in formal English. **Figurative language** is language that communicates meaning beyond the literal meaning of the words. Use context clues to figure out the meanings of idioms, slang, and figurative language.

Button your lip about the party. (idiom; means "keep quiet")

That's a really bad jacket; I want one. (slang; means "good-looking, excellent")

My brother had tried to make dinner. The kitchen was a battleground of dirty dishes, stains, spills, and potato peels. (figurative language; battleground, dirty dishes, stains, spills, and potato peels represent a messy scene)

Specific Context Clues		
Type of Clue	**Key Words/ Phrases**	**Example**
Definition or restatement of the meaning of the word	or, which is, that is, in other words, also known as, also called	Most chemicals are *toxic*, or **poisonous.**
Example following an unfamiliar word	such as, like, as if, for example, especially, including	*Amphibians,* such as **frogs and salamanders,** live in the pond by our house.
Comparison with a more familiar word or concept	as, like, also, similar to, in the same way, likewise	Like the rest of my *frugal* family, I always **save** most of the money I earn.

continued

Contrast with a familiar word or experience	unlike, but, however, although, on the other hand, on the contrary	I wish I had more *ingenuity* in making money instead of simply relying on the **same old** babysitting jobs.
Cause-and-effect relationship in which one term is familiar	because, since, when, consequently, as a result, therefore	Because the chemicals are *flammable*, the scientists wear special **fireresistant** clothing.

2 Analyzing Word Structure

Many words can be broken into smaller parts. These word parts include base words, roots, prefixes, and suffixes.

2.1 BASE WORDS

A **base word** is a word part that by itself is also a word. Other words or word parts can be added to base words to form new words.

2.2 ROOTS

A **root** is a word part that contains the core meaning of the word. Many English words contain roots that come from older languages such as Greek, Latin, Old English (Anglo-Saxon), and Norse. Knowing the meaning of the word's root can help you determine the word's meaning.

Root	Meaning	Example
photo (Greek)	light	photography
therm (Greek)	heat	thermometer
cred (Latin)	believe	credit

continued

mot (Latin)	move	motion
hēadfod (Old English)	head, top	headfirst

2.3 PREFIXES

A **prefix** is a word part attached to the beginning of a word. Most prefixes come from Greek, Latin, or Old English.

Prefix	Meaning	Example
mal-	bad or wrong	**mal**function
micro-	small or short	**micro**scope
semi-	half	**semi**circle

2.4 SUFFIXES

A **suffix** is a word part that appears at the end of a root or base word to form a new word. Some suffixes do not change word meaning. These suffixes are:

- added to nouns to change the number of persons or objects
- added to verbs to change the tense
- added to modifiers to change the degree of comparison

Suffix	Meaning	Example
-s, -es	to change the number of a noun	lock + s = locks
-d, -ed, -ing	to change verb tense	stew + ed = stewed
-er, -est	to indicate comparison in modifiers	mild + er = milder soft + est = softest

Other suffixes can be added to the root or base to change the word's meaning. These suffixes can also determine a word's part of speech.

Suffix	Meaning	Example
-er	one who does	teacher
-able	capable of	readable
-ly	in what manner	slowly

2.5 CONTENT-AREA VOCABULARY

Knowing the meaning of Greek, Latin, and Anglo-Saxon word parts can help you figure out the meaning of content-area vocabulary.

Word Part	Meaning	Example
derm	skin	dermatologist
logy	study of	astrology
bio	life	biography
hydr	water	hydrant
hypo	below, beneath	hypodermic
vid/vis	to see	visual
fract	to break	fraction

Strategies for Understanding Unfamiliar Words

- Look for any prefixes or suffixes. Remove them so that you can concentrate on the base word or the root.
- See if you recognize any elements—prefix, suffix, root, or base—of the word. You may be able to guess its meaning by analyzing one or two elements.
- Think about the way the word is used in the sentence. Use the context and the word parts to make a logical guess about the word's meaning.
- Look in a dictionary to see whether you are correct.

Practice and Apply

Use the strategies in this section and the vocabulary lessons in this book to help you figure out the meanings of the following content-area words.

forefathers	vision	microfilm
biology	fracture	import
auditory	ecology	hypothermia

3 Understanding Word Origins

3.1 ETYMOLOGIES

Etymologies show the origin and historical development of a word. When you study a word's history and origin, you can find out when, where, and how the word came to be.

ge·om·e·try (jē-ŏmʹĭ-trē) *n.,* pl. **-tries 1.** The mathematics of the properties, measurement, and relationships of points, lines, angles, surfaces, and solids. **2.** Arrangement. **3.** A physical arrangement suggesting geometric lines and shapes. [from Greek *geōmetriā,* from *geōmetrein,* to measure land].

3.2 WORD FAMILIES

Words that have the same root make up a word family and have related meanings. The following chart shows a common Greek root and a common Latin root. Notice how the meanings of the example words are related to the meanings of their roots.

Latin Root	*sens: "sense or feel"*
English	**sensory** relating to the senses **sensitive** responsive to sensations **sensation** a perception or feeling

continued

Greek Root	ast(e)r: "star"
English	**asteroid** a small object in outer space
	asterisk a star-shaped punctuation mark
	astronomy the study of outer space

3.3 FOREIGN WORDS

The English language includes words from diverse languages, such as French, Dutch, Spanish, Italian, and Chinese. Many words have stayed the way they were in their original languages.

French	Dutch	Spanish	Italian
ballet	boss	canyon	diva
vague	caboose	rodeo	cupola
mirage	dock	bronco	spaghetti

4 Synonyms and Antonyms

4.1 SYNONYMS

A **synonym** is a word with a meaning similar to that of another word. You can find synonyms in a thesaurus or a dictionary. In a dictionary, synonyms are often given as part of the definition of the word. The following word pairs are synonyms:

satisfy/please   occasionally/sometimes

rob/steal   schedule/agenda

4.2 ANTONYMS

An **antonym** is a word with a meaning opposite that of another word. The following word pairs are antonyms:

accurate/incorrect similar/different

fresh/stale   unusual/ordinary

5 Denotation and Connotation

5.1 DENOTATION

A word's dictionary meaning is called its **denotation.** For example, the denotation of the word *thin* is "having little flesh; spare; lean."

5.2 CONNOTATION

The images or feelings you connect to a word add a finer shade of meaning, called **connotation.** The connotation of a word goes beyond its basic dictionary definition. Writers use connotations of words to communicate positive or negative feelings.

Positive	Negative
slender	scrawny
thrifty	cheap
young	immature

Make sure you understand the denotation and connotation of a word when you read it or use it.

6 Analogies

An **analogy** is a comparison based on similarities between some things. Analogies can be used to explain unfamiliar words, subjects, or ideas in terms of familiar ones. An **analogy problem** shows a relationship between pairs of words. The relationship between the first pair of words is the same as the relationship between the second pair. Two relationships that analogy problems can express are part to whole and whole to part.

Part to Whole

handle : mug :: hilt : _____

a. hammer **b.** jewelry **c.** plate **d.** sword

*Read this analogy as "handle **is to** mug as hilt **is to** _____."*

What is the relationship between a *handle* and a *mug*? (A *handle* is the part designed for holding a *mug*.)

A *hilt* is part of which item? (A *hilt* is the handle of a *sword*.)

Whole to Part

horse : mane :: pheasant : _____

a. bird **b.** feather **c.** paw **d.** animal

What is the relationship between a *horse* and a *mane*? (A *horse* has a *mane,* the long hair along the top and sides of its neck.)

Which item is part of a *pheasant*? (The bird called a *pheasant* has a *feather* covering.)

7 Homonyms, Homographs, and Homophones

7.1 HOMONYMS

Homonyms are words that have the same spelling and sound but have different meanings.

> *The snake shed its skin in the shed behind the house.*

Shed can mean "to lose by natural process," but an identically spelled word means "a small structure."

If only one of the meanings of a homonym is familiar to you, use context clues to help you define the word if it is used in an unfamiliar way.

7.2 HOMOGRAPHS

Homographs are words that are spelled the same but have different meanings and origins. Some are also pronounced differently, as in these examples.

> *Please close the door. (klōz)*
>
> *That was a close call. (klōs)*

If you see a word used in a way that is unfamiliar to you, check a dictionary to see if it is a homograph.

7.3 HOMOPHONES

Homophones are words that sound alike but have different meanings and spellings. The following homophones are frequently misused:

it's/its   they're/their/there

to/too/two   stationary/stationery

Many misused homophones are pronouns and contractions. Whenever you are unsure whether to write *your* or *you're* and *who's* or *whose,* ask yourself if you mean *you are* and *who is/has.* If you do, write the contraction. For other homophones, such as *fair* and *fare,* use the meaning of the word to help you decide which one to use.

8 Words with Multiple Meanings

Some words have acquired additional meanings over time that are based on the original meaning.

> *I had to be replaced in the cast of the play because of the cast on my arm.*

The word *cast* has two meanings here, but both have the same origin. All of the meanings of *cast* are listed in one entry in the dictionary.

9 Specialized Vocabulary

Specialized vocabulary refers to terms used in a particular field of study or work. For example, science and mathematics each has its own technical or specialized vocabulary. You can use context clues, dictionaries on specific subjects, atlases, or manuals to help you define these terms.

10 Using Reference Sources

10.1 DICTIONARIES

A **general dictionary** will tell you a word's definitions, spelling, syllables, pronunciation, parts of speech, and history and origin.

① **tan·gi·ble** **②** (tăn´jə-bəl) *adj.* **③**
④ **1a.** Discernible by the touch; palpable. **b.** Possible to touch. **c.** Possible to be treated as fact; real or concrete. **2.** Possible to understand or realize. **3.** *Law* Relating to or being property, such as land, objects, and goods. [Late Latin *tangibilis,* from Latin *tangere,* to touch.] **⑤**

① Entry word syllabication
② Pronunciation
③ Part of speech
④ Definitions
⑤ Etymology

A **specialized dictionary** focuses on terms related to a particular field of study or work.

10.2 THESAURI

A **thesaurus** (plural, *thesauri*) is a dictionary of synonyms. A thesaurus can be especially helpful when you find yourself using the same modifiers over and over again.

10.3 SYNONYM FINDERS

A **synonym finder** is often included in wordprocessing software. It enables you to highlight a word and be shown a display of its synonyms.

10.4 GLOSSARIES

A **glossary** is a list of specialized terms, their definitions, and sometimes their pronunciations. Many textbooks contain glossaries, which are found at the back of the book. In fact, this text has three glossaries: the **Glossary of Literary and Informational Terms,** the **Glossary of Academic Vocabulary,** and the **Glossary of Critical Vocabulary.** Use these glossaries to help you understand how terms are used in this textbook. You can find electronic versions of many reference sources on the Internet, or in software programs at your school or library.

11 Spelling Rules

11.1 WORDS ENDING IN A SILENT *E*

Before adding a suffix beginning with a vowel or *y* to a word ending in a silent *e,* drop the *e* (with some exceptions).

> amaze + -ing = amazing
> love + -able = lovable
> create + -ed = created
> nerve + -ous = nervous

Exceptions: *change + -able = changeable; courage + -ous = courageous*

When adding a suffix beginning with a consonant to a word ending in a silent *e,* keep the *e* (with some exceptions).

> late + -ly = lately
> spite + -ful = spiteful
> noise + -less = noiseless
> state + -ment = statement

Exceptions: *truly, argument, ninth, wholly, awful,* and others

When a suffix beginning with *a* or *o* is added to a word with a final silent *e,* the final *e* is usually retained if it is preceded by a soft *c* or a soft *g.*

> bridge + -able = bridgeable
> peace + -able = peaceable
> outrage + -ous = outrageous
> advantage + -ous = advantageous

When a suffix beginning with a vowel is added to words ending in *ee* or *oe,* the final, silent *e* is retained.

> agree + -ing = agreeing   free + -ing = freeing
> hoe + -ing = hoeing   see + -ing = seeing

11.2 WORDS ENDING IN *Y*

Before adding most suffixes to a word that ends in *y* preceded by a consonant, change the *y* to *i.*

> easy + -est = easiest
> crazy + -est = craziest
> silly + -ness = silliness
> marry + -age = marriage

Exceptions: *dryness, shyness,* and *slyness*

However, when you add *-ing,* the *y* does not change.

> empty + -ed = emptied   but
> empty + -ing = emptying

When adding a suffix to a word that ends in *y* preceded by a vowel, the *y* usually does not change.

> play + -er = player
> employ + -ed = employed
> coy + -ness = coyness
> pay + -able = payable

11.3 WORDS ENDING IN A CONSONANT

In **one-syllable** words that end in one consonant preceded by one short vowel, double the final consonant before adding a suffix beginning with a vowel, such as

-ed or *-ing.* These are sometimes called 1+1+1 words.

dip + -ed = dipped   **set + -ing = setting**

slim + -est = slimmest   **fit + -er = fitter**

The rule does not apply to words of one syllable that end in a consonant preceded by two vowels.

feel + -ing = feeling   **peel + -ed = peeled**

reap + -ed = reaped   **loot + -ed = looted**

In words of more than one syllable, double the final consonant when (1) the word ends with one consonant preceded by one vowel and (2) when the word is accented on the last syllable.

be•gin´   per•mit´   re•fer´

In the following examples, note that in the new words formed with suffixes, the accent remains on the same syllable:

be•gin´ + -ing = be•gin´ning = beginning

per•mit´ + -ed = per•mit´ted = permitted

Exceptions: In some words with more than one syllable, though the accent remains on the same syllable when a suffix is added, the final consonant is nevertheless not doubled, as in the following examples:

tra´vel + er = tra´vel•er = traveler

mar´ket + er = mar´ket•er = marketer

In the following examples, the accent does not remain on the same syllable; thus, the final consonant is not doubled:

re•fer´ + -ence = ref´er•ence = reference

con•fer´ + -ence = con´fer•ence = conference

11.4 PREFIXES AND SUFFIXES

When adding a prefix to a word, do not change the spelling of the base word. When a prefix creates a double letter, keep both letters.

dis- + approve = disapprove

re- + build = rebuild

ir- + regular = irregular

mis- + spell = misspell

anti- + trust = antitrust

il- + logical = illogical

When adding *-ly* to a word ending in *l,* keep both *l's.* When adding *-ness* to a word ending in *n,* keep both *n's.*

careful + -ly = carefully

sudden + -ness = suddenness

final + -ly = finally

thin + -ness = thinness

11.5 FORMING PLURAL NOUNS

To form the plural of most nouns, just add *-s.*

prizes   dreams   circles   stations

For most singular nouns ending in *o,* add *-s.*

solos   halos   studios   photos   pianos

For a few nouns ending in *o,* add *-es.*

heroes   tomatoes   potatoes   echoes

When the singular noun ends in *s, sh, ch, x,* or *z,* add *-es.*

waitresses   brushes   ditches

axes   buzzes

When a singular noun ends in *y* with a consonant before it, change the *y* to *i* and add *-es.*

army—armies   **candy—candies**

baby—babies   **diary—diaries**

ferry—ferries   **conspiracy—conspiracies**

When a vowel (*a, e, i, o, u*) comes before the *y,* just add *-s.*

boy—boys   **way—ways**

array—arrays   **alloy—alloys**

weekday —weekdays **jockey—jockeys**

For most nouns ending in *f* or *fe,* change the *f* to *v* and add *-es* or *-s.*

life—lives   **thief—thieves**

calf—calves   **shelf—shelves**

knife—knives   **loaf—loaves**

For some nouns ending in *f,* add *-s* to make the plural.

roofs   chiefs   reefs   beliefs

Some nouns have the same form for both singular and plural.

deer   sheep   moose   salmon   trout

For some nouns, the plural is formed in a special way.

man—men	goose—geese
ox—oxen	woman—women
mouse—mice	child—children

For a compound noun written as one word, form the plural by changing the last word in the compound to its plural form.

stepchild—stepchildren	firefly—fireflies

If a compound noun is written as a hyphenated word or as two separate words, change the most important word to the plural form.

brother-in-law—brothers-in-law

life jacket—life jackets

11.6 FORMING POSSESSIVES

If a noun is singular, add **'s.**

mother—my mother's car

Ross—Ross's desk

Exception: The **s** after the apostrophe is dropped after *Jesus', Moses',* and certain names in classical mythology (*Zeus'*). These possessive forms can thus be pronounced easily.

If a noun is plural and ends with **s,** add an apostrophe.

parents—my parents' car

the Santinis—the Santinis' house

If a noun is plural but does not end in **s,** add **'s.**

people—the people's choice

women—the women's coats

11.7 SPECIAL SPELLING PROBLEMS

Only one English word ends in **-sede:** *supersede.* Three words end in **-ceed:** *exceed, proceed,* and *succeed.* All other verbs ending in the sound "seed" are spelled with **-cede.**

concede	precede	recede	secede

In words with **ie** or **ei,** when the sound is long **e** (as in *she*), the word is spelled **ie** except after **c** (with some exceptions).

i before *e*	thief	relieve	field
	piece	grieve	pier
except after *c*	conceit	perceive	ceiling
	receive	receipt	
Exceptions:	either	neither	weird
	leisure	seize	

12 Commonly Confused Words

Words	Definitions	Examples
accept/ except	The verb *accept* means "to receive or believe"; *except* is usually a preposition meaning "excluding."	Did the teacher **accept** your report? Everyone smiled for the photographer **except** Jody.
advice/ advise	*Advise* is a verb; *advice* is a noun naming that which an *adviser* gives.	I **advise** you to take that job. Whom should I ask for **advice**?
affect/ effect	As a verb, *affect* means "to influence." *Effect* as a verb means "to cause." If you want a noun, you will almost always want *effect*.	How deeply did the news **affect** him? The students tried to **effect** a change in school policy. What **effect** did the acidic soil produce in the plants?
all ready/ already	*All ready* is an adjective meaning "fully ready." *Already* is an adverb meaning "before or by this time."	He was **all ready** to go at noon. I have **already** seen that movie.

continued

Words	Definitions	Examples
desert/ dessert	*Desert* (dĕz´ərt) means "a dry, sandy, barren region." *Desert* (dĭ-zûrt´) means "to abandon." *Dessert* (dĭ-zûrt´) is a sweet, such as cake.	The Sahara, in North Africa, is the world's largest **desert.** The night guard did not **desert** his post. Alison's favorite **dessert** is chocolate cake.
among/ between	*Between* is used when you are speaking of only two things. *Among* is used for three or more.	**Between** ice cream and sherbet, I prefer the latter. Gary Soto is **among** my favorite authors.
bring/take	*Bring* is used to denote motion toward a speaker or place. *Take* is used to denote motion away from such a person or place.	**Bring** the books over here, and I will **take** them to the library.
fewer/less	*Fewer* refers to the number of separate, countable units. *Less* refers to bulk quantity.	We have **less** literature and **fewer** selections in this year's curriculum.
leave/let	*Leave* means "to allow something to remain behind." *Let* means "to permit."	The librarian will **leave** some books on display but will not **let** us borrow any.
lie/lay	To *lie* is "to rest or recline." It does not take an object. *Lay* always takes an object.	Rover loves to **lie** in the sun. We always **lay** some bones next to him.
loose/lose	*Loose* (lo͞os) means "free, not restrained"; *lose* (lo͞oz) means "to misplace or fail to find."	Who turned the horses **loose?** I hope we won't **lose** any of them.
passed/ past	*Passed* is the past tense of *pass* and means "went by." *Past* is an adjective that means "of a former time." *Past* is also a noun that means "time gone by."	We **passed** through the Florida Keys during our vacation. My **past** experiences have taught me to set my alarm. Ebenezer Scrooge is a character who relives his **past.**
than/then	Use *than* in making comparisons. Use *then* on all other occasions.	Ramon is stronger **than** Mark. Cut the grass and **then** trim the hedges.
two/too/to	*Two* is the number. *Too* is an adverb meaning "also" or "very." Use *to* before a verb or as a preposition.	Meg had **to** go **to** town, **too.** We had **too** much reading **to** do. **Two** chapters is **too** many.
their/there/ they're	*Their* means "belonging to them." *There* means "in that place." *They're* is the contraction for "they are."	**There** is a movie playing at 9 P.M. **They're** going to see it with me. Sakara and Jessica drove away in **their** car after the movie.

Glossary of Literary and Informational Terms

Act An act is a major division within a play, similar to a chapter in a book. Each act may be further divided into smaller sections, called scenes. Plays can have as many as five acts or as few as one.

Adventure Story An adventure story is a literary work in which action is the main element. An **adventure novel** usually focuses on a main character who is on a mission and is facing many challenges and choices.

Alliteration Alliteration is the repetition of consonant sounds at the beginning of words. Note the repetition of the *b* sound in this line: The *b*oy's dog *b*egan *b*egging for *b*iscuits.

Allusion An allusion is a reference to a famous person, place, event, or work of literature.

Analogy An analogy is a point-by-point comparison between two things that are alike in some respect. Often, writers use analogies in nonfiction to explain unfamiliar subjects or ideas in terms of familiar ones.

See also Extended Metaphor; Metaphor; Simile.

Anecdote An anecdote is a short account of an event that is usually intended to entertain or make a point.

Antagonist The antagonist is a force working against the protagonist, or main character, in a story, play, or novel. The antagonist is usually another character but can be a force of nature, society itself, or an internal force within the main character.

See also Protagonist.

Argument An argument is speaking or writing that expresses a position on a problem and supports it with reasons and evidence. An argument often takes into account other points of view, anticipating and answering objections that opponents might raise.

See also Claim; Counterargument; Evidence.

Assonance Assonance is the repetition of vowel sounds within nonrhyming words. An example of assonance is the repetition of the *i* sound in the following line: Into the ink-filled jar she inserted the brush.

Assumption An assumption is an opinion or belief that is taken for granted. It can be about a specific situation, a person, or the world in general. Assumptions are often unstated.

Author's Message An author's message is the main idea or theme of a particular work.

See also Main Idea; Theme.

Author's Perspective An author's perspective is the unique combination of ideas, values, feelings, and beliefs that influences the way the writer looks at a topic. Tone, or attitude, often reveals an author's perspective.

See also Author's Purpose; Tone.

Author's Position An author's position is his or her opinion on an issue or topic.

See also Claim; Writer's Point of View.

Author's Purpose A writer usually writes for one or more of these purposes: to express thoughts or feelings, to inform or explain, to persuade, and to entertain.

See also Author's Perspective; Writer's Point of View.

Autobiography An autobiography is a writer's account of his or her own life. In almost every case, it is told from the first-person point of view. Generally, an autobiography focuses on the most significant events and people in the writer's life over a period of time.

See also Memoir.

Ballad A ballad is a type of narrative poem that tells a story and was originally meant to be sung or recited. Because it tells a story, a ballad has a setting, a plot, and characters. **Folk ballads** were composed orally and handed down by word of mouth from generation to generation.

Bias In a piece of writing, the author's bias is the side of an issue that he or she favors. Words with extremely positive or negative connotations are often a signal of an author's bias.

Biography A biography is the true account of a person's life, written by another person.

As such, biographies are usually told from a third-person point of view. The writer of a biography usually researches his or her subject in order to present accurate information. The best biographers strive for honesty and balance in their accounts of their subjects' lives.

Bibliography A bibliography is a list of related books and other materials used to write a text. Bibliographies can be good sources for further study on a subject.

See also Works Consulted.

Business Correspondence Business correspondence is written business communications such as business letters, e-mails, and memos. In general, business correspondence is brief, to the point, clear, courteous, and professional.

Cast of Characters In the script of a play, a cast of characters is a list of all the characters in the play, usually in order of appearance. It may include a brief description of each character.

Cause and Effect Two events are related by cause and effect when one event brings about, or causes, the other. The event that happens first is the **cause**; the one that follows is the **effect.** Cause and effect is also a way of organizing an entire piece of writing. It helps writers show the relationships between events or ideas.

Character Characters are the people, animals, or imaginary creatures who take part in the action of a work of literature. Like real people, characters display certain qualities, or **character traits,** that develop and change over time, and they usually have **motivations,** or reasons, for their behaviors.

> **Central character:** Central or main characters are the most important characters in literary works. Generally, the plot of a short story focuses on one main character, but a novel may have several main characters.

> **Minor characters:** The less important characters in a literary work are known as minor characters. The story is not centered on them, but they help carry out the action of the story and help the reader learn more about the main character.

Dynamic character: A dynamic character is one who undergoes important changes as a plot unfolds. The changes occur because of the character's actions and experiences in the story. The changes are usually internal and may be good or bad. Main characters are usually, though not always, dynamic.

Static character: A static character is one who remains the same throughout a story. The character may experience events and have interactions with other characters, but he or she is not changed because of them.

See also Characterization; Character Traits.

Characterization The way a writer creates and develops characters is known as characterization. There are four basic methods of characterization.

- The writer may make direct comments about a character through the voice of the narrator.
- The writer may describe the character's physical appearance.
- The writer may present the character's own thoughts, speech, and actions.
- The writer may present thoughts, speech, and actions of other characters.

See also Character; Character Traits.

Character Traits Character traits are the qualities shown by a character. Traits may be physical (brown eyes) or expressions of personality (shyness). Writers reveal the traits of their characters through methods of characterization. Sometimes writers directly state a character's traits, but more often readers need to infer traits from a character's words, actions, thoughts, appearance, and relationships. Examples of words that describe traits include *courageous, humble, generous,* and *wild.*

Chronological Order Chronological order is the arrangement of events by their order of occurrence. This type of organization is used in fictional narratives and in historical writing, biography, and autobiography.

Claim In an argument, a claim is the writer's position on an issue or problem. Although an argument focuses on supporting one claim, a writer may make more than one claim in a text.

Clarify Clarifying is a reading strategy that helps readers understand or make clear what they are reading. Readers usually clarify by rereading, reading aloud, or discussing.

Classification Classification is a pattern of organization in which objects, ideas, and/or information are presented in groups, or classes, based on common characteristics.

Cliché A cliché is an overused expression. "Better late than never" and "hard as nails" are common examples. Good writers generally avoid clichés unless they are using them in dialogue to indicate something about a character's personality.

Climax The climax stage is the point of greatest interest in a story or play. The climax usually occurs toward the end of a story, after the reader has understood the **conflict** and become emotionally involved with the characters. At the climax, the conflict is resolved and the outcome of the plot usually becomes clear.

See also Plot.

Comedy A comedy is a dramatic work that is light and often humorous in tone, usually ending happily with a peaceful resolution of the main conflict.

Compare and Contrast To compare and contrast is to identify the similarities and differences of two or more subjects. Compare and contrast is also a pattern of organizing an entire piece of writing.

Conclusion A conclusion is a statement of belief based on evidence, experience, and reasoning. A valid conclusion is one that logically follows from the facts or statements upon which it is based.

Conflict A conflict is a struggle between opposing forces. Almost every story has a main conflict—a conflict that is the story's focus. An **external conflict** involves a character who struggles against a force outside him- or herself, such as nature, a physical obstacle, or another character. An **internal conflict** is one that occurs within a character.

See also Plot.

Connect Connecting is a reader's process of relating the content of a text to his or her own knowledge and experience.

Connotation A word's connotations are the ideas and feelings associated with the word, as opposed to its dictionary definition. For example, the word *mother,* in addition to its basic meaning ("a female parent"), has connotations of love, warmth, and security.

Consumer Documents Consumer documents are printed materials that accompany products and services. They usually provide information about the use, care, operation, or assembly of the product or service they accompany. Some common consumer documents are applications, contracts, warranties, manuals, instructions, labels, brochures, and schedules.

Context Clues When you encounter an unfamiliar word, you can often use context clues to understand it. Context clues are the words or phrases surrounding the word that provide hints about the word's meaning.

Counterargument A counterargument is an argument made to oppose another argument. A good argument anticipates opposing viewpoints and provides counterarguments to disprove them.

Couplet A couplet is a rhymed pair of lines. A couplet may be written in any rhythmic pattern: Follow your heart's desire/And good things may transpire.

See also Stanza.

Credibility Credibility is the believability or trustworthiness of a source and the information it provides.

Critical Essay *See* Essay.

Critical Review A critical review is an evaluation or critique by a reviewer, or critic. Types of reviews include film reviews, book reviews, music reviews, and art show reviews.

Database A database is a collection of information that can be quickly and easily accessed and searched and from which information can be easily retrieved. It is frequently presented in an electronic format.

Debate A debate is basically an argument—but a very structured one that requires a good deal of preparation. In school settings, debate usually is a formal contest in which two opposing teams defend and attack a proposition.

See also Argument.

Deductive Reasoning Deductive reasoning is a way of thinking that begins with a generalization, presents a specific situation, and then moves forward with facts and evidence toward a logical conclusion. The following passage has a deductive argument embedded in it: "All students in the math class must take the quiz on Friday. Since Lana is in the class, she had better show up." This deductive argument can be broken down as follows: generalization—All students in the math class must take the quiz on Friday; specific situation—Lana is a student who is in the math class; conclusion—Therefore, Lana must take the math quiz.

Denotation A word's denotation is its dictionary definition.

See also Connotation.

Description Description is writing that helps a reader to picture events, objects, and characters. To create descriptions, writers often use **imagery**—words and phrases that appeal to the reader's senses.

Dialect A dialect is a form of a language that is spoken in a particular place or by a particular group of people. Dialects may feature unique pronunciations, vocabulary, and grammar.

Dialogue Dialogue is written conversation between two or more characters. Writers use dialogue to bring characters to life and to give readers insights into the characters' qualities, traits, and reactions to other characters. In fiction, dialogue is usually set off with quotation marks. In drama, stories are told primarily through dialogue.

Diary A diary is a daily record of a writer's thoughts, experiences, and feelings. As such, it is a type of autobiographical writing. The terms *diary* and *journal* are often used synonymously.

Dictionary *See* Reference Works.

Drama A drama, or play, is a form of literature meant to be performed by actors in front of an audience. In a drama, the characters' dialogue and actions tell the story. The written form of a play is known as a script. A script usually includes dialogue, a cast of characters, and stage directions that give instructions about performing the drama. The person who writes the drama is known as the playwright or dramatist.

Draw Conclusions To draw a conclusion is to make a judgment or arrive at a belief based on evidence, experience, and reasoning.

Dynamic Character *See* Character.

Editorial An editorial is an opinion piece that usually appears on the editorial page of a newspaper or as part of a news broadcast. The editorial section of the newspaper presents opinions rather than objective news reports.

See also Op/Ed Piece.

Either/Or Fallacy An either/or fallacy is a statement that suggests that there are only two choices available in a situation when in fact there are more than two.

Emotional Appeals Emotional appeals are messages that create strong feelings to make a point. An appeal to fear is a message that taps into people's fear of losing their safety or security. An appeal to pity is a message that taps into people's sympathy and compassion for others to build support for an idea, a cause, or a proposed action. An appeal to vanity is a message that attempts to persuade by tapping into people's desire to feel good about themselves.

Encyclopedia *See* Reference Works.

Epic Poem An epic poem is a long narrative poem about the adventures of a hero whose actions reflect the ideals and values of a nation or a group of people.

Essay An essay is a short work of nonfiction that deals with a single subject. There are many types of essays. An **expository essay** presents or explains information and ideas. A **personal essay** usually reflects the writer's experiences, feelings, and personality. A **persuasive essay** attempts to convince the reader to adopt a certain viewpoint. A **critical essay** evaluates a situation or a work of art.

Evaluate To evaluate is to examine something carefully and to judge its value or worth. Evaluating is an important skill. A reader can evaluate the actions of a particular character, for example. A reader can also form opinions about the value of an entire work.

Evidence Evidence is a specific piece of information that supports a claim. Evidence can take the form of a fact, a quotation, an example, a statistic, or a personal experience, among other things.

Exaggeration An extreme overstatement of an idea is called an exaggeration. It is often used for purposes of emphasis or humor.

Exposition Exposition is the first stage of a typical story plot. The exposition provides important background information and introduces the setting and the important characters. The conflict the characters face may also be introduced in the exposition, or it may be introduced later, in the rising action.

See also Plot.

Expository Essay *See* Essay.

Extended Metaphor An extended metaphor is a figure of speech that compares two essentially unlike things at some length and in several ways. It does not contain the words *like* or *as*.

See also Metaphor.

External Conflict *See* Conflict.

Fable A fable is a brief tale told to illustrate a moral or teach a lesson. Often the moral of a fable appears in a distinct and memorable statement near the tale's beginning or end.

See also Moral.

Fact Versus Opinion A fact is a statement that can be proved, or verified. An opinion, on the other hand, is a statement that cannot be proved because it expresses a person's beliefs, feelings, or thoughts.

See also Generalization; Inference.

Fallacy A fallacy is an error—usually in reasoning. Typically, a fallacy is based on an incorrect inference or a misuse of evidence.

See also Either/Or Fallacy; Logical Appeal; Overgeneralization.

Falling Action The falling action is the stage of the plot in which the story begins to draw to a close. The falling action comes after the climax and before the resolution. Events in the falling action show the results of the important decision or action that happened at the climax. Tension eases as the falling action begins; however, the final outcome of the story is not yet fully worked out at this stage.

See also Climax; Plot.

Fantasy Fantasy is a type of fiction that is highly imaginative and portrays events, settings, or characters that are unrealistic. The setting might be a nonexistent world, the plot might involve magic or the supernatural, and the characters might have superhuman powers.

Farce Farce is a type of exaggerated comedy that features an absurd plot, ridiculous situations, and humorous dialogue. The main purpose of a farce is to keep an audience laughing. Comic devices typically used in farces include mistaken identity, wordplay (such as puns and double meanings), and exaggeration.

Faulty Reasoning *See* Fallacy.

Feature Article A feature article is a main article in a newspaper or a cover story in a magazine.

Fiction Fiction is prose writing that tells an imaginary story. The writer of a fictional work might invent all the events and characters or might base parts of the story on real people and events. The basic elements of fiction are plot, character, setting, and theme. Fiction includes short stories, novellas, and novels.

See also Novel; Novella; Short Story.

Figurative Language In figurative language, words are used in an imaginative way to express ideas that are not literally true. "Tasha's money is burning a hole in her pocket" is an example of figurative language. The sentence does not really mean that Tasha's pocket is on fire.

Instead, it means that Tasha is anxious to spend her money. Figurative language is used for comparison, emphasis, and emotional effect.

See also Metaphor; Onomatopoeia; Personification; Simile.

First-Person Point of View *See* Point of View.

Flashback In a literary work, a flashback is an interruption of the action to present events that took place at an earlier time. A flashback provides information that can help a reader better understand a character's current situation.

Foil A foil is a character who provides a striking contrast to another character. By using a foil, a writer can call attention to certain traits possessed by a main character or simply enhance a character by contrast.

Folklore The traditions, customs, and stories that are passed down within a culture are known as its folklore. Folklore includes various types of literature, such as legends, folk tales, myths, trickster tales, and fables.

See Fable; Folk Tale; Myth.

Folk Tale A folk tale is a story that has been passed from generation to generation by word of mouth. Folk tales may be set in the distant past and involve supernatural events. The characters in them may be animals, people, or superhuman beings.

Foreshadowing Foreshadowing occurs when a writer provides hints that suggest future events in a story. Foreshadowing creates suspense and makes readers eager to find out what will happen.

Form The structure or organization of a work of writing is often called its form. The form of a poem includes the arrangement of its words and lines on the page.

Free Verse Poetry without regular patterns of rhyme and rhythm is called free verse. Some poets use free verse to capture the sounds and rhythms of ordinary speech.

See also Rhyme.

Generalization A generalization is a broad statement about a class or category of people, ideas, or things based on a study of, or a belief about, some of its members.

See also Overgeneralization; Stereotyping.

Genre The term *genre* refers to a category in which a work of literature is classified. The major genres in literature are fiction, nonfiction, poetry, and drama.

Government Publications Government publications are documents produced by government organizations. Pamphlets, brochures, and reports are just some of the many forms these publications take. Government publications can be good resources for a wide variety of topics.

Graphic Aid A graphic aid is a visual tool that is printed, handwritten, or drawn. Charts, diagrams, graphs, photographs, and maps are examples of graphic aids.

Graphic Organizer A graphic organizer is a "word picture"—a visual illustration of a verbal statement—that helps a reader understand a text. Charts, tables, webs, and diagrams can all be graphic organizers. Graphic organizers and graphic aids can look the same. However, graphic organizers and graphic aids do differ in how they are used. Graphic aids help deliver important information to students using a text. Graphic organizers are actually created by students themselves. They help students understand the text or organize information.

Haiku Haiku is a form of Japanese poetry in which 17 syllables are arranged in three lines of 5, 7, and 5 syllables. The rules of haiku are strict. In addition to following the syllabic count, the poet must create a clear picture that will evoke a strong emotional response in the reader. Nature is a particularly important source of inspiration for Japanese haiku poets, and details from nature are often the subjects of their poems.

Hero A hero is a main character or protagonist in a story. In older literary works, heroes tend to be better than ordinary humans. They are typically courageous, strong, honorable, and intelligent. They are protectors of society who hold back the forces of evil and fight to make the world a better place. In modern literature, a hero may simply be the most important character in a story. Such a hero is often an ordinary person with ordinary problems.

Historical Documents Historical documents are writings that have played a significant role in human events. The Declaration of Independence, for example, is a historical document.

Historical Dramas Historical dramas are plays that take place in the past and are based on real events. In many of these plays, the characters are also based on real historical figures. The dialogue and the action, however, are mostly created by the playwright.

Historical Fiction A short story or a novel can be called historical fiction when it is set in the past and includes real places and real events of historical importance.

How-To Book A how-to book explains how to do something—usually an activity, a sport, or a household project.

Humor Humor is a quality that provokes laughter or amusement. Writers create humor through exaggeration, amusing descriptions, irony, and witty and insightful dialogue.

Hyperbole Hyperbole is a figure of speech in which the truth is exaggerated for emphasis or humorous effect.

Idiom An idiom is an expression that has a meaning different from the meaning of its individual words. For example, "to go to the dogs" is an idiom meaning "to go to ruin."

Imagery Imagery consists of words and phrases that appeal to a reader's five senses. Writers use sensory details to help the reader imagine how things look, feel, smell, sound, and taste.

Implied Main Idea *See* Main Idea.

Index The index of a book is an alphabetized list of important topics covered in the book and the page numbers on which they can be found. An index can be used to quickly find specific information about a topic.

Inductive Reasoning Inductive reasoning is the process of logical reasoning that starts with observations, examples, and facts and moves on to a general conclusion or principle.

Inference An inference is a logical guess that is made based on facts and one's own knowledge and experience.

Informational Text Informational text is writing that provides factual information. Examples include news reports, a science textbook, manuals, lab reports, and signs. Informational text also includes literary nonfiction, such as personal essays, opinion pieces, speeches, biographies, and historical accounts.

Internal Conflict *See* Conflict.

Internet The Internet is a global, interconnected system of computer networks that allows for communication through e-mail, listservs, and the World Wide Web. The Internet connects computers and computer users throughout the world.

Interview An interview is a conversation conducted by a writer or reporter in which facts or statements are elicited from another person, recorded, and then broadcast or published.

Journal A journal is a periodical publication issued by a legal, medical, or other professional organization. The term may also be used to refer to a diary or daily record.

Legend A legend is a story handed down from the past about a specific person, usually someone of heroic accomplishments. Legends usually have some basis in historical fact.

Limerick A limerick is a short, humorous poem composed of five lines. It usually has the rhyme scheme *aabba,* created by two rhyming couplets followed by a fifth line that rhymes with the first couplet. A limerick typically has a sing-song rhythm.

Loaded Language Loaded language consists of words with strongly positive or negative connotations intended to influence a reader's or listener's attitude.

Logical Appeal A logical appeal is a way of writing or speaking that relies on logic and facts. It appeals to people's reasoning or intellect rather than to their values or emotions. Flawed logical appeals—that is, errors in reasoning—are called logical fallacies.

See also Fallacy.

Logical Argument A logical argument is an argument in which the logical relationship between the support and claim is sound.

Lyric Poetry Lyric poetry is poetry that presents the personal thoughts and feelings of a single speaker. Most poems, other than narrative poems, are lyric poems. Lyric poetry can be in a variety of forms and cover many subjects, from love and death to everyday experiences.

Main Idea The main idea, or central idea, is the most important idea about a topic that a writer or speaker conveys. It can be the central idea of an entire work or of just a paragraph. Often, the main idea of a paragraph is expressed in a topic sentence. However, a main idea may just be implied, or suggested, by details. A main idea is typically supported by details.

Make Inferences *See* Inference.

Memoir A memoir is a form of autobiographical writing in which a writer shares his or her personal experiences and observations of significant events or people. Often informal or even intimate in tone, memoirs usually give readers insight into the impact of historical events on people's lives.

See also Autobiography.

Metaphor A metaphor is a comparison of two things that are basically unlike but have some qualities in common. Unlike a simile, a metaphor does not contain the words *like* or *as.*

See also Extended Metaphor; Figurative Language; Simile.

Meter In poetry, meter is the regular pattern of stressed (´) and unstressed (˘) syllables. Although poems have rhythm, not all poems have regular meter. Each unit of meter is known as a **foot** and is made up of one stressed syllable and one or two unstressed syllables.

See also Rhythm.

Minor Character *See* Character.

Monitor Monitoring is the strategy of checking your comprehension as you read and modifying the strategies you are using to suit your needs. Monitoring often includes the following strategies: questioning, clarifying, visualizing, predicting, connecting, and rereading.

Mood Mood is the feeling or atmosphere that a writer creates for the reader. Descriptive words, imagery, and figurative language all influence the mood of a work.

See also Tone.

Moral A moral is a lesson that a story teaches. A moral is often stated at the end of a fable.

See also Fable.

Motivation *See* Character.

Myth A myth is a traditional story that attempts to answer basic questions about human nature, origins of the world, mysteries of nature, and social customs.

Narrative Nonfiction Narrative nonfiction is writing that reads much like fiction, except that the characters, setting, and plot are real rather than imaginary. Narrative nonfiction includes autobiographies, biographies, and memoirs.

Narrative Poetry Poetry that tells a story is called narrative poetry. Like fiction, a narrative poem contains characters, a setting, and a plot. It might also contain such elements of poetry as rhyme, rhythm, imagery, and figurative language.

Narrator The narrator is the voice that tells a story. Sometimes the narrator is a character in the story. At other times, the narrator is an outside voice created by the writer. The narrator is not the same as the writer.

An **unreliable narrator** is one who tells a story or interprets events in a way that makes readers doubt what he or she is saying. An unreliable narrator is usually a character in the story. The narrator may be unreliable for a number of different reasons. For example, the narrator may not have all the facts or may be too young to understand the situation.

See also Point of View.

News Article A news article is writing that reports on a recent event. In newspapers, news articles are usually brief and to the point, presenting the most important facts first, followed by more detailed information.

Nonfiction Nonfiction is writing that tells about real people, places, and events. Unlike fiction, nonfiction is mainly written to convey factual information. Nonfiction includes a wide range of writing—newspaper articles, textbooks, instructional manuals, letters, essays, biographies, movie reviews, speeches, true-life adventure stories, advertising, and more.

Novel A novel is a long work of fiction. Like a short story, a novel is the product of a writer's imagination. Because a novel is considerably longer than a short story, a novelist can develop the characters and story line more thoroughly.

See also Fiction.

Novella A novella is a short prose tale, or short novel. It is longer than a short story and often teaches a moral, or satirizes a subject.

See also Short Story; Novel.

Ode An ode is a type of lyric poem that deals with serious themes, such as justice, truth, or beauty.

Onomatopoeia Onomatopoeia is the use of words whose sounds echo their meanings, such as *buzz, whisper, gargle,* and *murmur.*

Op/Ed Piece An op/ed piece is an opinion piece that typically appears opposite ("op") the editorial page of a newspaper. Unlike editorials, op/ed pieces are written and submitted by readers.

Oral Literature Oral literature consists of stories that have been passed down by word of mouth from generation to generation. Oral literature includes folk tales, legends, and myths. In more recent times, some examples of oral literature have been written down or recorded so that the stories can be preserved.

Organization *See* Pattern of Organization.

Overgeneralization An overgeneralization is a generalization that is too broad. You can often recognize overgeneralizations by the appearance of words and phrases such as *all, everyone, every time, any, anything, no one,* or *none.* An example is "None of the city's workers

really cares about keeping the environment clean." In all probability, there are many exceptions. The writer can't possibly know the feelings of every city worker.

Overview An overview is a short summary of a story, a speech, or an essay.

Paraphrase Paraphrasing is the restating of information in one's own words.

See also Summarize.

Pattern of Organization The term *pattern of organization* refers to the way ideas and information are arranged and organized. Patterns of organization include cause and effect, chronological, compare and contrast, classification, and problem-solution, among others.

See also Cause and Effect; Chronological Order; Classification; Compare and Contrast; Problem-Solution Order; Sequential Order.

Periodical A periodical is a magazine or another type of publication that is issued on a regular basis.

Personal Essay *See* Essay.

Personification The giving of human qualities to an animal, object, or idea is known as personification. For example, animals are personified when they have conversations with each other as if they were human.

See also Figurative Language.

Persuasion Persuasion is the art of swaying others' feelings, beliefs, or actions. Persuasion normally appeals to both the minds and the emotions of readers.

See also Emotional Appeals; Loaded Language; Logical Appeal.

Persuasive Essay *See* Essay.

Play *See* Drama.

Playwright *See* Drama.

Plot The series of events in a story is called the plot. The plot usually centers on a **conflict,** or struggle, faced by the main character. The action that the characters take to solve the problem builds toward a climax in the story. At this point, or shortly afterward, the problem is solved and the story ends. Most story plots have five stages: exposition, rising action, climax, falling action, and resolution.

See also Climax; Conflict; Exposition; Falling Action; Rising Action.

Poetry Poetry is a type of literature in which words are carefully chosen and arranged to create certain effects. Poets use a variety of sound devices, imagery, and figurative language to express emotions and ideas.

See also Alliteration; Assonance; Ballad; Free Verse; Imagery; Meter; Narrative Poetry; Rhyme; Rhythm; Stanza.

Point of View Point of view refers to how a writer chooses to narrate a story. When a story is told from the **first-person** point of view, the narrator is a character in the story and uses first-person pronouns, such as *I, me,* and *we.* In a story told from the **third-person** point of view, the narrator is not a character. Third-person narration makes use of pronouns such as *he, she, it,* and *they.* A writer's choice of narrator affects the information readers receive.

It is also important to consider whether a writer is writing from a **subjective** or an **objective** point of view. When writing from a subjective point of view, the writer includes personal opinions, feelings, and beliefs. When writing from an objective point of view, the writer leaves out personal opinions and instead presents information in a straightforward, unbiased way.

See also Narrator.

Predict Predicting is a reading strategy that involves using text clues to make a reasonable guess about what will happen next in a story.

Primary Source *See* Sources.

Prior Knowledge Prior knowledge is the knowledge a reader already possesses about a topic. This information might come from personal experiences, expert accounts, books, films, and other sources.

Problem-Solution Order Problem-solution order is a pattern of organization in which a problem is stated and analyzed and then one or more solutions are proposed and examined.

Prop The word *prop,* originally an abbreviation of the word *property,* refers to any physical object that is used in a drama.

Propaganda Propaganda is a form of communication that may use false or misleading information.

Prose The word *prose* refers to all forms of writing that are not in verse form. The term may be used to describe very different forms of writing—short stories as well as essays, for example.

Protagonist A protagonist is the main character in a story, play, or novel. The protagonist is involved in the main conflict of the story. Usually, the protagonist undergoes changes as the plot runs its course.

Public Documents Public documents are documents that were written for the public to provide information that is of public interest or concern. They include government documents, speeches, signs, and rules and regulations.

See also Government Publications.

Radio Play A radio play is a drama that is written specifically to be broadcast over the radio. Because the audience is not meant to see a radio play, sound effects are often used to help listeners imagine the setting and the action. The stage directions in the play's script indicate the sound effects.

Recurring Theme *See* Theme.

Reference Works Reference works are sources that contain facts and background information on a wide range of subjects. Most reference works are good sources of reliable information because they have been reviewed by experts. The following are some common reference works: encyclopedias, dictionaries, thesauri, almanacs, atlases, and directories.

Refrain A refrain is one or more lines repeated in each stanza of a poem.

See also Stanza.

Repetition Repetition is a technique in which a sound, word, phrase, or line is repeated for emphasis or unity. Repetition helps to reinforce meaning and create an appealing rhythm.

See also Alliteration; Sound Devices.

Resolution *See* Falling Action.

Review *See* Critical Review.

Rhetorical Questions Rhetorical questions are those that have such obvious answers that they do not require a reply. Writers often use them to suggest that their claim is so obvious that everyone should agree with it.

Rhyme Rhyme is the repetition of sounds at the end of words. Words rhyme when their accented vowels and the letters that follow have identical sounds. *Cat* and *hat* rhyme, as do *feather* and *leather.* The most common type of rhyme in poetry is called **end rhyme,** in which rhyming words come at the ends of lines. Rhyme that occurs within a line of poetry is called **internal rhyme.**

Rhyme Scheme A rhyme scheme is a pattern of end rhymes in a poem. A rhyme scheme is noted by assigning a letter of the alphabet, beginning with *a,* to each line. Lines that rhyme are given the same letter.

Rhythm Rhythm is a pattern of stressed and unstressed syllables in a line of poetry. Poets use rhythm to bring out the musical quality of language, to emphasize ideas, and to create moods. Devices such as alliteration, rhyme, assonance, and consonance often contribute to creating rhythm.

See also Meter.

Rising Action The rising action is the stage of the plot that develops the **conflict,** or struggle. During this stage, events occur that make the conflict more complicated. The events in the rising action build toward a **climax,** or turning point.

See also Plot.

Scanning Scanning is the process used to search through a text for a particular fact or piece of information. When you scan, you sweep your eyes across a page, looking for key words that may lead you to the information you want.

Scene In drama, the action is often divided into acts and scenes. Each scene presents an episode of the play's plot and typically occurs at a single place and time.

See also Act.

Scenery Scenery is a painted backdrop or other structures used to create the setting for a play.

Science Fiction Science fiction is fiction in which a writer explores unexpected possibilities of the past or the future, using known scientific data and theories as well as his or her creative imagination. Most science fiction writers create believable worlds, although some create fantasy worlds that have familiar elements.

See also Fantasy.

Screenplay A screenplay is a play written for film.

Script The text of a play, film, or broadcast is called a script.

Secondary Source *See* Sources.

Sensory Details Sensory details are words and phrases that appeal to the reader's senses of sight, sound, touch, smell, and taste. Note the sensory details in the following line. The morning sun shone brightly as a light breeze gently blew and rustled the poplar leaves. These details appeal to the senses of touch and smell.

See also Imagery.

Sequential Order Sequential order is a pattern of organization that shows the order of steps or stages in a process.

Setting The setting of a story, poem, or play is the time and place of the action. Sometimes the setting is clear and well defined. At other times, it is left to the reader's imagination. Elements of setting include geographic location, historical period (past, present, or future), season, time of day, and culture.

Setting a Purpose The process of establishing specific reasons for reading a text is called setting a purpose. Readers can look at a text's title, headings, and illustrations to guess what it might be about. They can then use these guesses to figure out what they want to learn from reading the text.

Short Story A short story is a work of fiction that centers on a single idea and can be read in one sitting. Generally, a short story has one main conflict that involves the characters and keeps the story moving.

See also Fiction.

Sidebar A sidebar is additional information set in a box alongside or within an article. Popular magazines often make use of sidebars.

Signal Words In a text, signal words are words and phrases that help show how events or ideas are related. Some common examples of signal words are *and, but, however, nevertheless, therefore,* and *in addition.*

Simile A simile is a figure of speech that makes a comparison between two unlike things using the words *like* or *as*: The calm lake was smooth as glass.

See also Figurative Language; Metaphor.

Sonnet A sonnet is a poem that has a formal structure, containing 14 lines and a specific rhyme scheme and meter. The sonnet, which means "little song," can be used for a variety of topics.

See also Rhyme Scheme.

Sound Devices Sound devices are ways of using words for the sound qualities they create. Sound devices can help convey meaning and mood in a writer's work. Some common sound devices include **alliteration, assonance, meter, onomatopoeia, repetition, rhyme,** and **rhythm.**

See also Alliteration; Assonance; Meter; Onomatopoeia; Repetition; Rhyme; Rhythm.

Sources A source is anything that supplies information. **Primary sources** are materials written by people who witnessed or took part in an event. Letters, diaries, autobiographies, and speeches are primary sources. Unlike primary sources, **secondary sources** are made by people who were not directly involved in an event or present when it occurred. Encyclopedias, textbooks, biographies, and most newspaper and magazine articles are examples of secondary sources.

Speaker In poetry the speaker is the voice that "talks" to the reader, similar to the narrator in fiction. The speaker is not necessarily the poet.

Speech A speech is a talk or public address. The purpose of a speech may be to entertain, to explain, to persuade, to inspire, or any combination of these purposes.

Stage Directions In the script of a play, the instructions to the actors, director, and stage crew are called the stage directions. Stage directions might suggest scenery, lighting, sound effects, and ways for actors to move and speak. Stage directions often appear in parentheses and in italic type.

Stanza A stanza is a group of two or more lines that form a unit in a poem. Each stanza may have the same number of lines, or the number of lines may vary.

See also Couplet; Form; Poetry.

Static Character *See* Character.

Stereotype In literature, characters who are defined by a single trait are known as stereotypes. Such characters do not usually demonstrate the complexities of real people. Familiar stereotypes in popular literature include the absent-minded professor and the busybody.

Stereotyping Stereotyping is a dangerous type of overgeneralization. It can lead to unfair judgments of people based on their ethnic background, beliefs, practices, or physical appearance.

Structure The structure of a work of literature is the way in which it is put together. In poetry, structure involves the arrangement of words and lines to produce a desired effect. One structural unit in poetry is the stanza. In prose, structure involves the arrangement of such elements as sentences, paragraphs, and events.

Style A style is a manner of writing. It involves how something is said rather than what is said.

Summarize To summarize is to briefly retell the main ideas of a piece of writing in one's own words.

See also Paraphrase.

Support Support is any information that helps to prove a claim.

Supporting Detail *See* Main Idea.

Surprise Ending A surprise ending is an unexpected plot twist at the end of a story. The surprise may be a sudden turn in the action or a piece of information that gives a different perspective to the entire story.

Suspense Suspense is a feeling of growing tension and excitement experienced by a reader. Suspense makes a reader curious about the outcome of a story or an event within a story. A writer creates suspense by raising questions in the reader's mind. The use of **foreshadowing** is one way that writers create suspense.

See also Foreshadowing.

Symbol A symbol is a person, a place, an object, an animal, or an activity that stands for something beyond itself. For example, a flag is a colored piece of cloth that stands for a country. A white dove is a bird that represents peace.

Synthesize To synthesize information means to take individual pieces of information and combine them in order to gain a better understanding of a subject.

Tall Tale A tall tale is a humorously exaggerated story about impossible events, often involving the supernatural abilities of the main character.

Teleplay A teleplay is a play written for television. In a teleplay, scenes can change quickly and dramatically. The camera can focus the viewer's attention on specific actions. The camera directions in teleplays are much like the stage directions in stage plays.

Text Features Text features are elements of a text, such as boldface type, headings, and subheadings, that help organize and call attention to important information. Italic type, bulleted or numbered lists, sidebars, and graphic aids such as charts, tables, timelines, illustrations, and photographs are also considered text features.

Theme A theme is a message about life or human nature that the writer shares with the reader. In many cases, readers must infer what the writer's message is. One way of figuring out a theme is to apply the lessons learned by the main characters to people in real life.

Recurring themes: Themes found in a variety of works. For example, authors from different backgrounds might express similar themes having to do with the importance of family values.

Universal themes: Themes that are found throughout the literature of all time periods.

See also Moral.

Thesaurus *See* Reference Works.

Thesis Statement A thesis statement, or controlling idea, is the main proposition that a writer attempts to support in a piece of writing.

Third-Person Point of View *See* Point of View.

Title The title of a piece of writing is the name that is attached to it. A title often refers to an important aspect of the work.

Tone The tone of a literary work expresses the writer's attitude toward his or her subject. Words such as *angry, sad,* and *humorous* can be used to describe different tones.

See also Author's Perspective; Mood.

Topic Sentence The topic sentence of a paragraph states the paragraph's main idea; all other sentences in the paragraph provide supporting details.

Tragedy A tragedy is a dramatic work that presents the downfall of a dignified character or characters who are involved in historically or socially significant events. The events in a tragic plot are set in motion by a decision that is often an error in judgment on the part of the hero. Succeeding events are linked in a cause-and-effect relationship and lead inevitably to a disastrous conclusion, usually death. William Shakespeare's *Romeo and Juliet* is a famous tragedy.

Traits *See* Character.

Treatment The way a topic is handled in a work is referred to as its treatment. Treatment includes the form the writing takes as well as the writer's purpose and tone.

Turning Point *See* Climax.

Understatement Understatement is a technique of creating emphasis by saying less than is actually or literally true. It is the opposite of **hyperbole,** or exaggeration. Understatement is often used to create a humorous effect.

Universal Theme *See* Theme.

Unreliable Narrator *See* Narrator.

Visualize Visualizing is the process of forming a mental picture based on written or spoken information.

Voice The term *voice* refers to a writer's unique use of language that allows a reader to "hear" a human personality in the writer's work. Elements of style that contribute to a writer's voice can reveal much about the author's personality, beliefs, and attitudes.

Website A website is a collection of "pages" on the World Wide Web, usually devoted to one specific subject. Pages are linked together and accessed by clicking hyperlinks or menus, which send the user from page to page within a website. Websites are created by companies, organizations, educational institutions, branches of the government, the military, and individuals.

Word Choice The success of any writing depends on the writer's choice of words. Words not only communicate ideas but also help describe events, characters, settings, and so on. Word choice can make a writer's work sound formal or informal, serious or humorous. A writer must choose words carefully depending on the goal of the piece of writing. For example, a writer working on a science article would probably use technical, formal words; a writer trying to establish the setting in a short story would probably use more descriptive words.

See also Style.

Workplace Documents Workplace documents are materials that are produced or used within a work setting, usually to aid in the functioning of the workplace. They include job applications, office memos, training manuals, job descriptions, and sales reports.

Works Cited The term *works cited* refers to a list of all the works a writer has referred to in his or her text. This list often includes not only books and articles but also Internet sources.

Works Consulted The term *works consulted* refers to a list of all the works a writer consulted in order to create his or her text. It is not limited just to those cited in the text.

See also Bibliography.

Writer's Point of View A writer's point of view is the writer's opinion about a topic.

Using the Glossary

This glossary is an alphabetical list of vocabulary words found in the selections in this book. Use this glossary just as you would a dictionary—to determine the meanings, parts of speech, pronunciation, and syllabication of words. (Some technical, foreign, and more obscure words in this book are not listed here but are defined for you in the footnotes that accompany many of the selections.)

Many words in the English language have more than one meaning. This glossary gives the meanings that apply to the words as they are used in the selections in this book. Words closely related in form and meaning are listed together in one entry (for instance, *consumption* and *consume*), and the definition is given for the first form.

The following abbreviations are used to identify parts of speech of words:

adj. adjective   *adv.* adverb   *n.* noun   *v.* verb

Each word's pronunciation is given in parentheses. A guide to the pronunciation symbols appears in the Pronunciation Key below. The stress marks in the Pronunciation Key are used to indicate the force given to each syllable in a word. They can also help you determine where words are divided into syllables.

For more information about the words in this glossary or for information about words not listed here, consult a dictionary.

Pronunciation Key

Symbol	Examples	Symbol	Examples	Symbol	Examples
ă	pat	m	mum	v	valve
ā	pay	n	no, sudden	w	with
ä	father	ng	thing	y	yes
âr	care	ŏ	pot	z	zebra, xylem
b	bib	ō	toe	zh	vision, pleasure, garage
ch	church	ô	caught, paw		
d	deed, milled	oi	noise	ə	about, item, edible, gallop, circus
ĕ	pet	ŏŏ	took		
ē	bee	ōō	boot	ər	butter
f	fife, phase, rough	ou	out		
g	gag	p	pop		

Sounds in Foreign Words

Symbol	Examples	Symbol	Examples	Symbol	Examples
h	hit	r	roar	KH	*German* ich, ach; *Scottish* loch
hw	which	s	sauce		
ĭ	pit	sh	ship, dash	N	*French,* bon
ī	pie, by	t	tight, stopped	œ	*French* feu, œuf; *German* schön
îr	pier	th	thin		
j	judge	*th*	this	ü	*French* tu; *German* über
k	kick, cat, pique	ŭ	cut		
l	lid, needle*	ûr	urge, term, firm, word, heard		

* In English the consonants *l* and *n* often constitute complete syllables by themselves.

Stress Marks

The relevant emphasis with which the syllables of a word or phrase are spoken, called stress, is indicated in three different ways. The strongest, or primary, stress is marked with a bold mark (´). An intermediate, or secondary, level of stress is marked with a similar but lighter mark (´). The weakest stress is unmarked. Words of one syllable show no stress mark.

Glossary of Academic Vocabulary

abnormal (ăb-nôr′məl) *adj.* not typical, usual, or regular; not normal

affect (ə-fĕkt′) *v.* to have an influence on or effect a change in something

aspect (ăs′pəkt) *n.* a characteristic or feature of something

attitude (ăt′ĭ-tōōd′) *n.* a way of thinking or feeling about something or someone

complex (kŏm′plĕks′) *adj.* consisting of many interwoven parts that make something difficult to understand

consume (kən sōōm′) *v.* to buy things for your own use or ownership

contrast (kŏn′trăst′) *v.* to show differences between two or more things that are being compared

cultural (kul′chər-əl′) *adj.* of or relating to culture or cultivation

despite (dĭ-spīt′) *prep.* in spite of; even though

element (ĕl′ə-mənt) *n.* a part or aspect of something

ensure (ĕn-shŏŏr′) *v.* to make sure or certain

error (ĕr′ər) *n.* a mistake

evaluate (ĭ-văl′yoo-āt′) *tr.v.* to examine something carefully to judge its value or worth

feature (fē′-chər) *n.* a prominent or distinctive part, quality, or characteristic

focus (fō′kəs) *v.* to direct toward a specific point or purpose

goal (gōl) *n.* the object toward which your work and planning is directed; a purpose

inadequate (ĭn-ăd′ĭ-kwĭt) *adj.* not enough or sufficient to fulfill a need or meet a requirement

interact (ĭn′tər-ăkt′) *v.* to act upon each other

participate (pär-tĭs′ə-pāt′) *v.* to be active and involved in something or to share in something

perceive (pər-sēv′) *v.* to become aware of something directly through any of the senses

potential (pə-tĕn′shəl) *adj.* capable of doing or being something; having possibility

purchase (pûr′chĭs) *v.* to buy

rely (rĭ-lī) *v.* to depend on something or someone for support, help, or supply

resource (re′-sors′) *n.* something that can be used for support or help

specify (spĕs′ə-fī′) *v.* to state exactly or in detail what you want or need

stress (strĕs) *v.* to put emphasis on something

task (tăsk) *n.* an assignment or work done as part of one's duties

technology (tĕk-nŏl′ə-jē) *n.* the application of science and engineering as part of a commercial or industrial undertaking

text (tĕkst) *n.* a literary work that is regarded as an object of critical analysis

valid (văl′ĭd) *adj.* convincing or having a sound reason for something

Glossary of Critical Vocabulary

addiction (ə-dĭk´shən) *n.* An *addiction* is a habit one is dependent on.

anxiety (ăng-zī´ĭ-tē) *n.* *Anxiety* is an uneasy, worried feeling.

apathy (ăp´ə-thē) *n.* *Apathy* is indifference or the lack of interest or concern.

arboretum (är´bə-rē´təm) *n.* An *arboretum* is a place where many trees are grown for educational or viewing purposes.

avalanche (ăv´ə-lănch) *n.* An *avalanche* is a large mass of snow, ice, dirt, or rocks falling quickly down the side of a mountain.

bedrock (bĕd´rŏk´) *n.* *Bedrock* is the solid rock that lies under sand, soil, clay, and gravel.

cache (kăsh) *n.* A *cache* is an amount of something that has been hidden away.

capacity (kə-păs´ĭ-tē) *n.* A person's *capacity* is his role or position.

coincidence (kō-ĭn´sĭ-dəns) *n.* A *coincidence* is a sequence of events that although accidental seems to have been planned.

conscience (kŏn´shəns) *n.* *Conscience* is the conforming to or living up to one's own sense of what is right.

corridor (kôr´ĭ-dər) *n.* A *corridor* is a narrow hallway or passageway.

croon (krōōn) *v.* When someone *croons,* that person hums or sings softly.

cynic (sĭn´ĭk) *n.* A *cynic* is a person who has negative opinions about other people and what they do.

deck (dĕk) *n.* The *deck* is the platform on a ship or boat where people stand.

decompose (dē´kəm-pōz´) *v.* When things *decompose,* they decay and break down into their basic parts.

diplomat (dĭp´lə-măt) *n.* A *diplomat* is a person appointed by a government to interact with other governments.

eloquence (ĕl´ə-kwəns) *n.* If someone behaves or speaks with *eloquence,* she uses persuasive powerful expression.

enact (ĕn-ăkt´) *v.* If you *enact* something, you make it into a law.

enterprising (ĕn´tər-prī´zĭng) *adj.* An *enterprising* person is someone who accepts challenges and takes initiative.

ethereal (ĭ-thîr´ē-əl) *adj.* If something is *ethereal,* it is light and airy.

exasperate (ĭg-zăs´pə-rāt´) *v.* If you *exasperate* someone, you make the person very angry.

exhibition (ĕk´sə-bĭsh´ən) *n.* An *exhibition* is an organized presentation or show.

exhort (ĭg-zôrt´) *v.* If you *exhort,* you make an urgent appeal to others.

exploit (ĕk´sploit´) *v.* If you *exploit* something, you use it selfishly.

exploitation (ĕk´sploi-tā´shən) *n.* *Exploitation* is the unfair treatment or use of something or someone for selfish reasons.

flammable (flăm´ə-bəl) *adj.* If something is *flammable,* it is easy for it to catch on fire and burn.

frantic (frăn´tik) *adj.* If you do something in a *frantic* way, you do it quickly and nervously.

geyser (gī´zər) *n.* A *geyser* is a natural hot spring that shoots hot water and steam into the air.

gradual (grăj´ōō-əl) *adj.* If something is *gradual,* it advances little by little.

gully (gŭl´ē) *n.* A *gully* is a deep ditch cut in the earth by running water.

haggard (hăg´ərd) *adj.* If you're *haggard,* you are worn out and exhausted.

hypothesis (hī-pŏth´ĭ-sĭs) *n.* A *hypothesis* is an explanation or theory for something that can be tested for validity.

ignorance (ĭg´nər-əns) *n.* *Ignorance* is the condition of being uneducated or uninformed.

impairment (ĭm-pâr´mənt) *n.* An *impairment* is an injury or weakness.

impetus (ĭm´pĭ-təs) *n.* The *impetus* is the driving force or motivation behind an action.

inexplicable (ĭn-ĕk´splĭ-kə-bəl) *adj.* If something is *inexplicable,* it is difficult to understand.

inquire (ĭn-kwīr´) *v.* If you *inquire* about something, you ask about it.

inspection (ĭn-spĕk´shən) *n.* An *inspection* is an official examination or review.

insulate (ĭn´sə-lāt´) *v.* When you *insulate* something, you prevent the passage of heat through it.

intangible (ĭn-tăn´jə-bəl) *n.* An *intangible* is something that is hard to describe because it cannot be perceived by the senses.

inundate (ĭn´ŭndāt´) *v.* To *inundate* is to give a huge amount of something.

judicious (jōō-dĭsh´əs) *adj.* If you are *judicious,* you have good judgment.

mandatory (măn´də-tôr´ē) *adj.* If something is *mandatory,* it is required.

maroon (mə-rōōn´) *v.* To *maroon* is to abandon or leave someone in a place that is hard to get away from.

marvel (mär´vəl) *v.* If you *marvel* at something, you are surprised or astonished by it.

meager (mē´gər) *adj.* If something is *meager,* it is small or deficient in quantity.

median (mē´dē-ən) *n.* A *median* is a dividing area between opposing lanes of traffic on a highway or road.

metabolism (mĭ-tăb´ə-lĭz´əm) *n.* The *metabolism* of a living thing is all the processes that allow for growth and life.

mischievous (mĭs´chə-vəs) *adj.* If someone is *mischievous,* the person is naughty.

misjudge (mĭs-jŭj´) *v.* If you *misjudge* something, you form an incorrect opinion about it.

moderate (mŏd´ər-ĭt) *adj.* When something is kept *moderate,* it is kept within a certain limit.

municipal (myōō-nĭs´ə-pəl) *adj.* If something is *municipal,* it relates to a city or town.

navigation (năv´ĭ-gā´shən) *n.* The *navigation* of a ship or boat is the act of guiding it along a planned course.

neural (nŏor´əl) *adj.* Anything that is *neural* is related to the nervous system.

neuron (nŏor´ŏn´) *n.* A *neuron* is a cell in the nervous system that carries messages between the brain and other body parts.

neuroscience (nŏor´ō-sī´əns) *n. Neuroscience* is any of the sciences that study the nervous system.

neuroscientist (nŏor´ō-sī´ən-tĭst) *n.* A *neuroscientist* is a person who studies the brain and the nervous system.

obituary (ō-bĭch´ōō-ĕr´ē) *n.* An *obituary* is a public notice of a death.

observation (ŏb´zər-vā´shən) *n.* An *observation* is the act of watching something.

plantation (plăn-tā´shən) *n.* A *plantation* is a large farm or estate on which crops are raised.

ponderous (pŏn´dər-əs) *adj.* If something is *ponderous,* it is very heavy.

portable (pôr´tə-bəl) *adj.* If something is *portable,* it can be carried or moved easily.

porthole (pŏrt´hōl) *n.* A *porthole* is a circular window on a boat or ship.

possession (pə-zĕsh´ən) *n.* A *possession* is something you own.

precarious (prĭ-kâr´ē-əs) *adj.* If something is *precarious,* it is dangerous and unstable.

precaution (prĭ-kô´shən) *n.* A *precaution* is an action taken to avoid possible danger.

precipitous (prĭ-sĭp´ĭ-təs) *adj.* When something is *precipitous,* it is very steep, like a cliff.

proliferation (prə-lĭf´ər-rā´shən) *n.* A *proliferation* is the fast growth of something.

prowess (prou´ĭs) *n. Prowess* is the strength and courage someone has.

reign (rān) *v.* If some things *reign* over something else, it means they dominate it.

reprove (rĭ-pro͞ov´) *v.* If you *reprove* someone, you express disapproval.

restrictive (rĭ-strĭk´tĭv) *adj.* When something is *restrictive*, it is limiting in some way.

scorn (skôrn) *n.* *Scorn* is disrespect or disdain.

sextant (sĕk´stənt) *n.* A *sextant* is an instrument used to determine location by measuring the position of the stars and sun.

shuffle (shuf´əl) *v.* When you *shuffle*, you move with short sliding steps.

singe (sĭnj) *v.* If you *singe* something, you slightly burn it.

snag (snăg) *v.* If you *snag* something, you catch it quickly and unexpectedly.

splinter (splĭn´tər) *v.* To *splinter* means to break up into sharp, thin pieces.

spyglass (spī´glăs´) *n.* A *spyglass* is a small telescope.

steward (sto͞o´ərd) *n.* A *steward* is a person who supervises and manages something.

stifle (stī´fəl) *v.* If you *stifle* something, you hold it back.

submerge (səb-mûrj´) *v.* When something *submerges*, it becomes covered by water.

superfluity (so͞o´pər-flo͞o´ĭ-tē) *n.* *Superfluity* is overabundance or excess.

sustain (sə-stān´) *v.* If things *sustain*, they remain in existence.

sustenance (sŭs´tə-nəns) *n.* *Sustenance* is the food needed to live.

swell (swĕl) *n.* A *swell* is a long, unbroken wave.

syringe (sə-rĭnj´) *n.* A *syringe* is a medical instrument used to inject fluids into the body.

taper (tā´pər) *v.* When things *taper*, they gradually get thinner.

tectonic (tĕk-tŏn´ĭk) *adj.* If something is *tectonic*, it relates to the deformation of Earth's rocky crust.

tedious (tē´dē-əs) *adj.* Something that is *tedious* is boring.

wistful (wĭst´fəl) *adj.* If you're *wistful*, you are thoughtful and longing for something.

Index of Skills

Key:

Teacher's Edition page numbers and subject entries are printed in **boldface** type.
Subject entries and page references that apply to both the Student Edition and the Teacher's Edition appear in lightface type.
There is no content from the Close Reader in this index.

159, 161, 162, 163, 166, **170**, 171, **172,** 173, 174, **185, 186, 187, 188,** 190, **194, 195, 196,** 198, **203, 204, 207, 208,** 210, **213,** 214, **221, 222, 223, 224, 225, 226, 227, 228,** 230, **233, 236,** 238, **242, 243,** 244, **245,** 246, 248, **249, 250, 252, 253,** 254, 256, **266, 267, 268, 269, 272, 273,** 275, 276, **284, 285, 287, 288, 289, 291, 292, 294, 296, 297, 299, 300, 302, 307, 308, 309, 311, 312, 321, 322, 327, 328, 330, 331, 332**

citing textual evidence, 15, **46,** 49, **207, 214a, 223,** 229, **232a**

claims, 27, 189, 197, R23, R65
  development of, R2
  in editorials, **24,** 27
  evidence to support, 27, 189, 197, R23, R25, R29, R68
  factual, R16
  in persuasive speech, 215–217
  reasons/reasoning to support, 189, R2–R3, R23
  by speaker, 189, 218
  vague, R2

clarification, 57, 217, 274, R2, R4, R66, R71

clauses, 18, R48
  adjective, 200, R31, R40, R49, R50
  adverb, 88, R49–R50
  combining, 156
  defined, 200, 240
  dependent, 52, R48
  independent, 52, 156
  main, 18, 52, 88, 156, R48–R50
  as modifier, 336, R40
  noun, 240, R49
  in predicates, 88, 200, 240, R48
  subordinate, 52, 88, 156, 240, R48, R49, R50
  transitional, R3

cliché, R66

climax, 15, 54, **123, 124,** 126, **336a,** R6–R7, R66, R68, R72–R73

Close Read Screencasts, 3, 31, 63, 111, 137, 169, 185, 221, 265, 307

close-up shot, 320a

collaborative discussion, R12

Collaborative Discussions, 14, **18a,** 28, 34, 40, **42a,** 48, 67, 74, 84, 91, 106, 124, 140, 146, 152, 172, 188, 196, 208, 213, 228, 236, 245, 254, 277, 302, 312, 318, 323, 332

collective nouns, R30, R54

colon, R34

combining sentences with phrases, 326

comedy, R66, R68

comma, 18, 38, R33–R34

commas and coordinate adjectives, 38

comma splice, R51

common nouns, R30, R37

commonplace assertion, R16

comparative forms, R386

compare-and-contrast organization, 165, **168a,** R19–R21, R66

Compare Media, 19

Compare Text, 71, 169, 265

comparisons, 303
  analogies as, 305, R58, R64

of arguments, 196
  figurative language and, 141, 214
  of genres, 284, 285, 288, 289, 290, 294, 296, 297, 300, 301, 306a
  metaphor as, 76, 174, R71
  of modifiers, R44
  in poetry, 214, 247
  simile as, 76, 141, 174, R75
  of speeches, 192a

complete predicate, 18, R32

complete sentences, 88, R51

complete subject, 18, R32

complex sentences, 156, R50

compound adjectives, R35

compound-complex sentences, 156, R50

compound nouns, R30, R62

compound predicate, R46

compound sentences, 18, 156, R33, R34, R50

compound subjects, R46, R52

concluding statements, 217, R5, R66

conclusions, R66
  in arguments, R3
  drawing, **43, 46,** 49, 229, R67
  in expository essays, 132, 339
  in informative texts, R5
  in memoirs, 176–177
  in multimedia presentations, 261
  in narratives, R7
  in opinion essays, 128
  in oral commentary, 58
  in persuasive texts, 217, 342–343, R25–R26
  in poetry analysis, 181
  supporting, 49

concrete details, 132–133, 339, 342, R5

concrete nouns, R30

conflict, **6,** 15, **18a,** 125, R66, R72. *See also* plot
  action and setting up, 55
  climax and, 15, R66
  dialogue for, 55
  in drama, **113, 114,** 125
  external, **6, 10, 18a,** R66, R68
  internal, **18a,** R66, R70
  main, R66
  plot and, 336a
  in short story, 53–55
  summary of, **64,** 68

conjunctions, 52, 88, 156, R31, R48, R51. *See also* coordinating conjunction; subordinating conjunction

conjunctive adverbs, R51

connecting
  compound sentences, 18
  conclusions in persuasive speech, 217
  ideas, 181, R3, R4
  to personal experience, R71

connotations, 51, R58, R66

consonants, R60–R61

consumer documents, R66

context clues, 191, **212a,** 257, 315, 335, R55, R59, R66

coordinate adjectives, 38

coordinating conjunction, 156, R31, R46
  in compound predicates, R46
  in compound sentences, 18, 156, R31, R34, R50, R51

correlative conjunction, R31, R52

counterarguments, **26,** 27, 189, 197, R23, R29, R66

counterclaims, R2, R29

couplet, 75, R66, R70. *See also* stanza

credibility, R5, R24, R66

critical essays, R66, R68

critical review, R66

Critical Vocabulary, **4, 5,** 17, **32, 33,** 37, **44, 45, 47,** 51, **64, 65, 66,** 70, **78, 79, 80,** 87, **94, 95, 96, 101,** 109, **138, 139, 140,** 143, **150, 151, 152,** 155, **160, 161, 163,** 167, **186, 187, 188,** 191, **194,** 199, **203, 204, 206,** 211, **224, 225, 226, 227, 228,** 231, **234, 235, 236,** 239, **250, 251,** 257, **266, 268, 270, 272, 275, 277,** 281, **284, 285, 287, 288, 291, 292, 295, 298,** 305, **308, 309, 311, 312,** 315, **328, 329, 330, 332,** 335, R80–R82. *See also* Glossary of Critical Vocabulary

critique, 314, R66

D

dangling modifiers, 316, R45

dangling participles, R48

dash, R34

debates, **200a,** R14–R15, R67. *See also* arguments

debate teams, R14

declarative sentences, R46

deductive arguments, R25–R26, R67

deductive mode, R25–R26

deductive reasons/reasoning, R25–R26, R67

demonstrations, 86

demonstrative pronouns, R30, R39

denotations, 51, R58, R67. *See also* connotations

dependent clause, 52, R33, R48. *See also* subordinate clauses

description, **32,** 126, R6–R7, R67

descriptive details, 141, 153, 175, 177

descriptive words, 336b

details, 209, 274
  analyzing, 107
  concrete, 132–133, 339, 342, R5
  descriptive, 141, 153, 175, 177
  determining, 209, **240a,** 274
  factual, 279, 303–304
  gathering, R6–R7
  in informational texts, 49, 237
  for narrative, R6–R7
  in news stories, 23
  organizing, 165
  sensory, 55, 176, R7, R70, R74
  of a setting, 15
  in summaries, 68, 85
  supporting, **21,** 23, **52a,** 165, **202, 205, 206, 240a, 266, 267, 268, 269, 270,** 274, R16, R76

diagram, 232a

dialect, **65,** 68, R67

dialogue, 55, **96, 112, 117,** 125, **126a,** 177, **292,** 303, R67

diary, R67, R70

diction, **72,** 73, 173, 237

dictionary, 109, 335, R59–R60

direct characterization, 110a

direct object, 240, R32, R38, R46, R48

direct quotations, R9

direct statements, 279

discussion, 29, 76, 238, R12–R13

diversity, 30, **90, 91,** 92, **92a**

documentary, **164, 318,** 319–320, **320a**

domain-specific words, 231

double comparisons, R45

double negatives, R45

drafts
  expository essay, 132–133, 339
  informative essay, 260–261
  memoirs, 176–177
  opinion essay, 128–129
  oral commentary, 58–59
  personal essay, 342–343
  persuasive speech, 216–217
  poetry analysis, 180–181
  research project, R9
  short story, 55

drama, **111,** 125–126, R67
  acts, R64
  cast of characters, **111,** 125, R65
  character development in, 117, 118, 119, 145
  dialogue in, 112, 117, 121, 122
  media and, 126a
  plot, **113, 114, 115, 116,** 125
  rising and falling action in, 115, 120, 123, 124
  scenes, 303, R64, R74
  sound effects, 119
  typography conventions, 112

dramatic irony, 198

dramatic reading, 69, 148

drawing conclusions. *See also* conclusions

dynamic character, R65

E

eBook, 16, 23, 27, 36, 42, 50, 69, 73, 75, 86, 108, 126, 142, 148, 154, 166, 171, 174, 190, 198, 210, 214, 230, 238, 244, 246, 256

editorial, **24,** 27, 49, R67

either/or fallacy, 197, R27–R28, R67

eliminate redundancy, 232

ellipses, R35

emotional appeals, R24, R67

emotional response, 319, R69

emphasis, **192a,** 279, **282a,** R79

encyclopedia. *See* reference works

end marks, R33

end rhyme, **72,** 73, 244, R74

epic poems/poetry, R67

essays, 154, 165, 230, R67–R68. *See also* expository essays
  author's message in, 165
  critical, R66, R68
  opinion, 127–130
  personal, **307, 308, 311,** 313, **316a,** 341–344, R67
  persuasive, 210
  structure of, **157, 159, 160, 161, 162, 163, 164,** 165, **168a**

establishing shot, 320a

ethical appeals, R24

etymologies, R57

Index of Titles and Authors

Key:

Authors and titles that appear in the Student Edition are in lightface type.

Authors and titles that appear in the Close Reader are in **boldface** type.

Names of authors who appear in both the Student Edition and the Close Reader are lightface.

For these authors, Student Edition page references are lightface and Close Reader page references are **boldface.**

Student Edition Acknowledgments

"Allied with Green" from *There is No Long Distance Now: Very Short Stories* by Naomi Shihab Nye. Text copyright © 2011 by Naomi Shihab Nye. Reprinted by permission of HarperCollins Publishers.

"Always Wanting More" from *I Want That: How We All Became Shoppers* by Thomas Hine. Text copyright © 2002 by Thomas Hine. Reprinted by permission of HarperCollins Publishers.

The American Heritage Dictionary of the English Language, Fifth Edition. Text copyright © 2011 by Houghton Mifflin Harcourt. Adapted and reprinted by permission from *The American Heritage Dictionary of the English Language, Fifth Edition.*

"Another Place, Another Time" by Cory Doctorow from *The Chronicles of Harris Burdick* by Chris Van Allsburg. Text copyright © 2011 by Cory Doctorow. Illustrations copyright © 1984 by Chris Van Allsburg. Reprinted by permission of Houghton Mifflin Harcourt.

"Big rocks' balancing acts" by Douglas Fox from *Science News for Kids,* October 19, 2011. Text copyright © 2011 by the Society for Science and the Public. Reprinted by permission of Science News for Kids.

"Dump" from *In a Prominent Bar in Secaucus: New and Selected Poems, 1955–2007* by X. J. Kennedy. Text copyright © 2007 by X. J. Kennedy. Reprinted by permission of Johns Hopkins University Press.

"Earth (A Gift Shop)" by Charles Yu from *Shadow Show,* edited by Sam Weller and Mort Castle. Text copyright © 2012 by Sam Weller and Mort Castle. Reprinted by permission of Charles Yu.

Excerpt from *Flesh & Blood So Cheap: The Triangle Fire and Its Legacy* by Albert Marrin. Text copyright © 2011 by Albert Marrin. Reprinted by permission of Alfred A. Knopf, a division of Random House, Inc.

"The Flight of Icarus" from *Stories of the Gods and Heroes* by Sally Benson. Text copyright 1940, renewed © 1968 by Sally Benson. Reprinted by permission of Dial Books for Young Readers, a division of Penguin Group (USA) Inc.

"How Things Work" from *Black Hair* by Gary Soto. Text copyright © 1985 by Gary Soto. Reprinted by permission of Houghton Mifflin Harcourt and BookStop Literary Agency, LLC, on behalf of the author. All rights reserved.

"Icarus's Flight" from *Mystery, So Long* by Stephen Dobyns. Text copyright © 2006 by Stephen Dobyns. Originally published by Penguin. Reprinted by permission of Stephen Dobyns.

Excerpt from Julianbeever.net. Text copyright © by Julian Beever. Reprinted by permission of Julian Beever.

Excerpt from *Life at Home in the 21st Century: 32 Families Open Their Doors* by Jeanne E. Arnold, Anthony P. Graesch, Enzo Ragazzini and Elinor Ochs. Text copyright © 2012 by the Regents of the University of California. Reprinted by permission of the Regents of the University of California, Cotsen Institute and Jeanne Arnold. All rights reserved.

"Living in the Dark" by Cheryl Bardoe from *Muse,* vol. 16, no. 2. Text copyright © 2012 by Carus Publishing Company. Reprinted by permission of Carus Publishing Company.

"Magic and the Brain" by Susana Martinez-Conde and Stephen L. Macknik, from *Scientific American,* December 2008. Text copyright © 2008 by Scientific American, Inc. Reprinted by permission of Scientific American, Inc.

Excerpt from *Mississippi Solo* by Eddie Harris. Text copyright © 1988 by Eddie Harris. Reprinted by permission of Lyons Press.

"Ode to Enchanted Light" from *Odes to Opposites* by Pablo Neruda, translated by Ken Krabbenhoft, selected and illustrated by Ferris Cook. Spanish text copyright © 1995 by Pablo Neruda and Fundación Pablo Neruda. English translation text copyright © 1995 by Ken Krabbenhoft. Text compilation copyright © 1995 by Ferris Cook. Reprinted by permission of Bullfinch and Agencia Literaria Carmen Balcells S.A. All rights reserved.

"Parents of rescued teenage sailor Abby Sunderland accused of risking her life" by Paul Harris from *The Observer,* June 13, 2010. Text © 2012 Guardian News and Media Limited or its affiliated companies. Reprinted by permission of Guardian News Media.

"The People Could Fly" from *The People Could Fly: American Black Folktales* by Virginia Hamilton. Text copyright © 1985 by Virginia Hamilton. Reprinted by permission of Alfred A. Knopf, a division of Random House, Inc.

"A Poem for My Librarian, Mrs. Long" from *Acolytes* by Nikki Giovanni. Text copyright © 2007 by Nikki Giovanni. Reprinted by permission of HarperCollins Publishers.

"Reflections on Working Toward Peace" by Craig Kielburger from *Architects of Peace: Visions of Hope in Words and Images,* edited by Michael Collopy and Jason Gardner. Text copyright © 2000 by Michael Collopy. Reprinted by permission of New World Library.

"Rogue Wave" from *Rogue Wave and Other Red-Blooded Sea Stories* by Theodore Taylor. Text copyright © 1996 by Theodore Taylor. Reprinted by permission of the Theodore Taylor Estate and the Watkins/Loomis Agency.

"Ship of Fools" by Joanna Weiss from *The Boston Globe,* June 15, 2010. Text copyright © 2010 by Globe Newspaper Company. Reprinted by permission of PARS International on behalf of The Boston Globe.

"Sleeping in the Forest" from *Twelve Moons* by Mary Oliver. Text copyright © 1972, 1973, 1974, 1976, 1977, 1978, 1979 by Mary Oliver. Reprinted by permission of Little, Brown and Company and Charlotte Sheedy Literary Agency on behalf of the author.

"The Song of Wandering Aengus" from *The Wind in the Reeds* by William Butler Yeats. Text copyright © in Spain. Reprinted by permission of United Agents, LLP, a subsidiary of A.P. Watt.

"Sorry, Wrong Number" by Lucille Fletcher. Text copyright © 1948 by Lucille Fletcher. Reprinted by permission of William Morris Endeavor Entertainment, LLC.

Excerpt from *The Story of the Triangle Factory Fire* by Zachary Kent. Text copyright © 1989 by Children's Press, Inc. Reprinted by permission of Children's Press, an imprint of Scholastic Library Publishing, Inc. All rights reserved.

"Train Time" by D'Arcy McNickle from *Voice of the Turtle: American Indian Literature 1900–1970* edited by Paula Gunn Allen. Text copyright © 1994 by Paula Gunn Allen. Reprinted by permission of Ballantine Books, a division of Random House, Inc.

Excerpt from *Uprising* by Margaret Peterson Haddix. Text copyright © 2007 by Margaret Peterson Haddix. Reprinted by permission of Simon & Schuster Books for Young Readers, an imprint of Simon & Schuster's Children's Publishing Division and Adams Literary.

"Why Exploring the Ocean is Mankind's Next Giant Leap" by Phillippe Cousteau from *Light Years Blog,* March 13, 2012. Text copyright © Philippe Cousteau. Reprinted by permission of Philippe Cousteau.

Excerpt from "Women in Aviation" from *Red-Tail Angels* by Frederick and Patricia McKissack. Text copyright © 1995 by Frederick and Patricia McKissack. Reprinted by permission of Walker & Co.

"Your World" from *Share My World* by Georgia Douglas Johnson. Text copyright © 1962 by Georgia Douglas Johnson. Reprinted by permission of the Moorland-Spingarn Research Center, Howard University.

Close Reader Acknowledgments

"Always Wanting More" from *I Want That: How We All Became Shoppers* by Thomas Hine. Text copyright © 2002 by Thomas Hine. Reprinted by permission of HarperCollins Publishers.

Text copyright © 2011 by Houghton Mifflin Harcourt. Adapted and reprinted by permission from *The American Heritage Dictionary of the English Language, Fifth Edition*.

"Arachne" from *Greek Myths* by Olivia E. Coolidge. Text copyright © 1949 by Olivia E. Coolidge. Reprinted by permission of Houghton Mifflin Harcourt Publishing Company.

"Big Things Come in Small Packages" from *Don't Split the Pole: Tales of Down-Home Folk Wisdom* by Eleanora E. Tate. Text copyright © 1997 by Eleanora E. Tate. Reprinted by permission of Eleanora E. Tate.

Excerpt from *A Christmas Carol: Scrooge and Marley* by Israel Horovitz. Text copyright © 1979 by Israel Horovitz. Reprinted by permission of William Morris Endeavor Entertainment, LLC.

"Doris Is Coming" from *Drinking Coffee Elsewhere* by ZZ Packer. Text copyright © 2003 by ZZ Packer. Reprinted by permission of Riverhead Books, an imprint of Penguin Group (USA) Inc. and Canongate Books.

"Heartbeat" by David Yoo. Text copyright © 2005 by David Yoo. Reprinted by permission of Writers House, LLC, on behalf of the author.

"He—y, Come On O—ut!" by Shinichi Hoshi from *The Best Japanese Science Fiction Stories*. Text copyright © 1989 by Shinichi Hoshi. Reprinted by permission of Barricade Books.

Excerpt from "The Hidden Southwest: The Arch Hunters" by James Vlahos from Adventure.nationalgeographic.com. Text copyright © 2008 by National Geographic Society. Reprinted by permission of National Geographic Society.

Excerpt by Joan Vernikos from "Is Space Exploration Worth the Cost?" by Stephen Dubner from www.freakonomics.com, January 11, 2008. Text copyright © by Freakonomics, LLC. Reprinted by permission of William Morris Endeavor Entertainment LLC, on behalf of Freakonomics, LLC.

Excerpt from "John Bergmann runs a special zoo for older, exploited, and abused animals," retitled "Difference Maker: John Bergmann and Popcorn Park" by David Karas, October 25, 2012 from www.csmonitor.com. Text copyright © by The Christian Science Monitor. Reprinted by permission of David Karas.

Excerpt from Julianbeever.net. Text copyright © by Julian Beever. Reprinted by permission of Julian Beever.

"The Most Daring of Our Leaders" from *Freedom's Daughters: The Unsung Heroines of the Civil Rights Movement from 1830 to 1970* by Lynne Olson. Text copyright © 2001 by Lynne Olson. Reprinted by permission of Charles Scribner, an imprint of Simon & Schuster Children's Publishing Division.

Excerpt from *Polar Dream* by Helen Thayer. Text copyright © 1993 by Helen Thayer. Reprinted by permission of Millikan Swanson Weiss.

"Prayer to the Pacific" from *Storyteller* by Leslie Marmon Silko. Text copyright © 1981, 2012 by Leslie Marmon Silko. Reprinted by permission of Viking Penguin, a division of Penguin Group (USA) Inc. and Wylie Agency Inc.

"Problems with Hurricanes" from *Maraca: New and Selected Poems 1965–2000* by Victor Hernández Cruz. Text copyright © 1991 by Victor Hernández Cruz. Reprinted by permission of Coffee House Press.

Excerpt from *Stan Lee Presents A Christmas Carol by Charles Dickens*. Copyright © 2007 by Marvel Characters, Inc. Reprinted by permission of Marvel Entertainment.

"Stinging Tentacles Offer Hint to Oceans' Decline" by Elisabeth Rosenthal from *The New York Times*, August 3, 2008, www.nytimes.com. Text copyright © 2008 by The New York Times Company. Reprinted by permission of PARS International on behalf of The New York Times.

"Tornado at Talladega" from *Blacks* by Gwendolyn Brooks. Text copyright © 1945, 1949, 1953, 1960, 1963, 1968, 1969, 1970, 1971, 1975, 1981, 1987 by Gwendolyn Brooks. Reprinted by permission of Brooks Permissions.